ENCYCLOPEDIA OF
ROSES

ENCYCLOPEDIA OF ROSES

Charles & Brigid Quest-Ritson

LONDON, NEW YORK, MUNICH, MELBOURNE, DELHI

Senior Editor Jill Hamilton
Editor Jane Perlmutter
Editorial Assistant Madeline Farbman
Senior Art Editor Ursula Dawson
Senior Managing Art Editor Lee Griffiths
Senior Managing Editor Anna Kruger
DTP Designer Louise Waller
Production Mandy Inness

Produced for Dorling Kindersley by **Cooling Brown**
Creative Director Arthur Brown
Managing Editor Amanda Lebentz
Art Director Derek Coombes
Designers Tish Jones, Elly King, Alison Gardner
Editors Alison Bolus, Monica Byles, Elizabeth Haldane, Carole McGlynn, Patsy North, Helen Ridge, Fiona Wild

First American Edition, 2003
This edition published in 2011

03 04 05 06 10 9 8 7 6 5 4 3 2 1
001–AE804–July/2011

Published in the United States by DK Publishing
375 Hudson Street, New York, New York 10014

A catalog record for this book is available from the Library of Congress

ISBN 978-0-7566-8868-4

Reproduced by Colourscan, Singapore
Printed and bound Toppan, China

Discover more at
www.dk.com

NOTES ON NOMENCLATURE

Some of the roses in this encyclopedia have more than one name. Those alternative names may be synonyms or trade names, which differ between countries. The rose which is widely grown in Britain and the United States as 'Iceberg' is properly known as 'Schneewittchen', the name first given to it by its German breeder. Some authorities take the view that 'Iceberg' should be treated as a trade name and written as Iceberg. Writers and publishers need to know which names take effect as "correct" and which should be regarded as synonyms. In this encyclopedia, the authors have tended to follow the example of the American Rose Society, which is the official registrar for new roses. This means that some of the names in this encyclopedia and the way they are written are different from the ones what are widely used in other publications. The position is complicated by differences of opinion arising from the International Convention on the Nomenclature of Cultivated Plants and by the failure of many major rose breeders to register their roses with American Rose Society. There is an ongoing dialogue between the Royal Horticultural Society and the American Rose Society concerning both the principles of rose-naming and their application to individual cultivars. It is to be expected that these discussions will result in greater agreement and uniformity in the future. It should however be said that there is substantial agreement on the correct naming of the vast majority of roses listed in this encyclopedia.

CONTENTS

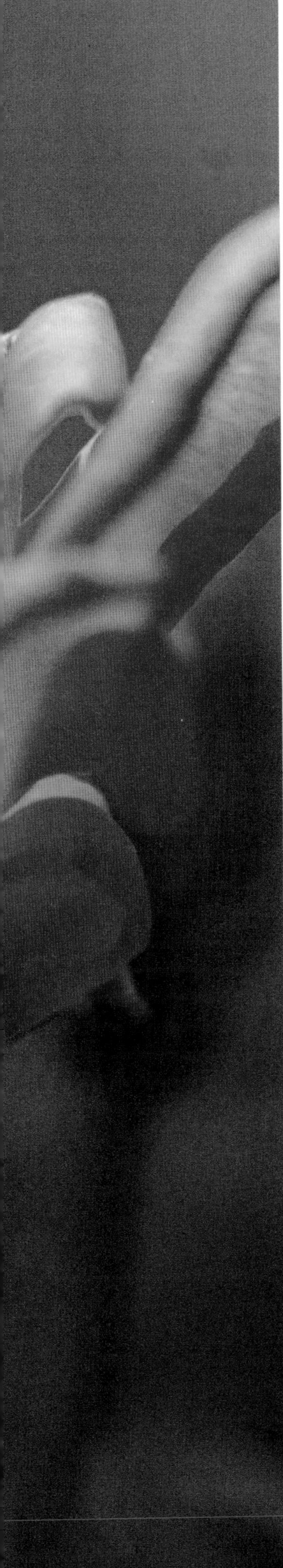

Authors' Introduction

THERE ARE ROSES for every soil and position. There are roses for tropical climates and roses that will flourish in the Arctic Circle. Most roses bloom nonstop until the first frost of winter; in warm climates, they flower for 12 months of the year. They tolerate neglect, but respond generously to extra care. For lazy gardeners – and busy people with little time to waste – roses cannot be beaten.

Their variability is astounding. Their height can be anything from 33in (10cm) to 40ft (10m). Their scent can be sweet, fruity, musky, or tealike – and complex combinations of all of these different fragrances. They come in every shade and color, except true blue. Roses are immensely useful plants in mixed plantings, yet may be spectacularly displayed with only fellow roses for company, as at the great gardens of Bagatelle in Paris.

We have loved roses, grown and collected them, for many years. The roses we have chosen for this encyclopedia are those that are most widely available throughout the world. A few are grown only in one or two countries, where their popularity proves that they deserve to be better known elsewhere. Turning the pages of this encyclopedia reminds us of their infinite beauty – their shape, scent, color, and size. We hope it will help you share our passion for this most beautiful of flowers.

Charles Quest-Ritson
Brigid Quest-Ritson

CHARLES AND BRIGID QUEST-RITSON

History of the Rose

THE ROSE is the most popular garden flower today, highly valued all over the world for its form, its scent, and its color. This is a recent phenomenon: roses only acquired their present popularity after about 1820. Pinks and auriculas, for example, were more highly esteemed flowers in the 18th century. Nevertheless, the last two centuries have seen tremendous progress in the raising of new roses by crossbreeding and selection. New types have arisen and the season has been prolonged to such an extent that many modern roses flower continuously.

The development of rose breeding started with the import of a handful of Chinese garden roses into Europe some 200 years ago. These roses were crossed with European cultivars to produce the great variety that emerged in the 19th century. The unsung heroes of rose breeding are the gardeners of ancient China who made it all possible.

Types of Rose

Garden roses are grouped in two ways: according to their habits of growth (for example, shrub roses, climbers, groundcover roses), and to their ancestry (Teas, Hybrid Teas, Hybrid Sweetbriars). These groups are not always clear, and they often overlap. They do, however, have a convenient and practical logic which it is worth trying to understand. One of the most useful divisions, though somewhat arbitrary, is between old roses and new, or modern, ones.

ROSA SPINOSISSIMA
The Scotch rose in this etching by Mary Lawrence (1796–1810) is an ancient ancestor of our modern garden roses.

Old roses are those introduced before 1867, or 1900, or 1945, according to an individual's point of view. Sometimes they are called Old Garden Roses, Old-fashioned Roses, Antique Roses, Heritage Roses, or Historic Roses. Many types are once-flowering, including the Albas, Boursaults, Centifolias, Damasks, Gallicas, and Moss roses. The repeat flowerers are the Bourbons, Chinas, Hybrid Perpetuals, Noisettes, Portlands, and Tea roses. They vary enormously between classifications and it is worth studying the characteristics of each classification, so that you know what to expect of them.

The ancestors of our garden roses are the **wild roses** from which all our cultivated varieties are descended. Examples include *Rosa canina*, the dog rose, and *Rosa spinosissima*, the Scotch rose. It is more correct to call them "rose species," rather than "species roses." Wild roses occur all over the northern hemisphere; there are about 150 distinct species. They are naturally variable, even within a single species. *Rosa canina*, for example, can have flowers of dark pink, mid-pink, pale pink, or white.

Old Oriental Roses

Old roses tend to make bushy plants, and their flowers are often most beautiful when fully opened out. They also have thinner petals and do not stand up so well to rain. Opinion is divided on whether they are naturally healthier than modern roses or not, and whether they are more strongly scented, and there are exceptions to every rule – old roses excite passion. Almost every country has a society or group dedicated to them.

China roses are the oldest of the old roses. They are ancient hybrids raised, selected, and grown in China for many centuries. Examples are 'Old Blush' and 'Slater's Crimson', which can be traced back at least 1,000 years. They are the result of hybridization between *Rosa gigantea, Rosa chinensis,* and, probably, *Rosa multiflora.* They are short bushes whose flowers repeat constantly: in hot climates they are ever-blooming. When they were introduced to the West and widely distributed, from about 1750 onward, they gave rise to a European-raised clutch of hybrids which are known as China roses. Examples include 'Fabvier' and 'Hermosa'.

Tea roses are similar to China roses, and share their hybrid ancestry. The most important cultivars for the history of roses were called 'Hume's Blush Tea-scented China' and 'Parks' Yellow Tea-scented China'; both were introduced to Europe from southern China early in the 19th century. They get their name from their characteristic scent of China tea leaves, which is also found in many China roses. They tend to be very tender (only a few are hardy in Zone 7), but are tolerant of drought. Tea roses make medium-sized bushes that need minimal pruning and flower constantly in hot climates: they are popular in Mediterranean climates, especially in California and Australia. They were widely grown in greenhouses as winter-flowering cut flowers in the 19th century. Crossbreeding between them, and sometimes with the China roses and European garden roses, led to the development of thousands of hybrids. Examples are 'Anna Oliver', 'Catherine Mermet', and 'Général Schablikine'.

The **Noisette roses** are a race of roses derived from 'Champneys' Pink Cluster', an American hybrid between the wild *Rosa moschata* and the China rose

SLATER'S CRIMSON
This repeat flowering rose was brought to Europe from China in the mid-18th century.

'Old Blush'. They are hardy climbing roses or semiclimbers, with masses of small flowers in large clusters, produced all through the growing season, or continuously in hot climates. Good examples are 'Noisette Carnée' and 'Bougainville'. Crosses were later made, mostly in France, with Tea roses, which increased the flower size of the Noisette but made them more tender. Examples include 'Mme. Alfred Carrière', 'Maréchal Niel', and 'Bouquet d'Or'. Many of them have large flowers and a tea-like scent. Some were even known as Tea-Noisettes.

OLD EUROPEAN ROSES

Unlike the oldest China roses, no European rose cultivar can be traced back before about 1400. There is nothing to link the simple Gallicas and Albas that can be identified in late medieval paintings to the roses of ancient Greece, Rome, or Persia.

Gallica roses may indeed have been cultivated 2,500 years ago, but we can put no names to them. They are selections and hybrids of *Rosa gallica*, a short suckering rose which is native to southern and central Europe from Spain to Slovakia and eastward to Turkey. They were greatly developed by French hybridists in the early years of the 19th century, and their large, sweetly scented flowers place them among the most lovely of all garden plants. They make medium-sized bushes – very hardy, once-flowering, and tolerant of poor soils.

Alba roses are early hybrids between the Gallicas and a relation of the dog rose, perhaps *Rosa villosa*. Because of a genetic oddity associated with the Caninae roses, the Albas are actually two-thirds dog rose and only one-third Gallica. They too were hybridized early in the 19th century, but less extensively than the Gallicas. Albas have pink or white flowers that are medium-sized and strongly scented. The plants are tall (6–10ft/2–3m), with a lanky habit of growth and gray or glaucous leaves. They are very hardy, but once-flowering. Examples include: 'Alba Maxima', 'Great Maiden's Blush', and 'Königin von Dänemark'.

No one knows the origins of the **Centifolia roses**, or how to define them. They certainly have similarities to the Gallica roses, and to the Damasks (see below). All we know is that they are hybrids, and that they first occurred in the Netherlands in about 1600. They have large, globular, pink flowers, very sweetly scented. The bushes are lax, open and prickly, growing to about 4–5ft (1.5m). Good examples include 'Centifolia' itself and its sports, 'Unique' and 'Spong'. Many of the other roses sometimes classified as Centifolias, including 'Fantin Latour' and 'Tour de Malakoff', are best regarded as hybrids with China roses.

While all the above old European roses are once-flowering, some of the **Damasks** are repeat flowering. We know from recent DNA tests that the early Damask roses like 'Kazanlik' and 'York and Lancaster' result from the cross (*Rosa gallica* x *Rosa moschata*) x *Rosa fedtschenkoana*, which means that they probably originated in central Asia and only found their way to Europe as economic migrants. They are very hardy and prickly, with a lax habit of growth and soft green or grey-green leaves. They grow to 4–6ft (1.5–2m). Forms were selected over the years for their larger flowers and greater number of petals, but an important new form occurred in about 1620 – 'Quatre Saisons'. This was genetically almost identical to other Damasks, but possessed of the miraculous gift of flowering more than once, known as "remontancy." The Damasks were widely crossed with other roses in the early 19th century, giving rise to such exquisite beauties as 'Mme. Hardy' and "Ville de Bruxelles."

The autumn-flowering Damasks, sometimes known as '**Damask Perpetuals**', gave rise to two very important developments – the Moss roses and the Portlands.

Mossiness is mutation that has occurred several times in the history of the rose, whereby the sepals, calyces and pedicels are covered in a growth that resembles moss. This moss is hard to the touch and sticky, and it smells of resin. **Moss roses** were widely bred and selected by French breeders in the middle of the 19th century,

"CABBAGE" ROSES IN ART
Centifolia roses, or old "cabbage" roses, appeared frequently in 17th- and 18th-century flower paintings, such as this "Roses in a Glass Vase on a Ledge" by Cornelis van Spaendonck (1756–1840)

especially by the nursery of Moreau & Robert. Some are repeat flowerers, others only once-flowering. Good examples are 'William Lobb', 'Henri Martin', and 'Salet'.

The **Portland roses** are repeat flowering roses that descend either from the original 'Portland Rose' or from hybrids between Gallicas and repeat flowering Damasks. 'Rose du Roi' and 'Yolande d'Aragon' are good examples, though many of the later Portland roses (like 'Comte de Chambord') are thought to have a touch of China rose in their ancestry. They originated in England, and were named after a Duchess of Portland. 'Portland Rose' is low and spreading, like a feeble Gallica, but later hybrids tend to be upright and stocky, with very short nodes which give them a dense, leafy look.

When the European roses were crossed with the Chinas and the Teas, the first recognizably modern roses began to emerge, though the Bourbons and the Hybrid Perpetuals are generally categorized as "old" rather than "new." The **Bourbon roses** get their name from the Île de Bourbon (now Réunion) where the original 'Bourbon Rose' is said to have occurred as a spontaneous hybrid between 'Old Blush' and 'Quatre Saisons'. They are repeat flowering roses that descend either from the original or from similar crosses between China roses and repeat flowering Damasks. They are 6–10ft (2–3m) tall, with an open habit, glossy leaves, and large, beautiful, sweet-scented flowers. They are reliably repeat flowering, but not as hardy as the European roses. They are also the most susceptible of all roses to blackspot and mildew, though they respond well to good cultivation. Some famous examples include 'Louise Odier' and 'Souvenir de la Malmaison'.

The **Hybrid Perpetual roses** are closely related to the Bourbons, but descended from crosses between China roses and Portlands rather than Damasks. 'Gloire des Rosomanes' is generally thought of as the forerunner of the Hybrid Perpetuals, which were the most popular garden roses until the end of the 19th century. They generally have very large flowers and indeed were bred for their size as cut flowers, to win competitive prizes at exhibitions – horticultural shows were a great innovation of the 19th century. Thousands of Hybrid Perpetuals were introduced, of which less than 600 survive today, mainly in specialist collections. They make coarse, open, vigorous plants, best pegged down to maximize their flowering. All flower more than once, though the second flowering is often sparse. Good examples of Hybrid Perpetuals are 'Général Jacqueminot' and 'Jules Margottin'.

THE ROSE OF MALMAISON
The Empress Josephine with her courtiers, in a section reproduced from 'The Rose of Malmaison', oil on canvas, painted c.*1867 by Jean Louis Victor (1819–79).*

Unusual 19th-century Hybrids

The rose industry as we know it was invented by the French from about 1815 onward. French breeders and growers produced a strong stream of new roses of every type throughout the 19th century. The industry quickly became driven by novelty, and has remained the creature of fashion ever since. By the last quarter of the 19th century, it was dominated by French Hybrid Perpetuals and Tea roses. Then a change began to take place. Plant hunters had for centuries introduced new plants into cultivation from other parts of the world. The expeditions and their botanical booty increased enormously toward the end of the century, and introduced a large number of new rose species from eastern Asia. Horticulturists in Europe and America, both amateur and professional, started to cross these Asian species with the Hybrid Perpetuals and Tea roses to produce new races and groups of garden roses. **Rugosa roses** are a good example. *Rosa rugosa* is a large-flowered, hardy, thrifty, perpetually flowering species from Japan, Korea, Siberia, and China. When it was crossed with European roses, it produced large (7–8ft/2.5m) shrubby plants, which were extremely hardy and floriferous with large, scented flowers and big, red hips. They are repeat-flowering and easy to grow: 'Mme. Georges Bruant' and 'Mrs. Anthony Waterer' are good examples from the 1890s, but *Rosa rugosa* has continued to be used in rose breeding ever since and some of our best modern shrub roses are derived from it.

Sir Joseph Banks
This portrait of the prodigious plant hunter who discovered Rosa banksiae *was painted by Sir Joshua Reynolds (1732–92).*

Meanwhile, in England, Lord Penzance bred **Hybrid Sweetbriars** by crossing the native *Rosa rubiginosa*, mainly with Hybrid Perpetuals. A little later, in the 1920s, Wilhelm Kordes in Germany started – somewhat more successfully – to raise dog-rose hybrids from the native *Rosa canina*. They are called the **Macrantha roses**: 'Daisy Hill' and 'Raubritter' are among the best known.

From the late 1890s onward, two climbing species were extensively hybridized and completely transformed our gardens. *Rosa multiflora* gave us the **Multiflora ramblers** and *Rosa wichurana* the **Wichurana ramblers**. Many were bred from 'Turner's Crimson Rambler', a Chinese hybrid between the two species with a dose of *Rosa chinensis* in its makeup. They burst into gardens in the early years of the 20th century and changed their design to incorporate rose-covered arches, pergolas, walls, and trelliswork: thus were their long, flexible branches shown to best advantage. Most bore large clusters of small flowers in extraordinary profusion and flowered only once, though some repeated and others had larger flowers. To this day, there is nothing to match their floriferousness when in full flower: it quite surpasses any other type of rose. Many of the best Wichurana ramblers were raised by Barbier in France, but many more – and Multiflora ramblers too – by rose breeders in Germany, England, and the US. From 1890 onward, France's position as the leading producer of roses was challenged. Good examples of the Wichurana ramblers are 'Albéric Barbier' and 'Dr. W. Van Fleet'; leading Multiflora ramblers include 'Tausendschön' and Goldfinch, while the 'Turner's Crimson Rambler' types are represented by 'Dorothy Perkins' and 'Excelsa'.

Some of the seedlings of Multiflora and Wichurana ramblers turned out not to be climbers but dwarf shrubs, with large clusters of small flowers which were borne perpetually all through the growing season. These were known as **Polyanthas** – hardy, floriferous, and sometimes showy. Good examples include 'Katharina Zeimet' and 'Maman Turbat'.

The Birth of Modern Roses

Modern roses begin with the **Hybrid Teas**. These arose as crosses between the hardy, vigorous Hybrid Perpetuals and the tender, perpetually flowering Tea roses.

The first hybrids were accidents of birth caused by the transfer of pollen by bees or wind – 'La France', for example, which some maintain is the first "modern" rose. From about 1880 onward, Henry Bennett in England and Joseph Pernet-Ducher in France raised new Hybrid Teas by deliberate cross-pollination. Peter Lambert in Germany soon followed. The results were spectacularly better than anything that had gone before, and so the future of the Hybrid Teas was assured. They combined the elegance of the Tea roses with the constitution of the Hardy Perpetuals. They were hardy in most of western and central Europe and they flowered perpetually. Early examples include 'Mme. Caroline Testout' and 'Lady Mary Fitzwilliam'. Soon the Northern Irish firms of Dickson and McGredy joined Lambert and Pernet-Ducher as leading breeders of Hybrid Teas.

In the 21st century they remain the most widely grown and popular of all roses – and, many would say, the best. Their flowers are large (up to 7in/18cm across), exquisitely shaped, and borne singly on long, sturdy stems, perfect for cutting. Most are strongly scented. Thanks to Joseph Pernet-Ducher's efforts in breeding yellow roses with *Rosa foetida*, the Hybrid Teas now come in every color except pure blue. They are upright shrubs with thick, stiff stems – less attractively shaped than the old roses, but fine when massed on their own account and easy to blend into mixed plantings. In hot climates they flower year-round. The history of roses from 1900 onward is the story of crossing and back-crossing the Hybrid Teas to every other class of rose.

Hybrid Musk roses were first raised by Pemberton in England and Lambert in Germany, by crossing bushy Multiflora ramblers with Hybrid Teas. They are loose shrubs in northern Europe but strong climbers in hot climates: 'Penelope' and 'Felicia' are the best-known examples. They have large clusters of strongly scented, medium-sized flowers all through the growing season. **Hybrid Polyanthas** were the result of crossing Hybrid Teas with dwarf Polyanthas, and were sometimes known as the Poulsen roses after the Danish firm that bred them – 'Else Poulsen' is one of the most popular.

Further back-crossing to Hybrid Teas turned the Polyanthas into the **Floribunda roses**, which gained in popularity after about 1950 and are second only to the Hybrid Teas in public esteem today. They have the same range of bright colors as Hybrid Teas but their flowers are smaller and borne in clusters. This makes them effective as roses for mass plantings, whether in public or private gardens, but they also combine well with other plants and have a very long season of flower – 12 months of the year in hot climates. The early Floribundas were often scentless, but these days most are scented. Likewise, early Floribundas tended to have single or semidouble flowers, while the best modern cultivars have large clusters of fully double flowers which are individually shaped like Hybrid Teas. In fact, the line between modern Hybrid Teas and Floribundas is hard to draw. In America there is a class for intermediates – roses of unusual vigor, with clusters of Hybrid Tea type flowers – called Grandifloras. No other country follows this precedent and, in any case, the Grandifloras merge imperceptibly into both Hybrid Teas and Floribundas.

Climbing Roses

Climbing roses are popular both with people whose enthusiasm is for old roses and with lovers of the new. Most derive from a group of wild species called the Synstylae, which have a lot of small white flowers in large clusters. Most of the hybrid groups are small, including the **Ayrshire roses** from *Rosa arvensis*, **Banksian roses** from *Rosa banksiae*, **Hybrid Sempervirens** or Evergreen roses from *Rosa sempervirens* and **Hybrid Setigera** or Prairie roses from *Rosa setigera*.

It was discovered early on that China roses and Tea roses sometimes produce **climbing sports** of great vigor. A bush-rose throws out a shoot that is much taller than the rest of the bush and produces no flowers until the following year. These sports are sometimes noticed, propagated, and introduced as a "climbing" form of the original bush-rose. The first were climbing Chinas and climbing Teas: examples are 'Climbing Pompon de Paris' and 'Climbing Devoniensis'. During the 19th century these sports appeared from time to time among other hybrid groups with China roses and Tea roses in their ancestry – hence climbing Bourbons and climbing Hybrid Perpetuals. Later came climbing Polyanthas, climbing Hybrid Teas ('Climbing Peace'), climbing Floribundas ('Climbing Iceberg'), climbing Grandifloras, and even climbing miniatures. The climbing Hybrid Teas, in particular, were issued in great numbers from 1930 onward, and tended to replace the old ramblers in popularity. They were exactly the same as the bush roses from which they sported in all respects except their

'Paul's Lemon Pillar' and 'Dr. Huey'

The light yellow 'Paul's Lemon Pillar' and dark red 'Dr. Huey' are fine examples of modern large-flowered climbers. Here they are shown growing together at David Ruston's garden in Renmark, Australia.

height: the flowers too were always slightly larger, though less freely repeated. Some were reputed to flower only once, though abundantly.

Rose breeders sought to create large-flowered climbers that repeated reliably throughout the season. Many **modern climbers** (or "large-flowered" climbers) were bred by crossing the larger-flowered Wichurana ramblers like 'New Dawn' with modern Floribundas and Hybrid Teas. The best of the seedlings would have large flowers, a climbing habit, and nonstop flowers: 'Parade' and Penny Lane are good examples. Other climbers were selected from unusually vigorous seedlings of Hybrid Teas and Floribundas – those that grew to 10ft (3m) or more, and flowered continuously. There might be a trace of the Wichurana ramblers a long way back, but only as distant ancestors: these super-vigorous modern climbers include 'Handel' and Compassion. The shorter ones might also be introduced as pillar roses. Some modern climbers were bred for specific purposes with new genes from little-used species: the Kordesii hybrids like 'Parkdirektor Riggers' and 'Dortmund' were bred for hardiness and the Hybrid Giganteas like 'Nancy Hayward' for their adaptability to hot climates.

'MME. A MEILLAND'
This historic rose, also known as 'Peace', was introduced in France in 1942. It became the world's favorite rose, and did much to advance the popularity of roses as garden plants.

THE DEVELOPMENT OF MODERN ROSES

Miniature roses arose from the 1930s onward through crossing short China roses with Polyanthas. Ralph Moore in California then crossed them with many other types of rose, so they now resemble miniature Hybrid Teas and Mosses – and we even have miniature climbers.

During the 1970s, the frontier between the larger miniature roses (larger in flower size and height) and the smaller Floribundas seemed to merge; the intermediates are now sometimes lumped together as patio roses. At about the same time, breeders realized that new markets were opening for groundcover roses, especially in public landscaping designs where hundreds of roses, all of one cultivar, are planted in vast masses to provide cheerful color and smother weeds. They had to be easy to grow and dense in their habit, wider than tall, and handsome in leaf. Many had *Rosa wichurana* or *Rosa sempervirens* in their background. Roses like Sommerwind and Bonica 82 have been immensely successful as landscape roses, but they also make good individual plants for gardens.

Any rose raised in the last 100 years that does not fit neatly into a defined category is called a **shrub rose**. This includes primary hybrids like 'Dupontii', overly large Floribundas like 'Fred Loads' and most of the superhardy Buck, Explorer, and Parkland roses. The definition of a shrub rose incorporates no indication of size, flowering habit, hardiness, or other essential characteristic. It follows that, before acquiring a shrub rose, you need to know what you are letting yourself in for. They include, however, some of the most rewarding of all roses. Some are separated out and given distinct names, like the early Scotch Roses, bred from *Rosa spinosissima*. The best were bred by Wilhelm Kordes in the 1930s and 1940s – 'Frühlingsmorgen' and 'Karl Förster' in particular.

MARY ROSE
Combining fragrance and vigor, Mary Rose, one of David Austin's English Roses, is a modern shrub that is popular worldwide.

By far the most famous shrub roses now are the English Roses bred by David Austin over the past 25 years. These are intended to combine the best of the old roses (Damask scent, complex blooms) with the best of the new (health, vigor, thick petals, repeat flowering). Many consider beauties like Abraham Darby, Graham Thomas, and Mary Rose as the best of the Austin roses. It is also true to describe them as the best of the new.

ROSES IN THE 21ST CENTURY

New roses are always seen at the time as an improvement on what has gone before, and many see the history of roses over the last two centuries as a steady progress toward perfection. Nevertheless, the charms of such old garden roses as the Gallicas and Damasks have generated specialized societies in many countries dedicated to the conservation and enjoyment of "historic" or "heritage" roses.

Rose breeders claim that their main preoccupation is to raise new roses that are resistant to mildew and blackspot, the fungal diseases that plague existing cultivars in cool, wet climates. As businessmen, they are concerned with making money too, which means that other traits are often more highly valued: floriferousness, drought resistance, winter hardiness, and continuous flowering. But the biggest rewards, more likely to result from genetic manipulation than natural mutation, are no doubt reserved for the raiser of the first truly blue rose.

How To Use This Book

ENCYCLOPEDIA OF ROSES is an authoritative guide to choosing and growing roses. It contains three main sections. The first section provides a brief history of the rose – its origins and development through the centuries – and describes the various types and groups of roses found in gardens around the world today. The 400-page main section is devoted to the A–Z of roses, an alphabetical listing of internationally popular and widely available wild and cultivated roses. Almost every rose in the A–Z is illustrated with a color photograph. Within the A–Z, also listed alphabetically by name, illustrated feature boxes provide supplementary information on associated topics of interest. The final section, cultivating roses, gives practical, straightforward information on caring for these easy to grow garden plants.

There are approximately 2,000 roses of every kind, photographed all over the world, featured within this encyclopedia. The authors hope this will become an invaluable reference for rose lovers and gardeners everywhere.

A–Z OF ROSES

Within the A–Z, roses are listed under the name by which they were first introduced in their country of origin. The famous rose 'Peace', for example, was introduced in France by its breeder, Meilland, as 'Mme. A. Meilland', and so can be found in its alphabetical position within the "M" section of the A–Z. Because so many roses are known by different names in different countries, the A–Z contains cross-references throughout to take readers to the rose they are looking for. Occasionally, the author and other plant finder resources differ on rose names. For this reason, readers should read the notes on nomenclature on p.4 and refer to the species index on p.445 if they are unable to locate a rose.

COLOR MAGIC

C

Color Magic

syn. 'JACMAG'
Hybrid Tea

ORIGIN **Warriner, US, 1978**
PARENTAGE **seedling x 'Spellbinder'**
FLOWER SIZE **5.9in (15cm)**
SCENT **Medium and sweet**
FLOWERING **Repeats**
HEIGHT/SPREAD **4.9ft (1.5m)/3.3ft (1m)**
HARDINESS **Zone 6**
AWARDS **AARS 1978**

Some roses change color in response to light and heat: the exact color of Color Magic at any given time depends upon both. It also grows in size as it opens, becoming largest in cool weather. The flowers are pale pink at first, but darken with age from the outside, so that the center is always paler than the outer petals, which finish almost crimson. The shape of the flowers is beautiful at all stages of growth, so it is a great pleasure to watch an individual flower develop

COLOR MAGIC

over several days. The flowers have large petals and are borne singly on very long stems. The plant has medium-dark leaves and quite a lot of prickles.

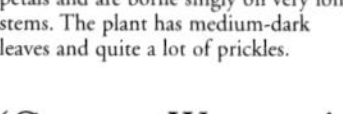

'Colour Wonder'

see 'KÖNIGIN DER ROSEN'

'Commandant Beaurepaire'

Bourbon

ORIGIN **Moreau-Robert, France, 1874**
FLOWER SIZE **2.8in (7cm)**
SCENT **Strong and sweet**
FLOWERING **Once only**
HEIGHT/SPREAD **5.7ft (1.75m)/4.9ft (1.5m)**
HARDINESS **Zone 5**

It is usually described as a Bourbon rose, but 'Commandant Beaurepaire' is in some ways closer to two other striped roses – 'Honorine de Brabant' and 'Variegata di Bologna' – than to any of the better-known Bourbons. All three striped cultivars have the same cupped flowers, the same penetrating lemony sweet scent, the same large, pale leaves, and the same long, pointed leaflets. 'Commandant Beaurepaire' has stripes and splashes of purple and white on a pink base. The pattern of colors is

'COMMANDANT BEAUREPAIRE'

completely irregular, but the overall effect is pinker than 'Honorine de Brabant' and 'Variegata di Bologna'.

Coloma

…OF A FLEMISH CASTLE, THE ROSE GARDEN AT COLOMA IN …STS A COLLECTION OF NEARLY 60,000 PLANTS

…the Environment and Infrastructure of the Flemish Community – is imaginatively designed and its collections are excellent. Nearly 3,000 different roses and 60,000 rose plants are displayed within its 5.5 acres (2.2 hectares) in three principal areas. One area features a complete collection of Belgian-raised roses, with dozens of first-rate cultivars that are little known outside the country. The Belgians – no matter how good their roses – have to work hard to earn recognition. This is because nurseries in countries with small home markets often have difficulty competing with the well-capitalized operations of rivals in larger countries. At Coloma, the work of Hippolite Delforge and Louis Lens is especially well-represented – here are the splendid Floribunda 'Hortiflora' (Delforge, 1974) and Lens's ground-breaking species hybrids 'Pink Surprise' (1987) and 'Jelena de Belder' (1996). The magnificent roses from the government experimental breeding station, RVS, include the golden Hybrid Tea 'Enghien' (1989).

Another area of the rose garden is dedicated to historical roses of every sort, systematically and stylishly displayed. They include such rarities as the Hybrid Perpetual 'Charlemagne' (Dubreuil, 1888).

The largest collection of the three, however, features roses from all over the world. This displays a representative selection arranged country by country and breeder by breeder. German and British roses are especially comprehensive, but countries such as Israel, Hungary, and Switzerland each have their place. The Netherlands occupies a large area, where the fine 'Mies Bouwman' (Buisman, 1973) grows, and there are extensive collections from the rose-growing nations of Canada and Australia, whose roses are rarely seen in western Europe.

'ENGHIEN'

COLOMA CASTLE

'Complicata'

Gallica

PARENTAGE ***Rosa gallica* x *Rosa canina***
FLOWER SIZE **4.7in (12cm)**
SCENT **Light and sweet**
FLOWERING **Once only**
HEIGHT/SPREAD **8.2ft (2.5m)/4.9ft (1.5m)**
HARDINESS **Zone 5**

The name is a tease: 'Complicata' is the most sublimely simple of all cultivated roses. DNA tests have proved it to be a hybrid between the French rose *Rosa gallica* and the dog rose *Rosa canina*. It is most …

Commandant Cousteau

syn. 'ADHARMAN'
Hybrid Tea

ORIGIN **Adam, Franc…**
FLOWER SIZE **2.8in (7…**
SCENT **Very strong a…**
FLOWERING **Repeats…**
HEIGHT/SPREAD **2.7ft…**
HARDINESS **Zone 6**
AWARDS **Nantes FA… de France 1993**

Commandant Cousteau – named after the French marine explorer and oceanographer – was Michel Adam's first great success as a breeder. It won not only the top prize in the Bagatelle trials but also a special biennial award for the most strongly scented new rose: the Prix International de la Ville de Nantes. "Fruity, raspberry, classic, vinous" were some of the adjectives in the winning citation. The shapely flowers are bright crimson, with dark pink petal backs, occasionally splashed or streaked with white. They have short petals and come in clusters of 3–7 …

Rose names
The rose's botanical or cultivar name is given here. Cultivar names are in Roman type with single quotes. Registered or trade names appear in sans serif typeface without quotes. All species of Rosa *are given in italics.*

Synonyms and code names
These are other names under which a rose may be sold or described. Code names are usually composed of three capital letters (usually an abbreviation of the breeder's name) and lower case letters to give a unique word that identifies the rose.

Classification group
Roses have been widely hybridized to produce many different groups of shrubs suitable for different purposes in the garden (see pp.8–13).

Origin and parentage
For wild roses, the origin tells you where the rose species occurs naturally in the wild. For cultivars, the breeder, country, and date of introduction, or the rose's appearance are given. Where this information is unknown or in doubt, it has been omitted.

Flower size and scent
The average size of the flowers is given and their scent is described. Please note that perceptions of scent differ: readers may not always agree.

Flowering
The continuity of flowering is described here, with details (where relevant) on when this occurs – early, mid-, or late in the season.

Height and spread
The average height and spread are given, though these details may vary according to site, growing conditions, climate, and the age of the plant.

Feature panels
Through special articles, such as this feature panel on one of Belgium's finest rose gardens, the authors provide an insight into places and people of interest throughout the rose world.

CARE AND CULTIVATION

Roses should be low-maintenance garden plants, and the section on caring for and cultivating roses reflects this. From choosing and buying to planting, pruning, feeding, and watering roses, and keeping them disease-free, this 10-page practical section gives gardeners all the information they need in order to grow roses sucessfully and obtain maximum rewards for minimum effort.

CULTIVATING ROSES

PLANTING AND GROWING ROSES

Planting Bare-root Roses

Planting Container-grown Roses

GROWING IN CONTAINERS

Planting and Staking Standard Roses

Feeding and Routine Care

DETACHING SUCKERS

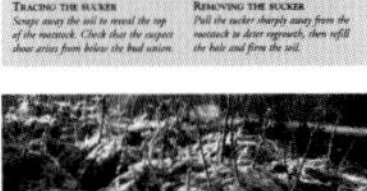

Awards

Where a rose has won several awards (see box, below right) these are listed in date order, according to the year in which the award was given.

COMMANDANT COUSTEAU

'COMPLICATA'

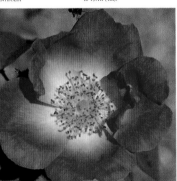

'COMTE DE CHAMBORD'

'COMPASSION'

'HIGHFIELD'

Hardiness zone

For each rose, a minimum hardiness zone is given to indicate the preferred climate of the plant (see box, right).

Special entry boxes

Where roses have produced sports, or mutations caused by spontaneous genetic changes, the parent plant and the sport (or sports) are featured together in special boxes to highlight their similarities.

Family tree

Arrows are used to help readers recognize the relationship between a rose "parent" and its sport (or sports) at a glance.

Cross-references

Where a rose has another name, or synonym, cross-references have been included to refer you to the name under which the rose is listed.

Information on sports

Most sports, being genetic mutations of the parent plant, share very similar characteristics. Where these differ, the details are given here.

HARDINESS ZONES

For each rose, the minimum hardiness zone is indicated, for example, Zone 6 for 'Mme. A. Meilland' ('Peace'). This means that the rose will survive winter temperatures of 0 to -10°F (-18 to -23°C), but not colder conditions than this. The information is based on the Plant Hardiness Zones system developed by the US Department of Agriculture.

Minimum average temperature

°C	Zone	°F
-40 to -35	3	-40 to -30
-35 to -29	4	-30 to -20
-29 to -23	5	-20 to -10
-23 to -18	6	-10 to 0
-18 to -12	7	0 to 10
-12 to -7	8	10 to 20
-1 to 5	9	30 to 40

ROSE AWARDS

New roses are tested in trial grounds throughout the world. European trial centers are situated in Belfast, Dublin, Geneva, Lyon, Madrid, Paris, Rome, and The Hague. Roses are judged on their reliability and excellence over two or more years, and if deemed worthy of merit, may qualify for gold medals or fragrance medals. Also important are the French and German trials, the former at Bagatelle and the latter leading to the ADR award.

In the US, the All-America Rose Selections (AARS) trials take place all over the country, from Florida to Minnesota and Arizona, and awards are given to only a few roses that have performed exceptionally well.

In the UK, the Royal National Rose Society stages exhaustive tests of roses' suitability for English conditions. The President's International Trophy is the top award, followed by gold medals.

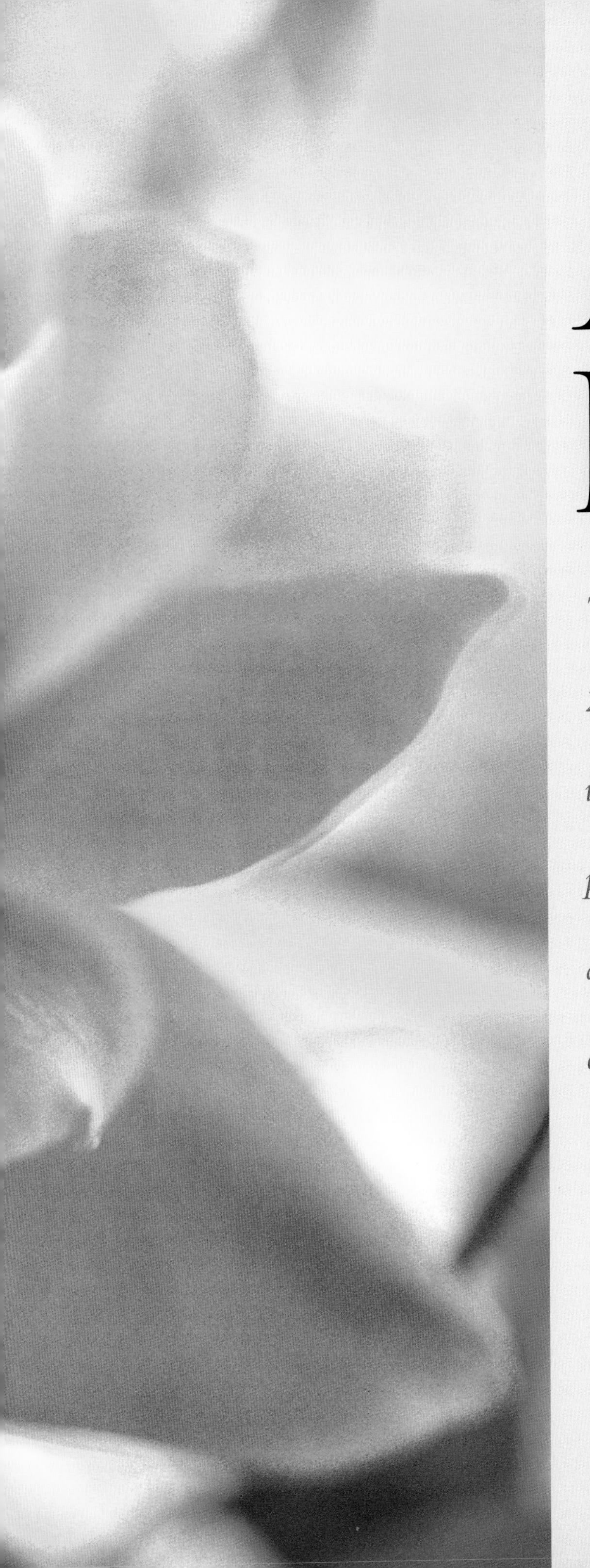

A–Z *of* ROSES

This directory features approximately 2,000 different roses from around the world. Some are already internationally popular, others are less well-known but are available in most countries and deserve to be more widely grown.

A Caen la Paix

syn. 'ORAKAH'

Hybrid Tea

ORIGIN **Orard, France, 1990**
FLOWER SIZE **3.9in (10cm)**
SCENT **Light and sweet**
FLOWERING **Recurrent**
HEIGHT/SPREAD **3.9ft (1.2m)/2.7ft (80cm)**
HARDINESS **Zone 6**

All Hybrid Teas are pretty in the bud but only a few are pretty when they open out. A Caen la Paix starts with the long, elegant, conical shape that is the hallmark of the Hybrid Teas, but its later shape is unusual for its neat circular outline and closely overlapping ("imbricated") petals. Its color is out of the ordinary too: deep cyclamen pink, with a hint of mauve. The purple shade intensifies with age, as the bright pink fades away. The flowers are usually carried singly, on long stems, and last well once cut. A Caen la Paix is the name of an annual arts festival in May in Caen in Normandy, France.

'A. MacKenzie'

syn. 'Alexander MacKenzie'

Shrub Rose

ORIGIN **Svejda, Canada, 1985**
PARENTAGE **'Queen Elizabeth' x ('Red Dawn' x 'Suzanne')**
FLOWER SIZE **2.4in (6cm)**
SCENT **Very light and fruity**
FLOWERING **Repeats**
HEIGHT/SPREAD **5.7ft (1.75m)/4.9ft (1.5m)**
HARDINESS **Zone 4**

'A. MacKenzie' is one of the Explorer roses bred by Dr. Felicitas Svejda in Ottawa to survive the bitter Canadian winters. It commemorates Sir Alexander MacKenzie (1763–1820), the Scottish-born explorer who was the first man to travel overland to the Pacific coast in British Columbia. Its flowers come in clusters of 5–15 and open from elegant buds. They are bright, pale crimson and fully double, set off by large, medium-dark, glossy leaves, which are reddish when young. The plant has an arching habit of growth and can be grown either as a loose shrub or as a short climber. In cool climates, it produces a second flush of flowers in autumn, but it grows surprisingly well in hot climates too, where it will reach 6.6ft (2m) and flower on and off throughout the year. It sometimes acquires a little blackspot late in the year.

'A. MacKenzie'

A Caen la Paix

A Shropshire Lad

syn. 'AUSled'

Shrub Rose

ORIGIN **Austin, Britain, 1996**
FLOWER SIZE **3.1in (8cm)**
SCENT **Strong and fruity**
FLOWERING **Repeats**
HEIGHT/SPREAD **4.1ft (1.25m)/2.7ft (80cm)**
HARDINESS **Zone 6**

The soft peachy pink colors of this beautiful English Rose from David Austin combine beautifully with other plantings. The flower opens out into a lightly cupped rosette, full of many small quilled petals at the center. The flowers are strongly peach colored, but paler toward the edge of the flower, and at the edge of the petals themselves, where they are mother-of-pearl or almost white. The petal backs are deep rose-red, which gives the flower its rich tones. The flowers come in clusters of 3–10 and are set off by dark, healthy leaves. The plant is vigorous and upright: in hot climates it will reach 6.6ft (2m). *A Shropshire Lad* is a collection of poems by the English poet A. E. Housman.

A Shropshire Lad

Abbaye de Cluny

syn. 'MEIbrinpay'

Hybrid Tea

ORIGIN **Meilland, France, 1993**
PARENTAGE **'Just Joey' x (Louis de Funès x Sun King '74)**
FLOWER SIZE **3.9in (10cm)**
SCENT **Very light, but said to be spicy**
FLOWERING **Repeats well**
HEIGHT/SPREAD **4.1ft (1.25m)/3.3ft (1m)**
HARDINESS **Zone 5**
AWARDS **Monza GM 1993; Belfast GM 1994; Lyon GM 1994; Plus Belle Rose de France 1994**

Abbaye de Cluny is one of Meilland's Romantica series – a new rose in the old-fashioned style. The flowers are a gentle apricot color, with somewhat more orange or copper toward the tips of the petals and creaminess toward the base – a very beautiful combination. The double flowers have an attractive cabbagelike shape, and come usually singly but occasionally in twos and threes. The bush makes vigorous growth, with masses of handsome leaves that are exceptionally healthy and resistant to blackspot. It repeats well, so that the flowers are almost continuously borne, and will grow to about 3.3ft (1m) in France but almost twice that height in hot climates. It is named after the great Benedictine Abbey at Cluny near Mâcon, which was largely destroyed during the French Revolution.

Abbeyfield Rose

syn. 'COCbrose'

Hybrid Tea

ORIGIN **Cocker, Britain, 1983**
PARENTAGE **'National Trust' x 'Silver Jubilee'**
FLOWER SIZE **4.7in (12cm)**
SCENT **Medium and sweet**
FLOWERING **Repeats**
HEIGHT/SPREAD **3.3ft (1m)/2.7ft (80cm)**
HARDINESS **Zone 6**
AWARDS **Glasgow GM 1990**

The flowers of Abbeyfield Rose are rich, dark pink, with even darker backs to the petals – dark enough to be described as cherry or pale crimson. The petals are large – both long and broad – but not too numerous, so that the flower is elegantly shaped as it opens out, and stands up well to heavy rain. The petals eventually reflex quite strongly, and reveal a mass of deep yellow stamens at the centre. Abbeyfield Rose has dark green, glossy leaves (crimson when young) and may need protection from blackspot late in the year. The plant is of average height, bushy, and very prickly. It is popular in Great Britain, but little known elsewhere.

Abbaye de Cluny

Abbeyfield Rose

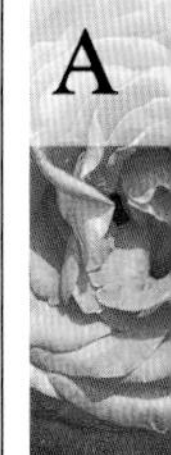

'ABBOTSWOOD'

'ABBOTSWOOD'

Hybrid Canina

ORIGIN **Hilling, Britain, 1954**
PARENTAGE ***Rosa canina* × unknown**
FLOWER SIZE **2–2.4in (5–6cm)**
SCENT **Light and sweet**
FLOWERING **Once, midseason**
HEIGHT/SPREAD **8.2ft (2.5m)/8.2ft (2.5m)**
HARDINESS **Zone 5**

'Abbotswood' was found as a seedling in the kitchen garden attached to the Abbotswood estate in Gloucestershire. It was introduced by Hilling through the good offices of their then employee, the rosarian Graham Thomas. To all intents, 'Abbotswood' resembles a semi-double form of the British native dog rose *Rosa canina*. The flowers open clear rose pink and fade to pale pink. The petal backs are slightly paler and there is a whitish patch at the center of the flower. This forms a good foil for the golden stamens, which are splayed out around the edge of the circular stigma. The flowers come in clusters, usually of 3–6, and have very long sepals. The leaves are fairly small and light green, with very toothed leaflets. The plant is vigorous, arching, and thorny, with long lasting hips in autumn and winter. If seed is sown, the resultant plants come true to their parent. Opinion is divided as to whether 'Abbotswood' is a naturally occurring double-flowered form of the wild dog rose, or whether it is a hybrid. Most species of the *Caninae* section of the genus experience an irregular form of meiosis, or cell division. Instead of splitting equally, four-fifths of a cell creates the seed embryo and only one-fifth turns into pollen. This, and a tendency to self-pollination, may explain why 'Abbotswood' so closely resembles the wild *Rosa canina* and why it comes true from seed. In any case, a mature plant in full flower is more than a match for any other shrub rose.

ABRAHAM DARBY

syn. 'AUSCOT'

Shrub Rose

ORIGIN **Austin, Britain, 1985**
PARENTAGE **'Yellow Cushion' × 'Aloha'**
FLOWER SIZE **4.3in (11cm)**
SCENT **Strong, spicy, and fruity**
FLOWERING **Repeats well**
HEIGHT/SPREAD **4.9ft (1.5m)/4.1ft (1.25m)**
HARDINESS **Zone 6**

Abraham Darby is one of the most successful and popular of David Austin's English Roses, and unusually, it was entirely bred from modern roses. The flowers are a glowing coppery apricot (a color never seen in old roses) with pinker outer petals, fading to soft peach pink and cream. They are more coppery in hot weather, and pinker in cool, and they open from yellow buds. The flowers are large, lightly cupped, and very full of petals, which they hold on to for too long, even when they have turned brown and died. They are borne singly or in small clusters (typically of three flowers). The plant has good, dark, glossy leaves and many large prickles. Rust may be a problem. The plant will reach 6.6ft (2m) in all directions in hot climates, or 9.8ft (3m) as a climber. It is one of the first to bloom and most continuous. Abraham Darby (1678–1717) was an English pioneer of the Industrial Revolution.

ABRAHAM DARBY

ACAPELLA

syn. 'TANALLEOA'

Hybrid Tea

ORIGIN **Tantau, Germany, 1994**
FLOWER SIZE **5.5in (14cm)**
SCENT **Very strong and sweet**
FLOWERING **Repeats well**
HEIGHT/SPREAD **4.9ft (1.5m)/3.3ft (1m)**
HARDINESS **Zone 6**
AWARDS **Le Rœulx GM 1998**

The flowers of Acapella are very large and full of petals. They open from large buds and are distinctly cupped at first but, once the petals have unfurled completely, they sometimes exhibit a button eye. Nevertheless, Acapella is a true Hybrid Tea rose, with flowers that are borne individually at the ends of long, strong, upright stems. The flowers are deepest pink or pale crimson, with silver white petal backs, and they keep their color well. The plant is very vigorous, with large leaves, an upright habit of growth, and quite a lot of prickles. In hot climates it will reach 6.6ft (2m). The vigor, size, color, and scent of the flowers amount to a powerful combination of attractions.

ACAPELLA

ACE OF HEARTS

see ASSO DI CUORI

ROSA ACICULARIS

Wild Rose

FLOWER SIZE **2in (5cm)**
SCENT **Light and sweet**
FLOWERING **Once, early in season**
HEIGHT/SPREAD **4.9ft (1.5m)/3.3ft (1m)**
HARDINESS **Zone 3**

Hardiness is the outstanding quality of *Rosa acicularis*, and it is native to some of the coldest areas of the northern hemisphere. Botanists sometimes describe its natural distribution as "circumpolar," for it grows in the most northerly parts of Alaska, Canada, Scandinavia, Russia, and Japan. Like most wild roses, it is very variable in its characteristics, but it generally forms a suckering thicket of wiry, russet colored stems. The flowers are a good rich pink, with white centers and quite a lot of magenta, and borne in clusters of 5–15 somewhat early in the season. They are followed by round hips, 1in (2.5cm) across. The plant has gray green leaves, good autumn color, and a mass of small, brown prickles.

ROSA ACICULARIS

'ADAM'

syn. 'PRESIDENT'

Tea Rose

ORIGIN **Adam, France, 1838**
FLOWER SIZE **3.1in (8cm)**
SCENT **Strong and tealike**
FLOWERING **Repeats well**
HEIGHT/SPREAD **6.6ft (2m)/4.9ft (1.5m)**
HARDINESS **Zone 7**

'Adam' is sometimes described as "the first Tea rose" bred in Europe; it is still one of the best of all Tea roses. The beautiful dark pink buds open out into muddled flowers, sometimes quartered. The petals are pink on the outside and peachy on the inside, with hints of buff, apricot, and salmon between them. The flowers come usually singly but sometimes in clusters of up to four, on long stems that last well when cut. The leaves are large and eventually dark green but, like the new growth, are beet red and bloomy at first. The height of the plant depends entirely upon the growing conditions: no more than 3.3ft (1m) as a bush in cool climates, but a 16.4ft (5m) climber in hot ones. 'Adam' is healthy, apart from a little mildew, and it is among the hardier Tea roses. It is easily propagated by cuttings.

'ADAM'

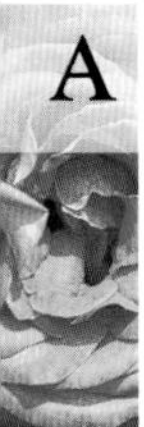
A

'ADAM MESSERICH'

'ADAM MESSERICH'

Hybrid China

ORIGIN **Lambert, Germany, 1920**
PARENTAGE **'Frau Oberhofgärtner Singer' × ('Louise Odier' seedling × 'Louis Philippe')**
FLOWER SIZE **4.7in (12cm)**
SCENT **Moderate and sweet**
FLOWERING **Recurrent**
HEIGHT/SPREAD **8.2ft (2.5m)/6.6ft (2m)**
HARDINESS **Zone 5**

Peter Lambert was an immensely innovative rose breeder, and many of his introductions fit into no clear category. The grandparents of 'Adam Messerich' are respectively a Hybrid Perpetual, a Hybrid Tea, a Bourbon Hybrid, and a China rose. So there is nothing quite like 'Adam Messerich'. The large, satiny, loose-petaled flowers tend to hang down, so the plant is best supported on a trellis or grown as a climber. In hot climates, or up a wall, it will reach 16.4ft (5m), but in a cool garden, pruned as a shrub, it will barely reach 3.3ft (1m). The flowers are a particularly dark, bright, loud pink at first, then fade to mid-pink. They tend to look a little messy as they age, but make excellent cut flowers.

'ADÉLAÏDE D'ORLÉANS'

syn. 'PRINCESSE ADÉLAÏDE D'ORLÉANS'

Sempervirens Hybrid

ORIGIN **Jacques, France, 1826**
PARENTAGE ***Rosa sempervirens* × 'Old Blush'**
FLOWER SIZE **2.4in (6cm)**
SCENT **Strong and musky**
FLOWERING **Once only, mid–late season**
HEIGHT/SPREAD **16.4ft (5m)/9.8ft (3m)**
HARDINESS **Zone 6**

'Adélaïde d'Orléans' is an extremely vigorous and handsome once-flowering rambler, with very long, slender, lax shoots that are ideal for training over arches and trellises. The semidouble flowers open from small crimson or dark pink buds, and retain a crimson mark on their backs. They open pale pink but quickly turn to pure white, by which time they are almost flat, with a distinctive wave or frill to the petals. The flower stalks are long and slender, so that the flowers hang down in graceful clusters. It flowers only once,

'ADÉLAÏDE D'ORLÉANS'

but the last few flowers are produced over a long period. The plant has small, dark, evergreen leaves and fierce prickles – red at first, then later brown. Recent DNA tests by Professor Maurice Jay in Lyon have shown that its parents were *R. sempervirens* × 'Old Blush'. It was named after Princesse Adélaïde d'Orléans (1777–1847), the adored twin sister of King Louis-Philippe of France. Antoine Jacques, the raiser, was his head gardener.

'ADELAIDE HOODLESS'

Shrub Rose

ORIGIN **Marshall, Canada, 1972**
PARENTAGE **'Fire King' × (*Rosa arkansana* 'J. W. Fargo' × 'Assiniboine')**
FLOWER SIZE **2.4in (6cm)**
SCENT **Light or slight**
FLOWERING **Repeats**
HEIGHT/SPREAD **6.6ft (2m)/5.7ft (1.75m)**
HARDINESS **Zone 3**

'Adelaide Hoodless' was bred to survive the Canadian winters: it is hardy even in Montréal. Its flowers are crimson or red, lightly double, and carried in large clusters (of 5–15 flowers, but more in autumn), which tend to bow down the long, lax branches. The plant has thin, slender stems, and may need support, but it is a vigorous grower and has fine, dark, glossy leaves. These are strongly resistant to fungal infection in the Canadian prairies but not always in other climates. The first flowering is fairly heavy, and is succeeded by a few sporadic blooms until a second, moderate flush in autumn. Adelaide Hoodless (1857–1910) was a Canadian social reformer.

'ADELAIDE HOODLESS'

'ADMIRAL RODNEY'

Hybrid Tea

ORIGIN **Trew, 1973**
FLOWER SIZE **5.9in (15cm)**
SCENT **Strong and sweet**
FLOWERING **Repeats**
HEIGHT/SPREAD **3.3ft (1m)/2.5ft (75cm)**
HARDINESS **Zone 5**

'Admiral Rodney' is a favorite exhibition rose in England and a fine garden plant in hotter climates. Its buds are long and elegant, and retain their elegance as they unfold into huge, long-petaled flowers. They are pale pink, with darker petal reverses – pale crimson – and dark pink shadows between the petals. They come singly or in clusters of three, which are disbudded when grown for show. The plant is large and vigorous, reaching 4.9ft (1.5m) in hot conditions. It has large glossy leaves and repeats well, the autumn flowers being slightly darker than earlier flushes. The strong, sweet scent makes it popular as a cut flower. Admiral George Brydges, Lord Rodney (1719–92), was a British naval hero.

ADMIRED MIRANDA

ADMIRED MIRANDA

syn. 'AUSMIR'

Shrub Rose

ORIGIN **Austin, Britain, 1982**
PARENTAGE **'The Friar' × seedling**
FLOWER SIZE **3.5in (9cm)**
SCENT **Strong and fruity**
FLOWERING **Repeats**
HEIGHT/SPREAD **3.3ft (1m)/2.7ft (80cm)**
HARDINESS **Zone 6**

David Austin's English Roses tend to grow tall in hot climates, even when short in England. Admired Miranda is an exception to this rule – short and compact in any part of the world. The flowers are a beautiful mixture of apricot, pink, and buff, deeper towards the center, and paling to ivory or white at the edges. They are very full of small petals – some of them pleated and quilled – and roughly quartered in shape. They come singly or in small clusters of 2–5 on a neat, sturdy plant with small, dark green leaves and large prickles. It is susceptible to fungal infections, but these are a problem in only some areas. Admired Miranda was Prospero's daughter in *The Tempest*.

'ADMIRAL RODNEY'

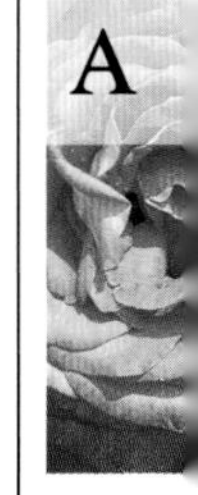

'Adolf Horstmann'

'Adolf Horstmann'

Hybrid Tea

ORIGIN **Kordes, Germany, 1971**
PARENTAGE **'Königin der Rosen' x 'Dr. A. J. Verhage'**
FLOWER SIZE **5.1in (13cm)**
SCENT **Medium and sweet**
FLOWERING **Repeats**
HEIGHT/SPREAD **4.1ft (1.25m)/3.3ft (1m)**
HARDINESS **Zone 5**

'Adolf Horstmann' is pretty at every stage of its flowering – an unusual quality among Hybrid Teas. The buds are somewhat small, but open up into large flowers. When fully open, they are sometimes said to resemble a double peony; they hold their petals for a long time, even in hot weather. Their color is a mixture of deep yellow and pink, though the overall effect starts apricot colored, then turns to yellow and finally to pink. The flowers are almost always carried singly, on long, upright stems, which makes it an excellent rose for cutting. The bush is shapely, and has good, dark green, healthy foliage. It is very floriferous. Although bred in Germany, and one of the hardiest Modern roses, 'Adolf Horstmann' also does well in mild climates like England's and hot areas like the southern US.

'Agatha'

syn. 'Agatha Francofurtana'

Gallica

ORIGIN **France, c.1818**
FLOWER SIZE **3.9in (10cm)**
SCENT **Strong and sweet**
FLOWERING **Once only**
HEIGHT/SPREAD **6.6ft (2m)/5.7ft (1.75m)**
HARDINESS **Zone 5**

The Agatha roses are a group of closely related Gallica hybrids, most of them bred or introduced in western Europe between 1760 and 1830. Their individual names and identities are still the subject of research and analysis by historians and collectors. They all have loosely double flowers in shades of pink or light crimson, paler petal backs, and a messy shape toward the center when they open out. Their soft, thin petals cause the flowers to ball in damp weather. The leaves of Agatha roses are usually bluer or grayer than other Gallica hybrids, with ridged leaflets like a hornbeam's. The more distinct cultivars include the Frankfurt rose 'Impératrice Joséphine', but there is confusion in nurseries, gardens, and reference books about the others. Gallica roses expert Professor François Joyaux considers that the original 'Agatha' has pink flowers with a hint of purple, beautiful golden stamens, and somewhat ragged petals. The plant is vigorous and strong growing, with large, gray green leaves. Roses under the name of 'Agatha' are sold and grown worldwide.

'Agatha'

Agatha Christie

see Ramira

'Agatha Francofurtana'

see 'Agatha'

'Agathe Incarnata'

Gallica

ORIGIN **Netherlands, c.1800**
FLOWER SIZE **3.9in (10cm)**
SCENT **Strong and sweet**
FLOWERING **Once, midseason**
HEIGHT/SPREAD **4.9ft (1.5m)/3.3ft (1m)**
HARDINESS **Zone 5**

A widely available Agatha rose, 'Agathe Incarnata' is believed by Gallica roses authority François Joyaux to be of Dutch origin and possibly a Damask hybrid. The flowers are flesh pink at the edges and a little darker toward the center, with quilled petals, a quartered shape, and usually a button eye. The long sepals are notably foliolate. All the Agatha roses are vigorous and healthy, but perform best in dry weather.

'Agathe Incarnata'

'Aglaia'

syn. 'Yellow Rambler'

Hybrid Multiflora

ORIGIN **Schmitt, Germany, 1896**
PARENTAGE ***Rosa multiflora* (or hybrid) x 'Rêve d'Or'**
FLOWER SIZE **2.4in (6cm)**
SCENT **Strong and musky**
FLOWERING **Once**
HEIGHT/SPREAD **6.6ft (2m)/8.2ft (2.5m)**
HARDINESS **Zone 6**

An important rose historically, 'Aglaia' was the foundation of the brilliant Peter Lambert's breeding lines, which gave us many of the best Hybrid Musks and Polyanthas. The double flowers are cupped, and open a bright pale yellow, but quickly fade to cream and white. They come in tight clusters, typically of 20–40 flowers. The bush has bright green leaves and flowers both early and profusely, but does not repeat. It clambers up to 16.4ft (5m) on a wall, but can be grown as a thin, freestanding shrub no more than 6.6ft (2m) high.

'Agnes'

Rugosa Hybrid

ORIGIN **Saunders, Canada, 1900**
PARENTAGE ***Rosa rugosa* x *Rosa foetida* 'Persiana'**
FLOWER SIZE **3.1in (8cm)**
SCENT **Light and fruity**
FLOWERING **Once, early in season**
HEIGHT/SPREAD **6.6ft (2m)/8.2ft (2.5m)**
HARDINESS **Zone 4**

Although 'Agnes' was bred in 1900, it was not introduced until 1922, when it was named after the raiser's wife. It is extremely useful because it flowers so early and is very hardy, which makes it especially popular in Canada and Scandinavia. The flowers are pale yellow, sometimes with buff tints, but deeper colored, almost amber at first, toward the center. The double flowers are lightly cupped and open in shape, with thin petals that tend to collapse in very wet weather, but are borne over a long period. They come on short stalks, usually singly, all along the arching stems of the bush. The leaves are clear green, small, rough, and ribbed; toward the end of the season they may show symptoms of blackspot and rust, but neither disease prevents 'Agnes' from flowering well again next year. There are sometimes a few flowers later on.

'Agnes'

'Aglaia'

'Agrippina'

see 'Climbing Cramoisi Supérieur'

'Aïcha'

Spinosissima Hybrid

ORIGIN **Petersen, Denmark, 1959**
PARENTAGE **'Souvenir de Jacques Verschuren' x 'Guldtop'**
FLOWER SIZE **3.5in (9cm)**
SCENT **Strong**
FLOWERING **Early, and repeats throughout the season**
HEIGHT/SPREAD **5.7ft (1.75m)/6.6ft (2m)**
HARDINESS **Zone 4**

'Aïcha' was bred as a shrub rose to survive the rigors of a Scandinavian winter, and is also hardy in much of central Europe and Canada. The flower buds are a particularly rich yellow at first, but the open flowers are lemon yellow and eventually cream. They have a loose and distinctive arrangement of petals, set off by long maroon stamens. The flowers come all along the arching branches, which are long enough for it to be trained as a short climber. It flowers early, and an established bush usually has a few flowers on it until autumn. The pale leaves sometimes attract blackspot, but this never seems to affect the bush's vigor and sheer flower power.

'Aïcha'

A

'Aimée Vibert'

'Aimée Vibert'

Noisette

ORIGIN **Vibert, France, 1828**
PARENTAGE **'Champney's Pink Cluster' x *Rosa sempervirens* hybrid**
FLOWER SIZE **2in (5cm)**
SCENT **Strong and musky**
FLOWERING **One long flowering**
HEIGHT/SPREAD **16.4ft (5m)/9.8ft (3m)**
HARDINESS **Zone 5**

Vibert knew this was a good rose as soon as it flowered for the first time, so he named it after his daughter and told his agents in England that everyone would soon be genuflecting before it. The buds of 'Aimée Vibert' are pink, and the flowers sometimes retain a trace of pink, but they open out into white rosettes with their stamens visible at the center. They come in small, dainty clusters, typically of 5–12 flowers, whose delicate beauty is best seen illuminated by sunlight. The petals are thin and spoil in rain or humid weather. The plant is vigorous, hardy, and healthy, with only a few prickles, and darkly handsome, semievergreen leaves. It flowers only once, but for such a long time that many believe it to be a repeat flowerer. It is still one of the best old ramblers.

'Alain Blanchard'

Gallica Hybrid

ORIGIN **Vibert, France, 1839**
FLOWER SIZE **3.9in (10cm)**
SCENT **Light**
FLOWERING **Once, midseason**
HEIGHT/SPREAD **4.9ft (1.5m)/2.7ft (80cm)**
HARDINESS **Zone 5**

Of all the simple, dark red Gallicas, 'Alain Blanchard' is the best. Its flowers are bright crimson at first, with a hint of scarlet, but they soon pass to pure crimson, enlivened by very dark (almost black) blotches and mottling, and occasional white flecks. The markings darken as the flowers fade. The petals unfurl completely, so that the flowers open out flat, enhanced by a lot of long, bright, golden yellow stamens. They come in twos and threes on a slender, upright bush, whose thin, wiry stems tend to keel over unless pruned back or propped up by other plantings. The stems are covered with many small dark bristles (too small to be called prickles) and bear neat, small, dark, tough leaves toward the top. It is fairly resistant to fungal infections. Alain Blanchard was a French soldier executed by the English after the siege of Rouen in 1418.

'Alain Blanchard'

'Alain'

Floribunda

ORIGIN **Meilland, France, 1948**
PARENTAGE **('Guinée' x 'Wilhelm') x 'Orange Triumph'**
FLOWER SIZE **3.1in (8cm)**
SCENT **Light**
FLOWERING **Repeats well**
HEIGHT/SPREAD **2.7ft (80cm)/2ft (60cm)**
HARDINESS **Zone 5**
AWARDS **Geneva GM 1948**

'Alain' has been a popular and reliable red Floribunda ever since it was first introduced. It was named after Alain Meilland, then a young boy but now head of the huge Meilland rose firm. The flowers are bright red and open out flat, so that their bright yellow stamens provide a contrast and a focal point. They come in open clusters of up to nine, and are very freely borne: the plant repeats regularly through until late autumn. It has dark leaves and a vigorous habit of growth.

Delforge introduced a climbing form, **'Climbing Alain'**, in 1957. It is also a strong grower and, in full flower, is among the most eye-catching of roses.

Sport of 'Alain'

'Climbing Alain'

Climbing Floribunda
ORIGIN **Delforge, Belgium, 1957**
FLOWER SIZE **3.5in (9cm)**
FLOWERING **Repeats intermittently after first spectacular flowering**
HEIGHT/SPREAD **13.1ft (4m)/6.6ft (2m)**

'Alain'

'Climbing Alain'

'Alba Maxima'

syn. Rosa alba maxima, 'Great Double White'

Alba Rose

ORIGIN **c.1700**
FLOWER SIZE **2.4in (6cm)**
SCENT **Sweet and strong**
FLOWERING **Once, midseason**
HEIGHT/SPREAD **8.2ft (2.5m)/4.9ft (1.5m)**
HARDINESS **Zone 4**

The Jacobite Rose probably arose as a mutation of 'Alba Semi-Plena' and shares the same sleek gray green leaves and lanky habit. The fully double flowers have a pink flush at first, which shows off their ruffled shape prettily, then turn to cream and white, finishing with a brown coloring at the center made by the dying stamens. 'Alba Maxima' has a few large prickles and is somewhat susceptible to rust, but it is a thrifty grower and, if well watered in the weeks before flowering, makes a display of supreme loveliness. In the US, it can reach a height of 10–12ft (3–3.7m). It is at its best when trained horizontally, so that flowering shoots break out all along the otherwise somewhat naked stems.

'Alba Maxima'

Alba Meidiland

syn. 'MEIcoublan', Alba Meillandécor, Alba Sunblaze, Meidiland Alba, White Meidiland

Ground Cover

ORIGIN **Meilland, France, 1987**
PARENTAGE **'Temple Bells' x Coppélia 76**
FLOWER SIZE **3.5in (9cm)**
SCENT **Little or none**
FLOWERING **Repeats**
HEIGHT/SPREAD **4.9ft (1.5m)/4.9ft (1.5m)**
HARDINESS **Zone 5**
AWARDS **Frankfurt GM 1989**

Alba Meidiland is quite simply the best of all white modern shrub roses. It has the virtues of the Meilland landscape roses

Alba Meidiland

A

in large measure – health, hardiness, and ease of cultivation – but allied to great floral beauty and floriferousness. The buds are ivory colored, but the flowers open pure white and very full, with a mass of wavy petals in an old-fashioned arrangement. They are among the largest flowers produced by roses of this type, and profusely carried in a spectacular display. They come in clusters of 3–5, but borne so close together that the whole bush is covered in flowers. Alba Meidiland has large, dark, shiny leaves and a dense, twiggy habit that makes it effective as a groundcover rose. It is a lax, vigorous, fast-growing shrub, broader than tall, and makes a very good weeping standard. It also repeats well, especially in mild climates or when watered. In fact, it is rarely out of flower.

'Alba Semi-Plena'

syn. Rosa alba semi-plena

Alba Rose

ORIGIN **c.1500**
FLOWER SIZE **2.8in (7cm)**
SCENT **Strong and sweet**
FLOWERING **Once, midseason**
HEIGHT/SPREAD **8.2ft (2.5m)/3.3ft (1m)**
HARDINESS **Zone 4**

This is one of the oldest of the roses that evolved in the western world. It can be traced back to the 14th century in old paintings, but there is no evidence (as is sometimes alleged) to link it to the Ancient Romans. On the other hand, it was probably the "white rose of York" in the Wars of the Roses in 15th-century England, and it is still used to produce attar of roses in Bulgaria. The flowers are semidouble and pure white, with small petals and dark yellow stamens. They come in clusters of 3–15, and have a fresh, lemony scent. Scarlet hips follow in the autumn. The long, lanky stems bear their flowers and gray green leaves only toward the top, but they respond well to hard pruning by producing flowers and leaves much lower down. They also break into flower and leaf all along their length if trained sideways or pegged down. They have a few large thorns. The plant is a tough and thrifty grower, often found in old gardens throughout western Europe. It flourishes in most climates where there is a cool snap in winter for its annual rest – in the US, it can grow to 10–12ft (3–3.7m).

'Alba Semi-Plena'

'Alba Suaveolens'

'Alba Suaveolens'

Alba Rose

ORIGIN **c.1750**
FLOWER SIZE **2.8in (7cm)**
SCENT **Strong and sweet**
FLOWERING **Once**
HEIGHT/SPREAD **6.6ft (2m)/4.1ft (1.25m)**
HARDINESS **Zone 4**

The semidouble rose known as 'Alba Suaveolens' is mixed up commercially with 'Alba Semi-Plena' and often sold in its place. The two are really quite distinct – 'Alba Suaveolens' has slightly larger flowers and more petals. The flowers are cream colored, fading quickly to white, with only a few anthers visible at the center. The Alba roses set viable seed, and a number of cultivars have been raised and distributed over the centuries. The plant has beautiful blue green leaves, a scattering of large prickles, and a vigorous, lanky habit. Rust may be a problem, as with 'Alba Semi-Plena' and 'Alba Maxima'.

Alba Sunblaze

see Alba Meidiland

'Albéric Barbier'

Wichurana Rambler

ORIGIN **Barbier, France, 1900**
PARENTAGE ***Rosa wichurana* × 'Shirley Hibberd'**
FLOWER SIZE **3.1in (8cm)**
SCENT **Strong, delicious, and musky**
FLOWERING **Once, midseason**
HEIGHT/SPREAD **23ft (7m)/13.1ft (4m)**
HARDINESS **Zone 7**

'Albéric Barbier' is a popular old rambler, widely grown in mild and warm areas, but not hardy in colder parts of the world. Its flowers open from rich apricot yellow buds, but fade first to cream and then to white. They are quite variable in their shape – sometimes semidouble, with a golden brush of stamens at the center, and sometimes more fully double, with a muddled display of petals that resembles a Tea rose. The overall effect is better than the close-up: this is a rambler to grace a small tree, a pergola, an archway, or a wall. The flowers are borne singly or in small clusters, but very profusely, and with an occasional flower or two later in the year. The small, dark, glossy leaves are almost evergreen, and the slender new growths are crimson: both are a beautiful foil to the flowers. The plant is healthy and vigorous, and thrives in the most unpromising situations.

'Alberich'

syn. 'Happy'

Polyantha

ORIGIN **de Ruiter, Belgium, 1954**
PARENTAGE **'Robin Hood' × 'Katharina Zeimet'**
FLOWER SIZE **1in (2.5cm)**
SCENT **Little or none**
FLOWERING **Repeats well**
HEIGHT/SPREAD **1.6ft (50cm)/1.6ft (50cm)**
HARDINESS **Zone 6**

The Belgian rose breeder Gerritt de Ruiter experimented widely with Polyantha roses at a time when they were fast losing popularity to the Floribundas. 'Alberich' was promoted as a Compacta rose, along with several others named after fictional German dwarfs (Alberich stole the Rhinemaidens' gold in Wagner's *Das Rheingold*). In England and North America, it was distributed as 'Happy', named after one of Walt Disney's seven dwarfs in the cartoon film *Snow White*. 'Alberich' and its siblings sold well, mainly on the strength of their names. 'Alberich' has very small, double, cupped flowers, which are crimson with quite a number of white streaks at the center. The flowers take on a blue tint as they age. The bush is small, fairly compact, and useful as a container plant, but somewhat susceptible to mildew. There are better small roses than 'Alberich'.

'Alberich'

'Albéric Barbier'

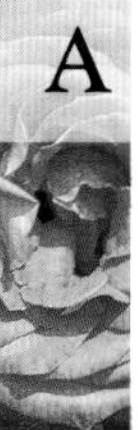

A

'ALBERTINE'

'ALBERTINE'

Wichurana Rambler

ORIGIN **Barbier, France, 1921**
PARENTAGE ***Rosa wichurana* (or hybrid) × 'Mrs. Arthur Robert Waddell'**
FLOWER SIZE **3.1in (8cm)**
SCENT **Strong and sweet**
FLOWERING **Once, plus occasional later flowers**
HEIGHT/SPREAD **13.1ft (4m)/9.8ft (3m)**
HARDINESS **Zone 7**

In mild climates, 'Albertine' is one of the most popular and widely grown of all climbing roses. Its floriferousness is astounding, it thrives upon neglect, and it roots very easily from cuttings – all factors that help to explain its dispersal around the world. The double or semidouble flowers are salmon pink, opening from darker buds, and much of their charm lies in the contrast between the pink petals and the coral backs. They are also intensely scented: 'Albertine' has a fragrance that carries on the air. The flowers have a loose mass of irregular petals and come in short-stemmed clusters of 3–7. The foliage is dark, shiny green, with crimson leaf tips and new growths – a good foil for the flowers. The plant is notably rigid and thick stemmed for a Wichurana, and its plentiful prickles help it to clamber through small trees and shrubs. If grown as a freestanding shrub, it attains a height of about 6.6ft (2m) and a diameter of 13.1ft (4m). It is susceptible to mildew and blackspot in cool climates, but the diseases never seem to affect its vigor or its capacity to flower next year. It is not choosy as to soil or aspect, but is less hardy than many Wichuranas.

ALCANTARA

syn. 'NOARE', Red Flower Carpet, Red Heidetraum, Vesuvia

Ground Cover

ORIGIN **Noack, Germany, 2000**
PARENTAGE **('Evelyn Fison' × 'Paprika') × Heidetraum**
FLOWER SIZE **2in (5cm)**
SCENT **Light and musky**
FLOWERING **Repeats constantly**
HEIGHT/SPREAD **2.7ft (80cm)/4.1ft (1.25m)**
HARDINESS **Zone 6**

ALCANTARA

Some of Noack's groundcover roses are branded and sold abroad as the Flower Carpet series. Alcantara is known in English-speaking countries as Red Flower Carpet, but it helps to think of each of the roses as an individual and to consider it on its own merits. Alcantara has very bright red, single flowers, with a few white streaks running out into the lightly ruffled petals, and a boss of golden yellow stamens. They are freely produced in clusters of 5–15, more or less continuously, and followed by red hips. In hot climates, such as in parts of Australia, Alcantara will flower year-round. Its leaves are small, dark, and shiny (*Rosa wichurana* is in its ancestry), and healthy in most situations. The plant is bushy and very prickly, not a true groundcover rose that smothers weeds, but more like a lax Floribunda. It is useful for containers as well as a forward position in mixed plantings.

'ALCHYMIST'

Shrub Rose

ORIGIN **Kordes, Germany, 1956**
PARENTAGE **'Golden Glow' × *Rosa rubiginosa* hybrid**
FLOWER SIZE **3.9in (10cm)**
SCENT **Strong and fruity**
FLOWERING **Once, early in season**
HEIGHT/SPREAD **16.4ft (5m)/6.6ft (2m)**
HARDINESS **Zone 5**

The alchemy in 'Alchymist' refers to its coloring: in some weather conditions the overall color turns to rich gold. The color is always variable but the outer petals tend to be yellow and the inner ones pink, giving an overall impression of apricot. With age, the yellow parts fade and the pink parts deepen in color, especially in hot weather. The flowers are cupped at first, later reflexing like a snowball, and very full of quilllike petals, which give it an old-fashioned, quartered look. They come in long-stemmed clusters of 3–7 flowers, starting early in the season and flowering for a long time, but only once. The plant is a stiff, upright, vigorous grower, slightly ungainly, with a lot of large prickles. It performs well in heat and survives cold winters. The foliage is unexciting – glossy, mid-green, and susceptible to blackspot. But it is one of the most beautiful and rewarding of all once-flowering climbers.

'ALEC'S RED'

'ALEC'S RED'

Hybrid Tea

ORIGIN **Cocker, Britain, 1970**
PARENTAGE **Duftwolke × 'Dame de Coeur'**
FLOWER SIZE **5.5in (14cm)**
SCENT **Light**
FLOWERING **Repeats well, from early to late in season**
HEIGHT/SPREAD **2.7ft (80cm)/2.7ft (80cm)**
HARDINESS **Zone 5**
AWARDS **Edland FA 1969; RNRS GM & PIT 1970; Belfast FA 1972; ADR 1973; Baden-Baden FA 1973**

'Alec's Red' was one of the first roses raised by Alec Cocker of Scotland. It was given its name by other breeders who trialed it before Cocker released it. It is a very large, red Hybrid Tea, with a strong, sweet scent. The flowers are deep red with a somewhat somber hue, globular, and many petaled. Instead of the classic conical, unfurling bloom of the Hybrid Tea, the buds tend to produce "split" flowers, making it unpopular with exhibitors, but it is an excellent and long-lasting cut flower. The flowers are borne on strong, upright stems, usually singly but sometimes in clusters of 3–5. The first flowering comes early in the season, but there may be a long wait for the next flush to follow. The plant is vigorous, with a lot of thorns, a weakness for blackspot, and a tendency to spread sideways. For such a many-petaled rose it is very rain resistant and is at its best in cool, moist conditions, making it especially popular in England.

'ALEXANDER'

'ALEXANDER'

Hybrid Tea

ORIGIN **Harkness, Britain, 1972**
PARENTAGE **'Super Star' × ('Ann Elizabeth' × 'Allgold')**
FLOWER **5.1in (13cm)**
SCENT **Slight**
FLOWERING **Reliably remontant**
HEIGHT/SPREAD **6.6ft (2m)/3.9ft (1.2m)**
HARDINESS **Zone 6**
AWARDS **ADR 1973; Hamburg GM 1973; Belfast GM 1974; James Mason GM 1987**

Jack Harkness named this rose after Field Marshal Earl Alexander of Tunis (1891–1969). It has two outstanding qualities: its vigor and its brilliant coloring. 'Alexander' is a sensational, unfading, bright vermilion, more vividly colored than any rose before or since. Individually, the flowers, which are Hybrid Tea-shaped, can be quite large: the secret is good cultivation – good feeding in particular. The flowers are usually borne singly in the first flush of flowers and in clusters of up to seven thereafter. The long stems make them good for cutting. The bush has small, dull leaves, which used to be a model of health but are now susceptible to mildew and blackspot. It is fairly free-flowering, rain resistant, and excessively prickly.

'ALEXANDER MACKENZIE'

see 'A. MACKENZIE'

'ALCHYMIST'

ALEXANDRA RENAISSANCE

ALEXANDRA RENAISSANCE

syn. 'POULDRA', Princess Alexandra

Shrub Rose

ORIGIN **Poulsen, Denmark, 1997**
FLOWER SIZE **3.9in (10cm)**
SCENT **Strong and sweet**
FLOWERING **Repeats**
HEIGHT/SPREAD **4.9ft (1.5m)/4.1ft (1.25m)**
HARDINESS **Zone 6**

Poulsen's Renaissance roses seek to combine the shape and fragrance of old roses, with the floriferousness and health of the new varieties. Alexandra Renaissance (named after Princess Alexandra of Denmark, b.1964) has large, pale crimson flowers that open out to a muddled form and a button eye. The wavy petals fade slightly as they age, and the flower picks up shades of magenta, pink, and mauve. They are usually borne singly (sometimes in clusters of three) on a strong, upright plant with medium-dark leaves and a fair scattering of prickles. Deadheading helps it to flower again quickly. The scent is delicious.

ALEXANDRA ROSE

see THE ALEXANDRA ROSE

'ALEXANDRE GIRAULT'

Wichurana Rambler

ORIGIN **Barbier, France, 1909**
PARENTAGE ***Rosa wichurana* x 'Papa Gontier'**
FLOWER SIZE **2.8in (7cm)**
SCENT **Light or slight**
FLOWERING **Once, early in season, with a few later flowers**
HEIGHT/SPREAD **16.4ft (5m)/8.2ft (2.5m)**
HARDINESS **Zone 6**

There is a famous planting of 'Alexandre Girault' covering the central trelliswork at L'Haÿ-les-Roses in Paris, the prettiest of Europe's historic rose gardens. Its long, slender, flexible stems have been woven back and forth to present a glittering mass of color in late May. The flowers are deep cherry pink at first, with yellow tints at the center and almost pure white petal backs, which create quite a contrast, especially when ruffled by wind. The flowers hang down in loose clusters (typically of 5–9) and open to a mass of little pointed petals. The foliage is dark, small, and shiny in the Wichurana way, and healthy too. It is one of the most vigorous Wichuranas, capable of reaching 26.2ft (8m) along a support, and sending out long new branches that lengthen so quickly that they seem to grow as you look at them.

'ALEXANDRE GIRAULT'

'ALFRED COLOMB'

Hybrid Perpetual

ORIGIN **Lacharme, France, 1865**
PARENTAGE **'Général Jacqueminot' seedling**
FLOWER SIZE **3.9in (10cm)**
SCENT **Strong and sweet**
FLOWERING **Remontant**
HEIGHT/SPREAD **4.9ft (1.5m)/5.7ft (1.75m)**
HARDINESS **Zone 5**

The popularity of 'Alfred Colomb' rests upon its sweet scent and its reliability as a reflowerer. The flowers are crimson – rich red on the upper surfaces of the petals and paler underneath – and they have a lightly cupped shape that is very "modern," being found among many English Roses and their rivals. They come singly or in small clusters and last well as cut flowers: their brilliant color and superb scent are perfect in a specimen vase. The prickly, leafy plant thrives especially well in hot, dry climates, where it will grow with extra vigor, but 'Alfred Colomb' also tolerates rain.

'ALFRED DE DALMAS'

'ALFRED DE DALMAS'

syn. 'MOUSSELINE'

Perpetual Moss

ORIGIN **Laffay, France, 1855**
FLOWER SIZE **3.1in (8cm)**
SCENT **Strong and sweet**
FLOWERING **Remontant**
HEIGHT/SPREAD **3.9ft (1.2m)/4.9ft (1.5m)**
HARDINESS **Zone 5**

The synonym for 'Alfred de Dalmas' is 'Mousseline', and the same rose is sold under both names. They were originally two different roses: only one has survived, but the experts cannot say which. Either way, this is one of the best repeat-flowering Moss roses. Its flowers are a beautiful flesh pink, fading to pale creamy pink, and distinctly cup-shaped, with a wisp of stamens at the center. They are sweetly scented, and the moss (brownish, and not too thick) has a resinous smell when touched. The flowers come in tight clusters (typically of 3–5) on short, leafy stems like a Portland rose. The plant is not very vigorous but, when well grown, it eventually makes a tall, upright plant and reaches 5.7ft (1.75m). Normally it is smaller – small enough for containers. The reflowering is stronger if the bush is lightly cut back after each flowering. The leaves are small, with rounded, gray green leaflets, and fairly healthy except for occasional blackspot.

'ALIDA LOVETT'

'ALIDA LOVETT'

Wichurana Rambler

ORIGIN **Van Fleet, US, 1905**
PARENTAGE **'Souvenir du Président Carnot' x *Rosa wichurana***
FLOWER SIZE **2.8in (7cm)**
SCENT **Moderate and sweet**
FLOWERING **Midseason and intermittently thereafter**
HEIGHT/SPREAD **13.1ft (4m)/6.6ft (2m)**
HARDINESS **Zone 6**

'Alida Lovett' is one of three roses bred by Dr. Walter Van Fleet in about 1905. Some years later, they were introduced by New Jersey nurseryman J. T. Lovett, who named them after his three daughters 'Alida Lovett', 'Bess Lovett', and 'Mary Lovett'. All are still available in North America, but only 'Alida Lovett' is widely grown elsewhere. The flowers open from coral pink buds and are rose pink with darker undersides to the petals; eventually they fade to palest pink. They open out fairly flat to reveal an attractive mass of loose petals inside. The flowers come in strong clusters of 3–11. 'Alida Lovett' has dark Wichurana leaves, large prickles, and a stiffer habit than most ramblers, which makes it more suitable for running up a tree or the side of a house than for tying in. It is a very attractive rose, with large flowers and a good scent.

'ALFRED COLOMB'

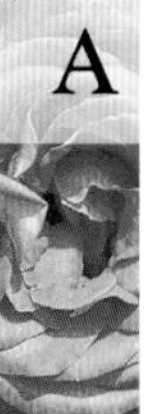
A

'Alister Stella Gray'

'Alister Stella Gray'

Noisette

ORIGIN **Gray, Britain, 1894**
PARENTAGE **'William Allen Richardson' x 'Mme Pierre Guillot'**
FLOWER SIZE **2.4in (6cm)**
SCENT **Strong and musky**
FLOWERING **Repeats well**
HEIGHT/SPREAD **13.1ft (4m)/6.6ft (2m)**
HARDINESS **Zone 7**

This beautiful and popular Noisette was named after his son by a rich Scottish amateur who moved to Bath, in the south of England, where the climate was better for growing Tea roses. Nevertheless, 'Alister Stella Gray' grows better still in a warm, dry climate, where its soft petals are unspoiled by English drizzle. The flowers open deep buff and fade to cream and white. Some are scrolled or quartered around a button eye, but most open loosely, even messily. All are complemented by the small, neat, dense, glossy foliage, which is occasionally a little susceptible to mildew and blackspot. The flowers are carried in small clusters of up to eight in the first flowering and as many as 35 on the vigorous new growth that flowers in autumn. The colors are also richer then, with short-lived patches of apricot and sometimes gold at the center. The wood is smooth, with slender stems and few thorns, and the leaves fresh green and fairly glossy. It may be grown either as a climber reaching up to 16.4ft (5m) or as a 6.6ft (2m) shrub or hedge.

All That Jazz

syn. 'TWOadvance'
Shrub Rose

ORIGIN **Twomey, US, 1991**
PARENTAGE **Gitte seedling**
FLOWER SIZE **4.7in (12cm)**
SCENT **Strong and sweet**
FLOWERING **Repeats well**
HEIGHT/SPREAD **4.9ft (1.5m)/4.1ft (1.25m)**
HARDINESS **Zone 5**
AWARDS **AARS 1991**

Health, vigor, and brilliant colors explain the popularity of All That Jazz. It was an unusual winner of America's top rose award and one of only a handful of shrub roses to score against the fashionable Hybrid Teas and Floribundas. The flowers are a dazzling combination of red, yellow, and pink – essentially coral colored with hints of salmon and lemon. The flowers are at best semidouble, but possessed of an elegant wave to their petals, and held aloft all over the surface of the bush. They are prolifically borne in clusters of 3–10 until late in the season. When the sun shines through them, there is no more brilliant rose in the garden. The plant has dark, shiny leaves and is very healthy. It has the vigorous, upright habit of an outsize Floribunda and is tolerant of both heat and cold – another reason for its popularity.

'Allgold'

Floribunda

ORIGIN **Le Grice, Britain, 1956**
PARENTAGE **'Goldilocks' x 'Ellinor Le Grice'**
FLOWER SIZE **2.8in (7cm)**
SCENT **Light and fruity**
FLOWERING **Repeats well**
HEIGHT/SPREAD **2.7ft (80cm)/2.7ft (80cm)**
HARDINESS **Zone 6**
AWARDS **NRS GM 1956**

'Allgold' was an important rose in the history of rose breeding: it was the first yellow Floribunda that kept its color and did not fade – at least, not in England, where it was bred. It is a rose that does better in cool climates, and its flowers stand up well to rain. They open from globular buds into loosely and lightly double flowers of pure, uniform, bright buttercup yellow. They are borne singly and in clusters of up to about ten. 'Allgold' has small, glossy, dark, healthy leaves, and, though never very tall or bushy, is a very vigorous grower, pushing out flush after flush of flowers in quick succession. It responds best to light pruning. The climbing sport, known as 'Climbing Allgold', flowers early, but has only a few flowers now and again thereafter. It is not as vigorous, in its way, as the bush form, but has the same deep, unfading yellow flowers.

Sport of 'Allgold'

'Climbing Allgold'

Climbing Floribunda
ORIGIN **Gandy, Britain, 1961**
FLOWER SIZE **3.1in (8cm)**
FLOWERING **Once liberally, then intermittently**
HEIGHT/SPREAD **13.1ft (4m)/6.6ft (2m)**

'Allgold'

'Climbing Allgold'

'Allen Chandler'

Climbing Hybrid Tea

ORIGIN **Chandler, Britain, 1923**
PARENTAGE **'Hugh Dickson' x seedling**
FLOWER SIZE **4.7in (12cm)**
SCENT **Light and sweet**
FLOWERING **Repeats**
HEIGHT/SPREAD **13.1ft (4m)/8.2ft (2.5m)**
HARDINESS **Zone 6**

In the 1920s and 1930s, 'Allen Chandler' was universally considered the best red climber in the Hybrid Tea style, and it keeps its popularity today. The long buds open to brilliant, dark red flowers. They have large, wavy petals, sometimes with a white patch at the base, and a broad boss of bright yellow stamens. They come in clusters, typically of 3–5 flowers, on long, upright stems. The plant has dark, healthy leaves and can be grown either as a 16.4ft (5m) climber against a wall, or as a 6.6ft (2m) bush. It flowers abundantly fairly early in the season, and more modestly in autumn, with always a few flowers in between. The autumn show is improved by deadheading during the summer, but then you lose the large scarlet hips.

All in One

see Exploit

All That Jazz

'Allen Chandler'

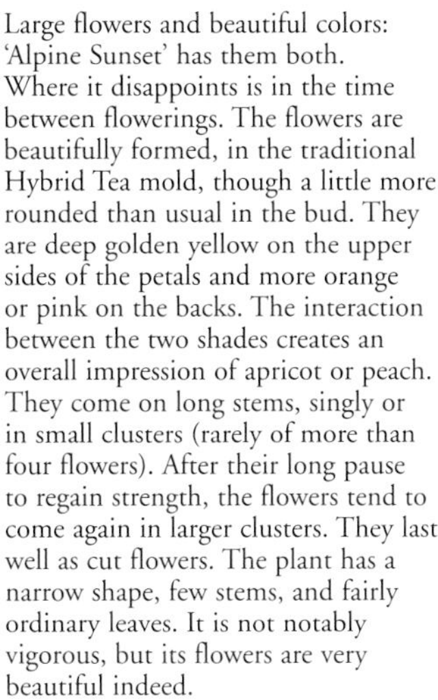

A

'ALLOTRIA'

'ALOHA'

ALPHONSE DAUDET

'ALLOTRIA'

Floribunda

ORIGIN **Tantau, Germany, 1958**
PARENTAGE **'Fanal' × 'Tantau's Triumph'**
FLOWER SIZE **3.1in (8cm)**
SCENT **Light and sweet**
FLOWERING **Repeats**
HEIGHT/SPREAD **3.3ft (1m)/2.7ft (80cm)**
HARDINESS **Zone 6**

There are better Floribundas these days, but 'Allotria' was far ahead of its contemporaries when Tantau first introduced this handsome red rose in 1958. Its flowers are large for a Floribunda, lightly double, and pretty at every stage of their development. They are vermilion when they first open, sometimes almost orange, but darken to scarlet as they age. The petals have quite a number of small white streaks running out from the center, which provide the flowers with contrast and character. They stand up well to rain. The flowers come in clusters of 3–7, and are good for cutting and exhibition. The plant has fairly large prickles and dark, bronzy green, glossy leaves. It is a reliable repeat flowerer.

'ALOHA'

Climbing Hybrid Tea

ORIGIN **Boerner, US, 1949**
PARENTAGE **'Mércèdes Gallart' × 'New Dawn'**
FLOWER SIZE **3.5in (9cm)**
SCENT **Strong, fruity, and sweet**
FLOWERING **Repeats well**
HEIGHT/SPREAD **9.8ft (3m)/6.6ft (2m)**
HARDINESS **Zone 5**

Many would say that 'Aloha' is the best of all climbing roses. The flowers open slowly from Hybrid Tea-shaped buds that give no indication of the great number of petals they display when they reflex and open out flat. The overall appearance of the flowers is deep rose pink, but the coloring is more complex than that: the inner petals are red and fade to pale crimson with a hint of terracotta or salmon, while the outer petals start dark pink and pass to rose pink. All the petals have pale edges, darker backs, and darker bases, giving rise to a two-tone effect. The flowers drop their petals well and do not ball in damp weather. They come in small clusters, occasionally singly, and last well when cut. The plant has very glossy leaves, which are dark bronze when young and dark green later, but always tough and leathery. It is free flowering, repeats well, and can be grown as a climber, pillar rose, or freestanding shrub. It sometimes attracts a little mildew or rust. 'Aloha' tolerates poor soil but is slow growing even on rich soils. It performs better in hot climates, but is very hardy and resists rain well.

ALPHONSE DAUDET

syn. 'MEIrouve'

Hybrid Tea

ORIGIN **Meilland, France, 1997**
FLOWER SIZE **4.7in (12cm)**
SCENT **Medium and fruity**
FLOWERING **Repeats**
HEIGHT/SPREAD **4.1ft (1.25m)/3.3ft (1m)**
HARDINESS **Zone 6**

In the 1990s, Meilland developed a range of large-flowered roses in the Hybrid Tea mold that show a complex old-fashioned arrangement of petals when they open out. Alphonse Daudet is a good example. The double flowers develop from large, elegant, mid-yellow buds in the classical Hybrid Tea style. The open flowers are quartered in shape and full of quilled petals until they open out completely to show their golden stamens at the center. The inner petals are a much richer color: golden or apricot, with darker backs and deeper shadows between the petals. Alphonse Daudet is a vigorous, upright plant, with large, medium-dark leaves and a fair scattering of prickles. Its flowers come in a series of flushes. Blackspot may be a problem in autumn.

'ALPINE SUNSET'

Hybrid Tea

ORIGIN **Cants, Britain, 1973**
PARENTAGE **'Dr. A. J. Verhage' × 'Grandpa Dickson'**
FLOWER SIZE **6.7in (17cm)**
SCENT **Medium and sweet**
FLOWERING **Repeats**
HEIGHT/SPREAD **3.3ft (1m)/2.3ft (70cm)**
HARDINESS **Zone 6**

'ALPINE SUNSET'

Large flowers and beautiful colors: 'Alpine Sunset' has them both. Where it disappoints is in the time between flowerings. The flowers are beautifully formed, in the traditional Hybrid Tea mold, though a little more rounded than usual in the bud. They are deep golden yellow on the upper sides of the petals and more orange or pink on the backs. The interaction between the two shades creates an overall impression of apricot or peach. They come on long stems, singly or in small clusters (rarely of more than four flowers). After their long pause to regain strength, the flowers tend to come again in larger clusters. They last well as cut flowers. The plant has a narrow shape, few stems, and fairly ordinary leaves. It is not notably vigorous, but its flowers are very beautiful indeed.

'ALTAICA'

syn. 'GRANDIFLORA', *Rosa spinosissima* 'ALTAICA'

Wild Rose

ORIGIN **1820**
FLOWER SIZE **2in (5cm)**
SCENT **Light and fruity**
FLOWERING **Once, early in season**
HEIGHT/SPREAD **6.6ft (2m)/3.3ft (1m)**
HARDINESS **Zone 4**

This is a cultivar of *Rosa spinosissima*, but much more vigorous and larger in all its parts. 'Altaica' has creamy flowers in small, short-stemmed clusters all along the long growth. They start to open early in the season and continue for a long time, with an occasional extra flower or two in late summer. The large, round, black hips are also very eye-catching. 'Altaica' has dainty leaves, a slender, upright habit of growth, and fewer prickles than *Rosa spinosissima* itself. In fact, its new growth is almost smooth, and the prickles develop only later as the wood hardens. It is very hardy and fairly healthy. It suckers attractively if grown on its own roots, and is widely planted as a landscaping plant to consolidate embankments on highways in Germany. It has proved an important rose for breeders, being the parent of the glorious series of "Frühling" shrub roses bred by Wilhelm Kordes in the 1930s and 1940s.

'ALTAICA'

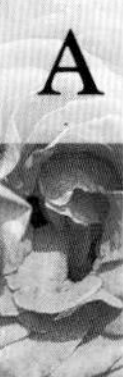

'ALTISSIMO'

Modern Climber

ORIGIN **Delbard-Chabert, France, 1966**
PARENTAGE **'Ténor' seedling**
FLOWER SIZE **3.9in (10cm)**
SCENT **Little or none**
FLOWERING **Repeats well**
HEIGHT/SPREAD **9.8ft (3m)/6.6ft (2m)**
HARDINESS **Zone 6**

This blood red modern climber is extremely popular worldwide, and one of the best in cool temperate climates, where its color glows intensely. The flowers are single, with dark stamens and just an occasional extra petal or two. They are uniformly red, with no white center and no difference in color between the upper side of the petals and the back. They come in small clusters (occasionally singly), on long stems, and flower almost constantly, and are then followed by large orange hips. They also last well as cut flowers. The plant is vigorous and healthy, with large dark leaves and purplish new growths. Cool weather produces the largest flowers and the richest colors.

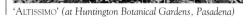

'ALTISSIMO' *(at Huntington Botanical Gardens, Pasadena)*

'AMADIS'

syn. 'CRIMSON BOURSAULT'

Boursault

ORIGIN **Laffay, France, 1829**
FLOWER SIZE **2.4in (6cm)**
SCENT **Little or none**
FLOWERING **Once, early in season**
HEIGHT/SPREAD **13.1ft (4m)/6.6ft (2m)**
HARDINESS **Zone 5**

The Boursault roses are extremely hardy and thornless. 'Amadis' is the most floriferous of them. Its loosely double, cup-shaped flowers open purple red and fade to a more lilac tone. Almost every flower has one or two conspicuous white stripes that run through from the center to the edge of the petals. This would be a defect in a midseason rose, but 'Amadis' opens so early that its flowers are welcome, stripes and all. However, the flowers hold on to their petals when they have finished flowering, so a plant looks messy and unattractive toward the end of its season. The flowers come in small, open, pendulous clusters. The plant is a fairly vigorous climber, but can also be grown as a freestanding shrub. Its leaves are thin and pale, while the thornless stems are green at first and maroon later, especially on their sunny sides.

'AMADIS'

AMALIA

syn. 'MEICAUF', Fiord

Hybrid Tea

ORIGIN **Meilland, France, 1986**
PARENTAGE **('Queen Elizabeth' × 'Karl Herbst') × 'Papa Meilland'**
FLOWER SIZE **4.7in (12cm)**
SCENT **Medium and sweet**
FLOWERING **Repeats**
HEIGHT/SPREAD **4.9ft (1.5m)/3.3ft (1m)**
HARDINESS **Zone 6**

It is fairly popular in France and available in the US, but Amalia has not had the worldwide success it deserves. There are many first-rate red Hybrid Teas on the market, and sometimes the competition is tough. Amalia has large, well-formed flowers that are pretty both in the bud and when they open out, though they spoil in rain. They are a good dark red, without even a hint of crimson, and borne singly on long stems that are perfect for cutting. Amalia has strong, vigorous stems, quite a covering of prickles, and large, healthy, medium-dark leaves. In hot climates it will quickly reach 6.6ft (2m).

AMALIA

AMANDA

syn. 'BEESIAN'

Floribunda

ORIGIN **Bees, Britain, 1979**
PARENTAGE **'Arthur Bell' × 'Zambra'**
FLOWER SIZE **3.5in (9cm)**
SCENT **Medium**
FLOWERING **Repeats**
HEIGHT/SPREAD **3.3ft (1m)/2.7ft (80cm)**
HARDINESS **Zone 6**

AMANDA

Amanda is an excellent deep yellow Floribunda, with an unusual, circular outline when it opens out flat. The flowers fade to lemon yellow and acquire an orange or crimson tint on the edge of the petals where they have been exposed to sunlight. This coloring emphasizes the neat wave in the petals, which is one of their attractions. The flowers produced in the autumn flush have more petals, often packed into tight rings around the central stamens. The flowers come in clusters of 3–9 on a stiff, prickly, upright plant with blue green, glossy leaves and red new growths. Amanda has never been widely grown outside England, where it remains fairly popular with exhibitors and private gardeners.

'AMATSU-OTOME'

Hybrid Tea

ORIGIN **Teranishi, Japan, 1960**
PARENTAGE **'Chrysler Imperial' × 'Doreen'**
FLOWER SIZE **5.1in (13cm)**
SCENT **Light and fruity**
FLOWERING **Repeats**
HEIGHT/SPREAD **4.9ft (1.5m)/4.1ft (1.25m)**
HARDINESS **Zone 6**

Japanese-raised roses seldom succeed in foreign markets, but 'Amatsu-Otome' is grown worldwide as an exhibition rose. The flowers are pale yellow with a hint of peach at the center and a lot of firm, broad, shapely petals. They are always borne singly on long stems and look splendid as garden roses during their first flowering, when the bush is covered in glowing blooms. The plant does, however, take some time to produce its next flush of flowers. 'Amatsu-Otome' is dense, vigorous, and fairly healthy, with glossy, medium-dark leaves. The Amatsu-Otome are spirits of the Japanese mountains.

'AMATSU-OTOME'

A

AMBASSADOR

syn. 'MEINUZETEN'

Hybrid Tea

ORIGIN **Meilland, France, 1979**
PARENTAGE **seedling x 'Whisky'**
FLOWER SIZE **3.9in (10cm)**
SCENT **Light and sweet**
FLOWERING **Repeats**
HEIGHT/SPREAD **4.1ft (1.25m)/3.3ft (1m)**
HARDINESS **Zone 6**

This handsome Hybrid Tea is beautiful both as an opening bud and when the flower is fully expanded. The flowers are orange, with golden yellow backs, and a yellow patch at the center when they open to display their stamens. Some of the inner petals have yellow stripes running up into the orange. The flowers may turn to salmon pink at the edges as they age, but they always give out an overall impression of orange or apricot. The flowers are borne singly on long stems, and are good for cutting. Ambassador is tall, upright, and vigorous, with large dark leaves. It is not the most generous bloomer, but its flowers are very eye-catching. Mildew and blackspot may be a problem in autumn and the flowers spoil in rain, so this is a rose that does best in hot, dry climates.

AMBASSADOR

AMBER QUEEN

syn. 'HARROONY', Prinz Eugen von Savoyen

Floribunda

ORIGIN **Harkness, Britain, 1983**
PARENTAGE **'Southampton' x 'Typhoon'**
FLOWER SIZE **3.1in (8cm)**
SCENT **Fairly strong and spicy**
FLOWERING **Almost continuous**
HEIGHT/SPREAD **2.7ft (80cm)/3.9ft (1.2m)**
HARDINESS **Zone 6**
AWARDS **ROTY 1984; Belfast GM 1986; Genoa GM 1986; Orléans GM 1987; AARS 1988; FA & Golden Rose of The Hague 1991; James Mason GM 1993**

Many would claim that Amber Queen is the best Floribunda rose of its color in cool climates. It is somewhat variable in color – sometimes its flowers are more yellow or pink than amber – but more usually a rich apricot shade that is very close to amber itself. It opens from squat buds to flowers that are large for a Floribunda and widely spaced in their clusters, so that there is always room for the individual flowers to expand. There are usually 3–7 flowers in a cluster, sometimes more, and the first flower of the cluster to open is often larger than the others, with more petals and a more complex shape. The leaves are unusually large, crimson at first but later dark green, and richly glossy. The bush has a spreading habit of growth, and reddish prickles to start with. Amber Queen is disease-resistant and repeats quickly – a consistently good performer.

AMBER QUEEN

'AMBOSSFUNKEN'

see 'SIGNORA PIERO PURICELLI'

AMBRIDGE ROSE

syn. 'AUSWONDER'

Shrub Rose

ORIGIN **Austin, Britain, 1990**
PARENTAGE **'Charles Austin' x 'Wife of Bath'**
FLOWER SIZE **3.1in (8cm)**
SCENT **Strong, sweet, and myrrhlike**
FLOWERING **Repeats well**
HEIGHT/SPREAD **2.5ft (75cm)/2ft (60cm)**
HARDINESS **Zone 5**

Ambridge Rose is a David Austin rose that does not grow too tall, even in hot climates. Its small, neat, compact habit, makes it very useful at the front of a border. The flowers are pale shell pink, with a hint of apricot at the center, fading to mother-of-pearl: the contrast between the pale outer petals and the warm pink center is very attractive. They are quite strongly cupped at first, but later open out into a rosette shape. The flowers come singly or in clusters of up to five, and shed their petals neatly when they have finished flowering. The plant has dark leaves (bronzy at first) and a lot of prickles. It is a quick repeat flowerer, better than most English Roses, so that it is seldom without flowers. It is hardy, and healthy, in most areas. Ambridge is the name of a fictional village in a popular British radio serial.

AMBRIDGE ROSE

AMERICA

syn. 'JACCLAM'

Modern Climber

ORIGIN **Warriner, US, 1976**
PARENTAGE **'Duftwolke' x 'Tradition'**
FLOWER SIZE **3.9in (10cm)**
SCENT **Strong and sweet**
FLOWERING **Repeats**
HEIGHT/SPREAD **9.8ft (3m)/6.6ft (2m)**
HARDINESS **Zone 6**
AWARDS **AARS 1976**

This climber is almost unknown outside the US, where it is very popular. America has strongly scented, double flowers of Hybrid Tea shape at first, opening out cupped and imbricated. They come in small clusters (typically of 4–5). They are salmon pink with paler reverses, and later fade to pink. Although a repeat flowerer, America is late to flower for the first time, and has long periods between flowerings. It is a neat, sturdy, upright plant of moderate vigor. The leaves are healthy, semiglossy, and mid-green. Pearly Gates is a very attractive, soft pink sport, with darker shadows between the petals. Likewise, the rarely seen Royal America (Cooper, 1994) is a white sport. Both are identical to America except for their color.

AMERICA

PEARLY GATES

Sport of America

PEARLY GATES

syn. 'JACCLAM'
ORIGIN **Meyer, US, 1999**

'AMÉLIA'

Alba Rose

ORIGIN **Vibert, France, 1823**
FLOWER SIZE **2.8in (7cm)**
SCENT **Strong, sweet, and fruity**
FLOWERING **Once only**
HEIGHT/SPREAD **4.1ft (1.25m)/3ft (1m)**
HARDINESS **Zone 5**

Most Alba roses are tall and lanky: 'Amélia' is an exception, rarely reaching 4.9ft (1.5m) even in hot climates. It is also one of the pinkest of the "White Roses." The flowers open rose pink with slightly paler reverses and a flutter of petals around a fringe of golden stamens. They come in small clusters, typically of 3–5, on long stems that are good for picking, and are followed by long, red hips. The plant is healthy, with mid-green leaves and a few prickles. It is useful for its neat habit and tolerates poor soils and difficult positions, but it flowers only once. A good rose, if not a classic.

'AMÉLIA'

A

'American Beauty'

'American Beauty'

syn. 'Mme. Ferdinand Jamin'
Hybrid Perpetual

ORIGIN **Lédéchaux, France, 1885**
FLOWER SIZE **4.3in (11cm)**
SCENT **Strong and sweet**
FLOWERING **Repeats a little**
HEIGHT/SPREAD **6.6ft (2m)/4.1ft (1.25m)**
HARDINESS **Zone 5**

This crimson Hybrid Perpetual owes its popularity to its name. It is rarely seen and little esteemed outside the US. The irony is that, in all probability, 'American Beauty' is an old French rose, renamed for the American market. If so, it should correctly be called 'Mme. Ferdinand Jamin'. The flowers open from fat, round buds. They are globular, full, pale crimson, and carried on long, straight stems. It was a popular cut-flower rose in late 19th-century America. The plant has a vigorous, upright habit, prickly stems, and dark leaves. Unfortunately, it is susceptible to all the fungal diseases that affect roses: blackspot, mildew, and rust. It is not a reliable repeater, but deadheading does improve the chance of enjoying a few late flowers.

'American Heritage'

Hybrid Tea

ORIGIN **Lammerts, US, 1965**
PARENTAGE **'Queen Elizabeth' x 'Yellow Perfection'**
FLOWER SIZE **5.5in (14cm)**
SCENT **Light and sweet**
FLOWERING **Repeats well**
HEIGHT/SPREAD **5.7ft (1.75m)/4.1ft (1.25m)**
HARDINESS **Zone 6**
AWARDS **AARS 1996**

The name is a help, but 'American Heritage' is still a popular Hybrid Tea in the US. The flowers are large, very full, and borne singly on long stems, which makes it a useful rose for picking. The buds are cream colored, with dark pink edges to their petals, and an attractive conical shape as they open out. The open flower, however, has a mass of small petals at its center, many of them quilled like an old-fashioned rose. The petals at the center of the flower have a rich suffusion of yellow, with hints of buff and pink to contrast with the ivory and crimson outer petals. The plant has prickly stems, large dark leaves, and crimson new growths. It is an upright grower and in hot climates can be trained as a pillar rose. Mildew may be a problem in cooler climates.

'American Heritage'

'American Home'

Hybrid Tea

ORIGIN **Morey, US, 1960**
PARENTAGE **'Chrysler Imperial' x 'New Yorker'**
FLOWER SIZE **4.7in (12cm)**
SCENT **Very rich, sweet, and Damasklike**
FLOWERING **Repeats**
HEIGHT/SPREAD **4.9ft (1.5m)/4.1ft (1.25m)**
HARDINESS **Zone 6**

'American Home' is a traditional crimson Hybrid Tea, with large, fat flowers and a sumptuous scent. The flowers are a good deep crimson and hold their color well, even when they have opened out fully to reveal a muddle of petals. Sometimes the petals have a white streak running out from the center of the flower. The flowers are borne singly or in clusters of up to four on strong stems. The plant has large, dull leaves and crimson new growths. It is fairly vigorous and upright and repeats well, but the flowers are sensitive to rain damage.

'American Home'

'American Pillar'

Wichurana Rambler

ORIGIN **Van Fleet, US, 1902**
PARENTAGE **(*Rosa wichurana* x *Rosa setigera*) x unidentified red Hybrid Perpetual**
FLOWER SIZE **2.2in (5.5cm)**
SCENT **Moderate and musky**
FLOWERING **Once, somewhat late in season**
HEIGHT/SPREAD **13.1ft (4m)/6.6ft (2m)**
HARDINESS **Zone 5**

'American Pillar' has been immensely popular ever since it was introduced. It never fails to flower exuberantly, though somewhat late in the season, after most roses have already given of their best. It roots quickly from cuttings, is easy to grow, and is the hardiest of Dr. Walter Van Fleet's "dooryard" roses. The flowers are a cheerful crimson, with a glowing white center and a large clump of bright golden stamens. They are paler in hot weather and bright sunlight, so this is a rose that looks better in cool conditions, but nevertheless grows and flowers spectacularly in widely different climates – from very hot to very cold. The flowers come in large clusters and are followed by a handsome crop of scarlet hips in autumn. The plant grows very vigorously, building up a lot of slender branches with a fair covering of large prickles. The British rosarian T. C. Mansell wrote in 1946 that "it can provide as impenetrable a thicket as ever Christian had to surmount" (referring to the trials facing Christian in John Bunyan's allegory *The Pilgrim's Progress*). The handsome leaves turn slightly purple in late autumn and last a long time, usually until after the birds have taken the hips.

America's Choice

see H. C. Andersen

'Améthyste'

Hybrid Wichurana

ORIGIN **Nonin, France, 1911**
PARENTAGE **'Non Plus Ultra' seedling**
FLOWER SIZE **1.2in (3cm)**
SCENT **Little or none**
FLOWERING **Once**
HEIGHT/SPREAD **13.1ft (4m)/8.2ft (2.5m)**
HARDINESS **Zone 6**

Many purple ramblers were introduced in the early years of the 20th century, mostly by French or German breeders. Nonin's 'Améthyste' is not among the best, though pleasant enough and still quite widely grown. Its flowers are crimson purple, fading to mauve, with a lot of white streaks and flashes to the petals. They are neat and pretty at first, but open out fairly loosely, and fail to shatter until late, so that eventually there is somewhat more brown among the flowers than purple. If you do not study them in close up, they manage to create a good overall effect. They are borne in large, open, airy, conical clusters, which are held strongly erect. The plant has bright green leaves and fairly smooth wood (only a few prickles), and it roots quickly from cuttings.

'Améthyste'

'American Pillar' ▶

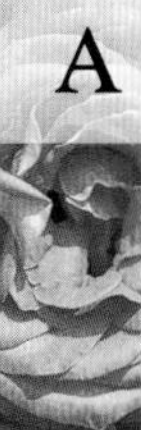

AMULETT

AMULETT

syn. 'TANALUMA'

Miniature Rose

ORIGIN **Tantau, Germany, 1991**
FLOWER SIZE **1.6in (4cm)**
SCENT **Light and fruity**
FLOWERING **Repeats well**
HEIGHT/SPREAD **1.3ft (40cm)/2ft (60cm)**
HARDINESS **Zone 6**

There is nothing quite like Amulett, which may explain why rose experts cannot decide whether to classify it among the Floribundas, miniatures, or shrub roses. It can grow to as much as 3.3ft (1m) in hot climates, but is little more than half that height in its native Germany. The flowers are exquisite: they have rows and rows of little petals lying neatly in circles like a chrysanthemum, in an arrangement termed "imbricated" by botanists. The flowers are dark pink or cherry colored, and fade only a little. They are borne in open clusters of 5–20. Amulett makes a very neat and pretty short plant, with small, shapely, dark, glossy leaves. It is an excellent rose for containers or the front of a border, and very free flowering.

'AMY JOHNSON'

Modern Climber

ORIGIN **Clark, Australia, 1931**
PARENTAGE **'Souvenir de Gustav Prat' x unknown**
FLOWER SIZE **3.1in (8cm)**
SCENT **Moderate and sweet**
FLOWERING **Recurrent**
HEIGHT/SPREAD **13.1ft (4m)/6.6ft (2m)**
HARDINESS **Zone 6**

'AMY JOHNSON'

'AMY ROBSART'

This vigorous Australian climber has lightly double, long-stemmed, silky pink flowers that pale slightly with age, especially at the tips. The petals are distinctly wavy, with occasional white streaks. The flowers open out flat and imbricated, but the red anthers are often obscured by little petaloids. The leaves have somewhat rounded leaflets with a corrugated surface. The aviatrix Amy Johnson (1903–41) made the first solo flight from England to Australia.

'AMY ROBSART'

Rubiginosa Hybrid

ORIGIN **Penzance, Britain, 1894**
PARENTAGE ***Rosa rubiginosa* x unknown**
FLOWER SIZE **1.6in (4cm)**
SCENT **Light**
FLOWERING **Once, fairly late in season**
HEIGHT/SPREAD **9.8ft (3m)/6.6ft (2m)**
HARDINESS **Zone 5**

'Amy Robsart' is one of Lord Penzance's sweetbriar hybrids, all of which have largely lost the distinguishing fragrance of the leaves of *Rosa rubiginosa*, which fills the air in humid weather. It has sticky, resinous buds and lightly scented flowers that open pale crimson with creamy stamens, a white center, and a notch in the edge of each petal. The flowers are single, with an occasional extra petal or petaloid, and come in clusters of 3–11. The leaves and leaflets are small, mid-green, serrated, and shiny. The plant is vigorous and unrefined, good for little except hedging (its stems are very prickly) and for its fine autumn hips. Amy Robsart was the neglected first wife of Lord Robert Dudley, a favorite of Queen Elizabeth I of England.

'ANAÏS SÉGALAS'

'ANAÏS SÉGALAS'

Gallica Hybrid

ORIGIN **Vibert, France, 1837**
FLOWER SIZE **3.9in (10cm)**
SCENT **Strong and sweet**
FLOWERING **Once only**
HEIGHT/SPREAD **4.9ft (1.5m)/4.1ft (1.25m)**
HARDINESS **Zone 5**

'ANEMONENROSE'

syn. R. x *anemonoides*, 'ANEMONE', 'PINK CHEROKEE'

Laevigata Hybrid

ORIGIN **Schmidt, Germany, 1896**
PARENTAGE ***Rosa laevigata* x unknown**
FLOWER SIZE **3.1in (8cm)**
SCENT **Light**
FLOWERING **Once, very early in season**
HEIGHT/SPREAD **9.8ft (3m)/6.6ft (2m)**
HARDINESS **Zone 7**

'Anemonenrose' has pretty, single, mid-pink flowers that fade to silver pink. Its petals are irregularly shaped, but broad, and sometimes have a white patch toward the center of the flower, where there is a handsome circle of wispy stamens. The plant has attractive dark leaves and lanky, thorny stems – it is best grown as a climber. It is not as vigorous as *Rosa laevigata*, but is slightly more hardy. A much darker pink sport of 'Anemonenrose' was introduced as **'Ramona'** by Dietrich & Turner in 1913. It remains a popular rose in warm climates, where the flowers are rich cherry crimson, though always paler on the petal backs. It is a popular wall climber, and flowers, like 'Anemonenrose', early in the season.

'ANEMONENROSE'

'RAMONA'

Sport of 'Anemonenrose'

'RAMONA'

Laevigata Hybrid
ORIGIN **Dietrich & Turner, US, 1913**
FLOWERING **Once, early in season**

'ANDENKEN AN ALMA DE L'AIGLE'

This handsome old rose is probably a hybrid between a Gallica and a Centifolia. The flowers of 'Anaïs Ségalas' are dark pink, fading fairly quickly to pale pink at the edges, so that for much of its life, every flower offers an attractive contrast between its dark pink center (almost crimson) and its pale pink outer petals. The petals also have paler backs. The flowers are very full, flat, and roughly quartered: sometimes they display a button eye. They come singly and in clusters of up to five. 'Anaïs Ségalas' has small, pale leaves and a lot of small, hooked prickles. It is a pleasant enough cultivar, but perhaps not outstanding: 'Gloire de France', for example, is better all-around. Anaïs Ségalas (1814–95) was a French poet.

'ANDENKEN AN ALMA DE L'AIGLE'

syn. 'ISABELLA', 'SOUVENIR D'ALMA DE L'AIGLE'

Hybrid Musk

ORIGIN **Kordes, Germany, 1948**
FLOWER SIZE **2.8in (7cm)**
SCENT **Strong and sweet**
FLOWERING **Repeats well**
HEIGHT/SPREAD **4.9ft (1.5m)/4.9ft (1.5m)**
HARDINESS **Zone 6**

The large and beautiful flowers of 'Andenken an Alma de l'Aigle' are a reminder of how closely the later Hybrid Musks resemble shrubby Floribundas. They are creamy white, or mother-of-pearl, with rose pink backs that give an overall impression of soft pink. The stamens create a hint of pale salmon-pink toward the center of the flowers. The flowers come in loose clusters of 3–15 (good for cutting) in a series of flushes right through until late autumn, with occasional flowers in between. The plant has mid-green leaves and somewhat roundish leaflets. It makes a rounded bush, excellent for landscaping or the back of a border. It grows just as well in hot, dry climates as in its native northern Germany. Alma de l'Aigle (1889–1959) was an educational reformer who wrote an influential meditation on roses, *Begegnungen mit Rosen* (1957).

'ANDERSONII'

Hybrid Canina

ORIGIN **Hillier, Britain, 1912**
PARENTAGE ***Rosa canina* x *Rosa gallica* (probably)**
FLOWER SIZE **2.4in (6cm)**
SCENT **Medium, sweet, and fresh**
FLOWERING **Once only**
HEIGHT/SPREAD **8.2ft (2.5m)/6.6ft (2m)**
HARDINESS **Zone 5**

'ANDERSONII'

'ANGEL FACE'

Floribunda

ORIGIN **Swim & Weeks, US, 1968**
PARENTAGE **('Circus' x 'Lavender Pinocchio') x 'Sterling Silver'**
FLOWER SIZE **3.9in (10cm)**
SCENT **Strong, sweet, and lemony**
FLOWERING **Almost continuous**
HEIGHT/SPREAD **2.7ft (80cm)/2.3ft (70cm)**
HARDINESS **Zone 6**
AWARDS **AARS 1969**

'Angel Face' may have been introduced over 30 years ago, but it is still the best mauve Floribunda – living proof that old roses are sometimes better than new. Its flowers are large for a Floribunda and carried in clusters of 3–9. They open out quickly to reveal a mass of strong, ruffled petals in pure lilac, apart from the occasional hint of crimson (especially along the edge of the petals), which gives the flowers a particular sumptuousness. They are very strongly scented: 'Angel Face' has a fragrance that carries on the air and has won several prizes for scent alone. It is popular with exhibitors as well as those who grow their roses mostly for garden display. The bush needs time to build up a framework, so prune it lightly, but an established plant will produce its flowers almost without interruption in mild climates. It has dark green, semiglossy foliage. A beautiful sport known as **'Climbing Angel Face'** was introduced in 1981. It is exactly same as the bush form but larger, with slightly larger flowers. It flowers early and profusely, then has lesser flushes until autumn.

'ANGEL FACE'

'CLIMBING ANGEL FACE'

Sport of 'Angel Face'

'CLIMBING ANGEL FACE'

Climbing Floribunda
ORIGIN **Haight, US, 1981**
FLOWER SIZE **4.3in (11cm)**
FLOWERING **Very well at first, then intermittently**
HEIGHT/SPREAD **9.8ft (3m)/6.6ft (2m)**

This vigorous shrub most resembles a dog rose with exceptionally large flowers. They are bright pink at first, fading to rosepink in the sun, with scalloped petal edges, a white patch at the center, and a ring of dark yellow stamens. They come in clusters of 3–5 and are followed by oval hips like *Rosa canina.* The plant has long, arching growths, large prickles, and mid-green leaves – all very like a dog rose. 'Andersonii' is a good shrub for a wild or woodland garden, but the plant is somewhat too vigorous (and its season too brief) for small gardens.

ANDRÉ LE NÔTRE

syn. 'MEIceppus'

Hybrid Tea

ORIGIN **Meilland, France, 2001**
FLOWER SIZE **4.7in (12cm)**
SCENT **Rich and sweet**
FLOWERING **Repeats well**
HEIGHT/SPREAD **4.1ft (1.25m)/2.7ft (80cm)**
HARDINESS **Zone 6**

This is not at all like traditional Hybrid Teas – pretty buds and messy flowers – but a truly modern large-flowered rose that is at its best when fully expanded. The flowers open from globular buds to reveal a muddled center in the "old-fashioned" style. The colors – and the way they change – are especially attractive, because the outer petals are almost white (pearly-pink at most) while the center of the flower is a rich, deep pink with apricot shadings at the base. The plant also has medium-dark green leaves, which are said to be very healthy, but André le Nôtre is too recent an introduction for gardeners to know how it will fare over the years ahead. Nevertheless, its colors, its exquisite shape, and its delicious scent created a sensation when it was introduced.

ROSA x *ANEMONOIDES*

see 'ANEMONENROSE'

ANDRÉ LE NÔTRE

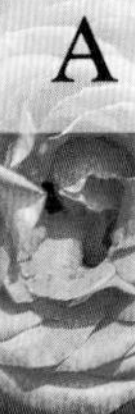
A

ANGELA

ANGELA

syn. 'KORDAY', Angelica

Shrub Rose

ORIGIN **Kordes, Germany, 1984**
PARENTAGE **'Yesterday' x 'Peter Frankenfeld'**
FLOWER SIZE **2in (5cm)**
SCENT **Little or none**
FLOWERING **Very free flowering**
HEIGHT/SPREAD **4.9ft (1.5m)/3.3ft (1m)**
HARDINESS **Zone 5**
AWARDS **ADR 1982**

Angela is an excellent and unusual shrub rose, whose popularity around the world continues to grow. It flourishes in widely different climates, from cool continental to Mediterranean. The flowers of Angela are pale pink, with crimson reverses – a striking combination – and very cupped, like no other rose, except perhaps 'Raubritter'. The flowers never open out completely but come in very large, tight clusters, where the contrast between their red outsides and their pink insides is well-displayed. They also remain in their clusters for a long time. The bush has good, mid-green, glossy leaves and is robust and healthy. It is fairly upright in cool climates, but mounds itself up to a lax 6.6ft (2m) bush in warmer areas, where it makes a good pillar rose that is never without flowers.

ANISLEY DICKSON

syn. 'DICKIMONO', Dicky, Münchner Kindl

Floribunda

ORIGIN **Dickson, Northern Ireland, 1983**
PARENTAGE **'Coventry Cathedral' x Memento**
FLOWER SIZE **2.8in (7cm)**
SCENT **Light**
FLOWERING **Repeats almost constantly**
HEIGHT/SPREAD **3.3ft (1m)/3.3ft (1m)**
HARDINESS **Zone 6**
AWARDS **RNRS PIT 1984**

When a rose breeder names a rose after his wife, you know he thinks it is a good one. Anisley was Pat Dickson's much-loved wife. Her rose is a bright salmon pink, almost coral, with palest pink petal backs and a white patch at the center. It is probably the best known and most grown of all the Dickson roses in North America. The lightly double, cupped flowers come in neat, upright clusters of 5–15, carried on long stems that make them popular for exhibition and as cut flowers. It is immensely floriferous. The plant is moderately vigorous, with very healthy, mid-green, glossy leaves and a bushy habit of growth.

ANISLEY DICKSON

ANITA PEREIRE

syn. 'ORAWICHKAY', 'ORADIWI', Starry Night

Shrub Rose

ORIGIN **Orard, France, 1996**
PARENTAGE **Anisley Dickson x *Rosa wichurana***
FLOWER SIZE **2.4in (6cm)**
SCENT **Light, musky, and pleasant**
FLOWERING **Continuous**
HEIGHT/SPREAD **3.3ft (1m)/6.6ft (2m)**
HARDINESS **Zone 6**
AWARDS **Paris GM 1996; AARS 2002**

The Orard brothers, Jean-Charles and Pierre, of Feyzin, near Lyon in France, bred this rose and introduced it quietly in 1996, naming it after the distinguished French garden historian Anita Pereire. Some years later it won top awards in the US, where it has been rechristened Starry Night. It is said that over 200,000 plants were sold in its first year in North America. The flowers are single and brilliant white, with a small boss of pale yellow stamens at the center, but they are borne continuously in amazing profusion, so that at times they seem to cover the dark, glossy leaves completely. Each petal reflexes a little at its edges, which gives an attractive and distinctive roll to the flowers. The flowers come in large clusters of 5–20 with 10in (25cm) stems and drop their petals cleanly. The plant is a lax shrub, wider than high, and originally bred for ground-cover and landscaping, but it makes a splendid plant in gardens, too. Anita Pereire is healthy in hot, dry climates, but suffers from blackspot and mildew in cool, wet ones.

ANNA FORD

ANNA FORD

syn. 'HARPICCOLO'

Miniature Rose

ORIGIN **Harkness, Britain, 1980**
PARENTAGE **'Southampton' x 'Darling Flame'**
FLOWER SIZE **2in (5cm)**
SCENT **Light and sweet**
FLOWERING **Repeats well**
HEIGHT/SPREAD **2ft (60cm)/2ft (60cm)**
HARDINESS **Zone 6**
AWARDS **RNRS PIT 1981; Genoa GM 1987; Glasgow GM 1989**

Popular in England, but little known elsewhere, Anna Ford was one of the first "patio" roses. Its flowers are a very bright orange, with a yellow patch toward the center, and turning to red and pink as they age. They are semidouble, and open out to reveal a circle of red filaments and yellow anthers. They come in medium-sized clusters, of 3–10 flowers in the first flush but with up to 20 later in the year. They are followed by pale orange, tomato-shaped hips. Anna Ford has small, shiny, rich green leaves, and is fairly healthy. It has a spreading habit, which makes it useful for front of the border plantings and use in containers. It was named after an English television journalist (b.1943).

ANITA PEREIRE

ANNA LIVIA

see TRIER 2000

'ANNA OLIVIER'

Tea Rose

ORIGIN **Ducher, France, 1872**
FLOWER SIZE **3.1in (8cm)**
SCENT **Strong tea scent**
FLOWERING **Repeats constantly**
HEIGHT/SPREAD **4.9ft (1.5m)/3.3ft (1m)**
HARDINESS **Zone 7**

Although its color is basically cream, 'Anna Olivier' manages to cram many other tints and shades into its shapely flowers. The petals have pale yellow backs, and sometimes there are hints of buff and pink within the flowers too. The colors are darker in cool weather. The petals are broad and reflex elegantly along their edges, but suffer in rain. The flowers are usually carried singly, but occasionally come in small clusters. Their scent is delicious. The leaves are medium-dark, large, and generally healthy, especially if well-grown. 'Anna Olivier' has bronzy crimson new growth and a few large prickles on its stems. In hot climates it will flower all year-round.

'ANNA OLIVIER'

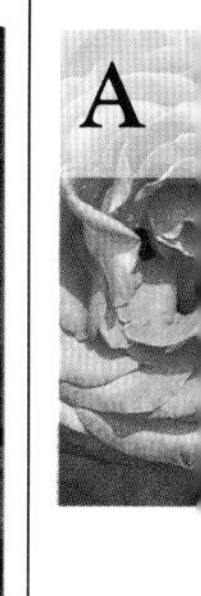

A

'ANNA PAVLOVA'

'ANNA PAVLOVA'

Hybrid Tea

ORIGIN **Beales, Britain, 1981**
FLOWER SIZE **5.5in (14cm)**
SCENT **Very strong, sweet, and Damasky**
FLOWERING **Repeats**
HEIGHT/SPREAD **4.9ft (1.5m)/3.3ft (1m)**
HARDINESS **Zone 6**

The 100th anniversary of the Russian ballerina's birth in 1881 and the 50th anniversary of her death in 1931 were well-commemorated by the issue of the exquisite 'Anna Pavlova' in 1981. The flowers are pale pink, darker toward the center and toward the base of the many petals, but paler, almost silvery pink, at the edges and darker again on the backs of the petals. They are beautiful at all stages: the petals reflex gently and the flowers keep their neat, concentric shape right from bud to fully open flower. They are usually borne singly on strong, stout stems. The bush has medium-dark leaves (watch out for blackspot in autumn) and a noticeably upright habit. The scent is ravishing.

ANNA ZINKEISEN

syn. 'HARQUHLING'

Spinosissima Hybrid

ORIGIN **Harkness, Britain, 1982**
PARENTAGE **seedling x 'Frank Naylor'**
FLOWER SIZE **3.1in (8cm)**
SCENT **Musky and spicy**
FLOWERING **Repeats well**
HEIGHT/SPREAD **4.9ft (1.5m)/3.3ft (1m)**
HARDINESS **Zone 5**

Anna Zinkeisen was introduced as a hybrid of the Scotch rose *Rosa spinosissima*, whose influence may be seen in the mass of somewhat thin petals and the way in which flowers are produced all over the bush, almost down to ground level. But *R. spinosissima* is actually quite a long way back in its ancestry, and Anna Zinkeisen also counts *R. californica* among its forebears. The flowers are creamy white, with a few lemon yellow hints toward the center. Usually the flowers open to show their golden stamens, but sometimes the center of the flower is obscured by petals. The flowers come in tight clusters of 3–15, occasionally singly, on a dense, prickly bush. The leaves are small, light green, semiglossy, and a little susceptible to blackspot.

ANNA ZINKEISEN

Though popular in Great Britain and New Zealand, Anna Zinkeisen grows particularly well in warm, dry climates so long as it is well-watered.

ANNE BOLEYN

syn. 'AUSECRET'

Shrub Rose

ORIGIN **Austin, Britain, 1999**
FLOWER SIZE **3.5in (9cm)**
SCENT **Light and sweet**
FLOWERING **Repeats**
HEIGHT/SPREAD **4.1ft (1.25m)/4.1ft (1.25m)**
HARDINESS **Zone 6**

The flowers of Anne Boleyn are very attractive. They open out almost flat to reveal a mass of short petals arranged as a rosette. They are basically pink – an attractive pale, rich pink – though the distribution of their coloring is somewhat inconstant. Sometimes part of an individual flower will be much darker than the rest. The petals also have darker backs. The flowers come singly or in handsome clusters of up to ten and are regularly produced until well into autumn. Anne Boleyn has dark leaves, and slender stems; it makes rather a lax shrub. Henry VIII of England had six wives: Anne Boleyn, Marchioness of Pembroke, was his second wife, whom he had executed for adultery in 1536.

ANNE HARKNESS

ANNE HARKNESS

syn. 'HARKARAMEL'

Floribunda

ORIGIN **Harkness, Britain, 1979**
PARENTAGE **'Bobby Dazzler' x (['Manx Queen' x 'Prima Ballerina'] x ['Chanelle' x 'Piccadilly'])**
FLOWER SIZE **2.8in (7cm)**
SCENT **Light and fruity**
FLOWERING **Repeats**
HEIGHT/SPREAD **4.9ft (1.5m)/3.3ft (1m)**
HARDINESS **Zone 6**

This stunning rose has one unusual feature, which is that it starts to flower very late, long after the first flowering of all other Floribundas. Anne Harkness produces its enormous clusters of flowers at a time when most roses are pausing between their first and second flowerings. They are deep apricot, with darker backs and a patch of deepest yellow at the center, and they all have the distinctive Harkness roll to their petals. The clusters have 6–20 flowers, are widely spaced, and flower (almost all of them) simultaneously, which makes this a very popular rose with exhibitors and flower arrangers. The plant has healthy, mid-green leaves and repeats well.

ANNE BOLEYN

'ANNE OF GEIERSTEIN'

Sweetbriar Hybrid

ORIGIN **Penzance, Britain, 1894**
PARENTAGE ***Rosa rubiginosa* seedling**
FLOWER SIZE **1.6in (4cm)**
SCENT **Medium and sweet**
FLOWERING **Once**
HEIGHT/SPREAD **9.8ft (3m)/6.6ft (2m)**
HARDINESS **Zone 5**

The sweetbriar hybrids, which Lord Penzance bred in the 1890s, are very large, prickly shrubs of little garden value. 'Anne of Geierstein' is the best of the bunch, because it has rich crimson flowers with a white patch at the center set off by a ragged circle of stamens. The bush is too big and the flowers too small for most gardens, but it may look good in a wild or woodland garden. Its flowers are fleeting and its leaves have only a faint scent of sweetbriar, but its vermilion hips make a cheerful display for a month or so in autumn before the birds take them. *Anne of Geierstein* (1829) is the only one of Sir Walter Scott's novels in which the plot is set outside Britain.

'ANNE OF GEIERSTEIN'

A

ANNELIESE ROTHENBERGER

ANNELIESE ROTHENBERGER

syn. 'TANOLG', Miss Harp, Oregold

Hybrid Tea

ORIGIN **Tantau, Germany, 1970**
PARENTAGE **'Piccadilly' × 'Königin der Rosen'**
FLOWER SIZE **5.5in (14cm)**
SCENT **Light and fruity**
FLOWERING **Repeats**
HEIGHT/SPREAD **4.9ft (1.5m)/3.3ft (1m)**
HARDINESS **Zone 6**
AWARDS **AARS 1975**

The original German name of this ravishing Hybrid Tea honors the great soprano (b.1926). However, Anneliese Rothenberger is more commonly grown these days in North America, where it is known as Oregold. The flowers are very large and almost cabbagelike at first, with large buds and many unusually long petals. They are a very beautiful, pale, golden yellow color, before fading to buff. The color is richest in cool climates or autumn weather, when the largest flowers are also borne. Anneliese Rothenberger has small, dark, healthy, glossy leaves and a vigorous, bushy habit. One unusual feature is the way it grows as a bush in its native Germany, but as a climber in hot climates. So it can be anything between a 3.3ft (1m) bush and a 13.1ft (4m) climber.

ANTHONY MEILLAND

syn. 'MEIBALTAZ'

Floribunda

ORIGIN **Meilland, France, 1990**
PARENTAGE **'Landora' × 'Mitzi'**
FLOWER SIZE **3.1in (8cm)**
SCENT **Little or none**
FLOWERING **Fairly continuous**
HEIGHT/SPREAD **3.3ft (1m)/2.7ft (80cm)**
HARDINESS **Zone 6**

The great attraction of Anthony Meilland is the unfading cheerful chrome yellow of its flowers. Even in hot climates and strong sunlight, they keep their color when other yellows have faded to white. The flowers are pretty in bud, and each flower is shaped like a Hybrid Tea until it opens out. They are also large for a Floribunda, with strong, short petals, though the clusters (usually of 3–5 flowers) can become a little congested. The leaves are dark green, glossy, and tough: they stand up well to disease. The plant has a compact habit and a sturdy growth. It is not without prickles. Anthony is the son of French rose breeder Alain Meilland.

ANTIKE 89

syn. 'KORDALEN'

Modern Climber

ORIGIN **Kordes, Germany, 1988**
PARENTAGE **('Grand Hotel' × 'Sympathie') × (seedling × 'Arthur Bell')**
FLOWER SIZE **5.1in (13cm)**
SCENT **Light and sweet**
FLOWERING **Repeats well**
HEIGHT/SPREAD **9.8ft (3m)/6.6ft (2m)**
HARDINESS **Zone 5**

In introducing Antike 89, Kordes have given us one of the best large-flowered modern climbers. It has large, full flowers of a very striking color, which flourish as well in heat as rain, and are produced most abundantly until late autumn. The flowers are white or palest pink, with crimson edges, but, since they have so many petals, the overall effect is more crimson than white. The flowers are cupped, with a muddled arrangement of thick, strong petals jostling for space within, closer to old garden roses in shape than modern ones. They come singly or in clusters of up to five and make excellent long lasting cut flowers. Antike 89 has lots of large, dark, tough,

ANTIKE 89

healthy leaves and thick stems. It builds up slowly as a climber, but also makes a good, freestanding shrub.

ANTIQUE SILK

see CHAMPAGNER

'ANTOINE RIVOIRE'

Hybrid Tea

ORIGIN **Pernet-Ducher, France, 1895**
PARENTAGE **'Dr. Grill' × 'Lady Mary Fitzwilliam'**
FLOWER SIZE **10cm (3.9in)**
SCENT **Strong, sweet, and tealike**
FLOWERING **Repeats well throughout season**
HEIGHT/SPREAD **1m (3.3ft)/1m (3.3ft)**
HARDINESS **Zone 6**

'Antoine Rivoire' was one of the first Hybrid Tea roses, bred toward the end of the 19th century. Its delicate coloring and repeat-flowering made it popular right from the start, and it is still widely grown in warmer climates. The flowers are pale pearl pink with a hint of darker coloring at the center. They are large, elegantly shaped, and full of petals – its Tea rose ancestors are very much in evidence. The plant has dark leaves, a scattering of prickles, and only moderate vigor, but it quickly repeats – all its energies seem to go into the production of flowers. It became an important parent for the production of other roses, so that 'Antoine Rivoire'

ANTHONY MEILLAND

'ANTOINE RIVOIRE'

turns up somewhere in the ancestry of almost every modern rose. Isaac Antoine Rivoire (1858–1924) was a nurseryman and politician in Lyon, France.

'ANTONINE D'ORMOIS'

Gallica

ORIGIN **Vibert, France, 1835**
FLOWER SIZE **2.4in (6cm)**
SCENT **Light and sweet**
FLOWERING **Once only**
HEIGHT/SPREAD **4.9ft (1.5m)/4.1ft (1.25m)**
HARDINESS **Zone 5**

The flowers of 'Antonine d'Ormois' (also known in some countries as 'Antonia d'Ormois') are fully double and cupped, though later they open out nearly flat and their soft blush pink color fades almost to white, starting at the edges. The outer guard petals are slightly recurved, but the inner ones form a quartered mass around a green style at the center. The flowers come singly or in twos and threes. 'Antonine d'Ormois' has slender stems, medium-dark leaves, and few prickles. It is not the most floriferous of Gallica roses, and starts into bloom somewhat late in the season.

'ANVIL SPARKS'

see 'SIGNORA PIERO PURICELLI'

'ANTONINE D'ORMOIS'

'APPLE BLOSSOM'

Multiflora Rambler

ORIGIN **Burbank, US, 1932**
PARENTAGE **'Dawson' x 'Dawson' seedling**
FLOWER SIZE **1.2in (3cm)**
SCENT **Musky**
FLOWERING **Once, midseason**
HEIGHT/SPREAD **13.1ft (4m)/9.8ft (3m)**
HARDINESS **Zone 5**

Several different cultivars are grown and sold as 'Apple Blossom', but the "true" cultivar was bred by Jackson Dawson at the Arnold Arboretum in the 1890s and introduced by the great American plant breeder Luther Burbank many years later. It is a fine, vigorous rambler. Seen from a distance, the mass of scented pink and white flowers closely resembles apple blossom. The buds are neat and pink, but, once the flowers open (the sepals reflex to a sharp-pointed star), they start to fade, ending up almost white. The petals have a ruffled edge that is quite unmistakable and gives the flowers their character and charm. The plant is easy to grow, roots quickly from cuttings, and tolerates a wide variety of soils, growing conditions, and climates. It has large pale leaves and some fair-sized prickles. It may suffer from fungal diseases, but not until after it has flowered, when such weaknesses may go unnoticed.

APPLEBLOSSOM

see SOMMERMELODIE

'APPLEJACK'

Shrub Rose

ORIGIN **Buck, US, 1973**
PARENTAGE **'Goldbusch' x ('Josef Rothmund' x *Rosa laxa*)**
FLOWER SIZE **3.5in (9cm)**
SCENT **Medium, sweet, and spicy**
FLOWERING **Repeats**
HEIGHT/SPREAD **8.2ft (2.5m)/8.2ft (2.5m)**
HARDINESS **Zone 4**

'APPLE BLOSSOM'

The American rose hybridizer Griffith Buck used 'Applejack' to bring hardiness to the roses he bred to survive the Iowa winters, but it is an excellent rose in its own right. Buck attributed its hardiness to the form of *Rosa laxa* he used to develop 'Applejack', which had been collected in Siberia. *Rosa laxa* also endowed 'Applejack' with its beautiful, small, gray green leaves. The flowers are semidouble, loose, and pink, with darker veins and stippling. They come in clusters of up to five, drop their petals cleanly, and are followed by scarlet hips. A bush in full flower is a vision of beauty. The plant is vigorous, prickly, and upright at first, before arching over as it matures. Its leaves have an applelike scent derived from *Rosa rubiginosa*, which is also to be found among its ancestors. Sometimes there is a second flush of flowers in autumn, but usually the main flowering continues for several months into late summer. 'Applejack' has only one weakness, which is that it needs a period of winter dormancy. Iowa suits it: Florida does not.

'APPLEJACK'

'APRICOT NECTAR'

'APRICOT NECTAR'

Floribunda

ORIGIN **Boerner, US, 1965**
PARENTAGE **seedling x 'Spartan'**
FLOWER SIZE **3.9in (10cm)**
SCENT **Strong and fruity**
FLOWERING **Recurrent**
HEIGHT/SPREAD **3.9ft (1.2m)/3.3ft (1m)**
HARDINESS **Zone 6**
AWARDS **AARS 1966**

'Apricot Nectar' remains a firm favorite all over the world nearly 40 years after it was introduced. It is easy to grow, strongly scented, very floriferous, and a very beautiful pale apricot pink color. The flowers have slightly darker petal backs and a yellow flush at the center, and fade eventually to cream, but the many shades and tints are attractive at every stage of their development. They stand out particularly well in the evening light and give of their best in warm, dry climates. Each has the shape of a classic Hybrid Tea and is good as a cut flower, too. They are abundantly borne in clusters of 3–11 (occasionally singly) and show up well against the dark, glossy, disease-resistant leaves. Sometimes the clusters are so large that they become congested or weigh the stems down. Growth is vigorous, upright, and bushy – it will reach 6.6ft (2m) if unpruned.

'APRIL HAMER'

Hybrid Tea

ORIGIN **Bell, Australia, 1983**
PARENTAGE **'Mount Shasta' x 'Prima Ballerina'**
FLOWER SIZE **4.3in (11cm)**
SCENT **Moderate**
FLOWERING **Recurrent**
HEIGHT/SPREAD **4.9ft (1.5m)/3.3ft (1m)**
HARDINESS **Zone 6**

'April Hamer' is a magnificent Australian rose of exhibition quality and great beauty. The flowers are large, with lots of ruffled petals, which open slowly even in hot climates. White with a pink edge at first, they then acquire a pale pink flush and darken further as they age – especially at the petal tips. It is a fair weather rose: the flowers blotch in rain. The plant makes purplish new growth that develops into handsome dark foliage.

'AQUARIUS'

'AQUARIUS'

Grandiflora

ORIGIN **Armstrong, US, 1971**
PARENTAGE **('Charlotte Armstrong' x 'Contrast') x ('Minna Kordes' x 'Floradora')**
FLOWER SIZE **3.9in (10cm)**
SCENT **Light and sweet**
FLOWERING **Repeats**
HEIGHT/SPREAD **4.9ft (1.5m)/4.1ft (1.25m)**
HARDINESS **Zone 6**
AWARDS **Geneva GM 1970; AARS 1971**

In some ways 'Aquarius' is a straightforward pink Grandiflora – vigorous, healthy, long-stemmed, and uncomplicated. But the flowers have an unusual way of changing color. They are pure medium pink at first, but take on a paler shade and fade to rose pink as they open. Then the tips of the petals start to darken again, until they are almost crimson. The darkening is triggered by sunlight and common in yellow roses (which sometimes turn red as they age), but seldom seen in pink. The flowers of 'Aquarius' are fully double, and borne singly or, more usually, in clusters of up to five. They are good for cutting, and splendid as garden roses. 'Aquarius' has large, coarse leaves, a scattering of prickles, and a vigorous, upright habit of growth. It remains a popular garden rose, especially in the US.

ARCADIAN

see NEW YEAR

'APRIL HAMER'

A

'Archiduc Charles'

'Archiduc Charles'

China Rose

ORIGIN **Laffay, France, c.1837**
PARENTAGE **'Old Blush' seedling**
FLOWER SIZE **2.8in (7cm)**
SCENT **Medium and musky**
FLOWERING **Continuous**
HEIGHT/SPREAD **4.9ft (1.5m)/3.3ft (1m)**
HARDINESS **Zone 6**

The most remarkable attribute of 'Archiduc Charles' is the way its flowers change from pink to crimson. They open palest pink, but darken (from the outside inward) until the flower is a true bicolor. In hot weather, the whole flower will turn crimson before it drops its petals; in cooler conditions, the contrast between pink and red is very arresting, both between different flowers and within an individual bloom. As a further refinement, the petal tips are always slightly paler and the petal backs are always slightly darker. The flowers open out loosely cupped, and reflex their petals. The foliage is small, dark green, and glossy. The plant is fairly healthy, apart from mildew, moderately vigorous, twiggy, bushy, and a very consistent bloomer, never without flowers. Archiduc Charles of Austria (1771–1847) was a distinguished soldier, a brother of Francis I, and great-uncle of Emperor Franz-Joseph.

'Archiduc Joseph'

'Archiduc Joseph'

Tea Rose

ORIGIN **Nabonnand, France, 1892**
PARENTAGE **'Mme. Lombard' seedling**
FLOWER SIZE **3.1in (8cm)**
SCENT **Strong and tealike**
FLOWERING **Continuous**
HEIGHT/SPREAD **6.6ft (2m)/5.7ft (1.75m)**
HARDINESS **Zone 7**

This rose is often confused with 'Monsieur Tillier' and sometimes with 'Duchesse de Brabant'. All are excellent roses, but 'Archiduc Joseph' is the best of the three. Its buds are dark pink and its flowers open pink, paler at the edges, and somewhat more raspberry red at the center. Sometimes there are hints of orange and bronze in the petals too. The petal backs are always a slightly darker pink. The petals start to reflex as the bud opens, and almost all of them end up reflexed along their edges into a pointed quill, like a starburst. The flowers are borne singly or in clusters of 3–6. The plant has pale, healthy, matte leaves and only a few prickles. It should be pruned very little or not at all. Archduke Joseph of Austro-Hungary (1833–1905) was a scholar (he published a Romany grammar) and agricultural reformer who founded the island park of Margitsziget in Budapest. He was a great plant collector and a patron of Nabonnand.

'Ardoisée de Lyon'

'Ardoisée de Lyon'

Hybrid Perpetual

ORIGIN **Damaizin, France, 1858**
FLOWER SIZE **3.9in (10cm)**
SCENT **Strong and sweet**
FLOWERING **Repeats**
HEIGHT/SPREAD **4.9ft (1.5m)/4.1ft (1.25m)**
HARDINESS **Zone 5**

This is one of the best 19th-century Hybrid Perpetuals. 'Ardoisée de Lyon' is vigorous, healthy, and very strongly scented. It color is very beautiful – brilliant cerise at first, fading at the edges to magenta, purple, plum, and slate. The flowers are full of petals and quartered, with a rough button eye at the center. They come singly or in rather tight clusters of up to seven in a series of flushes through until late autumn. Deadheading helps to bring on the next flush, but the plant produces handsome, elongated, orange hips if it is left unattended. 'Ardoisée de Lyon' is not as lanky as many Hybrid Perpetuals, but its prickly stems are best tied down so that they break into flower all along their lengths. Its leaves are large, gray green, and rather coarse.

'Archiduchesse Elisabeth d'Autriche'

Hybrid Perpetual

ORIGIN **Moreau-Robert, France, 1881**
FLOWER SIZE **4.7in (12cm)**
SCENT **Medium and sweet**
FLOWERING **Remontant**
HEIGHT/SPREAD **3.9ft (1.2m)/3.9ft (1.2m)**
HARDINESS **Zone 5**

Archiduchesse Elisabeth d'Autriche (1831–1903) was the daughter of the Austrian Archduke Charles Louis. Her rose is remarkable for its size and its reliable reflowering – so many Hybrid Perpetuals are far from perpetual flowering. The flowers are soft pale pink with mid-pink reverses. As they open out, they are paler at the edges and a richer pink in the center. Cabbage-like at first, they eventually open fairly flat, with a few rows of guard petals around the edges and a mass of many little petals within – reminiscent of some of the modern "heritage" roses bred by David Austin.

'Archiduchesse Elisabeth d'Autriche'

'Vick's Caprice'

The flowers come singly or in small clusters of up to 4–5. Although especially popular in Scandinavia (it is very hardy) and Britain, 'Archiduchesse Elisabeth d'Autriche' tends to ball in wet weather; it does better in countries with a warm, dry spring and summer. A striped form known as **'Vick's Caprice'** was introduced in 1891. It is identical in every detail, but with the addition of soft pink stripes.

Sport of 'Archiduchesse Elisabeth d'Autriche'

'Vick's Caprice'

ORIGIN **Vick, Britain, 1891**

'Arethusa'

China Tea

ORIGIN **William Paul, Britain, 1903**
FLOWER SIZE **3.1in (8cm)**
SCENT **Light**
FLOWERING **Remontant**
HEIGHT/SPREAD **3.3ft (1m)/3.3ft (1m)**
HARDINESS **Zone 8**

'Arethusa' made quite a sensation when it was first introduced, because its bright orange tints were then very unusual.

'Arethusa'

The orange color is seen only in the bud, because the flowers unfurl caramel colored, then lose their yellow tinges and end up pale buff pink or mother-of-pearl. The petal backs are darker. As they open out, the petals reflex along their sides, making a loose, messy flower. The flowers come on slender, nodding pedicels in clusters of 3–9 and are set off well by dark, lustrous leaves. But it is a dull rose by modern standards. In Greek mythology, Arethusa was one of the Nereïds.

'ARIANNA'

Hybrid Tea

ORIGIN **Meilland, France, 1968**
PARENTAGE **'Charlotte Armstrong' x ('Mme. A. Meilland' x 'Michèle Meilland')**
FLOWER SIZE **4.7in (12cm)**
SCENT **Light and sweet**
FLOWERING **Repeats well until late in season**
HEIGHT/SPREAD **4.9ft (1.5m)/4.1ft (1.25m)**
HARDINESS **Zone 6**
AWARDS **Bagatelle GM 1965; The Hague GM 1965; Rome GM 1965**

Although popular ever since it was introduced, 'Arianna' has proved to be especially successful in hot climates, where its large, many-petaled flowers can open out slowly. The flowers are a very attractive and unusual color – "orange pink" and "coral rose" were two early descriptions of it. In fact, the petals are deep rose pink with darker backs, which are overlaid with orange. This is reflected in the shadows that form between the petals and give the flower its unusual hue. The flowers are elegant in the bud (shapely and big enough for exhibition) and as they open out, though the color eventually fades to pink as they age. The plant has medium-sized, mid-green leaves and a scattering of large prickles. 'Arianna' is a good and reliable repeater, flowering late into autumn in warm climates.

ARIELLE DOMBASLE

ARIELLE DOMBASLE

syn. 'MEIHOURAG'

Modern Climber

ORIGIN **Meilland, France, 1991**
FLOWER SIZE **2.8in (7cm)**
SCENT **Medium, fruity, and musky**
FLOWERING **Repeats well**
HEIGHT/SPREAD **8.2ft (2.5m)/6.6ft (2m)**
HARDINESS **Zone 6**

Much of the success of this rose may be attributed to the popularity of the French actress after whom it was named. Arielle Dombasle is not one of Meilland's best roses, although it is a cheerful, short climber and does repeat well in autumn. Its flowers are orange, with a yellow center and a scattering of yellow flecks within the orange parts of the petals. The petal backs, too, are somewhat more yellow. The yellow tones fade completely as the flowers age, until the overall effect is more pink than orange. The flowers are rarely more than semidouble. They come singly or, more often, in small, erect clusters, typically of 5–7 but occasionally more. Arielle Dombasle has green leaves (red when young), which are somewhat susceptible to blackspot. The stems are covered in fierce prickles.

ARMADA

ARIZONA

syn. 'WERINA', Tocade

Grandiflora

ORIGIN **Weeks, US, 1975**
PARENTAGE **seedling x 'Geheimrat Duisberg'**
FLOWER SIZE **4.7in (12cm)**
SCENT **Strong and sweet**
FLOWERING **Repeats well**
HEIGHT/SPREAD **4.9ft (1.5m)/4.1ft (1.25m)**
HARDINESS **Zone 6**
AWARDS **AARS 1975**

There are as many colors in the flowers of this beautiful Hybrid Tea-style Grandiflora rose as in all the deserts of Arizona. The buds are almost orange at first, but the flowers open out warm pink, with apricot backs to the petals and a yellow suffusion at the base of the petals. The colors vary and (though always beautiful) are at their richest in cool weather and in the autumn. The double flowers are usually borne singly, occasionally in threes, on long stems that are good for cutting, and are elegant both in bud and as fully open blooms. Arizona is vigorous, compact, and upright, with tough, mid-green leaves and long prickles.

ARMADA

syn. 'HARUSEFUL'

Shrub Rose

ORIGIN **Harkness, Britain, 1988**
PARENTAGE **'New Dawn' x 'Silver Jubilee'**
FLOWER SIZE **3.9in (10cm)**
SCENT **Light**
FLOWERING **Repeats**
HEIGHT/SPREAD **5.7ft (1.75m)/4.1ft (1.25m)**
HARDINESS **Zone 5**
AWARDS **ADR 1993**

Armada is a useful shrub rose; healthy and vigorous. Its pale crimson buds open out into cupped, mid-pink flowers with darker reverses. They are profusely borne in clusters of 3–9 all over the surface of the bush and are followed by rounded orange fruits that stay on the bush well into winter. The plant makes a vigorous, branching, spreading shrub, with medium-dark, green, and glossy leaves that also show good disease resistance. It can be trained as a short climber in hot climates, and makes a good hedging plant. It is one of several interesting new roses bred by Harkness in recent years by crossing the Wichurana rambler 'New Dawn' with the best of modern Hybrid Teas and Floribundas.

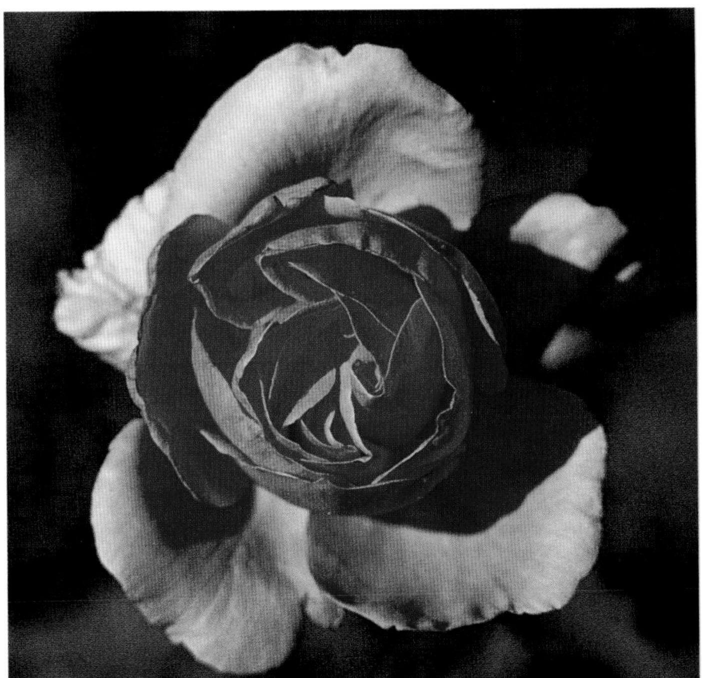
'ARIANNA'

ARIZONA

Arnaud Delbard

syn. 'DELtep', First Edition

Floribunda

ORIGIN **Delbard, France, 1976**
PARENTAGE **('Zambra' x ['Orléans Rose' x 'Goldilocks']) x ('Orange Triumph' seedling x 'Floradora')**
FLOWER SIZE **2.8in (7cm)**
SCENT **Light**
FLOWERING **Repeats well**
HEIGHT/SPREAD **3.9ft (1.2m)/2.7ft (80cm)**
HARDINESS **Zone 6**
AWARDS **AARS 1977**

Arnaud Delbard is a neat Floribunda in shades of light orange, vermilion, and coral. The flowers open flat, and pale quite attractively as they begin to fade. They open from scrolled buds and make a pretty arrangement with their petals, which are short, broad, and not too many. They come in nicely spaced clusters of 5–20. The leaves are mid-green, glossy, and healthy. The plant is vigorous and upright in habit. When introduced – it is a very 1970s rose – Arnaud Delbard was seen as an improvement on 'Fashion', being brighter and healthier. It was named after a member of the breeder's family and is still a popular rose in North America today.

Arnaud Delbard

'Arthur de Sansal'

'Arthur de Sansal'

Portland

ORIGIN **Cochet, France, 1855**
PARENTAGE **'Géant des Batailles' seedling**
FLOWER SIZE **3.1in (8cm)**
SCENT **Medium and sweet**
FLOWERING **Remontant**
HEIGHT/SPREAD **2.7ft (80cm)/2ft (60cm)**
HARDINESS **Zone 5**

Armstrong Nurseries

SEVERAL DISTINGUISHED ROSE BREEDERS, INCLUDING DR. WALTER LAMMERTS, HAVE CONTRIBUTED TO THE LEGACY OF FINE ROSES RAISED BY ARMSTRONG NURSERIES

John Armstrong left his home town in Ontario, Canada, in 1889 and moved to southern California in search of a cure for tuberculosis. Here, in what was to become Ontario, California, he started his own nursery. His first crops were olive trees and eucalyptus: roses did not become a major speciality until the 1920s.

John Armstrong and his son John S. Armstrong were plant breeders as well as growers. In the 1930s, Armstrong Nurseries created a rose research and development unit to breed new cultivars, and appointed Dr. Walter Lammerts to head it. Lammerts was a fastidious breeder who bred for size, scent, health, and strong colors. He introduced no more than 46 roses between 1940 and 1981, but they were all roses of remarkable quality. Many won prizes in the annual All-America Rose Selections. 'Charlotte Armstrong' was his first great success, issued in 1940 and named for John S. Armstrong's first wife. It is now the official flower of the city of Ontario. Lammerts' best-known rose is probably 'Queen Elizabeth', which combined the qualities of Hybrid Teas and Floribundas in such good measure that the American Rose Society introduced a new category of 'Grandiflora' roses to accommodate it. Other Lammerts successes include 'Chrysler Imperial', the rich yellow climber 'High Noon' (1946), the pink Hybrid Tea 'Show Girl' (1946), and the orange Floribunda 'Bahia' (1974).

'High Noon'

'Show Girl'

Lammerts was followed at Armstrong Nurseries by three more breeders of distinction – Herb Swim, Jack Christensen, and Tom Carruth. Swim's greatest roses were mainly Hybrid Teas: 'Sutter's Gold' (1950), 'Helen Traubel' (1951), the yellow 'Buccaneer' (1952), the white 'Matterhorn' (1965) and the dark red Grandiflora 'John S. Armstrong' (1961), which he named for his employer.

John Armstrong

Armstrong Nurseries was taken over by Jackson and Perkins in the 1980s, leaving Jack Christensen and Tom Carruth to give their greatest work as breeders to other employers. However, the legacy of Armstrong Nurseries in the middle years of the 20th century includes some of the finest roses, and their descendants, ever introduced.

'Arthur de Sansal', named after a French amateur horticulturist, is a typical Portland rose. The flowers are a rich, deep purple crimson with slightly paler backs. They open slowly until they are completely flat. Then they reveal a mass of quilled petals, a roughly quartered shape, and sometimes a button eye. The flowers come in small clusters (typically of 3–5) but have short pedicels and often look somewhat crammed up against each other as they expand. The flowers are surrounded by leaves. This happens with all Portland roses, because they have shorter and shorter internodes as they push up their buds, so that the flowers seem surrounded by a dense ruff of leaves. Plants of 'Arthur de Sansal' also have the short, compact, V-shaped outline of the Portland roses, with stout stems and smooth, dark green leaves – red for a while when young, especially around the edges of the leaflets. It is, unfortunately, susceptible to mildew and blackspot, so it prospers in hot, dry climates, where fungal diseases are not a problem, and where it will grow to 4.9ft (1.5m). It is reliably remontant, and repeats its flowering every six weeks or so.

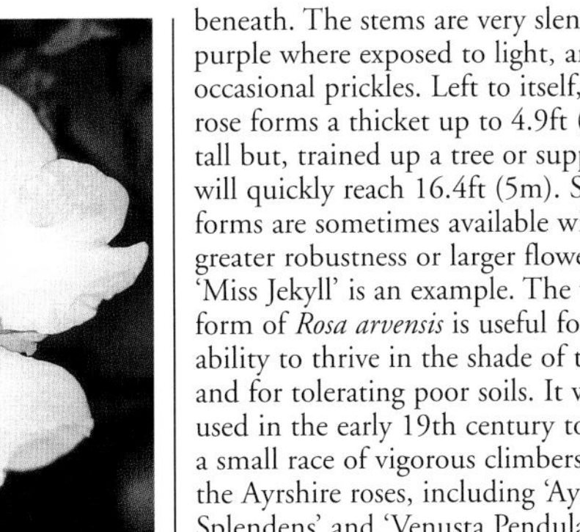

ROSA ARVENSIS

ARTISTRY

syn. 'JACIRST'

Hybrid Tea

ORIGIN **Zary, US, 1998**
FLOWER SIZE **4.7in (12cm)**
SCENT **Light and sweet**
FLOWERING **Repeats**
HEIGHT/SPREAD **4.9ft (1.5m)/4.1ft (1.25m)**
HARDINESS **Zone 6**
AWARDS **AARS 1997**

The color of Artistry is very variable. It opens a coral shade of orange and fades through crimson lake to dark pink, but it changes according to the weather, with the brightest colors appearing when it is hot. The petal backs are pale, sometimes no more than cream colored. Nevertheless, this excellent Hybrid Tea is always instantly recognizable. The flowers are classically long and conical at first, which makes Artistry a favorite among exhibitors, and they are borne singly on long stems, which also endears them to flower arrangers. The plant has large dark leaves, and a lot of them. It is vigorous, and repeats well and quickly. In hot climates it will grow to 6.6ft (2m).

ARTISTRY

ROSA ARVENSIS

Wild Rose

FLOWER SIZE **0.8in (2cm)**
SCENT **Strong and musky**
FLOWERING **Once only, fairly late in season**
HEIGHT/SPREAD **6.6ft (2m)/13.1ft (4m)**
HARDINESS **Zone 6**

Rosa arvensis is a trailing shrub or climbing rose, native to western and central Europe. Its flowers are pure white, with notched petals, exserted stigmas, and a strong musky scent: it is almost certainly the "original Shakespeare's Musk rose." The flowers are borne singly or in clusters of up to eight and are followed in autumn by round red hips. The leaves are thin, dark green above and slightly paler beneath. The stems are very slender, purple where exposed to light, and carry occasional prickles. Left to itself, the rose forms a thicket up to 4.9ft (1.5m) tall but, trained up a tree or support, it will quickly reach 16.4ft (5m). Selected forms are sometimes available with greater robustness or larger flowers: 'Miss Jekyll' is an example. The wild form of *Rosa arvensis* is useful for its ability to thrive in the shade of trees and for tolerating poor soils. It was used in the early 19th century to breed a small race of vigorous climbers called the Ayrshire roses, including 'Ayrshire Splendens' and 'Venusta Pendula'.

'ASCHERMITTWOCH'

'ASCHERMITTWOCH'

syn. 'ASH WEDNESDAY'

Modern Climber

ORIGIN **Kordes, Germany, 1955**
PARENTAGE ***Rosa rubiginosa* hybrid × 'Fashion'**
FLOWER SIZE **3.9in (10cm)**
SCENT **Medium and sweet**
FLOWERING **Once only**
HEIGHT/SPREAD **16.4ft (5m)/6.6ft (2m)**
HARDINESS **Zone 5**

Wilhelm Kordes used *Rosa rubiginosa* as a way of breeding greater hardiness into European roses. 'Aschermittwoch' was a surprising result – a rose whose outstanding quality is its remarkable and unique coloring. It is slightly variable and may on occasions have tints of lilac, pink, or yellow, but in most gardens, in most seasons, it is a stunning ghostly gray. The backs of the petals are more silvery, and this gives rise to dark gray shadows between the petals – all the more striking because the flower is so full of petals. The flowers come in clusters of 3–15 and are fairly abundantly borne. Unfortunately, it flowers only once, but 'Aschermittwoch' is one of those roses that ought to be in every rose lover's garden. The plant is very vigorous and fairly prickly. Its nondescript leaves may need protection against blackspot.

'ASH WEDNESDAY'

see 'ASCHERMITTWOCH'

'ARTHUR BELL'

Floribunda

ORIGIN **McGredy, Northern Ireland, 1965**
PARENTAGE **'Cläre Grammerstorf' × 'Piccadilly'**
FLOWER SIZE **3.9in (10cm)**
SCENT **Strong, rich, and fruity**
FLOWERING **Repeats very well**
HEIGHT/SPREAD **3.3ft (1m)/2.7ft (80cm)**
HARDINESS **Zone 5**
AWARDS **Belfast FA 1967**

This hardy, cheerful yellow Floribunda has proved exceptionally popular in England and the rest of northern Europe. It flowers early and repeats quickly. The flowers have a good, strong scent. Its weakness is the way its color fades: the flowers are a wonderful, deep yellow at first, but change quickly to primrose, lemon, and cream. This is most noticeable in hot or sunny weather, which explains why 'Arthur Bell' is not more widely grown in other parts of the world. The flowers are lightly double, with crimson stamens when they open out. They come in medium-sized clusters on thick, sturdy, prickly stems and stand up well to rain. The leaves are large, dark, healthy, and glossy.

Colin Pearce introduced a climbing form in 1979, which is widely grown in England but little known elsewhere. **'Climbing Arthur Bell'** is a stiff, stout grower and repeats well. Arthur Bell was the name of a Scotch whisky manufacturer; several of Sam McGredy IV's roses are named after alcoholic beverages.

'ARTHUR BELL'

'CLIMBING ARTHUR BELL'

Sport of 'Arthur Bell'

'CLIMBING ARTHUR BELL'

Climbing Floribunda
ORIGIN **Pearce, Britain, 1978**
FLOWER SIZE **4.3in (11cm)**
HEIGHT/SPREAD **11.5ft (3.5m)/6.6ft (2m)**

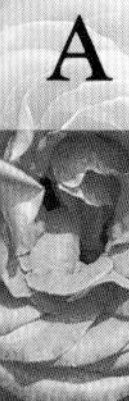

ASPIRIN ROSE

ASPIRIN ROSE

syn. 'TANIRIPSA'
Floribunda

ORIGIN **Tantau, Germany, 1997**
FLOWER SIZE **3.1in (8cm)**
SCENT **Light and sweet**
FLOWERING **Repeats well**
HEIGHT/SPREAD **2.7ft (80cm)/2.7ft (80cm)**
HARDINESS **Zone 5**
AWARDS **ADR 1996**

A rose called Aspirin? This one was chosen by Bayer to celebrate the 100th anniversary of the "wonder drug." It is a splendid short rose for almost any situation – part floribunda, part miniature, part shrub or groundcover – and particularly useful as individual plants in small gardens, as well as in large numbers in landscaping designs. When they first open, especially in cool weather, the flowers have a hint of blush pink at the center. Later they turn to pure glittering white. They are immensely freely borne in clusters of 3–15, so that the bush seems covered in flowers. They also drop their petals cleanly before they turn brown, so the bush always looks fresh. The bush is a good, dense shape, sometimes broader than high, and covered in small Wichurana-type leaves. They are very healthy apart from an occasional susceptibility to rust in affected areas. But Aspirin Rose is worth growing, even where this disease is prevalent.

'ASSEMBLAGE DE BEAUTÉ'

Gallica

ORIGIN **Delaage, 1823**
FLOWER SIZE **3.5in (9cm)**
SCENT **Light and sweet**
FLOWERING **Once only**
HEIGHT/SPREAD **4.9ft (1.5m)/3.3ft (1m)**
HARDINESS **Zone 5**

The name alone should guarantee the popularity of this beautiful Gallica. When it was first introduced (it was bred by a retired general), 'Assemblage de Beauté' was widely praised for the depth of its crimson coloring. The flowers are fully double, with quilled petals around a button eye. They are borne singly or, more usually, in sturdy clusters of up to five. The plant is upright, healthy, and fairly vigorous, but the leaves are a little darker and glossier than most Gallicas, suggesting some hybridity in its breeding.

ASSO DI CUORI

syn. 'KORRED', Ace of Hearts, Toque Rouge
Hybrid Tea

ORIGIN **Kordes, Germany, 1981**
FLOWER SIZE **4.7in (12cm)**
SCENT **Little or none**
FLOWERING **Repeats well**
HEIGHT/SPREAD **4.1ft (1.25m)/3.3ft (1m)**
HARDINESS **Zone 6**

This beautiful dark red Hybrid Tea has every virtue except strong scent. However, people's sense of smell varies, and some say they can detect a slight, sweet scent in Asso di Cuori. Its large, conical buds and reflexing petals make it a popular rose for cutting and exhibition, as well as a good choice for bedding. The flowers are borne on long stems, singly or in clusters of up to three, and keep their deep red coloring well. Sometimes it produces "split" buds, but these open out well as garden flowers. The tough petals stand up well to rain. Asso di Cuori has small, dark, glossy leaves and dark green prickles. A good, dependable rose.

'ASSEMBLAGE DE BEAUTÉ'

ASSO DI CUORI

'ASTRA DESMOND'

see 'WHITE FLIGHT'

'ASTRÉE'

Hybrid Tea

ORIGIN **Croix, France, 1956**
PARENTAGE **'Mme. A. Meilland' x 'Blanche Mallerin'**
FLOWER SIZE **5.1in (13cm)**
SCENT **Very strong and sweet**
FLOWERING **Repeats well**
HEIGHT/SPREAD **4.1ft (1.25m)/3.3ft (1m)**
HARDINESS **Zone 6**
AWARDS **Plus Belle Rose de France 1956**

Any Hybrid Tea that was bred as long ago as 1956 and is still widely available must be exceptional. 'Astrée' is outstanding in many ways. Its scent is one of the richest and most delicious of all roses. Its flowers are large, shapely, and beautiful at every stage of their development, starting as elegant buds. They are deep pink, with a hint of orange on the petal backs at first, and a suffusion of yellow toward the base of the petals. When they open out fully, and the petals roll back their edges, they reveal a pale gold center and dark crimson stamens – a beautiful contrast with the dark pink petals. They come singly or in clusters of up to four, and are held upright on a strong, vigorous bush with large, dark, healthy leaves.

'ASTRÉE'

ASTRID LINDGREN

syn. 'POULDUF', Dream Sequence
Shrub Rose

ORIGIN **Poulsen, Denmark, 1989**
FLOWER SIZE **3.5in (9cm)**
SCENT **Light and fruity**
FLOWERING **Repeats well**
HEIGHT/SPREAD **5.7ft (1.75m)/4.1ft (1.25m)**
HARDINESS **Zone 6**

Astrid Lindgren is a tall, bushy, Floribunda-type of shrub. It has pretty, creamy pink flowers with slightly darker petal backs. They come in clusters of 10–15, sometimes fewer. The flowers are loose, not too full, and open out well. They fade a little in the sun – the richest colors come in cool weather and autumn. It has great vigor

ASTRID LINDGREN

ATLANTIC STAR

and flowers very abundantly. The plant has masses of mid-green, healthy foliage and a good shrubby habit. It reaches 3.3ft (1m) in a really cold climate like Ontario (where it will need some winter protection), and as much as 8.2ft (2.5m) in warm climates. The name of this rose commemorates Swedish author Astrid Lindgren (1907–2002), who invented the popular children's character Pippi Långstrump (Pippi Longstocking).

ATHENA

syn. 'RÜHKOR'
Hybrid Tea

ORIGIN **Kordes, Germany, 1981**
PARENTAGE **Seedling x Helmut Schmidt**
FLOWER SIZE **4.3in (11cm)**
SCENT **Medium and sweet**
FLOWERING **Repeats**
HEIGHT/SPREAD **4.1ft (1.25m)/3.3ft (1m)**
HARDINESS **Zone 6**

One of the strange anomalies about the rose trade is the way a new variety may be introduced not in its country of origin but somewhere else instead. Athena is a good example – unknown in its native Germany, or in the rest of Europe, or anywhere in North America, but very popular and widely grown in Australia. The flowers are large and crystalline white, with pink edges to the petals. They have long petals and elegant buds that open out slowly. They are borne singly or in small clusters (rarely of more than five flowers) on long stems, which makes them good for cutting, though Athena is also a good bedding rose. The plant is upright and fairly vigorous, with large dark leaves.

ATHENA

ATLANTIC STAR

syn. 'FRYWORLD'
Floribunda

ORIGIN **Fryer, Britain, 1993**
FLOWER SIZE **3.5in (9cm)**
SCENT **Medium and sweet**
FLOWERING **Repeats well**
HEIGHT/SPREAD **3.3ft (1m)/2.7ft (80cm)**
HARDINESS **Zone 6**

Apricot Floribunda roses were fashionable in the 1990s. Atlantic Star is a good example. When the flowers open out, they are more pink than apricot, but the backs of their petals are orange, and the interaction between the pink and the orange produces the rich overall apricot effect. That said, the flowers tend to become more pink as they age. They are full of petals, which later develop an attractive wave. They are borne in clusters of up to seven on long, straight stems – perfect for cutting. The plant has thick, dark, glossy foliage, prickly stems, and a good health record. The flowers stand up well to rain.

AUCKLAND METRO

syn. 'MACPUCPAL', Métro, Precious Michelle
Hybrid Tea

ORIGIN **McGredy, New Zealand, 1987**
PARENTAGE **Sexy Rexy x (seedling x 'Ferry Porsche')**
FLOWER SIZE **4.7in (12cm)**
SCENT **Strong and sweet**
FLOWERING **Repeats**
HEIGHT/SPREAD **4.1ft (1.25m)/3.3ft (1m)**
HARDINESS **Zone 6**

For sheer beauty, it is difficult to beat Auckland Metro. The flowers are large, exquisitely shaped, deliciously scented, and palest pink. The buds have a greenish tinge at first, but they open out almost white – the coloring comes from a hint of pink on the backs of the innermost petals. The flowers come singly or in clusters of up to five on fairly long stems, which makes them good for cutting – as does their ability to keep their beautiful shape for much longer than most roses. Auckland Metro makes a sturdy, vigorous, bushy plant, with healthy, dark green leaves that provide a good foil for the translucent flowers. It is a quick repeater. The flowers sometimes turn green in hot sun, so 'Auckland Metro' produces its bes flowers in cool weather, or when it is well-irrigated and shaded in hotter weather.

'AUGUSTE GERVAIS'

Wichurana Rambler

ORIGIN **Barbier, France, 1918**
PARENTAGE ***Rosa wichurana* x 'Le Progrès'**
FLOWER SIZE **4.3in (11cm)**
SCENT **Medium, sweet, and fruity**
FLOWERING **Once exuberantly and then intermittently**
HEIGHT/SPREAD **16.4ft (5m)/9.8ft (3m)**
HARDINESS **Zone 7**

This exquisite large-flowered Wichurana rambler is popular still (and rightly so) in its native France, and much of the rest of Europe, but not well-known elsewhere. 'Auguste Gervais' has unusually large flowers, full of pale apricot pink petals that fade to cream at the edges. The undersides of the petals and, more noticeably, the center of the flower always retain richer tints than the outer petals, especially in cool climates. When they open out, the lightly cupped flowers have a rosette shape and a muddle of petals at the center. The flowers are borne in open clusters of 5–12, and make a fine display during their first big flowering. However, you can usually find a few flowers on an established plant until well into autumn. 'Auguste Gervais' has large, dark, glossy, Wichurana leaves and a long, flexible habit of growth. It is very vigorous, and will quickly reach 16.4ft (5m) or more.

'AUGUSTE GERVAIS'

AUGUSTE RENOIR

syn. 'MEITOIFAR'
Hybrid Tea

ORIGIN **Meilland, France, 1992**
PARENTAGE **(Versailles x Pierre de Ronsard) x 'Kimono'**
FLOWER SIZE **4.3in (11cm)**
SCENT **Strong and sweet**
FLOWERING **Repeats**
HEIGHT/SPREAD **4.9ft (1.5m)/3.3ft (1m)**
HARDINESS **Zone 5**

Although classed as a Hybrid Tea, Auguste Renoir belongs to Meilland's Romantica series of roses, which seeks to evoke the scent and beauty of 19th-century roses. The flowers are a swirling mass of rich pink opulence, sometimes reminiscent of a peony but always full of petals displayed in a loose arrangement. The color and sense of movement are intensified by the petals having slightly darker backs. The flowers are borne usually singly and their long stems are ideal for large cut flower arrangements. The plant has healthy, mid-green leaves and lots of prickles. It is vigorous, and will grow to 6.6ft (2m) in a hot climate – but elsewhere to no more than3.3ft (1m). It produces its flowers in heavy flushes, but does best in hot, dry climates: the flowers spoil in rain.

AUCKLAND METRO

AUGUSTE RENOIR

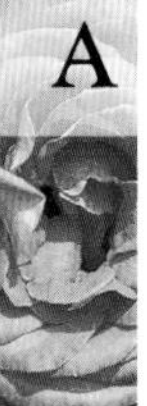

'Aunt Honey'

'Autumn Delight'

Ave Maria

'Aunt Honey'

Shrub Rose

ORIGIN **Buck, US, 1984**
PARENTAGE **'Music Maker' × 'Habanera'**
FLOWER SIZE **4.7in (12cm)**
SCENT **Medium, fruity, and sweet**
FLOWERING **Repeats well**
HEIGHT/SPREAD **4.1ft (1.25m)/3.3ft (1m)**
HARDINESS **Zone 4**

It is classified as a shrub rose, but 'Aunt Honey' looks for all the world like a pink Hybrid Tea. Griffith Buck's achievement was to breed a rose of such beauty that would flourish in the unpromising climate of Iowa. The buds are large and high-centered in the Hybrid Tea style. Its flowers open large and pink, full of petals, and neatly arranged like a camellia. Later they reflex along their sides and assume a more spiky shape. They are borne singly and in clusters of up to seven on a strong-growing, prickly, bushy plant. 'Aunt Honey' has pale green leaves and large, rounded leaflets. It flowers repeatedly until the first frost.

'Australia Felix'

Polyantha

ORIGIN **Clark, Australia, 1919**
PARENTAGE **'Jersey Beauty' × 'La France'**
FLOWER SIZE **2.4in (6cm)**
SCENT **Strong and sweet**
FLOWERING **Recurrent**
HEIGHT/SPREAD **3.3ft (1m)/3.3ft (1m)**
HARDINESS **Zone 6**

'Australia Felix'

This beautiful and very floriferous Polyantha rose should be much more widely known and grown outside its native Australia. Its loosely cupped, semidouble flowers open from neat little buds and come in long, well-spaced clusters of 10–30. The flowers have short petals, with a heart-shaped outline. They open rich mid-pink, with a white center and occasional white flecks, and fade to mother-of-pearl and nearly white. They are much paler on the reverses, with even an occasional greenish tinge. The plant sheds its old flowers slowly. The new growth is dark red, giving way to reddish stems and good, dark green, glossy Wichurana foliage. The plant has a few prickles and occasionally suffers from mildew, but it is very pretty, especially when well grown. It is not unlike (but superior to) some of the better-known Poulsen Polyanthas of the same period. Australia Felix was the name given to the early settlements in Victoria.

'Austrian Briar'

see Rosa foetida

'Austrian Copper'

see Rosa foetida 'Bicolor'

'Autumn Damask'

see 'Quatre Saisons'

'Autumn Delight'

Hybrid Musk

ORIGIN **Bentall, Britain, 1933**
FLOWER SIZE **2in (5cm)**
SCENT **Strong, sweet, and musky**
FLOWERING **Repeats**
HEIGHT/SPREAD **4.9ft (1.5m)/4.1ft (1.25m)**
HARDINESS **Zone 6**

The name of 'Autumn Delight' indicates that this Hybrid Musk rose is better in autumn than summer. The hips are of no great merit (they are rarely any color other than green), but the color of the flowers is much richer and more intense in the cool weather of an English autumn. Then the rich apricot buds open out to shades of buff, cream, and pink. In summer, and in the hot climates where Hybrid Musk bushes grow so well, the flowers are much paler – rarely more than cream – and quickly turn to white. The golden stamens and red filaments are attractive at all times. The flowers come in large clusters of 10–30 (but twice as many in autumn). The plant has small, dark, healthy leaves, smooth stems (often completely thornless), and an upright habit. It is fairly vigorous. Little or no pruning suits it best.

'Autumn Fire'

see 'Herbstfeuer'

'Avandel'

Miniature Rose

ORIGIN **Moore, US, 1977**
PARENTAGE **'Little Darling' × 'New Penny'**
FLOWER SIZE **1.2in (3cm)**
SCENT **Light, sweet, and fruity**
FLOWERING **Repeats well**
HEIGHT/SPREAD **1.6ft (50cm)/1ft (30cm)**
HARDINESS **Zone 6**
AWARDS **AoE 1978**

The flowers of 'Avandel' are very attractive. They are golden yellow, with orange tips to the petals and hints of pink, apricot, and crimson at different stages of their development. The petal backs are always slightly darker in color. In hot climates or strong sunlight, the yellow fades almost to white, leaving the flowers cream colored with crimson edges. As if in compensation for this, the flowers then open out completely to show their golden stamens at the center. The petals reflex attractively and the flowers come in clusters of 5–25. 'Avandel' has small, dark leaves and a bushy habit of growth. It is not a prolific flowerer – you may have to wait a while between flushes – but the clusters of bright, shapely flowers are very handsome.

'Avandel'

Ave Maria

syn. 'KORav', Sunburnt Country

Hybrid Tea

ORIGIN **Kordes, Germany, 1981**
PARENTAGE **'Uwe Seeler' × Sonia Meilland**
FLOWER SIZE **4.7in (12cm)**
SCENT **Medium, sweet, and fruity**
FLOWERING **Repeats**
HEIGHT/SPREAD **4.9ft (1.5m)/3.3ft (1m)**
HARDINESS **Zone 6**

The buds of Ave Maria are pale vermilion with a hint of orange, long, and classically shaped. When they open out to reveal their large petals, the flowers are more salmon pink. Though it is classed among the Hybrid Teas, the flowers of Ave Maria often come in clusters of 3–7. They are borne on long stems that are useful for cutting. They also stand up well to rain and have a brilliance that catches the eye from a distance – a good bedding rose where brightness is required. The plant has medium-sized, glossy leaves, lots of small prickles, and an upright habit of growth.

A

David Austin

THE GENIUS AND INVENTION OF DAVID AUSTIN, ONE OF THE MOST IMPORTANT ROSE BREEDERS OF MODERN TIMES, HAVE BROUGHT HIM HUGE INTERNATIONAL SUCCESS

In the 1950s, David Austin set out to breed roses that combined the shapes and scents of old-fashioned roses with the perpetually flowering habit of modern ones. The result was a change of fashion and a worldwide demand for his roses.

Austin, a farmer's son, was brought up in Albrighton in the English Midlands. His first introductions were vigorous once-flowering shrubs – first-generation crosses between Gallicas and Floribundas – 'Constance Spry' in 1961 and 'Chianti' in 1967. It was in 1969 that he issued his first repeat-flowering roses, a series named after characters in Chaucer's *The Canterbury Tales*, including 'Dame Prudence', 'The Prioress', and 'Wife of Bath'. The following year, Austin started his own nursery, David Austin Roses, which specialized in selling heritage and historic roses. But it was not until the early 1980s that sales of his own-raised roses started to exceed old-fashioned ones.

David Austin

It was at this time that Austin started to brand his roses "English Roses," but the phrase has been slow to catch the public's imagination, and in much of the world his roses are known simply as "David Austins". His international commercial success gained impetus with the release of 'Mary Rose' and 'Graham Thomas' in 1983. Since then, growth has been exponential and distribution controlled through a worldwide system of licensing that has ensured that Austin's roses are seen as a premium product in every market. Even in 1980, Austin was sowing no more than 20,000 seeds a year: his annual tally these days is 300,000 – and 4 million plants are sold every year.

There are certain points to remember when growing David Austin roses. They rarely repeat their flowering as frequently as Floribundas, Teas, and Hybrid Teas. Yet they actually seem more floriferous because they reach their greatest beauty at the fully open stage. They tend to be less hardy – few will accept greater cold than Zone 6 – and less disease-resistant than genuinely old roses. None of Austin's roses – even ones like 'Mistress Quickly', which was introduced as "totally disease resistant" – is free of fungal infection everywhere. Their vigor is stupendous. They tend to grow much taller in hot climates than in England: people in Texas or New South Wales who buy 'Leander' or 'Graham Thomas' expecting a 3.3ft (1m) shrub are often surprised to find that they have acquired a 9.8ft (3m) climber.

These days Austin's roses – like **Alnwick Castle** – can compete with all on health and floriferousness. Every year, in every way, Austin's roses get better and better. The proof lies in the competition that his success has provoked – like Generosa roses from Guillot and Romantica roses from Meilland in France: none of them has come close to matching Austin's creations for sheer excellence.

Alnwick Castle

Back on the farm at Albrighton, David Austin has laid out a demonstration garden. It is very well designed and planted to show roses of all kinds alongside his own creations. The standard of maintenance is excellent. It is a beautiful rose garden in Britain, open every day of the year – and free.

AUSTIN'S ROSE GARDEN AT ALBRIGHTON, SHROPSHIRE

A

‘AVEU’

‘AVEU’

Hybrid Tea

ORIGIN **Croix, France**
FLOWER SIZE **4.7in (12cm)**
SCENT **Medium and sweet**
FLOWERING **Repeats well**
HEIGHT/SPREAD **4.1ft (1.25m)/3.3ft (1m)**
HARDINESS **Zone 6**

This rich, dark pink Hybrid Tea is popular in France. ‘Aveu’ has large, plump buds of classical shape, rolling back their petals as they expand. The petals have silvery pink backs, and fade to pale pink as the flowers open out to reveal their dark yellow stamens. The flowers are borne singly (occasionally in twos and threes) on long, strong stems that are good for cutting and exhibition. ‘Aveu’ has large, dark, healthy leaves, a sturdy, upright habit of growth, and large prickles. It is a good rose that should be much more widely known and grown internationally.

‘AVIATEUR BLÉRIOT’

Wichurana Rambler

ORIGIN **Fauque, France, 1910**
PARENTAGE ***Rosa wichurana* × ‘William Allen Richardson’**
FLOWER SIZE **2.4in (6cm)**
SCENT **Light and fruity**
FLOWERING **Once, early in season**
HEIGHT/SPREAD **13.1ft (4m)/6.6ft (2m)**
HARDINESS **Zone 6**

‘Aviateur Blériot’ is a pretty and popular Wichurana rambler, though not the most floriferous. When first introduced, it was considered the best yellow Wichurana available. In fact, the flowers open apricot and fade to pale yellow, cream, and white. They then stay white for a long time, becoming increasingly messy until the petals turn brown. The flowers are fairly double, though the stamens are visible as they age, and come in clusters of 3–7. The small, dark, neat, glossy Wichurana leaves are very attractive. The plant has the flexible, trailing, sprawling habit that makes Wichuranas so suited to training over structures and grafting as weeping standards. The name commemorates

‘AVON’

Louis Blériot (1872–1936), the inventor of the monoplane and the first man to fly across the English Channel (31 miles/50km in 37 minutes) in 1909.

‘AVON’

Hybrid Tea

ORIGIN **Morey, US, 1961**
PARENTAGE **'Nocturne' × 'Chrysler Imperial'**
FLOWER SIZE **4.7in (12cm)**
SCENT **Strong and sweet**
FLOWERING **Repeats well**
HEIGHT/SPREAD **4.9ft (1.5m)/3.3ft (1m)**
HARDINESS **Zone 6**

This sumptuous crimson Hybrid Tea – with a scent to match its color – has retained its popularity over many years, despite the efforts of newer roses to dislodge it. The reason is that ‘Avon’ is a most reliable performer, especially in California and much of Australia, where its many-petaled flowers can open without damage from rain or mildew – both of which spoil it in cooler, wetter climates. It is a popular exhibition rose – the flowers are produced singly on long, strong stems – and a good, vigorous grower, constantly putting out more flowers. They keep their color and last well both as cut flowers and on the bush.

AVON

AVON

syn. ‘POULMULTI’, Niagara

Ground Cover

ORIGIN **Poulsen, Denmark, 1992**
FLOWER SIZE **1.4in (3.5cm)**
SCENT **Light and musky**
FLOWERING **Repeats well**
HEIGHT/SPREAD **4.9ft (1.5m)/6.6ft (2m)**
HARDINESS **Zone 5**

The Danish rose dynasty of Poulsen introduced this white groundcover rose in 1992. The flowers of Avon are small, semidouble, and white – little more than a miniature – but borne with wonderful freedom. Actually, the flowers open from pale pink buds and may be palest pink at first, but they quickly fade to white. They come in small clusters, typically of 5–10, all over the surface of the lax bush. The plant is usually said to reach no more than about 1.3ft (40cm) high and 3.3ft (1m) across, but in hot climates, if allowed to grow unchecked, it will attain a much greater size. It flowers almost continuously. The leaves are small, neat, dark, and healthy. Young plants are good for containers but will need to be planted in the ground in late autumn.

‘AWAKENING’

see ‘DR. W. VAN FLEET’

‘AYRSHIRE SPLENDENS’

syn. ‘SPLENDENS’

Ayrshire

ORIGIN **Rivers, Britain, 1835**
FLOWER SIZE **2.4in (6cm)**
SCENT **Strong and myrrhlike**
FLOWERING **Once only**
HEIGHT/SPREAD **16.4ft (5m)/9.8ft (3m)**
HARDINESS **Zone 5**

The Ayrshire roses are old hybrids of *Rosa arvensis*, the only Musk rose native to northwestern Europe. They are vigorous, once-flowering ramblers with long, flexible stems. ‘Ayrshire Splendens’ is one of the best, and looks spectacular when its heavy, crimson-splashed buds open up to reveal the pale flesh pink flowers inside. Later the flowers fade to white, with just a tinge of pink at the edges. They are semidouble, medium-sized, strongly and pungently scented of myrrh, and borne in small clusters (but in very great quantities). Orange red hips follow in due course. ‘Ayrshire Splendens’ is very hardy and vigorous, though the plant may take a few years to build up to its full size. The leaves are glossy and plentiful, though sometimes a little susceptible to mildew. Its hardiness has made it popular in central Europe, but it is regrettably little known in the US.

‘AVIATEUR BLÉRIOT’

‘AYRSHIRE SPLENDENS’

B

BABY BLANKET

see SOMMERMORGEN

'BABY FAURAX'

Polyantha

ORIGIN **Lille, France, 1924**
FLOWER SIZE **1.6in (4cm)**
SCENT **Light and musky**
FLOWERING **Repeats constantly**
HEIGHT/SPREAD **2ft (60cm)/1.3ft (40cm)**
HARDINESS **Zone 5**

'Baby Faurax' has stunning, little, double, purple flowers that are perfect in containers and mix well with almost every other plant in a garden border. The color depends on the weather – it is deeper and richer in cool weather, more lilac or mauve in hot. The petal backs are pale and the individual blooms fade as they age, turning brown before dropping their petals. The flowers come in small, loose clusters, typically of 5–10 blooms, sometimes more. 'Baby Faurax' has a dense, compact habit of growth, small, dark leaves, and quite a few prickles. The stems have dark glands on the surface that emit an attractive scent when rubbed.

'BABY FAURAX'

BABY LOVE

syn. 'SCRIVLUV'

Miniature Rose

ORIGIN **Scrivens, Britain, 1992**
PARENTAGE **Sweet Magic seedling x (Landora x *Rosa davidii elongata* seedling)**
FLOWER SIZE **2in (5cm)**
SCENT **Light and fruity**
FLOWERING **Almost continuous**
HEIGHT/SPREAD **3.3ft (1m)/2.5ft (75cm)**
HARDINESS **Zone 5**
AWARDS **RNRS GM 1993**

Baby Love was bred by an English amateur who had the patience to experiment with species roses: his quest for disease resistance led him to use *Rosa davidii*. The result is a neat, free-flowering patio rose that is practically immune to disease. Baby Love has small, single flowers of sunny yellow that appear all over the surface of the bush and are followed by small orange hips. It is densely clothed with small, dark, glossy leaves right down to ground level. It performs well in all climates – hot and cold, wet and dry – but grows tall in hot areas, where it may be as much as 5.7ft (1.75m). Its dense growth makes it equally useful as a small hedge or as a solid looking shrub in a mixed border.

BABY LOVE

PARC DE BAGATELLE

DESIGNED BY THE GREAT FORESTIER TO HONOR THE CITY OF PARIS, THIS MAGNIFICENT ROSE GARDEN IS SET IN THE GROUNDS OF A ROYAL CHATEAU

THE CHÂTEAU AT BAGATELLE was built in 1777 by the future King Charles X to win a wager with his sister-in-law Queen Marie-Antoinette. When the city of Paris acquired the 60-acre (24-hectare) estate in 1905, the city fathers instructed the great designer Jean-Claude Nicolas Forestier (1861–1930) to lay out a rose garden at its southern end.

Forestier centered his design around two axes – a long view to the magnificent 19th-century orangery and a cross-view from an oriental kiosk from which the Empress Eugénie had once watched the Prince Imperial learn to ride. This charming folly is set on a mound to the southeast of the grounds and offers a beautiful vista of the garden.

Forestier's rose garden has a firm design, with geometric beds edged in neatly trimmed box and sown with grass. Clumps of roses are planted in circles cut out of the grass, often surrounding a handsome standard rose. This pattern is repeated all over the garden to stunning effect. Huge obelisks of climbing roses also feature in the design. Several plants of a single cultivar are wound around supports and kept well trimmed and trained so that they are spectacular in full flower. A long pergola thickly covered with climbing and rambling roses fills the far end of the rose garden. More climbers are trained as garlands on rope swags that give form to the beds, while large cones of perfectly clipped yew give further structure to the design.

Bagatelle has some 20,000 roses, in about 2,500 different cultivars. In front of the orangery is a collection of historic roses – notably the early Hybrid Teas and Floribundas. The importance of Bagatelle lies in its stylish design and its popularity as much as in its collection of roses. It was Forestier's masterpiece, and one of two gardens – the other is La Roseraie du Val de Marne at L'Haÿ-les-Roses – that have made Paris famous for its roses.

ROSES ARE GROWN IN MANY WAYS IN THE VIEW UP TO THE EMPRESS'S KIOSK

CLIPPED CONES OF YEW

B

'BABY MASQUERADE'

'BABY MASQUERADE'

syn. 'BABY CARNIVAL'

Miniature Rose

ORIGIN **Tantau, Germany, 1955**
PARENTAGE **'Tom Thumb' × 'Masquerade'**
FLOWER SIZE **1in (2.5cm)**
SCENT **Light**
FLOWERING **Repeats very well**
HEIGHT/SPREAD **9.8in (25cm)/1.3ft (40cm)**
HARDINESS **Zone 6**

'Baby Masquerade' has long enjoyed great popularity as a miniature rose, with the inconstant coloring of its parent 'Masquerade'. Its flowers open yellow, with coral pink edges. As they open, the petals fold back, lose their yellowness, and acquire redder tints, until they end up dull crimson. Sometimes the flowers also bleach as they age. The petal backs are always paler and the outer petals take on more color than the inner ones, but this array of different colors is what distinguishes 'Baby Masquerade'. The plant is healthy and has little Polyantha leaves, but it is grown for its flowers and is very floriferous.

'BALLERINA'

Hybrid Musk

ORIGIN **Bentall, Britain, 1937**
FLOWER SIZE **1.2in (3cm)**
SCENT **Musky**
FLOWERING **Almost continuous**
HEIGHT/SPREAD **4.9ft (1.5m)/5.7ft (1.75m)**
HARDINESS **Zone 6**

'Ballerina' has one of the simplest – and least sophisticated – flowers of all shrub roses, and yet is also one of the most popular. The sheer quantity of its flowers explain all: 'Ballerina' blooms ceaselessly through until early winter, and its flower trusses get larger and larger as it does so. The individual flowers open dark pink and fade away quickly, enlarging and developing their white eye until only a hint of pale pink remains at the edge of the petal. The stamens are pretty to start with, but they too fade away and brown very quickly. The flowers come in perfectly spaced clusters and are followed by small orange hips, useful for decoration. The plant is tough and healthy, with mid-green leaves and a few large prickles. It is best allowed to grow to its natural size and shape, which is rounded and mounded, rather than clipped, though it can be trained as a short climber against a hot wall. It is equally good when grown as a border plant or specimen shrub (it is pictured, above, grown as a short standard) and when planted as a hedge. It is also very easy to grow. In hot climates it will flourish in shade, where it keeps its coloring longer.

'BALLERINA'

'BALTIMORE BELLE'

ROSA BANKSIAE

Wild Rose

FLOWER SIZE **0.4in (1cm)**
SCENT **Strong and violetlike**
FLOWERING **Once only, very early in season**
HEIGHT/SPREAD **23ft (7m)/9.8ft (3m)**
HARDINESS **Zone 7**

The Banksian roses are always among the first to flower, several weeks before the main flush of other roses. They are vigorous climbing plants, very popular in warm climates, where they thrive with little attention even in the hottest and driest of positions. Their long growths are covered with clusters of small flowers, often violet scented, and always white or yellow. The wild species is known as *Rosa banksiae* var. *normalis*. Its single flowers have distinctive white petals and long, wispy stamens. It comes from subtropical China, where it is widely used in agricultural areas as a boundary hedge between fields.

The double white form is a popular garden plant in China. It was the first Banksian rose to be introduced to the West in 1807 by William Kerr, who worked for the director of Kew, Sir Joseph Banks (1743–1820). It was named after Banks's wife Dorothea (1758–1828) and is known to gardeners as ***Rosa banksiae* var. *banksiae***. It has large clusters of very double flowers and is enormously vigorous and enduring: the largest rose bush in the world is a specimen of *Rosa banksiae* var. *banksiae* in Tombstone, Arizona, which was planted in 1886. The circumference of its trunk is now about 11.5ft (3.5m) and its canopy, supported by wires and scaffolding, covers an area of 6,600sq ft (800sq m).

The double yellow Banksian rose, ***Rosa banksiae* var. *lutea***, was introduced to the West from Nankin by John Parks for the Horticultural Society of London in 1824. It has large clusters of straw yellow flowers with a green eye. It is the only Banksian rose without a scent, but its profusion so early in the season compensates abundantly. It is probably an old Chinese garden hybrid between the wild species and a yellow China rose. It is the hardiest of the Banksians. The single yellow form, *Rosa banksiae* f. *lutescens*, has slightly larger flowers and turquoise blue hips.

Other forms and hybrids of *Rosa banksiae* are commonly found in Chinese gardens, including 'Fortuniana'. Western hybrids of the Banksian rose are less commonly seen, but include the ever-blooming 'Purezza' bred by Quinto Mansuino in Italy, which is pure white, loosely double and 1.6in (4cm) in diameter.

Banksian Hybrids

BANKSIAE VAR. *BANKSIAE*

BANKSIAE VAR. *LUTEA*

SCENT **Little or none**
HARDINESS **Zone 6**

ROSA BANKSIAE VAR. *NORMALIS*

ROSA BANKSIAE VAR. *BANKSIAE*

ROSA BANKSIAE VAR. *LUTEA*

'BALTIMORE BELLE'

Setigera Hybrid

ORIGIN **Feast, US, 1843**
PARENTAGE ***Rosa setigera* × unknown**
FLOWER SIZE **1.4in (3.5cm)**
SCENT **Light and musky**
FLOWERING **Once only, late in season**
HEIGHT/SPREAD **13.1ft (4m)/9.8ft (3m)**
HARDINESS **Zone 5**

The pollen parent of 'Baltimore Belle' was probably a Noisette rose, which has given it a few autumn flowers and means that it is slightly less hardy than most of the ironclad Prairie roses. It is, however, a most spectacular sight in full flower. The flowers have a charming shape – very double, with a button center and sometimes a green eye. The outer petals are slightly incurved. In some years, the buds are richly touched with crimson. The flowers are pale pink at first, and fade to white, but retain an occasional dark pink petal toward the center. They have long pedicels, like cherry blossom, and the clusters (of up to 30 flowers) droop down while the individual pedicels curve up and carry their flowers toward the sun. It has a long flowering season, starting somewhat late. The leaves are rough, large, handsome, fresh mid-green, and comparatively resistant to disease. The plant has very pliable stems, and roots easily from cuttings.

'BANTRY BAY'

Modern Climber

ORIGIN **McGredy, Northern Ireland, 1967**
PARENTAGE **'New Dawn' × 'Korona'**
FLOWER SIZE **3.5in (9cm)**
SCENT **Light and sweet**
FLOWERING **Repeats well**
HEIGHT/SPREAD **11.5ft (3.5m)/6.6ft (2m)**
HARDINESS **Zone 5**

'Bantry Bay' is one of the short, floriferous modern climbers that Sam McGredy bred in the 1960s and 1970s, using the ever-blooming rambler 'New Dawn' as his foundation. They lack the flexibility of 'New Dawn', being stout-stemmed and upright in habit, but they all have large flowers and are rarely out of bloom. The flowers of 'Bantry Bay'

B

'BANTRY BAY'

open from long buds. They are rich pink at first, with slightly darker petal backs and a hint of salmon, but they fade eventually to pale pink, especially in hot sunshine. On the other hand, their strong petals stand up well to rain. They come singly or in clusters of 3–5 on long stems. Many of the flowers come on old wood, breaking out at every level, but later in the year they are borne on new wood. The plant has a lot of leaves with dark, broad leaflets, coppery at first.

BARBARA AUSTIN

syn. 'AUSTOP'

Shrub Rose

ORIGIN **Austin, Britain, 1997**
PARENTAGE **Fair Bianca x seedling**
FLOWER SIZE **3.1in (8cm)**
SCENT **Medium and sweet**
FLOWERING **Repeats**
HEIGHT/SPREAD **4.9ft (1.5m)/4.1ft (1.25m)**
HARDINESS **Zone 5**

The flowers of Barbara Austin are mid-pink at first, but fade to a very beautiful blush pink with occasional hints of mauve. They are lightly cupped, and show a mass of petals arranged as an informal rosette. They are borne usually singly but sometimes in clusters of up to six. But the real strength of this rose is the profusion with which it covers itself: the bush is studded with glorious shapely flowers. It grows into a strong, twiggy, upright shrub, but may need a little staking as it matures, to keep the mass of flowers from tumbling over. It has healthy, mid-green leaves. Barbara Austin is David's younger sister, and a distinguished nurserywoman in her own right.

BARBARA AUSTIN

THE BARBIERS

THE FAMOUS FRENCH BARBIER NURSERY INTRODUCED WICHURANA RAMBLERS TO EUROPE OVER A CENTURY AGO

RENÉ BARBIER AND his partners in the Barbier nursery – Léon, Georges, and Albert – were based near Orléans in Olivet, where Albert was mayor. René produced hybrids that were everything Wichurana ramblers should be: vigorous, flexible, floriferous, and healthy. Their flowers were large, scented, and beautifully shaped. There are 33 Barbier hybrids still in existence, all introduced between 1900 and 1930. Together they amount to the single most impressive group of Wichurana ramblers ever produced, and include such universal and perennial favourites as 'François Juranville' (1906) and 'Albertine' (1921).

'FRANÇOIS FOUCARD'

In fact, the Barbiers introduced so many Wichurana ramblers that the market could not absorb them properly. As a result, some of the best cultivars, including 'Joseph Liger' (1909), 'François Poisson' (1902), 'Désiré Bergera' (1910), 'Jules Levacher' (Barbier, 1908), and 'Valentin Beaulieu' (1902), are now extremely rare in cultivation. Specimens survive only in the great European collections at L'Haÿ-les-Roses and Sangerhausen. However, the modern interest in conservation, choice, and variety means that others have recently been reintroduced to commerce, including the exquisite 'Alexandre Tremouillet' (1903) and 'François Foucard' (1901).

Most of the Barbier ramblers were crosses between *Rosa wichurana* and Tea roses – and, later, of Hybrid Teas. They are more floriferous but less hardy than ramblers that have Hybrid Perpetuals as one of their parents. (Nevertheless, the later Barbier ramblers like 'Jacotte' (1920) and 'Primevère' (1929) are hardy and popular all through New England.)

The Barbier family also bred and introduced the first Wichurana Polyantha, 'Renoncule', in 1911 as well as a number of "way-out" hybrids: 'Rustica' (1929) was a seedling of 'Harison's Yellow', and 'Wichmoss' (1911) came from a cross between *Rosa wichurana* and 'Salet'. But it is for their spectacular, early-flowering Wichurana ramblers that the Barbiers are best remembered today.

'DÉSIRÉ BERGERA'

BARBARA BUSH

syn. 'JACBUSH'

Hybrid Tea

ORIGIN **Warriner, US, 1990**
PARENTAGE **Pristine x 'Antigua'**
FLOWER SIZE **5.5in (14cm)**
SCENT **Light and sweet**
FLOWERING **Repeats**
HEIGHT/SPREAD **4.9ft (1.5m)/4.1ft (1.25m)**
HARDINESS **Zone 6**

The flowers of Barbara Bush are large and very full of petals – fat in the bud and opulent when opened out. Their coloring is exquisite, but also somewhat variable. The petals are essentially white, with pale, smoky pink edges, but the pink coloring intensifies as the flower ages. In hot weather the coloring is much more extensive than usual, so that the rose may appear pink all over, and make you wonder whether it has undergone a mutation. The flowers come singly and in clusters of up to five on long, strong stems – excellent for cutting and exhibition. Barbara Bush has sturdy, stiff, upright stems and a very great number of large prickles. The leaves are dark green and glossy, and may need protection against mildew and blackspot in certain areas. This rose was named after the wife of George Bush, the former American president.

BARBARA BUSH

B

Rose Barni

THE BARNI FAMILY OWNS ITALY'S MOST IMPORTANT HYBRIDIZING HOUSE WHICH OPERATES FROM FAMOUS ROSE-CLAD PREMISES IN PISTOIA, TUSCANY

Italy has a long history of rose breeding, from Mazzetti and Manetti in the 19th century to Mansuino and Aicardi in the 20th. The Barni family firm dates back to the 19th century but it was not until the mid-20th century that it began to specialize in roses. Its first new rose was a climbing sport of 'Dr. Debat', a sumptuous cross between 'Mme. A. Meilland' and 'Mrs. John Laing'. Barni's 'Climbing Dr. Debat' has flowers as large as 7in (18cm) in diameter.

Bella di Todi

In the 1970s, the Barni family embarked on its modern breeding program. Its first international success came in 1987 with the issue of two Hybrid Musks, Castor and Pollux, named after the heavenly twins. Through the 1980s and 90s, Barni bred every class of rose suitable to the Mediterranean climate, from Hybrid Teas and Floribundas to miniatures and groundcover roses.

The family also took a lead in the production of striped roses: Rinascimento was by far the best striped rose anywhere in the world when it was introduced in 1989. Rosita Missoni, issued in 1998, is a very handsome red and yellow striped rose. Recent successes include several roses that combine the shape and scent of old roses with the vigor and repeat flowering of modern roses: among Barni's best are Stile '800 (1999) and Bella di Todi (2000).

'Climbing Dr. Debat'

Breeding is now managed under the young Beatrice Barni, who has once again begun to concentrate on the production of new Hybrid Teas of exceptional size and vigor – some of these recent introductions have flowers as large as 7.8in (20cm) across. She raises some 60,000 seedlings a year, which places Barni among the top producers of roses worldwide.

The Barni Nursery

Barkarole

syn. 'TANelorak', Taboo, Grand Château

Hybrid Tea

ORIGIN **Evers/Tantau, Germany, 1988**
FLOWER SIZE **2.8in (7cm)**
SCENT **Moderate to good and sweet**
FLOWERING **Repeats well**
HEIGHT/SPREAD **3.3ft (1m)/2.7ft (80cm)**
HARDINESS **Zone 6**

This magnificent Hybrid Tea is very popular worldwide, but especially in its native Germany, where it is extensively used as a bedding rose in large plantings. The flowers open from black buds into perfectly formed Hybrid Tea roses, although they come in well-spaced clusters of up to 7–9. They are rich Turkey red in color, with a velvety sheen on the outer petals (which are darker still), and they keep their color well. The clusters have long stems, making them ideal for cutting. The leaves are red at first, then dark green and glossy ('Kordesii' must feature in the ancestry of Barkarole), although occasionally susceptible to powdery mildew. The bush is medium-tall and slender, reaching 2.3ft (70cm) in a cool climate and at least twice that height in a warm one. The color of the flowers is usually best in cool weather.

Barkarole

'Baron de Bonstetten'

Hybrid Perpetual

ORIGIN **Liabaud, France, 1871**
PARENTAGE **'Général Jacqueminot' x 'Géant des Batailles'**
FLOWER SIZE **4.3in (11cm)**
SCENT **Medium and sweet**
FLOWERING **Repeats a little**
HEIGHT/SPREAD **6.6ft (2m)/4.9ft (1.5m)**
HARDINESS **Zone 5**

More than one rose is sold as 'Baron de Bonstetten'. The "true" cultivar is a wonderful, rich, velvety crimson, and its flowers open out lightly cupped to reveal a mass of small petals within. It would need an immense effort of will not to try smelling it – unfortunately, the scent is sometimes difficult to detect. The flowers lose their intense, freshly opened brilliance as they age, turning to purple and lilac. In hot weather, however, they may crumple

B

'BARON DE BONSTETTEN'

up and die prematurely. 'Baron de Bonstetten' is not a reliable repeat flowerer, but its autumn blooms can be exceptionally large and richly colored. The plant has somewhat lanky stems and is very thorny. Its dark leaves are susceptible to rust and mildew in some climates. The Baron de Bonstetten, after whom this rose was named, was a wealthy amateur archeologist who lived in Switzerland.

'BARON DE WASSENAER'

Moss Rose

ORIGIN **Verdier, France, 1854**
FLOWER SIZE **3.9in (10cm)**
SCENT **Strong and sweet**
FLOWERING **Once only**
HEIGHT/SPREAD **5.7ft (1.75m)/4.9ft (1.5m)**
HARDINESS **Zone 5**

It is not the most exciting of old garden roses, but 'Baron de Wassenaer' has its admirers. The flowers are bright magenta crimson, with slightly paler petal backs, and fade to cerise pink. They open distinctly cupped, with rounded, incurved petals. When they are fully expanded, the straggly inner petals are framed by the large guard petals. The flowers are borne in clusters of up to five. The sepals, receptacles, and flower stalks are well covered by dark, brown moss, which transmutes into a dense covering of short prickles on the main stems of the plant. 'Baron de Wassenaer' has an upright habit of growth. The somewhat sparse leaves are pale green, with a dark outline when young. Blackspot can be somewhat a problem.

'BARON DE WASSENAER'

'BARON GIROD DE L'AIN'

see 'EUGEN FÜRST'

'BARON J-B. GONELLA'

Bourbon Rose

ORIGIN **Guillot père, France, 1859**
PARENTAGE **'Louise Odier' seedling**
FLOWER SIZE **3.1in (8cm)**
SCENT **Strong and sweet**
FLOWERING **Remontant**
HEIGHT/SPREAD **5.7ft (1.75m)/4.1ft (1.25m)**
HARDINESS **Zone 5**

This typical Bourbon rose has the classic sweet scent of the group, although it starts off with somewhat unimpressive, dumpy, rose red buds. When they start to open, they reveal their true glory as large, elegant, clear, bright pink flowers (darker in cool weather), which reflex gradually as more and more petals unfurl. The petals have silvery pink backs and take on a hint of mauve as they age. The flower shape also changes, from globular to somewhat more lightly cupped, and they are so large and heavy that they sometimes hang down despite having sturdy stalks. The effect is very charming. 'Baron J-B. Gonella' makes an otherwise upright shrub with green leaves, healthier than most Bourbons, and with only a few prickles.

'BARON J-B. GONELLA'

'BARONNE ADOLPHE DE ROTHSCHILD'

syn. 'BARONESS ROTHSCHILD'

Hybrid Perpetual

ORIGIN **Pernet père, France, 1868**
PARENTAGE **Sport of 'Souvenir de la Reine d'Angleterre'**
FLOWER SIZE **4.7in (12cm)**
SCENT **Moderate and tealike**
FLOWERING **Occasionally repeats**
HEIGHT/SPREAD **5.7ft (1.75m)/4.1ft (1.25m)**
HARDINESS **Zone 5**

Most roses are fairly stable, but from time to time a particular cultivar will produce a whole range of sports, which are then propagated, tested, and introduced under new names. The most sportive of Hybrid Perpetuals was 'Souvenir de la Reine d'Angleterre' (Cochet, 1855), which is now quite a rare rose, but its most famous sport, 'Baronne Adolphe de Rothschild', was responsible for several more. 'Baronne Adolphe de Rothschild', named after the wife of a rich banker, has large, pretty, rose pink flowers, which are palest pink at the tips and darker at the base of the petals. The petal backs are always slightly darker too. The outer petals reflex and the inner ones recurve, but all have a silky sheen to them that is quite distinctive. 'Baronne Adolphe de Rothschild' is also quite unlike other roses in its habit of growth. It has thick, stiff, prickly, upright, short-jointed stems with plenty of large leaves like a Portland rose. It is very late to flower but, when well grown, produces its flowers on long stems. Most are borne singly, but a few come in twos and threes, in tight clusters. Mildew may be a visitor in areas where this is a problem. The two most widely grown sports of 'Baronne Adolphe de Rothschild' are identical in everything except their color: **'Merveille de Lyon'** is white with a pink flush, which intensifies in hot weather, while **'Mabel Morrison'**, named after the wife of a Wiltshire landowner, opens palest pink but quickly fades to white. **'Spencer'** is also said to be a sport of 'Merveille de Lyon', though it differs from its putative parent more than usually. Its flowers are soft pink with paler silky reverses but, being inherently unstable, many of the petals show considerable variation: some are much darker than others (deepest pink, even pale crimson), while others (especially at their edges) are so pale as to be almost white. The petals are irregular in shape: some are quilled, others pleated, yet others reflexed. Sometimes the flower has a rough button eye: they are usually very full and flat. The plant has the stiff habit, short internodes, and ruff of leaves that show its relationship to the Portland roses. It is somewhat prickly and the wood is brittle, easy to break off carelessly.

'BARONNE ADOLPHE DE ROTHSCHILD'

'MABEL MORRISON'

'MERVEILLE DE LYON'

'SPENCER'

Sports of 'Baronne Adolphe de Rothschild'

'MABEL MORRISON'

ORIGIN **Bennett, Britain, 1878**

'MERVEILLE DE LYON'

ORIGIN **Pernet père, France, 1882**

Sport of 'Merveille de Lyon'

'SPENCER'

ORIGIN **W. Paul, Britain, 1892**
FLOWER SIZE **4.3in (11cm)**
SCENT **Strong and sweet**
FLOWERING **Remontant**
HEIGHT/SPREAD **4.1ft (1.25m)/2.5ft (75cm)**

'BARONNE HENRIETTE DE SNOY'

'BARONNE HENRIETTE DE SNOY'

Tea-Noisette

ORIGIN **Bernaix, France, 1897**
PARENTAGE **'Gloire de Dijon' x 'Mme. Lombard'**
FLOWER SIZE **3.5in (9cm)**
SCENT **Light and tealike**
FLOWERING **Repeats very well**
HEIGHT/SPREAD **8.2ft (2.5m)/8.2ft (2.5m)**
HARDINESS **Zone 7**

'Baronne Henriette de Snoy' is one of those Tea roses that can be grown as a 3.3ft (1m) bush in cool climates or a 13.1ft (4m) climber elsewhere. The flowers are creamy pink, with darker petal backs, and many subtle hints of flesh, buff, and mother-of-pearl as they open out to reveal a mass of small petals. They spoil in wet weather and damp off in humid conditions, so 'Baronne Henriette de Snoy' attains its greatest beauty in warm, dry areas, where it will flower almost continuously. The flowers come in small clusters (of up to five) on dark red stems, and open successively over a long period rather than flowering all at once. The new wood, too, is dark red, and fairly thick and lush, before it hardens and branches. The foliage is large, moderately glossy, and somewhat susceptible to mildew, though this does not prevent the plant from flowering right through to early winter.

'BARONNE PRÉVOST'

Hybrid Perpetual

ORIGIN **Desprez, France, 1842**
FLOWER SIZE **4.3in (11cm)**
SCENT **Strong and sweet**
FLOWERING **Repeats well**
HEIGHT/SPREAD **4.9ft (1.5m)/3.3ft (1m)**
HARDINESS **Zone 5**

Some experts still argue about whether to classify 'Baronne Prévost' as a Hybrid Perpetual or a Portland rose. It is one of the most beautiful and remontant of all old roses. The flowers are a deep rich pink, fading to rose pink, and possess a delicious scent. They open out to display small petals roughly quartered around a rudimentary button eye. The flowers come singly or in somewhat tight clusters of up to four and have a

'BARONNE PRÉVOST'

ruff of leaves beneath them. The plant has a sturdy, upright habit of growth and extremely prickly stems. The bright green leaves are susceptible to blackspot, but this is not a problem in the hot, dry areas where 'Baronne Prévost' grows best. It is also very hardy, and should be among everyone's Top Ten old roses in any climate.

BARRY FEARN

see SCHWARZE MADONNA

BASSINO

syn. 'KORMIXAL', Suffolk

Ground Cover

ORIGIN **Kordes, Germany, 1988**
PARENTAGE **('Sea Foam' x Rote Max Graf) x seedling**
FLOWER SIZE **1.6in (4cm)**
SCENT **Light and musky**
FLOWERING **Continuous**
HEIGHT/SPREAD **2.7ft (80cm)/4.9ft (1.5m)**
HARDINESS **Zone 5**

BASSINO

Known as Suffolk in Britain (where it is most popular) but Bassino everywhere else, this is an excellent modern ground-cover rose and typical of Kordes' best. The flowers are deep, bright red, with occasional streaks of white, which serve to increase the brilliance of the red – as do the deep yellow stamens. The flowers come in large clusters (typically of 10–30) all over the surface of the neat, compact plant. All you see for months on end is vivid flowers and beautiful, small, dark, glossy leaves. The flowers continue until well into autumn, and are followed by small red hips. The plant is very healthy, hardy, and thrifty, and useful in containers or at the front of a border.

'BASYE'S PURPLE ROSE'

Shrub Rose

ORIGIN **Basye, US, 1968**
PARENTAGE ***Rosa rugosa* form x *Rosa foliolosa***
FLOWER SIZE **2.4in (6cm)**
SCENT **Strong, rich, and sweet**
FLOWERING **Repeats intermittently**
HEIGHT/SPREAD **6.6ft (2m)/4.9ft (1.5m)**
HARDINESS **Zone 5**

Dr. Robert Basye made the cross that brought us 'Basye's Purple Rose' as part of his experiments in raising

'BARONNE EDMOND DE ROTHSCHILD'

Hybrid Tea

ORIGIN **Meilland, France, 1969**
PARENTAGE **('Baccará' x 'Crimson Queen') x 'Mme. A. Meilland'**
FLOWER SIZE **4.7in (12cm)**
SCENT **Very strong and sweet**
FLOWERING **Repeats well**
HEIGHT/SPREAD **3.9ft (1.2m)/3.3ft (1m)**
HARDINESS **Zone 6**
AWARDS **Lyon GM 1968; Rome GM 1968**

'Baronne Edmond de Rothschild' is a sumptuous Hybrid Tea in possession of three great virtues: vigor, scent, and beauty. The flowers are deep pink, with silvery pink reverses, very large and full-petaled. This – and their thick petals – makes them very useful for cutting and exhibition. They last well in water, even if picked fully open. They are borne usually singly, but sometimes in clusters, especially in autumn. The leaves are large, glossy, and tough, but susceptible to blackspot, although this is not a problem in hot, dry climates. The plant is vigorous and easy to grow.

Its climbing sport **'Climbing Baronne Edmond de Rothschild'** is a fine, lusty grower with very large flowers and vigorous glossy foliage. It is identical to the bush form in everything except its larger flowers and its climbing habit. A plant in full flower is a very handsome and impressive sight, but its flowering is only intermittent after the first spectacular flush.

Sport of 'Baronne Edmond de Rothschild'

'CLIMBING BARONNE EDMOND DE ROTHSCHILD'

ORIGIN **Meilland, France, 1974**
FLOWER SIZE **5.9in (15cm)**
FLOWERING **Once well, then intermittently**
HEIGHT/SPREAD **13.1ft (4m)/6.6ft (2m)**
HARDINESS **Zone 6**

'BARONNE EDMOND DE ROTHSCHILD'

'CLIMBING BARONNE EDMOND DE ROTHSCHILD'

thornless roses. 'Basye's Purple Rose' has masses of prickles, but its extraordinary dark flowers well justify its introduction. They are rich wine red or purple, in a particular tint that no other rose can match exactly. Even the filaments are the same intense dark color, though the stamens at the end are bright golden yellow. The flowers are single, and come in clusters of 3–7 blooms right through until the first frost, starting with a magnificent initial display early in the season. Hips are rarely produced. 'Basye's Purple Rose' is a vigorous grower, with thick, sturdy stems and an arching habit. The long, bright green, healthy leaves have narrow leaflets like *Rosa foliolosa*. If grown on its own roots, the plant will sucker around agreeably and form a good thicket.

'BEAUTÉ'

Hybrid Tea

ORIGIN **Mallerin, France, 1953**
PARENTAGE **'Mme. Joseph Perraud' seedling**
FLOWER SIZE **4.7in (12cm)**
SCENT **Medium and fruity**
FLOWERING **Repeats**
HEIGHT/SPREAD **3.3ft (1m)/2.7ft (80cm)**
HARDINESS **Zone 6**

Its striking color brought instant popularity for 'Beauté', and it remains a widely grown rose half a century later. Its flowers are a wonderful rich apricot color, with hints of orange and gold, opening from long, slender, orange buds. They are not overly full of petals but loosely double, so that they stand up well to rain. They come singly and in clusters of up to four. The plant has dark green, semiglossy leaves and is reasonably healthy. 'Beauté' is not overly vigorous, but responds to care and good cultivation by flowering again quickly. It performs best if it is only lightly pruned and allowed to build up a permanent structure of branches.

BEAUTIFUL BRITAIN

syn. 'DICFIRE'
Floribunda

ORIGIN **Dickson, Northern Ireland, 1983**
PARENTAGE **'Red Planet' × 'Eurorose'**
FLOWER SIZE **3.1in (8cm)**
SCENT **Good, sweet, and fruity**
FLOWERING **Repeats well**
HEIGHT/SPREAD **2.7ft (80cm)/2ft (60cm)**
HARDINESS **Zone 6**
AWARDS **ROTY 1983**

This eye-catching, short Floribunda is widely grown in Britain, but nowhere else: a good name in one market may not sell roses in another. Beautiful Britain has deep orange, lightly double flowers that fade fairly quickly to end up pale apricot with a yellow flush at the center. The petal backs are darker at all stages. The flowers are lightly cupped and stand up well to rain. They are very freely borne, singly and in clusters of up to five. Beautiful Britain makes a bushy plant with fairly ordinary leaves – mid-green and semiglossy, but bronze tinted when new – which are healthy except for a little blackspot in autumn. It is a useful plant for the front of a border, early to flower, and quick to repeat.

BEAUTIFUL BRITAIN

'BEAUTY OF GLAZENWOOD'

see 'FORTUNE'S DOUBLE YELLOW'

'BEAUTY SECRET'

Patio Rose

ORIGIN **Moore, US, 1965**
PARENTAGE **'Little Darling' × 'Magic Wand'**
FLOWER SIZE **1.2in (3cm)**
SCENT **Medium and sweet**
FLOWERING **Repeats quickly and abundantly**
HEIGHT/SPREAD **2ft (60cm)/1.3ft (40cm)**
HARDINESS **Zone 6**
AWARDS **AoE 1975**

Few roses have been so consistently popular for nearly 40 years as this neat, bushy, award winner from Ralph Moore. Its reputation both as a garden plant and on the show bench is unsurpassed among enthusiasts for miniature roses. The flowers of 'Beauty Secret' are distinctive in the way they open out into a flat mass of tightly quilled petals. The shapely rosettes of bright vermilion petals have slightly darker petal backs and open from redder buds. In hot weather the color is paler but still an attractive and unusual shade. The flowers come in clusters of 3–5 and contrast well with the crimson new growth and leaves. The plant is bushy, healthy, and hardy.

BEAUTY STAR

syn. 'FRYSTAR', Liverpool Remembers
Hybrid Tea

ORIGIN **Fryer, Britain, 1990**
PARENTAGE **'Corso' × seedling**
FLOWER SIZE **3.9in (10cm)**
SCENT **Strong**
FLOWERING **Repeats well**
HEIGHT/SPREAD **4.9ft (1.5m)/3.3ft (1m)**
HARDINESS **Zone 6**

Although bred for the British market – it won an award in the Belfast Trials – Beauty Star does best in California, where it grows to 8.2ft (2.5m), which is three times its height in England. The flowers are orange – somewhat more vermilion in cool weather and pinker in hot – with paler, silvery petal backs. They usually come singly on long stems, but are sometimes carried in small, well-spaced clusters. The plant has glossy, mid-green leaves and is susceptible to mildew, but only in cool climates. It is extremely prickly.

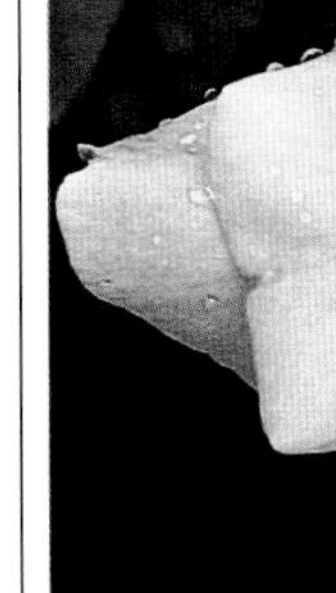

'BEAUTÉ'

'BEAUTY SECRET'

BEAUTY STAR

B

ROSA BEGGERIANA

ROSA BEGGERIANA

Wild Rose

FLOWER SIZE **1.6in (4cm)**
SCENT **Fetid**
FLOWERING **Once, somewhat late in season**
HEIGHT/SPREAD **9.8ft (3m)/6.6ft (2m)**
HARDINESS **Zone 5**

Rosa beggeriana is a variable species that occurs naturally from Turkey through to Central Asia. Keen botanists have split it up into as many as 50 subspecies. Others, who prefer to group them together as one aggregate species, argue that *Rosa fedtschenkoana* should be regarded as part of the *Rosa beggeriana* group. *Rosa beggeriana* is a fine shrub of considerable horticultural merit. It has small, white flowers in clusters of 5–12 at the ends of the new shoots. They have pale yellow stamens and a smell designed to attract flies to pollinate them. They are followed by round hips. The leaves are gray or blue gray, very attractive, and sometimes fragrant like the leaves of sweetbriars. *Rosa beggeriana* needs a climate with hot summers and cold winters to flower well. Then it makes a handsome, vigorous, useful shrub that suckers around agreeably.

BELAMI

syn. 'KORPRILL', Woods of Windsor

Hybrid Tea

ORIGIN **Kordes, Germany, 1985**
PARENTAGE **(Prominent x 'Carina') x 'Emily Post'**
FLOWER SIZE **5.1in (13cm)**
SCENT **Light, sweet, and musky**
FLOWERING **Repeats**
HEIGHT/SPREAD **5.7ft (1.75m)/4.1ft (1.25m)**
HARDINESS **Zone 6**

BELAMI

The flowers of Belami are large and peach colored. As they age, the yellow tints fade away and the flowers turn a little more pink. It is an attractive transformation, not least because the flowers are large and shapely as they spiral out of their buds. They are usually borne singly on long, strong stems, which makes them good for cutting. Belami has large, dark, glossy, healthy leaves, with wide, rounded leaflets. The new growths are a very rich crimson and the prickles (few, but large) remain purple for a long time. It makes a very vigorous and strong plant, with upright, bushy growth. It is especially free flowering.

'BELINDA'

Hybrid Musk

ORIGIN **Bentall, Britain, 1936**
FLOWER SIZE **1.6in (4cm)**
SCENT **Strong, sweet, and musky**
FLOWERING **Repeats well**
HEIGHT/SPREAD **5.7ft (1.75m)/6.6ft (2m)**
HARDINESS **Zone 6**

Although not among the best-known Hybrid Musks, 'Belinda' has a considerable following, especially in warmer parts of the US. The flowers are dark bright pink – fading to rose pink unless grown partially in shade – with yellow stamens and white centers. They are individually small, but borne in very large clusters – typically of 30–60 flowers – so that sometimes the branches are bowed down by their weight. Each of the clusters comes at the end of a long stem and lasts well if cut for the house. The leaves are bright, pale green, but seem completely lost in a froth of pink when the bush is in full flower. The plant repeats well and makes an excellent short climbing rose in hot climates, quickly reaching 13.1ft (4m).

'BELINDA'

'BELINDA'S DREAM'

Shrub Rose

ORIGIN **Basye, US, 1992**
PARENTAGE **'Jersey Beauty' x 'Tiffany'**
FLOWER SIZE **4.3in (11cm)**
SCENT **Very strong and sweet**
FLOWERING **Repeats all through the growing season**
HEIGHT/SPREAD **9.8ft (3m)/13.1ft (4m)**
HARDINESS **Zone 6**

Many of the best modern climbers have been bred by crossing old rambling roses with modern Hybrid Teas. 'Belinda's Dream' is an outstanding example: it combines beauty and floriferousness with hardiness and a fair degree of disease resistance. The flowers are mid-pink, with pale pink undersides. They come in small clusters and last well when cut. They do not form hips, so there is no need for deadheading, but the plant responds well to light pruning from time to time. It is prickly, and only lightly covered in small, blue green leaves. Its vigorous, arching habit of growth makes it useful for hedges: it tends to look lanky when trained as a climber. It was bred by a Texan academic and excels in hot climates, but also grows well in temperate regions. It may need some protection against blackspot in cool, damp weather, but its vigor and floriferousness are unaffected by disease.

BELLA RENAISSANCE

syn. 'POULJILL', Child of Achievement

Shrub Rose

ORIGIN **Poulsen, Denmark, 1995**
FLOWER SIZE **4.3in (11cm)**
SCENT **Light**
FLOWERING **Repeats well**
HEIGHT/SPREAD **3.9ft (1.2m)/2.7ft (80cm)**
HARDINESS **Zone 5**

'BELINDA'S DREAM'

The flowers of Bella Renaissance respond to good cultivation. Sometimes no more than semidouble, they have the fuller, muddled shape of a David Austin rose when well-fed and watered. All the roses in Poulsen's Renaissance series combine the best of old-fashioned roses with modern ones. The flowers of Bella Renaissance are a very rich yellow at the center, with sometimes a hint of gold or orange too, and lemon yellow at the edges. They open out lightly cupped, and are borne singly or in clusters of up to five flowers. The leaves are handsome, dark, and glossy, and have good disease resistance. The plant repeats regularly, flush after flush, until well into autumn – all in all, a sound performer.

BELLA RENAISSANCE

B

BELLA ROSA

BELLA ROSA

syn. 'KORWONDER', Toynbee Hall

Floribunda

ORIGIN **Kordes, Germany, 1981**
PARENTAGE **Seedling x Träumerei**
FLOWER SIZE **2in (5cm)**
SCENT **Light**
FLOWERING **Almost continuous**
HEIGHT/SPREAD **2.3ft (70cm)/2.3ft (70cm)**
HARDINESS **Zone 4**
AWARDS **Copenhagen GM 1982; Baden-Baden GM 1983**

Bella Rosa has three outstanding qualities: it is very compact, very hardy, and very floriferous. The small, lightly double flowers come in large, tight, flat clusters. They open deep pink and fade eventually to pale pink, acquiring a red spotting in wet weather, but the overall impression is always of rich pink coloring. The flowers are borne in clusters of 4–10 on short stems, quite close to the leaves, which are small, dark, glossy, and very handsome. The plant is very healthy and makes neat bushy growth. In hot climates it will grow to 4.9ft (1.5m) but still keep its compact habit. In cool climates it is a popular bedding rose and combines well in mixed plantings. Its adaptability has ensured that Bella Rosa is popular and successful all over the world.

'BELLE AMOUR'

Gallica Hybrid

ORIGIN **France, c.1840**
FLOWER SIZE **7cm (2.8in)**
SCENT **Medium and musky**
FLOWERING **Once**
HEIGHT/SPREAD **4.9ft (1.5m)/4.1ft (1.25m)**
HARDINESS **Zone 5**

No one knows the origins of 'Belle Amour': it has been variously classed as an Alba and a Damask. However, it seems best to call it a Gallica hybrid and to enjoy its unique qualities. Its color, for example, is unlike any old garden rose, for it is distinctly salmon pink at first and turns to rose pink only later on. Its petals open out flat around a tuft of bright yellow stamens, like a semidouble camellia. Some people say that they can discern a whiff of myrrh in its scent. The flowers usually come in small clusters, typically of 3–5. The plant has an upright habit of growth, quite a lot of prickles, and healthy, mid-green leaves. It flowers profusely, but only once.

'BELLE AMOUR'

'BELLE DE CRÉCY'

Gallica

ORIGIN **Hardy, France, 1829**
FLOWER SIZE **2.8in (7cm)**
SCENT **Strong and sweet**
FLOWERING **Once**
HEIGHT/SPREAD **3.3ft (1m)/3.3ft (1m)**
HARDINESS **Zone 5**

The popularity of 'Belle de Crécy' rests upon the way its color changes as it opens from a crimson bud and reflexes through cerise, dark pink, magenta, lilac, and mauve, until its petals are almost gray. The transformation starts with the outer petals, so there is always an attractive contrast between the center and the edges of a flower. The double flowers have a roughly quartered shape and a mass of small petals, which are quilled, tucked, and pleated around a green eye. They come singly or in clusters of up to four blooms. The plant has dark leaves, long leaflets, and a lot of prickles, so small as to be little more than bristles. Mildew can be a problem.

'BELLE DE CRÉCY'

BELLE ÉPOQUE

BELLE ÉPOQUE

syn. 'FRYYABOO'

Hybrid Tea

ORIGIN **Fryer, Britain, 1994**
PARENTAGE **Remember Me x Helmut Schmidt**
FLOWER SIZE **3.9in (10cm)**
SCENT **Light and fruity**
FLOWERING **Repeats**
HEIGHT/SPREAD **4.9ft (1.5m)/3.3ft (1m)**
HARDINESS **Zone 6**

This is one of many modern beauties produced by Gareth Fryer in England that show how infinitely capable of further development are the Hybrid Teas. The flowers of Belle Époque are a pale bronze yellow, with darker backs to the petals – orange with a tint of russet brown and pink. Both are unusual colors, and the combination is very handsome, especially when the buds are expanding and the effect is clearly seen. The buds are elegant and conical, and eventually open into lightly cupped flowers. They come singly or in small clusters on a vigorous, tall plant, which flowers early and repeats quickly. The tough, healthy, bright green leaves are attractive in their own right. Belle Époque is excellent all-around.

'BELLE ISIS'

Gallica

ORIGIN **Parmentier, France, 1845**
FLOWER SIZE **3.1in (8cm)**
SCENT **Strong, musky, and myrrhlike**
FLOWERING **Once only**
HEIGHT/SPREAD **5.7ft (1.75m)/4.1ft (1.25m)**
HARDINESS **Zone 5**

'Belle Isis' is a beautiful, pale pink Gallica – rich mid-pink at the center of the flowers and palest pink toward the edges. The flowers are roughly quartered around a small green eye and held well clear of the bush on slender stems, singly or in clusters of up to five. The plant has lush, pale green leaves and a few prickles. Its stems are slender, and they sometimes keel over under the weight of their flowers, so a little staking is advisable. 'Belle Isis' is not a pure Gallica, but probably a hybrid with *Rosa arvensis* or one of the Ayrshire roses. This has endowed it with a distinct bitter scent, which is generally described as "myrrh-like" but which most people find attractive. 'Belle Isis' has also passed this scent on to its seedling 'Constance Spry', the first of David Austin's English Roses and the ancestor of many of them.

'BELLE ISIS'

B

BELLE OF BERLIN

'BELLE POITEVINE'

'BELLE SANS FLATTERIE'

BELLE OF BERLIN

syn. 'TANIREB'

Hybrid Tea

ORIGIN **Tantau, Germany, 1994**
FLOWER SIZE **4.3in (11cm)**
SCENT **Strong and sweet**
FLOWERING **Repeats well**
HEIGHT/SPREAD **6.6ft (2m)/4.1ft (1.25m)**
HARDINESS **Zone 6**

Belle of Berlin is popular as a garden rose (and for cutting) throughout Australia, but has never been released elsewhere. It is an excellent rose, with the shape and vigor of a Grandiflora. The buds are long and slim, with stout, thick petals, and a greenish tinge. As they open out, the flowers are seen to be pale pink with salmon pink backs, but at all stages they are large, strongly scented, and perfect for picking – they have stems 1.6–2ft (50–60cm) long and last very well in water. When they open out completely, they reveal an old-fashioned, muddled arrangement of petals. The plant is very vigorous, almost thornless, healthy, and hardy. It has a particularly upright habit and attractive crimson new growth.

'BELLE OF PORTUGAL'

see 'BELLE PORTUGAISE'

'BELLE POITEVINE'

Rugosa Hybrid

ORIGIN **Bruant, France, 1894**
FLOWER SIZE **3.5in (9cm)**
SCENT **Strong and sweet**
FLOWERING **Continuous**
HEIGHT/SPREAD **5.7ft (1.75m)/4.9ft (1.5m)**
HARDINESS **Zone 5**

Here we have one of the oldest and loveliest of Rugosa roses. The flowers of 'Belle Poitevine' open from long buds. They are large and loosely double, with long petals and a cluster of pale stamens visible between the magenta ruffles. They come in clusters of 3–7 and are sometimes followed by large, red hips. The plant has typical Rugosa leaves and prickly stems, but is both healthy and very hardy. If grown on its own roots, it suckers around and makes an excellent hedge. Its first flowering is very generous, but it continues to produce clusters of flowers thereafter right through until late autumn.

'BELLE PORTUGAISE'

syn. 'BELLE OF PORTUGAL'

Hybrid Gigantea

ORIGIN **Cayeux, France, 1903**
PARENTAGE **'Reine Marie Henriette' x *Rosa gigantea***
FLOWER SIZE **4.7in (12cm)**
SCENT **Light and tealike**
FLOWERING **Once, early in season**
HEIGHT/SPREAD **16.4ft (5m)/9.8ft (3m)**
HARDINESS **Zone 9**

'Belle Portugaise' was a famous and important rose because it was the first hybrid of *Rosa gigantea* to be bred in the West. It was the creation of Henri Cayeux, a young Frenchman in charge of the Botanic Garden in Lisbon, whose ambition was to breed Hybrid Giganteas that would be hardy in Paris. As with the first-generation hybrids later developed by such breeders as Alister Clark in Australia and Georg Schoener in California, it has proved a very vigorous climber, flowering very early in the season, but only once. The flowers are very large – sometimes as much as 5.9in (15cm) across – and open from elegant, slender, crimson buds to a beautiful, pale, creamy pink with darker, rose pink reverses. The flowers have a few very large petals, and several smaller ones that tend to fold over and obscure the center, where there is a large circle of long, pale stamens. The outer petals sink down under their own weight, so that the flower as a whole is always lopsided and collapses in rain. The foliage is very like *Rosa gigantea*: long, slender, pale green leaflets that droop elegantly when young. 'Belle Portugaise' is extremely vigorous, reaching as much as 10m (32.8ft) up a tree, and has been popular in California for many years. A white-flowered sport called 'Belle Blanca' has recently been introduced.

'BELLE PORTUGAISE'

'BELLE SANS FLATTERIE'

Gallica

ORIGIN **France, 1820**
FLOWER SIZE **3.1in (8cm)**
SCENT **Light and sweet**
FLOWERING **Once only**
HEIGHT/SPREAD **3.3ft (1m)/2.7ft (80cm)**
HARDINESS **Zone 5**

It seems that the rose now known as 'Belle sans Flatterie' does not entirely match the one grown by the Empress Joséphine 200 years ago. Nevertheless, it is an excellent garden rose throughout its one long season of flower. Its buds are large and full and its flowers are very shapely when they open, round in outline and usually quartered at the center. They are a good, clear, rich pink but with pale petal backs and much paler outer petals around the rim. They are abundantly borne in large clusters. The plant has few prickles and an attractive, mounded shape. The leaves are mid-green and small, but have conspicuously long terminal leaflets. It is one of the healthiest of Gallicas.

BELLE STORY

syn. 'AUSELLE'

Shrub Rose

ORIGIN **Austin, Britain, 1984**
PARENTAGE **('Chaucer' x 'Parade') x ('The Prioress' x 'Schneewittchen')**
FLOWER SIZE **3.5in (9cm)**
SCENT **Strong and myrrhlike**
FLOWERING **Remontant**
HEIGHT/SPREAD **3.9ft (1.2m)/3.9ft (1.2m)**
HARDINESS **Zone 6**

Belle Story is a pretty rose, and quite unusual. Its flowers are cupped at first, but, when they open out, they are dominated by a huge boss of stamens – which is interesting because the individual stamens are of different lengths and the filaments are red. The flowers open a charming shade of peach pink, and fade to pale pink, but the petal backs are always paler. The flowers are double, but appear to be only semidouble because the petals lie neatly on top of each other. The flowers come in spacious clusters of up to ten; the one at the tip of the cluster is always larger than those that open later. The plant makes strong, slender growth and has dark, semi-glossy foliage. Belle Story was an early nursing officer with the British navy.

BENSON & HEDGES SPECIAL

syn. 'MACSHANA', Dorola

Patio Rose

ORIGIN **McGredy, New Zealand, 1982**
PARENTAGE **'Darling Flame' x Mabella**
FLOWER SIZE **1.6in (4cm)**
SCENT **Light and fruity**
FLOWERING **Repeats well**
HEIGHT/SPREAD **1.6ft (50cm)/1.3ft (40cm)**
HARDINESS **Zone 6**

BELLE STORY

Benson & Hedges Special

The flowers of Benson & Hedges Special are a good, rich yellow when they first open, and keep their color better than most, but in hot climates they do eventually fade to lemon and cream. They are shapely and double, but open out lightly cupped to display their golden stamens. They come in clusters of 5–20 and are profusely produced during the first flowering, but thereafter somewhat more intermittently. They last well as cut flowers. The light green foliage is a good foil, if a little sparsely produced, and the short, sturdy bush is more vigorous than many miniatures. Blackspot may be a problem later in the year.

Berkshire

see Sommermärchen

Bernsteinrose

syn. 'TANeitber', Ambra Rosata

Floribunda

Origin **Tantau, Germany, 1987**
Flower size **3.5in (9cm)**
Scent **Light and fruity**
Flowering **Late in season; repeats very well**
Height/Spread **2.5ft (75cm)/2ft (60cm)**
Hardiness **Zone 5**

"Bernstein" is the German word for amber, which well describes the color of this sumptuous, short-growing Floribunda. The flowers are most beautiful when they have opened out to reveal a muddled mass of petals that is reminiscent of David Austin's English Roses. They are borne in clusters of 3–7 and are produced in great quantities until late in the season. They stand up well to rain and come on a neat, compact plant that is notably hardy. German nurserymen sometimes describe Bernsteinrose as a shorter, hardier version of Amber Queen. The leaves are medium-dark and glossy – a good foil for the flowers – and usually very healthy.

Bernsteinrose

Henry Bennett

KNOWN AS "THE FATHER OF THE HYBRID TEA," HENRY BENNETT WAS A PROGRESSIVE VICTORIAN WHO INVENTED MODERN ROSES

When he was a yeoman farmer at Manor Farm, Stapleford, in Wiltshire, Henry Bennett (1823–90) regarded roses and their improvement as no more than a hobby. However, as a progressive Victorian, Bennett believed that scientists had a duty to improve upon God's handiwork for the benefit of mankind. Knowing that scientific breeding practices were being used for food crops and livestock, he assumed that the same principles of hybridization and selection applied to roses. In the early 1870s he paid visits to the leading French rose breeders but left disillusioned, believing that they relied too much on nature.

Henry Bennett

Bennett continued to ponder how roses might be improved. He set about breeding a hardy yellow rose by crossing Hybrid Perpetuals with yellow Tea roses and choosing the parents with care. He never succeeded, but he introduced his seedlings, mainly pink or red, as "Pedigree Hybrids of the Tea Rose." When ten came out at the same time in 1879, they created a sensation. The best were 'Beauty of Stapleford', named after his Wiltshire village, and the shapely pink 'Duke of Connaught', which was popular as a cut flower under glass. The *Société Lyonnaise d'Horticulture* promptly called Bennett's pedigree roses "Hybrid Teas," and the term has been attached to the class ever since.

In the late 1870s, the collapse of the grain market – the biggest in English history – prompted Bennett to surrender his tenancy of Manor Farm and establish himself as a rose grower. A whole succession of bestsellers followed: the sumptuous 'Lady Mary Fitzwilliam' and the opulent 'Heinrich Schultheis' in 1882; the excellent garden rose 'Grace Darling' in 1884; 'Her Majesty' in 1885 – a rose so large it was guaranteed to win first prize at any rose show for years to come; the elegant 'Viscountess Folkestone' in 1886; culminating in Bennett's masterpiece 'Mrs. John Laing' in 1887.

'Grace Darling'

Henry Bennett invented modern roses, the Hybrid Teas that flower repeatedly, not as delicate greenhouse treasures, but as hardy garden plants. There is scarcely a rose in our gardens today that does not descend from the Hybrid Teas of the Wiltshire "wizard."

Manor Farm, Stapleford

B

BEROLINA

BEROLINA

syn. 'KORPRIWA', Selfridges

Hybrid Tea

ORIGIN **Kordes, Germany, 1984**
PARENTAGE **seedling x Mabella**
FLOWER SIZE **4.3in (11cm)**
SCENT **Light and fruity**
FLOWERING **Repeats well**
HEIGHT/SPREAD **5.7ft (1.75m)/4.1ft (1.25m)**
HARDINESS **Zone 6**
AWARDS **ADR 1986**

Tall, vigorous, and easy to grow, Berolina is an excellent Hybrid Tea. Its high-centered flowers are a rich yellow at first, with shades of amber and gold, and even a suggestion of red on the buds. They fade during the next few days to pale lemon. They are borne both singly and in large clusters, so that the overall display is more like that of a Floribunda. Their long, strong stems are useful for cutting and large flower arrangements. The long petals tend to spoil in rain, but in good conditions Berolina is also a fine exhibition rose. It has very handsome, dark, glossy leaves, which are resistant to blackspot and powdery mildew. The bush is very tall: in hot climates, if left unpruned, it will reach 8.2ft (2.5m).

BERRIES 'N' CREAM

see CALYPSO

BETTY BOOP

syn. 'WEKPLAPIC'

Floribunda

ORIGIN **Carruth, US, 1999**
PARENTAGE **Playboy x Picasso**
FLOWER SIZE **3.5in (9cm)**
SCENT **Light**
FLOWERING **Repeats well**
HEIGHT/SPREAD **4.9ft (1.5m)/3.3ft (1m)**
HARDINESS **Zone 6**
AWARDS **AARS 1999**

Betty Boop is a cheerful, energetic cartoon character in the US, well matched by this bright, floriferous rose. The flowers are lightly semidouble and open out quickly from nearly black buds. They are bright yellow at first, with broad coral edges; then the yellow fades to white and disappears from the edges too, so that the coral turns to crimson. The colors and patterns on the individual flowers are striking at all stages of development, even though the stamens turn quickly brown before the flowers fade. The bush has dark, glossy, healthy leaves and a naturally bushy habit. It is very floriferous, and produces its flushes of flowers so quickly that a bed of it is never without flowers. Although bred in California, Betty Boop is hardy in a wide range of climates and, because of its light petalage, tolerates rain as well as heat and cold.

BETTY BOOP

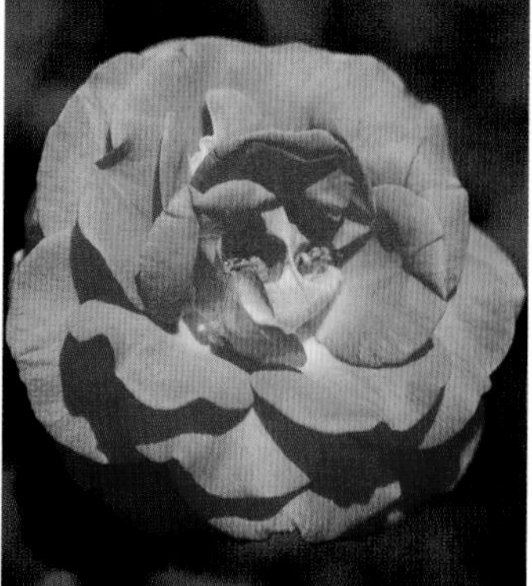

BETTY HARKNESS

BETTY HARKNESS

syn. 'HARETTTE'

Floribunda

ORIGIN **Harkness, Britain, 1998**
FLOWER SIZE **3.1in (8cm)**
SCENT **Medium and sweet**
FLOWERING **Repeats**
HEIGHT/SPREAD **3.3ft (1m)/2.7ft (80cm)**
HARDINESS **Zone 6**
AWARDS **Golden Rose of Courtrai 1997**

This eye-catching Floribunda is an instant success with all who see it in flower. The neat, rounded, handsome blooms are dark orange, with brown shadows between the petals at first and yellow on the petal backs. The flowers come in large, spacious clusters (typically of 5–15), and the brilliant orange color attracts attention and stays in the memory. The yellow fades as the flower ages, so that eventually the color takes on a salmon pink tinge. The plant has healthy, dark green leaves and a good bushy habit. It repeats well and quickly. Betty Harkness is an excellent rose, stunning when thickly planted in a massed display.

'BETTY PRIOR'

Floribunda

ORIGIN **Prior, Britain, 1935**
PARENTAGE **'Kirsten Poulsen' x unknown**
FLOWER SIZE **2in (5cm)**
SCENT **Light**
FLOWERING **Late in season; very floriferous**
HEIGHT/SPREAD **3.3ft (1m)/2.7ft (80cm)**
HARDINESS **Zone 5**
AWARDS **NRS GM 1933**

This tough, enduring rose was one of the first Polyanthas to be recognized as a Floribunda. Its flowers are single and nearly scentless – often said to be a weakness of the early Floribundas – but they are produced in great profusion, almost unceasingly through to late autumn. They open deep pink, with a paler base to the petals and pale crimson reverses, but the colors fade with age, and they end up a ghostly white, with crimson blotches developing where they have been hit by raindrops. Even at this stage, however, 'Betty Prior' remains a rose to enjoy. The flowers come in clusters of 5–15 and keep their petals well. The plant is very hardy, and performs better in cool climates like its native England, where its color is deeper and more intense.

'BETTINA'

Hybrid Tea

ORIGIN **Meilland, France, 1953**
PARENTAGE **'Mme. A. Meilland' x ('Mme. Joseph Perraud' x 'Demain')**
FLOWER SIZE **3.5in (9cm)**
SCENT **Medium and fruity**
FLOWERING **Repeats well**
HEIGHT/SPREAD **3.3ft (1m)/2.7ft (80cm)**
HARDINESS **Zone 5**

When it was first introduced, there was nothing to match 'Bettina' for its bright orange coloring. The flowers are still a beautiful and unusual shade, with slightly more yellow toward the center and a tinge of red on the petal tips as they age. The petal backs are redder, too, but the overall effect is of pure, brilliant orange. The opening buds are handsome in the traditional Hybrid Tea manner, and remain so as they open out, but the flowers lose their elegant shape when fully expanded. 'Bettina' is a good repeater, and very hardy. The plant also has very few prickles. Its leaves are dark and handsome, bronzy when young, but susceptible to blackspot and occasionally mildew too, in areas where these fungal diseases are a problem.

'BETTINA'

Meilland introduced a climbing sport, known as **'Grimpant Bettina'**, in 1953. Its flowers are slightly larger, but it is otherwise exactly the same as the original. It flowers very freely at the start of the season, and then no more than occasionally.

Sport of 'Bettina'

'GRIMPANT BETTINA'

syn. 'CLIMBING BETTINA'

Climbing Hybrid Tea

ORIGIN **Meilland, France, 1958**
FLOWER SIZE **3.9in (10cm)**
FLOWERING **Once very well, then occasionally**
HEIGHT/SPREAD **11.5ft (3.5m)/6.6ft (2m)**

'BETTY PRIOR'

B

'BETTY UPRICHARD'

BIBI MAIZOON

'BETTY UPRICHARD'

Hybrid Tea

ORIGIN **Dickson, Northern Ireland, 1922**
FLOWER SIZE **4.3in (11cm)**
SCENT **Strong and sweet**
FLOWERING **Repeats well**
HEIGHT/SPREAD **4.1ft (1.25m)/3.3ft (1m)**
HARDINESS **Zone 6**
AWARDS **NRS GM 1921**

In the cooler parts of the world, and especially in Britain, 'Betty Uprichard' was one of the most popular garden roses of the 1920s and 1930s. Like many of the classic Dickson Hybrid Teas, its flowers are only lightly double, which helps them to perform well in wet weather. They are salmon pink, with darker petal backs (almost pale crimson), but always pinker toward the edge of the petals and paler toward the center of the flower. The petals are large and loosely held, which also explains part of its charm. It is very vigorous, a quick repeater, and fairly healthy even today. Betty Uprichard was an Irish gentlewoman who died in a hunting accident.

'BEWITCHED'

Hybrid Tea

ORIGIN **Lammerts, US, 1967**
PARENTAGE **'Queen Elizabeth' × 'Tawny Gold'**
FLOWER SIZE **4.7in (12cm)**
SCENT **Strong and sweet**
FLOWERING **Repeats well**
HEIGHT/SPREAD **4.9ft (1.5m)/3.3ft (1m)**
HARDINESS **Zone 5**
AWARDS **AARS 1967; Portland GM 1967**

'Bewitched' is a sumptuous pink Hybrid Tea with beautiful flowers on a somewhat dreary, stiff, upright bush. The flowers are large – the petals themselves are large and long – and bright candy pink with slightly darker backs. The petals are prettily ruffled, and this gives the open flower much of its character. They hold their color well, so this is a good rose for hot climates, although 'Bewitched' does produce its largest flowers in cool weather. The flowers are usually borne singly, on long, strong stems, and last for many days when cut. The bush repeats well, and in warm climates is almost continuously in flower. It grows up in a tall, narrow V-shape, like its parent 'Queen Elizabeth', and flowers most profusely if it is allowed to build up a structure and is pruned only lightly.

BIBI MAIZOON

syn. 'AUSDIMINDO'

Shrub Rose

ORIGIN **Austin, Britain, 1989**
PARENTAGE **'The Reeve' × 'Chaucer'**
FLOWER SIZE **3.1in (8cm)**
SCENT **Strong, sweet, and fruity**
FLOWERING **Repeats**
HEIGHT/SPREAD **3.3ft (1m)/3.3ft (1m)**
HARDINESS **Zone 6**

The flowers of Bibi Maizoon are globular and incurved: even in hot climates they remain tightly cupped and rarely open out fully. It is a shape that many find especially attractive. The flowers are deep pink within and paler toward their outsides, with a rich, sweet scent. They tend to nod on the end of their stems, and are borne usually singly but sometimes in twos and threes. The plant is a moderate grower even in hot climates, but is prone to mildew and blackspot in damp ones. David Austin no longer lists Bibi Maizoon, but it remains popular in the hotter, drier parts of North America.

'BEWITCHED'

'BICOLETTE'

Hybrid Tea

ORIGIN **Tschanz, France, 1980**
FLOWER SIZE **4.3in (11cm)**
SCENT **Medium and sweet**
FLOWERING **Late in season; repeats well**
HEIGHT/SPREAD **3.3ft (1m)/2.7ft (80cm)**
HARDINESS **Zone 6**

This striking Hybrid Tea remains popular in France and deserves to be better known elsewhere. The flowers are bright dark red, with no hint of crimson, but have a tinge of yellow toward the edge of the petals. Their pale petal backs also have a yellow sheen – hence the name 'Bicolette'. They open slowly from classically elegant Hybrid Tea buds, and are borne singly on long, sturdy stems. The plant has a lot of prickles and shiny, mid-green leaves. It repeats well and, in warm areas, continues flowering into early winter, although it may by then show signs of its susceptibility to mildew.

BIG PURPLE

see STEPHENS' BIG PURPLE

'BICOLETTE'

BINGO MEIDILAND

syn. 'MEIPOTAL', Carefree Delight

Shrub Rose

ORIGIN **Meilland, France, 1994**
PARENTAGE **(Eyepaint × Nirvana) × Smarty**
FLOWER SIZE **2in (5cm)**
SCENT **Light and sweet**
FLOWERING **Almost continuous**
HEIGHT/SPREAD **3.3ft (1m)/3.9ft (1.2m)**
HARDINESS **Zone 4**
AWARDS **Paris GM 1992; The Hague GM 1993; ADR 1994; AARS 1996**

Bingo Meidiland is an excellent all-around shrub rose. It was introduced as suitable for hedging, massed planting, or groundcover, but it also makes a fine specimen shrub and a useful plant in mixed borders. Its pale pink flowers have a hint of cream at the center, as well as a large puff of pale yellow stamens. They are exquisite when seen with the sun shining through them against the background of the dark leaves. The flowers of Bingo Meidiland have long stems and come in large, airy clusters of 10–30, followed by little red hips later in the year. The plant is very prickly, but sends up stem after stem of reddish new growth, which bursts into a large spray of flowers until early winter. The leaves are shiny in the Wichurana manner and very healthy.

BINGO MEIDILAND

'BIRDIE BLYE'

'BISCHOFSSTADT PADERBORN'

'BLACK BEAUTY'

'BIRDIE BLYE'

Shrub Rose

ORIGIN **Van Fleet, US, 1904**
PARENTAGE **'Hélène' x 'Bon Silène'**
FLOWER SIZE **3.5in (9cm)**
SCENT **Light and musky**
FLOWERING **Repeats constantly**
HEIGHT/SPREAD **4.9ft (1.5m)/4.9ft (1.5m)**
HARDINESS **Zone 6**

This beautiful and floriferous shrub is typical of the inventive breeding undertaken by Dr. Walter Van Fleet in the 1890s and 1900s. 'Hélène' is a hardy, small-flowered, once-flowering Multiflora rambler, and 'Bon Silène' a large-flowered, repeat flowering Tea rose. 'Birdie Blye' combines the best of both parents. It is a large-flowered, hardy, ever-blooming shrub – a prototype of the Pemberton Hybrid Musks. The flowers are dark pink, fading to pale pink, and fully double, with long buds and long petals that reflex as they open. They come in clusters of 3–7, and are well set off by the glossy, healthy, mid-green leaves. 'Birdie Blye' makes a twiggy bush with arching stems. In hot climates it will grow to 6.6ft (2m) and can be trained as a pillar rose. The stems are covered in a lot of little prickles.

BIRTHDAY GIRL

see COCORICO '89

'BISCHOFSSTADT PADERBORN'

syn. 'PADERBORN'

Shrub Rose

ORIGIN **Kordes, Germany, 1964**
PARENTAGE **'Korona' x 'Spartan'**
FLOWER SIZE **2.8in (7cm)**
SCENT **Little or none**
FLOWERING **Repeats continuously**
HEIGHT/SPREAD **4.9ft (1.5m)/4.1ft (1.25m)**
HARDINESS **Zone 6**
AWARDS **ADR 1968**

This cross between two popular 1950s Floribundas has produced a rose of such vigor that 'Bischofsstadt Paderborn' is classified as a shrub. The lightly cupped flowers are vermilion, with a tiny pale patch behind the yellow stamens and an occasional white streak running up from the center. They are semidouble, and open out quickly, but are carried in great profusion in loose, upright clusters of 5–12. A plant of 'Bischofsstadt Paderborn' makes a tremendous impact from quite a distance, and is especially useful for creating colorful effects in public plantings. The flowers stand up well to rain but also shed their petals cleanly in due course. They continue in bloom until the first frost. The plant is bushy and upright, but twiggy, with healthy, medium-dark leaves. The name commemorates a fine cathedral city in Westphalia, Germany.

'BISHOP DARLINGTON'

Hybrid Musk

ORIGIN **Thomas, US, 1926**
PARENTAGE **'Aviateur Blériot' x 'Moonlight'**
FLOWER SIZE **3.5in (9cm)**
SCENT **Musky**
FLOWERING **Repeats well, until early winter**
HEIGHT/SPREAD **9.8ft (3m)/4.9ft (1.5m)**
HARDINESS **Zone 6**

'Bishop Darlington' is one of those roses that tends to look better from a distance than close-up. It has elegant, slender, coral pink buds that open to semidouble, creamy pink flowers, with much darker petal backs and a yellow glow at the center. But one or two small petals toward the center of the flower usually fold themselves over and obscure the fine, long stamens – a trait that spoils its beauty. The flowers come in stiff, well-spaced, long-stemmed clusters, typically of 5–7, followed by small orange hips. The plant is vigorous, slender (almost gawky), and upright in its habit. The leaves are large, dark green, and healthy, but few. The plant tolerates poor soils and cold climates, but performs much better in warm ones, where it grows much taller and makes a good climber. It is easily propagated from cuttings and is especially suited to the back of a border, where its lanky naked stems are hidden by companion plantings. Its quoted parentage ('Aviateur Blériot' x 'Moonlight') is questionable, but it does have the Hybrid Musks' characteristic of releasing its scent upon the air – delicious in humid weather.

'BISHOP DARLINGTON'

'BLACK BEAUTY'

Hybrid Tea

ORIGIN **Delbard, France, 1973**
PARENTAGE **('Gloria di Roma' x 'Impeccable') x 'Papa Meilland'**
FLOWER SIZE **3.1in (8cm)**
SCENT **Light and sweet**
FLOWERING **Repeats**
HEIGHT/SPREAD **4.9ft (1.5m)/3.3ft (1m)**
HARDINESS **Zone 6**

The flowers of 'Black Beauty' are no more than medium-sized, but they are a very dark and attractive crimson color. The outer petals are indeed nearly black, while the inner ones are dark red, with velvety markings. The flowers are attractive when opening (though the petals are short) but somewhat formless when fully expanded. They are borne singly or in clusters of 2–3 on long stems, making them good for cutting – they would be even better if their scent were stronger. The plant is a bushy grower, but performs best in hot climates, where it can build up a structure and flower almost continuously. Mildew may be a problem in cool climates.

'BLACK BOY'

'BLACK BOY'

Climber

ORIGIN **Clark, Australia, 1919**
PARENTAGE **'Etoile de Hollande' x 'Bardou Job'**
FLOWER SIZE **4.7in (12cm)**
SCENT **Strong, fresh, and appley**
FLOWERING **Early season; repeats in late season**
HEIGHT/SPREAD **13.1ft (4m)/6.6ft (2m)**
HARDINESS **Zone 6**

'Black Boy' is still the most popular crimson climber in its native Australia. It is not actually black but a very striking color combination: the outer petals are purplish crimson, the inner ones a light, bright crimson. As it fades, the purplish color of the outer petals becomes stronger and acquires blackish pink markings. Sometimes there is a white edge to the petaloids in the middle. The buds are long and elegant, but open quickly to reveal a large, bright boss of stamens. The flowers come early in the season in small, long-stemmed clusters of 3–5. They are impressive for their size, especially when the stems are tied down so that a whole branch is covered in flowers. The plant has somewhat few leaves and is susceptible to blackspot, but it will survive years of neglect in hot, dry Australian conditions. Its moderate vigor makes it suitable for small gardens.

BLACK JADE

BLACK JADE

syn. 'BENBLACK'

Miniature Rose

ORIGIN **Benardella, US, 1985**
PARENTAGE **Sheri Anne x Laguna**
FLOWER SIZE **1.6in (4cm)**
SCENT **Little or none**
FLOWERING **Repeats well**
HEIGHT/SPREAD **2ft (60cm)/2ft (60cm)**
HARDINESS **Zone 6**
AWARDS **AoE 1985**

Some say that Black Jade is the deepest of all red roses. It is certainly the darkest miniature rose, and its flowers are exquisitely formed like scaled-down Hybrid Teas. It is not without faults: the plant has a stiffly upright habit and a weakness for mildew and blackspot. And the flowers are scentless – very unusual for a dark crimson rose of any kind. The buds are nearly black, and open very dark red. The flowers eventually expand to a cupped shape, with paler red petals clustered around a tuft of tiny golden stamens. The flowers come singly and in small clusters on stems that are long enough to be worth picking. Black Jade has glossy, dark green leaves and repeats well. Its flowers tend to burn in sun, and in hot climates it is often grown in partial shade, where it keeps its color better.

BLACK MAGIC

syn. 'TANKALGIC'

Hybrid Tea

ORIGIN **Tantau, Germany, 1997**
FLOWER SIZE **9cm (3.5in)**
SCENT **Light and sweet**
FLOWERING **Repeats well**
HEIGHT/SPREAD **4.9ft (1.5m)/3.3ft (1m)**
HARDINESS **Zone 6**

BLACK MAGIC

'BLAIRII NO. 2'

Although mainly a florist's variety, Black Magic is also popular as a garden rose in hot, dry climates, including much of Australia, California, and South Africa. The buds are so dark as to be nearly black. Even when they start to expand, the flowers are a blackish red, and only their innermost petals can truly be said to be red or, rather, very dark crimson. The flowers are medium-sized, with fairly reflexed petals, and borne singly or, occasionally, in clusters of up to four. The plant is vigorous, with tall, upright growth, dark, healthy leaves, and bronzy new growth. It is widely grown in the Netherlands to supply the European cut-flower trade: the individual flowers have a vase life of over 14 days.

'BLACK VELVET'

Hybrid Tea

ORIGIN **Morey, US, 1960**
PARENTAGE **'New Yorker' x 'Rouge Meilland'**
FLOWER SIZE **5.5in (14cm)**
SCENT **Medium and sweet**
FLOWERING **Repeats**
HEIGHT/SPREAD **4.1ft (1.25m)/3.3ft (1m)**
HARDINESS **Zone 6**

"Black" is somewhat an exaggeration, but 'Black Velvet' is certainly a good dark red. Introduced more than 40 years ago, it is still widely grown in Australia and New Zealand. The flowers are large, classically shaped, and of exhibition quality, though not too full of petals. Sometimes dark markings appear on the tips of the petals, which give them a velvety sheen. The flowers are usually borne singly on long stems, which make them suitable for cutting. Then they open out, fairly quickly, to a cupped shape with golden stamens at the center. Finally the flowers turn dull purple as they age. 'Black Velvet' has large, dull, dark leaves and is healthy in hot, dry climates. It has a strong, upright habit, thick stems, and a fair scattering of large prickles.

'BLACK VELVET'

'BLAIRII NO. 2'

Hybrid China

ORIGIN **Blair, Britain, c.1835**
FLOWER SIZE **4.7in (12cm)**
SCENT **Strong and sweet**
FLOWERING **Once only**
HEIGHT/SPREAD **9.8ft (3m)/6.6ft (2m)**
HARDINESS **Zone 6**

No one knows the parentage of 'Blairii No. 2', but it is assumed to be a cross between the Tea rose 'Parks' Yellow' and a Gallica or Bourbon rose. The name of the rose also calls for explanation. Mr. Blair was an amateur who lived in the London suburbs. He raised three seedlings from his cross, and named them 'Blairii No. 1', 'Blairii No. 2', and 'Blairii No. 3'. 'Blairii No. 3' is lost to cultivation, and 'Blairii No. 1' is quite rare, although it is a better rose than 'Blairii No. 2' and repeat-flowering. Which leaves us with the ever popular 'Blairii No. 2'. Its flowers are unusually large and they open out neatly, so that the petals lie flat over each other in neat circles around the center. They are pink at the edges, where they pale to shades of lilac, gray, and off-white, and dark purple-pink or crimson toward the center. The plant is tall, vigorous, lanky, and susceptible to mildew and blackspot, but beautiful when its surface is completely covered by clusters of large, scented flowers.

'BLANC DE VIBERT'

Portland

ORIGIN **Vibert, France, 1847**
FLOWER SIZE **2.8in (7cm)**
SCENT **Medium and Damasklike**
FLOWERING **Repeats**
HEIGHT/SPREAD **4.9ft (1.5m)/3.3ft (1m)**
HARDINESS **Zone 5**

This white-flowered Autumn Damask is capable of producing flowers of exquisite and shapely loveliness. The only trouble is that the petals are so thin and soft that the flowers ball in damp weather and spoil in rain. So 'Blanc de Vibert' fares best in dry, warm climates, which also minimize its susceptibility to blackspot and mildew. The flowers are fully double, with a mass of papery petals around a button eye, and pure white except for a hint of pink on the outermost petals. They come singly or in tight clusters of up to seven. The foliolate sepals and long, slender receptacles are typical of the Damasks. 'Blanc de Vibert' is bushy, narrow, and upright in habit, with a lot of bristles but no really thorny prickles. Its leaves are pale, matte, gray green, and rather unrefined.

'BLANC DE VIBERT'

Les Jardins du Prieuré Notre Dame d'Orsan, France ▶

'Blanc Double de Coubert'

Rugosa Hybrid

ORIGIN **Cochet-Cochet, France, 1892**
PARENTAGE ***Rosa rugosa* × 'Sombreuil'**
FLOWER SIZE **3.5in (9cm)**
SCENT **Strong, rich, and sweet**
FLOWERING **Almost continuous**
HEIGHT/SPREAD **4.9ft (1.5m)/4.9ft (1.5m)**
HARDINESS **Zone 4**

Vita Sackville-West made this rose popular: the name of 'Blanc Double de Coubert' trips easily off the lips of well-bred English lady gardeners. It is now widely grown all over the world, and has proved so hardy in such places as Ontario and Austria that it is now smart to say that it cannot be a hybrid of the tender Tea rose 'Sombreuil', but a double form of *Rosa rugosa* 'Alba'. 'Blanc Double de Coubert' has many good qualities – vigor, health, scent, and beautiful, crinkly white flowers, followed by large squat, orange hips. It tolerates poor soils and desiccation, and is very healthy. The leaves are wrinkled and pleated in texture and turn a brilliant yellow in autumn. It blooms continually. On the other hand, it spoils in rain, is extremely prickly, and may look coarse in small gardens. Nevertheless, it is a remarkably useful shrub, especially for cold climates. Coubert is the village southeast of Paris where Philémon and Scipion Cochet had their nursery.

Three years after Philémon Cochet's death in 1896, his son Charles Cochet-Cochet introduced a fully double sport of 'Blanc Double de Coubert', which he named **'Souvenir de Philémon Cochet'**. It has a mass of small petals packed into a dense arrangement like an old Damask rose. It is even more susceptible to rain damage, but in all other respects it resembles 'Blanc Double de Coubert'.

Sport of 'Blanc Double de Coubert'

'Souvenir de Philémon Cochet'

ORIGIN **Cochet-Cochet, France, 1899**

'Blanc Double de Coubert'

'Souvenir de Philémon Cochet'

'Blanchefleur'

'Blanche de Belgique'

Hybrid Alba

ORIGIN **c.1830**
FLOWER SIZE **3.1in (8cm)**
SCENT **Strong and sweet**
FLOWERING **Once only**
HEIGHT/SPREAD **6.6ft (2m)/4.9ft (1.5m)**
HARDINESS **Zone 4**

This beautiful, compact Alba rose was probably raised in Belgium and introduced by one of the Paris nurserymen of the day. The flowers of 'Blanche de Belgique' are pure white, strongly scented, and full of petals in a muddled arrangement around a coarse button eye. They open from greenish buds with elegant, long sepals. As the flowers age, the petals crumple, spoil, and turn brown, somewhat unattractively. That said, it is one of the most ravishing of all old roses as it starts into bloom. The flowers come singly or in clusters of up to six on a compact, twiggy bush, not as lanky as most Albas. 'Blanche de Belgique' also has handsome, healthy, glaucous, gray green leaves. The flowers are very freely borne, but the plant is strictly once-flowering. It is extremely hardy, and tolerant of poor soils.

'Blanche Moreau'

Moss Rose

ORIGIN **Moreau-Robert, France, 1880**
PARENTAGE **'Comtesse de Murinais' × 'Quatre Saisons Blanc Mousseux'**
FLOWER SIZE **2.8in (7cm)**
SCENT **Strong and sweet**
FLOWERING **Once only**
HEIGHT/SPREAD **5.7ft (1.75m)/3.3ft (1m)**
HARDINESS **Zone 5**

'Blanche Moreau' flowers so rarely more than once that it is best regarded as once-flowering. Its flowers are pure white (with just a hint of pink as they open), fully double, somewhat rain sensitive, and thickly covered with hard, dark moss on the sepals, receptacles, and flower stems. The flowers come in small, tight clusters, typically of 3–5. 'Blanche Moreau' is not the most exciting of old garden roses, but the best way to justify its place in the garden is to bend down its long, slender, lanky stems and tie them low to the ground. Then they will break into flower all along their length. The plant is very prickly, with dark green foliage, somewhat sensitive to mildew.

'Blanchefleur'

Centifolia

ORIGIN **Vibert, France, 1835**
FLOWER SIZE **3.9in (10cm)**
SCENT **Rich, strong, and sweet**
FLOWERING **Once, somewhat early in season**
HEIGHT/SPREAD **4.9ft (1.5m)/6.6ft (2m)**
HARDINESS **Zone 5**

'Blanchefleur' is a great favorite among lovers of old roses – its flowers glow with brightness. Palest pink at first (they open from round, crimson-tipped buds with leafy sepals), they soon fade to white – hence the name – and reflex right back into great globes of ruffled petals. They are not consistent in their shape, but sometimes have a button eye and a green carpel at the center. The flowers come in clusters of 3–11 on somewhat short stems, which can lead to some congestion. They are borne prolifically on a vigorous, prickly plant with healthy, pale green leaves. The new growths come up strongly from the base but arch over during their second year under the weight of their blooming, so that the bush becomes a sprawling mass of fresh leaves and scented flowers. It responds well to training on a pillar or post, but looks even better intermixed with strong-growing herbaceous plants.

Rosa blanda

Wild Rose

FLOWER SIZE **5cm (2in)**
SCENT **Light and sweet**
FLOWERING **Once only**
HEIGHT/SPREAD **2m (6.6ft)/1.5m (4.9ft)**
HARDINESS **Zone 5**

Rosa blanda is a North American relation of *Rosa cinnamomea* – early-flowering and thornless, with handsome single flowers and large hips. It is native to eastern and central North America and has been used in the US to breed thornless roses. Its rich pink flowers are borne singly or in clusters of up to six. They are followed by bright vermilion hips. *Rosa blanda* has long, thin, glaucous leaves and long, smooth stems. It is not entirely thornless, but the prickles that do appear are few and confined to the base of the plant. An excellent rose for wild gardens.

'Blanche de Belgique'

'Blanche Moreau'

Rosa blanda

'BLAZE'

'BLAZE'

Modern Climber

ORIGIN **Callay, US, 1932**
PARENTAGE **'Paul's Scarlet Climber' x 'Gruss an Teplitz'**
FLOWER SIZE **2.8in (7cm)**
SCENT **Light**
FLOWERING **Repeats when well established**
HEIGHT/SPREAD **13.1ft (4m)/8.2ft (2.5m)**
HARDINESS **Zone 5**

There has always been strong competition for the unofficial position of being the world's most popular red climbing rose. 'Blaze' was promoted as an improved 'Paul's Scarlet Climber', but, in the event, has never been as widely planted and grown as its parent. Its flowers are bright dark red, although the exact shade was considered, when first introduced, a brilliant, blazing scarlet novelty. They are somewhat rounded or cupped in shape, and usually borne in upright clusters of 3–10. The first, abundant flowering is followed by smaller flushes later in the season. The plant is of only moderate vigor, but its large mid-green leaves (with fairly rounded leaflets) shrug off disease. It is easy to grow and propagates quickly from hardwood cuttings taken in the autumn.

'BLAZE SUPERIOR'

see 'DEMOKRACIE'

BLENHEIM

see SCHNEESTURM

'BLESSINGS'

Hybrid Tea

ORIGIN **Gregory, Britain, 1967**
PARENTAGE **'Queen Elizabeth' seedling**
FLOWER SIZE **4.3in (11cm)**
SCENT **Medium and sweet**
FLOWERING **Repeats well**
HEIGHT/SPREAD **80cm (2.7ft)/60cm (2ft)**
HARDINESS **Zone 6**

'Blessings' was introduced as a Floribunda rose, which explains why it tends to produce its flowers in clusters of 3–7, and why it is pretty at all stages of growth. The flowers open from long, slender, Hybrid Tea buds at the end of long purple stems. They are pale salmon pink, with coral petal backs, and not overly full – this rose was bred for the English climate – and eventually open out like a Floribunda. The plant is vigorous, with handsome, large, dark leaves. It is an excellent bedding rose, very free-flowering, and easy to grow.

'BLEU MAGENTA'

Multiflora Rambler

ORIGIN **c.1920**
FLOWER SIZE **2in (5cm)**
SCENT **Light or slight**
FLOWERING **Once, somewhat late in season**
HEIGHT/SPREAD **13.1ft (4m)/6.6ft (2m)**
HARDINESS **Zone 5**

The origins of this popular purple climber are obscure. All we know is that it came from L'Haÿ-les-Roses in the 1950s as a rose without a name.

'BLEU MAGENTA'

It is probably an older rose whose original name has been lost. 'Bleu Magenta' was L'Haÿ's description of its color: it remains the richest colored and "bluest" of the purple 'Veilchenblau' ramblers. The individual flowers open dark pink or crimson, then change first to purple, then to violet, and finally to slate blue; some petals have white flecks in them. The flowers are very double, but open out flat. They are borne in clusters of 10–30, which become somewhat congested when in full bloom. The wood is nearly thornless, but the leaves are much smaller than those of other blue or Veilchenblau ramblers. There is a famous planting of 'Bleu Magenta' around a circular trellis in the rose garden at Mottisfont Abbey in England, interspersed with the pink-flowered 'Debutante'.

'BLOOMFIELD ABUNDANCE'

see 'CÉCILE BRUNNER'

'BLOOMFIELD COURAGE'

Wichurana Rambler

ORIGIN **Thomas, US, 1925**
FLOWER SIZE **1.2in (3cm)**
SCENT **Little or none**
FLOWERING **Once, early in season**
HEIGHT/SPREAD **19.7ft (6m)/13.1ft (4m)**
HARDINESS **Zone 6**

The flowers of 'Bloomfield Courage' have dark crimson edges, a vivid white center, and yellow stamens. Individually, they are fairly ordinary, but they come in extraordinary quantities in large, loose clusters of 15–40, all along the stems. When the plant is in full flower, fairly early in the season, it is impossible to see the leaves, which are dark and glossy in the way of most Wichurana ramblers. Small scarlet hips follow in autumn. The plant is immensely vigorous, easy to cultivate, almost thornless, and simple to propagate from cuttings. 'Bloomfield Courage' needs a lot of space, but can be wound around a support, or tied down horizontally to maximize the production of flowers.

'BLOOMFIELD DAINTY'

Hybrid Musk

ORIGIN **Thomas, US, 1924**
PARENTAGE **'Danaë' x 'Mme. Edouard Herriot'**
FLOWER SIZE **2in (5cm)**
SCENT **Strong and musky**
FLOWERING **Repeats constantly**
HEIGHT/SPREAD **6.6ft (2m)/5.7ft (1.75m)**
HARDINESS **Zone 6**

This handsome Hybrid Musk is popular in hot climates, where it flowers for months on end. 'Bloomfield Dainty' has orange buds that open canary yellow but quickly fade to pink from the petal tips inward. The flowers are single and have a strong, carrying scent of musk. At their center is a boss of stamens, deep yellow at first, before they turn brown. 'Bloomfield Dainty' is only moderately vigorous: it makes a slender, arching shrub but can, with difficulty, be trained as a short climber. The leaves are dark and glossy, and somewhat susceptible to blackspot. However, this is not such a problem in the dry Mediterranean climates where 'Bloomfield Dainty' does best.

'BLESSINGS'

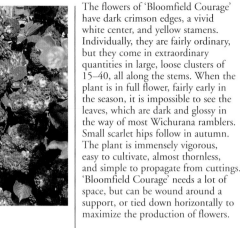

'BLOOMFIELD COURAGE'

'BLOOMFIELD DAINTY'

'Blossomtime'

Blue Parfum

Blueberry Hill

'Blossomtime'

Modern Climber

ORIGIN **O'Neal, US, 1951**
PARENTAGE **'New Dawn' x unknown**
FLOWER SIZE **3.5in (9cm)**
SCENT **Strong and sweet**
FLOWERING **Repeats well**
HEIGHT/SPREAD **11.5ft (3.5m)/6.6ft (2m)**
HARDINESS **Zone 5**

'Blossomtime' is a somewhat shrubby climber or pillar rose. The flowers open from elegant, pointed buds. The petals are silvery pink, with darker reverses, which means that the flower has deep pink shadows between the petals. The flowers have somewhat muddled centers and come in clusters of 3–7. The plant is healthy, with glossy leaves, and never without some flowers after its first, most generous flowering.

'Blue Girl'

see 'Kölner Karneval'

'Blue Moon'

see 'Mainzer Fastnacht'

'Blue Nile'

see 'Nil Bleu'

Blue Parfum

syn. 'TANfifum'
Hybrid Tea

ORIGIN **Tantau, Germany, 1977**
FLOWER SIZE **4.3in (11cm)**
SCENT **Strong and sweet**
FLOWERING **Repeats well**
HEIGHT/SPREAD **3.9ft (1.2m)/2.7ft (80cm)**
HARDINESS **Zone 6**

Many of the modern "blue" roses have a very strong scent, but only Blue Parfum celebrates its color and its fragrance in its name. Its flowers are purple at first, but the outer petals turn more crimson as they open, while the inner ones remain mauve or lavender. Although the buds are long and elegant, the flowers are only semidouble when they open out, and sometimes their petals develop ragged edges. The scent, however, is rich and pervasive. The plant has a dense, compact habit and good dark leaves as a foil for the flowers.

Blue River

syn. 'KORsicht'
Hybrid Tea

ORIGIN **Kordes, Germany, 1984**
PARENTAGE **'Mainzer Fastnacht' x 'Zorina'**
FLOWER SIZE **3.9in (10cm)**
SCENT **Very strong and sweet**
FLOWERING **Repeats well**
HEIGHT/SPREAD **3.3ft (1m)/2.5ft (75cm)**
HARDINESS **Zone 6**

The color of Blue River is both attractive and unusual – pale lavender, with crimson shadings all along the edges of the petals. Better still is its sumptuous scent, quite a feature of modern "blue" roses. The flowers have many incurved petals and a fairly globular shape, but they are abundantly borne (singly or in clusters of 2–5) on a densely bushy, vigorous plant. Blue River has been popular in Europe since its introduction, but in recent years its renown has spread to North America and Australia. It fares particularly well in hot, dry climates where its flowers can open out slowly and change color as they age, taking on shades of silver, gray, and mauve.

Blue River

Blueberry Hill

syn. 'WEKcryplag'
Floribunda

ORIGIN **Carruth, US, 1997**
PARENTAGE **Crystalline x Playgirl**
FLOWER SIZE **3.5in (9cm)**
SCENT **Light and fruity**
FLOWERING **Almost continuous**
HEIGHT/SPREAD **2.7ft (80cm)/2.7ft (80cm)**
HARDINESS **Zone 6**

Blueberry Hill is a very pretty, compact Floribunda. The flowers open out quickly from nicely shaped crimson buds. They are lightly double, slightly wavy (a style that is popular in the US), and lightly scented – the scent is most noticeable in the morning. The flowers are pale lilac pink with much darker backs. The outer petals are much darker than the inner ones at first, so that the flowers look like a mixture of blueberries and cream, but they are uniformly pale later on. The flowers are enhanced by golden stamens that keep their color well. They come singly or in clusters of up to nine (generally about five) on long stems that are good for cutting. They are produced in great profusion both at the first flowering and thereafter almost continuously until early winter. The bush has healthy, glossy foliage and a stocky, rounded habit. In warm climates it will grow to 3.9ft (1.2m), but half that is more normal in cold areas. Apart from its height, the performance of Blueberry Hill is consistent in all climates.

Blühwunder

syn. 'KORedan', Flower Power, Ponderosa
Floribunda

ORIGIN **Kordes, Germany, 1994**
PARENTAGE **'Mazurka' x unknown**
FLOWER SIZE **2.4in (6cm)**
SCENT **Light and fruity**
FLOWERING **Almost continuous**
HEIGHT/SPREAD **3.3ft (1m)/2.7ft (80cm)**
HARDINESS **Zone 6**
AWARDS **Bagatelle GM 1993; ADR 1995**

It is unusual for a German-bred rose to be more popular in France than in its country of origin, but that has proved to be the fate of Blühwunder, better known to the French as Ponderosa. Although classed as a Floribunda, it is a very cheerful, short, shrub rose whose profuse flowering makes it suitable for mass plantings and landscaping. The individual flowers are fairly ordinary, with short, broad petals that open out around a lightly cupped flower, but they come in large clusters (of 5–20) on a neat and very healthy bush with small, dark, glossy leaves. Clearly, it has *Rosa wichurana* somewhere in its ancestry. The flowers are pale salmon pink at first, fading first to rose pink and then to palest pink in hot weather. The petal backs are always slightly darker. Blühwunder should certainly be more widely grown elsewhere.

Blühwunder

B

'BLUSH DAMASK'

'BLUSH DAMASK'

Gallica-Damask Hybrid

ORIGIN **Britain, 1759**
FLOWER SIZE **2.8in (7cm)**
SCENT **Medium and sweet**
FLOWERING **Once, early or midseason**
HEIGHT/SPREAD **6.6ft (2m)/6.6ft (2m)**
HARDINESS **Zone 5**

'Blush Damask' is an ancient and beautiful rose with a somewhat short season of flower. The flowers are filled with thin petals and are often lopsided and misshapen: sometimes it is difficult to find a "perfect" flower on a whole bush. Their color, too, is uneven, since every flower has patches of pale pink and dark pink – and lilac tints too – although the edges are usually paler than the center, and the petal backs are also paler. The flowers open out to a swirl of petals and sometimes reflex to a pompon. They come singly or in clusters of 2–3 on short, slender stalks, weighed down by their carrige. The bush grows tall and leafy: it has a lax habit of growth, and the pale green of its leaves increases the impression of delicacy that the flowers radiate. In fact the bush is tough, frugal, and vigorous – especially when grown on its own roots and allowed to make a twiggy thicket of stems. Despite the misshapen flowers, the overall effect is very attractive.

'BLUSH HIP'

Alba Hybrid

ORIGIN **1840**
FLOWER SIZE **2.8in (7cm)**
SCENT **Strong and sweet**
FLOWERING **Once only**
HEIGHT/SPREAD **9.8ft (3m)/6.6ft (2m)**
HARDINESS **Zone 4**

No one knows the origins of 'Blush Hip', but it is thought to have occurred in England during the 1840s. It is an Alba rose, but a pink one, and the turbinate receptacles suggest that it may be a hybrid with a Frankfurt rose. The flowers open out flat from dark pink buds. They are bright pink at first, fading to rose pink as they age. They have a mass of small petals, often quartered, around a button eye and a green stigma. They are sometimes borne singly but more usually in clusters of up to seven, starting fairly

'BLUSH HIP'

early in the season in cool climates but late in hot ones. Despite its name, it never sets hips. 'Blush Hip' has the gray green leaves of Alba roses and Frankfurt roses, and a fair scattering of prickles. Its slender, flexible stems are sometimes trained upward like a climbing rose.

'BLUSH NOISETTE'

see 'NOISETTE CARNÉE'

'BLUSH RAMBLER'

Hybrid Multiflora

ORIGIN **Cant, Britain, 1903**
PARENTAGE **'Turner's Crimson Rambler' × 'The Garland'**
FLOWER SIZE **1.6in (4cm)**
SCENT **Strong and musky**
FLOWERING **Once, somewhat late in season**
HEIGHT/SPREAD **13.1ft (4m)/9.8ft (3m)**
HARDINESS **Zone 6**

This is one of the loveliest of the Hybrid Multifloras – a very vigorous plant that will climb as much as 26.2ft (8m) up a tree. The flowers of 'Blush Rambler' are almost single, and open bright pink, before fading to white, but the overall impression they give is of pale blush pink. They come in large, lax, open clusters (typically of 20–50 flowers) and have the inestimable quality of shedding their petals as soon as they fade. This means that the flower trusses always appear clean and fresh. The plant has large, pale green leaves, few prickles, and a vigorous, upright habit of growth. The new stems that shoot up from the base are very strong and thick: the whole plant radiates health and vigor. It is especially floriferous in hot climates and is at its best in dry weather because the flowers, even though simple, tend to blotch in rain.

'BLUSH RAMBLER'

'BOBBIE JAMES'

'BOBBIE JAMES'

Hybrid Multiflora

ORIGIN **Sunningdale, Britain, 1961**
FLOWER SIZE **1.6in (4cm)**
SCENT **Strong and musky**
FLOWERING **Once, midseason**
HEIGHT/SPREAD **16.4ft (5m)/9.8ft (3m)**
HARDINESS **Zone 6**

'Bobbie James' is the best of the small-flowered ramblers that closely resemble a wild rose but have larger flowers and more petals. The English rosarian Graham Thomas (then working for Sunningdale Nurseries) discovered it as a seedling in Lady Serena James's garden at St. Nicholas near Richmond, Yorkshire, and named it after her husband, the Hon. Robert James, who died in 1960. Its flowers are lightly double, reminiscent of cherry blossom, but carried with amazing profusion in large clusters bursting with flowers. They are followed by innumerable small orange red hips in autumn. The leaves are bright green and glossy, but almost invisible when the plant is in full bloom – such is the foaming mass of its flowers. The flowers have bright yellow stamens and a very strong scent of musk. Best grown up into a tree, 'Bobbie James' will grow as much as 26.2ft (8m) in ideal conditions.

'BOBBY CHARLTON'

Hybrid Tea

ORIGIN **Fryer, Britain, 1974**
PARENTAGE **'Royal Highness' × 'Prima Ballerina'**
FLOWER SIZE **5.5in (14cm)**
SCENT **Very strong and sweet**
FLOWERING **Repeats**
HEIGHT/SPREAD **5.7ft (1.75m)/4.1ft (1.25m)**
HARDINESS **Zone 6**
AWARDS **Baden-Baden GM 1976; Portland GM 1980**

In hot climates, 'Bobby Charlton' is an outsized plant,6.6ft (2m) tall, with huge flowers – a peerless example of perfection among the Hybrid Teas. It is popular as an exhibition rose in England, but rarely is at its best there. The flowers are pink with slightly paler, silver pink backs to the large, long petals. Their great size and supreme elegance of shape are one of the marvels of the world of roses. The flowers are usually borne singly, occasionally in clusters of up to four, on long, strong stems that have a few large prickles. A vigorous, strapping plant with large, tough leaves, it repays good cultivation. Blackspot may be a problem later in the season. It is named after an English soccer hero.

'BOBBY CHARLTON'

BOLCHOÏ

BOLCHOÏ

syn. 'MEIZUZES', Madam Speaker

Hybrid Tea

ORIGIN **Meilland, France, 1996**
FLOWER SIZE **5.1in (13cm)**
SCENT **Very strong and fruity**
FLOWERING **Repeats well**
HEIGHT/SPREAD **3.3ft (1m)/2.5ft (75cm)**
HARDINESS **Zone 6**

Scent, beauty, and an unusual combination of colors are all present in this splendid modern rose. The flowers – almost always borne singly on long, strong stems – are scarlet and yellow when they first open: the upper sides are scarlet, while the petal backs are pure yellow. As they open out, the yellow fades away to leave the flowers crimson on one side and pink underneath. The petals then acquire a distinctive wave, which once again highlights the contrast of colors. The flower is beautiful at all stages of its growth, making it valuable both in the garden and as a cut flower. The scent is a bonus, but so strong and delicious that it won top prize at the international trials at Le Roeulx, Belgium, in 1996. The plant is healthy, with plenty of bright green leaves.

'BON SILÈNE'

Tea Rose

ORIGIN **Hardy, France, c.1837**
FLOWER SIZE **3.1in (8cm)**
SCENT **Strong and tealike**
FLOWERING **Continuous**
HEIGHT/SPREAD **8.2ft (2.5m)/8.2ft (2.5m)**
HARDINESS **Zone 7**

It may have a little China rose in its background, but 'Bon Silène' was one of the first Tea roses to be bred in the West. It has the large flowers, long buds, profuse flowering, and intense scent that we associate with the great Tea roses. The flowers are dark pink and double, with a hint of cream at the base of their petals. They fade to rose pink as they age and open out somewhat loosely, even messily, but the color is still among the richest and deepest of all the Teas. 'Bon Silène' builds up into a big, bulky plant, full of somewhat prickly, little, twiggy stems. Its leaves are healthy, small, and mid-green (crimson when young). It roots easily from cuttings and grows more vigorously than most Tea roses. It responds well to good cultivation, feeding, and watering, but old bushes of 'Bon Silène' have been known to survive neglect for decades in old abandoned gardens. A winner.

'BON SILÈNE'

'BONFIRE NIGHT'

Floribunda

ORIGIN **McGredy, Northern Ireland, 1971**
PARENTAGE **'Tiki' x 'Variety Club'**
FLOWER SIZE **3.1in (8cm)**
SCENT **Light and fruity**
FLOWERING **Repeats well**
HEIGHT/SPREAD **4.1ft (1.25m)/3.3ft (1m)**
HARDINESS **Zone 6**

'Bonfire Night' is an excellent, vigorous 1970s Floribunda, with the mixture of red, orange, and yellow in its flowers that was then fashionable. It looks for all the world like a seedling of 'Masquerade', with the same small dark leaves and the same tendency for the flowers to open yellow and turn by degrees to red, though the petal backs are yellow at all times. The flowers are lightly double with fairly long petals and a Hybrid Tea shape when they first open. The plant grows vigorous and tall and tolerates bad growing conditions, including poor soil and some degree of shade.

'BONFIRE NIGHT'

'BONN'

Hybrid Musk

ORIGIN **Kordes, Germany, 1950**
PARENTAGE **'Hamburg' x 'Kordes' Sondermeldung'**
FLOWER SIZE **3.5in (9cm)**
SCENT **Light and musky**
FLOWERING **Repeats well**
HEIGHT/SPREAD **5.7ft (1.75m)/4.9ft (1.5m)**
HARDINESS **Zone 5**

Although traditionally classed among the Hybrid Musks, 'Bonn' is a good example of the brightly colored, hardy, repeat flowering shrub roses that Kordes produced in the middle years of the 20th century. They were known as Park roses and were very popular in the public gardens of Germany and northern Europe, where high horticultural standards are always expected. 'Bonn' has bright orange vermilion flowers that fade to pale crimson and bleach at their edges with age. They come in large clusters (typically of 7–15 flowers) on long stems that sometimes bend over under their weight but always make a conspicuous display. They are useful for giving bulk to large flower arrangements. The plant has large, mid-green leaves and a vigorous habit of growth. Bonn is a Rhineland town that was once the capital of West Germany.

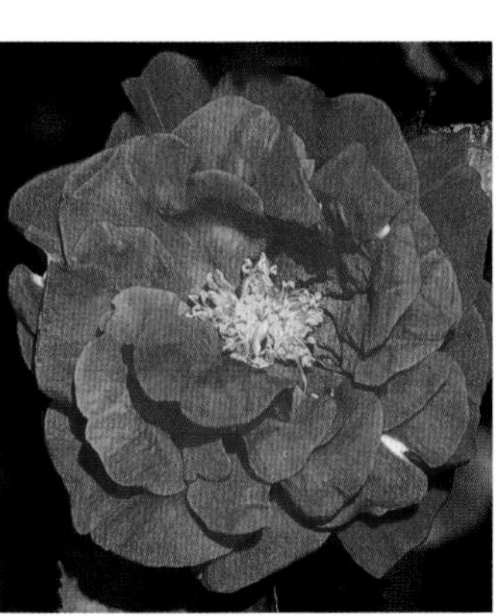

'BONN'

BONICA 82

syn. 'MEIDOMONAC'

Shrub Rose

ORIGIN **Meilland, France, 1985**
PARENTAGE **(*Rosa sempervirens* x 'Mlle. Marthe Carron') x 'Picasso'**
FLOWER SIZE **2.4in (6cm)**
SCENT **Light and sweet**
FLOWERING **Repeats**
HEIGHT/SPREAD **3.3ft (1m)/4.1ft (1.25m)**
HARDINESS **Zone 5**
AWARDS **ADR 1983; AARS 1987**

Bonica 82 is one of the most successful and widely planted of all modern roses. It owes its popularity partly to its remarkable vigor and floriferousness, and partly to its suitability for so many purposes. It is equally useful and easy to grow as a shrub rose, groundcover rose, landscaping plant, and container rose. The flowers are bright, pale pink, opening from rich pink buds and fading eventually almost to white in hot climates. They have ruffled petals and a lightly cupped shape. The flowers usually come in clusters of 5–15. Although their stalks are short, they are useful, long-lasting roses to cut for the house. Bonica 82 has a very long and spectacular main flowering. Thereafter, it continues to produce a few flowers until late autumn. They are followed by bright red hips that usually persist until the following spring. The plant makes a thick, rounded bush, capable of reaching 4.9ft (1.5m), but is best pruned back to about half its size every other year or so. Its leaves are handsome, dark, and glossy and contribute much to its overall beauty. Blackspot often afflicts it later in the year, but seems not to affect the plant's growth, flowering, or vigor.

In 1994 Meilland introduced a fully double sport of Bonica 82, which it named Royal Bonica. The increased number of petals means that the flowers are also larger and slightly darker in color. Some people say that it also grows a little bigger and bushier than Bonica 82 but in all other respects, Royal Bonica is identical to its parent. It is a classic example of a sport which, though clearly an improvement, has never proved as popular as the rose from which it arose. That said, it is widely grown and sold all over the world. It would be difficult, however, to find any true match for the popularity of Bonica 82.

BONICA 82

ROYAL BONICA

Sport of Bonica 82

ROYAL BONICA

syn. 'MEIMODAC'
ORIGIN **Meilland, France, 1994**
FLOWER SIZE **2.8in (7cm)**
HEIGHT/SPREAD **4.1ft (1.25m)/4.9ft (1.5m)**

B

'BORDERER'

'BORDURE ROSE'

'BOTZARIS'

'BORDERER'

Polyantha

ORIGIN **Clark, Australia, 1918**
PARENTAGE **'Jersey Beauty' × unknown**
FLOWER SIZE **2.4in (6cm)**
SCENT **Light and musky**
FLOWERING **Recurrent**
HEIGHT/SPREAD **1.6ft (50cm)/3.3ft (1m)**
HARDINESS **Zone 7**

'Borderer' is one of the best dwarf-growing Polyanthas bred by Australian amateur Alister Clark from the Wichurana rambler 'Jersey Beauty'. It is extremely floriferous, and the flowers have the charming mixture of pink, cream, and buff that is common to the Barbier ramblers. The coloring is darker on newly opened petals and paler on the petal backs. The center is cream colored, sometimes displaying good yellow stamens and sometimes a button eye. Some of the petals are quill-shaped. The flowers come in clusters of 5–20 on a lax, spreading plant that has only a few prickles. This habit makes it excellent for the front of a border and particularly effective when planted in masses. It has good, dark, glossy Wichurana leaves. Like many of the Wichurana Polyanthas, 'Borderer' seems to anticipate by 80 years the modern groundcover and landscape roses.

'BORDURE ROSE'

syn. 'STRAWBERRY ICE'

Floribunda

ORIGIN **Delbard, France, 1975**
PARENTAGE **(['Goldilocks' × 'Virgo'] × ['Orange Triumph' × 'Yvonne Rabier']) × 'Fashion'**
FLOWER SIZE **2.8in (7cm)**
SCENT **Little or none**
FLOWERING **Repeats constantly**
HEIGHT/SPREAD **2.7ft (80cm)/3.3ft (1m)**
HARDINESS **Zone 6**
AWARDS **Baden-Baden GM 1973; Madrid GM 1974**

The Delbard family has introduced several 'Bordure' roses, which are low-growing, compact Floribundas for landscaping and prominent positions at the front of a border. 'Bordure Rose' is the most popular, and perhaps the best. It has very pretty pink flowers, shaped like camellias and graded toward a white patch at the center. The petal backs are also white, except for a pink tinge toward their tips. The flowers come in clusters of 5–10 on short stems. They do not flourish in cool weather or wet conditions, but the first flowering in spring or summer produces flowers of great beauty. The plant has fairly ordinary leaves and a dense habit of growth. It looks best when several plants are grown close together.

BOSSA NOVA

syn. 'POULOMA', My Granny, The Fawn

Polyantha

ORIGIN **Poulsen, Denmark, 1992**
PARENTAGE **'The Fairy' × 'New Dawn'**
FLOWER SIZE **2.8in (7cm)**
SCENT **Light and musky**
FLOWERING **Repeats**
HEIGHT/SPREAD **3.3ft (1m)/6.6ft (2m)**
HARDINESS **Zone 5**

Although it was introduced as a groundcover plant, Bossa Nova is best treated as a climber. Otherwise it makes a loose, creeping shrub that tangles in and out of other plants and fails to suppress the weeds. Bossa Nova came from a cross between two famous and popular roses, each introduced as long ago as the 1930s. Its flowers are pink, fading to white at the edges, and full of petals. They usually have an attractive quartered shape, but their petals are thin and do not stand up well to rain. Bossa Nova does best in dry, warm climates where its flowers can open undamaged and where the risk of blackspot and mildew is minimized. The plant has medium-dark, glossy leaves and quite a scattering of prickles.

'BOTZARIS'

Damask Rose

ORIGIN **Robert, France, 1856**
FLOWER SIZE **3.1in (8cm)**
SCENT **Strong and sweet**
FLOWERING **Once, midseason**
HEIGHT/SPREAD **3.9ft (1.2m)/3.9ft (1.2m)**
HARDINESS **Zone 5**

One of the best of all Damask roses, 'Botzaris' has extremely beautiful flowers that are deliciously sweet-scented. They are pure white, with hints and tints of cream and pink at the center at first, and they open out flat and quartered. They have a great number of petals, of which a fair few toward the center roll over into a fat button eye. The flowers also have a hint of a green carpel at the center, although this is not so conspicuous as in 'Mme. Hardy'. The flowers are backed by long, leafy sepals and lush, bright green leaves – in both these features, 'Botzaris' is a typical Damask. The shrub is very healthy and not very prickly. It may be pruned as a low bush at 2.6ft (80cm) or allowed to grow up to twice that height as a more lax shrub. The traditional formula for pruning Damasks is to cut them back by a third, after they have flowered, to keep them compact. Marcos Botzaris (1790–1823) was a hero of Greek independence.

'BOUGAINVILLE'

Noisette

ORIGIN **Cochet, France, c.1822**
FLOWER SIZE **1.6in (4cm)**
SCENT **Light and musky**
FLOWERING **Constant**
HEIGHT/SPREAD **8.2ft (2.5m)/6.6ft (2m)**
HARDINESS **Zone 6**

This excellent ever-blooming Noisette rose is probably a seedling of 'Noisette Carnée', which it resembles closely in all but its deeper pink coloring. The flowers open from round, crimson purple buds and are bright pink at first, before fading to pale pink. The backs of the petals are always paler. The petals are numerous, bursting somewhat messily out of the flowers, which are carried in erect clusters of up to 50. 'Bougainville' produces a mass of long, slender basal stems. The leaves are light, bright green, and very healthy, with somewhat elongated leaflets. The plant is more prickly than 'Noisette Carnée' and slightly less vigorous, growing to about 6.6ft (2m) as a dense, leafy shrub, but more against a wall. In hot climates it is constantly in flower; elsewhere it flowers until the first frost of winter.

'BOUGAINVILLE'

B

'Boula de Nanteuil'

'Boula de Nanteuil'

syn. 'Comte de Nanteuil'

Gallica

ORIGIN **Roeser, France, 1834**
FLOWER SIZE **3.1in (8cm)**
SCENT **Medium and sweet**
FLOWERING **Once, midseason**
HEIGHT/SPREAD **3.3ft (1m)/3.9ft (1.2m)**
HARDINESS **Zone 5**

Although not one of the most stunning of Gallicas, 'Boula de Nanteuil' has a distinct charm. Its flowers are a pale purple crimson, and fade to shades of Parma violet in hot weather. The outer petals are larger than the inner ones, which are sometimes folded over to make a rough button eye. All the petals are paler on their reverses, while the innermost ones are often flecked with white – both features that add character to the open flower. In hot weather the petals reflex into a ball. The plant has small, medium-dark leaves and thin, dark stems. It is fairly healthy, but not notably vigorous, taking some years to build up a twiggy structure. 'Boula de Nanteuil' is a good Gallica for small gardens.

'Boule de Neige'

Noisette

ORIGIN **Lacharme, France, 1867**
PARENTAGE **'Mlle. Blanche Lafitte' x 'Sapho'**
FLOWER SIZE **2.8in (7cm)**
SCENT **Strong and sweet**
FLOWERING **Remontant**
HEIGHT/SPREAD **9.8ft (3m)/6.6ft (2m)**
HARDINESS **Zone 6**

This cross between a Noisette and a Hybrid Perpetual is remarkably hardy, but it needs a hot climate to grow to its true size and give of its best. It is one of several crosses that Lacharme made between the same parents. 'Boule de Neige' has fat, crimson tipped buds, and a hint of pink as it opens, before revealing a mass of short, brilliant white petals. The double flower is very full at first, and slightly cabbagelike in shape, before the outer petals reflex completely to form a ball – hence the name. The petals, although many, are thin and delicate, which means that they spoil in rain. The flowers come in large clusters of 5–20, somewhat tightly held together, on an upright plant with dark green, slightly glaucous leaves. It has short internodes, which give the impression of dense growth, and a stiffness that makes the wood brittle – it is easy to snap off a piece accidentally.

'Bouquet d'Or'

Noisette

ORIGIN **Ducher, France, 1872**
PARENTAGE **'Gloire de Dijon' seedling**
FLOWER SIZE **3.5in (9cm)**
SCENT **Fairly strong and tealike**
FLOWERING **Almost continuous**
HEIGHT/SPREAD **11.5ft (3.5m)/6.6ft (2m)**
HARDINESS **Zone 8**

'Bouquet d'Or' is a widely grown short climber that flowers continuously in warm climates. The flowers are fully double, and open out from dumpy buds into a flat mass of somewhat broad, intricately folded petals. They are variable in shape, mostly muddled but occasionally quartered. Their color, too, is inconsistent – usually buff yellow, with a very occasional hint of pink, plus peach pink petal backs and a tendency to fade at the edges to cream and pale apricot. However, all the petals reflex along their edges, while keeping a crease down their middles – a distinctive characteristic. The flowers come singly or in clusters of up to four blooms. The leaves are fairly dark green and the plant is fairly prickly, but it is a good grower.

'Bouquet d'Or'

'Bourbon Queen'

see 'Reine de l'Isle de Bourbon'

Bow Bells

syn. 'AUSbells'

Shrub Rose

ORIGIN **Austin, Britain, 1991**
PARENTAGE **('Chaucer' x 'Conrad Ferdinand Meyer') x Graham Thomas**
FLOWER SIZE **3.1in (8cm)**
SCENT **Light and sweet**
FLOWERING **Repeats well**
HEIGHT/SPREAD **3.9ft (1.2m)/3.3ft (1m)**
HARDINESS **Zone 5**

Closer in style to a Floribunda than to David Austin's other English Roses, Bow Bells has red buds that open out to pure pink flowers, lightly cupped, with paler pink edges to the petals. There is a pretty cluster of stamens inside, but this is sometimes obscured by petals folding over the center. The double flowers come in clusters of 3–9, sometimes more, on long, slender stems that tend to flop down under their own weight. The plant is prickly, vigorous, and leafy, reaching as much as 6.6ft (2m) in hot climates, but the flowers are larger and keep their color longer in cool climates. It is a good repeater, again more like a Floribunda. Bow Bells is named after the church of St. Mary-le-Bow in London.

Rosa bracteata

Rosa bracteata

Wild Rose

FLOWER SIZE **2.4in (6cm)**
SCENT **Light and fruity**
FLOWERING **Once, somewhat late in season**
HEIGHT/SPREAD **9.8ft (3m)/16.4ft (5m)**
HARDINESS **Zone 8**

There is no mistaking *Rosa bracteata*: every flower has several large, gray green bracts beneath it. The flowers are large for a wild species, and have long, golden stamens. They are usually borne singly, on very short stems, and the calyx and bracts are covered in velvety down. The plant is most noted for its handsome, dense, bright green, glittering leaves. It is very healthy and vigorous, best grown as a wide, freestanding shrub, but capable of clambering to 16.4ft (5m) or more if encouraged to climb up a tree. Although native to warm, subtropical, coastal parts of China, it has also naturalized in Florida and Louisiana. It has not been much used for hybridization, though the incomparable 'Mermaid' was bred from it, and *Rosa bracteata* could still be used to breed new shrub roses for hot, humid climates.

'Boule de Neige'

Bow Bells

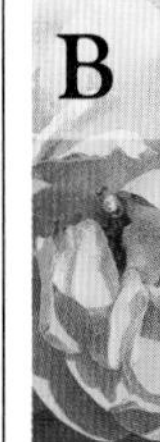

B

BRANDY

BRANDY

syn. 'AROcad'

Hybrid Tea

ORIGIN **Swim & Christensen, US, 1981**
PARENTAGE **'First Prize' x 'Dr A. J. Verhage'**
FLOWER SIZE **5.1in (13cm)**
SCENT **Medium and tealike**
FLOWERING **Early in season; repeats well**
HEIGHT/SPREAD **4.9ft (1.5m)/4.1ft (1.25m)**
HARDINESS **Zone 6**
AWARDS **AARS 1982**

This popular and beautiful Hybrid Tea has long, elegant buds and large, rich apricot flowers or, more accurately, buff colored flowers with orange apricot undersides to the petals. The color varies a little, and is usually stronger in cool weather and in autumn. The flowers are usually borne singly, but occasionally in twos and threes, on long, strong, stiff stems, so Brandy is good both as a garden plant and for cutting. The leaves are dark and slightly glaucous, but the new growths are a beautiful crimson. The plant is vigorous and healthy: it repeats well and is rarely out of flower for long, especially if lightly pruned and allowed to build up a more shrubby structure.

BRASS BAND

BRASS BAND

syn. 'JACcofl'

Floribunda

ORIGIN **Christensen, US, 1993**
PARENTAGE **Rimosa 79 x seedling**
FLOWER SIZE **3.1in (8cm)**
SCENT **Light and fresh**
FLOWERING **Repeats regularly throughout the growing season**
HEIGHT/SPREAD **3.9ft (1.2m)/3.3ft (1m)**
HARDINESS **Zone 6**
AWARDS **AARS 1995**

"Brassy" is the word most often used to describe the color of this spectacular Floribunda, but the colors are both beautiful and clean, while the short, ruffled petals (much loved by American breeders) give it a bouncy charm. The flowers are deep orange, although slightly paler at the edges of the thick, waxy petals. The petal backs are pure yellow, but the yellow fades from every part of the flower, so that the orange coloring becomes redder with age – ending up pale coral or deep salmon, while always brighter and darker at the center. The flowers come in large clusters of 5–9 blooms and show up well against the large, dark green, semi-glossy leaves. The plant makes sturdy growth and repeats freely throughout the season. The colors are strongest in cool weather, and the flowers are noticeably larger if the plants are well-watered when it is hot and dry.

BRAVEHEART

see GORDON'S COLLEGE

BREATH OF LIFE

syn. 'HARquanne'

Shrub Rose

ORIGIN **Harkness, Britain, 1980**
PARENTAGE **'Red Dandy' x 'Alexander'**
FLOWER SIZE **3.5in (9cm)**
SCENT **Medium, sweet, and musky**
FLOWERING **Repeats well**
HEIGHT/SPREAD **6.6ft (2m)/4.1ft (1.25m)**
HARDINESS **Zone 6**

Although often sold as a climber, Breath of Life is a bushy, upright shrub that rarely grows taller than 6.6ft (2m), unless it is planted against a wall. The flowers are plump and full of petals. They open pale coral or apricot colored, paler at the edges, and fade to mother-of-pearl. The contrast of colors within the large, half-open bud is exquisite, especially if the central petals are neatly spiraled. The flowers do not, however, drop their petals before turning brown, and they tend to spot in rain. The flowers usually come singly, sometimes in twos or threes, on long, stout stems, which makes them excellent in cut-flower arrangements.

BREATH OF LIFE

Breath of Life is vigorous, upright, and branching in habit, with a few big prickles and large, medium-dark leaves. Blackspot may be a problem in autumn. It is a lanky grower: the bottom half of an established plant has no flowers or leaves and needs complementary planting to hide its nakedness.

BREDON

syn. 'AUSbred'

Shrub Rose

ORIGIN **Austin, Britain, 1984**
PARENTAGE **'Wife of Bath' x 'Lilian Austin'**
FLOWER SIZE **2.8in (7cm)**
SCENT **Light and fruity**
FLOWERING **Repeats well**
HEIGHT/SPREAD **3.3ft (1m)/2.5ft (75cm)**
HARDINESS **Zone 6**

The flowers of Bredon are very full, flat, and imbricated. They have masses of little petals radiating out from the center with a distinctive rhythm. The flowers are peach colored at the center, grading through lemon, buff, and cream to white at the edges. The petals are actually cream colored, and it is the backs that carry the color: this gives rise to wonderful reflected tones in the depths of the flower. They are borne in clusters of 3–9 on a gawky, open, prickly plant with dark glossy leaves. It may need deadheading, not to encourage repeat flowering (which is good) but because it does not shed its dead petals cleanly. Mildew may be a problem. Bredon is a hill in Shropshire.

BREDON

'BREEZE HILL'

Wichurana Hybrid

ORIGIN **Van Fleet, US, 1926**
PARENTAGE ***Rosa wichurana* x 'Beauté de Lyon'**
FLOWER SIZE **3.1in (8cm)**
SCENT **Moderate and fruity**
FLOWERING **Once, midseason**
HEIGHT/SPREAD **13.1ft (4m)/9.8ft (3m)**
HARDINESS **Zone 5**

Many regard 'Breeze Hill' as the best of all the once-flowering ramblers. Its flowers are unusually large, exquisitely ruffled, and a very beautiful mixture of colors. They are generously borne, singly or in clusters of up to seven, opening amber or apricot at the center, but buff pink at the edges, and fading to cream and pink. In hot climates and sunny positions they eventually pass to white, but they keep their color in cool climates or in shade. The flowers unfurl slowly to quilled and quartered centers. The leaves are small and tough, with rounded leaflets. The plant is vigorous, bushy, and thick-stemmed: there are a few flowers in autumn to follow the ravishing midseason display.

'BREEZE HILL'

B

'BRENDA COLVIN'

'BRIDAL PINK' *(at Werribee Park, Victoria, Australia)*

BRIGADOON

'BRENDA COLVIN'

Filipes Rambler

ORIGIN **Colvin, Britain, 1970**
PARENTAGE ***Rosa filipes* × unknown**
FLOWER SIZE **1.2in (3cm)**
SCENT **Sweet and musky**
FLOWERING **Once, late in season**
HEIGHT/SPREAD **16.4ft (5m)/16.4ft (5m)**
HARDINESS **Zone 6**

This is the best of the simpler Filipes hybrids. It occurred in Oxfordshire at Filkins, the garden of influential designer Brenda Colvin. Its flowers are small, but they are carried in large, spacious clusters with such abundance that the massed effect is impressive. Its lightly semidouble flowers are white, with mid-pink petal backs that fade to pale pink, reminiscent of apple blossom. The plant is extremely vigorous, healthy, and well-furnished with handsome, rich green leaves. It is not overly armored, but carries enough medium-sized, down-curving prickles to haul itself quickly up into trees (the best way to grow it), from which it cascades with clusters all along its long growths. It bears a few small red hips in autumn. 'Brenda Colvin' is fairly widely grown in the gardens of northern Europe, especially in Scandinavia, but also flourishes in Mediterranean climates.

'BRIDAL PINK'

syn. 'JACBRI'

Floribunda

ORIGIN **Boerner, US, 1967**
PARENTAGE **'Summertime' seedling × 'Spartan' seedling**
FLOWER SIZE **3.1in (8cm)**
SCENT **Good and sweet**
FLOWERING **Repeats quickly**
HEIGHT/SPREAD **2.7ft (80cm)/2ft (60cm)**
HARDINESS **Zone 6**

'Bridal Pink' is cultivated widely as a cut flower: the sprays of pink and cream roses are perfect for mixed bouquets and floral arrangements. The flowers have long, slender buds like small Hybrid Teas, and open only slowly, so that their life as a cut flower – and in the garden – is a long one. They are occasionally borne singly, but usually in clusters of up to about ten. They are gentle pink in color, although the petal backs are slightly darker and the outer petals eventually fade to pale pink or cream. When 'Bridal Pink' is treated as a garden rose, its color is best in cool weather, but the flowers are borne with great profusion in flush after flush all through the growing season. The bush grows quickly, but not too tall – some authorities maintain that a good cut-flower rose should not waste its energies on producing long stems and a lot of foliage. The leaves are leathery, quite dark, and sometimes susceptible to mildew.

BRIDE

syn. 'FRYYEARN'

Hybrid Tea

ORIGIN **Fryer, Britain, 1995**
FLOWER SIZE **3.9in (10cm)**
SCENT **Light and sweet**
FLOWERING **Repeats well**
HEIGHT/SPREAD **4.1ft (1.25m)/3.3ft (1m)**
HARDINESS **Zone 6**

Gareth Fryer, the breeder of this exquisite Hybrid Tea, insists that this rose takes its name from a village on the Isle of Man, and has nothing to do with marriage. Bride does, however, have a very beautiful soft pink color and a delicious scent. The petal backs have a slightly apricot tinge at first, which suffuses the flower as it opens; later it fades to pure pink. The flowers are borne singly, occasionally in small clusters, on long stems that are particularly good for cutting. Bride is also valued by exhibitors. The flowers are, however, produced freely enough for it to be used successfully as a bedding rose. The plant has large, healthy, dark leaves that are crimson when young.

BRIDE'S DREAM

see MARCHENKÖNIGIN

BRIGADOON

syn. 'JACPAL'

Hybrid Tea

ORIGIN **Warriner, US, 1991**
PARENTAGE **seedling × Pristine**
FLOWER SIZE **5.9in (15cm)**
SCENT **Medium and fruity**
FLOWERING **Repeats well**
HEIGHT/SPREAD **4.1ft (1.25m)/3.3ft (1m)**
HARDINESS **Zone 6**
AWARDS **AARS 1992**

Size and elegance: it is the perfection of the individual flowers that is the strong point of Brigadoon. Each opens from a long, pointed bud and curls back its petals to create a classically beautiful shape, borne on long stems that are perfect for cutting. The bicolor flowers are smoky orange or pale vermilion at their tips, but almost pure white on the backs of the petals and also at the center. The color runs down into the paler parts and intensifies with age. The flowers come singly or occasionally in small clusters. The plant has large, dark green leaves and grows vigorously, sending up new flowers in rapid succession. A modern classic.

BRIGHT SMILE

syn. 'DICDANCE'

Floribunda

ORIGIN **Dickson, Northern Ireland, 1980**
PARENTAGE **'Eurorose' seedling**
FLOWER SIZE **3in (8cm)**
SCENT **Light and fruity**
FLOWERING **Repeats well**
HEIGHT/SPREAD **2ft (60cm)/1.3ft (40cm)**
HARDINESS **Zone 6**
AWARDS **Belfast GM 1982**

The popularity of this short Floribunda rests upon its cheerful abundance. Each semidouble flower is a bright mid-yellow, with a hint of richer yellow at the center. When it opens out, the golden orange stamens are visible, and they infuse the flower with yet more yellow richness. The flowers come singly or in clusters of up to five blooms and appear almost without interruption until late in the season. The plant is vigorous and healthy, with somewhat ordinary mid-green leaves. It is small enough to be grown in a pot and used in annual bedding plans, or to provide a ribbon of color along the edge of a bed.

BRIDE

BRIGHT SMILE

'Brilliant Pink Iceberg'

see 'Schneewittchen'

'Britannia'

Polyantha

ORIGIN **Burbage, Britain, 1929**
PARENTAGE **'Coral Cluster' x 'Éblouissant'**
FLOWER SIZE **1.6in (4cm)**
SCENT **Light and musky**
FLOWERING **Almost continuous**
HEIGHT/SPREAD **1.3ft (40cm)/2ft (60cm)**
HARDINESS **Zone 6**

The fashion for shrub roses has led many rose growers to reevaluate the old Polyantha roses, which seem to flower endlessly in every imaginable color. 'Britannia' is one that has recently been rescued from obscurity and has attracted a distinct following. Its single flowers are bright crimson, with a pure white center and cheerful yellow stamens. They come in neat, spacious clusters of 7–20 on a small shrub that tirelessly pushes up flowering stems for months on end. The leaves are pale green and healthy, with somewhat narrow leaflets.

Brite Lites

see Princess Alice

Broadlands

see Sonnenschirm

Broadway

syn. 'BURway'

Hybrid Tea

ORIGIN **Anthony Perry, US, 1985**
PARENTAGE **('First Prize' x 'Gold Glow') x 'Sutter's Gold'**
FLOWER SIZE **4.7in (12cm)**
SCENT **Strong, sweet, and fruity**
FLOWERING **Repeats well**
HEIGHT/SPREAD **3.9ft (1.2m)/3.3ft (1m)**
HARDINESS **Zone 6**
AWARDS **AARS 1986**

Anthony Perry from California was one of the few amateurs to win the top award from the All-America Rose Selections. Broadway is an excellent bicolor Hybrid Tea, full of long petals and elegantly

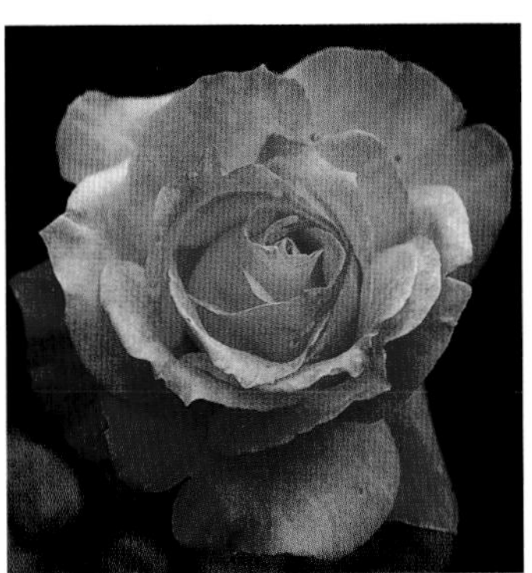

Broadway

'Britannia'

shaped at all stages. The center of the double flower is a rich amber yellow, but the petals have pink tinges that deepen and turn to crimson as they age. Then the yellow fades to cream and pink patches develop farther down the petals. It is an attractive transformation, best seen in hot dry weather – Broadway is especially recommended for such areas as the Central Valley of California, where it is also very healthy. The plant has large, dark green leaves and a vigorous, narrow, upright habit.

Brother Cadfael

syn. 'AUSglobe'

Shrub Rose

ORIGIN **Austin, Britain, 1990**
PARENTAGE **'Charles Austin' seedling**
FLOWER SIZE **4.7in (12cm)**
SCENT **Strong, sweet, and fruity**
FLOWERING **Occasionally re-blooms**
HEIGHT/SPREAD **4.9ft (1.5m)/3.3ft (1m)**
HARDINESS **Zone 6**

Brother Cadfael is a vigorous shrub with some of the largest flowers among David Austin's English Roses. They open from dark pink or crimson buds into rose pink double flowers (slightly darker on the petal backs) which are very full, cupped, and globular at first, but later open out so that the outer petals reflex downward. They are borne singly or in clusters of up to five on an upright, sturdy plant. The flowers have short stalks and plenty of leaves around them, like Portland roses. Brother Cadfael has few thorns. It is vigorous and quick to grow, but sometimes slow to repeat its flowering. In hot climates, it will make a short climber, 8.2ft (2.5m) tall.

Brother Cadfael

Brown Velvet

Brown Velvet

syn. 'MACultra', Colorbreak

Floribunda

ORIGIN **McGredy, New Zealand, 1983**
PARENTAGE **'Mary Sumner' x Kapai**
FLOWER SIZE **2.8in (7cm)**
SCENT **Light and fruity**
FLOWERING **Repeats well**
HEIGHT/SPREAD **3.3ft (1m)/2.5ft (75cm)**
HARDINESS **Zone 6**
AWARDS **NZ GM 1979**

The flowers of this excellent orange Floribunda take on a distinctly brown flush in cool weather. The petals are always more yellow toward the center, but the brown coloring, when it occurs, is very striking. The flowers are of good size and double, and open out nearly flat, with distinctive, ruffled petals. They come in clusters of up to 12 (sometimes more in autumn). Brown Velvet has unusually dark and shiny leaves, crimson when young and generally healthy. The plant is fairly vigorous but short-growing. However, if grown in a hot climate and left unpruned, it will reach 6.6ft (2m).

Rosa brunonii

Wild Rose

FLOWER SIZE **1.2in (3cm)**
SCENT **Strong and musky**
FLOWERING **Once, midseason**
HEIGHT/SPREAD **23ft (7m)/13.1ft (4m)**
HARDINESS **Zone 6**

There are many different forms of *Rosa brunonii*: botanists tell us that it is a species currently undergoing rapid development. It occurs throughout the Himalayas, from Kashmir and Afghanistan to the mountains of western Szechwan, and has given rise to many horticultural hybrids and selections, including the rose known as *Rosa moschata*. It is an excellent, vigorous climber for a garden where it can be allowed to clamber up a medium or tall tree – it is capable of reaching as much as 49.2ft (15m). The flowers are creamy white at first, passing to pure white when they open, with rich yellow stamens and a prominent style at the center. They come in large, open, billowing clusters of up to 100, and are succeeded by small (0.4in/1cm) round hips. The leaves are large, with narrow, drooping leaflets. The plant is extremely vigorous, growing quickly and hooking itself up on short, stout prickles. It is not for the faint hearted, but a supreme beauty when well-placed.

Rosa brunonii

B

Bucks Fizz

see Gavno

'Buff Beauty'

Hybrid Musk

ORIGIN **Bentall, Britain, 1939**
PARENTAGE **'William Allen Richardson' x unknown**
FLOWER SIZE **3.1in (8cm)**
SCENT **Strong and sweet**
FLOWERING **Repeats well**
HEIGHT/SPREAD **6.6ft (2m)/4.9ft (1.5m)**
HARDINESS **Zone 6**

This is the most widely grown of the Hybrid Musks. The flowers are variable in their color: apricot yellow, soft orange, honey, and, above all, a rich buff. Its color is deeper in shade or in cooler weather (especially in autumn), and tends to fade to cream in hot, sunny weather. The flowers are fully double and held in loose clusters that cut well; they also tend to be larger in autumn. The plant has a lax habit of growth, and is often trained up as a climber in hot areas. In cool climates, it eventually turns into a broad shrub with long, arching, flexible stems. Its leaves are large, dark green (red when young), and healthy, and it makes a vigorous and easy to grow plant. Its flowers come in a series of flushes, with a particularly large one in early autumn but continuing until early winter in mild climates.

'Buff Beauty'

Buffalo Gal

see Foxi

'Bullata'

see 'Centifolia'

Burgund 81

syn. 'KORgund', Loving Memory
Hybrid Tea

ORIGIN **Kordes, Germany, 1981**
PARENTAGE **'Henkell Royal' x seedling**
FLOWER SIZE **4.7in (12cm)**
SCENT **Slight**
FLOWERING **Repeats well**
HEIGHT/SPREAD **4.9ft (1.5m)/2.7ft (80cm)**
HARDINESS **Zone 6**

The buds of Burgund 81 are nearly black, and held on long, strong stems. They have an elegantly conical shape, which is emphasized as they slowly unfurl their blooms – the outer petals reflex from their tips, which adds to the beauty of the opening flower. They are dark crimson, in contrast to the inner petals, which are eventually revealed as bright red. When the flowers open out fully, they lose their shape and collapse into a formless mass of petals. The flowers come singly or in small clusters. The plant has dark, healthy, glossy leaves and a bushy, upright habit of growth. In hot climates it will reach 6.6ft (2m), but is normally pruned to half that height.

Burgund 81

'Burgundy'

see 'Pompon de Bourgogne'

Burning Sky

see Paradise

Griffith Buck

THE SUPERHARDY ROSES RAISED BY PROFESSOR GRIFFITH BUCK HAVE ACHIEVED CULT STATUS, ESPECIALLY IN COLD PARTS OF NORTH AMERICA AND SCANDINAVIA

Professor Griffith Buck (1915–91) taught horticulture at Iowa State College for more than 30 years. His research work aimed to breed garden roses that would survive the long cold winters and hot humid summers of the American Midwest. He introduced 88 roses into commerce, of which some 60 are still grown.

Buck's interest in roses began at school when he struck up a friendship with a pen pal – the niece of the Spanish rose nurseryman, Pedro Dot. It was Dot who told the young Buck how to hybridize roses and encouraged him to try it.

When Buck started work at Iowa State College, he chose an extremely hardy form of *Rosa laxa* from Russia to bring hardiness into his hybrids. Wilhelm Kordes sent him an equally hardy sweetbriar hybrid called 'Josef Rothmund', and it was a cross between the two that formed the basis of Buck's breeding lines.

'Prairie Flower'

Crosses with commercial Hybrid Teas and Floribundas (not hardy in Iowa) enabled Buck to introduce vigorous, hardy shrubs with large, handsome, richly colored flowers. The tall 'Applejack' (1973) was one of his early successes. Other cultivars that he used very widely as parents for further breeding were 'Prairie Princess' (1972) and 'Prairie Flower' (1975).

Buck's method was to grow his seedlings under glass and plant them outside in the field after their first winter. Those that survived the following winters without protection were then considered for introduction. Because his research program could not afford to spray against diseases, Buck also pulled out any infected plants. As a result he developed healthy shrubs, with flowers like Floribundas and Hybrid Teas, that were extremely hardy as well as tolerant of summer heat. 'Wild Ginger' (1978) is a good example of his Hybrid Teas.

Later introductions, like 'Distant Drums' (1984), produced some unusual colors and floral forms.

Buck's roses flourish both in temperate and hot climates. They are now very widely available. Good collections can be found in special display gardens at the University of Minnesota and at the Reiman Gardens, both in Buck's home state of Iowa.

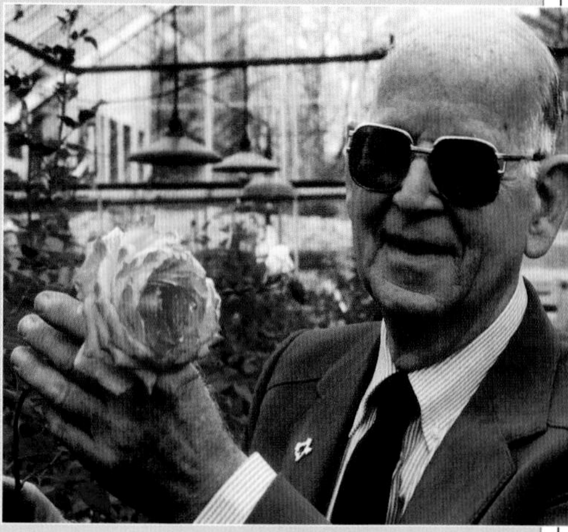

Griffith Buck in 1984

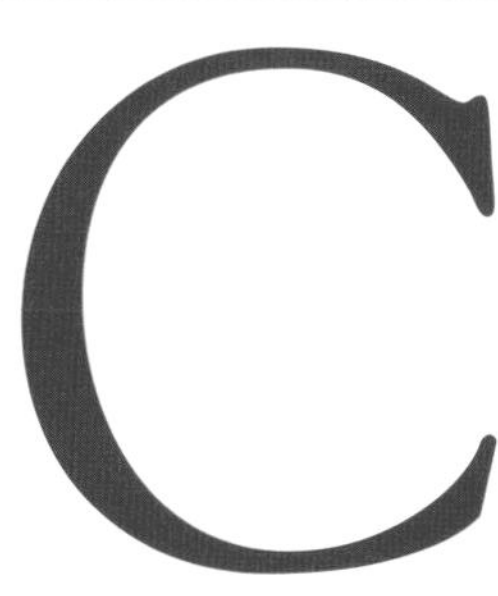

CABARET

syn. 'LAPED'
Hybrid Tea

ORIGIN **Laperrière, France, 1992**
FLOWER SIZE **4.3in (11cm)**
SCENT **Light and sweet**
FLOWERING **Repeats well**
HEIGHT/SPREAD **4.1ft (1.25m)/3.3ft (1m)**
HARDINESS **Zone 6**

The flowers of Cabaret have a white ground, but are deeply dipped in red. The petal tips are dark pink, but paler toward the center of the flower and rich scarlet on the outer petals. The flowers have large, long buds that open to reveal a very great number of petals, each of them reflexing at its tips and edges. The flowers are somewhat more muddled when fully open. They are borne singly, occasionally in twos and threes, on stout stems that are good for cutting and last well in water. Cabaret has somewhat small, medium-dark leaves.

'CABBAGE ROSE'

see 'CENTIFOLIA'

CADILLAC DE VILLE

see MOONSTONE

'CAFÉ'

Floribunda

ORIGIN **Kordes, Germany, 1956**
PARENTAGE **('Golden Glow' x 'Kordesii') x 'Lavender Pinocchio'**
FLOWER SIZE **3.1in (8cm)**
SCENT **Light and sweet**
FLOWERING **Repeats**
HEIGHT/SPREAD **3.3ft (1m)/2.7ft (80cm)**
HARDINESS **Zone 6**

'CAFÉ'

CABARET

'Café' was a by-product of Wilhelm Kordes's experiments in breeding hardy garden roses from 'Kordesii'. It was considered a unique color at the time – a mixture of brown, yellow, and tan that resembled *café-au-lait*. The color differs from season to season, but it remains one of the best of the "brown" roses. The flowers are fuller than most Floribundas, but open out flat, with a lot of small ruffled or quilled petals within a lightly cupped shape. They are usually borne in small clusters (typically of 3–5 flowers) but sometimes also singly, and they tend to nod their heads. The leaves are dark, glossy, and healthy. It is not a very vigorous rose in cool climates, but may lose its color in hot ones. Nevertheless, it is worth persisting with and responds well to good cultivation.

ROSA CALIFORNICA

Wild Rose

FLOWER SIZE **1.6in (4cm)**
SCENT **Light and sweet**
FLOWERING **Once heavily, then intermittently**
HEIGHT/SPREAD **6.6ft (2m)/4.9ft (1.5m)**
HARDINESS **Zone 6**

Botanists tell us that *Rosa californica* is a group of closely related species all in a rapid state of evolution. They grow wild from Oregon to Baja California in the US, and eastward into Columbia. They tolerate considerable drought and cold. The flowers are small, single, and variable in color, but usually rose-pink, and borne in clusters of 5–10, occasionally many more. The plants produce flowers over a long season and, after the first main flowering, continue well into autumn, so that flowers and fruits sometimes appear together. The hips are small (0.4in/1cm), round, and red. The plant has a suckering, thicketing habit, with long, straight stems, a lot of prickles (especially on the old wood), and dull, mid-green leaves. It is very healthy, except for a little blackspot where this is a problem. It has been widely used in recent years to breed garden roses with unusual colors – especially browns and purples.

'CALIFORNICA PLENA'

Species Hybrid

ORIGIN **Geschwind, Hungary, 1894**
FLOWER SIZE **1.6in (4cm)**
SCENT **Light and sweet**
FLOWERING **Once only**
HEIGHT/SPREAD **8.2ft (2.5m)/6.6ft (2m)**
HARDINESS **Zone 5**

There is some uncertainty whether the rose we grow today as 'Californica Plena' is the same one that Rudolf Geschwind introduced in 1894 or whether it is another of his hybrids, called 'Theano'. In any case, it is a first-rate shrub, somewhat too vigorous for small gardens, but stupendous in a wild or woodland setting. The flowers are loosely semidouble and deepest pink, with white streaks at the center and yellow stamens. They come in small clusters (typically of 5–7 flowers) and contrast beautifully with the gray green leaves and crimson new wood. The plant is tall, prickly, and naturally stoloniferous, though never enough to be a nuisance. It is very hardy, healthy, and tolerant of both drought and poor soils.

CALYPSO

CALYPSO

syn. 'POULCLIMB', Berries 'n' Cream
Modern Climber

ORIGIN **Poulsen, Denmark, 1997**
PARENTAGE **Evita seedling**
FLOWER SIZE **2in (5cm)**
SCENT **Light and fruity**
FLOWERING **Repeats**
HEIGHT/SPREAD **9.8ft (3m)/6.6ft (2m)**
HARDINESS **Zone 5**

This modern climber, bred in Denmark, has become very popular in the US, where it is known as Berries 'n' Cream. Calypso has clusters of somewhat small, semidouble flowers whose coloring is reminiscent of the old striped Gallica rose 'Versicolor' – a striking mixture of crimson and white, randomly splashed and irregularly striped across the petals. The flowers tend to bear more red in hot weather and white in cool. The plant too shows the effect of different growing conditions, for it grows much taller (13.1ft/4m) in hot climates and shorter (6.6ft/2m) in temperate. The flowers have prettily ruffled petals and come in clusters of 5–15 on strong, 9.8in (25cm) stems, followed by red hips. Calypso has large, dark, healthy, glossy leaves and very few prickles. When well fed and watered, it flowers almost continuously.

ROSA CALIFORNICA

'CALIFORNICA PLENA'

C

'CAMAÏEU'

'CAMAÏEU'

Gallica

ORIGIN **Vibert, France, 1830**
FLOWER SIZE **2.8in (7cm)**
SCENT **Very strong and sweet**
FLOWERING **Once only**
HEIGHT/SPREAD **3.3ft (1m)/3.3ft (1m)**
HARDINESS **Zone 5**

Although not as well-known as *Rosa gallica* 'Versicolor', this is an extremely attractive, neat, small Gallica, whose opening flowers have bright crimson and white stripes on a rose pink ground. The colors then fade over a period of several days to wonderful shades of lilac, lavender, and gray, against a white background. Meanwhile, each flower reflexes like a small pompon around the green pointel, which creates a focal point at the center. The plant has fairly small, rough, dull green leaves and a compact, thrifty, twiggy habit of growth. It does well in almost any conditions except wet soils, and suckers around agreeably. The name 'Camaïeu' alludes to the contrasting tones in cameo work, which was the height of fashion in the 1820s and 1830s.

CAMBRIDGE

see LAVENDER COVER

CAMBRIDGESHIRE

syn. 'KORHAUGEN', Carpet of Color

Shrub Rose

ORIGIN **Kordes, Germany, 1994**
FLOWER SIZE **1.6in (4cm)**
SCENT **Light and sweet**
FLOWERING **Repeats well**
HEIGHT/SPREAD **1.6ft (50cm)/4.1ft (1.25m)**
HARDINESS **Zone 6**

This is a small shrub rose, wider than it is tall. The flowers are small, cupped, and semidouble – and a somewhat garish color. They are bright orange, with yellow at the center and yellow again on the backs of the petals. They fade slowly to pink, and lose their yellow, so that eventually the flowers end up dark pink and cream, with hints of in-between shades as they age. The clusters are large (typically of 10–20 flowers) and the flowers last a long time on the plant. A single cluster has every shade of orange, pink, and yellow, all irradiating color in a single eyeful. The plant has small, bright green leaves, a few sharp prickles, and a fairly compact habit.

CAMP DAVID

CAMP DAVID

Hybrid Tea

ORIGIN **Tantau, Germany, 1984**
FLOWER SIZE **5.1in (13cm)**
SCENT **Light**
FLOWERING **Repeats well**
HEIGHT/SPREAD **4.9ft (1.5m)/4.1ft (1.25m)**
HARDINESS **Zone 6**

Camp David is one of those roses that attained its greatest popularity not in its homeland, but in quite a different part of the world. This large, heavy-petaled Hybrid Tea was never introduced in Germany, but proved very popular in Australia, where it is a notable exhibition rose. It has a large number of thick petals, unfurls slowly, and holds its crimson coloring even in hot sun. The flowers open from nearly black buds, and their outer petals are very dark indeed. The inner petals are a little paler on opening and reflex nicely. Eventually the flowers open right out and flat. They lack a scent to match their rich coloring, but the flowers are almost always borne singly and are splendid for cutting. The plants are strong, well-branched, and healthy. Camp David is the American presidential retreat in Maryland where Israel and Egypt signed the Camp David Peace Agreement in 1978.

'CAMPANILE'

Modern Climber

ORIGIN **Delbard-Chabert, France, 1967**
PARENTAGE **('Queen Elizabeth' x 'Provence') x ('Sultane' seedling x 'Mme. Joseph Perraud')**
FLOWER SIZE **4.3in (11cm)**
SCENT **Strong and fruity**
FLOWERING **Repeats**
HEIGHT/SPREAD **9.8ft (3m)/6.6ft (2m)**
HARDINESS **Zone 6**

CAMBRIDGESHIRE

'CAMPANILE'

Although it was introduced many years ago, this modern climber is still widely grown in western Europe, especially in France and Germany. It flowers tirelessly and never climbs too high. It helps to think of 'Campanile' as an exceptionally tall-growing Hybrid Tea: it has a bushy habit of growth and produces its flowers in a series of flushes. The flowers are very full of petals and open dark pink, taking on a crimson tinge as they open and age. They are usually borne in clusters (typically of 3–5 flowers) but occasionally singly. The opening buds are fat and globular. 'Campanile' is a lush and vigorous grower, with large, dark, healthy leaves, bronzy when young.

CANARY

syn. 'TANCARY'

Hybrid Tea

ORIGIN **Tantau, Germany, 1976**
FLOWER SIZE **12cm (4.7in)**
SCENT **Medium**
FLOWERING **Repeats**
HEIGHT/SPREAD **3.3ft (1m)/2.7ft (80cm)**
HARDINESS **Zone 5**

Although "old" for a "modern" rose, Canary is still popular in Europe, and almost unknown elsewhere. It is a good mid-yellow Hybrid Tea, with a pink flush suffusing its buds as they open out. Then the petals acquire a red edging as they age – scarlet at first, fading to crimson and pink as the rich yellow also passes to lemon. The flowers are carried on long stems in small clusters (typically of 3–7) but occasionally singly, and eventually open out to reveal a mass of golden stamens. The plant is vigorous and healthy, with nondescript leaves that are bronzy at first before turning dark green.

CANARY

'CANARY BIRD'

'CANARY BIRD'

syn. ROSA XANTHINA 'CANARY BIRD'

Shrub Rose

ORIGIN **Britain, 1907**
PARENTAGE ***Rosa xanthina* x *Rosa hugonis***
FLOWER SIZE **2in (5cm)**
SCENT **Light and fruity**
FLOWERING **Once, very early in season**
HEIGHT/SPREAD **8.2ft (2.5m)/13.1ft (4m)**
HARDINESS **Zone 5**

There is something of a mystery surrounding the origins of this beautiful early-flowering rose – it was bred in England, perhaps as part of Dr. Hurst's experiments with rose species. The flowers are pure bright yellow, fading to cream in hot sunny weather, with long coppery stamens. They are borne singly on short stems all along the long, arching, prickly branches. Each flower is supported by a tuft of dainty, bright green leaves, which emerge just as the buds are formed. They have 9–11 very small leaflets. Later come round, purplish black hips. 'Canary Bird' is healthy and grows into a large rounded bush. It needs plenty of space to develop because it resents pruning, but makes a handsome specimen shrub when underplanted with late-flowering daffodils.

CANDELABRA

syn. 'JACCINGO'

Grandiflora

ORIGIN **Zary, US, 1999**
PARENTAGE **Tournament of Roses seedling**
FLOWER SIZE **4.7in (12cm)**
SCENT **Medium, sweet, and musky**
FLOWERING **Repeats well**
HEIGHT/SPREAD **4.9ft (1.5m)/3.3ft (1m)**
HARDINESS **Zone 6**
AWARDS **AARS 1999**

The flowers of this vigorous American Grandiflora are attractive at all stages, whether as buds or as fully open blooms. The buds are notably long and elegantly pointed. The flowers are vermilion-lake at first, and fade gently to salmon pink, but their exact coloring does depend upon the weather – deeper and richer in cool temperatures, when the flowers are also larger. They come in small clusters (typically of 3–5 flowers, but occasionally singly) on a thickly bushy but upright plant. The new growths, purple at first, develop into handsome, dark green, glossy leaves and moderately prickly stems. Candelabra has so far proved very healthy and an abundant flowerer, but is rarely seen outside the US.

CANDELLA

CANDELLA

syn. 'MACSPEEDO', Eternally Yours

Hybrid Tea

ORIGIN **McGredy, New Zealand, 1990**
PARENTAGE **Howard Morrison x Esmeralda**
FLOWER SIZE **5.1in (13cm)**
SCENT **Light and sweet**
FLOWERING **Repeats**
HEIGHT/SPREAD **4.9ft (1.5m)/4.1ft (1.25m)**
HARDINESS **Zone 6**

The color contrasts within a perfect flower of Candella are remarkable – red petals and white backs. When the buds are opening out, the effect is electrifying: the petals are a rich Turkey red with a velvety sheen, but their undersides are pure, ghostly, silvery white. Not all the flowers are perfect: sometimes they are all red, and at other times some of the petals will have white backs but not others. Some may even bear a suggestion of "hand painting." Candella is a vigorous grower, with strong, upright stems – although the flowers may droop if the plant is not properly fed. The leaves are dark and healthy, apart from an occasional brush with mildew.

'CANDY CANE'

Climbing Miniature

ORIGIN **Moore, US, 1958**
PARENTAGE **seedling x 'Zee'**
FLOWER SIZE **1.2in (3cm)**
SCENT **Light**
FLOWERING **Repeats well**
HEIGHT/SPREAD **4.9ft (1.5m)/2ft (60cm)**
HARDINESS **Zone 6**

'Candy Cane' is a miniature climber – it has the scrambling growth of all climbers and ramblers, but the whole plant is miniaturized, including the flowers. It owes its name to their pink and white stripes. In fact, the color is more complicated than that: the flowers open crimson but fade to pink, with white centers. They have an unusual pattern of white streaks and sparks that extend through the colored part of the petals almost to their tips. They also have paler petal backs. The flowers come in loose clusters of 5–15 on a vigorous, upright, healthy plant with thin, wiry stems that make it useful for training along low fences in small gardens. If the plant is promptly deadheaded, it flowers freely and almost continuously.

CANDELABRA

'CANDY CANE'

'CANDY STRIPE'

see 'PINK PEACE'

ROSA CANINA

Wild Rose

FLOWER SIZE **1.6in (4cm)**
SCENT **Light, sweet, and fresh**
FLOWERING **Once only**
HEIGHT/SPREAD **13.1ft (4m)/9.8ft (3m)**
HARDINESS **Zone 5**

For many people in Europe and southwest Asia, and in those parts of North America and Australia where it has naturalized, *Rosa canina* (also known as "dog rose") is the archetypal wild rose. Its short-lived flowers are offerings of ethereal beauty, but its prickles are fierce and uninviting. The flowers come singly or in small clusters and are any shade from deep pink to near white, but usually pale rose pink. The petals have a distinct notch in the middle of their outer edge. The hips are conical and bright vermilion: in many countries they remain untouched by birds until well into winter. The sepals have a curious attribute, which is that they bear a crest along those sides that are not overlapped by other sepals. Thus two sepals are bearded, two smooth, and one bearded on one side only. *Rosa canina* has pale green leaves, usually with seven leaflets, and a vigorous, arching habit. It is not a suitable garden plant, although some of its hybrids, such as 'Kiese', are invaluable. It is commonly used as a rootstock for budding in temperate climates. It is very variable in the wild, and has sometimes been split up by overenthusiastic botanists into many species and subspecies, but it is best treated as one aggregate species in a rapid state of evolution.

ROSA CANINA

C

CANNES FESTIVAL 83

CANNES FESTIVAL 83

syn. 'MEILICAFAL'

Hybrid Tea

ORIGIN **Meilland, France, 1983**
FLOWER SIZE **4.7in (12cm)**
SCENT **Light and fruity**
FLOWERING **Repeats**
HEIGHT/SPREAD **4.9ft (1.5m)/4.1ft (1.25m)**
HARDINESS **Zone 6**

This is a handsome and dependable Hybrid Tea in an unusual and attractive combination of colors. The flowers of Cannes Festival 83 are basically yellow, with amber colored shadows between the petals. These come from the slightly darker, pinker petal backs. As the flowers open out, neatly and imbricated, the petals take on a hint of buff and the stamens at the center are seen to be red. The flowers are borne singly or in small clusters, and the plant repeats its flowerings well into autumn. Cannes Festival 83 has dark, somewhat ordinary leaves and a vigorous habit of growth. If left unpruned it will quickly reach 6.6ft (2m) and turn itself into a big bush with flowers produced at every level.

'CANTABRIGIENSIS'

Shrub Rose

ORIGIN **Cambridge Botanic Garden, Britain, c.1931**
PARENTAGE ***Rosa hugonis* × *Rosa sericea***
FLOWER SIZE **1.6in (4cm)**
SCENT **Light and sweet**
FLOWERING **Once only, fairly early in season**
HEIGHT/SPREAD **2m (6.6ft)/2m (6.6ft)**
HARDINESS **Zone 5**

This beautiful shrub rose occurred as a self-sown seedling in the Cambridge Botanic Garden in England. It has deeper yellow flowers than *Rosa sericea* and opens much better than *Rosa hugonis*. Because it flowers so early in the season, it deserves a more prominent position than most wild or near wild roses. In England it is often seen underplanted with primroses, bluebells, and late-flowering narcissi. The flowers of 'Cantabrigiensis' are a clear, light yellow and distinctively cupped, seeming almost to be folded into shape by the petals. They are very copiously carried all over the surface of the plant and

'CANTABRIGIENSIS'

followed by attractive, small vermilion hips. 'Cantabrigiensis' is vigorous and upright (at first – later it broadens out) and densely twiggy with a lot of small bristly prickles. The leaves are very small and bright green. They may attract blackspot later in the year, but it never affects the next year's flowering.

'CANTERBURY'

Shrub Rose

ORIGIN **Austin, Britain, 1969**
PARENTAGE **('Monique' × 'Constance Spry') × seedling**
FLOWER SIZE **5.5in (14cm)**
SCENT **Medium**
FLOWERING **Repeats**
HEIGHT/SPREAD **2.5ft (75cm)/2.5ft (75cm)**
HARDINESS **Zone 6**

'Canterbury' is not for impatient gardeners: it needs a few years to build up to a fair size and give generously of its flowers, but it is worth waiting for.

'CAPITAINE BASROGER'

The flowers are almost single, very large, and peach pink at first (fading to pure rose pink), with pretty stamens and creamy petal backs. They sit lightly among the dark green leaves and glow with color when the sun shines through them. In cool climates the plant responds to feeding and a sheltered position, growing into a lax, rounded shrub, but in warmer climates it is more robust and reaches 4.9ft (1.5m) high and wide.

CANYONLANDS

see FREDENSBORG

'CAPITAINE BASROGER'

Moss Rose

ORIGIN **Moreau-Robert, France, 1890**
FLOWER SIZE **3.1in (8cm)**
SCENT **Medium and sweet**
FLOWERING **Repeats a little**
HEIGHT/SPREAD **6.6ft (2m)/4.1ft (1.25m)**
HARDINESS **Zone 5**

'Capitaine Basroger' is a handsome, repeat flowering Moss rose. It is also one of the deepest in color – a rich purple. The buds are small and globular, but open into medium-sized flowers, full of small petals and roughly quartered. The petal backs are paler, almost light crimson, as can be seen when they fold over to create a prominent button eye. Sometimes the petals have a white fleck in them toward the center. The sepals, receptacles, and flower stems are thickly covered in olive-green moss. The plant has small, rough leaves that are somewhat susceptible to blackspot; mildew can also be a problem. It is a vigorous, lanky grower that needs support and can even be trained as a pillar rose.

'CAPITAINE JOHN INGRAM'

Moss Rose

ORIGIN **Laffay, France, 1854**
FLOWER SIZE **2.4in (6cm)**
SCENT **Strong and sweet**
FLOWERING **Once only**
HEIGHT/SPREAD **4.1ft (1.25m)/4.9ft (1.5m)**
HARDINESS **Zone 5**

Small-flowered and once-flowering, 'Capitaine John Ingram' is nevertheless a very widely grown and valued Moss rose. Its flowers are a splendid deep crimson purple, though the petal backs are much paler. The exact color depends upon the weather, but it fades to lilac in hot sunshine. The flowers are loosely double and roughly quartered, although their petals tend to recurve. The buds, sepals, and receptacles are covered in red brown moss; the same reddish color is seen on the many bristles and prickles. The flower may make a lax button eye, but it sometimes fails to turn enough petals over to do so successfully. 'Capitaine John Ingram' makes a dense, sprawling shrub of moderate vigor. It flowers only once, but for quite a long period. Some people say that it produces a few flowers in autumn for them. Its dark green leaves are small and often show a thin crimson edging. Mildew and blackspot are a constant problem later in the year.

'CANTERBURY'

'CAPITAINE JOHN INGRAM'

CAPRICE DE MEILLAND

CAPRICE DE MEILLAND

syn. 'MEIsionver'

Hybrid Tea

ORIGIN **Meilland, France, 1998**
FLOWER SIZE **4.3in (11cm)**
SCENT **Very strong, sweet, and fruity**
FLOWERING **Repeats well**
HEIGHT/SPREAD **3.3ft (1m)/2.7ft (80cm)**
HARDINESS **Zone 6**
AWARDS **Bagatelle FA 1997; Geneva FA 1997; Rome 1997**

Meilland has been an innovative breeder of new roses for many years: the family that gave us 'Mme A. Meilland' is still introducing new Hybrid Teas of stunning quality. Caprice de Meilland has traditional Hybrid Tea buds (long, conical, and elegant), which are singly borne on long, sturdy stems. They open out slowly, showing a rich cerise in the outer petals and a paler pink toward the center of the flower. The petals are thick and strong, making it very rain resistant and a useful cut rose for home arrangements; it has also been grown commercially. The plant is vigorous and healthy, with medium-dark leaves. But its scent is remarkable: the jury of one international competition where it won a prize noted "spicy nuances of cloves, allied to a fruity scent, including blackcurrants, apples, and lychees…".

'CAPTAIN CHRISTY'

Hybrid Tea

ORIGIN **Lacharme, France, 1873**
PARENTAGE **'Victor Verdier' x 'Safrano'**
FLOWER SIZE **5.1in (13cm)**
SCENT **Light and sweet**
FLOWERING **Repeats well**
HEIGHT/SPREAD **4.1ft (1.25m)/4.1ft (1.25m)**
HARDINESS **Zone 6**

'Captain Christy' was one of the earliest Hybrid Teas to be bred, in 1873, before they were even described as a new group of roses. Contemplate its beauty today, and you may wonder whether there has been any real progress in the intervening years. The flowers are simply enormous and beautifully formed, not with long, elegant buds like modern Hybrid Teas, but fat and full, with row upon row of petals. The flowers open from cabbagelike buds and, with so many petals, they fare best in hot, dry weather. The petals are silvery pink, with deeper backs, which creates rich pink shades at the center. The flowers are borne usually singly, with short, sturdy, upright stems on a vigorous, leafy bush. There is a climbing form with even larger flowers. Captain Christy was an English amateur rose lover, and a founder member of the National Rose Society of Great Britain.

'CAPTAIN CHRISTY'

'CAPTAIN HAYWARD'

Hybrid Perpetual

ORIGIN **Bennett, Britain, 1893**
PARENTAGE **'Triomphe de l'Esposition' seedling**
FLOWER SIZE **3.9in (10cm)**
SCENT **Medium and sweet**
FLOWERING **Early in season; remontant**
HEIGHT/SPREAD **6.6ft (2m)/4.9ft (1.5m)**
HARDINESS **Zone 6**

'Captain Hayward' is not the perfect crimson Hybrid Perpetual, but it has some very attractive qualities. The color of its flowers is irresistible: a glowing carmine (true crimson in cool weather) with a hint of scarlet and a silky sheen to the petals. The flowers are not especially large, nor overly full of petals, but they are a very beautiful and inviting shape, both as high-centered, opening buds and as fully expanded, lightly cupped, and loosely held flowers. Sometimes the petals have a slightly mottled or striped pattern. 'Captain Hayward' makes a good cut flower. It starts early in the season and repeats well after a somewhat long interval. Sometimes the flowers are followed by large orange hips. The plant is vigorous and slightly gawky, with smooth, mid-green leaves and a fair scattering of prickles. Blackspot may be problem later in the year.

'CAPTAIN HAYWARD'

'CAPTAIN SAMUEL HOLLAND'

Modern Climber

ORIGIN **Ogilvie, Canada, 1991**
PARENTAGE **'Kordesii' x ('Red Dawn' x 'Suzanne')**
FLOWER SIZE **2.8in (7cm)**
SCENT **Light and musky**
FLOWERING **Repeats very well**
HEIGHT/SPREAD **6.6ft (2m)/3.3ft (1m)**
HARDINESS **Zone 4**

'Captain Samuel Holland' is one of many excellent roses bred by the Canadian Department of Agriculture to survive the Canadian winters. The flowers open out flat from neatly pointed buds, which quickly turn into loosely double rosettes around a small splash of stamens at the center. They are a deep magenta or pale crimson, and keep their color well before fading slightly to dark pink. They come singly or in clusters of up to 12 on stems that are long enough to cut. The influence of 'Kordesii' is clearly seen in its dark, glossy leaves and lax, rambling habit, as well as its strong resistance to blackspot and mildew. It is also propagated quickly and easily from softwood cuttings. Captain Samuel Holland (1717–1801) was a Dutchman who was George III's Surveyor General in Canada and carried out the first survey of Prince Edward Island.

'CAPTAIN SAMUEL HOLLAND'

'CARABELLA'

Floribunda

ORIGIN **Riethmuller, Australia, 1960**
PARENTAGE **'Gartendirektor Otto Linne' x unknown**
FLOWER SIZE **2in (5cm)**
SCENT **Light**
FLOWERING **Recurrent**
HEIGHT/SPREAD **6.6ft (2m)/3.3ft (1m)**
HARDINESS **Zone 6**

'Carabella' is the best of the billowing shrub roses bred from the old Lambertiana 'Gartendirektor Otto Linne' by the Australian amateur Frank Riethmuller (1885–1966). Its flowers are small, single, and somewhat more white than pink: the broad apricot pink edges fade first to pink and then almost to white. The stamens, which are showy at first, soon turn brown and wither. But the flowers are borne abundantly and continuously in large clusters of 10–30 right through the year in warm climates. The autumn flowering clusters on vigorous, arching new stems may have up to 80 flowers on them. The thornless plant is lushly clothed with neat foliage and roots very easily from cuttings.

'CARABELLA'

C

'CARDINAL DE RICHELIEU'

'CARDINAL DE RICHELIEU'

Hybrid China

ORIGIN **Parmentier, France, c.1845**
FLOWER SIZE **2.4in (6cm)**
SCENT **Light, green, and herby**
FLOWERING **Once only**
HEIGHT/SPREAD **5.7ft (1.75m)/4.9ft (1.5m)**
HARDINESS **Zone 5**

Cardinals wear red (mere bishops wear purple), but no rose is more purple than 'Cardinal de Richelieu' in a good year. It also has an unusual chromosome count, being triploid where most Gallicas are tetraploid: this suggests that 'Cardinal de Richelieu' is probably a hybrid with a diploid China rose. The flowers are not large, but full of short, incurved petals – purple, with near white undersides. When they curl over to make a button eye, the contrast between the white and the purple is very striking. The base of the petals is also very pale, with occasional white streaks. Later the color fades to mauve and lilac, before the flower drops its petals and shatters tidily. The flowers usually come in clusters of about three. The plant has thornless stems and small, shiny, China leaves. It flowers better than most Gallicas in hot climates.

CARDINAL HUME

syn. 'HARregale'

Shrub Rose

ORIGIN **Harkness, Britain, 1984**
PARENTAGE **([seedling × ('Orange Sensation' × 'Allgold') × *R. californica*]) × 'Frank Naylor'**
FLOWER SIZE **2.4in (6cm)**
SCENT **Light and spicy**
FLOWERING **Early in season and recurrently**
HEIGHT/SPREAD **4.9ft (1.5m)/6.6ft (2m)**
HARDINESS **Zone 6**

Jack Harkness introduced Cardinal Hume as a shrub rose, and considered it similar to David Austin's English Roses, but it is much more distinct and unusual. It has a complicated ancestry that involves *Rosa californica*, though it has not been much used for further breeding. The flowers are crimson at first, turning to purple later, with much paler reverses. They come in large clusters (typically of 15–20 flowers) and have a mass of short petals. They are followed by beautiful, round, deep glowing scarlet hips, which contrast with the autumn flowers. The leaves are dark, and liable to blackspot in damp, cool climates, but the plant grows very well in hot, dry climates like California, where it makes a vigorous, well-branched, sprawling shrub, wider than it is tall. Pruned hard at Descanso Gardens in California, it still makes a bush about 6.6ft (2m) wide and 4.9ft (1.5m) high. Cardinal George Basil Hume (1923–99) was Archbishop of Westminster.

CARDINAL HUME

CARDINAL SONG

see JACQUES PRÉVERT

CAREFREE BEAUTY

syn. 'BUCbi', Audace

Shrub Rose

ORIGIN **Buck, US, 1977**
PARENTAGE **seedling × 'Prairie Princess'**
FLOWER SIZE **4in (10cm)**
SCENT **Light and fruity**
FLOWERING **Repeats well**
HEIGHT/SPREAD **5.7ft (1.75m)/4.9ft (1.5m)**
HARDINESS **Zone 4**

Carefree Beauty is one of the best of the Carefree shrub roses bred by Griffith Buck to withstand the freezing winters of the American Midwest. Its flowers are pink (the petal backs are paler) and lightly double, like a Floribunda, but opening from long buds that are closer to the Hybrid Teas. The flowers open flat with a few irregular, loose petals at the center and an occasional white stripe running through them. They come singly or in small clusters of up to five on a vigorous, healthy, leafy, sprawling shrub that is very floriferous and repeats well. Later in the year come large orange hips.

CAREFREE BEAUTY

CAREFREE DELIGHT

see BINGO MEIDILAND

CAREFREE WONDER

see DYNASTIE

'CARIBIA'

see 'HARRY WHEATCROFT'

'CARINA'

Hybrid Tea

ORIGIN **Meilland, France, 1963**
PARENTAGE **'Message' × ('Rouge Meilland' × 'Kordes' Sondermeldung')**
FLOWER SIZE **4.7in (12cm)**
SCENT **Medium and sweet**
FLOWERING **Repeats very well**
HEIGHT/SPREAD **3.3ft (1m)/2.7ft (80cm)**
HARDINESS **Zone 5**
AWARDS **ADR 1966**

In France, 'Carina' is one of the most famous and widely grown of Hybrid Teas. It is a classic rose pink color with slightly darker, mid-pink backs to the petals. As it ages, the outer petals fade slightly while the inner ones remain richly colored. If hit by heavy rain, they turn spotty and blotchy. The flowers are borne sometimes singly and sometimes in clusters of up to five. It is an excellent show rose that repays careful cultivation by producing individual blooms of exceptional size, beauty, and perfection of shape. The plant has large leaves and an upright habit of growth. 'Carina' was the first Meilland rose to win the top prize at the German rose trials, though its susceptibility to rust and mildew might be counted against it today.

'CARINA'

'CARLA'

Hybrid Tea

ORIGIN **de Ruiter, Belgium, 1963**
PARENTAGE **'Queen Elizabeth' × 'The Optimist'**
FLOWER SIZE **4.3in (11cm)**
SCENT **Medium and sweet**
FLOWERING **Repeats**
HEIGHT/SPREAD **4.9ft (1.5m)/4.1ft (1.25m)**
HARDINESS **Zone 6**

This beautiful Hybrid Tea has had a long stay among the world's most popular garden roses. The flowers of 'Carla' are rose pink with deeper backs to the petals. They have the classic shape of the perfect modern rose as they open from long, conical buds. When fully expanded, their shape is looser. Then they have a touch of salmon pink toward the center and start to fade to palest pink at the edges. The flowers come almost invariably singly, though sometimes in twos or threes. They last well as cut flowers and were once popular for exhibition. The plant has dark green leaves and a few large prickles.

'CARLA'

'CARMENETTA'

'CARMENETTA'

Shrub Rose

ORIGIN Central Experimental Farm, Canada, 1923
PARENTAGE *Rosa glauca* x *Rosa rugosa*
FLOWER SIZE 1.6in (4cm)
SCENT Light
FLOWERING Once only
HEIGHT/SPREAD 8.2ft (2.5m)/8.2ft (2.5m)
HARDINESS Zone 3

Isabella Preston bred 'Carmenetta' at the Canadian Central Experimental Farm to withstand the rigors of a Canadian winter. It strongly resembles *Rosa glauca*, with slightly larger flowers and long, elegant sepals, which make them seem larger still. The flowers are rich pink, with a white center and creamy stamens, but neither conspicuous nor beautiful. They come in clusters of 5–20 and are quickly followed by dark red hips, which usually stay on the bush, untouched by birds, for several months. The chief asset of 'Carmenetta' is its dusky purple foliage, which is very similar to several naturally occurring forms of *R. glauca*. It is useful in areas with very cold winters but no real improvement on *R. glauca* itself. Its popularity can in part be explained by the ease with which nurserymen propagate it from softwood cuttings. The plant is vigorous and healthy, apart from an occasional close encounter with rust.

ROSA CAROLINA

Wild Rose

ORIGIN 1826
FLOWER SIZE 1.8in (4.5cm)
SCENT Strong and sweet
FLOWERING Once only
HEIGHT/SPREAD 3.3ft (1m)/2.5ft (75cm)
HARDINESS Zone 5

Americans call this the "pasture" rose, because it is commonly found in grassy meadows. Its low height is unusual among wild roses of the eastern US. *Rosa carolina* is a suckering shrub that rarely reaches more than 3.3ft (1m), even in cultivation. The flowers are usually bright, rich pink, with a ring of dark yellow stamens. Paler forms, including a white one, and double forms are also known. The flowers are usually borne singly at the ends of short new growths, somewhat late in the season. Their scent carries and can be sensed from quite a distance. They are followed by small (less than 0.4in/1cm), roundish hips that last well into the winter. *Rosa carolina* has a covering of bristly prickles on its older stems, but the young growths are smooth at first. The leaves are mid-green and shiny, typically with five leaflets. It grows wild from Nova Scotia to Texas and Wisconsin, but New England is the heartland of its natural distribution.

ROSA CAROLINA

CAROLINE DE MONACO

syn. 'MEIPIERAR', Cameo Cream, Marcellin Champagnat

Hybrid Tea

ORIGIN Meilland, France, 1988
PARENTAGE Chicago Peace x Tchin-Tchin
FLOWER SIZE 4.7in (12cm)
SCENT Light and sweet
FLOWERING Repeats well
HEIGHT/SPREAD 4.1ft (1.25m)/2.7ft (80cm)
HARDINESS Zone 6

The flowers of Caroline de Monaco are the essence of loveliness. They have the large, elegant buds and gently reflexing petals that characterize the best of Chicago Peace and its descendants. They open out white, with cream colored or ivory petal backs, and are borne singly or, occasionally, in clusters of up to five. The long, sturdy stems make it a good rose for cutting: Caroline de Monaco has also proved popular with exhibitors. The flowers are well set off by unusually handsome leaves – large, healthy, dark green (bronzy when young), and copious. The name of the rose honors the elder daughter of Prince Rainier and Princess Grace of Monaco.

CAROLINE DE MONACO

CARROT TOP

see TOP HIT

CARTE D'OR

syn. 'MEIDRESIA'

Floribunda

ORIGIN Meilland, France, 2002
FLOWER SIZE 3.5in (9cm)
SCENT Light and fruity
FLOWERING Repeats well
HEIGHT/SPREAD 3.3ft (1m)/2.5ft (75cm)
HARDINESS Zone 6

Carte d'Or has large clusters of large flowers, which are repeated so quickly that the plant seems always to be in flower. It is this sheer productivity that most commends it. The flowers are full of short petals and beautifully formed, especially when they open out. They are rich, deep yellow at first, but Carte d'Or is one of those yellow roses that loses its color as it ages, so the flowers pass fairly quickly to pale yellow, cream, and white – and brown too, because they do not shed their petals neatly. The plant has fine, neat, medium-dark leaves, which may need to be protected against blackspot in autumn. But these shortcomings do not detract from the overall excellence of Carte d'Or.

CARTE D'OR

'CASINO'

syn. 'GERBE D'OR'

Modern Climber

ORIGIN McGredy, Northern Ireland, 1963
PARENTAGE 'Coral Dawn' x 'Buccaneer'
FLOWER SIZE 4.3in (11cm)
SCENT Medium and fruity
FLOWERING Repeats
HEIGHT/SPREAD 11.5ft (3.5m)/6.6ft (2m)
HARDINESS Zone 6
AWARDS NRS GM 1963

For a few years after its introduction, 'Casino' was widely considered the best yellow climber. It is still popular and widely grown. The flowers are large, and shaped like Hybrid Teas, at least during the first (and best) flush of blooms: later flushes tend to produce clusters of shallower flowers with fewer petals, like a Floribunda. They are deep yellow in bud, mid-yellow as they open, pale yellow when fully expanded, and creamy white as they fade. This process is triggered by heat and sun: the flowers keep their color well if cut in bud and taken indoors. They are at their best in cool, dry weather, when they can open fully and the mass of small, loose, dark yellow inner petals contrasts with the larger, paler outside ones. The upright, hardy plant has large, glossy leaves and grows vigorously to 9.8–13.1ft (3–4m).

'CASINO'

C

CASSANDRE

CASSANDRE

syn. 'MEIDENJI'

Modern Climber

ORIGIN **Meilland, France, 1989**
FLOWER SIZE **2.8in (7cm)**
SCENT **Light and sweet**
FLOWERING **Repeats**
HEIGHT/SPREAD **8.2ft (2.5m)/4.9ft (1.5m)**
HARDINESS **Zone 6**

Some of the best modern climbing roses are actually Floribundas or Hybrid Teas possessed of unusual vigor and height. Cassandre is a pale crimson Floribunda-type rose that happens to grow to about 9.8ft (3m). The great advantage of such roses is that they flower repeatedly or even continuously, like the best bush roses. The flowers of Cassandre come in small clusters (typically of 3–5). They have a beautiful circular outline and prettily ruffled petals, which fade to dark pink as they age. They are loosely held, which means that you can look up at them and see into the flowers, though they are also borne quite low down on the plant. Cassandre has fairly glossy, dark green foliage and a scattering of prickles. It is reasonably healthy.

CASTORE

syn. 'BARCAST'

Shrub

ORIGIN **Barni, Italy, 1987**
FLOWER SIZE **1.6in (4cm)**
SCENT **Musky**
FLOWERING **Almost continuous**
HEIGHT/SPREAD **2.7ft (80cm)/3.9ft (1.2m)**
HARDINESS **Zone 5**

Barni introduced Castore and Polluce simultaneously; in Greek legend, Castor and Pollux were the twin sons of Leda and Zeus. Castore has pink and white flowers – dark peach pink at first, fading quickly to pale pink, with a white patch at the center – and their color is best in cool climates. They come in large, spacious sprays, typically of 30–50 flowers, that combine very well with herbaceous plants in a mixed border. Castore has a very long flowering season and repeats so quickly that there are always a few flowers on some part of the bush, as well as heavy flushes of flowers every few weeks. The plant has small, glossy, Wichurana leaves and a lax habit, so that the long flowering sprays arch out sideways, but

CASTORE

it can also be trained as a 6.6ft (2m) pillar rose. In cool climates it may attract a little mildew in autumn, but it is generally a healthy rose and a vigorous grower.

CATHERINE DENEUVE

syn. 'MEIPRASERPI'

Hybrid Tea

ORIGIN **Meilland, France, 1981**
FLOWER SIZE **4.7in (12cm)**
SCENT **Medium and sweet**
FLOWERING **Repeats**
HEIGHT/SPREAD **4.1ft (1.25m)/3.3ft (1m)**
HARDINESS **Zone 6**
AWARDS **Rome GM 1979**

This handsome, salmon pink Floribunda is popular in western Europe, but little known elsewhere. Catherine Deneuve (named after the French actress) has pale red flowers that fade to an attractive shade of salmon pink. They have long, large petals and eventually open out to reveal a cluster of stamens and a patch of rich yellow at the base of the petals. The flowers come on fairly long stems, and last well when cut. Catherine Deneuve is vigorous, but puts most of its energies into quick re-flowering. Although it will grow to as much as 4.9ft (1.5m) if left unpruned, it is normally seen as a bedding rose of about half that height. The plant has healthy, mid-green, shiny leaves and an upright habit. It is very adaptable, surviving cold winters but also faring especially well in Mediterranean climates.

CATHERINE DENEUVE

'CATHERINE MERMET'

Tea Rose

ORIGIN **Guillot fils, France, 1869**
FLOWER SIZE **3.9in (10cm)**
SCENT **Medium and tealike**
FLOWERING **Repeats well**
HEIGHT/SPREAD **3.9ft (1.2m)/2.7ft (80cm)**
HARDINESS **Zone 7**

The long, elegant, pointed buds of 'Catherine Mermet' were forerunners of the classic conical shape that became the model of beauty for Hybrid Tea roses in the early 20th century. The tips of their petals start to scroll back while the buds are still unopened. The petals are pale peach pink, with slightly darker backs, which create subtly beautiful tones within the heart of each flower. Eventually the flower opens out completely, but the individual flowers last for many days. They are borne singly or in small clusters (typically of 2–3 flowers) on long, stout, upright stems. The leaves are dark, thin, often misshapen, and susceptible to mildew in cool climates. 'Catherine Mermet' grows to its greatest perfection in hot, dry climates such as California and much of Australia. It was immensely popular and widely grown in the late 19th century as a cut-flower rose.

CELEBRITY

CELEBRITY

Hybrid Tea

ORIGIN **Weeks, US, 1988**
PARENTAGE **('Sunbonnet' x 'Mister Lincoln') x seedling**
FLOWER SIZE **6.7in (17cm)**
SCENT **Strong and fruity**
FLOWERING **Repeats well**
HEIGHT/SPREAD **4.9ft (1.5m)/3.3ft (1m)**
HARDINESS **Zone 6**

Its color varies a little according to the weather, but in cool conditions Celebrity is the richest of all the yellow Hybrid Teas. Deep yellow or mid-yellow, it holds its color well, whatever the season. Sometimes there is a hint of red on the petal backs. The unusually big, pointed buds are elegant, and open into lustrous, shapely flowers. These too are remarkably large, especially if borne singly, which is usual, though sometimes they come in clusters of up to five. They have long stems, excellent for cutting and for exhibition. The plant is vigorous and quite outsized, with large hooked prickles and large, dark, glossy, healthy leaves.

'CATHERINE MERMET'

C

'CÉLESTE'

syn. 'CELESTIAL'

Hybrid Alba

ORIGIN **France, c.1759**
FLOWER SIZE **2.8in (7cm)**
SCENT **Strong and sweet**
FLOWERING **Once only**
HEIGHT/SPREAD **6.6ft (2m)/4.9ft (1.5m)**
HARDINESS **Zone 5**

No one knows the origins of 'Céleste', though it is one of several roses that claim to be the "Minden Rose," plucked by British soldiers and worn at the battle of Minden, Germany, in 1759. 'Céleste' is a cool rose pink, with semidouble, cupped flowers and a big boss of dark yellow stamens. Simple but exquisite, it is one of the most beautiful of all old roses. Why that should be the case, when many are larger, or have more petals, or display brighter colors and more complex forms, is hard to say. It has something to do with the clarity of its color, merging to cream at the center, and the fresh fragility with which the petals seem bathed. And the scent, so sweet and so pure. But 'Céleste' is a tough shrub, with gray green leaves, and healthy, hardy, and shade tolerant too.

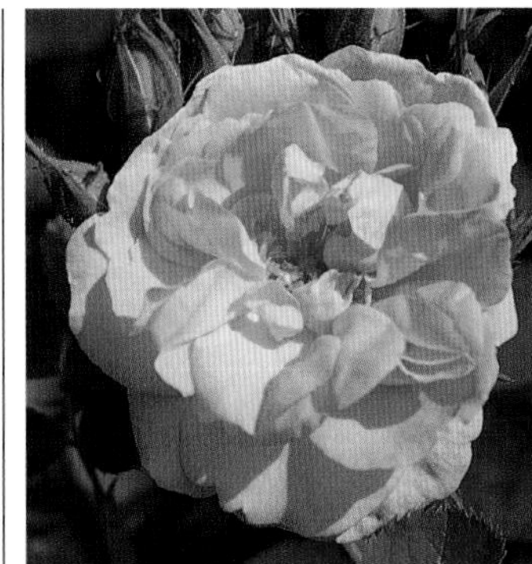
'CÉLESTE'

CELINA

syn. 'NOASUN', Sunshine, Yellow Flower Carpet

Shrub Rose

ORIGIN **Noack, Germany, 1997**
FLOWER SIZE **2in (5cm)**
SCENT **Light and sweet**
FLOWERING **Almost continuous**
HEIGHT/SPREAD **2.7ft (80cm)/2.7ft (80cm)**
HARDINESS **Zone 6**

There are few really first class ground-cover roses with yellow flowers: Celina is one of the best. In English speaking countries, Noack has promoted it as Yellow Flower Carpet. It is not a carpeting rose, but a useful small shrub. Celina has mid-yellow buds and lemon yellow semidouble or double flowers, which fade to cream. Sometimes they have a few red patches on the outside of the outer petals. They come in loose clusters of 10–25, drop their petals cleanly, and are followed in due course by small greenish hips. The plant has handsome, glossy Wichurana leaves, a few prickles, and a compact habit of growth. It is useful in large plantings as a shrub or landscape rose, provided you plant enough of it. It also combines well with most other colors in mixed plantings and containers. The first flowering is prolific; subsequent ones are less abundant but still valuable.

CELINA

'CÉCILE BRUNNER'

syn. 'MLLE CÉCILE BRUNNER'

Polyantha

ORIGIN **Ducher, France, 1881**
PARENTAGE **Unnamed Polyantha × 'Mme. de Tartras'**
FLOWER SIZE **2in (5cm)**
SCENT **Medium, sweet, and musky**
FLOWERING **Continuous**
HEIGHT/SPREAD **3.3ft (1m)/3.3ft (1m)**
HARDINESS **Zone 6**

Nicknamed the "sweetheart rose," 'Cécile Brunner' conquered the world of roses as soon as it was introduced, and has remained uniquely popular ever since. The flowers are carried in large, airy clusters like a Polyantha, typically with 10–25 flowers, but each resembles a miniature Hybrid Tea. They open from the most elegant and slender buds imaginable, which develop into perfect, small flowers, usually with reflexed petals and sometimes with a button eye. The flowers are coral pink in the center and pinky white at the edges, fading especially quickly in sun, and strongly scented. The plant is healthy, vigorous, easy to grow, and almost thornless.

'**White Cécile Brunner**' is exactly the same as 'Cécile Brunner' except for its coloring, which is pure white except for a hint of yellow at the center at first. There is also a deep pink form called 'Mme. Jules Thibaud'. '**Climbing Cécile Brunner**' is remarkable for its vigor and floriferousness. Most climbing sports are not as free-flowering as the bush roses from which they sported, but 'Climbing Cécile Brunner' will grow to at least 26.2ft (8m) and an established plant is rarely out of flower. Its flowers and leaves are slightly larger than those of the original. The flowers are borne in large clusters of up to 100 (typically 20–30). '**Spray Cécile Brunner**', better known as 'Bloomfield Abundance', is a larger, more vigorous form of 'Cécile Brunner'. It starts into flower later and flowers repeatedly rather than continuously. It produces very large clusters, which may contain as many as 200 well-spaced flowers, and can be impressive in full flower. It has one curious attribute, which is that the sepals are often foliolate – they are transformed into long, narrow, leaflike structures, more a curiosity than a thing of beauty.

'CÉCILE BRUNNER'

Sports of 'Cécile Brunner'

'WHITE CÉCILE BRUNNER'

ORIGIN **Fauque, France, 1909**

'CLIMBING CÉCILE BRUNNER'

Climbing Polyantha
ORIGIN **Hosp, US, 1894**
FLOWER SIZE **2.4in (6cm)**
HEIGHT/SPREAD **19.7ft (6m)/9.8ft (3m)**

'SPRAY CÉCILE BRUNNER'

syn. 'BLOOMFIELD ABUNDANCE'
ORIGIN **Howard, US, 1941**
FLOWERING **Almost continuous**
HEIGHT/SPREAD **9.8ft (3m)/6.6ft (2m)**

'WHITE CÉCILE BRUNNER'

'CLIMBING CÉCILE BRUNNER'

'SPRAY CÉCILE BRUNNER'

'CÉLINA'

Moss Rose

ORIGIN **Hardy, France, 1855**
FLOWER SIZE **3.5in (9cm)**
SCENT **Medium and sweet**
FLOWERING **Once only**
HEIGHT/SPREAD **4.1ft (1.25m)/3.3ft (1m)**
HARDINESS **Zone 5**

This dainty little rose is one of the best once-flowering Mosses. The flowers are semidouble, with very dark violet purple petals arranged around a brilliant yellow mass of stamens. Closer examination reveals that the petals have a mottled coloring, the result of purple highlights on a crimson ground. They also have an occasional white streak running out from the center. The buds, sepals, and stalks are generously covered with dark moss. 'Célina' is dense and compact, and its mid-green leaves have purple edges when young. Mildew can be a problem on the mossy parts, but not usually until after the plant has finished flowering. The red hips, still bearing traces of moss, are a bonus.

'CÉLINA'

'Céline Forestier'

'Céline Forestier'

Noisette

ORIGIN **Leroy, France, 1858**
PARENTAGE **'Champney's Pink Climber' x 'Parks' Yellow'**
FLOWER SIZE **2.8in (7cm)**
SCENT **Strong and tealike**
FLOWERING **Early in season; repeats**
HEIGHT/SPREAD **13.1ft (4m)/6.6ft (2m)**
HARDINESS **Zone 7**

This popular old Noisette is a rose of unique beauty. Its buds are dark pink, but the flowers of 'Céline Forestier' open pale yellow with hints of buff, apricot, and pink. Their color is always deeper at the center and paler toward the edges, which fade to cream as they age, so that the silky guard petals are almost white. The flowers are fully double, with quilled petals toward the center, and often quartered around a green eye. Their scent is delicious. The flowers are borne sometimes singly, but usually in small clusters (typically of 3–5), starting early in the season and continuing almost without cease. 'Céline Forestier' makes a large, loose shrub, 6.6ft (2m) high, but twice that when grown as a climber. Its leaves are bright, glossy green, and very healthy, apart from an occasional bout of mildew in autumn. It is easily propagated from cuttings and will tolerate poorer soils.

'Celsiana'

Damask Rose

ORIGIN **Spanish Netherlands, c.1750**
FLOWER SIZE **3.1in (8cm)**
SCENT **Strong and sweet**
FLOWERING **Once only**
HEIGHT/SPREAD **6.6ft (2m)/4.9ft (1.5m)**
HARDINESS **Zone 5**

The name 'Celsiana' commemorates the French plantsman Jacques-Martin Cels (1743–1806), but the rose is thought to be an older cultivar renamed by the French botanist Claude-Antoine Thory (1757–1827) in his memory. It has thin, rose pink petals, which appear crinkled and delicate when they first open but quickly fade to palest pink, while all the time exuding a wonderfully rich fragrance that carries in the air.

'Celsiana'

The flowers open from pale red buds, which provide a contrast with the changing colors of the petals. They also grow in size from 2.4in (6cm) to nearer to 3.5in (9cm) as they open to reveal the big brush of golden stamens at the center. They come in somewhat large, well-spaced clusters, typically of 7–15 flowers, which extend the season of flowering, making 'Celsiana' one of the longest flowering of the once-flowering roses. The plant is tall and strong, with a lot of small prickles and gray green leaves, but arches over under the weight of its flowers: it benefits from a light trim immediately after flowering.

'Centenaire de Lourdes'

Floribunda

ORIGIN **Delbard-Chabert, France, 1958**
PARENTAGE **'Frau Karl Druschki' x unknown**
FLOWER SIZE **4in (10cm)**
SCENT **Medium**
FLOWERING **Starting somewhat late in season; remontant**
HEIGHT/SPREAD **4.9ft (1.5m)/5.7ft (1.75m)**
HARDINESS **Zone 6**

'Centenaire de Lourdes' is an unusual shrub whose reputation as a good garden rose is still growing. It has remarkable vigor (inherited from its Druschki parent) and good disease resistance. Moreover, it is a well-shaped, rounded shrub with a lot of excellent foliage. The flowers open pale crimson, and fade to mid-pink, especially at the edge of the somewhat wavy petals, which are paler on their backs, with a white patch toward the center. The flowers are large and heavy, so that they tend to hang down in their clusters (usually of 3–15). The clusters make excellent cut flowers, and last well. By early autumn, the bush is covered with conspicuous clusters of orange fruits, making 'Centenaire de Lourdes' one of the best roses for hips. The name commemorates the centenary of the visions of St. Bernadette of Lourdes in 1858.

Centenary

see NDR 1 Radio Niedersachsen

'Century Two'

Hybrid Tea

ORIGIN **Armstrong, US, 1971**
PARENTAGE **'Charlotte Armstrong' x 'Duet'**
FLOWER SIZE **4.7in (12cm)**
SCENT **Strong and rich**
FLOWERING **Repeats well**
HEIGHT/SPREAD **4.3ft (1.3m)/3.3ft (1m)**
HARDINESS **Zone 6**

'Century Two' is closely related to 'Queen Elizabeth' and shares many of its qualities: it is a fine exhibition Hybrid Tea that performs very well as a garden plant. The flowers are large, elegantly shaped, and full of thick, sturdy petals, mid-pink in color with slightly darker backs to the petals. They are borne singly or in small clusters (rarely more than three at a time) on long stems. The plant is well shaped, vigorous, and healthy, and produces its flowers almost continuously. In hot, dry climates it is a rose without fault.

'Centenaire de Lourdes'

'Century Two'

'Cerise Bouquet'

Shrub Rose

ORIGIN **Tantau, Germany, c.1937**
PARENTAGE ***Rosa multibracteata* x 'Crimson Glory'**
FLOWER SIZE **2.4in (6cm)**
SCENT **Light**
FLOWERING **Once, spectacularly, followed by a few later**
HEIGHT/SPREAD **9.8ft (3m)/16.4ft (5m)**
HARDINESS **Zone 5**

Two famous German rose breeders combined to give us 'Cerise Bouquet'. It was actually bred by Matthias Tantau of Uetersen in the 1930s, as part of his experiments with unusual species. Tantau gave some plants to Wilhelm Kordes of Sparrieshoop but decided that it was not good enough to introduce commercially. Kordes also experimented with breeding roses from rarely used species and forgot that 'Cerise Bouquet' (which he esteemed very highly) had come originally from Tantau, so he introduced it himself some 20 years later. It has been popular ever since as a huge, once-flowering shrub rose. The cherry crimson flowers appear in clusters all along the long, thick, arching branches of last year's growth. A plant in full flower is an awesome sight – and awesomely prickly too, which makes it useful for hedges and boundaries. The grayish leaves are small but healthy and the plant has somewhat pale wood densely studded with large prickles. It is a very strong grower and makes a stupendous specimen set in an expanse of mown grass or on the edge of a lake.

'Cerise Bouquet'

'CENTIFOLIA'

'CENTIFOLIA'

syn. 'CABBAGE ROSE'

Centifolia

ORIGIN **Spanish Netherlands, 1596**
FLOWER SIZE **3.5in (9cm)**
SCENT **Strong and sweet**
FLOWERING **Once, slightly late in season**
HEIGHT/SPREAD **4.9ft (1.5m)/4.9ft (1.5m)**
HARDINESS **Zone 4**

No one knows the origins of the famous old cabbage rose, 'Centifolia'. The most plausible account is that it occurred as a hybrid between Gallicas and Damasks late in the 16th century, probably in the Netherlands. Its popularity was immediate and immense, and it is clearly identifiable in Dutch flower paintings from the 17th century onward. It was valued above all for the size of its flowers and the sweetness of their scent. Eighteenth-century botanists considered it a species and made it the "type" species of the genus *Rosa*. Modern botanists know better. 'Centifolia' got its name because of its many petals: critics were quick to point out that it should have been called 'Centipetala'. It has well over 100 petals, the outer ones large and eventually reflexing but for most of the time curving in to make a large goblet of pure rose pink. The flowers are borne singly and in clusters of up to seven on a lax, open shrub. The plant has lots of prickles, leafy sepals, and coarse green leaves, which droop attractively. It is vigorous and healthy, roots easily from cuttings, and clumps up nicely if grown on its own roots.

'Centifolia' turned out to be unusually sportive. In 1777, a white form was discovered and distributed as **'Unique'** by an English nurseryman: it is exactly the same as 'Centifolia' except for its color. A striped variant was distributed as **'Unique Panachée'** by Vibert in 1821: it has rose pink stripes on a white background, but the coloring is weak and the plant often reverts to simple 'Centifolia'. Meanwhile, a sport of 'Centifolia' had been in circulation since about 1800 under the name **'Bullata'**. This rose differs from 'Centifolia' only in its leaves, which are very large, crinkly, and ridged – "bullate" is the botanical word. The sections between the leaf veins resemble a gathered piece of fabric. The young leaves are often reddish brown. A short, compact form known as **'Spong'** was introduced in 1804; it sometimes reverts to plain 'Centifolia'.

By far the most interesting sports of 'Centifolia' were the first Moss rose **'Common Moss'** and the "winged Moss" known as **'Cristata'**. All the Centifolia roses have aromatic glands on their sepals, calyces, and pedicels. In 'Common Moss', those glands are overdeveloped and build up into a strange growth that resembles moss. It is highly aromatic and sticky to the touch. In 'Cristata', the edges of the sepals have developed a dense, leafy, bright green growth that projects like a crest from the undersides of the flower. It is a structure of great complexity and beauty, and steals the eye away from the flower. But in all other respects, both 'Common Moss' and 'Cristata' resemble plain 'Centifolia'. 'Common Moss' has produced a white sport on at least two occasions: the best known is **'Shailer's White Moss'**, which is widely available and resembles 'Common Moss' in everything except its color.

All the Centifolia roses and their sports are highly infertile, and rarely produce seeds. They do, however, carry small quantities of viable pollen, which led to them spawning a small race of Centifolia hybrids early in the 19th century. Perhaps the best known is 'Gros Choux d'Hollande', which most authorities place with the Bourbon roses. But these problems of taxonomy can be ignored: the important thing is to enjoy Centifolias for the unique qualities they offer – huge, cabbagelike flowers with a superb scent and an interesting chunk of horticultural history attached to them.

'COMMON MOSS'

'SHAILER'S WHITE MOSS'

'UNIQUE'

'UNIQUE PANACHÉE'

'BULLATA'

'SPONG'

'CRISTATA'

Sports of 'Centifolia'

'COMMON MOSS'

syn. 'CENTIFOLIA MUSCOSA'
ORIGIN **France, c.1700**

'UNIQUE'

syn. 'VIÈRGE DE CLÉRY'
ORIGIN **Grimwood, Britain, 1777**

'BULLATA'

syn. 'CENTIFOLIA BULLATA'
ORIGIN **c.1800**
FLOWERING **Once, midseason**

'SPONG'

ORIGIN **Spong, Britain, 1804**
FLOWER SIZE **2.4in (6cm)**
HEIGHT/SPREAD **4.1ft (1.25m)/3.3ft (1m)**

'CRISTATA'

syn. 'CRESTED MOSS', 'CHAPEAU DE NAPOLÉON'
Moss Rose
ORIGIN **Hilzer-Kirche, Switzerland, 1827**

Sport of 'Common Moss'

'SHAILER'S WHITE MOSS'

syn. 'WHITE BATH'
ORIGIN **Shailer, Britain, 1788**

Sport of 'Unique'

'UNIQUE PANACHÉE'

syn. 'CENTIFOLIA VARIEGATA', 'VILLAGE MAID'
ORIGIN **Vibert, France, 1821**

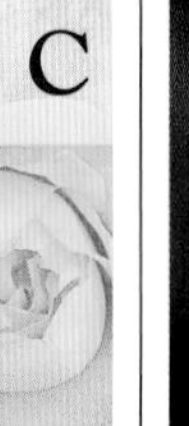

CÉSAR

CÉSAR

syn. 'MEISARDAN'

Pillar Rose

ORIGIN **Meilland, France, 1993**
FLOWER SIZE **2.8in (7cm)**
SCENT **Slight**
FLOWERING **Remontant**
HEIGHT/SPREAD **6.6ft (2m)/8.2ft (2.5m)**
HARDINESS **Zone 6**

César, named after the French artist and sculptor César Baldaccini (1921–98), is a vigorous Floribunda that can be grown as a short climber or trained as a shrub. It looks distinctly modern: the broad, very frilly petals fold themselves over the center of the flower, so that there is a startling contrast between the dark pink upper surfaces and pale apricot backs. The flowers open quickly, and are round and flat, but they seldom open out completely. They fare surprisingly well in wet weather, but still give their best display in warm, dry conditions. The yellow tinge fades so that the older flowers develop a contrast of pink and white that is very marked. The plant grows lankily to 6.6ft (2m) as a shrub, but arches over under the weight of its flowers, which come in clusters of 3–9, so it is best pruned as a shrub or trained over a support. It makes a fine short climber in hot climates. It has healthy foliage and is a reliable repeat flowerer.

CHACOK

see PIGALLE 84

CHAMPAGNE COCKTAIL

syn. 'HORFLASH'

Floribunda

ORIGIN **Horner, Britain, 1983**
PARENTAGE **'Old Master' x Southampton**
FLOWER SIZE **3.5in (9cm)**
SCENT **Light**
FLOWERING **Repeats well**
HEIGHT/SPREAD **3.3ft (1m)/2.7ft (80cm)**
HARDINESS **Zone 6**
AWARDS **Glasgow GM 1990**

Hailed as the first yellow "hand-painted" rose, Champagne Cocktail also owes something to 'Masquerade' for its coloring. Its flowers are rich yellow at first, then apricot, and finally deep strawberry pink. The petals have a large area marked with red – orange red at first, but crimson later – in flecks and patches, which shows its descent from 'Old Master'. The petal backs are always much paler, while the petals themselves have a crinkled shape. The flowers open out to display their color well and come in clusters of 4–11. The plant has dark green leaves and a tendency to blackspot in cool climates. In hot climates its flowers are more fleeting.

CHAMPAGNER

syn. 'KORAMPA', Antique Silk

Floribunda

ORIGIN **Kordes, Germany, 1985**
PARENTAGE **Anabell seedling**
FLOWER SIZE **3.1in (8cm)**
SCENT **Light and sweet**
FLOWERING **Repeats well**
HEIGHT/SPREAD **2.7ft (80cm)/2ft (60cm)**
HARDINESS **Zone 6**

CHAMPAGNE COCKTAIL

CHAMPAGNER

Champagner is a very distinct and unusual color, selected for the cut-flower market but also good in the garden. The flowers are basically white, with a flush of buff on the petal backs. The petals are very neatly arranged. When they are unfurling, you can see champagne colored shadows between them. The flowers are usually borne in clusters of 3–7. They come on a short, sturdy bush, with medium-dark, healthy leaves and few prickles. Champagner is a most elegant rose, whose subtle color is much appreciated for flower arrangements.

'CHAMPION OF THE WORLD'

Hybrid Perpetual

ORIGIN **Woodhouse, 1894**
PARENTAGE **'Hermosa' x 'Magna Charta'**
FLOWER SIZE **3.1in (8cm)**
SCENT **Light and sweet**
FLOWERING **Repeats**
HEIGHT/SPREAD **5.7ft (1.75m)/4.1ft (1.25m)**
HARDINESS **Zone 5**

This pink Hybrid Perpetual is altogether too modest to be called a champion. Its flowers are medium-sized and mid-pink, with darker petal backs toward the edge. The petals form a loose rosette and fade slightly to rose pink as they age. The flowers are usually carried in clusters of 3–5. 'Champion of the World' makes a shrubby, lax, and slender plant,

'CHAMPION OF THE WORLD'

mounding up to 6.6ft (2m) in hot climates but usually pruned to half that height in cooler areas. It has very few prickles and repeats reliably – but a champion it is not.

'CHAMPLAIN'

Shrub Rose

ORIGIN **Svejda, Canada, 1982**
PARENTAGE **'Kordesii' seedling x ('Red Dawn' x 'Suzanne')**
FLOWER SIZE **2.4in (6cm)**
SCENT **Light and musky**
FLOWERING **Repeats constantly**
HEIGHT/SPREAD **4.1ft (1.25m)/3.3ft (1m)**
HARDINESS **Zone 5**

In full flower, 'Champlain' is one of the most floriferous of all roses. Although bred to survive the worst of a Canadian winter, it looks more like a Floribunda than the other Explorer roses. The flowers are bright, deep red, and semidouble, their color enhanced by a large cluster of bright yellow stamens. They come in small clusters (typically of 5–7 flowers) almost continuously until the first frosts. 'Champlain' is compact, with small, pale, glossy leaves (bronzy when young) and quite a lot of prickles. It is very healthy in cool climates, but mildew may be a problem in damp areas. Samuel de Champlain (1567–1635) was a French adventurer who explored the Northwest Passage and died as Governor of New France.

'CHAMPLAIN'

'Champneys' Pink Cluster'

'Champneys' Pink Cluster'

Noisette

ORIGIN **Champneys, US, 1811**
PARENTAGE ***Rosa moschata* × 'Old Blush'**
FLOWER SIZE **2in (5cm)**
SCENT **Light and musky**
FLOWERING **Once only**
HEIGHT/SPREAD **13.1ft (4m)/6.6ft (2m)**
HARDINESS **Zone 6**

John Champneys (1743–1820) was a small-time rice planter in Charleston, South Carolina. The vigorous and once-flowering hybrid that he first saw in about 1802 was the ancestor of all the Noisette roses. Its flowers are pale pink, neatly double, and borne in large, loose clusters, typically of 5–20 flowers. They have long receptacles, like *Rosa moschata*, but smaller, pale, glossy leaves like the China roses. 'Champneys' Pink Cluster' grows quickly and is fairly healthy, except for an occasional touch of mildew or blackspot in susceptible areas. It has quite a scattering of large prickles. It flowers only once, but is followed by small red hips, and is still widely grown and appreciated for its hardiness and ease of growing.

'Chapeau de Napoléon'

see 'CENTIFOLIA'

'Chaplin's Pink Climber'

Modern Climber

ORIGIN **Chaplin, Britain, 1928**
PARENTAGE **'Paul's Scarlet Climber' × 'American Pillar'**
FLOWER SIZE **2.4in (6cm)**
SCENT **Light and musky**
FLOWERING **Once only**
HEIGHT/SPREAD **16.4ft (5m)/9.8ft (3m)**
HARDINESS **Zone 5**

This vigorous, easy to grow rambler was popular right from its introduction, but later became less fashionable. The semidouble flowers are a particularly vivid shade of dark pink or carmine, with occasional white flecks. They hold their color well, with almost no fading as they age, though they blotch badly in rain. The petal reverses are much paler pink and the flowers have conspicuous pale yellow stamens. They come in medium-sized clusters (of 5–15 flowers) but, because of the size of the individual flowers, seem much larger. They are borne in such profusion that a well-grown specimen in full glory is an unforgettable sight. The leaves are bright, dark green, and glossy and the plant grows to 13.1–16.4ft (4–5m). 'Chaplin's Pink Climber' is propagated very easily from hardwood cuttings in the autumn. It is still very popular in Europe – and seldom seen elsewhere.

'Chaplin's Pink Climber'

Charisma

SYN. 'JELROGANOR', Surprise Party

Floribunda

ORIGIN **Jelly, US, 1977**
PARENTAGE **'Gemini' × 'Zorina'**
FLOWER SIZE **3.1in (8cm)**
SCENT **Medium and fruity**
FLOWERING **Repeats well**
HEIGHT/SPREAD **2.7ft (80cm)/2.7ft (80cm)**
HARDINESS **Zone 6**
AWARDS **Portland GM 1976; AARS 1978**

Charisma

This excellent Floribunda has been popular for many years, and deservedly so. Its flowers are a startling combination of orange, vermilion, and yellow, and they open well to show the contrasts between those colors. The base and center are yellow, as are the petal backs, but the petals also have vermilion tips, which blend to orange at the edges. The petals are short but shapely, and there are a lot of them: the flower is very full and very double, while still managing to open out well. The colors are particularly strong in hot, dry conditions. The flowers are carried sometimes singly, often in clusters of three, and occasionally in groups of nine together. The rich green, glossy leaves are disease-resistant, and the plant makes a spectacular first display, followed by smaller flushes almost continuously through to late autumn.

Charity

syn. 'AUSCHAR'

Shrub Rose

ORIGIN **Austin, Britain, 1994**
PARENTAGE **Graham Thomas × seedling**
FLOWER SIZE **2.8in (7cm)**
SCENT **Strong and myrrhlike**
FLOWERING **Repeats well**
HEIGHT/SPREAD **3.3ft (1m)/2.5ft (75cm)**
HARDINESS **Zone 6**

Charity is a none too vigorous saffron yellow English Rose from David Austin, useful in mixed plantings. The lightly cupped flower is enclosed by large, white guard petals around the outside. Inside is a mass of small petals, many of them quill-shaped. They are a rich fawn yellow or butterscotch at first, and slightly darker on the petal backs, but tend to fade gently from the outside. They come singly or in clusters of up to seven. Their strong scent of myrrh is a great bonus. The plant is stout-growing and upright, but occasionally liable to blackspot. Charity takes its name from the National Gardens Scheme, the leading charitable foundation in England and Wales for public gardens.

Charity

'Charles Albanel'

Rugosa Hybrid

ORIGIN **Svejda, Canada, 1982**
PARENTAGE **'Souvenir de Philémon Cochet' seedling**
FLOWER SIZE **3.1in (8cm)**
SCENT **Strong and sweet**
FLOWERING **Early in season; repeats well**
HEIGHT/SPREAD **2.5ft (75cm)/4.1ft (1.25m)**
HARDINESS **Zone 4**

Some of the early Explorer roses were introduced from open-pollinated and self-pollinated seedlings: 'Charles Albanel' is among them. It is a semidouble, magenta Rugosa descended from the many-petaled, white 'Souvenir de Philémon Cochet'. Its flowers have a handsome boss of yellow stamens and come in clusters of 3–7, followed by large, tomato-shaped hips. The plant has typical crinkly Rugosa leaves – pale green and healthy – and lots of prickles. It tends to grow more sideways than upward, and is sometimes promoted as a low-maintenance or shrub rose. It flowers freely, somewhat early in the season, and then sporadically until the first frost. Charles Albanel was a French Jesuit, the first European to travel overland to Hudson's Bay, in 1672.

'Charles Albanel'

CHARLES DE GAULLE

CHARLES DE GAULLE

syn. 'MEIIANEIN', Katherine Mansfield

Hybrid Tea

ORIGIN **Meilland, France, 1974**
PARENTAGE **('Mainzer Fastnacht' x 'Prélude') x ('Kordes' Sondermeldung' x 'Caprice')**
FLOWER SIZE **3.9in (10cm)**
SCENT **Very strong and sweet**
FLOWERING **Repeats well**
HEIGHT/SPREAD **3.3ft (1m)/2.7ft (80cm)**
HARDINESS **Zone 6**

One can but wonder how France's greatest soldier and statesman of the 20th century would react to being commemorated by a frilly, fragrant, lilac mauve Hybrid Tea. Charles de Gaulle is, however, a stupendously beautiful rose, and rightly very popular even today. The flowers have short petals, broad and wavy, and very pretty when they open out. The petals have slightly darker backs, especially in shady positions, which reinforces the coolness of the overall color. The flowers come singly or in clusters of up to five, on a compact, healthy plant that bears a lot of mid-green leaves. The scent is glorious – a deep, intense mixture of damask sweetness and Tea-rose spice. Its color and scent, together with its long stems, make it an excellent cut flower for the house. It does not like wet weather, but is very floriferous and you can be certain of many nearly perfect flowers right through until late autumn.

'CHARLES DE MILLS'

syn. 'BIZARRE TRIOMPHANT'

Gallica

ORIGIN **France, c.1790**
FLOWER SIZE **4.3in (11cm)**
SCENT **Light and sweet**
FLOWERING **Once only**
HEIGHT/SPREAD **4.9ft (1.5m)/5.7ft (1.75m)**
HARDINESS **Zone 5**

No one knows the correct name for the sumptuous crimson purple Ga'lica known as 'Charles de Mills', although the leading French authority Professor François Joyaux believes it may be the same as 'Bizarre Triomphant' – one of the few Gallicas to date from the 18th century. It is one of the most widely grown of all old-fashioned roses, and this popularity rests upon its magnificent flowers, vigor, color, and easiness to grow. The flowers are large and lightly cupped at first, but filled with a mass of small petals that arrange themselves so that they radiate out from an empty receptacle at the center. When the flower reflexes, it resembles an overblown mushroom. The flowers are slightly variable in color but always a glorious shade of purple or crimson, often with hints of black, plum, and Parma violet. The individual flowers last well on the bush and as cut flowers; they come, almost invariably, in clusters of three. The almost thornless plant has fresh, green, matte, rugged leaves and a naturally arching habit, the result of the individual branches being weighed down by the flowers. It benefits from a gentle support or staking, but makes a fine suckering thicket. It may get a little mildew late in the season.

'CHARLES DE MILLS'

'CHARLES AUSTIN'

syn. 'AUSLES'

Shrub Rose

ORIGIN **Austin, Britain, 1973**
PARENTAGE **'Chaucer' x 'Aloha'**
FLOWER SIZE **3.1in (8cm)**
SCENT **Light and fruity**
FLOWERING **Repeats**
HEIGHT/SPREAD **6.6ft (2m)/4.1ft (1.25m)**
HARDINESS **Zone 5**

'Charles Austin' is one of David Austin's earliest roses, named after his father, and it remains among the most popular. The flowers are very pretty: they come in small clusters of 3–5 on long stalks and open out lightly cupped or flat. Sometimes the little petals at the center are quilled and quartered. They are soft orange at the center, richer toward the base of the petals, and more creamy at the edges. It is an excellent cut flower and responds well to hard pruning. Indeed, it is a slow repeat flowerer unless properly cut back after its first flowering. 'Charles Austin' is a lanky grower that will quickly attain 9.8ft (3m) in a hot climate, and reach the roof, even in cool climates, if planted against a house. The leaves are large and the plant has fine red prickles. It is fairly healthy, except for a little blackspot or mildew on occasions. A colour sport, introduced as **'Yellow Charles Austin'** in 1981, is almost as universally grown. It is the same as the orange original in every detail except that its flowers are lemon yellow on the outside and golden yellow at the center, fading to cream and buff.

'CHARLES AUSTIN'

'YELLOW CHARLES AUSTIN'

Sport of 'Charles Austin'

'YELLOW CHARLES AUSTIN'

syn. 'AUSYEL'
ORIGIN **Austin, Britain, 1981**

'CHARLES MALLERIN'

Hybrid Tea

ORIGIN **Meilland, France, 1951**
PARENTAGE **('Gloria di Roma' x 'Congo') x 'Tassin'**
FLOWER SIZE **3.9in (10cm)**
SCENT **Very strong and sweet**
FLOWERING **Repeats**
HEIGHT/SPREAD **4.1ft (1.25m)/3.3ft (1m)**
HARDINESS **Zone 6**

A famous crimson rose in its day, 'Charles Mallerin' was named by Meilland to honor the great French amateur breeder. It is one of the darkest red roses and one of the most fragrant, but it is difficult to grow well. At their best, the flowers open slowly from elegant, long-petaled buds. All too often, however, the buds are misshapen and the open flowers a mess of loosely held petals. The bush is none too vigorous and the flowers sparse. Mildew and blackspot can be a problem. But anyone who has seen and smelled a perfect bloom will want to grow it. The secret seems to be lots of feeding and watering while the plant is growing and the buds are developing, then dry, warm weather while they open.

'CHARLES MALLERIN'

CHARLES RENNIE MACKINTOSH

syn. 'AUSREN'

Shrub Rose

ORIGIN **Austin, Britain, 1988**
PARENTAGE **('Chaucer' x 'Conrad Ferdinand Meyer') x Mary Rose**
FLOWER SIZE **2.4in (6cm)**
SCENT **Moderate and musky**
FLOWERING **Repeats very well**
HEIGHT/SPREAD **3.3ft (1m)/2.7ft (80cm)**
HARDINESS **Zone 5**

Charles Rennie Mackintosh is an exceptional rose, unique among David Austin's for its soft lilac pink coloring. This is more pronounced in cool weather – it is pinker in hot climates – but the plant is happy in all conditions, holding up well to rain in England and flowering incessantly even in the hot, dry summers of California or Australia. The flowers open out so that a ring of large guard petals encloses a shallowly cupped mass of quilled petals, arranged in quarters around a neat button eye. The color is always attractive and full of variety, because the petals fade to gray pink at the edges and because the petal backs (including the parts that turn over to make the eye) are always slightly paler. The flowers come in nodding clusters of 3–9 on a twiggy, bushy, extremely prickly plant with small mid-green leaves and somewhat rounded leaflets. It is a tireless flowerer and, despite its wiry appearance, very vigorous, continually sending up new flowering stems from the base of the plant. The name commemorates the Scottish architect and Art Nouveau designer Charles Rennie Mackintosh (1868–1928).

CHARLES RENNIE MACKINTOSH

CHARLES AZNAVOUR

syn. 'MEIBEAUSAI', Matilda, Seduction, Pearl of Bedfordview

Floribunda

ORIGIN **Meilland, France, 1988**
PARENTAGE **Coppélia 76 x Nirvana**
FLOWER SIZE **3.5in (9cm)**
SCENT **Little or none**
FLOWERING **Repeats well**
HEIGHT/SPREAD **2.7ft (80cm)/2.3ft (70cm)**
HARDINESS **Zone 6**
AWARDS **Bagatelle GM 1987; Courtrai 1987**

The popularity of Charles Aznavour – the rose – comes from the sheer profusion of its flowers and the speed with which it repeats. The flowers are semisingle, with gently wavy petals and a small boss of pale stamens. They open ivory white with a pink center and then acquire a dark pink edging as they age and the ivory fades to pure white. The color is bleached by the sun in hot areas, so that it is almost completely white in high summer. On the other hand, the flowers need dry weather to look their best. They come in clusters of 5–15 and last very well as cut flowers, keeping their color. The leaves are dark green, semiglossy, and disease resistant. The plant is compact, thrifty, and a very prolific flowerer. Although very hardy, it is especially widely planted as a landscaping rose in warm areas, where it will grow to 3.9ft (1.2m). It is named after the husky Franco-Armenian singer (b.1924). Meilland introduced a different (but fairly similar) rose as Gala Charles Aznavour in 1997. Rather confusingly, they ceased offering it for sale after 2001, while still listing the original Charles Aznavour. Gala Charles Aznavour has slightly larger, semidouble flowers, with white centers, white petal backs, and broad pink edges. It is still quite widely grown in France, and flourishes in Australia.

GALA CHARLES AZNAVOUR

syn. 'MEISAZY'
ORIGIN **Meilland, France, 1997**
FLOWER SIZE **3.9in (10cm)**
SCENT **Light, sweet**
FLOWERING **Repeats**
HEIGHT/SPREAD **2.7ft (80cm)/2ft (60cm)**
HARDINESS **Zone 6**

CHARLES AZNAVOUR

GALA CHARLES AZNAVOUR

CHARLOTTE RAMPLING

CHARLOTTE

syn. 'AUSPOLY', Elgin Festival

Shrub Rose

ORIGIN **Austin, Britain, 1993**
PARENTAGE **'Chaucer' x 'Conrad Ferdinand Meyer' x Graham Thomas**
FLOWER SIZE **3.1in (8cm)**
SCENT **Medium and tealike**
FLOWERING **Repeats well**
HEIGHT/SPREAD **3.3ft (1m)/2.5ft (75cm)**
HARDINESS **Zone 5**

Charlotte is a slimmer, paler seedling of Graham Thomas. The flowers are very pretty as individual blooms: each has a globular mass of small, rich yellow petals surrounded by pale yellow guard petals which lie flat. The colors fade to lemon yellow at the center and cream or even white at the edges. The flowers are not so striking at a distance, and in hot climates they keep their colors better in a slightly shady position. The petals are always slightly paler on their backs. The flowers come singly or in clusters of up to five. The leaves are bright, pale green, and large. The plant has bushy, branching growth and is rather upright in habit. It reflowers sporadically, and a light prune between flowerings will encourage the production of more flowers and keep the bush in shape. In hot climates it will reach 4.9ft (1.5m) or more. It may need a little preventive treatment against mildew and blackspot.

CHARLOTTE

'CHARLOTTE ARMSTRONG'

Hybrid Tea

ORIGIN **Lammerts, US, 1940**
PARENTAGE **'Sœur Thérèse' x 'Crimson Glory'**
FLOWER SIZE **5.9in (15cm)**
SCENT **Medium and sweet**
FLOWERING **Repeats well**
HEIGHT/SPREAD **4.9ft (1.5m)/3.3ft (1m)**
HARDINESS **Zone 6**
AWARDS **AARS 1940; Portland GM 1941; NRS GM 1950**

For a rose first introduced more than 60 years ago, 'Charlotte Armstrong' has unusually large flowers. The long petals are tough and weather resistant, with the result that it was probably used for hybridizing in the 1940s and 1950s more than any other American rose. The buds are red, but the flowers open rich mid-pink with darker backs. They are borne singly on long, straight stems, only occasionally in twos or threes. The plant is upright, loose, gawky, and exceptionally vigorous, with tough, dark leaves. The Armstrongs were based in southern California, and 'Charlotte Armstrong' is the official flower of the City of Ontario (part of the Los Angeles sprawl), but it does very well in temperate climates too. Charlotte was the first wife of John S. Armstrong.

'CHARLOTTE ARMSTRONG'

CHARLOTTE RAMPLING

syn. 'MEIHIRVIN', Thomas Barton

Hybrid Tea

ORIGIN **Meilland, France, 1988**
FLOWER SIZE **3.9in (10cm)**
SCENT **Strong and sweet**
FLOWERING **Repeats well**
HEIGHT/SPREAD **4.1ft (1.25m)/3.3ft (1m)**
HARDINESS **Zone 5**
AWARDS **Monza GM 1987; Glasgow FA 1995**

Its flowers are not among the largest, but Charlotte Rampling is a popular red Hybrid Tea in France. The flowers are an unusual shade of pale crimson or dark red – "wine red" is one description – with a velvety sheen to the petals and an occasional white streak toward the center. The flowers come singly, or in clusters of up to five, on long stems that are good for cutting. They are very strongly scented and free with their scent in such a way that they fill a room with their fragrance. The plant has large, dark leaves (crimson when young) and is hardy, vigorous, and healthy. It repeats well. Charlotte Rampling (b.1945) is an English actress, popular in France.

CHARMIAN

syn. 'AUSMIAN'

Shrub Rose

ORIGIN **Austin, Britain, 1982**
PARENTAGE **seedling x 'Lilian Austin'**
FLOWER SIZE **2.8in (7cm)**
SCENT **Very strong and sweet**
FLOWERING **Repeats fairly well**
HEIGHT/SPREAD **4ft (1.25m)/3.3ft (1m)**
HARDINESS **Zone 6**

In cool climates, Charmian is a large, lax shrub, but in warmer parts of the world it is a handsome climber reaching 9.8ft (3m). The flowers open out as deep pink rosettes and are usually carried in clusters of 3–7 on long stems, well clear of the leaves. If hard pruned, however, the plant comes back with enormous clusters of 20 flowers or more. It has large, dark leaves, a fair number of prickles, and a lax habit of growth. It is healthy and vigorous, and very amenable to training. Its long, slender stems are best trained horizontally so that they break into flower all along their length. Charmian was Cleopatra's attendant in Shakespeare's *Antony and Cleopatra*.

CHATSWORTH

see MIRATO

CHARMIAN

C

'CHAUCER'

'CHAUCER'

Shrub Rose

ORIGIN **Austin, Britain, 1970**
PARENTAGE **'Duchesse de Montebello' × 'Constance Spry'**
FLOWER SIZE **4.3in (11cm)**
SCENT **Strong and myrrhlike**
FLOWERING **Repeats well**
HEIGHT/SPREAD **3.3ft (1m)/2.7ft (80cm)**
HARDINESS **Zone 5**

'Chaucer' is a repeat flowering shrub rose bred from two once-flowering parents, a good example of how a recessive gene can be hidden for one or more generations. Its flowers are large, cupped, and packed with petals, rose pink at first with slightly darker reverses and paler edges. Sometimes its stamens are visible at the center; sometimes it has a button eye. The flowers come on long stems in clusters of 3–7 and are very freely borne right through until late autumn. The leaves are bronze green at first, and pale green later, with large leaflets, but they are very susceptible to mildew. Nevertheless, 'Chaucer' is worth growing for its vigor, its glorious scent, and the sheer beauty of its flowers.

CHERISH

syn. 'JACSAL'

Floribunda

ORIGIN **Warriner, US, 1980**
PARENTAGE **'Bridal Pink' × 'Matador'**
FLOWER SIZE **3.1in (8cm)**
SCENT **Slight**
FLOWERING **Repeats well**
HEIGHT/SPREAD **3.3ft (1m)/3.3ft (1m)**
HARDINESS **Zone 6**
AWARDS **AARS 1980**

CHERISH

CHERRY BRANDY '85

Cherish is halfway between a Floribunda and a Hybrid Tea. The flowers are too short-petaled to be a good Hybrid Tea but come too few in a cluster to qualify as a proper Floribunda. Their color is good: the delightful buds are vermilion and the flowers are coral pink at first, eventually opening out to beautiful full, flat flowers, shrimp pink with a creamy salmon center and slightly darker petal backs. They are borne singly or in clusters of up to three and are pretty both in the garden and as long-lasting cut flowers. The leaves are large and dark but susceptible to blackspot, and the plant makes a good, compact, spreading bush.

CHERRY BRANDY '85

syn. 'TANRYRANDY'

Hybrid Tea

ORIGIN **Tantau, Germany, 1985**
FLOWER SIZE **4.3in (11cm)**
SCENT **Light to moderate**
FLOWERING **Repeats well**
HEIGHT/SPREAD **3.3ft (1m)/2.7ft (80cm)**
HARDINESS **Zone 5**

Cherry Brandy '85 has large flowers that open a very striking burnt apricot, with darker petal backs – a rich combination of shades. They come on long stems in open clusters of 3–9, and in this respect more closely resemble a Floribunda than a Hybrid Tea. They have a hint of yellow at the center at first, but eventually lose some of their yellow coloring and fade to a pale salmon pink. The petals are short and broad, which gives the flowers a good shape when they open out, but the buds expand very slowly and take a long time to reach that stage. This makes Cherry Brandy '85 a good cutting rose, as well as being useful in the garden, provided it is not spoiled by rain. The plant is healthy, vigorous, and well covered by large, bright leaves.

'CHESHIRE LIFE'

Hybrid Tea

ORIGIN **Fryer, Britain, 1972**
PARENTAGE **'Prima Ballerina' × 'Princess Michiko'**
FLOWER SIZE **4.3in (11cm)**
SCENT **Light and fruity**
FLOWERING **Repeats well**
HEIGHT/SPREAD **5.7ft (1.75m)/4.1ft (1.25m)**
HARDINESS **Zone 6**

'CHESHIRE LIFE'

The flowers of 'Cheshire Life' are as bright as any Floribunda's, but blessed with many petals and much beauty of shape at every stage of their development. The flowers open pale orange, losing their yellow tones and darkening with age, so that they end up red, though close examination reveals that each flower has shades of orange, vermilion, and even crimson in it. They are borne singly or in spacious, well-held clusters of up to five. 'Cheshire Life' makes a vigorous plant, with crimson new growth, thick stems, dark leaves, and a very great number of ferocious prickles. Blackspot and mildew may visit it in autumn, but it also flowers especially well during that season.

'CHEVY CHASE'

Multiflora Rambler

ORIGIN **Hansen, US, 1939**
PARENTAGE ***Rosa soulieana* × 'Éblouissant'**
FLOWER SIZE **1.2in (3cm)**
SCENT **Little or none**
FLOWERING **Once only, fairly late in season**
HEIGHT/SPREAD **16.4ft (5m)/9.8ft (3m)**
HARDINESS **Zone 6**

'Chevy Chase' is an unusual climber. It is one of very few bred from *Rosa soulieana*, though the influence of that species is not obvious. DNA analysis may one day reveal the truth: it is estimated that at least 15 percent of rose parentages are erroneous. The densely petaled flowers of 'Chevy Chase' are much neater and darker than other ramblers. They also keep their color for a long time before eventually turning cherry red. The flowers are each a perfectly shaped, flat rosette. They are very profusely borne in clusters of 10–20 and have the ability to be both very darkly colored and very brilliant at the same time. The plant's leaves are pale green, with a wrinkled surface, but healthy – much healthier than other popular Multiflora Ramblers, like 'Turner's Crimson Rambler' and 'Excelsa'. The plant is only moderately vigorous and may be slow to establish itself, but it will eventually grow to a great size.

'CHEVY CHASE'

'CHIANTI'

'CHIANTI'

Shrub Rose

ORIGIN **Austin, Britain, 1965**
PARENTAGE **'Dusky Maiden' × 'Tuscany'**
FLOWER SIZE **3.1in (8cm)**
SCENT **Strong and sweet**
FLOWERING **Once only**
HEIGHT/SPREAD **4.9ft (1.5m)/4.9ft (1.5m)**
HARDINESS **Zone 5**

'Chianti' was a landmark rose: its wonderful rich purple coloring flaunted the inherent potential of breeding from old roses like 'Tuscany'. Its flowers are purplish crimson (later maroon – though the color does differ a little from year to year) and open out lightly cupped before reflexing into great ruffled pompons. They come in long-stemmed clusters of 3–5 and are excellent cut flowers. Pretty vermilion hips follow, and often last right through the winter. 'Chianti' makes an arching shrub, best when its long, prickly stems are bent over so that it breaks into flower all along its length. The leaves are pale green and liable to get blackspot later in the year, after it has flowered. It roots easily from cuttings, but does not sucker when grown on its own roots. Chianti is the wine of Tuscany.

'CHICAGO PEACE'

see 'MME. A. MEILLAND'

CHILTERNS

see MAINAUFEUER

'CHINA DOLL'

Polyantha

ORIGIN **Lammerts, US, 1946**
PARENTAGE **'Mrs. Dudley Fulton' × 'Tom Thumb'**
FLOWER SIZE **2in (5cm)**
SCENT **Light and musky**
FLOWERING **Repeats constantly**
HEIGHT/SPREAD **1.6ft (50cm)/3.3ft (1m)**
HARDINESS **Zone 5**

There are three forms of 'China Doll' – the original pink Polyantha, introduced in 1946, and two climbing sports. The first of the sports was introduced in the US in 1977 and is known as 'Weeping China Doll'; the second is known as 'Climbing China Doll' and was

'CHINA DOLL'

introduced by Melville in Western Australia. They are all very similar except for their habit of growth. The flowers are small, semidouble, and pink, with white petal backs, a hint of white at the center, and yellow stamens when the flowers open out. Their petals have a distinct ruffled edge, which gives each flower its distinctive character and charm. The flowers come in large clusters and are most exuberantly borne. They are long lasting and repeat so quickly that the plant seems always to be in flower. 'China Doll' has few prickles (often none) and healthy, matte, dark green leaves. It is easy to grow, tolerates poor soil, and grows quickly from cuttings. The bush form is short, compact, and useful for containers and front of the border plantings in small gardens. 'Weeping China Doll' has a trailing habit and is popular for weeping standards and as a landscape plant. 'Climbing China Doll' tends to be grown in Australia as a conventional rambler, but flowers in a series of flushes, unlike the old-fashioned, once-flowering climbing Polyanthas.

'CHINATOWN'

Shrub Rose

ORIGIN **Poulsen, Denmark, 1963**
PARENTAGE **'Columbine' × 'Cläre Grammerstorf'**
FLOWER SIZE **4.7in (12cm)**
SCENT **Strong**
FLOWERING **Recurrent**
HEIGHT/SPREAD **5.7ft (1.75m)/6.6ft (2m)**
HARDINESS **Zone 5**
AWARDS **NRS GM 1962**

When a Hybrid Tea or Floribunda rose has a lot of stems and leaves, instead of the usual scraggy growth, it is often called a shrub rose. 'Chinatown' is best thought of as an exceptionally bushy shrub which carries some of its flowers in clusters. It produces large quantities of shapely flowers through until late autumn. They open bright canary yellow but fade to pale yellow and cream, and acquire a pink tinge, especially along the petal edges. Some are borne singly and others in clusters of up to nine. The bush is always shapely, with a lot of large, dark leaves. Its vigor ensures that it makes a good show even on poor soils. The flowers fade somewhat quickly in hot sunshine, so 'Chinatown' performs best in cool climates or in partial shade. In hot climates it will climb to 13.1ft (4m). In California, many regard it as the best of all yellow climbers.

'CHLORIS'

'CHLORIS'

Hybrid Alba

ORIGIN **Descemet, France, c.1820**
FLOWER SIZE **2.8in (7cm)**
SCENT **Strong and sweet**
FLOWERING **Once only**
HEIGHT/SPREAD **6.6ft (2m)/4.9ft (1.5m)**
HARDINESS **Zone 3 or 4**

'Chloris' is an unusual rose – an Alba that is nearly thornless and has fairly dark green leaves. Most Albas have stout prickles and grayish leaves, so it is probably a hybrid with a Gallica. The flowers are a very pretty pale pink, paler at the edges (pearl, or nearly white), with a lot of thin, translucent, incurved petals arranged in rough quarterings around a green eye. They come in small clusters (typically of 3–5) and flower for several weeks, though only once. 'Chloris' has long, arching stems, which will break into flower the whole way along if they are trained horizontally. The plant is healthy and tolerates poor soil. It also grows easily from cuttings.

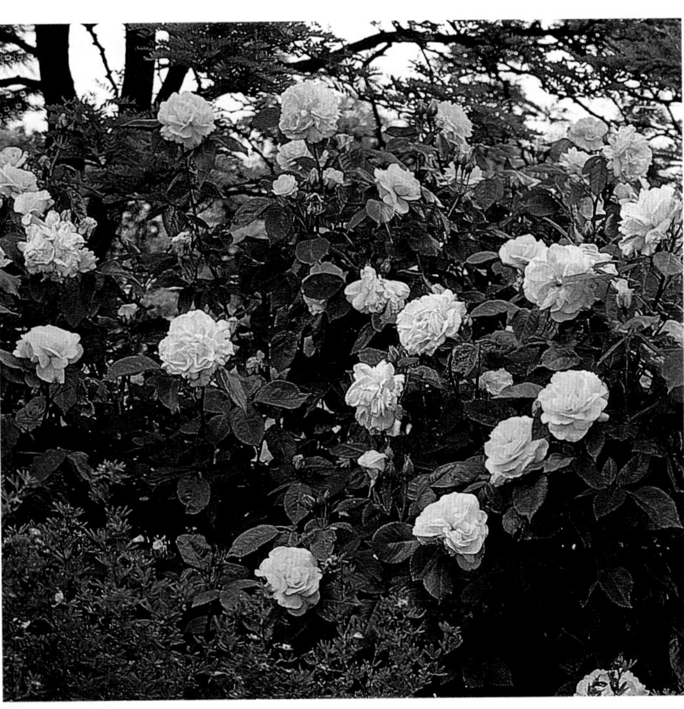

'CHINATOWN'

C

CHORUS

CHORUS

syn. 'MEIJULITA'

Floribunda

ORIGIN **Paolino, in France, 1975**
PARENTAGE **'Tamango' x ('Sarabande' x 'Zambra')**
FLOWER SIZE **3.5in (9cm)**
SCENT **Light and sweet**
FLOWERING **Repeats well**
HEIGHT/SPREAD **3.3ft (1m)/2.5ft (75cm)**
HARDINESS **Zone 5**
AWARDS **ADR 1977**

Although usually seen as a short-growing bedding rose, Chorus will reach at least 4.9ft (1.5m) if grown in a hot climate and left unpruned. It is, however, more frequently seen as a compact and neatly pruned bush. Its flowers are bright vermilion at first, later turning scarlet and picking up a hint of dark salmon. The flowers are double and full of short petals that stand up well to rain. They open from small buds and come in clusters of 3–10. Chorus has dark, glossy leaves (reddish at first). The plant is healthy, and shows very little susceptibility to blackspot or mildew, though in some climates it may be advisable to take precautions to prevent the spread of rust. It is very hardy, free flowering, and tolerant of poor soils.

CHRIS EVERT

syn. 'WEKJUVOO', Raymond Kopa

Hybrid Tea

ORIGIN **Carruth, US, 1996**
PARENTAGE **Voodoo x ('Katherine Loker' x 'Prince Abricot')**
FLOWER SIZE **5.1in (13cm)**
SCENT **Light and fruity**
FLOWERING **Repeats**
HEIGHT/SPREAD **4.1ft (1.25m)/2.7ft (80cm)**
HARDINESS **Zone 6**

This strapping orange Hybrid Tea is actually a mixture of yellow and crimson. The petal backs and bases are yellow and the petal tips red – it is the combination that gives an overall impression of orange. The flowers of Chris Evert are large and showy, shapely, and long-petaled. They usually come singly, but occasionally in twos and threes, and last well as cut flowers. Like many of the most sumptuous Hybrid Teas, Chris Evert is at its best in cool weather, when its flowers are largest and most full of petals. The flowers are, however, susceptible to rain damage. The plant has an upright, vigorous but compact habit of growth, large mid-green leaves, and deep red new foliage. It was named after the American ladies' tennis champion.

'CHRISTIAN DIOR'

Hybrid Tea

ORIGIN **Meilland, France, 1958**
PARENTAGE **'Mme. A. Meilland' x 'Rouge Meilland'**
FLOWER SIZE **4.7in (12cm)**
SCENT **Light and fruity**
FLOWERING **Repeats**
HEIGHT/SPREAD **4.9ft (1.5m)/4.1ft (1.25m)**
HARDINESS **Zone 6**
AWARDS **Geneva GM 1958; AARS 1962**

Rich, dark crimson Hybrid Teas have been bred for more than a century, but breeders have found that bright red ones are much more difficult to produce. 'Christian Dior' was a good attempt at a real Turkey red rose, and remains popular more than 40 years later. The flowers are large, full, and classically shaped at first, but open out later, and fade very slightly, taking on a cherry colored tint. They often have a few white stripes stretching into the petals from the center of the flower. The flowers come singly, but occasionally in small clusters, on long stems that make them useful for cutting. 'Christian Dior' has strong, glossy leaves, copper colored at first before turning to a fairly dark green. They may suffer a little from mildew and blackspot in circumstances where these diseases are rife. In any event, 'Christian Dior' performs best in hot, dry weather.

CHRISTOPHE COLOMB

syn. 'MEIRONSSE', Columbus, Christopher Columbus

Hybrid Tea

ORIGIN **Meilland, France, 1991**
PARENTAGE **Coppélia 76 x (Ambassador x seedling)**
FLOWER SIZE **4.7in (12cm)**
SCENT **Slight**
FLOWERING **Repeats well**
HEIGHT/SPREAD **4.9ft (1.5m)/3.9ft (1.2m)**
HARDINESS **Zone 6**
AWARDS **Durbanville, 1990**

This rose was timed to come out for the 500-year celebrations of Christopher Columbus's voyage to America in 1492. It is variously known in different countries as Christoph Colombus, Christopher Columbus, Cristobal Colón, and Cristóforo Colombo. Columbus was Genoese, so it is appropriate that this commemorative rose won a gold medal at the Genoa trials in 1992. The flowers are vermilion, with a yellow sheen on the backs of the petals. The petals are very broad, not especially long, but attractive. They have the classic shape of the Hybrid Tea, but usually come in clusters of 3–7; only occasionally are they borne on a single stem. The leaves are large, glossy, and fairly dark green, carried on a prickly plant that grows strongly and slenderly to as much as 6.6ft (2m) in a hot climate.

'CHROMATELLA'

'CHROMATELLA'

syn. 'CLOTH OF GOLD'

Noisette

ORIGIN **Coquereau, France, 1843**
PARENTAGE **'Lamarque' seedling**
FLOWER SIZE **3.9in (10cm)**
SCENT **Light and tealike**
FLOWERING **Constantly**
HEIGHT/SPREAD **13.1ft (4m)/9.8ft (3m)**
HARDINESS **Zone 8**

Some roses need hot, dry weather to give of their best, and 'Chromatella' is undoubtedly among them. Quite apart from its extreme tenderness, it needs heat to set its flower buds and dryness for them to expand. Rain smashes the soft petals, and damp weather induces mildew and balling. But, at its best, 'Chromatella' has always been a sight to remember. The flowers were "like large golden bells." wrote the English nurseryman Thomas Rivers in 1867, recalling his first vision of it in 1843. The flowers open from cream colored buds with a green tinge. They produce a couple of rows of broad outer petals, and a mass of small, short ones within. They are a rich mid-yellow, with lemon or sulphur yellow undersides to the petals. The plant grows quickly and vigorously, with a lot of dark leaves, crimson tinted at first. It will flower continuously in hot climates, provided it is watered all through the summer; otherwise, it is dormant until autumn.

CHRIS EVERT

'CHRISTIAN DIOR'

CHRISTOPHE COLOMB ▶

C

'CHUCKLES'

Floribunda

ORIGIN **Shepherd, US, 1958**
PARENTAGE **('Jean Lafitte' x 'New Dawn') x 'Orange Triumph'**
FLOWER SIZE **3.5in (9cm)**
SCENT **Medium, sweet, and fruity**
FLOWERING **Repeats constantly**
HEIGHT/SPREAD **4.1ft (1.25m)/4.1ft (1.25m)**
HARDINESS **Zone 5**

Its flowers are pink and white, and no more than single, but 'Chuckles' is an unusual rose, and still popular many years after it was introduced. The long buds open up to deep pink flowers with white centers and golden stamens. The color fades to pale pink as the flowers age. The flowers come in clusters of 3–15 (twice as many in autumn), and are succeeded by orange hips. 'Chuckles' has a lot of dark, shiny leaves and a vigorous, arching habit of growth which makes it a prototype landscaping rose. It flowers in flushes until late autumn, with a few individual flowers in between. Deadheading speeds up the next flush. 'Chuckles' is usually seen pruned low as a 2.5ft (75cm) bush, but in hot climates will easily reach 5.7ft (1.75m).

'CICELY LASCELLES'

'CICELY LASCELLES'

Climber

ORIGIN **Clark, Australia, 1937**
PARENTAGE **'Frau Obergärtner Singer' x 'Scorcher'**
FLOWER SIZE **4.3in (11cm)**
SCENT **Slight**
FLOWERING **Remontant**
HEIGHT/SPREAD **9.8ft (3m)/4.9ft (1.5m)**
HARDINESS **Zone 8**

The rose now grown as 'Cicely Lascelles' in Australia is a Gigantea Hybrid: it may be a different rose from the original introduction. The buds are dark pink or pale crimson. The loosely semidouble flowers are sugar pink, but darker on the petal backs. Each has about ten large, broad petals. They are borne singly or in clusters of up to eight on long, slender, upright stems. The plant has a lot of leaves, which droop down in the Gigantea way when young. Its moderate height and great vigor make it very suitable for small gardens. It flowers early and then recurrently right through to autumn.

'CHRYSLER IMPERIAL'

Hybrid Tea

ORIGIN **Lammerts, US, 1952**
PARENTAGE **'Charlotte Armstrong' x 'Mirandy'**
FLOWER SIZE **4.3in (11cm)**
SCENT **Very strong and sweet**
FLOWERING **Repeats**
HEIGHT/SPREAD **5.7ft (1.75m)/3.3ft (1m)**
HARDINESS **Zone 6**
AWARDS **Portland GM 1951; AARS 1953; Gamble FA 1965**

The Chrysler Imperial motor car has long since ceased production, but the sumptuous 'Chrysler Imperial' rose, after which it was named, remains a widely popular Hybrid Tea. Its strengths are a strong, rich scent and a floriferousness that makes it one of the most productive of all roses. The flowers are crimson, full, shapely, and borne individually on long stems. The color is slightly paler on the undersides of the petals, and the true depth of its crimson is revealed only when the large, high-centered buds open out to velvety globular flowers. They are excellent for cutting. The plant has dull, dark green leaves and may need some protection against mildew. It grows best in hot climates, but produces its most beautiful flowers in cooler weather, especially in autumn.

The American Paul Begonia introduced a climbing sport in 1957. This is exactly the same as the bush form, but grows vigorously to 13.1ft (4m). **'Climbing Chrysler Imperial'** flowers prolifically at the start of the rose season but has only a few flowers thereafter.

'CHRYSLER IMPERIAL'

'CLIMBING CHRYSLER IMPERIAL'

Sport of 'Chrysler Imperial'

'CLIMBING CHRYSLER IMPERIAL'

Climbing Hybrid Tea
ORIGIN **Begonia, US, 1957**
FLOWER SIZE **4.7in (12cm)**
HEIGHT/SPREAD **13.1ft (4m)/6.6ft (2m)**

CIDER CUP

syn. 'DICLADIDA'

Patio Rose

ORIGIN **Dickson, Northern Ireland, 1987**
PARENTAGE **Memento x ('Liverpool Echo' x 'Woman's Own')**
FLOWER SIZE **1.6in (4cm)**
SCENT **Light and fruity**
FLOWERING **Repeats well**
HEIGHT/SPREAD **2.5ft (75cm)/2ft (60cm)**
HARDINESS **Zone 6**

This cheerful and attractive short Floribunda is a great asset. The flowers of Cider Cup have such a Hybrid Tea shape when young that they can be used as buttonholes. Later they open out in clusters that create a substantial splash of garden color. It is the best sort of patio rose – compact, free-flowering, and easy to grow. The flowers are pale orange when freshly expanded, fading later to a beautiful soft shade of apricot. There is a hint of the "hand-painted" roses in the way the coloring pales toward the edges of the petals. The flowers are freely produced in clusters (typically of 5–10) right through until late autumn. Cider Cup has small, medium-dark leaves and a sturdy, vigorous habit of growth. An excellent rose.

'CINDERELLA'

'CINDERELLA'

Miniature Rose

ORIGIN **de Vink, Netherlands, 1953**
PARENTAGE **'Cécile Brunner' x 'Tom Thumb'**
FLOWER SIZE **0.8in (2cm)**
SCENT **Light and musky**
FLOWERING **Repeats well**
HEIGHT/SPREAD **11.8in (30cm)/7.8in (20cm)**
HARDINESS **Zone 6**

When 'Cinderella' was first introduced, it was seen to be so small that, for a while, it was allocated to a new class of rose – the "micromini." The flowers are freely borne, almost continuously, on a very healthy and attractive plant. Their color differs according to the climate – pure white in hot weather but mother-of-pearl, with flesh pink tints, in cool. The flowers also have a silky sheen, which greatly enhances their beauty. They come in long clusters of 5–20 flowers and are very freely borne all over the surface of the plant. 'Cinderella' has small, dark, healthy leaves, smooth stems (no prickles), and a neat, upright habit of growth. It is a classic beauty and a significant rose.

CIDER CUP

ROSA CINNAMOMEA

syn. ROSA MAJALIS

Wild Rose

FLOWER SIZE **2in (5cm)**
SCENT **Little or none**
FLOWERING **Once only, somewhat early in season**
HEIGHT/SPREAD **8.2ft (2.5m)/4.9ft (1.5m)**
HARDINESS **Zone 4**

Although it has been cultivated in European gardens since at least Renaissance times, *Rosa cinnamomea* is not as commonly seen as it should be. It comes from central and eastern Europe, often in mountainous areas, and stretches into Siberia. It is therefore very hardy. In temperate climates *Rosa cinnamomea* also has the advantage of flowering early in the season, several weeks before the main burst of roses. It has dark pink flowers (sometimes paler – all roses vary in the wild) with a small white patch at the center and pale yellow stamens. These are followed by small, round, red hips. *Rosa cinnamomea* has slender stems that are smooth when young but may develop hooked prickles at the nodes as they age and turn to russet brown. The leaves are dull gray green and slender. The plant is vigorous and tends to form a suckering clump. There are several double-flowered forms or hybrids known as ***Rosa cinnamomea* 'Plena'**. Sometimes they form a hemispherical mound of petals at the center, like a camellia or hollyhock. On other occasions, they have a mass of small, quilled petals in a quartered flower. *Rosa cinnamomea* 'Plena' is more widely grown than the single type, but its petals are thin and it does bruise easily in rain.

ROSA CINNAMOMEA

ROSA CINNAMOMEA 'PLENA'

Possible hybrid of ROSA CINNAMOMEA

ROSA CINNAMOMEA 'PLENA'

ORIGIN **1600**
HARDINESS **Zone 5**

'CITY OF BELFAST'

'CIRCUS'

Floribunda

ORIGIN **Swim, US, 1956**
PARENTAGE **'Fandango' x 'Rosenmärchen'**
FLOWER SIZE **2.8in (7cm)**
SCENT **Light and fruity**
FLOWERING **Repeats well**
HEIGHT/SPREAD **4.1ft (1.25m)/3.3ft (1m)**
HARDINESS **Zone 6**
AWARDS **Geneva GM 1955; AARS 1956; NRS GM 1956**

There are several forms of 'Circus' in cultivation: it seems to have undergone a number of small mutations. The original form, still widely available, has flowers that are orange with reddish edges and a hint of pink when they first open, and then fade to yellow – an unusual change of color. The flowers are very full and somewhat round in outline, with ruffled petals. They come in clusters of 3–11. 'Circus' has small, dark, healthy leaves and large prickles. It makes a short, dense plant, easy to grow and always full of color. For this reason, and its cheerful endurance of both sun and rain, 'Circus' is a popular and valuable bedding rose.

'CIRCUS'

'CITY OF BELFAST'

Floribunda

ORIGIN **McGredy, Northern Ireland, 1968**
PARENTAGE **'Evelyn Fison' x ('Korona' x 'Circus')**
FLOWER SIZE **7cm (2.8in)**
SCENT **Light**
FLOWERING **Repeats well**
HEIGHT/SPREAD **2.5ft (75cm)/2.5ft (75cm)**
HARDINESS **Zone 6**
AWARDS **NZ GM 1967; RNRS PIT 1967; Belfast GM 1970; The Hague GM 1976**

Few roses hold their color as well as 'City of Belfast' – a compact Floribunda whose flowers remain scarlet almost until they drop. The petals are short, but have a small white patch at the base and a distinct roll to their outline, which gives the flower much of its character. They also have more petals than was usual for Floribundas in 1968, when 'City of Belfast' was introduced. The flowers come in clusters of 5–15 and hold themselves upright, so that it makes a very useful, cheerful, short bedding rose – and, above all, a very reliable performer, more often in full bloom than not. The leaves are mid-green (bronzy when young), and may attract blackspot late in the season.

'CITY OF LEEDS'

Floribunda

ORIGIN **McGredy, Northern Ireland, 1966**
PARENTAGE **'Evelyn Fison' x ('Spartan' x 'Schweizer Gruss')**
FLOWER SIZE **2.8in (7cm)**
SCENT **Light and sweet**
FLOWERING **Repeats well**
HEIGHT/SPREAD **4.9ft (1.5m)/3.3ft (1m)**
HARDINESS **Zone 6**
AWARDS **RNRS GM 1965**

The 1960s produced far too many indifferent Floribundas, and a few real treasures. 'City of Leeds' is one of the best. It has the form of a Hybrid Tea, the large, open clusters of a good Floribunda, and a hybrid vigor all of its own. The flowers are salmon pink, with darker petal backs. They are pretty in the bud, and striking too as they open out. They last well on the bush and drop their petals cleanly when they fade. Their only real weakness is a tendency for the petals to spot badly in wet weather. 'City of Leeds' repeats both freely and well, being more orange in color during the autumn. It is, however, a fine bedding rose at any season. The leaves are dark, tough, and fairly healthy. Though usually seen as a hard-pruned bedding rose, 2.7ft (80cm) tall, 'City of Leeds' will naturally reach 6.6ft (2m) in a cool climate and more elsewhere.

'CITY OF LEEDS'

CITY OF LONDON

syn. 'HARUKFORE'

Floribunda

ORIGIN **Harkness, Britain, 1986**
PARENTAGE **Radox Bouquet x Margaret Merrill**
FLOWER SIZE **3.1in (8cm)**
SCENT **Medium and sweet**
FLOWERING **Repeats well**
HEIGHT/SPREAD **5.7ft (1.75m)/4.1ft (1.25m)**
HARDINESS **Zone 6**
AWARDS **Le Rœulx GM 1985; Belfast GM 1990; The Hague GM & FA 1993**

The flowers of City of London develop from somewhat small buds and continue to grow and expand as they open out. They are creamy white, with rose pink backs, and their semidouble form is enhanced by a ring of golden stamens at the center. The colors and shape are reminiscent of the famous old rambler 'New Dawn'. The flower has a very clean, fresh look, and the petals are somewhat more loosely held as they age, which gives an extra grace to the whole flower. The contrast between the nearly white flowers and the pink buds is especially attractive. The flowers come singly or, more usually, in clusters of up to seven. City of London has large, glossy, medium-dark leaves and bronzy new growth. Blackspot can be a problem in autumn. The stems are thick and sturdy, with a few large thorns. It is a lusty grower, and in hot climates it can be trained as a pillar rose.

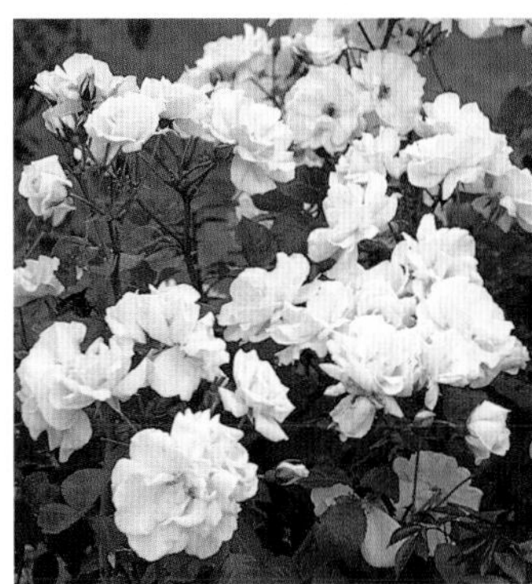

CITY OF LONDON

C

'CITY OF YORK'

see 'DIREKTOR BENSCHOP'

'CLAIR MATIN'

Modern Climber

ORIGIN **Meilland, France, 1960**
PARENTAGE **'Fashion' × (['Kordes' Sondermeldung' × 'Orange Triumph'] × 'Phyllis Bide')**
FLOWER SIZE **2.8in (7cm)**
SCENT **Medium and sweet**
FLOWERING **Repeats very well**
HEIGHT/SPREAD **9.8ft (3m)/8.2ft(2.5m)**
HARDINESS **Zone 6**
AWARDS **Bagatelle GM 1960**

The sheer profusion and abundance of 'Clair Matin' is without equal. It starts into flower early and is never without a large number of flowers until winter sets in. It is a rose that responds to good cultivation – feeding and spraying mean larger flowers and more new growth. The flowers have pretty coral colored buds but open out salmon pink at first, later pale pink. The petal backs are always darker than the open flower. The flowers are lightly cupped, carried in small clusters, typically of 3–7, and sweetly scented.

CLAIR RENAISSANCE

'CLAIRE JACQUIER'

The plant has prickly crimson new growth and reaches 6.6ft (2m) as a shrub (13.1ft/4m as a climber). It is susceptible to mildew and blackspot, but this will offend only the most fastidious gardeners, since the plant grows and flowers with complete disregard for such afflictions.

'CLAIR MATIN'

CLAIR RENAISSANCE

syn. 'POULSUNG'

Shrub Rose

ORIGIN **Poulsen, Denmark, 1995**
FLOWER SIZE **3.9in (10cm)**
SCENT **Medium and sweet**
FLOWERING **Repeats**
HEIGHT/SPREAD **4.9ft (1.5m)/3.3ft (1m)**
HARDINESS **Zone 6**

Poulsen's Renaissance roses aim to combine the beautiful floral forms of old roses with the health and floriferousness of the new. Clair Renaissance is a good example – and a rose of great beauty. Its flowers open like classic, large-flowered Hybrid Teas. They come both singly and in clusters of up to five. They are milky pink with palest salmon petal backs; the overall effect is of pale apricot pink, fading to white at the edges. As the flowers expand, so they take on the appearance of an old-fashioned rose, with masses of small petals arranged in a loose rosette. They last well as cut flowers and make a fine display as a garden rose. Clair Renaissance also has an upright habit and healthy, dark green leaves.

'CLAIRE JACQUIER'

syn. 'MLLE. CLAIRE JACQUIER'

Noisette

ORIGIN **Bernaix, France, 1888**
FLOWER SIZE **1.2in (3cm)**
SCENT **Strong and musky**
FLOWERING **Once only**
HEIGHT/SPREAD **16.4ft (5m)/6.6ft (2m)**
HARDINESS **Zone 7**

'Claire Jacquier' is popular for its sheer floriferousness and its willingness to grow: in ideal conditions it will reach as much as 32.8ft (10m). The neat, scrolled buds give way to flowers that are somewhat messy, but dainty. They are buff yellow at first, but soon change to cream and milk white from the edges inward. Once the stamens at the center turn brown, the whole flower is a dull white. The flowers are borne in fairly tight clusters, typically of 5–9. The plant has masses of shiny, dark leaves, and is a vigorous, exuberant grower. Very occasionally it produces a few flowers late in the season. It is hardier than most Noisettes.

CLAIRE ROSE

syn. 'AUSLIGHT'

Shrub Rose

ORIGIN **Austin, Britain, 1990**
PARENTAGE **'Charles Austin' × 'Schneewittchen' seedling**
FLOWER SIZE **3.9in (10cm)**
SCENT **Strong and sweet**
FLOWERING **Repeats**
HEIGHT/SPREAD **4.9ft (1.5m)/4.1ft (1.25m)**
HARDINESS **Zone 6**

Claire Rose is a very pretty, traditional English rose – soft-colored and full of petals – like an updated 'Souvenir de la Malmaison'. The flowers open out to reveal a mass of small pink petaloids, roughly gathered into quarters within a frame of nearly white outer guard petals. They come sometimes singly, but usually in clusters of up to five, which weigh down the branches. Their color is always deeper toward the center of the flower, where the shadows between the petals take on a dark pink hue. They make wonderful cut flowers. The plant is fairly vigorous and will grow to 8.2ft (2.5m) in hot climates, where it responds well to pegging down. It may get mildew in damp climates.

CLAIRE ROSE

C

Class Act

syn. 'JACARE', First Class
Floribunda

ORIGIN **Warriner, US, 1988**
PARENTAGE **Sun Flare x seedling**
FLOWER SIZE **3.5in (9cm)**
SCENT **Medium and fruity**
FLOWERING **Repeats very well**
HEIGHT/SPREAD **3.3ft (1m)/2.7ft (80cm)**
HARDINESS **Zone 5**
AWARDS **AARS 1989; Portland GM 1989; NZ GM 1990**

CLASS ACT

Some growers regard Class Act as a rival to Kordes' 'Schneewittchen', but it has never enjoyed comparable popularity. The flowers open from pale yellow buds. They have a flush of gentle yellow at the center at first, but quickly turn to creamy white. They are particularly attractive at the half-open stage, when they are elegantly cupped. Later, the petals are more loosely held. The long, wispy, golden stamens are pretty, but brown quite quickly. The flowers are borne, sometimes singly but more usually in clusters of 3–7 (occasionally up to 15), on long stems. The plant is vigorous, prickly, well shaped, and floriferous, with neat, glossy, medium or dark green leaves. An excellent garden rose, it is best in hot, dry climates, where it is free of mildew.

Claude Monet

syn. 'JACDESA'
Floribunda

ORIGIN **Jackson & Perkins, US, 1992**
FLOWER SIZE **3.5in (9cm)**
SCENT **Light and fruity**
FLOWERING **Repeats well**
HEIGHT/SPREAD **4ft (1.25m)/3.3ft (1m)**
HARDINESS **Zone 6**

CLAUDE MONET

This vividly striped Floribunda is vigorously promoted as one of Delbard's Painter roses, though (as Delbard is the first to admit) it was actually bred by Jackson & Perkins in the US. The flowers are among the best of their type – lemon yellow splashed with crimson when opening, then cream and pink as they age. There is usually more yellow than red, though occasionally the red coloring predominates in a particular flower. It is a most handsome and striking combination of colors, and every flower has a different pattern of splashes and stripes. The flowers come singly or, more commonly, in clusters of up to five, and are well shaped, with a lot of broad, short petals. They are pretty in the bud but later open out attractively. Claude Monet is a reliable repeat flowerer.

Alister Clark

ONE OF THE MOST DISTINGUISHED PLANT BREEDERS AUSTRALIA HAS PRODUCED, ALISTER CLARK INTRODUCED MORE THAN 130 NEW ROSE CULTIVARS

Alister Clark (1864–1949) began to hybridize roses at his family estate, "Glenara," near Melbourne, in about 1905. Clark was not a professional nurseryman, but a rich amateur, whose other passions were racing and fox hunting. Over the next 40 years, he introduced more than 130 new cultivars, almost all of which are still grown today. Clark's aim was to breed roses that would thrive in the Victorian climate and survive the long, hot, dry summers without watering. Above all, he insisted that they should be strongly scented.

Clark developed several different lines of breeding. He used the Wichurana rambler 'Jersey Beauty' to breed drought tolerant Polyantha roses, including 'Australia Felix' (1919), 'Borderer' (1918), and 'Mary Guthrie' (1929). One of his first roses was a many-petaled Hybrid Tea, called 'Lady Medallist' (1912) which opens slowly even in the Australian heat. Clark continued to raise unusual Hybrid Teas for many years: his later achievements included such beauties as 'Lady Huntingfield' (1937). Some of his Hybrid Teas were large shrubs like 'Restless' (1938), or even climbers like 'Norah Cunningham' (1920). Clark used the thornless Bourbon 'Zéphirine Drouhin' to raise the stunning climber Emily Roberts (1937).

ALISTER CLARK

Clark's greatest success came with his Gigantea Hybrids, the race of beautiful once-flowering climbing roses like 'Cicely Lascelles' (1937). Nevertheless, Clark's supreme achievement was the perpetually flowering bush-roses which had *Rosa gigantea* for one of their grandparents, with foliage that was immune to disease and an ability to survive the hot, dry Australian summer without water: roses like 'Lorraine Lee' (1924) and 'Squatter's Dream' (1923) are still among the most popular and successful of all roses in Australia today.

'LADY MEDALLIST'

'NORAH CUNNINGHAM'

C

CLIFFS OF DOVER

CLIFFS OF DOVER

syn. 'POULEMB', Dover

Shrub Rose

ORIGIN **Olesen, Denmark, 1995**
FLOWER SIZE **0.8in (2cm)**
SCENT **Light and musky**
FLOWERING **Continuous**
HEIGHT/SPREAD **2ft (60cm)/3.3ft (1m)**
HARDINESS **Zone 6**

The two great qualities of Cliffs of Dover are its health and floriferousness. It is widely used for landscaping and mass plantings where low maintenance is required. The flowers are small, dull white, with stamens that turn quickly brown. They are borne in conical clusters of 10–40 and are succeeded by tiny, round red hips, which are 0.2in (0.5cm) across, and usually long lasting. The plant has long, dark leaves with small, glossy leaflets, and a flat, low, floppy habit of growth.

'CLIMBING AMERICAN BEAUTY'

Modern Climber

ORIGIN **Hoopes Bros & Thomas, US, 1909**
PARENTAGE **(*Rosa wichurana* x 'Marion Dingee') x 'American Beauty'**
FLOWER SIZE **2.8in (7cm)**
SCENT **Strong and Damasky**
FLOWERING **Once**
HEIGHT/SPREAD **13.1ft (4m)/9.8ft (3m)**
HARDINESS **Zone 6**

Despite its name, 'Climbing American Beauty' is not a climbing sport at all, but a large-flowered Wichurana Rambler. It is popular for its deep color, its large flowers, and its attractive name. The flowers are pale crimson when they first open, but they fade to mid-pink and are always paler on the undersides of the petals. They are usually borne in small pendulous clusters (typically of 3–5 flowers) on long stems. The petals are only loosely held, but the flowers hold on to them after they have turned brown and died, so that the plant eventually looks somewhat messy unless it is scrupulously deadheaded. The leaves are healthy, dense, and glossy in the Wichurana manner, and the plant grows quickly and vigorously.

'CLIMBING BLUE MOON'

see 'MAINZER FASTNACHT'

CLIMBING GOLD BUNNY

see RIMOSA 79

'CLIMBING GOLDEN SCEPTER'

see 'CLIMBING SPEK'S YELLOW'

'CLIMBING ICEBERG'

see 'SCHNEEWITTCHEN'

'CLIMBING LADY SYLVIA'

see 'OPHELIA'

'CLIMBING MME. BUTTERFLY'

see 'OPHELIA'

'CLIMBING AMERICAN BEAUTY'

'CLIMBING MME. EDOUARD HERRIOT'

'CLIMBING MME. EDOUARD HERRIOT'

Climbing Hybrid Tea

ORIGIN **Ketten Bros, Luxembourg, 1921**
PARENTAGE **Sport of 'Mme. Edouard Herriot'**
FLOWER SIZE **4.7in (12cm)**
SCENT **Medium and fruity**
FLOWERING **Repeats well in autumn**
HEIGHT/SPREAD **13.1ft (4m)/9.8ft (3m)**
HARDINESS **Zone 6**

Few people grow the bush form of 'Mme. Edouard Herriot' these days and fewer still remember the lady whose name it bears: her husband was French Foreign Minister in the 1920s. However, the climbing form of her rose, 'Climbing Mme. Edouard Herriot', is widely grown throughout the world for its wonderfully bright and beautiful flowers. They are coral pink, fading to salmon, with darker, redder backs to the petals and somewhat more yellow toward the center. The overall effect has variously been described as salmon-pink, terracotta, strawberry rose, prawn red, and flame pink. However, each flower has many shades and hues within it and no two are alike, though the coloring is usually most intense toward the center. The flowers are lightly double and elegant in bud but somewhat loose and messy when open. They are profusely borne very early in the season and then intermittently until another good display in autumn. 'Climbing Mme. Edouard Herriot' has mid-green leaves (bronzy red when young), and a weakness for blackspot. The plant is prickly and lanky but easy to grow in almost all soils and situations.

'CLIMBING PAUL LÉDÉ'

Climbing Tea

ORIGIN **Low, 1913**
PARENTAGE **Sport of 'Paul Lédé'**
FLOWER SIZE **3.1in (8cm)**
SCENT **Strong and tealike**
FLOWERING **Repeats a little**
HEIGHT/SPREAD **16.4ft (5m)/8.2ft (2.5m)**
HARDINESS **Zone 7**

This is a climbing sport of a Tea rose that was introduced by Pernet-Ducher in Lyon in 1902. The bush form of 'Paul Lédé' is rarely seen these days, but the climbing sport is popular and widely grown. Its flowers are a very beautiful mixture of rich pink and buff, and full of long petals. The edges of the flowers age to pale yellow, but the center remains almost raspberry pink. The flowers are usually borne singly on weak stems, so that they hang down – a great asset in a climbing rose. 'Climbing Paul Lédé' is unforgettable when it flowers, very abundantly, and somewhat early in the season. There are a few later blooms. The plant has a lot of dark green leaves and grows with considerable vigor, especially in hot climates. 'Climbing Paul Lédé' can, however, be successfully grown against the wall of a house in cool climates. It tends to be sold as 'Paul Lédé' these days, rather than 'Climbing Paul Lédé', but more than one cultivar circulates under the name and it is wrongly named in several major rose collections.

'CLIMBING PEACE'

see 'MME. A MEILLAND'

'CLOTH OF GOLD'

see 'CHROMATELLA'

'CLIMBING PAUL LÉDÉ'

'Clothilde Soupert'

'Clothilde Soupert'

Polyantha

ORIGIN **Soupert & Notting, Luxembourg, 1890**
PARENTAGE **'Mignonette' x 'Mme. Damaizin'**
FLOWER SIZE **1.5in (4cm)**
SCENT **Strong and sweet**
FLOWERING **Repeats continually**
HEIGHT/SPREAD **2.7ft (80cm)/2ft (60cm)**
HARDINESS **Zone 5**

Sweetly scented Polyantha roses are few, but 'Clothilde Soupert' is one of the best, and one of the oldest. The flowers have a very pretty combination of colors – milk white at the edges and pale pink within. Actually, the petals are white with pink undersides, and it is the shadows between them that give the flowers their pinkness. The petals are small and soft, which means that the flowers tend to ball in damp weather and crumple in rain. They come in clusters of 3–9 flowers on a neat, thrifty plant that seems to be permanently in flower. Mildew can be a problem, so 'Clothilde Soupert' does best in dry, warm climates, where it will flower all the year round. It makes a pretty houseplant in less favorable climates and roots easily from cuttings.

'Clytemnestra'

Hybrid Musk

ORIGIN **Pemberton, Britain, 1915**
PARENTAGE **'Trier' x 'Liberty'**
FLOWER SIZE **2.4in (6cm)**
SCENT **Strong and fruity**
FLOWERING **Repeats well**
HEIGHT/SPREAD **6.6ft (2m)/6.6ft (2m)**
HARDINESS **Zone 7**
AWARDS **NRS GM 1914**

Despite its many qualities, 'Clytemnestra' has never been as popular as most of the Pemberton Hybrid Musks. It is a fine, free flowering shrub that repeats well, and the bright, coral pink buds are very pretty. The loosely double flowers open bright apricot, with dark yellow toward the center, but fade until they are no more than pearl pink, with peachy petal backs. Their most distinctive quality, however, is the way the petals curl back their edges like quills as they age and also reflex back from the center. Not everyone finds this attractive. However, the flower has a large boss of wispy stamens, which keep their color well.

'Clytemnestra'

The flowers come in small clusters at first (sometimes no more than 3–5) and larger ones later in the year. The lax, spreading bush has few prickles, dark leaves and long, pointed leaflets. It is healthy and easy to grow.

'Cocktail'

Shrub Rose

ORIGIN **Meilland, France, 1957**
PARENTAGE **('Kordes' Sondermeldung' x 'Orange Triumph') x 'Phyllis Bide'**
FLOWER SIZE **2.2in (5.5cm)**
SCENT **Medium and fruity**
FLOWERING **Recurrent**
HEIGHT/SPREAD **9.8ft (3m)/6.6ft (2m)**
HARDINESS **Zone 5**

'Cocktail' is either a shrubby climber or a vigorous pillar rose, ideal for smaller gardens. The flowers are very bright and attractive when they first open: they are shining crimson, infused with a yellow of remarkable brilliance. The yellow extends from the base of the petals to their backs, but soon fades completely, so that for most of their lives the flowers appear a somewhat dull crimson and white. They also blotch in rain, though they last well as cut flowers. The clusters of 20–40 flowers are on long, slender, upright stems. The plant is bushy, with handsome, glossy leaves and many prickles. It is a very profuse flowerer that continues to send out flush after flush of flowers almost continuously. It is tolerant of poor soils and grows well against buildings, but perhaps does best as a loose shrub tied into an archway, where its new flowers look dazzling when shot through by sunlight.

'Cocktail'

Cocorico '89

Cocorico '89

syn. 'MEIlasso', Birthday Girl, The Karnival

Floribunda

ORIGIN **Meilland, France, 1989**
FLOWER SIZE **2.4in (6cm)**
SCENT **Light**
FLOWERING **Almost continuous**
HEIGHT/SPREAD **2.7ft (80cm)/3.9ft (1.2m)**
HARDINESS **Zone 6**
AWARDS **Bagatelle GM 1989; Monza GM 1989; Rome GM 1989; Saverne GM 1989; Baden-Baden GM 1990; Belfast GM 1991**

Cocorico '89 is a cheerful, strong, thrifty rose, as useful in mixed plantings as it is in big landscaping designs. The flowers are semidouble, cupped, with distinctly wavy petals (very pretty), mainly crimson at first, with a little cream at the base of the petals. Then the cream turns to white and the crimson to pink, which starts to recede, so that little remains except a pink margin around the edge of the petals. The flowers tend to become spotty in rain. The bush has tough, deep green, glossy foliage and a spreading habit, but the sheer profusion of its flowers is unsurpassed.

Colette

syn. 'MEIroupis', John Keats

Shrub Rose

ORIGIN **Meilland, France, 1994**
PARENTAGE **(Fiona x 'Friesia') x 'Prairie Princess'**
FLOWER SIZE **3.1in (8cm)**
SCENT **Strong and sweet**
FLOWERING **Repeats**
HEIGHT/SPREAD **5.7ft (1.75m)/4.1ft (1.25m)**
HARDINESS **Zone 6**

The Meilland family has developed its Romantica series of roses in response to the demand for roses that combine the shape and scent of old roses with the colors and repeat flowering of new. Colette is a good example. The flowers are very full of short, broad, wavy petals. They are cupped at first, then later they open out and the flowers acquire a roughly quartered shape. They are pale apricot pink in color, with a hint of mustard yellow at the center, but fading to lighter tones at the edges, and always with paler undersides to the petals. The flowers are borne singly or in small clusters, rarely more than three at a time. The plant grows vigorously, and has small, dark green leaves.

Meilland brought out a sport of Colette in 1999 called Yellow Romantica. It is exactly the same as Colette in all respects except for its soft yellow coloring.

Colette

Yellow Romantica

Sport of Colette

Yellow Romantica

syn. 'MEIjacolet'
ORIGIN **Meilland, France,1999**

Color Magic

syn. 'JACMAG'

Hybrid Tea

ORIGIN **Warriner, US, 1978**
PARENTAGE **seedling × 'Spellbinder'**
FLOWER SIZE **5.9in (15cm)**
SCENT **Medium and sweet**
FLOWERING **Repeats**
HEIGHT/SPREAD **4.9ft (1.5m)/3.3ft (1m)**
HARDINESS **Zone 6**
AWARDS **AARS 1978**

Some roses change color in response to light and heat: the exact color of Color Magic at any given time depends upon both. It also grows in size as it opens, becoming largest in cool weather. The flowers are pale pink at first, but darken with age from the outside, so that the center is always paler than the outer petals, which finish almost crimson. The shape of the flowers is beautiful at all stages of growth, so it is a great pleasure to watch an individual flower develop over several days. The flowers have large petals and are borne singly on very long stems. The plant has medium-dark leaves and quite a lot of prickles.

COLOR MAGIC

'Colour Wonder'

see 'KÖNIGIN DER ROSEN'

'Commandant Beaurepaire'

Bourbon

ORIGIN **Moreau-Robert, France, 1874**
FLOWER SIZE **2.8in (7cm)**
SCENT **Strong and sweet**
FLOWERING **Once only**
HEIGHT/SPREAD **5.7ft (1.75m)/4.9ft (1.5m)**
HARDINESS **Zone 5**

It is usually described as a Bourbon rose, but 'Commandant Beaurepaire' is in some ways closer to two other striped roses – 'Honorine de Brabant' and 'Variegata di Bologna' – than to any of the better-known Bourbons. All three striped cultivars have the same cupped flowers, the same penetrating lemony sweet scent, the same large, pale leaves, and the same long, pointed leaflets. 'Commandant Beaurepaire' has stripes and splashes of purple and white on a pink base. The pattern of colors is completely irregular, but the overall effect is pinker than 'Honorine de Brabant' and 'Variegata di Bologna'.

'COMMANDANT BEAUREPAIRE'

Coloma

SET IN THE GROUNDS OF A FLEMISH CASTLE, THE ROSE GARDEN AT COLOMA IN BELGIUM BOASTS A COLLECTION OF NEARLY 60,000 PLANTS

COLOMA IS A BEAUTIFUL CASTLE in the Flemish style, built of brick in the early 1500s and surrounded by a moat. It lies in the village of Sint-Pieters-Leeuw, some 6 miles (10km) south of Brussels.

Within Coloma's 37 acres (15 hectares) of landscaped park is an important modern rose garden. The garden – a Flemish enterprise, backed by funding from the Department of the Environment and Infrastructure of the Flemish Community – is imaginatively designed and its collections are excellent. Nearly 3,000 different roses and 60,000 rose plants are displayed within its 5.5 acres (2.2 hectares) in three principal areas. One area features a complete collection of Belgian-raised roses, with dozens of first-rate cultivars that are little known outside the country. The Belgians – no matter how good their roses – have to work hard to earn recognition. This is because nurseries in countries with small home markets often have difficulty competing with the well-capitalized operations of rivals in larger countries. At Coloma, the work of Hippolite Delforge and Louis Lens is especially well-represented – here are the splendid Floribunda 'Hortiflora' (Delforge, 1974) and Lens's ground-breaking species hybrids 'Pink Surprise' (1987) and 'Jelena de Belder' (1996). The magnificent roses from the government experimental breeding station, RVS, include the golden Hybrid Tea 'Enghien' (1989).

COLOMA CASTLE

'ENGHIEN'

Another area of the rose garden is dedicated to historical roses of every sort, systematically and stylishly displayed. They include such rarities as the Hybrid Perpetual 'Charlemagne' (Dubreuil, 1888).

The largest collection of the three, however, features roses from all over the world. This displays a representative selection arranged country by country and breeder by breeder. German and British roses are especially comprehensive, but countries such as Israel, Hungary, and Switzerland each have their place. The Netherlands occupies a large area, where the fine 'Mies Bouwman' (Buisman, 1973) grows, and there are extensive collections from the rose-growing nations of Canada and Australia, whose roses are rarely seen in western Europe.

The plant is fairly vigorous, prickly, and healthy. Every so often, but not every year, it produces a few flowers in autumn; otherwise, it is strictly a once-flowering rose.

Commandant Cousteau

syn. 'ADHARMAN', Le Grand Huit

Hybrid Tea

ORIGIN **Adam, France, 1993**
FLOWER SIZE **2.8in (7cm)**
SCENT **Very strong and sweet**
FLOWERING **Repeats well**
HEIGHT/SPREAD **2.7ft (80cm)/2.7ft (80cm)**
HARDINESS **Zone 6**
AWARDS **Nantes FA 1991; Plus Belle Rose de France 1993**

Commandant Cousteau – named after the French marine explorer and oceanographer – was Michel Adam's first great success as a breeder. It won not only the top prize in the Bagatelle trials but also a special biennial award for the most strongly scented new rose: the Prix International de la Ville de Nantes. "Fruity, raspberry, classic, vinous" were some of the adjectives in the winning citation. The shapely flowers are bright crimson, with dark pink petal backs, occasionally splashed or streaked with white. They have short petals and come in clusters of 3–7. The leaves are tough, dark, and glossy, indicating *Rosa wichurana* in its recent ancestry, and a vivid beet red at first. The plant is very healthy. It is widely grown in France and increasingly in southern Europe, but its qualities have yet to be fully recognized elsewhere in the world.

'Common Moss'

see 'CENTIFOLIA'

COMMANDANT COUSTEAU

'Complicata'

Gallica

PARENTAGE ***Rosa gallica* x *Rosa canina***
FLOWER SIZE **4.7in (12cm)**
SCENT **Light and sweet**
FLOWERING **Once only**
HEIGHT/SPREAD **8.2ft (2.5m)/4.9ft (1.5m)**
HARDINESS **Zone 5**

The name is a tease: 'Complicata' is the most sublimely simple of all cultivated roses. DNA tests have proved it to be a hybrid between the French rose *Rosa gallica* and the dog rose *Rosa canina*. It is most popular in England, but is probably French in origin. Its flowers are large, single, and lightly cupped, rose pink with a white center and a large crown of stamens. The flowers fade slightly as they age, and close up at night. They come in clusters of 2–5 flowers, typically in threes, and are followed by red hips. 'Complicata' is a vigorous plant with bright green leaves (which are not dropped until well into winter), only a few prickles, and a lax, open habit. 'Complicata' can scramble up to 13.1ft (4m).

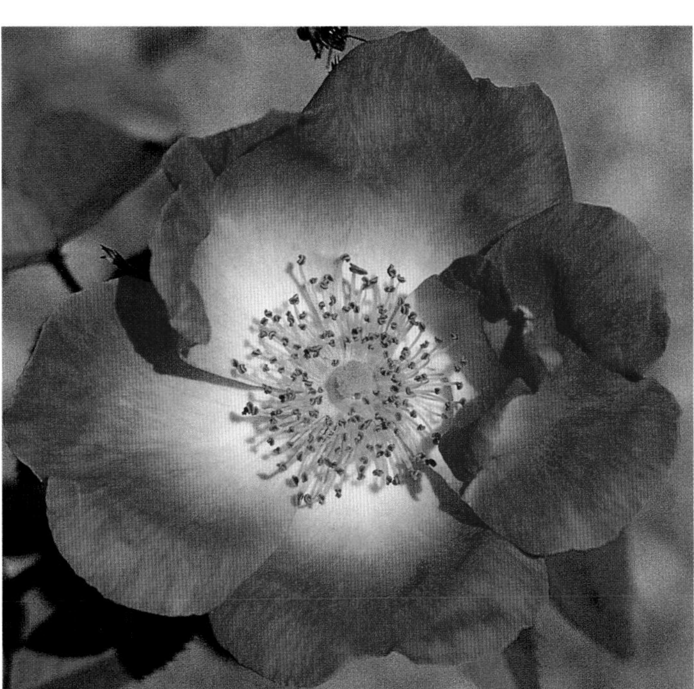

'COMPLICATA'

'Comte de Chambord'

Portland

ORIGIN **Moreau-Robert, France, 1860**
PARENTAGE **'Baronne Prévost' x 'Portland Rose'**
FLOWER SIZE **3.1in (8cm)**
SCENT **Strong and sweet**
FLOWERING **Repeats well**
HEIGHT/SPREAD **5.7ft (1.75m)/4.1ft (1.25m)**
HARDINESS **Zone 5**

'Comte de Chambord' is among the most popular and widely available of 19th-century roses – and with good reason, for it is by any reckoning one of the best. Its flowers are deep pink at the center and pale, translucent pink at the edges. They are cupped, but the outer petals reflex prettily while the inner ones form a rough quartered shape. The petals are frail, so the flowers may ball in humid weather and spoil in rain, but they are so liberally borne that you will enjoy many perfect specimens during the course of a season. They come in small, tight clusters (typically of 3–5 flowers) on sturdy, prickly, leafy stems. The bush is stiff and upright in habit, and sometimes susceptible to blackspot. The Comte de Chambord (1820–83) was the last legitimist king of France, known to his supporters as Henri V.

'COMTE DE CHAMBORD'

'Compassion'

syn. 'BELLE DE LONDRES'

Modern Climber

ORIGIN **Harkness, Britain, 1972**
PARENTAGE **'White Cockade' x 'Prima Ballerina'**
FLOWER SIZE **4.7in (12cm)**
SCENT **Strong, fruity, and sweet**
FLOWERING **Repeats well**
HEIGHT/SPREAD **9.8ft (3m)/6.6ft (2m)**
HARDINESS **Zone 6**
AWARDS **Baden-Baden GM 1973; Edland FA 1973; ADR 1976; Geneva GM 1979; Orléans GM 1979**

'Compassion' is a very popular modern climber. When its flowers first open, they are extraordinarily beautiful: a mixture of salmon pink, apricot, and orange, with pink on the upper sides of the petals. They develop from classic Hybrid Tea buds into a pretty, ruffled confection of petals. Then the color fades to a dirty white and the flowers omit to drop their petals, so that the loveliest of roses turns into one of the ugliest. The flowers are borne singly or in clusters of up to five. The plant has large, healthy, dark green, glossy leaves, quite a lot of prickles, and a thick, coarse, gawky, upright habit of growth.

A sport of 'Compassion' called **'Highfield'** is also popular. Its yellow flowers are smaller, with fewer petals. It loses its color quickly and shows the same weaknesses as 'Compassion' as it ages. There are better modern yellow climbers: 'Golden Showers' and Goldener Olymp, for example.

'COMPASSION'

Sport of 'Compassion'

'Highfield'

syn. 'HARcomp'
ORIGIN **Harkness, Britain, 1980**
SCENT **Medium, fruity, and sweet**
FLOWERING **Repeats**

'HIGHFIELD'

C

'Comtesse Cécile de Chabrillant'

'Comtesse Cécile de Chabrillant'

Hybrid Perpetual

ORIGIN **Marest, France, 1858**
PARENTAGE **'Jules Margottin' seedling**
FLOWER SIZE **3.1in (8cm)**
SCENT **Strong and sweet**
FLOWERING **Repeats well**
HEIGHT/SPREAD **4.9ft (1.5m)/4.9ft (1.5m)**
HARDINESS **Zone 5**

'Comtesse Cécile de Chabrillant' has neat, rounded, cabbagelike flowers, a shape unusual among the Hybrid Perpetuals. They have many rows of short, broad, incurved petals, which curl back just a little at their edges as they age. They are rich pink with paler, silver pink backs and streaks and shadows of many other shades of pink. They come singly or (especially during the first flowering) in close clusters of up to four and repeat well in autumn, with always a flower or two in between. 'Comtesse Cécile de Chabrillant' has matte, midsized, medium-dark leaves. Its stout stems have a scattering of small prickles. It makes a compact 3.3ft (1m) plant when grown as a shrub, but reaches twice as high and wide when trained as a lanky climber against a wall.

'Comtesse de Murinais'

Moss Rose

ORIGIN **Vibert, France, 1843**
FLOWER SIZE **2.4in (6cm)**
SCENT **Strong and sweet**
FLOWERING **Once only**
HEIGHT/SPREAD **8.2ft (2.5m)/4.9ft (1.5m)**
HARDINESS **Zone 5**

'Comtesse de Murinais'

'Comtesse du Caÿla'

Vibert introduced very few dull roses, but 'Comtesse de Murinais' is not among his best. It is a lanky grower, sending up long, prickly, bare stems that will reach as much as 13.1ft (4m) up a wall – it is an example of a Moss rose climber. The flowers are small, and tend to be perched in small clusters (typically of 3–5) on the end of the long stems, but much greater blooming may be obtained by tying the long stems down horizontally in winter so that all the axils produce short laterals and flowers. The flowers are white, with a hint of pink at first, and muddled centers. The plant has pale green leaves and is covered in dark red bristles that later metamorphose into brown prickles. Mildew and blackspot are its constant companions. Yet 'Comtesse de Murinais' is widely grown throughout the world.

'Comtesse du Caÿla'

China Rose

ORIGIN **Guillot, France, 1902**
PARENTAGE **'Rival de Paestum' x 'Mme. Falcot'**
FLOWER SIZE **2.8in (7cm)**
SCENT **Strong and tealike**
FLOWERING **Continuous**
HEIGHT/SPREAD **6.6ft (2m)/4.1ft (1.25m)**
HARDINESS **Zone 7**

Variously described as a Tea rose, a China rose, or a "China Tea," 'Comtesse du Cayla' is one of those roses that do best in a warm climate where it can be fed, watered, and pampered. Then the flowers are large and many-petaled, instead of the thin, small, semisingle blooms it puts out under conditions of stress. The flowers are a spectacular mixture of orange and pink, with flashes of coral and scarlet, fading to salmon pink as they age. They are borne singly or in small clusters (typically of three flowers) on a neat, twiggy bush that has small, bright green leaves and fierce hooked prickles. The bush builds up slowly into a large mass (up to 6.6ft/2m) of small zigzag branches, which are best pruned lightly, if ever. The flowers nod on their slender stems and the new growths are rich crimson. Mildew can be a problem. There have been many historic Comtesses du Caÿla: best known was Zoé Talon, born in 1784, who became the mistress of Louis XVIII.

'Comtesse Vandal'

Hybrid Tea

ORIGIN **Leenders, Netherlands, 1932**
PARENTAGE **('Ophelia' x 'Mrs. Aaron Ward') x 'Souvenir de Claudius Pernet'**
FLOWER SIZE **3.5in (9cm)**
SCENT **Light and sweet**
FLOWERING **Repeats**
HEIGHT/SPREAD **3.3ft (1m)/2.5ft (75cm)**
HARDINESS **Zone 6**
AWARDS **Bagatelle GM 1931**

Although bred in Belgium, 'Comtesse Vandal' fares better in climates where mildew is less prevalent. It was, for example, extremely popular in Spain during the 1950s. It is very beautiful in bud, somewhat charmless when opened out, and unattractive when finally its

'Comtesse Vandal'

petals reflex abruptly into a spiky ball. Its coloring continues to fascinate and delight: orange or dark buff on the upper side of the petals, and deep apricot pink on the reverses, fading in hot climates to dirty white. The flowers usually come in clusters of 3–7 and are very freely borne.

Concerto '94

syn. 'MEIhaitoil'

Shrub Rose

ORIGIN **Meilland, France, 1994**
FLOWER SIZE **3.5in (9cm)**
SCENT **Light**
FLOWERING **Repeats well**
HEIGHT/SPREAD **3.3ft (1m)/3.3ft (1m)**
HARDINESS **Zone 6**

Concerto '94 has large, open clusters of very pretty flowers. These are a pale peach color in the overall impression they give, but they have a pale yellow center and pale yellow petal backs. When the flowers open out, the petals are sometimes quilled, but more often imbricated. At that stage, too, there are pretty tints of deep apricot in the center, making a combination of unusual shapes and soft colors that is very attractive. The flowers come in clusters of 5–9 and are set off by a lot of dark, glossy leaves. The plant is healthy, and looks good as a specimen rose in a mixed border and in mass plantings. Like many French roses, it is grown too little in other countries.

Concerto '94

CONCORDE

CONCORDE

syn. 'MEIRELBAT'
Floribunda

ORIGIN **Meilland, France, 1993**
FLOWER SIZE **3.5in (9cm)**
SCENT **Light**
FLOWERING **Repeats well**
HEIGHT/SPREAD **2.7ft (80cm)/2.3ft (70cm)**
HARDINESS **Zone 6**

Concorde is a very pretty "hand-painted" Floribunda, too rarely seen outside France. Its flowers have a large patch of dark pink or pale crimson on a pale buff pink background. The petal backs confirm this distribution of color by being almost white, as are the unopened buds. The flowers open out almost flat and come in clusters of 5–15. The plant has good dark leaves and prickles.

'CONDESA DE SÁSTAGO'

Hybrid Tea

ORIGIN **Dot, Spain, 1932**
PARENTAGE **('Souvenir de Claudius Pernet' × 'Maréchal Foch') × 'Margaret McGredy'**
FLOWER SIZE **4.3in (11cm)**
SCENT **Strong, sweet, and fruity**
FLOWERING **Repeats**
HEIGHT/SPREAD **4.1ft (1.25m)/3.3ft (1m)**
HARDINESS **Zone 6**
AWARDS **Rome GM 1933**

'CONDITORUM'

Spanish breeders were quick to develop the strong red, orange, and yellow colors that suit the gardens of the Mediterranean. 'Condesa de Sástago' is an excellent example that was also very popular in the US. It is almost bicolor, being deep raspberry red on the upper side of the petals and deep yellow underneath. Unfortunately, it tends to fade fairly quickly and end up a dull parchment pink. However, the flowers are very full of petals, so there is usually more color at the center of the flower than at the edges. The plant is vigorous and erect, with dark, glossy, healthy leaves, and repeats well.

'CONDESA DE SÁSTAGO'

'CONDITORUM'

Gallica

ORIGIN **Hungary**
FLOWER SIZE **3.9in (10cm)**
SCENT **Strong and sweet**
FLOWERING **Once only**
HEIGHT/SPREAD **5.7ft (1.75m)/4.1ft (1.25m)**
HARDINESS **Zone 5**

'Conditorum' is sometimes known as "The Hungarian Rose" because it was widely planted in Hungary for the production of rose water. It is certainly one of the oldest Gallicas and, as with all other ancient roses, of unknown origin, though it has been cultivated in Western Europe since at least 1600. Its flowers are bright crimson at first, fading to purple, with ruffled petals surrounding a cluster of bright yellow stamens and a small green button eye. They are carried – very profusely – in clusters of 3–7 and are complemented by lush, mid-green leaves. The prickly bush grows taller than most Gallicas, and is vigorous even on poor soils.

CONGRATULATIONS

see SYLVIA

CONSERVATION

syn. 'COCDIMPLE'
Patio Rose

ORIGIN **Cocker, Britain, 1986**
PARENTAGE **(['Sabine' × 'Circus'] × 'Maxi') × 'Darling Flame'**
FLOWER SIZE **2.4in (6cm)**
SCENT **Light, sweet, and musky**
FLOWERING PERIOD **Repeats well**
HEIGHT/SPREAD **3.3ft (1m)/1.6ft (50cm)**
HARDINESS **Zone 6**
AWARDS **Dublin GM 1986**

CONSERVATION

Conservation is somewhere between a Miniature and a Patio rose, although its narrow, upright habit sets it apart from both. The semisingle flowers are pretty, with orange petals grading to yellow at the center. They keep their color fairly well as they age, fading only very slightly from pale orange to salmon. The flowers come in compound clusters of up to 40, and the whole stem seems to burn with color. Conservation has small, healthy, glossy leaves and compact, upright stems. It is a useful container plant and responds well to pruning.

'CONRAD FERDINAND MEYER'

Rugosa Hybrid

ORIGIN **Müller, Germany, 1929**
PARENTAGE ***Rosa rugosa* × 'Gloire de Dijon'**
FLOWER SIZE **3.9in (10cm)**
SCENT **Very strong and sweet**
FLOWERING **Repeats**
HEIGHT/SPREAD **8.2ft (2.5m)/4.9ft (1.5m)**
HARDINESS **Zone 4**

Dr. Müller named this glorious Rugosa rose after the Swiss poet who had died the year before. 'Conrad Ferdinand Meyer' is a leggy shrub or pillar rose, best pegged down so that it flowers all along its branches. The buds are elegant and high-centered at first. The flowers are large and full of petals – large, lightly reflexed petals at the edges, and a mass of smaller, paler petals at the center. They are silver pink with darker rose pink backs, sometimes quartered, and always early flowering. The penetrating scent is delicious. 'Conrad Ferdinand Meyer' is, however, a temperamental repeater – one of those roses that is definitely helped by deadheading after the first flowering. The plant is excessively vigorous, fast growing, and prickly, with coarse, pale, Rugosa leaves and red midribs – all a great contrast to its beautiful flowers. David Austin has used it extensively in recent years to breed English Roses. Its great shortcoming is a weakness for rust, which can defoliate it even before the first flowering has finished. There is a white sport called **'Nova Zembla'**, which is exactly the same as 'Conrad Ferdinand Meyer' in all respects except its color.

'CONRAD FERDINAND MEYER'

'NOVA ZEMBLA'

Sport of 'Conrad Ferdinand Meyer'

'NOVA ZEMBLA'

ORIGIN **Mees, 1907**

'Constance Spry'

Shrub Rose

ORIGIN **Austin, Britain, 1961**
PARENTAGE **'Belle Isis' x 'Dainty Maid'**
FLOWER SIZE **5.1in (13cm)**
SCENT **Strong and myrrhlike**
FLOWERING **Once only**
HEIGHT/SPREAD **8.2ft (2.5m)/4.9ft (1.5m)**
HARDINESS **Zone 6**

This is an iconic rose. Constance Spry (1886–1960) was the founder of modern flower arrangement. "Her" rose, introduced posthumously, was David Austin's first ever hybrid, and the ancestor (often literally) of all the modern roses that combine the best of old roses and new. It was the archetype of what became known as the English Rose. The flowers are round and globular, with so many incurved petals that the flowers never really open out. Instead, they resemble throughout their long flowering the cabbagelike roses of 17th-century Dutch flower paintings. The flowers of 'Constance Spry' are a pale, clear pink on the outside and a more modern, deeper pink within. They are borne both singly and in clusters of up to six, typically in threes. A plant in full flower is a fine sight, especially if its long growth is trained against a wall plant or wound around a support. It is a vigorous, lanky grower, with slender stems and a lot of small prickles. The leaves and leaflets are large (especially the terminal leaflet) and matte mid-green (paler, and bronze tinted when young), with short, almost sessile petioles on the leaflets. Mildew and blackspot may affect it later in the season. It roots easily from cuttings and, if grown on its own roots, forms a small, suckering thicket. Although 'Constance Spry' blooms only once, the flowers have an unusual scent of myrrh that has passed to many of its repeat flowering descendants.

'Coquette des Blanches'

'Coral Satin'

'Coquette des Blanches'

Noisette

ORIGIN **Lacharme, France, 1871**
PARENTAGE **'Mlle. Blanche Laffitte' x 'Sapho'**
FLOWER SIZE **3.9in (10cm)**
SCENT **Medium and sweet**
FLOWERING **Repeats well**
HEIGHT/SPREAD **9.8ft (3m)/6.6ft (2m)**
HARDINESS **Zone 6**

'Coquette des Blanches' is a short climber or pillar rose, with surprisingly large flowers, and a lot of them. The fat buds open to very full, cupped flowers, almost bursting with the great number of small quilled petals inside. The flowers of 'Coquette Des Blanches' are white, with a hint of pink at the center, and are very abundantly produced, though they do not drop their petals when they have finished flowering. It is a leafy plant – the leaves are dark and glossy, with a slightly glaucous hue – because the stems have very short internodes and every flower seems to have a lot of leaves below it. Nevertheless, it is an excellent rose, especially in hot, dry climates.

'Coral Dawn'

Modern Climber

ORIGIN **Boerner, US, 1952**
PARENTAGE **'New Dawn' seedling x unknown**
FLOWER SIZE **2.8in (7cm)**
SCENT **Strong, sweet, and musky**
FLOWERING **Repeats well**
HEIGHT/SPREAD **9.8ft (3m)/6.6ft (2m)**
HARDINESS **Zone 5**

The name is somewhat a misnomer – 'Coral Dawn' is not at all coral colored, but a good, deep pink instead. It has the dark, healthy, glossy leaves of 'New Dawn', but fuller flowers and a denser, shrubbier habit of growth. The flowers are globular, with a muddled mass of short petals and a good scent. They fare better in dry weather, because the petals are soft and damage in rain. They come singly or in clusters of up to seven (typically three), and fade to pale pink as they age. Strong sunlight may bleach them unattractively. The plant has many prickles. It makes a good pillar rose, flowering nonstop until the first frost.

'Constance Spry'

'Coral Dawn'

Coral Meidiland

see Douceur Normande

'Coral Satin'

Climber

ORIGIN **Zombory, US, 1960**
PARENTAGE **'New Dawn' x 'Fashion'**
FLOWER SIZE **3.5in (9cm)**
SCENT **Medium and sweet**
FLOWERING **Repeats well**
HEIGHT/SPREAD **9.8ft (3m)/4.9ft (1.5m)**
HARDINESS **Zone 6**

'Coral Satin' is a coral colored version of 'New Dawn' – not a sport, but a hybrid with that popular coral Floribunda 'Fashion'. Although the flowers open coral, they do eventually turn to deep pink, with slightly paler shades on the petal backs, and may fade to mid-pink in hot sun. They open from pretty, Hybrid Tea type buds. They are occasionally borne singly but usually in long-stemmed, open, pendulous clusters of 5–9 flowers, and are very good for cutting. 'Coral Satin' has beautiful crimson new growth, which turns into large, dark, heavy foliage. It is somewhat prickly but vigorous, and pushes out its flowers almost constantly until well into autumn.

'Cornelia'

Hybrid Musk

BREEDER **Pemberton, Britain, 1925**
FLOWER SIZE **2in (5cm)**
SCENT **Strong, sweet, and musky**
FLOWERING **Repeats very well**
HEIGHT/SPREAD **4.9ft (1.5m)/5.7ft (1.75m)**
HARDINESS **Zone 6**

The parents of 'Cornelia' are not recorded, but we can assume that 'Trier' was one of them, and a dark Hybrid Tea the other. The neat, lightly double flowers are smaller than 'Felicia' and 'Penelope' but very freely borne. They open from coral red buds and

'CORNELIA'

keep a deep salmon pink color on the petal backs, though the inner ones are pure pink. They have a distinctive ripple that is unique among the Hybrid Musks. The color fades in hot weather, but is superb in autumn and especially in cool climates like England. The flowers come in large, spacious clusters, typically of 25 at the first flowering, but at least twice that in autumn. The plant has healthy, dark green leaves, smooth stems (few prickles), and a mounding habit. In hot climates it can be trained up as a 13.1ft (4m) climber, but it is easy to grow anywhere.

'COSIMO RIDOLFI'

Gallica

ORIGIN **Vibert, France, 1842**
FLOWER SIZE **3.5in (9cm)**
SCENT **Light and sweet**
FLOWERING **Once only**
HEIGHT/SPREAD **3.3ft (1m)/3.3ft (1m)**
HARDINESS **Zone 5**

The Marchese Cosimo Ridolfi (1794–1865) was an influential agricultural improver and Italian politician. The rose named after him is a fine crimson purple Gallica. The flower opens out from a dumpy bud to display a lightly cupped flower, very full of petals, often quartered around a button eye. The color fades to lilac and the undersides of the petals are silvery pink. There are always white flecks toward the center, especially in the folded petals that create the eye, but sometimes on the edges of the petals too. The flowers come singly or in clusters of up to four. 'Cosimo Ridolfi' has stout, upright branches, few prickles (if any), a bushy habit of growth, and large, healthy, medium-dark leaves.

'COSIMO RIDOLFI'

COSMOS

COSMOS

syn. 'COMSAN'

Hybrid Tea

ORIGIN **Combe, France, 1993**
FLOWER SIZE **3.9in (10cm)**
SCENT **Medium and sweet**
FLOWERING **Repeats**
HEIGHT/SPREAD **4.1ft (1.25m)/2.7ft (80cm)**
HARDINESS **Zone 6**

This beautiful Hybrid Tea is especially popular in France, where it was bred. Cosmos has flowers of purest, glacial white. The large petals (both broad and long) reflex elegantly from a classically conical bud. Later the flowers open out completely to show their dark yellow stamens, but they are at their loveliest when no more than partly expanded. They are usually borne singly (sometimes in clusters of up to four) and last well when cut. Cosmos is best as a bedding rose in dry weather, when the petals are not susceptible to rain damage. The plant has healthy, medium-dark green leaves, and a vigorous, upright habit. It is usually seen pruned to 2.7ft (80cm) but it will grow to at least twice that height if left unpruned.

CÔTÉ JARDINS

syn. 'ORAPENT'

Hybrid Tea

ORIGIN **Orard, France, 2001**
PARENTAGE City of London x Penthouse
FLOWER SIZE **4.7in (12cm)**
SCENT **Light and sweet**
FLOWERING **Repeats well**
HEIGHT/SPREAD **4.1ft (1.25m)/3.3ft (1m)**
HARDINESS **Zone 6**

This large-flowered Hybrid Tea was introduced in 2001 and became one of France's best-selling roses overnight. Côté Jardins is a classically beautiful specimen rose, bred from two established champions. It has rose pink flowers with darker petal backs, which slowly unscroll their petals. Later they open out flat, but not completely, because the innermost petals tend to fold themselves over at the center: their dark pink backs contrast pleasantly with the pale pink outer petals. The flowers, usually borne singly, are good for cutting, but sometimes they come in clusters of up to five. The leaves are large, dark, and healthy and the plant is vigorous. Côté Jardins repeats well, though the best flowers are produced in warm weather.

COTTAGE ROSE

syn. 'AUSGLISTEN'

Shrub Rose

ORIGIN **Austin, Britain, 1991**
PARENTAGE **'Wife of Bath'** x Mary Rose
FLOWER SIZE **2.8in (7cm)**
SCENT **Medium and sweet**
FLOWERING **Repeats**
HEIGHT/SPREAD **3.3ft (1m)/2.7ft (80cm)**
HARDINESS **Zone 6**

The charm of Cottage Rose is its informality. The flowers are not the fullest, which makes it possible for them to open out in such a way that the petals have a ragged roll to them, like an old Damask rose. They are a good rose pink to start with, with deep, warm pink petal backs, which remain darker than the upper sides – the contrast enhances the loose arrangement of petals. Sometimes they have a rough button eye. They are borne singly and in clusters of up to five. The plant has slender stems, a lot of prickles, mid-green leaves, and an arching habit. It may pick up a little mildew and blackspot, but it is a very good shrub for a mixed border.

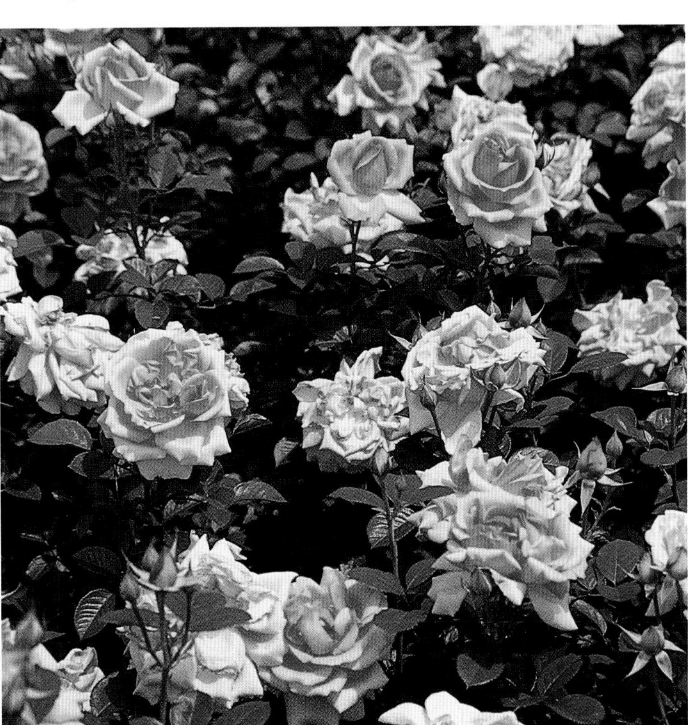

CÔTÉ JARDINS

COTTAGE ROSE

'COUNTRY DANCER'

Shrub Rose

ORIGIN **Buck, US, 1973**
PARENTAGE **'Prairie Princess' x 'Johannes Boettner'**
FLOWER SIZE **3.9in (10cm)**
SCENT **Medium and fruity**
FLOWERING **Repeats**
HEIGHT/SPREAD **4.9ft (1.5m)/3.3ft (1m)**
HARDINESS **Zone 5**

Although it is capable of reaching 4.1ft (1.25m), 'Country Dancer' is usually seen as a shrub, pruned to about 2.5ft (75cm). It is one of the most compact of the roses bred by Griffith Buck in Iowa to survive the cold winters of the American prairies. The flowers are a bright, rich pink at first, with a hint of cherry red at the center, and fading slowly to rose pink as they age. The petals have a papery quality, but are very tough and stand up well to bad weather: 'Country Dancer' does better in cool climates than hot. The flowers are good for cutting and shed their petals cleanly. The plant has large, glossy, healthy, dark leaves and makes a vigorous, bushy shrub.

'COUNTRY DANCER'

C

COUNTRY LIVING

COUNTRY LIVING

syn. 'AUSCOUNTRY'

Shrub Rose

ORIGIN **Austin, Britain, 1991**
PARENTAGE **'Wife of Bath'** x Graham Thomas
FLOWER SIZE **2.8in (7cm)**
SCENT **Light and sweet**
FLOWERING **Repeats**
HEIGHT/SPREAD **4.9ft (1.5m)/2.7ft (80cm)**
HARDINESS **Zone 6**

At its best, Country Living is one of David Austin's most beautiful roses. The flowers are rose pink, cupped and full of soft petals, fading to palest pink as they age and sometimes displaying a button eye or a few stamens. They come singly or in small clusters (rarely of more than three flowers at a time) on a small, twiggy bush with small, light green leaves and a lot of prickles. In cool climates it needs nurturing to reach 3.3ft (1m) and is somewhat prone to mildew and balling. In hot climates it grows to 6.6ft (2m) and is very narrow and upright in shape, almost fastigiate.

COUNTRYMAN

see THE COUNTRYMAN

'COUPE D'HÉBÉ'

Hybrid Bourbon

ORIGIN **Laffay, France, 1840**
FLOWER SIZE **3.1in (8cm)**
SCENT **Strong and sweet**
FLOWERING **Once only**
HEIGHT/SPREAD **8.2ft (2.5m)/4.9ft (1.5m)**
HARDINESS **Zone 5**

The flowers of 'Coupe d'Hébé' are deep pink and globular, like the old cabbage roses: the layers and layers of petals seem to circulate around the center without the slightest wave to their shape. They usually come in tight clusters of 3–5 with long stems that are good for cutting. Their scent is delicious. 'Coupe d'Hébé' flowers only once, but very profusely, and the flowers are followed by large red hips.

'COUPE D'HÉBÉ'

The plant has a vigorous, erect habit of growth, and does well even in poor soils. Its leaves are medium-pale and glossy, but they are susceptible to mildew later in the year.

'CRAMOISI SUPÉRIEUR'

China Rose

ORIGIN **Coquereau, France, 1832**
FLOWER SIZE **2in (5cm)**
SCENT **Light and tealike**
FLOWERING **Almost continuous**
HEIGHT/SPREAD **3.3ft (1m)/3.3ft (1m)**
HARDINESS **Zone 6**

'Cramoisi Supérieur' was one of the first China roses to be bred in Europe. It combines the hardiness of 'Old Blush' with the brilliant crimson of 'Slater's Crimson China'. Its flowers are bright, dark crimson, with paler petal tips and backs, and paler colors toward the center, where the petals have white flecks. The flowers are distinctively cupped, and produced in loose clusters almost continuously. The plant is a twiggy mass of small stems, mounding up to about 3.3ft (1m), but more in hot climates. The leaves are small, sparse, dark, shiny, and sensitive to blackspot, though the disease seems to have no effect on the plant's vigor or its amazing flower production. It is an extremely useful garden plant because it flowers so freely and can be relied upon to provide color almost all year-round. It is also tolerant of hot, dry climates, where it is often found thriving in old, abandoned, or neglected gardens.

A climbing form, **'Climbing Cramoisi Supérieur'**, sometimes known as 'Agrippina', was introduced in 1885 and is still a popular rose, especially in Italy. Its flowers are slightly larger than the bush form and, although not as constantly colorful, it too is never completely out of flower. Both root easily from cuttings and grow with vigor.

'CRAMOISI SUPÉRIEUR'

'CLIMBING CRAMOISI SUPÉRIEUR'

A strange mutation of 'Cramoisi Supérieur' was introduced in 1912 and named **'Serratipetala'**. Its petals are crimped, fringed, and cut in the manner of a carnation and are slightly smaller as a result, but in all other respects it resembles 'Cramoisi Supérieur' exactly. Breeders have tried to cross 'Serratipetala' with "normal" roses to produce hybrids with its distinctive shape, but always unsuccessfully. It seems that the mutation is somatic rather than genetic, since 'Serratipetala' also reverts quite readily. It is at best a curiosity.

Sports of 'Cramoisi Supérieur'

'CLIMBING CRAMOISI SUPÉRIEUR'

syn. 'AGRIPPINA'
ORIGIN **Couturier, France, 1885**
FLOWER SIZE **2.8in (7cm)**
FLOWERING **Flowers very freely**
HEIGHT/SPREAD **13.1ft (4m)/6.6ft (2m)**

'SERRATIPETALA'

ORIGIN **Vilfray, France, 1912**
FLOWER SIZE **4cm (1.6in)**

'SERRATIPETALA'

'CRAMOISI PICOTÉ'

Gallica

ORIGIN **Vibert, France, 1834**
FLOWER SIZE **2in (5cm)**
SCENT **Light and sweet**
FLOWERING **Once only**
HEIGHT/SPREAD **5.7ft (1.75m)/2.7ft (80cm)**
HARDINESS **Zone 5**

Late flowering, with small and oddly shaped flowers, 'Cramoisi Picoté' is not everyone's favorite Gallica rose. However, it has for many rose lovers a distinct charm and value. The flowers open from small, dark, red buds that look as if they have had their tops cut off. As they unfold, their petals are seen to be dark pink, with purple streaks and splotches, and an irregular crimson edge. There are many of them, and the outer petals fold back until the flowers are complete pompons, occasionally even deeper than wide. They also expose a green eye at the center. The flowers sometimes come singly but usually in clusters of 2–4. The plant has thin, upright stems and a narrow habit of growth. The small dark leaves may attract mildew and blackspot, but these never seem to do permanent damage.

CRAZY FOR YOU

see FOURTH OF JULY

'CRAMOISI PICOTÉ'

'Crépuscule'

'Crépuscule'

Noisette

ORIGIN **Dubreuil, France, 1904**
FLOWER SIZE **3.5in (9cm)**
SCENT **Strong, sweet, and musky**
FLOWERING **Almost continuous**
HEIGHT/SPREAD **8.2ft (2.5m)/4.9ft (1.5m)**
HARDINESS **Zone 7**

'Crépuscule' was one of the last Tea-Noisettes to be introduced before our ancestors' gardens were swamped by the craze for Multiflora and Wichurana ramblers. It is also one of the most beautiful of all roses. The flowers open deep rich copper or butterscotch, and usually slightly darker on the petal backs and at the center of the flower. They fade to buff and even to cream as they age, but the exact coloring depends upon conditions: it is darker in autumn, shade, cool weather, and rain, and paler in summer, sunshine, hot weather, and drought. The flowers come singly or in clusters of 3–5 and have a delicious scent. The nearly thornless plant has long, dark green leaves (crimson at first, as is the new growth) which droop attractively. It is healthy but only moderately vigorous: it can be trained either as a sprawling bush or as a slow-growing climber.

Cressida

syn. 'AUSCRESS'

Shrub Rose

ORIGIN **Austin, Britain, 1983**
PARENTAGE **'Conrad Ferdinand Meyer' x 'Chaucer'**
FLOWER SIZE **5.1in (13cm)**
SCENT **Strong, rich, and fruity**
FLOWERING **Repeats**
HEIGHT/SPREAD **4.9ft (1.5m)/3.3ft (1m)**
HARDINESS **Zone 6**

This is one of those English Roses whose published height was intended for English customers. Cressida will grow to 9.8ft (3m) or even more in hot climates and can then be trained as a bushy climber. The flowers are showy and beautiful, a rich apricot, fading to buff and almost to white at the edge of the outer petals. They are large and cupped, with sometimes a button eye and occasionally a glimpse of stamens at the center. They come singly or in clusters of up to seven on a vigorous, gawky, larger than life shrub. In autumn,

Cressida

the flowers may be borne in multiple clusters of up to 20. Cressida has large, fairly dark leaves, very thick stems, and a dense covering of ferocious prickles. It is acquainted with mildew, though nothing diminishes its vigor.

'Crested Moss'

see 'Centifolia'

Crimson Bouquet

syn. 'KORbeteilich'

Floribunda

ORIGIN **Kordes, Germany, 1999**
PARENTAGE Bad Füssing x Ingrid Bergman
FLOWER SIZE **3.5in (9cm)**
SCENT **Light and sweet**
FLOWERING **Continuous**
HEIGHT/SPREAD **3.9ft (1.2m)/3.3ft (1m)**
HARDINESS **Zone 5**
AWARDS **AARS 2000**

Crimson Bouquet is a spectacular modern red Floribunda in the great German tradition of vivid bedding roses. The flowers are bright, dark scarlet – a brilliant and bold color – with darker reverses (the buds are almost black at first). The colors fade only a little as they open out to a pretty shape with a long-lasting brush of yellow stamens at the center. The flowers come in long-stemmed clusters of 5–11. They are complemented by beautiful large, glossy foliage that is dark green when mature and red when young. The bush is too short to be classified as a Grandiflora, which is how it was introduced in the US, but it is vigorous with large prickles. It flowers abundantly, and responds well to watering and feeding in hot, dry conditions; but the flower size and petalage are improved by cool weather.

Crimson Bouquet

'Crimson Glory'

Hybrid Tea

ORIGIN **Kordes, Germany, 1935**
PARENTAGE **'Cathrine Kordes' seedling x 'W. E. Chaplin'**
FLOWER SIZE **3.9in (10cm)**
SCENT **Very strong and sweet**
FLOWERING **Repeats**
HEIGHT/SPREAD **4.1ft (1.25m)/4.1ft (1.25m)**
HARDINESS **Zone 5**
AWARDS **NRS GM 1936; Gamble FA 1961**

'Crimson Glory' probably had the longest reign as the world's favorite crimson Hybrid Tea, popular everywhere for its dark color and its amazing Damask fragrance. The flowers open from nearly black buds, shapely enough to make it popular with exhibitors. They are crimson, with darker velvety markings toward the tips of the petals, and not especially full, sometimes little more than semidouble. They hang their heads, because the flower necks are weak, but this was seen as an asset in wet countries like England, because the rain ran down the upturned petals and dripped away from the petal tips, leaving the flowers undamaged. As a plant it grows best in warm climates, reaching as much as 6.6ft (2m) and showing none of the weakness for mildew and blackspot that plagues 'Crimson Glory' in cool climates. On the other hand, the flowers tend to turn an ugly purple color in hot climates, and, although 'Crimson Glory' was widely grown and liked in the southern US, it was less popular in Italy and Spain. It is still an excellent rose, with a scent to die for. The plant is prickly and bushy,

'Crimson Glory'

'Climbing Crimson Glory'

with leaves that are nearly evergreen but rich crimson when young. The climbing sport, known as **'Climbing Crimson Glory'**, is also still popular. It is not among the most vigorous or tall-growing of climbers, but its flowers are larger than the bush form's and their pendulous habit is an advantage.

Sport of 'Crimson Glory'

'Climbing Crimson Glory'

Climbing Hybrid Tea
ORIGIN **Millar, US, 1941**
FLOWERING **Once spectacularly, then intermittently**
HEIGHT/SPREAD **2.5m (8.2ft)/1.5m (4.9ft)**

Crimson Meidiland

syn. 'MEIouscki', 'Crimson Meillandécor'

Shrub Rose

ORIGIN **Meilland, France, 1996**
FLOWER SIZE **2.8in (7cm)**
SCENT **Little or none**
FLOWERING **Repeats constantly**
HEIGHT/SPREAD **4.9ft (1.5m)/4.1ft (1.25m)**
HARDINESS **Zone 6**
AWARDS **ADR 1996**

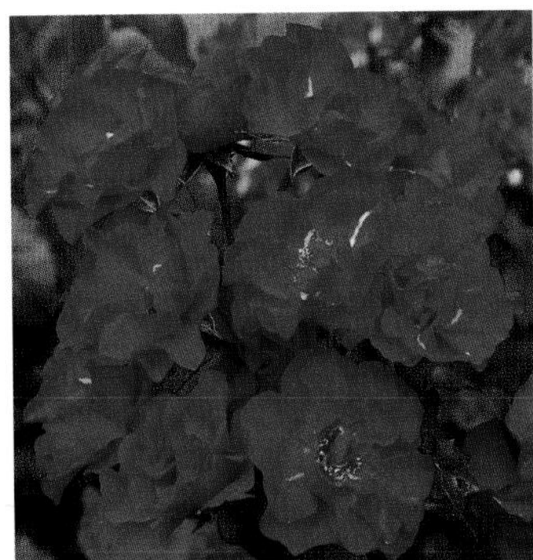
Crimson Meidiland

This member of the Meidiland series is not crimson, but bright scarlet, with occasional white flecks at the base of some of the petals. The Meidiland roses are bred for health, ease of cultivation, and hardiness: Crimson Meidiland is a magnificent rose for mass plantings and landscaping, provided its brilliant red color fits in well. It also makes a good subject for small gardens or containers. The flowers are semidouble, roughly cupped, and stand up well to rain or sun. They come singly or in clusters of up to about five. The dark, glossy leaves are exceptionally healthy, and the plant is vigorous and hardy. Its first flowering is prolific, and is followed until late autumn by repeat flowerings, with usually a few flowers in between the flushes.

'Crimson Meillandécor'

see Crimson Meidiland

'Crimson Rambler'

see 'Turner's Crimson Rambler'

C

'CRIMSON SHOWER'

'CRIMSON SHOWER'

Wichurana Rambler

ORIGIN **Norman, Britain, 1951**
PARENTAGE **'Excelsa' x unknown**
FLOWER SIZE **1.2in (3cm)**
SCENT **Light**
FLOWERING **Once only, late in season**
HEIGHT/SPREAD **11.5ft (3.5m)/4.9ft (1.5m)**
HARDINESS **Zone 6**

'Crimson Shower' was bred by an English amateur named Albert Norman, a retired London diamond cutter who had the good fortune to breed two excellent Bush roses – 'Ena Harkness' and 'Frensham'. It is, however, not much of an improvement on the ramblers that were bred in the 1900s and 1910s. The flowers are a good bright crimson, with slightly paler petal backs, and borne in long, loose clusters of 20–60. They last a long time both on the bush and as cut flowers. The plant is useful in cool climates because it flowers very late, as indeed does its parent 'Excelsa'. The leaves are small, dark, and glossy – a good foil to the crimson flowers. It makes a good weeping standard.

'CRISTATA'

see 'CENTIFOLIA'

'CRITÉRION'

Hybrid Tea

ORIGIN **de Ruiter, Netherlands, 1966**
PARENTAGE **'Kordes' Sondermeldung' x 'Signal Red'**
FLOWER SIZE **4.7in (12cm)**
SCENT **Strong and sweet**
FLOWERING **Repeats**
HEIGHT/SPREAD **4.9ft (1.5m)/3.3ft (1m)**
HARDINESS **Zone 6**

Pale crimson or cerise, the flowers of 'Critérion' are a rich, unfading color. They have broad petals and are held erect on long, strong stems. Their buds are elegant but open quickly. The flowers are still pretty when they are fully expanded and display a muddled arrangement of petals at the center. They are almost always carried singly – just occasionally in twos or threes. 'Critérion' has a vigorous, branching habit of growth and good, large, healthy, medium-dark leaves. Blackspot may make an appearance later in the season. 'Critérion' is a good repeater, almost continuously in flower. It is especially popular in France, where a climbing form is also sold and grown.

'CRITÉRION'

CROWN PRINCESS MARGARETA

syn. 'AUSWINTER'

Shrub Rose

ORIGIN **Austin, Britain, 1999**
FLOWER SIZE **4.3in (11cm)**
SCENT **Strong and fruity**
FLOWERING **Repeats well**
HEIGHT/SPREAD **5.7ft (1.75m)/4.9ft (1.5m)**
HARDINESS **Zone 6**

It is sometimes said that David Austin's latest English Roses are very like his earlier ones. Crown Princess Margareta, however, shows how consistent has been the steady improvement in quality that Austin has set out to achieve. It is a magnificent rose, and fully deserves the instant popularity it has enjoyed. The flowers are large and completely full of quilled and folded petals splayed out around the half-hidden yellow stamens at the center. Their color is variable: apricot at the center and golden yellow at the edges in hot weather, but richer and more coppery in cool. Whatever the weather, the effect is exquisite. The flowers are borne singly and in clusters of up to four on a tall, vigorous, arching shrub with a dense structure and a lot of dark, healthy leaves. It is no more than bushy in cool climates but can be trained as a pillar rose elsewhere. The rose was named after Princess Margaret of Connaught (1882–1920), Queen Victoria's granddaughter.

CROWN PRINCESS MARGARETA

CRYSTAL PALACE

syn. 'POULREK'

Patio Rose

ORIGIN **Olesen, Denmark, 1995**
FLOWER SIZE **2.4in (6cm)**
SCENT **Light and fruity**
FLOWERING **Repeats well**
HEIGHT/SPREAD **2.7ft (80cm)/2.7ft (80cm)**
HARDINESS **Zone 5**

It is no wonder that Crystal Palace quickly proved so popular: its flowers are exquisitely formed and colored, and the bush is neat, small, and vigorous. It can be considered either as a small Floribunda or as a patio rose. It also grows well in containers. The flowers, however, are full of little petals neatly arranged in an old-fashioned imbricated shape. The overall impression they give is of buff pink, but closer examination reveals that the petals are creamy white on their upper sides and pale peach pink on their backs. They come singly or, more often, in small clusters (typically of 3–5 flowers) in a series of flushes until late autumn, with usually a few flowers in between. The leaves of Crystal Palace are mid-green, glossy, and healthy, and the plant has a neat, bushy habit. In hot climates, if left unpruned, it will reach 4.9ft (1.5m).

CRYSTAL PALACE

CRYSTALLINE

syn. 'AROBIPY', Valerie Swane

Hybrid Tea

ORIGIN **Christensen-Carruth, US, 1987**
PARENTAGE **'Deep Purple' x ('Ivory Tower' x 'Angel Face')**
FLOWER SIZE **5.1in (13cm)**
SCENT **Light, sweet, and fruity**
FLOWERING **Repeats constantly**
HEIGHT/SPREAD **4.9ft (1.5m)/4.1ft (1.25m)**
HARDINESS **Zone 6**

Here is one of the most successful white roses for hot, dry climates. Crystalline is a consistent show winner and an excellent garden rose. The flowers are supremely elegant as the buds unfurl and their long petals curve back from a perfect cone. They are pure white, except for a hint of green at the base of the outer petals and perhaps a suggestion of pink on the petal edges. The flowers clusters come in twos and threes, at the end of a long, strong stem. In the garden, Crystalline may produce clusters with as many as 7–15 flowers, so that the heavy stems then need support. If not deadheaded, the flowers are followed by large vermilion hips. The plant has healthy, pale green leaves, very prickly stems, and a vigorous, upright habit.

'CUISSE DE NYMPHE EMUE'

see 'GREAT MAIDEN'S BLUSH'

CRYSTALLINE

Cumbaya

Cumbaya

syn. 'MEIzabo'

Ground Cover

ORIGIN **Meilland, France, 2000**
PARENTAGE **(Fiona x Sommerwind) x Smarty**
FLOWER SIZE **1.2in (3cm)**
SCENT **Light and musky**
FLOWERING **Repeats well**
HEIGHT/SPREAD **2.7ft (80cm)/3.3ft (1m)**
HARDINESS **Zone 6**

Meilland describes Cumbaya as a rose for rock gardens, but it is a good plant in any type of garden, and useful in containers too. Its flowers are single and very simple: dark pink or pale crimson, fading to pink, and with a pure white eye. The petal backs are also white. Sometimes the petals are slightly crimped, but usually the flower is a cheerful, open saucer of color. The flowers come in clusters of 3–7. Cumbaya is a low, neat, compact plant, with small, medium-dark Wichurana leaves. It is very healthy and very floriferous, carrying its flowers almost without interruption until late into autumn. The sheer quantity and flower power of its first flowering is quite exceptional.

Cupcake

syn. SPIcup

Miniature Rose

ORIGIN **Spies, US, 1981**
PARENTAGE **'Gene Boerner' x ('Gay Princess' x 'Yellow Jewel')**
FLOWER SIZE **1.4in (3.5cm)**
SCENT **Light and sweet**
FLOWERING **Repeats**
HEIGHT/SPREAD **1.3ft (40cm)/11.8in (30cm)**
HARDINESS **Zone 5**
AWARDS **AoE 1981**

Cupcake

This vigorous miniature rose is an all-American speciality, rarely seen elsewhere. The flowers of Cupcake are a very beautiful, clear, fresh pink – darker in cool weather and paler in hot. They have a lot of tiny, neat, imbricated petals. The outer ones are longer than the inner, and they fade slightly (and attractively) as the flowers age. The flowers come singly or in small clusters and last a long time on the bush. The plant repeats fairly quickly, so that the display is almost continuous. Cupcake has a lot of healthy, glossy, gray green leaves and a neat, rounded, compact habit. It tolerates both heat and cold, and is often recommended for containers, where it can be studied and appreciated more easily than in a mixed planting.

'Cupid'

Modern Climber

ORIGIN **Cant, Britain, 1915**
FLOWER SIZE **4.7in (12cm)**
SCENT **Light and sweet**
FLOWERING **Once only**
HEIGHT/SPREAD **16.4ft (5m)/9.8ft (3m)**
HARDINESS **Zone 6**

Many of the Hybrid Tea type climbers bred in the early years of the 20th century were once-flowering. 'Cupid' is typical, though its flowers are followed by unusually large, orange, pear-shaped hips that last well into winter. The flowers are large, almost single, and very beautiful when they open pale apricot, with crinkly petals, though they fade quickly to shell pink and white. They come in small, long-stemmed clusters (typically of 3–5 flowers) and are prettily set off by their pale stamens. The plant is vigorous, prickly, gawky, and somewhat susceptible to late spring frosts. On the other hand, the flowers keep their colors best in cool climates. It remains popular in England.

'Cupid'

'Cuthbert Grant'

'Cuthbert Grant'

Arkansana Hybrid

ORIGIN **Marshall, US, 1967**
PARENTAGE **('Crimson Glory' x 'Assiniboine') x 'Assiniboine'**
FLOWER SIZE **3.1in (8cm)**
SCENT **Moderate**
FLOWERING **Repeats after a pause**
HEIGHT/SPREAD **4.9ft (1.5m)/3.9ft (1.2m)**
HARDINESS **Zone 4**

This is one of the best and most distinctive of the Explorer roses bred by Henry Marshall at the Department of Agriculture at Ottawa to withstand the cold winters of the Canadian prairies. The bush owes its hardiness to 'Assiniboine' – a cross between the early Floribunda 'Donald Prior' and the native Arctic rose *R. arkansana* – and its color comes from the famous crimson Hybrid Tea 'Crimson Glory'. The flowers of 'Cuthbert Grant' are a wonderful deep reddish purple, beautifully set off by the pale glaucous green leaves. They are cupped in shape and borne in clusters of 3–9 on long, slender pedicels. They arch out from the center of the cluster, and their delicacy contrasts with the thick, stiff, and vigorous stems on which they grow. The plant is one of the first to bloom, and then has a long rest before producing a splendid second flowering in the autumn, when the flowers are more purple and less crimson. It is very resistant to blackspot, powdery mildew, and rust. In hot climates – for which it was most certainly not intended – it will shoot up to 8.2ft (2.5m).

Cymbeline

syn. 'AUSlean'

Shrub Rose

ORIGIN **Austin, Britain, 1982**
PARENTAGE **seedling x 'Lilian Austin'**
FLOWER SIZE **3.1in (8cm)**
SCENT **Strong and fruity**
FLOWERING **Repeats**
HEIGHT/SPREAD **4.1ft (1.25m)/4.9ft (1.5m)**
HARDINESS **Zone 5**

Cymbeline is popular for its unusual color: the flowers are a pale gray pink, with hints of buff at the center and nearly white edges. They open out to display a mass of small petals, which get darker and smaller toward the center of the flower. They come in loose, nodding clusters of 3–7. The plant produces a lot of dark green, healthy foliage and reddish new growth. It is a vigorous grower, broader than it is tall, with long, arching shoots that will reach nearly 6.6ft (2m) in hot climates and flower at the tips. If pegged down, or grown as a hedge, it flowers along the length of these shoots. It is, in any event, a good repeat flowerer, and especially pretty when trained up a pillar.

Cymbeline

'D'AGUESSEAU'

Gallica

ORIGIN **Vibert, France, 1836**
FLOWER SIZE **2.8in (7cm)**
SCENT **Light and sweet**
FLOWERING **Once only**
HEIGHT/SPREAD **4.1ft (1.25m)/3.3ft (1m)**
HARDINESS **Zone 5**

There is something of a mystery surrounding the name and origin of 'd'Aguesseau'. It may have been bred by Parmentier, and only introduced by Vibert, but the d'Aguesseau family were not prominent in the 1830s, their best-known member being a judge who died in 1751. The rose is small for a Gallica, and bright rich crimson in color – paler at the center, and more purple at the edges, with dark pink petal backs. It is full of petals, usually gathered up into a coarse button eye around a small green style. The flowers come singly or in clusters of up to four and are well set off by the mid-green, wrinkly leaves. The plant is fairly healthy and easy to grow, but it is perhaps not among the top rank of Gallicas.

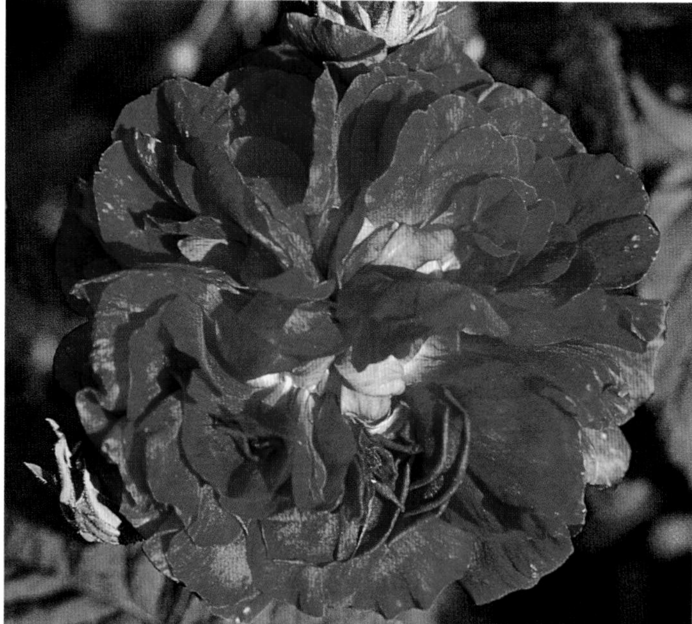

'D'AGUESSEAU'

'DAINTY BESS'

Hybrid Tea

ORIGIN **Archer, Britain, 1925**
PARENTAGE **'Ophelia' × 'Kitchener of Khartoum'**
FLOWER SIZE **4.3in (11cm)**
SCENT **Light and fruity**
FLOWERING **Repeats well**
HEIGHT/SPREAD **3.3ft (1m)/3.3ft (1m)**
HARDINESS **Zone 5**
AWARDS **NRS GM 1925**

Rose breeders will tell you that they get any number of seedlings like 'Dainty Bess' and that none is worth keeping: all the more surprising, therefore, is the continuing popularity of this beautiful single-flowered Hybrid Tea. It is pale pink, an unremarkable color in a rose, with slightly darker petal backs. The petals are long, strong, broad, and wavy, but it is the purple filaments that give 'Dainty Bess' its distinctive character and charm. Without their color and pattern of growth, the flower would indeed be worthless. As it is, the stamens transform the flower into a thing of great beauty. The flowers come on long stems in airy clusters of 3–5, followed by large red hips. The plant has dull leaves, prickly stems, and an occasional weakness for blackspot. It is a thrifty, unfussy grower and an almost continuous bloomer.

Van Barneveld introduced a climbing form in 1935. It is exactly the same as the bush form but grows eventually to 9.8ft (3m). **'Climbing Dainty Bess'** flowers prolifically at the start of the rose season, and intermittently thereafter.

'DAINTY BESS'

'CLIMBING DAINTY BESS'

Sport of 'Dainty Bess'

'CLIMBING DAINTY BESS'

Climbing Hybrid Tea
ORIGIN **Van Barneveld, US, 1935**
FLOWERING **Repeats**
HEIGHT/SPREAD **9.8ft (3m)/6.6ft (2m)**

'DAINTY MAID'

Floribunda

ORIGIN **Le Grice, Britain, 1940**
PARENTAGE **'D. T. Poulsen' seedling**
FLOWER SIZE **2.4in (6cm)**
SCENT **Light, sweet, and musky**
FLOWERING **Repeats well**
HEIGHT/SPREAD **4.1ft (1.25m)/3.3ft (1m)**
HARDINESS **Zone 5**
AWARDS **Portland GM 1941**

This classic early Floribunda has outlived almost all its contemporaries. It was considered a great improvement upon the Poulsen Floribundas at the time because its flowers do not spot and blotch in the rain. They were also free from mildew and blackspot. The flowers open from coral red buds and are nearly single – pale pink, at first, with a pale yellow patch toward the center, around the large ring of stamens. They fade fairly quickly but the backs of the petals are darkest pink, even carmine, and keep their color well. They come in spacious clusters of 5–15 flowers and are supported by dark, healthy leaves. 'Dainty Maid' flowers especially well in autumn.

'DAINTY MAID'

'DAISY HILL'

'DAISY HILL'

Shrub Rose

ORIGIN **Daisy Hill Nursery, Ireland, c.1906**
FLOWER SIZE **2.8in (7cm)**
SCENT **Light and sweet**
FLOWERING **Once only**
HEIGHT/SPREAD **6.6ft (2m)/6.6ft (2m)**
HARDINESS **Zone 5**

Little is known of the origins of 'Daisy Hill', except that it was introduced by the Daisy Hill Nursery near Newry in Ireland, which introduced two other famous foundlings: 'Rambling Rector' and 'Narrow Water'. It resembles 'Macrantha' but is slightly larger and has a few more petals. Wilhelm Kordes uses it to breed his Canina hybrids. It shares the lax, vigorous, scandent, or scrambling habit of 'Macrantha', and produces its beautiful rose pink flowers (with silvery backs) in small, spacious clusters of up to seven. They are followed by vermilion red hips, reminiscent of a dog-rose's. The leaves are thin, medium-dark, and last well into winter. But it is the peerless beauty of the flower that most recommends it.

ROSA DAMASCENA 'VERSICOLOR'

see 'YORK AND LANCASTER'

'DAME DE COEUR'

syn. 'QUEEN OF HEARTS'
Hybrid Tea

ORIGIN **Lens, Belgium, 1958**
PARENTAGE **'Mme. A. Meilland' × 'Kordes' Sondermeldung'**
FLOWER SIZE **4.7in (12cm)**
SCENT **Light and sweet**
FLOWERING **Repeats well**
HEIGHT/SPREAD **4.1ft (1.25m)/3.3ft (1m)**
HARDINESS **Zone 6**

This classic 1950s Hybrid Tea is still very widely grown in western Europe. 'Dame de Coeur' has large, pale crimson or cherry red flowers, which keep their color well and fade only slightly with age. They are borne usually singly but occasionally in clusters of up to four flowers, on long, strong stems which make them good for cutting (they last well, too). The plant has ordinary, medium-dark, semiglossy leaves but is vigorous, sturdy, upright,

'Dame de Coeur'

and healthy. It is a good and reliable repeater. It is also a good garden plant which mixes well with other roses and herbaceous plants.

'Dame Edith Helen'

Hybrid Tea

ORIGIN **Dickson, Northern Ireland, 1926**
PARENTAGE **'Mrs. John Laing' seedling**
FLOWER SIZE **5.1in (13cm)**
SCENT **Very strong and sweet**
FLOWERING **Repeats**
HEIGHT/SPREAD **4.9ft (1.5m)/3.3ft (1m)**
HARDINESS **Zone 6**

This classic Hybrid Tea has been a firm favorite with exhibitors ever since it was introduced. It grows best as a garden plant in hot climates, where its many layers of petals can unfold slowly, though the flowers will also tolerate a certain amount of rain. The flowers are a rich pink, very full and perfectly shaped. They are borne singly on stout, upright stems and last a long time, both as cut flowers and in the garden. The scent is delicious. The bush is strong and vigorous, with a lot of prickles and leaves, which are healthy except for an occasional brush with mildew. It is not the quickest of roses to flower again, but will provide crop after crop of flowers in areas where there is a long growing season. Dame Edith Helen (1879–1959) was the formidable Marchioness of Londonderry who created the gardens at Mount Stewart in Northern Ireland.

'Dame Edith Helen'

'Dame Prudence'

'Dame Prudence'

Shrub Rose

ORIGIN **Austin, Britain, 1969**
PARENTAGE **'Ivory Fashion' x ('Constance Spry' x 'Ma Perkins')**
FLOWER SIZE **3.9in (10cm)**
SCENT **Medium and sweet**
FLOWERING **Repeats**
HEIGHT/SPREAD **2.7ft (80cm)/2ft (60cm)**
HARDINESS **Zone 6**

This early hybrid is no longer offered by David Austin, but 'Dame Prudence' is still quite widely sold and grown. Its flowers are soft, pale pink, with nearly white petal backs and deeper apricot pink shadows toward the center. It is only loosely double, and may lack shape, although it opens out to show its stamens nicely in warm weather. The petals are ruffled but somewhat fragile, and may be damaged by wind and rain. The plant is not very vigorous, with short, twiggy stems, but will respond to heat by reaching 4.9ft (1.5m) in countries such as Australia, where it is widely grown. The leaves are small, mid-green, and may be susceptible to blackspot in areas where this is a problem.

'Danaë'

'Danaë'

Hybrid Musk

ORIGIN **Pemberton, Britain, 1913**
PARENTAGE **'Trier' x 'Gloire de Chédane-Guinoiseau'**
FLOWER SIZE **2.4in (6cm)**
SCENT **Strong, musky, and fruity**
FLOWERING **Repeats well**
HEIGHT/SPREAD **5.7ft (1.75m)/4.1ft (1.25m)**
HARDINESS **Zone 6**

It is not the best of the Pemberton Hybrid Musks, but 'Danaë' has many virtues – health, fragrance, and floriferousness. The buds are deep apricot at first, but change to buff yellow as they open out. In hot climates, the flowers then fade very quickly to white as they expand: they keep their color longer in cool climates and under overcast skies. They have a distinctive wave to their petals, which accounts for much of their charm and character. The flowers come in clusters of 10–20 at first, but up to 50 later in the year – the plant repeats constantly, so that it is rarely completely out of flower. It has slender stems and glossy, dark leaves, which sometimes show a little susceptibility to mildew. In hot climates it can be trained as a 16.4ft (5m) climber.

'Danse des Sylphes'

Modern Climber

ORIGIN **Mallerin, France, 1959**
PARENTAGE **'Danse du Feu' x 'Toujours'**
FLOWER SIZE **2.4in (6cm)**
SCENT **Little or none**
FLOWERING **Repeats quite well**
HEIGHT/SPREAD **9.8ft (3m)/6.6ft (2m)**
HARDINESS **Zone 5**

Brightly colored Floribundas were the fashion in the 1950s: 'Danse des Sylphes' was their climbing equivalent, and a commercial success right from the start. The flowers open out fully double, with a shapely, rounded outline. They are a rich red color, with brighter, scarlet markings toward the center of the flower. They come in small clusters, typically 3–5 in a bunch, but often singly, especially later in the year. The first flowering is spectacular – a brilliant display of the brightest hues – and is followed by lesser flushes through until autumn. The plant is vigorous, with its fair share of thorns and glossy, healthy leaves. Cheerful, rather than sophisticated.

'Danse des Sylphes'

'DANSE DU FEU'

'DANSE DU FEU'

syn. 'SPECTACULAR'

Modern Climber

ORIGIN **Mallerin, France, 1953**
PARENTAGE **'Paul's Scarlet Climber' x *Rosa multiflora* seedling**
FLOWER SIZE **2.8in (7cm)**
SCENT **Light**
FLOWERING **Once abundantly, then intermittently**
HEIGHT/SPREAD **9.8ft (3m)/6.6ft (2m)**
HARDINESS **Zone 5**

Hardiness, nonstop flowering, and a real color break at the time – 'Danse du Feu' has always been popular. Its vermilion color is so bright that it was renamed 'Spectacular' in North America. The flowers eventually fade to red, but they also have occasional streaks of white on the inmost petals. They open out semidouble, and come in small clusters (typically of 5–7 flowers) in great profusion during the long first flowering and then intermittently right through until autumn. The plant is vigorous, with large prickles and large, shiny, dark green leaves, bronzy when young. It is still a good choice for a bright red climber.

DAPPLE DAWN

see 'RED COAT'

'DAVID THOMPSON'

Rugosa Hybrid

ORIGIN **Svejda, Canada, 1979**
PARENTAGE **'Schneezwerg' x 'Fru Dagmar Hastrup'**
FLOWER SIZE **2.8in (7cm)**
SCENT **Strong and sweet**
FLOWERING **Repeats well**
HEIGHT/SPREAD **6.6ft (2m)/4.9ft (1.5m)**
HARDINESS **Zone 3**

'David Thompson' was bred to withstand a Canadian winter, as did the English-born geographer and explorer (1770–1857), whose achievements it commemorates. It is very much a Rugosa hybrid, with the prickly stems and wrinkled leaves of the species, as well as its tendency to go on flowering throughout the growing season. The flowers are purple pink, with white flashes and pale anthers. They open so that they are lightly cupped but still fairly double, with petals pressed together around the edges. The flowers come in short-stalked clusters of 3–7. It is not an exciting rose, but its hardiness makes it extremely valuable in the coldest areas of the rose-growing world. It grows to about 6.6ft (2m) in warm climates, but to no more than half that in cold areas, with a well-rounded shape. The leaves have a tendency for the leaflets to brown at the edges, but they are very resistant to blackspot and mildew.

ROSA DAVIDII

ROSA DAVIDII

Wild Rose

FLOWER SIZE **1.6in (4cm)**
SCENT **Light and sweet**
FLOWERING **Once, somewhat late in season**
HEIGHT/SPREAD **6.6ft (2m)/4.9ft (1.5m)**
HARDINESS **Zone 5**

This wild rose from China is one of the best species to grow. It is handsome both in flower and in fruit, and makes a fine show in the woodland or wild garden. The flowers are rose pink, usually with a patch of white and a ring of golden stamens at the center, although, like all wild roses, it is variable both in nature and in cultivation. The flowers come in loose corymbs, and each petal is subtended by long sepals, which frame the flower and make it seem larger. The sepals have a resinous smell if you rub them. The plant has pleasant leaves with narrow leaflets, but its best feature is its hips, which are flagon-shaped, scarlet, and pendulous, borne all along the main branches.

DAWN CHORUS

syn. 'DICQUASAR'

Hybrid Tea

ORIGIN **Dickson, Northern Ireland, 1991**
PARENTAGE **Wishing x 'Peer Gynt'**
FLOWER SIZE **3.1in (8cm)**
SCENT **Medium and fruity**
FLOWERING **Repeats constantly**
HEIGHT/SPREAD **2.7ft (80cm)/2ft (60cm)**
HARDINESS **Zone 6**
AWARDS **Dublin GM 1991; ROTY 1993**

'DAVID THOMPSON'

DAWN CHORUS

The floriferousness of Dawn Chorus is remarkable: it seems miraculous that such a small plant can produce so many large flowers. Although classed as a Hybrid Tea, its flowers also come in clusters of up to five. They are vivid orange, with yellow backs and bases to the petals. Eventually they fade to a mixture of pink, cream, and pale yellow. The flowers have short stems, so they are of little value as cut flowers, but Dawn Chorus is a splendid, short-growing bedding rose. It has small, dark, glossy leaves with a reddish tint when young. The plant is compact, fairly prickly, and very healthy, except for a little blackspot sometimes in autumn.

'DAYBREAK'

Hybrid Musk

ORIGIN **Pemberton, Britain, 1918**
PARENTAGE **'Trier' x 'Liberty'**
FLOWER SIZE **2in (5cm)**
SCENT **Medium, sweet, and musky**
FLOWERING **Repeats well**
HEIGHT/SPREAD **4.9ft (1.5m)/4.1ft (1.25m)**
HARDINESS **Zone 6**

Not all the Pemberton Musk roses are equally good: some owe their survival to the group's reputation rather than their own merits. Many would say that 'Daybreak' is among them – a popular rose, but not of outstanding worth. The semidouble flowers are pale yellow at first, but quickly fade to cream and white. They open out to reveal a small cluster of long, wispy stamens. The leaves are dark and handsome, and bronzy when young – a pretty foil for any rose. The plant is vigorous, neat, and bushy. 'Daybreak' is pleasant, but unexceptional – but the scent of its flowers is that true, rich mixture of musk and sweetness that is one of the best among all roses.

'DAYBREAK'

'DAYDREAM'

'DAYDREAM'

Modern Climber

ORIGIN **Clark, Australia, 1924**
PARENTAGE **'Souvenir de Gustave Prat' x 'Rosy Morn'**
FLOWER SIZE **4.3in (11cm)**
SCENT **Light**
FLOWERING **Repeat flowering**
HEIGHT/SPREAD **9.8ft (3m)/6.6ft (2m)**
HARDINESS **Zone 6**

'Daydream' is a handsome and sweetly scented climbing rose, bred for the Australian market but hardy in much colder climates. Its flowers are mother-of-pearl pink, but slightly darker toward the center, though the petals have flushes of rose pink on their upper sides even when faded. The flowers show a handsome circle of reddish gold stamens at first, and quite resemble a semidouble peony before the stamens turn brown. They are sometimes borne singly, but usually in clusters of 3–5 flowers. The plant grows bushily and flowers intermittently after its first profuse blossoming. Pruned hard, it makes a good shrub.

'DE LA GRIFFERAIE'

Hybrid Gallica

ORIGIN **Vibert, France, 1845**
FLOWER SIZE **3.1in (8cm)**
SCENT **Medium and sweet**
FLOWERING **Once, midseason**
HEIGHT/SPREAD **9.8ft (3m)/6.6ft (2m)**
HARDINESS **Zone 5**

'De la Grifferaie' was probably bred from *Rosa multiflora* 'Platyphylla' and a Gallica rose – which makes it an unusual and experimental hybrid. It was widely used as a rootstock in the 19th century, and is still often found as a garden relic. It roots extremely easily from cuttings. The flowers open deep cherry pink and fade slowly through shades of pink and lilac almost to white. The coloring and the way it fades are uneven, so that parts of an individual flower may be darker or paler than others, and sometimes the petals have paler stripes on them too. The flowers are full, round, and flat, like a Gallica, and borne in airy clusters of 5–15. The lanky plant has almost thornless stems and large, round, rugose leaflets. It can hold its own with the best of the old garden roses. It takes its name from a domaine near Vibert's nursery in the Loire valley.

'DE LA MAÎTRE D'ECOLE'

'DE LA MAÎTRE D'ECOLE'

syn. 'DU MAÎTRE D'ECOLE'

Gallica

ORIGIN **Coquereau, France, 1831**
FLOWER SIZE **4.7in (12cm)**
SCENT **Strong and sweet**
FLOWERING **Once only**
HEIGHT/SPREAD **3.3ft (1m)/3.3ft (1m)**
HARDINESS **Zone 5**

Many experts call this sumptuous Gallica rose 'du Maître d'Ecole', but the correct name is 'de la Maître d'Ecole'. It was raised by an amateur who lived at La Maître d'Ecole in Angers. It has some of the largest and most beautiful flowers of all roses, each of them quartered around a small green carpel. The flowers are crimson purple at first, but reflex and fade over several days through dark pink, lilac, and Parma violet, almost to gray at the edges, so that a fully mature flower presents a stunning contrast between the ash mauve edges and the rich purple center. The petals are folded, tucked, and quilled as they swirl around the center of the flower, sometimes forming a button eye when the silvery pink of the petals' undersides is revealed. The flowers come singly or in clusters of up to four. The plant has large, healthy, bright, pale green leaves, a few tiny prickles, and an upright habit of growth until bent over by the weight of the flowers.

'DE LA GRIFFERAIE'

'DE MONTARVILLE'

'DE MONTARVILLE'

Kordesii Hybrid

ORIGIN **Agriculture Canada, Canada, 1998**
PARENTAGE **('Queen Elizabeth' x 'Arthur Bell') x ('Kordesii' seedling x ['Joanna Hill' x 'Altaica'])**
FLOWER SIZE **2.8in (7cm)**
SCENT **Light and fruity**
FLOWERING **Repeats well**
HEIGHT/SPREAD **3.3ft (1m)/3.3ft (1m)**
HARDINESS **Zone 4**

Recent Explorer roses, such as 'De Montarville', from Agriculture Canada's Research Station at Morden in Manitoba, are an improvement on the older ones. The new cultivars are more resistant to disease and they flower for much longer periods. 'De Montarville' has crimson buds and dark pink flowers with substantial petals that stand up well to rain. They open out flat and imbricated like a camellia, with paler inner petals and a circle of stamens at the center. They are borne usually singly, sometimes in small clusters, fairly constantly until the first frost. The plant has small, dark, healthy leaves, a few prickles, and a compact, bushy habit of growth. In warm climates, it will grow to 6.6ft (2m). The de Montarville family were French landowners in Quebec.

'DEAREST'

Floribunda

ORIGIN **Dickson, Northern Ireland, 1960**
PARENTAGE **seedling x 'Spartan'**
FLOWER SIZE **2.8in (7cm)**
SCENT **Medium and sweet**
FLOWERING **Repeats well**
HEIGHT/SPREAD **2.7ft (80cm)/2ft (60cm)**
HARDINESS **Zone 5**

Although introduced as long ago as 1960, 'Dearest' remains popular in Britain and Australia. It is almost unknown in North America, which is a shame, because it is a fine, short-growing Floribunda. Its flowers open bright salmon pink and fade to a duller pinker shade with a white patch toward the center. They are fully double, but this is not obvious because the petals lie flat around a tuft of golden stamens. They come in large clusters and repeat well – the plant throws out a series of flushes right through until late autumn. 'Dearest' has dark, glossy leaves and is fairly vigorous. In hot climates it will reach 4.9ft (1.5m). Its flowers spoil in rain.

'DEAREST'

D

DÉBORAH

DÉBORAH

syn. 'MEINOIRAL', Play Rose

Patio Rose

ORIGIN **Mouchotte, France, 1988**
PARENTAGE **Anne de Bretagne x ('Prairie Princess' x 'Playboy')**
FLOWER SIZE **2.4in (6cm)**
SCENT **Slight**
FLOWERING **Almost continuous**
HEIGHT/SPREAD **2.7ft (80cm)/2ft (60cm)**
HARDINESS **Zone 6**
AWARDS **ADR 1989**

Déborah – now better known as Play Rose – has very pretty semidouble, pink flowers with an open shape almost like a wild rose, and wavy petals. They come in tightly bunched clusters but have the great asset of dropping their petals cleanly. They are also resistant to rain damage and are followed by bright orange hips. The plant has dark, glossy leaves and is very useful for poor soils and partly shaded positions. Déborah occasionally gets a little mildew.

DEBUT

see DOUCE SYMPHONIE

'DEBUTANTE'

Wichurana Rambler

ORIGIN **Walsh, US, 1902**
PARENTAGE **'Turner's Crimson Rambler' seedling**
FLOWER SIZE **1.6in (4cm)**
SCENT **Light and musky**
FLOWERING **Once only**
HEIGHT/SPREAD **16.4ft (5m)/9.8ft (3m)**
HARDINESS **Zone 5**

'DEBUTANTE' *(with purple 'Bleu Magenta' at Mottisfont Abbey, England)*

Many Wichurana ramblers with small, pink flowers were introduced in the early years of the 20th century: 'Debutante' is one of the best. Its flowers are a beautiful clear pink at first, and fade to creamy pink with just a hint of lilac in hot weather. They are profusely borne in loose clusters (typically of 5–10 flowers) so that the whole plant seems to cascade with prettiness. The flowers are cupped and fully double, but eventually open out to a rosette. Then the outer petals start to fold back so that the full-blown flower forms an irregular ball of reflexed petals. They are produced midseason on a vigorous, slender plant that grows quickly but does not repeat. The stems are flexible and the leaves are neat, dark and glossy in the Wichurana manner. There is a famous planting of 'Debutante' at Mottisfont Abbey in England, where it graces a circular trellis alternating with 'Bleu Magenta'.

GEORGES DELBARD

AS WELL KNOWN FOR INTRODUCING NEW VARIETIES OF FRUIT AS FOR HIS ROSES, DELBARD SINGLE-HANDEDLY BUILT UP ONE OF THE LARGEST NURSERIES IN EUROPE

THE FAMOUS NURSERY established by Georges Delbard (1906–99) is still based in his native village of Malicorne, in the remote Allier department of France. Roses were only one of his interests: his greatest impact was as a breeder of new varieties of fruit, especially apples, pears, and cherries.

GEORGES DELBARD

The most spectacular of Delbard's early rose hybrids was 'Centenaire de Lourdes' (1958). He also introduced a series of fine modern climbing roses, which are healthy and repeat well: 'Altissimo' (1966) and 'Obélisque' (1967) are early examples. Later climbers include 'Blanche Colombe' and his masterpiece 'Papi Delbard', both introduced in 1995.

The Delbard nursery has developed several lines in recent years: the Sauvageonne, or "wild-style," roses, including 'Pur Caprice' and 'Pimprenelle'; the Souvenir of Love roses, which are scented and evocative, like 'Chartreuse de Parme'; the race of striped "Roses des Peintres," or Painters' roses, which includes such excellent roses as 'Henri Matisse' (1995) and 'Camille Pisarro' (1996); classic bedding roses with strong colors, like 'Fêtes Galantes' (1994) and 'Jardins de Villandry' (1995); and landscaping roses of supreme floriferousness, including 'Bordure Blanc' (1997). Delbard also has a stake in the burgeoning floristry market, for roses as cut flowers.

The Delbard family are innovative breeders and we can expect some distinct and original developments in years to come. Their policy is to select a new seedling first for its color and shape – the plants may not be suitable for introduction but they may display genetic possibilities for further development – and then, only later, assess them for their habit and health.

The display garden at Malicorne is a showcase for their achievements, past and present. As well as roses, there are stupendous herb gardens and dahlia displays, and an extensive "jardin verger" where roses and herbaceous plants grow in among rows of trained fruit trees – spectacular in autumn.

'OBÉLISQUE'

'Delicata'

Della Balfour

Denise Grey

'Deep Secret'

see 'Mildred Scheel'

'Delicata'

Rugosa Hybrid

ORIGIN **Cooling, US, 1898**
FLOWER SIZE **3.1in (8cm)**
SCENT **Light**
FLOWERING **Repeats well**
HEIGHT/SPREAD **4.1ft (1.25m)/4.1ft (1.25m)**
HARDINESS **Zone 4**

Most Rugosa roses are tall and lanky, but 'Delicata' is neat and compact, sometimes a little broader than it is high. The flowers are not large, but they are full of ruffled petals, and have a shape and form that is unique and unmistakable. They open out to display their pale stamens and are attractive at every stage of their development. The flowers are a rich, slightly mauvey pink, but paler in hot weather. They come in clusters, typically of 3–5 flowers. 'Delicata' has handsome, pale green, wrinkled leaves and a lot of prickles. It is one of the first roses to start into flower, and is also a good repeater; later flushes are borne alongside large, vermilion hips. It is very hardy, but not as adaptable as some Rugosas, though it responds well to good cultivation and is a rewarding rose to grow.

Della Balfour

syn. 'HARblend', Desert Glo, Renown's Desert Glo, Royal Pageant

Modern Climber

ORIGIN **Harkness, Britain, 1994**
PARENTAGE **Rosemary Harkness x Elina**
FLOWER SIZE **3.9in (10cm)**
SCENT **Strong and fruity**
FLOWERING **Repeats well**
HEIGHT/SPREAD **9.8ft (3m)/6.6ft (2m)**
HARDINESS **Zone 6**

Harkness has bred several of its modern climbers by crossing two vigorous bush roses: Della Balfour gets its height from Elina. It is a bushy climber, which can certainly be pruned back and grown as a bush, but reaches 9.8ft (3m) in hot climates and 13.1ft (4m) against a wall. The flowers are a good, rich yellow when they first open, with crimson edges to the petals, but the colors fade with age and end up a dirty cream with traces of pink. The flowers have large petals, and come singly or in clusters (typically of 3–5) on long, stiff, upright stems – sometimes too far up to appreciate. Della Balfour has large, medium-dark leaves, large prickles, and a stiff, upright habit of growth. The coarseness of its growth contrasts with the bright promise of its flowers.

'Demokracie'

syn. 'Blaze Superior'

Wichurana Rambler

ORIGIN **Böhm, Czechoslovakia, 1935**
PARENTAGE **'Blaze' x unknown**
FLOWER SIZE **3.1in (8cm)**
SCENT **Little or none**
FLOWERING **Once spectacularly, then intermittently**
HEIGHT/SPREAD **13.1ft (4m)/9.8ft (3m)**
HARDINESS **Zone 5**

This is by far the best known of Jan Böhm's roses, and especially popular in the US, where it is known as 'Improved Blaze'. Böhm built up one of the largest nurseries in Europe at Blatná in southern Bohemia, and introduced over 100 new roses between 1925 and 1950. 'Improved Blaze' is a large-flowered Wichurana rambler, promoted as an improved form of 'Blaze', with larger, fewer, deeper-colored flowers. The flowers are an intense vermilion red, round, double, and freely borne, singly or in clusters of up to about seven. It continues to produce flowers on and off after the first spectacular flowering. It is a fairly vigorous grower, with large, dark leaves and an ability to shrug off fungal infections. Its hardiness makes it popular from central Europe to Scandinavia, and the American Midwest.

'Demokracie'

Denise Grey

syn. 'MEIxetal', Caprice, Make-Up

Shrub Rose

ORIGIN **Meilland, France, 1988**
FLOWER SIZE **2.2in (5.5cm)**
SCENT **Light**
FLOWERING **Repeats well**
HEIGHT/SPREAD **3.9ft (1.2m)/4.9ft (1.5m)**
HARDINESS **Zone 6**
AWARDS **Frankfurt GM 1989; Bagatelle GM 1992**

Denise Grey is a very attractive shrub rose, which has proved particularly popular in Australia and mainland Europe. It is immensely floriferous in its first and most splendid display, when it is covered in large clusters, bursting with 20–50 flowers, but it continues to flower right through to early winter. The flowers are a bright, clear pink at first, fading as they age (especially in the sun), so that the overall impression is of a mass of pink and white. They are best in cool climates, where they keep their color longer. The plant has dark, glossy leaves and a tendency to grow more sideways than upward. The new growths develop vertically at first, then start to arch over, so that in hot climates Denise Grey forms a ground-covering mass 4.9ft (1.5m) high and twice as wide.

'Dentelle de Malines'

Shrub Rose

ORIGIN **Lens, Belgium, 1986**
PARENTAGE ***Rosa filipes* x ('Robin Hood' x 'Baby Faurax')**
FLOWER SIZE **1.2in (3cm)**
SCENT **Light and musky**
FLOWERING **Once only**
HEIGHT/SPREAD **8.2ft (2.5m)/8.2ft (2.5m)**
HARDINESS **Zone 6**

Louis Lens was a very adventurous hybridizer, and the first to bring *Rosa filipes* into mainstream rose breeding. One of the early results was 'Dentelle de Malines', a shrub rose of extraordinary floriferousness, which can also be used as a short climber. The individual flowers are small, flat, and double, like a Noisette. Their color is rich pink at first, before fading by degrees to white; the petal backs are paler and fade first. 'Dentelle de Malines' carries its flowers in very large clusters (typically of 30–60), and this sheer profusion is one of its greatest qualities, especially when the branches arch over under the sheer weight of their flowers. These are followed by pretty vermilion hips in autumn. The plant has long, thin leaves and a vigorous, spreading habit, sending up long, new growth in all directions.

'Dentelle de Malines'

D

'DESPREZ À FLEURS JAUNES'

'DEUIL DE PAUL FONTAINE'

'DESPREZ À FLEURS JAUNES'

syn. 'JAUNE DESPREZ'

Noisette

ORIGIN **Desprez, France, 1830**
PARENTAGE **'Blush Noisette' x 'Parks' Yellow'**
FLOWER SIZE **2.4in (6cm)**
SCENT **Strong and sweet**
FLOWERING **Light but continuous**
HEIGHT/SPREAD **16.4ft (5m)/9.8ft (3m)**
HARDINESS **Zone 7**

Despite its name, 'Desprez à Fleurs Jaunes' is not really yellow: the color is variable and includes hints of buff and salmon pink as well as pale yellow, but is usually little more than cream or white. The flowers open somewhat messily, only occasionally quartered, and often have split centers. They hang down in clusters of 3–7. It is a popular, easy to grow climber in hot, dry climates, but a mildewed, stingy bloomer in cool ones and a disaster in rain. It makes a very vigorous, fast-growing plant, with lots of lush, pale green, nearly evergreen leaves. It was the first of the "Tea-Noisettes."

'DEUIL DE PAUL FONTAINE'

Moss Rose

ORIGIN **Fontaine, France, 1873**
FLOWER SIZE **3.5in (9cm)**
SCENT **Light and sweet**
FLOWERING **Repeats**
HEIGHT/SPREAD **4.1ft (1.25m)/3.3ft (1m)**
HARDINESS **Zone 5**

Dark crimson roses are always popular, and 'Deuil de Paul Fontaine' has the added attraction of being a Moss rose. The lightly cupped flowers lose their crimson shade as they age, and turn first to purple, then to dark lilac. They have a mass of small, muddled petals, golden stamens, and sometimes a button eye. The petal backs are mauve-pink, which provides a nice contrast. The moss is red brown and thick, which is very beautiful, but also attracts mildew. Poorly grown, in damp climates, the flower stems, stalks, receptacles, and sepals are white with mold. 'Deuil de Paul Fontaine' is very prickly and moderately vigorous, growing well in warm, dry climates, where it can also be fed and watered: then it will reach 5.7ft (1.75m) and flower regularly every 5–6 weeks until late autumn. Its leaves are long and dark with an attractive red tinge to the outline of the leaflets.

DIADEM

syn. 'TANMEDA', Royal Favourite

Floribunda

ORIGIN **Tantau, Germany, 1986**
FLOWER SIZE **2.8in (7cm)**
SCENT **Light**
FLOWERING **Repeats well**
HEIGHT/SPREAD **2.5ft (75cm)/1.6ft (50cm)**
HARDINESS **Zone 5**

Diadem is a really useful short Floribunda, very floriferous and tolerant of wet weather – it is especially popular in northwestern Europe. The flowers are a pretty, pale, fresh pink, which fades almost to white. The petal backs are always darker and the flowers are naturally somewhat full and cupped, so the contrast between pale pink and dark pink is a constant and attractive feature. The flowers tend to nod over in small clusters, typically of 3–5. The plant is bushy, upright, and compact, with dark, healthy leaves. It is also very hardy.

DIADEM

'DEVONIENSIS'

Tea Rose

ORIGIN **Foster, Britain, 1838**
PARENTAGE **'Smith's Yellow' x 'Parks' Yellow'**
FLOWER SIZE **3.1in (8cm)**
SCENT **Very strong and tealike**
FLOWERING **Continuous**
HEIGHT/SPREAD **2.7ft (80cm)/2ft (60cm)**
HARDINESS **Zone 8**

'Devoniensis' was a chance seedling raised by an English amateur called Captain Foster, who lived at Stone in Devon. It is the oldest surviving Tea rose to come from England, and still one of the most beautiful. Its elegant buds are pale pink, but their color fades to creamy white shortly after the flowers open out, while always retaining hints and tints of pink and buff toward the center of the flower. This coloration set the standard for perfection among the Tea roses.

The flowers are very variable in their shape, but their petals always roll back just at the tips so that the whole flower is built from layer after layer of petals. The scent is simply delicious. The leaves are dark and the crimson new growths very handsome. 'Devoniensis' was instantly and widely popular, and still grown as a commercial cut flower in Florida in the 1920s.

A climbing sport introduced as **'Climbing Devoniensis'** by Pavitt in 1858 occasioned considerable interest: it was the first climbing sport to be widely sold, at a time when the phenomenon was little understood. It is an even better rose than the bush form, with larger flowers (3.9in/10cm), a dense habit of growth, and masses of pendulous flowers borne on short stems singly, or occasionally in twos and threes. Its main flowering is long-lasting and spectacular, but it is never out of flower thereafter. Both 'Devoniensis' and its climbing sport are healthy and vigorous and respond to good cultivation.

Sport of 'Devoniensis'

'CLIMBING DEVONIENSIS'

Climbing Tea Rose

ORIGIN **Pavitt, 1858**
FLOWER SIZE **3.9in (10cm)**
FLOWERING **A big main flush followed by intermittent flowers**
HEIGHT/SPREAD **13.1ft (4m)/6.6ft (2m)**

'DEVONIENSIS'

'CLIMBING DEVONIENSIS'

'DIAMOND JUBILEE'

'DIAMOND JUBILEE'

Hybrid Tea

ORIGIN **Boerner, US, 1947**
PARENTAGE **'Maréchal Niel' x 'Feu Pernet-Ducher'**
FLOWER SIZE **4.7in (12cm)**
SCENT **Medium**
FLOWERING **Repeats well**
HEIGHT/SPREAD **3.9ft (1.2m)/3.3ft (1m)**
HARDINESS **Zone 6**
AWARDS **AARS 1948**

This famous, classic Hybrid Tea is still popular, and deservedly so. The flowers are pale gold with many thick petals and apricot reverses, fading to cream at the edges. They have the elegant, pointed Hybrid Tea shape, and gently unscroll themselves as they open. Even when fully open, they continue to glow with color and good health, though they do spoil easily in rain. The bush is vigorous and erect, with tough, ordinary looking leaves. Its disease-resistance is good. If the weather is dry and warm, 'Diamond Jubilee' is also one of the most rewarding Hybrid Teas in autumn.

DIANA, PRINCESS OF WALES

syn. 'JACshaq'

Hybrid Tea

ORIGIN **Zary, US, 1998**
PARENTAGE **Anne Morrow Lindbergh x Sheer Elegance**
FLOWER SIZE **6.7in (17cm)**
SCENT **Light and sweet**
FLOWERING **Repeats**
HEIGHT/SPREAD **6.6ft (2m)/3.3ft (1m)**
HARDINESS **Zone 6**

The death of Diana, Princess of Wales, triggered the issue of a number of commemorative roses. Keith Zary's Hybrid Tea is the best by far. It is very much an exhibition type rose with huge flowers that are always borne singly on long stems (1.6–2ft/50–60cm). They are basically pink and white – ivory white, with deep pink edges to the petals and a hint of yellow at the center. The petals are very long, and their color piping emphasizes the beauty of the unscrolling buds. They fade eventually to palest pink or mother-of-pearl. The plant has dark leaves, crimson at first, and a lot of them. It makes a bushy plant with large prickles. It is not the most floriferous of roses, but it sacrifices quantity for quality. In hot climates the plant will reach 8.2ft (2.5m).

DICKY

see ANISLEY DICKSON

DIANA, PRINCESS OF WALES

'DICK KOSTER'

Polyantha

ORIGIN **Koster, Netherlands, 1929**
PARENTAGE **Sport of 'Anneke Koster'**
FLOWER SIZE **1.6in (4cm)**
SCENT **Light**
FLOWERING **Repeats very well**
HEIGHT/SPREAD **1.6ft (50cm)/2.5ft (75cm)**
HARDINESS **Zone 5**

Once upon a time there was a repeat flowering Polyantha rose called 'Echo' (Lambert, 1914). It was an unusual rose, because it started life as a sport from a once-flowering Multiflora rambler called 'Tausendschön', and there are very few examples of roses sporting from a tall once-flowerer to a dwarf repeat flowerer. But the sporting did not stop with 'Echo', because 'Echo' sported to 'Greta Kluis' (Kluis, 1916), 'Greta Kluis' sported to 'Anneke Koster' (Koster, 1927), and 'Anneke Koster' sported to 'Dick Koster'. 'Dick Koster' sported many times – its offspring include **'Margo Koster'** and **'Morsdag'**; and 'Morsdag' sported twice, to **'Orange Morsdag'** and to **'Vatertag'**. There is nothing to choose between them except their color: 'Dick Koster' is deep pink, 'Margo Koster' is bright orange with silvery-pink undersides (quite a novelty when it first came out), 'Morsdag' is dark red, 'Orange Morsdag' is rich orange, and 'Vatertag' is also orange. Their flowers are not especially attractive close-up: the petals curve over so far that the globular flowers do not open out until shortly before petal fall. They tend to ball in humid weather and are easily bruised by rain. 'Morsdag' and 'Vatertag' are widely sold as potted plants to celebrate Mother's Day and Father's Day. All are widely available and popular in every part of the world, flowering abundantly and rooting very easily from cuttings. There were other sports along the way, and some of them, like 'Sneprinsesse' (Grootendorst, 1946), are still grown in great rose gardens and sold by specialized nurseries.

Sports of 'Dick Koster'

'MARGO KOSTER'

ORIGIN **Koster, Netherlands, 1931**

'MORSDAG'

syn. 'MOTHER'S DAY', 'MUTTERTAG', 'FÊTE DES MÈRES'
ORIGIN **Grootendorst, Netherlands, 1949**

Sports of 'Morsdag'

'ORANGE MORSDAG'

ORIGIN **Grootendorst, Netherlands, 1956**

'VATERTAG'

syn. 'FATHER'S DAY', 'FÊTE DES PÈRES'
ORIGIN **Tantau, Germany, 1959**

'DICK KOSTER'

'MARGO KOSTER'

'MORSDAG'

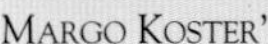

'VATERTAG'

'ORANGE MORSDAG'

DIE WELT

'DIREKTOR BENSCHOP'

DIE WELT

syn. 'DIEKOR', The World

Hybrid Tea

ORIGIN **Kordes, Germany, 1976**
PARENTAGE **seedling x 'Peer Gynt'**
FLOWER SIZE **4.3in (11cm)**
SCENT **Light and sweet**
FLOWERING **Repeats**
HEIGHT/SPREAD **1.6ft (50cm)/3.3ft (1m)**
HARDINESS **Zone 5**

Die Welt is a large Hybrid Tea with flowers so fat that they only narrowly escape grossness. They are creamy yellow, with hints of salmon and bright, dark pink edges, but, as the cream appears more on the back of the petals, the overall impression is of pink. They come singly or in clusters of up to three, and open slowly, which makes them wonderful for picking and exhibition. The leaves too are very large: glossy, mid-green, and occasionally susceptible to mildew. The plant is thick-stemmed, vigorous, upright, and bushy. All things considered, a splendid rose.

'DIREKTOR BENSCHOP'

syn. 'CITY OF YORK'

Wichurana Rambler

ORIGIN **Tantau, Germany, 1945**
PARENTAGE **'Dorothy Perkins' x 'Professor Gnau'**
FLOWER SIZE **2in (5cm)**
SCENT **Light and musky**
FLOWERING **Once only, with a few later blooms**
HEIGHT/SPREAD **16.4ft (5m)/9.8ft (3m)**
HARDINESS **Zone 5**

Matthias Tantau introduced 'Direktor Benschop' just as World War II was ending and wanted to change its name to 'City of York', in honor of the invading English armies. However, the original name has priority under the rules that apply to the naming of all cultivated plants. 'Direktor Benschop' is a good example of the Floribunda type of climber that comes from crossing the old ramblers with modern Hybrid Teas. The flowers open from buff yellow buds into semidouble, creamy white flowers with prominent stamens at the center. They come in small clusters and are most abundantly borne. They are too small and cupped to be attractive close-up, but a plant in full flower attracts attention over quite a distance. The plant has handsome, dark, glossy leaves and a fair number of prickles. It is especially popular still in Germany, and mixes very well with other roses and such perennials as delphiniums.

'DIRIGENT'

syn. 'THE CONDUCTOR'

Floribunda

ORIGIN **Tantau, Germany, 1956**
PARENTAGE **'Fanal' x 'Karl Weinhausen'**
FLOWER SIZE **2.8in (7cm)**
SCENT **Light**
FLOWERING **Repeats well**
HEIGHT/SPREAD **3.9ft (1.2m)/3.3ft (1m)**
HARDINESS **Zone 5**

DICKSON ROSES

THE DICKSON FAMILY OF NORTHERN IRELAND HAS A DISTINGUISHED HISTORY OF ROSE BREEDING THAT SPANS SIX GENERATIONS

THE DICKSON FAMILY is the oldest rose breeding dynasty in the UK. Colin Dickson (b.1956), who now heads the breeding program in Newtownards, near Belfast, is the sixth generation to occupy himself with raising new roses.

'K. OF K.'

The Dicksons have proved prolific. Brothers frequently part company and set up firms of their own, but the main Dickson trading names over the years have been Alexander Dickson & Sons, Royal Nurseries, Dicksons of Hawlmark, and Dickson Nurseries Ltd.

George Dickson (1832–1914) was the first Briton to follow the lead of Henry Bennett and breed roses. His first introductions in 1886 were undistinguished, but he bred a real moneymaker with his lilac pink Hybrid Tea 'Mrs. W. J. Grant' (1892). It was followed by 'Liberty' (1902), and 'George Dickson' (1912). Meanwhile the Hybrid Perpetuals were not forgotten: the fine pale crimson 'Tom Wood' was issued in 1896, and 'J. B. Clark' and 'Hugh Dickson' in 1905.

'TOM WOOD'

During this period, the Dickson style of Hybrid Tea began to emerge: not too full of petals (Irish rain made that essential), but as long-petaled and elegant in the bud as possible. It was a style that Dickson sought above all others, and it became the standard for Hybrid Teas all over the world. 'K. of K.' (1917), 'Betty Uprichard' (1922), and 'Shot Silk' (1924) are fine examples of this style.

When Patrick Dickson began breeding roses in 1957, he adhered to the family's concern for good form, but sought his greatest successes in brightly colored roses of all types. His first success was 'Grandpa Dickson' (1966), followed by such beauties as the crimson 'Precious Platinum' (1974), the stupendous pale yellow 'Elina' (1983), and the rich yellow 'Freedom' (1984). But his taste, and his son Colin's, for bright colors shows in such roses as 'Disco Dancer' (1984), 'Laughter Lines' (1987), 'Tequila Sunrise' (1988), 'Gypsy Dancer' (1994), and the cut-flower cultivar 'Acapulco' (1997).

ALEXANDER AND PATRICK DICKSON

'DIRIGENT'

This vigorous Floribunda is sometimes called a shrub rose because it makes a big, broad bush. The flowers have an occasional hint of white at the center but are otherwise a very uniform color – bright blood red. They come in large, loose clusters of 20–40, held upright on slender stems, and stand up well to rain, hence the continued popularity of 'Dirigent' in northern Europe. The plant is healthy, with large, reddish green leaves, and grows to as much as 6.6ft (2m) high in a hot climate.

'DOLCE VITA'

Hybrid Tea

ORIGIN **Delbard, France, 1971**
PARENTAGE **'Voeux de Bonheur' × (['Chic Parisien' × 'Michèle Meilland'] × 'Mme. Joseph Perraud')**
FLOWER SIZE **4.7in (12cm)**
SCENT **Medium and sweet**
FLOWERING **Repeats**
HEIGHT/SPREAD **4.9ft (1.5m)/3.3ft (1m)**
HARDINESS **Zone 6**

The flowers of 'Dolce Vita' open pale salmon pink, but lose their yellow tint as they age. The effect is that the flowers seem to change to pure pink as they develop. They have a paler patch toward the center. The opening flowers are long and attractive, unfurling their petals from elegant buds, but the flowers also remain shapely when eventually they open out completely. They are borne singly or in clusters of up to four on fairly long stems, which make them useful for cutting. 'Dolce Vita' was also a popular exhibition rose when it was first introduced. The plant has dull, medium-dark leaves and a vigorous, upright habit of growth. If unpruned, it will reach over 6.6ft (2m).

'DOLLY PARTON'

'DOLLY PARTON'

Hybrid Tea

ORIGIN **Winchel, US, 1983**
PARENTAGE **'Duftwolke' × 'Oklahoma'**
FLOWER SIZE **5.1in (13cm)**
SCENT **Very strong and sweet**
FLOWERING **Repeats**
HEIGHT/SPREAD **4.9ft (1.5m)/3.3ft (1m)**
HARDINESS **Zone 5**

This vermilion Hybrid Tea is named after the American country-western singer (b.1946). It is fairly popular in the US and Australia, but unknown in Europe. The flowers of 'Dolly Parton' are a very bright, luminescent color, large and full of petals, and borne singly on long, strong stems. They make excellent cut flowers, but their color is somewhat difficult to blend with others. 'Dolly Parton' has large, mid-green leaves and a vigorous, upright habit of growth. It's never been one of the healthier Hybrid Teas and shows some susceptibility to mildew and blackspot. Better roses now exist in this color.

DOMAINE DE COURSON

syn. 'MEIDRIMY'

Modern Climber

ORIGIN **Meilland, France, 1995**
FLOWER SIZE **3.1in (8cm)**
SCENT **Light and sweet**
FLOWERING **Repeats well**
HEIGHT/SPREAD **8.2ft (2.5m)/8.2ft (2.5m)**
HARDINESS **Zone 6**

Although Domaine de Courson is listed as a climber, it is probably best treated as a shrub: it is a thick and bushy grower and makes a splendid strong-growing, spreading plant. The flowers are exceptionally beautiful: they are pale pink, with much darker patches on the upper sides of the petals, which create a two-tone effect. The petals are short but plentiful, with a mass of small, nibbed petals backed by broader guard petals. The flowers are borne in loose clusters of 3–15 and make a fine show. Sometimes the new growth produces clusters of extraordinary size with long stems that are perfect for large arrangements. The plant has healthy, medium-dark leaves, a few prickles and a sturdy habit of growth. Courson, near Paris, is the site of France's premier flower show, held twice a year in May and October.

DOMSTADT FULDA

syn. 'KORTANKEN', Cathedral City

Floribunda

ORIGIN **Kordes, Germany, 1994**
FLOWER SIZE **2.8in (7cm)**
SCENT **Light**
FLOWERING **Repeats constantly**
HEIGHT/SPREAD **2.7ft (80cm)/2ft (60cm)**
HARDINESS **Zone 6**
AWARDS **Dublin GM 1993; Belfast GM 1996**

Kordes has introduced many fine Floribundas with bright red or orange colors, but Domstadt Fulda is one that has never quite had the popularity it deserves. The flowers are dark vermilion – in a very bright shade – with occasional white streaks. They open round and flat from short Hybrid Tea-type buds. They come in clusters of 5–15 flowers on a vigorous, short, healthy plant with fine, dark, shiny, healthy leaves. The plant is stocky and dense and repeats its flowering very quickly, so that it is rarely without flowers. In hot climates it will grow to as much as 4.1ft (1.25m). Its name commemorates the 1,250th anniversary of the founding of the city of Fulda in Hessen, Germany.

DOMSTADT FULDA

'DON JUAN'

Modern Climber

ORIGIN **Malandrone, US, 1958**
PARENTAGE **'New Dawn' seedling × 'New Yorker'**
FLOWER SIZE **3.9in (10cm)**
SCENT **Strong and sweet**
FLOWERING **Repeats**
HEIGHT/SPREAD **13.1ft (4m)/8.2ft (2.5m)**
HARDINESS **Zone 6**

'Don Juan' was for several years the leading dark crimson-flowered climber in the US: it is still widely available around the world. The flowers have the form of a Hybrid Tea and last well, both as cut flowers and on the bush. They are carried singly or in small clusters on long, strong stems and are followed by orange hips. The tough, dark green foliage is a good foil, though it may need protection against blackspot. The plant is vigorous, prickly, and upright, but not especially tall-growing, which means that it can be used as a pillar rose. It does especially well in hot areas. Its scent is delicious.

'DOLCE VITA'

DOMAINE DE COURSON

'DON JUAN'

D

D

'Dorothy Perkins'

Wichurana Rambler

ORIGIN **Jackson & Perkins, US, 1901**
PARENTAGE **'Turner's Crimson Rambler' seedling**
FLOWER SIZE **1.4in (3.5cm)**
SCENT **Light to medium**
FLOWERING **Once, late in season, for a long time**
HEIGHT/SPREAD **13.1ft (4m)/6.6ft (2m)**
HARDINESS **Zone 5**

'Dorothy Perkins' was once the most famous rambling rose in the world. "It is literally everywhere" wrote the Englishman George Taylor in 1936. Part of its success is due to the ease with which it grows from cuttings, so that it has always been passed from garden to garden until whole neighborhoods were decorated with 'Dorothy Perkins'. Its flowers are little, bright pink rosettes, carried in enormous, long, open clusters very late in the season – it is one of the last roses to start into bloom. The flowers fade to pale pink, but survive a long time. The plant has small, dark, glossy leaves (somewhat susceptible to mildew) and long, flexible stems that make it perfect for draping around pergolas, arches, and other supports.

'Dorothy Perkins'

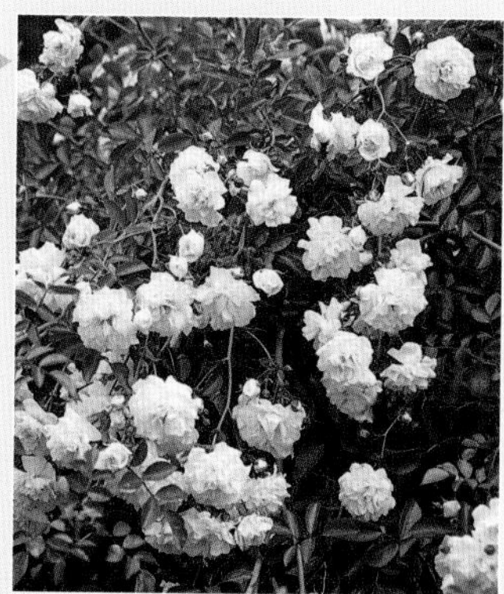
'White Dorothy'

'White Dorothy' is a pure white sport of the pink 'Dorothy Perkins', identical to its parent in all things except color: it has exactly the same vigour, floriferousness, grace, and susceptibility to mildew. It is a somewhat unstable sport, and tends to revert back to 'Dorothy Perkins', which means that there are often branches of pink on the plant. Some consider this instability a shortcoming; others think that it adds contrast and interest. But most would agree that 'White Dorothy' is surpassed in beauty by 'Sander's White Rambler'.

Sport of 'Dorothy Perkins'

'White Dorothy'

ORIGIN **Cant, Britain, 1908**

'Doris Tysterman'

'Doris Tysterman'

Hybrid Tea

ORIGIN **Wisbech, Britain, 1975**
PARENTAGE **'Peer Gynt' seedling**
FLOWER SIZE **3.5in (9cm)**
SCENT **Light and fruity**
FLOWERING **Repeats**
HEIGHT/SPREAD **4.9ft (1.5m)/3.3ft (1m)**
HARDINESS **Zone 6**

'Doris Tysterman' is a popular orange Hybrid Tea. Actually, its flowers are mainly yellow on the upper sides of the petals and crimson underneath, but the colors reflected in the shadows between the petals give an overall impression of orange. Sometimes the

Pedro Dot

THIS MAN OF VISION PUT SPAIN'S ROSE INDUSTRY ON THE MAP WITH HIS REMARKABLE LEGACY OF WORLD-CLASS MINIATURE ROSES AND OTHER FAVORITES

Many Spaniards have been active as rose breeders over the years – Aldrufeu, Camprubí, Ferrer, Munné, and Pahissa are honored among Spanish rose lovers. But, until recently, Spain offered only a small home market for roses, and it was difficult for Spanish breeders to compete abroad with the well-financed, large international growers. Against this background, Pedro Dot (1885– 1976) stands out as a man who made his name as a rose breeder all over the world, especially where miniature roses are cherished.

Pedro Dot

Dot was a Catalan, the son of a nurseryman from Sant Feliu de Llobregat, but he started his own nursery and began to breed roses. There are two reasons for Dot's success. First, he traveled widely as a young man in search of practical experience and useful contacts. Second, his breeding was unusually wide-ranging and innovative.

His first successes were with Hybrid Teas – not the delicate, lightly petaled roses of northern Europe, but thick, sturdy, brightly colored flowers that were suitable to the Mediterranean climate and sold well in the southern US. The bright cerise 'Director Rubió' came out in 1926 and was followed by a series of scorching orange roses: 'Duquesa de Peñaranda' and 'Luis Brinas' in 1931, 'Condesa de Sástago' in 1932, and 'Angels Mateu' in 1934, followed by 'Charles Farges' in 1935.

Meanwhile, Dot had introduced three completely different roses, which are all still grown worldwide: his white shrub rose 'Nevada' (1927), his once-flowering climber 'Mme. Grégoire Staechelin' (1927), and his vigorous yellow 'Golden Moss' rose (1932).

'Luis Brinas'

Then Dot turned his attention to miniature roses, crossing them with Hybrid Teas to breed miniature flowers with better shapes. His masterpieces were the yellow 'Estrellita de Oro' (1940), the carmine 'Perla de Alcañada' (1944), and the white 'Para Ti' (1946).

In 1999 at Sant Feliu de Llobregat, a new rose garden was planted to celebrate the work of Pedro Dot and other Spanish breeders. It boasts 20,000 roses and more than 400 cultivars. It is here, too, that the annual Spanish National Rose Show takes place during the second weekend in May.

'Duquesa de Peñaranda'

flowers are more tangerine or apricot, but the color is always attractive and cheerful. The outer petals of the flower are much larger than the inner, which means that it opens out well. The flowers have long stems, which make them good for cutting. The plant is vigorous and tall – if left unpruned it will reach 6.6ft (2m) – with a few large prickles and an upright habit of growth. The leaves are healthy, dark, and glossy. The new growth is crimson.

Dorola

see Benson & Hedges Special

'Dortmund'

Kordesii Hybrid

ORIGIN **Kordes, Germany, 1955**
PARENTAGE **seedling x 'Kordesii'**
FLOWER SIZE **4.3in (11cm)**
SCENT **Light and pleasant**
FLOWERING **Heavy flowering midseason, thereafter sporadic**
HEIGHT/SPREAD **6.6ft (2m)/4.9ft (1.5m)**
HARDINESS **Zone 5**
AWARDS **ADR 1954; GM Portland, 1971**

'Dortmund' is an invaluable short climber for small gardens. The flowers are deep cherry red, set off by a large central patch of white and a big boss of bright yellow stamens – the combination is very striking. The flowers come in clusters of 3–11, which are large because the individual flowers are themselves large. A heavy crop of orange hips follows, but this reduces the reblooming in autumn, so deadheading the spent blooms is essential for those who would sacrifice the hips for more flowers. The leaves are very dark and glossy. They are also very healthy. The plant makes a leafy, bushy climber up to about 9.8ft (3m), less if grown and pruned as a shrub.

Douce Symphonie

syn. 'MEIbarke', Debut

Miniature Rose

ORIGIN **Mouchotte, France, 1988**
PARENTAGE **Coppélia 76 x Magic Carrousel**
FLOWER SIZE **1.4 in (3.5cm)**
SCENT **Little or none**
FLOWERING **Repeats well**
HEIGHT/SPREAD **2ft (60cm)/1.6ft (50cm)**
HARDINESS **Zone 6**
AWARDS **AARS 1989**

Douce Symphonie

'Dortmund'

Douce Symphonie is a very pretty, compact, and unusual miniature rose. Its flowers are basically red and white, but the pattern of their coloration is somewhat unusual. The petals are pale yellow at first with nearly white backs, but laced with thick crimson edges, like an old-fashioned pink. As the flower opens and ages, the yellow and cream fade to white, while the crimson fades to pink and runs down into the white parts of the petals. The effect at all times is very striking. The flowers come in small clusters (typically of 3–7) and are well set off by the small, glossy, dark leaves. Douce Symphonie is bushy and healthy. It starts into flower early and continues until the first frost. It is sometimes promoted as a groundcover plant, but it is actually better in containers or planted out in small gardens, where it mixes well with other plants.

Douceur Normande

syn. 'MEIpopul', Amstelveen, Coral Meidiland, Stadt Hildesheim

Shrub Rose

ORIGIN **Meilland, France, 1993**
PARENTAGE **(Immensee x Serpent Vert) x ('Temple Bells' x 'Red Cascade')**
FLOWER SIZE **2.2in (5.5cm)**
SCENT **Light or slight**
FLOWERING **Continuous, if well cultivated**
HEIGHT/SPREAD **3.3ft (1m)/3.3ft (1m)**
HARDINESS **Zone 6**
AWARDS **Bagatelle GM 1995**

Few roses have so many synonyms as Douceur Normande, but they are a measure of its success worldwide. It is an excellent landscaping rose and is widely planted on roadside verges in hot climates, where its annual maintenance consists of a winter trim back to 1.6ft (50cm). But it is also planted in cold winter areas and tolerates rain well, though the flower covers itself in red spots where heavy rain has hit it. The flowers open pale crimson or dark, rich pink, and have a small white patch at the center. The petal backs are slightly darker. They keep their petals and their color for a long time, acquiring a coral or salmon pink tint as they age. In hot weather the flowers bleach and are reluctant to drop their petals. They come in clusters of 5–11 and are borne both freely and continuously. In hot climates Douceur Normande will grow to 6.6ft (2m) high and as much across, but only half that height is normal elsewhere. The plant has many prickles, dark, shiny leaves, and a bushy habit of growth. It is an excellent groundcover or patio plant in small gardens.

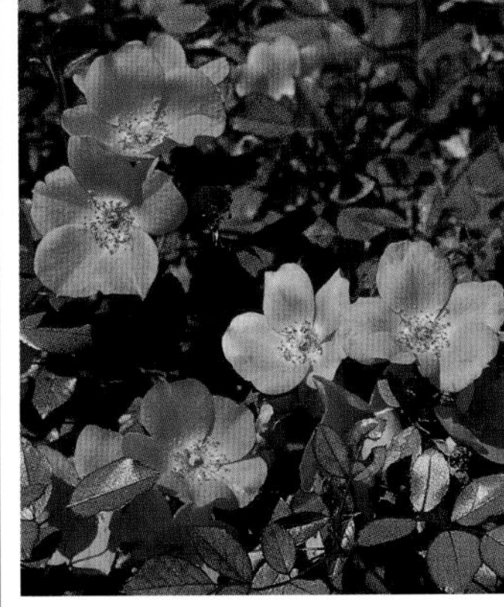

Douceur Normande

Double Delight

syn. 'ANDeli'

Hybrid Tea

ORIGIN **Swim & Ellis, US, 1977**
PARENTAGE **'Granada' x 'Garden Party'**
FLOWER SIZE **5.1in (13cm)**
SCENT **Very sweet, fruity, and strong**
FLOWERING **Repeats constantly**
HEIGHT/SPREAD **3.3ft (1m)/2.5ft (75cm)**
HARDINESS **Zone 5**
AWARDS **Baden-Baden GM 1976; Rome GM 1976; AARS 1977; World's Favourite Rose 1985; Gamble FA 1986**

Double Delight is one of the best-known and most widely grown modern roses throughout the world. No one knows whether its name refers to the two contrasting colors in its blooms, or whether the "double delight" is its color and its scent. The opening bud sets the standard: it is a perfect Hybrid Tea, unfurling slowly from a long, conical shape. It also makes a long-lasting cut rose and, provided the buds are not "split," a first-class exhibition rose too. The flowers are creamy white at first, with just a red tinge on the outer petals, but as they mature so the extent of the crimson coloring grows, especially in hot climates. This results in the startling contrast between the layers of bright crimson outer petals and the creamy white heart. The flowers are very large and usually borne singly, though occasionally in twos and threes, on long, sturdy, thick, prickly stems. The plant has large dark leaves and an upright habit, but is more bushy (a better shape) than many Hybrid Teas. It is also very easy to grow, though not immune from mildew and blackspot. The red coloring is created by the action of ultraviolet light on the natural pigments in the petals. This means that no two flowers are identical, because the weather that conditions them is always different. It also explains why the flowers remain pure white if Double Delight is grown in a greenhouse where ultraviolet light is filtered out by the glass.

The climbing sport, known as Climbing Double Delight, has also become popular. It is exactly the same as the bush form, except that it climbs quickly to a considerable height. An established plant flowers very profusely once a year and thereafter is never without a few flowers. Like the bush form, its bright color blends wonderfully with other plants in the garden: silver and blues are best.

Double Delight

Climbing Double Delight

Sport of Double Delight

Climbing Double Delight

syn. 'AROclidd'

Climbing Hybrid Tea

ORIGIN **Christensen, US, 1982**
FLOWER SIZE **5.5in (14cm)**
FLOWERING **Repeats well**
HEIGHT/SPREAD **13.1ft (4m)/3.3ft (1m)**

D

D

Dove

Dove

syn. 'AUSdove'

Shrub Rose

ORIGIN **Austin, Britain, 1984**
PARENTAGE **'Wife of Bath' x ('Schneewittchen' x unknown)**
FLOWER SIZE **3.5in (9cm)**
SCENT **Medium and tealike**
FLOWERING **Repeats almost constantly**
HEIGHT/SPREAD **2.5ft (75cm)/3.3ft (1m)**
HARDINESS **Zone 6**

David Austin considers Dove so prone to blackspot that he would not have introduced it these days, but it remains a favorite – and a great performer – in dry climates where disease is not a problem. The buds of Dove are like a Hybrid Tea's, but open out to a fully imbricated rosette. The flowers are white, with a hint of mother-of-pearl at the heart, and come singly in open, lax clusters of up to seven. The coloring comes from the petal backs, which are pale apricot at the centre. Dove drops its petals cleanly as soon as the flowers have finished. The dark leaves are a good foil for the flowers.

Dover

see Cliffs of Dover

'Dr. Eckener'

Rugosa Hybrid

ORIGIN **Berger, Czechoslovakia, 1930**
PARENTAGE **'Golden Emblem' x *Rosa rugosa* seedling**
FLOWER SIZE **4.3in (11cm)**
SCENT **Strong and sweet**
FLOWERING **Repeats**
HEIGHT/SPREAD **8.2ft (2.5m)/8.2ft (2.5m)**
HARDINESS **Zone 5**

Many first generation Rugosa hybrids were introduced around 1900, but very few were then backcrossed to the Hybrid Teas. 'Dr. Eckener' is one of those exceptions, and shows how splendid was the potential for further development. Its flowers are large, semidouble, and salmon pink at first, with a yellow flush to the center and shades of apricot and peach in the petals. It is a very striking combination, especially when the sun shines through the petals. Later the yellow tints fade away to leave a pale pink flower with a creamy white center. 'Dr. Eckener' has large, pale, crinkly leaves and a lot of large prickles. It tends to grow somewhat tall and lanky, but responds well to pruning or pegging down. Its hardiness has made it very popular in Scandinavia. Dr. Hugo Eckener (1868–1954) was the designer of the first Zeppelin airships.

'Dr. Eckener'

'Dr. Grill'

'Dr. Grill'

Tea Rose

ORIGIN **Bonnaire, France, 1886**
PARENTAGE **'Ophirie' x 'Souvenir de Victor Hugo' [Bonnaire]**
FLOWER SIZE **3.9in (10cm)**
SCENT **Fairly strong and tealike**
FLOWERING **Repeats well**
HEIGHT/SPREAD **3.3ft (1m)/2ft (60cm)**
HARDINESS **Zone 7**

'Dr. Grill' is pretty at every stage of its development. The buds are long and elegant, copper colored with dark pink markings, especially on the backs of the petals. The open flowers fade to pale buff and light pink, with attractive honey colored tones at the center. Although they open wide, the flowers often have their centers obscured by petals folding over the stigma. The outer petals meanwhile curl back their petal edges to form a pointed tip. The flowers come singly, or in clusters of 3–5, and repeat very consistently – the autumn flowers are the best for both color and size. The bush is prickly and slender, with red new growth and a degree of susceptibility to mildew.

Dr. Herbert Gray

Dr. Herbert Gray

syn. 'AUSfar'

Shrub Rose

ORIGIN **Austin, Britain, 1998**
PARENTAGE **Heritage seedling**
FLOWER SIZE **3.1in (8cm)**
SCENT **Strong and sweet**
FLOWERING **Repeats well**
HEIGHT/SPREAD **4.1ft (1.25m)/3.3ft (1m)**
HARDINESS **Zone 6**

This new pink English Rose from David Austin is extremely pretty. The flowers of Dr. Herbert Gray are not especially large, but they are profusely borne in small clusters (typically of 3–5). They are a charming, deep, rose pink at first, fading to pale pink, with darker petal backs, which set up attractive dark shadows between the many folds of the open rosette-shaped flowers. The petals often have a wavy, scalloped edge, which adds to the overall beauty. The scent is delicious. Dr. Herbert Gray has small, medium-dark leaves, few prickles, and a lax, spreading habit. It is a particularly good repeat flowerer.

'Dr. Huey'

syn. 'Shafter'

Wichurana Rambler

ORIGIN **Thomas, US, 1914**
PARENTAGE **'Ethel' x 'Gruss an Teplitz'**
FLOWER SIZE **2in (5cm)**
SCENT **Light and musky**
FLOWERING **Once only, midseason**
HEIGHT/SPREAD **13.1ft (4m)/8.2ft (2.5m)**
HARDINESS **Zone 6**
AWARDS **ARS GM 1924**

'Dr. Huey' is widely grown, especially in hot climates, as an understock on which to bud other roses. It roots very quickly and surely from cuttings, grows very fast, and is nearly thornless. It is also a good rose in its own right, with an amazing profusion of small, ruffled, dark crimson petals and a pleasantly rounded flower enlivened by yellow stamens. The flowers come in small clusters, usually of 5–10, but tend to scorch badly in sun, and do not drop their petals when they turn brown and die. So it looks best either at a distance, or in the early stages of flowering. The glossy, rich green leaves are a good foil for the flowers. The plant is so vigorous that it will grow

'DR. HUEY'

26.2–32.8ft (8–10m) up a tree. Dr. Robert Huey, who died aged 85 in 1928, was a famous Philadelphia amateur rosarian who inspired many Americans to try growing roses, including Capt. Thomas. The synonym 'Shafter' takes its name from a rose-growing town in California's Central Valley.

DREAM SEQUENCE

see ASTRID LINDGREN

'DREAMING SPIRES'

Modern Climber

ORIGIN **Mattock, Britain, 1973**
PARENTAGE **'Arthur Bell' seedling × 'Allgold'**
FLOWER SIZE **3.1in (8cm)**
SCENT **Medium, fruity, and sweet**
FLOWERING **Repeats**
HEIGHT/SPREAD **9.8ft (3m)/8.2ft (2.5m)**
HARDINESS **Zone 6**
AWARDS **Belfast GM 1977**

The flowers of this dependable and attractive yellow climber appear early in the season. Its lightly double flowers are a strong, bright yellow with bronzy backs at first, but fading quickly as they open out to reveal red filaments. The hotter the climate, the quicker they fade, ending up almost white. However, they come in small clusters, so there is always a succession of flowers, and they open from elegant buds of Hybrid Tea shape. The plant has a vigorous and upright habit of growth and handsome, dark green leaves, which are fairly healthy. It repeats well, and produces some especially large, richly colored flowers in autumn.

'DREAMING SPIRES'

'DR. W. VAN FLEET'

Wichurana Rambler

ORIGIN **Van Fleet, US, 1910**
PARENTAGE **(*Rosa wichurana* × 'Safrano') × 'Souvenir du Président Carnot'**
FLOWER SIZE **3.5in (9cm)**
SCENT **Medium and sweet**
FLOWERING **Once only, followed by sporadic flowers**
HEIGHT/SPREAD **16.4ft (5m)/6.6ft (2m)**
HARDINESS **Zone 5**

'DR. W. VAN FLEET'

'NEW DAWN'

'PROBUZENÍ'

'WEISSE NEW DAWN'

'Dr. W. Van Fleet' was an epoch-making rose: "an heroic rose, of noble size and perfect form, borne on a rampant plant, first of the new race of climbers" wrote G. A. Stevens in 1933. It was, moreover, the "father" of 'New Dawn', and thus the grandfather of many of our best modern climbers. 'Dr. W. Van Fleet' has large, pale pink flowers, even paler at the edges of the petals, in large, loose clusters. They are perfectly shaped, both as long, elegant buds and as full-petaled, wavy flowers, and are excellent as picking roses; indeed, the original stock was bought as a cutting rose by a New York florist. The attractive, glossy foliage is bronze green, turning to dark green, and healthy.

The sole weakness of 'Dr. W. Van Fleet' is that it flowers only once, but that was repaired by its perpetual-flowering sport **'New Dawn'**, which was introduced in 1930. The flowers are identical, but it continues to flower right through until winter. Its hardiness and vigor match those of 'Dr. W. Van Fleet': its only distinction is its perpetual flowering. Modern climbers begin with 'New Dawn'. Crossed with Hybrid Teas, 'New Dawn' passed on its characteristic long-flowering, its prolific flower production, and, usually, its hardiness too. The most successful breeder was Eugene Boerner, who worked for the large firm of Jackson & Perkins and was responsible for 'Aloha', 'Coral Dawn', 'Parade', and 'Pink Cloud'. One other factor made 'New Dawn' a rose of immense significance to the well-being of the horticultural industry: it was the first plant ever to be patented (U.S. Patent No. 1, 1930).

It has produced only two sports of its own: the many-petaled **'Probuzení'** and **'Weisse New Dawn'**. This is a pure white sport of 'New Dawn', and should not be confused with 'White New Dawn', which is a distinct seedling. 'Weisse New Dawn' has crimson tipped buds and opens palest pink, but it quickly fades to pure white. It is popular in Europe.

'Probuzení' is a fully double sport of 'New Dawn', introduced by that indefatigable promoter of unusual mutations, Jan Böhm of Blatná. This is the correct name for the rose that was reintroduced in England by Beales in 1992 as 'Awakening', which is the English translation of "probuzení." The flowers are very pretty, usually quartered, with hundreds of small quilled or irregular petals at the center. The color at the center of the flower is a mixture of dark apricot and pink, which contrasts with the silvery pink of the outer petals. The dark coloring comes from the petal backs and is reflected between the petals at the center. In hot weather, the flower opens out completely into a pink pompon, but its petals are soft, so they ball in humid conditions and blotch in rain. It is, in all other respects, identical to 'New Dawn' and is especially valued in central Europe for its hardiness.

Sport of 'Dr. W. Van Fleet'

'NEW DAWN'

syn. 'THE NEW DAWN'
ORIGIN **Dreer, US, 1930**
FLOWER SIZE **2.8in (7cm)**
FLOWERING **Repeats continuously**
HEIGHT/SPREAD **13.1ft (4m)/6.6ft (2m)**
AWARDS **World's Favourite Rose 1997**

Sports of 'New Dawn'

'PROBUZENÍ'

syn. 'AWAKENING'
ORIGIN **Böhm, Czechoslovakia, 1935**
HEIGHT/SPREAD **9.8ft (3m)/6.6ft (2m)**

'WEISSE NEW DAWN'

ORIGIN **Berger, Germany, 1959**

'DRESDEN DOLL'

Miniature Moss Rose

ORIGIN **Moore, US, 1975**
PARENTAGE **'Fairy Moss' seedling**
FLOWER SIZE **1.4in (3.5cm)**
SCENT **Light and sweet**
FLOWERING **Repeats well**
HEIGHT/SPREAD **1.3ft (40cm)/11.8in (30cm)**
HARDINESS **Zone 6**

One of the greatest achievements of the American breeder Ralph Moore was the development of miniature roses that were also mossy. He achieved this by crossing the old, once-flowering, purple Moss rose William Lobb with a repeat flowering rose, and by backcrossing the offspring to one of his miniature roses. 'Dresden Doll' is the offspring of the next generation. It has beautiful, rose pink flowers, full of petals but able to open out completely to reveal its tiny yellow stamens. The buds, sepals, and pedicels are all thickly covered with bright green, pine-scented moss. It repeats well, but the mossy parts do attract mildew, so 'Dresden Doll' does best in dry climates like California. It is perfect for small containers, where its conspicuous moss and charming flowers can be appreciated.

'DRESDEN DOLL'

D

Dronning Margrethe

'Duc de Cambridge' *(with proliferating bud behind)*

Dronning Margrethe

syn. 'POULskov', Enchantment, Queen Margrethe, Königin Margrethe

Shrub Rose

ORIGIN **Poulsen, Denmark, 1991**
PARENTAGE **seedling x 'Egeskov'**
FLOWER SIZE **2.8in (7cm)**
SCENT **Medium and fruity**
FLOWERING **Repeats well**
HEIGHT/SPREAD **2ft (60cm)/2ft (60cm)**
HARDINESS **Zone 5**
AWARDS **NZ GM 1993**

Dronning Margrethe – personally chosen to bear her name by the Danish Queen – is a very pretty, neat, and shapely shrub. The flowers are pale pink, with deeper coloring on the petal backs and toward the center. They open quartered, and have a pretty arrangement of petals, with large guard petals surrounding a lightly cupped mass of smaller ones. They come in clusters of 3–9 flowers and have a tendency to hang on and die badly in wet weather or cool climates. They are abundantly produced and repeat so quickly that the bush is seldom out of flower. The foliage is very dark and glossy, indicating Wichurana antecedents, and healthy too. Dronning Margrethe combines well with other plants in mixed plantings but is also splendid as a massed planting on its own.

'Du Maître d'École'

see 'De la Maître d'École'

'Dublin Bay'

Modern Climber

ORIGIN **McGredy, New Zealand, 1974**
PARENTAGE **'Bantry Bay' x 'Altissimo'**
FLOWER SIZE **3.9in (10cm)**
SCENT **Little or none**
FLOWERING **Repeats constantly**
HEIGHT/SPREAD **9.8ft (3m)/6.6ft (2m)**
HARDINESS **Zone 5**

'Dublin Bay' is one of the most widely grown roses throughout the world. Its flowers are a rich dark red, with crimson markings on the petal tips, which increase its air of velvety sumptuousness. The flowers, which are attractive both as buds and when opened out, come in long-stemmed clusters of 3–9. The plant may be a bit slow to start climbing: it tends to form a Floribunda type bush at first, before sending up its first really long, strong stem. Once established, however, it is quick to grow and quick to repeat, almost never out of flower. The plant is prickly, healthy, tolerant of both heat and cold, and covered with shiny, dark green foliage. It looks particularly good when massed as a hedge. If only it were scented, it would be the perfect red rose.

'Duc de Cambridge'

Damask Rose

ORIGIN **c.1815**
FLOWER SIZE **3.9in (10cm)**
SCENT **Medium and sweet**
FLOWERING **Once only**
HEIGHT/SPREAD **8.2ft (2.5m)/5.7ft (1.75m)**
HARDINESS **Zone 5**

When well grown, 'Duc de Cambridge' is one of the best of old garden roses, but it has one significant weakness: in some years almost all the flowers are lost to the strange phenomenon known as proliferation. This means that the carpels are enlarged into a huge, green, disfiguring growth at the center. However, a normal flower is a thing of beauty, with a mass of dark quilled petals radiating from the center, crimson on top, and paler underneath. The flower opens out flat and starts to reflex further before shattering its petals. The bush has large, pale green leaves with long leaflets and stout stems, fairly thickly covered with prickles. They grow upright at first, but bow down when the flowers are opening. Blackspot can be a problem. The Duke of Cambridge (1774–1850) was the 7th and youngest surviving son of George III of England.

'Duc de Fitzjames'

Gallica

ORIGIN **c.1840**
FLOWER SIZE **3.5in (9cm)**
SCENT **Medium and sweet**
FLOWERING **Once only**
HEIGHT/SPREAD **5.7ft (1.75m)/4.1ft (1.25m)**
HARDINESS **Zone 5**

Some modern authorities assert that 'Duc de Fitzjames' is a Centifolia, but the old catalogues invariably class it among the Gallicas. It has pale purple flowers with palest pink reverses, which create an unusual and attractive effect when some of the petals turn over and show their backs. Later the colors fade to mauve pink. The flower is lightly cupped and full of petals, but the inner ones are broader than usual among the Gallicas – never narrow enough to be described as "quill-shaped" – so they fold over in their distinctive way. The flowers come singly or in clusters of up to four on a vigorous, rounded bush. It has long, sturdy branches, some prickles, and mid- or pale green leaves. Édouard, Duc de Fitzjames (1776–1839) was a leader of the legitimist party under the July monarchy.

'Duc de Guiche'

Gallica

ORIGIN **Prévost, France, c.1810**
FLOWER SIZE **3.1in (8cm)**
SCENT **Strong and sweet**
FLOWERING **Once only**
HEIGHT/SPREAD **4.1ft (1.25m)/3.3ft (1m)**
HARDINESS **Zone 5**

'Duc de Guiche' is an excellent, short-growing Gallica. Its dark crimson buds open out to fully double flowers, with a nice circular outline, a quartered shape, and a green pistil at the center. The exact color of the flowers differs considerably according to the climate and season. The overall color is strong cherry crimson, with paler petal backs, but in some years it may be no more than dark pink. In any event, the flowers fade to pale purple, mauve, and lilac, when eventually they expand into many-petaled pompons. They are borne singly or in clusters of 2–3. The plant is neat, with short, arching stems, healthy, light green, rough Gallica leaves, and a lot of small prickles or bristles. It is a stout, thrifty grower and spreads around very satisfactorily if grown on its own roots. Antoine, Duc de Guiche, was a royalist politician whose activities spanned the reigns of Louis XVI through to Louis-Philippe.

'Duc de Fitzjames'

'Duc de Guiche'

D

'DUCHER'

'DUCHER'

China Rose

ORIGIN **Ducher, France, 1869**
FLOWER SIZE **1.6in (4cm)**
SCENT **Fruity**
FLOWERING **Repeats well**
HEIGHT/SPREAD **6.6ft (2m)/6.6ft (2m)**
HARDINESS **Zone 7**

The Ducher family of Lyon bred many good roses, but the one they chose to bear their own name is one of the most modest. It is a small-flowered China rose, almost the only pure white one ever raised. The flowers are long and slender, and droop down on the bush, but occasionally open out to show a muddle of small petals within and a hint of palest pink. They come throughout the season, usually singly but later in clusters, on long new growth; in hot climates they continue coming all the year round. The bush is rounded and twiggy, with small, dark leaves that are a good foil to the brilliant white flowers.

'DUCHESS OF PORTLAND'

see 'PORTLAND ROSE'

DUCHESS OF YORK

syn. 'DICRACER', Sunseeker

Miniature Rose

ORIGIN **Dickson, Northern Ireland, 1992**
PARENTAGE Little Prince x Gentle Touch
FLOWER SIZE **1.6in (4cm)**
SCENT **Light**
FLOWERING **Repeats well**
HEIGHT/SPREAD **2ft (60cm)/2ft (60cm)**
HARDINESS **Zone 6**
AWARDS **Belfast GM 1994**

Pat Dickson introduced Duchess of York at the Chelsea Flower Show in 1992 in honor of Sarah Ferguson, the daughter-in-law of Queen Elizabeth II of England. That year it was the third most popular of all miniature roses in the UK. Sales plummeted in 1993, when embarrassing photographs of the Duchess appeared in several British newspapers. Dickson changed the name to Sunseeker in January 1994, and the rose became popular worldwide. It is an excellent small Floribunda or patio rose. The flowers open from neat buds: they are orange at first, then fade to vermilion and, eventually, to pink. They have a white center and often a white stripe down the center of the petals; together with the yellow stamens, these create a glow that suffuses the entire flower. The flowers come singly or in clusters of 3–5 and are perfectly matched by small, dark, neat Wichurana-type leaves. The plant has a few prickles and does better in warm climates than in its country of origin. It is a most prolific flowerer and useful for summer bedding plans.

DUCHESS OF YORK

'DUCHESSE D'ANGOULÊME'

Gallica

ORIGIN **Vibert, France, 1821**
FLOWER SIZE **3.5in (9cm)**
SCENT **Strong and sweet**
FLOWERING **Once only**
HEIGHT/SPREAD **4.1ft (1.25m)/3.3ft (1m)**
HARDINESS **Zone 5**

Historians of the rose argue about the origins of 'Duchesse d'Angoulême' – is it a Gallica or a Centifolia? – but it has always been the same rose that we grow under that name today. Its flowers have beautiful, thin, translucent petals, rose pink toward the center and milky white at the edges. They are globular at first, before opening out into a roughly quartered shape. They come in nodding clusters, typically of 3–5 flowers. The plant has wrinkled, mid-green leaves and a rounded habit. It is shorter than many Gallicas, and nearly thornless. The Duchesse d'Angoulême was the eldest child of Louis XVI and Marie-Antoinette.

'DUCHESSE D'ANGOULÊME'

'DUCHESSE D'AUERSTÄDT'

Tea-Noisette

ORIGIN **Bernaix, France, 1888**
PARENTAGE **'Rêve d'Or' x unknown**
FLOWER SIZE **4.3in (11cm)**
SCENT **Strong and tealike**
FLOWERING **Continuous**
HEIGHT/SPREAD **16.4ft (5m)/8.2ft (2.5m)**
HARDINESS **Zone 7**

Alexandre Bernaix bred many climbing Tea-Noisettes at his Lyon nursery in the 1880s and 1890s. Every one of them is still a supremely satisfactory garden plant: 'Duchesse d'Auerstädt' remains the best yellow climber for Mediterranean conditions. The flowers are very large, very double, and usually quartered. They are strongly scented and carried singly or in small clusters on long stems. The leaves and new growth are rich deep purple at first, a good foil to the unfading golden yellow of the flowers themselves. The plant flowers most profusely early in the season but is never without a flower thereafter until well into winter. It is a thorny, gaunt grower, but this does not create a problem because the flowers have weak stems and hang down toward the admirer. It is a sumptuous beauty, but not for cool, wet climates.

'DUCHESSE D'AUERSTÄDT'

'DUCHESSE DE BRABANT'

Tea Rose

ORIGIN **Bernède, France, 1857**
FLOWER SIZE **2.8in (7cm)**
SCENT **Strong and tealike**
FLOWERING **Repeats constantly**
HEIGHT/SPREAD **4.9ft (1.5m)/4.9ft (1.5m)**
HARDINESS **Zone 7**

In warmer parts of the world, 'Duchesse de Brabant' has been a popular and widely grown rose ever since it was introduced. In some places it is the first and last to flower, while in others it is truly continuous and never out of bloom. Then it mounds up slowly and bushily until it reaches as much as 8.2ft (2.5m), covered in attractive, pale pink flowers. The color is actually somewhat variable, and can be a bright mid-pink with a hint of salmon. The flowers are cupped or tulip-shaped, borne singly or (more usually) in clusters of up to ten. They last well if cut. Their petals are somewhat thin, so this is a rose that does best in dry climates. 'Duchesse de Brabant' is moderately vigorous, with a much-branched structure and a tendency to grow as wide as it is tall. Its leaves are mid-green, and slightly wavy. It is propagated from cuttings and is easy to grow in hot, dry climates. Mildew may be a problem elsewhere. Schwartz introduced a white-flowered sport in 1880 and called it **'Mme. Joseph Schwartz'**, though it is also known as 'White Duchesse de Brabant'. The flowers are mother-of-pearl, fading quickly to white, and the petals almost transparent. In all other details, it is exactly the same as 'Duchesse de Brabant'.

'DUCHESSE DE BRABANT'

'MME. JOSEPH SCHWARTZ'

Sport of 'Duchesse de Brabant'

'MME. JOSEPH SCHWARTZ'

syn. 'WHITE DUCHESSE DE BRABANT'
ORIGIN **Schwartz, France, 1880**

'DUCHESSE DE MONTEBELLO'

'DUCHESSE DE BUCCLEUGH'

Gallica

ORIGIN **Vibert, France, 1837**
FLOWER SIZE **3.5in (9cm)**
SCENT **Medium and sweet**
FLOWERING **Once only**
HEIGHT/SPREAD **5.7ft (1.75m)/4.1ft (1.25m)**
HARDINESS **Zone 5**

The flowers of this beautiful, many-petaled Gallica are almost exactly the same shade of bright, rich crimson as *Rosa gallica* 'Officinalis', and it helps to think of 'Duchesse de Buccleugh' as a full-petaled version of that well-known rose. The flowers have paler, pinker petal backs, which help to give them character when they curl over their petals. They open fully double and cupped, with a roughly quartered shape and a pretty mass of small petals. The flowers come singly or in clusters of up to four and are well set off by the dark, wrinkly leaves. The plant is vigorous and nearly thornless, with fairly slender, erect stems, which bow down under the weight of the flowers. The Duchess was Lady Charlotte Anne Thynne, daughter of the 2nd Marquess of Bath and wife of the 5th Duke of Buccleugh.

'DUCHESSE DE MONTEBELLO'

Gallica Hybrid

ORIGIN **Laffay, France, 1829**
FLOWER SIZE **2.4in (6cm)**
SCENT **Strong and sweet**
FLOWERING **Once only, but abundantly**
HEIGHT/SPREAD **5.7ft (1.75m)/6.6ft (2m)**
HARDINESS **Zone 5**

This charming old rose is a thrifty grower that will tolerate thin soil and survive years of neglect, though proper cultivation brings greater rewards. The flowers come in small clusters (usually of 3–5) and open from round, erect buds. They are bright pink at first, with a large button eye, before fading almost immediately to flesh pink and ending up mother-of-pearl with white edges. The bush is nearly thornless and has

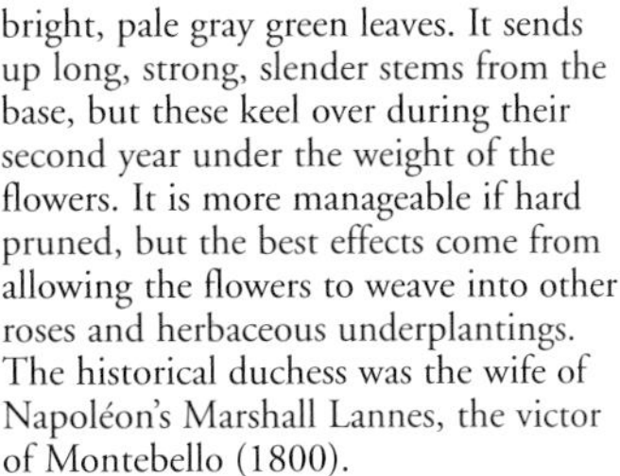

bright, pale gray green leaves. It sends up long, strong, slender stems from the base, but these keel over during their second year under the weight of the flowers. It is more manageable if hard pruned, but the best effects come from allowing the flowers to weave into other roses and herbaceous underplantings. The historical duchess was the wife of Napoléon's Marshall Lannes, the victor of Montebello (1800).

'DUCHESSE DE ROHAN'

Portland

ORIGIN **Lévêque, France, 1847**
FLOWER SIZE **3.1in (8cm)**
SCENT **Strong, rich, sweet, and Damask**
FLOWERING **Repeats**
HEIGHT/SPREAD **5.7ft (1.75m)/3.3ft (1m)**
HARDINESS **Zone 5**

The origins of the rose we grow as 'Duchesse de Rohan' are unknown. It is often described as a Centifolia rose, but Centifolias flower only once, while 'Duchesse de Rohan' is a reliable repeater. So the attribution to Lévèque may not be accurate. Nevertheless, 'Duchesse de Rohan' is an excellent rose. The flowers open deep pink and fade to a pretty pale pink, with a mass of small petals in a roughly quartered shape around a button eye. They come singly, but sometimes in small clusters, especially during the first flowering. The plant has a narrow shape and slender, upright growths, which arch over under the weight of flowers. The leaves are pale and rather wrinkly, but the plant is thornless apart from a very few bristles. Blackspot and mildew may make an appearance later in the year, but do no lasting damage. Deadheading helps to promote the next flowering, and the plant responds well to feeding and watering.

'DUCHESSE DE ROHAN'

'DUCHESSE DE VERNEUIL'

Moss Rose

ORIGIN **Portemer, France, 1856**
FLOWER SIZE **3.1in (8cm)**
SCENT **Strong and sweet**
FLOWERING **Once only**
HEIGHT/SPREAD **4.9ft (1.5m)/3.3ft (1m)**
HARDINESS **Zone 5**

'Duchesse de Verneuil' is an excellent, sturdy, once-flowering Moss rose. The lightly double flowers open bright, clear rose pink with paler petal backs, and are nearly flat in shape. They come in clusters of 3–7 and are well set off by golden stamens and a lot of healthy, matte, light green foliage. The moss too is light green: there is a lot of it and it extends a long way down the stems. The plant is sturdy and upright, hardy and thrifty, and does well even in poor soils in cold climates. The rose takes its name either from the original Duchesse de Verneuil, who was a mistress of King Henri IV of France, or from one of her semifictional descendants, who appear as characters in the novels of Honoré de Balzac.

'DUCHESSE DE BUCCLEUGH'

'DUCHESSE DE VERNEUIL'

D

'DUET'

'DUET'

Hybrid Tea

ORIGIN **Swim, US, 1960**
PARENTAGE **'Fandango' x 'Roundelay'**
FLOWER SIZE **3.9in (10cm)**
SCENT **Moderate and fruity**
FLOWERING **Repeats well**
HEIGHT/SPREAD **4.9ft (1.5m)/3.3ft (1m)**
HARDINESS **Zone 5**
AWARDS **Baden Baden GM 1959; AARS 1961**

'Duet' is a popular, attractive, and easy to grow rose that does best in warm climates. The flowers are most remarkable for the contrast between their two colors: they are pale rose pink (with a hint of coral at first) on the upper surfaces of the petals and dark purple pink on the backs. The petals are large, broad, thick, and slightly ruffled. As the flowers age, the outer petals lose their remaining color, which has the effect of intensifying the rich reflected hues at the center of the bloom. The flowers are borne singly or in clusters of up to five (these blooms resemble those of a Floribunda) almost without interruption until early winter. The leaves are mid-green, glossy, of medium size, and disease resistant. The plant makes a strapping, upright bush and gives best results when lightly pruned and allowed to build up to its full height.

DUFTRAUSCH

syn. 'TANSCHAUBUD', Old Fragrance, Senteur Royale

Hybrid Tea

ORIGIN **Tantau, Germany, 1985**
FLOWER SIZE **5.1in (13cm)**
SCENT **Strong, sweet, rich, and fruity**
FLOWERING **Repeats**
HEIGHT/SPREAD **3.3ft (1m)/2.5ft (75cm)**
HARDINESS **Zone 6**

Although it is sometimes listed as a purple rose, Duftrausch is closer in color to pale crimson or cerise. It is a brilliant and distinctive tint, which catches the eye from far away. The flowers are notably large, and have been known to reach 5.9in (15cm) when eventually they open out to reveal their golden stamens. They are borne, almost invariably, singly on strong stems. Their scent is rich and delicious. Duftrausch

DUFTRAUSCH

responds well to good cultivation and prefers only a light pruning – then it grows vigorously and produces its flowers abundantly in a series of flushes until late autumn. The plant has dark, matte and very healthy leaves and a strong, bushy habit of growth.

'DUFTWOLKE'

syn. 'TANELLIS', 'FRAGRANT CLOUD', 'NUAGE PARFUMÉ'

Hybrid Tea

ORIGIN **Tantau, Germany, 1967**
PARENTAGE **seedling x 'Prima Ballerina'**
FLOWER SIZE **5.1in (13cm)**
SCENT **Very strong, rich, fruity, and sweet**
FLOWERING **Repeats well**
HEIGHT/SPREAD **4.9ft (1.5m)/3.3ft (1m)**
HARDINESS **Zone 5**
AWARDS **NRS PIT 1964; Portland GM 1966; Gamble FA 1970; World's Favourite Rose 1981**

Beauty, size, and an amazing scent – 'Duftwolke' has all the qualities you could ask for in a rose. It is also vigorous, strong-growing, healthy, and almost continuously in flower. Only its color is not to everyone's taste – a bright vermilion sometimes described as orange, coral, or geranium. It is a shade not found in any other rose, and assumes a strange purplish tint as the flowers age. The individual flowers are shapely and large. The plant is classified as a Hybrid Tea, but the flowers usually come in fat clusters of 3–7. They last well as cut flowers, though they have somewhat short stems. The plant is fairly prickly, with large leaves and a good branching habit. In hot climates it will easily reach 6.6ft (2m).

DUFTZAUBER 84

syn. 'KORZAUN', Fragrant Charm, Royal William

Hybrid Tea

ORIGIN **Kordes, Germany, 1984**
PARENTAGE **'Feuerzauber' seedling**
FLOWER SIZE **5.1in (13cm)**
SCENT **Strong, sweet, and fruity**
FLOWERING **Repeats well**
HEIGHT/SPREAD **4.1ft (1.25m)/3.3ft (1m)**
HARDINESS **Zone 6**
AWARDS **ROTY 1987; The Hague FA 1987**

This immensely popular red Hybrid Tea is one of the best of all roses bred in the last quarter of the 20th century. Duftzauber 84 is a rose without faults. The flowers are large, perfectly formed, and a beautiful deep, unfading turkey red color. Sometimes the petals have dark velvety markings on their tips. The flowers are shapely and attractive, both as high-centered, opening buds and as fully expanded, cupped blooms. They are usually borne singly, but sometimes in twos and threes, on long, strong, upright

'DUFTWOLKE'

DUFTZAUBER 84

stems that are excellent for cutting. The scent carries on the air, and is delicious. Duftzauber 84 has large, handsome, healthy, dark green, semi-glossy leaves. It has a strong, vigorous, upright habit of growth and repeats quickly, which makes it an excellent bedding rose.

'DUKE OF WINDSOR'

see 'HERZOG VON WINDSOR'

'DUNWICH'

syn. Rosa spinosissima 'DUNWICHENSIS'

Wild Rose

ORIGIN **Britain, 1950**
FLOWER SIZE **1.2in (3cm)**
SCENT **Medium and fetid**
FLOWERING **Once, usually very early in season**
HEIGHT/SPREAD **4.1ft (1.25m)**
HARDINESS **Zone 5**

The Dunwich rose is a cultivar of *Rosa spinosissima*, which is a variable species. 'Dunwich' is distinct in two principal ways. First, it is extremely floriferous, covering itself with flowers in a way that no other Scottish rose does. Second, it has a neat, low, dense habit of growth, with small leaves and branches that spread out in fan-shaped tiers. The flowers are creamy white at first, with handsome dark yellow stamens. The bush is very prickly and, if grown on its own roots, suckers energetically, so that within a short time there is enough 'Dunwich' to make a low hedge. It is very tolerant of poor soils and is thought to have been found on the sand dunes of the Suffolk village of Dunwich, most of which has now been lost to coastal erosion.

'DUNWICH'

'Duplex'

'Duplex'

syn. 'Wolley-Dod's Rose'
Species Hybrid

Origin **Wolley-Dod, Britain**
Parentage ***Rosa villosa* hybrid**
Flower size **2in (5cm)**
Scent **Light and sweet**
Flowering **Once only**
Height/spread **6.6ft (2m)/6.6ft (2m)**
Hardiness **Zone 5**

'Duplex' is a double-flowered hybrid of *Rosa villosa*, which probably arose from pollination by an Old Garden rose. It has been known since at least the 18th century, but variously attributed since then to Vibert (in the 1820s) and Charles Wolley-Dod (in the 1900s). Its flowers open pastel pink, from pale red buds. They are lightly and neatly double, with a hint of white toward the center of the flower and a ring of golden stamens. They come in short-stemmed clusters of 3–7 and sit very prettily among the lush, gray green leaves. Later in the year come dark red, hairy hips. The plant is vigorous, healthy, and very hardy. If grown on its own roots, it suckers around agreeably.

'Dupontii'

syn. Rosa x *dupontii*
Shrub Rose

Origin **c.1817**
Flower size **2.8in (7cm)**
Scent **Strong and sweet**
Flowering **Once, fairly early in season**
Height/spread **9.8ft (3m)/8.2ft (2.5m)**
Hardiness **Zone 6**

No one knows the origins of this rose, though it is sometimes attributed to André Dupont (1756–1817), who advised Empress Josephine on her rose garden at Malmaison. The flowers are single, sometimes with an extra petal or petaloid at the center, and creamy white (later pure white) with pink buds and pink petal backs. The petals are broad and overlapping, and encircle a crown of long, wispy stamens. At the center is a long projecting stigma, suggesting that one of 'Dupontii's parents was a Synstylae rose like *Rosa moschata*, perhaps crossed with an Alba rose. The flowers come in small clusters (typically of 3–5), and are followed by shining, scarlet, oval hips. The handsome leaves are soft, gray green. The plant is vigorous and very beautiful during its all too brief flowering.

'Dupontii'

'Dusky Maiden'

'Dusky Maiden'

Floribunda

Origin **Le Grice, Britain, 1947**
Parentage **('Daily Mail Scented Rose' x 'Etoile de Hollande') x 'Else Poulsen'**
Flower size **3.1in (8cm)**
Scent **Light**
Flowering **Repeats well**
Height/spread **3.3ft (1m)/2.5ft (75cm)**
Hardiness zone **6**
Awards **NRS GM 1948**

This cross between a Hybrid Tea and a Polyantha was one of the first true Floribunda roses. Its simple flowers are borne in great profusion, so that it seems never to be out of bloom. The flowers are a rich, unfading scarlet crimson – uniformly colored with no paling toward the center and no white flecks in the petals, just a small boss of pale yellow stamens to light them up at the center. They come in clusters of 3–9 on a bushy plant that grows easily in a wide variety of situations and climates .

'Dwarf Pavement'

see 'Rosa Zwerg'

Dynamite

syn. 'JACsat'
Kordesii

Origin **Warriner, US, 1992**
Parentage **seedling x 'Sympathie'**
Flower size **4.3in (11cm)**
Scent **Slight**
Flowering **Repeats well**
Height/spread **9.8ft (3m)/6.5ft (2m)**
Hardiness **Zone 5**

Scent is the only quality that Dynamite does not possess in abundance – it is hardy, healthy, floriferous, and easy to grow. The flowers are bright turkey red with large petals and come in small clusters, typically of 3–5. They keep their color and shape well. The plant is forever putting out new flowering stems. If these are pegged down or tied in horizontally after flowering, they will break into flower again along their length. The foliage is dark green and glossy. Like many Kordesii climbers, Dynamite is handsome rather than beautiful.

Dynamite

Dynastie

syn. 'MEIpitac', Carefree Wonder
Shrub Rose

Origin **Meilland, France, 1990**
Parentage **('Prairie Princess' x Nirvana) x (Eyepaint x Rustica)**
Flower size **4in (10cm)**
Scent **Light**
Flowering **Continuous**
Height/spread **2.3ft (70cm)/2.3ft (70cm)**
Hardiness **Zone 4**
Awards **AARS 1991**

This excellent neat shrub rose combines large flowers with great hardiness and an enormous potential for landscaping. The flowers are bright shocking pink, with a white center, yellow stamens, and white petal backs: it is a stunning contrast of colors, especially when the buds are opening, but even later on when the flowers open out flat. They come singly or in tight clusters of up to five and are followed by dull red hips. The plant naturally blooms right through until winter but, if deadheaded, the flowers come much more freely. The plant is neat, bushy, and low-growing, forming a thicket of stems if grown on its own roots. It reaches 1.6ft (50cm) high in cold climates, but as much as 4.9ft (1.5m) where it can grow unchecked. The leaves are small, glossy, and free from disease. It is very popular in the US, where it is grown as Carefree Wonder, and in its native France, but should be grown much more widely in other parts of Europe.

Dynastie

D

E

'EARTH SONG'

Grandiflora

ORIGIN **Buck, US, 1975**
PARENTAGE **'Music Maker' × 'Prairie Star'**
FLOWER SIZE **5.1in (13cm)**
SCENT **Medium**
FLOWERING **Repeats well**
HEIGHT/SPREAD **8.2ft (2.5m)/3.3ft (1m)**
HARDINESS **Zone 4**

Dr. Griffith Buck bred 'Earth Song' from two roses that he had introduced himself, both of them steps on the road toward his ultimate goal – top-quality garden roses that would survive the freezing winters and hot humid summers of Iowa. 'Earth Song' resembles a more slender version of 'Queen Elizabeth'. Its small, narrow buds open into surprisingly large flowers, sometimes as much as 5.5–5.9in (14–15cm) across. They are rich ruby pink at first, then paler as they age and open to reveal their stamens, but they never lose their original richness of hue. They are borne singly or in clusters of up to five on a slim, upright shrub, which has dark, tough, healthy leaves, reddish when young. It has proved hardy not just in Iowa but in even colder areas, while also flourishing in much warmer climates, such as southern California.

'EARTH SONG'

'EASLEA'S GOLDEN RAMBLER'

Wichurana Rambler

ORIGIN **Easlea, Britain, 1932**
FLOWER SIZE **3.9in (10cm)**
SCENT **Strong and sweet**
FLOWERING **Once only, early in season**
HEIGHT/SPREAD **9.8ft (3m)/6.6ft (2m)**
HARDINESS **Zone 6**
AWARDS **NRS GM 1932**

This beautiful yellow climber was bred by Walter Easlea, who started his own nursery near Leigh-on-Sea, England, in 1900 and specialized in Hybrid Teas. It has the largest flowers of all once-flowering yellow ramblers. They open flat from pointed buds, with a mass of frilled outer petals enclosing a muddled arrangement of smaller ones at the center. They are dark yellow at first, with coppery hints and occasional streaks of orange on the outer petals, and keep their color well, though they do fade first to lemon and then to cream at the edges of the flowers, while always retaining a darker yellow at the center. The individual flowers are very weatherproof and last well both in the garden and when cut for the house. They are carried either singly or in clusters of up to seven, sometimes more. The leaves are olive green and glossy, with a slightly ridged surface to the leaflets. The plant is very vigorous, with large prickles, and inclined to legginess.

'EASLEA'S GOLDEN RAMBLER'

EASY GOING

see 'FELLOWSHIP'

ROSA ECAE

Wild Rose

FLOWER SIZE **1.2in (3cm)**
SCENT **Little or none**
FLOWERING **Once only, early in season**
HEIGHT/SPREAD **6.6ft (2m)/4.9ft (1.5m)**
HARDINESS **Zone 5**

The bright flowers of *Rosa ecae* are one of the joys of spring. They are small, but intensely golden yellow, and they cover the length of the branches, one appearing at every node. Each is backed by a cluster of tiny, fresh green, scented leaves, seldom more than 1in (2.5cm) long, and composed of up to nine rounded leaflets. The flowers are followed by small (0.2in/0.5cm), round, red hips, which fall to the ground when ripe. *Rosa ecae* is a thicketing shrub, with a mass of slender branches and branchlets, sometimes growing at somewhat odd angles. The stems are slender and brown and develop long, flat prickles as they age. It is a native of central Asia from northwestern Pakistan to the Tien Shan and Pamir mountains, where it tolerates hot summers and cold winters.

ROSA ECAE

'ECLIPSE'

'ECLIPSE'

Hybrid Tea

ORIGIN **Nicolas, US, 1935**
PARENTAGE **'Joanna Hill' × 'Federigo Casas'**
FLOWER SIZE **3.9in (10cm)**
SCENT **Strong, sweet, and fruity**
FLOWERING **Repeats well**
HEIGHT/SPREAD **4.9ft (1.5m)/3.3ft (1m)**
HARDINESS **Zone 5**
AWARDS **Portland GM 1935; Rome GM 1935; Bagatelle GM 1936**

Jean Henri Nicolas, who bred this striking yellow rose, was a wealthy Frenchman who emigrated to the US when he met and married a girl from Chicago. Later, he worked as a breeder for Jackson & Perkins, America's largest rose growers. Nicolas sought roses that would be hardy and healthy in New England. 'Eclipse' has remained a popular garden rose not merely for its health and hardiness, but also because it produces a continuous succession of flowers until well into autumn. The long, elegant buds open quickly into lightly double flowers, which are a splendid rich yellow before fading to lemon. The large brush of red stamens adds greatly to their beauty, and the flowers stand up well to rain, though their petals are few and have ragged edges. The original plant first flowered on August 31 1932, the day of a total solar eclipse in New England.

'EDDIE'S JEWEL'

'EDDIE'S JEWEL'

Shrub Rose

ORIGIN **Eddie, US, 1962**
PARENTAGE **'Donald Prior' × *Rosa moyesii***
FLOWER SIZE **3.5in (9cm)**
SCENT **Light and sweet**
FLOWERING **Once only**
HEIGHT/SPREAD **11.5ft (3.5m)/8.2ft (2.5m)**
HARDINESS **Zone 5**

There are only a few hybrids of *Rosa moyesii*, the stately "flagon-hip" species: 'Eddie's Jewel' is the best of them. Its flowers are a rich, bright crimson, keeping their color but losing their brightness as they age, and often highlighted by white streaks flaring out from the center. The golden stamens are also very noticeable. The flowers come singly or in clusters of up to five and are followed by a few hips – not every flower seems to form them. The plant is tall, healthy, and vigorous, with crimson stems, few prickles, and handsome foliage that resembles a larger edition of the leaves of *Rosa moyesii*. It is an excellent rose that, though long loved by the cognoscenti, should be much more widely known and grown.

'EDELWEISS'

'EDELWEISS'

syn. 'SNOWLINE'

Floribunda

ORIGIN **Poulsen, Denmark, 1970**
PARENTAGE **'Pernille Poulsen' × 'White Jewel'**
FLOWER SIZE **3.1in (8cm)**
SCENT **Light and musky**
FLOWERING **Repeats well**
HEIGHT/SPREAD **2.3ft (70cm)/1.6ft (50cm)**
HARDINESS **Zone 6**
AWARDS **ADR 1970**

Short-growing Floribundas are excellent bedding roses. If they are also white and unusually free flowering, they are useful in any planting and any color scheme. 'Edelweiss' is a fine example and has been popular ever since it was introduced. The flowers are pure white with a hint of yellow at the center, which is reflected by the half-hidden stamens. By the time the petals have opened out completely, the stamens are brown. The flowers come in large but rather tight clusters, typically of 5–10, and stand up to rain better than most white roses. 'Edelweiss' is a compact, bushy grower, but fairly vigorous. Its medium-sized leaves are dark and glossy. It is a reliable repeat flowerer, almost constantly in bloom.

EDEN ROSE 88

see PIERRE DE RONSARD

'EDITH CAVELL'

see 'MISS EDITH CAVELL'

'EDITH DE MARTINELLI'

Floribunda

ORIGIN **Arles, France, 1958**
PARENTAGE **('Gruss an Teplitz' × 'Sondermeldung') × 'Floradora'**
FLOWER SIZE **4.3in (11cm)**
SCENT **Medium and fruity**
FLOWERING **Repeats well**
HEIGHT/SPREAD **3.3ft (1m)/2ft (60cm)**
HARDINESS **Zone 6**
AWARDS **Geneva GM 1958**

Although almost unknown elsewhere, 'Edith de Martinelli' has been a firm favorite in France and very widely grown ever since it was first introduced. The surprise is that this excellent Floribunda should have remained such a French speciality: 'Edith de Martinelli' is an outstanding rose by any standards, and performs well in both hot and cold climates, and wet or dry weather. The flowers are vermilion lake in color, slightly pinker on the petal backs, and fading to salmon pink at the edges. They are borne very profusely in well-spaced clusters of 3–9: they tend to nod slightly on their pedicels as they age, so that the older flowers look out slightly sideways and the younger ones somewhat more upward. The flowers are cup-shaped and very full of petals. 'Edith de Martinelli' is a small, compact plant, never more than 3.3ft (1m) high, and often only half that height, but the climbing form, now rather rare, known as 'Grimpant Edith de Martinelli' (Orard, 1983) climbs vigorously to 16.4ft (5m).

'EDITH DE MARTINELLI'

'EDITOR STEWART'

EDITH HOLDEN

syn. 'CHEWLEGACY'

Floribunda

ORIGIN **Warner, Britain, 1988**
PARENTAGE **'Belinda' × ('Elizabeth of Glamis' × ['Galway Bay' × 'Sutter's Gold'])**
FLOWER SIZE **3.5in (9cm)**
SCENT **Light and fruity**
FLOWERING **Repeats**
HEIGHT/SPREAD **6.6ft (2m)/3.3ft (1m)**
HARDINESS **Zone 6**

Edith Holden was bred by Chris Warner before he became a professional rose breeder. It is a unique color, even among the growing range of roses that are described as "tan" or "brown." The flowers are dark, burnt orange, with a brown wash, fading to dusty pink. They have a hint of yellow at the center and pretty stamens. Later they fade to gray and fawn. The petal backs are always slightly paler. The flowers come in long-stemmed clusters of 5–11 (good for flower arrangements) and are followed in autumn by small, round, orange hips. Flowering is almost continuous. The bush has medium-dark, glossy leaves (bronzy at first) and few prickles. It grows vigorously and makes a fine 9.8ft (3m) pillar rose in hot climates, though it is sturdy enough to grow as a bush without support. Edith Holden was author of *The Country Diary of an Edwardian Lady.*

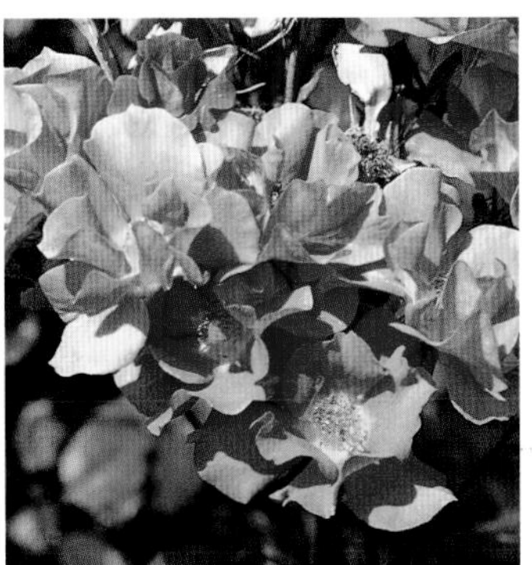
EDITH HOLDEN

'EDITOR STEWART'

Hybrid Tea-type Pillar Rose

ORIGIN **Clark, Australia, 1939**
FLOWER SIZE **3.5in (9cm)**
SCENT **Light**
FLOWERING **Fully recurrent**
HEIGHT/SPREAD **9.8ft (3m)/4.9ft (1.5m)**
HARDINESS **Zone 6**

'Editor Stewart' is a good-looking and vigorous bush or pillar rose, with red young growths and striking semidouble flowers. In Australia, after a spectacular spring flowering, it always has a few flowers until early winter. The flowers are cherry crimson, fading only slightly as they age. They are set off by brilliant yellow stamens and white flashes in the petals – Alister Clark's roses often owe their charm to such irregularities. The flowers are borne on slender stems in large, elegant sprays of up to 15 (typically of three or five), or occasionally singly. They open out flat at first, but later acquire a ruffled or wavy effect.

ROSA EGLANTERIA

see ROSA RUBIGINOSA

EGLANTYNE

syn. 'AUSMAK'

Shrub Rose

ORIGIN **Austin, Britain, 1994**
PARENTAGE **seedling × Mary Rose**
FLOWER SIZE **3.1in (8cm)**
SCENT **Strong**
FLOWERING **Repeats well**
HEIGHT/SPREAD **4.9ft (1.5m)/4.1ft (1.25m)**
HARDINESS **Zone 6**

Eglantyne is one of the prettiest, most floriferous, and most popular of David Austin's English Roses. The flowers are pale pink with mid-pink backs and paler edges; later they fade to palest pink and white. They are beautifully old-fashioned in shape: lightly cupped, quilled rosettes, with masses of petals, and sometimes a button eye or a green pointel. They are carried in fairly dense, nodding, long-lasting clusters of 3–9. The plant is bushy, slender, upright, and prickly, with medium-sized, matte green leaves. Blackspot can be a problem, but repeat flowering is not: Eglantyne is almost always in bloom. It was named after Eglantyne Jebb, who founded the Save the Children Fund during World War I.

EGLANTYNE

'Eiffel Tower'

Hybrid Tea

ORIGIN **Armstrong & Swim, US, 1963**
PARENTAGE **'First Love' seedling**
FLOWER SIZE **4.7in (12cm)**
SCENT **Strong and sweet**
FLOWERING **Repeats**
HEIGHT/SPREAD **4.9ft (1.5m)/3.3ft (1m)**
HARDINESS **Zone 5**
AWARDS **Geneva 1963; Rome 1963**

The first thing you notice about 'Eiffel Tower' is its long and slender buds. They usually come singly at the end of a long, upright stem, which seems to increase the length of the flower itself. However, they also open out attractively, at which stage they are a slightly mauve pink, with darker petal backs, before fading to pale pink. They are very popular for cutting. The plant is slender and upright, with large, mid-green leaves, which are fairly resistant to blackspot and mildew. 'Eiffel Tower' grows best in warm climates and repeats regularly. The flowers tend to spoil in rain, but their scent is delicious – some say it is the sweetest and richest of all the Hybrid Teas.

'Electron'

see 'Mullard Jubilee'

'Elegance'

Wichurana Rambler

ORIGIN **Brownell, US, 1937**
PARENTAGE **'Glenn Dale' x ('Mary Wallace' x 'Miss Lolita Armour')**
FLOWER SIZE **4.7in (12cm)**
SCENT **Medium and sweet**
FLOWERING **Repeats intermittently**
HEIGHT/SPREAD **16.4ft (5m)/9.8ft (3m)**
HARDINESS **Zone 5**

Dr. and Mrs. Brownell bred roses to survive the cold winters of New England. Although difficult to find now in the US, this vigorous, yellow climber is still popular in Europe. The flowers of 'Elegance' live up to their name – long-stemmed, large, and scented, perfect for cutting. They open a pure rich yellow, but fade quickly to lemon, with cream at the edges. The petal backs are darker, which gives rise to very pretty shades within the flower as it opens out. The foliage is beautiful – large, dark, and glossy in the Wichurana manner – with crimson new growth and large prickles on the slender, fast-growing branches. It flowers fairly well in midseason and sporadically (if at all) thereafter. It is immensely vigorous and will quickly reach 32.8ft (10m) up a tree.

'Elegance'

'Eiffel Tower'

Elina

syn. 'Dicjana', Peaudouce

Hybrid Tea

ORIGIN **Dickson, Northern Ireland, 1983**
PARENTAGE **'Nana Mouskouri' x 'Lolita'**
FLOWER SIZE **5.9in (15cm)**
SCENT **Medium and sweet**
FLOWERING **Repeats**
HEIGHT/SPREAD **4.9ft (1.5m)/3.3ft (1m)**
HARDINESS **Zone 5**
AWARDS **ADR 1987; NZ GM 1987; James Mason GM 1994**

Only superlatives can do justice to the size and beauty of the flowers of Elina. They are perfectly formed Hybrid Teas, full of elegantly reflexing petals, and carried singly on very long stems. Their exact color depends upon the weather and climate. In their native Northern Ireland, they are lemon yellow fading to cream at the edges. In hotter conditions, they are rarely more than ivory or off-white. Nevertheless, Elina is a top exhibition rose all over the world and splendid to pick for arrangements because its flowers are so large and its stems so long. The plant has large, dark, glossy leaves and is very healthy except for a little mildew in damp conditions. Thrips like it, too. It is extraordinarily vigorous and will grow to 9.8ft (3m) in a season in hot climates.

Elina

'Elizabeth Harkness'

'Elizabeth Harkness'

Hybrid Tea

ORIGIN **Harkness, Britain, 1969**
PARENTAGE **'Red Dandy' x 'Piccadilly'**
FLOWER SIZE **4.7in (12cm)**
SCENT **Strong and sweet**
FLOWERING **Repeats well**
HEIGHT/SPREAD **3.3ft (1m)/2.5ft (75cm)**
HARDINESS **Zone 6**

Jack Harkness named this elegant Hybrid Tea after his only daughter on her 21st birthday. It is a slender beauty under English skies, but a hefty stunner in hot climates, where it quickly reaches 8.2ft (2.5m). The flowers are always an exquisite mixture of pale colors – pearly white overall, but with pale pink, buff, and apricot reflected within the opening flowers. In hot weather they fade quickly to ivory-white. They come on long stems, usually singly but sometimes in twos and threes. The long petals are susceptible to rain damage, but the flower opens out attractively in dry weather. The plant has dark leaves and an upright habit of growth. Blackspot and rust can be a problem in some areas.

'Elizabeth of Glamis'

syn. 'Irish Beauty'

Floribunda

ORIGIN **McGredy, Northern Ireland, 1964**
PARENTAGE **'Spartan' x 'Highlight'**
FLOWER SIZE **3.9in (10cm)**
SCENT **Medium and sweet**
FLOWERING **Repeats well**
HEIGHT/SPREAD **3.3ft (1m)/2.7ft (80cm)**
HARDINESS **Zone 7**
AWARDS **NRS PIT 1963**

'Elizabeth of Glamis' is very free flowering and unusual for the size of its individual flowers. Their color is a bright salmon pink, fading to a pinker pink, but always darker in the center – more the color of smoked salmon. They open out from elegant, well-formed, Hybrid Tea type buds. The open flowers also have a very pleasing shape, with a slight wave to the petals. They come in clusters of 3–7, held well above the foliage. The leaves – and there are a lot of them – are dark green and fairly glossy, while the plant is vigorous, compact, and bushy. It is an excellent bedding rose that responds to good cultivation and seems to do best in warm situations. It deserves its continuing popularity. It was named after Queen Elizabeth, wife of King George VI of England, whose father owned Glamis Castle in Scotland.

'Elizabeth of Glamis'

ELLE

ELLE

syn. 'MEIBDÉROS'

Hybrid Tea

ORIGIN **Meilland, France, 2000**
FLOWER SIZE **4.7in (12cm)**
SCENT **Very strong and sweet**
FLOWERING **Repeats well**
HEIGHT/SPREAD **4.1ft (1.25m)/2.7ft (80cm)**
HARDINESS **Zone 6**

Elle is a high circulation fashion magazine: its rose is equally stylish. Elle is a very beautiful combination of yellow, orange, and pink. The petals are pink, with creamy backs, but the whole flower is suffused with yellow at first, so it appears orange until the yellow starts to fade from the outer petals and the pink predominates. The flowers are large, strongly scented (it won a prize for scent at Bagatelle in 1999), and full of petals arranged in an old-fashioned shape. They come singly, occasionally in twos and threes, on long, strong stems that are perfect for cutting. The leaves are dark, shiny, and healthy. An excellent rose.

ELLEN

syn. 'AUSCUP'

Shrub Rose

ORIGIN **Austin, Britain, 1984**
PARENTAGE **'Charles Austin' x seedling**
FLOWER SIZE **3.9in (10cm)**
SCENT **Strong and fruity**
FLOWERING **Repeats slowly**
HEIGHT/SPREAD **4.1ft (1.25m)/3.3ft (1m)**
HARDINESS **Zone 6**

Ellen Drew was an employee of Austin's who retired in 1984, and Ellen was named after her. The flowers give an overall appearance of apricot at first, though they are, in fact, fawn or buff, with dark apricot petal backs. Then the yellow tinge fades to leave a pale pink and creamy white flower. The flowers open cup-shaped, with a somewhat loose and shapeless mass of petals that spoil in the rain. They come in large clusters of 3–15 (typically 9), tightly packed together on short stems. The plant has handsome dark leaves and a lot of prickles. It is not very recurrent, but reflowering definitely improves with deadheading.

'ELLEN POULSEN'

Polyantha

ORIGIN **Poulsen, Denmark, 1911**
PARENTAGE **'Mme. Norbert Levavasseur' x 'Dorothy Perkins'**
FLOWER SIZE **1in (2.5cm)**
SCENT **Little or none**
FLOWERING **Almost continuous**
HEIGHT/SPREAD **3.3ft (1m)/3.3ft (1m)**
HARDINESS **Zone 5**

This cheerful and floriferous Polyantha was one of the first to be bred by the Poulsen family, whose hybrids came to dominate the development of Floribunda roses in the 1920s and 1930s. The flowers are dark pink, with a white center, fully double, but cupped in shape. Later they fade to rosepink. The flowers come in clusters of 5–15 and are backed by a lot of dark, glossy, healthy, sturdy leaves. The plant is bushy and compact, but this does not stop it from growing to as much as 4.1ft (1.25m) high and 5.7ft (1.75m) across in hot climates. In its native Denmark, it is more commonly seen as a low, dense shrub, 1.6ft (50cm) high and eventually 2.3ft (70cm) across. Its health, vigor, and flower production make it an excellent choice for a wide range of climates and positions.

ELLEN

'ELLEN POULSEN'

'ELLEN WILLMOTT'

Hybrid Tea

ORIGIN **Archer, Britain, 1936**
PARENTAGE **'Dainty Bess' x 'Lady Hillingdon'**
FLOWER SIZE **8cm (3.1in)**
SCENT **Light and fruity**
FLOWERING **Repeats well**
HEIGHT/SPREAD **4.9ft (1.5m)/3.3ft (1m)**
HARDINESS **Zone 6**

It is a little surprising that the English horticulturist Ellen Willmott should be commemorated by a single-flowered Hybrid Tea rose, when her greatest interest was in wild rose species and old roses. However, Archer introduced this rose two years after Wilmott's death, when she was unable to refuse the honor. 'Ellen Willmott' is a pleasant rose that relies entirely for its effect upon the stupendous stamens at the center. They have crimson filaments and gold anthers, and some of them are very lengthy, so that they stretch a long way out from the center of the flower. Those flowers are pale pink, fading to ivory white, but with darker, peach colored petal backs and a slight wave to the petals, which confers a distinctive charm upon the whole flower. They come in clusters of 3–12, which more closely resemble the Floribundas that were to be bred in the 1940s and 1950s than any Hybrid Tea. 'Ellen Willmott' is vigorous and healthy, with dark green leaves and beautiful crimson new growth.

'ELLEN WILLMOTT'

'ELMSHORN'

Shrub Rose

ORIGIN **Kordes, Germany, 1951**
PARENTAGE **'Hamburg' x 'Verdun'**
FLOWER SIZE **1.6in (4cm)**
SCENT **Light or slight**
FLOWERING **Repeats well**
HEIGHT/SPREAD **6.6ft (2m)/5.7ft (1.75m)**
HARDINESS **Zone 5**
AWARDS **ADR 1950**

'Elmshorn' is an excellent shrub rose, particularly useful where a massed display is needed on a large scale but also pretty as a long flowering specimen shrub in a mixed border. The flowers are pale crimson at first, then deep, intense pink, and fading at the edges in hot weather to pale pink. They have masses of short petals in a cupped shape (later turning into a pompon) and have the great attribute of dropping those petals cleanly when they finish flowering. They are carried in stout, open clusters of 10–20 flowers, held well above the bush. The foliage is dark and glossy and the bush is very vigorous. As a freestanding specimen, it is usually about 6.6ft (2m) tall, but hard pruning can bring it down to about 4.9ft (1.5m). If encouraged to climb, it will reach 16.4ft (5m) in a hot climate. It is immensely floriferous and recurrent flowering, especially good in autumn, and continuing until winter. Elmshorn is a town near the Kordes nursery in northern Germany.

'ELMSHORN'

'Else Poulsen'

Floribunda

ORIGIN **Poulsen, Denmark, 1924**
PARENTAGE **'Orléans Rose' x 'Red Star'**
FLOWER SIZE **2in (5cm)**
SCENT **Little or none**
FLOWERING **Almost continuous**
HEIGHT/SPREAD **3.3ft (1m)/3.9ft (1.2m)**
HARDINESS **Zone 5**

'Else Poulsen' was an immensely popular rose when it was introduced, and did much to create a market for vigorous, large-flowered Polyantha roses. These were hybrids between Polyanthas and Hybrid Teas and tended to be called "Hybrid Polyanthas". The flowers of 'Else Poulsen' are actually quite small, but carried in great profusion in rather tight clusters of 8–15, so that they make a considerable impact. They are pale pink, opening from dark pink buds, with mid-pink petal backs and a white patch at the center. The petals curve inward, but are also slightly wavy. They are very long lasting, both in the garden and as cut flowers. The leaves are dark and glossy, and the plant makes shrubby, upright growth. It flowers ceaselessly until early winter, and, though fairly weatherproof, the petals do acquire little red spots after heavy rain. It is susceptible to mildew, especially late in the year, though the disease never seems to affect its vigor. In hot climates it will grow to 6.6ft (2m).

In 1932, the Dutch nurseryman Matthias Leenders introduced a pale crimson sport of 'Else Poulsen', which he named **'Mevrouw van Straaten van Nes'**. It is exactly the same as its parent in all respects except for its rich color. It is popular in North America, where it is known as 'Permanent Wave', and in Australia.

'Else Poulsen'

'Mevrouw van Straaten van Nes'

Sport of 'Else Poulsen'

'Mevrouw van Straaten van Nes'

syn. 'PERMANENT WAVE'
ORIGIN **Leenders, Netherlands, 1932**
AWARDS **Bagatelle GM 1932; Rome GM 1934**

Elveshörn

syn. 'KORbotaf'

Polyantha

ORIGIN **Kordes, Germany, 1985**
PARENTAGE **'The Fairy' seedling**
FLOWER SIZE **2.8in (7cm)**
SCENT **Light and musky**
FLOWERING **Almost continuous**
HEIGHT/SPREAD **3.3ft (1m)/3.3ft (1m)**
HARDINESS **Zone 5**

The bright, dark pink or pale crimson flowers of Elveshörn are both conspicuous and attractive. They glow with color, while also having a silvery sheen to their petals. They are often borne singly, but also in clusters of up to five, occasionally more. They come on short stems and are well set off by the hard, glossy, handsome, mid-green leaves. Elveshörn is a compact shrub rose of Polyantha origins, so it has a dense, branching structure, lots of prickles, and a spreading habit of growth – sometimes it is wider than high. It is very hardy and healthy, and flowers profusely until late autumn. It is often recommended as a landscaping rose and a short hedging rose, but it is useful, above all, as a free flowering, rain-resistant garden rose.

Elveshörn

Emanuel

syn. 'AUSuel'

Shrub Rose

ORIGIN **Austin, Britain, 1985**
PARENTAGE **('Chaucer' x 'Parade') x (seedling x 'Schneewittchen')**
FLOWER SIZE **3.9in (10cm)**
SCENT **Strong and sweet**
FLOWERING **Repeats**
HEIGHT/SPREAD **4.9ft (1.5m)/4.9ft (1.5m)**
HARDINESS **Zone 6**

David Austin once said that Emanuel would be one of his best roses were it not for its tendency to blackspot. Fortunately, blackspot is not a problem everywhere: Emanuel can safely be grown without any preventive spraying in many parts of the US, Australia, South Africa, and the Mediterranean. The flowers are large, luscious, flat rosettes of delicate apricot pink, and deliciously scented. The color is variable – deeper in cool weather, pinker in hot – because the yellow flush that creates its delicate apricot tones fades quickly in hot sun. The flowers have a lot of petals and nod their heads agreeably. They come singly or in twos and threes, and break easily from every node if pegged down. The plant is thick and bushy, with a scattering of prickles and a lot of dark green leaves.

Emanuel

Emily

syn. 'AUSburton'

Shrub Rose

ORIGIN **Austin, Britain, 1992**
PARENTAGE **'The Prioress' x Mary Rose**
FLOWER SIZE **3.1in (8cm)**
SCENT **Strong and sweet**
FLOWERING **Repeats well**
HEIGHT/SPREAD **2.7ft (80cm)/2ft (60cm)**
HARDINESS **Zone 6**

The great strength (and weakness, too) of Emily is its lack of vigor. It is slow-growing and short, even in hot climates, where some of David Austin's roses grow too tall for small gardens. Emily is always of modest dimensions. Its flowers are exquisite – very full and palest pink, with a hint of ivory on the outer petals, and beautiful at every stage of their development. They are cupped at first, but later the outer petals reflex so that the inner petals develop and expand first as a rosette and later as a loose mass of pale, translucent petals. The flowers come singly and in small clusters, seldom of more than five together, and are set off by the bright red tips of the unopened buds. Emily makes a slender, prickly plant with glossy, mid-green leaves. It needs a sheltered position in cool climates and responds well everywhere to feeding and watering.

Emily

'Emily Gray'

'Emily Gray'

Wichurana Rambler

ORIGIN **Williams, Britain, 1918**
PARENTAGE **'Jersey Beauty' x 'Comtesse du Caÿla'**
FLOWER SIZE **2.8in (7cm)**
SCENT **Strong and tealike**
FLOWERING **Once only, fairly early in season**
HEIGHT/SPREAD **16.4ft (5m)/6.6ft (2m)**
HARDINESS **Zone 7**

This beautiful Wichurana rambler was raised by an amateur and named after his sister. It flowers only once, but there is nothing to match the beauty of its flowers and, above all, its leaves. The flowers are cupped, and full of long, dark stamens, apricot at first before fading to golden yellow and buff: the color is beautiful at all stages. The flowers are somewhat loosely petaled and borne early in the season, in small, long-stemmed clusters (typically of 3–5). The leaves are large, dark, glossy, and bronze green with crimson stalks – a wonderful foil for any rose. 'Emily Gray' is a stout but leggy grower that requires a minimum of pruning while it is building up. Eventually it covers itself with flowers.

'Empereur du Maroc'

Hybrid Perpetual

ORIGIN **Guinoiseau, France, 1858**
PARENTAGE **'Géant des Batailles' x unknown**
FLOWER SIZE **3.9in (10cm)**
SCENT **Very strong and sweet**
FLOWERING **Remontant**
HEIGHT/SPREAD **4.9ft (1.5m)/4.1ft (1.25m)**
HARDINESS **Zone 5**

'Empereur du Maroc' is one of the darkest, most sumptuous, most intensely scented, velvety, black and crimson roses ever raised. The flowers open out to reveal a mass of petals, and are occasionally quartered. So dark is their coloring that they seem to absorb light rather than emit it. In hot climates, the dark color cannot reflect heat, and the petals therefore tend to scorch and turn brown. The flowers come singly or in clusters of up to seven. The bush is prickly, with dark green leaves and a tendency to attract mildew and blackspot. It is not reliably remontant, but the chances of getting a second crop of flowers are greatly increased if the plant is pruned back to the base of the current season's growth immediately after it has flowered for the first time – well worth the effort.

'Empress Joséphine'

see 'Impératrice Joséphine'

'Enfant de France'

Hybrid Perpetual

ORIGIN **Lartay, France, 1860**
FLOWER SIZE **4.7in (12cm)**
SCENT **Strong and sweet**
FLOWERING **Repeats quickly**
HEIGHT/SPREAD **3.3ft (1m)/3.3ft (1m)**
HARDINESS **Zone 5**

The plant now sold as 'Enfant de France' (the experts say it is really something else) is a first-rate old-fashioned rose – almost a rose without fault. Its flowers are large and strongly scented. They open out to a very full, flat shape, quilled and quartered, occasionally reflexing yet further into a pompon. Sometimes there is a button eye at the center of the flower. The silky coloring is very distinctive: bright rose pink at the center, and paler at the edge of the flower, but the unusual feature is that it has much darker patches of color that occur irregularly anywhere within the flower. The flowers come singly or in clusters of 3–5, opening from erect, round buds. The leaves are long, and there are a lot of them. The plant has the habit, inherited from the Portland roses, of producing ever-shorter internodes on its stout flowering stems, so that the flower seems surrounded by a ruff of pale green leaves. The leaves are beautiful too, with long, drooping leaflets. The plant is healthy, compact, tolerant of both great heat and cold, and a reliable repeat-flowerer. It will grow to 4.1ft (1.25m) in a hot climate, but is one of those old roses that responds well to pruning by sending up yet another flush of flowers within a few weeks.

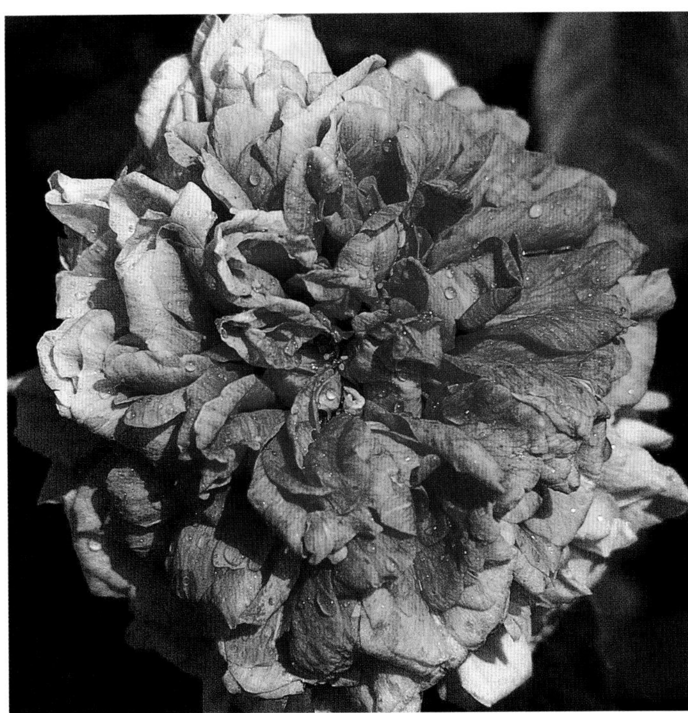
'Enfant de France'

'Empereur du Maroc'

'Ena Harkness'

Hybrid Tea

ORIGIN **Norman, Britain, 1946**
PARENTAGE **'Crimson Glory' x 'Southport'**
FLOWER SIZE **4.3in (11cm)**
SCENT **Medium and sweet**
FLOWERING **Repeats well**
HEIGHT/SPREAD **2.7ft (80cm)/2ft (60cm)**
HARDINESS **Zone 6**
AWARDS **NRS GM 1945; Portland GM 1955**

This was the rose that made the fortune of the Harkness family, one of England's largest nurseries. Everyone came to know the name of Ena Harkness. It was actually bred by an amateur, Albert Norman, who was later to become president of the National Rose Society of Great Britain. Harkness introduced it, and never looked back. 'Ena Harkness' was seen as an improved 'Crimson Glory', with larger, shapelier flowers that kept their bright crimson coloring longer. It suffers, however, from the same weak neck as its parent, so that the flowers nod over instead of standing erect. It withstands rain very well, and is immensely productive, its flowers starting early in the season, and continuing through until late autumn.

The weak flower stalk, which may be a defect in the bush form, becomes an asset in the climbing form, **'Climbing Ena Harkness'**, which was introduced by the distinguished nursery of Gurteen & Ritson in 1954. It does not flower as continuously as the bush form, but the first flush is spectacular and you are seldom without flowers on an established plant thereafter. The flowers are slightly larger, too.

'Ena Harkness'

'Climbing Ena Harkness'

Sport of 'Ena Harkness'

'Climbing Ena Harkness'

Climbing Hybrid Tea
ORIGIN **Gurteen & Ritson, Britain, 1954**
FLOWER SIZE **5.1in (13cm)**
FLOWERING **Once spectacularly, then intermittently**
HEIGHT/SPREAD **9.8ft (3m)/5.7ft (1.75m)**

E

ENGLAND'S ROSE

ENGLAND'S ROSE

syn. 'AUSRACE'

Shrub Rose

ORIGIN **Austin, Britain, 1995**
PARENTAGE **Graham Thomas x Heritage**
FLOWER SIZE **3.9in (10cm)**
SCENT **Strong and fruity**
FLOWERING **Repeats**
HEIGHT/SPREAD **3.3ft (1m)/2.7ft (80cm)**
HARDINESS **Zone 6**

The Royal National Rose Society of Great Britain sponsored this rose when it was first issued: it was intended as one of a series of branded roses to commemorate Diana, Princess of Wales. With or without this romantic royal connection, England's Rose is a very beautiful and desirable rose. The flowers open palest apricot, a most attractive shade, and pale to buff as they fade, with white outer petals. Sometimes the flowers are button-eyed, and sometimes imbricated like a camellia, but the many petals are always neatly arranged and lightly cupped, with deeper hues reflected by their slightly darker petal backs. They come in clusters of 3–7 on a vigorous, upright bush with handsome, dark leaves.

ENGLISH ELEGANCE

syn. 'AUSLEAF'

Shrub Rose

ORIGIN **Austin, Britain, 1985**
FLOWER SIZE **2.4in (6cm)**
SCENT **Medium and sweet**
FLOWERING **Repeats**
HEIGHT/SPREAD **6.6ft (2m)/4.9ft (1.5m)**
HARDINESS **Zone 6**

ENGLISH ELEGANCE

Although no longer promoted by David Austin, English Elegance is still fairly popular among garden owners in hot, dry climates. In the UK, it is a short climber, weaving its way up to 9.8ft (3m); elsewhere it makes a loose, open bush. The flowers are a mixture of apricot, yellow, and pink – darker and more coppery toward the center. They are loosely double and somewhat disorganized in shape – lightly blowsy. Occasionally they come singly, but more usually in clusters of up to seven. The stems are short and do not last long as cut flowers. On the bush, the flowers tend to hold on to their dead petals instead of dropping them. English Elegance has medium-dark leaves, sometimes susceptible to mildew and blackspot, and is nearly thornless. It responds well to feeding and watering; deadheading also helps it to reflower.

ENGLISH GARDEN

syn. 'AUSBUFF', Schloss Glücksburg

Shrub Rose

ORIGIN **Austin, Britain, 1990**
PARENTAGE **('Lilian Austin' x seedling) x ('Schneewittchen' x 'Wife of Bath')**
FLOWER SIZE **3.9in (10cm)**
SCENT **Strong and fruity**
FLOWERING **Repeats well**
HEIGHT/SPREAD **2.7ft (80cm)/2.7ft (80cm)**
HARDINESS **Zone 6**

English Garden is a very reliable rose, always compact and neat in habit, which produces an almost continuous stream of beautiful, scented roses through until late autumn. The flowers are rich yellow, with a deeper apricot on the petal backs: they fade to cream at their edges. They open into lightly cupped rosettes (later almost flat), sometimes quartered, with quilled petals, and apricot reflections at the center. They are held up well on strong stems, usually singly but occasionally in small clusters, and last well as cut flowers. The plant has tough, mid-green leaves that occasionally suffer from blackspot and mildew.

ENGLISH GARDEN

'ENGLISH MISS'

'ENGLISH MISS'

Floribunda

ORIGIN **Cants, Britain, 1977**
PARENTAGE **'Dearest' x 'The Optimist'**
FLOWER SIZE **2in (5cm)**
SCENT **Strong, fruity, and sweet**
FLOWERING **Repeats very well**
HEIGHT/SPREAD **2.7ft (80cm)/2.7ft (80cm)**
HARDINESS **Zone 6**

The delicate coloring of the flowers of 'English Miss' explains its long popularity. They are pale buff pink at first, an exquisite shade that sets up very beautiful shadows between the petals, because the petal backs are darker than the topsides. Later they fade to palest pink as the flowers open out and, especially in hot weather, the petal tips acquire a reddish tinge. The flowers have a great number of short, broad petals toward the center, surrounded by larger guard petals with a slight ripple to their carriage. The flowers come in spacious clusters of 3–15. The plant is small and compact, sometimes broader than high. It has crimson new growth and small, healthy, dark green leaves.

'ERFURT'

Shrub Rose

ORIGIN **Kordes, Germany, 1931**
PARENTAGE **'Eva' x 'Reveil Dijonnais'**
FLOWER SIZE **2.8in (7cm)**
SCENT **Strong, sweet, and musky**
FLOWERING **Repeats well**
HEIGHT/SPREAD **4.9ft (1.5m)/4.9ft (1.5m)**
HARDINESS **Zone 5**

This cross between a Hybrid Musk and a Hybrid Fetida resembles neither of its parents: 'Erfurt' is a simple, unsophisticated beauty wih a charm of its own and a floriferousness that makes it welcome in any garden. The flowers open deep pink, with a cream center, and fade to pale rose pink and white. They are semidouble, with a large boss of stamens that gives great character to the flower. There is quite a range of color on the bush at any one time. The flowers come in clusters of 5–10 and are followed by good-sized orange hips that last well into winter. The plant has healthy, dark, glossy leaves and makes a broad, loose shrub. Erfurt is a cathedral city in Germany.

'ERFURT'

'ERINNERUNG AN BROD'

'ERINNERUNG AN BROD'

Rambler

ORIGIN **Geschwind, Hungary, 1886**
PARENTAGE ***Rosa setigera*** **hybrid × 'Génie de Châteaubriand'**
FLOWER SIZE **3.1in (8cm)**
SCENT **Strong and sweet**
FLOWERING **Remontant**
HEIGHT/SPREAD **8.2ft (2.5m)/5.7ft (1.75m)**
HARDINESS **Zone 4**

Rudolf Geschwind used the American Prairie rose *Rosa setigera* to introduce hardiness into his hybrids, so that they would survive the bitter winds and low temperatures of winter in central Europe. 'Erinnerung an Brod' combines that hardiness with good repeat flowering and a violet purple color that was second to none when it was first introduced. The flowers are slightly paler toward the center, very full and flat, with neatly imbricated petals and slightly paler petal backs. They come singly or in clusters of 3–9 on a vigorous, healthy plant with flexible branches and lush green leaves. It is very floriferous and, in warm climates, will flower all through the winter. It is the parent of 'Veilchenblau' (Kiese, 1908) and thus the grandparent of all the "blue" roses. Brod is a spa town in Slovenia.

'ERNEST H. MORSE'

syn. 'E. H. MORSE'

Hybrid Tea

ORIGIN **Kordes, Germany, 1964**
PARENTAGE **'Prima Ballerina' × 'Brillant'**
FLOWER SIZE **4.3in (11cm)**
SCENT **Strong and sweet**
FLOWERING **Repeats**
HEIGHT/SPREAD **5.7ft (1.75m)/3.3ft (1m)**
HARDINESS **Zone 6**
AWARDS **RNRS GM 1965**

The Kordes family named this rich red Hybrid Tea after their agent in England, and 'Ernest H. Morse' has always been more popular in Britain than Germany. The flowers are bright blood red, not notably shapely in bud, but well-formed and handsome as they open out. The flowers have slightly shorter petals than many Hybrid Teas, but they also stand up well to rain.

'ERNEST H. MORSE'

They open out quickly to reveal a loose center. The inner petals are slightly paler and often conspicuously streaked with white. In fact, all the petals lose their brilliance as they age, though they keep their mid-red coloring well. They come singly and in small clusters (seldom of more than four flowers) on strong stems, and repeat their flowering quickly. 'Ernest H. Morse' has dark, matte, healthy leaves, and grows vigorously in all conditions. A real workhorse among red Hybrid Teas.

'EROTIKA'

syn. 'EROICA'

Hybrid Tea

ORIGIN **Tantau, Germany, 1968**
PARENTAGE **seedling × 'Dr. A. J. Verhage'**
FLOWER SIZE **4.7in (12cm)**
SCENT **Strong and sweet**
FLOWERING **Repeats well**
HEIGHT/SPREAD **4.1ft (1.25m)/3.3ft (1m)**
HARDINESS **Zone 6**
AWARDS **ADR 1969**

It is still widely grown in Germany, but in other countries the popularity of 'Erotika' suffered from its name. It is almost unknown in North America. 'Erotika' is a classic, dark red Hybrid Tea, with large flowers and a superb scent. Its petals are not long enough for it to be a good exhibition rose, but its flowers last well if cut and have an attractive, rippled outline when they open out. Sometimes there are darker, velvetlike markings on the petals. The flowers usually come singly, but sometimes in clusters of 3–4. They stand up well to rain, but the plant may freeze back in winter in cool areas where the wood does not receive enough summer heat to ripen properly. 'Erotika' has dark, glossy leaves and a vigorous, upright habit of growth. It is a reliable bedding rose and a good repeater.

'EROTIKA'

'ESCAPADE'

Floribunda

ORIGIN **Harkness, Britain, 1967**
PARENTAGE **'Pink Parfait' × 'Baby Faurax'**
FLOWER SIZE **2.8in (7cm)**
SCENT **Light and musky**
FLOWERING **Continuous**
HEIGHT/SPREAD **4.1ft (1.25m)/3.3ft (1m)**
HARDINESS **Zone 5**
AWARDS **Baden-Baden GM 1969; Belfast GM 1969; ADR 1973**

Jack Harkness called this dainty and floriferous rose 'Escapade' because its flowers seemed always to be on an escapade with the bees. It is a cross between a pink Floribunda and a purple Polyantha. The semidouble flowers are lilac pink with white centers and bright yellow stamens. The color fades quickly in heat and sun, so it is often no more than pale pink in hot climates. However, the unopened buds are always bright crimson, providing a pretty contrast to the open flowers, which appear almost continuously. The plant is bushy and leafy, with pale, glossy leaves. It is exceptionally healthy and free from fungal diseases in hot climates and cold; only in mild, humid ones does it ever show the slightest hint of blackspot. 'Escapade' is a first-rate rose and a real charmer all over the world.

'ESCAPADE'

ESMERALDA

syn. 'KORMALDA', Keepsake

Hybrid Tea

ORIGIN **Kordes, Germany, 1981**
PARENTAGE **seedling × 'Red Planet'**
FLOWER SIZE **5.1in (13cm)**
SCENT **Medium and fruity**
FLOWERING **Repeats**
HEIGHT/SPREAD **5.7ft (1.75m)/4.1ft (1.25m)**
HARDINESS **Zone 6**
AWARDS **Portland GM 1987**

This stout and vigorous Hybrid Tea is a firm favorite in every corner of the world. Esmeralda has all the desirable qualities you could want: health, strength, elegance, and scent. The flowers are large and shapely, with long buds whose outer petals roll back as they expand. They are pink, with deeper, brighter pink edges – a most unusual and attractive combination of shades. The flowers also have patches of cream or white at the base of the petals and toward the center of the flower. They are usually borne singly, but sometimes in small clusters, and are good for cutting. Everything about Esmeralda is outsize – not only the flowers, but also the large, stout prickles, the broad leaflets, and the large, healthy, dark, glossy leaves. The plant too is vigorous and almost always in flower.

ESMERALDA

Especially for You

syn. 'FRYworthy'

Floribunda

ORIGIN **Fryer, Britain, 1996**
FLOWER SIZE **3.5in (9cm)**
SCENT **Strong, sweet, and fruity**
FLOWERING **Repeats well**
HEIGHT/SPREAD **4.1ft (1.25m)/3.3ft (1m)**
HARDINESS **Zone 6**

E

The flowers of Especially For You are intermediate between a Hybrid Tea and a Floribunda: fairly large and shapely as they open out, but not overly full of petals and usually borne in clusters. They are pale yellow, with darker petal backs, and they fade at the edges as they age, so that the center of the flower is always a rich egg yolk yellow but the outer parts are closer to cream. The flowers have an attractive shape at all stages, because the inner petals tend to remain folded over the center of the flower when the outer petals have expanded. The scent of the flowers is delicious. The plant is vigorous, upright, and healthy, with large, dark leaves and quite a lot of prickles. It flowers freely and almost continuously.

Especially for You

'Étoile de Hollande'

Hybrid Tea

ORIGIN **Verschuren, Netherlands, 1919**
PARENTAGE **'General MacArthur' × 'Hadley'**
FLOWER SIZE **4.3in (11cm)**
SCENT **Very strong, rich, sweet, and delicious**
FLOWERING **Repeats well**
HEIGHT/SPREAD **3.3ft (1m)/2.7ft (80cm)**
HARDINESS **Zone 6**

'Étoile de Hollande'

'Climbing Étoile de Hollande'

There are comparatively few examples of a bush rose producing a climbing sport that is more popular than the original: climbing sports have to compete against "real" climbing roses. But 'Étoile de Hollande' is a case in point. The bush form was a popular bedding rose in the 1920s and 1930s, and indeed is still quite widely grown, but it cannot match its climbing sport for worldwide popularity today. 'Étoile de Hollande' has slender, not too double, loosely petaled flowers, which are a rich, velvety crimson and intensely fragrant. It is a prickly bush of moderate vigour, and seldom reaches more than 3.3ft (1m), even in hot climates. The flowers come singly or in small clusters of 2–5 on slightly drooping stems. They open quickly and repeat well.

'Climbing Étoile de Hollande' has the same flowers (but slightly larger) and the same powerful scent, but is very impressive when covered in crimson clusters during its first, most exuberant flowering. 'Climbing Étoile de Hollande' is also a good repeater: an established plant will produce a few flowers continuously here and there until winter sets in. It is a lanky, prickly, erect grower, which means that it benefits from being taken down in winter and trained sideways to break into flower all along its length. This also produces more leaves: both the bush and the climber are sparsely foliaged, though such leaves as they have are large. The gawkiness of the vigorous climbing form can be softened by companion planting – clematis are the usual complement. Both forms are susceptible to mildew in climates where this is a problem.

Sport of 'Etoile de Hollande'

'Climbing Étoile de Hollande'

Climbing Hybrid Tea

ORIGIN **Leenders, Netherlands, 1931**
FLOWER SIZE **4.7in (12cm)**
HEIGHT/SPREAD **13.1ft (4m)/8.2ft (2.5m)**

Essex

Essex

syn. 'POULnoz', Aquitaine, Pink Cover

Shrub Rose

ORIGIN **Poulsen, Denmark, 1987**
PARENTAGE **'The Fairy' seedling**
FLOWER SIZE **1.2in (3cm)**
SCENT **Light and sweet**
FLOWERING **Repeats**
HEIGHT/SPREAD **2.5ft (75cm)/4.9ft (1.5m)**
HARDINESS **Zone 6**
AWARDS **Dublin GM 1987**

The flowers of Essex are small and simple, but it nevertheless won several prizes when it was first introduced. It is still a popular shrub rose in England. Since it tends to spread sideways rather than growing upward, it is a useful space filler in a mixed planting. The flowers are pink and single, with a white patch at the center and a tuft of dark yellow stamens. They come in neatly spaced clusters of 3–15 on and off until late autumn, and are followed by small red hips. The leaves are small, healthy, dark, and glossy. Essex is a rose that sometimes looks better in photographs than in reality.

'Étendard'

syn. 'Red New Dawn'

Modern Climber

ORIGIN **Robichon, France, 1956**
PARENTAGE **'New Dawn' × seedling**
FLOWER SIZE **3.1in (8cm)**
SCENT **Light and sweet**
FLOWERING **Repeats**
HEIGHT/SPREAD **9.8ft (3m)/6.6ft (2m)**
HARDINESS **Zone 5**

'Étendard' is known as 'Red New Dawn', but shows little resemblance to its distinguished parent. Its flowers are bright red, with the shape and form of a Hybrid Tea. They are borne in upright, long-stemmed clusters of 3–9. The plant has dark, glossy, healthy leaves, a lot of prickles, and a stiff manner of growth. It lacks the Wichurana habit of producing flowers and leaves down to ground level, but is nevertheless a pleasant rose and excellent for cutting.

Eternally Yours

see Candella

'Étendard'

'ÉTOILE DE LYON'

'ÉTOILE DE LYON'

Tea Rose

ORIGIN **Guillot, France, 1881**
PARENTAGE **'Mme. Charles' x unknown**
FLOWER SIZE **4.3in (11cm)**
SCENT **Strong and tealike**
FLOWERING **Repeats constantly**
HEIGHT/SPREAD **4.9ft (1.5m)/4.9ft (1.5m)**
HARDINESS **Zone 8**

'Etoile de Lyon' was a popular "deep yellow" Tea rose when it was first introduced, though to our modern eyes it appears little more than pale buff yellow. Nevertheless, it is an excellent garden rose – elegant, floriferous, and strongly scented – that deserves a place in every Zone 8 or 9 garden. The flowers have hints of lemon yellow and buff in them as they open out, and the large petals curl gently back in the manner of Teas and Hybrid Teas. Later they fade to milky white, while always darker on the petal backs. The flowers have weak stems and the attractive drooping habit which follows. However, they eventually open out to reveal an attractively muddled center surrounded by circles of flat guard petals. They come singly or in clusters of up to seven. The plant has dark, evergreen leaves and beautiful red new growth. In hot, dry climates it will flower non-stop, if irrigated, and reach 9.8ft (3m).

'EUGEN FÜRST'

Hybrid Perpetual

ORIGIN **Soupert & Notting, Luxembourg, 1875**
PARENTAGE **'Baron de Bonstetten' x unknown**
FLOWER SIZE **3.1in (8cm)**
SCENT **Strong and sweet**
FLOWERING **Remontant**
HEIGHT/SPREAD **4.9ft (1.5m)/4.1ft (1.25m)**
HARDINESS **Zone 5**

'Eugen Fürst' is a sumptuous crimson Hybrid Perpetual: its glowing color and classical shape call for admiration. The crimson coloring is actually fairly variable, and differs from year to year and according to climate and season. At its best a red dark crimson with a bright red flush at first, it is sometimes no more than dark pink or cherry colored, and fades to mauve in hot weather. The flowers come in small clusters – 3–9 at a time – but their pedicels are short, which means that the clusters get very congested and the flowers do not have room to expand completely without pushing up against each other. They perform best in dry weather and dry climates, where the pale green leaves and broad leaflets are not so vulnerable to blackspot. After the first big flush there is always a flower or two on the bush right through until late autumn. Eugen Fürst was a German horticulturist, best remembered for breeding new fruit cultivars.

Even more widely grown is a striped sport of 'Eugen Fürst' called **'Baron Girod de l'Ain'**, which makes an interesting contrast. The nature of its striping is very unusual. Instead of flecks and splashes across the whole flower, it consists of narrow, irregular white piping just along the tips of the petals, as if their edges had been torn off to reveal a layer of pure white cells beneath. When the petals stretch out and the outer ones reflex, the effect is very pronounced and charming, since the inner petals remain a disorganized mass, but their white edging curls and twists in all directions across the center of the flower.

Sport of 'Eugen Fürst'

'BARON GIROD DE L'AIN'

ORIGIN **Reverchon, France, 1897**

'EUGEN FÜRST'

'BARON GIROD DE L'AIN'

'EUGÈNE DE BEAUHARNAIS'

China Rose

ORIGIN **Hardy, France, 1838**
FLOWER SIZE **3.1in (8cm)**
SCENT **Strong and sweet**
FLOWERING **Repeats well**
HEIGHT/SPREAD **3.3ft (1m)/2.7ft (80cm)**
HARDINESS **Zone 6**

'EUGÈNE DE BEAUHARNAIS'

Although popular in the US, 'Eugène de Beauharnais' is no longer seen in Europe. This is a pity, because it is an excellent, floriferous, short rose for small gardens. The flowers are a wonderful bright, rich cherry crimson, with hints of purple and pink, and much paler reverses, sometimes showing a flash of white at the center. The petals are quilled, ruffled, muddled, and roughly quartered, sometimes around a button center. They come in slightly nodding, congested clusters, usually surrounded by a ruff of leaves like Portland roses. The bush is short, stout, compact, and erect, with seriously prickly stems. The dark green leaves have crimson edges. It blooms almost continuously. Rust, mildew, and blackspot can each be a problem. Eugène de Beauharnais, Prince of Eichstadt (1781–1824), was the son of Empress Joséphine.

'EUGÉNIE GUINOISEAU'

Moss Rose

ORIGIN **Guinoiseau, France, 1864**
FLOWER SIZE **3.1in (8cm)**
SCENT **Light and sweet**
FLOWERING **Remontant**
HEIGHT/SPREAD **5.7ft (1.75m)/4.1ft (1.25m)**
HARDINESS **Zone 5**

The perpetual-flowering Mosses are excellent shrub roses, and 'Eugénie Guinoiseau' is one of the best. Its flowers are a sumptuous crimson purple – bright crimson at first, then somewhat more purple later, with slightly paler petal backs. The flowers form a rough rosette and sometimes a button eye. The petals, though plentiful, are quite narrow. The flowers come singly and in small clusters (rarely of more than four) and are followed by orange hips. The sepals, peduncles, and stems of the flowers are covered in dark moss, which turns into bristly prickles as it runs down on to the branches of the bush itself. The leaves are dark green and fairly healthy, though the plant as a whole is susceptible to mildew. Nevertheless, 'Eugénie Guinoiseau' is a vigorous, upright grower and a very reliable repeat flowerer.

'EUPHROSYNE'

Hybrid Multiflora

ORIGIN **Schmitt, Germany, 1896**
PARENTAGE **'Mignonette' x unknown**
FLOWER SIZE **1.2in (3cm)**
SCENT **Light and musky**
FLOWERING **Once only**
HEIGHT/SPREAD **13.1ft (4m)/6.6ft (2m)**
HARDINESS **Zone 5**

'EUGÉNIE GUINOISEAU'

'Euphrosyne' was one of three roses bred by Schmitt in Alsace, when Alsace was part of Germany, and bought by Peter Lambert of Trier, who used them as the basis for his extensive breeding. It is pretty when the flowers are starting to open out – they are then bright rose pink – but they lose their charm when they fade quickly to white and the yellow stamens turn brown. The flowers come in large clusters of 20–50, which eventually get congested because the individual flowers have short stalks. In wet weather, the flowers pick up red splash marks and the clusters begin to rot. The plant has fine, large, pale green leaves and a weakness for mildew. It roots very quickly and easily from cuttings.

'EUPHROSYNE'

E

'EUROPEANA'

'EUROPEANA'

Floribunda

ORIGIN **de Ruiter, Belgium, 1963**
PARENTAGE **'Ruth Leuwerik' x 'Rosemary Rose'**
FLOWER SIZE **2.4in (6cm)**
SCENT **Little or none**
FLOWERING **Repeats well**
HEIGHT/SPREAD **2.7ft (80cm)/2.7ft (80cm)**
HARDINESS **Zone 5**
AWARDS **The Hague GM 1962; AARS 1968; Portland GM 1970**

Many years after its first introduction, 'Europeana' remains an exceptional rose. There is nothing to match its large clusters of glowing crimson flowers set off by new leaves of beet red. The colors are intensified if it is interplanted with white Polyanthas or gray-leaved herbaceous plants. The individual flowers are quite small, but they are profusely borne in large, flat-topped clusters of 10–30. They are rosette-shaped (full of neat little petals), and last a long time. The plant repeats well and the flowers neither fade nor brown in the sun, so 'Europeana' is widely grown in much hotter climates than its native Belgium. Its leaves are dark green and glossy, and the plant is both healthy and vigorous.

EUROSTAR

see MARSELISBORG

'EUTIN'

Floribunda

ORIGIN **Kordes, Germany, 1940**
PARENTAGE **'Eva' x 'Solarium'**
FLOWER SIZE **2in (5cm)**
SCENT **Light**
FLOWERING **Repeats well**
HEIGHT/SPREAD **4.9ft (1.5m)/4.1ft (1.25m)**
HARDINESS **Zone 5**

'Eutin' was introduced by Kordes in 1940, when Europe was already well into World War II, yet this rose remains popular even now in North America. This is due to its floriferousness and its ability to survive and perform well with very little maintenance. It was one of the earliest Floribundas, though bred from a Hybrid Musk, and most resembles a Hybrid Polyantha, which shows just how difficult it can sometimes be to categorize a rose. 'Eutin' has crimson flowers that open from little buds. The flowers are double and globular, but open up enough to show their stamens. The petals are slightly pinker on their backs and have occasional white stripes. The flowers come in large clusters of 15–30 (like those of its parent 'Eva'). The flowers last well and are useful as cut flowers in arrangements. The plant has dark, glossy, healthy foliage and an open habit. It is good all-around, suitable for bedding and hedging, as well as mixed plantings. It is a great survivor in old, deserted gardens, too. Eutin is a small town in northern Germany, near the city of Lübeck.

'EUTIN'

'EVA'

'EVA'

Hybrid Musk

ORIGIN **Kordes, Germany, 1933**
PARENTAGE **'Robin Hood' x 'J. C. Thornton'**
FLOWER SIZE **2.4in (6cm)**
SCENT **Medium, sweet, and musky**
FLOWERING **Repeats**
HEIGHT/SPREAD **8.2ft (2.5m)/6.6ft (2m)**
HARDINESS **Zone 6**

The continued popularity of 'Eva' is testimony to the conservatism of the rose trade. It is a sound performer, but outclassed by many modern roses. Its flowers are almost single, but messy. They open and close with the sun, and their petals seem to become twisted and irregular as they do so. They are a good bright crimson, fading to dark carmine, with a paler, nearly white patch toward the center and a small cluster of stamens, which quickly turn brown. However, 'Eva' bears its flowers in large, open clusters, typically of 20–30, but occasionally twice that size, especially in autumn when the new growths develop into unusually large trusses. Then its color and sheer flower power are both impressive. The flowers are followed by small, round, pale red hips. 'Eva' makes a vigorous, open shrub, with large, healthy, mid-green leaves appearing somewhat sparsely. It was an important parent, and can count thousands of modern roses among its descendants, including 'Queen Elizabeth'.

'EVANGELINE'

Wichurana Rambler

ORIGIN **Walsh, US, 1906**
PARENTAGE ***Rosa wichurana* x 'Turner's Crimson Rambler'**
FLOWER SIZE **1.6in (4cm)**
SCENT **Medium and musky**
FLOWERING **Once only, late in season**
HEIGHT/SPREAD **16.4ft (5m)/6.6ft (2m)**
HARDINESS **Zone 6**

'Evangeline' has large quantities of small, pretty, pink and white flowers, with a characteristic notch in the middle of each petal edge. They are delightful when they first open out, and the yellow stamens shine at the center. But this stage does not last long: the flowers fade to dirty white, the stamens turn brown, and the flowers hang for so long that the clusters begin to look congested. The long-stemmed clusters are long and large (20–50 flowers) and very profusely borne. Small orange hips follow in autumn. It makes a very vigorous plant, somewhat liable to mildew, but capable of reaching as much as 26.2ft (8m).

'EVANGELINE'

EVELYN

syn. 'AUSSAUCER', Apricot Parfait

Shrub Rose

ORIGIN **Austin, Britain, 1991**
PARENTAGE Graham Thomas x Tamora
FLOWER SIZE **4.7in (12cm)**
SCENT **Very strong and sweet**
FLOWERING **Repeats**
HEIGHT/SPREAD **4.1ft (1.25m)/4.1ft (1.25m)**
HARDINESS **Zone 5**

Evelyn is popular for the size of its flowers and their wonderful scent: David Austin considers it one of the most fragrant roses he has ever bred. The flowers are somewhat variable in color: usually peach pink at the center while, on the petal backs, they fade to creamy pink at the edges. In fact, the whole flower becomes pinker and paler as it ages. It opens out lightly cupped, often with a button eye, but its exact shape, though always attractive, varies almost as much as its color. The plant has pale green leaves (blackspot can be a problem) and tall, upright growth. It reaches about 3.3ft (1m) in cool climates, but at least twice that in hot weather. Deadheading encourages reflowering.

EVELYN

'EVELYN FISON'

'EVELYN FISON'

Floribunda

ORIGIN **McGredy, Northern Ireland, 1962**
PARENTAGE **'Moulin Rouge' x 'Korona'**
FLOWER SIZE **2.8in (7cm)**
SCENT **Light and sweet**
FLOWERING **Repeats well**
HEIGHT/SPREAD **3.3ft (1m)/2.7ft (80cm)**
HARDINESS **Zone 6**
AWARDS **NRS GM 1963**

Few roses are as versatile as 'Evelyn Fison'. It keeps its glorious, bright red color in hot sun and seems quite unaffected by heavy rain. It is a born survivor. The flowers are dark scarlet and fully double, but the inner petals are smaller, and the flowers do eventually open out to reveal a patch of yellow stamens at the center. They come in large, well-spaced clusters, typically of 7–15 flowers, and are almost continuously borne until late autumn. 'Evelyn Fison' was, and still is, a popular bedding rose for its compact growth, brilliant color, and reliability, but it also makes a useful contribution of bright color to mixed plantings. It has healthy, dark green leaves, a scattering of prickles, and crimson new growth.

'EVEREST DOUBLE FRAGRANCE'

Floribunda

ORIGIN **Beales, Britain, 1980**
PARENTAGE **'Dearest' x 'Elizabeth of Glamis'**
FLOWER SIZE **3.5in (9cm)**
SCENT **Strong and sweet**
FLOWERING **Repeats**
HEIGHT/SPREAD **4.1ft (1.25m)/3.3ft (1m)**
HARDINESS **Zone 6**

'Everest Double Fragrance' is a fairly ordinary Floribunda. Its flowers open from pointed buds and are a pretty pale peach pink at first, before fading to pure soft pink, mother-of-pearl, and white. They come in clusters of 3–7 and have fine stamens at the center, though these turn brown soon after the flowers open out. The plant has lots of large prickles, dark, rugose leaves, and a tall, lanky habit of growth. In hot climates it will grow to 6.6ft (2m). It appears to be fairly resistant to disease.

'EVEREST DOUBLE FRAGRANCE'

'EXCELLENZ VON SCHUBERT'

Polyantha

ORIGIN **Lambert, Germany, 1909**
PARENTAGE **'Mme. Norbert Levavasseur' x 'Frau Karl Druschki'**
FLOWER SIZE **1.2in (3cm)**
SCENT **Light and musky**
FLOWERING **Continuous**
HEIGHT/SPREAD **4.9ft (1.5m)/4.9ft (1.5m)**
HARDINESS **Zone 5**

Few shrub roses are more deserving of garden space than this vigorous hybrid between a truly dwarf Polyantha and the famous white Hybrid Tea 'Frau Karl Druschki'. The proportions of 'Excellenz von Schubert' are intermediate between the two. It makes a large bush or a short climber, anticipating the Hybrid Musks that Pemberton was later to develop in Britain. The flowers are small, dark pink pompons, with hints of mauve as they fade. They are borne in fairly large clusters (of 5–30 flowers), starting late in the season but continuing through until autumn. The plant has dark leaves, narrow leaflets, long flowering canes, and few prickles. It will make 8.2ft (2.5m) on a pillar, but more up a wall or through a small tree.

'EXCELLENZ VON SCHUBERT'

'EXCELSA'

Wichurana Rambler

ORIGIN **Walsh, US, 1909**
PARENTAGE **'Turner's Crimson Rambler' x unknown**
FLOWER SIZE **1.2in (3cm)**
SCENT **Little or none**
FLOWERING **Once only, late in season**
HEIGHT/SPREAD **13.1ft (4m)/6.6ft (2m)**
HARDINESS **Zone 5**

'Excelsa' is the red counterpart to 'Dorothy Perkins', which is a small-flowered, late-flowering rambler that carries its flowers in spectacular profusion when almost every other rose has finished. The flowers of 'Excelsa' are bright crimson red, a brilliant glowing color, with white streaks toward the center. They come in long, open sprays of 10–30. The foliage is mid-green, small, tough, and glossy, and the stems are prickly. 'Excelsa' was introduced as an improved, healthier 'Turner's Crimson Rambler', but in fact it is a martyr to mildew, especially when grown against a wall. The disease disfigures the leaves and flower stems, but it does not seem to affect the vigor of 'Excelsa' and its ability to send out long new growth to flower all along their length next year. It roots very easily from cuttings, which has helped to ensure its popularity, especially in rural areas, all over the world.

'EXCELSA'

EXPLOIT

syn. 'MEILIDER', All in One, Colonia

Modern Climber

ORIGIN **Meilland, France, 1985**
PARENTAGE **'Fugue' x 'Iskra'**
FLOWER SIZE **2.8in (7cm)**
SCENT **Little or none**
FLOWERING **Once spectacularly, then intermittently**
HEIGHT/SPREAD **9.8ft (3m)/6.6ft (2m)**
HARDINESS **Zone 5**

Few roses are more spectacular during their first flowering than Exploit: its brilliant, dark scarlet Floribunda type flowers catch the eye from a great distance. It is less exciting close-up, because the flowers are short on character and scentless. They are fairly double, and open out to show their yellow stamens, but they are not among the most charming of roses. However, they keep their color well, and stand up well to both sun and rain. They come singly or in small, upright clusters, typically of 3–5. Exploit grows vigorously and not too tall. The leaves are dark (bronzy when young), healthy, and glossy, with somewhat round leaflets. After its first flowering, there are always a few flowers on the plant until late autumn. It is especially popular in France.

EXPLOIT

Eyeopener

syn. 'INTEROP', Tapis Rouge
Ground Cover

ORIGIN **Interplant, Netherlands, 1987**
PARENTAGE **'Eyepaint' seedling x 'Dortmund' seedling**
FLOWER SIZE **1.6in (4cm)**
SCENT **Little or none**
FLOWERING **Repeats well**
HEIGHT/SPREAD **1.6ft (50cm)/4.9ft (1.5m)**
HARDINESS **Zone 5**

This groundcover rose combines the hardiness of the Kordesii hybrid 'Dortmund' with a brightness that comes from Sam McGredy's "hand-painted" roses. The flowers are bright, dark red, with a small white eye and vivid golden brown stamens. They are small individually, but carried in large multiple clusters, each made up of smaller clusters and all arranged on the same plane. Their impact comes from having so many brilliant flowers staring up at the beholder. The plant is a lax shrub, with small, dark, glossy, Wichurana leaves and a spreading habit of growth. It starts late into flower, but then continues on and off until late autumn. Blackspot may sometimes make an appearance, but it does not seem to have any effect on the plant's vigor.

EYEOPENER

Eyepaint

syn. 'MACEYE'
Floribunda

ORIGIN **McGredy, New Zealand, 1975**
PARENTAGE **seedling x 'Picasso'**
FLOWER SIZE **2in (5cm)**
SCENT **Light**
FLOWERING **Repeats well**
HEIGHT/SPREAD **3.3ft (1m)/2.7ft (80cm)**
HARDINESS **Zone 5**
AWARDS **Baden-Baden GM 1974; Belfast GM 1978**

Eyepaint is more of a shrub than a Floribunda: it covers itself in large clusters of brilliant scarlet flowers (typically 10–30) and will grow to 6.6ft (2m) or more in all directions in hot climates. The flowers have a distinct white eye at the center and conspicuous yellow stamens: the combination is startlingly bright. The temptation is to look at the flowers close-up instead of the bush as a whole. The plant has beautiful, glossy, hard green leaves and a billowing habit of growth. It is vigorous and disease-free, and is always one of the most cheerful roses in the garden, and fairly overpowering as a landscaping rose.

EYEPAINT

Explorer and Parkland Roses

CANADA'S DEPARTMENT OF AGRICULTURE DEVELOPED THE SUPERHARDY EXPLORER AND PARKLAND ROSES TO FLOURISH IN THE COLDEST OF CONDITIONS

For over a century now, the Canadian government has been committed to breeding plants that will survive and flourish in the bitter climate of its inland provinces. 'Agnes' was the first rose to be distributed, and was bred as long ago as 1900. More recently, a stream of superhardy hybrids was issued from Department of Agriculture research stations in Manitoba and Quebec, and promoted as Explorer and Parkland roses. They are hardy down to -31°F (-35°C) – with natural snow protection – but are also required to be disease-resistant, repeat flowering, and easy to grow in Canadian conditions. Most require minimal pruning and are easily raised from softwood cuttings. All are grown on their own roots, so that in borderline conditions when they are frozen back to ground level they will come again from the roots.

'MORDEN SUNRISE'

The Explorer roses are raised in Ottawa and tested both there and in Quebec. Such is their popularity among people who live in cold climates that almost all have separate entries in this encyclopedia: they include 'Alexander MacKenzie', 'George Vancouver', 'Henry Kelsey', 'John Davis', and 'Martin Frobisher'. Two recent cultivars, 'Nicolas' (1996) and 'Quadra' (1995), are also worth growing. The Parkland Roses come from Morden in Manitoba and almost all are likewise described in this book, including 'Adelaide Hoodless', 'Cuthbert Grant', 'Morden Blush', and 'Morden Centennial'. Other good cultivars are 'Morden Cardinette' (1980), 'Morden Snowbeauty' (1999), and 'Morden Sunrise' (1999).

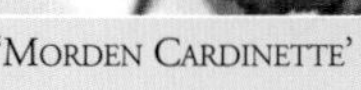

'MORDEN CARDINETTE'

All the Explorer and Parkland roses also do well in milder climates, and even in hot ones like Texas or California. They tend to grow much taller in such conditions and are sometimes not as resistant to disease as they are in cold climates. But these roses have revolutionized the gardening possibilities not only for rose growers in Canada and the colder US states but also for those in Scandinavia and central Europe.

'Fabvier'

China Rose

ORIGIN **Laffay, France, 1832**
FLOWER SIZE **2in (5cm)**
SCENT **Little or none**
FLOWERING **Almost continuous**
HEIGHT/SPREAD **2.5ft (75cm)/3.3ft (1m)**
HARDINESS **Zone 6**

The brilliant crimson flowers of 'Fabvier' were a great novelty when this China rose was introduced in the 1830s. Nothing among the old European roses could match the bright sheen of its petals. Although individually quite small, the flowers come in fair-sized clusters of 3–15, and their brilliance is enhanced by bright yellow stamens and the presence of two or three long white streaks, which run from the center right to the edge of the petals. There is a small patch of white flashing at the base of the petals too. The plant is compact, with neat, small leaves and a tendency to develop mildew on the pedicels. Its slender stems carry a few large prickles. From the start it was grown not for cuttings or for exhibition but as a garden rose, valued for its luminous flowers and almost continuous flowering. Baron Charles-Nicolas Fabvier (1782–1855) was a French general and hero of Greek Independence.

'Fabvier'

Fair Bianca

syn. 'AUSca'

Shrub Rose

ORIGIN **Austin, Britain, 1982**
FLOWER SIZE **3.1in (8cm)**
SCENT **Strong and myrrhlike**
FLOWERING **Repeats well**
HEIGHT/SPREAD **3.3ft (1m)/2.5ft (75cm)**
HARDINESS **Zone 5**

Fair Bianca

Fair Bianca is a very pretty English rose, still the best David Austin in white. The flowers open from small, red brown buds, and are pure white with just a hint of cream at the center. They are also very double, with masses of neat, small petals held within a circle of outer guard petals – shallowly cupped at first, later flat. Sometimes they have a button eye, but they are always a very pretty shape. They come in clusters of 3–9 and last well as cut flowers. The plant has dark, semiglossy leaves that are somewhat susceptible to disease, especially blackspot. The habit of the shrub is neat, short, strong, and upright: it never reaches more than 3.3ft (1m) high, which makes Fair Bianca a very good plant for small gardens. The stems are covered in small, fine prickles. Fair Bianca was the kindly sister of Katherine in *The Taming of the Shrew*.

'F. J. Grootendorst'

Rugosa Hybrid

ORIGIN **de Goey, 1918**
PARENTAGE ***Rosa rugosa* seedling x unknown Polyantha**
FLOWER SIZE **1.4in (3.5cm)**
SCENT **Little or none**
FLOWERING **Constantly in flower**
HEIGHT/SPREAD **5.7ft (1.75m)/4.1ft (1.25m)**
HARDINESS **Zone 4**

There are four "Grootendorst" roses. The first – from which the others are sports (or sports of sports) – was bred by an amateur, and introduced by the Boskoop nursery of F. J. Grootendorst & Sons, who named it after the patriarch of the family, 'F. J. Grootendorst'. Its flowers are bright red. It has produced two color sports: **'Pink Grootendorst'** in 1923 and the deep red **'Grootendorst Supreme'** in 1936. 'Pink Grootendorst' then produced its own sport, **'White Grootendorst'**, in 1962. All are identical except for their coloring and all revert quite frequently to their begetters – 'White Grootendorst' to 'Pink Grootendorst', and 'Pink Grootendorst' and 'Grootendorst Supreme' in turn to the grandaddy of them all, 'F. J. Grootendorst'.

They are unusual among Rugosa roses for their scentlessness and among all roses for the crimped edges of their petals – matched only by another Rugosa hybrid, 'Fimbriata,' and by the China rose, 'Serratipetala'. The flowers come in dense clusters, typically of 7–15, and are surrounded by rich, pale green, wrinkled leaves. The thick, green stems and gray brown branches are extremely prickly, and the plants make densely leafy growth when young. Later they may become somewhat bare and lanky, but they respond very well to pruning and return quickly to lush bushiness. All will grow to 5.7ft (1.75m) if left unpruned and all are unusually hardy, healthy, and free flowering. They look extremely good as cut flowers, either alone or with other flowers, and are useful in mixed beds because they are never out of flower until late into autumn.

'F. J. Grootendorst'

'Pink Grootendorst'

'White Grootendorst'

Sports of 'F. J. Grootendorst'

'Grootendorst Supreme'

ORIGIN **Grootendorst, Netherlands, 1936**

'Pink Grootendorst'

ORIGIN **Grootendorst, Netherlands, 1923**

Sport of 'Pink Grootendorst'

'White Grootendorst'

ORIGIN **Eddy, US, 1962**

'FAIRLIE REDE'

'FAIRLIE REDE'

Hybrid Tea or Pillar Rose

ORIGIN **Clark, Australia, 1937**
PARENTAGE **'Mrs. E. Willis' × seedling**
FLOWER SIZE **4.3in (11cm)**
SCENT **Medium**
FLOWERING **Fully recurrent**
HEIGHT/SPREAD **4.9ft (1.5m)/3.3ft (1m)**
HARDINESS **Zone 7**

'Fairlie Rede' makes an elegant and vigorous shrub, with very thorny stems. Its pretty, dark pink buds open to smoky pink flowers with crimson filaments and messy centers. The shell-shaped petals have a darker shade of apricot pink on their backs, and this produces a beautiful deep suffusion at the center of the flower. The flowers are occasionally borne singly, but usually in clusters of up to 12, typically 3–5. The leaves are mid-green and large, but have fairly narrow leaflets. Fairlie Rede was a commercial rose grower near Melbourne.

'FAIRY DANCE'

Ground Cover

ORIGIN **Harkness, Britain, 1980**
FLOWER SIZE **1.2in (3cm)**
SCENT **Light and musky**
FLOWERING **Repeats well**
HEIGHT/SPREAD **1.6ft (50cm)/1.3ft (40cm)**
HARDINESS **Zone 5**

Jack Harkness introduced a series of Wichurana miniature roses in the late 1970s. Most were seedlings of 'The Fairy' and bore the prefix 'Fairy' in their names – including 'Fairy Dance', which has proved the most enduring. The flowers of 'Fairy Dance' are dark scarlet, semidouble, and very freely borne in clusters of 5–15. The plant has small, healthy, glossy, dark leaves, and a compact habit in its native England, but in hot climates it grows much taller and can be trained as a miniature climber. It repeats well and comes very easily from cuttings. It is useful in the garden as a splash of foreground color, and flourishes in containers.

'FAIRY DANCE'

FALSTAFF

syn. 'AUSVERSE'

Shrub Rose

ORIGIN **Austin, Britain, 1999**
FLOWER SIZE **3.5in (9cm)**
SCENT **Strong and sweet**
FLOWERING **Repeats**
HEIGHT/SPREAD **4.9ft (1.5m)/4.9ft (1.5m)**
HARDINESS **Zone 6**

The color of Falstaff is a splendid dark crimson – bright and rich at first, before passing to dull purple. The flowers are cupped, with a mass of small petals held within broader guard petals. All the petals are short and slightly incurved: they are usually arranged within the flower as a loose rosette, but on other occasions in a more quartered form with a rough button eye. They come singly or in tight clusters of up to five on fairly long stems, but sometimes the individual pedicels within a cluster are weak and the flowers hang down. Falstaff has dark leaves (watch for blackspot) and a fair covering of prickles. In hot climates it can be trained as a 9.8ft (3m) climber. It responds well to deadheading.

FALSTAFF

FAME!

FAME!

syn. 'JACZOR'

Grandiflora

ORIGIN **Zary, US, 1998**
PARENTAGE **Tournament of Roses × 'Zorina'**
FLOWER SIZE **5.1in (13cm)**
SCENT **Light**
FLOWERING **Repeats well**
HEIGHT/SPREAD **4.9ft (1.5m)/3.3ft (1m)**
HARDINESS **Zone 6**
AWARDS **AARS 1998**

Although Fame! has done well since it was introduced, its renown has not spread as widely as it deserves. The flowers open from elegant cherry pink buds. They keep the same dark pink for a long time before fading to mid-pink. The flowers are semidouble with a hint of yellow at the base, reflected from the stamens, which do not brown until the flower is almost finished. The petals are distinctly notched at their tips. The flowers are borne, usually singly, occasionally in clusters of up to five, on long, straight stems. This makes them useful for exhibition and for cutting. The plant has clean, healthy foliage – large and dark – and a broad, bushy habit of growth.

'FANTIN-LATOUR'

Shrub Rose

ORIGIN **c.1940**
FLOWER SIZE **3.5in (9cm)**
SCENT **Strong and sweet**
FLOWERING **Once only, midseason**
HEIGHT/SPREAD **5.7ft (1.75m)/6.6ft (2m)**
HARDINESS **Zone 5**

'Fantin-Latour' turned up as a seedling in an English garden in the middle of the 20th century. Although often classified among the Centifolias, it is clearly a modern hybrid, a prototype of David Austin's English Roses. The flowers are a beautiful rose pink, with a mass of small petals contained within a quartered rosette, and a rough button eye at the center. They come in large clusters, flowering over a long period, but only once. The leaves have short joints, so that the leaflets tend to overlap each other. They are susceptible to mildew and blackspot. The plant is vigorous and grows quickly, reaching 13.1ft (4m) if trained against a wall. It has large thorns and a tendency to lankiness, but responds very well to horizontal training by breaking into flower all along the stems. It has no connection with the French painter Ignace-Henri-Théodore Fantin-Latour (1836–1904), except for its name.

ROSA FARRERI 'PERSETOSA'

see ROSA PERSETOSA

FASCINATION

see FREDENSBORG

'FANTIN-LATOUR'

'FASHION'

'FASHION'

Floribunda

ORIGIN **Boerner, US, 1949**
PARENTAGE **'Rosenmärchen' x 'Crimson Glory'**
FLOWER SIZE **3.1in (8cm)**
SCENT **Medium and sweet**
FLOWERING **Repeats well**
HEIGHT/SPREAD **3.3ft (1m)/2.7ft (80cm)**
HARDINESS **Zone 6**
AWARDS **NRS GM 1948; Bagatelle GM 1949; Portland GM 1949; AARS 1950; ARS GM 1954**

This cross between a famous mauve Floribunda and an even more famous crimson Hybrid Tea produced a remarkable orange pink flower that combined the best of both parents. 'Fashion' was immediately welcomed for its bright, unusual colur, variously described as a combination of coral, peach, orange, and salmon. But its fall from popularity came as quickly as its ascent when it was discovered to be highly susceptible to rust, which it then spread among other roses. However, that was in the 1960s, when the world rose industry was dominated by breeders and producers in cool climates. Rust is a lesser problem in dry climates, and rust prone roses flourish in places like Australia and California without any sign of disease. So 'Fashion' is still a great rose for Mediterranean climates, and hotter. The flowers are full of petals, but come in clusters, and repeat quickly. It is very free flowering and scented, with glossy leaves and a vigorous, bushy habit of growth.

'FATHER'S DAY'

see 'DICK KOSTER'

ROSA *FEDTSCHENKOANA*

Wild Rose

FLOWER SIZE **2in (5cm)**
SCENT **Fetid**
FLOWERING **Continuous**
HEIGHT/SPREAD **8.2ft (2.5m)/4.9ft (1.5m)**
HARDINESS **Zone 4**

Although *Rosa fedtschenkoana* has been grown in gardens for a long time, only recently have DNA tests shown that it is a parent of all the original Damask roses, like 'Quatre Saisons' and 'Kazanlik'. Since *Rosa fedtschenkoana* flowers almost continuously until late autumn, this discovery answers the question that has long puzzled historians – from where did Western roses get their first remontant genes? *Rosa fedtschenkoana* is in any case an attractive and unusual rose. Its leaves are gray, its new stems are white, and its new prickles are crimson – a very striking combination, especially since the prickles are long, slender, and many. The flowers are white, with pale yellow stamens, and are tip-borne (singly, or in twos and threes) at the end of new growth. They are followed by long, bright red, pear-shaped hips. The plant is hardy and healthy, and suckers around, building up into a thicketing mass.

ROSA FEDTSCHENKOANA

'FELICIA'

Hybrid Musk

ORIGIN **Pemberton, Britain, 1928**
PARENTAGE **'Ophelia' x 'Trier'**
FLOWER SIZE **2.4in (6cm)**
SCENT **Strong, sweet, and musky**
FLOWERING **Continuous**
HEIGHT/SPREAD **4.9ft (1.5m)/5.7ft (1.75m)**
HARDINESS **Zone 6**

Many gardeners consider 'Felicia' the best of the Pemberton Hybrid Musks. It has the most beautiful colors, the largest flowers, and the most continuous flowering. It is also very healthy. The flowers are loosely double, with long petals, rose pink in color, with apricot petal backs and a patch of cream toward the center: the overall impression is of pale salmon pink. The flowers come in large, loose, open clusters, 5–15 at the first flowering, but in larger clusters in autumn – as many as 50 on the end of the new growth, which comes up from near ground level. They cut very well for the vase and their scent is freely dispersed. The plant makes a lax bush, which requires minimal pruning for several years until it has built up to a good size. It has large, medium-dark leaves and some large prickles. It is very popular in England, where it combines well with herbaceous plants in mixed borders. It grows taller in hot climates, but the colors fade somewhat quickly.

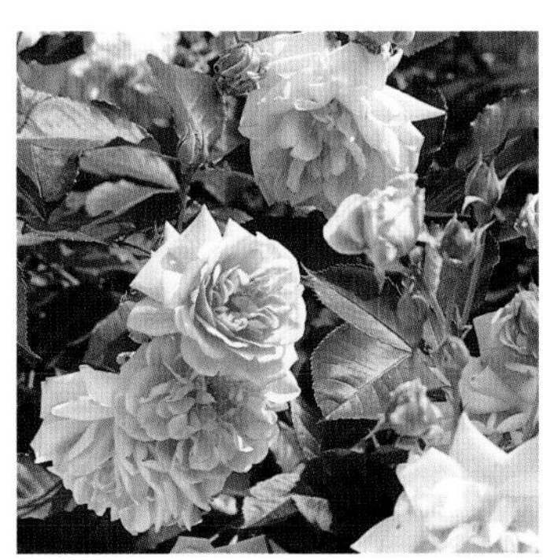
'FELICIA'

'FÉLICITÉ ET PERPÉTUE'

Sempervirens Hybrid

ORIGIN **Jacques, France, 1828**
PARENTAGE ***Rosa sempervirens* x 'Old Blush'**
FLOWER SIZE **1.6in (4cm)**
SCENT **Strong and musky**
FLOWERING **Once only, midseason**
HEIGHT/SPREAD **16.4ft (5m)/9.8ft (3m)**
HARDINESS **Zone 5**

'Félicité et Perpétue' is the best known of the Sempervirens climbers, a rose of great vigor and beauty. Its flowers open pale rose pink, from crimson buds, but soon pass to cream and then to pure white. They are brimming with petals, formed into a neat rosette around a button eye: "each petal in place, each flower in place, exactly right," according to the English rose breeder Jack Harkness. The flowers are carried in large, open clusters – typically of 20–40 – well set off by very dark, small, healthy evergreen leaves. Their only shortcoming is the way the flowers turn brown as they age and do not shed their petals cleanly. The plant is a thick, vigorous, leafy climber with a few very large prickles and a lax habit, which makes it easy to train over arches and along other structures. St. Felicity and St. Perpetua were early Christian martyrs.

In 1879, the New York florist Peter Henderson introduced a dwarf, repeat flowering sport, which he named **'White Pet'**. Climbing sports of bush roses are fairly frequent occurrences, but the opposite phenomenon, which produced 'White Pet', is very rare indeed. 'White Pet' forms a short, dense, evergreen bush, and flowers continuously. The flowers are slightly smaller than 'Félicité et Perpétue' but freely borne in upright clusters. It is a popular front of the border rose and combines well with most other plants. Its only weakness, shared with 'Félicité et Perpétue', is a tendency to hold on to its flowers until they are brown.

'FÉLICITÉ ET PERPÉTUE'

'WHITE PET'

Sport of 'Félicité et Perpétue'

'WHITE PET'

syn. LITTLE WHITE PET
ORIGIN **Henderson, US, 1879**
FLOWER SIZE **1.2in (3cm)**
FLOWERING **Continuous, starting fairly late**
HEIGHT/SPREAD **2ft (60cm)/2ft (60cm)**

'FÉLICITÉ PARMENTIER'

Alba Rose

ORIGIN **Parmentier, France, 1834**
FLOWER SIZE **2.4in (6cm)**
SCENT **Medium and sweet**
FLOWERING **Once, midseason**
HEIGHT/SPREAD **4.9ft (1.5m)/3.3ft (1m)**
HARDINESS **Zone 5**

Like 'Königin von Dänemark', 'Félicité Parmentier' is thought to be a hybrid between an Alba rose and a Damask. It has round buds that open into neat, small flowers, which are lightly cupped, usually quartered, and sometimes blessed with a button eye, but always full of a great number of small petals. They are a very pretty, soft, translucent pink at first, but later fade to white. The petal backs too are white. Later the flowers reflex into a pompon. They come in somewhat tight clusters of 3–9 and are carried in great abundance. The plant is dense, stiff, and upright (useful for small gardens), and has slightly bluish leaves. It is fairly healthy, except for occasional patches of rust on some of the leaves. Of all the once-flowering old roses, it has one of the longest seasons of bloom.

'FÉLICITÉ PARMENTIER'

F

F

'FELLEMBERG'

'FELLEMBERG'

China Rose

ORIGIN **c.1835**
FLOWER SIZE **2in (5cm)**
SCENT **Medium and sweet**
FLOWERING **Repeats almost continuously**
HEIGHT/SPREAD **8.2ft (2.5m)/6.6ft (2m)**
HARDINESS **Zone 6**

The origins of this excellent rose are obscure. It is sometimes known as 'Fellenberg' and attributed to the agricultural improver Philipp Emanuel von Fellenberg (1771–1844). It is a very profuse and perpetually flowering China-Noisette hybrid. Its crimson buds open out to dark carmine-pink flowers, which fade to mauve pink but always retain a distinct satiny brightness. They are sweetly scented, cupped, with bright yellow stamens, and carried in clusters of 5–15. The buds are liable to ball, so it grows best in warm, dry weather, when the color of the flowers is much darker too. The plant has healthy, dark, bluish leaves, small and neat, but densely borne because the internodes are short. It has quite a number of large prickles and a bushy, spreading habit – making it a good pillar rose. It grows easily and quickly from cuttings.

FERDY

FERDINAND PICHARD

FERDINAND PICHARD

Hybrid Perpetual

ORIGIN **Tanne, France, 1921**
FLOWER SIZE **2.8in (7cm)**
SCENT **Strong and sweet**
FLOWERING **Repeats**
HEIGHT/SPREAD **8.2ft (2.5m)/4.9ft (1.5m)**
HARDINESS **Zone 5**

For many years, Ferdinand Pichard was far and away the best and most remontant of striped roses. Only when rose breeders used its genes in the 1970s to create more striped roses did it lose its preeminent position. Its origins are unknown: Rémy Tanne was an amateur from Rouen. The flowers are lightly double, elegant in bud, but open up to show their yellow stamens. They are pale pink, with crimson stripes and splashes irregularly distributed through the petals. No two flowers are ever alike. They come singly or in somewhat congested clusters of up to five, and the plant repeats well, producing a series of secondary flushes after the first main flowering. The plant has large, pale leaves and leaflets, and pale, thick, prickly stems. It is one of the healthiest of old roses and one whose growth responds to heat – making 3.3ft (1m) in England but reaching two or three times that height on the French Riviera.

FERDY

syn. 'KEItoly'

Ground Cover or Shrub Rose

ORIGIN **Suzuki, Japan, 1984**
PARENTAGE **seedling x 'Petite Folie' seedling**
FLOWER SIZE **1.2in (3cm)**
SCENT **Little or none**
FLOWERING **Once only, late in season, for a long time**
HEIGHT/SPREAD **4.9ft (1.5m)/4.9ft (1.5m)**
HARDINESS **Zone 6**

Ferdy is a very striking rose with only one fault – it flowers but once. That flowering is, however, long and spectacular: the bush truly covers itself with flowers, perhaps more than any other rose. The flowers are neat, semi-double, and coral pink at first, but darken (especially in hot weather) to red as they age, before fading and dying almost to white. A hedge or massed planting of Ferdy at its peak is an unforgettable sight. The flowers are accompanied by small, neat, shiny, healthy, mid-green leaves. The plant has wiry stems, short internodes, and a very dense, bushy, upright habit of growth. It is this mounded mass of tiny branches that explains its floriferousness. The flowers tend not to drop their petals when eventually they die, and then the temptation is to prune the rose back to make it look neater. In fact, little or no pruning suits it best, and anything more than the lightest of trims may result in a serious loss of flowers next year.

FESTIVAL

syn. 'KORdialo'

Floribunda

ORIGIN **Kordes, Germany, 1994**
PARENTAGE **Regensberg seedling**
FLOWER SIZE **2.4in (6cm)**
SCENT **Little or none**
FLOWERING **Repeats well**
HEIGHT/SPREAD **2.5ft (75cm)/1.6ft (50cm)**
HARDINESS **Zone 6**
AWARDS **ROTY 1994**

You can see the influence of Regensberg in this short-growing, semidouble, "hand-painted" Floribunda. Festival's striking red flowers and compact habit of growth are great assets in a small garden. The flowers are blood red, with much paler (almost white) reverses and white streaks that run up into the petals. Actually, the petal backs are a pure silvery white, but you can see the crimson coming through from the other side, so the overall effect is palest pink. The flowers come in small clusters, typically of 3–5, and occasionally singly. The small, dark, neat, glossy leaves are a good complement, as are the crimson edges to the leaflets. The plant is very prickly. It is useful as a container plant and for front of the border plantings.

FESTIVAL

FELLOWSHIP

syn. 'HARwelcome', Livin' Easy

Floribunda

ORIGIN **Harkness, Britain, 1992**
PARENTAGE **'Southampton' x Remember Me**
FLOWER SIZE **3.9in (10cm)**
SCENT **Moderate, a mixture of fruit and sweetness**
FLOWERING **Repeats quickly and well**
HEIGHT/SPREAD **3.3ft (1m)/2ft (60cm)**
HARDINESS **Zone 6**
AWARDS **RNRS GM 1990; AARS 1996**

Fellowship is a striking Floribunda, especially good in massed plantings. The flowers are gleaming pale orange or dark apricot, with slightly paler backs to the petals and more yellow toward the center. The thick, sturdy petals are slightly wavy and shield-shaped (they have little pointed tips) and the flowers come in clusters of 3–7. The flowers open slightly cupped, showing their stamens at the center, and acquire crimson edges as they age. The leaves are mid-green, glossy, and healthy, and the plant grows well in a wide variety of climates – from California to England, and from Germany to Louisiana. It is, however, very well armed, with spiky prickles all around the stem. That aside, it is one of the best Floribundas to come out of the 1990s.

Easy Going is a sport of Fellowship, and is exactly the same as its parent in every way, except for its color, which is paler apricot (with sometimes a hint of pink), instead of the oranges and yellows of Fellowship. Otherwise it has all the strengths of that excellent Floribunda, including thick petals, a sturdy habit, health, and adaptability.

FELLOWSHIP

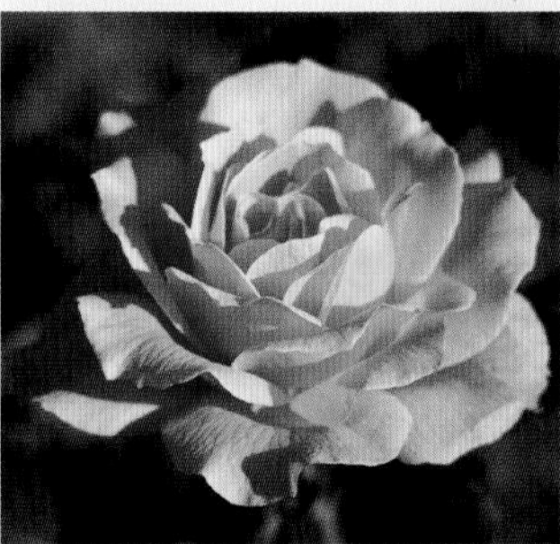

EASY GOING

Sport of Fellowship

EASY GOING

syn. 'HARflow'
ORIGIN **Harkness, Britain, 1999**

The Fineschi Garden

THE LARGEST COLLECTION OF ROSES EVER ASSEMBLED BY AN AMATEUR CAN BE SEEN AT PROFESSOR GIANFRANCO FINESCHI'S GARDEN IN TUSCANY, ITALY

The Fineschi garden in Tuscany is extraordinary in that it has been created solely by Professor Gianfranco Fineschi over the past 40 years – the 100-year-old European Rosarium at Sangerhausen has only a few more hundred roses than can be found in Fineschi's private collection.

Professor Gianfranco Fineschi

The Fineschi house, "Casalone," near Cavriglia, is the center of an agricultural estate of vines and olive groves and is surrounded by the hills and woods of the Chianti region. It was first acquired by Fineschi's grandfather in the early 1900s. The professor has made his collection among the olive trees themselves. Its future is secured by a charitable foundation, the Fondazione Roseto Botanico Carla Fineschi, which is dedicated to his late wife.

The garden has grown ever larger over the years as it has gained more land to accommodate more roses. It now extends to about 8.6 acres (3.5 hectares). Its design is organic, with areas dedicated to different sections of the genus *Rosa*, including Gallicas, Moss roses, and Hybrid Perpetuals. Smaller areas celebrate lesser-known byways of rose breeding, like the many hybrids of *Rosa banksiae* bred by Quinto Mansuino and his followers in Italy in the 1960s and 1970s.

Modern roses, starting from about 1900, are arranged according to breeder. Extensive areas are dedicated to the work of single families, like the Meillands of France, the Kordes of Germany, and the McGredys of Northern Ireland and New Zealand. Here it is possible to see the whole history of roses displayed in microcosm. Smaller areas of the garden display the work of breeders from Argentina, Brazil, South Africa, and other countries whose roses are rarely seen in Europe. The Polish collection includes the striking orange Hybrid Tea called 'Warszawa', introduced by the little-known Grabczewski in 1957. There are similar surprises and novelties to discover among the collections of roses from Czechoslovak or Portuguese breeders.

'Warszawa'

There are sections that display roses and their sports: **Festival Fanfare** (Ogilvie, 1982), for example, can be found alongside its parent 'Fred Loads' (Holmes, 1968). Elsewhere are raised beds brimming with miniature roses, and several roses that Fineschi himself has saved from extinction, like the elegant Wichurana ramblers: pink 'Lyon Rambler' (1908), and white 'Mme. Portier-Durel' (1910), and the exquisite foundling Hybrid Tea that goes by the name of 'Gloria di Roma'.

Around the outside of the garden is a stupendous display of climbing roses and ramblers, fan trained to display their flowers to advantage, like the old Wichurana rambler 'Snowflake' (Cant, 1922). Within the garden, some of the roses are grown as exceptionally high standards, sometimes grafted as much as 8.2–9.8ft (2.5–3m) high: the orange Floribunda 'Guitare' (Gaujard, 1963) has an olive tree as its background. Tall shrub roses like the Penzance Briars are grown within wooden box fences, with their flowers spilling out over the top.

The Fineschi garden is open daily in May and June: the peak display usually comes during the last week in May. Visitors should remind themselves that this is the fruit of one man's passion, an extraordinary achievement in a single lifetime, particularly since Fineschi worked as an orthopedic surgeon in Rome during the week, and escaped to his garden only at weekends.

Rose-covered Pergola at Casalone

F

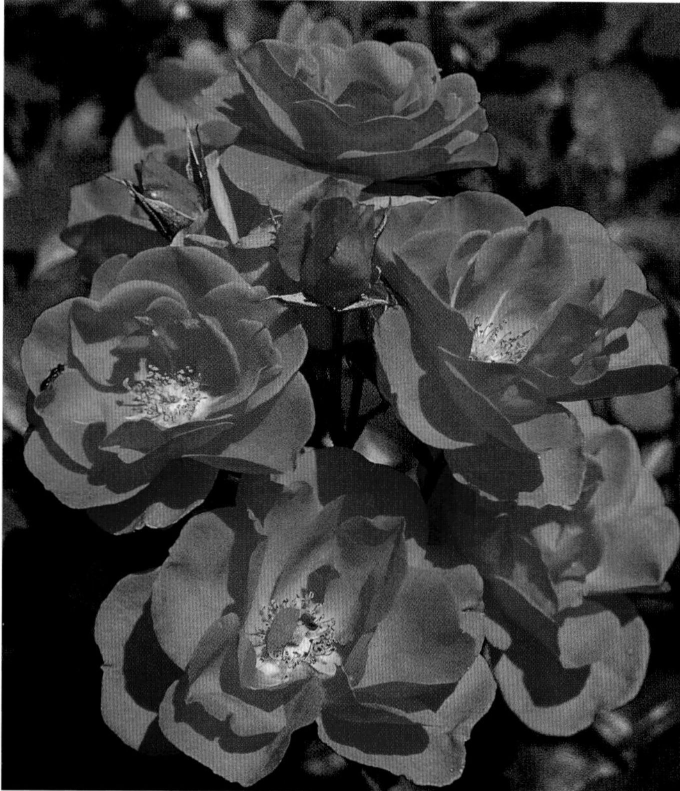

'FEUERWERK'

'FEUERWERK'

syn. 'FEU D'ARTIFICE'

Shrub Rose

ORIGIN **Tantau, Germany, 1962**
FLOWER SIZE **2.8in (7cm)**
SCENT **Medium and fruity**
FLOWERING **Repeats well**
HEIGHT/SPREAD **5.7ft (1.75m)/4.1ft (1.25m)**
HARDINESS **Zone 5**

This handsome shrub is best thought of as a very vigorous Floribunda. The flowers of 'Feuerwerk' occasionally come singly, but are usually borne in loose clusters (typically of 3–7). The flowers are semidouble, with strong, wavy petals that stand up well to rain. They open orange, or coral pink, and fade by degrees to salmon pink, with a pale patch around the golden stamens at the center. They are very pretty at all stages – even the long, slender buds are unusually attractive. 'Feuerwerk' makes an upright, bushy shrub, with large, medium-pale, glossy leaves. It is a very abundant flowerer and a prompt reflowerer. It has been widely planted in public gardens throughout Europe, but it also makes a useful shrub rose in private gardens.

'FIMBRIATA'

Rugosa Hybrid

ORIGIN **Morlet, France, 1891**
PARENTAGE ***Rosa rugosa* × 'Mme. Alfred Carrière'**
FLOWER SIZE **2.4in (6cm)**
SCENT **Light and sweet**
FLOWERING **Midseason, then intermittently until late autumn**
HEIGHT/SPREAD **6.6ft (2m)/6.6ft (2m)**
HARDINESS **Zone 4**

The unique characteristic of 'Fimbriata', from which it gets its name, is the ragged edge to its petals, like a dianthus or pink. The broad outer petals are feathered and frilly in an irregular way: "fimbriated" is the botanical word for it. The effect is very attractive. The flowers open a soft, pale pink and fade to white. Clearly visible are the stamens, which are very pale yellow and long lasting. The flowers come in loose clusters of 5–15 and are useful for cutting. They are well set off by the pale, rugose leaves. The plant is healthy, free flowering, and vigorous.

FIONA

syn. 'MEIBELUXEN'

Ground Cover

ORIGIN **Meilland, France, 1979**
PARENTAGE **'Sea Foam' × 'Picasso'**
FLOWER SIZE **3.1in (8cm)**
SCENT **Light and sweet**
FLOWERING **Repeats very well**
HEIGHT/SPREAD **3.3ft (1m)/6.6ft (2m)**
HARDINESS **Zone 5**

'FIMBRIATA'

FIONA

This was one of Meilland's first landscaping roses and made a great impression all over the world. Fiona has masses of semidouble flowers of a startling, bright red – a dark scarlet that draws attention to itself from a great distance. The flowers have a very small patch of white at the base of their petals, behind the ring of yellow stamens, which helps to intensify the brilliant color. They come in clusters of 5–15 all over the surface of the bush and are followed by vermilion hips. Fiona is a lax, prickly grower, wider than it is high, and good for sites where it can scramble up and down the surface of the soil; it is also good for hiding eyesores. Like all landscaping roses it is an invaluable garden plant. Its leaves are small, medium-dark, and glossy (*Rosa wichurana* is in its ancestry). It is extremely healthy. It may get a touch of blackspot in some situations, but this never does any lasting damage.

FIRST CLASS

see CLASS ACT

FIRST EDITION

see ARNAUD DELBARD

'FIRST PRIZE'

Hybrid Tea

ORIGIN **Boerner, US, 1970**
PARENTAGE **'Golden Masterpiece' seedling × 'Enchantment' seedling**
FLOWER SIZE **6.7in (17cm)**
SCENT **Medium and fruity**
FLOWERING **Repeats well**
HEIGHT/SPREAD **4.9ft (1.5m)/3.3ft (1m)**
HARDINESS **Zone 6**
AWARDS **AARS 1970**

The name says it all: 'First Prize' is a whopping exhibition rose. The flowers may be as much as 7in (18cm) in size, and there exists a climbing form whose flowers are even larger. They have the classic high, conical shape of the exhibition Hybrid Tea, and unfurl their long petals very slowly, even in the hot, dry climates where this rose grows best. The buds are pale crimson, but open to soft pink centers, sometimes with a hint of ivory or cream within, and always with a gentle contrast between the dark outer petals and the pale inner ones, though all the colors fade in hot weather. The flowers are usually borne singly

'FIRST PRIZE'

(occasionally in clusters of up to four), at the end of long, strong stems. The bush has vicious thorns, red new growth, and dark tough leaves, which are no strangers to blackspot and powdery mildew. It hot areas it will grow gawkily to 8.2ft (2.5m).

'FISHER HOLMES'

Hybrid Perpetual

ORIGIN **Verdier, France, 1865**
PARENTAGE **'Maurice Bernardin' seedling**
FLOWER SIZE **3.9in (10cm)**
SCENT **Strong and sweet**
FLOWERING **Remontant**
HEIGHT/SPREAD **4.9ft (1.5m)/4.1ft (1.25m)**
HARDINESS **Zone 5**

Few Hybrid Perpetuals have so much to offer as 'Fisher Holmes' – good repeat flowering, a sumptuous color, and a vigor to match. Its flowers are not among the largest, but they are freely produced, both singly and in clusters of up to five. They are a brilliant dark red at first, with a bright color much prized in the 19th century, with a darker sheen and hints of velvety crimson on the outer petals. The petal backs are slightly paler. As the flowers open out, they turn to pale crimson or purple, and develop a beautiful imbricated shape like a camellia. They are excellent, long-lasting cut flowers. 'Fisher Holmes' makes a vigorous plant, with thin, mid-green leaves, that are unfortunately somewhat susceptible both to mildew and blackspot. In hot, dry climates, however, these diseases are not a problem, and here 'Fisher Holmes' makes an outstanding shrub rose, best pegged down so that it flowers all along its branches.

'FISHER HOLMES'

FISHERMAN'S FRIEND

FISHERMAN'S FRIEND

syn. 'AUSCHILD'

Shrub Rose

ORIGIN **Austin, Britain, 1988**
PARENTAGE **'Lilian Austin' × 'The Squire'**
FLOWER SIZE **3.5in (9cm)**
SCENT **Very strong and sweet**
FLOWERING **Repeats**
HEIGHT/SPREAD **4.1ft (1.25m)/3.3ft (1m)**
HARDINESS **Zone 6**

Some of David Austin's English Roses are more highly prized outside England: Fisherman's Friend is a good example – very popular in North America and Australia. Its lightly cupped flowers are deep crimson, with paler backs, and fade slightly to ruby, magenta, or cerise, but they are packed with petals and rich with an intensely sweet Damask fragrance. They come fairly late in the season and tend to flower only at the end of the stems, so this is a rose that responds to pegging down. The plant has dark leaves, a very thick covering of prickles, and a stiff, upright habit. It is strong, vigorous, and healthy: in hot climates it will grow to 6.6ft (2m). Its name, Fisherman's Friend, was bought at a charity auction by a manufacturer of throat lozenges.

FLAMINGO

syn. KORFLÜG, Margaret Thatcher

Hybrid Tea

ORIGIN **Kordes, Germany, 1979**
PARENTAGE **seedling × 'Lady Like'**
FLOWER SIZE **3.9in (10cm)**
SCENT **Light and sweet**
FLOWERING **Repeats well**
HEIGHT/SPREAD **4.1ft (1.25m)/3.3ft (1m)**
HARDINESS **Zone 5**

The color of Flamingo recalls the pink of the European flamingo, though it fades eventually to silvery pink at the edges. Flamingo also has a very elegant, attractive, and long-lasting shape. It was bred for the cut-flower market, but has never enjoyed such success under glass as it does as a garden plant. The buds are ivory colored and high centered in the Hybrid Tea fashion, but not too full. The flowers are borne singly and in clusters of up to seven on long, strong stems, that are perfect for picking. Flamingo is a most vigorous grower, constantly pushing up new flowering stems. The bush is healthy, with medium-dark leaves.

FLAMINGO

'FLAMMENTANZ'

'FLAMMENTANZ'

syn. KORFLATA

Modern Climber

ORIGIN **Kordes, Germany, 1955**
PARENTAGE ***Rosa rubiginosa* hybrid × 'Kordesii'**
FLOWER SIZE **3.1in (8cm)**
SCENT **Light**
FLOWERING **Once only, midseason**
HEIGHT/SPREAD **8.2ft (2.5m)/6.6ft (2m)**
HARDINESS **Zone 4**
AWARDS **ADR 1952**

'Flammentanz' is a descendant of 'Kordesii' and *Rosa rubiginosa*, both of which were used by the Kordes family to breed many of their best shrub roses. Wilhelm Kordes regarded it as his best crimson sweetbriar hybrid, but also disparaged it because it flowered only once. It is extremely hardy, and therefore popular in Scandinavia, where the climate means that repeat flowering is less important than in countries where roses have a longer growing season. The flowers are 3.1in (8cm) across, Turkey red, and come in clusters of 3–7 on a stiff, prickly bush. It makes a coarse shrub or a short climber. It has mid-green leaves, which sometimes show signs of chlorosis (a chlorophyll deficiency), but it is a thrifty grower and very tough.

FLORA DANICA

syn. 'POULRIM', Garden News, Spellbound

Hybrid Tea

ORIGIN **Poulsen, Denmark, 1996**
FLOWER SIZE **3.1in (8cm)**
SCENT **Moderate**
FLOWERING **Repeats well**
HEIGHT/SPREAD **2.5ft (75cm)/2.5ft (75cm)**
HARDINESS **Zone 5**

A very handsome Hybrid Tea, Flora Danica is a swirling mixture of orange and pink. The inner petals tend to be orange or apricot in color, while the outer ones – the guard petals – are deep pink and the petal backs are yellow. All these colors combine to create a sumptuous variety of nuances in the shadows between the sturdy petals. The flowers come singly or in clusters of

FLORA DANICA

3–9, and are excellent for cutting. The plant has dark, glossy leaves. *Flora Danica* is a famous illustrated work, consisting of 3,240 engravings, that was published in 51 parts between 1761 and 1874.

'FLORA MCIVOR'

Rubiginosa Hybrid

ORIGIN **Penzance, Britain, 1894**
PARENTAGE ***Rosa rubiginosa* × unknown**
FLOWER SIZE **1.2in (3cm)**
SCENT **Light and sweet**
FLOWERING **Once only**
HEIGHT/SPREAD **9.8ft (3m)/8.2ft (2.5m)**
HARDINESS **Zone 5**

Of all the sweetbriar hybrids that Lord Penzance introduced in the 1890s, 'Flora McIvor' most closely resembles its parent *Rosa rubiginosa*. The flowers are a little larger, and the leaves have lost some of the distinctive sweetbriar scent, but it is a large, prickly bush whose short flowering is followed by scarlet hips. It is too large and coarse for most gardens, but useful in a wild garden and for hedging.

'FLORA MCIVOR'

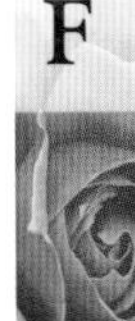

Gardens of the Rose, Royal National Rose Society, Hertfordshire, England ▶

'Flore'

syn. Flora

Hybrid Sempervirens

ORIGIN **Jacques, France, 1830**
PARENTAGE **(*Rosa sempervirens* x *Rosa arvensis*) x 'Old Blush'**
FLOWER SIZE **2.4in (6cm)**
SCENT **Strong and musky**
FLOWERING **Once only**
HEIGHT/SPREAD **13.1ft (4m)/9.8ft (3m)**
HARDINESS **Zone 6**

The Hybrid Sempervirens are among the hardiest and best of ramblers. 'Flore' is outstanding: its crimson buds open to ruffled flowers, which have pink petals toward the outside and are creamy white toward the center. Crimson stains remain on the outside of the outer petals and create a charming effect. Sometimes the flowers have a button eye. They come in loose clusters of 5–20 and have a delicious musky scent, tinged with that distinctive bitterness which is described as "myrrh." Their only weakness is a tendency not to shed their petals when they have finished flowering but to retain their brown relics forever. The plant is easy to grow: it flourishes in almost all soils and situations. In warm climates, its small, neat, shining green leaves are evergreen.

'FLORE'

Flower Carpet

see Heidetraum

Flower Power

see Blühwunder

Flutterbye

syn. 'WEKplasol'

Shrub Rose

ORIGIN **Carruth, US, 1995**
PARENTAGE **'Playboy' x 'Mutabilis'**
FLOWER SIZE **2in (5cm)**
SCENT **Medium and fruity**
FLOWERING **Continuous**
HEIGHT/SPREAD **4.9ft (1.5m)/4.9ft (1.5m)**
HARDINESS **Zone 6**

Flutterbye is a very unusual rose. The surface of the shrub is covered with bright yellow, nearly single flowers, tinged with orange, pink, and every imaginable in-between shade. They open pale yellow, but darken and take on pink and orange tones as they age, starting with the petal backs and the petal tips. The flowers are not large, but they are copiously borne, almost continuously, in small clusters. The flowers are backed by dark, glossy green leaves – an excellent foil, and disease resistant too. Flutterbye makes a fine, rounded shrub in cool climates but can be trained as a pillar rose or short climber in hot ones.

FLUTTERBYE

Folklore

syn. 'KORlore'

Hybrid Tea

ORIGIN **Kordes, Germany, 1977**
PARENTAGE **'Duftwolke' x seedling**
FLOWER SIZE **4.3in (11cm)**
SCENT **Strong and sweet**
FLOWERING **Repeats**
HEIGHT/SPREAD **4.9ft (1.5m)/3.3ft (1m)**
HARDINESS **Zone 5**

Folklore is an elegant, long-lasting cutting rose of tremendous vigor, blessed with one of the strongest, sweetest scents. Its flowers open from long, pointed buds. They are usually dark orange pink at first, fading to salmon pink with creamy yellow reverses, but the exact color differs according to the season and the weather – bright coral, solid orange, or soft salmon. They have thick, rain proof petals and long sepals, and come singly or in clusters of up to nine. The plant has large, glossy leaves and rich crimson new growth, with a slight tendency to attract mildew. It is, however, extremely vigorous, growing to as much as 8.2ft (2.5m) in one season in hot climates. It is a much prized exhibition rose, heavy blooming, a reliable repeater, and responds to being well-fed.

FOLKLORE

Rosa foetida

syn. 'Austrian Briar'

Wild Rose

FLOWER SIZE **2.4in (6cm)**
SCENT **Strong and fetid**
FLOWERING **Once, fairly early in season**
HEIGHT/SPREAD **6.6ft (2m)/6.6ft (2m)**
HARDINESS **Zone 4**

The origins of *Rosa foetida* are obscure. It is probably a species and perhaps a native of central and southwestern Asia, where it is widely naturalized. The name of the species refers to its fetid scent, which is more attractive to flies, wasps, and beetles than to humans. The flowers are a very pure, bright yellow, fading only very slightly at the edges of the petals as they age. The filaments and anthers remain yellow and do not turn brown, an unusual and attractive characteristic. The flowers are borne, usually singly, on short spurs and are sometimes followed by round, red brown hips. The plant has thin brown wood and prickles, which later turn gray. The leaves are small, with bright green, toothed leaflets. They have a reputation not only for attracting blackspot but also, somewhat unfairly, for introducing it into modern roses. *Rosa foetida* is very much a denizen of climates that enjoy a hot summer and a cold winter.

The sport of *Rosa foetida* known as **'Bicolor'** has been known since the 16th century. It is exactly the same as the yellow species in all details except that the upper sides of its petals are nasturtium red. The flowers are also very slightly larger than the yellow form. The backs of the petals remain yellow. Individual flowers of 'Bicolor' are variable in hue and in the extent to which the bottom of the petal is yellow. They often have flashes and flecks of yellow in them: the orange coloring is only a few cells thick. They have the yellow stamens as the type. 'Bicolor' is an unstable mutation, and commonly reverts to *Rosa foetida*.

There is a second sport of *Rosa foetida* called **'Persiana'**, which is a form with double flowers. These are the brightest egg yolk yellow imaginable, with occasional hints of gold refracted by the petals toward the center of the flower. The flowers are variable in shape: although always cupped, the pattern into which the petals arrange themselves differs considerably from flower to flower. All have thin petals, which makes them subject to balling in wet climates and humid conditions.

It was 'Persiana' that Joseph Pernet-Ducher used to breed the first truly yellow garden rose, 'Soleil d'Or', introduced in 1900. All modern yellow and orange roses owe their coloring to this ancestral hybrid and thus to the bright colors of *Rosa foetida*.

ROSA FOETIDA

Sports of *Rosa foetida*

Rosa foetida 'Bicolor'

syn. 'Austrian Copper'
ORIGIN **1590**
FLOWER SIZE **2.8in (7cm)**

Rosa foetida 'Persiana'

Species (Double Form)
ORIGIN **1837**
FLOWER SIZE **2.8in (7cm)**

ROSA FOETIDA 'BICOLOR'

ROSA FOETIDA 'PERSIANA'

'FOLKSINGER'

ROSA FORRESTIANA

'FORTUNIANA'

'FOLKSINGER'

Shrub Rose

ORIGIN **Buck, US, 1984**
PARENTAGE **Carefree Beauty x 'Friesia'**
FLOWER SIZE **3.9in (10cm)**
SCENT **Good and sweet**
FLOWERING **Repeats**
HEIGHT/SPREAD **4.1ft (1.25m)/3.3ft (1m)**
HARDINESS **Zone 4**

'Folksinger' is one of the Floribunda type shrub roses bred by Dr. Griffith Buck to withstand the cold winters in Iowa. It is vigorous and very hardy, but it also has a very good display of beautiful pale yellow flowers. They fade to mother-of-pearl and almost to white, with pale buff tints at the center and pale tan or dark buff on the petal backs. They are shaped like Hybrid Teas at first, but later open out cupped and loosely double. They come singly or in clusters – as many as 15 flowers at a time, but more commonly 5–7 – and continue flowering until late autumn. The bush is strong-growing, upright, and prickly, with dark, glossy, healthy, coppery leaves.

'FONTAINE'

syn. 'FOUNTAIN', 'RED PRINCE'

Shrub Rose

ORIGIN **Tantau, Germany, 1970**
PARENTAGE **'Olala' x 'Duftwolke'**
FLOWER SIZE **4.3in (11cm)**
SCENT **Strong and sweet**
FLOWERING **Repeats constantly**
HEIGHT/SPREAD **6.6ft (2m)/4.1ft (1.25m)**
HARDINESS **Zone 6**
AWARDS **ADR 1971; RNRS PIT 1971**

'FONTAINE'

'Fontaine' is a rose without equal, with the abundance and energy of a Floribunda and the toughness of a real shrub rose. The flowers can be as much as 5.1in (13cm) in diameter and come in large, loose clusters of up to ten on a single, long, strong stem. The flowers are sometimes semidouble, sometimes semisingle, but always large, with ruffled petals, and beautiful at all stages of their development. The petals keep their color and their brightness well. 'Fontaine' makes a shrubby plant, with dark, glossy leaves and a clean bill of health. It is extremely free flowering. Despite its size, it makes an excellent bedding rose.

FOOTLOOSE

see MIRATO

ROSA FORRESTIANA

Wild Rose

FLOWER SIZE **1.2in (3cm)**
SCENT **Little or none**
FLOWERING **Once only**
HEIGHT/SPREAD **8.2ft (2.5m)/8.2ft (2.5m)**
HARDINESS **Zone 6**

This dainty and vigorous species comes from southwestern China. It has small leaves studded with small, dark pink flowers, which are borne either singly or in clusters of up to five. Each flower is subtended by a leafy bract, which frames it and adds to its charm. The flowers are followed by small (0.4in/1cm), round, bristly, vermilion hips. It is a good plant for large, wild gardens and woodland plantings, but lacks ornamental value among more intensive garden plantings.

'FORTUNE'S DOUBLE YELLOW'

syn. 'BEAUTY OF GLAZENWOOD'

China Rose

ORIGIN **Britain, 1845**
FLOWER SIZE **3.1in (8cm)**
SCENT **Light and tealike**
FLOWERING **Once, early in season**
HEIGHT/SPREAD **9.8ft (3m)/13.1ft (4m)**
HARDINESS **Zone 8**

This rose owes its name to Robert Fortune, an English plant hunter who brought samples of it from Ningpo in China to Europe. In hot climates, like southern California, it is one of the most outstandingly floriferous of all roses. The flowers are variable in color, but are usually pale peach or buff yellow, later cream, with pink tinges on the petal backs. Neat in bud, the flowers open out somewhat shapelessly, but in such quantity that the overall impression is always of massed color. They come in small clusters, usually of 3–5 flowers. The leaves are small and neat – very close to typical *Rosa chinensis* foliage. The plant grows rampantly, forming a dense thicket of slender stems and innumerable hooked prickles.

'FORTUNE'S DOUBLE YELLOW'

'FORTUNIANA'

Banksian Hybrid

ORIGIN **c.1850**
PARENTAGE ***Rosa banksiae* x *Rosa laevigata* (probably)**
FLOWER SIZE **2.4in (6cm)**
SCENT **Medium, of violets**
FLOWERING **Spectacularly and early, then intermittently**
HEIGHT/SPREAD **16.4ft (5m)/6.6ft (2m)**
HARDINESS **Zone 7**

John Lindley named this handsome Banksian rose after the English plant collector Robert Fortune (1812–80). It is a spectacular flowering plant in hot climates, but best seen from a distance, since its flowers are somewhat messy close-up. They are much larger than other Banksians and sometimes display a button eye. They are carried in small, airy, pendulous clusters and start into flower very early in the year. The main flowering continues for up to three months, but an established plant is never out of flower. The leaves are small, dark, and evergreen, and the plant grows into a straggling, scrambling climber. It is widely used in tropical areas with sandy soils as a rootstock, especially in parts of Australia and the southeastern corner of the US. It thrives in heat, resists drought, and is perfectly happy in poor soil.

'FOUNTAIN'

see 'FONTAINE'

F

FOURTH OF JULY

FOURTH OF JULY

syn. 'WEKROALT', Crazy for You

Modern Climber

ORIGIN **Carruth, US, 1999**
PARENTAGE **Roller Coaster x 'Altissimo'**
FLOWER SIZE **2.2in (5.5cm)**
SCENT **Light and fruity**
FLOWERING **Almost continuous**
HEIGHT/SPREAD **9.8ft (3m)/6.6ft (2m)**
HARDINESS **Zone 5**
AWARDS **ARS GM 1999**

Fourth of July is a red and white splashed climber of the Floribunda type. It was the first climbing rose to win an AARS award in 23 years. The flowers open crimson and pink but fade to oxblood red and white. The colored stripes are so bold that the small size of the flowers and their lack of petals go quite unnoticed. The striped markings on the individual blooms vary considerably – some are mostly red and others mostly white. This adds to their impact, as do the golden stamens and the fact that individual flowers last for a long time on the bush. They come in open clusters of 5–20: the central flower of a cluster opens first and is larger. The plant has nice clean foliage, small and dark with slightly rounded leaflets and a larger terminal leaflet. It is very prickly and rather gawky, but growth is vigorous and quick, and these good qualities are constant across a wide variety of conditions and climates. The name Fourth of July commemorates Independence Day.

FOXI

syn. 'UHLWE', Buffalo Gal

Rugosa Hybrid

ORIGIN **Uhl, Germany, 1989**
FLOWER SIZE **3.1in (8cm)**
SCENT **Strong, sweet, and spicy**
FLOWERING **Almost continuous**
HEIGHT/SPREAD **4.9ft (1.5m)/4.9ft (1.5m)**
HARDINESS **Zone 4**
AWARDS **Edland FA 1991; ADR 1992**

Although it will grow in warm climates to 4.9ft (1.5m) high, Foxi is a compact Rugosa rose and seldom reaches as much as 3.3ft (1m) in its native Germany. Its flowers are semidouble and stand up better to rain than most Rugosas. They are deep mauve pink or pale magenta,

FOXI

with a large boss of yellow stamens at the center. They come in tight clusters of 3–10 and are followed by large, red hips. Foxi has a dense, mounded habit of growth and masses of healthy, mid-green, pleated leaves, which turn bright yellow in autumn. The plant has two outstanding qualities: it is amazingly hardy, and it will tolerate poor soils and difficult growing conditions, including salt. Thus it is an excellent landscaping rose for cold climates, as well as a versatile garden plant.

'FRAGRANT CLOUD'

see 'DUFTWOLKE'

'FRAGRANT DELIGHT'

Floribunda

ORIGIN **Wisbech, Britain, 1978**
PARENTAGE **'Chanelle' x 'Whisky'**
FLOWER SIZE **2.8in (7cm)**
SCENT **Strong, rich, and sweet**
FLOWERING **Repeats well**
HEIGHT/SPREAD **4.1ft (1.25m)/3.3ft (1m)**
HARDINESS **Zone 6**
AWARDS **Edland FA 1976; James Mason GM 1988**

You can see the influence of 'Whisky' in 'Fragrant Delight': it has the same large, loose petals and intense fragrance. The flowers are pink, with coppery petal backs, and the shadows that form between the petals are a mixture of raspberry red and orange. Although technically a Floribunda, the flowers are full of petals. They come singly and in clusters of up to seven, and are well set off by dark, glossy foliage and crimson new growths. In the right conditions, the plant is a healthy, bushy grower and is rarely out of flower. In hot weather, however, it tends to open out rather quickly and drop its petals shortly thereafter, so 'Fragrant Delight' is best in cool climates, where the color of the flowers is as sumptuous as their scent.

'FRAGRANT HOUR'

Hybrid Tea

ORIGIN **McGredy, New Zealand, 1973**
PARENTAGE **'Arthur Bell' x ('Spartan' x 'Grand Gala')**
FLOWER SIZE **4.3in (11cm)**
SCENT **Strong and sweet**
FLOWERING **Repeats fairly well**
HEIGHT/SPREAD **4.1ft (1.25m)/3.3ft (1m)**
HARDINESS **Zone 6**
AWARDS **Belfast GM 1975; Gamble FA 1997**

'Fragrant Hour' is intensely sweet scented and won the James Alexander Gamble award for fragrance, yet some people find it only lightly scented. The flowers are an unusual combination of orange and pink – orange toward the center and pink at the edges, but merging into each other to create an attractive overall effect of salmon pink. The petal backs are always slightly darker in color. The flowers are elegant in bud, and keep their shape as they open out into a mass of ruffled petals. The plant grows strongly and upright in form, with dark green leaves. It is healthy, except for perhaps a little blackspot later in the year.

FRAGRANT MEMORIES

see SEBASTIAN KNEIPP

'FRAGRANT MEMORY'

see 'JADIS'

FRAGRANT PLUM

FRAGRANT PLUM

syn. 'AROPLUMI'

Grandiflora

ORIGIN **Christensen, US, 1990**
PARENTAGE **'Shocking Blue' x ('Nil Bleu' x ['Ivory Tower' x 'Angel Face'])**
FLOWER SIZE **4.3in (11cm)**
SCENT **Very strong, sweet, and fruity**
FLOWERING **Repeats**
HEIGHT/SPREAD **4.9ft (1.5m)/3.3ft (1m)**
HARDINESS **Zone 6**

With vigor, scent, and an unusual combination of rich colors, Fragrant Plum is a splendid rose for hot climates. It is popular in the warmer parts of North America and throughout Australia, but has never been introduced into Europe. Its buds are long and elegant, but deep magenta or crimson in color, giving no hint of the pinks, mauves, and purples that distinguish the open flowers. These are a mixture of lavender and similar pale shades of purple, with deep, rich, plum colored edgings. The upper sides of the petals are always pinker, and the backs usually darker. The flowers are borne singly and in clusters of up to seven on long, strong stems, which last well and are very good for cutting. Fragrant Plum has large, dark leaves and a vigorous, upright habit of growth. It responds well to feeding, watering, and deadheading by repeat flowering regularly until late autumn. The best colors are produced in hot weather, but the largest flowers in cool weather.

'FRAGRANT DELIGHT'

'FRAGRANT HOUR'

'FRANCESCA'

Hybrid Musk

ORIGIN **Pemberton, Britain, 1922**
PARENTAGE **'Danaë' × 'Sunburst'**
FLOWER SIZE **3.5in (9cm)**
SCENT **Medium, rich, fruity, and musky**
FLOWERING **Repeats continuously**
HEIGHT/SPREAD **6.6ft (2m)/6.6ft (2m)**
HARDINESS **Zone 6**

Of all the Pemberton Hybrid Musks, 'Francesca' has the largest flowers and the richest color. The flowers are glowing amber colored in the bud (long and elegant) and as they open out, before fading to buff and cream. They are loosely but lightly double, with enough petals to droop under their weight – a very attractive feature, since the flowers come in large, open, pendulous sprays (typically of 5–10 flowers). The leaves are an excellent foil for this rich coloring – dark green, glossy, almost modern looking, and very healthy. The plant has very few prickles and a lax habit of growth. It is not the most vigorous of Musks, but takes a few years to grow to maturity, after which it sends out long annual new growth of 6.6ft (2m) or so. It is a reliable repeater, seldom out of flower, and capable of producing very large clusters of flowers in autumn.

FRANCINE AUSTIN

syn. 'AUSRAM'

Shrub Rose

ORIGIN **Austin, Britain, 1988**
PARENTAGE **'Alister Stella Gray' × 'Ballerina'**
FLOWER SIZE **1.6in (4cm)**
SCENT **Strong and musky**
FLOWERING **Constantly in flower**
HEIGHT/SPREAD **3.9ft (1.2m)/4.9ft (1.5m)**
HARDINESS **Zone 6**

Francine Austin is an unusual rose. Its pink-tipped buds produce large, airy clusters of small, pure white flowers in great profusion right through until early winter. It is best thought of as a modern Hybrid Musk, with pretty flowers in the shape of a rosette or pompon and occasionally with stamens visible at the center. The clusters average 10–30 flowers – more in autumn – and are somewhat hard to distinguish against the very pale green foliage. The plant is naturally rather lanky and awkward in shape – broader than tall – and should be either pruned to a stout bush or supported by other plantings. In hot positions, it can be trained as a 6.6ft (2m) climber: the stems are flexible and have their fair share of prickles. Francine Austin is named after David Austin's daughter-in-law.

'FRANCESCA'

'FRANCIS DUBREUIL'

Tea Rose

ORIGIN **Dubreuil, France, 1894**
FLOWER SIZE **3.1in (8cm)**
SCENT **Strong and sweet**
FLOWERING **Repeats well**
HEIGHT/SPREAD **2.7ft (80cm)/3.3ft (1m)**
HARDINESS **Zone 7**

'Francis Dubreuil' is one of the darkest crimson roses ever raised, and certainly the most elegant. Its buds have the classic long, conical shape of the Tea roses, and the flowers are so dark as to appear almost black at first. As the bud unfurls, it becomes apparent that the flower is slightly paler crimson on its petal backs and is redder toward the center, though always dark and velvety.

'FRANCIS DUBREUIL'

'Francis Dubreuil' is not a strong grower: the flowers have thin petals and slender stems, so that the flowers nod at the end of their pedicels. They are carried singly or in small clusters of seldom more than five. The foliage is slightly wavy, thin, and susceptible to mildew. The bush is twiggy and tolerates poor soil. Although best in hot, dry weather, the flowers do sometimes burn in the heat. Francis Dubreuil was a tailor from Lyon who took to rose breeding late in life. His daughter married Antoine (Papa) Meilland and gave her name to the 20th century's most famous rose – 'Mme. A. Meilland'.

'FRANCIS E. LESTER'

Hybrid Musk

ORIGIN **Lester, US, 1946**
PARENTAGE **'Kathleen' × unknown**
FLOWER SIZE **2in (5cm)**
SCENT **Strong, fruity, and musky**
FLOWERING **Once only**
HEIGHT/SPREAD **13.1ft (4m)/8.2ft (2.5m)**
HARDINESS **Zone 6**

'Francis E. Lester' was introduced as a seedling from 'Kathleen', but it differs from other Hybrid Musks because it flowers only once. In fact, it is a very handsome and vigorous once-flowering climber. Its flowers open apple blossom pink, with a creamy center set off at first by bright yellow stamens. The flowers then fade to white. They are carried in spacious clusters of 20–30, which, because the individual flowers are comparatively large, seem enormous. It has an occasional cluster of flowers later, after the first spectacular burst, followed by large, open clusters of small hips, which normally last well into winter. The plant has bright, rich green leaves and a few large prickles. Francis E. Lester was born in England but made his name as a rose grower in Watsonville, California. His book *My Friend, the Rose* is a classic.

F

'FRANCOFURTANA'

see 'IMPÉRATRICE JOSÉPHINE'

'FRANÇOIS JURANVILLE'

Wichurana Rambler

ORIGIN **Barbier, France, 1906**
PARENTAGE ***Rosa wichurana* × 'Mme. Laurette Messimy'**
FLOWER SIZE **2.8in (7cm)**
SCENT **Strong and fruity**
FLOWERING **Once, spectacularly, then only occasionally**
HEIGHT/SPREAD **16.4ft (5m)/9.8ft (3m)**
HARDINESS **Zone 6**

'François Juranville' is one of the best-known Wichurana ramblers bred by Barbier, and is especially popular in cooler climates, where its flowers retain their rich coppery pink color longest. The flowers are loosely double, opening flat and occasionally quartered, with slightly quilled and twisted petals. The dark, glossy foliage is small, tough, and bronzy green when young, later turning dark green and glossy. The plant has long, slender, flexible stems, which are a dusky purple crimson color when young. 'François Juranville' is a rampant grower with only a few thorns, but is capable of climbing 26.2ft (8m) up a tree. In hot, dry positions, the flowers are rarely more than soft pink, with a hint of buff at the center, and are somewhat evanescent.

FRANCINE AUSTIN

'FRANCIS E. LESTER'

'FRANÇOIS JURANVILLE'

FRANÇOIS RABELAIS

FRANÇOIS RABELAIS

syn. 'MEINUSIAN', Rabelais
Floribunda

ORIGIN **Meilland, France, 1996**
PARENTAGE **(Tchin-Tchin x Matthias Meilland) x 'Lilli Marleen'**
FLOWER SIZE **3.1in (8cm)**
SCENT **Light and fruity**
FLOWERING **Repeats well**
HEIGHT/SPREAD **3.3ft (1m)/3.3ft (1m)**
HARDINESS **Zone 6**

Although capable of growing to 3.3ft (1m) in height, François Rabelais is usually pruned hard and trained as a low edging plant, little more than 11.8in (30cm) high. Its large, blood red flowers look all the more striking for growing out of such short twiggy stems. The flowers are very full and have an old-fashioned shape when they open out, with lots of little, quill-shaped petals. However, it is their massed effect that generally catches the eye. François Rabelais makes a healthy plant, especially in hot, dry climates, with medium-dark leaves and a compact, bushy habit of growth. It is useful in small gardens and especially popular for containers. It flowers almost continuously until late autumn. Satirist François Rabelais (1483–1553) was the creator of *Gargantua* and *Pantagruel*.

'FRAU ASTRID SPÄTH'

see 'JOSEPH GUY'

'FRAU DAGMAR HARTOPP'

see 'FRU DAGMAR HASTRUP'

'FRAU KARL DRUSCHKI'

syn. 'REINE DES NEIGES'
Hybrid Perpetual

ORIGIN **Lambert, Germany, 1901**
PARENTAGE **'Merveille de Lyon' x 'Mme. Caroline Testout'**
FLOWER SIZE **4.7in (12cm)**
SCENT **Little or none**
FLOWERING **Repeats well**
HEIGHT/SPREAD **5.7ft (1.75m)/4.1ft (1.25m)**
HARDINESS **Zone 5**

'FRAU KARL DRUSCHKI'

Although generally classed as a Hybrid Perpetual, 'Frau Karl Druschki' is best regarded as a Hybrid Tea, possessed of remarkable vigor and hardiness. Its flowers are large, elegantly pointed in bud, with a tinge of pink at first that fades very quickly so that, by the time the bud starts to expand into a flower, its color is pure glistening white. Eventually, the flower opens out completely and shows its stamens, but it is more attractive as an opening bud. Its petals spoil in rain, so it gives of its best in dry weather and dry climates. It was a famous exhibition rose in its day, the most popular of all for several years, but it is also an elegant cut flower for decorations and a dependable, easy to grow garden plant. The flowers are complemented by dark leaves. Sometimes there are red hips in autumn. Frau Karl Druschki was the wife of a president of the German Rose Society, a businessman from Görlitz. She died in 1921.

'FRED LOADS'

Shrub Rose

ORIGIN **Holmes, Britain, 1968**
PARENTAGE **'Dorothy Wheatcroft' x 'Orange Sensation'**
FLOWER SIZE **2.8in (7cm)**
SCENT **Light**
FLOWERING **Repeats well**
HEIGHT/SPREAD **4.9ft (1.5m)/4.1ft (1.25m)**
HARDINESS **Zone 5**

'Fred Loads' is an unusual rose for two reasons. First, it has exceptionally large clusters of flowers. Second, its vivid orange vermilion color makes it difficult to blend with other plants in the garden. The flowers turn to dusty orange and eventually to peach, but the overall impression is of bright orange. The color runs right to the center of the flower, leaving no white patch at the base of the petals, but the petals often have white streaks running out from the center a long way into the petals. The flowers are lightly cupped and the stamens have notably long filaments. The flowers usually come in clusters of 10–30 – more, if the bush is pruned hard. In hot climates, 'Fred Loads' will grow to 9.8ft (3m) or more, and makes a fine, bushy pillar rose. It is always taller than it is wide, and tends to flower at the ends of its long stems, but also arches over and then breaks into flower all along the stems. In a border, it needs something in front to hide its bare base. The foliage is mid-green, glossy, and healthy. 'Fred Loads' performs equally well in hot, cold, wet, and dry climates. It has also sported to produce a striped form called 'Festival Fanfare', whose hard orange is almost completely changed to a soft peaches and cream coloring – worth looking out for. Fred Loads was a gardener in England who starred in a radio program called *Gardeners' Question Time*.

'FRED LOADS'

FREDENSBORG

syn. 'POULMAX', Canyonlands, Fascination
Shrub Rose

ORIGIN **Poulsen, Denmark, 1995**
FLOWER SIZE **2.4in (6cm)**
SCENT **Light**
FLOWERING **Almost continuous**
HEIGHT/SPREAD **2.5ft (75cm)/4.9ft (1.5m)**
HARDINESS **Zone 5**
AWARDS **ROTY 1999**

Fredensborg is a very floriferous small shrub rose with beautiful dark, glossy, healthy leaves. The flowers are coral pink at first, with darker petal backs, but they fade unattractively to shell pink. Nevertheless, they flower almost continuously right through until early winter. They are not too full, and open out almost flat, but tend to acquire red blotches in the rain. The flowers come in clusters of 7–20. The bush is healthy, with handsome, bronzy new leaves. The rose is named after the royal castle of Fredensborg in Denmark.

FREDENSBORG

FRÉDÉRIC MISTRAL

FRÉDÉRIC MISTRAL

syn. 'MEITEBROS', The Children's Rose
Hybrid Tea

ORIGIN **Meilland, France, 1993**
PARENTAGE **('Perfume Delight' x 'Prima Ballerina') x The McCartney Rose**
FLOWER SIZE **3.5in (9cm)**
SCENT **Strong and rich**
FLOWERING **Repeats well**
HEIGHT/SPREAD **3.3ft (1m)/2.7ft (80cm)**
HARDINESS **Zone 6**
AWARDS **Baden-Baden FA 1993; Le Rœulx FA 1994; Monza FA 1994; Belfast FA 1996**

Frédéric Mistral looks at first like an elegant Hybrid Tea, until it opens out to reveal a mass of inner petals in the old-fashioned style. This combination is reminiscent of some of David Austin's English Roses: Frédéric Mistral belongs to Meilland's Romantica series, which aims to combine the best of the old roses with the health and vigor of the new. The flowers are rose pink, with slightly darker petal backs. The outer petals act as guards, while the inner ones are very variable in the pattern they make. The flowers are usually borne singly, but sometimes in clusters of 3–5. They are very free with their scent, an old damask fragrance, which fills the air. The plant is vigorous and upright, with rich green, healthy, semiglossy foliage and a habit of sending up more flowers in quick succession. It will grow to as much as 6.6ft (2m) high in a hot climate, and its flowers keep best in dry weather. It is named in honor of Frédéric Mistral (1830–1914), the Provençal poet.

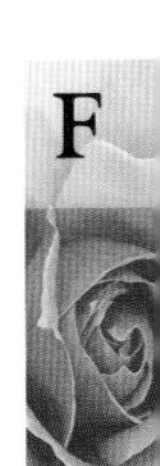

FREEDOM

FREEDOM

syn. 'DICJEM'

Hybrid Tea

ORIGIN **Dickson, Northern Ireland, 1984**
PARENTAGE **('Eurorose' × 'Taifun') × Bright Smile**
FLOWER SIZE **3.5in (9cm)**
SCENT **Light and sweet**
FLOWERING **Repeats well**
HEIGHT/SPREAD **2.7ft (80cm)/2ft (60cm)**
HARDINESS **Zone 6**
AWARDS **RHRS GM 1983; The Hague GM 1992; James Mason GM 1997**

Freedom is a handsome, classic, large-flowered Hybrid Tea – of a good, rich yellow color that fades only very slightly. It has almost a golden glow between its petals. The flowers are not too full, which may explain its popularity in damp climates such as in England, but it reveals a very pretty flower as it unfurls. The flowers are usually borne singly on long, thick, erect stems. The bush has large, healthy, dark leaves and makes strong, upright growth.

FREISINGER MORGENROTE

syn. 'KORMARTER', Sunrise

Shrub Rose

ORIGIN **Kordes, Germany, 1988**
PARENTAGE **seedling × 'Lichtkönigin Lucia'**
FLOWER SIZE **3.1in (8cm)**
SCENT **Medium to strong**
FLOWERING **Repeats well**
HEIGHT/SPREAD **6.6ft (2m)/4.9ft (1.5m)**
HARDINESS **Zone 5**

Freisinger Morgenrote is a beautiful shrub rose, or short climber, with a remarkable mixture of colors within its flowers: the outer petals are a bright cherry color, while the inner ones are apricot – it is difficult to think of a greater contrast. Later, the flowers lose their yellow tints and the apricot coloring changes to pink. The flowers come in clusters of 3–7 and are shaped like those of a pretty Floribunda. The plant has small, dark leaves, which are glossy and bronzy when young: they contrast beautifully with the opening flowers. It grows vigorously, reaching 6.6ft (2m) high and wide as a shrub, and 9.8ft (3m) if trained as a climber. There are always a few flowers on the bush after the first spectacular flowering. The name commemorates the Bavarian town of Freising, which is recognized as a "*Rosenstadt*" (see p.343) by the German Rose Society.

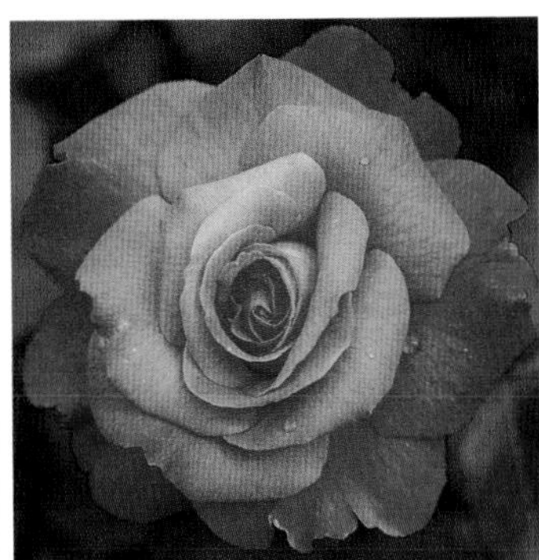

FREISINGER MORGENROTE

FRENCH LACE

syn. 'JACLACE'

Floribunda

ORIGIN **Warriner, US, 1980**
PARENTAGE **'Dr. A. J. Verhage' × 'Bridal Pink'**
FLOWER SIZE **4.3in (11cm)**
SCENT **Light and fruity**
FLOWERING **Repeats well**
HEIGHT/SPREAD **3.3ft (1m)/2.7ft (80cm)**
HARDINESS **Zone 5**
AWARDS **AARS 1982; Portland GM 1984**

This is a rose of great beauty. Its buds are long, slender, and elegant – creamy white with a hint of apricot at the center. When they open out, the petals have a uniquely graceful ruffled carriage and are surprisingly thick for such an ethereally lovely rose. They come singly or in long-stemmed clusters of up to seven flowers – excellent for picking. French Lace also makes a good border plant. The leaves are small, dark, glossy, and healthy. Although very hardy, it is at its best in warm climates, and forms the centerpiece of the rose gardens at the Huntington Botanical Gardens in Pasadena, California.

FRENCH LACE

'FRENSHAM'

'FRENSHAM'

Floribunda

ORIGIN **Norman, Britain, 1946**
PARENTAGE **('Miss Edith Cavell' × 'Edgar Andreu') × 'Crimson Glory'**
FLOWER SIZE **3.1in (8cm)**
SCENT **Light and musky**
FLOWERING **Repeats very well**
HEIGHT/SPREAD **4.1ft (1.25m)/2.7ft (80cm)**
HARDINESS **Zone 5**
AWARDS **NRS GM 1943; ARS GM 1955**

Bred by an English amateur, 'Frensham' was so successful when first introduced by Harkness that it wiped out the sales of all competitors. Its great qualities in 1946 were its vigor, its rich red coloring, and its beautiful shape. After about ten years, however, it suddenly succumbed to mildew, probably caused by a mutant form of the fungus. 'Frensham' is still widely grown, but does benefit from good cultivation and efforts to prevent infection. The flowers are a brilliant dark red and semidouble. There is little or no trace of any paler shade at the center; this gives the flowers an extraordinary richness. They are borne in clusters of 5–15 and stand up well to rain. The plant is vigorous and well branched, with mid-green, glossy leaves. It repeats regularly until late autumn.

FRIEND FOR LIFE

syn. 'COCNANNE'

Floribunda

ORIGIN **Cocker, Britain, 1993**
PARENTAGE **seedling × ('Anne Cocker' × 'Silver Jubilee')**
FLOWER SIZE **2.4in (6cm)**
SCENT **Light**
FLOWERING **Repeats well**
HEIGHT/SPREAD **2.7ft (80cm)/2ft (60cm)**
HARDINESS **Zone 6**
AWARDS **Glasgow GM 1997**

The flowers of Friend for Life are salmon pink at first, with darker petal backs and edges, and a paler patch toward the center. As they age, the petals lose their yellow tint and pass to pure pink. Sometimes one or two long white stripes run up into the flower from the center. The stamens are beautiful: long, but all of different lengths, with red filaments and golden yellow anthers. It is the stamens, and the curled-back petal tips (like a clematis) that give the semidouble flowers their character. The flowers come in clusters of 5–12 and cover the short, compact bush when in full bloom. Friend for Life has dark, glossy leaves and quite a lot of prickles. Its neat stature makes it a useful container plant, but for sheer floriferousness it can hold its own in any position.

FRIEND FOR LIFE

FRIESIA

FRIESIA

syn. 'KORRESIA', Sun Sprite

Floribunda

ORIGIN **Kordes, Germany, 1977**
PARENTAGE **'Friedrich Wörlein' x 'Spanish Sun'**
FLOWER SIZE **3.1in (8cm)**
SCENT **Strong and sweet**
FLOWERING **Starts early and repeats well**
HEIGHT/SPREAD **2.7ft (80cm)/2.7ft (80cm)**
HARDINESS **Zone 5**
AWARDS **Baden-Baden 1972; ADR 1973; Gamble FA 1979; James Mason GM 1988**

Friesia was the best yellow Floribunda to come out of the 1970s and has remained deservedly popular. The flowers are a good mid-yellow, with darker yellow on the backs of the petals. They fade only slightly and are shapely at all stages. When they open out and display their stamens, the red anthers add considerably to their beauty. They are borne singly or in clusters of 3–7 and keep their strong scent throughout their long flowering. The plant is compact and healthy, with dark green, glossy foliage. Growth is vigorous and bushy, and the plant is almost always in flower. It is equally at home in hot weather or cool, and tolerates rain well. It thrives even in poor soils, and is still the best yellow rose for bedding.

'FRITZ NOBIS'

Shrub Rose

ORIGIN **Kordes, Germany, 1940**
PARENTAGE **'Joanna Hill' x 'Magnifica'**
FLOWER SIZE **3.5in (9cm)**
SCENT **Strong and spicy**
FLOWERING **Once only**
HEIGHT/SPREAD **6.6ft (2m)/5.7ft (1.75m)**
HARDINESS **Zone 5**

This once-flowering shrub rose is a magnificent sight when its long branches arch over under the weight of its flowers. It blooms luxuriantly. The flowers are rose pink, with coppery backs to the petals, and a pale yellow flush at the center – an extremely attractive combination of colors which is enhanced by the wavy petals and the old-fashioned muddled arrangement as the flowers open out. They come in long-stemmed clusters of 3–9, and are excellent for cutting. They are followed by large orange hips, which last well into winter. The leaves are small, thin, and susceptible to blackspot, but its abundance and hardiness guarantee 'Fritz Nobis' a place in any cold climate

'FRITZ NOBIS'

garden with the space to accommodate it. It is less of an attraction for gardeners in warm climates, who have so many repeat flowering shrub roses to choose from. Fritz Nobis was a friend and colleague of the breeder Wilhelm Kordes.

FROHSINN 82

syn. 'TANSINNROH', Joyfulness, Peccato di Gioia

Hybrid Tea

ORIGIN **Tantau, Germany, 1982**
FLOWER SIZE **5.5in (14cm)**
SCENT **Light or medium, and sweet**
FLOWERING **Repeats**
HEIGHT/SPREAD **4.9ft (1.5m)/3.3ft (1m)**
HARDINESS **Zone 6**

The color of Frohsinn 82 is variable. The overall impression is of pale coral flowers with slightly paler shades on the petal backs, but it also has a tendency for the edges to darken considerably. This darkening is triggered by heat, which turns the flowers apricot colored, with crimson edges. In cool weather, they remain creamy white, with pink edges and a hint of yellow at the center. This variability is attractive and delightful, but Frohsinn 82 also has some very fine qualities, notably the large size of its flowers and the long time they remain in good condition. They are excellent for cutting, being borne, usually singly, on long, straight stems. The plant is very hardy, healthy, and strong-growing, with a lot of branches and dark, shiny leaves.

FROHSINN 82

'FRONTENAC'

Shrub Rose

ORIGIN **Ogilvie, Canada, 1992**
PARENTAGE **('Queen Elizabeth' x ['Arthur Bell' x 'Von Scharnhorst']) x ('Kordesii' x ['Red Dawn' x 'Suzanne'])**
FLOWER SIZE **3.1in (8cm)**
SCENT **Light**
FLOWERING **Repeats**
HEIGHT/SPREAD **4.1ft (1.25m)/3.3ft (1m)**
HARDINESS **Zone 4**

The flowers of 'Frontenac' are brilliant light crimson or deep pink. When they open out fully they have an irregular patch of white at the center, with streaks of white running out into the petals and a small circle of dark stamens. They are lightly double but cup-shaped, and very pretty when you look at them individually. However, they are most valued for their massed effect when a bush is covered in flowers during its first flowering. They come in small clusters (typically of 3–5 flowers) and continue intermittently until the first frost. The plant has dark, healthy, glossy leaves and a dense, shrubby habit of growth. 'Frontenac' is named after the Comte de Frontenac (1620–98), an equally colorful governor general of New France.

'FRU DAGMAR HASTRUP'

'FRU DAGMAR HASTRUP'

syn. 'FRAU DAGMAR HARTOPP'

Rugosa Hybrid

ORIGIN **Denmark, 1914**
FLOWER SIZE **3.1in (8cm)**
SCENT **Strong and sweet**
FLOWERING **Repeats well**
HEIGHT/SPREAD **3.3ft (1m)/3.3ft (1m)**
HARDINESS **Zone 4**

'Fru Dagmar Hastrup' is not the most exciting Rugosa rose, but it has some excellent qualities: it is compact, healthy, and sweetly scented. The flowers are a pretty shade of silvery pink, and single. They have a fringe of pale stamens at the center and are quickly followed by large, tomatolike hips, which usually stay on the bush long after the leaves have turned bright yellow and fallen. As the plant is a consistent bloomer, throwing out flowers until well into autumn, the later flowers are often seen against a background of mature hips. The plant has bright green, crinkled leaves and a low-growing, slightly spreading habit of growth. 'Fru Dagmar Hastrup' is sometimes used as an informal hedge, which, although not tall, has ferocious prickles on all its stems. If planted on its own roots (it roots easily from cuttings), it suckers and presents a yet more formidable barrier.

'FRONTENAC'

'FRÜHLINGSDUFT'

'FRÜHLINGSMORGEN'

'FRÜHLINGSDUFT'

Spinosissima Hybrid

ORIGIN **Kordes, Germany, 1949**
PARENTAGE **'Joanna Hill' x 'Altaica'**
FLOWER SIZE **3in (8cm)**
SCENT **Strong, sweet, and fruity**
FLOWERING **Early, and intermittently thereafter**
HEIGHT/SPREAD **9.8ft (3m)/8.2ft (2.5m)**
HARDINESS **Zone 5**

Of all the Frühling roses bred by Wilhelm Kordes in the 1930s and 1940s, none has such a beautiful color or so rich a scent as 'Frühlingsduft'. The flowers vary according to the weather, but are basically pale buff yellow, overlaid with pink. The pink tends to cover the upper sides of the petals, and the buff (fading to cream) remains on the undersides, which gives rise to very beautiful shades and shadows between the petals. The flowers come on short stems, singly or in clusters of up to five, and continue to flower intermittently all through the summer and autumn, as well as being one of the first of all roses to start into flower. The leaves have small, dull, thin leaflets and a slight weakness for blackspot. The bush makes long, arching stems, which are covered in red prickles when young, although these fall off as the wood matures. It is very hardy and, as a result, popular in Scandinavia.

'FRÜHLINGSGOLD'

Spinosissima Hybrid

ORIGIN **Kordes, Germany, 1937**
PARENTAGE **'Altaica' x 'Joanna Hill'**
FLOWER SIZE **4.3in (11cm)**
SCENT **Light and fruity**
FLOWERING **Once early, then intermittently**
HEIGHT/SPREAD **8.2ft (2.5m)/9.8ft (3m)**
HARDINESS **Zone 5**

The Frühling roses are fine, early flowering, arching shrubs. In Germany, they finish flowering long before most roses open their first blooms in summer: the Frühling roses are for spring. The buds have streaks of orange on them, but the flowers are great saucers of gleaming primrose yellow, paling to cream at the edges as they open and expand, but always deeper toward the center, where large, dark stamens intensify the yellow. The flowers are carried, usually singly but sometimes in short clusters, all along the long, arching stems of last year's growth, and so abundantly that the plant seems bowed over by them. This is a hardy and thrifty rose that does best in cool climates, for its yellow flowers fade quickly in hot areas where many roses flower earlier than the 'Frühling' tribe. The plant has small, thin, pale green leaves, somewhat susceptible to blackspot, and a fair sprinkling of prickles. Sometimes black, round hips appear later in the season.

'FRÜHLINGSMORGEN'

Spinosissima Hybrid

ORIGIN **Kordes, Germany, 1942**
PARENTAGE **('E.G. Hill' x 'Cathrine Kordes') x 'Altaica'**
FLOWER SIZE **4.3in (11cm)**
SCENT **Strong and sweet**
FLOWERING **Once early, then intermittently**
HEIGHT/SPREAD **6.6ft (2m)/8.2ft (2.5m)**
HARDINESS **Zone 5**

The great beauty of 'Frühlingsmorgen' lies in the way the large single flowers perch on top of the long, arching branches. They are deep pink at first, with creamy centers and rich crimson stamens, fading over the next few days to pale pink and white. The long dark stamens give great character to the open flower. The plant has small, thin leaves, which are susceptible to blackspot, and a few prickles on its stems. It never looks quite as vigorous or healthy as 'Frühlingsgold', though many would argue that 'Frühlingsmorgen' is yet more beautiful in flower. In Germany, where it was bred, its first flowering takes place in late spring and is followed by a few flowers on and off until well into autumn.

FUCHSIA MEIDILAND

syn. 'MEIPELTA'

Ground Cover

ORIGIN **Meilland, France, 1991**
PARENTAGE ***Rosa wichurana* seedling x 'Clair Matin'**
FLOWER SIZE **2in (5cm)**
SCENT **Light and musky**
FLOWERING **Repeats constantly**
HEIGHT/SPREAD **2.5ft (75cm)/4.1ft (1.25m)**
HARDINESS **Zone 5**

Meilland has given us many fine groundcover roses, which are just as valuable in the smallest garden as in the largest landscaping plans. Fuchsia Meidiland has vast quantities of pale crimson flowers all over the surface of a dense, mounded bush. They are semi-double, with a white circle at the center and paler petal backs. They are produced in small clusters (typically of 5–7 flowers) very profusely during their first flush and thereafter more intermittently until late autumn. Fuchsia Meidiland is

FUCHSIA MEIDILAND

hardy, healthy, and semievergreen. Its leaves are small, neat, medium-dark green, and shiny. It makes a lax shrub, wider than high.

'FULGENS'

see 'MALTON'

FULTON MACKAY

syn. 'COCDANA', Maribel, Senteur des Iles

Hybrid Tea

ORIGIN **Cocker, Britain, 1988**
PARENTAGE **'Silver Jubilee' x 'Jana'**
FLOWER SIZE **4.7in (12cm)**
SCENT **Medium and fruity**
FLOWERING **Repeats well**
HEIGHT/SPREAD **3.3ft (1m)/2.7ft (80cm)**
HARDINESS **Zone 6**
AWARDS **Glasgow GM 1992**

Fulton MacKay is a fine Hybrid Tea, whose long, elegant buds open into large and beautiful flowers. It makes an outstanding exhibition rose and cut flower. The opening flowers are a deep apricot orange, with crimson edges to the petals. Later they fade to buff and pink, starting with the outer petals, which are almost coral at first. The colors and the contrasts within the flowers are always very attractive, but the size of the petals and the way they reflex as they unfurl are also very distinctive and help to give this rose its particular charm. The leaves are dark and glossy, though somewhat susceptible to blackspot. The plant is sturdy and bushy, grows quickly, and stays in flower right through until early winter. The rose is named after the Scottish actor Fulton MacKay (1922–87).

'FRÜHLINGSGOLD'

FULTON MACKAY

'Gabrielle Noyelle'

Moss Rose

ORIGIN **Buatois, France, 1933**
PARENTAGE **'Salet' x 'Souvenir de Mme. Krenger'**
FLOWER SIZE **3.9in (10cm)**
SCENT **Medium and sweet**
FLOWERING **Remontant**
HEIGHT/SPREAD **5.7ft (1.75m)/5.7ft (1.75m)**
HARDINESS **Zone 5**

This cross between a pink Moss rose and a salmon pink Hybrid Tea has produced a very beautiful hybrid. 'Gabrielle Noyelle' has the conspicuous moss of 'Salet' but the long petals and elegant flowers of the Hybrid Teas. The flowers are pale salmon pink, fading to cream and white, with slightly pinker, darker petal backs, but they also have a large patch of deep golden stamens at the center, which suffuses a yellow flush and reflects it off the petals. The effect is delicate and charming, as is the somewhat loose way the flowers hold their petals. They come in clusters, typically of 3–8, but sometimes singly (and occasionally more). The plant has dark, glossy leaves and narrow leaflets, and grows vigorously. It is essentially a fair-weather rose that grows best in heat. The petals spoil in rain and the mossy parts quickly acquire a coating of white mildew in cool conditions. That said, it is a shrub of outstanding beauty, which can be trained as a short climber or allowed to develop a twiggy, bushy shape.

GALAXY

Galaxy

syn. 'MEIHUTERB'

Floribunda

ORIGIN **Meilland, France, 1995**
FLOWER SIZE **3.1in (8cm)**
SCENT **Moderate**
FLOWERING **Repeats well**
HEIGHT/SPREAD **3.3ft (1m)/2.5ft (75cm)**
HARDINESS **Zone 6**

Galaxy is a very floriferous and attractive creamy pink Floribunda. The buds are buff yellow with red tips, but open into pretty, round, creamy yellow flowers, which fade to white at the edges while retaining a tint of yellow or buff at the center. The colors are constantly changing – paler in summer and pinker in autumn – but always have soft hues. The flowers come in fairly tight clusters of 3–9, sometimes more. The plant has small, mid-green, healthy leaves and an upright habit of growth. In hot climates it will reach 4.9ft (1.5m).

'GABRIELLE NOYELLE'

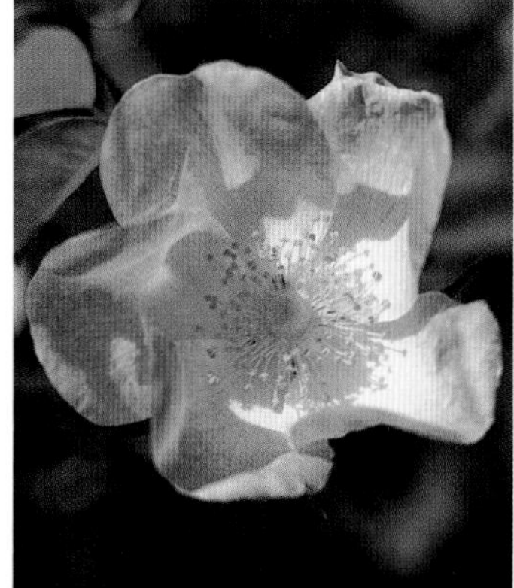

ROSA GALLICA VAR. *PUMILA*

Rosa gallica

Wild Rose

FLOWER SIZE **2.4in (6cm)**
SCENT **Medium and sweet**
FLOWERING **Once only**
HEIGHT/SPREAD **3.3ft (1m)/3.3ft (1m)**
HARDINESS **Zone 5**

Rosa gallica is one of the most important wild species of roses: its genes are present in almost all our modern roses. It grows naturally from France through central Europe, Ukraine, Turkey, and Iraq, and its horticultural forms have long had an economic importance. The European form, *Rosa gallica* var. *pumila*, is shown above, photographed on a plant from Tuscany. The flowers are single, lightly cupped, and bright pink at first, fading to pale pink, with a white eye and golden stamens. They are borne, usually singly but sometimes in clusters of up to five, and beautifully held on short, stout stems – exquisite when illuminated by sun. They are followed by round, dull vermilion hips. The sepals and receptacles exude a sticky resin scent. The leaves are fairly small, mid-green, and rough to the touch. *Rosa gallica* is a short, thicketing plant in the wild, often no more than 1.6ft (50cm) high. It is taller and lusher in cultivation, but retains a wiry, upright habit of growth.

'Galway Bay'

Modern Climber

ORIGIN **McGredy, Northern Ireland, 1966**
PARENTAGE **'Gruss an Heidelberg' x 'Queen Elizabeth'**
FLOWER SIZE **3.5in (9cm)**
SCENT **Medium and fruity**
FLOWERING **Repeats well**
HEIGHT/SPREAD **9.8ft (3m)/8.2ft (2.5m)**
HARDINESS **Zone 6**

The buds of 'Galway Bay' are apricot colored, but the flowers lose their yellow tinges when they open and exhibit instead a combination of pinks – dark pink on the outsides of the petals and toward their edges but much paler toward the center. The flowers open, sometimes from split buds, into cupped or cabbagelike shapes. They are medium-large (3.9in/10cm) and borne, sometimes singly but more usually in small clusters, on a vigorous plant. The plant is healthy, with rich, red, new growths and dark green, glossy foliage. It is an excellent repeater, almost constantly in bloom.

'GALWAY BAY'

Garden News

see FLORA DANICA

'Garden Party'

Hybrid Tea

ORIGIN **Swim, US, 1959**
PARENTAGE **'Charlotte Armstrong' x 'Mme. A. Meilland'**
FLOWER SIZE **4.3in (11cm)**
SCENT **Light and lemony**
FLOWERING **Repeats well**
HEIGHT/SPREAD **3.9ft (1.2m)/2.5ft (75cm)**
HARDINESS **Zone 5**
AWARDS **Bagatelle GM 1959; AARS 1960**

'Garden Party' is a large-flowered Hybrid Tea for hot climates. The flowers are cool, creamy white, with buff and lemon hints at the center and pink edges to the outer petals – a very pretty combination. They are borne singly but most abundantly throughout the season. The plant has red new growths and neat, dark leaves with a glaucous bloom. It is a popular exhibition rose for its good shape and large flowers, but its preference for heat and its vigorous growth also make it a good garden rose in hot climates. The plant is upright, slender, and occasionally subject to mildew. 'Garden Party' will grow to as much as 6.6ft (2m) if it is left unpruned.

'GARDEN PARTY'

'GARDENIA'

'GARDENIA'

Wichurana Rambler

ORIGIN **Manda, US, 1899**
PARENTAGE ***Rosa wichurana* x 'Perle des Jardins'**
FLOWER SIZE **2.2in (5.5cm)**
SCENT **Light and musky**
FLOWERING **Once, early in season**
HEIGHT/SPREAD **16.4ft (5m)/9.8ft (3m)**
HARDINESS **Zone 6**

'Gardenia' was the first large-flowered Wichurana rambler to be introduced, and it is still widely grown, despite competition from the fairly similar 'Albéric Barbier'. It was hailed as a yellow rambler ("a hardy 'Maréchal Niel'"), although the flowers are rich buff yellow at first, and fade quickly to cream and white, so that the overall impression of the plant in flower is of whiteness. The flowers are usually lightly cupped, quartered (with a passing resemblance to a gardenia), and borne in clusters of 3–9 on short, sturdy stems. There are usually a few flowers on an established plant after the big main flowering. The leaves are small, dark, and glossy, with red new growths and the long, flexible stems of the best Wichuranas.

'GARTENDIREKTOR OTTO LINNE'

Polyantha

ORIGIN **Lambert, Germany, 1934**
PARENTAGE **'Robin Hood' x 'Rudolph Kluis'**
FLOWER SIZE **1.2in (3cm)**
SCENT **Light**
FLOWERING **Repeats quickly**
HEIGHT/SPREAD **8.2ft (2.5m)/4.9ft (1.5m)**
HARDINESS **Zone 5**

'GARTENDIREKTOR OTTO LINNE'

GAVNO

'Gartendirektor Otto Linne' is a very reliable, floriferous, and easy to grow shrub rose, slightly short on character. The flowers open deep pink, with a little white patch at the center, and fade to palest pink. They have ruffled petals and come in slightly pendulous, long-stemmed, conical clusters of 20–50 flowers. The yellow stamens fade quickly to brown. The plant has handsome, healthy, large leaves, with long leaflets. Its stems are almost thornless. It mounds up into a thick bushy mass, but can also be trained as a short climber in hot climates. Otto Linne was the first director of gardens and cemeteries in Hamburg.

GAVNO

syn. 'POULGAV', Bucks Fizz

Floribunda

ORIGIN **Olesen, Denmark, 1988**
PARENTAGE **seedling x Mary Sumner**
FLOWER SIZE **3.9in (10cm)**
SCENT **Medium and fruity**
FLOWERING **Repeats well**
HEIGHT/SPREAD **4.9ft (1.5m)/4.1ft (1.25m)**
HARDINESS **Zone 5**

The flowers of Gavno are shapely and richly colored. They open pale orange, with a yellow base to the petals, and paler backs. As they age and mature, they lose all trace of yellow but take on somewhat more red, so that they end up a deep salmon pink. The stamens at the center are green yellow. The flowers have the beautiful shape of a Hybrid Tea at first, but continue to hold their petals attractively as they open out lightly cupped, and take on a slight wave. The flowers come singly or in well-spaced clusters of up to seven. The plant has mid-green leaves, crimson new growths, and prickly stems. Blackspot and mildew may make their appearance in autumn, but do no lasting damage. The plant grows vigorously and repeats well: a good rose.

GEMINI

syn. 'JACNEPAL'

Hybrid Tea

ORIGIN **Zary, US, 1999**
PARENTAGE **Anne Morrow Lindbergh x New Year**
FLOWER SIZE **4.3in (11cm)**
SCENT **Strong and sweet**
FLOWERING **Repeats well**
HEIGHT/SPREAD **5.7ft (1.7m)/4.1ft (1.25m)**
HARDINESS **Zone 5**
AWARDS **AARS 2000**

Gemini is a new Hybrid Tea with a very striking coloring, which is proving popular as a rose for cutting and exhibition. The flowers are elegant at all stages of their development. The very long, pointed buds have large outer petals, which reflex at their tips as they slowly start to unfurl. The flowers are creamy white at the center, with a hint of yellow on the petal backs, and a broad, dusty, pink band of coloring on the edges of the swirling petals. It is a very pretty combination. The flowers are abundantly carried on long stems, usually singly but sometimes in clusters of up to five. The bushes are sturdy, tall, and upright, with a few prickles and lots of very handsome, healthy, dark, glossy leaves.

GEMINI

'GENE BOERNER'

Floribunda

ORIGIN **Boerner, US, 1968**
PARENTAGE **'Ginger' x ('Ma Perkins' x 'Garnette Supreme')**
FLOWER SIZE **3.1in (8cm)**
SCENT **Light**
FLOWERING **Repeats well**
HEIGHT/SPREAD **4.9ft (1.5m)/2.5ft (75cm)**
HARDINESS **Zone 5**
AWARDS **AARS 1969**

'Gene Boerner' is the perfect pink Floribunda rose with every flower shaped like a perfect Hybrid Tea. They open out from crimson buds and have a uniform mid-pink color with deeper strawberry pink tones at the base of the petals. The flowers open very prettily and the petals eventually reflex to reveal attractive stamens. The plant is very tolerant of heat, but starts to pale at the edges. The color is best in cool weather, though the flower holds its form in any conditions. The flowers come singly and in clusters of up to five. The foliage is mid-green, glossy, and very healthy, except for an occasional brush with blackspot. The plant makes vigorous, slender, upright growth, and grows as high as 8.2ft (2.5m) if unchecked. It is best pruned lightly, and will repeat so quickly that flowering is effectively continuous. Gene Boerner (1893–1966) was director of research at Jackson & Perkins: the rose was issued posthumously and released as a tribute to his developmental work on Floribunda roses. When he died, Boerner left his estate to Cornell University to fund graduate research into roses.

'GENE BOERNER'

'GÉNÉRAL GALLIÉNI'

'GÉNÉRAL JACQUEMINOT'

'GÉNÉRAL GALLIÉNI'

Tea Rose

ORIGIN **Nabonnand, France, 1899**
PARENTAGE **'Souvenir de Thérèse Levet' x 'Reine Emma des Pays-Bas'**
FLOWER SIZE **2.8in (7cm)**
SCENT **Light and tealike**
FLOWERING **Early and almost continuous**
HEIGHT/SPREAD **3.3ft (1m)/2.7ft (80cm)**
HARDINESS **Zone 7**

Love him or hate him – there is no middle ground with 'Général Galliéni'. The flowers are muddled to the extent of being confused and misshapen, seldom showing a handsome bud or opening to a regular shape. They are pale apricot cream at first, but the petals darken with age. In cool weather, it is only the outer guard petals that take on a crimson tint, while the inner petals remain pink, buff, and cream. In hot weather, the whole flower changes color and the outer petals assume a strange brown tint. Whatever their color, the petals often have large, unsightly white streaks. The plant has few thorns and neat, glaucous leaves. It starts into flower very early, and in hot climates will flower without cease. Joseph Galliéni (1849–1916) was Governor of Madagascar when the rose was introduced, and organized the defense of Paris at the start of World War I.

'GÉNÉRAL JACQUEMINOT'

Hybrid Perpetual

ORIGIN **Roussel, France, 1846**
PARENTAGE **'Gloire des Rosomanes' x unknown**
FLOWER SIZE **3.5in (9cm)**
SCENT **Strong and sweet**
FLOWERING **Repeats well**
HEIGHT/SPREAD **4.9ft (1.5m)/4.1ft (1.25m)**
HARDINESS **Zone 5**

For 50 years, 'Général Jacqueminot' was the most widely grown and popular crimson rose in the world. It was popular both as a garden plant for its free-flowering habit and as a rose for cutting and exhibition. It was also widely used for floristry and for hybridizing, so that 'Général Jacqueminot' appears as an ancestor of almost every crimson rose today. The flowers are prettiest in bud, when they are bright crimson red. Later they open out into globular flowers, when the color takes on a duller purple hue. The petal backs have a paler sheen, and some of the petals have white streaks. The flowers are not too full – somewhat lightly double, in fact – and tend to nod their heads. They come singly or in twos and threes. The plant has a lot of prickles and bright green leaves. Blackspot and mildew may sometimes appear, but this is a rose that responds particularly well to good cultivation – and is healthier when well grown. Its second flowering is improved by deadheading the first. Général J.-F. Jacqueminot (1787–1865) was a French army officer under King Louis-Philippe, who took up several commercial directorships on retirement.

'GÉNÉRAL KLÉBER'

Moss Rose

ORIGIN **Robert, France, 1856**
FLOWER SIZE **3.9in (10cm)**
SCENT **Strong and sweet**
FLOWERING **Once only**
HEIGHT/SPREAD **5.7ft (1.7m)/4.1ft (1.25m)**
HARDINESS **Zone 5**

'Général Kléber' is one of the most satisfactory of all old roses. It is vigorous and healthy and, if grown on its own roots, suckers around enough to provide you with an extra plant or two to give away every year. The flowers are a pure rose pink, with just a hint of salmon at first. They are fully double, with a lot of small petals, which form a shallow, quartered rosette and sometimes a button eye at the center. The undersides of the petals are a more silvery pink, which gives a pretty contrast to the folds and tucks within the flower. The flowers are very sweetly scented and borne singly or in small clusters, rarely more than three together. The buds, sepals, and flower stalks are covered in bright green moss, which reemerges as small, bristly prickles further down the plant – but feebly, because 'Général Kléber' is mostly smooth-stemmed. The leaves are beautiful, lush, and pale. Général Joseph Kléber (1752–1800) was one of Napoléon I's generals in Egypt; he was murdered shortly after the French victory.

'GÉNÉRAL KLÉBER'

'GÉNÉRAL SCHABLIKINE'

'GÉNÉRAL SCHABLIKINE'

Tea Rose

ORIGIN **Nabonnand, France, 1878**
FLOWER SIZE **3.1in (8cm)**
SCENT **Medium and tea-scented**
FLOWERING **Almost continuous**
HEIGHT/SPREAD **5.7ft (1.75m)/4.1ft (1.25m)**
HARDINESS **Zone 7**

'Général Schablikine' is the best of all Tea roses, being the hardiest and the most floriferous. Its flowers are an extraordinary mixture of cherry and copper in color, but pretty at all stages. They start as long, elegant, slightly pendulous buds and end up as fully open and quartered flowers with rolled-back petals. They are borne singly or in clusters of up to five, both generously and ceaselessly. The compact, healthy, vigorous plant has crimson stems, a lot of dark leaves, coppery young growths, a slightly angular habit of branching, and a few large thorns. It requires minimum pruning and comes easily from cuttings. 'Général Schablikine' was once widely planted in Italy for the cut-flower market and is still extremely popular as a garden rose in its native south of France.

ROSA GENTILIANA

see 'POLYANTHA GRANDIFLORA'

GENTLE TOUCH

syn. 'DICLULU'

Miniature Rose

ORIGIN **Dickson, Northern Ireland, 1986**
PARENTAGE **('Liverpool Echo' x 'Woman's Own') x Memento**
FLOWER SIZE **2.8in (7cm)**
SCENT **Light and musky**
FLOWERING **Repeats well**
HEIGHT/SPREAD **1.6ft (50cm)/1.3ft (40cm)**
HARDINESS **Zone 6**

Rose categories merge into each other: Gentle Touch has been described as both a miniature and a Floribunda; it also fits with the intermediates known as patio roses. The flowers are beautiful and dainty – pale pink with a hint of salmon on the upper side of the petals and paler toward the center. The backs are pearly white. The flowers start as elegant little buds, each a perfect buttonhole. Then they open out very quickly and nearly flat, apart from a distinctive wave to the edges. The flowers come in clusters, typically of 3–10. Gentle Touch has neat, small, mid-green, semiglossy leaves and a bushy habit of growth. It is a strong and sturdy grower, and repeats well. It is an excellent plant for containers or the front of a border.

GENTLE TOUCH

GEOFF HAMILTON

GEOFF HAMILTON

syn. 'AUSHAM'

Shrub Rose

ORIGIN **Austin, Britain, 1997**
PARENTAGE **Heritage seedling**
FLOWER SIZE **2.8in (7cm)**
SCENT **Strong and sweet**
FLOWERING **Repeats well**
HEIGHT/SPREAD **4.9ft (1.5m)/4.1ft (1.25m)**
HARDINESS **Zone 6**

This is one of the best modern David Austin roses, named in memory of an English gardening television host. The flowers are exceptionally neat and beautiful in their shape, each forming a perfect rosette, with masses of tiny, ranked petals cupped within larger guard petals. They are a delicate, uniform, pale pink until eventually the outer petals start to fade, to palest pink in mild climates but almost to white in hot ones. The scent is delicious. The flowers come singly or (more usually) in small clusters on fairly long stems, which are good for cutting. Geoff Hamilton repeats regularly right through until late autumn, and, if well grown, is never without flowers. The plant has a strong, dense habit of growth and somewhat ordinary, healthy, mid-green leaves.

'GEORG ARENDS'

Hybrid Tea

ORIGIN **Hinner, Germany, 1910**
PARENTAGE **'Frau Karl Druschki' × 'La France'**
FLOWER SIZE **5.1in (13cm)**
SCENT **Strong and sweet**
FLOWERING **Repeats well**
HEIGHT/SPREAD **6.6ft (2m)/4.9ft (1.5m)**
HARDINESS **Zone 5**

'GEORG ARENDS'

The size and elegance of the flowers of 'Georg Arends' are impressive even by today's standards. They open from long buds with enormous, scrolled petals. They are a beautiful, pure pink – a soft, silky color, which is enhanced by a silvery sheen. The flowers come sometimes singly, but more usually in somewhat tight clusters, and are very freely produced in a series of flushes through until late autumn. Deadheading helps to speed up the arrival of the next flush, but the interval before flowerings is always short. The flowers have long receptacles like a Damask rose and a strong resemblance to 'Frau Karl Druschki'. The plant is vigorous, with long stems and very few prickles. The leaves are large, pale, and susceptible to mildew in areas where this is a problem, but not in dry climates. Its flowers are susceptible to rain damage. It was once grown for the cut-flower trade, but its flowers drop their petals and do not last well in water. Georg Arends (1862–1952) was a very distinguished German nurseryman and raiser of herbaceous plants.

GEORGE BURNS

syn. 'WEKCALROC'

Floribunda

ORIGIN **Carruth, US, 1996**
PARENTAGE **'Calico' x Roller Coaster**
FLOWER SIZE **3.5in (9cm)**
SCENT **Strong and sweet**
FLOWERING **Repeats well**
HEIGHT/SPREAD **2.7ft (80cm)/2ft (60cm)**
HARDINESS **Zone 6**

The cheerful colors of George Burns are very striking: the upper sides of the petals are lemon yellow, fading to cream and splashed with crimson or pink stripes, while the backs of the petals are creamy white with no other coloring at all. The yellow is brightest in cool weather but the stripes are stronger when it is hot. The flowers take on a distinctive ruffled shape as they open out. They come in large clusters (typically of 3–11 flowers) on a sturdy, compact bush. The leaves are large, glossy, dark green, and occasionally susceptible to blackspot. George Burns (1896–1996) was a wisecracking comedian.

GEORGE BURNS

'GEORGE DICKSON'

'GEORGE DICKSON'

Hybrid Tea

ORIGIN **Dickson, Northern Ireland, 1912**
FLOWER SIZE **4.3in (11cm)**
SCENT **Medium and sweet**
FLOWERING **Repeats**
HEIGHT/SPREAD **5.7ft (1.75m)/6.6ft (2m)**
HARDINESS **Zone 6**
AWARDS **NRS GM 1911**

There have been many Hybrid Teas like 'George Dickson': large, crimson flowers, which nod their heads and have a scent to match the richness of their color. The popularity of 'George Dickson' has survived for nearly a century, partly because it is a very strong grower whose long, arching stems can be pegged down so that it blooms profusely all along its lengths. It has also been used as a short climber, whose flowers are best seen and smelled from below. These are large, cupped, and cabbagelike when young, but later they turn their petals back and dissolve into an irregular mass of petals. They are liberally produced, singly or in small, congested clusters, on a lanky, prickly bush. The leaves are large, dull, and attractive to mildew.

'GEORGE VANCOUVER'

Shrub Rose

ORIGIN **Ogilvie, Canada, 1994**
FLOWER SIZE **2.4in (6cm)**
SCENT **Fetid**
FLOWERING **Repeats well**
HEIGHT/SPREAD **3.3ft (1m)/4.1ft (1.25m)**
HARDINESS **Zone 4**

This Kordesii shrub was bred to survive the winters in central Canada and named after the explorer who mapped much of the west coast of North America in the 1790s. 'George Vancouver' could be described as an improved 'Champlain' – hardier and healthier. The flowers open from crimson buds. They are medium-red at first, but fade eventually to dark pink. They come singly or in small clusters (of up to seven) and are followed by handsome red hips. 'George Vancouver' is compact and upright in Canada, but lanky and gawky in warmer climates. Likewise its foliage – dark, glossy, and handsome – is almost immune to fungal diseases in cold areas but liable to get blackspot, and occasionally mildew, in temperate climates. The bush is vigorous and prickly. It flowers abundantly at its first blooming and thereafter continuously but on a lesser scale.

'GEORGE VANCOUVER'

'GEORGES VIBERT'

'GEORGES VIBERT'

Gallica

ORIGIN **Robert, France, 1853**
FLOWER SIZE **2.4in (6cm)**
SCENT **Very strong and sweet**
FLOWERING **Once only**
HEIGHT/SPREAD **5.7ft (1.75m)/4.1ft (1.25m)**
HARDINESS **Zone 5**

Georges Vibert (1840–1902) was a playwright and academic painter. His grandfather was the famous rose hybridist Jean-Pierre Vibert (1777–1866). The rose was named after the 13-year-old Georges by Jean-Pierre Vibert's head gardener Robert, who took over his employer's business. It is not the most showy of Gallicas, but it makes up with charm and scent what it lacks in size. The flowers are cupped, with a button eye and a green pointel at the center. The neatly arranged petals are rose pink, minutely striped with dark pink – a very pretty combination, which is rendered even more intriguing when the colors fade to palest pink and lilac. The flowers are somewhat irregular in outline and have elongated stipules. They are usually borne in clusters (typically of 3–5) on a vigorous bush with small, mid-green leaves.

'GERANIUM'

Wild Rose

ORIGIN **Royal Horticultural Society, Britain, 1938**
FLOWER SIZE **2in (5cm)**
SCENT **Light and sweet**
FLOWERING **Once only**
HEIGHT/SPREAD **13.1ft (4m)/13.1ft (4m)**
HARDINESS **Zone 5**

'GERANIUM'

This is best regarded as a cultivar of *Rosa moyesii*, from which it differs only in the color of its flowers. It is said to be shorter and more compact too, but the size and shape of 'Geranium' is well within the natural variation that the species exhibits in the wild. The flowers are a brilliant geranium red, without the fluorescence of a pelargonium but rendered even brighter by yellow stamens. The hips are pendulous and flagon-shaped, perhaps a little broader than most other forms of *Rosa moyesii*, but the same bright vermilion red. 'Geranium' was selected at the Royal Horticultural Society's gardens at Wisley in England, and was probably grown from wild-collected seed.

'GERANIUM RED'

Floribunda

ORIGIN **Boerner, US, 1947**
PARENTAGE **'Crimson Glory' seedling**
FLOWER SIZE **3.1in (8cm)**
SCENT **Strong, sweet, and fruity**
FLOWERING **Repeats well**
HEIGHT/SPREAD **3.3ft (1m)/2.7ft (80cm)**
HARDINESS **Zone 6**

The only thing wrong with 'Geranium Red' is that it came out in 1947, when old-fashioned flower shapes were distinctly unfashionable. It has now been rediscovered and shown to be an excellent rose. The flowers are an

GERLEV ROSENPARK

TWO IMPORTANT COLLECTIONS FEATURING HISTORIC, WILD, AND POULSEN-RAISED ROSES FORM THE BASIS OF ONE OF DENMARK'S FINEST ROSE GARDENS

THERE ARE MANY fine rose gardens in Denmark: one of the most interesting is at Gerlev, near Frederikssund. It is based on two important collections of roses. One was built up over many years by Valdemar Petersen, who was largely responsible for reviving Danish interest in historic roses. Petersen bred 'Aïcha' and 'Menja' and founded the impressive old-rose nursery, Rosenplanteskolen i Løve, near Høng. In 1981, he presented plants of some 800 cultivars to the foundation that owns Gerlev.

Petersen was not just interested in old cultivars, such as Gallicas and Damask roses, but also assembled a great number of wild rose species and primary hybrids. These now occupy a magnificent double border, nearly 656ft (200m) long, at the center of the garden at Gerlev. They flower before the cultivars, starting in May, and produce fine hips from July onward, so they have the effect of extending the season of interest. One of the last to flower is the rarely seen *Rosa wichurana* var. *grandiflora*.

THE ROSE BEDS AT GERLEV ROSENPARK

The other collection at Gerlev is a complete inventory of roses bred by the Poulsen family, by far the most important rose breeders in Scandinavia. These are displayed in a series of free-form beds in which the roses are planted according to the year in which they were introduced. This works surprisingly well, and makes it possible to study the whole history of Poulsen's rose breeding from 1912 right up to their latest novelties. An early rarity is the Multiflora Rambler 'Grevinde Rose Daneskjold Samsoë' (1914). An early Floribunda, popular in its day, is 'Karen Poulsen' (1932). At the other end of the sequence are modern beauties like Alexandra Renaissance (1997) and Kalmar (1998).

'KAREN POULSEN'

'GERANIUM RED'

'GERBE ROSE'

unmistakable bright scarlet – not the exact color of geraniums, but fairly close to it, with hints of orange at the center and a trace of bright pink at the edges. They are intensely sweet-scented and carried both singly and in loose clusters of up to five. But it is their fully double shape that is so unusual and attractive – a swirling mass of quilled petals in a quartered form, which, even today, is unusual in a rose of such fiery coloration. 'Geranium Red' has small, dark, glossy leaves and slender, twiggy branches, suggestive of China rose ancestry. It is not the most vigorous grower but responds well to good cultivation and fares best in hot weather. Its moderate height makes it a great garden plant, though its color can be difficult to combine with others.

'Gerbe Rose'

Wichurana Rambler

ORIGIN **Fauque, France, 1904**
PARENTAGE ***Rosa wichurana*** **x 'Baronne Adolphe de Rothschild'**
FLOWER SIZE **3.1in (8cm)**
SCENT **Very strong and sweet**
FLOWERING **Once only**
HEIGHT/SPREAD **13.1ft (4m)/6.6ft (2m)**
HARDINESS **Zone 6**

'Gerbe Rose' has large flowers – for a Wichurana rambler – and they are among the most sweetly scented of all roses. The flowers are pure pink, darker toward the center and paler at the petal tips, which are attractively ruffled. They are lightly cupped, with a muddled arrangement of petals within, sometimes roughly quartered. They are borne singly, or more commonly in short-stemmed clusters of 3–7. The plant has nearly thornless stems, a stiff habit of growth (not typical of the Wichuranas as a whole), red new growth, and dense, glossy, healthy, evergreen foliage. It flowers fairly early in the season and repeats on and off until midautumn, so that it is rarely without at least a few flowers.

Rudolph Geschwind

THE ROSES RAISED BY HUNGARIAN BREEDER RUDOLPH GESCHWIND REPRESENT A GENE POOL OF ENORMOUS VALUE AND BEAUTY

RUDOLF GESCHWIND (1829–1910) was one of the most important rose breeders of all time. Geschwind was a Hungarian, and roses were his hobby, though they had also been the basis of his early academic career, culminating in his *Die Hybridation und Sämmlingszucht der Rosen* (Vienna, 1865).

Geschwind's abiding preoccupations were winter hardiness, health, and freedom of flowering. He employed no fewer than 35 rose species in his search for hardiness, including such American roses as *Rosa acicularis, R. arkansana, R. blanda, R. californica*, and *R. carolina*. Eventually, Geschwind developed a race of shapely "Nordlandrosen," which he called "Die Rosen der Zukunft," the roses of the future. They were hardy to -34.6°F (-37°C), flowered continuously throughout the summer and autumn, and were vigorous and healthy. Fortunately, most of his 140 introductions have survived to this day.

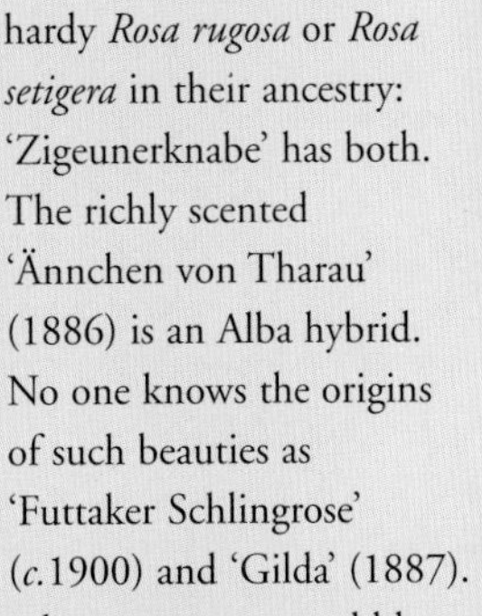
'GILDA'

Geschwind's hybrids fit into no easy categories. His best-known rose is 'Gruss an Teplitz', a mixture of Chinas, Bourbons, Teas, and Hybrid Perpetuals. The stunning 'Geschwinds Schönste' is probably a seedling of it. Many have the super-hardy *Rosa rugosa* or *Rosa setigera* in their ancestry: 'Zigeunerknabe' has both. The richly scented 'Ännchen von Tharau' (1886) is an Alba hybrid. No one knows the origins of such beauties as 'Futtaker Schlingrose' (*c.*1900) and 'Gilda' (1887). One can but wonder how our roses would have evolved in the 20th century had Geschwind found a disciple to continue his work. Even today, Geschwind's roses represent a gene pool of enormous value (and beauty) to draw on for the future development of the rose.

'GESCHWINDS SCHÖNSTE'

G

GERTRUDE JEKYLL

GERTRUDE JEKYLL

syn. 'AUSBORD'
Shrub Rose

ORIGIN **Austin, Britain, 1986**
PARENTAGE **'Wife of Bath' x 'Comte de Chambord'**
FLOWER SIZE **4.3in (11cm)**
SCENT **Very strong**
FLOWERING **Repeats well**
HEIGHT/SPREAD **4.1ft (1.25m)/3.3ft (1m)**
HARDINESS **Zone 5**

Gertrude Jekyll is one of the best and most popular of David Austin's English roses: its name commemorates the English writer and garden designer (1843–1932). The flowers are rich, dark pink, pale crimson at the center, fading to palest pink at the edges. They open out almost flat to reveal a mass of small petals, sometimes forming a quartered shape, and occasionally revealing a few golden stamens at the center. The flowers come in small clusters, typically of 3–5. The plant is very prickly and leafy, with long, pointed leaflets. Like its Portland parent, its internodes shorten toward the top of each stem, so that the flowers are surrounded by a leafy ruff. Gertrude Jekyll is immensely vigorous and will grow quickly to 9.8ft (3m) in a hot climate. Pruning and deadheading are essential if it is to rebloom.

'GESCHWIND'S ORDEN'

syn. 'DÉCORATION DE GESCHWIND'
Multiflora Hybrid

ORIGIN **Geschwind, Hungary, 1886**
FLOWER SIZE **2.4in (6cm)**
SCENT **Light and sweet**
FLOWERING **Repeats occasionally**
HEIGHT/SPREAD **8.2ft (2.5m)/4.9ft (1.5m)**
HARDINESS **Zone 4**

The rose we grow now as 'Geschwind's Orden' may be different from the original. Nevertheless, it is one of the prettiest of all the remarkable roses bred by Rudolph Geschwind in Hungary

'GESCHWIND'S ORDEN'

in the 19th century. Its parentage is uncertain, but it is thought to be a cross between 'de la Grifferaie' and 'Louise Odier'. The flowers open from round buds, cupped and roughly quartered. The outer petals are broad, flat, and eventually palest pink, while the many inner ones are crimson or purple, curved and narrow. All are somewhat thin, but the overall effect is exquisite. The flowers come singly or in clusters of up to seven. The plant has long branches, smooth at first but acquiring prickles during their second year, and rough and wrinkled leaves – watch out for blackspot.

'GHISLAINE DE FÉLIGONDE'

Multiflora Rambler

ORIGIN **Turbat, France, 1916**
PARENTAGE **'Goldfinch' x unknown**
FLOWER SIZE **1.8in (4.5cm)**
SCENT **Sweet and musky**
FLOWERING **Repeats a little in autumn**
HEIGHT/SPREAD **9.8ft (3m)/6.6ft (2m)**
HARDINESS **Zone 6**

'Ghislaine de Féligonde' is one of the best Multiflora ramblers – not overly vigorous but healthy and repeat flowering. It can be grown as a 9.8–13.1ft (3–4m) climber or as a 6.6ft (2m) bush. The flower buds are bright nasturtium orange, but the color of the flowers is immensely variable. In hot weather, they open pale apricot and fade quickly to white, but in cool weather (and autumn) they are much pinker, and retain their color. The flowerings come in long flushes, with gaps of several weeks between when only a few flowers appear. The clusters are long and spacious, with 6–12 flowers in summer but twice as many in autumn. The plant is almost thornless, although many of its flowering shoots carry a mass of tiny crimson bristles. The leaves are light green, large, and handsome. Comtesse Ghislaine de Féligonde was the wife of a wounded French cavalry officer who dragged her husband to safety in the dead of night from the no-man's-land between the opposing trenches in World War I.

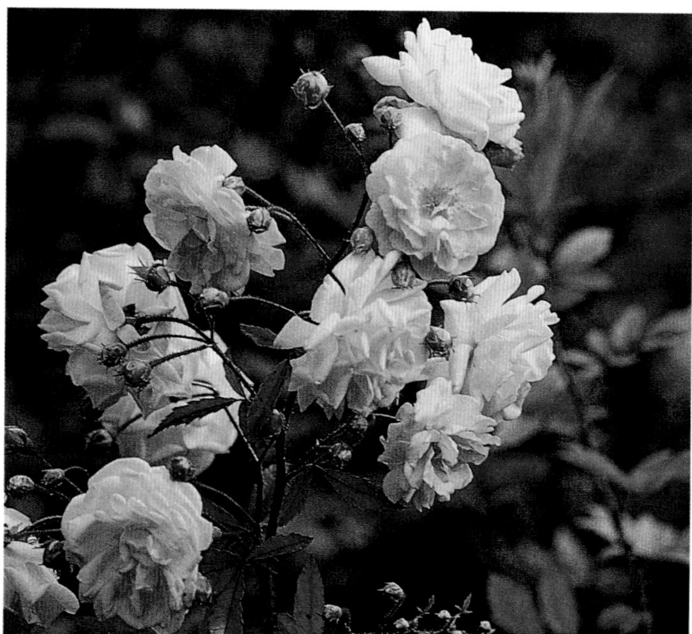

'GHISLAINE DE FÉLIGONDE' *(in cool autumn weather)*

GIFT OF LIFE

see POETRY IN MOTION

ROSA GIGANTEA

Wild Rose

FLOWER SIZE **4.7in (12cm)**
SCENT **Light and sweet**
FLOWERING **Once, very early in season**
HEIGHT/SPREAD **32.8ft (10m)/16.4ft (5m)**
HARDINESS **Zone 8**

The name of this wild rose – *Rosa gigantea* – indicates that the flowers are unusually large. It is also one of the most vigorous species, capable of reaching 82ft (25m) up a tree. The flowers are pure white, opening from creamy buds and sometimes splashed with pink on the backs of the petals. They are carried singly all along the long growths and are succeeded in due course by large (1.6in/4cm), round orange hips like little apples. The flowers develop a wave to their petals,

ROSA GIGANTEA

which is very elegant. *Rosa gigantea* comes from the mountains of Indo-China and is hardy only in warm climates. Nevertheless, it is one of the most important ancestors of our garden roses, being present in many of the early garden roses brought out of China in the 18th and 19th centuries and used to breed modern roses.

GINA LOLLOBRIGIDA

syn. 'MEILIVAR', The Children's Rose
Hybrid Tea

ORIGIN **Meilland, France, 1989**
PARENTAGE **Laura 81 x Tchin-Tchin**
FLOWER SIZE **5.1in (13cm)**
SCENT **Light and sweet**
FLOWERING **Repeats**
HEIGHT/SPREAD **4.9ft (1.5m)/3.3ft (1m)**
HARDINESS **Zone 6**

The glamorous Italian actress is well commemorated by this tall, elegant rose. Gina Lollobrigida is a large yellow Hybrid Tea, with masses of beautifully shaped petals. The petals are a fine mid-yellow on their upper sides and a deep golden yellow on their backs. They keep their color well. The flowers are produced, almost always singly, on very long stems, which are excellent for large flower arrangements. The plant is very vigorous and tall, almost gawky if allowed to grow unpruned, but well furnished with large, healthy, dark green foliage. In some countries, Gina Lollobrigida is also known as The Children's Rose, which is a pity because Frédéric Mistral (Meilland, 1993) bears the same synonym in several other countries. A ridiculous situation exists in Australia, where both roses circulate as The Children's Rose.

GINA LOLLOBRIGIDA

Gîtes de France

'Gipsy Boy'

see 'Zigeunerknabe'

Gîtes de France

syn. 'MEIwaton', Hagenbecks Tierpark

Modern Climber

ORIGIN **Meilland, France, 1994**
FLOWER SIZE **3.1in (8cm)**
SCENT **Medium and sweet**
FLOWERING **Repeats**
HEIGHT/SPREAD **8.2ft (2.5m)/4.9ft (1.5m)**
HARDINESS **Zone 6**
AWARDS **ADR 1993**

Although classified as a climber, Gîtes de France can also be grown as a tall shrub. It has a stupendous first flowering, fairly early in the season, but flowers are more sparsely borne thereafter. The semidouble flowers are pale crimson with a rather ragged outline and white flashes at the base of the petals. The deep yellow stamens give a focal point to the open flower. They sometimes come singly, but usually in slightly congested clusters of 3–10, and stand up well to rain. The plant occasionally produces much larger clusters, of up to 25 flowers. Gîtes de France is very vigorous, with thick stems and a lot of prickles. Its medium-dark leaves stand up well to mildew and rust, but not to blackspot. It is very hardy and easy to grow, and tolerates poor soil. It is popular in Germany, where it is known as Hagenbecks Tierpark.

Glad Tidings

see Lübecker Rotspon

'Gladsome'

Multiflora Rambler

ORIGIN **Clark, Australia, 1937**
FLOWER SIZE **1.4in (3.5cm)**
SCENT **Musky**
FLOWERING **Once, late in season**
HEIGHT/SPREAD **16.4ft (5m)/11.5ft (3.5m)**
HARDINESS **Zone 5**

This charming Multiflora rambler exudes good health and vigor. 'Gladsome' has lush, thick stems and mounds of bright, pale green leaves. The flowers are simple, with a glowing pink edge around a clear white eye. The pink fades and the bright yellow stamens turn brown, but the flowers are borne very generously in clusters of 15–100, and display themselves very prettily. Sometimes the branches tumble to the ground under the weight of the flowers, but the plant still holds its clusters up well. 'Gladsome' flowers only once, somewhat late in the season, but the flowering is followed by masses of small ovoid hips.

Glamis Castle

syn. 'AUSlevel'

Shrub Rose

ORIGIN **Austin, Britain, 1992**
PARENTAGE **Graham Thomas x Mary Rose**
FLOWER SIZE **2.4in (6cm)**
SCENT **Strong, a mixture of myrrh and sweetness**
FLOWERING **Repeats well**
HEIGHT/SPREAD **2.7ft (80cm)/2.7ft (80cm)**
HARDINESS **Zone 6**

Many consider Glamis Castle to be the best white rose ever bred by David Austin. It is certainly one that responds to good feeding and mulching, and to irrigation also in hot climates. The flowers are pure white, with a hint of buff or cream at first, and shallowly cupped with a mass of small ruffled petals – very attractive. They come in small clusters and are unusually rain resistant. The plant has a short, twiggy habit of growth, with mid-green leaves and many prickles. Glamis Castle is a good reflowerer, excellent at the front of a border. Its only weakness is an occasional brush with mildew and blackspot.

'Gladsome'

Rosa glauca

syn. Rosa rubrifolia

Wild Rose

FLOWER SIZE **0.8in (2cm)**
SCENT **Little or none**
FLOWERING **Once, midseason**
HEIGHT/SPREAD **6.6ft (2m)/4.9ft (1.5m)**
HARDINESS **Zone 4**

Rosa glauca is an invaluable garden rose, not for its flowers but for the beauty of its purple leaves and its copious crop of hips. It is the perfect foil for other roses, shrubs, and herbaceous plants because it combines well with every color. The flowers are small, bright crimson or carmine, fading to mid-pink, and backed by very long, slender sepals. They come in clusters of 5–15 and are quickly followed by scarlet hips, round and 0.6in (1.5cm) in diameter, which last well into the winter. The plant has wonderful foliage: plum purple in the sun and slate gray in shade, bluer on the upper sides of the leaflets and more crimson underneath. The exact shade differs genetically between different plants. The young stems are purple, covered in a white bloom, which gives an overall appearance of blueness. They are entirely smooth when young, but prickles develop on the old wood in the second year. *Rosa glauca* is very hardy, but, since it comes from the mountains of central Europe – from the Pyrenees through the Alps to the Carpathians – it does not grow well in climates where there are prolonged periods of summer heat and no cold snap in winter. In the gardens of northern Europe it seeds around well.

Glamis Castle

Rosa glauca

'GLENFIDDICH'

G

'GLENFIDDICH'

Floribunda

ORIGIN **Cocker, Britain, 1976**
PARENTAGE **'Arthur Bell' x ('Sabine' x 'Circus')**
FLOWER SIZE **3.5in (9cm)**
SCENT **Light and sweet**
FLOWERING **Repeats well**
HEIGHT/SPREAD **3.3ft (1m)/3.3ft (1m)**
HARDINESS **Zone 6**

The name of 'Glenfiddich' is especially appropriate for a rose bred from 'Arthur Bell': both are named after Scotch whiskies. Its color is golden amber, slightly darker on the petal backs, but fading eventually to yellow. The individual flowers have quite a lot of Hybrid Tea in their ancestry, so they are large and shapely. They are sometimes borne singly and never in very large clusters – typically of 3–5. The flowers have beautiful golden stamens and red filaments when they open out. 'Glenfiddich' is extremely free flowering, starting early and continuing late into autumn almost without interruption. The leaves are dark, glossy, and healthy, and the plant fares especially well in cool climates, where it keeps its color best. It is extremely prickly.

'GLOIRE DE DIJON'

'GLOIRE DE DIJON'

Climbing Tea Rose

ORIGIN **Jacotot, France, 1853**
FLOWER SIZE **3.9in (10cm)**
SCENT **Strong and tealike**
FLOWERING **Repeats constantly**
HEIGHT/SPREAD **16.4ft (5m)/9.8ft (3m)**
HARDINESS **Zone 6**

No one knows the origins of 'Gloire de Dijon', but it was popular right from the start – one of the most widely grown of all roses – and an important ancestor of our modern roses. It was a chance seedling, but the Jacotot family believed that the seed parent was probably 'Desprez à Fleurs Jaunes' and the pollen parent 'Souvenir de la Malmaison'. The flowers of 'Gloire de Dijon' open out lightly cupped, to show a mass of irregularly quartered petals. They are buff yellow, fading to pale yellow and fawn, but tinged at first with salmon in the center, especially on the undersides of the petals. The flowers spoil in rain but last well when cut for the house. In tropical and subtropical climates it flowers all through the year. Elsewhere it starts early and continues until stopped by frost. The plant should be pruned lightly and its leggy growths trained horizontally so that they break at the axils and produce flowering spurs all along their length. 'Gloire de Dijon' is the hardiest of all Tea roses, and one of the most beautiful. The English rose writer Graham Stuart Thomas described it as "the most popular and satisfactory of all old climbing roses, an epoch making rose."

'GLOIRE DE DUCHER'

Hybrid Perpetual

ORIGIN **Ducher, France, 1865**
FLOWER SIZE **3.9in (10cm)**
SCENT **Strong and sweet**
FLOWERING **Repeats well**
HEIGHT/SPREAD **6.6ft (2m)/6.6ft (2m)**
HARDINESS **Zone 5**

'Gloire de Ducher' is widely grown in Europe for its very large, full, crimson purple flowers. Their beautiful shape and strong scent anticipate some of the best English Roses of David Austin. The outer petals are plummy violet at first, and the inner ones maroon, with hints of velvety crimson, but the petal backs are paler – almost silvery. The flowers open flat, but the petals are wavy and loosely held, informally arranged around a rough button eye. The plant is a lanky grower, with a lot of bright green leaves. It is best wound around a pillar or pegged down to encourage it to break into flower all along its stems, but it should not be grown against a wall because it is susceptible to mildew. Blackspot is also a constant presence, but 'Gloire de Ducher' is most certainly worth growing for its sumptuous flowers. The name commemorates Claude Ducher (1820–74), who began his nursery at Chemin des Quatre Maisons 25, Guillotière, Lyon, in 1845.

'GLOIRE DE DUCHER'

'GLOIRE DE FRANCE'

'GLOIRE DE FRANCE'

Gallica

ORIGIN **Bizard, France, 1828**
FLOWER SIZE **4.7in (12cm)**
SCENT **Strong, rich, and sweet**
FLOWERING **Once only**
HEIGHT/SPREAD **4.9ft (1.5m)/4.1ft (1.25m)**
HARDINESS **Zone 5**

Seldom are roses so aptly named as 'Gloire de France'. It is the very quintessence of the glorious Gallica roses. Its flowers are enormous, brilliant pink, deliciously scented, and swirling with neatly arranged little petals. The color may be slightly paler, more silvery, at the edges, but 'Gloire de France' is the purest pink of all the Gallicas. The flowers open flat and are borne usually singly, only occasionally in twos and threes, which is just as well, because they come in such quantities that they weigh the branches down. Before they flower, the stems are stout and upright, and rather prickly for a Gallica. The leaves are a soft, fresh green and very healthy.

'GLOIRE DE GUILAN'

Damask Rose

ORIGIN **Lindsay/Hilling, Britain, 1949**
FLOWER SIZE **2.8in (7cm)**
SCENT **Very strong and sweet**
FLOWERING **Once only**
HEIGHT/SPREAD **5.7ft (1.75m)/4.9ft (1.5m)**
HARDINESS **Zone 4**

Nancy Lindsay claimed to have found this rose in Guilan in Persia, where it was grown for attar of roses; it was introduced by the English nursery of Thomas Hilling. 'Gloire de Guilan' is an old-fashioned Damask, fairly closely related to 'Kazanlik'. Its flowers open rich pink and fade to clear rose pink, with a paler patch toward the center, and deep yellow stamens. The flowers have fewer petals than most Damasks, being only lightly double, like 'Celsiana'. 'Gloire de Guilan' makes a lax, prickly shrub, and suckers when grown on its own roots. The leaves are pale green and very attractive when young. The stems tend to bow down under the weight of their flowers, and are perhaps best cut back by about one-third in winter. The scent of the flowers is delicious.

'GLOIRE DE GUILAN'

'Gloire des Mousseux'

'Gloire des Mousseux'

Moss Rose

ORIGIN **Laffay, France, 1852**
FLOWER SIZE **4.7in (12cm)**
SCENT **Strong and sweet**
FLOWERING **Repeats occasionally**
HEIGHT/SPREAD **4.9ft (1.5m)/4.1ft (1.25m)**
HARDINESS **Zone 5**

Many would say that 'Gloire des Mousseux' is the finest of all Moss roses. It has the largest flowers, and they are richly scented, with a beautiful color and shape. The buds, sepals, and receptacles are all well covered in bright green moss. The flowers are clear, bright pink with a silky sheen to their petals. They fade a little at the edges, but the overall effect radiating from the rumpled, imbricated petals is of brilliant, pure pink. The flowers come sometimes singly but usually in clusters of 3–7. 'Gloire des Mousseux' has a lot of small bristles and pale green leaves that exude both lushness and freshness. It is a vigorous grower, and can reach as much as 6.6ft (2m), but is normally pruned back to half that height. Sometimes – but not every year – it produces a few flowers in autumn.

'Gloire des Rosomanes'

China Rose

ORIGIN **Vibert, France, 1825**
FLOWER SIZE **2.8in (7cm)**
SCENT **Moderate**
FLOWERING **Repeats continuously**
HEIGHT/SPREAD **8.2ft (2.5m)/6.6ft (2m)**
HARDINESS **Zone 5**

'Gloire des Rosomanes' is an important rose: it was one of the first fertile hybrids between the old European roses derived from *Rosa gallica* and the old Chinese cultivars descended from *Rosa chinensis*. It appears – a long way back – in the pedigree of almost every modern rose. Its flowers are very striking but because the petals are inconsistent in their shape and arrangement, they look somewhat loose, ragged, and unbalanced. They are bright cherry crimson, with a white center and a lot of white stripes, which run through the crimson part of the petals and cause them to twist and look deformed. Yet the effect of a bush in

'Gloire des Rosomanes'

flower is spectacular from a distance, and, when freshly opened, the flowers have a brilliance that was never seen again among 19th-century roses. The flowers appear in large clusters (of up to 20 at a time) on thin, upright stems and in great profusion. Later come a lot of slightly urn-shaped hips, and more flowers too, for 'Gloire des Rosomanes' is very floriferous, almost continuously in flower in hot climates. The plant reaches 8.2ft (2.5m) high as a dense, vigorous bush, or twice that height as a climber in hot climates – but will reach less than 3.3ft (1m) tall in the cooler parts of the globe, where it has proved remarkably hardy.

'Gloire Lyonnaise'

Hybrid Perpetual

ORIGIN **Guillot fils, France, 1887**
PARENTAGE **'Baronne Adolphe de Rothschild' × 'Mme. Falcot'**
FLOWER SIZE **3.9in (10cm)**
SCENT **Light and tealike**
FLOWERING **Remontant**
HEIGHT/SPREAD **4.9ft (1.5m)/4.1ft (1.25m)**
HARDINESS **Zone 7**

'Gloire Lyonnaise'

Gloriana 97

'Gloire Lyonnaise' has a somewhat 20th-century look: though classified as a Hybrid Perpetual, its ancestry declares it a genuine Hybrid Tea. The flowers are large and pure white, with a hint of lemon or cream at the base of the petals. They open slowly from long buds – very full and cupped at first but later opening out. They are best in dry weather, when the flower can expand without rain damage to the thin, sensitive petals. The flowers come singly or in small clusters of 3–5 on strong, upright stems. The plant is stiff and stout, with a lot of fierce prickles and tough, dark leaves. Mildew can be a problem, but it is more unsightly than serious. The flowers come in flushes, separated by about six weeks.

Gloriana 97

syn. 'CHEWpope'

Climbing Miniature

ORIGIN **Warner, Britain, 1997**
PARENTAGE **Laura Ford × Stephens' Big Purple**
FLOWER SIZE **2.4in (6cm)**
SCENT **Medium, sweet, and musky**
FLOWERING **Almost constant**
HEIGHT/SPREAD **8.2ft (2.5m)/4.9ft (1.5m)**
HARDINESS **Zone 6**

It has taken a while for the good qualities of this unusual short climbing rose to be appreciated, but its worldwide popularity is now growing fast. The rich purple coloring of Gloriana 97 is remarkable, as is its extraordinary floriferousness. The flowers are pale crimson at first, with a purple tone that intensifies as they age. They have slightly paler backs and eventually open to show their yellow stamens. The flowers are round and, though not large, have a look of solidity about them. The petals often display a pointed tip. The flowers come singly or in clusters of up to ten (typically 3–5) all over the plant, almost to ground level. Gloriana 97 has the small, dark, shiny leaves of the miniature ramblers and a scattering of little, bristly prickles. Its leaves are small and dainty, and may pick up a little blackspot late in the year.

'Glory of Edsell'

Spinosissima Hybrid

ORIGIN **Britain, c.1900**
FLOWER SIZE **1.2in (3cm)**
SCENT **Light and sweet**
FLOWERING **Once only**
HEIGHT/SPREAD **8.2ft (2.5m)/8.2ft (2.5m)**
HARDINESS **Zone 5**

The flowers of 'Glory of Edsell' have the characteristic marbled coloring of a Spinosissima Hybrid. They are bright pink, with a white patch at the center, but close examination reveals that the white runs into the pink to give it a streaked effect. The flowers are single, and come at the end of little spurs all the way along the long, slender, arching branches. In cool climates it is an early flowerer. 'Glory of Edsell' is a tall, upright, vigorous bush with few prickles, though they are quite long and pointed. Its leaves are small and dark and the new wood has an attractive pale russet color in winter.

Glowing Peace

see Philippe Noiret

'Glory of Edsell'

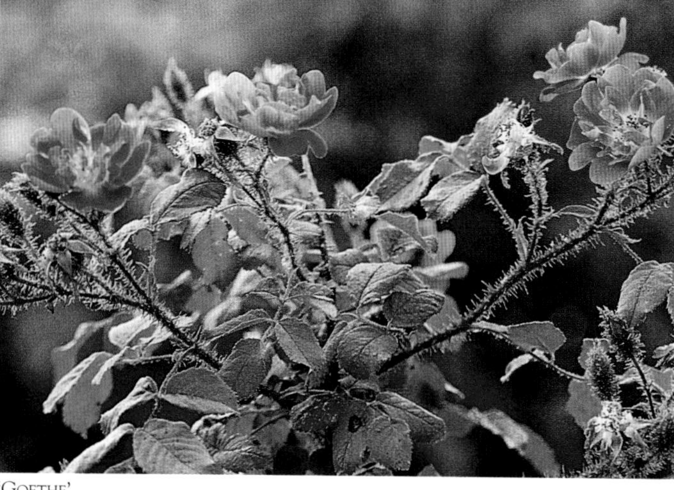
'GOETHE'

'GOETHE'

Moss Rose

ORIGIN **Lambert, Germany, 1911**
FLOWER SIZE **1.6in (4cm)**
SCENT **Strong and sweet**
FLOWERING **Once, midseason**
HEIGHT/SPREAD **8.2ft (2.5m)/6.6ft (2m)**
HARDINESS **Zone 5**

Named after the German writer Johann Wolfgang von Goethe (1749–1832), 'Goethe' is something of a mystery rose. It is probably a cross between a Multiflora rambler and a Moss rose. It makes a shrubby climber, whose heavily mossed buds, stems, and sepals are a remarkable contrast to the small, lightly cupped, dark pink flowers. These have a white center and occasional white flashes on some of the petals, as well as very pale stamens. They come in clusters of up to 15, elegantly spaced so that each flower can be studied clearly. The bristly moss starts on the buds and pedicels, then runs down on to the stems, where it emerges as a dense covering of long, slender prickles. They form an attractive pink haze on the outline of the new growth and a hard, discouraging defense around the older stems. This formidable armature has led to 'Goethe' being recommended as a hedging rose. The leaves have a blue cast and are no strangers to blackspot and mildew.

GOLD BUNNY

see RIMOSA 79

'GOLD GLOW'

Hybrid Tea

ORIGIN **Anthony Perry, US, 1959**
PARENTAGE **'Fred Howard' x 'Sutter's Gold'**
FLOWER SIZE **4.3in (11cm)**
SCENT **Medium and fruity**
FLOWERING **Repeats**
HEIGHT/SPREAD **4.1ft (1.25m)/3.3ft (1m)**
HARDINESS **Zone 6**

This beautiful yellow Hybrid Tea was bred by an American amateur. 'Gold Glow' has bright yellow flowers, so richly colored when newly open that they do indeed appear golden at the center. However, the color fades, as is often the case with yellow roses, through lemon yellow to cream and even to white. This change starts with the petals at the edge of the flowers, so that there is often a charming contrast between the outer rings of paler yellow and the deeper, glowing yellow of the center. The flowers are very full of petals, which tend to lie back in an imbricated shape but are occasionally quilled in the old-fashioned style. The flowers come singly and in clusters of up to four. 'Gold Glow' makes a vigorous, sturdy, upright bush, with large, healthy, handsome, dark leaves. It repeats quickly, so that the bush is almost continuously in flower.

'GOLD GLOW'

'GOLD MEDAL'

'GOLD MEDAL'

syn. 'AROYQUELI'

Grandiflora

ORIGIN **Christensen, US, 1982**
PARENTAGE **'Yellow Pages' x ('Granada' x 'Garden Party')**
FLOWER SIZE **4.3in (11cm)**
SCENT **Light and fruity**
FLOWERING **Repeats well**
HEIGHT/SPREAD **4.9ft (1.5m)/3.3ft (1m)**
HARDINESS **Zone 6**
AWARDS **NZ GM 1993**

The flowers of 'Gold Medal' open slowly from elegant orange yellow buds. They are a good golden yellow at first, with a coral pink edge to the petals, but they fade to a much paler yellow and eventually almost to white. They retain the pink edge as a slight color wash. The long-stemmed flowers are borne either singly or, especially in autumn, in clusters of up to seven. They are excellent for cutting and last well in water. The bush makes tall, upright, bushy growth and carries large, dark, handsome, clean foliage. 'Gold Medal' fares best in hot climates: it is very much at home in California, where it was bred.

'GOLDBUSCH'

Shrub Rose

ORIGIN **Kordes, Germany, 1954**
PARENTAGE **'Golden Glow' x 'Obergärtner Wiebicke' seedling**
FLOWER SIZE **3.9in (10cm)**
SCENT **Moderate and fruity**
FLOWERING **Remontant**
HEIGHT/SPREAD **8.2ft (2.5m)/4.9ft (1.5m)**
HARDINESS **Zone 6**

'GOLDBUSCH'

Although sometimes classed among the Briar Hybrids, 'Goldbusch' is far removed from its wild ancestors and resembles more closely a vigorous Floribunda. It is what the Germans call a "Park Rose" – a tall, floriferous, low-maintenance shrub rose – and it is excellent even today. The buds are coral pink and the flowers are peachy yellow before fading to cream, but then they darken as they age and take on a pink tone. They open out to reveal their red brown stamens, which are surrounded by somewhat irregular inner petals. Then all the petals acquire a ruffled outline as they age. The flowers come in large clusters, typically of 5–15, and are followed by large hips. The plant has mid-green leaves and an occasional weakness for blackspot. Its height differs according to the climate: in hot areas it reaches 8.2ft (2.5m) and is capable of reaching 13.1ft (4m); in cooler climates it may struggle to 4.1ft (1.25m).

GOLDEN CELEBRATION

syn. 'AUSGOLD'

Shrub Rose

ORIGIN **Austin, Britain, 1992**
PARENTAGE **'Charles Austin' x Abraham Darby**
FLOWER SIZE **3.1in (8cm)**
SCENT **Strong**
FLOWERING **Repeats well**
HEIGHT/SPREAD **4.1ft (1.25m)/3.3ft (1m)**
HARDINESS **Zone 5**

Golden Celebration is deservedly popular. Its beautiful arching stems are smothered in gorgeous golden flowers of a very unusual hue. They have golden apricot centers, with paler petal backs and paler edges. Occasionally they are more yellow at first, but there is always a rich suffusion of gold at the center. The flowers are cupped and full of petals, sometimes with a button eye. They come in nodding clusters of 3–7, occasionally singly. The bush has pleasant, large, mid-green leaves, nearly thornless stems, and a lax, rounded habit. It is also fairly healthy, except for a little blackspot. In hot climates it will reach 6.6ft (2m), but rarely more than 4.1ft (1.25m) in cool climates.

'Golden Chersonese'

'Golden Chersonese'

Shrub Rose

ORIGIN **Allen, Britain, 1967**
PARENTAGE ***Rosa ecae* x 'Canary Bird'**
FLOWER SIZE **1.6in (4cm)**
SCENT **Light and resinous**
FLOWERING **Once only, very early in season**
HEIGHT/SPREAD **6.6ft (2m)/6.6ft (2m)**
HARDINESS **Zone 6**

Ted Allen, who bred this rose, was an English amateur: the name 'Golden Chersonese' (by which the Malayan peninsula is sometimes known) refers as much to his years as an agronomist in Malaya as to its rich color. Allen succeeded in combining the deep yellow coloring of *Rosa ecae* with the larger flowers and greater hardiness of 'Canary Bird'. The flowers come singly at the nodes of the old wood, all along the long branches, very early in the season. They are set off by neat, dainty, bright green leaves, which have the aromatic scent of *Rosa ecae.* The plant is healthy and vigorous, with long arching stems and a thick armature of long prickles. It roots easily from softwood cuttings.

'Golden Delight'

Floribunda

ORIGIN **Le Grice, Britain, 1955**
PARENTAGE **'Goldilocks' x 'Ellinor Le Grice'**
FLOWER SIZE **2.8in (7cm)**
SCENT **Strong, sweet, and fruity**
FLOWERING **Repeats well**
HEIGHT/SPREAD **2ft (60cm)/2ft (60cm)**
HARDINESS **Zone 6**

Edward Le Grice regarded 'Golden Delight' as a useful step toward breeding the perfect yellow Floribunda. It is short, compact, and a good repeat flowerer. The flowers are borne in fairly tight clusters of 3–7, though sometimes also singly. The flowers are slightly cupped and very full of small, incurved petals – an unusual shape when 'Golden Delight' was first introduced. They are a good mid-yellow, not such a deep shade as its sister seedling 'Allgold', but they keep their color well. The plant grows strongly and repeats quickly. It may show a touch of blackspot in autumn, but is usually fairly healthy.

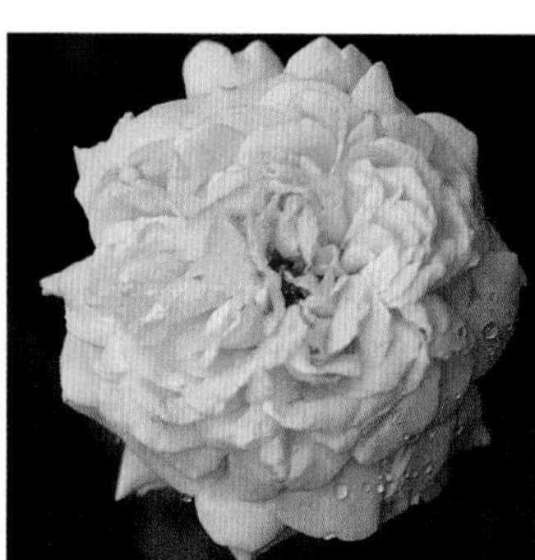
'Golden Delight'

Golden Holstein

syn. 'KORtikel', Goldyla

Floribunda

ORIGIN **Kordes, Germany, 1989**
FLOWER SIZE **3.1in (8cm)**
SCENT **Light and fruity**
FLOWERING **Repeats constantly**
HEIGHT/SPREAD **4.1ft (1.25m)/4.1ft (1.25m)**
HARDINESS **Zone 6**

Golden Holstein is the yellowest of all Floribundas: its semidouble flowers are the richest, deepest yellow imaginable, without the slightest hint of orange or red. They have slightly wavy petals and are borne in large, somewhat tightly packed clusters, typically of 5–15 flowers. The stamens remain yellow for a long time, and although the color eventually fades in hot weather, the flowers stand up sturdily to rain. The plant has clean, healthy leaves (mildew is only rarely a problem) and repeats constantly, so that it seems never without flowers. It grows vigorously, but the height of the plant depends upon climate and training. In its native Holstein, it rarely exceeds 2.5ft (75cm), but in hot climates it reaches at least twice that height.

Golden Holstein

Golden Jubilee

Golden Jubilee

syn. 'COCagold'

Hybrid Tea

ORIGIN **Cocker, Britain, 1981**
PARENTAGE **'Peer Gynt' x 'Gay Gordons'**
FLOWER SIZE **4.7in (12cm)**
SCENT **Strong, fruity, and musky**
FLOWERING **Repeats well**
HEIGHT/SPREAD **4.1ft (1.25m)/3.3ft (1m)**
HARDINESS **Zone 6**

It is not exactly golden, but Golden Jubilee is a very good rose. It has large flowers of perfect shape and it is a vigorous grower. The flowers are pale yellow, with a pink flush on the tips of the petals and deeper yellow toward the center. They are borne singly (occasionally in twos and threes) on long stems, making them popular for cutting and exhibition. The petals reflex sharply and form a starry shape when they open out fully to reveal their yellow stamens. Golden Jubilee has large, mid-green leaves and long, strong, prickly stems. Mildew and blackspot may visit it later in the year, but never affect its vigor. In fact, some of its most sumptuous flowers appear in autumn.

'Golden Masterpiece'

Hybrid Tea

ORIGIN **Boerner, US, 1954**
PARENTAGE **'Mandalay' x 'Spek's Yellow'**
FLOWER SIZE **6.3in (16cm)**
SCENT **Medium, sweet, and fruity**
FLOWERING **Repeats**
HEIGHT/SPREAD **4.9ft (1.5m)/3.3ft (1m)**
HARDINESS **Zone 6**

The Masterpiece roses were produced as a branding exercise by Jackson & Perkins in the 1950s and 1960s. 'Golden Masterpiece' is a fair representative, selected for the size and beauty of its Hybrid Tea flowers. They are not, however, golden in color – more creamy yellow with lemon yellow petal backs and a deeper yellow patch toward the center when they open out. They are popular exhibition roses because they are almost always borne singly and have been known to reach as much as 7in (18cm). They come on long stems that also make them good for cutting. 'Golden Masterpiece' is still sometimes sold as "the biggest yellow rose." It is vigorous, with large, dark leaves. Blackspot may be a problem in autumn, and the flowers ball in damp weather, but it is a good rose in hot, dry climates.

'Golden Masterpiece'

GOLDEN MEDAILLON

GOLDEN MEDAILLON

syn. 'KORIKON', Limelight

Hybrid Tea

ORIGIN **Kordes, Germany, 1984**
PARENTAGE **'Gitte' × seedling**
FLOWER SIZE **4.3in (11cm)**
SCENT **Strong**
FLOWERING **Repeats well**
HEIGHT/SPREAD **2.5ft (75cm)/2.5ft (75cm)**
HARDINESS **Zone 6**

The flowers of Golden Medaillon are pretty at all stages of their development: the tall, pointed buds open out into full flowers with a lot of neatly arranged petals with slightly crimped edges. They are not golden, but rich buttercup yellow toward the center of the flower and paler toward the outside, fading fairly evenly as they age to lemon yellow. They are borne singly or in small clusters (usually fewer than seven) and flower particularly well in autumn. Two outstanding features are the strong scent of the flowers and the beautiful dark, glossy leaves, crimson when young. The bush is otherwise fairly ordinary, though the flowers last well if cut for the house.

'GOLDEN MOSS'

Moss Rose

ORIGIN **Dot, Spain, 1932**
PARENTAGE **'Frau Karl Druschki' × ('Souvenir de Claudius Pernet' × 'Blanche Moreau')**
FLOWER SIZE **2.8in (7cm)**
SCENT **Medium and sweet**
FLOWERING **Once only, with an occasional late straggler**
HEIGHT/SPREAD **13.1ft (4m)/16.4ft (5m)**
HARDINESS **Zone 5**

Pedro Dot (1885–1976) was a very inventive breeder, and 'Golden Moss' was the result of one of his early experiments in breeding modern Moss roses. 'Golden Moss' opens apricot colored before fading to pale buff and mother-of-pearl. The flowers are borne singly or in clusters of up to three on short stems. The moss covers the sepals and runs some way down the stems. It is represented farther down the branches by a very thick covering of prickles. The plant is a lanky, lax shrub with a naturally thicketing habit when grown on its own roots. It grows very vigorously to at least 9.8ft (3m) (more in warm or hot climates), arching over and filling a large area. It has mid-green, matte leaves and a propensity for mildew, especially on the flower buds.

'GOLDEN SCEPTER'

see 'SPEK'S YELLOW'

'GOLDEN MOSS'

'GOLDEN SHOWERS'

'GOLDEN SHOWERS'

Modern Climber

ORIGIN **Lammerts, US, 1956**
PARENTAGE **'Charlotte Armstrong' × 'Captain Thomas'**
FLOWER SIZE **3.5in (9cm)**
SCENT **Medium and sweet**
FLOWERING **Repeats well**
HEIGHT/SPREAD **9.8ft (3m)/6.6ft (2m)**
HARDINESS **Zone 7**
AWARDS **AARS 1956; Portland GM 1957**

'Golden Showers' is an excellent, early flowering, yellow climber for mild climates. The flowers open golden yellow from pointed buds and fade gently to lemon and eventually to cream. They are lightly double, with a distinct ruffle to their petals and beautiful red stamens at the center – a lovely combination. They come singly or in small, long-stemmed clusters, typically of 3–5 flowers. After the magnificent first flowering of the year, they are produced in ones and twos until a memorable reflowering starts in autumn. They are excellent for cutting. The plant has thick stems and glossy, mid-green foliage, sometimes susceptible to blackspot. It can also be pruned back and grown as a shrub. It is popular in England, where its flowers stand up well to rain, and will accept quite a lot of shade in hot climates.

'GOLDEN UNICORN'

Shrub Rose

ORIGIN **Buck, US, 1984**
PARENTAGE **'Paloma Blanca' × ('Carefree Beauty' × 'Antike')**
FLOWER SIZE **3.9in (10cm)**
SCENT **Light and sweet**
FLOWERING **Repeats**
HEIGHT/SPREAD **4.1ft (1.25m)/3.3ft (1m)**
HARDINESS **Zone 5**

The color of 'Golden Unicorn' is very striking when it starts to open out. The buds are orange, tinged with vermilion, and the opening bloom is deep apricot yellow. However, the fully open flower fades to become cream colored, with pink edges and only a suggestion of yellow at the center. It is a good example of the inconsistancy of yellow roses, which generally produce their richer colors in cool weather. Griffith Buck selected 'Golden Unicorn' because it was hardy in Iowa, where he lived and worked. The flowers are cupped, with handsome orange stamens, and are borne singly or in clusters of up to seven. 'Golden Unicorn' makes a vigorous, strong-growing, bushy plant, tolerant of poor soils and very hardy. Its leaves are lush, dark green, its stems prickly. It repeats well, and produces flowers until the first frost of winter. Buck served with the US paratroopers in World War II: Golden Unicorn was the name of his division.

'GOLDEN VISION'

Hybrid Gigantea

ORIGIN **Clark, Australia, 1922**
PARENTAGE **'Maréchal Niel' × *Rosa gigantea***
FLOWER SIZE **2.8in (7cm)**
SCENT **Medium**
FLOWERING **Early, with only a few later flowers**
HEIGHT/SPREAD **13.1ft (4m)/9.8ft (3m)**
HARDINESS **Zone 9**

'Golden Vision' is a very early flowering rambler for warm climates. Its flowers are lemon and cream, fading to white, but the color is unevenly distributed so that each flower has darker yellow patches within a pale background – an unusual and charming feature. The flowers are pretty when newly open but messy when the petals open out. They are borne in small clusters on a very vigorous plant with few prickles, light green foliage, and reddish new growth.

'GOLDEN UNICORN'

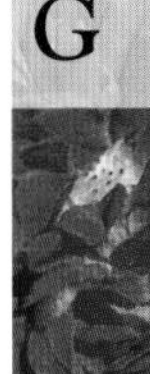

GOLDEN WEDDING

GOLDEN WEDDING

syn. 'AROKRIS'
Floribunda

ORIGIN **Bear Creek, US, 1990**
FLOWER SIZE **3.1in (8cm)**
SCENT **Light and fruity**
FLOWERING **Repeats**
HEIGHT/SPREAD **4.9ft (1.5m)/3.3ft (1m)**
HARDINESS **Zone 6**

This is a good rose with a big-selling name. It is extremely popular in England, where Golden Wedding is a natural choice to give couples who have achieved 50 years of marriage. However, it is virtually unknown in the US, where it was raised. Its flowers are a good, rich yellow, with darker (almost golden) backs to the petals. They are shapely and full of petals, and borne in well-spaced clusters of 3–10. Unfortunately, their scent is on the light side. Golden Wedding makes a vigorous, tall-growing plant, with fairly healthy, medium-dark green leaves. It is usually seen as a hard-pruned border plant, 2.7ft (80cm) high, but will grow to twice that height and produce more flowers if lightly pruned.

'GOLDEN WINGS'

Shrub Rose

ORIGIN **Shepherd, US, 1958**
PARENTAGE **'Soeur Thérèse' x ('Altaica' x 'Ormiston Roy')**
FLOWER SIZE **4.7in (12cm)**
SCENT **Medium and fruity**
FLOWERING **Repeats well**
HEIGHT/SPREAD **6.6ft (2m)/4.9ft (1.5m)**
HARDINESS **Zone 5**

Roy Shepherd, who bred 'Golden Wings', was an American amateur who wanted to employ the good qualities of 'Altaica' to produce hardy, continually flowering shrub roses. He was also the author of the classic *History of the Rose* (New York, 1954). 'Golden Wings' has long, slender, pointed buds, which open first as large, cupped flowers and later more loosely. They are pale lemon at first (later creamy white), with 5–10 petals, lit up by glowing amber stamens and crimson anthers – ravishing when the sun shines through them. The flowers come singly or in clusters of 2–5, and, despite their apparent fragility, stand up well to wind and rain. They are followed by handsome, large, round orange hips, which last well into winter. The leaves are light green, unexciting, and occasionally susceptible to blackspot. The plant needs a few years to build up to a good size, during which time it should be pruned little or not at all. 'Golden Wings' is one of the first and last roses to flower every year.

'GOLDEN WINGS'

GOLDEN YEARS

syn. 'HARWEEN'
Floribunda

ORIGIN **Harkness, Britain, 1988**
PARENTAGE **'Landora' x Amber Queen**
FLOWER SIZE **3.1in (8cm)**
SCENT **Light and fruity**
FLOWERING **Repeats constantly**
HEIGHT/SPREAD **3.3ft (1m)/2.5ft (75cm)**
HARDINESS **Zone 6**
AWARDS **Hradec Golden Rose 1989; Orléans GM 1990**

Golden Years is typical of modern Harkness roses at their best: it has dark leaves, a rich color, a circular shape when the flower opens out, and a movement to the petals that gives it a distinctive character. The flowers are pale orange, with gold and apricot hints. Darker shades on the petal backs give rise to rich golden shadows within the flowers, even when they are fully open. It keeps its color in hot sun and, though it opens out very wide, possesses so many rows of imbricated petals that the stamens are never seen. The plant has dark green, glossy leaves and quite a lot of prickles. Harkness has said that the name celebrates the centenary of the girls' school in its home town of Hitchin, but naturally it also has other commercial possibilities. Golden Years is popular in Britain as a retirement gift.

GOLDEN YEARS

GOLDENER OLYMP

GOLDENER OLYMP

syn. 'KORSCHUPPE', Olympic Gold
Modern Climber

ORIGIN **Kordes, Germany, 1984**
PARENTAGE **seedling x 'Goldstern'**
FLOWER SIZE **4.7in (12cm)**
SCENT **Strong and sweet**
FLOWERING **Repeats**
HEIGHT/SPREAD **8.2ft (2.5m)/6.6ft (2m)**
HARDINESS **Zone 5**

The finest short-growing, yellow, modern climber is Goldener Olymp. Its gorgeous flowers are unusually large for a rose that bears its blooms in clusters as well as singly. Sometimes they bend over the long, strong stems that bear them. The flowers have wavy petals and open a rich, bronzy color, then fade to butterscotch and pale yellow, especially at the petal edges. However, the color is variable, and sometimes the flowers seem more yellow than golden. They stand up well to rain and also have a delicious scent, though some people say they can barely detect any scent at all. The leaves are large, dark green, dull, and healthy. The plant is fairly vigorous, upright, bushy, and occasionally somewhat lanky. Its first flowering is spectacular: subsequent flushes more modest.

'GOLDFINCH'

Hybrid Multiflora

ORIGIN **George Paul, Britain, 1907**
PARENTAGE **'Helene' x unknown**
FLOWER SIZE **1.4in (3.5cm)**
SCENT **Moderate and fruity**
FLOWERING **Once only, early in season**
HEIGHT/SPREAD **9.8ft (3m)/6.6ft (2m)**
HARDINESS **Zone 6**

'GOLDFINCH'

'Goldfinch' made quite an impact when it was first introduced as a "yellow rambler", but its color fades so quickly that its flowers are yellow only for a few hours. The buds are apricot colored and the flowers open rich yellow, before fading to white. They change color most quickly in hot, sunny weather. The flowers are abundantly borne in clusters of 15–25 and have rich yellow stamens. The bush is stout, vigorous, and thrifty: it survives neglect, and, though it may suffer from blackspot and mildew, fungal disease does not affect its flowering. The leaves are small, bright green, and shiny, and the stems are almost thornless. 'Goldfinch' can be grown as a short climber or a large, spreading bush.

'Goldilocks'

Floribunda

ORIGIN **Boerner, US, 1945**
PARENTAGE **seedling x 'Doubloons'**
FLOWER SIZE **2.8in (7cm)**
SCENT **Little or none**
FLOWERING **Repeats well**
HEIGHT/SPREAD **2.7ft (80cm)/2ft (60cm)**
HARDINESS **Zone 5**

When 'Goldilocks' first appeared, there was no Floribunda to match its yellow flowers. Boerner used it for many years to breed more roses, and it has remained popular since. It suffers, however, from the tendency of almost all yellow roses to fade as they age: the buds are deep golden yellow, but the flowers quickly pass to lemon yellow. The buds are like small Hybrid Teas, but open out very full of petals, with a muddled center. The flowers are globular at first, later cupped, then flat, and finally completely reflexed, when the petals take on a spiky shape like a cactus dahlia. 'Goldilocks' has dark leaves like a Wichurana, though its only declared parent, 'Doubloons', was a Setigera Hybrid.

Goldmarie 82

Goldmarie 82

syn. 'KORfalt'
Floribunda

ORIGIN **Kordes, Germany, 1984**
PARENTAGE **(['Arthur Bell' x Zorina] x ['Honigmond' x 'Dr. A.J. Verhage']) x (seedling x 'Friesia')**
FLOWER SIZE **3.1in (8cm)**
SCENT **Light, but distinct**
FLOWERING **Repeats well**
HEIGHT/SPREAD **3.3ft (1m)/3.3ft (1m)**
HARDINESS **Zone 5**
AWARDS **Golden Rose of the Hague 1986**

Goldmarie 82 – so-called to distinguish it from an earlier rose called simply 'Goldmarie' – is a fine, bold, shrub rose in the Floribunda style. It carries long-stemmed clusters (of 5–11 flowers) of lightly double, rich yellow gold flowers, fading eventually to mid-yellow with a hint of pink on their petal tips. The deep yellow color is particularly strong and long lasting. The flowers open out to a round outline and have distinctly wavy petals. They are well complemented by dark, lush, glossy leaves and dense, neat, bushy growth. In hot climates the plant will grow 4.9ft (1.5m) high and wide, but the flowers are larger, and the colours more intense, in cool climates.

'Goldilocks'

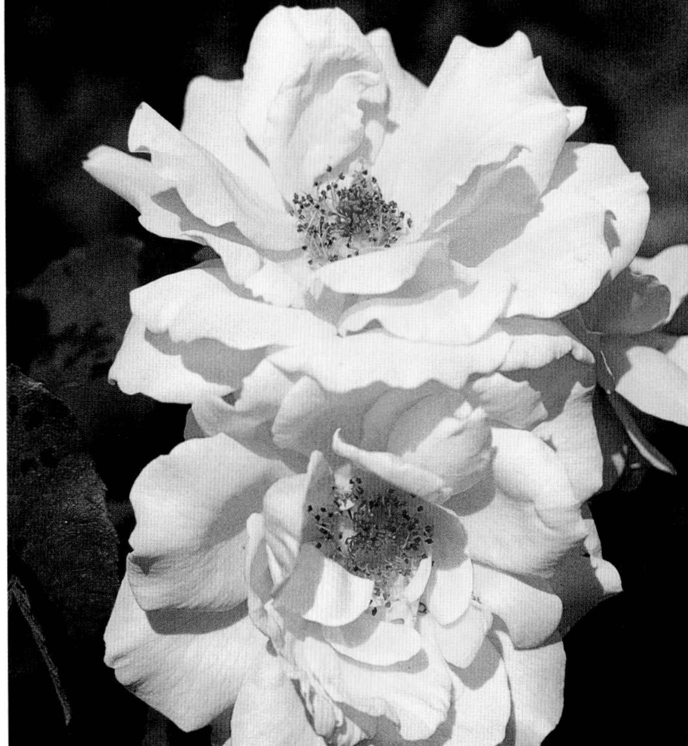

'Goldstern'

Goldsmith

see Helmut Schmidt

'Goldstern'

Kordesii Hybrid

ORIGIN **Tantau, Germany, 1966**
FLOWER SIZE **3.9in (10cm)**
SCENT **Strong, sweet, and fruity**
FLOWERING **Repeats**
HEIGHT/SPREAD **9.8ft (3m)/6.6ft (2m)**
HARDINESS **Zone 5**

The Tantau family rarely published the parentages of their roses, but 'Goldstern' is probably a Kordesii climber: it has the large, dark, shiny leaves and hardy demeanor of the race. Its flowers are large, full, and cupped, opening out to reveal their golden stamens. The petals are deep golden yellow, fading slightly to lemon yellow at the edges as they age. The flowers come singly or in small clusters (seldom of more than four) and stand up well to rain. They are carried in profusion in the first flowering, and then more intermittently until the first frosts of winter. 'Goldstern' is a short climber in hot areas and a sprawling shrub in cold ones – it is extremely hardy. The plant is vigorous and bushy. The leaves are said to be very healthy, but blackspot can be a problem.

Good as Gold

Good as Gold

syn. 'CHEWsunbeam'
Climbing Miniature

ORIGIN **Warner, Britain, 1994**
PARENTAGE **Anne Harkness x Laura Ford**
FLOWER SIZE **1.6in (4cm)**
SCENT **Light and fruity**
FLOWERING **Repeats constantly**
HEIGHT/SPREAD **8.2ft (2.5m)/6.6ft (2m)**
HARDINESS **Zone 6**
AWARDS **NZ GM 1996**

It is hard to fault this beautiful patio climber: Good as Gold is the most constant in flower of all. The flowers are not especially large, but they are well- shaped and a brilliant, clear, deep, sunny yellow, with slightly darker petal backs. They come in small clusters on long, slender stems (good for cutting) and, like all Warner's patio climbers, are carried all over the plant, from top to bottom. The plant is also clothed in small, dark, neat leaves right down to ground level, though Good as Gold is not without prickles. The plant is a slender, upright grower and very healthy. Its shortness, dense shape, and constant flowering make it a very useful rose for small gardens and confined spaces.

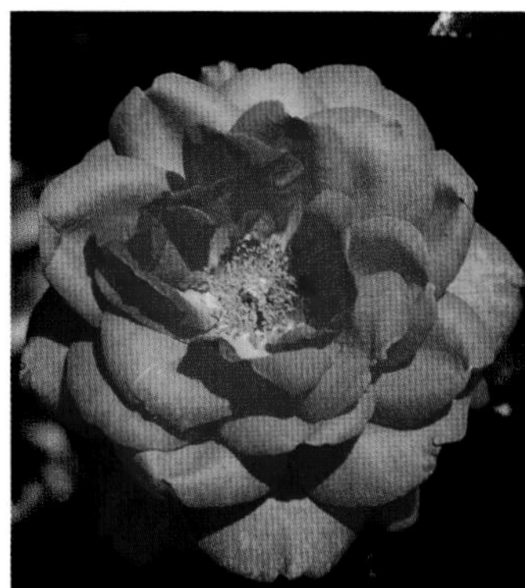
GORDON'S COLLEGE

GORDON'S COLLEGE

syn. 'COCJABBY', Braveheart
Floribunda

ORIGIN **Cocker, Britain, 1992**
PARENTAGE Abbeyfield Rose x Roddy McMillan
FLOWER SIZE **4.7in (12cm)**
SCENT **Strong, fruity, and sweet**
FLOWERING **Repeats well**
HEIGHT/SPREAD **4.9ft (1.5m)/3.3ft (1m)**
HARDINESS **Zone 6**

This excellent Floribunda owes part of its popularity to its second name, Braveheart, but stands on its own merit. Gordon's College is a beautiful, vigorous, free-flowering rose. The flowers are large, pink, and shaped like Hybrid Teas. They are borne singly or in long compound clusters of up to ten, their pinkness tinged with coral and salmon. Gordon's College makes a stout, upright plant with a good, bushy habit and a very large number of prickles. It has a lot of dark green, glossy leaves and is healthy, except for a little blackspot in autumn. The new growths are beet red and very beautiful. It is a very vigorous plant, which will grow to 6.6ft (2m) if left unpruned, even in its native Scotland, but can be pruned back to any height – almost to ground level if required, from which it grows back evenly and vigorously. It is also quick to repeat its flowering. Alec Cocker attended Robert Gordon's College in Aberdeen.

GOURMET POPCORN

see 'POPCORN'

GRAHAM THOMAS

syn. 'AUSMAS'
Shrub Rose

ORIGIN **Austin, Britain, 1983**
PARENTAGE **seedling x ('Charles Austin' x 'Schneewittchen' seedling)**
FLOWER SIZE **4.3in (11cm)**
SCENT **Strong, rich, and fruity**
FLOWERING **Repeats very well**
HEIGHT/SPREAD **5.7ft (1.75m)/5.7ft (1.75m)**
HARDINESS **Zone 5**

This is an iconic rose. Not only is it the biggest and best yellow of all David Austin's English Roses, but its name commemorates the man who did more than anyone in the 20th century to reintroduce old roses to popularity. The flowers of Graham Thomas are rich, bright, golden yellow, fading to lemon, especially in hot sunshine. Sometimes the flowers have hints of apricot or buff toward the center. They are cupped and full of irregularly arranged petals – but not overly full, because sometimes you can see the red filaments at the center. The flowers are sometimes borne singly, but usually in long-stemmed clusters of 3–9. They open out and drop their petals fairly quickly, so the flowers are short-lived and not much use as cut flowers. Graham Thomas has large leaves, bright mid-green or pale, which occasionally suffer from blackspot. The plant grows to 13.1–16.4ft (4–5m) in hot climates, but is difficult to train as a climber because it has a very upright habit and brittle stems, which snap off at the joints. It responds well to feeding and watering, especially in hot climates, by producing ever-larger flowers so frequently as to be perpetual flowering.

GRAHAM THOMAS

'GRANADA'

Hybrid Tea

ORIGIN **Lindquist, US, 1963**
PARENTAGE **'Tiffany' x 'Cavalcade'**
FLOWER SIZE **4.3in (11cm)**
SCENT **Strong and fruity**
FLOWERING **Repeats well**
HEIGHT/SPREAD **4.9ft (1.5m)/3.3ft (1m)**
HARDINESS **Zone 6**
AWARDS **AARS 1964; Gamble FA 1968**

'Granada' is an unusual rose with many outstanding qualities. Its large, shapely flowers usually come singly in the first flowering and in clusters in autumn. It is one of the first to flower in hot climates and an excellent cut flower. And its scent is stupendous. Its coloring is also unusual because it is so variable. The buds (very beautiful) are coral pink, but the flowers are orange, gold, pink, and yellow, varying from flower to flower and according to the weather. The swirling edges tend to be pink rather than yellow, and the colors are strongest in cool conditions, but the greatest variety of shades is seen when it is hot. 'Granada' is healthy (except for occasional mildew in autumn) and repeats very well, producing crop after crop of long-stemmed roses through until early winter. It cannot be beaten for massed plantings, but it rarely fits easily into the sort of garden that prizes coordinated color schemes.

'GRAND HOTEL'

syn. 'HOTEL ROYAL'
Modern Climber

BREEDER **McGredy, Northern Ireland, 1972**
FLOWER SIZE **3.9in (10cm)**
SCENT **Little or none**
FLOWERING **Repeats**
HEIGHT/SPREAD **16.4ft (5m)/9.8ft (3m)**
HARDINESS **Zone 6**
AWARDS **ADR 1977**

The flowers of 'Grand Hotel' are a rich dark red, with velvety crimson patches, almost black, toward the tips. There are even darker shadows in the spaces between the thick, tough petals. The flowers come singly or in clusters of up to five, on long, stiff stems, and last well. They are good for cutting and of elegant, conical, Hybrid Tea shape. Large red hips follow; if you want the plant to flower until late autumn, it is best to deadhead it. It has tough, dark, glossy leaves and grows with vigor, though it is quite lanky and stiff in its habit.

'GRANADA'

'GRAND HOTEL'

GRAND SIÈCLE

syn. 'DELEGRAN', Great Century
Hybrid Tea

ORIGIN **Delbard-Chabert, France, 1986**
PARENTAGE **(['Queen Elizabeth' x 'Provence'] x ['Michèle Meilland' x 'Bayadère']) x (['Vœux de Bonheur' x 'Grace de Monaco'] x ['Mme. A. Meilland' x 'Dr. Debat'])**
FLOWER SIZE **6.7in (17cm)**
SCENT **Medium and fruity**
FLOWERING **Repeats**
HEIGHT/SPREAD **4.1ft (1.25m)/3.3ft (1m)**
HARDINESS **Zone 6**

Size is everything with Grand Siècle: it is one of the largest flowered of all roses. If well fed and watered, and grown in cool, dry conditions, its flowers can reach 7.8in (20cm) across. They open from large, long buds and are rich pink at the center, fading to pale pink at the edges. In hot climates – hotter than the central uplands of France where Grand Siècle was bred – the flowers are paler, sometimes no more than pearl pink with creamy edges. When eventually they open out, they have rich, red stamens. Grand Siècle bears its flowers singly, on long, strong stems that are good for cutting and for exhibition. Later in the season, the flowers sometimes come in clusters of up to six. The plant has large, healthy, mid-green leaves, large prickles, thick stems, and a vigor to match the greatness of its flowers.

GRAND SIÈCLE

'GRAND'MÈRE JENNY'

'GRAND'MÈRE JENNY'

Hybrid Tea

ORIGIN **Meilland, France, 1950**
PARENTAGE **'Mme. A. Meilland' x ('Julien Potin' x 'Sensation')**
FLOWER SIZE **4.7in (12cm)**
SCENT **Medium and sweet**
FLOWERING **Repeats well**
HEIGHT/SPREAD **4.1ft (1.25m)/3.3ft (1m)**
HARDINESS **Zone 6**
AWARDS **NRS GM 1950; Rome GM 1955**

"A more refined version of Mme. A. Meilland ('Peace')" was one description of 'Grand'mère Jenny', when it was first introduced in France in 1950. It is a fair description because, although 'Grand'mère Jenny' has inherited the vigor, health, size, and beauty of its illustrious parent, it is a much more compact grower and especially suitable for small gardens. The flowers are rich golden yellow at first, with a hint of copper or orange toward the center, and a broad band of crimson at the edge of the petals. As they open up and age, the flowers fade to buff yellow and pink. The buds are large and shapely and the open flowers no less attractive. They come both singly and in clusters of up to about six, and are regularly repeated until late autumn. 'Grand'mère Jenny' is a good rose in almost all conditions: it performs well in hot climates and its flowers stand up well to rain. The large, dark, glossy leaves are a good complement to the flowers, but watch out for blackspot.

'GRANDPA DICKSON'

syn. 'IRISH GOLD'

Hybrid Tea

ORIGIN **Dickson, Northern Ireland, 1966**
PARENTAGE **('Kordes' Perfecta' x 'Governador Braga da Cruz') x 'Piccadilly'**
FLOWER SIZE **4.7in (12cm)**
SCENT **Light and fruity**
FLOWERING **Repeats well**
HEIGHT/SPREAD **4.1ft (1.25m)/3.3ft (1m)**
HARDINESS **Zone 6**
AWARDS **RNRS PIT 1965; Golden Rose of the Hague 1966; Belfast GM 1968; Portland GM 1970**

It is known in North America as 'Irish Gold', but the original Irish name of this rose is 'Grandpa Dickson'. It was named after Alexander Dickson (1893–1975), for many years head of the Dickson family of Ulster rose breeders. The flowers of 'Grandpa Dickson' are pale yellow – primrose yellow at the center and lemon yellow or cream at the edges, with a touch of pink on the buds and the backs of the outer petals. The flowers of 'Grandpa Dickson' are elegantly shaped both in the bud and as open flowers. They usually come in small clusters (typically of three flowers) on fairly long stems, which are held well above the dark, glossy leaves. 'Grandpa Dickson' is usually healthy, if somewhat susceptible to blackspot. However, it is not very vigorous, and this is especially the case if it is hard pruned over several years. It repeats well.

'GRANDPA DICKSON'

GREAT CENTURY

see GRAND SIÈCLE

'GREAT MAIDEN'S BLUSH'

syn. 'CUISSE DE NYMPHE EMUE'

Alba Rose

ORIGIN **Britain, c.1550**
FLOWER SIZE **2.4in (6cm)**
SCENT **Strong and sweet**
FLOWERING **Once only**
HEIGHT/SPREAD **5.7ft (1.75m)/11ft (3.4m)**
HARDINESS **Zone 5**

Historians cannot agree whether this beautiful rose is French, with the name of 'Cuisse de Nymphe Emue', or English (from Kew) in origin, in which case its name should more properly be 'Great Maiden's Blush'. It is an early Alba rose and one of the most beautiful. Its flowers are the palest rose pink at first but soon fading to white at the edges, with a pretty arrangement of its many petals and a strong, penetrating scent. The globular or deeply cupped flowers come in small clusters, seldom of more than five together, and are succeeded by long, orange hips. The plant is tall and slender, with few prickles and pale blue green leaves with gray undersides. It is tough, hardy, and adaptable. Sometimes it may fall prey to rust, but the plant is vigorous enough to shrug it off. If grown on its own roots, it suckers around mildly – a great asset.

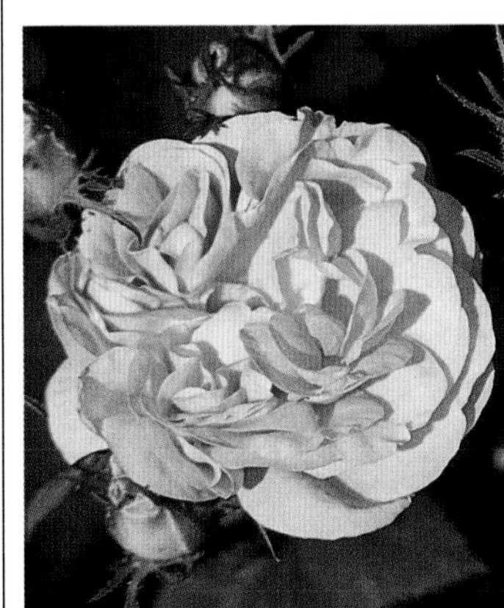

'GREAT MAIDEN'S BLUSH'

'GREAT WESTERN'

Hybrid Bourbon

ORIGIN **Laffay, France, 1840**
FLOWER SIZE **3.1in (8cm)**
SCENT **Strong and sweet**
FLOWERING **Once only**
HEIGHT/SPREAD **8.2ft (2.5m)/4.9ft (1.5m)**
HARDINESS **Zone 5**

The *Great Western* was a famous transatlantic mail boat, which held several speed records. The rose that Laffay chose to commemorate it is a pale purple crimson hybrid, which fades to mauve pink, starting at the edges. It is still widely available, despite being only once-flowering. The flowers open large, full, flat, and loosely quartered. They are occasionally borne singly, but usually in clusters of 3–7, and freely produced over a long season. Their scent is delicious – strong, sweet, and rich. The plant is sturdy, prickly, and tough: the stems bow down under the weight of the flowers. The dark leaves are sometimes susceptible to blackspot.

'GREEN ICE'

'GREEN ICE'

Miniature Rose

ORIGIN **Moore, US, 1971**
PARENTAGE **(*Rosa wichurana* x 'Floradora') x 'Jet Trail'**
FLOWER SIZE **1.6in (4cm)**
SCENT **Light and musky**
FLOWERING **Repeats well**
HEIGHT/SPREAD **2ft (60cm)/2.7ft (80cm)**
HARDINESS **Zone 6**

The buds of this pretty little miniature are pink, and the flower has pink outer petals at first. But as it ages, the flower turns to white and assumes a cold green tinge – hence its name 'Green Ice'. The effect is most pronounced when the plant is grown in partial shade. The flowers open flat and full of neat petals like an old-fashioned rose. They are arranged as a rosette, with a green pistil at their center, and sometimes a button eye. The flowers come in small clusters, typically of 3–7, and are well complemented by the dark, glossy, healthy leaves. 'Green Ice' is free flowering, with a lax, low, spreading habit of growth.

'GREAT WESTERN'

'GREENMANTLE'

'GREENMANTLE'

Rubginosa Hybrid

ORIGIN **Penzance, Britain, 1895**
PARENTAGE ***Rosa rubiginosa* x unknown**
FLOWER SIZE **1.2in (3cm)**
SCENT **Light and sweet**
FLOWERING **Once only**
HEIGHT/SPREAD **9.8ft (3m)/8.2ft (2.5m)**
HARDINESS **Zone 5**

It is hard to explain the popularity of the Penzance Briars. 'Greenmantle' is the result of an unexciting experiment in hybridization by a British Law Lord. The flowers are small and single, with a dark pink edge and a white center. They are produced in moderate quantities on a very vigorous, prickly bush and are followed by vermilion hips. The leaves are said to have a faint scent of sweetbriar. Greenmantle was a character in Sir Walter Scott's *Redgauntlet*.

GREENSLEEVES

syn. 'HARLENTEN'

Floribunda

ORIGIN **Harkness, Britain, 1980**
PARENTAGE **('Rudolph Timm' x 'Arthur Bell') x (['Pascali' x 'Elizabeth of Glamis'] x ['Sabine' x 'Violette Dot'])**
FLOWER SIZE **2.8in (7cm)**
SCENT **Little or none**
FLOWERING **Repeats well**
HEIGHT/SPREAD **4.1ft (1.25m)/2.5ft (75cm)**
HARDINESS **Zone 6**

GREENSLEEVES

There is only one reason to grow Greensleeves: its flowers turn pale green as they age and last a long time in cut-flower arrangements. Its buds are dark dusky pink, but the flowers open out parchment colored before fading to white and assuming their curious green shade. The stamens turn brown and the wavy petals take on an artificial appearance, like a thick paper rose, as if nature were imitating art. The flowers come in crowded clusters of up to 15, which are best cut while young and allowed to develop their green coloring in water. The plant is frankly ugly – stiff, prickly, and rigidly upright, with bright green leaves. But flower arrangers will forgive Greensleeves all its shortcomings for the fascinating potential in its extraordinary flowers.

GREETINGS

syn. 'JACDRECO'

Shrub Rose

ORIGIN **Zary, US, 1999**
PARENTAGE **Lavender Dream x Minnie Mouse**
FLOWER SIZE **2in (5cm)**
SCENT **Light and fruity**
FLOWERING **Repeats very well**
HEIGHT/SPREAD **4.9ft (1.5m)/6.6ft (2m)**
HARDINESS **Zone 6**
AWARDS **RNRS PIT 1997**

Sometimes a rose is much more successful abroad than in its own country. Greetings is a good example. It was bred in California but has not yet been introduced in the US.

'GREVILLEI'

GREETINGS

On the other hand, it won the top award of the Royal National Rose Society in England, where it has been widely distributed and sold. The flowers are a splendid purplish crimson, with paler petal backs (lavender pink) and a prominent white center, from which several white stripes run out into the petals. They are not large, and only semidouble, but they come in large clusters (typically of 5–25), which catch the eye from quite a distance. Greetings makes a thick, twiggy shrub, wider than high, with healthy, medium-dark, shiny leaves. It grows vigorously and quickly, and tolerates difficult growing conditions. It makes a fine, tall landscaping rose, but its distinctive, zany charm is even more effective in a garden setting.

'GREVILLEI'

syn. ROSA MULTIFLORA VAR. PLATYPHYLLA, 'SEVEN SISTERS'

Multiflora Rambler

ORIGIN **Britain, 1817**
FLOWER SIZE **1.2in (3cm)**
SCENT **Strong, sweet, and musky**
FLOWERING **Once only**
HEIGHT/SPREAD **13.1ft (4m)/8.2ft (2.5m)**
HARDINESS **Zone 6**

Several different roses circulate under the names of 'Grevillei' and 'Seven Sisters'. Botanists advise that they should all be regarded as forms of *Rosa multiflora* var. *platyphylla*. They are garden hybrids of *Rosa multiflora*, originally from China but also grown as seedlings in Europe. They get their 'Seven Sisters' name from the way the flowers change color: "white, light blush, deeper blush, light red, darker red, scarlet and purple," according to the English writer John Loudon in 1838. In fact, the flowers open dark pink – dark enough on occasions to appear as red or purple – and fade through pink to white. The flowers are borne in large clusters of 25–50. The plants are vigorous and healthy, except for a little mildew in situations where this is a problem. They have large leaves, with somewhat wrinkled leaflets, and can be rooted very easily from cuttings.

'GROOTENDORST SUPREME'

see 'F. J. GROOTENDORST'

'GROS CHOUX D'HOLLANDE'

Bourbon Rose

ORIGIN **Vibert, France, c.1840**
FLOWER SIZE **4.7in (12cm)**
SCENT **Medium and sweet**
FLOWERING **Once only**
HEIGHT/SPREAD **6.6ft (2m)/6.6ft (2m)**
HARDINESS **Zone 5**

There is some debate about whether 'Gros Choux d'Hollande' is a once-flowering Bourbon or a Centifolia hybrid. It is also possible that the rose we now grow under this name is not the same as the one that Vibert introduced. Nevertheless, it is a sumptuous pink cabbage rose with a rich scent and considerable vigor. The flowers open rich dark pink from fat, red buds. They fade gently to mid-pink and slightly paler pink at the edges. They are lightly cupped, sometimes with button eyes, and very full of petals. They have large, elongated calyces and short sepals, and come in clusters of 3–7. The plant has large leaves and leaflets, somwhat wrinkled and light green. The flowers are among the most beautiful of all old roses, but 'Gros Choux d'Hollande' does make an outsize shrub, large in all its parts.

'GROS CHOUX D'HOLLANDE'

'Gruss an Aachen'

Grouse

see Immensee

'Gruss an Aachen'

Floribunda

ORIGIN **Geduldig, Germany, 1909**
PARENTAGE **'Frau Karl Druschki' x 'Franz Deegen'**
FLOWER SIZE **3.1in (8cm)**
SCENT **Light and sweet**
FLOWERING **Repeats well**
HEIGHT/SPREAD **2.7ft (80cm)/2.7ft (80cm)**
HARDINESS **Zone 6**

Many people see 'Gruss an Aachen' as a forerunner of the Floribundas or the English Roses, but in some countries the rose grown under this name is actually a China rose called 'Irène Watts'. The true 'Gruss an Aachen' opens from orange buds into a full-petaled, rose pink flower, with darker apricot pink backs to the petals. The shadows that form between the petals reflect some of these darker colors and account for much of their beauty, especially when the outer petals fade to cream and white. The colors are strongest in cool climates and autumn weather. The petals usually form themselves into a rosette, occasionally with a button eye, but there are always plenty of them and together they combine to give the flower a substantial look. The flowers come singly or, more usually, in clusters of up to seven, on a compact, neat plant. The leaves are dark and healthy (watch out for blackspot late in the year) and the plant is reliably remontant. It is only moderately vigorous, and requires minimal pruning, but responds well to feeding and watering.

'Gruss an Coburg'

'Gruss an Heidelberg'

'Gruss an Coburg'

Hybrid Tea

ORIGIN **Felberg-Leclerc, 1927**
PARENTAGE **'Alice Kaempff' x 'Souvenir de Claudius Pernet'**
FLOWER SIZE **3.5in (9cm)**
SCENT **Strong, fruity, and tealike**
FLOWERING **Repeats well**
HEIGHT/SPREAD **3.3ft (1m)/3.3ft (1m)**
HARDINESS **Zone 6**

'Gruss an Coburg' is one of the few early Hybrid Teas that have remained popular ever since their original introduction. It is not hard to see why: 'Gruss an Coburg' has flowers of unique shape, color, and beauty. It is elegant at all stages from bud to fully open flower, and a very modern combination of colors. The petals are pale apricot, fading to dusky pink, but their backs are dark copper colored – setting up a dramatic and beautiful contrast. The petals lie flat and imbricated, but also reflex along their sides. The plant is a good grower, with deep bronze green leaves, occasionally touched by blackspot, but apparently immune to mildew.

'Gruss an Heidelberg'

syn. 'Heidelberg'

Kordesii Hybrid

ORIGIN **Kordes, Germany, 1959**
PARENTAGE **'Minna Kordes' x 'Floradora'**
FLOWER SIZE **3.9in (10cm)**
SCENT **Light and musky**
FLOWERING **Repeats well**
HEIGHT/SPREAD **9.8ft (3m)/6.6ft (2m)**
HARDINESS **Zone 5**

Wilhelm Kordes said that 'Gruss an Heidelberg' grew best as a shrub in cool climates, but it develops into a handsome climber in hot ones. The buds are long and elegant, opening out into bright crimson flowers, which hold their color well, fading only slightly as they age. The petal backs are paler. The flowers have muddled centers, full of petals, but open out enough to reveal small dark stamens. They are freely produced, singly and in clusters of up to ten, right through until late autumn. 'Gruss an Heidelberg' has dark, shiny leaves, which suggest an undeclared trace of Kordesii in its ancestry. It is a vigorous, upright grower, and fairly healthy except for a weakness for blackspot. It flowers freely and repeats well, especially in autumn.

'Gruss an Teplitz'

China Rose

ORIGIN **Geschwind, Hungary, 1897**
PARENTAGE **('Sir Joseph Paxton' x 'Fellenberg') x ('Papa Gontier' x 'Gloire des Rosomanes')**
FLOWER SIZE **2.4in (6cm)**
SCENT **Light and fruity**
FLOWERING **Continuous**
HEIGHT/SPREAD **6.6ft (2m)/4.9ft (1.5m)**
HARDINESS **Zone 5**

'Gruss an Teplitz'

No "old-fashioned" rose has such brilliant coloring as 'Gruss an Teplitz' – the flowers are bright scarlet crimson with white flecks on the inner petals. Nevertheless, when first introduced it was even more valued for its combination of floriferousness and hardiness. It was bred to flower continuously until late autumn and to survive the brutal winters of central Europe. The flowers are cupped, loosely double, and borne in clusters of 3–7. The leaves are thin and susceptible in some climates to blackspot and mildew, though neither affects the ability of 'Gruss an Teplitz' to go on growing and flowering without interruption. It is a most dependable and unfussy rose, which makes a lax shrub – all the better for a little staking – or a 6.6ft (2m) pillar, but there also exists a climbing form, which will grow to 13.1ft (4m).

'Gruss an Zabern'

Multiflora Rambler

ORIGIN **Lambert, Germany, 1903**
PARENTAGE **'Euphrosyne' x 'Mme. Ocker Ferencz'**
FLOWER SIZE **1.2in (3cm)**
SCENT **Strong, sweet, and spicy**
FLOWERING **Once, very early in season**
HEIGHT/SPREAD **13.1ft (4m)/6.6ft (2m)**
HARDINESS **Zone 5**

'Gruss an Zabern' is one of the best Multiflora ramblers – certainly the first to flower and one of the most free flowering. Its early flowering means that it makes a vivid impression long before other roses have started to bloom. It remains in flower for an unusually long time, but does not repeat. The cheerful, highly scented flowers are pure white (with just a hint of cream as they open) and come in thick, flat clusters of 20–60. The plant is very prickly but healthy, vigorous, remarkably hardy, and resistant to late frost damage. The rose breeder Ludwig Walter summed up its qualities in 1918: "this is the first to flower, the most beautiful, and the most free flowering of the white ramblers." It is still widely available today, and deservedly so. The name is a salutation to the town of Zabern, now Saverne in Alsace.

'Gruss an Zabern'

'GUINÉE'

Modern Climber

ORIGIN **Mallerin, France, 1938**
PARENTAGE **'Souvenir de Claudius Denoyel' x 'Ami Quinard'**
FLOWER SIZE **3.5in (9cm)**
SCENT **Strong and sweet**
FLOWERING **Once generously, thereafter stingily**
HEIGHT/SPREAD **11.5ft (3.5m)/8.2ft (2.5m)**
HARDINESS **Zone 6**

The market for deep crimson roses is insatiable, and 'Guinée' has enjoyed many years of popularity as a strongly scented climber with flowers like a Hybrid Tea. The crimson is especially dark when the flowers are in bud, when yet darker, velvety patches appear toward the petal tips. The inner petals are often paler, no more than dark scarlet, but 'Guinée' does require careful placing because the overall color is so dark and recessive that it needs a pale background to show it up; it is unbeatable when planted against a whitewashed wall. That said, it has its shortcomings, including a weakness for blackspot and a gawky, prickly habit. The flowers are only medium-sized, and their production after the main flowering hovers between stingy and miserly. They come singly or in clusters of up to five, and are attractive when picked for the house. They mix well with gray leaves in flower arrangements.

GUIRLANDE D'AMOUR

syn. 'LENALBI'

Multiflora Rambler

ORIGIN **Lens, Belgium, 1993**
FLOWER SIZE **1.2in (3cm)**
SCENT **Strong and musky**
FLOWERING **Repeats in autumn**
HEIGHT/SPREAD **9.8ft (3m)/8.2ft (2.5m)**
HARDINESS **Zone 5**
AWARDS **Madrid 1994**

'GUINÉE' *(at L'Haÿ-les-Roses)*

Guirlande d'Amour is a modern rose with a distinctly historic look: it has quickly become popular in northern Europe, whether as a vigorous bush or as a bushy climber. The semidouble flowers are pure white, with distinctly irregular petals: they vary in their shape and in the direction in which they develop, but they all have an unusual roll, which makes the flowers quite unmistakeable. It is very floriferous, producing large, long clusters of up to 80, which cover the whole plant from ground level up to its highest point. Unlike most of the old Multiflora and Wichurana ramblers, it repeats well.

GUY DE MAUPASSANT

syn. 'MEIsocrat'

Shrub Rose

ORIGIN **Meilland, France, 1994**
PARENTAGE **(Anne de Bretagne x 'Mrs. John Laing') x 'Egeskov'**
FLOWER SIZE **3.1in (8cm)**
SCENT **Strong and fruity**
FLOWERING **Repeats**
HEIGHT/SPREAD **6.6ft (2m)/4.1ft (1.25m)**
HARDINESS **Zone 6**

GUY DE MAUPASSANT

Guy de Maupassant (named for the writer, 1850–93) is a very strongly scented Floribunda rose in the old-fashioned style. The flowers have a swirling mass of innumerable small petals, some of them quilled, within a circle of guard petals. The petals are dark pink with pale pink reverses, but broad and short, so that the effect is of cupped flowers, sometimes roughly quartered. The flowers are borne singly or, more usually, in clusters of up to five. The plant has healthy, mid-green, glossy leaves, and flowers in a series of flushes. It can be trained as a short climber, but it is more often grown as a bush and sometimes pruned to less than 3.3ft (1m).

'GWEN NASH'

Modern Climber

ORIGIN **Clark, Australia, 1920**
PARENTAGE **'Rosy Morn' x unknown**
FLOWER SIZE **3.9in (10cm)**
SCENT **Slight**
FLOWERING **Recurrent**
HEIGHT/SPREAD **13.1ft (4m)/9.8ft (3m)**
HARDINESS **Zone 6**

'Gwen Nash' has medium-large, lightly scented, elegantly semidouble flowers. They open mother-of-pearl, with occasional white stripes and a white

'GWEN NASH'

center, and fade to palest rose. The petals reflex along their sides to create an effect that is very characteristic. The flowers have a big, airy boss of stamens, though this is sometimes obscured by petaloid stamens, and are borne in clusters of 3–6 on long stems. The plant is moderately thorny and has slightly wrinkled leaves. It is floriferous and repeats well. It was described by a writer in the *American Rose Annual* in 1931 as "the most beautiful rose I ever saw; the sheer beauty of a plant in full bloom is enough to take one's breath away."

GWENT

syn. 'POULurt', Aspen

Ground Cover

ORIGIN **Olesen, Denmark, 1992**
FLOWER SIZE **1.2in (3cm)**
SCENT **Little or none**
FLOWERING **Repeats well**
HEIGHT/SPREAD **1.6ft (50cm)/3.3ft (1m)**
HARDINESS **Zone 6**

Gwent is one of those low, lax-growing shrub roses that are wider than they are tall. Its flowers open semidouble, lightly cupped, and rich, buttercup yellow, before fading to lemon. The petals have a distinctive (and attractive) ruffle, and surround a cluster of golden stamens. The flowers are not large, but come in large clusters of 5–20, which make a considerable impact. The leaves are small, dark, and glossy (*Rosa wichurana* is not far back in its ancestry) but sometimes susceptible to blackspot. Gwent is a quick and good repeater, and small enough to be an effective plant in containers.

'GIPSY CARNIVAL'

see 'KIBOH'

GWENT

GUIRLANDE D'AMOUR *(at André Eve's garden, Pithiviers, France)*

H

H. C. Andersen

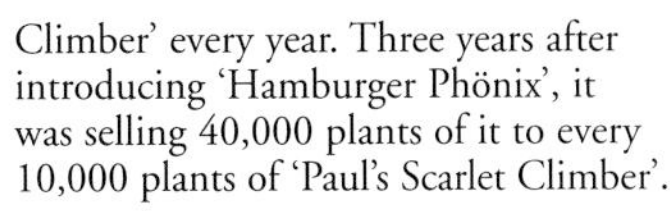

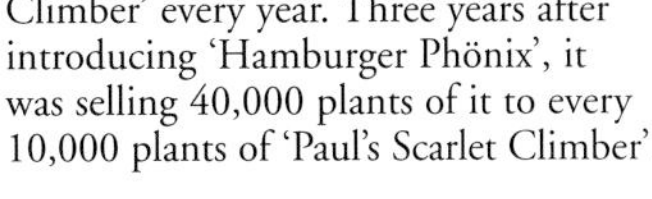

'Hamburger Phönix'

H. C. Andersen

syn. 'POULander', America's Choice

Floribunda

ORIGIN **Olesen, Denmark, 1986**
PARENTAGE **'Montana' x seedling**
FLOWER SIZE **3.1in (8cm)**
SCENT **Light**
FLOWERING **Repeats constantly**
HEIGHT/SPREAD **2.5ft (75cm)/2.5ft (75cm)**
HARDINESS **Zone 5**

H. C. Andersen is a short Floribunda or large-flowered minature, named after the Danish writer of fairytales. The flowers open bright scarlet or blood red, and keep their color well, before eventually they fade to a duller red. They are lightly double, with ruffled petals and pale stamens at the center. They come in clusters of 5–11 and are very freely borne. The plant has healthy, dark green leaves, bronzy at first. In Denmark, where it was bred, it is usually a short (even dumpy) but sturdy grower, but it will reach 4.9ft (1.5m) if grown in a hot climate and left unpruned.

Hacienda

syn. 'ORAdel'

Hybrid Tea

ORIGIN **Orard, France, 2000**
PARENTAGE **seedling x Michel Hidalgo**
FLOWER SIZE **4.3in (11cm)**
SCENT **Very strong, rich, fruity, and sweet**
FLOWERING **Repeats well**
HEIGHT/SPREAD **5.7ft (1.75m)/3.3ft (1m)**
HARDINESS **Zone 6**
AWARDS **Bagatelle FA 1998; Geneva FA 1998; Madrid FA 1998; Monza FA 1998; Rome GM & FA 1998; Saverne FA 1998**

This recent introduction has won many prizes in Europe for its superb scent. It also produces fine roses – large, shapely, crimson Hybrid Teas. In South Africa, its name is Red 'n Fragrant – which says it all. Hacienda has handsome buds that open out eventually to rather an irregular shape with wavy-edged petals. They lose some of their crimson glow as they age, but preserve it when cut for the house: the flowers usually come singly on long stems, which make them especially good for cutting. Hacienda makes a rugged, vigorous, healthy plant with dark green, semiglossy leaves. It repeats quickly and abundantly, so that the bush is rarely out of flower.

'Hakuun'

syn. 'White Cloud'

Patio Rose

ORIGIN **Poulsen, Denmark, 1962**
PARENTAGE **seedling x 'Rosenmärchen'**
FLOWER SIZE **3.1in (8cm)**
SCENT **Light and musky**
FLOWERING **Repeats very well**
HEIGHT/SPREAD **2.5ft (75cm)/2ft (60cm)**
HARDINESS **Zone 6**

You cannot go wrong with 'Hakuun' at the front of a border. It is short, floriferous and combines with any color scheme. The flowers are lightly double and open palest yellow before fading quickly to buff, cream, and white. The backs of the petals are always slightly darker, though they too fade to creamy white. The flowers come in clusters of 3–10, sometimes more. The bush is especially free flowering in its first burst of bloom, but it is never out of flower thereafter until late autumn. The plant is vigorous, short and spreading in habit, with mid-green leaves. It also grows well and flowers heavily under glass.

'Hamburger Phoenix'

Kordesii Hybrid

ORIGIN **Kordes, Germany, 1954**
PARENTAGE **'Kordesii' x seedling**
FLOWER SIZE **3.1in (8cm)**
SCENT **Light and sweet**
FLOWERING **Repeats well**
HEIGHT/SPREAD **9.8ft (3m)/6.6ft (2m)**
HARDINESS **Zone 5**

This splendid repeat-flowering climber was the first Kordesii Hybrid. Its name commemorates the city of Hamburg's extraordinary rise from the ashes of World War II. The flowers open from bronzy black buds. They are semidouble and dark, unfading blood red in color, with a small patch of white at the base of the petals. They are profusely carried in loose, open clusters of 3–15 and followed in due course by large orange hips. The shrub has healthy, glossy, dark green foliage, and repeats well, especially if the earlier flowers are deadheaded. The plant soon became one of Wilhelm Kordes bestsellers. In the early 1950s, Kordes had been selling 30,000–50,000 plants of 'Paul's Scarlet Climber' every year. Three years after introducing 'Hamburger Phönix', it was selling 40,000 plants of it to every 10,000 plants of 'Paul's Scarlet Climber'.

Handel

Modern Climber

ORIGIN **McGredy, Northern Ireland, 1965**
PARENTAGE **'Columbine' x 'Gruss an Heidelberg'**
FLOWER SIZE **3.5in (9cm)**
SCENT **Medium and sweet**
FLOWERING **Repeats constantly**
HEIGHT/SPREAD **9.8ft (3m)/6.6ft (2m)**
HARDINESS **Zone 6**
AWARDS **Portland GM 1975**

Handel created a sensation when it came out. It was the first repeat-flowering climber to have the distinctive dark pink edging of 'Mme. A. Meilland', and it heralded a new interest in raising short climbing roses for small gardens. Its flowers are creamy white at first, with a pale golden flush at the center of the flower and a pale crimson band all around the edge of the petals. The elegantly ruffled petals give an extra bounce to the flower as a whole. The flowers come in long-stemmed clusters of 3–9 and are good for cutting. They open from long, slender buds and are at their best half open. They then change and develop according to the weather: in cool climates the colors fade; in hot climates the color intensifies and seeps into the pale parts of the flower, so that the contrast is lost. In wet weather the flowers crumple. The plant has dark, glossy leaves and may attract a little blackspot. It grows slowly, though an established plant throws up new growth from ground level almost continuously.

Hacienda

'Hakuun'

Handel

'HANNAH GORDON'

'HANNAH GORDON'

syn. 'KORWEISO'

Floribunda

ORIGIN **Kordes, Germany, 1983**
PARENTAGE **seedling x Bordure Rose**
FLOWER SIZE **3.9in (10cm)**
SCENT **Light or slight**
FLOWERING **Repeats well**
HEIGHT/SPREAD **3.9ft (1.2m)/3.3ft (1m)**
HARDINESS **Zone 5**

'Hannah Gordon' is a free flowering Floribunda in a striking combination of red and white. The flowers have a distinct edging of rich cherry around a white center. That edging is usually thick and heavily pronounced, but may on occasions be more delicate – especially in hot weather. The flowers have the shape of a perfect Hybrid Tea at first, but develop a distinct wave to their petals when they open out. They are borne singly or in clusters of up to nine. The leaves are dark and glossy, bronzed at first, then green – a good foil for the flowers. The bush is upright and fairly healthy. It was named after the Scottish actress Hannah Gordon (b.1941).

'HANSA'

Rugosa Hybrid

ORIGIN **Schaum & Van Tol, 1905**
FLOWER SIZE **3.9in (10cm)**
SCENT **Strong and sweet**
FLOWERING **Repeats well**
HEIGHT/SPREAD **6.6ft (2m)/4.9ft (1.5m)**
HARDINESS **Zone 4**

This is one of the best Rugosa hybrids, which means it is one of the best of all garden roses. 'Hansa' has all the qualities one could ever ask for, except for elegance and thornlessness: the flowers have a loose and crumpled look that is far from classic, and the prickles are ferocious. The buds are long and elegant, and open into muddled, semi-double masses of silky magenta around a thick cluster of golden stamens. They come in small clusters (of 3–5 flowers) and all are followed by large vermilion hips like small tomatoes. The plant has healthy, pale green, crinkled leaves, and grows very vigorously. It is one of the first and last to flower, and continues in flower all through the summer. It is a leafy grower, and seems immune to disease. It makes a big shrub, and suckers around energetically if grown on its own roots. It is good for hedging, but also deserves a prominent position in the garden, provided its size is not too great.

'HAPPY'

see 'ALBERICH'

HAPPY CHILD

syn. 'AUSCOMP'

Shrub Rose

ORIGIN **Austin, Britain, 1993**
PARENTAGE **'Schneewittchen' x (seedling x Hero)**
FLOWER SIZE **3.1in (8cm)**
SCENT **Strong and tealike**
FLOWERING **Repeats quite well**
HEIGHT/SPREAD **3.3ft (1m)/3.3ft (1m)**
HARDINESS **Zone 5**

The flowers of Happy Child are an unusually bright dark yellow at first, but fade quickly to lemon, cream, and white. They open into lightly cupped rosettes of variously shaped petals, sometimes with a button eye. The petals reflex somewhat more than most David Austin roses, giving it quite a modern appearance. This is enhanced by the very glossy, dark leaves, like a modern Floribunda's. The flowers come in small clusters (typically of 3–5) on a bushy plant which has a sprinkling of prickles. Although sometimes a little slow to establish, Happy Child eventually makes a handsome plant with a slightly lax habit of growth. It repeats well, but suffers occasionally from blackspot.

'HARISON'S YELLOW'

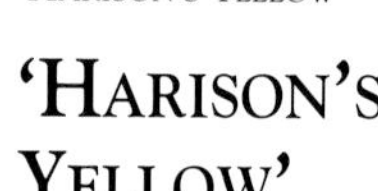

'HARISON'S YELLOW'

syn. Rosa x *harisonii*

Foetida Hybrid (probably)

ORIGIN **Harison, US, 1830**
FLOWER SIZE **2.4in (6cm)**
SCENT **Medium and fruity**
FLOWERING **Once, early in season**
HEIGHT/SPREAD **5.7ft (1.75m)/5.7ft (1.75m)**
HARDINESS **Zone 4**

Known as the "yellow rose of Texas," this rose was in fact introduced from a garden in New York City, belonging to a Mr. George Harison. Its exact parentage is uncertain. It has the very prickly stems, small, gray green leaves, and handsome black hips of *Rosa spinosissima*, but probably owes its flower color to *Rosa foetida*. The flowers are a rich, clear yellow, slightly paler at the petal edges, but matched by stamens of exactly the same bright hue. They are cupped in shape, but only lightly, so that it is easy to look into the flowers. 'Harison's Yellow' is extremely adaptable and easy to grow. It thrives in poor soil or rich, dry climates or wet, hot areas or cold: within the US it grows well from Texas to Alaska. It attracts blackspot, but grows and flowers unabashed. It makes a dense shrub at first, but later throws up long, open, arching stems. If only it flowered more than once a year...

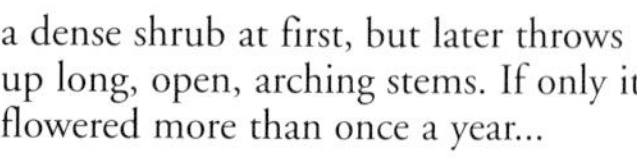

HARLEKIN

syn. 'KORLUPO', Arlequin, Kiss of Desire

Modern Climber

ORIGIN **Kordes, Germany, 1986**
FLOWER SIZE **3.9in (10cm)**
SCENT **Light and sweet**
FLOWERING **Repeats constantly**
HEIGHT/SPREAD **9.8ft (3m)/6.6ft (2m)**
HARDINESS **Zone 6**

The three leading bicolored modern climbers are Harlekin, Antike 89, and 'Handel'. Many would agree that Harlekin is the best of the three. Its flowers are deeply tinged with bright crimson, on a creamy white or pale pink ground, and it keeps those colors right through until the petals drop. The large, cupped flowers come singly and in clusters of up to five, and are very freely borne. They are very full of petals and tend to nod their heads slightly – an attractive characteristic in a climbing rose. Harlekin makes a bushy climber with very handsome, dark green, healthy, glossy foliage. It is a quick repeater, rarely out of flower.

'HANSA'

HAPPY CHILD

HARLEKIN

Harmonie

Harmonie

syn. 'KORtember'

Hybrid Tea

ORIGIN **Kordes, Germany, 1981**
PARENTAGE **'Duftwolke' x 'Uwe Seeler'**
FLOWER SIZE **4.7in (12cm)**
SCENT **Strong and sweet**
FLOWERING **Repeats well**
HEIGHT/SPREAD **4.9ft (1.5m)/3.3ft (1m)**
HARDINESS **Zone 6**
AWARDS **Baden-Baden GM 1981**

You would expect a 'Duftwolke' seedling to have a stupendous scent, and Harmonie is no exception. This tall, vigorous Hybrid Tea has wonderfully elegant and strongly scented flowers. The large petals unfurl from long buds into classically shaped flowers that keep their symmetry as they open out. They are salmon pink overall, but on close examination the petal backs are slightly darker and there is somewhat more yellow toward the center when the flowers open out fully. They come singly and in small clusters on long, strong stems and are good for cutting. Harmonie makes a strong, vigorous plant with large, handsome, healthy, dark green leaves. It is a reliable repeat flowerer: its autumn flowers are exceptionally large and richly colored.

'Harry Wheatcroft'

see 'Piccadilly'

Harvest Fayre

syn. 'DICnorth'

Floribunda

ORIGIN **Dickson, Northern Ireland, 1989**
PARENTAGE **seedling x Bright Smile**
FLOWER SIZE **3.1in (8cm)**
SCENT **Light and fruity**
FLOWERING **Repeats well**
HEIGHT/SPREAD **3.3ft (1m)/2.7ft (80cm)**
HARDINESS **Zone 6**
AWARDS **ROTY 1990**

Harvest Fayre

Although the British rose trade chose Harvest Fayre as their Rose of the Year in 1990, it remains little known outside England. This is a shame, because Harvest Fayre is a good rose and its flowers glow with color. They are a deep, bright yellow, with apricot backs to the petals, and they keep their colors well. The flowers are borne in great profusion, occasionally singly but more usually in spacious clusters of up to about ten flowers. Harvest Fayre has a somewhat upright habit of growth and healthy, glossy, pale green leaves. It starts into flower a little later than most roses, but then continues until late autumn. The brilliance of its flowers catches your eye from far away.

Harkness Roses

THE ENGLISH COMPANY THAT INTRODUCED THE FAMOUS 'ENA HARKNESS' IN THE 1950s IS STILL AT THE FOREFRONT OF THE MARKET TODAY

The rose company of R. Harkness & Co. has a dominant position in the British market and a worldwide reputation because of the roses bred by Jack Harkness (1918–1994).

Jack Harkness

There were other introductions before that time, starting with a pale pink sport of 'Heinrich Schultheis' which the Harkness family introduced as 'Mrs. Harkness' in 1893. They were also responsible for introducing two important mid-20th century roses bred by an amateur called Albert Norman – 'Frensham' and 'Ena Harkness'. During the 1950s, 'Ena Harkness' was the world's favorite crimson Hybrid Tea, and so the family name became well-known.

Jack Harkness started raising roses in 1962. He was an intellectual among rose breeders and had studied the history of roses in depth. He wanted to breed healthier roses, and to employ new genes from species which had not yet found their way into the hybridizers' palette. Working with species takes time to deliver results: Harkness's early successes were all Hybrid Teas like 'Alexander' (1972), or Hybrid Tea type climbers like 'Compassion' (1972).

These were followed by Floribundas with large, Hybrid Tea-shaped flowers: good examples are Margaret Merril (1977), Amber Queen (1983), and Bill Slim (1987).

When the work that Jack Harkness had done with new species began to bear fruit, he was able to introduce some remarkable advances, starting with the purple Polyantha (classed as a Floribunda) 'Yesterday' (1974). This was followed by the Spinosissima hybrid Anna Zinkeisen (1982), the Californica hybrid Cardinal Hume (1984) and the Hultheimia hybrids like Euphrates (1986).

Harkness has continued to breed and issue new roses since Jack Harkness's death in 1994. It remains to be seen, however, whether roses like Bridge of Sighs (2000) will enjoy the popularity and renown of their predecessors years earlier.

Bill Slim

L'HAŸ-LES-ROSES

THE ROSERAIE DU VAL-DE-MARNE AT L'HAŸ-LES-ROSES IS THE MOST FAMOUS ROSE GARDEN IN FRANCE

THE ROSE GARDEN at L'Haÿ in the southern suburbs of Paris was laid out in 1899 for Monsieur Jules Gravereaux. He was a rich businessman who cofounded the chain of Bon Marché department stores. The designer was the prestigious landscape architect Edouard André. By 1914, the garden was famous enough for President Poincaré to allow the commune of L'Haÿ to rename itself L'Haÿ-les-Roses. Following a reorganization of local government in Paris, the garden is now known as the Roseraie du Val-de-Marne.

'HARRY KIRK'

Gravereaux's rose garden was the first to be built with the express intention of growing every rose in the world. In its glory days before World War I, the garden could boast some 7,000 different rose cultivars. These days its 4.2 acres (1.7 hectares) supports about 16,000 roses, made up of some 200 species and 3,000 cultivars. Eighty-five percent of them date back to before 1950.

The garden at L'Haÿ-les-Roses was also the first to be made on such a scale with roses as the only ornamental plants. It was a revolutionary idea at the time to suggest that roses alone could successfully be used to make a garden. There are roses in beds and massed plantings; roses grafted as low standards, and magnificent tall weepers; Hybrid Perpetuals tied nearly horizontally along low ropes; rambling roses tumbling over trellises, pylons, and archways.

The design of the garden is tightly geometric. Long tunnels draped with climbers give an extraordinary illusion of size. Cross-paths and box-edged beds conceal tiny, densely planted, collections of old roses – Gallicas, Damasks, Moss roses, and so on. A sheltered wall protects the tender Tea roses. Wild rose species have their own place and yet are integrated into the layout. The central pool is surrounded by mass plantings of colorful modern roses. The famous trellis above the rose theater is hung with 'Alexandre Girault'.

The Roseraie du Val-de-Marne at l'Haÿ-les-Roses appeals at every level. Students of old roses are drawn by the biggest and best collection in France. The fine assembly of modern roses is displayed in unconventional ways to show them to advantage. To lovers of beauty with no pretensions to horticultural knowledge, the Roseraie is a place of intense and romantic beauty. And the sheer panache and style of its design are unmistakably French.

THE ROSERAIE DU VAL-DE-MARNE AT L'HAŸ-LES-ROSES

'HAWKEYE BELLE'

'HAWKEYE BELLE'

Shrub Rose

ORIGIN **Buck, US, 1975**
PARENTAGE **('Queen Elizabeth' x 'Pizzicato') x 'Prairie Princess'**
FLOWER SIZE **3.9in (10cm)**
SCENT **Strong and sweet**
FLOWERING **Repeats well**
HEIGHT/SPREAD **4.9ft (1.5m)/4.1ft (1.25m)**
HARDINESS **Zone 5**

The flowers of 'Hawkeye Belle' are beautifully shaped like a Hybrid Tea rose – creamy white at the edges and a rich pink at the center. Yet this is a shrub that was bred for hardiness, with shape and color as secondary considerations. The flowers are high-centered at first, their petals arranged in a concentric swirl. They are borne singly and in clusters of up to about seven (typically 3–5) on long stems, which make them good as cut flowers. The individual flowers last a long time, both in water and on the bush. 'Hawkeye Belle' is a thick, bushy, vigorous shrub and repeats its flowering right through until the first frost. It has quite a covering of prickles and a lot of large, medium-dark leaves, bronzy when young.

HEATHER AUSTIN

syn. 'AUSCOOK'

Shrub Rose

ORIGIN **Austin, Britain, 1997**
FLOWER SIZE **2.8in (7cm)**
SCENT **Medium, sweet, and spicy**
FLOWERING **Repeats**
HEIGHT/SPREAD **6.6ft (2m)/5.7ft (1.75m)**
HARDINESS **Zone 6**

The flowers of Heather Austin – named after one of David Austin's sisters – are unusually globular. Indeed, they are so rounded and enclosed that they rarely open out fully, which may explain why it has not become as popular as most of his English Roses. The flowers are very full of mid-pink petals, ringed in imbricated circles like tiling on a dome. The petal backs (which are all that you generally see) are slightly darker pink, and, if you lift up the drooping stems and push open the mouth of the flower, you will see that they also have golden stamens. The flowers come singly and in clusters of up to five, and the plant repeats later in the year. Heather Austin is a vigorous grower, quickly reaching

HEATHER AUSTIN

6.6ft (2m), even in the cool climate of its native England. Its stems are extremely prickly and its leaves are mid-green, matte, and fairly healthy.

HEIDEKÖNIGIN

HEAVENLY ROSALIND

syn. 'AUSMASH'

Shrub Rose

ORIGIN **Austin, Britain, 1995**
PARENTAGE **'Shropshire Lad' x Heritage**
FLOWER SIZE **2.8in (7cm)**
SCENT **Medium and sweet**
FLOWERING **Repeats**
HEIGHT/SPREAD **6.6ft (2m)/6.6ft (2m)**
HARDINESS **Zone 5**

Not all of David Austin's roses have many-petaled, old-fashioned shapes: Heavenly Rosalind is a sweet and simple flower. The five-petaled flowers are creamy white, fading to pure white, with a pink edging and pinker petal reverses – the whole effect is set off by a crown of crimson stamens at the center. In fact, Heavenly Rosalind resembles a wild rose, though the flowers are, of course, much bigger than those of most species. The flowers come in clusters of 3–10 and are followed by orange hips. The plant has medium-sized, mid-green leaves and a scattering of prickles. It is healthy, except for some brushes with blackspot in autumn. Heavenly Rosalind looks best in large gardens and semi-wild plantings.

'HEBE'S LIP'

see 'RUBROTINCTA'

HECTOR BERLIOZ

syn. 'HARZELT'

Hybrid Tea

ORIGIN **Harkness, Britain, 1998**
PARENTAGE **seedling x Dr. Darley**
FLOWER SIZE **5.1in (13cm)**
SCENT **Light and sweet**
FLOWERING **Repeats**
HEIGHT/SPREAD **4.9ft (1.5m)/3.3ft (1m)**
HARDINESS **Zone 6**

Sometimes a rose is released not in its country of origin but in another part of the world, where it has fared especially well in public and private trials. Hector Berlioz is a case in point: Harkness's agents in France were so impressed by its performance that it is now widely grown throughout that country, but not at all in England. The flowers are large, shapely, and scarlet, with a classic Hybrid Tea elegance as they open and long petals that catch the eye from a great distance. They are borne usually singly (just occasionally in twos or threes) on long, strong stems, which make them useful for cutting and, in particular, for large arrangements. It is an excellent garden rose, especially in warm climates, and should certainly be grown in Mediterranean conditions around the world. The plant has large, healthy, medium-dark leaves and an angular, branching habit. Hector Berlioz grows vigorously and repeats well.

HEIDEKÖNIGIN

syn. 'KORDAPT', Pheasant

Wichurana Rambler

ORIGIN **Kordes, Germany, 1985**
PARENTAGE **Zwergkönig '78 x *Rosa wichurana* seedling**
FLOWER SIZE **2.4in (6cm)**
SCENT **Light and musky**
FLOWERING **Once only, late in season**
HEIGHT/SPREAD **11.5ft (3.5m)/6.6ft (2m)**
HARDINESS **Zone 6**

Heidekönigin was introduced as a groundcover rose, and some years passed before people realized that it grew even better as a climbing rose. Its flowers open a slightly coral pink color, before changing to mid-pink and rose pink, but their petals are very prettily arranged in a frilly mound that gives them both style and substance. This is enhanced by their round outline. They come in the long, loose, open clusters typical of Wichurana ramblers, each with 10–30 flowers, and arch out gracefully as they develop. The leaves are dark, small, evergreen, and healthy. The plant has very flexible stems, which means you can train it to do almost anything, and it covers itself with an immense profusion of flowers at a time when most roses have finished their main flowering. Although it is supposed to be once-flowering, there are a few flowers later in the season.

'HEIDELBERG'

see 'GRUSS AN HEIDELBERG'

HEIDESOMMER

syn. 'KORLIRUS', Cévennes

Ground Cover

ORIGIN **Kordes, Germany, 1985**
PARENTAGE **'The Fairy' x seedling**
FLOWER SIZE **2.4in (6cm)**
SCENT **Very strong and sweet**
FLOWERING **Continuous**
HEIGHT/SPREAD **2.7ft (80cm)/3.3ft (1m)**
HARDINESS **Zone 5**

Groundcover shrub roses have proliferated over the last 20 years, and none is so sweetly scented as Heidesommer. It has a rich, powerful fragrance which catches you from a long distance away. Bees love it, too. Heidesommer has handsome, weather resistant flowers – cream fading quickly to pure white and opening from pale buff buds. The petals retain a creamy tinge on their backs. They are loosely semidouble, with a circle of dark yellow stamens at the center, and very prolifically borne in clusters of 5–25. Heidesommer starts into flower late, but remains in flower almost constantly thereafter. The clusters cut well for the house. The bush has a lax habit and a mass of beautiful, small, dark, shiny, healthy Wichurana leaves. It is an excellent plant for the front of a border, quite beyond its use as a groundcover and landscaping rose. It can also be used to lighten a dark corner.

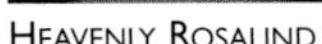
HEAVENLY ROSALIND

HECTOR BERLIOZ

HEIDESOMMER

'HEINRICH MÜNCH'

'HEINRICH MÜNCH'

Hybrid Tea

ORIGIN **Hinner, Germany, 1911**
PARENTAGE **'Frau Karl Druschki' x ('Mme. Caroline Testout' x 'Mrs. W. J. Grant')**
FLOWER SIZE **5.5in (14cm)**
SCENT **Strong, rich, and sweet**
FLOWERING **Repeats**
HEIGHT/SPREAD **4.9ft (1.5m)/4.1ft (1.25m)**
HARDINESS **Zone 5**

Although sometimes classified as a Hybrid Perpetual, 'Heinrich Münch' belongs in every way among the Hybrid Teas. It was raised by a leading German amateur and introduced (by a nursery in Dresden) as a dual-purpose rose for exhibition and garden display. Its flowers are simply sumptuous, both in their abundance and in their delicious scent. 'Heinrich Münch' has long, large petals of exquisite silver pink, with a slightly darker pink on their backs. The flowers are huge, and take a long time to unfurl and unroll their many petals, so this is a rose that does best in warm, dry climates. The flowers come singly on long, strong stems, but occasionally in clusters of up to four. 'Heinrich Münch' makes a vigorous, leafy bush, with thick stems and a scattering of prickles. It responds well to feeding and watering and, when well grown, is still one of the most beautiful of all early 20th-century roses.

'HEINRICH SCHULTHEIS'

'HEINRICH SCHULTHEIS'

Hybrid Perpetual

ORIGIN **Bennett, Britain, 1882**
PARENTAGE **'Mabel Morrison' x unknown**
FLOWER SIZE **4.7in (12cm)**
SCENT **Strong and sweet**
FLOWERING **Repeats well**
HEIGHT/SPREAD **4.1ft (1.25m)/3.3ft (1m)**
HARDINESS **Zone 5**

Heinrich Schultheis (1846–99) was the founder of Germany's first rose nursery. It is still one of the largest in Europe, and has turned his native town of Steinfurth into a center for rose growing. By 1970 the village had 210 growers producing 14 million roses every year. Heinrich Schultheis's rose was bred by Henry Bennett and is an excellent, strong-growing, compact Hybrid Perpetual. Its flowers open from rounded buds and are cupped, but opulently full of deep pink petals. They are borne singly, but sometimes in tight clusters of 2–3, on short, stout stems, which hold the flowers strongly erect. They are surrounded by leaves, as Portland roses are, and are one of the first Hybrid Perpetuals to flower. It was a famous exhibition rose in its day, but is valuable still because it repeats much better than many so-called Hybrid Perpetuals. 'Heinrich Schultheis' has produced a number of paler sports over the years: most commonly seen are 'Paul's Early Blush' (Paul, 1893) and 'Mrs. Harkness' (Harkness, 1893).

HEINZELMÄNNCHEN

syn. 'KORNUMA', Red Pixie
Floribunda

ORIGIN **Kordes, Germany, 1983**
PARENTAGE **'Satchmo' seedling x ('Messestadt Hannover' x 'Hamburg')**
FLOWER SIZE **2.4in (6cm)**
SCENT **Light and sweet**
FLOWERING **Repeats well**
HEIGHT/SPREAD **2.7ft (80cm)/2ft (60cm)**
HARDINESS **Zone 6**

As well as being popular in Germany, where it was raised and introduced, Heinzelmännchen is also widely grown in the very different climate of Australia, where it is known as Red Pixie. It should be tried in other parts of the world. Heinzelmännchen is a short-growing Floribunda with very full flowers, bright blood red in color. They come in clusters of 3–10 and hold their color well. Sometimes the inner petals are crinkled and form an old-fashioned shape when the flowers open out wide. The flowers are borne generously and repeatedly until late autumn. They stand up well to rain. Heinzelmännchen makes a sturdy, compact, bushy plant in Germany, where it grows to about 1.3ft (40cm), but is also considered compact in Australia, where it reaches twice that height. The leaves are healthy, dark, and glossy. The *Heinzelmännchen* is a creature of German folklore.

HEIDETRAUM

syn. 'NOATRAUM', Flower Carpet
Ground Cover

ORIGIN **Noack, Germany, 1989**
PARENTAGE Immensee x Amanda
FLOWER SIZE **2in (5cm)**
SCENT **Light and musky**
FLOWERING **Almost continuous**
HEIGHT/SPREAD **2.7ft (80cm)/3.3ft (1m)**
HARDINESS **Zone 5**
AWARDS **L'Haÿ GM 1988; ADR 1990; Boskoop GM 1990; The Hague GM 1990; Dortmund GM 1991; Glasgow GM 1993**

Heidetraum is a magnificent rose, extremely healthy and very floriferous, that functions as a short climber, as groundcover, or as a small sprawling shrub in borders. It was vigorously marketed in the English-speaking world as Flower Carpet, and, more than any other rose, showed gardeners what modern roses were capable of. It flowers over a very long season, even when its first flowers have produced ripe, orange hips. The flowers are deep pink, almost crimson at first (the buds are red), and open cupped, loosely double, with a small white eye. They fade to mid-pink and palest lilac pink, before dropping their petals cleanly. They come in open clusters of 10–20. The dark, glossy leaves come from the super healthy *Rosa wichurana*: Heidetraum is unmoved by mildew, blackspot, or rust. In 1997 Noack introduced a paler sport, Sommermelodie. It is the same as the original, with all its good qualities: only its color is different.

HEIDETRAUM

SOMMERMELODIE

Sport of Heidetraum

SOMMERMELODIE

syn. 'NOAMEL', Appleblossom
ORIGIN **Noack, Germany, 1997**

HEINZELMÄNNCHEN

'HEIRLOOM'

'HEIRLOOM'

Hybrid Tea

ORIGIN **Warriner, US, 1972**
FLOWER SIZE **3.9in (10cm)**
SCENT **Very strong and sweet**
FLOWERING **Repeats**
HEIGHT/SPREAD **4.9ft (1.5m)/4.1ft (1.25m)**
HARDINESS **Zone 6**

Although classed as a Hybrid Tea, 'Heirloom' also blooms in clusters of up to seven like a Floribunda. The flowers are lilac pink with magenta backs to the petals – a combination that gives great depth to the flowers. The flowers of 'Heirloom' open out lightly cupped, but full of quite short, broad petals. Their scent is delicious. The petal edges are darker, but gray purple shadows fill the spaces in between. The clusters have short stems and show up well against the dark leaves. 'Heirloom' is healthy and hardy, but grows faster in hot climates. It blooms in a series of flushes, which can be speeded up by deadheading.

'HELEN TRAUBEL'

Hybrid Tea

ORIGIN **Swim, US, 1951**
PARENTAGE **'Charlotte Armstrong' x 'Wilhelm Breder'**
FLOWER SIZE **5.5in (14cm)**
SCENT **Strong and sweet**
FLOWERING **Repeats well**
HEIGHT/SPREAD **4.9ft (1.5m)/3.3ft (1m)**
HARDINESS **Zone 6**
AWARDS **Rome GM 1951; AARS 1952**

'HELEN TRAUBEL'

ROSA HELENAE

Nothing could be lovelier than a perfect flower of 'Helen Traubel' – and there are always plenty of them – but it is also a fickle and inconstant performer. There are two main problems: first, the color varies considerably, veering between an exquisite apricot and a dowdy pink; second, the slender flower stems tend to bend over and break, especially in wet weather. But its qualities greatly outweigh its weaknesses, and 'Helen Traubel' has remained a firm favorite throughout the world for more than 50 years. The flowers are large, long, and slender in bud, before opening out into vast glowing goblets of color. They are borne singly, occasionally in small clusters, on long, elegant stems. The petals are huge and always look fresh, even when they age and develop a slight wave. The bush is healthy, with beautiful crimson new growths. Helen Traubel (1899–1972) was a great Wagnerian opera singer from St. Louis, Missouri.

ROSA *HELENAE*

Wild Rose

FLOWER SIZE **1.6in (4cm)**
SCENT **Strong and musky**
FLOWERING **Once only, fairly early in season**
HEIGHT/SPREAD **16.4ft (5m)/9.8ft (3m)**
HARDINESS **Zone 5**

Rosa helenae is one of the best of all the wild roses that climb. It carries large clusters of pure white flowers, but the clusters are more spacious than those of most species, and the flowers are larger. It has two more gifts – less excessive vigor than most climbers, and greater hardiness. The plant mounds up slowly until it can find a tree or similar support, whereupon it will climb quickly to a great height and festoon the branches of the tree with its long stems and airy clusters. It is helped by hooked prickles, which curve backward and enable it to get a hold. The long leaves are pale green, with grayer undersides. The flowers have unusually pale stamens and a long stigma at the center. They are followed by small (0.4in/1cm), orange, oval hips. *Rosa helenae* is widespread throughout western and central China, through to Indo-China. It was introduced to the West by Ernest Wilson for the Arnold Arboretum in 1900, and named after his wife, Helen.

HELMUT SCHMIDT

syn. 'KORBELMA', Goldsmith, Simba

Hybrid Tea

ORIGIN **Kordes, Germany, 1979**
PARENTAGE **Mabella x seedling**
FLOWER SIZE **4.3in (11cm)**
SCENT **Light**
FLOWERING **Repeats well and frequently**
HEIGHT/SPREAD **3.3ft (1m)/2.7ft (80cm)**
HARDINESS **Zone 6**
AWARDS **Belgium GM 1979; Geneva GM 1979**

Helmut Schmidt is a good, easy to grow Hybrid Tea, which flowers almost continuously. The flowers are lemon yellow at first, fading to lemon cream, and always paler at the edges of the petals. They are carried singly or in clusters of up to four. They are most elegant as half-opened buds, and are still popular for exhibition and as a cut flower – they last a long time in water. The petals are broad and strong and stand up well to rain, though the plant also does well in sun and will reach 4.9ft (1.5m) or more in hot climates. The bush has large, healthy leaves, medium-dark and glossy, and few thorns. Helmut Schmidt (b.1918) was Chancellor of West Germany from 1974 to 1982.

HELMUT SCHMIDT

H

ROSA *HEMISPHAERICA*

Wild Rose

FLOWER SIZE **2.8in (7cm)**
SCENT **Foetid**
FLOWERING **Once only, fairly early in season**
HEIGHT/SPREAD **5.7ft (1.75m)/4.9ft (1.5m)**
HARDINESS **Zone 5**

By a strange quirk of the rules of botanical nomenclature, *Rosa hemisphaerica* is the double-flowered form of the species, not the simple, single-flowered form that grows wild in parts of Turkey and Armenia. However, the double-flowered form has a long history in cultivation: it has been known since at least 1625 and appears in many old Dutch flower paintings, as well as being drawn by Redouté. It was the only double yellow rose in cultivation until well into the 19th century. Its flowers are cupped and full of bright, pale yellow stamens, which nod down slightly. The bush has small, gray green leaves and a thin, twiggy, prickly structure. It has acquired a reputation for being difficult to grow well, because its flowers ball and its leaves suffer terrible blackspot in mild, damp climates. However, it is a vigorous and spectacular rose in hot, dry climates where its beautiful flowers can open out properly and the gray foliage makes a splendid foil.

ROSA HEMISPHAERICA

'Henri Foucquier'

'Henri Martin'

Henry Fonda

'Henri Foucquier'

Gallica

ORIGIN **France, c.1850**
FLOWER SIZE **4.7in (12cm)**
SCENT **Very strong and sweet**
FLOWERING **Once only**
HEIGHT/SPREAD **4.9ft (1.5m)/4.1ft (1.25m)**
HARDINESS **Zone 5**

Huge flowers, rich scent, great vigor, and no prickles – 'Henri Foucquier' is a star among the Gallica roses. Its flowers open from crimson buds. They are cherry red at first, but fade fairly quickly, starting at the edges, through magenta, mauve, and lilac pink to palest gray, so that the center of each flower remains bright cerise while the edges are already nearly white. The transformation is a magnificent performance, made better because of the great size of the outstretched flower and its stupendous scent. The flowers have a mass of small petals (which lie flat, without quilling or pleating) and sometimes a rough button eye. The plant has darker leaves than many Gallicas but is one of the healthiest. The name has no connection with the polemicist and politician Henry Fouquier (1838–1901).

'Henri Martin'

Moss Rose

ORIGIN **Laffay, France, 1862**
FLOWER SIZE **2.4in (6cm)**
SCENT **Strong and sweet**
FLOWERING **Once, midseason**
HEIGHT/SPREAD **4.9ft (1.5m)/4.1ft (1.25m)**
HARDINESS **Zone 5**

'Henri Martin' (named after the French historian, 1810–83), is a vigorous, healthy, and floriferous red Moss rose. The flowers open out quickly and have a very round outline. Sometimes a few dark yellow stamens are visible at the center, but usually they are obscured by petals. The flower is a light crimson red at first, but quickly takes on a more purple hue, especially in hot weather. Sometimes – it depends on the weather – it is no more than dark pink. The flowers come in clusters of 3–9 and are followed in autumn by small, round, red hips. The receptacles and flower stalks are covered in good light green moss, which looks like little bristles but is soft to the touch, and sticky. It also smells of resin. The plant is thrifty, fast-growing, and tolerant of poor soils. It has bright green, medium-dark foliage, few prickles, and a lax, arching habit of growth, which means that it performs best when staked to a tripod or other support.

Henri Matisse

syn. 'DELSTROBLA'

Hybrid Tea

ORIGIN **Delbard, France, 1995**
PARENTAGE **('Lara' x Candia) x seedling**
FLOWER SIZE **4.3in (11cm)**
SCENT **Light**
FLOWERING **Repeats**
HEIGHT/SPREAD **4.1ft (1.25m)/3.3ft (1m)**
HARDINESS **Zone 6**

Despite a somewhat complex ancestry, Henri Matisse is very similar to the famous striped Hybrid Perpetual 'Ferdinand Pichard'. Its flowers have the same shade of crimson, slashed with irregular pale pink splashes. The elegant flowers are borne singly or in rather tight clusters of up to seven. They have moderately long stems and have been grown commercially on a limited scale to provide an unusual cut flower, but growers find that Henri Matisse does not produce the number of flowers expected of a commercial rose. That said, it is a good performer in the garden, and fairly healthy. Henri Matisse is one of Delbard's Painter series of roses.

Henry Fonda

syn. 'JACYES'

Hybrid Tea

ORIGIN **Christensen, US, 1995**
FLOWER SIZE **4.7in (12cm)**
SCENT **Light and sweet**
FLOWERING **Repeats**
HEIGHT/SPREAD **4.9ft (1.5m)/3.3ft (1m)**
HARDINESS **Zone 6**

This is a rich yellow Hybrid Tea, but it lacks the timeless good looks of the movie star whose name it commemorates. The flowers often have a ragged shape, so that their petal edges look as if they were torn (the photograph shown here is a flattering resemblance). Henry Fonda is almost golden yellow toward the center of the flower and in the shadows that form between the petals. The shape of the flowers is pretty at all stages, from bud to the fully blown bloom. The flowers are borne singly, occasionally in twos and threes, on strong stems. The plant is fairly vigorous, with healthy, medium-dark green leaves. This is a good rose, but not a great one.

'Henry Hudson'

Rugosa Hybrid

ORIGIN **Svejda, Canada, 1976**
PARENTAGE **'Schneezwerg' (open pollinated)**
FLOWER SIZE **2.8in (7cm)**
SCENT **Strong and sweet**
FLOWERING **Constant**
HEIGHT/SPREAD **3.3ft (1m)/3.3ft (1m)**
HARDINESS **Zone 4**

Some of the earliest Explorer roses to be introduced were not the result of controlled hybridization but of the experimental work that preceded it. 'Henry Hudson' was a spin-off from tests to discover the genetic possibilities of 'Schneezwerg'. The outcome is a very handsome, hardy, and healthy shrub with exceptionally pretty flowers. The buds are pink at first – so are the outer petal tips – but the flowers are pure white in hot weather and have a hint of pink in autumn. They are semi-double and open out to display the stamens at the center. The petals have a tissue paper freshness, and sparkle when the sun shines through them, but later they turn brown and wither on the bush. The plant is a typical Rugosa – rough, pale leaves, a lot of fierce prickles, a dense habit of growth, and a tendency to sucker. Henry Hudson (d.1611) was the English navigator who discovered Hudson Bay.

Henri Matisse

'Henry Hudson'

'HENRY KELSEY'

'HENRY KELSEY'

Kordesii Hybrid

ORIGIN **Svejda, Canada, 1984**
PARENTAGE **'Kordesii' seedling**
FLOWER SIZE **2.8in (7cm)**
SCENT **Strong and fruity**
FLOWERING **Repeats well**
HEIGHT/SPREAD **8.2ft (2.5m)/6.6ft (2m)**
HARDINESS **Zone 4**

This Kordesii hybrid is one of the tallest Explorer roses introduced by Agriculture Canada to widen the range of roses that will survive Canadian winters. 'Henry Kelsey' is not the hardiest, nor the most resistant to blackspot, but its flowers are among the brightest – sparkling crimson, enhanced by a large mop of brilliant golden stamens at the center. They are semi-double, cupped, and borne in medium-sized clusters (typically of 5–15 flowers), starting with a spectacular first flowering and continuing on a lesser scale until the first frost. The plant has dark green, glossy leaves. In warmer climates it will quickly grow to 13.1ft (4m) as a climber. Henry Kelsey explored inland Canada for the Hudson Bay Company in the 1680s.

'HENRY NEVARD'

Hybrid Perpetual

ORIGIN **Cant, Britain, 1924**
FLOWER SIZE **4.7in (12cm)**
SCENT **Strong and sweet**
FLOWERING **Remontant**
HEIGHT/SPREAD **6.6ft (2m)/5.7ft (1.75m)**
HARDINESS **Zone 6**

When the plant is well grown, the flowers of 'Henry Nevard' may be as much as 5.9in (15cm) across. This is all the more surprising when you examine the petals and see how short they are. But the cupped flowers are full of petals and have a stupendous, rich scent as well. They come sometimes singly and sometimes in somewhat tight clusters of up to four, on long, stout, prickly stems. They are bright crimson at first, later losing their brightness and passing to a paler shade. 'Henry Nevard' is a demanding rose to grow well. Its dull, dark leaves are very susceptible both to mildew and blackspot, and it tends to grow bare and lanky. It is not a natural reflowerer, but is at its best if pruned hard after its first flowering. Then the new growths will flower well in autumn, after which they can be tied down to flower all along their lengths next year.

'HENRY NEVARD'

HERITAGE

'HERBSTFEUER'

syn. 'AUTUMN FIRE'

Shrub Rose

ORIGIN **Kordes, Germany, 1961**
FLOWER SIZE **3.9in (10cm)**
SCENT **Light and sweet**
FLOWERING **Repeats**
HEIGHT/SPREAD **8.2ft (2.5m)/5.7ft (1.75m)**
HARDINESS **Zone 6**

No one knows the ancestry of 'Herbstfeuer', but its enormous, flagon-shaped hips suggest that *Rosa moyesii* is among its antecedents. Nevertheless, it is a strong-growing, repeat flowering rose that could pass as a vigorous Floribunda. Its flowers are semidouble and dark red, without a hint of crimson. At the center is a ring of golden stamens and a tiny patch of white, from which occasional white streaks run up into the petals. It is not an especially shapely or neat flower, but has a velvety sheen which is attractive. Then come the wonderful, long, vermilion hips. 'Herbstfeuer' has large, dark leaves, huge prickles (but not too many of them), and thick crimson stems. It is a good repeater, and the autumn flowers come at the same time as the hips, though not as plentifully as in the first flush. It is a strong, upright grower which, if it is not pruned to about 3.3ft (1m), will need staking or the protection of other shrubs.

'HERBSTFEUER'

HERITAGE

syn. 'AUSBLUSH'

Shrub Rose

ORIGIN **Austin, Britain, 1984**
PARENTAGE **seedling x ('Schneewittchen' x 'Wife of Bath')**
FLOWER SIZE **3.5in (9cm)**
SCENT **Strong and sweet**
FLOWERING **Repeats well**
HEIGHT/SPREAD **3.9ft (1.2m)/3.3ft (1m)**
HARDINESS **Zone 6**

Heritage is one of the most popular of David Austin's English Roses. It is very floriferous, carrying two or three full flushes of flowers, with a scattering in between, and continuing until early winter. The flowers are pale salmon pink at the centrt and cream or white towards the outside. The globular flowers rarely open out: they are full of petals, which means that they do not like rain or overhead watering. The flowers shatter early, so Heritage makes a disappointing cut flower, but it always looks clean and fresh in the garden. The flowers come in clusters of 3–7 and are carried all over the bush, right down to ground level. The long, lax stems (almost thornless) tend to flop over and then flower all along their length. If left unchecked (it prefers only the lightest pruning regimen), it eventually builds up into a stout, bushy, upright shrub. The leaves are few, but large, dark green, glossy, and healthy – only occasionally liable to a little blackspot. It is at its best in cool climates and owes its popularity to its health, floriferousness, and the sheer prettiness of its flowers.

'HERMOSA'

China Rose or China Hybrid

ORIGIN **Marchesseau, France, 1834**
FLOWER SIZE **2.4in (6cm)**
SCENT **Fairly strong and tealike**
FLOWERING **Repeats well; almost constant**
HEIGHT/SPREAD **2.7ft (80cm)/2.7ft (80cm)**
HARDINESS **Zone 6**

'Hermosa' – the name means "beautiful" – is classified as a China rose, but is probably a hybrid between 'Old Blush' and a European rose. The flowers open from long, elegant buds, which start to nod gently as they grow heavier. The flowers are pink with a subtle hint of lilac and slightly darker petal backs. They have rather delicate petals – and a lot of them – which unroll at their tips. The flowers eventually open out to a muddled center but are prettiest in bud or half open. They come in clusters of 3–7. The bush has delicate, light green leaves, slender growths, and a tidy habit, with lots of small, thin branches. It enjoys good disease resistance in hot, dry climates, but is a martyr to mildew and blackspot in cool ones. It looks good at the front of a mixed border but prefers a sheltered position, where it will flower almost incessantly until early winter. It roots easily from cuttings. There is a climbing sport called 'Setina', which has larger flowers, but fewer of them after its first splendid blooming early in the season.

'HERMOSA'

HERO

HERO

syn. 'AUSHERO'

Shrub Rose

ORIGIN **Austin, Britain, 1982**
PARENTAGE **'The Prioress' x seedling**
FLOWER SIZE **3.5in (9cm)**
SCENT **Strong and myrrhlike**
FLOWERING **Repeats well**
HEIGHT/SPREAD **4.9ft (1.5m)/4.1ft (1.25m)**
HARDINESS **Zone 6**

Hero (named after Leander's girlfriend) is a tall, fragrant, heavy-blooming shrub rose. The flowers are pure pink, deeper toward the center of the flower and paler on the outer petals. There is also a hint of coral at the center, partly reflected by the golden anthers and crimson filaments. The first flowers are incurved and globular, but later ones are more shallowly cupped. They come in very long-stemmed clusters of 3–7. The plant is lightly clad with pale green leaves. It has an open habit of growth, which means that it is best interplanted with tall herbaceous plants. In hot climates, it will reach 9.8ft (3m) as a climber. Several sports have occurred in cultivation: best known is 'Huntington Hero', which was found at the Huntington Botanical Gardens in San Marino, California. It has fewer petals and a paler color than Hero.

HERTFORDSHIRE

see TOMMELISE

'HERZOG VON WINDSOR'

syn. 'DUKE OF WINDSOR'

Hybrid Tea

ORIGIN **Tantau, Germany, 1969**
PARENTAGE **'Spartan' x 'Montezuma'**
FLOWER SIZE **4.3in (11cm)**
SCENT **Very strong, sweet, and delicious**
FLOWERING **Repeats well**
HEIGHT/SPREAD **4.1ft (1.25m)/3.3ft (1m)**
HARDINESS **Zone 6**
AWARDS **Edland FA 1968; ADR 1970**

This handsome Hybrid Tea commemorates the Duke of Windsor (1894–1972), better known as King Edward VIII of England. Like the Duke himself, the rose has always been popular in Germany. The flowers are a distinct shade of salmon orange, with slightly paler backs to the petals.

'HERZOG VON WINDSOR'

Sometimes they appear a little more vermilion or pink, but they are always bright, attractive, and deliciously scented. They come singly or in clusters of up to five. 'Herzog von Windsor' is moderately vigorous but should not be pruned too hard. In order to avoid die-back, it should be allowed to build up a good structure of branches. It has medium-dark leaves and crimson new growths: mildew, rust, and blackspot may all be visitors, but rarely do any serious damage. The plant is very prickly.

'HI, NEIGHBOR'

Grandiflora

ORIGIN **Buck, US, 1981**
PARENTAGE **('Queen Elizabeth' x 'Prairie Princess') x 'Portrait'**
FLOWER SIZE **4.3in (11cm)**
SCENT **Medium and sweet**
FLOWERING **Repeats well**
HEIGHT/SPREAD **4.9ft (1.5m)/4.1ft (1.25m)**
HARDINESS **Zone 5**

It is not quite as hardy as most of Griffith Buck's roses, but the flowers of 'Hi, Neighbor' are good enough for it to be classified not as a shrub rose but as a Grandiflora. They are large, somewhat globular, and full of petals – so full that they tend to hang down under their own weight. They are a rich pale crimson or dark pink in color, and fade a little as they open. The flowers come singly and in clusters of up to five, and the plant repeats regularly through until the first frosts. 'Hi, Neighbor' has large, strong, dark leaves and an upright habit of growth. It reaches about 1–1.25m (3.3–4.1ft) in cold areas, but as much as 5.7ft (1.75m) in hot parts: like many of the Buck roses, it was bred for cold climates but also performs splendidly in hot ones. Blackspot may be a problem.

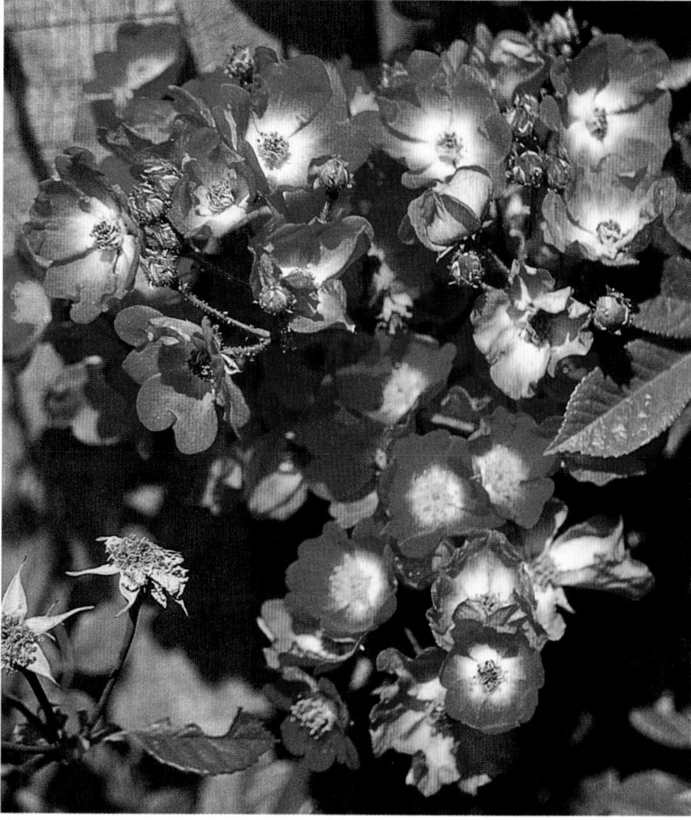
'HIAWATHA'

'HIAWATHA'

Wichurana Rambler

ORIGIN **Walsh, US, 1904**
PARENTAGE **'Turner's Crimson Rambler' x unknown**
FLOWER SIZE **1.8in (4.5cm)**
SCENT **Little or none**
FLOWERING **Once only, late in season**
HEIGHT/SPREAD **13.1ft (4m)/6.6ft (2m)**
HARDINESS **Zone 5**

'Hiawatha' is probably the best-known Wichurana rambler of its type, with large trusses of scentless red and white flowers. They glow with color when they first open – the rich crimson flowers are illuminated by a white center and golden stamens – but they look much duller when the crimson turns to maroon pink and the stamens to brown. The flowers are borne in clusters, typically of 15–40, very late in the season. 'Hiawatha' has been popular ever since its introduction, partly because it roots so easily from cuttings. The foliage is dark green and glossy, in the Wichurana way, and liable to attract mildew, especially if grown against a wall.

HIDALGO

see MICHEL HIDALGO

HIGH HOPES

syn. 'HARYUP'

Modern Climber

ORIGIN **Harkness, Britain, 1992**
PARENTAGE Compassion x Congratulations
FLOWER SIZE **3.1in (8cm)**
SCENT **Medium and sweet**
FLOWERING **Repeats well**
HEIGHT/SPREAD **13.1ft (4m)/9.8ft (3m)**
HARDINESS **Zone 6**
AWARDS **Tokyo GM 1992**

The flowers on High Hopes are an elegant Hybrid Tea shape. They open mid-pink and fade to pale pink or

'HI, NEIGHBOR'

HIGH HOPES

mother-of-pearl, while always retaining a deeper pink at the center. They are, however, only medium-sized and are somewhat overwhelmed by the copious quantities of large, dark green leaves that the plant produces. They are borne usually singly, occasionally in small clusters of 2–5, at the end of long stems. The plant is vigorous, stiff, very upright, and not excessively floriferous. It suffers occasionally from blackspot.

'HIGHDOWNENSIS'

syn. Rosa x *highdownensis*

Moyesii Hybrid

ORIGIN **Stern, Britain, 1928**
PARENTAGE ***Rosa moyesii*** **x unknown**
FLOWER SIZE **2in (5cm)**
SCENT **Light and sweet**
FLOWERING **Once only**
HEIGHT/SPREAD **11.5ft (3.5m)/13.1ft (4m)**
HARDINESS **Zone 5**

There is a steady demand from people with large gardens for unusual shrub roses. 'Highdownensis' satisfies this need by producing striking flowers, large hips, and very exuberant growth. It is a form or hybrid of *Rosa moyesii*. Its bright, cherry crimson single flowers are borne in clusters over several weeks in mid-season. The leaves are late to emerge, and still small when flowering begins, so the flowers stand out against the pale brown stems and large prickles. Later come the pale orange hips – 2.4in (6cm) long and shaped like fat flagons. In most areas, they tend to be taken by birds after only a few weeks. The leaves, when fully expanded, are long and slender, with many small, red-edged leaflets. The prickles on the new wood are a glistening crimson. 'Highdownensis' grows fast in all directions and is only really suitable for wild and woodland areas.

HIGHFIELD

see 'COMPASSION'

HILDA MURRELL

HILDA MURRELL

syn. 'AUSMURR'

Shrub Rose

ORIGIN **Austin, Britain, 1984**
PARENTAGE **'The Squire' x ('Parade' x 'Chaucer')**
FLOWER SIZE **4.3in (11cm)**
SCENT **Strong, sweet, and damasky**
FLOWERING **Repeats a little**
HEIGHT/SPREAD **4.9ft (1.5m)/4.1ft (1.25m)**
HARDINESS **Zone 6**

The flowers of Hilda Murrell are sumptuous, rich pink rosettes at first, full of petals and eventually opening out lightly cupped and roughly quartered. They are mid-pink, with darker petal backs, and a hint of peach or apricot at the center. As they age, the colors fade slightly, so that a fully open flower has a beautiful contrast between the center and the edges of the flower. The flowers are borne singly or, occasionally, in clusters. Hilda Murrell has large, mid-green leaves: the broad leaflets are set close to each other and have wrinkled surfaces. The plant has stout stems and a fair scattering of prickles. It is fairly vigorous and its reputation for miserly flowering is not justified: it is a reliable autumn flowerer as well as an abundant producer of flowers earlier in the year. Hilda Murrell was a nurserywoman who pioneered interest in old garden roses in Britain. She was murdered in mysterious circumstances in 1984.

'HIGHDOWNENSIS'

'HIPPOLYTE'

Gallica

ORIGIN **France, c.1840**
FLOWER SIZE **2.8in (7cm)**
SCENT **Light and sweet**
FLOWERING **Once only**
HEIGHT/SPREAD **5.7ft (1.75m)/6.6ft (2m)**
HARDINESS **Zone 5**

No one knows who bred 'Hippolyte', but it is probably French and has a dash of China rose genes alongside its Gallica ancestry. The flowers (small for a Gallica) are tight, round rosettes of dark violet petals when they open out. The petal backs are much paler, as is the button eye that they form around the center. The purple fades to deep mauve as it ages. The flowers come in clusters of 2–5 (occasionally more, or singly), which are very abundantly borne all along the lax, arching growths. The plant is thornless, with smooth leaves that come from its China ancestors, and supple stems which may need some support. Mildew can be a problem later in the year.

'HOMÈRE'

'HOMÈRE'

Tea Rose

ORIGIN **Robert & Moreau, France, 1858**
FLOWER SIZE **2in (5cm)**
SCENT **Light and tealike**
FLOWERING **Repeats constantly**
HEIGHT/SPREAD **3.3ft (1m)/2.7ft (80cm)**
HARDINESS **Zone 7**

The hardiness of 'Homère' sets it apart from other Tea roses and suggests that it has more in common with the Chinas. The flowers are long, slender, elegant, and full of petals, which means that they open slowly. Basically white, they have the ability – common to both Teas and Chinas – to suggest a great variety of other hues and tints. The outer petals often have pink or crimson tips, but the innermost ones throw out hints of pale salmon, flesh, and mother-of-pearl. The flowers usually come singly, occasionally in twos, and seldom open out fully, hanging down under the weight of their many petals, so that rain washes off the outsides and the heart of the flower is untouched. The plant has small, dark leaves, few prickles, and a mass of twiggy branches. It will grow to 6.6ft (2m) against a wall and is less susceptible to mildew and blackspot than many of its kind.

'HIPPOLYTE'

'HONEYFLOW'

HONORÉ DE BALZAC

'HONEYFLOW'

Lambertiana

ORIGIN **Riethmuller, Australia, 1957**
PARENTAGE **'Spring Song' x 'Gartendirektor Otto Linne'**
FLOWER SIZE **1.8in (4.5cm)**
SCENT **Strong**
FLOWERING **Fully recurrent, almost perpetually in flower**
HEIGHT/SPREAD **4.9ft (1.5m)/4.1ft (1.25m)**
HARDINESS **Zone 5**

'Honeyflow' is a vigorous shrub, with billowing masses of pale pink flowers in large clusters – typically of 20–30. They fade almost to white as they age, but their sheer quantity is remarkable. They are well set off by smooth, shiny, dark green leaves – pretty, with long leaflets – and arching, nearly thornless stems. This rose is almost unknown outside its native Australia, and is perhaps less deserving of space in the garden than its rival 'Carabella'.

HONOR

syn. 'JACOLITE', Michèle Torr
Hybrid Tea

ORIGIN **Warriner, US, 1980**
FLOWER SIZE **5.5in (14cm)**
SCENT **Medium, sweet, and Damask**
FLOWERING **Repeats well**
HEIGHT/SPREAD **5.7ft (1.75m)/4.1ft (1.25m)**
HARDINESS **Zone 6**
AWARDS **Portland GM 1978; AARS 1980**

Its long, rain sensitive petals make Honor a rose for hot, dry climates: it is seen to perfection in its native California. The flowers open slowly from elegantly formed buds. Their petals are pure white, with just a hint of cream reflected in the shadows at the base of each flower. They are attractive even when they open out fully and reveal their golden stamens. Sometimes the outer petals have a tinge of pink on their undersides. The flowers are borne singly, occasionally in twos and threes, on very long stems, which make them perfect for cutting and popular for exhibition. The plants are vigorous, and make sturdy growth – the stems are unusually thick – which is purple crimson at first. The plant is healthy, rarely troubled by disease.

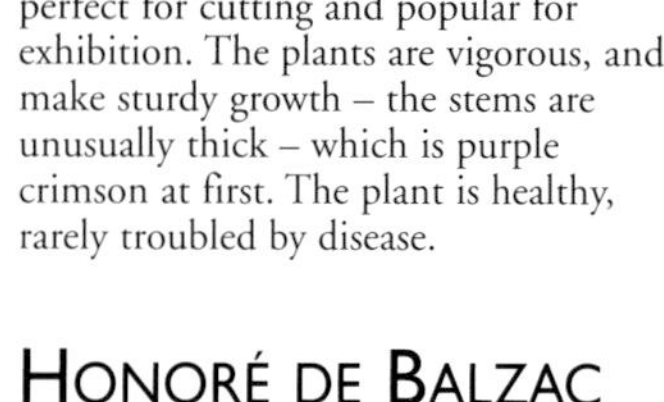

HONORÉ DE BALZAC

syn. 'MEIPARNIN', Romantic Days
Hybrid Tea

ORIGIN **Meilland, France, 1993**
PARENTAGE **Fiorella 82 seedling x Lancôme**
FLOWER SIZE **5.5in (14cm)**
SCENT **Good and fruity**
FLOWERING **Repeats**
HEIGHT/SPREAD **4.1ft (1.25m)/3.3ft (1m)**
HARDINESS **Zone 5**

The Romantica series of Meilland roses – to which Honoré de Balzac belongs – is intended to combine the form and scent of old roses with the vigor and colors of modern ones. Honoré de Balzac is best thought of as a Hybrid Tea which expands into a cabbagelike mass of petals held in a rounded flower. They are rose pink at first but fade to cream and white, starting with the outer petals, so that the flower appears two-toned by the time it has opened out. The petals have pale crimson edges and slightly darker backs. The flowers are large, strongly scented, and usually borne singly on long stems. Honoré de Balzac is a lanky grower, with very large, healthy, dark, glossy leaves. It flowers in a series of flushes and does best in hot, dry conditions, where its flowers can expand without being damaged by rain.

HONOR

'HONORINE DE BRABANT'

Bourbon Rose

FLOWER SIZE **2.4in (6cm)**
SCENT **Strong and sweet**
FLOWERING **Repeats well**
HEIGHT/SPREAD **5.7ft (1.75m)/5.7ft (1.75m)**
HARDINESS **Zone 6**

No one knows the origins of 'Honorine de Brabant' – who bred this beautiful striped rose, when they did so, or whom the name commemorates. It is very popular and widely grown, valued both for its hardiness and its tolerance of hot sun. The flowers are cupped, with a somewhat muddled arrangement of small petals within. The flowers are pale pink, with irregular, pale crimson stripes and slashes, though later the pink fades to white and the crimson to lilac. They come in short-stemmed clusters of 3–7. The plant is very vigorous, with a lot of healthy, large, pale green leaves, a shrubby, branching structure, and a few prickles. It is a good repeater: the first flowering is always the most abundant, but 'Honorine de Brabant' carries many flowers in autumn too. It is one of the best of the old roses.

'HONORINE DE BRABANT'

'Hope for Humanity'

'Hope for Humanity'

Shrub Rose

ORIGIN **Collicutt & Davidson, Canada, 1996**
PARENTAGE **('Prairie Princess' x 'Morden Amorette') x 'Morden Cardinette' seedling**
FLOWER SIZE **2.8in (7cm)**
SCENT **Medium and sweet**
FLOWERING **Repeats well**
HEIGHT/SPREAD **4.9ft (1.5m)/4.1ft (1.25m)**
HARDINESS **Zone 4**

The name is a tribute to the Canadian Red Cross, whose centenary 'Hope for Humanity' commemorates. It is a fine shrub rose in the Morden series, developed to survive the cold winters of Manitoba. The flowers are deep purple crimson, full of petals, and shapely: the opening buds resemble Hybrid Teas but the fully open flowers expand to reveal a white patch at the center. They are borne in spacious clusters, typically of 3–5 flowers, but occasionally more, or less. 'Hope for Humanity' flowers until the first frost. In cool climates it rarely exceeds 2.5ft (75cm) in height, but, as with most of the Morden roses, it flourishes even in hot climates like the American South, where it will quickly reach 4.9ft (1.5m). The leaves are medium-dark, handsome, and healthy, except for occasional blackspot.

'Hot Chocolate'

syn. 'SIMcho'

Floribunda

ORIGIN **Simpson, New Zealand, 1986**
PARENTAGE **Princess x ('Tana' x Mary Sumner)**
FLOWER SIZE **3.1in (8cm)**
SCENT **Light and appley**
FLOWERING **Repeats well**
HEIGHT/SPREAD **3.3ft (1m)/2.7ft (80cm)**
HARDINESS **Zone 6**
AWARDS **NZ GM 1986**

The name says it all: this rose sells on its color. It is popular in New Zealand and Australia, but scarcely known elsewhere. The flowers are orange and brown, with occasional white streaks, and sections of white piping along the edge of the petals. This gives them an irregular shape that is unattractive in close-up. The color turns browner as

'Hot Chocolate'

the flowers age but 'Hot Chocolate' is very eye-catching at all stages. The flowers are usually borne in clusters of 3–5 and give their deepest coloring in cool autumn weather. The leaves are very large and dark green.

Hot Tamale

syn. 'JACpoy'

Miniature Rose

ORIGIN **Zary, US, 1993**
FLOWER SIZE **2.4in (6cm)**
SCENT **Light and fruity**
FLOWERING **Repeats well**
HEIGHT/SPREAD **2ft (60cm)/1.3ft (40cm)**
HARDINESS **Zone 6**
AWARDS **AoE 1994**

The flowers of Hot Tamale are perfect miniature Hybrid Teas, with long, elegant buds and neatly turned petals. They open bright orange, with yellow bases to the petals and yellow petal backs. Over the next few days the yellow starts to fade to white, which means that the orange also loses its yellow and turns first to salmon and then to pink. At the same time, the tips of the petals take on a deeper hue, and end up almost crimson. Since the flowers are at all times very shapely, this whole transformation is a beautiful performance to watch. The flowers of Hot Tamale are borne singly and in small clusters on a neat, prickly bush with small, dark green, glossy leaves. It is a popular rose both for cutting and for growing in containers.

'Hugh Dickson'

Hybrid Perpetual

ORIGIN **Dickson, Northern Ireland, 1905**
PARENTAGE **'Lord Bacon' x 'Gruss an Teplitz'**
FLOWER SIZE **3.1in (8cm)**
SCENT **Medium and sweet**
FLOWERING **Repeats**
HEIGHT/SPREAD **9.8ft (3m)/6.6ft (2m)**
HARDINESS **Zone 5**

Hugh Dickson was a member of the Northern Ireland family of rose breeders. "His" rose is still popular, though rarely as good as 'George Dickson'. 'Hugh Dickson' has pale crimson flowers, which are pretty as the buds unfurl, for the petals are long. When well grown, the flowers have a lot of petals and an attractive shape. If a plant is not fed and watered, its flowers can become short of petals and fail to open wide, so that they end up strongly cupped around an empty center. They come singly or, more often, in tight clusters of 3–5. 'Hugh Dickson' has very long, prickly stems and medium-sized, mid-green, fairly healthy leaves. It is vigorous, and sends up a constant stream of new growth from near the base, which keeps the flowers coming until well into autumn. Its lanky habit makes it a good subject for pegging down.

'Hugh Dickson'

Rosa hugonis

Wild Rose

FLOWER SIZE **2in (5cm)**
SCENT **Little or none**
FLOWERING **Once only, early in season**
HEIGHT/SPREAD **6.6ft (2m)/8.2ft (2.5m)**
HARDINESS **Zone 5**

In cool climates, *Rosa hugonis* is often the earliest rose to bloom. The pale, primrose yellow flowers are carried on short stems all along the long, arching growth, and emphasize the graceful shape of the plant itself. They are simple and lightly cupped, with attractive golden stamens at the center. They are followed by red hips that fall to the ground as soon as they are ripe. *Rosa hugonis* has dark brown stems, a lot of small prickles, and tiny, fernlike leaves that turn to crimson in autumn. It is both healthy and vigorous. Some botanists suggest that *Rosa hugonis* may have originated as a naturally occurring hybrid between *Rosa sericea* and *Rosa xanthina*. Nevertheless, it is native to a large area of central China and Szechwan.

Hot Tamale

Rosa hugonis

'HULA GIRL'

'HULA GIRL'

Miniature Rose

ORIGIN **Williams, US, 1975**
PARENTAGE **'Miss Hillcrest' x 'Mabel Dot'**
FLOWER SIZE **1.2in (3cm)**
SCENT **Light and fruity**
FLOWERING **Repeats well**
HEIGHT/SPREAD **2ft (60cm)/1.3ft (40cm)**
HARDINESS **Zone 6**
AWARDS **AoE 1976**

This splendid miniature has very beautiful flowers, carried in great abundance. The buds of 'Hula Girl' resemble a tiny Hybrid Tea, but open out quickly to reveal a mass of imbricated petals, neatly reflexed along their edges. They are orange at first, but fade quickly to salmon pink as they expand – they end up more pink than salmon. The petals tend to fade to white at the edges, which emphasizes the beautiful shape of the flower. The flowers come in clusters of 3–10 and are profusely carried. 'Hula Girl' has small, dark, neat, glossy leaves and makes a small, open plant that benefits from deadheading in summer and shaping in winter. It is an excellent bedding rose, but even better in a container.

'HUNTER'

syn. 'THE HUNTER'
Rugosa Hybrid

ORIGIN **Mattock, Britain, 1961**
PARENTAGE ***Rosa rugosa* 'Rubra' x 'Kordes' Sondermeldung'**
FLOWER SIZE **2.4in (6cm)**
SCENT **Light and sweet**
FLOWERING **Repeats well**
HEIGHT/SPREAD **4.9ft (1.5m)/4.9ft (1.5m)**
HARDINESS **Zone 5**

Bright red is unusual among the Rugosa roses. 'Hunter' was a good attempt at achieving it, but the flowers lose their brilliance quickly and end up dull crimson. They are double, not especially large, but profusely carried in their first flush and thereafter on a lesser scale until well into autumn. The petals are fairly thick, and stand up well to rain. They form a solid rosette with only a hint of stamens at the center. The flowers of 'Hunter' come in small clusters, typically of three, on short, prickly stems. The leaves are closer to a Floribunda's than normal – glossy and dark, with only a slight wrinkling to betray their Rugosa ancestry.

HURDY GURDY

syn. 'MACPLUTO', Pluto
Miniature Rose

ORIGIN **McGredy, New Zealand, 1986**
PARENTAGE **'Matangi' x 'Stars 'n' Stripes'**
FLOWER SIZE **2in (5cm)**
SCENT **Light and fruity**
FLOWERING **Repeats well**
HEIGHT/SPREAD **2.5ft (75cm)/1.6ft (50cm)**
HARDINESS **Zone 6**

Hurdy Gurdy is an unusual and eye-catching miniature. The flowers are dark red and white, but very variable in the pattern and occurrence of their striping: no two flowers are the same, though the petal backs are always white. They are cupped at first. They come in clusters of 5–15 (occasionally more), and shed their petals cleanly. There is quite a crop of small red hips in autumn, but this does not interfere with the almost continuous flowering. The leaves are small, healthy, dark, and fairly glossy. Normally Hurdy Gurdy is no more than a low bush, but in hot climates it will climb to 8.2ft (2.5m). Although good as a specimen plant, and excellent in landscaping schemes, it is sometimes difficult to find the right place for it in mixed plantings.

ICE CREAM

see 'MEMOIRE'

ICE MEIDILAND

syn. 'MEIVAHYN'
Shrub Rose

ORIGIN **Meilland, France, 1996**
PARENTAGE **'Katharina Zeimet' x ('Schneewittchen' x Alba Meidiland)**
FLOWER SIZE **2.4in (6cm)**
SCENT **Light and musky**
FLOWERING **Repeats well**
HEIGHT/SPREAD **2.7ft (80cm)/4.1ft (1.25m)**
HARDINESS **Zone 5**

This fine shrub rose has a lax, floppy, mounding habit and nearly evergreen foliage, which enable it to smother any weeds that get in its way. Ice Meidiland was bred as a landscaping plant – hardy, hearty, and healthy – but also makes an excellent rose for the front of a border or for a weeping effect in a container. The flowers are semidouble and white, with just a hint of pink at first and a neat circle of pale yellow stamens. They usually come in somewhat tight clusters of 4–7 (but sometimes more or fewer) and look nice against the small, neat, dark, glossy leaves. Ice Meidiland is a good repeater but, like its parent 'Katharina Zeimet', it tends to hold on to its petals after the flower has faded.

ICE MEIDILAND

'ICED GINGER'

Floribunda

ORIGIN **Dickson, Northern Ireland, 1971**
PARENTAGE **'Anne Watkins' x seedling**
FLOWER SIZE **4.3in (11cm)**
SCENT **Light and sweet**
FLOWERING **Repeats well**
HEIGHT/SPREAD **4.9ft (1.5m)/4.1ft (1.25m)**
HARDINESS **Zone 6**

The flowers of 'Iced Ginger' are large and shapely, like a Hybrid Tea, but borne in Floribunda clusters, thus combining the best of both types of modern garden rose. The buds are red, but the flowers are an especially beautiful color – palest pink, with darker backs and an apricot suffusion at the base of the petals. The coloring produces ginger shadows within the flowers, to contrast with the pale, frosted tips of the petals. The flowers are generously produced on long, erect stems, though the plant as a whole has an open habit of growth and a tendency to grow sideways rather than upward. The leaves are rich red at first, mid-green later, and may pick up a little blackspot in areas where this is a problem. The long petals are somewhat susceptible to rain damage, so 'Iced Ginger' fares best in hot, dry climates.

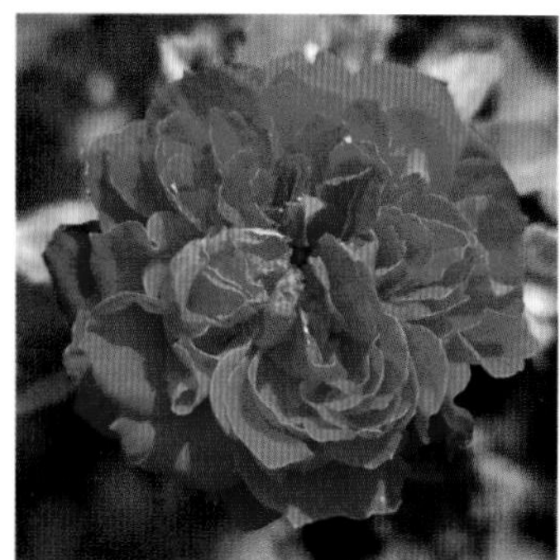

'HUNTER'

HURDY GURDY

'ICED GINGER'

'ICED PARFAIT'

'ICED PARFAIT'

Floribunda

ORIGIN **Lewis-Hickman, Australia, 1972**
PARENTAGE **'Pink Parfait' × 'Iceberg'**
FLOWER SIZE **3.5in (9cm)**
SCENT **Strong**
FLOWERING **Fully recurrent**
HEIGHT/SPREAD **3.3ft (1m)/3.3ft (1m)**
HARDINESS **Zone 6**

'Iced Parfait' is pretty at all stages – first when in bud, then as it expands, and finally when it is fully opened out to show its large boss of pale stamens. The flowers are pale creamy pink, fading to white, and come singly or, more usually, in clusters of up to six. The plant is bushy and compact, with light to mid-green leaves, broad leaflets, and red prickles. It was bred by Sister Mary-Xavier Lewis-Hickman (1910–95), a nun in Launceston, Tasmania.

'ILLUSION'

Kordesii Hybrid

ORIGIN **Kordes, Germany, 1961**
FLOWER SIZE **3.5in (9cm)**
SCENT **Light**
FLOWERING **Repeats well**
HEIGHT/SPREAD **9.8ft (3m)/6.6ft (2m)**
HARDINESS **Zone 5**

The Kordesii climbers are tough, hardy, vigorous, and brightly colored – their introduction in the 1950s and 1960s entirely changed people's perception of what a climbing rose should be. 'Illusion' is typical of the class, with good clusters of rich scarlet flowers (5–10), freely produced early in the growing season and then continuously, but in smaller numbers, right through until late autumn. The leaves are dark green and shiny, and often remain on the plant until well into winter. The orange hips are a bonus. Although not the most exciting choice for warmer climates, its hardiness makes 'Illusion' an outstanding climbing rose for cold climates, including central Europe and the American Midwest.

'ILSE KROHN SUPERIOR'

'ILSE KROHN SUPERIOR'

Kordesii Hybrid

ORIGIN **Kordes, Germany, 1964**
PARENTAGE **Sport of 'Ilse Krohn'**
FLOWER SIZE **4.3in (11cm)**
SCENT **Medium and sweet**
FLOWERING **Repeats well**
HEIGHT/SPREAD **9.8ft (3m)/6.6ft (2m)**
HARDINESS **Zone 5**

'Ilse Krohn Superior' is an interesting rose, because it is a repeat flowering climber that sported from a once-flowerer: normally the sport would be a dwarf shrub, but this is a vigorous, short climber, perfect for small gardens. It is still the best large-flowered white climber for cold climates. Its buds are long, elegant, and creamy white, with large petals that start to reflex as they open – very much like a large Hybrid Tea, in fact. The open flowers seem full of petals, tiered up like layers of strong taffeta. The large petals are thick and substantial, and seem to glow with color rather than reflecting it. There is just a hint of buff yellow at the center. The flowers come singly or in small clusters, typically three together, nodding slightly. They stand up well to rain and are well set off by the dark, lustrous, Kordesii foliage. It has slender stems and good resistance to disease.

'ILLUSION'

IMMENSEE

syn. 'KORIMRO', Grouse, Lac Rose

Shrub Rose

ORIGIN **Kordes, Germany, 1982**
PARENTAGE **'The Fairy' × *Rosa wichurana* seedling**
FLOWER SIZE **1.6in (4cm)**
SCENT **Strong, sweet, and musky**
FLOWERING **Once only, late in season**
HEIGHT/SPREAD **1.6ft (50cm)/16.4ft (5m)**
HARDINESS **Zone 5**
AWARDS **RNRS GM 1984**

Immensee was the first of the fast-growing shrub and landscaping roses: it set a standard for vigor and health that has never been equaled. The flowers open palest mother-of-pearl, with a blush pink edge, and fade quickly to white. They have prominent golden stamens, which turn brown after a day or so. They are very attractive to bees and butterflies. The single flowering is very profuse, followed occasionally by a few later flowers here and there. The flowers come in small clusters, typically of 3–5, and are followed by lots of tiny vermilion hips. It is very lax in its habit and, like its parent *Rosa wichurana*, is naturally a sprawling ground-covering plant, layering and rooting as it grows – as much as 13.1ft (4m) in a season. Its leaves are healthy, dark, small, evergreen, and glossy. It is a shrub rose in the sense that it covers a large area, but it does not exclude weeds. It does, however, make a wonderful late-flowering rambling rose. Immensee is a small lake in northern Switzerland.

IMMENSEE

'IMMORTAL JUNO'

syn. 'AUSJUNO'

Shrub Rose

ORIGIN **Austin, Britain, 1983**
FLOWER SIZE **3.1in (8cm)**
SCENT **Very strong and sweet**
FLOWERING **Repeats well**
HEIGHT/SPREAD **4.9ft (1.5m)/3.9ft (1.2m)**
HARDINESS **Zone 6**

'Immortal Juno' is still popular all over the world, except in its native England, where its heavy flowers spoil in the rain. It is an excellent shrub rose for drier climates. The flowers are a rich, warm, glowing rose pink, with slightly paler edges on the petals. They open out almost flat from globular buds to reveal a circular outline, a glimpse of stamens at the center, and a muddled mass of quilled petals. They come singly or in clusters of up to seven and tend to hang down under their own weight. The plant has somewhat small, smooth, pale leaves and an upright habit of growth, but sometimes the stems flop over under the weight of the flowers: discreet staking is the answer. It is a prickly rose and may suffer from mildew occasionally but it is usually healthy. Immortal Juno – the phrase comes from Ovid's *Metamorphoses* – was the wife (and sister) of Jupiter.

'IMMORTAL JUNO'

'IMP'

'IMPÉRATRICE JOSÉPHINE'

INDIAN SUMMER

I

'IMP'

Floribunda

ORIGIN **Dawson, Australia, 1971**
PARENTAGE **'Daily Sketch' x 'Impeccable'**
FLOWER SIZE **2.8in (7cm)**
SCENT **Light**
FLOWERING **Repeats reliably**
HEIGHT/SPREAD **3.9ft (1.2m)/3.3ft (1m)**
HARDINESS **Zone 6**

The flowers of 'Imp' are immensely variable and yet also very distinctive. Basically greenish white in color, the backs of the petals have thick crimson edges, which later become thinner and paler, developing irregular bands, stripes, and splotches of crimson, pink, and lilac. The flowers also open out flat as they age, so that more white is visible, contrasting with the crimson backs of the globular, unopened buds. They come in somewhat tight clusters of up to 15 flowers (very occasionally singly, but most usually in clusters of 3–7) and have thick stems. The plant is bushy, stout, compact, and healthy, with the usual Floribunda foliage, but the flowers are very handsome and unusual. An individual bloom makes a striking buttonhole. George Dawson (1904–91) was a retired market gardener from Fern Gully in Victoria, Australia. 'Imp' appeared in the Australian Roses postage stamp series in 1983.

IMPÉRATRICE FARAH

syn. 'DELIVOUR', Empress Farah, Kaiserin Farah, Strawberry Parfait

Hybrid Tea

ORIGIN **Delbard, France, 1992**
FLOWER SIZE **4.7in (12cm)**
SCENT **Light**
FLOWERING **Repeats**
HEIGHT/SPREAD **4.1ft (1.25m)/2.7ft (80cm)**
HARDINESS **Zone 6**
AWARDS **Geneva GM 1992; Rome GM 1992**

The opening buds of Impératrice Farah are unusually elegant. The petal edges are decked out in pale crimson, and curl back in the classic manner of the Hybrid Teas, so that only the colored tips seem to be reflexed. They appear mainly crimson at first but, as the flowers open out fully, they are seen to be more white than red. Nevertheless, the contrast between the white petals and their crimson edges is attractive at all stages of the flowers' development. They are large, with long petals, and are usually borne singly, though occasionally in clusters of up to five. Their stems are long, and perfect for cutting. Impératrice Farah has large, shiny leaves, which stand up well to blackspot, and a vigorous, upright habit of growth.

'IMPÉRATRICE JOSÉPHINE'

syn. 'EMPRESS JOSEPHINE', 'FRANCOFURTANA'

Gallica

ORIGIN **Descemet, France, c.1815**
FLOWER SIZE **4.3in (11cm)**
SCENT **Strong and sweet**
FLOWERING **Once only**
HEIGHT/SPREAD **4.9ft (1.5m)/5.7ft (1.75m)**
HARDINESS **Zone 5**

This is the best of the Agatha or Frankfurt roses, widely considered as hybrids between *Rosa gallica* and *Rosa cinnamomea*. 'Impératrice Joséphine' is the largest and fullest and, of course, named after a great rose lover. The flowers are purplish pink, with brighter veining toward the center and a paler, silvery tinge toward the edge of the large, delicate, papery, crinkly petals. The flower as a whole fades to lilac pink as it ages. The flowers are fully double and loosely quartered, with a mass of frilly petals through which the stamens are quite visible when fully open. They are borne singly and in clusters of up to seven, and are followed by orange hips. The hips, and the receptacles before them, have a distinctive "turbinate" (meaning turnip-shaped) outline. 'Impératrice Joséphine' has a lot of handsome, healthy, ribbed, pale gray green leaves and is almost thornless. It makes a fine, dense, lax shrub. Its only weakness is a tendency for the flowers to ball in damp weather and spoil in rain.

INDIAN SUMMER

syn. 'PEAPERFUME'

Hybrid Tea

ORIGIN **Pearce, Britain, 1991**
FLOWER SIZE **3.9in (10cm)**
SCENT **Strong, sweet, and fruity**
FLOWERING **Repeats well**
HEIGHT/SPREAD **4.1ft (1.25m)/3.3ft (1m)**
HARDINESS **Zone 6**
AWARDS **Glasgow FA 1993**

Vigor, scent, and color are what make Indian Summer an excellent rose. The flowers are a rich peachy yellow color, with slightly darker, more apricot colored petal backs. It is a very pretty combination, and the flowers keep their colors unusually well, though they eventually fade to buff at the edges. The flowers are shaped like Hybrid Teas at first, though they open out to show how their fairly short petals surround the attractive red filaments. They come in clusters of up to seven and their scent is delicious. The plant has a dense covering of dark leaves, bronzy new growth, and quite a lot of prickles.

'INDIGO'

Portland

ORIGIN **Laffay, France, 1830**
FLOWER SIZE **2.8in (7cm)**
SCENT **Light and sweet**
FLOWERING **Repeats**
HEIGHT/SPREAD **6.6ft (2m)/4.1ft (1.25m)**
HARDINESS **Zone 5**

"Purple" is a better description, but the color of 'Indigo' is variable. Sometimes its flowers are very dark, but at other times they are mid-purple, crimson, or deep mauve, and they tend to fade with age. The flowers are fully double, with slightly paler petal backs. Most have a button eye, some a cluster of bright yellow stamens at the center: all reflex fully into pompons. They are borne on short, stout stems in the Portland manner, thickly surrounded by dark leaves. They come singly or in clusters of up to three and are followed in hot climates by orange hips. The plant has dark stems, a lot of long, narrow prickles, an upright habit of growth, and a certain familiarity with mildew.

IMPÉRATRICE FARAH

'INDIGO'

'Inermis Morletii'

syn. 'Morletii'

Boursault

ORIGIN **Morlet, France, 1883**
FLOWER SIZE **1.8in (4.5cm)**
SCENT **Little or none**
FLOWERING **Once only, very early**
HEIGHT/SPREAD **9.8ft (3m)/6.6ft (2m)**
HARDINESS **Zone 5**

'Inermis Morletii' is a hybrid between a Boursault rose and a Noisette. Its red, smooth, thornless stems show its descent from the Boursaults. The flowers are dark purple pink or pale crimson, fading to mid-pink, but there is always a slightly lilac or purple tinge to the petals. The petals also have occasional white stripes running through the colored parts. The flowers come in clusters of up to about ten, and open out flat. They are rarely attractively shaped and are almost scentless, but the plant enjoys considerable hardiness: the flowers are among the earliest in cold climates, flowering a good month before the main season.

Ingrid Bergman

syn. 'POULman'

Hybrid Tea

ORIGIN **Poulsen, Denmark, 1984**
PARENTAGE **'Precious Platinum' x seedling**
FLOWER SIZE **3.9in (10cm)**
SCENT **Medium and sweet**
FLOWERING **Repeats well**
HEIGHT/SPREAD **2.7ft (80cm)/2.3ft (70cm)**
HARDINESS **Zone 5**
AWARDS **Madrid GM 1986; Golden Rose of the Hague 1987; Belfast GM 1995**

The classic red flowers of Ingrid Bergman have made it very popular all over the world. The flowers spiral open from long, elegant buds that are almost black. They are deep Turkey red all over, with the same unfading rich red shade on both sides of the petals – no white center, no white stripes, just pure dark red. They are usually borne singly, and are excellent for cutting but equally good for garden display. They are fully double, but stand up well to rain. Ingrid Bergman is sturdy, vigorous, and compact, with lacquered, shiny leaves and crimson new growth. It is very healthy and unusually hardy for a Hybrid Tea. Ingrid Bergman (1915–1982) was a popular Hollywood movie actress of Swedish origin.

Ingrid Bergman

'Inermis Morletii'

Ingrid Weibull

syn. 'TANweieke', Showbiz

Floribunda

ORIGIN **Tantau, Germany, 1981**
FLOWER SIZE **2.8in (7cm)**
SCENT **Light**
FLOWERING **Almost constant**
HEIGHT/SPREAD **2.5ft (75cm)/2.5ft (75cm)**
HARDINESS **Zone 5**
AWARDS **AARS 1985**

Ingrid Weibull is the perfect dark red Floribunda – neat, floriferous, healthy, and compact. It has large clusters of perfect flowers that cover the ground and appear almost incessantly right through until late autumn. The flowers open out quickly until they are almost flat, with a neat round outline and a small tuft of yellow stamens at the center. They are a very good bright dark red, enlivened by an occasional white stripe in the petals. The plant has dark, glossy leaves and is very healthy. It is a magnificent bedding rose, not least because, as well as coming so frequently, the flowers last a very long time.

Ingrid Weibull

International Herald Tribune

syn. 'HARquantum', Margaret Isobel Hayes, Violetta

Shrub Rose

ORIGIN **Harkness, Britain, 1984**
PARENTAGE **seedling x (['Orange Sensation' x 'Allgold'] x *Rosa californica*)**
FLOWER SIZE **2in (5cm)**
SCENT **Medium**
FLOWERING **Continuous**
HEIGHT/SPREAD **2ft (60cm)/2ft (60cm)**
HARDINESS **Zone 6**
AWARDS **Geneva GM 1983; Monza GM 1984**

International Herald Tribune is an extremely useful shrub for small gardens, mixed borders, and containers. Its cupped flowers are rich purple – a very unusual shade – with white centers and a lot of white streaks, and crooked white petaloids toward the center. This combination of purple petals, white petaloids, and a cupped shape gives the flowers their distinctive appearance. There is nothing else like them. The flowers are semidouble, with pale yellow anthers, and come in clusters of 5–25 on a bush that is too small to be called a shrub rose but too nonconformist to be classified among the Polyanthas.

International Herald Tribune

The leaves are glossy, mid-green, and fairly healthy, though blackspot may be a problem.

Intrigue *(Kordes, 1978)*

see Lavaglut

Intrigue

syn. 'JACum'

Floribunda

ORIGIN **Warriner, US, 1982**
PARENTAGE **'White Masterpiece' x 'Heirloom'**
FLOWER SIZE **3.1in (8cm)**
SCENT **Strong, rich, and sweet**
FLOWERING **Repeats well**
HEIGHT/SPREAD **5.7ft (1.75m)/4.1ft (1.25m)**
HARDINESS **Zone 6**
AWARDS **AARS 1984**

The color of Intrigue is its first attraction – a good rich purple when the flowers first open – but it also has scent, vigor, and floriferousness. The flowers are a stunning color at all times, even when they fade to magenta, and very full of neatly arranged petals. The petals have paler backs and the flowers come in large clusters, typically of 5–15, on long stems that are good for cutting. The plant is tall, lanky, and upright in growth, but can be pruned to 3.3ft (1m) or less if required. Its leaves are healthy, medium-dark, and fairly glossy. In short, Intrigue is an excellent rose and deservedly popular, but far too rarely seen outside North America.

Intrigue

INVINCIBLE

INVINCIBLE

syn. 'RUNTRU', Fennica

Floribunda

ORIGIN **de Ruiter, Belgium, 1983**
PARENTAGE **'Rubella' x 'National Trust'**
FLOWER SIZE **3.1in (8cm)**
SCENT **Light and sweet**
FLOWERING **Repeats well**
HEIGHT/SPREAD **3.3ft (1m)/2.5ft (75cm)**
HARDINESS **Zone 5**

It is classed among the Floribundas, but Invincible has many Hybrid Teas in its ancestry. Its flowers have a lot of petals, though these are on the short side, and the open flower certainly resembles a Hybrid Tea. The flowers come in small clusters (typically of 3–7) on strong, thick, sturdy stems that are good for cutting. They are a brilliant, dark red – blood red or Turkey red – and keep their color well right through until they drop their petals. Invincible is a good repeater, and its nearly continuous flowering makes it useful as a bedding rose. The individual flowers also stand up well to rain and wind. The leaves are large, dark, healthy, and fairly glossy, and the plant is a vigorous grower.

'IPSILANTÉ'

see 'YPSILANTI'

'IRENE AV DENMARK'

Floribunda

ORIGIN **Poulsen, Denmark, 1948**
PARENTAGE **'Orléans Rose' x ('Mme. Plantier' x 'Edina')**
FLOWER SIZE **2.8in (7cm)**
SCENT **Fairly strong and sweet**
FLOWERING **Almost continuous, from midseason until winter**
HEIGHT/SPREAD **2ft (60cm)/2ft (60cm)**
HARDINESS **Zone 5**

'Irene av Denmark' was the most widely grown white Polyantha rose for about 20 years after its introduction in 1948. It is a very pretty and floriferous rose, and most useful for bedding. The flowers have just a hint of pink at first, but soon turn pure white. The petals are somewhat thin and delicate, so they do not fare well in wet weather, but they are produced most abundantly and are especially pretty when they are unfurling their petals. They come in clusters of 3–9. The plant is low-growing, vigorous, and compact. The foliage is dark and a good foil for the flowers, but susceptible to blackspot. Nevertheless, 'Irene av Denmark' is still popular, and rightly so.

'IRENE AV DENMARK'

'IRÈNE WATTS'

China Rose

ORIGIN **Guillot, France, 1896**
PARENTAGE **'Mme. Laurette Messimy' x unknown**
FLOWER SIZE **2.8in (7cm)**
SCENT **Light but fruity**
FLOWERING **Repeats well**
HEIGHT/SPREAD **2.7ft (80cm)/2ft (60cm)**
HARDINESS **Zone 7**

The flowers of 'Irène Watts' are mother-of-pearl, with slightly darker and pinker petal backs and hints of apricot and salmon toward the center. They often retain patches of darker colour as the petal edges fade to pale pink. They open from somewhat dumpy buds and come in clusters of 3–11. The plant is twiggy, and short on vigor. Its height depends upon the warmth it receives, but rarely exceeds 3.3ft (1m). It should be allowed to build up to its natural height, with no pruning other than the removal of dead or dying wood. The leaves are pale and thin, with elegantly slender leaflets, somewhat susceptible to blackspot in damp climates. It flowers continuously.

'IRISH BEAUTY'

see 'ELIZABETH OF GLAMIS'

'IRÈNE WATTS'

'IRISH ELEGANCE'

'IRISH ELEGANCE'

Hybrid Tea

ORIGIN **Dickson, Northern Ireland, 1905**
FLOWER SIZE **3.1in (8cm)**
SCENT **Strong and sweet**
FLOWERING **Repeats well**
HEIGHT/SPREAD **4.9ft (1.5m)/4.1ft (1.25m)**
HARDINESS **Zone 7**

In the early 1900s, the Dickson family of rose breeders issued a number of single-flowered Hybrid Teas. They were extremely floriferous and, as garden roses, can be considered forerunners of the Floribundas. 'Irish Elegance' is one that has remained popular. It has flowers of apricot and yellow, fading to pink and cream, opening from scarlet buds. It grows vigorously, repeats well and tolerates poor soil. If left unpruned and allowed to build up its natural size it will reach as much as 8.2ft (2.5m).

IRISH EYES

syn. 'DICWITNESS'

Floribunda

ORIGIN **Dickson, Northern Ireland, 1999**
PARENTAGE **Mr. J C B x Gypsy Dancer**
FLOWER SIZE **2in (5cm)**
SCENT **Light and fruity**
FLOWERING **Repeats well**
HEIGHT/SPREAD **2.7ft (80cm)/2ft (60cm)**
HARDINESS **Zone 6**

The flowers of Irish Eyes are bright orange at first with yellow undersides. As they age, the yellow starts to fade and the orange turns to vermilion. Look carefully and you can see scarlet veins running through the petals too. It is a very striking combination of colors and one that has ensured instant popularity for this neat Floribunda since its release in 1999. The flowers are individually carried on long stalks, but they all emanate from a long, upright stem, so that the overall effect is of a cluster. The plant has small, healthy, medium-dark leaves, a scattering of prickles, and a neat, upright habit of growth. It is a reliable and quick repeater.

IRISH EYES

'IRISH FIREFLAME'

Hybrid Tea

ORIGIN **Dickson, Northern Ireland, 1914**
FLOWER SIZE **2.8in (7cm)**
SCENT **Medium and sweet**
FLOWERING **Repeats constantly**
HEIGHT/SPREAD **3.3ft (1m)/2.7ft (80cm)**
HARDINESS **Zone 6**

'Irish Fireflame' is the best of the single-flowered Hybrid Teas introduced by the Dicksons in the early 1900s. It is very similar to 'Irish Elegance' (pictured above) but its flowers open dark orange pink with a yellow center and golden stamens. Later they fade to mid-pink and white. The flowers are five-petaled and carried singly or in clusters of up to seven. The plant is healthy and fairly vigorous, with typical Hybrid Tea prickles and leaves.

'IRISH GOLD'

see 'GRANDPA DICKSON'

'IRISH FIREFLAME'

IRRESISTIBLE

IRRESISTIBLE

syn. 'TINRESIST'

Miniature Rose

ORIGIN **Bennett, US, 1989**
PARENTAGE **'Tiki' x Brian Lee**
FLOWER SIZE **1.6in (4cm)**
SCENT **Medium and fruity**
FLOWERING **Repeats well**
HEIGHT/SPREAD **2.7ft (80cm)/1.6ft (50cm)**
HARDINESS **Zone 6**

Dee Bennett was an amateur rose lover in California who was so successful in breeding roses that she turned professional. Irresistible is one of her best miniatures. Its flowers are white, with a hint of pink at the center at first, and greenish markings on the outer petals. They are perfect scaled-down Hybrid Teas, very full of petals, and usually borne singly on long, strong stems but occasionally in quite large clusters. It is popular with exhibitors, but also makes a good garden rose, standing up to rain and lasting well as a cut flower. Irresistible is taller than most miniature roses and can reach as much as 3.3ft (1m) high, though the flowers are always small. It makes a vigorous, healthy plant. Its height is an asset in the garden, where it combines well with almost everything and is seldom out of flower.

'ISABELLA SPRUNT'

see 'SAFRANO'

ISABELLE RENAISSANCE

syn. 'POULISAB', Isabella

Shrub Rose

ORIGIN **Poulsen, Denmark, 1995**
FLOWER SIZE **3.9in (10cm)**
SCENT **Medium and sweet**
FLOWERING **Repeats**
HEIGHT/SPREAD **4.9ft (1.5m)/4.1ft (1.25m)**
HARDINESS **Zone 6**

This is a fine example of Poulsen's Renaissance roses, which appeal to those who also like David Austin's English Roses. The flowers of Isabelle Renaissance are a very rich, dark red – a pure color that needs to be planted where its dark tones show up against paler contrasting shades. The red is enlivened by occasional streaks of white toward the center. The flowers are very full, laid out with masses of small, quilled petals in a rosette form and sometimes roughly quartered. Later the flowers expand even further, lose their neat shape and show their yellow stamens at the center. They come singly and in rather tight clusters of 3–4. Isabelle Renaissance makes a vigorous plant, with large, dark, healthy leaves and the upright habit of a Hybrid Tea.

ISABELLE RENAISSANCE

'ISKRA'

syn. 'SPARKLING SCARLET'

Modern Climber

ORIGIN **Meilland, France, 1970**
PARENTAGE **'Danse des Sylphes' x 'Zambra'**
FLOWER SIZE **2.8in (7cm)**
SCENT **Little or none**
FLOWERING **Repeats a little**
HEIGHT/SPREAD **11.5ft (3.5m)/8.2ft (2.5m)**
HARDINESS **Zone 6**

Cheerful, simple, and almost scentless, 'Iskra' is very much a 1960s rose. The breeder's intention was to combine the free flowering vigor of the climber 'Danse des Sylphes' with the bright orange coloring of 'Zambra'. The flowers open quickly, and keep their bright vermilion color well. They are borne in small clusters, typically of 3–7 flowers, sometimes much larger, and stand up well to rain. The plant is fairly vigorous, if a little lanky, and has large, glossy leaves with somewhat rounded leaflets.

'ISKRA'

'ISPAHAN'

'ISPAHAN'

Damask Rose

ORIGIN **c.1832**
FLOWER SIZE **3.5in (9cm)**
SCENT **Very strong and sweet**
FLOWERING **Once only, over a long period**
HEIGHT/SPREAD **6.6ft (2m)/6.6ft (2m)**
HARDINESS **Zone 5**

'Ispahan' is the best of all the once-flowering old garden roses. If you have room for no more than one old rose, 'Ispahan' should be your choice. It is hardy, healthy, and sweetly scented. It is the first of the Damasks to start into flower and the last to stop. Its flower clusters are larger than any other's, often containing as many as 15 flowers. It is handsome even in winter because, unique among all Damask roses, 'Ispahan' is semievergreen. Its origins are obscure, because it was introduced into wider cultivation by an English gardener named Norah Lindsay, who claimed to have found it in Persia. There is nothing to match its large, mid-pink flowers, full of petals arranged around a rough button eye, as they unfold for week after week in high season. And the scent is delicious.

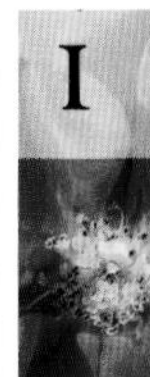

I

'IVORY FASHION'

Floribunda

ORIGIN **Boerner, US, 1958**
PARENTAGE **'Sonata' x 'Fashion'**
FLOWER SIZE **5.1in (13cm)**
SCENT **Light and fruity**
FLOWERING **Repeats well**
HEIGHT/SPREAD **4.1ft (1.25m)/2.7ft (80cm)**
HARDINESS **Zone 6**
AWARDS **AARS 1959**

This beautiful, pale Floribunda is elegant both as a long, expanding bud and later, when it has opened out its flowers fully to reveal its long stamens and red filaments. 'Ivory Fashion' is indeed ivory colored or pale buff at first, but later it fades to white, while always retaining a hint of ivory or buff at the center of the flower. The flowers are borne singly or in clusters of up to five, and seem to grow in size as they age. They are often damaged by rain, so this is a rose that does best in dry weather, though it is worth growing even in damp climates. The dark, healthy leaves are a good foil for the flowers, and there is a beautiful climbing form, now very rare.

'IVORY FASHION'

J

'J. P. Connell'

Shrub Rose

ORIGIN **Svejda, Canada, 1987**
PARENTAGE **'Arthur Bell' x 'Von Scharnhorst'**
FLOWER SIZE **3.1in (8cm)**
SCENT **Medium, musky, and fruity**
FLOWERING **Repeats**
HEIGHT/SPREAD **4.9ft (1.5m)/4.1ft (1.25m)**
HARDINESS **Zone 4**

This remarkable rose was bred to survive Canadian winters. 'J. P. Connell' is one of the few yellow roses in the Explorer series. It has no trace of *Rosa rugosa* in its ancestry, which explains why it has "proper" rose flowers like a Hybrid Tea as it opens out, and resembles a Floribunda when fully expanded. The flowers are mid-yellow or lemon yellow, and fade to cream as they open, though the inner petals stay yellow longer. Lightly cupped and fully double, the flowers have an attractive circle of red stamens at their center. They come singly or in small clusters (of up to seven). 'J. P. Connell' has nearly thornless stems and an upright habit, with mid-green leaves. Blackspot may be a problem in damp climates. The bush is not very vigorous and takes several years to build up its size and strength. Its blooming habit reflects this: once-flowering at first, then with a few later flowers, and eventually a reliable repeat bloomer. Patience pays off.

JACQUELINE DU PRÉ

Jacqueline du Pré

syn. 'HARWANN'
Shrub Rose

ORIGIN **Harkness, Britain, 1988**
PARENTAGE **'Radox Bouquet' x 'Maigold'**
FLOWER SIZE **3.1in (8cm)**
SCENT **Light and musky**
FLOWERING **Early in season, and repeats well**
HEIGHT/SPREAD **5.7ft (1.75m)/4.1ft(1.25m)**
HARDINESS **Zone 6**
AWARDS **Le Rœulx GM 1988**

The lightly cupped flowers of Jacqueline du Pré have an ethereal beauty. Creamy white, with pale pink reverses, the petals show a translucent quality in dull weather and glow with illumination when the sun shines through them. The long, pink filaments – all of different lengths – provide a focal point for the whole flower. The flowers come in clusters of 3–11 and are backed by good, dark, healthy leaves. The bush is quite prickly but grows stoutly and fills out with age. It does best with minimum pruning and a little deadheading after flowering. It was named after the talented cellist who was born in Oxford, England, in 1945 and died of multiple sclerosis in 1987. Jack Harkness considered this one of the best of all his introductions.

'J. P. CONNELL'

JACQUELINE NEBOUT

Jacqueline Nebout

syn. 'MEICHOIJU', City of Adelaide
Floribunda

ORIGIN **Meilland, France, 1989**
FLOWER SIZE **2.8in (7cm)**
SCENT **Light and sweet**
FLOWERING **Repeats well**
HEIGHT/SPREAD **4.9ft (1.5m)/4.1ft (1.25m)**
HARDINESS **Zone 6**
AWARDS **Dublin GM 1988**

After it was given the extra name of City of Adelaide in 1993, Jacqueline Nebout quickly became as popular in Australia as in its native France. It stands up very well to the hot temperatures and long, dry months that characterize Australian life. The flowers are pink – a good, rich pink, with slightly darker petal backs. They open slightly paler in hot weather – a more silvery pink – but keep their color well, always with deeper shades on the reverses, so that the flower is full of rich pink shades and shadows. The flowers come in clusters of 3–10 and are produced continuously in warm climates. Jacqueline Nebout has a dense, bushy habit of growth and rich, dark green leaves. It was named after a high profile Parisian politician.

Jacquenetta

syn. 'AUSJAC'
Shrub Rose

ORIGIN **Austin, Britain, 1983**
PARENTAGE **seedling x 'Charles Austin'**
FLOWER SIZE **3.5in (9cm)**
SCENT **Strong and fruity**
FLOWERING **Repeats well**
HEIGHT/SPREAD **4.9ft (1.5m)/4.9ft (1.5m)**
HARDINESS **Zone 5**

Jacquenetta is best considered (and treated) as a very attractive Floribunda, rather than a shrub rose. The flowers open pale apricot, fading to mother-of-pearl, with slightly darker petal backs and, at first, a pale yellow flush toward the center. Each flower has quite a large central spray of stamens and a delicious scent. Although often described as single, the flowers usually have more than five petals, especially in cool climates. The flowers come singly or in clusters of up to nine. The plant has dark leaves, (sometimes liable to attract mildew and rust) and a somewhat lax, open habit. Jacquenetta is a character in William Shakespeare's *Love's Labour's Lost*.

JACQUENETTA

'Jacques Cartier'

syn. 'MARCHESA BOCCELLA'
Portland

ORIGIN **Moreau-Robert, France, 1868**
FLOWER SIZE **3.5in (9cm)**
SCENT **Strong and sweet**
FLOWERING **Repeats very well**
HEIGHT/SPREAD **4.9ft (1.5m)/3.3ft (1m)**
HARDINESS **Zone 5**

If you live in a cold climate and have room for only one old rose, 'Jacques Cartier' should be your choice. It is hardy, healthy, floriferous, and exquisitely beautiful. The flowers are deep rose pink (slightly paler on the petal backs) and stuffed with small petals arranged in a swirling mass around a neat button eye. Unlike many old roses, 'Jacques Cartier' stands up well to rain – the petals are arranged in such a way that rain just runs off them. The flowers come singly or in tight clusters of up to five, and are attractive when cut for the house. The plant flowers generously and repeatedly every six weeks or so until winter sets in: deadheading helps to speed up the next flush. 'Jacques Cartier' is also a rose that responds well to feeding and watering. The plant is upright, narrow, and compact, with pale leaves and long, narrow leaflets. It mixes well with other plants and can be pruned short and grown in containers too.

'JACQUES CARTIER'

Jackson and Perkins

THE US ROSE BREEDING FIRM OF JACKSON & PERKINS BEGAN ITS EXTRAORDINARY RISE TO THE TOP IN THE 1940S WITH THE WORK OF EUGENE BOERNER

JACKSON & PERKINS, known in the trade as "J & P," was founded in 1872 in Newark, New York. Roses were not part of its business at first, but became its main line after the success of its pink rambler 'Dorothy Perkins'. J & P then expanded to become the largest wholesale rose grower in the US – and, indeed, the world. In the 1930s, Jean Henri Nicolas, a French agronomist and a director of the company, tried his hand at rose breeding. His yellow Hybrid Tea 'Eclipse' (1935) remains popular in Europe and the US, while his pink Floribunda 'Smiles' was both attractive and fairly advanced when introduced in 1937.

EUGENE BOERNER

The glory days of J & P as rose breeders began with the work of Eugene Boerner (1893–1966), who took over from Nicolas in 1937. Boerner bred some fine climbers, such as 'Aloha', 'Coral Dawn', and 'Parade', and a handful of excellent Hybrid Teas, including the ever-popular 'First Prize' and 'John F. Kennedy'. However, it was Floribundas above all that Boerner developed, pouring out a stream of first-rate cultivars throughout the 1940s, 1950s, and 1960s. 'Apricot Nectar', 'Lavender Pinocchio', and the remarkable 'Masquerade' remain bestsellers many years after they were first introduced, but some of Boerner's finest Floribundas are now rarely seen, including 'Golden Fleece' (1954), 'Jiminy Cricket' (1954), 'Gold Cup' (1957), and 'Fashionette' (1958).

During the 1960s, ownership of the company finally passed away from the Perkins family. Boerner was followed in 1963 by Bill Warriner, who won no fewer than 20 All-America Rose Selection awards over the next 20 years. He bred somewhat more Hybrid Teas than his predecessor – Honor and Pristine are among the best-known – and several very fine modern climbers, including the brilliant red 'Tempo' (Warriner, 1975) and the extraordinarily colored Butterscotch (1986). But, like Boerner, he is probably best remembered for his Floribundas, most of which have fully petaled flowers in the Hybrid Tea mould: some of the best are French Lace and Intrigue and his later cultivars Pleasure (1988), Neon Lights (1991), and Señorita (1991).

PLEASURE

The present hybridizer at Jackson & Perkins, Dr. Keith Zary, raises 300,000–400,000 seedlings every year. He joined the company in 1985 and is best known for introducing a run of sumptuous, prizewinning Hybrid Teas, like Opening Night (1998) and Gemini (1999). Zary has also bred a number of fine Floribundas, including Honey Bouquet (1999), and Amber Waves (2000), and the excellent purple and white shrub rose Greetings (1999), which won the top prize at the English trials in 1997. Zary runs the research center at Somis, California, though some of the trialing is done at the company's extensive growing fields near Bakersfield.

J & P is part of a much bigger group these days. It merged with Armstrong Nurseries in the late 1980s and its ultimate holding company today is a Japanese corporation. It still produces up to nine million roses every year but, as throughout the US, the number is falling. Some people think that what the industry needs to reverse the trend is a rose as radical and universally attractive as the original 'Dorothy Perkins'.

'SMILES'

JACQUES PRÉVERT

JACQUES PRÉVERT

syn. 'MEIMOUSLIN', Cardinal Song
Grandiflora

ORIGIN **Meilland, France, 1992**
PARENTAGE **Olympiad x (Michel Lis le Jardinier x 'Red Lady')**
FLOWER SIZE **5.1in (13cm)**
SCENT **Light**
FLOWERING **Repeats well**
HEIGHT/SPREAD **6.6ft (2m)/4.1ft (1.25m)**
HARDINESS **Zone 6**
AWARDS **Lyon GM 1993**

Vigor, elegance, size, and good health are abundantly present in Jacques Prévert; all it lacks to match its other qualities is a strong scent. The flowers are large, perfectly formed, and borne either singly or in small clusters on a tall, upright plant. The long stems last for many days in flower, which also makes them useful for cutting. The flowers keep their color well, even when they open out to a broad, lightly cupped shape. The leaves are dark, glossy, and healthy. The name commemorates a poet (1900–77) who is highly regarded by some people in France. A good rose, but slightly short on character.

'JADIS'

syn. 'FRAGRANT MEMORY'
Hybrid Tea

ORIGIN **Warriner, US, 1974**
PARENTAGE **'Chrysler Imperial' x 'Virgo'**
FLOWER SIZE **4.3in (11cm)**
SCENT **Very strong and sweet**
FLOWERING **Repeats**
HEIGHT/SPREAD **4.1ft (1.25m)/3.3ft (1m)**
HARDINESS **Zone 6**

Long appreciated for its amazingly rich scent, 'Jadis' has kept its popularity in the face of competition from healthier modern roses. Its flowers are a deep, rich pink, with a hint of magenta toward the center and paler petal edges. When they open out, the flowers grade from deepest pink around the stamens to nearly white at the edges. They are borne singly or in small clusters (typically of three flowers) on long, strong stems, which make them perfect for cutting. 'Jadis' grows into an open, upright plant, sending up flush after flush of its large, elegant flowers. It is a martyr to mildew and blackspot in areas where these diseases are a problem, but still one of the all-around best in dry climates.

'JAMES MASON'

'JAMES MASON'

Gallica

ORIGIN **Beales, Britain, 1982**
PARENTAGE **'Scharlachglut' x 'Tuscany Superb'**
FLOWER SIZE **4.7in (12cm)**
SCENT **Medium and sweet**
FLOWERING **Once, midseason**
HEIGHT/SPREAD **5.7ft (1.75m)/4.9ft (1.5m)**
HARDINESS **Zone 4**

No one breeds Gallica roses any more: the last were introduced over 150 years ago. Yet 'James Mason' is as close to a Gallica as any shrub rose can be, in both looks and breeding. It has a modern brilliance to its coloring – the petals shine with a scarlet overlay – but the shape of the flower, the bright boss of stamens, and the healthy, light green leaves all show it to be a reproduction Gallica. It flowers abundantly, usually in clusters of three, and makes a vivid splash in the garden; in color schemes it belongs more closely to the reds than the crimsons. The scarlet hips are a bonus. It commemorates the English actor James Mason (1909–84), a great lover of roses.

'JAMES MITCHELL'

Moss Rose

ORIGIN **Verdier, France, 1861**
FLOWER SIZE **2in (5cm)**
SCENT **Strong and sweet**
FLOWERING **Once only**
HEIGHT/SPREAD **4.9ft (1.5m)/4.9ft (1.5m)**
HARDINESS **Zone 5**

The flowers of 'James Mitchell' are small but more than compensated by their rich scent. The flowers are a rich rose pink, with masses of long petals rayed out from a rough button eye. They fade slightly as they age and the petal backs are slightly paler, so there is always a pretty contrast of shades within each flower. However, the real contrast comes between the pink flowers and the thick layer of dark moss that covers the buds, sepals, and receptacles, and then runs down the stems, where it transmutes into little prickles. 'James Mitchell' makes a vigorous, dense shrub with soft green leaves that are unusually healthy among old roses. It flowers only once, but profusely and earlier than most Mosses.

'JADIS'

'JAMES MITCHELL'

'JAMES VEITCH'

Moss Rose

ORIGIN **Verdier, France, 1865**
FLOWER SIZE **3.1in (8cm)**
SCENT **Strong and sweet**
FLOWERING **Remontant**
HEIGHT/SPREAD **4.1ft (1.25m)/4.1ft (1.25m)**
HARDINESS **Zone 5**

The Veitches were by far the most successful English nurserymen of the 19th century, and one of the collectors they employed is also commemorated by a Moss rose, 'William Lobb'. The mossiness of 'James Veitch' runs down from the buds, the sepals, and the flower stems until it meets the branches of the bush itself, where there are ferocious little prickles. The flowers are crimson at first, then violet, before changing to lilac, lavender, and gray as they age. The petals have much paler undersides at all times and fold back abruptly along their sides, giving the flower a quilled effect. They come in clusters, typically of 3–5, and will repeat more quickly if deadheaded. The bush has dark green leaves and the susceptibility to mildew from which no Moss rose is free.

'JANET'S PRIDE'

Rubiginosa Hybrid

ORIGIN **G. Paul, Britain, 1892**
PARENTAGE ***Rosa rubiginosa* x unknown**
FLOWER SIZE **2in (5cm)**
SCENT **Medium and sweet**
FLOWERING **Once, midseason**
HEIGHT/SPREAD **8.2ft (2.5m)/6.6ft (2m)**
HARDINESS **Zone 5**

'JAMES VEITCH'

'JANET'S PRIDE'

'Janet's Pride' was found as a seedling in a hedgerow in Cheshire, England. It is a hybrid of the sweet briar *Rosa rubiginosa* and, though the other parent is unknown, it was probably a Hybrid Perpetual. The great attraction of *Rosa rubiginosa* itself is the sweet scent of its leaves, but 'Janet's Pride' has little or no fragrance to its leaves. Its unique characteristic is the unusual coloring of its semidouble flowers. Depending on how you look at them, they are either white with thick pink edges or pink with a large white patch at the center. The coloring is also irregular, and white streaks run right through to the edges of the petals. When in full bloom, this is one of the most arresting of all flowers. 'Janet's Pride' is a rose for large gardens and wild gardens, with small leaves, very prickly stems, and a tendency to blackspot. It is usually a shy flowerer, but in some years the bloom is abundant and followed by a crop of orange hips. It deserves to be more widely grown outside Europe.

'JANINA'

Hybrid Tea

ORIGIN **Tantau, Germany, 1974**
FLOWER SIZE **4.3in (11cm)**
SCENT **Medium and fruity**
FLOWERING **Repeats**
HEIGHT/SPREAD **4.1ft (1.25m)/3.3ft (1m)**
HARDINESS **Zone 6**

'JANINA'

The overall color of 'Janina' is orange, but closer examination shows a multitude of beautiful shades. The petals are bright orange vermilion when they first open, with yellow backs to the petals and an occasional yellow streak running through the inner petals. When the flowers open out, they reveal a bright yellow patch at the center and handsome golden stamens. Later the yellow tints fade, leaving the flower more salmon pink with creamy undersides. The flowers are shapely at all stages, though the petals are not notably long, and they come on long, strong stems, which are good for cutting. 'Janina' also makes a good bedding rose. It is vigorous and not too prickly, and its dark leaves are fairly healthy except for a little blackspot later in the year.

JARDINS DE BAGATELLE

syn. 'MEIMAFRIS', Drottning Silvia, Sarah, Ibu Tien Suharto, Karl Heinz Hanisch

Hybrid Tea

ORIGIN **Meilland, France, 1986**
PARENTAGE **('Queen Elizabeth' x 'Arturo Toscanini') x Laura**
FLOWER SIZE **4.7in (12cm)**
SCENT **Strong and sweet**
FLOWERING **Repeats well**
HEIGHT/SPREAD **4.1ft (1.25m)/3.3ft (1m)**
HARDINESS **Zone 6**
AWARDS **Bagatelle FA 1984; Geneva GM 1984; Madrid FA 1986; Poitiers GM 1986; Genoa GM 1987**

JARDINS DE BAGATELLE

The flowers of Jardins de Bagatelle are large and shapely, but it is their color that first attracts attention – cream with a hint of pink or buff at first, and dark apricot petal backs. The colors fade a little over the next few days, but the flowers retain a suggestion of buff or peach pink at the center right through until they drop their petals. They are also very strongly scented. The flowers are borne both singly and in clusters of up to five on long, strong stems that are good for cutting. Jardins de Bagatelle also makes a fine display in the garden. It is very adaptable and has proved successful in many different climates and conditions – cold and hot, damp and dry. The plant has large, dark, healthy leaves and a broad upright habit. It is a profuse flowerer and a good repeater.

JARDINS DE FRANCE

syn. 'MEIZEBUL'

Floribunda

ORIGIN **Meilland, France, 1998**
FLOWER SIZE **3.5in (9cm)**
SCENT **Light and sweet**
FLOWERING **Repeats well**
HEIGHT/SPREAD **4.1ft (1.25m)/3.3ft (1m)**
HARDINESS **Zone 6**
AWARDS **Bagatelle GM 1998; Dublin GM 1998**

This handsome, shrubby Floribunda has won many prizes in Europe as a rose for garden effect. The flowers of Jardins de France are full of short, incurved petals, which stand up very well to wind and rain. They are rich pink with a hint of salmon at first, and paler, more silvery pink backs to the petals. The coloring is not uniform, however, because every flower has patches of darker pink, and also of white in places, creating an unusual effect. The flowers come in dense clusters, typically of 3–8, but sometimes more. They are produced in great quantity and fairly continuously right through until late autumn. Jardins de France makes a broad, bushy plant with very handsome, healthy, dark, glossy leaves. It is generally seen cut back and growing to about 3.3ft (1m), but will reach twice that height if left unpruned.

JARDINS DE FRANCE

'JAUNE DESPREZ'

see 'DESPREZ À FLEURS JAUNES'

JAYNE AUSTIN

syn. 'AUSBREAK'

Shrub Rose

ORIGIN **Austin, Britain, 1990**
PARENTAGE **Graham Thomas x Tamora**
FLOWER SIZE **2in (5cm)**
SCENT **Strong and spicy**
FLOWERING **Repeats well**
HEIGHT/SPREAD **4.1ft (1.25m)/2.7ft (80cm)**
HARDINESS **Zone 6**

Jayne Austin is a very attractive rose but tends to produce somewhat more leaves than flowers. It is named after David Austin's daughter-in-law. The flowers are buff yellow at first, but fade to cream and then white, especially at their edges, though the petal backs are darker and the inner petals also keep their apricot color much longer. The outer petals are large and flat, the inner ones smaller and more irregularly shaped. The flowers usually form a rosette around a button eye. They come in clusters (typically of 3–5 flowers) held upright on fairly long stems. The plant has quite a lot of large prickles, and the long stems keel over to create a rounded shape out of a naturally narrow, upright habit. The mid-green, glossy leaves are susceptible to mildew in cool weather and occasionally to rust. Nevertheless, Jayne Austin fares best in mild climates like its native England, since it tends to scorch in the sun.

JAYNE AUSTIN

JAZZ

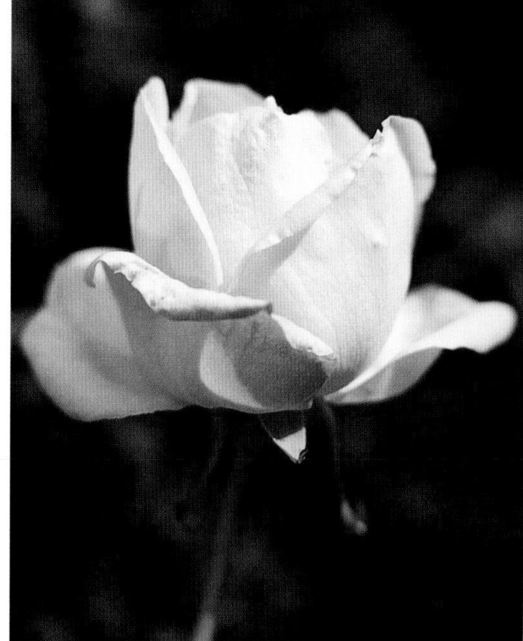

'JEAN DUCHER'

JAZZ

syn. 'POULNORM', Naheglut, That's Jazz

Modern Climber

ORIGIN **Poulsen, Denmark, 1997**
FLOWER SIZE **3.1in (8cm)**
SCENT **Very light**
FLOWERING **Repeats**
HEIGHT/ SPREAD **9.8ft (3m)/6.6ft (2m)**
HARDINESS **Zone 5**

Crimson climbers have always been popular, even when they have little or no scent. Jazz is bidding to take over from 'Dublin Bay' as the world's favorite, though it is not such a good rose. The flowers are prettily shaped, fairly full, and unfurl slowly. They are a good crimson, but not a very distinctive shade, and they come singly or in clusters of up to five. The plant has prickly, sturdy, upright growth, dark, glossy leaves, and small, round leaflets. It grows stoutly, building up to about 9.8ft (3m). Jazz is popular in Denmark and France, but 'Dublin Bay' has held its ground elsewhere.

'JEAN DUCHER'

Tea Rose

ORIGIN **Ducher, France, 1873**
FLOWER SIZE **3.1in (8cm)**
SCENT **Strong and tealike**
FLOWERING **Repeats constantly**
HEIGHT/SPREAD **4.9ft (1.5m)/4.9ft (1.5m)**
HARDINESS **Zone 7**

This famous old Tea rose is widely grown all over the world in hot, dry climates, where 'Jean Ducher' blooms all the year round. The flowers open pale flesh pink with a buff yellow wash and hints of apricot or peach toward the center: the combination of muted pinks and yellows is very typical of the Tea roses. The flowers are lightly and loosely double, and generally borne singly. 'Jean Ducher' has fairly soft petals, which are sensitive to rain damage. In damp climates the elegant, pointed, evergreen leaves may also be susceptible to blackspot and mildew. Elsewhere, it is trouble-free and flowers without interruption. It tolerates poor soil and neglect, but responds well to good cultivation. Like many Tea roses, 'Jean Ducher' is best left unpruned, except for removing dead wood. Then it grows into a tall, twiggy bush, which is covered in flowers for months on end. It is easy to grow from cuttings.

JEAN GIONO

syn. 'MEIROKOI'

Hybrid Tea

ORIGIN **Meilland, France, 1994**
PARENTAGE **('Yakimour' x 'Landora') x** Graham Thomas
FLOWER SIZE **3.5in (9cm)**
SCENT **Light and fruity**
FLOWERING **Repeats**
HEIGHT/SPREAD **4.9ft (1.5m)/3.3ft (1m)**
HARDINESS **Zone 6**

The influence of Graham Thomas is immediately apparent in this blowsy beauty, although its striking tangerine color is quite unlike the David Austin roses. Actually the coloring is variable: sometimes the outer petals are bright yellow while the inner ones are more apricot or even pink. The flowers come singly or in small clusters and take several days to unfold all their ruffled petals, so this is a rose that fares better in dry climates. The petals fade to buff or cream at their edges, which serves to emphasize their ruffled shape. The long stems make it very useful for cutting, though they do have large prickles. Jean Giono (1895–1970) was a French poet and novelist who wrote lyrically of the countryside of his native Provence.

JEAN GIONO

JEAN KENNEALLY

syn. 'TINEALLY'

Miniature Rose

ORIGIN **Bennett, US, 1984**
PARENTAGE **'Futura' x 'Party Girl'**
FLOWER SIZE **1.2in (3cm)**
SCENT **Light and musky**
FLOWERING **Repeats well**
HEIGHT/SPREAD **3.3ft (1m)/2.7ft (80cm)**
HARDINESS **Zone 5**
AWARDS **AoE 1986**

In hot climates, Jean Kenneally will eventually grow to 3.3ft (1m) tall, but it is most definitely a miniature rose in every detail except its height. The flowers are small, neat, elegant miniature Hybrid Teas, though they usually come in large clusters (of up to 15) like a Floribunda. The buds are exquisitely shapely and very popular at rose competitions in the US. The flowers are pink, with a peachy wash to the petal backs, creating an apricot color overall. Jean Kenneally has glaucous green leaves and a vigorous, upright habit. Its first flowering is profuse, but it continues to flower on a lesser scale until late in the season. It was bred by Dee Bennett of San Diego, California, and named after her friend, the chairman of the San Diego Rose Society. It is now popular all over the world.

JEAN KENNEALLY

'JEAN MERMOZ'

Polyantha

ORIGIN **Chenault, France, 1937**
FLOWER SIZE **0.8in (2cm)**
SCENT **Light and musky**
FLOWERING **Repeats well**
HEIGHT/SPREAD **1.6ft (50cm)/3.3ft (1m)**
HARDINESS **Zone 6**

This pretty Polyantha rose commemorates the famous French aviator (1901–36), who died a few months before it was issued. 'Jean Mermoz' bears small, deep pink flowers in long, loose clusters almost continuously until late autumn. They are very full of neatly imbricated petals, which are slightly darker on their reverses than their upsides, and keep their color best in cool weather. The clusters have 5–15 flowers, which last a long time, but tend to hold on to their petals for too long – until after they have withered and turned brown. The plant has small, dark, glossy leaves – *Rosa wichurana* is one of its ancestors – and is very healthy. 'Jean Mermoz' flourishes in containers and makes a good edging for the front of a border. It is easy to propagate from cuttings. It is one of the few Polyanthas from the 1930s to remain popular today.

'JEAN MERMOZ'

'JEANNE DE MONTFORT'

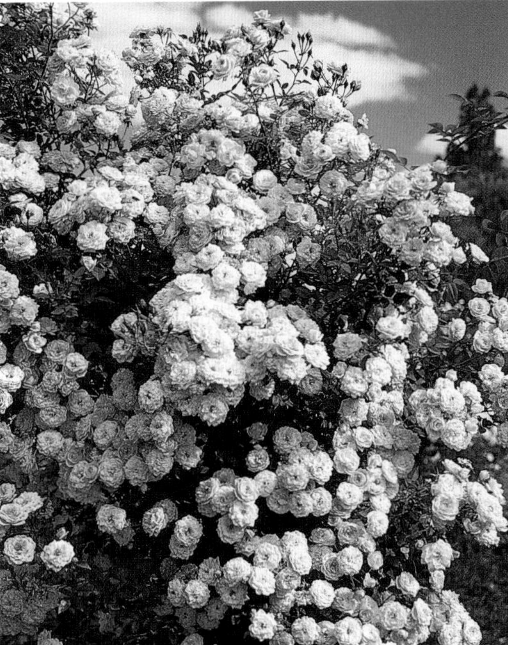

'JEANNE LAJOIE'

'JENS MUNK'

'JEANNE DE MONTFORT'

Moss Rose

ORIGIN **Robert, France, 1851**
FLOWER SIZE **3.5in (9cm)**
SCENT **Strong and sweet**
FLOWERING **Once only**
HEIGHT/SPREAD **9.8ft (3m)/8.2ft (2.5m)**
HARDINESS **Zone 5**

One of the tallest and mossiest of roses, 'Jeanne de Montfort' is an excellent shrub for gardens with space for it. The flowers open from red buds to a very pretty rose pink color; a couple of rows of guard petals lie flat around the outside, while a few smaller petals fill the center around a heavy brush of golden stamens. They come in clusters of 3–7, sometimes more. The buds and flower stalks are heavily covered with brown green moss. The plant makes a lanky, sprawling shrub that is best tied down so that it will break into flower all along its length. The leaves are fresh, pale green, and healthy, though the mossy buds may attract mildew. Jeanne de Montfort, nicknamed "La Flamme," was a Breton princess who fought a series of brilliant campaigns against the French kings in the 1340s and 1350s.

'JEANNE LAJOIE'

Climbing Miniature

ORIGIN **Sima, US, 1975**
PARENTAGE **('Casa Blanca' × 'Kordes' Sondermeldung') × 'Midget'**
FLOWER SIZE **1.6in (4cm)**
SCENT **Little or none**
FLOWERING **Continuous**
HEIGHT/SPREAD **6.6ft (2m)/4.9ft (1.5m)**
HARDINESS **Zone 5**

'Jeanne Lajoie' must be one of the most floriferous roses ever bred; it is also immensely attractive and adaptable. The flowers are small – rich mid-pink, fading to pale pink and eventually to white – but carried in such profusion that the plant seems obliterated by them. They are very full of petals, neat, flat, and round, and carried in clusters of 10–40. The bushy plant has dark, glossy leaves (there is *Rosa wichurana* in its ancestry), red new growth, and a dense, compact shape. Although technically a climber, it is equally well grown as a freestanding shrub. It is long-flowering, continuing until early winter, when the blooms assume a very dark pink hue. The name commemorates a French-Canadian folk heroine of the 1920s.

JENNIFER

syn. 'BENJEN'

Miniature Rose

ORIGIN **Benardella, US, 1985**
PARENTAGE **'Party Girl' × 'Laguna'**
FLOWER SIZE **2.4in (6cm)**
SCENT **Medium and sweet**
FLOWERING **Repeats well**
HEIGHT/SPREAD **2ft (60cm)/2ft (60cm)**
HARDINESS **Zone 6**
AWARDS **AoE 1985**

The flowers of Jennifer are quite large for a miniature rose. They open from purplish buds with purple petal tips, but the flowers themselves are soft pink and, in hot climates, fade to pale mauve and almost to white. They are exquisitely scrolled like miniature Hybrid Teas at first, but open out fully and, in hot climates, fairly quickly, though they still have an elegant and graceful shape when open. They are lightly double and borne in clusters of 5–10. Jennifer has long, large prickles and a spreading habit of growth. Its leaves are medium-dark, semiglossy, and healthy. The plant grows vigorously and is quick to repeat.

JENNIFER

'JENS MUNK'

Rugosa Hybrid

ORIGIN **Svejda, Canada, 1974**
PARENTAGE **'Schneezwerg' × 'Fru Dagmar Hastrup'**
FLOWER SIZE **2.8in (7cm)**
SCENT **Strong, penetrating, and sweet**
FLOWERING **Repeats well**
HEIGHT/SPREAD **4.1ft (1.25m)/4.1ft (1.25m)**
HARDINESS **Zone 3**

This Rugosa hybrid is one of the hardiest of the Explorer roses, yet 'Jens Munk' will also grow quite happily in hot climates. It has lightly cupped, semidouble, rich pink flowers with pale stamens. The petal backs are slightly paler and sometimes there are white streaks at the base of the petals. The flowers come in small clusters of 2–5 on short stems and are followed by hips in autumn, though the plant flowers sporadically throughout summer and especially well in autumn. The bush is vigorous, and changes from a gawky young plant into a mature arching shrub, which is resistant to blackspot and only occasionally susceptible to mildew. The leaflets are veined in the Rugosa manner. 'Jens Munk' is particularly popular in Canada and Scandinavia but, like all the Explorer roses, is widely available in almost every country. It roots very easily from softwood cuttings.

'JERSEY BEAUTY'

Wichurana Rambler

ORIGIN **Manda, US, 1899**
PARENTAGE ***Rosa wichurana* × 'Perle des Jardins'**
FLOWER SIZE **2.4in (6cm)**
SCENT **Light and musky**
FLOWERING **Once, early in season, and then occasionally**
HEIGHT/SPREAD **16.4ft (5m)/9.8ft (3m)**
HARDINESS **Zone 7**

The popularity of 'Jersey Beauty' dates back to 1899. It was one of the first Wichurana ramblers to be introduced commercially, and, despite being much less impressive today than many later ramblers, it remains widely sold and grown. The short-lived flowers open pale buff yellow but fade almost immediately to white, set off by dark yellow stamens. They come in clusters of 3–7, sometimes more, and are followed by bright red hips. The plant has handsome foliage – dark, glossy, and disease resistant – and crimson new growth. It is vigorous and healthy. Its long, slender stems are very adaptable to training and can quickly be wound around any support. 'Jersey Beauty' grows best in hot climates, and may flower sparsely elsewhere. The name derives from New Jersey – Manda came from South Orange.

'JERSEY BEAUTY'

Polesden Lacey, Surrey, England ▶

'JESSIKA'

'JESSIKA'

Hybrid Tea

ORIGIN **Tantau, Germany, 1971**
PARENTAGE **'Königin der Rosen' x 'Piccadilly'**
FLOWER SIZE **4.7in (12cm)**
SCENT **Medium and sweet**
FLOWERING **Repeats well**
HEIGHT/SPREAD **4.1ft (1.25m)/3.3ft (1m)**
HARDINESS **Zone 6**

The flowers of 'Jessika' are a fine combination of colors: salmon pink at first, with creamy inner petals and buff petal backs. As the flower ages, however, the yellow shades fade and the petals turn darker, taking on a dark pink (almost crimson) tint along the edges. As the flowers are full of petals, the transformation is very attractive and prolonged over several days. The flowers are usually produced singly and always on long, strong stems, which are good for cutting. 'Jessika' makes a strong, upright plant and repeats well: the autumn flowers are often darker and more richly colored, but blackspot may be a problem by then.

JOHANN STRAUSS

syn. 'MEIOFFIC', Forever Friends, Sweet Sonata

Hybrid Tea

ORIGIN **Meilland, France, 1992**
PARENTAGE **Flamingo x ('Kalinka' x 'Tip Top')**
FLOWER SIZE **3.9in (10cm)**
SCENT **Light and fruity**
FLOWERING **Repeats well**
HEIGHT/SPREAD **4.1ft (1.25m)/3.3ft (1m)**
HARDINESS **Zone 6**

JOHANN STRAUSS

A modern classic, Johann Strauss is a superbly beautiful rose. The individual flowers are fat and full of petals, rounded and cabbagelike in their proportions. The petals are gleaming white on the upper sides and palest pink with a hint of apricot on the backs: this creates a pale pink suffusion in the shadows that form between the many layers of petals. The flowers are usually borne singly, but occasionally come in clusters of up to five, especially later in the season. Their stems are long, which makes them good for picking. The leaves are large, dark, and glossy – a splendid foil for the flowers – and extremely healthy. The plant does well in both hot climates and cool, and the flowers stand up well to rain. This is one of Meilland's best.

'JOHN CABOT'

Kordesii Hybrid

ORIGIN **Svejda, Canada, 1978**
PARENTAGE **'Kordesii' x ('Masquerade' x *Rosa laxa*)**
FLOWER SIZE **2.8in (7cm)**
SCENT **Light and musky**
FLOWERING **Repeats**
HEIGHT/SPREAD **8.2ft (2.5m)/6.6ft (2m)**
HARDINESS **Zone 4**

This was the first of the Explorer roses to be released. The pale crimson purple flowers open neatly semidouble, with occasional white streaks and fine stamens at the center. The flowers come in clusters of 3–10, and fade slightly as they age. They are borne in great profusion for some six or seven weeks at first, and then only sporadically before another big flowering in autumn. The plant is densely leafy, with lots of pale, glossy, green leaves, and long, curving prickles. It mounds up slowly into an arching shrub (good for hedging), but in warmer climates the individual growths can be trained up as a climber to at least 9.8ft (3m) high. The leaves are sometimes susceptible to blackspot, but it is a thrifty grower, and requires little maintenance, while also responding well to feeding. John Cabot (1450–98) was the Genoese sailor who first went looking for the Northwest Passage.

'JOHN CABOT'

JOHN CLARE

JOHN CLARE

syn. 'AUSCENT'

Shrub Rose

ORIGIN **Austin, Britain, 1994**
PARENTAGE **'Wife of Bath' x 'Conrad Ferdinand Meyer' seedling**
FLOWER SIZE **3.1in (8cm)**
SCENT **Light**
FLOWERING **Continuous**
HEIGHT/SPREAD **2.7ft (80cm)/3.3ft (1m)**
HARDINESS **Zone 5**

John Clare is a very floriferous English Rose, though it more closely resembles a dark pink Floribunda. The cupped flowers are full of short petals – mid-pink in color, with paler edges and darker backs. They come in long-stemmed clusters of 5–9, held clear of the leaves. They are borne in great quantity (David Austin regards this as the most floriferous of all his roses), but they do not drop their petals well, so John Clare grows better in a dry climate. The leaves are crimson when young, turning later to dark green. The bush is sturdy and healthy.

'JOHN DAVIS'

Kordesii Hybrid

ORIGIN **Svejda, Canada, 1986**
PARENTAGE **'Kordesii' x ('Red Dawn' x 'Suzanne')**
FLOWER SIZE **3.1in (8cm)**
SCENT **Light and musky**
FLOWERING **Repeats**
HEIGHT/SPREAD **8.2ft (2.5m)/6.6ft (2m)**
HARDINESS **Zone 4**

The flowers of 'John Davis' have an attractive, old-fashioned shape. Sometimes they are quartered, but usually they open out to show their golden centers. They are very bright pink at first, then fade to pale pink, with creamy bases to the petals. The flowers come in clusters of 10–15, and appear continuously until the first frosts. The dense, prickly plant is well covered with small, glossy, deep green leaves, which are rich red at first. 'John Davis' has short internodes and a naturally trailing habit, which makes it a good rambler for cold areas. It requires almost no pruning but

'JOHN DAVIS'

'JOHN F. KENNEDY'

responds well to good feeding and protection from mildew and blackspot. This was the best of the early Explorer roses. John Davis (1550–1605) was the first navigator to pass through the Davis Straight into Baffin Bay.

'JOHN F. KENNEDY'

Hybrid Tea

ORIGIN **Boerner, US, 1965**
PARENTAGE **seedling x 'White Queen'**
FLOWER SIZE **5.5in (14cm)**
SCENT **Medium and sweet**
FLOWERING **Repeats**
HEIGHT/SPREAD **4.9ft (1.5m)/3.3ft (1m)**
HARDINESS **Zone 6**

No rose is so rewarding or so difficult to grow well as 'John F. Kennedy'. It is a large-flowered Hybrid Tea of the sort that is sometimes cultivated to win prizes at shows. The flowers are cream colored at first, but soon change to pure white, with green markings on the backs of the outer petals. All the petals are large and long, with a classic curling back at the edges of the bud, followed by a slight wave to their outline when the flowers open fully. The flowers are borne singly or in clusters of up to four on long, straight stems – perfect for cutting. The first flowering of the year is spectacular, but the plant is slow to rebloom. Wind and rain spoil the flowers quickly – the tips of the petals turn brown and unsightly. The plant is fairly vigorous, with large, strong, dark leaves, though they are no strangers to mildew and blackspot. 'John F. Kennedy' is best in hot, dry climates.

'JOHN FRANKLIN'

Shrub Rose

ORIGIN **Svejda, Canada, 1980**
PARENTAGE **'Lilli Marleen' seedling**
FLOWER SIZE **2.4in (6cm)**
SCENT **Light and musky**
FLOWERING **Repeats**
HEIGHT/SPREAD **4.1ft (1.25m)/4.1ft (1.25m)**
HARDINESS **Zone 5**

Although popular and widely grown, 'John Franklin' is not the best of the Explorer roses. It is susceptible to disease in mild climates and not entirely hardy throughout Canada. The flowers are bright crimson, fairly double, and fringed or ragged at the edge of the petals – an attractive and unusual feature. They come in clusters of 3–7, though sometimes there are as many as 30 flowers in a vast cluster. The leaves are dark and glossy, and the plant has a dense, upright habit of growth. Like all the Explorer roses, 'John Franklin' propagates easily from softwood cuttings. Sir John Franklin (1786–1847) discovered the Northwest Passage, and then disappeared into it.

'JOHN HOPPER'

'JOHN HOPPER'

Hybrid Perpetual

ORIGIN **Ward, Britain, 1862**
PARENTAGE **'Jules Margottin' x 'Mme. Vidot'**
FLOWER SIZE **3.9in (10cm)**
SCENT **Rich and sweet**
FLOWERING **Midseason, and occasionally thereafter**
HEIGHT/SPREAD **4.9ft (1.5m)/4.1ft (1.25m)**
HARDINESS **Zone 5**

'JOHN FRANKLIN'

Ward of Ipswich was an undistinguished nurseryman who introduced about 20 roses: all are now lost except for 'John Hopper', one of the first British Hybrid Perpetuals. The flowers open from fat, globular buds to a full flower with a nice circular outline. Inside the large guard petals is a crush of small petals, sometimes quilled but usually shapeless. The flower is a deep shocking pink, and some of the color comes from unattractive patches of dark crimson veining on the petal tips; the petal backs are paler – creamy pink. The flowers hold their color well (which is a shame) and are borne singly or in tight, congested clusters of up to five – the pedicels are too short. The bush is stiff, prickly, and a bashful repeat flowerer. Its matte, green leaves are susceptible to blackspot. But its scent is stupendous.

JOHN KEATS

see COLETTE

'JOHN S. ARMSTRONG'

Grandiflora

ORIGIN **Swim, US, 1961**
PARENTAGE **'Charlotte Armstrong' seedling**
FLOWER SIZE **3.5in (9cm)**
SCENT **Light and sweet**
FLOWERING **Repeats well**
HEIGHT/SPREAD **4.9ft (1.5m)/3.3ft (1m)**
HARDINESS **Zone 6**
AWARDS **AARS 1962**

This prickly Grandiflora rose was bred in southern California, but flourishes all over the world and has proved especially popular in Australia. Outside North America, 'John S. Armstrong' is classified as a Floribunda. The flowers are large, and carried in small clusters (typically of 3–7) on long, strong, slender stems, perfect for cutting. They are a good, dark red and keep their color even in very hot weather. The

'JOHN S. ARMSTRONG'

petals are not especially long, but they are broad and plentiful, and acquire an attractive ripple when they open out. 'John S. Armstrong' grows tall and vigorously. Its leaves are large, dark, semiglossy, and fairly healthy: in dry climates it is one of the most resistant to fungal infections of all roses. It flowers profusely and repeats quickly.

'JOHN WATERER'

Hybrid Tea

ORIGIN **McGredy, Northern Ireland, 1970**
PARENTAGE **'King of Hearts' x 'Hanne'**
FLOWER SIZE **4.3in (11cm)**
SCENT **Medium and sweet**
FLOWERING **Repeats**
HEIGHT/SPREAD **4.9ft (1.5m)/3.3ft (1m)**
HARDINESS **Zone 6**

This handsome Hybrid Tea enjoyed considerable popularity in the 1970s and 1980s and is still seen and grown all over the world. 'John Waterer' – named after an English nurseryman – has long, elegant buds and long, large petals, though they are sometimes a little ragged at their edges. They also tend to burn and turn black in hot sunshine. However, the flowers are a beautiful deep crimson, occasionally enlivened by a white streak running out from the center. They are usually borne singly, though sometimes in small clusters, on long stems: 'John Waterer' is the ideal dark red rose for cutting, though it sometimes nods its head a little. People have always disagreed about the strength of its scent: some find it barely detectable, others very strong and sweet. Its leaves are large and fairly healthy (watch out for mildew in autumn) and it has a vigorous, upright, branching habit of growth.

'JOHN WATERER'

'JOSEPH GUY'

syn. 'LAFAYETTE'

Floribunda

ORIGIN **Nonin, France, 1924**
PARENTAGE **'Rödhätte' x 'Richmond'**
FLOWER SIZE **2in (5cm)**
SCENT **Light and musky**
FLOWERING **Repeats well**
HEIGHT/SPREAD **2.5ft (75cm)/1.6ft (50cm)**
HARDINESS **Zone 5**

Its substantial clusters of large (for a Polyantha) flowers made 'Joseph Guy' popular from the start. In fact, it was a prototype for the Floribunda roses, which were to change people's gardens all over the world from about 1950 onward. The flowers are semidouble, cupped, loosely petaled, and rich cherry pink or pale crimson. They stay on the bush a long time and fade to pink as they age. The bush has few thorns and lots of rich, healthy, shiny leaves. It is a very good repeat flowerer, rarely without flowers until the first frosts. In cold areas it is also unusually hardy and one of the first to flower every year. Wilhelm Kordes introduced a climbing sport in 1928, which he called 'Auguste Kordes' after his mother. It has slightly larger flowers and grows to about 8.2ft (2.5m). It is one of the most floriferous of all early-flowering ramblers.

In 1930, the Berlin nursery of Späth introduced a charming pale pink sport of the bush form as

'JOSEPH GUY'

'FRAU ASTRID SPÄTH'

'Frau Astrid Späth'. There is a rare further sport known as 'Striped Astrid Späth', in which the pale pink petals of 'Frau Astrid Späth' are overlaid with the darker stripes of the original 'Joseph Guy'.

Sport of 'Joseph Guy'

'FRAU ASTRID SPÄTH'

ORIGIN **Späth, Germany, 1930**

'JOSEPH'S COAT'

Modern Climber

ORIGIN **Armstrong & Swim, US, 1963**
PARENTAGE **'Buccaneer' x 'Circus'**
FLOWER SIZE **2.8in (7cm)**
SCENT **Light**
FLOWERING **Heavy, then intermittent**
HEIGHT/SPREAD **8.2ft (2.5m)/4.9ft (1.5m)**
HARDINESS **Zone 5**
AWARDS **Bagatelle GM 1964**

'JOSEPH'S COAT' *(plus delphiniums)*

This multicolored rose in the 'Masquerade' tradition may be grown as a small climber or a large, freestanding bush. In either case, 'Joseph's Coat' is an eye-catching plant, and its first flowering is always stunning. Subsequent blooming is intermittent, though the colors in autumn are particularly fine. The semi-double flowers are bright yellow at first, flushed with red, then change to orange and cherry red. They come in small, open clusters and are accompanied by beautiful dark, semiglossy leaves.

'JOSEPHINE BRUCE'

Hybrid Tea

ORIGIN **Bees, Britain, 1949**
PARENTAGE **'Crimson Glory' x 'Madge Whipp'**
FLOWER SIZE **4.7in (12cm)**
SCENT **Medium and sweet**
FLOWERING **Repeats well**
HEIGHT/SPREAD **2.7ft (80cm)/3.3ft (1m)**
HARDINESS **Zone 6**

The sumptuous, dark crimson flowers of 'Josephine Bruce' have guaranteed its popularity for more than half a century. This is slightly surprising, because it lacks the rich, sweet scent of so many crimson Hybrid Teas. It is also exceptionally prickly and has a peculiar habit of growth, sending its new growths curving out sideways instead of shooting heavenward. However, the flowers are elegantly shaped and the petals have a wonderful velvety bloom to their surfaces. The plant is susceptible to blackspot and powdery mildew, but grows well all over the world, even where fungal diseases are a problem. There is an excellent climbing sport that grows no higher than 9.8ft (3m) and is clothed with flowers from top to bottom.

JUBILÉ DU PRINCE DE MONACO

JOYFULNESS

see FROHSINN 82

JUBILÉ DU PRINCE DE MONACO

syn. 'MEIsponge'

Floribunda

ORIGIN **Meilland, France, 2001**
FLOWER SIZE **3.9in (10cm)**
SCENT **Strong and sweet**
FLOWERING **Repeats well**
HEIGHT/SPREAD **3.3ft (1m)/3.3ft (1m)**
HARDINESS **Zone 6**

Jubilé du Prince de Monaco is a showy rose, and quite unlike any other. The flowers have the size and shape of a Hybrid Tea, but come in clusters like a Floribunda. It is their color that is so remarkable: an extraordinary mixture of red and white. The flowers open mosty white, with pink edgings to their large, ruffled petals. The pink deepens to crimson, so that the center gives an impression of pale pink while the outer parts of the flower are rich crimson, but the exact color differs from rose to rose. The plant is healthy, grows vigorously, and flowers fairly continuously through until late autumn. It is a very effective rose for massed plantings, but equally eye-catching as a single specimen in a mixed border.

'JOSEPHINE BRUCE'

JUDE THE OBSCURE

syn. 'AUSjo'

Shrub Rose

ORIGIN **Austin, Britain, 1995**
PARENTAGE **Abraham Darby x Windrush**
FLOWER SIZE **4.7in (12cm)**
SCENT **Strong, sweet, and fruity**
FLOWERING **Repeats**
HEIGHT/SPREAD **4.9ft (1.5m)/4.1ft (1.25m)**
HARDINESS **Zone 6**
AWARDS **Monza FA 1996**

The flowers of Jude the Obscure have a lot of large, incurved petals: it gives them a globular shape. When eventually they open out a little, they take on a somewhat ruffled appearance. Their color is very beautiful – a mixture of pale apricot and buff toward the center, with pale, creamy white, outer petals. They are reminiscent of the subtle colors seen in 19th-century Tea roses. They come singly and in small clusters but tend to be damaged by rain and humidity. The plant is bushy and prickly, with somewhat lax stems and crimson new growths. The leaves are dull green and fairly healthy. It is a good repeater. *Jude the Obscure* is the name of a novel by the English writer Thomas Hardy.

JUDE THE OBSCURE

JUDY GARLAND

'JULES MARGOTTIN'

'JULIA'S ROSE'

JUDY GARLAND

syn. 'HARKING'
Floribunda

ORIGIN **Harkness, Britain, 1977**
PARENTAGE **(['Super Star' x 'Circus'] x ['Sabine' x 'Circus']) x 'Pineapple Poll'**
FLOWER SIZE **2.8in (7cm)**
SCENT **Medium, fruity, and musky**
FLOWERING **Repeats well**
HEIGHT/SPREAD **4.9ft (1.5m)/3.3ft (1m)**
HARDINESS **Zone 6**

The brilliant multicolored flowers of Judy Garland have a lot of petals, which change and darken as they age. They are yellow at first, with just a hint of orange on the petal tips, but as they develop and open out (showing their stamens), they acquire an orange or vermilion edge so that, by the time they die, the flowers look more red than yellow. They come singly or, more usually, in rather erect clusters of up to ten, so that all the colors and shades between are present in a single cluster and repeated all over the bush. They are useful as cut flowers and very pleasantly scented. Judy Garland makes a neat, bushy plant with small, mid-green leaves and quite a lot of prickles. Sometimes it may have a touch of blackspot in autumn, but it is generally healthy and vigorous.

'JULES MARGOTTIN'

Hybrid Perpetual

ORIGIN **Margottin, France, 1853**
PARENTAGE **'La Reine' seedling**
FLOWER SIZE **3.9in (10cm)**
SCENT **Strong and sweet**
FLOWERING **Remontant**
HEIGHT/SPREAD **4.9ft (1.5m)/4.1ft (1.25m)**
HARDINESS **Zone 5**

The flowers of 'Jules Margottin' are deep pink or pale crimson and possessed of a delicious, rich scent. Their petals are short, plentiful, and tightly incurved at first, so that the globular buds open out to a cabbagelike shape. Later the flowers expand further until they are almost flat, and the petals take on a great variety of twists and turns. The flowers often have foliolate sepals and are borne both singly and in tight clusters of up to five. Few roses are more spectacular than 'Jules Margottin' arching over under the weight of large flowers all along its stems. The plant is prickly, vigorous, and a good repeater: the later flowers come in clusters at the ends of the new growths. Mildew can be a problem. 'Jules Margottin' proved to be an important parent in the development of garden roses.

'JULIA'S ROSE'

Hybrid Tea

ORIGIN **Wisbech, Britain, 1976**
PARENTAGE **'Mainzer Fastnacht' x 'Dr. A. J. Verhage'**
FLOWER SIZE **3.5in (9cm)**
SCENT **Light**
FLOWERING **Repeats well**
HEIGHT/SPREAD **3.3ft (1m)/2.7ft (80cm)**
HARDINESS **Zone 6**
AWARDS **Baden-Baden 1983**

Julia is Julia Clements, a famous name among flower arrangers. Her rose is one of those subtle orange ones with hints of brown in it. The mahogany shades show up particularly well in the shadows that form between the petals, because the petal backs have a pink overlay, which interacts with the orange to create brown reflections. 'Julia's Rose' has to be well grown to be effective: the larger the flowers are and the more petals they have, the better the complex colors appear. They fade much too quickly to be worthwhile in hot weather: the best browns are for autumn. The flowers have a distinctive wave to their petals; the golden stamens have crimson filaments. The flowers are borne singly or in clusters of up to five on fairly long, straight stems, but a sharp flower arranger needs several bushes to supply enough cut flowers. Blackspot can be a challenge.

'JUNO'

Centifolia

ORIGIN **pre-1832**
FLOWER SIZE **3.5in (9cm)**
SCENT **Strong and sweet**
FLOWERING **Once only**
HEIGHT/SPREAD **4.9ft (1.5m)/4.1ft (1.25m)**
HARDINESS **Zone 5**

Several roses have been known as 'Juno' or 'Junon' over the centuries, but no one knows the origins of the one that is now grown and sold as 'Juno'. It is sometimes classified among the Centifolias and sometimes with the Gallicas. The pale pink flowers open slowly to reveal darker hints as they unfurl. They are globular at first, and at this stage resemble 'Centifolia', but later they open out almost flat to reveal a mass of quilled petals surrounding a large button eye. They take on a roughly quartered shape, with a slightly ragged outline. They are borne singly and in clusters of up to about four all along the branches of a lax and arching plant. 'Juno' has gray green leaves and is free flowering, though the flowers sometimes ball in cool, damp weather and mildew may be problem later on. It is a vigorous grower and tolerant of poor soil.

'JUST JOEY'

Hybrid Tea

ORIGIN **Cants, Britain, 1972**
PARENTAGE **'Duftwolke' x 'Dr. A. J. Verhage'**
FLOWER SIZE **5.5in (14cm)**
SCENT **Medium and sweet**
FLOWERING **Repeats well**
HEIGHT/SPREAD **3.3ft (1m)/2.5ft (75cm)**
HARDINESS **Zone 6**
AWARDS **James Mason GN 1986; World's Favourite Rose 1994**

The great strength of 'Just Joey' is its beauty at all stages of its development, whether as an elegantly unfurling bud or as a fully expanded flower with large, substantial, wavy petals delectably arranged around its crimson stamens. It makes one of the most spectacular and floriferous displays of all roses, with some of the largest flowers. The flowers appear creamy orange or buff in color, but the undersides of the petals are more apricot colored. All the petals fade to cream, almost to white, starting from the outside, so that there are many different shades within a single flower at any one time. 'Just Joey' does best in cool climates, where its colors are deepest and its scent strongest, but remains little known in hot areas. The plant is open and moderately vigorous, with glossy, healthy leaves. It was one of the first roses to be bred by Roger Pawsey of Cants: Joey is the name of his wife.

'JUNO'

'JUST JOEY'

K

'Kaiserin Auguste Viktoria'

Hybrid Tea

ORIGIN **Lambert, Germany, 1891**
PARENTAGE **'Lady Mary Fitzwilliam' x 'Coquette de Lyon'**
FLOWER SIZE **4.7in (12cm)**
SCENT **Strong and tealike**
FLOWERING **Repeats constantly**
HEIGHT/SPREAD **4.9ft (1.5m)/4.1ft (1.25m)**
HARDINESS **Zone 7**

This exquisite early Hybrid Tea was the foundation on which Peter Lambert built his career: he became the greatest rose hybridist of the early 20th century. 'Kaiserin Auguste Viktoria' was named after the German empress, wife of William II, and herself a great rose lover. It has flowers of great beauty. The buds are fairly globular, but each one opens to a perfect old-fashioned shape, often quartered, with a mass of quilled petals. They are pure ivory white at the edges, but pale apricot or buff yellow at the center, fading slightly as the flowers age. 'Kaiserin Auguste Viktoria' was for many years a popular florists' rose – it responds well to good cultivation and flowers continuously – and the most widely grown of all white roses in the American South. The flowers come singly or, occasionally, in twos and threes, and are well set off by dark, glossy leaves (crimson when young). The plant is vigorous and healthy, and grows strongly. 'Kaiserin Auguste Viktoria' also proved to be an important parent of modern roses.

'Kaiserin Auguste Viktoria'

Kaleidoscope

Kaleidoscope

syn. 'JACbow'

Floribunda

ORIGIN **Walden, US, 1998**
PARENTAGE **Pink Polyanna x Rainbow's End**
FLOWER SIZE **2.8in (7cm)**
SCENT **Little or none**
FLOWERING **Repeats well**
HEIGHT/SPREAD **4.1ft (1.25m)/3.3ft (1m)**
HARDINESS **Zone 6**
AWARDS **AARS 1999**

No winner of the top All-America Rose Selections award has such remarkable coloring as Kaleidoscope. The flowers change from green brown, tan, and yellow to grayed pink and mauve, with crimson tips to the petals. The color is very variable and depends also upon the weather and how much direct sunlight the individual petals receive. The flowers come in large clusters but make good buttonholes, because the buds are neat and shapely. They also have distinctive fimbriated sepals. The plant is very prickly and bushy, with small, glossy, mid-green leaves and a spreading, bushy habit of growth. It was actually introduced as a landscaping rose, though its ornamental value qualifies it for mixed plantings and containers.

'Kalinka'

syn. 'Pink Wonder'

Floribunda

ORIGIN **Meilland, France, 1970**
PARENTAGE **'Zambra' x ('Sarabande' x ['Goldilocks' x 'Fashion'])**
FLOWER SIZE **3.5in (9cm)**
SCENT **Strong and sweet**
FLOWERING **Repeats well**
HEIGHT/SPREAD **4.1ft (1.25m)/3.3ft (1m)**
HARDINESS **Zone 6**
AWARDS **Madrid GM 1969; Belfast GM 1972**

It was introduced as long ago as 1970, but 'Kalinka' is still a popular bedding Floribunda all over the world except North America. It grows quickly and easily in a wide choice of climatic conditions. The flowers are a beautiful mid-pink color, with a hint of salmon at first, which eventually fades to pure rose pink. The flowers have an old-fashioned shape, which is sometimes a mass of concentric round petals around a white center and on other occasions a muddle of smaller, quilled petals. The flowers come in clusters of 3–7 and are borne in amazing profusion, starting early in the season and repeating well. The plant has dark, glossy, healthy leaves and is almost thornless. There is also a climbing form, popular in Europe and Australia, known as 'Climbing Kalinka'. It grows to about 16.4ft (5m) and, unlike many climbing sports, is a reliable repeat flowerer.

Kardinal 85

Kardinal 85

syn. 'KORlingo'

Hybrid Tea

ORIGIN **Kordes, Germany, 1985**
PARENTAGE **Flamingo x seedling**
FLOWER SIZE **4.7in (12cm)**
SCENT **Light**
FLOWERING **Repeats well**
HEIGHT/SPREAD **4.1ft (1.25m)/2.5ft (75cm)**
HARDINESS **Zone 6**

'Kalinka'

Kardinal 85 is a superb, large-flowered, velvety crimson Hybrid Tea that was launched as a long-stemmed cut-flower rose but is an equally good garden plant, especially in warm areas. It is short on scent, but florists believe that fragrance shortens the life of a rose. The flower opens very slowly from nearly black buds. Its outer petals reflex into points, and the inner ones gently unswirl from a high, pointed tip: the classic shape of a Hybrid Tea as it opens. In a garden, the flower opens bright red and, after several days, becomes crimson pink. As a cut flower, it retains its bright dark redness and lasts a long time in water. The flowers have thick petals and come singly (occasionally in twos and threes) on very long stems. The plant has stout brown wood and quite a lot of prickles. It is very healthy. As with all commercial roses, it flowers again quickly and consistently – a true cut-and-come-again rose.

Karen Blixen

syn. 'POULari', Roy Black, Silver Anniversary

Hybrid Tea

ORIGIN **Poulsen, Denmark, 1992**
FLOWER SIZE **5.1in (13cm)**
SCENT **Light and sweet**
FLOWERING **Repeats**
HEIGHT/SPREAD **4.9ft (1.5m)/3.3ft (1m)**
HARDINESS **Zone 6**
AWARDS **Baden-Baden GM 1991**

Most exhibition roses do their best in dry weather. Karen Blixen is no exception: its thin petals collapse in rain and show their bruises by developing red spots. In good conditions, the flowers are very beautiful – white, with a hint of palest lemon at the center at

KAREN BLIXEN

first, and opening from long, classically shaped buds. They are usually borne singly, sometimes in small clusters, but not always on strong stems, so they tend to nod over instead of remaining sturdily erect. Karen Blixen has medium-green leaves, sometimes susceptible to blackspot, and a tall, vigorous, and somewhat lanky habit of growth. But in hot, dry conditions it is a star performer.

'KARL FÖRSTER'

Spinosissima Hybrid

ORIGIN **Kordes, Germany, 1930**
PARENTAGE **'Frau Karl Druschki' x 'Altaica'**
FLOWER SIZE **2.4in (6cm)**
SCENT **Light and fetid**
FLOWERING **Repeats well**
HEIGHT/SPREAD **8.2ft (2.5m)/9.8ft (3m)**
HARDINESS **Zone 4**

'Karl Förster' is an excellent shrub rose that presaged the better-known series of "Frühling" roses in the 1940s. In fact, it is a better rose than any of them, except for one characteristic – 'Karl Förster' has soft petals, which spoil in rain. For a dry climate, however, it is one of the best of all shrub roses. The flowers are fully double and pure white, with (very occasionally) a hint of pink at first. They have a very beautiful old-fashioned shape as they open out and are well complemented by the healthy, pale gray green leaves. 'Karl Förster' makes a bushy, arching, rounded shrub and flowers continuously: an established plant always has flowers on it after the first spectacular flowering. Karl Förster (1874–1970) was a large-scale nurseryman in Potsdam who promoted the natural style of gardening for which Germany is renowned.

'KARL FÖRSTER'

'KARL HERBST'

'KARL HERBST'

Hybrid Tea

ORIGIN **Kordes, Germany, 1957**
PARENTAGE **'Kordes' Sondermeldung' x 'Mme. A. Meilland'**
FLOWER SIZE **3.9in (10cm)**
SCENT **Medium and sweet**
FLOWERING **Repeats**
HEIGHT/SPREAD **4.9ft (1.5m)/4.1ft (1.25m)**
HARDINESS **Zone 6**

There is a paradox about 'Karl Herbst': ever since it was first introduced, people have said what a dull rose it is, and yet it remains widely grown all over the world some 50 years later. It was sometimes described as a "red 'Peace'," but it has a strange, recessive color, with none of the brightness that the word "red" evokes. However, the flowers are full-petaled and attractively shaped, borne usually singly but sometimes in clusters of up to four. The plant has glossy green leaves, crimson new growth, and quite a lot of prickles. It grows best if lightly pruned and allowed to build up a proper structure of branches. Karl Herbst (d.1962) worked as a salesman for Kordes for over 40 years.

'KATHARINA ZEIMET'

Polyantha

ORIGIN **Lambert, Germany, 1901**
PARENTAGE **'Étoile de Mai' x 'Marie Pavié'**
FLOWER SIZE **1.6in (4cm)**
SCENT **Medium, sweet, and pleasant**
FLOWERING **Repeats constantly**
HEIGHT/SPREAD **4.1ft (1.25m)/3.3ft (1m)**
HARDINESS **Zone 5**

Now that we realize what good, perpetually flowering shrubs they are, many of the early Polyantha roses are coming back into fashion. 'Katharina Zeimet' is a fine example – hardy, healthy, and tireless in flower. The flowers are pure white and loosely double, sometimes with a glint of yellow stamens at the center – pretty, but not outstanding as individual flowers. However, they are held high in long clusters (typically of 5–20) and carried so profusely that the bush makes an impact for months on end. Sadly, the bush does not shed its dead flowers cleanly, but holds on to the brown petals. 'Katharina Zeimet' is among the first and last roses to flower, and the blooms are enhanced by cheerful, elegantly pointed, bright green leaves. The plant

'KATHARINA ZEIMET'

is very hardy, healthy, and vigorous: it will reach 4.9ft (1.5m) if left unpruned – more in a hot climate. It associates with other plants, but is small enough to be grown in containers. It also roots quickly and easily from cuttings.

'KATHERINE MANSFIELD'

see 'CHARLES DE GAULLE'

'KATHLEEN'

Hybrid Musk

ORIGIN **Pemberton, Britain, 1922**
PARENTAGE **'Daphne' x 'Perle des Jardins'**
FLOWER SIZE **1.6in (4cm)**
SCENT **Medium and musky**
FLOWERING **Constantly in flower**
HEIGHT/SPREAD **8.2ft (2.5m)/4.9ft (1.5m)**
HARDINESS **Zone 6**

Of all the Pemberton Hybrid Musks, 'Kathleen' has the most simple and natural of outlines. Its reputed parentage ('Daphne' × 'Perle des Jardins') is probably wrong: 'Kathleen' is a true Musk rose, and needs to be enjoyed for

'KATHLEEN'

its vigor, floriferousness, and untamed beauty. The flowers are pale pink at the edges, fading to white, and single. They open from coral pink buds and each has a spray of yellow stamens at the center. The outline of the flowers is quite distinctive: anyone who knows 'Kathleen' can spot it instantly. The flowers come in large clusters (typically of 10–30) on long, elegant stems and are well complemented by dark, glossy, healthy leaves. Small red hips follow. The plant is tall and slender – it makes a fine pillar rose, but is also useful at the back of a border, where it will create a lot of interest without occupying too much space. It repeats well, and produces especially large clusters of flowers in autumn. It is the putative parent of the famous climbing rose 'Francis E. Lester'.

'KATHLEEN FERRIER'

Shrub Rose

ORIGIN **Buisman, Netherlands, 1952**
PARENTAGE **'Gartenstolz' x 'Shot Silk'**
FLOWER SIZE **2.4in (6cm)**
SCENT **Medium and sweet**
FLOWERING **Repeats**
HEIGHT/SPREAD **6.6ft (2m)/4.1ft (1.25m)**
HARDINESS **Zone 5**

'Kathleen Ferrier' is one of those vigorous Floribundas that grows so tall that it ends up being classified as a shrub rose. It was introduced over 50 years ago, in honor of the English contralto (1912–1953). The flowers open from red buds and are crimson, with a hint of salmon at first and a white patch at the center. Later it fades to pink and white, though the petal backs are slightly darker. The flowers are semi-double, with a ripple to their petals, and bright stamens at the center, which unfortunately turn quickly brown. They come in very large, well-spaced clusters on long, gawky, prickly stems. The plant has dark, glossy leaves (bronzy at first) and repeats well in autumn.

'KATHLEEN HARROP'

see 'ZÉPHIRINE DROUHIN'

'KATHLEEN FERRIER'

KATHRYN MCGREDY

syn. 'MACAUCLAD'

Hybrid Tea

ORIGIN **McGredy, New Zealand, 1995**
PARENTAGE **City of Auckland x Lady Rose**
FLOWER SIZE **5.5in (14cm)**
SCENT **Strong and sweet**
FLOWERING **Repeats well**
HEIGHT/SPREAD **3.3ft (1m)/2.7ft (80cm)**
HARDINESS **Zone 6**

Breeders always keep their best roses to bear their family name: Kathryn is the eldest daughter of Sam McGredy IV, the last in a long line of great Irish rosarians. The flowers of Kathryn McGredy are large, full of petals, and usually a very pretty, pale salmon pink. The color is variable, being rose pink, pastel, or blush pink, according to the climate and weather. However, the flowers are consistently well-formed and of high individual quality. Sam McGredy says that he knows no rose that produces quite so many perfect blooms. It is also among the quickest to repeat. The flowers are usually borne singly (and are enormous) in the first flowering, but smaller and in spacious clusters (typically of 3–5), later in the year. The plant has handsome, dark, healthy, glossy leaves and rich crimson new growths.

KATHRYN MORLEY

syn. 'AUSVARIETY'

Shrub Rose

ORIGIN **Austin, Britain, 1990**
PARENTAGE **Mary Rose x 'Chaucer'**
FLOWER SIZE **3.5in (9cm)**
SCENT **Strong and sweet**
FLOWERING **Repeats well**
HEIGHT/SPREAD **3.3ft (1m)/3.3ft (1m)**
HARDINESS **Zone 6**

Kathryn Morley was never one of David Austin's greatest creations, but its good qualities have been recognized by the rose-loving public. The flowers are a clear rose pink – paler at their edges and darker at the center – with richer pink coloring on the petal backs. The flowers are lightly cupped, very full and double, sometimes button-eyed and quartered, sometimes just a mass of curling, twisting petals surrounding a few stamens. They also have a translucent quality that seems to glow with soft color. The flowers come on long stems in small, loose clusters, which are set off by large dark leaves. The plant has tall, arching stems and lots of large prickles. In warm, dry climates Kathryn Morley is very healthy (powdery mildew can be a problem in cool, damp areas) and will grow to 6.6ft (2m), which is twice the height it attains in its native England. The flowers repeat well, coming in flushes every three or four weeks throughout the season. David Austin auctioned the right to name this rose for the benefit of a charity: the purchasers acquired it in memory of their daughter who died at the age of 18.

'KAZANLIK'

syn. 'TRIGINTIPETALA'

Damask Rose

ORIGIN **1689**
FLOWER SIZE **2.8in (7cm)**
SCENT **Strong and sweet**
FLOWERING **Once only**
HEIGHT/SPREAD **6.6ft (2m)/4.9ft (1.5m)**
HARDINESS **Zone 4**

Several different roses are grown as 'Kazanlik', which is the name of a town in Bulgaria where Damask roses are grown for attar of roses. The industry is an old one, and the roses have often been grown from seed as well as from cuttings, so that 'Kazanlik' is best regarded as a "group" name, to which cultivars like 'Trigintipetala', 'Gloire de Guilan', and 'Prof. Emile Perrot' belong. 'Kazanlik' is therefore an old Damask, usually with lightly double, rose pink flowers in a loose arrangement of petals, which sometimes incorporates a button eye. The flowers have long, leafy sepals and elongated receptacles (and, later, hips), and come in clusters of 3–7.

KENT

They are intensely sweet-scented. The plant is very prickly, with gray green leaves and slender stems.

KEEPSAKE

see ESMERALDA

KENT

syn. 'POULCOV', Pyrénées, Sparkler, White Cover

Shrub Rose

ORIGIN **Poulsen, Denmark, 1988**
FLOWER SIZE **1.2in (3cm)**
SCENT **Light and musky**
FLOWERING **Continuous**
HEIGHT/SPREAD **2.5ft (75cm)/4.1ft (1.25m)**
HARDINESS **Zone 6**
AWARDS **Baden-Baden GM 1990; RNRS PIT 1990**

Kent was a landmark rose. It won prizes against stiff competition from traditional Hybrid Teas and Floribundas. Kent showed that shrub roses could occupy the best places in every garden. Its flowers are small, lightly double, pure brilliant white, and lightly scented. However, they are abundantly and continuously borne in small clusters all over the surface of the plant right through until the first frosts. They are set off by small, dark, neat, glossy, healthy leaves, and the plant has a low, spreading habit. It is best massed as a landscaping plant, though it also makes an excellent front of the border shrub and is widely grown in containers. Its success encouraged breeders to produce more shrub type roses.

'KENTUCKY DERBY'

Hybrid Tea

ORIGIN **Armstrong, US, 1972**
PARENTAGE **'John S. Armstrong' x 'Grand Slam'**
FLOWER SIZE **5.9in (15cm)**
SCENT **Strong and sweet**
FLOWERING **Repeats well**
HEIGHT/SPREAD **6.6ft (2m)/4.9ft (1.5m)**
HARDINESS **Zone 6**

Good red Hybrid Teas have a strong following, and 'Kentucky Derby' has been popular for over 30 years. The flowers are enormous, beautifully shaped in bud, and still pretty when they open. They also hold their dark, blood red color right through until the petals drop. They are usually borne singly, though occasionally in twos and threes, on long, strong, straight stems, which make them good for cutting and exhibition. In the garden, 'Kentucky Derby' makes a very vigorous, outsize plant, which grows fast and repeats well. Once very healthy, it may now benefit from protection against blackspot and mildew. The annual Kentucky Derby is one of the highlights of the American horse racing season.

KATHRYN MORLEY

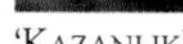

'KAZANLIK'

'KENTUCKY DERBY'

KATHRYN MCGREDY ▶

'Kew Rambler'

'Kiftsgate'

K

'Kew Rambler'

Modern Climber

ORIGIN **Kew, Britain, 1913**
FLOWER SIZE **1.6in (4cm)**
SCENT **Strong and musky**
FLOWERING **Once only, late in season**
HEIGHT/SPREAD **16.4ft (5m)/9.8ft (3m)**
HARDINESS **Zone 7**

'Kew Rambler' is said to be the result of an experimental cross carried out at the Royal Botanic Gardens, Kew, England, between *Rosa soulieana* and 'Hiawatha': if true, then this is one of the few hybrids yet developed from the beautiful, gray-leaved *Rosa soulieana*. Its flowers are a glowing flesh pink at first, with a creamy center, but soon fade to white. They come in large clusters of 20–60 flowers, which are retained for a long time. The plant is very vigorous, capable of reaching 26.2ft (8m), with a lot of large prickles, and glossy, dark leaves, which suggest the presence of *Rosa wichurana* in its ancestry. It flowers only once, but the large quantities of small, round, orange hips are an autumn and winter bonus.

'Kiese'

Hybrid Canina

ORIGIN **Kiese, Germany, 1910**
PARENTAGE ***Rosa canina* × 'Général Jacqueminot'**
FLOWER SIZE **2in (5cm)**
SCENT **Light and sweet**
FLOWERING **Once only, midseason**
HEIGHT/SPREAD **8.2ft (2.5m)/9.8ft (3m)**
HARDINESS **Zone 5**

The correct name for this shrub rose is 'Kiese's Unterlage', which means "Kiese's understock." The name commemorates Hermann Kiese (1865–1923), whose nursery at Vieselbach in Thüringen was the birthplace of many leading roses in the early 20th century. Kiese's intention was to breed a new rootstock that would guarantee a higher "take" for budded roses than the usual stock at that time, *Rosa canina*. The genes of 'Général Jacqueminot' would make it more acceptable to Hybrid Perpetuals and Hybrid Teas. In any event, 'Kiese' is a splendid once-flowering shrub rose with glowing crimson flowers. The bush is very vigorous and healthy, with dark, semiglossy leaves and large vermilion hips.

'Kiftsgate'

Wild Rose

ORIGIN **Murrell, Britain, 1954**
FLOWER SIZE **1.2in (3cm)**
SCENT **Strong and musky**
FLOWERING **Once, somewhat late in season**
HEIGHT/SPREAD **32.8ft (10m)/13.1ft (4m)**
HARDINESS **Zone 6**

'Kiftsgate' is believed to be a form of the Chinese climber *Rosa filipes*. It is named after Kiftsgate Court, the garden in Gloucestershire, England where it first occurred as a seedling. The original plant is now some 82ft (25m) up into a copper beech tree and may be the largest rose in Europe. Its flowers are small, single, and white, but are carried in huge, airy clusters, with as many as 100 flowers in them. These are followed in due course by equally impressive clusters of small orange hips. The flowers owe their distinctive elegance to their glorious golden stamens, their long, widely spaced pedicels, and their long, slender sepals. The pale green leaves (bronzy when young) are large, with long, slender leaflets. 'Kiftsgate' roots easily from cuttings, but also hybridizes with other roses, so there is more than one rose in cultivation under its name. Since it is very unsuitable for small gardens, it has become something of a status symbol among those who garden on a large scale.

'Kiese'

'Kimono'

Floribunda

ORIGIN **de Ruiter, Belgium, 1961**
PARENTAGE **'Cocorico' × 'Frau Anny Beaufays'**
FLOWER SIZE **2.8in (7cm)**
SCENT **Medium, sweet, and musky**
FLOWERING **Repeats**
HEIGHT/SPREAD **3.3ft (1m)/2.5ft (75cm)**
HARDINESS **Zone 6**

'Kimono' is a very pretty Floribunda, still widely grown more than 40 years after its introduction. Its flowers are salmon pink at first, and fade to a pretty pale pink. They come in large, upright clusters of 5–20 and are very generously borne – it is one of the most floriferous of all roses, and its cheerful, gleaming color pleases the eye from far away. 'Kimono' has a sturdy, upright habit of growth and is both vigorous and bushy. Blackspot may be a problem, but it is a very reliable performer.

'Kimono'

King Tut

see Laura Ford

'King's Ransom'

Hybrid Tea

ORIGIN **Morey, US, 1961**
PARENTAGE **'Golden Masterpiece' × 'Lydia'**
FLOWER SIZE **5.1in (13cm)**
SCENT **Medium and sweet**
FLOWERING **Repeats**
HEIGHT/SPREAD **4.1ft (1.25m)/3.3ft (1m)**
HARDINESS **Zone 6**
AWARDS **AARS 1962**

Deep, rich yellow roses that do not fade have always been sought by rose breeders. 'King's Ransom' holds its color even in the hottest climates, though the depth of its coloring varies. Sometimes the first flowering is surprisingly pale. That aside, 'King's Ransom' is a rose that cannot be faulted. The flowers are large, elegantly shaped, full of petals, and stand up well to all weather. They come on long stems, singly or in clusters of up to four, which makes them good for cutting and exhibition. 'King's Ransom' has a vigorous, upright habit of growth, a lot of prickles, and dark, glossy leaves. It flowers repeatedly, though you may have to wait for the next flush longer than with more modern roses.

'King's Ransom'

'KIRSTEN POULSEN'

'KIRSTEN POULSEN'

Hybrid Polyantha

ORIGIN **Poulsen, Denmark, 1924**
PARENTAGE **'Orléans Rose' x 'Red Star'**
FLOWER SIZE **2in (5cm)**
SCENT **Light and musky**
FLOWERING **Repeats constantly**
HEIGHT/SPREAD **2ft (60cm)/2ft (60cm)**
HARDINESS **Zone 6**

This is one of the roses that brought the Poulsen family to prominence in the 1920s and 1930s. 'Kirsten Poulsen' is a cross between a Polyantha and a Hybrid Tea, and represents a decisive step on the road toward breeding the first true Floribundas. It is still widely grown and seen today, and extremely easy to propagate from cuttings. The flowers of 'Kirsten Poulson' are cherry red, cupped, and single, with yellow stamens and a delicious musky scent. They come in loose sprays, which may contain anything between three or 30 flowers, hold their color well, and stand up well to rain. The plant grows energetically and tolerates poor soils.

KISS OF DESIRE

see HARLEKIN

'KITTY KININMONTH'

Modern Climber

ORIGIN **Clark, Australia, 1922**
PARENTAGE ***Rosa gigantea* seedling x unknown**
FLOWER SIZE **3.9in (10cm)**
SCENT **Medium and sweet**
FLOWERING **Occasionally recurrent**
HEIGHT/SPREAD **16.4ft (5m)/9.8ft (3m)**
HARDINESS **Zone 8**

The sweetly scented flowers of 'Kitty Kininmonth' are profusely borne very early in the season, either singly or in clusters of up to ten. They are large (4.7in/12cm), loose, semidouble, and bright lipstick pink, eventually fading to a more delicate shade of rose pink. The petals are occasionally flecked with white stripes, and the center is sometimes obscured by irregularly shaped petaloids. The plant is very vigorous and fast-growing, with only a few prickles, but lush young foliage and large round leaflets.

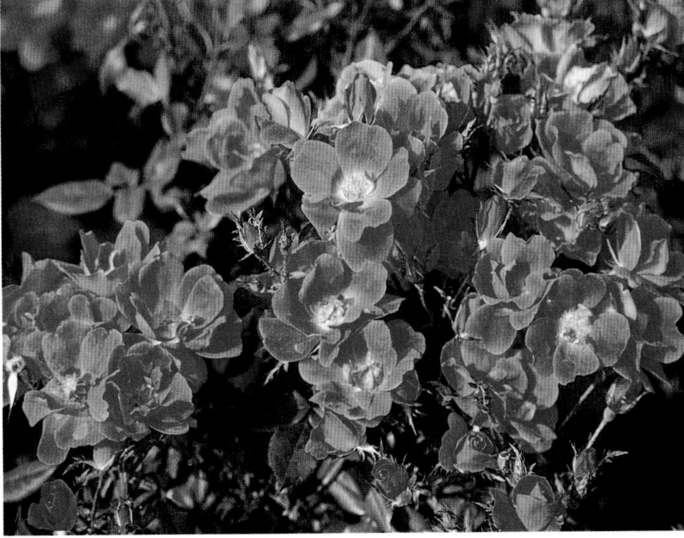
KNOCK OUT

KNOCK OUT

syn. 'RADRAZZ'

Shrub Rose

ORIGIN **Radler, US, 1999**
PARENTAGE **'Carefree Beauty' x Razzle Dazzle**
FLOWER SIZE **3.1in (8cm)**
SCENT **Medium, musky, and sweet**
FLOWERING **Almost continuous**
HEIGHT/SPREAD **3.3ft (1m)/4.1ft (1.25m)**
HARDINESS **Zone 5**
AWARDS **AARS 2000**

Many people consider Knock Out a good example of the type of rose that will be most popular in the future. It is a landscaping or shrub rose, in the Floribunda style, but totally disease-free, drought-tolerant, extremely hardy, and amazingly floriferous. The individual flowers are a cheerful light cherry color, cupped around a small patch of white at the center and a brush of green yellow stamens. They seem to glow with color, and keep this glow to the end. The flowers come with notably foliolate sepals in slightly congested clusters of 3–7, very abundantly borne. The plant has a branching, spreading habit – good for mixed plantings – with a dense covering of slightly glaucous leaves. The new stems and growths are purplish. And it flowers and flowers.

'KÖLNER KARNEVAL'

syn. 'BLUE GIRL'

Hybrid Tea

ORIGIN **Kordes, Germany, 1964**
FLOWER SIZE **5.1in (13cm)**
SCENT **Light, fruity, and sweet**
FLOWERING **Repeats well**
HEIGHT/SPREAD **4.1ft (1.25m)/3.3ft (1m)**
HARDINESS **Zone 6**
AWARDS **Rome GM 1964**

Bred in Germany, and named in honor of the famous carnival held at Cologne, 'Kölner Karneval' is rarely seen in Germany, but it is widely grown in the US, where it is known as 'Blue Girl'. Europe's loss is America's gain, for 'Kölner Karneval' is a splendid, large-flowered, lilac Hybrid Tea. The shapely flowers are borne singly on long stems and are pure lavender colored, with a slightly paler patch at the base of the petal backs. The large petals spoil in rain, but in good weather they open eventually to reveal a circle of red filaments. The bush has large, deep green leaves, bronzy when young and susceptible to blackspot in damp climates. 'Kölner Karneval' is vigorous and repeats well, but is at its best when grown in cool weather. It also responds well to feeding and watering.

'KITTY KININMONTH'

'KÖNIGIN DER ROSEN'

'KÖNIGIN DER ROSEN'

syn. 'COLOUR WONDER'

Hybrid Tea

ORIGIN **Kordes, Germany, 1964**
PARENTAGE **'Kordes' Perfecta' x 'Super Star'**
FLOWER SIZE **4.7in (12cm)**
SCENT **Medium and fruity**
FLOWERING **Repeats well**
HEIGHT/SPREAD **4.9ft (1.5m)/4.1ft (1.25m)**
HARDINESS **Zone 6**
AWARDS **ADR 1964; Belfast GM 1966**

The English name, 'Colour Wonder', points to the main attraction of this superb rose: there are many different tints in every flower of 'Königin der Rosen', and all of them are beautiful. Salmon pink is the main color, on a yellow ground. When sunlight shines through the newly opened flower, the colors are orange and gold, but the flowers darken as they age, becoming redder. The petals have much paler backs, but later take on a pink edge. Its changing color is not the only fascination of 'Königin der Rosen': the flowers also have an old-fashioned, muddled shape when they open out, very unusual in this color range and especially in a 1960s rose. They are usually borne singly (occasionally in clusters of up to seven) and last a very long time both on the bush and as a cut flower, provided they are not cut until fully open. 'Königin der Rosen' makes a vigorous, open shrub with strong, thick stems and plenty of large prickles. Its leaves are handsome, healthy, large, and dark – crimson when young. The plant is very floriferous and grows well in poor soils.

'KÖLNER KARNEVAL'

'KÖNIGIN VON DÄNEMARK'

KONRAD HENKEL

'KÖNIGIN VON DÄNEMARK'

syn. 'DRONNINGEN AV DANMARK', 'QUEEN OF DENMARK'

Alba Rose

ORIGIN **Booth, Britain, 1826**
FLOWER SIZE **3.1in (8cm)**
SCENT **Strong and sweet**
FLOWERING **Once only**
HEIGHT/SPREAD **4.9ft (1.5m)/3.3ft (1m)**
HARDINESS **Zone 4**

The famous old rose is thought to be a hybrid between an Alba and a Damask. It was certainly the first to be the subject of a legal action, when John Booth (a Scottish nurseryman in Schleswig-Holstein) was unfairly accused by a Hamburg professor of botany called Lehmann of reintroducing an older rose under a new name. An added embarrassment was the fact that Booth had received permission for its name from the Danish Queen, Marie Sophie Friederike of Hessen-Kassel (1767–1852), wife of Frederik VI. The flowers of 'Königin von Dänemark' are deep sugar pink at the center, with paler edges. They are flat and very full of petals, rosette-shaped, occasionally quartered, with button eyes and some quill-shaped petals. They also have long sepals. The flowers come in clusters of 3–9, sometimes so heavy that the branches arch over under their weight. The leaves are dark, glaucous green, greener than many Albas, and somewhat coarse. The plant is comparatively compact and very thorny.

KONRAD HENKEL

syn. 'KORJET'

Hybrid Tea

ORIGIN **Kordes, Germany, 1983**
PARENTAGE **seedling x 'Red Planet'**
FLOWER SIZE **4.7in (12cm)**
SCENT **Medium and sweet**
FLOWERING **Repeats well**
HEIGHT/SPREAD **4.9ft (1.5m)/3.3ft (1m)**
HARDINESS **Zone 6**

This rose commemorates the German industrialist who did much to reestablish the country's economic strength after World War II. Konrad Henkel is a fine, large Hybrid Tea. Its flowers are a deep, rich scarlet, with hints of crimson, and very beautifully shaped. They stand up well to both heat and rain – the petals are unusually thick and strong. They are borne singly or in small clusters (of never more than four flowers) on long, straight stems that are perfect for cutting. The plant is tall and upright with large, dark, semiglossy leaves, which are basically very healthy, though mildew may be a problem later in the year. It is free flowering and repeats well, which makes it one of the best Hybrid Teas for garden display.

KORDES' BRILLANT

syn. 'KORBISCH'

Shrub Rose

ORIGIN **Kordes, Germany, 1983**
PARENTAGE **'Sympathie' seedling**
FLOWER SIZE **3.5in (9cm)**
SCENT **Light**
FLOWERING **Repeats**
HEIGHT/SPREAD **6.6ft (2m)/4.1ft (1.25m)**
HARDINESS **Zone 5**

Kordes' Brillant is a tall, scarlet Shrub rose in the Floribunda mould. The buds open out to round, loose-petaled flowers with stamens visible in the middle. They are Turkey red at first, but later a little more scarlet, and they hold their color well – a penetrating, brilliant red. The flowers come in well-spaced clusters of 3–9. The plant has splendid, dark, healthy, glittering, Kordesii leaves. It flowers very prolifically in midseason, then puts out a series of smaller flushes until late autumn, though it is never completely without flowers. It is tall, vigorous, gawky, and lanky – one could even say that its stems are too long and too stiff – but it is simply magnificent in a mixed planting of hot colors.

'KORDES' PERFECTA'

Hybrid Tea

ORIGIN **Kordes, Germany, 1957**
PARENTAGE **'Spek's Yellow' x 'Karl Herbst'**
FLOWER SIZE **5.5in (14cm)**
SCENT **Strong and sweet**
FLOWERING **Repeats**
HEIGHT/SPREAD **4.9ft (1.5m)/3.3ft (1m)**
HARDINESS **Zone 6**
AWARDS **NRS PIT 1957; Portland GM 1959**

When Wilhelm Kordes first set eyes on this beautiful Hybrid Tea, he exclaimed "At last! My perfect rose!" It is easy to see why: no rose has such a combination of color, scent, size, and exquisite form. The flowers of 'Kordes' Perfecta' are creamy yellow with dark pink edges, though the colors may be darker in cool weather and fade in hot. They start from long buds, and the petals take several days to unfold but eventually unscroll in the classic Hybrid Tea manner: the effect is heightened by the pink edging. The flowers come singly on the end of long, strong stems but occasionally the plant produces an exceptionally vigorous new growth on which many long-stemmed flowers are borne individually all along the main stem. 'Kordes' Perfecta' was for years a famous and distinctive exhibition rose, and it is still excellent for cutting. The plant is vigorous, upright, prickly, and healthy, though the wood is sometimes a little brittle. The leaves are dark and glossy. It takes a while to repeat its flowering, but the autumn colors can be especially rich. The intense scent is a bonus.

KRONENBOURG

see 'MME. A. MEILLAND'

'KORDES' PERFECTA'

'KRONPRINZESSIN VIKTORIA'

see 'SOUVENIR DE LA MALMAISON'

KUPFERKÖNIGIN

syn. 'KORANDERER', Our Copper Queen

Hybrid Tea

ORIGIN **Kordes, Germany, 1996**
FLOWER SIZE **3.9in (10cm)**
SCENT **Moderate and sweet**
FLOWERING **Repeats well**
HEIGHT/SPREAD **3.3ft (1m)/2.5ft (75cm)**
HARDINESS **Zone 6**

Kupferkönigin is one of those handsome modern roses that reminds us how well the Hybrid Teas have continued to develop in recent years. Its flowers are very beautiful: a striking combination of pure mustard yellow with copper apricot backs. They come usually singly but sometimes in clusters of up to five, and they keep their color well. The leaves are very healthy and glossy – deep bronze at first, later darkest green, providing a wonderful foil for the flowers. The plant is vigorous and will grow to 4.9ft (1.5m) in hot climates, but it is likely to reach less than 3.3ft (1m) in its native Germany. It repeats well and stands up well to rain. The long stems make it an excellent rose for cutting.

KORDES' BRILLANT

KUPFERKÖNIGIN

THE KORDES FAMILY

THESE HIGHLY SUCCESSFUL GERMAN ROSE BREEDERS HAVE RAISED HUNDREDS OF ROSES, INCLUDING THE SUPERHARDY, HEALTHY KORDESII HYBRIDS

THE GERMAN FIRM of W. Kordes' Sohne belongs to the most distinguished rose-breeding family in Europe. There are more roses in this encyclopedia bred by Kordes than by any other breeder. The company dates from 1887, but its greatest expansion followed a move from Elmshorn to Sparrieshoop in 1918, and the return in 1919 of Wilhelm Kordes (1891–1976) from a four-and-a-half year internment in the Isle of Man. Kordes spent World War I reading every book about rose breeding he could lay his hands upon. By the time the war was over, he had amassed a detailed knowledge of rose parentages and ideas for the advancement of rose breeding that were second to none.

Kordes sought to develop new races of hardy, healthy roses using species and cultivars whose qualities had been overlooked by others. His experiments focused at first upon the native European species, including *Rosa canina*, *R. rubiginosa*, and *R. spinosissima*: the results include such important shrub roses as 'Harry Maasz' (1939), 'Louis Rödiger' (1935), 'Raubritter' (1936), 'Karl Förster' (1930), and the early flowering "Frühlings" series. He also experimented with the Hybrid Musks such as 'Elmshorn' (1950), 'Erfurt' (1931), and 'Eva' (1933). Hybrid Teas were not neglected: 'Crimson Glory' (1935) had an unusually long reign as the world's favorite crimson rose.

'HARRY MAASZ'

However, Kordes knew that it was through introducing new genes that all the great advances in plant breeding had been achieved: his son Reimer (1922–2000) bred the world's favorite white rose 'Schneewittchen', actually a Hybrid Musk.

The prosperity of W. Kordes' Sohne after World War II depended in part upon the success of the Kordesii Hybrids – a race of superhardy, healthy short climbers and shrub roses bred from a unique seedling known as 'Kordesii'. This was a spontaneous cross between 'Max Graf' and an unknown red Hybrid Tea, and it bred true from seed. It was a fertile parent that brought health, hardiness, vigor, and repeat flowering. 'Leverkusen' and 'Hamburger Phönix' were the first Kordesii Hybrids to be released in 1954. Thereafter, they followed in great numbers and made an indelible impression on the market over a period of ten years. The dark, glossy foliage of many modern roses can be traced back to 'Kordesii'.

REIMER KORDES

During the 1950s and 1960s, Kordes and his son Reimer were also introducing such important representatives of other breeding lines as 'Kordes' Sondermeldung' (1950), 'Kordes' Perfecta' (1957), its seedling 'Königin der Rosen' (1964), and 'Lilli Marleen' (1959). Reimer moved on from shrub roses to concentrate on brilliantly colored Hybrid Teas and Floribundas for private and public gardens. Nevertheless, he introduced roses of every type: large-flowered climbers such as 'Alchymist' (1956) and 'Antike 89' (1988); groundcover roses such as 'Immensee' and 'Sommerwind'; Hybrid Teas including 'Duftzauber 84' (1984) and 'Kupferkönigin' (1996); shrubs such as 'Charivari' (1970), Lucinde (1988), and 'Rosenstadt Zweibrücken' (1989); Floribundas such as 'Golden Holstein' (1989) and 'Crimson Bouquet' (1999); and cut-flower roses such as 'Champagner' (1985).

The company is still owned and managed by the Kordes family, with a fine show garden at Sparrieshoop and a substantial business throughout the world.

'ROSENSTADT ZWEIBRÜCKEN'

K

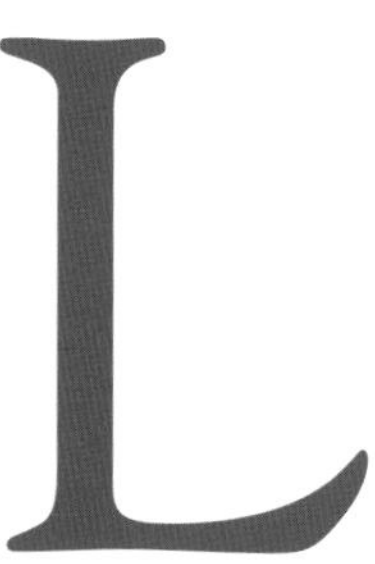

L. D. Braithwaite

syn. 'AUScrim'

Shrub Rose

ORIGIN **Austin, Britain, 1988**
PARENTAGE **Mary Rose × 'The Squire'**
FLOWER SIZE **3.1in (8cm)**
SCENT **Strong and sweet**
FLOWERING **Repeats well**
HEIGHT/SPREAD **3.3ft (1m)/3.3ft (1m)**
HARDINESS **Zone 6**

This is probably the best modern crimson rose in the old-fashioned style, though it is far from perfect and its color is perhaps a little too bright. The flowers are cupped and contained by broad outer petals that eventually reflex, but form a loosely petaled rosette within – a very attractive shape. Sometimes the stamens are visible at the center. The flower keeps its color well, though the deepest crimson is obtained in cool weather. The flowers come singly or in clusters of up to five, and the bush is a good repeater – flushes of flowers appear almost continuously. The bush has small dark leaves, but fairly few of them, so that the structure of the plant is in no way hidden. In hot climates, L. D. Braithwaite responds by growing much taller and more vigorously, reaching 5.7ft (1.75m) high and wide. The stems are very prickly and the internodes shorten as they grow toward the flower – a trait inherited from some distant Portland rose in its ancestry. It may suffer from mildew in autumn and blackspot in any season. The rose commemorates David Austin's father-in-law, Leonard Dudley Braithwaite.

L. D. Braithwaite

L'Aimant

L'Aimant

syn. 'HARzola', Oxford, Victorian Spice

Floribunda

ORIGIN **Harkness, Britain, 1994**
PARENTAGE **'Southampton' × (Radox Bouquet × Margaret Merril)**
FLOWER SIZE **3.5in (9cm)**
SCENT **Strong and sweet**
FLOWERING **Repeats well**
HEIGHT/SPREAD **3.3ft (1m)/2.5ft (75cm)**
HARDINESS **Zone 6**
AWARDS **Paris FA 1991; Edland FA 1992; Glasgow FA 1998**

L'Aimant is a modern classic, widely grown all over the world for its beautiful, frilly, pink flowers and its stupendous fragrance. The flowers open slowly to a mass of short, wavy, bright pink petals, slightly paler at the edges and with a hint of salmon at the center. They come singly or in clusters of up to five and are excellent for cutting. The unusual, informal shape of the flowers makes them useful in the garden, too. The plant stands up well to rain but grows best in warm weather. It has a bushy shape, so the flowers do not appear just at the tips of the tallest stems. It is vigorous, with dark green leaves that occasionally act as hosts to blackspot.

'La Belle Distinguée'

Rubiginosa Hybrid

ORIGIN **France, 1820**
FLOWER SIZE **2in (5cm)**
SCENT **Light and sweet**
FLOWERING **Once, early in season**
HEIGHT/SPREAD **3.3ft (1m)/2.7ft (80cm)**
HARDINESS **Zone 5**

'La Belle Distinguée' is one of the oddballs among old garden roses that do not fit easily into any established category. It is probably a hybrid of *Rosa rubiginosa*, an early Sweetbriar Hybrid whose origins are long since forgotten. The semidouble flowers are very striking, being an unusually bright crimson among old roses, the color set off by a dense ring of golden stamens. The bush is very compact, with lots of small, sharp prickles and small dark leaves that have more than just a hint of the distinctive, fruity, sweetbriar aroma. It lacks the leafy luxuriance of Gallicas and Damasks, but 'La Belle Distinguée' is a fine rose in its own right, and fits well into mixed plantings.

'La Belle Distinguée'

'La Belle Sultane'

syn. 'Violacea'

Gallica

ORIGIN **France, c.1810**
FLOWER SIZE **2.4in (6cm)**
SCENT **Light**
FLOWERING **Once only, midseason**
HEIGHT/SPREAD **5.7ft (1.75m)/4.9ft (1.5m)**
HARDINESS **Zone 5**

It has all the appearance of an ancient rose, but 'La Belle Sultane' cannot even be traced back to the time of Empress Joséphine. Ironically, some historians maintain that the beautiful Sultana was a distant cousin of the Empress, Aimée Dubucq de Rivery. The flowers of the rose now widely sold as 'La Belle Sultane' are almost single, sometimes with a few extra petals when well grown, and a handsome circle of long golden stamens. The petals are darkest crimson, almost black, toward the edges and more red toward the center and on the backs. There is a small white patch at the center, and white streaks occasionally leak out into the petals. The effect is surprisingly brilliant for such a dark rose: much of that brilliance comes from the stamens. The bush is tall, tough, thrifty, and wiry, with slender stems and small dark leaves that have a purple outline when young. The plant is almost thornless, but the stems are covered in small dark bristles – aromatic glands that rub off easily and smell of resin. 'La Belle Sultane' is not the most floriferous of Gallicas, but no collector of old roses would want to be without it.

'La Belle Sultane'

'La France'

Hybrid Tea

ORIGIN **Guillot fils, France, 1867**
FLOWER SIZE **4.3in (11cm)**
SCENT **Strong and sweet**
FLOWERING **Repeats well**
HEIGHT/SPREAD **4.9ft (1.5m)/4.1ft (1.25m)**
HARDINESS **Zone 6**

'La France' was the first Hybrid Tea ever introduced. It was called a Hybrid Tea because it was a cross between a Hybrid Perpetual and a Tea rose. Its importance was not apparent at first: the Hybrid Teas were not recognized as a distinct class of rose until 12 years later. It would have helped if 'La France' had been the result of a deliberate cross, but the most that can be said of its origins is that it may be the result of a dalliance between 'Mme. Victor Verdier' and 'Mme. Bravy', a Tea rose. Its flowers are large, beautifully pointed when they first open, silver pink in color (slightly darker on the outsides of the petals), elegantly reflexed, and powerfully scented with that sweet Damask scent that is so much appreciated by rose lovers. The flower stems are long, and it repeats very well. It is still one of the best of all Hybrid Teas. The petals are soft and the leaves are prone to fungal infections, which means that the plant performs best in warm, dry climates.

The New York nurseryman Peter Henderson introduced the climbing sport, which is still as widely grown and popular as the original. **'Climbing La France'** is a stiff, lanky grower with somewhat short internodes, but it thrives in almost any soil and position, and an established plant always has a few flowers after the first main, magnificent flowering.

'La France'

'Climbing La France'

Sport of 'La France'

'Climbing La France'

Climbing Hybrid Tea

ORIGIN **Henderson, US, 1893**
FLOWER SIZE **4.7in (12cm)**
FLOWERING **Once well, then intermittently**
HEIGHT/SPREAD **13.1ft (4m)/6.6ft (2m)**

'LA MARNE'

'LA MARNE'

Polyantha

ORIGIN **Barbier, France, 1915**
PARENTAGE **'Mme. Norbert Levavasseur' × 'Comtesse du Caÿla'**
FLOWER SIZE **2in (5cm)**
SCENT **Light and musky**
FLOWERING **Repeats constantly**
HEIGHT/SPREAD **4.1ft (1.25m)/2.7ft (80cm)**
HARDINESS **Zone 6**

This perky little Polyantha is popular still in the US, but largely forgotten in Europe. 'La Marne' is an excellent small shrub, valued for its thornlessness and tolerance of neglect. Its flowers are very attractive – semidouble, deep pink, with ruffled petals, a white center, and cheerful yellow stamens when it opens out. They come in loose clusters of 5–20 and are very freely produced all through the growing season. 'La Marne' has dark leaves and an upright habit of growth. It may get a little mildew in cool, damp weather, but these conditions also produce the brightest colors (the flowers fade in strong sun). 'La Marne' is vigorous, tolerant of poor soils, and useful for landscaping, but it is attractive close-up as well as at a distance.

'LA MORTOLA'

Species Climber

ORIGIN **Hanbury, Britain, 1955**
FLOWER SIZE **1.4in (3.5cm)**
SCENT **Strong and musky**
FLOWERING **Once, midseason**
HEIGHT/SPREAD **23ft (7m)/13.1ft (4m)**
HARDINESS **Zone 7**

'La Mortola' is a cultivar of *Rosa brunonii*. It was selected at the famous Hanbury garden on the Italian Riviera, and introduced through Graham Thomas when he worked for the British firm of T. Hilling & Co. in the 1950s. It has larger flowers than most forms of *Rosa brunonii*, and large, limp, gray green leaves. At the garden of La Mortola itself, it cascades irrepressibly out of the top of a 100-year-old Italian cypress.

'LA NOBLESSE'

Centifolia

ORIGIN **Soupert & Notting, Luxembourg, 1856**
FLOWER SIZE **3.5in (9cm)**
SCENT **Strong and sweet**
FLOWERING **Once only**
HEIGHT/SPREAD **4.9ft (1.5m)/4.1ft (1.25m)**
HARDINESS **Zone 5**

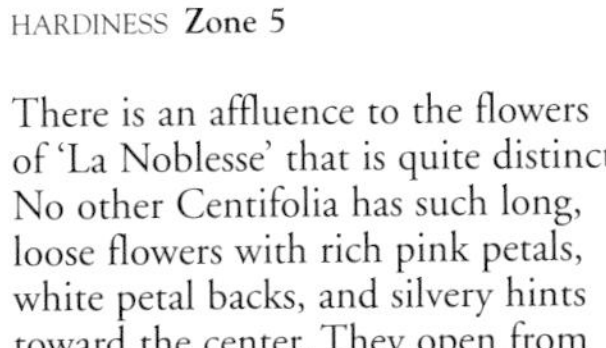

There is an affluence to the flowers of 'La Noblesse' that is quite distinct. No other Centifolia has such long, loose flowers with rich pink petals, white petal backs, and silvery hints toward the center. They open from red buds, are full, cupped, and almost blowsy in shape, with slightly wavy petals. The flowers come in clusters of 3–7, rather late in the season, and tend to nod under the weight of their petals. Their scent is delicious. 'La Noblesse' makes a bushy plant, with lush leaves that are somewhat rugose in texture and susceptible to blackspot. But this is a problem only in cool, damp climates and, even there, is never enough to detract from the beauty of the flowers. 'La Noblesse' was one of the last Centifolias to be introduced.

'LA MORTOLA'

LA PALOMA 85

'LA NOBLESSE'

LA PALOMA 85

syn. 'TANAMOLA', The Dove

Floribunda

ORIGIN **Tantau, Germany, 1985**
FLOWER SIZE **3.1in (8cm)**
SCENT **Little or none**
FLOWERING **Repeats well**
HEIGHT/SPREAD **2ft (60cm)/1.6ft (50cm)**
HARDINESS **Zone 6**

La Paloma 85 is a good white Floribunda, if not a match for the free flowering, pure white 'Schneewittchen'. Its buds are elegant, like a Hybrid Tea's, and are initially produced only singly or in small clusters. They open out fairly full and open, with a rounded outline. The flowers are cream colored at first, with a lemon heart, but later turn pure white. The autumn flowers are more obviously like a Floribunda's – larger clusters (of up to nine flowers) and smaller blooms. The plant has dark, glossy leaves and a strong, bushy habit of growth. It is very healthy and floriferous, and the flowers stand up well to rain.

'LA REINE'

syn. 'ROSE DE LA REINE'

Hybrid Perpetual

ORIGIN **Laffay, France, 1842**
PARENTAGE **'William Jesse' seedling**
FLOWER SIZE **3.9in (10cm)**
SCENT **Strong and sweet**
FLOWERING **Repeats**
HEIGHT/SPREAD **5.7ft (1.75m)/4.9ft (1.5m)**
HARDINESS **Zone 5**

Although one of the first Hybrid Perpetuals to be bred, 'La Reine' is still one of the best. The large, cupped flowers open from pointed buds. They are dark lilac pink with paler silky pink reverses, and open out to a mass of petals. The petals are thin and tend to ball in wet or humid weather: this is a rose that does better in hot, dry weather. The flowers come singly or in small clusters (of up to four) and repeat their flowering over a series of flushes. The individual flowers last a long time before fading. The plant has very few thorns and fairly long stems, which can be pegged down to increase their flowering. It is, however, smaller and more compact than many Hybrid Perpetuals. Mildew and blackspot may sometimes pose a problem.

'LA REINE VICTORIA'

see 'REINE VICTORIA'

'LA REINE'

LA SÉVILLANA

syn. 'MEIGEKANU'

Floribunda

ORIGIN **Meilland, France, 1978**
PARENTAGE **(['Jolie Madame' × 'Zambra'] × 'Super Star') × 'Rusticana'**
FLOWER SIZE **3.1in (8cm)**
SCENT **Light**
FLOWERING **Almost continuous**
HEIGHT/SPREAD **4.1ft (1.25m)/4.9ft (1.5m)**
HARDINESS **Zone 5**
AWARDS **ADR 1979; Orléans GM 1980**

The house of Meilland, often Europe's market leader, realized in the 1970s that it ought to be introducing roses for ground cover and landscaping. La Sévillana was one of their first – a blazing, iridescent, flaming, geranium-tinted red Floribunda, brilliant even on a dark, overcast day. It holds its color in hot sun and always looks fresh, although it remains an unusual color among landscaping roses. It is equally effective in the garden, where you can study its finer points, like the ruffled petals, the yellow flush at the base, and the freckles that develop in rainy weather. It is immensely free flowering, but needs deadheading (the hedge trimmer will do), unless you are willing to forego more flowers for masses of bright red hips in autumn. The plant has a dense, rounded habit, a lot of healthy, glossy, deep green leaves, and beautiful, dark red new growths.

Meilland also introduced a very fine climbing sport as Grimpant La Sévillana in 1997. It is vigorous and early-flowering, and makes a sheet of brilliant red for many weeks, but has only an occasional flower thereafter.

Pink La Sévillana is another sport of La Sévillana and identical to it in everything except its color. Instead of the glorious flame red tints of the original, Pink La Sévillana starts as a middling sort of pink and fades a little as it ages. In hot weather, however, it bleaches badly, so that the flowers fade to a dirty white – never a problem with the red form. In fact, this presents a problem only in hot areas; most people in cool or temperate climates consider Pink La Sévillana a good rose. It reverts occasionally to the red form. There is also a climbing form of Pink La Sévillana, rarely seen but a fine and vigorous plant.

LA SÉVILLANA

Sports of La Sévillana

GRIMPANT LA SÉVILLANA

syn. 'MEIGE-KANUSAR', CLIMBING LA SÉVILLANA

Climbing Floribunda

ORIGIN **Meilland, France, 1997**
FLOWERING **Once very strongly, then intermittently**
HEIGHT/SPREAD **13.1ft (4m)/9.8ft (3m)**

PINK LA SÉVILLANA

syn. 'MEIGEROKA'

ORIGIN **Meilland, France, 1984**
HEIGHT/SPREAD **4.1ft (1.25m)/4.9ft (1.5m)**
AWARDS **Baden-Baden GM 1985; ADR 1986**

GRIMPANT LA SÉVILLANA

PINK LA SÉVILLANA

LA VILLE DE BRUXELLES

see VILLE DE BRUXELLES

'LADY HUNTINGFIELD'

Shrub Rose

ORIGIN **Clark, Australia, 1937**
PARENTAGE **'Busybody' × 'Aspirant Marcel Rouyer'**
FLOWER SIZE **3.9in (10cm)**
SCENT **Strong and tealike**
FLOWERING **Fully recurrent**
HEIGHT/SPREAD **3.3ft (1m)/4.1ft (1.25m)**
HARDINESS **Zone 6**

'Lady Huntingfield' is a very beautiful shrub rose for a dry, warm climate: its petals are rain-sensitive and the flower buds ball in damp weather, even in its native Australia. When the plant is suited, however, the large, shapely flowers, with their broad, incurved petals, glow like goblets of apricot and gold. The outer petals and the petal backs are paler, but both keep a rich apricot tone at the base that suffuses the whole flower. The flowers are borne on long stems, either singly or in clusters of up to nine. The plant is vigorous and bushy, well-furnished with smooth, deep green foliage. It is one of many Alister Clark roses that should be grown wherever the climate is Mediterranean.

'LADY HUNTINGFIELD'

LADY LIKE

syn. 'TANEKILY'

Hybrid Tea

ORIGIN **Tantau, Germany, 1989**
PARENTAGE **seedling × 'Super Star'**
FLOWER SIZE **5.1in (13cm)**
SCENT **Strong and sweet**
FLOWERING **Repeats well**
HEIGHT/SPREAD **3.3ft (1m)/2.5ft (75cm)**
HARDINESS **Zone 5**

Although not destined for immortality among the great roses of all time, Lady Like is a very good rose, currently among the best of its color. The flowers are a rich, dark pink, with a hint of cream toward the center. The outer petals are especially large, and fold over the inner ones at first to create an attractive bud. Later the whole flower opens out in a loose arrangement of petals that stand up well to wind and rain. Lady Like is especially good as a cut flower because it lasts a long time in water and will open out fully before wilting away. The bush is of moderate height but vigorous, with dark, healthy, glossy leaves.

'LADY MARY FITZWILLIAM'

'LADY MANN'

see 'LORRAINE LEE'

'LADY MARY FITZWILLIAM'

Hybrid Tea

ORIGIN **Bennett, Britain, 1882**
PARENTAGE **'Devoniensis' × 'Victor Verdier'**
FLOWER SIZE **4.7in (12cm)**
SCENT **Strong and sweet**
FLOWERING **Almost continuous**
HEIGHT/SPREAD **2ft (60cm)/1.6ft (50cm)**
HARDINESS **Zone 6**

The importance of 'Lady Mary Fitzwilliam' is twofold: first, it was by far the most floriferous of the earliest Hybrid Teas bred by the English farmer Henry Bennett in Wiltshire; second, it proved a powerful parent whose genes turn up in almost every modern rose. In fact, it is a very feeble grower and puts all its efforts into producing its large, pendulous, elegant flowers. The English rosarian Jack Harkness commented with surprise that "such powers of procreation should lay within such weakly loins." The modern popularity of 'Lady Mary Fitzwilliam' is largely founded on this point of historical interest. Moreover, until the 1970s, it was thought to be extinct. Great was the excitement when it was reintroduced, though some observers have suggested that what we now grow as 'Lady Mary Fitzwilliam' again is actually 'Mrs. Wakefield Christie-Miller' (McGredy, 1909). All of which has simply added yet more to its popularity.

LADY LIKE

L

'LADY HILLINGDON'

Tea Rose

ORIGIN **Lowe & Shawyer, Britain, 1910**
PARENTAGE **'Papa Gontier' x 'Mme. Hoste'**
FLOWER SIZE **3.9in (10cm)**
SCENT **Strong and tealike**
FLOWERING **Continuous**
HEIGHT/SPREAD **3.3ft (1m)/3.3ft (1m)**
HARDINESS **Zone 8**

'Lady Hillingdon' was one of the last Tea roses to be bred, and it is by far the loveliest in its color range. The flowers are a rich dark amber color at first, before fading gently through buff to cream and ivory white at the edges, while always retaining a rich apricot at the heart. The long, slender, elegant buds open out to cupped flowers and are slightly pendulous. They come in clusters of 3–7 and last well when cut: they were once widely used for forcing in the US. The new growths are dark crimson – a most beautiful and eye-catching contrast to the color of the flowers – and the young stems have a purple bloom on top of the crimson. Later they turn to dark green. The plant grows slowly, with a thin, twiggy structure, somewhat ungainly, but it is very floriferous, especially if only lightly pruned.

The climbing form, **'Climbing Lady Hillingdon'**, is very vigorous, with flowers that are slightly larger and droop rather more – a distinct asset in any climber. It is popular in England, where it is often hardy against the wall of a house. It is one of the most continually flowering of all climbing sports. Lady Hillingdon (1857–1940), famous for her aphorisms, was born the Honorable Alice Marion Harbord and married the second Baron Hillingdon in 1886.

Sport of 'Lady Hillingdon'

'CLIMBING LADY HILLINGDON'

Climbing Tea Rose
ORIGIN **Hicks, Britain, 1917**
FLOWER SIZE **4.3in (11cm)**
FLOWERING **Repeats well**
HEIGHT/SPREAD **13.1ft (4m)/6.6ft (2m)**

'LADY HILLINGDON'

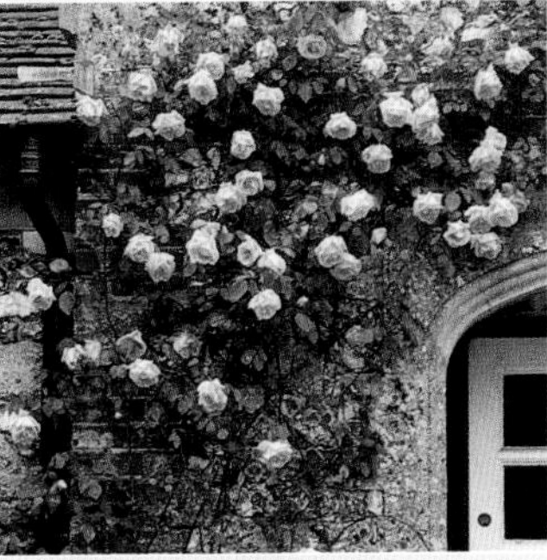

'CLIMBING LADY HILLINGDON'

LADY MEILLAND

syn. 'MEIALZONITE'

Hybrid Tea

ORIGIN **Meilland, France, 1986**
FLOWER SIZE **4.3in (11cm)**
SCENT **Strong and sweet**
FLOWERING **Repeats**
HEIGHT/SPREAD **4.1ft (1.25m)/2.7ft (80cm)**
HARDINESS **Zone 6**
AWARDS **NZ GM 1982**

Lady Meilland has long-petaled, medium to large flowers of classic Hybrid Tea form, but often borne in clusters of three, five, or even more. They are a handsome color – pale orange, with red petal backs, but losing their orange tints as they age and acquiring an overall tone of salmon pink. It is vigorous and fairly tall-growing, with an upright habit and long stems that make the flowers useful for cutting. The plant has medium-dark leaves, but blackspot and rust may be a problem in cool climates. The many-petaled flowers may also spoil in wet weather, so Lady Meilland is essentially a plant for warm, dry climates, where it is one of the most vigorous and satisfactory of all roses.

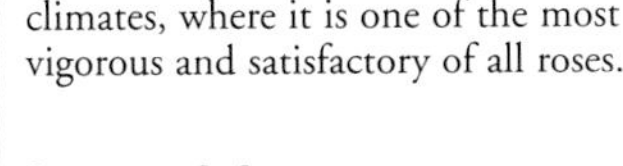

LADY MEILLANDINA

syn. 'MEILARCO'

Miniature Rose

ORIGIN **Meilland, France, 1985**
PARENTAGE **('Fashion' x 'Zambra') x Belle Meillandina**
FLOWER SIZE **1.6in (4cm)**
SCENT **Light**
FLOWERING **Repeats very well**
HEIGHT/SPREAD **1.6ft (50cm)/1.6ft (50cm)**
HARDINESS **Zone 6**

At its best, Lady Meillandina is one of the most beautiful of all patio or miniature Floribunda roses. The flowers are variable in shape, but usually open imbricated, with a lot of petals lying flat around a cupped center, and then expand until the whole center is filled with little petaloids. The color is a rich apricot or salmon pink, fading gradually from the outside toward the center, which gives rise to beautiful contrasts within the flower. The leaves are small, dark, and healthy, and the bush makes an excellent potted plant or container plant. It sometimes produces a large green eye, usually as a result of over-feeding. For rose-growers who consider this feature unattractive, Lady Meillandina does best in poor soils.

'LADY PENZANCE'

Rubiginosa Hybrid

ORIGIN **Penzance, Britain, 1894**
PARENTAGE ***Rosa rubiginosa* x *Rosa foetida* 'Bicolor'**
FLOWER SIZE **1.6in (4cm)**
SCENT **None**
FLOWERING **Once only, early in season**
HEIGHT/SPREAD **8.2ft (2.5m)/9.8ft (3m)**
HARDINESS **Zone 4**

Only its historic interest can explain the continuing popularity of 'Lady Penzance' today. It may have only a few insignificant flowers on a dull, bulky bush, but it was the Briar Hybrid that Lord Penzance selected from all his seedlings to honor his wife. It is also the first known example of a man-made hybrid of *Rosa foetida*. The flowers are pale coral with a patch of yellow at the center and creamy yellow backs, but are early and short-lived. The leaves have some of the aromatic qualities of *Rosa rubiginosa*; nonetheless, it is an unexciting rose, valuable only in collections and best in a semiwild garden.

'LADY PENZANCE'

LADY ROSE

syn. 'KORLADY'

Hybrid Tea

ORIGIN **Kordes, Germany, 1979**
PARENTAGE **seedling x 'Träumerei'**
FLOWER SIZE **4.7in (12cm)**
SCENT **Moderate and sweet**
FLOWERING **Repeats very well**
HEIGHT/SPREAD **3.3ft (1m)/2.5ft (75cm)**
HARDINESS **Zone 6**
AWARDS **Belfast GM 1981**

Lady Rose is one of the best vermilion Hybrid Teas. It is equally useful in the garden and as a cut flower. The flowers are vermilion orange, fading to coral pink. They start with an elegant bud, especially pretty at the half open stage, before they open out to a muddled and fairly formless mass of petals. They come in long, spacious clusters, typically of 5–9 flowers, but occasionally singly. The plant has beautiful, dark green, healthy, glossy foliage. It sends up flush after flush of flowers in such rapid succession that it must be among the most floriferous of all Hybrid Teas.

'LADY SYLVIA'

see 'OPHELIA'

LADY MEILLAND

LADY MEILLANDINA

LADY ROSE

'LADY WATERLOW'

'LADY WATERLOW'

Tea-Noisette

ORIGIN **Nabonnand, France, 1903**
PARENTAGE **'La France de '89' x 'Mme. Marie Lavalley'**
FLOWER SIZE **4.3in (11cm)**
SCENT **Strong**
FLOWERING **Repeats well**
HEIGHT/SPREAD **13.1ft (4m)/8.2ft (2.5m)**
HARDINESS **Zone 7**

'Lady Waterlow' was the last of the great Tea-Noisettes to be introduced before the world of climbing roses was swamped by a flood of Multiflora and Wichurana Ramblers. It is one of the earliest of all roses to flower, its buds as long and slender as any Hybrid Tea's. Its flowers are large, full of petals, pretty at all stages, and strongly scented. They open light salmon pink and fade to pure rose pink, but the exact color varies according to the season and the climate. They come singly or in clusters of up to five flowers on sturdy stems that invite picking. The plant is prickly, with large leaves, and is never without flowers from spring to late autumn. It is vigorous but needs a hot climate for good growth: it grows to 16.4ft (5m) in California but will reach only 6.6ft (2m) as a pillar rose in Britain. Lady Waterlow (née Margaret Hamilton) was a Californian from the Napa Valley who married Sir Sydney Waterlow in 1882.

'LADY X'

Hybrid Tea

ORIGIN **Meilland, France, 1965**
PARENTAGE **('Pigalle' x 'Tristeza') x 'Prélude'**
FLOWER SIZE **4.7in (12cm)**
SCENT **Medium and fruity**
FLOWERING **Repeats well**
HEIGHT/SPREAD **6.6ft (2m)/3.3ft (1m)**
HARDINESS **Zone 7**
AWARDS **Portland GM 1968**

'Lady X' is widely grown in the US and Australia, but no longer in Europe. It has very long, slender buds and long petals, which are pale mauve pink at first, with even paler petal backs and slightly darker edges to the petals. As the petals unscroll, the outer ones reflex to make a star shape, which enhances the beauty of the opening bud. They fade to pale pink and eventually open out loosely. The color is never very strong, so this is a rose that associates well with other soft colors. The plant has sparse foliage and few thorns. 'Lady X' grows strongly to a considerable height, flowers repeatedly, and is generally healthy.

ROSA LAEVIGATA

ROSA LAEVIGATA

Wild Rose

FLOWER SIZE **2.8in (7cm)**
SCENT **Sweet, like gardenias**
FLOWERING **Once only, very early in season**
HEIGHT/SPREAD **16.4ft (5m)/16.4ft (5m)**
HARDINESS **Zone 7**

The Cherokee rose gets its popular name because it appears to have naturalized over much of the American South, but it is actually a native of tropical lowland areas of southern China, Indochina, and Taiwan. It is a vigorous shrub that naturally clambers up trees to as much as 32.8ft (10m), though it is usually grown as a lax, freestanding shrub along a wall or boundary. Its shiny evergreen leaves are attractive at all times of the year. They usually have no more than three leaflets (occasionally five), which are somewhat variable in shape. The flowers are white, solitary, and borne on very bristly stalks, with bristly receptacles and bristly sepals, too. The handsome golden stamens are very striking, as are the bristly orange hips. *Rosa laevigata* is one of the best of all roses for gardens in warm climates.

'LADY X'

'LAFAYETTE'

see 'JOSEPH GUY'

'LAFTER'

Hybrid Tea

ORIGIN **Brownell, US, 1948**
PARENTAGE **('V for Victory' x ['General Jacqueminot' x 'Dr. W. Van Fleet']) x 'Pink Princess'**
FLOWER SIZE **3.9in (10cm)**
SCENT **Strong, fruity, and sweet**
FLOWERING **Repeats well**
HEIGHT/SPREAD **6.6ft (2m)/4.9ft (1.5m)**
HARDINESS **Zone 5**

'Lafter' not only thrives in cold climates but also gives an excellent performance in mild or hot areas. It makes a broad, leafy plant – much more of a shrub rose than a Hybrid Tea. The flowers are bright salmon, sometimes even coral colored at first, with yellow backs. It is a very vivid and modern coloring, which catches the eye from quite a distance. Later the petals fade to pink and cream, though there is still a pale yellow patch at the center when the semidouble flowers open out. The flowers come singly or in clusters of up to five, and are very freely borne right through until late autumn. 'Lafter' has large, glossy leaves, medium-dark and medium-sized, which color up well in autumn. It is usually very healthy, except for an occasional touch of blackspot in mild areas. The plant has quite a lot of prickles, and is sometimes recommended for hedging. It roots easily from cuttings.

'LAFTER'

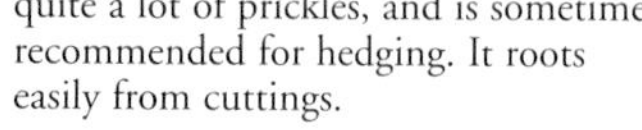

LAGERFELD

syn. 'AROLAQUELI', Starlight

Grandiflora

ORIGIN **Christensen, US, 1986**
PARENTAGE **'Nil Bleu' x ('Ivory Tower' x 'Angel Face')**
FLOWER SIZE **4.3in (11cm)**
SCENT **Strong and sweet**
FLOWERING **Repeats**
HEIGHT/SPREAD **4.9ft (1.5m)/3.3ft (1m)**
HARDINESS **Zone 6**

Lilac-flowered Hybrid Teas are popular in California, where Lagerfeld was bred, though the rose was named after the Parisian couturier, Karl Lagerfeld. It does extremely well in hot, dry climates. Its flowers have long petals and elegant buds, and remain attractive as they open out. Lagerfeld is a very pale mauve, with a silvery wash at the tips of the petals and cream toward the center of the flowers. The petal backs are darker – a true lilac mauve – but they fade from view as the flower reflexes and opens out. The flowers are good for cutting and exhibition, but spoil in rain. They are followed by large, round hips, but deadheading helps to bring on the next flush of flowers. Lagerfeld is upright, healthy, and open in habit, with somewhat ordinary, mid-green leaves and a lot of prickles.

LAGERFELD

'Lamarque'

Tea-Noisette

ORIGIN **Maréchal, France, 1830**
PARENTAGE **'Blush Noisette' x 'Parks' Yellow'**
FLOWER SIZE **2.8in (7cm)**
SCENT **Light and tealike**
FLOWERING **Early in season, then sporadically**
HEIGHT/SPREAD **16.4ft (5m)/9.8ft (3m)**
HARDINESS **Zone 8**

'Lamarque' is still a very popular rose in hot climates, where it grows to as much as 32.8ft (10m) and flowers spectacularly in spring. The flowers are creamy white, fading to pure white at the edges, fully double, with a disorganized mass of little petals at the center. They hang down on long stems, sometimes singly, but more often in clusters of 3–4. 'Lamarque' flowers early and profusely, and always carries a few flowers right through until early winter. It is one of only a few roses that release their scent into the air, so that you do not need to inhale a flower to smell it. The plant is notably healthy, almost thornless, and blessed with bright green leaves.

'LAMARQUE'

'Lambert Closse'

Shrub Rose

ORIGIN **Ogilvie, Canada, 1994**
PARENTAGE **'Arthur Bell' x 'John Davis'**
FLOWER SIZE **3.1in (8cm)**
SCENT **Light and fruity**
FLOWERING **Repeats well**
HEIGHT/SPREAD **3.3ft (1m)/2.7ft (80cm)**
HARDINESS **Zone 4**

The flowers of 'Lambert Closse' are much more "normal" than most of the roses bred in Canada. You have to go back several generations before you find *Rosa rugosa* – the ancestor that gives it its hardiness. Rugosa roses are prickly shrubs: 'Lambert Closse' looks like a Hybrid Tea. Its flowers are long-petaled, elegant, and a very pretty pink. It is a dark, rich pink at first, but fades to very pale pink, starting with the outer petals, so there is usually a stunning contrast of shades within the open flower. They are usually borne singly on strong, upright stems. The plant has pale, glossy leaves, which are healthy except for a little blackspot in mild climates. It has an upright habit of growth and flowers more or less continuously until the first frosts.

Peter Lambert

THE GERMAN ROSE INDUSTRY OWES MUCH TO PETER LAMBERT, A BREEDER OF GREAT DISTINCTION WHO WORKED WITH MANY DIFFERENT CLASSES OF ROSES

PETER LAMBERT (1859–1939) was the founder of the German rose industry. He was a third-generation nurseryman from Trier, and an educated and wealthy individual. He joined the German Rose Society in 1885 and was editor of its *Rosenzeitung* from 1890 to 1911. He was also one of the promoters of the German National Rosarium at Sangerhausen.

PETER LAMBERT

Lambert introduced his first rose hybrids in 1889. The following year he introduced a white Hybrid Tea that established his reputation as a rose breeder of international standing. 'Kaiserin Auguste Viktoria' was an immediate bestseller all over the world.

Lambert's career as a breeder spanned more than 50 years. A summary of its highlights shows how widely he worked with different classes of roses: they include the dwarf Polyantha roses 'Léonie Lamesch' (named after the woman Lambert married) and 'Eugénie Lamesch' (1899); the earliest Polyantha cross with a Hybrid Tea, 'Freiherr von Marschall' (1903); the *Rosa rugosa* cross 'Schneezwerg' (1912); the Pernetiana 'Von Scharnhorst' (1916); the Bourbon/ China rose 'Adam Messerich' (1920); and the Multiflora Rambler 'Mosel' (1920).

Lambert selected roses for good health by avoiding parents that displayed a weakness for mildew or rust. As a result, a century later his roses remain among the healthiest: the Hybrid Tea 'Frau Karl Druschki' (1901) still exemplifies the hardiness, health, vigor, and freedom of flower that Lambert admired, sought, and introduced to our gardens. Its many seedlings included 'Graf Silva Tarouca' (1915) and 'Reichspräsident von Hindenburg' (1931).

'REICHSPRESIDENT VON HINDENBURG'

In 1905 Lambert named the vigorous, free flowering, and remontant shrub 'Trier' in honor of his home town. He then used 'Trier' to develop a distinct class of large, repeat flowering, Hybrid Musk shrubs and climbers with wonderfully handsome leaves and a deliciously strong scent. These became known as the Lambertianas.

'MOSEL'

'LAMINUETTE'

'LANEII'

LANTERN

'LAMINUETTE'

syn. 'MINUETTE'
Floribunda

ORIGIN **Lammerts, US, 1969**
PARENTAGE **'Mme. A. Meilland' x 'Rumba'**
FLOWER SIZE **3.1in (8cm)**
SCENT **Light and sweet**
FLOWERING **Repeats well**
HEIGHT/SPREAD **2.5ft (75cm)/1.6ft (50cm)**
HARDINESS **Zone 6**

This very pretty bicolor rose has had a long career as a cut flower. The pale crimson edges of 'Laminuette' come from 'Mme. A. Meilland'; the ground color is creamy white, with a hint of pale yellow at the center. As they age, the crimson fades to pink and runs down into the petals from the edges. The flowers have a lot of petals, and they open very slowly – which explains their commercial success – and they keep their neat shape at all stages of their development. But 'Laminuette' also makes a good garden plant, especially in hot climates where mildew and blackspot do not present a problem. The plant is small, but bushy and vigorous, with glossy, dark green leaves that are a good complement to the dainty flowers.

LAND OF THE LONG WHITE CLOUD

see NEW ZEALAND

'LANDORA'

syn. 'SUNBLEST'
Hybrid Tea

ORIGIN **Tantau, Germany, 1970**
PARENTAGE **seedling x 'King's Ransom'**
FLOWER SIZE **4.7in (12cm)**
SCENT **Light and fruity**
FLOWERING **Repeats very well**
HEIGHT/SPREAD **4.1ft (1.25m)/3.3ft (1m)**
HARDINESS **Zone 5**
AWARDS **Japan GM 1971; NZ GM 1973**

'LANDORA'

More than 30 years since it first came onto the market in Germany, 'Landora' is still one of the most popular yellow roses, especially in Europe. Its flowers are pretty as they start to expand, but remain attractive when they open out fully to reveal their stamens. They keep their color well, too – pure bright yellow, with always a deeper suggestion of gold between the petals. Although this rose is classed as a Hybrid Tea, the flowers often come in clusters of up to seven, on long, strong stems that last well when cut. 'Landora' is vigorous, hardy, and healthy, and its popularity has been reinforced by the emergence of a first-rate climbing form known as **'Climbing Landora'**. It is exactly the same as the bush form, but climbs to 13.1ft (4m), and flowers only intermittently after its first splendid flush. It is one of the best yellow Climbing Hybrid Teas available.

Sport of 'Landora'

'CLIMBING LANDORA'

Climbing Hybrid Tea
ORIGIN **Orard, France, 1978**
FLOWER SIZE **5.1in (13cm)**
FLOWERING **Once richly, then lightly**
HEIGHT/SPREAD **13.1ft (4m)/6.6ft (2m)**

'LANEII'

Moss Rose

ORIGIN **Laffay, France, 1845**
FLOWER SIZE **4.3in (11cm)**
SCENT **Strong and sweet**
FLOWERING **Once only**
HEIGHT/SPREAD **5.7ft (1.75m)/4.9ft (1.5m)**
HARDINESS **Zone 5**

'Laneii' is a very distinctive Moss rose – and one of the best – yet never as widely grown as its qualities merit, partly because it is difficult to propagate. A well-grown plant in full flower is a sight of supreme beauty. The flowers expand from round, pink buds that glisten as they burst open the bright green, mossy sepals. The petals form a large, ruffled mass of brilliant dark pink or pale crimson. Some are pleated, and others have an occasional white stripe, but the overall impression is of a mass of shining color. The moss covers the turbinate receptacles and runs a long way down the stems before turning into brown prickles. The plant has rich, pale green leaves, a dense habit of growth, and great vigor. It can even be trained as a pillar rose.

LANTERN

syn. 'MACLANTER', Octoberfest
Grandiflora

ORIGIN **McGredy, New Zealand, 1996**
PARENTAGE Louise Gardner x New Zealand
FLOWER SIZE **4.7in (12cm)**
SCENT **Strong and fruity**
FLOWERING **Repeats well**
HEIGHT/SPREAD **4.9ft (1.5m)/3.3ft (1m)**
HARDINESS **Zone 6**

The large and elegant flowers of Lantern are an unusual color: pale salmon or apricot, with a hint of red on the tips of the petals. It is a rare combination of shades to find in a Hybrid Tea. The flowers have yellow petal backs, which fade quickly to cream, while the petal tips darken as they age and spread their color down into the rest of the petals. In fact, the color is always changing, and is noticeably darker in cool weather. The flowers come both singly and in long-stemmed clusters (of up to about seven, if well grown) and are good for cutting. They contrast well with the magnificent, dark, glossy leaves and crimson new growth of Lantern. The plants are vigorous, upright, sturdy, and healthy. They repeat well, and make a good show as a garden shrub.

LAS VEGAS

syn. 'KORGANE'
Hybrid Tea

ORIGIN **Kordes, Germany, 1981**
PARENTAGE **'Ludwigshafen am Rhein' x 'Feuerzauber'**
FLOWER SIZE **4.3in (11cm)**
SCENT **Light and fruity**
FLOWERING **Repeats well**
HEIGHT/SPREAD **4.1ft (1.25m)/3.3ft (1m)**
HARDINESS **Zone 6**
AWARDS **Geneva GM 1985; Portland GM 1989**

Las Vegas is as bright as its name suggests, but somewhat less glitzy. It is an orange and yellow bicolor, whose brilliant orange or vermilion petals have equally bright yellow undersides. The flowers open from long, shapely buds and are attractive even when fully open, with layer upon layer of petals. The flowers come singly, or in clusters of up to five, on slightly nodding stems. The plant is vigorous and healthy, with dark leaves and bronzy new growth. Las Vegas expands quickly, producing new growth from the base: it is a rose that is rarely without flowers.

LAS VEGAS

LAURA FORD

LAURA FORD

syn. 'CHEWARVEL', King Tut, Normandie

Climbing Miniature

ORIGIN **Warner, Britain, 1989**
PARENTAGE **Anna Ford x ('Elizabeth of Glamis' x ['Galway Bay' x 'Sutter's Gold'])**
FLOWER SIZE **2in (5cm)**
SCENT **Light or slight**
FLOWERING **Continuous**
HEIGHT/SPREAD **8.2ft (2.5m)/4.9ft (1.5m)**
HARDINESS **Zone 6**

Laura Ford is sometimes described as a climbing patio rose, because its flowers are larger than a miniature's, and it will grow to about 9.8ft (3m). Its flowers are bright yellow when they open, with a hint of red on the backs of the petals. As they open out, only lightly double, the petals change to lemon yellow and acquire a pretty pink edging. The flowers come singly or in small clusters, typically of 5–7, and are followed by small orange hips. The plant has small, dark, glossy leaves and a dense, compact habit of growth. It is comparatively healthy. Its prickly stems are very flexible, but it is an upright grower and manages to flower from top to bottom, starting early and continuing through until late autumn.

'LAURÉ DAVOUST'

Hybrid Noisette

ORIGIN **Laffay, France, 1834**
FLOWER SIZE **1.2in (3cm)**
SCENT **Strong and musky**
FLOWERING **Once only, midseason**
HEIGHT/SPREAD **9.8ft (3m)/6.6ft (2m)**
HARDINESS **Zone 6**

It is difficult to know how to categorize 'Lauré Davoust': some consider it an early Multiflora rambler, while others treat it as a hybrid between *Rosa sempervirens* and a Noisette. It has a unique charm of its own, because every one of its tiny pink flowers opens out into a perfect little rosette, usually with a button eye at the center. The flowers are exquisitely beautiful as they open and when their color fades from pink to white. However, the flowers then retain their petals until they are brown, and the clusters become ever more congested as successive flowers try to push their way through and open, so that toward the end of its flowering there are fewer, uglier roses. But it has handsome, neat, dark, healthy leaves, and, in warm climates, it grows very quickly and easily to 16.4ft (5m) or more. No one knows who Lauré Davoust was: French authorities speculate about her relationship to Napoléon I's Marshal Davoust.

'LAURÉ DAVOUST' *(at Mottisfont Abbey)*

LAURENCE OLIVIER

see WAPITI

LAVAGLUT

syn. 'KORLECH', Intrigue

Floribunda

ORIGIN **Kordes, Germany, 1978**
PARENTAGE **'Gruss an Bayern' x seedling**
FLOWER SIZE **2.4in (6cm)**
SCENT **Light**
FLOWERING **Repeats very well**
HEIGHT/SPREAD **2.5ft (75cm)/2.5ft (75cm)**
HARDINESS **Zone 5**

Lavaglut is the perfect small red Floribunda: healthy, floriferous, and a glorious color. It is a bit short on scent, but there is nothing to match the large heads of deep dark red flowers set off by dark, glossy leaves. The flowers open out neat, flat, and full of petals, though the golden stamens are usually visible at the center. They last a long time in their clusters of 10–20 flowers and will shrug off both heat and rain. The plant is vigorous, with leaves that start bronze green before turning darker and greener. It is a good exhibition rose and lasts a long time as a cut flower. It is occasionally susceptible to blackspot, but the leaves are so wonderfully dark that the infection is not always apparent.

LAVAGLUT

LAVENDER COVER

LAVENDER COVER

syn. 'POULRUST', Cambridge

Ground Cover

ORIGIN **Poulsen, Denmark, 1994**
FLOWER SIZE **1in (2.5cm)**
SCENT **Strong and musky**
FLOWERING **Repeats well**
HEIGHT/SPREAD **2.5ft (75cm)/3.3ft (1m)**
HARDINESS **Zone 5**

The main assets of this modern groundcover rose are its floriferousness and the cool color of its little flowers. They open from dark pink buds and are semidouble, with deep mauve pink flowers that have a white patch at the center around the yellow stamens. However, the color fades very quickly, and the stamens turn to brown, so that after a day or so the flowers are little better than off-white with a smudge of pale gray pink somewhere in the petals. They make up for this by flowering in great numbers and coming in large clusters almost continuously after the first big flush, so that there are always some flowers on the plant right through until late autumn. The leaves are small, neat, dark, and healthy, and the plant is wider than it is tall.

LAVENDER DREAM

syn. 'INTERLAV'

Shrub Rose

ORIGIN **Interplant, Netherlands, 1984**
PARENTAGE **'Yesterday' x 'Nastarana'**
FLOWER SIZE **1.2in (3cm)**
SCENT **Little or none**
FLOWERING **Repeats well**
HEIGHT/SPREAD **4.9ft (1.5m)/4.9ft (1.5m)**
HARDINESS **Zone 5**
AWARDS **ADR 1987**

Lavender Dream is a modern shrub rose closely related to the old Hybrid Musks. It has vast quantities of little, semidouble flowers on a vigorous, billowing bush. The flowers open bright dark pink then fade to pale pink purple, with golden stamens visible at the center: despite their name, they are not strongly lavender colored. They come in somewhat tight clusters of 10–40. The plant has small, dark leaves (watch out for mildew), a fair share of prickles, and a habit of sending out arching canes that reach up to 6.6ft (2m) in hot climates but half that height in cool countries. Lavender Dream is free flowering, rain resistant, and useful in massed plantings as a groundcover or landscaping rose, but is also easy to mix in garden plantings, where it combines well with soft colors.

LAVENDER DREAM

L

'Lavender Jewel'

Miniature Rose

ORIGIN **Moore, US, 1978**
PARENTAGE **'Little Chief' x 'Angel Face'**
FLOWER SIZE **1.6in (4cm)**
SCENT **Light and musky**
FLOWERING **Repeats quickly**
HEIGHT/SPREAD **1.6ft (50cm)/11.8in (30cm)**
HARDINESS **Zone 6**

Everyone agrees that 'Lavender Jewel' is the finest mauve colored miniature rose, but it is also one of the most useful garden plants. It flowers almost continuously and combines well with all other soft-colored plants. The flowers are attractive and usually borne in clusters (typically of 3–7) but sometimes also singly. They are shaped like dumpy Hybrid Teas at first, but open out later into miniature Floribundas. Their color is a good, clear lavender, with hints of mauve and lilac. As the flowers open out, they start to fade to palest Parma violet at the edges. 'Lavender Jewel' makes a vigorous plant – neat and compact in cool climates and rather more sprawling in hot ones. Its leaves are medium-dark and usually fairly free from disease.

'Lavender Jewel'

L

'Lavender Lassie'

Hybrid Musk

ORIGIN **Kordes, Germany, 1960**
PARENTAGE **'Hamburg' x 'Mme. Norbert Levavasseur'**
FLOWER SIZE **2.8in (7cm)**
SCENT **Strong and sweet**
FLOWERING **Almost continuous**
HEIGHT/SPREAD **6.6ft (2m)/6.6ft (2m)**
HARDINESS **Zone 6**

The name is a misnomer: 'Lavender Lassie' is closer to pink than lavender. Eventually the flowers fade to palest pink, keeping their color longest in partially shaded positions. Nevertheless, it is one of the best of all shrub roses, and wonderfully scented. The flowers have an old-fashioned shape but are borne in modern quantities – almost continuously in hot climates, where 'Lavender Lassie' can also be trained as a 13.1ft (4m) climber. The buds are small, and give no hint of the mass of petals within the open flower. The flowers come in small clusters at first, but in large trusses of up to 30 later in the year. The plant is vigorous and strong-growing, with healthy, mid-green, semiglossy foliage. 'Lavender Lassie' flowers early, especially in warm climates, and tolerates poor soil and neglect.

'Lavender Lassie'

'Lavender Pinocchio'

Floribunda

ORIGIN **Boerner, US, 1948**
PARENTAGE **'Rosenmärchen' x 'Grey Pearl'**
FLOWER SIZE **2.8in (7cm)**
SCENT **Strong and fruity**
FLOWERING **Repeats well**
HEIGHT/SPREAD **3.3ft (1m)/2.7ft (80cm)**
HARDINESS **Zone 6**

There had been several lavender mauve roses before this extraordinary rose came onto the market more than 50 years ago, and a few with hints of brown, but none that combined its shades of brown, mauve, and pink as brazenly as 'Lavender Pinocchio'. The outer petals and the tips of the individual petals are usually lavender, and the innermost petals and petal bases pale brown, but there are hints of chocolate, orange, tan, and gray too. The opening buds are shapely, with enough petals to intensify the color contrasts, and they open out cleanly into pretty, cupped flowers, before flattening and loosening their petals just before they drop. They come in clusters of 5–15 on a moderately vigorous and healthy but very prickly plant. 'Lavender Pinocchio' was extensively used to breed more roses with wacky colors, and still remains very widely grown and popular today.

'Lavender Pinocchio'

Lawinia

syn. 'TANklawi'

Modern Climber

ORIGIN **Tantau, Germany, 1980**
FLOWER SIZE **3.5in (9cm)**
SCENT **Strong and sweet**
FLOWERING **Repeats**
HEIGHT/SPREAD **9.8ft (3m)/6.6ft (2m)**
HARDINESS **Zone 5**

This is one of the best modern climbers. Lawinia has bright pink flowers of a particularly pure hue, slightly paler at the edge of the petals and darker toward the center of the flower. They are elegant in bud and open into long-petaled, loosely cupped flowers held in large, pendulous clusters of up to seven. They are most abundantly borne, so that a plant in full bloom is completely covered with large, scented, weatherproof flowers. Lawinia has large, mid- or dark green leaves and repeats so well as to be a continuous bloomer. It makes an upright, bushy, stout, and fairly vigorous plant that can be planted as a freestanding shrub as well as a climber.

Lawinia

'Lawrence Johnston'

'Lawrence Johnston'

Fetida Hybrid

ORIGIN **Pernet-Ducher, France, c.1900**
PARENTAGE **'Mme. Eugène Verdier' x *Rosa foetida***
FLOWER SIZE **3.1in (8cm)**
SCENT **Medium and fetid**
FLOWERING **Once only**
HEIGHT/SPREAD **16.4ft (5m)/6.6ft (2m)**
HARDINESS **Zone 5**

'Lawrence Johnston' was a neglected by-product of Joseph Pernet-Ducher's work on the development of yellow Hybrid Teas. Then, in about 1930, Lawrence Johnston saw it in flower and bought the original plant for his famous garden at Hidcote Manor in England. In 1950, Graham Stuart Thomas introduced it commercially through the nursery of Hilling, where he worked. The flowers are sulphur yellow, loosely and untidily double, with elongated sepals, and borne in long-stemmed clusters of 3–7. The plant is vigorous, prickly, and somewhat gaunt, with dull, thin, light green leaves, that are rather susceptible to blackspot. In cool countries it flowers very early, but this trait is less distinctive in hot climates. There is an occasional extra flower later in the year.

'Le Rêve'

Modern Climber

ORIGIN **Pernet-Ducher, France, 1923**
PARENTAGE **'Souvenir de Mme. Eugène Verdier' x 'Persiana'**
FLOWER SIZE **4.7in (12cm)**
SCENT **Light, fruity, and delicious**
FLOWERING **Once, early in season**
HEIGHT/SPREAD **16.4ft (5m)/9.8ft (3m)**
HARDINESS **Zone 5**

'Le Rêve' *(at Sangerhausen)*

Pernet-Ducher raised this rose more than 20 years before he introduced it commercially as part of his experiments with *Rosa foetida* to breed roses that were truly yellow and hardy. The flowers are a good, bright, deep yellow and keep their color longer than many later yellow hybrids. They are loosely and untidily semidouble, opening out lightly cupped, and are carried in clusters of 3–9 all along the previous year's branches. It flowers exceptionally early and keeps flowering for a long time, but the bright green leaves are very susceptible to blackspot. In mild, damp climates they often drop off shortly after the plant has flowered. This appears not to affect next year's flowering, but 'Le Rêve' certainly fares best in warm, dry climates.

'Le Rosier Évêque'

Leaping Salmon

'Le Rosier Évêque'

syn. 'L'Évêque', 'The Bishop'

Centifolia

ORIGIN **c.1790**
FLOWER SIZE **3.1in (8cm)**
SCENT **Medium and sweet**
FLOWERING **Once only, rather late**
HEIGHT/SPREAD **4.9ft (1.5m)/4.1ft (1.25m)**
HARDINESS **Zone 5**

'Le Rosier Évêque' is probably an old hybrid between a purple Gallica and a pink Centifolia. Its own color is variable, but is usually purple crimson at first, and magenta or lilac later. The petals are paler on their backs. The flowers open from short, fat buds and are very double, rosette-shaped, and full of little petals. They are lightly cupped, sometimes have a button eye, and come in clusters of about seven. The plant has bright green leaves and will grow to quite a height – up to 6.6ft (2m) if unpruned – though its habit is more lax than most Gallicas so its height is not obvious. But it is a splendid sight when cascading with its dark flowers, especially if they are interwoven with pale herbaceous flowers and silver leaves.

'Le Vésuve'

China Rose

ORIGIN **Laffay, France, 1825**
FLOWER SIZE **2.8in (7cm)**
SCENT **Strong and tealike**
FLOWERING **Continuous**
HEIGHT/SPREAD **4.9ft (1.5m)/3.3ft (1m)**
HARDINESS **Zone 7**

Although always presented as a China rose, 'Le Vésuve' has more in common with the Teas. Its flowers open from long, very elegant, dark pink buds. They are silvery pink at first, with hints of apricot in hot weather. Then they darken as their long petals expand and reflex, so that by the time they are fully open, the outer petals are turning to crimson. The flowers hold their petals loosely, sometimes even blowsily, and nod their heads. They come singly or in small clusters (typically of three flowers) on slender, crimson stems. 'Le Vésuve' has dark leaves, crimson when young, and slim but prickly stems. It makes a broad, twiggy bush, which is best pruned as little as possible. This is a most beautiful rose, with a stupendous tea scent.

'Leander'

syn. 'AUSlea'

Shrub Rose

ORIGIN **Austin, Britain, 1982**
PARENTAGE **'Charles Austin' x seedling**
FLOWER SIZE **2.4in (6cm)**
SCENT **Strong and fruity**
FLOWERING **Some repeat flowering**
HEIGHT/SPREAD **6.6ft (2m)/6.6ft (2m)**
HARDINESS **Zone 5**

'Leander' is a tall, vigorous shrub rose of great beauty. Its coral colored buds open out to small, nearly flat flowers, full of small petals. They are deep apricot at first, with darker petal backs, fading later to pale salmon pink, mother-of-pearl, and white. They come on long stems in clusters of 3–15. The plant naturally throws out long, arching stems from the base and is best treated as a short (8.2ft/2.5m) climber in hot climates. It has large, medium-dark leaves (bronzy at first), broad leaflets, and many prickles. Mildew may be a problem in autumn, and its reflowering is patchy, but 'Leander' is still an excellent rose overall.

LeAnn Rimes

see Perception

Leaping Salmon

syn. 'PEAmight'

Modern Climber

ORIGIN **Pearce, Britain, 1983**
PARENTAGE **(['Vesper' x 'Aloha'] x ['Paddy McGredy' x 'Maigold']) x 'Prima Ballerina'**
FLOWER SIZE **4.3in (11cm)**
SCENT **Strong and sweet**
FLOWERING **Repeats**
HEIGHT/SPREAD **9.8ft (3m)/6.6ft (2m)**
HARDINESS **Zone 6**

This is a popular Hybrid Tea-type climber in England and New Zealand. The flowers of Leaping Salmon are large, shapely, and pale coral pink or salmon colored. The color has a very remarkable vividness when the flowers are young, but fades as they age. The flowers are lightly double, and open out attractively in warm weather. They ball in rain. They are borne singly or in small clusters (typically of 3–4 flowers) on long stems that last well when cut. The plant has large, healthy, semiglossy dark leaves and a scattering of large prickles. Leaping Salmon has a somewhat stiff, upright habit of growth and may take a while to reflower. Its vigor and height depend on growing conditions: it climbs slowly to 9.8ft (3m) in cool London but quickly to 19.7ft (6m) in warm Auckland.

'Le Vésuve'

'Leander'

'LÉDA'

syn. 'PAINTED DAMASK'
Damask Rose

ORIGIN **France, c.1827**
FLOWER SIZE **3.1in (8cm)**
SCENT **Strong and sweet**
FLOWERING **Once only**
HEIGHT/SPREAD **4.1ft (1.25m)/4.9ft (1.5m)**
HARDINESS **Zone 5**

The great attraction of 'Léda' is the extraordinary contrast between the dark crimson bud and the pure white flower that it becomes. Only a few traces of crimson remain on the tips of the outermost petals. The flowers have a button eye and a somewhat indistinct pattern of little petals radiating out. They come in clusters of 3–7 and are wonderfully complemented by the large, green leaves. If pruned after flowering, it may produce a few later flowers. Léda was the mythological queen of Sparta to whom Zeus paid a visit disguised as a swan: the result of their liaison was the heavenly twins Castor and Pollux.

'LÉDA'

LÉONARD DE VINCI

LOUIS LENS

THE BELGIAN NURSERYMAN LOUIS LENS IS BEST REMEMBERED FOR HIS VALUABLE WORK WITH WILD ROSES

LOUIS LENS (1924–2001) was a third-generation nurseryman from Malines. The firm established by his father and grandfather in 1870 grew to become one of the largest in Belgium. Roses were its main concern: by 1930 the company was selling 1.5 million roses every year.

LOUIS LENS

Lens began breeding roses in the 1950s, and his first specialities were elegant Hybrid Teas: 'Dame de Coeur' (1958) and 'Pascali' (1963) are among his best known. Later he turned to breeding new Hybrid Musks from 'Ballerina' (Bentall, 1937). 'Schubert' (1984), 'Françoise Drion' (1995), 'Robe Fleurie' (1995), and 'Robe de Neige' (1995) are good examples of roses that produce their huge panicles of small flowers continuously on arching stems. Back-crosses to Floribundas brought larger-flowered shrubs, such as the "hand-painted" 'Pirouette' (1984) and the outstanding 'Omi Oswald' (1988).

Toward the end of his life, Lens was possessed by the beauty of wild roses and a desire to make them flower recurrently. *Rosa filipes* produced the wonderful, shrubby, once-flowering climbers 'Pleine de Grâce' (1983), 'Dentelle de Malines' (1986), and the stunning purple 'Dentelle de Bruxelles' (1988). *Rosa multiflora* var. *adenochaeta* brought him 'Pink Spray' (1980), 'White Spray' (1980), and 'Tapis Volant' (1982). The rarely used *Rosa bracteata* gave us 'Pink Surprise' (1987) and 'Jelena de Belder' (1996). All are roses of immeasurable value to future rose breeders. Unusual among nurserymen, Lens was not driven by commercial considerations: it was the beauty of the rose that mattered most.

His nursery is now owned by Rudy and Ann Velle-Boudolf and operates from Oudenburg, near Ostende. It is by far the most prestigious rose nursery in Belgium, with a fine display garden of over 800 different roses.

'SCHUBERT'

LÉONARD DE VINCI

syn. 'MEIDEAURI'
Shrub Rose

ORIGIN **Meilland, France, 1994**
PARENTAGE **Sommerwind x ('Milrose' x 'Rosamunde')**
FLOWER SIZE **2.8in (7cm)**
SCENT **Little or none**
FLOWERING **Repeats well**
HEIGHT/SPREAD **3.3ft (1m)/3.3ft (1m)**
HARDINESS **Zone 5**
AWARDS **Monza GM 1993**

Léonard de Vinci is one of Meilland's Romantica roses in the old-fashioned style. The inner petals are rosette-shaped (occasionally even quartered), like one of David Austin's English Roses. They are cyclamen pink with dark pink reverses and come in clusters of 5–15. Unfortunately, they do not drop their petals cleanly, so the fading flowers pass to off-white and brown pink as they die. They are also very cupped, so that they do not open out, and cannot shed rainwater naturally. So Léonard de Vinci fares best in a warm, dry climate. The plant is bushy, healthy, and fairly prickly, with medium-sized, dark, glossy leaves. Its height depends on the climate: a bushy Pillar rose 6.6ft (2m) high in warm areas, but less than 3.3ft (1m) in cool climates. It flowers almost continuously. It is named after Leonardo da Vinci (1452–1519).

'LÉONIE LAMESCH'

Polyantha

ORIGIN **Lambert, Germany, 1899**
PARENTAGE **'Aglaia' x ('Mignonette' x 'Shirley Hibberd')**
FLOWER SIZE **2in (5cm)**
SCENT **Strong, musky, and fruity**
FLOWERING **Continuous**
HEIGHT/SPREAD **2.5ft (75cm)/2.5ft (75cm)**
HARDINESS **Zone 6**

The Polyantha roses that were so popular 80 years ago are now enjoying a revival. 'Léonie Lamesch' is one of the earliest, and still among the best. The flowers are an unusual mixture of copper, orange, and red, with the darker colors occurring on the petal tips. The vivid

'LÉONIE LAMESCH'

yellow tints fade as they age, so that an aging flower ends up completely white, with crimson markings at the edges. The flowers are not especially shapely but they come in bright clusters of 3–15 and are strongly scented. 'Léonie Lamesch' has rich green foliage and considerable vigor. It is usually seen as a neat plant at the front of a border but, if left unpruned, is capable of growing to 6.6ft (2m) in all directions. Shortly after the rose was launched, Mlle. Léonie Lamesch became Frau Peter Lambert.

'LÉONTINE GERVAIS'

Wichurana Rambler

ORIGIN **Barbier, France, 1903**
PARENTAGE ***Rosa wichurana* x 'Souvenir de Catherine Guillot'**
FLOWER SIZE **2in (5cm)**
SCENT **Strong, sweet, and musky**
FLOWERING **Once, with a few late stragglers**
HEIGHT/SPREAD **16.4ft (5m)/6.6ft (2m)**
HARDINESS **Zone 7**

This famous and popular rambler has often been confused with 'François Juranville': 'Léontine Gervais' is paler and only semidouble. The buds are coppery red, but the flowers open apricot pink and fade to pale pink, cream, or white – quickly, in hot weather. The petal backs are slightly darker at all times. The overall effect is very similar to the Tea roses. The flowers are borne singly and in short-stemmed clusters of up to about seven. The crimson filaments are a fine foil,

LES AMOUREUX DE PEYNET

and the flowers are best seen close-up because they are not so profusely borne as some Barbier ramblers. The plant is healthy, sinuous, and vigorous. Its leaves are dark and lustrous, and the growing stems turn crimson in response to sun.

LES AMOUREUX DE PEYNET

syn. 'MEITOBLA', Simply Magic

Floribunda

ORIGIN **Meilland, France, 1992**
FLOWER SIZE **2.8in (7cm)**
SCENT **Light**
FLOWERING **Repeats well**
HEIGHT/SPREAD **2ft (60cm)/2.5ft (75cm)**
HARDINESS **Zone 5**
AWARDS **Bagatelle GM 1991; Lyon Rose of the Century 1992**

Les Amoureux de Peynet is classified as a Floribunda, but it is closer to a ground-cover shrub rose. It is immensely floriferous, with a spreading habit, and the shiny leaves that come from *Rosa wichurana* somewhere in its ancestry. The flowers are mid-pink, fading to pale pink, and occasionally bleaching in the sun. The petals are very uniformly colored, with exactly the same color on both sides, which is unusual. They come in large clusters of 10–40 and continue until early winter. The plant is very healthy and ideal for small gardens and patios, while frankly spectacular when planted in large masses.

'LEVERKUSEN'

'L'ÉVÊQUE'

see 'LE ROSIER ÉVÊQUE'

'LEVERKUSEN'

Kordesii Hybrid

ORIGIN **Kordes, Germany, 1954**
PARENTAGE **'Kordesii' x 'Golden Glow'**
FLOWER SIZE **2.8in (7cm)**
SCENT **Medium and sweet**
FLOWERING **Constantly in flower**
HEIGHT/SPREAD **9.8ft (3m)/6.6ft (2m)**
HARDINESS **Zone 4**

'Leverkusen' was the first yellow Kordesii hybrid: it is still the best, combining a pure shade of yellow with the hardiness for which the Kordesiis were bred. Its flowers have large outer petals that fade to cream, and shorter inner petals that are deep yellow right at the center, and paler as they fade slowly through sulphur, lemon, and butter yellow. The buds are pretty and the flowers eventually have a slight ruffle to their petals which is also very attractive. They come singly or in clusters of up to about ten, though 3–5 is the norm. The first crop is abundant, and the plant is never without flowers thereafter, but in hot climates it produces substantial second and third flushes. The leaves are small, dark, and glossy in the Kordesii way, but sometimes susceptible to blackspot later in the season. The hips stay green for a very long time, and only change to yellow somewhat late in the year. Leverkusen is a city in Germany.

'LEWESON GOWER'

see 'SOUVENIR DE LA MALMAISON'

'LICHTKÖNIGIN LUCIA'

syn. 'REINE LUCIA'

Modern Climber

ORIGIN **Kordes, Germany, 1966**
PARENTAGE **'Zitronenfalter' x 'Cläre Grammerstorf'**
FLOWER SIZE **3.5in (9cm)**
SCENT **Moderate and sweet**
FLOWERING **Repeats well**
HEIGHT/SPREAD **6.6ft (2m)/4.9ft (1.5m)**
HARDINESS **Zone 5**
AWARDS **ADR 1968**

The popularity of 'Lichtkönigin Lucia' is still increasing – an unusual paradox for a rose that has been in commerce for so long. Its long, elegant buds open slowly like a Hybrid Tea. The flowers are yellow, lightly cupped, with red tips and handsome, deep gold stamens. They open rich chrome yellow, and fade to lemon and then to cream. They come in clusters of 5–15. The bush has small, mid-green, healthy, glossy leaves. It flowers early and heavily, but is never out of flower thereafter until late autumn. It is naturally a shrub rose, growing broad and bushy, but can also be trained as a climber, for which its continuously flowering habit makes it valuable.

'LÉONTINE GERVAIS'

'LICHTKÖNIGIN LUCIA'

LIEBESZAUBER

LIEBESZAUBER

syn. 'KORMIACH'

Hybrid Tea

ORIGIN **Kordes, Germany, 1990**
PARENTAGE **'Panthère Rose' seedling**
FLOWER SIZE **4.7in (12cm)**
SCENT **Strong and sweet**
FLOWERING **Repeats**
HEIGHT/SPREAD **4.1ft (1.25m)/3.3ft (1m)**
HARDINESS **Zone 6**
AWARDS **The Hague FA 1994**

There is always a market for dark red roses with a good scent. Thousands have been introduced over the last two centuries. Liebeszauber is one of the better ones. Its flowers are large, shapely, and full of petals. Their color is best described as blood red – a clear, dark shade, with velvety tints. They are almost always borne singly, but sometimes come in clusters of up to five, on long, strong stems that are useful for cutting. They also make a good display in the garden and repeat so quickly as to be almost continually in flower. Liebeszauber makes a vigorous, spreading, branching shrub with strong, thick stems, large, dark, healthy leaves, and crimson new growths. In its native Germany it is usually seen as a pruned rose 2.7ft (80cm) high but, in hot climates, it has been known to grow as high as 8.2ft (2.5m).

'LILAC CHARM'

Floribunda

ORIGIN **Le Grice, Britain, 1962**
PARENTAGE **'Lavender Pinocchio' x unknown**
FLOWER SIZE **3.9in (10cm)**
SCENT **Medium and sweet**
FLOWERING **Repeats well**
HEIGHT/SPREAD **2.5ft (75cm)/1.6ft (50cm)**
HARDINESS **Zone 6**
AWARDS **NRS GM 1961**

'Lilac Charm' is an excellent short Floribunda that has remained popular ever since it was first introduced. The flowers are slightly more than single – they have about ten petals – and open out from neat, slender buds. They are a true lilac, a very clear shade that fades little, but what gives them their unique character is the mass of stamens with golden anthers and red filaments at the center. They become the focus of attention for the whole flower. The flowers come in clusters of 3–15 and repeat well right through until late autumn. The leaves are dark and healthy, and the small size of the bush makes it very useful at the front of a mixed border.

LILAC ROSE

syn. 'AUSLILAC'

Shrub Rose

ORIGIN **Austin, Britain, 1990**
PARENTAGE **seedling x Hero**
FLOWER SIZE **3.1in (8cm)**
SCENT **Strong**
FLOWERING **Repeats fairly well**
HEIGHT/SPREAD **3.3ft (1m)/2.5ft (75cm)**
HARDINESS **Zone 6**

The color of Lilac Rose does not live up to its name in hot climates, where it remains resolutely pink, but there is a hint of purple on the petal backs when it is grown in its native England. The flowers are large, neat, strongly scented, cupped and shaped like a rosette, pink at the center, with paler edges. They usually come in clusters of 3–7. The plant is prickly and sturdy with mid-green leaves that can be prone to fungal infections. However, Lilac Rose is a good choice for a mixed border, where its shape and color combine well with other plants.

'LILAC CHARM'

LILAC ROSE

'LILIAN AUSTIN'

'LILIAN AUSTIN'

Shrub Rose

ORIGIN **Austin, Britain, 1973**
PARENTAGE **'Aloha' x 'The Yeoman'**
FLOWER SIZE **3.5in (9cm)**
SCENT **Medium and fruity**
FLOWERING **Repeats well**
HEIGHT/SPREAD **3.3ft (1m)/4.1ft (1.25m)**
HARDINESS **Zone 6**

'Lilian Austin' is one of those David Austin roses that more closely resemble Floribundas. The flowers are lightly and loosely double, large, and agreeably scented. They are rich coral pink at first, with yellow centers, but then the yellow tinge fades from the whole flower and they end up rose pink with a hint of cream at the center. The petal backs are always slightly darker in color and give the flowers much of their character, though the ruffled petals sometimes impart a ragged look. The flowers come in clusters of 3–11 on a lax, prickly bush with healthy, dark green leaves. 'Lilian Austin' repeats well, but its relaxed habit of growth means that it is often wider than it is tall, unless it is staked and trained to make a more upright outline. Lilian Austin was David Austin's mother.

'LILLI MARLEEN'

Floribunda

ORIGIN **Kordes, Germany, 1959**
PARENTAGE **('Crimson Glow' x 'Rudolph Timm') x 'Ama'**
FLOWER SIZE **3.1in (8cm)**
SCENT **Strong and sweet**
FLOWERING **Almost continuous**
HEIGHT/SPREAD **2.7ft (80cm)/2.3ft (70cm)**
HARDINESS **Zone 5**
AWARDS **ADR 1960; Golden Rose of the Hague 1966**

The blood red, scented flowers of 'Lilli Marleen' have been popular for over 40 years. Even today, there is nothing to match it for color and neatness. The flowers come in clusters of 3–15 and hold their color extremely well, so that the bush seems always to be covered in

'CLIMBING LILLI MARLEEN'

fresh flowers. The plant has small, dark leaves and a neat habit: the compact plant carries its flowers all over its surface, like a modern groundcover rose. It may need a little protection against powdery mildew, but is otherwise both healthy and vigorous. There is a climbing form of 'Lilli Marleen' that is well worth seeking out – it makes a neat column of brilliant red early in the season.

Limelight

see Golden Medaillon

Linda Campbell

syn. 'MORten'

Rugosa Hybrid

ORIGIN **Moore, US, 1990**
PARENTAGE **'Anytime' x 'Rugosa Magnifica'**
FLOWER SIZE **2.4in (6cm)**
SCENT **Little or none**
FLOWERING **Repeats quickly**
HEIGHT/SPREAD **6.6ft (2m)/4.9ft (1.5m)**
HARDINESS **Zone 5**

This adventurous cross between a miniature rose and an old Rugosa hybrid is a lanky, prickly shrub, tall enough to be used as a climber in cold areas where its hardiness is a great asset. The flowers of Linda Campbell open from the pointed buds typical of Rugosa hybrids, borne at the tips of the branches. They are loosely double, slightly ruffled in the middle, and a very bright red, often with white streaks at the base of the petals. They are carried on short stems in tight clusters of 3–9 flowers, and last a long time before fading. The plant has long, arching branches that extend at least 4.9ft (1.5m) in a season. The leaves are less wrinkly than most Rugosa hybrids and usually healthy, especially in cold climates. Linda Campbell was editor of *The American Rose Annual*; she died young, of cancer.

Linda Campbell

Liselle

syn. 'RULis', Royal Romance

Hybrid Tea

ORIGIN **de Ruiter, Belgium, 1981**
PARENTAGE **'Whisky' x 'Matador'**
FLOWER SIZE **4.7in (12cm)**
SCENT **Light and fruity**
FLOWERING **Repeats well**
HEIGHT/SPREAD **4.1ft (1.25m)/3.3ft (1m)**
HARDINESS **Zone 6**

This handsome Hybrid Tea is a very beautiful color: apricot pink in the bud, pale orange and yellow as it opens out, and pink again as the yellow tints fade away. Liselle is also beautiful at every stage of the flower's development. It starts from a classically shaped bud but opens out into a symmetrical mass of large petals. The flowers come singly and in clusters of up to five, on long, strong stems that are good for cutting. The plant has handsome, dark green leaves and grows vigorously, so that it is seldom out of flower until late autumn. In northern Europe it is usually pruned back to about 2.7ft (80cm), but in hot climates it has been known to reach 5.7ft (1.75m).

Liselle

Little Bo-Peep

Little Artist

syn. 'MACmanley', Top Gear

Patio Rose

ORIGIN **McGredy, New Zealand, 1982**
PARENTAGE **Eyepaint x Ko's Yellow**
FLOWER SIZE **1.6in (4cm)**
SCENT **Light and fruity**
FLOWERING **Repeats well**
HEIGHT/SPREAD **1.6ft (50cm)/2.7ft (80cm)**
HARDINESS **Zone 6**

The newly open flowers of Little Artist are very eye-catching – semidouble, crimson and yellow, with white petal backs and a brilliant circle of dark yellow stamens. They seem to glisten in the sun. However, the yellow fades quickly to white and the flowers take on rather a hard red tone. It is best interplanted with gray-leaved plants that show the red color to advantage. The flowers of Little Artist are borne in great abundance on a vigorous bush with handsome, dark, glossy leaves and a useful habit of spreading sideways more than upward. It is tireless in its blooming: in hot climates it will flower year-round.

Little Bo-Peep

syn. 'POULlen', Gentle Cover, Natchez

Patio Rose

ORIGIN **Olesen, Denmark, 1991**
PARENTAGE **Pink Drift seedling**
FLOWER SIZE **1.2in (3cm)**
SCENT **Musky**
FLOWERING **Almost continuous**
HEIGHT/SPREAD **2.7ft (80cm)/3.3ft (1m)**
HARDINESS **Zone 6**
AWARDS **RNRS PIT 1991**

The great asset of Little Bo-Peep is its unusually dense and bushy habit. It builds up a mass of small, twiggy stems that are absolutely covered with small leaves and tiny, healthy, medium-dark leaflets. These are studded on and off throughout the season with tiny, pink, musk-scented flowers that open to reveal a ring of golden stamens at the center. They come in clusters of 5–10 and there is a nice contrast between the rose pink flowers and the darker, mid-pink buds. Little Bo-Peep is late to start into bloom but then continues long after most roses have stopped flowering. It tends to grow sideways more than upward and makes an excellent patio or groundcover rose which, by its sheer bulk, holds its own in any rose bed. It is also good in containers.

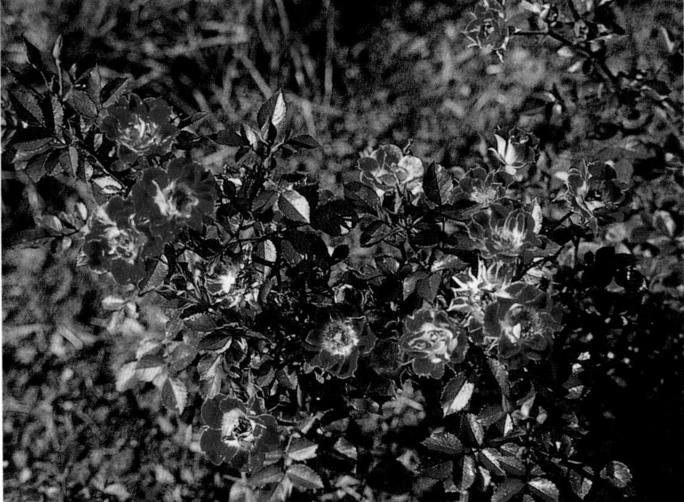

Little Artist

'LITTLE BUCKAROO'

Miniature Rose

ORIGIN **Moore, US, 1956**
PARENTAGE **(*Rosa wichurana* x 'Floradora') x ('Oakington Ruby' x 'Floradora')**
FLOWER SIZE **1.2in (3cm)**
SCENT **Medium and fruity**
FLOWERING **Repeats well**
HEIGHT/SPREAD **1.3ft (40cm)/1.6ft (50cm)**
HARDINESS **Zone 6**

This attractive little rose did much to establish a market for miniatures: 'Little Buckaroo' opened the eyes of garden owners to the charms of little roses. The crimson flowers are small and double, but open out to reveal a white patch and yellow stamens at the center. The flowers come in open clusters and may be followed by small, red hips. 'Little Buckaroo' has a loose habit of growth and tends to spread sideways at least as much as it reaches upward, which makes it a useful sprawler for mixed plantings and containers. The leaves are very handsome – dark, small, and glossy in the Wichurana way, and very healthy. It roots quickly and easily from cuttings.

'LITTLE BUCKAROO'

'LITTLE GEM'

Moss Rose

ORIGIN **W. Paul, Britain, 1880**
FLOWER SIZE **2in (5cm)**
SCENT **Strong and sweet**
FLOWERING **Remontant**
HEIGHT/SPREAD **3.3ft (1m)/2.7ft (80cm)**
HARDINESS **Zone 5**

The flowers of 'Little Gem' are a bright shade of cherry crimson, and full of petals. As they open out completely they start to reflex into little pompons. They are not large, but very attractive, with an old-fashioned, muddled arrangement of petals and a delicious scent. The buds, sepals, receptacles, and flower stalks are liberally covered in dark green moss. The flowers usually come in clusters of 5–12 and are seen at their best when the first flowers open against a background of mossy, unopened buds. 'Little Gem' is a neat, short-growing shrub, though it is in no sense a miniature rose and the bright green leaves are medium-sized. It is not reliably remontant but occasionally produces a few flowers in autumn.

LITTLE RAMBLER

syn. 'CHEWRAMB', Baby Rambler

Miniature Rambler

ORIGIN **Warner, Britain, 1994**
PARENTAGE **('Cécile Brunner' x 'Baby Faurax') x ('Marjorie Fair' x 'Nozomi')**
FLOWER SIZE **1.6in (4cm)**
SCENT **Strong, musky, and sweet**
FLOWERING **Repeats constantly**
HEIGHT/SPREAD **9.8ft (3m)/6.6ft (2m)**
HARDINESS **Zone 6**

In many ways, this modern patio rambler is closer to the Multiflora ramblers that were introduced in the early 20th century. Little Rambler has rather tight clusters of pale pink flowers which are full of short, neatly displayed petals – fully double, but opening out to display pale yellow stamens at the center. They are pale pink at first and fade to white as they age. The tiny, unopened buds are crimson. The flowers usually come in clusters of 10–30. Where Little Rambler differs from the true Multifloras is in its tiny, dark, glossy foliage, which more closely resembles a miniature rose. It is also healthy. The plant has few prickles on the long, slender branches, which respond well to training and tend to arch over unless given some support. That said, the plant is very bushy, quickly forming a mass of stems and apparently always in flower.

LITTLE RAMBLER

'LITTLE GEM'

'LITTLE WHITE PET'

see 'FÉLICITÉ ET PERPÉTUE'

LIVERPOOL REMEMBERS

see BEAUTY STAR

LIVIN' EASY

see FELLOWSHIP

'LOLITA'

syn. 'KORLITA'

Hybrid Tea

ORIGIN **Kordes, Germany, 1973**
PARENTAGE **'Königin der Rosen' x seedling**
FLOWER SIZE **4.7in (12cm)**
SCENT **Strong and sweet**
FLOWERING **Repeats well**
HEIGHT/SPREAD **5.7ft (1.75m)/3.3ft (1m)**
HARDINESS **Zone 6**
AWARDS **ADR 1973**

The beauty of 'Lolita' lies in its coloring, shape, and vigor. The flowers are attractive at all stages of development, first as buds, then as elegantly opening flowers, and finally when they have opened out fully to reveal their stamens and the petals take on a slight wave. The color changes too – coppery in the bud, fading to a most beautiful pale peach and later to cream, while the outer petals acquire a pink edge. The petal backs are always a little darker. The flowers are usually borne singly on long stems that are good for cutting. The tall, upright, healthy plant is useful in mixed borders.

'LOLITA'

'LONG JOHN SILVER'

Setigera Hybrid

ORIGIN **Horvath, US, 1934**
PARENTAGE ***Rosa setigera* seedling x 'Sunburst'**
FLOWER SIZE **3.9in (10cm)**
SCENT **Moderate, musky, and sweet**
FLOWERING **Once, late in season**
HEIGHT/SPREAD **16.4ft (5m)/9.8ft (3m)**
HARDINESS **Zone 4**

It is the size and vigor of 'Long John Silver' that distinguish it from most ramblers. The plant grows very fast, and uses its large prickles to quickly hook itself up to the top of any support. The flowers are a wonderful luminous white and very full of petals. They come in clusters of 3–15, with somewhat short stalks, and may get congested later, especially since the individual flowers last such a long time on the plant. The leaves are unusually large and distinctly convex in shape. The plant is a very gawky, stiff, upright grower and its vigor is hard to control, but it is outsize in all its features and the flowers are of astounding beauty.

'*ROSA LONGICUSPIS*'

see '*ROSA MULLIGANII*'

'LONG JOHN SILVER'

LORD BYRON

see POLKA 91

'LORD PENZANCE'

Rubiginosa Hybrid

ORIGIN **Penzance, Britain, 1894**
PARENTAGE ***Rosa rubiginosa* x 'Harison's Yellow'**
FLOWER SIZE **1.6in (4cm)**
SCENT **Light and sweet**
FLOWERING **Once only, early in season**
HEIGHT/SPREAD **6.6ft (2m)/8.2ft (2.5m)**
HARDINESS **Zone 5**

Lord Penzance (a cousin of Oscar Wilde) was a great Victorian politician and jurist. His hobby was breeding roses, and this is the hybrid that he chose to name after himself. It is a remarkably modest rose, whose small, pale yellow flowers have a touch of pink and come in small clusters (typically of 3–5). The leaves have just a little of the fragrance that graces *Rosa rubiginosa*, while the yellow tints come from 'Harison's Yellow'. It is a vigorous, rounded, prickly shrub, whose small leaves are susceptible to blackspot. It is not a rose for small gardens, but has its place in historical collections.

'LORD PENZANCE'

LORDLY OBERON

syn. 'AUSRON'

Shrub Rose

ORIGIN **Austin, Britain, 1982**
PARENTAGE **'Chaucer' x unknown**
FLOWER SIZE **3.5in (9cm)**
SCENT **Strong and sweet**
FLOWERING **Repeats eventually**
HEIGHT/SPREAD **6.6ft (2m)/8.2ft (2.5m)**
HARDINESS **Zone 6**

Although long ago superseded by better English Roses, **Lordly Oberon** is still extensively grown worldwide. Its rose pink flowers (paler at the edges and on the backs of the petals) are short, broad, and so incurved (in the manner of 'Constance Spry', only more so), that the heavily cupped flowers rarely open out fully. They come on long stems, singly and in clusters of two or three, all along the long, arching growth. The plant is lanky and slow to flower again, but grows vigorously, and in hot climates will reach as much as 11.5ft (3.5m).

LORDLY OBERON

LOUIS DE FUNÈS

syn. 'MEIRESTIF'

Hybrid Tea

ORIGIN **Meilland, France, 1987**
PARENTAGE **(Ambassador x 'Whisky') x ('Arthur Bell' x 'Kabuki')**
FLOWER SIZE **5.1in (13cm)**
SCENT **Light but fruity**
FLOWERING **Repeats well**
HEIGHT/SPREAD **4.1ft (1.25m)/2.7ft (80cm)**
HARDINESS **Zone 6**
AWARDS **Geneva GM 1983; Monza GM 1983**

This traditional orange Hybrid Tea commemorates the life and work of a great French actor. The flowers are large, classically elegant, and singly borne on long, strong stems. Their color is very attractive – a strong nasturtium shade that is slightly darker toward the tips of the petals and more yellow toward the base. The petal backs too are yellow, which gives rise to a very striking bicolor effect. However, the yellow tint then starts to fade from the flower, so that the petals seem to turn more red, and the tips are seen to be crimson. But at all stages the flower is supremely elegant and the colors both bold and harmonious. The plant is vigorous and fairly healthy, with mid-green leaves and a fair sprinkling of prickles.

LOUIS DE FUNÈS

'LORRAINE LEE'

Hybrid Gigantea Bush Rose

ORIGIN **Clark, Australia, 1924**
PARENTAGE **'Jessie Clark' x 'Capitaine Millet'**
FLOWER SIZE **3.1–3.5in (8–9cm)**
SCENT **Medium**
FLOWERING **Fully recurrent, almost perpetually in flower**
HEIGHT/SPREAD **6.6ft (2m)/4.9ft (1.5m)**
HARDINESS **Zone 9**

'LORRAINE LEE'

Sports of 'Lorraine Lee'

'CLIMBING LORRAINE LEE'

Climbing Tea Rose
ORIGIN **McKay, US, 1932**
FLOWERING **Profuse in spring, sparing thereafter**
HEIGHT/SPREAD **19.7ft (6m)/8ft (2.5m)**
HARDINESS **Zone 9**

'LADY MANN'

Hybrid Gigantea Bush Rose
ORIGIN **Clark, Australia, 1940**

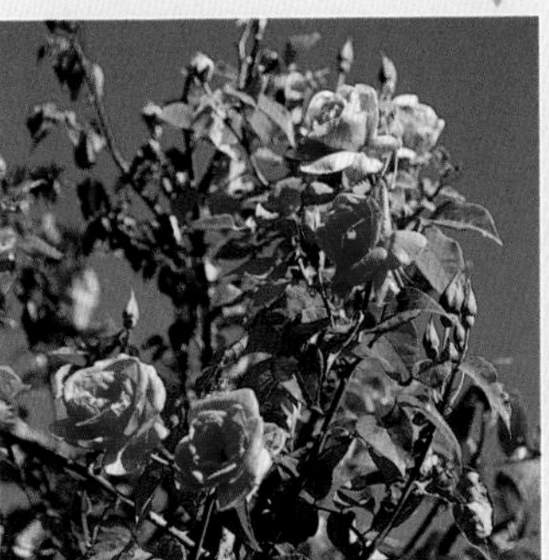

'CLIMBING LORRAINE LEE'

'LADY MANN'

'Lorraine Lee' was one of Alister Clark's first bush roses bred from *Rosa gigantea*. Its exotic ancestry can be seen in its slender, angular, bloomy, purple flower stems and the rich beet purple of its young leaves – which turn out to be evergreen. The semidouble flowers open from elegant, dark, pointed buds and are strong pink in color with a slight hint of coral and darker petal backs. They fade to pale pink, so that there is a lot of variation in color among the individual blooms upon a bush at any one time, but the effect of all the different shades is very pretty. The flowers are sometimes carried singly but more often in clusters of 3–5, and they are well spaced out within their clusters. The plant has beautiful bloomy stems and thick, vigorous new growths, sporting a few large prickles. It blooms throughout the year, but needs a warm place to flourish, even in Melbourne. Alister Clark considered 'Lorraine Lee' better than any of his later hybrids: "for its color and habit it is, in my opinion, unsurpassed by anything I have done." The Melbourne newspaper, *The Argus*, used to run an annual popularity poll among its readers: 'Lorraine Lee' constantly topped the list of bush roses. Lorraine Lee was a relation of Alister Clark's sister-in-law Mary (Minnie) Clark. Lorraine was born in Melbourne in 1890, moved to England as a child, lived at Frinton-on-Sea in Essex (where her rose did not survive the English winters), and died unmarried in 1974.

'Climbing Lorraine Lee' (McKay, 1932) is also a popular rose. It has slightly larger flowers than the original bush form, and they are profusely borne in early spring but much more sparingly thereafter. It is one of the most vigorous roses in existence and will easily reach 19.7ft (6m) – not a rose for low fences, but very pretty interwoven to flower at the same time as wisteria. Several color sports of 'Lorraine Lee' are popular in Australia. Best known is **'Lady Mann'** (Clark, 1940), which has flowers of a pure, deep, rich pink, with no hint of yellow or coral. Lady (Adeline) Mann was the wife of Sir Frederick Mann, a distinguished Australian lawyer who was Chief Justice of Victoria (1935–44) and Lieutenant-Governor (1936–45).

Other sports of 'Lorraine Lee' include the apricot colored 'Baxter Beauty' and 'Yellow Baxter Beauty'.

'Louis Gimard'

'Louis Jolliet'

'Louis Gimard'

Moss Rose

ORIGIN **Pernet père, France, 1877**
FLOWER SIZE **3.1in (8cm)**
SCENT **Strong and sweet**
FLOWERING **Once only**
HEIGHT/SPREAD **4.9ft (1.5m)/3.3ft (1m)**
HARDINESS **Zone 5**

The flowers of 'Louis Gimard' are very full of petals, which are crimson at the center, then mid-pink fading to lilac and palest gray pink at the edges. Cupped at first, they do eventually open out almost flat. The flowers come singly or, more often, in clusters of up to about five, and show a good covering of khaki colored moss on the buds, sepals, receptacles, and flower stems. The thin, shiny leaves suggest that 'Louis Gimard' has China roses among its ancestors, as does the way its petals turn back at their edges. The plant has slender stems, covered in crimson bristles when young, and a lax habit of growth. Sometimes the flowers hang down among the leaves, so the display is improved by careful pruning and training. It is a thrifty grower and fares well in poor soil.

'Louis Jolliet'

Kordesii Hybrid

ORIGIN **Ogilvie, Canada, 1992**
PARENTAGE **'Kordesii' seedling**
FLOWER SIZE **2.4in (6cm)**
SCENT **Light and fruity**
FLOWERING **Almost continuous**
HEIGHT/SPREAD **4.9ft (1.5m)/4.1ft (1.25m)**
HARDINESS **Zone 4**

This is one of the most floriferous Explorer roses. 'Louis Jolliet' is also exceptionally vigorous, with long, trailing growth that can be trained up as a short climber. The flowers are pale crimson or dark pink, and open to a somewhat formless mass of wavy petals. They are, however, very colorful from a distance, especially since they sometimes come in clusters of up to 30, though 5–10 is more usual. The plant flowers more or less continuously until the first frost. The leaves are glossy, dark green, and very healthy. Louis Jolliet, or Joliet (1645–1700), was a French Canadian traveler who explored the Mississippi, Fox, Wisconsin, and Illinois rivers.

'Louis Philippe'

China Rose

ORIGIN **Guérin, France, 1834**
FLOWER SIZE **2.4in (6cm)**
SCENT **Light and tealike**
FLOWERING **Continuous**
HEIGHT/SPREAD **4.9ft (1.5m)/4.1ft (1.25m)**
HARDINESS **Zone 6**

This popular China rose was named after the King of France who reigned from 1830 to 1848: his twin sister, Adélaïde d'Orléans, gave her name to another rose. 'Louis Philippe' is fairly similar to many of the first China roses introduced into Europe from China. Its flowers are double and bright crimson red, but open out to show a ring of yellow stamens and a pronounced white patch at the center. White streaks also run up from the center into the crimson petals – a very typical feature of China roses. The color darkens as the flowers age, but remains slightly paler at the edges. The plant has small, dark leaves and lots of prickles (it is still recommended for hedging and roots easily from cuttings), and tolerates drought and neglect. Its height depends upon how you grow it – sometimes no more than 2ft (60cm) as a bedding rose, it will reach nearly 6.6ft (2m) if allowed to build up its twiggy structure over the years. Several sports and forms are known, including a climbing form and the "Bermuda form" which is probably a seedling, not a mutation.

'Louis XIV'

China Rose

ORIGIN **Guillot fils, France, 1859**
PARENTAGE **'Général Jacqueminot' seedling**
FLOWER SIZE **2.8in (7cm)**
SCENT **Strong and sweet**
FLOWERING **Repeats very well**
HEIGHT/SPREAD **2ft (60cm)/2ft (60cm)**
HARDINESS **Zone 7**

If color and scent were all one sought in a rose, 'Louis XIV' would be in every garden. Its flowers are among the deepest, richest crimson imaginable, with nearly black shadings and a velvety sheen to the petals. They are elegantly shaped and freely produced, though somewhat small. The leaves are a good crimson when young, but susceptible to mildew and blackspot later. 'Louis XIV' is a weak, spindly grower – it needs lots of feeding and watering to perform well, though it does not always respond. Hot climates suit it best.

'Louise d'Arzens'

'Louise d'Arzens'

Noisette

ORIGIN **Lacharme, France, 1861**
PARENTAGE **'Mlle. Blanche Lafitte' x 'Sapho'**
FLOWER SIZE **3.1in (8cm)**
SCENT **Medium and sweet**
FLOWERING **Repeats very well**
HEIGHT/SPREAD **8.2ft (2.5m)/6.6ft (2m)**
HARDINESS **Zone 6**

'Louise d'Arzens' is one of five roses bred from the same parents and introduced by Lacharme at about the same time. They are 'Boule de Neige', 'Lady Emily Peel', 'Coquette des Blanches', 'Coquette des Alpes', and 'Louise Darzens' (as some authorities spell it). It is not surprising, therefore, that more than one rose is now grown under the name of 'Louise d'Arzens'. The correct cultivar has pink buds, opening to pure white flowers that later acquire hints of palest pink or buff. They usually come in clusters of 3–7. The leaves are dark and slightly glaucous. The plant makes a stout 6.6ft (2m) shrub – more as a climber.

'Louis Philippe'

'Louis XIV'

'LOUISE ODIER'

'LOUISE ODIER'

Bourbon Rose

ORIGIN **Margottin, France, 1851**
PARENTAGE **'Emile Courtier' seedling**
FLOWER SIZE **2.8in (7cm)**
SCENT **Rich and sweet**
FLOWERING **Repeats**
HEIGHT/SPREAD **9.8ft (3m)/6.6ft (2m)**
HARDINESS **Zone 5**

'Louise Odier' embodies all the charms and virtues of the Bourbon roses: it is vigorous, and produces its beautiful, sweet-scented flowers almost nonstop. The flowers are pale pink at the edges, but slightly darker and more richly pink toward the center. They open lightly cupped like Centifolias, with ranks of neatly arranged petals lying flat around the center. Later, the petals reflex like China roses, until the flowers flatten out and shed them cleanly. The flowers come singly or in rather tight clusters of up to five, and are freely borne in a succession of flushes, with one or two flowers in between. The plant has a lot of pale or mid-green leaves, which may need protection against mildew and blackspot in areas where those diseases are prevalent. The stems are thick, prickly, and vigorous. 'Louise Odier' performs best in hot climates, but is also extremely hardy, provided the new growth is well ripened by sun.

LOVE

syn. 'JACTWIN'
Grandiflora

ORIGIN **Warriner, US, 1980**
PARENTAGE **seedling × 'Redgold'**
FLOWER SIZE **4.3in (11cm)**
SCENT **Little or none**
FLOWERING **Repeats well**
HEIGHT/SPREAD **3.5ft (1.1m)/4.1ft (1.25m)**
HARDINESS **Zone 6**
AWARDS **AARS 1980; Portland GM 1980**

There was a fashion 20 or 30 years ago for roses that exhibited a strong contrast of color between the two sides of the petal. Love is typical of them – its petals are rich cherry pink on one side and silvery white on the back. Its individual petals unfold abruptly, from an arrangement in which they are curled over the center of the flower to a new position around the sides. At the first stage, the contrast between the crimson and the white is particularly strong. Later, when all the petals have unfurled, the flowers

LOVE

are seen to have a bright white patch at the center and the cherry red fades to dark pink. The flowers are usually borne singly on long, upright stems. The plant is vigorous and healthy, with dark leaves, large prickles, purplish stems, and crimson new growth.

LOVE AND PEACE

syn. 'BALPEACE'
Hybrid Tea

ORIGIN **Twomey, US, 2001**
PARENTAGE **seedling × 'Mme. A. Meilland'**
FLOWER SIZE **5.1in (13cm)**
SCENT **Medium and fruity**
FLOWERING **Repeats well**
HEIGHT/SPREAD **6.6ft (2m)/3.3ft (1m)**
HARDINESS **Zone 6**
AWARDS **AARS 2002**

If proof were ever needed of the importance of 'Mme. A. Meilland' ('Peace') nearly 60 years after it was introduced, you need only look at the seedlings it can still produce. Love and Peace won an All-America Rose Selection prize in 2002, and it is head and shoulders above many of the other Hybrid Teas of recent years. The flowers are deep buff yellow with crimson edges – both colors darker and richer than their parent's – and full of petals, while still producing, especially in hot climates, a peerless flower that is suitable for exhibition as well as making a good garden plant. The flowers are almost invariably borne singly, but sometimes in small clusters. The plant is vigorous, healthy, and covered from top to bottom with large, dark, glittering leaves – a splendid foil for the brilliant flowers.

LOVELY LADY

LOVELY FAIRY

see 'THE FAIRY'

LOVELY LADY

syn. 'DICJUBELL'
Hybrid Tea

ORIGIN **Dickson, Northern Ireland, 1986**
PARENTAGE **'Silver Jubilee' × ('Eurorose' × Anabel)**
FLOWER SIZE **3.9in (10cm)**
SCENT **Medium and sweet**
FLOWERING **Repeats**
HEIGHT/SPREAD **2.7ft (80cm)/2ft (60cm)**
HARDINESS **Zone 6**
AWARDS **Belfast GM 1988**

Lovely Lady has some of the coloring of its distinguished parent, 'Silver Jubilee'. It opens apricot pink, but fades to pure pink from the outside while always retaining a tinge of coral at the heart. The petal backs are slightly darker, which explains why the flower has such attractive shades and shadows as it opens. The flowers are classic Hybrid Tea-shaped, carried singly or in clusters of up to three at first, but in clusters worthy of a Floribunda later in the year. They also make good cut flowers. The plant is fairly compact, with healthy, average-sized, mid-green, glossy leaves. It repeats its flowering quickly.

'LOVERS' MEETING'

Hybrid Tea

ORIGIN **Gandy, Britain, 1980**
PARENTAGE **seedling × 'Egyptian Treasure'**
FLOWER SIZE **4.7in (12cm)**
SCENT **Little or none**
FLOWERING **Repeats**
HEIGHT/SPREAD **4.9ft (1.5m)/3.3ft (1m)**
HARDINESS **Zone 6**

A good name can help to make a rose popular. 'Lovers' Meeting' is a pleasant rose whose success has not been hindered by its suggestive name, even though it is almost scentless. The flowers are a rich orange, with a hint of a crimson flush along the edges of the petals. They are slender, pointed, and very traditional in shape. 'Lovers' Meeting' makes a good garden rose in cool, wet climates like that of England, where it is seen as an 2.7ft (80cm) bedding rose. Transplant it to Australia or South Africa, however, and it will reach as much as 2m (6.6ft). There the flowers open quickly and turn from orange to crimson in the sun. The plant has handsome, bronzy new leaves and is considered healthy.

LOVING MEMORY

see 'BURGUND 81'

LOVE AND PEACE

'LOVERS' MEETING'

LÜBECKER ROTSPON

LÜBECKER ROTSPON

syn. 'TANTIDE', Glad Tidings, Peter Wessel, Victoria

Floribunda

ORIGIN **Tantau, Germany, 1988**
FLOWER SIZE **3.5in (9cm)**
SCENT **Little or none**
FLOWERING **Repeats well**
HEIGHT/SPREAD **2.5ft (75cm)/2ft (60cm)**
HARDINESS **Zone 5**
AWARDS **ROTY 1989; Durbanville GM 1991**

Lübecker Rotspon celebrates the red wine of Lübeck, which is imported from Bordeaux and matured in that Hanseatic city: German writers invariably describe the rose as "Bordeaux red" in color. It is an excellent short-growing Floribunda. Its flowers are dark red, and exactly the same shade of red on both sides of the petals, later turning almost black. The flowers are medium-sized, lightly cupped, and packed with a lot of short petals. They come in clusters of 3–11 (typically 5–7), and shed their petals cleanly when they have finished flowering. Lübecker Rotspon is short and neat, with beautiful dark, glossy leaves that are very disease resistant, except for an occasional flirtation with blackspot. It is one of the last roses to come into flower, but then keeps up its flowering almost continuously until late autumn.

LUCETTA

syn. 'AUSEMI'

Shrub Rose

ORIGIN **Austin, Britain, 1983**
FLOWER SIZE **4.7in (12cm)**
SCENT **Strong**
FLOWERING **Repeats**
HEIGHT/SPREAD **4.1ft (1.25m)/4.1ft (1.25m)**
HARDINESS **Zone 5**

Lucetta is one of those roses that either makes a large, lax shrub or can be trained as a short climber or pillar rose. Its flowers are very large, lightly double, and open out as great globes of pale pink with darker petal backs and a yellow glow at the center. Later they fade to cream and then almost to white. Their simple prettiness is matched by the discreet paleness of their stamens, before these turn brown. The flowers come in clusters of 3–7. The bush is fairly prickly, with a spreading habit, and healthy mid-green leaves. It will grow to 6.6ft (2m) as a pillar rose – more in a hot climate. Lucetta was a character in William Shakespeare's *The Two Gentlemen of Verona*.

LUCETTA

LUTIN

syn. 'MEISECASO', Shady Lady

Shrub Rose

ORIGIN **Meilland, France, 1987**
FLOWER SIZE **1.6in (4cm)**
SCENT **Medium and fruity**
FLOWERING **Repeats constantly**
HEIGHT/SPREAD **3.3ft (1m)/3.3ft (1m)**
HARDINESS **Zone 6**

The flowers of Lutin are dark pink or pale crimson, fading to mid-pink, but the petals have a somewhat pointed shape and often have deep pink edges and white centers. They come in clusters of 3–15 and open out as attractive rosettes. Lutin has small, neat, glossy, mid-green leaves and very few prickles, and is fairly healthy. The plant is naturally upright in habit but forms a rounded bush, as high as it is wide. In hot climates it reaches 4.9ft (1.5m) in all directions, but is rarely more than half that in its native France. It is especially popular in Australia, where it is known as Shady Lady and recommended for mass plantings in shady places. Nevertheless, it grows much better in a sunny position and makes a fine specimen shrub in the garden.

LUTIN

'LYKKEFUND'

'LYKKEFUND'

Helenae Hybrid

ORIGIN **Olesen, Denmark, 1930**
PARENTAGE ***Rosa helenae* × unknown**
FLOWER SIZE **1.6in (4cm)**
SCENT **Strong mixture of musk and sweetness**
FLOWERING **Once, midseason**
HEIGHT/SPREAD **13.1ft (4m)/6.6ft (2m)**
HARDINESS **Zone 5**

'Lykkefund' is popularly known as the "thornless" rambler, but many better roses can claim the same title, including 'Tausendschön' and 'Veilchenblau'. That said, 'Lykkefund' produces beautiful clusters of small, loose, semidouble flowers of an exquisite pale mother-of-pearl color that turns quickly to white. They are set off by dark golden stamens (which give a rich flush to the whole of the flower at first), red pedicels, and lush, bright green leaves. The flowers come in clusters of 10–20 on a plant that is indeed thornless, though the leaves have barbs along their undersides. It roots quickly from cuttings, grows vigorously, and will reach as much as 32.8ft (10m) up a tree. When in full flower, the whole plant is a mass of fragrance and elegance.

LYNN ANDERSON

syn. 'WEKJOE'

Grandiflora

ORIGIN **Winchel, US, 1993**
PARENTAGE **seedling × 'Gold Medal'**
FLOWER SIZE **5.1in (13cm)**
SCENT **Medium and sweet**
FLOWERING **Repeats well**
HEIGHT/SPREAD **4.9ft (1.5m)/3.3ft (1m)**
HARDINESS **Zone 6**

The singer Lynn Anderson "never promised you a rose garden," but this is a beautiful rose to remember her by. Its flowers are full of petals, white with pink edges, and they open from classically long and elegant Hybrid Tea buds. In fact, they are almost at their best at the opening bud stage, when there is a hint of cream at the center but the pink piping has not yet started to age and fade. The flowers are borne singly or in clusters of up to five, on long stems that are good for cutting. The plant is healthy, and well-covered with matte, mid-green leaves. Although raised in California, it also flourishes in more temperate climates.

LYNN ANDERSON

M

'MABEL MORRISON'

see 'BARONNE ADOLPHE DE ROTHSCHILD'

MABELLA

syn. 'KORGOLD', New Day

Hybrid Tea

ORIGIN **Kordes, Germany, 1977**
PARENTAGE **'Arlene Francis' x 'Roselandia'**
FLOWER SIZE **5.1in (13cm)**
SCENT **Strong and fruity**
FLOWERING **Repeats well**
HEIGHT/SPREAD **4.1ft (1.25m)/3.3ft (1m)**
HARDINESS **Zone 6**

Mabella is a versatile, large-flowered, yellow Hybrid Tea: it makes a good display in the garden but is also beautiful as a cut flower. It has been grown as a florists' rose but is also popular with exhibitors. The flowers are golden yellow at first, though sometimes slightly paler at the center. Later they open out and fade to lemon yellow. The color is uniform – both sides of the petals are the same color. The flowers usually come singly on long, strong stems. The bush has big, dark leaves and an upright habit of growth. Its height depends upon the weather – 2.7ft (80cm) in cool climates, but twice that in hot. Though fairly disease-resistant, it may need some watching if spotless foliage is desired.

'MACRANTHA'

syn. 'WAITZIANA'

Species Hybrid

FLOWER SIZE **2.4in (6cm)**
SCENT **Sweet and musky**
FLOWERING **Once only**
HEIGHT/SPREAD **8.2ft (2.5m)/4.9ft (1.5m)**
HARDINESS **Zone 5**

'KRAUSE'S MACRANTHA'

MABELLA

Several different roses are grown under the name of 'Macrantha'. The original clone, pictured by Redouté as *Rosa canina* var. *grandiflora*, is no longer in cultivation. It was probably a hybrid between *Rosa canina* and *Rosa gallica*, but others suggest that *Rosa arvensis* or an Alba contributed to its makeup. All the cultivars now grown as 'Macrantha' are once-flowering roses of great beauty, whatever their parents. They have single or semisingle flowers on scrambling shrubs that look good both in the garden and in natural plantings. 'Macrantha' was widely used by German breeders between 1900 and 1950 to develop hardy garden roses. Among the best are 'Daisy Hill' (Kordes, 1906), 'Professor Ibrahim' (Krause, 1937), and 'Krause's Macrantha' (Krause, 1931), which has semidouble, pink and white flowers with beautiful red anthers.

MADAM SPEAKER

see BOLCHOÏ

'MADELEINE SELTZER'

Hybrid Multiflora

ORIGIN **Walter, France, 1926**
PARENTAGE **'Tausendschön' x 'Mrs. Aaron Ward'**
FLOWER SIZE **2in (5cm)**
SCENT **Strong and musky**
FLOWERING **Once only**
HEIGHT/SPREAD **9.8ft (3m)/6.6ft (2m)**
HARDINESS **Zone 5**

'Madeleine Seltzer' is a very beautiful Hybrid Multiflora that owes everything to 'Tausendschön' and nothing to 'Mrs. Aaron Ward'. The flowers are pure cream, fading to white, and full of neat, ruffled petals, just like 'Tausendschön'. They come in clusters of up to 20 on a strong, thornless plant, and are set off by pale, rich green foliage (bronzy when young). The petals are thin and spoil in rain, so 'Madeleine Seltzer' does better in dry weather. Unfortunately it flowers only once, and briefly, but its beauty and scent are magical.

'MADELEINE SELTZER'

'MAGENTA'

'MAGENTA'

Floribunda

ORIGIN **Kordes, Germany, 1954**
PARENTAGE **seedling x 'Lavender Pinocchio'**
FLOWER SIZE **2.8in (7cm)**
SCENT **Strong and sweet**
FLOWERING **Repeats well**
HEIGHT/SPREAD **4.9ft (1.5m)/4.1ft (1.25m)**
HARDINESS **Zone 6**

'Magenta' was one of many interesting oddities to come from the inventive Wilhelm Kordes in the 1950s. Technically a Floribunda, it grows more like a shrub rose, building up slowly into a lanky, open plant, 4.9–6.6ft (1.5–2m) tall. The flowers are not magenta so much as lavender purple, fading to soft gray mauve – a useful color for flower arranging. "Rosy-magenta", "soft deep mauve," "lilac, gray, magenta, and purple," "lavender mauve," and "lavender cerise" are other descriptions. When photographed, the color tends to come out pink. The flowers are medium-sized, charmingly disorganized, with a lot of petals in a loose rosette, and very strongly scented. They come in clusters of 5–15 and repeat every so often through to mid-autumn. The leaves are dark, and few. The plant is tall, open, and lax in habit, somewhat slow to grow at first, and better in protected sites.

MAGIC BLANKET

see SCHNEEKÖNIGIN

MAGIC CARPET

syn. 'JACLOVER', Tapis Magique

Shrub Rose

ORIGIN **Zary & Warriner, US, 1992**
PARENTAGE Immensee x Class Act
FLOWER SIZE **2in (5cm)**
SCENT **Light and musky**
FLOWERING **Repeats well**
HEIGHT/ SPREAD **3.3ft (1m)/5.7ft (1.75m)**
HARDINESS **Zone 6**
AWARDS **ROTY 1996**

This dainty little Wichurana Polyantha has become very popular. Its flowers open cherry crimson, with a circle of rich yellow stamens, a patch of white at the center, and a few streaks of white running into the petals. The color changes to very attractive shades of mauve, lilac, lavender, or Parma violet as it ages. The flowers are small, semidouble, lightly cupped, and borne in medium-sized clusters (typically of 10–20), well set off by small, dark, glossy, healthy leaves. But the main attraction of Magic Carpet is its adaptability in cultivation. Since it grows much wider than high, it is an excellent rose for groundcover and landscaping. It is also a good subject for a forward position in a garden (the purple flowers seem to combine with every other color) and also for containers and hanging baskets. It flowers almost continuously.

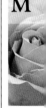

MAGIC CARPET

Magic Carrousel

Magic Carrousel

syn. 'MOORcar'
Miniature Rose

ORIGIN **Moore, US, 1972**
PARENTAGE **'Little Darling' x 'Westmont'**
FLOWER SIZE **2in (5cm)**
SCENT **Little or none**
FLOWERING **Repeats constantly**
HEIGHT/SPREAD **2ft (60cm)/1.3ft (40cm)**
HARDINESS **Zone 6**

This is a classic among miniature roses, a great advance when it first came out and still among the best. It has deep pink buds that open to a high-centered flower, for all the world a scaled-down Hybrid Tea. But the distinct charm of Magic Carrousel lies in its fully open, imbricated blooms, which are white or cream, heavily edged with deep pink or pale crimson. The flowers are popular both with gardeners (it is exceptionally floriferous) and with exhibitors. It also makes a long-lasting cut flower for the house. The plant is vigorous and fairly healthy, with small, glossy leaves and an upright habit of growth.

Magic Meidiland

syn. 'MEIbonrib'
Shrub Rose

ORIGIN **Meilland, France, 1993**
PARENTAGE ***Rosa sempervirens* hybrid x (Milrose x Bonica 82)**
FLOWER SIZE **1.2in (3cm)**
SCENT **Light and musky**
FLOWERING **Constantly in flower**
HEIGHT/SPREAD **1.6ft (50cm)/2.5ft (75cm)**
HARDINESS **Zone 6**
AWARDS **ADR 1993**

Magic Meidiland

The Meilland landscape roses have for long been the market leaders and Magic Meidiland is one of their best. Its flowers are small and little more than semi-double, but borne in great profusion in clusters of 3–10, right through until the first frost in cold climates. They are dark pink, with white patches toward the center, golden stamens, and red buds. The leaves are unusually beautiful: small, dark, very glossy, and very healthy. They also withstand extremes of heat and cold. Magic Meidiland makes a lax, mounding plant, often wider than it is tall but, in any event, its size depends upon the climate – 1.6ft (50cm) in its native France, but at least twice that in the hotter parts of Australia and the US.

'Magna Charta'

see 'Mme. Gabriel Luizet'

'Magnifica'

Rubiginosa Hybrid

ORIGIN **Hesse, Germany, 1916**
PARENTAGE **'Lucy Ashton' seedling**
FLOWER SIZE **2.8in (7cm)**
SCENT **Strong, sweet, and fruity**
FLOWERING **Once only**
HEIGHT/SPREAD **5.7ft (1.75m)/6.6ft (2m)**
HARDINESS **Zone 5**

The importance of 'Magnifica' lies in its history: the German breeder Wilhelm Kordes used it widely to produce superhardy shrub roses, including 'Fritz Nobis' (1940) and 'Sparrieshoop' (1953), while the most beautiful of pale pink Hybrid Teas 'Margaret Merril' is among its more distant descendants. 'Magnifica' is an open-pollinated seedling of 'Lucy Ashton', one of Lord Penzance's Hybrid Sweetbriars. It has larger flowers than its parent and more petals, so it is probably the result of a cross with a Hybrid Tea. The flowers are very handsome, with dark pink petals, a white center, and a thick ring of golden stamens. They are abundantly borne in clusters of 3–10, and followed by very dark hips which last well into winter. 'Magnifica' has a lot of barbed prickles, and gives off the strong apple scent of sweetbriars even in winter, though this delicious fragrance is strongest when emitted by the small, young leaves in early summer.

'Magnifica'

'Maigold'

Shrub Rose

ORIGIN **Kordes, Germany, 1953**
PARENTAGE **'Poulsen's Pink' x 'Frühlingstag'**
FLOWER SIZE **3.5in (9cm)**
SCENT **Strong, fruity, and slightly fetid**
FLOWERING **Early in the season and occasionally thereafter**
HEIGHT/SPREAD **9.8ft (3m)/4.9ft (1.5m)**
HARDINESS **Zone 5**

'Maigold' is very popular in cool climates for its hardiness and early flowering – its name ("May Gold") indicates that it flowers a month before other roses in Germany. Its buds are long and pointed and open to reveal coppery apricot flowers with golden yellow backs, quite a harsh color at first. The flowers are slightly ragged in outline but have a beautiful crown of crimson filaments and yellow anthers at the center. They fade to pale yellow, especially in hot climates: the colors are most vivid in cool weather. They are borne singly or in small clusters. The leaves are distinct and bright, pale green (bronzy at first), with strongly serrated leaflets. It is sometimes susceptible to blackspot. The plant is very well armed, and the prickles are long and thin.

'Maigold'

'Maigold' will grow to 13.1ft (4m) as a climber, and looks very fine from a distance. It tolerates poor soils and is easily propagated from cuttings.

'Mainzer Fastnacht'

syn. 'Blue Moon', 'Sissi'
Hybrid Tea

ORIGIN **Tantau, Germany, 1964**
PARENTAGE **'Sterling Silver' seedling x seedling**
FLOWER SIZE **4.3in (11cm)**
SCENT **Strong, fruity, and sweet**
FLOWERING **Repeats well**
HEIGHT/SPREAD **3.3ft (1m)/2.5ft (75cm)**
HARDINESS **Zone 6**
AWARDS **ADR 1964; Rome GM 1964**

'Mainzer Fastnacht'

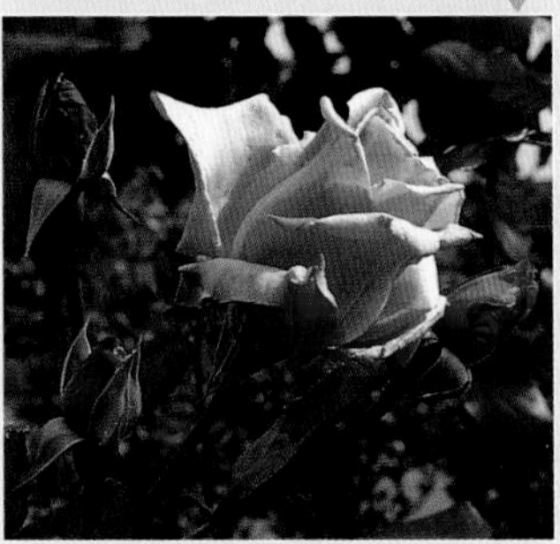
'Climbing Blue Moon'

'Mainzer Fastnacht', under its various different names, is probably the best-known and most widely grown of all lilac mauve roses. Many would say it was still the best. The flowers open slowly from large, elegant buds and are beautiful even when fully expanded. They are borne, usually singly, on long, strong stems and are excellent for cutting – they last a long time in water. The plant is healthy, vigorous, and easy to grow. It looks especially fine in large plantings, and can be difficult to place within a mixed bed with other plants. Although very hardy, it performs best in warm climates. Its German name (which means "Carnival of Mainz") recalls the fame of Mainz as a carnival city.

A climbing sport of 'Mainzer Fastnacht' was introduced by Mungia in the US in 1981 under the name of **'Climbing Blue Moon'**. It is exactly the same in all respects as the bush form, except that its flowers are slightly larger, and it flowers only intermittently after its first spectacular blooming. It grows to about 11.5ft (3.5m) and makes a vigorous, leggy, slightly stiff climber. The scent of both 'Mainzer Fastnacht' and 'Climbing Blue Moon' is delicious.

Sport of 'Mainzer Fastnacht'

'Climbing Blue Moon'

syn. 'Climbing Sissi'
Climbing Hybrid Tea
ORIGIN **Mungia, US, 1981**
FLOWER SIZE **4.7in (12cm)**
FLOWERING **Repeats a little**
HEIGHT/SPREAD **11.5ft (3.5m)/3.3ft (1m)**

MAINAUFEUER

syn. 'KORTEMMA', Chilterns, Red Ribbons, Canterbury, Fiery Sensation

Ground Cover

ORIGIN **Kordes, Germany, 1990**
PARENTAGE **Weisse Max Graf x Walzertraum**
FLOWER SIZE **3.1in (8cm)**
SCENT **Light and musky**
FLOWERING **Early and prolonged, some repeat**
HEIGHT/SPREAD **2.5ft (75cm)/4.1ft (1.25m)**
HARDINESS **Zone 6**
AWARDS **Baden-Baden 1991**

Few roses have so many synonyms as this excellent red groundcover rose. It is known in Germany (and most of Europe) as Mainaufeuer, as Chilterns in England, Red Ribbons in the US, Canterbury in New Zealand, and Fiery Sensation in South Africa. And it flourishes in all their very different climates and growing conditions. The semidouble flowers are bright blood red, with a fiery, luminous, velvety sheen to their petals and a few golden stamens at the center. They come in large clusters of 10–30 and make a considerable impact when in full bloom. They keep their color as they age, and drop their petals cleanly. The plant has dark, shiny, healthy leaves and a prostrate habit, sending up stems from the base which flower at the tips, arch over and flower again all along their length. Mainaufeuer is an extremely useful garden plant.

MAINAUFEUER

ROSA MAJALIS

see ROSA CINNAMOMEA

'MALTON'

syn. 'FULGENS'

Hybrid China

ORIGIN **Guérin, France, 1830**
FLOWER SIZE **2.4in (6cm)**
SCENT **Strong, sweet, and tealike**
FLOWERING **Repeats well**
HEIGHT/SPREAD **13.1ft (4m)/9.8ft (3m)**
HARDINESS **Zone 6**

This China rose is an underestimated garden plant, whether grown as a climber or as a freestanding shrub. The flowers are crimson, with much paler reverses (light pink, almost white) and white flecks at the center, and they keep their color well until the petals fall. The petals are rounded, short, incurved, and numerous. The flower stalks are long and slender, so that the flowers hang down elegantly in small clusters (typically of five flowers). The flowers appear intermittently throughout the season after the first abundant flush. The leaves are dark and small, and the plant makes long new wands of 9.8ft (3m) or so. Its ultimate height can be as much as 16.4ft (5m) up a wall. It roots easily from cuttings.

'MALTON'

MAINAU GARDEN

WITH STUNNING VIEWS OVER LAKE CONSTANCE, GERMANY'S PREMIER GARDEN IS AN ISLAND PARADISE THAT CONTAINS SOME 30,000 ROSE BUSHES

MAINAU IS EUROPE'S most popular garden, and it is wonderfully organized for the enjoyment of nearly 1.5 million tourists who visit it every year. Some 70 gardeners help to maintain this tropical island paradise, north of the Alps, and their hard work is reflected in the standards of neatness and cleanliness that are everywhere apparent.

The 110-acre (45-hectare) island rises steeply to a height of 131ft (40m) above the level of Lake Constance. At its eastern end, the baroque palace built in 1740 has splendid views across the lake. To the side of the palace is the rose garden, laid out in the Italian style by Grand Duke Friedrich I of Baden in 1871. It is surrounded on three sides by a pergola of centennial climbing roses, while the fourth is the balustraded garden of the palace itself. The varieties are mostly modern, with many repeat flowering climbers. Bush roses are pruned hard and planted very closely to maximize the display. Standard roses intensify the effects. The beauty of the Italian rose garden in early summer is overwhelming: palms and cypresses surround it and increase its exotic allure.

THE CHAPEL AND PALACE AT MAINAU

STATUE IN ROSE GARDEN

On the broad lower slopes of the island along its southern side is a huge informal garden of shrub roses, planted in 1969. Many of the roses are grown as unpruned shrubs: 'The Fairy' is 6.6ft (2m) tall and 'Variegata di Bologna' nearly twice that height.

Mainau has some 1,200 different cultivars and 30,000 rose bushes, but it is also famous for its displays of bedding – huge plantations of dahlias and millions of tulips grown in grass.

'Maman Cochet'

Tea Rose

ORIGIN **Cochet, France, 1893**
PARENTAGE **'Marie van Houtte' × 'Mme. Lombard'**
FLOWER SIZE **2.8in (7cm)**
SCENT **Strong, tealike, and delicious**
FLOWERING **Continuous**
HEIGHT/SPREAD **1.25m (4.1ft)/3.3ft (1m)**
HARDINESS **Zone 7**

'Maman Cochet' and its sports represent the highest achievements of which the Tea roses are capable. Not only are they supremely elegant and prolific, they also thrive on neglect to such an extent that they frequently turn up in abandoned gardens and old cemeteries, flowering and flourishing with nothing to sustain them. 'Maman Cochet' has large, long flowers, which hang down on their weak stems and open from buds which are cream colored, infused with raspberry pink. Further tints increase their loveliness as they open up – ivory, mother-of-pearl, lavender, and lemon. The flowers continue to grow and expand until they open out to a mass of long, overlapping petals, exquisitely arranged around the center, sometimes quartered, sometimes imbricated like a camellia. The flowers come singly, or in twos and threes, and are borne ceaselessly in hot climates, where they flower year-round. They have thin petals which spoil in rain, and ball in cool, humid climates. But they are supremely self-confident performers in hot, dry climates, where they are one of the mainstays of every garden.

There is a climbing form, which reaches 8.2ft (2.5m), and a white one called **'White Maman Cochet'**, whose flowers have lemon yellow centers and pink tips to the outer petals. Both are widely grown and look as enchanting in the vase as in the garden.

'MAMAN COCHET'

'WHITE MAMAN COCHET'

Sport of 'Maman Cochet'

'White Maman Cochet'

ORIGIN **Cook, US, 1896**

'Maman Turbat'

Polyantha

ORIGIN **Turbat, Germany, 1911**
PARENTAGE **'Mme. Norbert Levavasseur' × 'Katharina Zeimet'**
FLOWER SIZE **1.2in (3cm)**
SCENT **Light and musky**
FLOWERING **Repeats well**
HEIGHT/SPREAD **2.7ft (80cm)/2ft (60cm)**
HARDINESS **Zone 5**

The beauty and sheer profusion of the early Polyantha roses is a source of wonder, and 'Maman Turbat' is one of the best. The flowers open mid-pink and fade to pale pink – the buds, too, are very pale because the reverses of the petals are palest pink. They are full of petals, but tightly cupped, so that they seldom seem to open out completely. The flowers come in large clusters of 10–30 almost continuously until the first frosts – but well into the winter in warmer climates. 'Maman Turbat' has bright green leaves which are some of the healthiest among Polyanthas, and grows with great vigor. It is a very useful plant in containers or at the front of a mixed planting.

'MAMAN TURBAT'

MANDARIN

Mandarin

syn. 'KORcelin'

Miniature Rose

ORIGIN **Kordes, Germany, 1987**
FLOWER SIZE **1.4in (3.5cm)**
SCENT **Light and sweet**
FLOWERING **Almost continuous**
HEIGHT/SPREAD **2ft (60cm)/2ft (60cm)**
HARDINESS **Zone 5**
AWARDS **Glasgow GM 1994**

This is an excellent small rose, variously described as a patio rose, a miniature, and a Polyantha. Its flowers are like small pompon dahlias and a delightful color – a mixture of crimson pink, salmon, and orange, with paler centers, darker outer petals, and yellow backs. The overall effect is indeed mandarin- or tangerine colored. The flowers are borne singly or in small clusters from top to bottom of the plant. They are set off by neat, glossy leaves, which indicate *Rosa wichurana* somewhere among its ancestors and account for its hardiness and health. Mandarin makes a cheerful, compact plant, with a few long prickles. It is a strong and vigorous grower, certainly one of the most attractive short roses and, some would say, the best by a large margin.

Manita

syn. 'KORberuhig'

Modern Climber

ORIGIN **Kordes, Germany, 1996**
FLOWER SIZE **3.1in (8cm)**
SCENT **Light and sweet**
FLOWERING **Repeats**
HEIGHT/SPREAD **8.2ft (2.5m)/8.2ft (2.5m)**
HARDINESS **Zone 5**
AWARDS **ADR 1997**

The individual flowers of Manita are not its chief glory – they are semidouble and no more than pink and white – but its floriferousness and the overall effect of so many flowers both cry out for admiration. The flowers are mid-pink with a small white circle around a boss of dull gold stamens at the center. The petals are attractively ruffled and have an occasional white stripe running through to their tips. They come in clusters of 5–9, but the clusters run into each other, so that they appear to be much larger than they really are. The plant is vigorous and healthy, with mid-green, matte leaves. It flowers in flushes – two in a cool climate but three in a hot – with a few stragglers in between. It also makes a good specimen shrub.

MANITA

MANOU MEILLAND

syn. 'MEITULIMON'
Floribunda

ORIGIN **Meilland, France, 1979**
PARENTAGE **'Baronne Edmond de Rothschild' (self-pollinated seedling) × ('Ma Fille' × 'Love Song')**
FLOWER SIZE **3.9in (10cm)**
SCENT **Light**
FLOWERING **Repeats continually**
HEIGHT/SPREAD **3.3ft (1m)/3.3ft (1m)**
HARDINESS **Zone 6**
AWARDS **Paris GM 1977; Madrid GM 1978; NZ GM 1980**

When first introduced, Manou Meilland was promoted as a shorter-growing version of 'Baronne Edmond de Rothschild'. Although that was a Hybrid Tea, and Manou Meilland is more of a Floribunda, they do share the same deep rich cyclamen pink color, and each has paler silvery pink backs to its petals. The main difference is that the flowers of Manou Meilland come in clusters of 3–9, and open out their petals, which then develop an attractive ruffling. The plant has lots of healthy, glossy leaves and grows vigorously, quickly throwing out new flowering stems, though never exceeding 3.3ft (1m) in height. One effect of its floriferousness is that the plant tends to bulge out sideways as it ages, thus providing a launch pad for more flowering stems to develop.

Meilland introduced a climbing form in 1997 as Grimpant Manou Meilland. It has larger flowers (4.3in/11cm) and grows to 9.8ft (3m), but is otherwise similar to the bush form. After its first spectacular flowering, its subsequent flowerings are no more than intermittent.

GRIMPANT MANOU MEILLAND

Sport of Manou Meilland

GRIMPANT MANOU MEILLAND

syn. 'MEITULIMONSAR'
Climbing Floribunda
ORIGIN **Meilland, France, 1997**
FLOWER SIZE **4.3in (11cm)**
FLOWERING **Once abundantly, thereafter intermittently**
HEIGHT/SPREAD **9.8ft (3m)/6.6ft (2m)**

MANY HAPPY RETURNS

syn. 'HARWANTED'
Floribunda

ORIGIN **Harkness, Britain, 1991**
PARENTAGE **'Herbstfeuer' × 'Pearl Drift'**
FLOWER SIZE **3.5in (9cm)**
SCENT **Medium and fruity**
FLOWERING **Repeats well**
HEIGHT/SPREAD **2ft (60cm)/2.7ft (80cm)**
HARDINESS **Zone 6**
AWARDS **Geneva GM 1987**

Many Happy Returns is a pale pink shrub rose with the appearance of a somewhat spreading Floribunda. The flowers are rose pink at first, with slightly darker reverses, fading to palest creamy pink. They are gently cupped, lightly petaled, and exquisitely beautiful. They are borne in great profusion in clusters of 5–11. The stems of the plant bend down under their weight (the plant has a natural tendency to spread), so that they are covered in flowers from end to end, completely obscuring the leaves. They are followed in autumn by red hips. The plant has very healthy, dark, glossy leaves, and quite a few prickles. It continues to flower, somewhat more intermittently, after its first splendid burst of beauty. It is a particularly good garden plant.

'MARBRÉE'

Portland

ORIGIN **Robert & Moreau, France, 1858**
FLOWER SIZE **2.8in (7cm)**
SCENT **Medium and sweet**
FLOWERING **Remontant**
HEIGHT/SPREAD **3.3ft (1m)/2.7ft (80cm)**
HARDINESS **Zone 5**

Several old garden roses have dark flowers speckled and sprinkled with tiny, paler spots, but 'Marbrée' is the only one that can fairly claim to be a repeat flowerer. The flowers are semi-double, and open out so that their large, wavy petals lie flat around a handsome circle of rich golden stamens. They are pale crimson, maroon, or purple, according to the season, and every petal is dotted with little pointilist spots. In all other respects, 'Marbrée' is a typical Portland rose – thick-stemmed, sturdy, and compact, with a lot of long, pointed leaves, bristly stems, and a good remontant habit. The flowers come in tight, bunched clusters of 3–5 and are followed by hairy, orange hips.

MANY HAPPY RETURNS

'MARBRÉE'

'MARCEL BOURGOUIN'

Gallica

ORIGIN **Corboeuf, France, 1899**
FLOWER SIZE **3.9in (10cm)**
SCENT **Medium and sweet**
FLOWERING **Once only**
HEIGHT/SPREAD **4.1ft (1.25m)/3.3ft (1m)**
HARDINESS **Zone 5**

'Marcel Bourgouin' was one of the last Gallicas to be introduced: by 1899 the Hybrid Teas already dominated the market for garden roses. Nevertheless, it is not exceptional – a good rose, rather than a great one. The flowers are lightly double, with few enough petals to reveal a cluster of deep yellow stamens when they open out fully. The petals are deep crimson, overlaid with darker purple markings. They have paler, pinker backs, and occasional white streaks that work their way out of the center. They are borne singly or, more usually, in clusters of up to four or five, on strong stems that lift the flowers well clear of the foliage. The plant has a few small prickles and handsome, mid-green leaves.

'MARCEL BOURGOUIN'

MARCEL PAGNOL

syn. 'MEISOYRIS', Matilda, Red Cross
Hybrid Tea

ORIGIN **Meilland, France, 1994**
PARENTAGE **'Duftwolke' × ('Oklahoma' × Duftzauber 84)**
FLOWER SIZE **5.1in (13cm)**
SCENT **Strong, sweet, and fruity**
FLOWERING **Repeats**
HEIGHT/SPREAD **4.1ft (1.25m)/3.3ft (1m)**
HARDINESS **Zone 6**

You cannot go wrong with a red Hybrid Tea, especially if it also has a rich, sweet scent. Marcel Pagnol is currently one of the best-selling red roses all over the world. Its flowers are large, blood red, and velvety, with elegant buds and a good shape even when they open out. They are borne, usually singly but occasionally in clusters of up to four, on long, strong stems – perfect for cutting. Their scent is delicious. The flowers repeat quickly and well, so that Marcel Pagnol also makes a good garden rose, which will grow to at least 4.9ft (1.5m) in hot climates. The plant has tough, dark green, glossy leaves, and quite a lot of prickles. The rose is named after the French playwright and film director (1895–1974).

MARCEL PAGNOL

MÄRCHENKÖNIGIN

MÄRCHENKÖNIGIN

syn. 'KORoyness', Bride's Dream, Fairy Tale Queen

Hybrid Tea

ORIGIN **Kordes, Germany, 1985**
PARENTAGE **'Royal Highness' seedling**
FLOWER SIZE **4.7in (12cm)**
SCENT **Light and sweet**
FLOWERING **Repeats**
HEIGHT/SPREAD **5.7ft (1.75m)/4.1ft (1.25m)**
HARDINESS **Zone 6**

This rose was introduced as an improved form of 'Royal Highness', which is a fair description. Märchenkönigin has all the virtues of that famous exhibition Hybrid Tea, but with improved health and, in particular, better resistance to blackspot. The flowers are especially elegant as they unfurl slowly from large, pale pink buds. They are borne singly at the ends of very long, strong stems, making them perfect for large flower arrangements. Märchenkönigin is vigorous and healthy, with large dark leaves and only a few prickles. It fares best in warm weather, when it can grow without interruption – the flowers tend to ball in rain or humid conditions – and it does especially well in hot climates where it can be fed and irrigated.

'MÄRCHENLAND'

Floribunda

ORIGIN **Tantau, Germany, 1946**
PARENTAGE **'Swantje' x 'Hamburg'**
FLOWER SIZE **2.4in (6cm)**
SCENT **Medium and sweet**
FLOWERING **Repeats**
HEIGHT/SPREAD **4.1ft (1.25m)/2.7ft (80cm)**
HARDINESS **Zone 5**

These days this is usually listed as a Floribunda, but it helps to remember that 'Märchenland' was originally issued as a shrub rose, and commended for its hardiness, health, and floriferousness. The flowers open from vermilion red buds, and keep a darker salmon pink shade on their petal backs, but they are pure, fresh pink when they open out. They come in large clusters (typically of 10–30), and have a charming and distinctive wave. They make an impressive display in their first flowering and continue to produce flushes right through until late autumn, when the flowers are darker too. The leaves are an unexciting mid-green, but the plant has a bushy, shrubby habit. 'Märchenland' is still among the best of the shrub roses.

'MARCHESA BOCCELLA'

see 'JACQUES CARTIER'

'MARCHIONESS OF LONDONDERRY'

Hybrid Perpetual

ORIGIN **Dickson, Northern Ireland, 1893**
FLOWER SIZE **5.1in (13cm)**
SCENT **Moderate**
FLOWERING **Occasionally repeats**
HEIGHT/SPREAD **6.6ft (2m)/5.7ft (1.75m)**
HARDINESS **Zone 5**

Dickson introduced 'Marchioness of Londonderry' as a pure white Hybrid Perpetual, but the rose we grow under that name today is pale pink, with beautiful dark pink shadows between its many layers of petals. It is thought to be a seedling of 'Baronne Adolphe de Rothschild', a popular silver pink rose that is a good repeat bloomer, but 'Marchioness of Londonderry' is shy of flowering. Its flowers are enormous, with many ranks of short, broad petals which take a long time to expand and unfurl. They are held well on sturdy, upright stems, which makes them good roses for exhibition. The Londonderrys were immensely rich and powerful landowners in the Ards Peninsula, where the Dicksons had their nursery.

'MÄRCHENLAND'

MARCO POLO

MARCO POLO

syn. 'MEIpaleo'

Hybrid Tea

ORIGIN **Meilland, France, 1993**
PARENTAGE Ambassador x Anneliese Rothenberger
FLOWER SIZE **3.1in (8cm)**
SCENT **Strong, sweet, and fruity**
FLOWERING **Repeats well**
HEIGHT/SPREAD **4.9ft (1.5m)/4.1ft (1.25m)**
HARDINESS **Zone 6**
AWARDS **Belfast FA 1994; The Hague FA 1996**

Marco Polo is an exemplary yellow Hybrid Tea: tall, vigorous, healthy, and very strongly scented. The flowers are a deep, rich yellow on both sides of the petals, and keep their color well until just before they fall. They have the classic high-centered, conical shape of the Hybrid Tea, and unfurl their petals elegantly. The lightly double flowers are usually borne singly, but occasionally in twos and threes, on long, straight, upright stems, which makes them very useful for cutting. They also stand up well to rain. The plant has healthy, glossy foliage, which is a good foil for the bright and beautiful flowers.

'MARÉCHAL DAVOUST'

'MARÉCHAL DAVOUST'

Moss Rose

ORIGIN **Robert, France, 1853**
FLOWER SIZE **3.5in (9cm)**
SCENT **Strong and sweet**
FLOWERING **Once only**
HEIGHT/SPREAD **4.9ft (1.5m)/4.1ft (1.25m)**
HARDINESS **Zone 5**

There has only been one Maréchal Davoust in the history of France: Louis, Duke d'Auerstädt, one of Napoléon I's greatest commanders, who died in 1823. His rose is a rich crimson Moss, very similar in appearance to the purple Gallicas, apart from its mossiness. Its flowers are usually crimson, but sometimes more red or more purple, according to the weather. They are lightly cupped, and filled with small petals, many of them quill-shaped, with paler, pinker backs. The flowers are sometimes quartered and may display a button eye, but neither of these characteristics is constant. What really distinguishes 'Maréchal Davoust' is the light covering of very dark moss on the sepals, receptacle, and flower stem. This then runs down and appears as a mass of small, dark prickles. The flowers come singly or in clusters of up to four. The plant is a lax grower, with small leaves and narrow leaflets, often with a dark edge to them.

MARÉCHAL LECLERC

syn. 'KRIcarlo', Touch of Class

Hybrid Tea

ORIGIN **Kriloff, France, 1984**
PARENTAGE **'Micaëla' x ('Queen Elizabeth' x 'Romantica')**
FLOWER SIZE **5.1in (13cm)**
SCENT **Moderate and fruity**
FLOWERING **Repeats**
HEIGHT/SPREAD **5.7ft (1.75m)/4.1ft (1.25m)**
HARDINESS **Zone 6**
AWARDS **AARS 1986; Portland GM 1988**

MARÉCHAL LECLERC

This rose, known as Touch of Class in the US and voted top American exhibition rose for ten years in succession, is actually French. Its real name – Maréchal Leclerc – commemorates Maréchal Philippe Leclerc, hero of the liberation of Paris in 1945. The flowers spiral slowly open from elegantly pointed coral buds. They are mainly pink, but composed of several shades of pink, as well as orange and cream. When they open out they have attractively ruffled petals and a distinctive salmon pink glow. They are carried, usually singly, on very long stems, so Maréchal Leclerc is a splendid rose for large arrangements as well as being a prize winner. The plant is vigorous and healthy, except for a little mildew late in the season, with large, deep green leaves and crimson new growth.

'MARÉCHAL NIEL'

Noisette

ORIGIN **Pradel, France, 1864**
PARENTAGE **'Chromatella' x unknown**
FLOWER SIZE **4.3in (11cm)**
SCENT **Strong and tealike**
FLOWERING **Once, early**
HEIGHT/SPREAD **13.1ft (4m)/9.8ft (3m)**
HARDINESS **Zone 8**

Many who garden in warm climates consider 'Maréchal Niel' to be the best yellow climbing rose ever introduced. When well-grown, it is an astounding sight in spring, covered in long, pendulous flowers. The color is variable, from apricot to pale lemon cream, but usually with a patch of pure gold somewhere on every flower. It fades quite quickly, and the flowers sometimes take on a pink tinge too. They are usually borne singly, and hang down under their own weight. The petals, though many, are actually somewhat thin, so this is a rose for dry climates. Its foliage is pale green, large, handsome, and plentifully produced. The plant has some large red prickles and may be susceptible to blackspot, but grows vigorously nonetheless. It is best grown on its own roots, and comes easily from cuttings. 'Maréchal Niel' was named after Adolphe Niel (1802–69), the hero of the battles of Magenta and Solferino, who was a Marshal of France and Minister of War under Napoléon III.

'MARÉCHAL NIEL'

MARGARET MERRIL

syn. 'HARKULY'
Floribunda

ORIGIN **Harkness, Britain, 1977**
PARENTAGE **('Rudolph Timm' x 'Dedication') x 'Pascali'**
FLOWER SIZE **3.9in (10cm)**
SCENT **Very strong and sweet**
FLOWERING **Repeats constantly**
HEIGHT/SPREAD **4.9ft (1.5m)/3.3ft (1m)**
HARDINESS **Zone 6**
AWARDS **Edland FA 1978; Geneva GM 1978; Monza GM & FA 1978; Rome GM 1978; NZ GM & FA 1982; The Hague FA 1987; James Mason GM 1990; Auckland FA 1992**

It is one of the world's most popular roses, but no one can agree whether Margaret Merril is pink or white, a Hybrid Tea or a Floribunda. The truth is that the flowers are a beautiful pale pink in cool climates and white in hot. And the flowers come singly early in the year and then in ever larger clusters well into autumn. Individually they are large and elegant in the Hybrid Tea manner, with long, slender buds of exquisite shape. Then they open out to cupped flowers like a Floribunda, with prominent red stamens at the center. If you look at them closely, you see that the stamens have buff gray pollen – a very unusual color for roses. The flowers have an attractive roll to their petals, which increases the impression of delicacy they impart, though they are, in fact, unusually thick and strong, and stand up well to rain. The plant is tall, vigorous, slender, upright, and healthy, with large glossy leaves. It will grow as much as 8.2ft (2.5m) in hot climates and flower through 12 months of the year, but its ethereal beauty is perhaps even more enchanting in cool climates.

MARGARET MERRIL

'MARIA CALLAS'

MARGARET THATCHER

see FLAMINGO

'MARGO KOSTER'

see 'DICK KOSTER'

'MARGUERITE HILLING'

see 'NEVADA'

'MARIA CALLAS'

syn. 'MISS ALL-AMERICAN BEAUTY'
Hybrid Tea

ORIGIN **Meilland, France, 1965**
PARENTAGE **'Chrysler Imperial' x 'Karl Herbst'**
FLOWER SIZE **5.5in (14cm)**
SCENT **Strong and sweet**
FLOWERING **Repeats well**
HEIGHT/SPREAD **2.5ft (75cm)/3.3ft (1m)**
HARDINESS **Zone 6**
AWARDS **Portland GM 1966; AARS 1968**

'Maria Callas' is popular in the US, where it is known as 'Miss All-American Beauty'. It is an enormous, exhibition style Hybrid Tea, which may look good on a flower show bench but makes a poor showing in the garden. In actual fact, its flowers are too variable to fare well in competitions – their split buds and loose, muddled centers are too wayward for strict judges of rose beauty. However, 'Maria Callas' does make an excellent and long-lasting cut rose for the house. The flowers are huge (as much as 6.7in/17cm when they open out) and shocking pink in color – a shade of pale cerise that is the same all through the flower and fades only slowly. The flowers may burn in the sun. 'Maria Callas' is very prickly, and makes scraggy growth, producing a few stems right from the base, which take several weeks to develop, but eventually have a single enormous bloom at each tip. Although usually cut back to 2–2.5ft (60–75cm), the plant will reach 6.6ft (2m) if left unpruned. The leaves are large, and very healthy, especially in dry gardens. The name of the rose commemorates the Greek opera singer (1923–77).

'MARIA LIESA'

Wichurana Rambler

ORIGIN **Liebau, Germany, 1936**
FLOWER SIZE **1.2in (3cm)**
SCENT **Strong and musky**
FLOWERING **Once, midseason**
HEIGHT/SPREAD **13.1ft (4m)/8.2ft (2.5m)**
HARDINESS **Zone 5**

'Maria Liesa' is the best of many climbing roses raised by a German Augustinian monk, Bruder Alfons Brümmer (1874–1936), and the only one widely available. It has small, single, deep pink flowers with white centers and conspicuous stamens. It flowers only once, but it is valued for its hardiness, floriferousness, the length of that single flowering, and its sheer charm when in flower. The flowers come in large, loose clusters, typically of 25–60, and are much visited by bees. They are followed by masses of small hips. The leaves are dark and glossy (both *Rosa multiflora* and *Rosa wichurana* are probably in its ancestry), and the stems are almost thornless. Maria and Liesa were the names of two women who worked in Bruder Alfons's monastery at Germershausen.

'MARIA LIESA'

MARIA MATHILDA

MARIA MATHILDA

syn. 'LENMAR'

Floribunda

ORIGIN **Lens, Belgium, 1980**
PARENTAGE **seedling x ('New Penny' x 'Jour de Fête')**
FLOWER SIZE **2.8in (7cm)**
SCENT **Strong, musky, and delicious**
FLOWERING **Repeats well**
HEIGHT/SPREAD **2.7ft (80cm)/1.6ft (50cm)**
HARDINESS **Zone 6**
AWARDS **Golden Rose of the Hague 1981**

Although officially classified as a miniature, it is better to think of Maria Mathilda as a short Floribunda or patio rose – and one of the best. The pink buds open to beautiful, elegant flowers which are palest pink at first, then fade quickly to white. The pink coloring is on the backs of the petals: the upper sides are always white. The flowers are lightly double and come in clusters of 3–9. They are unusually long-lasting both as cut flowers and on the bush. The plant has fairly ordinary leaves, dark and glossy, and an upright habit of growth. It is only moderately vigorous, but very healthy, and it repeats so well that it is rarely out of flower. Louis Lens named this rose after his wife: it is very popular in Belgium and the Netherlands.

'MARIA STERN'

Hybrid Tea

ORIGIN **Brownell, US, 1969**
PARENTAGE **'Tip Toes' x 'Queen Elizabeth'**
FLOWER SIZE **4.3in (11cm)**
SCENT **Strong, a mixture of sweetness and fruit**
FLOWERING **Repeats well**
HEIGHT/SPREAD **5.7ft (1.75m)/4.1ft (1.25m)**
HARDINESS **Zone 4**

'MARIA STERN'

Most of the Brownells' "subzero roses" were bred from *Rosa wichurana*, but 'Maria Stern' owes its great hardiness to the little-known 'Tip Toes', which includes the ironclad 'Général Jacqueminot' and 'Dr. W. Van Fleet' among its ancestors. The vigor and floriferousness of 'Maria Stern' come from 'Queen Elizabeth', arguably the best American rose of the 1950s. 'Maria Stern' has beautifully shaped flowers of a particularly bright, unfading shade of orange or vermilion, with hints of coral. They come singly, or occasionally in twos and threes, on a healthy and vigorous plant. Bred by amateurs and introduced by small-time nurserymen in New York State, 'Maria Stern' enjoys a continuing popularity which can be attributed to its excellent color, hardiness, health, and adaptability to different climates.

MARIANDEL

syn. 'KORPEAHN', Carl Philip, Christian IV, The Times Rose

Floribunda

ORIGIN **Kordes, Germany, 1985**
PARENTAGE **'Tornado' x 'Redgold'**
FLOWER SIZE **2.8in (7cm)**
SCENT **Light and sweet**
FLOWERING **Repeats well**
HEIGHT/SPREAD **2.7ft (80cm)/2ft (60cm)**
HARDINESS **Zone 6**
AWARDS **RNRS PIT 1982; Golden Rose of the Hague 1990**

This fine, dark red Floribunda is extremely popular and widely grown in Europe. The flowers of Mariandel open from short, pointed buds. They are semidouble, with ruffled petals around a gleaming boss of golden stamens. They keep their deep red color well and are unaffected by rain or hot sun. They come in clusters of 3–7 on strong stems, which are useful for cutting. The leaves are bronze red at first, then dark green, glossy, and very healthy; their dark coloring is as striking as the darkness of the flowers. The plant is bushy, compact, vigorous, and very healthy. It is also very free flowering. All the best qualities of modern German Floribundas come together in wonderful Mariandel.

MARIANDEL

'MARIE BUGNET'

'MARIE BUGNET'

Rugosa Hybrid

ORIGIN **Bugnet, Canada, 1963**
PARENTAGE **'Thérèse Bugnet' seedling x 'Pink Grootendorst'**
FLOWER SIZE **3.5in (9cm)**
SCENT **Strong and sweet**
FLOWERING **Continuous, until first frosts**
HEIGHT/SPREAD **3.3ft (1m)/3.3ft (1m)**
HARDINESS **Zone 4**

Most of the super hardy shrub roses bred to survive a Canadian winter have come from the government experimental horticulture stations at Morden and Ottawa. 'Marie Bugnet' is an exception and, like 'Thérèse Bugnet', was bred by an Alberta nurseryman called Georges Bugnet. The flowers are pure white and very pretty, full of ruffled, papery petals in small clusters (typically of 3–5 flowers). They are easily spoiled by rain, and do not set hips, but the elegant buds and brilliant white flowers are exceptionally beautiful. The plant is unusual among Rugosa roses for its compactness. Its long, healthy, light green, crinkly leaves cover the neat plant, and have good autumn color. In winter the prickly stems are a rich russet brown. It starts into flower early and continues until the first frosts. If grown on its own roots, it will make a neat thicket and a fine low hedge.

MARIE CURIE

syn. MEILOMIT

Floribunda

ORIGIN **Meilland, France, 1996**
FLOWER SIZE **3.5in (9cm)**
SCENT **Light and spicy**
FLOWERING **Once only**
HEIGHT/SPREAD **2.7ft (80cm)/3.3ft (1m)**
HARDINESS **Zone 5**

Marie Curie has flowers like a Floribunda, but it is a bushy plant, wider than high, and it flowers only once, so it is best considered a shrub or groundcover rose. The flowers have a beautiful and unusual shape, with ruffled petals and frilly edges. The cherry pink buds open to reveal pink outer petals and apricot inner ones. The apricot then fades to cream, while the outer petals remain pink. The range and variability of colors within the flowers is especially attractive, both close-up and when seen as a mass of color. The flowers come in clusters of 5–15 and are backed by large, glossy, healthy leaves. The plant is compact and useful both at the front of a border and as a landscaping plant. Its name commemorates Marie Curie (1867–1934), the Franco-Polish physicist and discoverer of radioactivity.

MARIE CURIE

'MARIE DE BLOIS'

'MARIE DE BLOIS'

Moss Rose

ORIGIN **Robert, France, 1852**
FLOWER SIZE **3.9in (10cm)**
SCENT **Strong and sweet**
FLOWERING **Remontant**
HEIGHT/SPREAD **4.9ft (1.5m)/4.9ft (1.5m)**
HARDINESS **Zone 5**

It is best described as a mossy Centifolia but, like all old roses, 'Marie de Blois' has a distinctive shape and character of its own. The flowers are mid-pink and fade to palest pink with a tinge of lilac. They are large, with a somewhat disorganized mass of ruffled petals within, and a rich, sweet scent. They come singly and in clusters of up to five, starting early in the season and repeating fairly regularly until mid-autumn. The buds, sepals, and flower stems are covered in sticky, aromatic moss – bright crimson when young – which runs down the stems and transmutes into prickles, so that the older wood is very prickly indeed. 'Marie de Blois' is unusually healthy among the old roses, with attractive, fresh green leaves and considerable vigor. It is valuable for its ability to flower more than once.

'MARIE PAVIÉ'

Polyantha

ORIGIN **Alégatière, France, 1888**
FLOWER SIZE **2.2in (5.5cm)**
SCENT **Strong and musky**
FLOWERING **Repeats well**
HEIGHT/SPREAD **2ft (60cm)/2.5ft (75cm)**
HARDINESS **Zone 6**

'Marie Pavié' is one of the oldest Polyanthas, but is still capable of showing what this class of roses can offer. The neat, semidouble flowers open from small buds (flesh pink or mother-of-pearl), before fading to white. They come in nicely spaced clusters of 5–20 flowers, held well above the foliage, and are very free with their scent, which floats upon the air, especially on humid evenings. The flowers are set off by the medium-sized, bright green foliage, which is fairly disease-free, though mildew and blackspot do affect it occasionally. The plant is vigorous, compact, and thornless, and almost perpetually in flower – it throws up flush after flush with a few flowers in between. It is good at the front of a mixed border, and has been recently rediscovered as a landscape rose.

'MARIE VAN HOUTTE'

Tea Rose

ORIGIN **Ducher, France, 1871**
PARENTAGE **'Mme. Falcot' × 'Mme. de Tartras'**
FLOWER SIZE **3.5in (9cm)**
SCENT **Strong and tealike**
FLOWERING **Almost continuous**
HEIGHT/SPREAD **4.1ft (1.25m)/3.3ft (1m)**
HARDINESS **Zone 6**

Many consider 'Marie van Houtte' the best of all the Tea roses. The lightly cupped flowers are large, and full of neatly reflexed petals, which are creamy yellow at first, except for a few smudges of pink on the backs of the outer petals. However, the color is sensitive either to heat or to ultraviolet (scientists are not sure which, but 'Mutabilis' has the same property), so that the color changes in hot, sunny weather to pale crimson, starting with the edges of the older petals. The flowers sometimes come singly, but usually in clusters of 3–5. The plant has dull, green leaves and a somewhat loose habit of growth, but it is exceptionally healthy and free flowering. If left unpruned – and the most 'Marie van Houtte' ever needs is the lightest of trims – the plant will eventually grow to as much as 8.2ft (2.5m) and survive years of neglect. It is also fairly hardy as Tea roses go, and roots very easily from cuttings.

'MARIE VAN HOUTTE'

'MARIE-JEANNE'

Polyantha

ORIGIN **Turbat, France, 1913**
FLOWER SIZE **1.6in (4cm)**
SCENT **Medium, sweet, and musky**
FLOWERING **Repeats constantly**
HEIGHT/SPREAD **2.7ft (80cm)/2.7ft (80cm)**
HARDINESS **Zone 6**

The white buds of this highly attractive Polyantha open pale flesh pink but fade quickly to white. The flowers of 'Marie-Jeanne' are neatly circular in shape, and full of petals that tend to stay on the plant after they have withered. The stamens also turn quickly to brown. The flowers are very attractive, and large for a Polyantha, borne in thick clusters of 5–10. 'Marie-Jeanne' has bright green leaves, a sturdy habit of growth, and few thorns. It is a useful plant in beds and containers, especially in warm climates, where it will eventually reach 4.1ft (1.25m), and flower year-round.

'MARIE-LOUISE'

Damask Rose

ORIGIN **France, c.1811**
FLOWER SIZE **3.9in (10cm)**
SCENT **Strong and sweet**
FLOWERING **Once only**
HEIGHT/SPREAD **4.1ft (1.25m)/3.3ft (1m)**
HARDINESS **Zone 5**

The rose we know as 'Marie Louise' may be different from the original grown at Malmaison in 1811, but it is a very pretty and popular Damask. The flowers open rich dark pink from red buds, and fade in the sun as they age, starting with the outer petals, but they always have a paler pink on the backs of the petals, which provides an attractive contrast when they curl over. This is most apparent in the pale pink button eye that forms around the pistils at the center. The flowers are roughly quartered in shape and are borne singly or, more usually, in clusters of up to five, on slender stalks. They are intensely sweetly scented. The bush is a thicket of slender stems that are not strong enough to hold the flowers upright, and tend to keel over: 'Marie Louise' is a rose that really does need staking. The leaves are large, lush, pale green, and very handsome. Mildew may sometimes be a problem.

'MARIE PAVIÉ'

'MARIE-JEANNE'

'MARIE-LOUISE'

'Marie-Victorin'

'Marie-Victorin'

Kordesii Hybrid

ORIGIN **Agriculture Canada, Canada, 1999**
PARENTAGE **'Arthur Bell' x ('Kordesii' x 'Applejack')**
FLOWER SIZE **3.5in (9cm)**
SCENT **Little or none**
FLOWERING **Repeats well**
HEIGHT/SPREAD **4.9ft (1.5m)/4.1ft (1.25m)**
HARDINESS **Zone 4**

This is one of the few Explorer roses to show a hint of yellow in its coloring. The flowers of 'Marie-Victorin' have a peach pink flush at first, which comes from a yellow tinge on the petal backs. They open out to a semidouble shape, with a mass of yellow stamens. The yellow flush fades to white, so that the flowers then appear mid-pink before fading to pale pink. They are borne singly, but more often in small clusters – typically of 3–5 – and are followed by vermilion hips. The plant is hardy and healthy (except for a little blackspot) with glossy, dark leaves. Brother Marie-Victorin Kerouac (1885–1944) – priest, scientist, educator, and politician – was a symbol of French Canadian identity.

'Marijke Koopman'

Hybrid Tea

ORIGIN **Fryer, Britain, 1979**
FLOWER SIZE **4.7in (12cm)**
SCENT **Light and sweet**
FLOWERING **Repeats very well**
HEIGHT/SPREAD **4.9ft (1.5m)/3.3ft (1m)**
HARDINESS **Zone 6**
AWARDS **The Hague GM 1978**

This is one of the best and easiest to grow of all Hybrid Teas. The long, pointed buds of 'Marijke Koopman' expand into large, elegantly shaped flowers of a wonderful deep, rich pink. The outer petals are very large, which means that the flower is still attractive when it opens out completely. The flowers are borne singly and in small clusters (rarely of more than three) on long stems, which makes them perfect for picking. They are very long lasting. The plant is free flowering and keeps up its production even in the hot, dry, summer weather that sends most roses into dormancy. 'Marijke Koopman' has a lot of healthy, rich, dark green foliage and a vigorous, upright habit of growth.

'Marijke Koopman'

Marinette

Marinette

syn. 'AUScam'

Shrub Rose

ORIGIN **Austin, Britain, 1995**
PARENTAGE **Lucetta x 'Red Coat'**
FLOWER SIZE **3.5in (9cm)**
SCENT **Fairly strong and sweet**
FLOWERING **Repeats well**
HEIGHT/SPREAD **3.9ft (1.2m)/4.9ft (1.5m)**
HARDINESS **Zone 5**

This is not a typical David Austin rose: both its shape and its coloring are unusual. The flower opens from a slender, scrolled bud which has large outer petals and shows itself to be semi-double. The petals are pink-edged but cream or white at the base, where there is a pretty circle of very pale yellow stamens. The pink parts of the petals have white streaks in them, and the petal backs are paler. The flowers come singly or in small clusters on long stems held well above the foliage. Although it fades eventually to white and palest rose, the whole flower is pretty and distinct at all stages, and the bush in full flower resembles a cloud of butterflies. The leaves are small, glossy, and susceptible to blackspot. The bush is shrubby, graceful, upright, and nicely proportioned. It is named after the French-born wife of an English publisher, Viscount Camrose.

'Marjorie Fair'

syn. 'Red Ballerina', 'Red Yesterday'

Shrub Rose

ORIGIN **Harkness, Britain, 1977**
PARENTAGE **'Ballerina' x 'Baby Faurax'**
FLOWER SIZE **1.2in (3cm)**
SCENT **Light and musky**
FLOWERING **Continuous**
HEIGHT/SPREAD **4.9ft (1.5m)/4.9ft (1.5m)**
HARDINESS **Zone 5**
AWARDS **Rome GM 1977; Baden-Baden GM 1979**

This charming and cheerful shrub rose is deservedly popular all over the world. Its flowers are single, crimson with a white center, and set off by bright yellow stamens. They are small, but come in large clusters, typically of 20–60 flowers, so they make a considerable impact in a garden – it is a louder, more eye-catching plant than its parent 'Ballerina'. The flowers keep their color and last a long time, but are eventually succeeded by small, red hips. The leaves are mid-green, thin, and glossy. The plant is a bushy shrub, forever pushing out new flowering stems, but it can be trained to 9.8ft (3m) as a climber up a wall. It is fairly healthy apart from an occasional dab of mildew or blackspot, where this is a likely occurrence. It flowers tirelessly.

'Marjorie Fair'

'Marjory Palmer'

Polyantha-type Shrub Rose

ORIGIN **Clark, Australia, 1936**
PARENTAGE **'Jersey Beauty' x unknown**
FLOWER SIZE **2.8in (7cm)**
SCENT **Strong**
FLOWERING **Fully recurrent**
HEIGHT/SPREAD **2.7ft (80cm)/3.3ft (1m)**
HARDINESS **Zone 7**

'Marjory Palmer' is one of several excellent Polyantha roses bred by Alister Clark from the Wichurana rambler 'Jersey Beauty'. The overall impression it gives is of color – a mass of bright pink in rather a modern shade. In fact, the opening buds (small, fat, and somewhat flat-topped) are pale crimson, while the flowers are a rich mid-pink, with slightly darker reverses, fading eventually to rose pink. The flowers have lots of small petals which are paler at the edges, often with a tinge of white, not unlike some of the "hand-painted" roses developed by Sam McGredy more than 50 years later. They are also unusually large and flat for a Polyantha. They come in small, well-spaced clusters (typically of 5–12 flowers) right through until early winter. This floriferousness is complemented by dense, healthy, glossy, dark, Wichurana foliage and a sturdy, spreading habit of growth.

'Marjory Palmer'

'MARLENA'

'MARLENA'

Miniature Rose

ORIGIN **Kordes, Germany, 1964**
PARENTAGE **'Gertrud Westphal' x 'Lilli Marleen'**
FLOWER SIZE **2.8in (7cm)**
SCENT **Light**
FLOWERING **Repeats very well**
HEIGHT/SPREAD **1.3ft (40cm)/1.3ft (40cm)**
HARDINESS **Zone 5**
AWARDS **Baden-Baden GM 1962; ADR 1964; Belfast GM 1966**

'Marlena' is still one of the best short-growing Floribundas or miniatures, invaluable as a bedding rose and at the front of a low border. Its lightly cupped flowers are rich crimson scarlet, with occasional flashes of white in the petals that make the crimson appear all the more brilliant – so do its yellow stamens, which keep their color for a long time. The flowers come in clusters of 5–11 and are both rainproof and unaffected by strong sun. The plant is extremely floriferous. It has very beautiful, beet red new growth and large, medium-dark green leaves. It is hardy and healthy, and seems to flower nonstop until early winter, even in poor soils.

MARMALADE SKIES

syn. 'MEIMONBLAN'

Floribunda

ORIGIN **Meilland, France, 1999**
FLOWER SIZE **4.7in (12cm)**
SCENT **Light and sweet**
FLOWERING **Repeats well**
HEIGHT/SPREAD **4.9ft (1.5m)/3.3ft (1m)**
HARDINESS **Zone 6**
AWARDS **AARS 2001**

Oranges are not the only fruit in Marmalade Skies: most nurseries describe its color as a unique shade of tangerine. It is actually a fairly traditional, bright, vermilion lake color and slightly paler on the petal backs, but the flowers keep their color extremely well, for an unusually long time, and only fade to salmon pink right at the end. Marmalade Skies is a conventional large-flowered Floribunda. The flowers are double, but open out lightly cupped to show their stamens. The plant is vigorous and upright, with large prickles and dark green leaves. It is billed as a

MARRY ME

short grower, but will eventually reach a height of 6.6ft (2m) in hot climates. It may need protection against mildew and blackspot.

MARRY ME

syn. 'DICWONDER'

Miniature Rose

ORIGIN **Dickson, Britain, 1998**
PARENTAGE **seedling x Cider Cup**
FLOWER SIZE **2in (5cm)**
SCENT **Light and sweet**
FLOWERING **Repeats well**
HEIGHT/SPREAD **2.5ft (75cm)/2.5ft (75cm)**
HARDINESS **Zone 6**

This cheerful miniature is unlike most modern roses because it makes a very dense bush, with a lot of upright stems forming quite a thicket of flowers and leaves. Marry Me has mid-pink flowers which start as scaled-down Hybrid Teas then open out very neatly, each like a little camellia. They come in small clusters (typically of 5–10) and are carried in amazing profusion during their first flowering and then on a lesser scale almost continuously until late autumn. Marry Me has small, glossy leaves, bronzy when young, and quite a few prickles. It grows too tall to be a true miniature, but makes a very useful shrub in a mixed border. It is, however, one of those roses that are popular only in their own country, so that it is rarely seen outside Britain.

MARSELISBORG

MARSELISBORG

syn. 'POULREB', Eurostar, Summer Gold, Yellowstone

Floribunda

ORIGIN **Olesen, Denmark, 1995**
FLOWER SIZE **3.5in (9cm)**
SCENT **Moderate**
FLOWERING **Repeats well**
HEIGHT/SPREAD **2.7ft (80cm)/2ft (60cm)**
HARDINESS **Zone 5**

Marselisborg is a handsome Floribunda, not unlike a shorter version of Graham Thomas. The flowers are golden yellow, with hints of amber at the center that are reflected from the red filaments. The flowers eventually fade slightly at the edges. They open out to a cupped shape with attractive muddled centers, and look particularly good against the dark, shining leaves. They come singly or – more usually – in clusters of up to five. The plant is upright and bushy, though the flowers sometimes arch outward on their long stems, and it repeats quickly. It is generally healthy, though blackspot may be a problem. Marselisborg is the summer castle of the Danish royal family.

MARTHA'S VINEYARD

syn. 'POULANS', Gaby Cover

Shrub Rose

ORIGIN **Olesen, Denmark, 1995**
FLOWER SIZE **1.6in (4cm)**
SCENT **Little or none**
FLOWERING **Constantly in flower**
HEIGHT/SPREAD **2.5ft (75cm)/4.9ft (1.5m)**
HARDINESS **Zone 5**

It is late to start into flower, but there is no stopping Martha's Vineyard once it gets going. It is an extremely floriferous, low-growing landscaping rose – one of those loose mounding plants that is always wider than tall. The semidouble flowers are bright crimson at first, fading to pink as they age, with a white patch toward the middle when they open out, ruffled petals, and dark yellow stamens. They come in spacious clusters of 5–10 flowers, and have a lot of little bristles on their stems. They drop their petals cleanly when they die but do not produce hips. Martha's Vineyard has very healthy, medium-dark leaves on a vigorous plant which tolerates extremes of heat and cold. It makes a useful hedge – broad but impenetrable – and will reach as much as 4.9ft (1.5m) in hot climates.

'MARTHE'

see 'ZÉPHIRINE DROUHIN'

MARTHA'S VINEYARD

MARMALADE SKIES

'Martin Frobisher'

'Martin Frobisher'

Rugosa Hybrid

ORIGIN **Svejda, Canada, 1968**
PARENTAGE **'Schneezwerg' seedling**
FLOWER SIZE **2.4in (6cm)**
SCENT **Medium and sweet**
FLOWERING **Repeats well**
HEIGHT/SPREAD **5.7ft (1.75m)/3.3ft (1m)**
HARDINESS **Zone 4**

'Martin Frobisher' was the first of the Explorer series of super-hardy roses bred and released by Agriculture Canada. It is still one of the best and almost thornless. The flowers are a very pretty milky pink color, with pure white backs to the petals, most visible when they curl over to form a button eye. The pink coloring appears to be dabbed onto the flowers, and is strongest toward the center. The flowers usually come in clusters of 3–5, on fairly long, slender stems that are good for cutting. Unfortunately, they turn brown before shedding their petals. Nor are they followed by hips. The leaves are gray green, with a glaucous bloom, and healthy except for blackspot occasionally. The plant is an upright, vigorous shrub that flowers prolifically and almost continuously until the first frosts. It also performs surprisingly well in hot climates like the American South.

Marvelle

see Tropical Sunset

'Mary Guthrie'

Polyantha

ORIGIN **Clark, Australia, 1929**
PARENTAGE **'Jersey Beauty' × 'Scorcher'**
FLOWER SIZE **2.8in (7cm)**
SCENT **Light**
FLOWERING **Fully recurrent**
HEIGHT/SPREAD **3.3ft (1m)/4.1ft (1.25m)**
HARDINESS **Zone 6**

This is not the best of Alister Clark's Polyantha roses bred from 'Jersey Beauty', but it is still popular in Australia. The flowers are rich mid-pink, fading slightly to rose pink as they age, and single – the wispy, golden yellow stamens are attractive. The flowers come in large clusters (10–20 blooms) on a spreading bush with very handsome, healthy, glossy leaves.

'Mary MacKillop'

'Mary MacKillop'

Hybrid Tea

ORIGIN **Swane, Australia, 1989**
FLOWER SIZE **4.3in (11cm)**
SCENT **Light**
FLOWERING **Fully recurrent**
HEIGHT/SPREAD **3.3ft (1m)/2.3ft (70cm)**
HARDINESS **Zone 6**

'Mary MacKillop' is a short, sturdy bush, with handsome, dark, glossy foliage, reddish young growth and thick prickles. But the best thing about this rose is its color – pale clear pink (with a hint of coral in the bud), fading to white, with a slightly darker pink edge to the petals. The flowers are elegantly shaped at all stages, high centred at first, before opening out to reveal a circular pattern of overlapping petals. The flowers are stoutly and uprightly held, singly or in small clusters of two or three. St. Mary MacKillop (1842–1909) was Australia's first native-born saint.

Mary Magdalene

syn. 'AUSjolly'

Shrub Rose

ORIGIN **Austin, Britain, 1999**
FLOWER SIZE **3.5in (9cm)**
SCENT **Strong, tealike, and myrrhlike**
FLOWERING **Repeats**
HEIGHT/SPREAD **4.1ft (1.25m)/3.3ft (1m)**
HARDINESS **Zone 6**

Mary Magdalene is a charming English Rose in the China rose style – not too vigorous, but very floriferous. The flowers open a beautiful pearl pink, with slightly darker petal backs and a hint of pale coral at the center. They fade fairly quickly to mother-of-pearl, before ending ivory white. The petal backs are always paler. The flowers are very full, lightly cupped rosettes, with a mass of petals around a button eye. They are pretty at all stages of their development but keep their exquisite shape well. They come singly or in clusters of up to seven (typically three), and are well held. The leaves are small and medium-dark, with a crimson edge when young. The plant is dense, bushy, and healthy, except for an occasional touch of mildew. The stems have a scattering of prickles.

'Mary Marshall'

'Mary Marshall'

Miniature Rose

ORIGIN **Moore, US, 1970**
PARENTAGE **'Little Darling' × 'Fairy Princess'**
FLOWER SIZE **1.2in (3cm)**
SCENT **Light and musky**
FLOWERING **Repeats well**
HEIGHT/SPREAD **1.6ft (50cm)/1.3ft (40cm)**
HARDINESS **Zone 6**

The colors of 'Mary Marshall' are quite unusual for a miniature rose – pale coral or salmon pink, with paler edges to the quilled petals and a hint of yellow at the center to start with. Later they fade to pale pink. The buds have the look of

'Mary Guthrie'

Mary Magdalene

Mary Rose

syn. 'AUSMARY'

Shrub Rose

ORIGIN **Austin, Britain, 1983**
PARENTAGE **'Wife of Bath' x 'The Miller'**
FLOWER SIZE **2.8in (7cm)**
SCENT **Light and sweet**
FLOWERING **Repeats well**
HEIGHT/SPREAD **3.9ft (1.2m)/3.9ft (1.2m)**
HARDINESS **Zone 5**

Mary Rose remains one of the most enduringly popular of David Austin's English Roses. The flowers are bright pink, with slightly paler backs to their petals, and cupped at first. When they open out a little more to show their stamens, their petals are slightly loose and ruffled. The outer petals eventually reflex and fade to paler pink as they age, while the inner petals remain curved toward the center. The flowers come in clusters of 3–7 on long, prickly stems and are wonderful for cutting, though the petals tend to drop quite quickly. The plant is fairly loose in its habit of growth, reaching 4.9ft (1.5m) in warm climates, and flowering almost without interruption – it is among the first and last to flower every year. The leaves are mid-green, ordinary, and susceptible to blackspot. The *Mary Rose* was Henry VIII of England's flagship, named after his sister, who married King Louis XII of France. In 1982, it was raised to the surface after more than 400 years in the mud of the Solent.

David Austin introduced a white-flowered sport called Winchester Cathedral in 1988: it is exactly the same as Mary Rose in all its details, except for its color. It reverts easily, so that pink patches appear on almost every bush of Winchester Cathedral during the course of the year. It may be no more than a pink fleck or patch on a single petal, but sometimes a whole flower or a branch comes out pink. Although infuriating commercially, this instability is one of Winchester Cathedral's great charms.

In 1992, Austin also introduced a softer pink sport of Mary Rose called Redouté in honor of the painter (1759–1840) who catalogued the Empress Josephine's roses at Malmaison. It is identical to both Mary Rose and Winchester Cathedral in everything except its color, which is pale pink, fading almost to white.

MARY ROSE

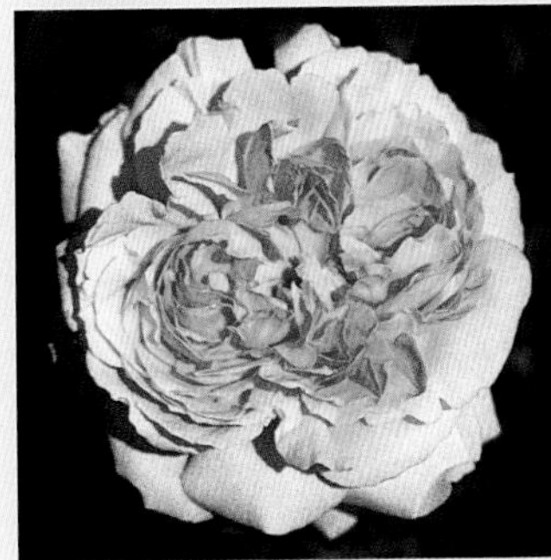
REDOUTÉ

WINCHESTER CATHEDRAL

Sports of Mary Rose

Redouté

syn. 'AUSPALE'
ORIGIN **Austin, Britain, 1992**

Winchester Cathedral

syn. 'AUSCAT'
ORIGIN **Austin, Britain, 1992**

miniature Hybrid Teas, but the flowers open up to an old-fashioned shape, with a lax, open arrangement of petals. They come in clusters of 3–11 and blend especially well with yellows and reds. The bush has neat, small, slightly glaucous leaves and purple stems. It is very healthy, with a somewhat lax habit of growth, but it flowers almost continuously until late autumn. In hot climates it may reach 2.7ft (80cm).

'Mary Wallace'

Wichurana Rambler

ORIGIN **Van Fleet, US, 1924**
PARENTAGE ***Rosa wichurana* hybrid x a pink Hybrid Tea**
FLOWER SIZE **4.3in (11cm)**
SCENT **Medium, sweet, and musky**
FLOWERING **Once spectacularly and then intermittently**
HEIGHT/SPREAD **16.4ft (5m)/9.8ft (3m)**
HARDINESS **Zone 6**

'MARY WALLACE'

'Mary Wallace' had the largest flowers of any Wichurana rambler when it was first introduced by the American Rose Society, two years after the death of its breeder Walter Van Fleet. This elegant beauty was named after the daughter of the then American Secretary of Agriculture, Henry C. Wallace, and proved such a success that by 1928, it was voted the most popular rose in the US. Its flowers are semidouble and open from long, pointed buds like a Hybrid Tea's. They are silvery pink with darker petal backs, but slightly paler at the edges, and with long, reflexing petals, though they retain them when eventually they wither and turn brown. The flowers are borne singly and in long-stemmed clusters of up to seven. 'Mary Wallace' has a scattering of large, thick leaves, more like a Hybrid Tea's than a Wichurana's, but glossy, rich green, and fairly disease resistant. The plant is very vigorous, with an open habit and few prickles.

Mary Webb

syn. 'AUSWEBB'

Shrub Rose

ORIGIN **Austin, Britain, 1984**
PARENTAGE **seedling x 'Chinatown'**
FLOWER SIZE **4.7in (12cm)**
SCENT **Strong and fruity**
FLOWERING **Repeats**
HEIGHT/SPREAD **4.1ft (1.25m)/3.3ft (1m)**
HARDINESS **Zone 5**

Mary Webb has large, lightly double flowers, so cupped as to resemble huge glowing peonies. They are a delicious shade of lemon yellow, sometimes soft apricot or buff at first, and usually fading to cream or white, but always with a hint of lemon or fawn at the center. They are very large and strongly scented, and come singly or in long-stemmed clusters of 3–5 flowers. The leaves, too, are large, but light green, crimson colored at first, matte, with somewhat round leaflets. As is the case with many of the David Austin roses, the plant responds to regular deadheading and seasonal pruning by flowering more abundantly in autumn. It does especially well in hot climates. It is named after Mary Webb (1881–1927), a Shropshire poet and novelist.

MARY WEBB

'Masquerade'

Floribunda

ORIGIN **Boerner, US, 1949**
PARENTAGE **'Goldilocks' x 'Holiday'**
FLOWER SIZE **2.8in (7cm)**
SCENT **Light and musky**
FLOWERING **Repeats well**
HEIGHT/SPREAD **3.3ft (1m)/3.3ft (1m)**
HARDINESS **Zone 5**
AWARDS **NRS GM 1952**

When 'Masquerade' appeared in 1949, it was immediately recognized as a completely new type of rose. The flowers opened bright yellow but turned first to pink and then to deep crimson before dropping their petals. It was a unique color change, and, given the brightness of the yellow shades, one with enormous potential for further development. Over the next 25 years, hundreds of seedlings and more remote descendants of 'Masquerade' were introduced all over the world: multicolored roses became a major fashion. The flowers of 'Masquerade' are semidouble but carried in spacious clusters, typically of 10–20, so that their display is always conspicuous. They are followed by round, red hips. The plant has small, dark, healthy leaves, grows vigorously, and repeats well, over a long period.

A climbing sport was introduced in 1958 and is now as popular as the bush form. **'Climbing Masquerade'** is similar in all respects except that its flowers are noticeably larger (up to 3.5in/9cm) and it climbs to at least 13.1ft (4m). It is much more floriferous than most climbing sports, and repeats very well.

'Masquerade'

'Climbing Masquerade'

Sport of 'Masquerade'

'Climbing Masquerade'

Climbing Floribunda
ORIGIN **Gregory, Britain, 1958**
FLOWER SIZE **3.5in (9cm)**
FLOWERING **Repeats**
HEIGHT/SPREAD **13.1ft (4m)/6.6ft (2m)**

M

'Matangi'

syn. 'MACman'
Floribunda

ORIGIN **McGredy, New Zealand, 1974**
PARENTAGE **seedling x 'Picasso'**
FLOWER SIZE **3.5in (9cm)**
SCENT **Light or slight**
FLOWERING **Repeats well**
HEIGHT/SPREAD **3.3ft (1m)/2.7ft (80cm)**
HARDINESS **Zone 6**
AWARDS **RNRS PIT 1974; Rome GM 1974; Belfast GM 1976; Portland GM 1982**

'Matangi' was long considered the best of Sam McGredy's "hand-painted" roses. The flowers are bright vermilion, fading to pale crimson, with much paler backs (almost white) and irregular margins of silvery white around the edge of the petals. The extent of the coloring, which gives the flower its "hand-painted" character, differs from year to year and season to season. The flowers open from elegant buds and are often borne singly, especially in the first flush of flowers, as well as in clusters of 3–9. They are also fairly rain resistant and shatter well when they have flowered. They are very freely produced on a tall plant with glossy, dark green leaves that are bronzy when young and may suffer from blackspot later. It is still an excellent bedding rose – and was the first of all roses to be patented in New Zealand. Matangi is an island resort in Fiji.

'Matangi'

Matthias Meilland

syn. 'MEIfolio'
Floribunda

ORIGIN **Meilland, France, 1985**
PARENTAGE **('Mme. Charles Sauvage' x 'Fashion') x ('Rusticana' x Tchin Tchin)**
FLOWER SIZE **3.5in (9cm)**
SCENT **Little or none**
FLOWERING **Repeats**
HEIGHT/SPREAD **2.7ft (80cm)/2ft (60cm)**
HARDINESS **Zone 6**
AWARDS **Frankfurt GM 1989**

Matthias Meilland has all the virtues one expects of a Meilland rose – including magnificent color, health, and vigor – but no scent. The flowers are a stunning dark geranium red, with occasional white flecks. They open out around the yellow stamens and appear to be only semidouble, but that is an illusion: there are a lot of petals, neatly rippling around and lying over each other. They come in clusters of up to seven. The bush has glossy, deep green leaves and is very disease resistant. It is a tip-flowerer, which means that it flowers again better if deadheaded between flushes. In hot climates it will grow to 4.9ft (1.5m), but is rarely more than half that height in its native France, where it is a high performance bedding rose.

Matthias Meilland

'Max Graf'

Rugosa Hybrid

ORIGIN **Bowditch, US, 1919**
PARENTAGE ***Rosa wichurana* x *Rosa rugosa***
FLOWER SIZE **2in (5cm)**
SCENT **Light and musky**
FLOWERING **Once only**
HEIGHT/SPREAD **1.6ft (50cm)/13.1ft (4m)**
HARDINESS **Zone 5**

The rose we call 'Max Graf' today is probably an older one, renamed when it was discovered by a worker (called Max Graf) in Bowditch's Nursery in Connecticut. It is a hybrid between *Rosa wichurana* and *Rosa rugosa*, with pretty, dark pink flowers (fading to rose pink) and a large brush of pale yellow stamens. The flowers come somewhat late in the season, but in clusters large enough to make an impact. Its branches normally trail like *Rosa wichurana*, from which it also inherits its dark, glossy leaves and a propensity to root as it creeps along the ground. Its stems are, however, thickly covered in fierce, brown bristles, a trait that comes from *Rosa rugosa*. It is widely sold as a groundcover plant, but it does not smother perennial weeds effectively and is itself very prickly to weed among. It is exceptionally hardy and completely immune to blackspot, perhaps best when grown and trained up as a climber.

'Max Graf'

Maxim

Maxim

syn. 'TANmixa', Joy of Life
Hybrid Tea

ORIGIN **Tantau, Germany, 1993**
FLOWER SIZE **3.5in (9cm)**
SCENT **Light**
FLOWERING **Repeats well**
HEIGHT/SPREAD **4.1ft (1.25m)/3.3ft (1m)**
HARDINESS **Zone 6**

Maxim is sold in Germany and popular in Australia, but rarely seen elsewhere. It is a red and white bicolor Hybrid Tea: the flowers are white, with crimson edges. The thickness of the crimson edging varies considerably: it tends to increase as the flowers age and leaches into the white parts. The outer petals have more color than the inner ones. The flowers are very pretty, dainty, and usually borne singly on long stems. It is a good cutting rose. The height of the plant is variable – rarely more than 3.3ft (1m) in Germany but usually more than 4.9ft (1.5m) in Australia. It is free flowering, vigorous, and healthy, with glossy, dark leaves.

'May Queen'

Wichurana Rambler

ORIGIN **Van Fleet, US, 1898**
PARENTAGE ***Rosa wichurana* hybrid × 'Mrs. de Graw'**
FLOWER SIZE **3.1in (8cm)**
SCENT **Medium and fruity**
FLOWERING **Once only**
HEIGHT/SPREAD **16.4ft (5m)/9.8ft (3m)**
HARDINESS **Zone 6**

Early-flowering and profuse, 'May Queen' was also the first of the large-flowered Wichurana ramblers to be introduced. The flowers have a distinctly old-fashioned look, opening out almost flat to show a mass of quilled petals in a roughly quartered shape. They are a good mid-pink and open from red buds. At their best, they are among the most beautiful of roses, but they often have a ragged outline and their soft petals are easily damaged by rain. They are borne singly but, more usually, in clusters of 3–5, on slender stalks that hang down under the weight of the petals. 'May Queen' is an extremely vigorous climber that has been known to reach as much as 26.2ft (8m). Its leaves are small and glossy with somewhat rounded leaflets, and the plant has quite a lot of hooked prickles.

'MAY QUEEN'

Mayor of Casterbridge

syn. 'AUSbrid'

Shrub Rose

ORIGIN **Austin, Britain, 1996**
PARENTAGE **'Charles Austin' × 'Louise Odier'**
FLOWER SIZE **3.5in (9cm)**
SCENT **Medium and sweet**
FLOWERING **Repeats well**
HEIGHT/SPREAD **4.9ft (1.5m)/4.1ft (1.25m)**
HARDINESS **Zone 6**

Much of the character of Mayor of Casterbridge comes from its parent, 'Louise Odier'. The flowers are very full, cupped, and pink, with incurved petals which are slightly paler pink on their undersides. They are borne singly or in short-stemmed clusters of two or three. The bush has long, prickly stems, a stiff, upright habit, and dull, mid-green leaves, which are somewhat susceptible to blackspot. The plant tends to send up long, gawky stems, which flower at their tips. If these are then bent downward, or trained sideways, they will break into flower all along their length. Mayor of Casterbridge repeats better than many of David Austin's English Roses. In hot climates it will reach as high as 8.2ft (2.5m).

MAYOR OF CASTERBRIDGE

The McGredy Family

FOUR GENERATIONS OF THE IRISH FAMILY OF McGREDY BECAME NURSERYMEN AND THEY ALL SPECIALIZED IN BREEDING HYBRID TEAS

Samuel McGredy set himself up as a nurseryman at Portadown in Northern Ireland in 1880. The McGredys were general nurserymen at first, but roses soon became a speciality. His son Samuel McGredy II, grandson Samuel McGredy III, and great-grandson Samuel McGredy IV all bred roses at Portadown.

The family raised Hybrid Teas, and from 1900 onward, the annals of rose history are littered with their successes: beauties like 'Mrs. Herbert Stevens' (1910) and 'Lady Alice Stanley' (1909); splendid red roses like 'Victory' (1920) and 'Lord Charlemont' (1922) interspersed with subtle novelties like 'Grey Pearl' (1945). When Sam McGredy IV took the reigns in 1953, it was bright-colored Hybrid Teas that followed, like 'Piccadilly' (1960) and 'Uncle Walter' (1963). But bright Floribundas were his speciality, and they came thickly over the years: Yellowhammer (1956), Orangeade (1959), Evelyn Fison (1962), Paddy McGredy (1962), Irish Mist (1966), City of Leeds (1966), Courvoisier (1970), Bonfire Night (1971), Tony Jacklin (1972), and Mary Sumner (1976).

SAM McGREDY IV

'LORD CHARLEMONT'

Early in his career, Sam McGredy IV turned his hand to breeding repeat flowering climbers: Casino (1963), Schoolgirl (1964), Handel (1965), Galway Bay (1966), Bantry Bay (1967), Swan Lake (1968), Santa Catalina (1970), Grand Hotel (1972), and Dublin Bay (1974). By breeding with the Hybrid Briar 'Frühlingsmorgen', he developed a range of "hand-painted" roses, with streaks and patches of white marbling set against a red background: 'Picasso' (1971), 'Matangi' (1974), 'Old Master' (1974), 'Regensberg' (1979), and 'Sue Lawley' (1980). This color break was later carried into miniature and patio roses with 'Little Artist' (1982) and 'Hurdy Gurdy' (1986).

After moving to New Zealand in 1972, Sam McGredy IV bred a great number of fine Hybrid Teas and Grandifloras that sold well in the US: bright yellow 'Jan Spek' (1986); 'Auckland Metro' (1987), 'Penthouse' (1987), 'Mount Hood' (1988), and 'New Zealand' (1989); the orange and yellow bicolor 'Today' (1990); 'Paddy Stephens' (1991); 'Kathryn McGredy' (1995), and 'Tropical Sunset' (1998).

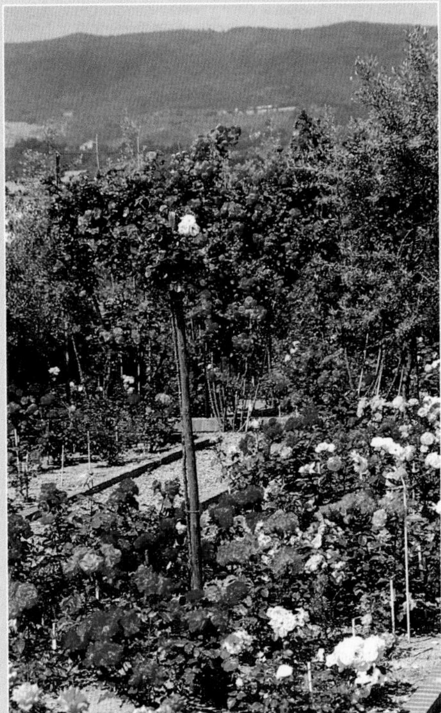

McGREDY HYBRID TEAS, FINESCHI GARDEN, ITALY

'MEDALLION'

'MEDALLION'

Hybrid Tea

ORIGIN Warriner, US, 1973
PARENTAGE 'South Seas' x 'King's Ransom'
FLOWER SIZE 6.3in (16cm)
SCENT Light and fruity
FLOWERING Repeats
HEIGHT/SPREAD 5.7ft (1.75m)/4.1ft (1.25m)
HARDINESS Zone 5
AWARDS Portland GM 1972; AARS 1973

Size is everything with 'Medallion': the flowers have been known to reach up to 7in (18cm) across. It is one of America's favorite exhibition roses, but quite unknown elsewhere in the world. The flowers open from very long, orange buds. They are pale apricot pink, with much darker backs to the petals. They also have a tendency to become more pink and less apricot as they age. In hot weather, the flowers are little more than lemon, fading to cream, with buff hints. They are not at all rain resistant – the flowers have very soft petals and hang their heads after rain – but the biggest blooms are produced in cool weather, like autumn. The flowers come singly on long stems, which make them good for cutting as well as for competitive exhibition (a popular activity in the US). 'Medallion' is tall, spreading, and vigorous, with large, dark leaves but few prickles. It repeats its flowers until well into autumn. Deadheading helps to speed up the next flush.

'MEG'

Modern Climber

ORIGIN Gosset, Britain, 1954
PARENTAGE 'Paul's Lemon Pillar' x 'Mme. Butterfly'
FLOWER SIZE 5.5in (14cm)
SCENT Light and sweet
FLOWERING Once only, with a few late flowers
HEIGHT/SPREAD 9.8ft (3m)/4.9ft (1.5m)
HARDINESS Zone 6

'Meg' has few of the qualities that rose breeders look for in a good commercial introduction: it was raised by an amateur. Its popularity may be attributed to its large, wide-open flowers with glorious stamens at the center. The flowers are pale peach pink at first, with a delicate amber yellow blush at the center and slightly darker petal backs. Later they fade to palest pink. The stamens have a slightly wispy look, which comes from their being all of different lengths. The flowers are borne in long-stemmed clusters of 3–9 and are followed by large hips in autumn. The plant is prickly, lanky, and stiff in its habit of growth. The wood is brittle: you can all too easily knock a branch off by accident. 'Meg' should not be grown as a freestanding shrub because the wind will break off the stems at ground level.

'MEG'

'MEG MERRILIES'

Rubiginosa Hybrid

ORIGIN Penzance, Britain, 1894
PARENTAGE *Rosa rubiginosa* seedling x Hybrid Perpetual
FLOWER SIZE 1.6in (4cm)
SCENT Light and sweet
FLOWERING Once only
HEIGHT/SPREAD 8.2ft (2.5m)/6.6ft (2m)
HARDINESS Zone 5

Lord Penzance's Hybrid Sweetbriars continue to have a following, though they are suitable only for wild gardens and woodlands. 'Meg Merrilies' has crimson flowers with a white center, paler petal backs, and a circle of golden stamens. Sometimes the flowers have an extra petal or two, but they are usually no more than five-petaled, with a notch in the middle of each petal edge. Scarlet hips follow the flowers. The plant has a lot of prickles, and mid-green leaves which retain just a hint of the sweetbriar scent if crushed. Meg Merrilies was the gypsy woman in Sir Walter Scott's *Guy Mannering.*

'MEG MERRILIES'

MÉLI-MÉLO

syn. 'ORAstrip'

Hybrid Tea

ORIGIN Orard, France, 1998
FLOWER SIZE 3.1in (8cm)
SCENT Strong and sweet
FLOWERING Repeats well
HEIGHT/SPREAD 3.3ft (1m)/2.7ft (80cm)
HARDINESS Zone 6

The flowers of Méli-Mélo are a very unusual combination of colors – blood red, streaked with butter yellow at first, but changing as the flower opens out and develops to dark pink and creamy white. The streaking is very irregular: some flowers turning out mostly red and others predominantly yellow. They are borne in clusters of 3–7 on a fairly vigorous bush. Méli-Mélo is a good rose which should be more widely grown outside France, where it is popular as a garden plant. It has a very strong scent and is quite healthy. However its flowers seem to collapse in rain, so it only opens out and looks its best in dry weather.

MÉLI-MÉLO

MEMENTO

syn. 'DICbar'

Floribunda

ORIGIN Dickson, Northern Ireland, 1978
PARENTAGE 'Bangor' x 'Anabel'
FLOWER SIZE 2.8in (7cm)
SCENT Light
FLOWERING Repeats continuously
HEIGHT/SPREAD 2.7ft (80cm)/2ft (60cm)
HARDINESS Zone 6
AWARDS Belfast GM 1980

Memento has all the best qualities of a modern Dickson Floribunda: health, bright color, and supreme floriferousness. The flowers are pale vermilion, with ruffled petals and a small white eye. They open out lightly cupped – later flat – and hold their color well, fading only slightly in hot sun. They also blotch in rainy weather, but manage to keep their petals in place. A massed bed in full flower is frankly dazzling. The flowers come in long clusters of 5–15, held well above the leaves. The plant makes a sturdy, healthy bush with large, matte, mid-green leaves. It seems to flower nonstop.

MEMENTO

The Meilland Family

FAME AND FORTUNE CAME TO THE MEILLAND FAMILY OF FRANCE BY WAY OF 'MME. A. MEILLAND' ('PEACE'), PROBABLY THE WORLD'S BEST-KNOWN ROSE

The Meillands have been rose growers for six generations, but their fame and fortune descend from a single rose – 'Mme. A. Meilland'. Royalties from the US, where it is known as 'Peace', brought them the dominant position within the French market that they still enjoy.

Marie Louise and Alain Meilland

Much of the credit for maintaining that eminence is due to the energy and foresight of Francis Meilland (1912–58) and his son Alain. It was Francis who first understood the importance of the American market, where plant patenting began in 1930. His US agents Conard-Pyle introduced Meilland's 'Golden State' to America in 1937. And the success of 'Mme. A. Meilland' should not overshadow two extremely important Floribundas of the period – 'Michèle Meilland' (1945) and 'Alain' (1948).

Meilland Logo

The vigor of 'Mme. A. Meilland' soon found its way into many more roses: 'Grand'mère Jenny' (1950) and 'Bettina' (1953) were two early seedlings that have endured. The 20 years that followed the introduction of 'Mme. A. Meilland' are dominated by its seedlings, so that almost every modern rose can claim it as an ancestor.

At the same time, the Meillands made a conscious effort to breed roses for the cut-flower trade: the success of 'Baccará' (1954) and its descendant **Sonia Meilland** (1974) fully justified this. Now they offer some 60 cultivars, including dual purpose (for the cut-flower trade and for the garden) roses like **Paris d'Yves Saint Laurent** (1994).

Hybrid Teas and Floribundas remain an important part of Meilland's work. The Floribunda **Marmalade Skies** and the Hybrid Tea **Philippe Noiret** both won All-America Rose Selection prizes in 2001. Recent successes include the Hybrid Tea style climber **Sorbet** (1993) and the Hybrid Teas **Paul Ricard** (1994), **Bolchoï** (1996), and **Puy du Fou** (1999).

The director of breeding since 1978, Jacques Mouchotte, says (with characteristic modesty) that he creates nothing, but just allows the genes that are already present to express themselves. Nevertheless, he has launched several new lines and initiatives, including the successful range of Romantica roses. These descend from **Yves Piaget** and can be seen as a French response to David Austin's English Roses. They are hardy, healthy, and vigorous shrubs or short climbers: they include **Abbaye de Cluny**, **Guy de Maupassant**, and **Johann Strauss**. Mouchotte has also been responsible for the remarkable success of the ironclad ground-cover roses known as the 'Meillandécor', or Meidiland series. Roses like **Alba Meillandécor** and **Rouge Meillandécor** are hardy, healthy, adaptable, and amazingly floriferous. Nor should the first generation of Meilland's landscaping roses be forgotten: **Bonica 82**, **La Sevillana**, and **Swany** are still bestsellers worldwide.

Meilland's rose-breeding station at Le Luc-en-Provence in southern France is backed up by five trial grounds and test stations in France, the US, and Germany. Every year Meilland makes 5–8,000 crosses on 100–120,000 flowers, and raises about 250,000 seedlings. It employs some 600 people in 34 acres (14 hectares) of glasshouses and 585 acres (240 hectares) of open-air production, and produces 12 million roses a year.

Sorbet at Meilland's nursery, Le Luc-en-Provence

MEMOIRE

MEMOIRE

syn. 'KORZURI', Ice Cream
Floribunda

ORIGIN **Kordes, Germany, 1992**
FLOWER SIZE **4.7in (12cm)**
SCENT **Strong and sweet**
FLOWERING **Repeats well**
HEIGHT/SPREAD **4.1ft (1.25m)/2.7ft (80cm)**
HARDINESS **Zone 6**
AWARDS **Belfast GM 1994**

This is one of the best of all modern roses, an improved Margaret Merril (if such a paragon were possible). Memoire is intermediate between the Hybrid Teas and the Floribundas: its beautiful white flowers are large and shapely, but they usually come in clusters. In cool weather they have a pink tint at the center; in hot climates there is a hint of cream instead. The flowers are full of neatly arranged petals, and open from elegant buds. They come on long stems, which makes them good for cutting. Exhibitors like their regular shape, too. The plant is strong, vigorous, and healthy, with shiny, dark green leaves, bronzy when young. The flowers spoil in rain, so Memoire does best in dry weather, but it is deservedly popular all over the world. The scent of its half open flowers is delicious.

M

'MEMORIAM'

Hybrid Tea

ORIGIN **Von Abrams, US, 1961**
PARENTAGE **('Blanche Mallerin' x 'Mme. A. Meilland') x ('Mme. A. Meilland' x 'Frau Karl Druschki')**
FLOWER SIZE **5.9in (15cm)**
SCENT **Strong and sweet**
FLOWERING **Repeats**
HEIGHT/SPREAD **2.7ft (80cm)/2ft (60cm)**
HARDINESS **Zone 6**
AWARDS **Portland GM 1960**

'Memoriam' is a classic exhibition rose, with huge flowers of perfect shape. The buds are long, and unroll their many petals slowly. Pink at first, they tend to fade to white as the flowers open, while keeping an exquisite pink tinge at the center. The flowers are borne singly on long stems, and have won many prizes over the years. They are also deliciously scented. 'Memoriam' is, however, one of those roses that fare best in hot, dry climates: those large flowers seem to dissolve in rain. It also grows much taller – as high as 4.9ft (1.5m). The plant is moderately vigorous, with big, dark, healthy leaves and large prickles.

'MENJA'

Hybrid Musk

ORIGIN **Petersen, Denmark, 1960**
FLOWER SIZE **0.8in (2cm)**
SCENT **Light and musky**
FLOWERING **Repeats well**
HEIGHT/SPREAD **6.6ft (2m)/6.6ft (2m)**
HARDINESS **Zone 5**

'Menja' is very popular in its native Scandinavia, and occasionally seen in Germany, but it is unknown and ungrown elsewhere. Its flowers are quite distinctive, because they are so tightly cupped as to appear bell-shaped, and never open out as other roses do. It is said to be a Hybrid Musk, but it is very different from those bred by Lambert, Pemberton, or Lens. The buds are pale crimson, opening to pink flowers (always darker on the back of the petals), and fade to white in hot weather. They do not drop their petals, which can be unsightly, but come in long, airy sprays – nicely spaced out – of 20–40 flowers. In autumn the clusters are much larger – great arching wands with more than 100 flowers. They keep their color better in the cool weather of autumn, too. The bush has healthy, light green leaves, short prickles, and tiny orange hips. Its autumn growths can be as much as 6.6ft (2m) long: it makes a good pillar rose in warm climates.

'MERMAID'

'MERMAID'

Bracteata Hybrid

ORIGIN **W. Paul, Britain, 1918**
PARENTAGE ***Rosa bracteata* x unknown**
FLOWER SIZE **3.9in (10cm)**
SCENT **Light**
FLOWERING **Continuous**
HEIGHT/SPREAD **16.4ft (5m)/13.1ft (4m)**
HARDINESS **Zone 6**

'Mermaid' was bred from crossing the evergreen *Rosa bracteata* with a yellow Tea rose. Its flowers are very beautiful: that beauty comes partly from the color and carriage of the soft yellow petals, but more from the handsome deep gold stamens, long and wispy, which keep their color and look good even after the petals have fallen. It flowers nonstop over a long period. The dark, glossy leaves are bright green, with olive green undersides, and evergreen in warm climates. The plant is slow to establish, and best grown on its own roots. It eventually builds up into a large plant, smothering everything else beneath it. It can be trained, but this must be done when the wood is young: old growths are brittle and will break off with the slightest careless handling. 'Mermaid' resents pruning: do nothing except to prevent it from going where it is not wanted.

'MERVEILLE DE LYON'

see 'BARONNE ADOLPHE DE ROTHSCHILD'

'MESSIRE DELBARD'

syn. 'GRANDESSA'
Modern Climber

ORIGIN **Delbard, France, 1976**
PARENTAGE **('Danse du Feu' x 'Guinée') x (['Ténor' x 'Fugue'] x ['Delbard's Orange Climber' x 'Gloire de Dijon'])**
FLOWER SIZE **4.3in (11cm)**
SCENT **Light and sweet**
FLOWERING **Repeats constantly**
HEIGHT/SPREAD **13.1ft (4m)/8.2ft (2.5m)**
HARDINESS **Zone 6**

Do not be put off by the complicated ancestry of 'Messire Delbard': it means that the parents were unnamed seedlings that Delbard considered unworthy of commercial introduction. The flowers of 'Messire Delbard' are bright, blood red and usually borne in clusters of 3–5 on long, strong stems. They would be more valuable if they had a rich red scent as well, but unfortunately they are almost scentless. They are, however, produced constantly until late autumn, after a fairly heavy first flowering. 'Messire Delbard' makes a vigorous, erect plant with very healthy, dark leaves. It is popular still in western Europe and a plant in full flower is a striking sight.

'MEMORIAM'

'MESSIRE DELBARD'

'MENJA' ▶

'Mevrouw Nathalie Nypels'

syn. 'Nathalie Nypels'
Polyantha

ORIGIN **Leenders, Netherlands, 1919**
PARENTAGE **'Orléans Rose' x ('Comtesse du Caÿla' x *Rosa foetida* 'Bicolor')**
FLOWER SIZE **2.4in (6cm)**
SCENT **Strong**
FLOWERING **Almost continuous**
HEIGHT/SPREAD **2ft (60cm)/2.5ft (75cm)**
HARDINESS **Zone 6**

'Mevrouw Nathalie Nypels' has remained a popular Polyantha ever since it was first introduced. Its great attributes are its neat, bushy habit and its almost perpetual flowering. The flowers are large for a Polyantha, short-petaled, semidouble, and lightly cupped. They are mid-pink at first, with a hint of salmon, then pale pink and eventually white. The flowers keep their color best in cool climates and autumn temperatures. They come in open, upright clusters of 3–15, well set off by healthy, dark, glossy leaves. The plant is low-growing and spreading, useful in massed plantings and as part of a mixed design. It starts to flower early in the season and continues off and on until early winter. Deadheading the spent flowers promotes further flowering. 'Mevrouw Nathalie Nypels' is among the easiest roses to propagate from cuttings.

'Mevrouw Nathalie Nypels'

M

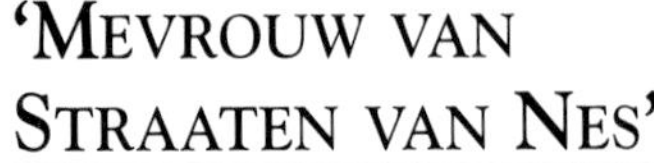

'Mevrouw van Straaten van Nes'

see 'Else Poulsen'

Michael Crawford

see Victor Borge

Michel Hidalgo

syn. 'MEItulandi', Hidalgo
Hybrid Tea

ORIGIN **Meilland, France, 1979**
PARENTAGE **seedling x 'Papa Meilland'**
FLOWER SIZE **5.5in (14cm)**
SCENT **Strong and sweet**
FLOWERING **Repeats**
HEIGHT/SPREAD **4.1ft (1.25m)/3.3ft (1m)**
HARDINESS **Zone 6**
AWARDS **Baden-Baden FA 1978**

Michel Hidalgo was chief trainer to the French national soccer team at the time this sumptuous red Hybrid Tea was introduced. It is one of the many richly scented, crimson roses that Meilland has produced over the years. The flowers are large, well-formed, and usually borne singly. They make excellent, long-lasting cut flowers and continue to open out in the vase. Sometimes there is a streak or two of white at the center of the flower. Michel Hidalgo shares a weakness common among red Hybrid Teas of hanging its head, which means it is not such a good garden plant. Nevertheless, it is a floriferous rose that repeats quickly and keeps on flowering right through until the first frost. Michel Hidalgo has a somewhat gaunt habit, with large dark leaves, bronzy at first, and a fair number of prickles.

Michel Hidalgo

Michelangelo

syn. 'MEItelov'
Hybrid Tea or Shrub Rose

ORIGIN **Meilland, France, 1997**
FLOWER SIZE **4.3in (11cm)**
SCENT **Very strong and sweet**
FLOWERING **Repeats well**
HEIGHT/SPREAD **4.9ft (1.5m)/2.5ft (75cm)**
HARDINESS **Zone 6**
AWARDS **Geneva GM 1997; Monza GM 1997; Bagatelle GM 1999; The Hague Fragrance Award 2001**

Michelangelo is one of Meilland's Romantica roses, bred to exhibit an "old-fashioned" shape and a strong scent. It is a handsome and very fragrant yellow Hybrid Tea, with attractively shaped flowers. They are a clear golden yellow at first, but fade to lemon or cream at the edges. They are cupped and fully double, containing a muddled mass of irregularly shaped petals – very pretty. They are borne singly or in clusters of up to seven. The plant thrives in a wide variety of climates, hot and cool. Its polished, dark green leaves are fairly disease free, but occasionally attract some blackspot. Michelangelo is a particularly fine cut flower: its scent will fill a room. It is named for the Renaissance artist and sculptor Michelangelo Buonarroti (1475–1564) and should not be confused with the striped McGredy rose called The Painter, which is known by the name of Michelangelo in New Zealand.

Michelangelo

'Michèle Meilland'

Floribunda

ORIGIN **Meilland, France, 1945**
PARENTAGE **'Joanna Hill' x 'Mme. A. Meilland'**
FLOWER SIZE **3.9in (10cm)**
SCENT **Light and sweet**
FLOWERING **Repeats well**
HEIGHT/SPREAD **3.3ft (1m)/2.7ft (80cm)**
HARDINESS **Zone 6**

The delicate beauty of 'Michèle Meilland' is an illusion – this is one of the toughest and most reliable of the older Hybrid Teas. It is also one of the most elegant: the flowers are a beautiful shape, both as slender, unfurling buds and as fully open blooms. However, it is their color which is most entrancing: pale pink, with hints of pale salmon or buff toward the center in cool weather. The plant has few prickles and pale green, healthy leaves. The flowers are very freely produced and at their best in autumn, when the colors are strongest. Definitely a rose which performs best in cooler climates. Meilland introduced a climbing sport in 1951 as **'Grimpant Michèle Meilland'**. It is similar in every way to the bush form, except that it grows to 11.5ft (3.5m). The flowers, too, are larger and may grow up to 4.7in (12cm). Its best flowering is the first of the year, but it also produces a useful number of flowers in subsequent flushes.

'Michèle Meilland'

Sport of 'Michèle Meilland'

'Grimpant Michèle Meilland'

Climbing Floribunda
ORIGIN **Meilland, France, 1951**
FLOWER SIZE **4.7in (12cm)**
FLOWERING **Repeats fairly well**
HEIGHT/SPREAD **11.5ft (3.5m)/6.6ft (2m)**

Michka

syn. 'MEIvaleir'
Modern Climber

ORIGIN **Meilland, France, 1998**
FLOWER SIZE **4.3in (11cm)**
SCENT **Light and fruity**
FLOWERING **Repeats well**
HEIGHT/SPREAD **6.6ft (2m)/4.1ft (1.25m)**
HARDINESS **Zone 6**

Meilland introduced Michka as a climbing rose but, since it rarely exceeds 6.6ft (2m) in height, it would be better

Michka

MIDAS TOUCH

treated as a Grandiflora or shrub rose – its habit of growth is entirely too stiff and bushy to be a climber. Its flowers are a wonderful rich yellow when they first open, with occasional pink streaks. It fades to cream as it ages, starting at the edges and, since the flowers have an attractive ruffle to their petals, their overall beauty is thereby enhanced. The flowers come in clusters of 3–7 and are very freely borne, but they spoil in rain so this is very much a fair weather rose. Michka has large leaves and extremely big prickles. It is a vigorous grower – and healthy.

MIDAS TOUCH

syn. 'JACTOU'

Hybrid Tea

ORIGIN **Christensen, US, 1992**
PARENTAGE **Brandy x Friesensonne**
FLOWER SIZE **3.5in (9cm)**
SCENT **Medium and fruity**
FLOWERING **Repeats well**
HEIGHT/SPREAD **4.9ft (1.5m)/3.3ft (1m)**
HARDINESS **Zone 6**
AWARDS **AARS 1994**

Midas Touch is a good, unfading, golden yellow Hybrid Tea. It is only lightly double, so the bud quickly opens out to show the golden stamens at the center of a cupped flower, but it has one of the strongest yellow colors of all roses. Both sides of the slightly wavy petals are the same pure yellow. The flowers are usually borne singly, but occasionally in small clusters, and stand up well to rain. The dark leaves are large and healthy. The bush is somewhat prickly, but it grows vigorously and repeats its flowering quickly and freely. Easy to grow in all climates, Midas Touch produces its best flowers in cool weather.

'MIKADO'

syn. 'KOH-SAI'

Hybrid Tea

ORIGIN **Suzuki, Japan, 1987**
PARENTAGE **'Duftwolke' x 'Kagayaki'**
FLOWER SIZE **4.3in (11cm)**
SCENT **Light and sweet**
FLOWERING **Repeats**
HEIGHT/SPREAD **3.3ft (1m)/2.7ft (80cm)**
HARDINESS **Zone 6**
AWARDS **AARS 1988**

You would expect a seedling of 'Duftwolke' to have a stronger scent, but 'Mikado' makes up for this deficiency

'MIKADO'

with health and beauty. The flowers (very full) are cherry red with a yellow flush. The red tints are strongest toward the tips of the petals. The yellow coloring is especially strong on the petal backs and gives the flowers an overall look of dark salmon pink or coral. The yellow tints fade away as the flowers age, leaving them pink and white. The flowers are usually produced singly, but sometimes in clusters of up to five, and not continuously but in a series of flushes. The plant has very handsome, dark green, glossy leaves, which are exceptionally healthy.

'MILDRED SCHEEL'

syn. 'DEEP SECRET'

Hybrid Tea

ORIGIN **Tantau, Germany, 1977**
FLOWER SIZE **3.9in (10cm)**
SCENT **Strong and sweet**
FLOWERING **Repeats well**
HEIGHT/SPREAD **2.7ft (80cm)/2.7ft (80cm)**
HARDINESS **Zone 5**
AWARDS **ADR 1978**

'Mildred Scheel' is a popular crimson Hybrid Tea, perhaps the best to have been introduced in the 1980s. Its flowers are borne singly and have the classic Hybrid Tea elegance in bud and as they open. When fully open, however, there are few roses with such a muddled and variable pattern of little petals – almost always charming, but invariably irregular in their disposition. The flowers are deep crimson and keep their color very well. They are very strongly scented (a "true" red rose scent), but somewhat rain sensitive. The leaves are dark, healthy, and glossy, and the plant grows vigorously, reaching over 3.3ft (1m) in a hot climate but producing better quality flowers in cool or shady

'MILDRED SCHEEL'

'MINNEHAHA' *(at Ninfa, Italy)*

positions. Mildred Scheel (1932–85) was the first wife of Walter Scheel, the German president.

'MILKMAID'

Hybrid Noisette

ORIGIN **Clark, Australia, 1925**
PARENTAGE **'Crépuscule' x unknown**
FLOWER SIZE **2.8in (7cm)**
SCENT **Strong, sweet, and musky**
FLOWERING **Once, early**
HEIGHT/SPREAD **16.4ft (5m)/13.1ft (4m)**
HARDINESS **Zone 8**

This climber is much admired in Australia for the sheer abundance of its first, main flowering in spring. The flowers come in medium-sized clusters (typically of 5–9 flowers). They change from fawn or cream to milk white,

'MILKMAID'

and tend to hang down in a disorderly but charming mass of petals. The plant is nearly evergreen, very vigorous, and has been known to grow as tall as 23ft (7m). In parts of South Australia, the rose grown as 'Milkmaid' is actually the Wichurana rambler 'Alberic Barbier'.

'MINNEHAHA'

Wichurana Rambler

ORIGIN **Walsh, US, 1905**
PARENTAGE **'Turner's Crimson Rambler' seedling**
FLOWER SIZE **1.6in (4cm)**
SCENT **Light and musky**
FLOWERING **Once only**
HEIGHT/SPREAD **13.1ft (4m)/6.6ft (2m)**
HARDINESS **Zone 5**

A great number of small-flowered Wichurana ramblers were introduced in the early years of the 20th century, most of them seedlings of 'Turner's Crimson Rambler'. The pink ones like 'Minnehaha' are indistinguishable today from 'Dorothy Perkins', and, even when newly introduced, few experts could tell them apart. The plant most often seen now as 'Minnehaha' has large, open clusters of small, neat, very double flowers. It blooms somewhat late in the season, and the color of its flowers fades slightly from rich pink to pale. Its leaves are small, dark, and shiny in the Wichurana way and it throws out new, slender growth, that can easily reach 13.1ft (4m) long in their first season.

MINNIE PEARL

MINNIE PEARL

syn. 'SAVAHOWDY'

Miniature Rose

ORIGIN **Saville, US, 1982**
PARENTAGE **('Little Darling' x 'Tiki') x 'Party Girl'**
FLOWER SIZE **1.8in (4.5cm)**
SCENT **Light and musky**
FLOWERING **Repeats constantly**
HEIGHT/SPREAD **2ft (60cm)/2ft (60cm)**
HARDINESS **Zone 6**

The elegant shape and long stems of Minnie Pearl have made it one of the most popular miniature roses in North America. The flowers are palest salmon pink, with slightly darker petal backs and a hint of yellow toward the center. They come singly or in clusters of up to five. Minnie Pearl has small, neat leaves, which are glossy and mid-green. The plant makes dense, bushy growth. It repeats well throughout the summer and autumn. Minnie Pearl (1912–96) was a country-western comedienne.

'MINUETTE'

see 'LAMINUETTE'

'MIRANDY'

Hybrid Tea

ORIGIN **Lammerts, US, 1945**
PARENTAGE **'Lady Sackville' x 'Charlotte Armstrong'**
FLOWER SIZE **5.5in (14cm)**
SCENT **Strong and sweet**
FLOWERING **Repeats**
HEIGHT/SPREAD **2.7ft (80cm)/1.6ft (50cm)**
HARDINESS **Zone 6**

'MIRANDY'

'Mirandy' has sumptuous, enormous Hybrid Tea flowers, perched on top of a scraggy bush. The flowers are very full, rather globular in bud, and open out quickly. They are garnet red at first, but tend to lose their brightness and turn to crimson and purple with age. They are also redder in hot weather and more purple in autumn or after a cool spring. The flowers are much larger and more substantial than the slow-growing bush suggests, which means that there is often a long wait for the second flowering. The soft, velvety petals tend to ball in cool climates, but produce flowers of outstanding beauty in warm, dry areas. They are almost always borne singly on long, strong, upright stems. The leaves are leathery and the bush is not vigorous, but it is easy to understand why it has remained so popular for so long when you find it covered in perfect flowers.

MIRATO

syn. 'TANOTAX', Chatsworth, Footloose

Shrub Rose

ORIGIN **Tantau, Germany, 1990**
FLOWER SIZE **2.8in (7cm)**
SCENT **Light**
FLOWERING **Almost continuous**
HEIGHT/SPREAD **3.3ft (1m)/3.3ft (1m)**
HARDINESS **Zone 5**
AWARDS **ADR 1993; ROTY 1995**

This is an excellent modern groundcover or shrub rose, equally useful in landscaping, mixed borders, or specimen plantings. It is one of those new shrubs bred from *Rosa wichurana*, and has the small, dark, glossy, and very healthy leaves that come with this ancestry. The flowers open out deep pink, round, and lightly double, and fade slightly as they age and blotch a little in rain. Sometimes the golden stamens are visible at the center of the flowers. They come in clusters of 3–15, first on the branch tips and then on every lateral growth, so that a bush in full flower is covered in color both at the top and down to ground level. The flowers shed their petals very cleanly when they are spent, and the plant flowers again rapidly, continuing until early winter. The leaves have a reddish tinge when young. The plant is very hardy and grows to about 6.6ft (2m) in all directions.

MIRATO

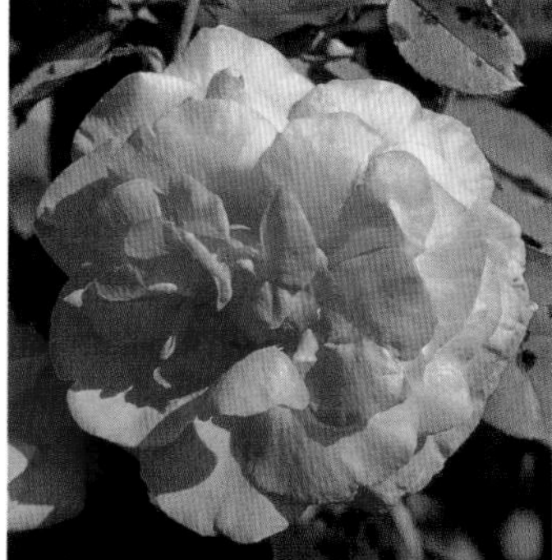
'MISCHIEF'

'MISCHIEF'

Hybrid Tea

ORIGIN **McGredy, Northern Ireland, 1961**
PARENTAGE **'Mme. A. Meilland' x 'Spartan'**
FLOWER SIZE **4.7in (11cm)**
SCENT **Strong and fruity**
FLOWERING **Repeats well**
HEIGHT/SPREAD **4.1ft (1.25m)/3.3ft (1m)**
HARDINESS **Zone 6**
AWARDS **NRS PIT 1961; Portland GM 1965**

The flowers of 'Mischief' open salmon pink and fade to pale pink, with darker petal backs – the buds are red. They have the classic, conical shape of traditional Hybrid Teas, and not too many petals, so that the flowers stand up very well to rain. They come singly and in clusters of up to four. 'Mischief' makes a vigorous plant, not too tall, which repeats its flowering with unusual speed, so that it appears to be never out of flower. It has mid-green leaves which are prone to blackspot and rust in areas where these diseases are a problem. Still, it remains an excellent rose.

'MISS ALL-AMERICAN BEAUTY'

see 'MARIA CALLAS'

'MISS EDITH CAVELL'

see 'ORLÉANS ROSE'

'MISS HARP'

see 'ANNELIESE ROTHENBERGER'

'MISS MARION MANIFOLD'

Hybrid Perpetual Climber

ORIGIN **Adamson, Australia, 1913**
FLOWER SIZE **3.9in (10cm)**
SCENT **Strong and sweet**
FLOWERING **Recurrent**
HEIGHT/SPREAD **13.1ft (4m)/9.8ft (3m)**
HARDINESS **Zone 6**

'Miss Marion Manifold' is one of those rich, glowing, crimson climbers that were developed from the old Hybrid

'MISS MARION MANIFOLD'

Perpetuals and selected for their vigour. The coloring does eventually fade to mid-pink in hot weather, and the petal backs are always slightly paler, but the flowers are intensely scented and borne in clusters of 1–4. The plant is nearly thornless and very hardy, but grows especially well, to about 13.1ft (4m), in warm climates. It has rather large leaves. It was raised by the gardener to the Manifold family at "Talindert," Camperdown, Victoria.

'MISTER LINCOLN'

Hybrid Tea

ORIGIN **Swim & Weeks, US, 1964**
PARENTAGE **'Chrysler Imperial' x 'Charles Mallerin'**
FLOWER SIZE **5.5in (14cm)**
SCENT **Strong and sweet**
FLOWERING **Repeats well**
HEIGHT/SPREAD **4.9ft (1.5m)/3.3ft (1m)**
HARDINESS **Zone 6**
AWARDS **AARS 1965**

'Mister Lincoln' was for many years the most popular crimson Hybrid Tea in the US. Like many successful roses, it is beautiful at every stage of its development. The buds are classic, elegant, and conical, and the large, thick petals unravel themselves slowly. Eventually they open out to show their darkest coloring toward the outside of the flower and a much brighter crimson around the stamens in the center. Sometimes it takes on a more purple shade as it fades. The long-stemmed flowers (almost always borne singly) are good for cutting and last well in water. The foliage is ordinary, except for being dark red when young. The plant is vigorous, upright, and inclined to

'MISTER LINCOLN'

MISTRESS QUICKLY

legginess in hot climates, where it benefits from discreet companion plantings. It is generally healthy, except for a susceptibility to blackspot. But its color and scent are stupendous.

MISTRESS QUICKLY

syn. 'AUSKY'

Shrub Rose

ORIGIN **Austin, Britain, 1995**
PARENTAGE **'Blush Noisette' × 'Martin Frobisher'**
FLOWER SIZE **2in (5cm)**
SCENT **Light**
FLOWERING **Repeats well**
HEIGHT/SPREAD **3.3ft (1m)/1.6ft (50cm)**
HARDINESS **Zone 5**

Mistress Quickly has a very interesting parentage: it is a cross between a Noisette rose from Charleston and a Hybrid Rugosa bred for hardiness in Ottawa. It has masses of small, bright pink flowers in long sprays. The flowers are neat, pretty rosettes, full of small petals, with splashes of dark pink on some of them, and paler backs. They come in clusters of 10–25. It is very hardy, but very heat resistant too, and is wonderful in areas with cold winters and hot summers. In cool climates it may stay as low as 1.6ft (50cm), but in hot ones it makes a very pretty pillar rose, 6.6ft (2m) high, with nearly continuous flowering. The leaves are small, gray green, glossy, and almost completely resistant to disease. Its flowers look good in mixed plantings, where they combine well with other plants.

'MLLE. CÉCILE BRUNNER'

see 'CÉCILE BRUNNER'

'MLLE. CLAIRE JACQUIER'

see 'CLAIRE JACQUIER'

'MME. A. MEILLAND'

syn. 'GIOIA', 'GLORIA DEI', 'PEACE'

Hybrid Tea

ORIGIN **Meilland, France, 1945**
PARENTAGE **'Joanna Hill' × ('Charles P. Kilham' × 'Margaret McGredy')**
FLOWER SIZE **5.5in (14cm)**
SCENT **Medium and sweet**
FLOWERING **Repeats very well**
HEIGHT/SPREAD **4.9ft (1.5m)/4.1ft (1.25m)**
HARDINESS **Zone 6**
AWARDS **Portland GM 1944; AARS 1946; ARS GM 1947; NRS GM 1947; Golden Rose of the Hague 1965; World's Favourite Rose 1976**

Everyone knows 'Mme. A. Meilland' – though it is called 'Gloria Dei' in Germany, 'Gioia' in Italy, and 'Peace' in English-speaking countries. It is simply the most famous rose in the world, and probably still the most widely grown. Its name commemorates the raiser's mother, who died young – as indeed did François Meilland himself. Its flowers are enormous: its vigor was so remarkable when it was first introduced that it ushered in a completely new standard for excellence in roses. The boom years of rose popularity in the 1950s and 1960s can single-handedly be attributed to 'Mme. A. Meilland'. The flowers are invariably large and beautiful at every stage of their development, from the elegant bud to the fully open bloom, though it is in fact immensely variable in cultivation. The color, for example, is basically pale yellow with a crimson edge, fading to cream and pink, but in practice the coloration differs from season to season and place to place. Its scent, too, is elusive. Many claim it is scentless; others describe its scent as strong, rich, sweet, and fruity. There is controversy, too, about its exact parentage. However, all are agreed on its vigor, the strength of its petals, the great size of its tough, dark leaves, the occasional large prickles, and its resistance to disease.

Being so widely grown, 'Mme. A. Meilland' has also sported many times, and all the sports are in their way as good as the original. First discovered in the Windy City, **'Chicago Peace'** is exactly the same as its parent in everything except its coloring, which is much brighter, deeper, and richer – the flowers are crimson and peach where the original is pink and yellow. Otherwise, its thick petals, attractive shape, and large, healthy leaves are all identical to those of its parent. The color of the flowers varies according to the weather and the season, and is best in cool climates – but it is an excellent rose, easy and rewarding, wherever it is grown.

By far the most striking sport of 'Mme. A. Meilland' is **'Kronenbourg'**, whose flowers are a dark, velvety red with pure yellow petal backs. The contrast is remarkable and, since the plant also possesses all the other good qualities of 'Mme. A. Meilland', ensured that 'Kronenbourg' became and remained a favorite all over the world. In due course, a climbing sport was also introduced as 'Climbing Kronenbourg'.

'MME. A. MEILLAND'

Sports of 'Mme. A. Meilland' (*syn.* 'Peace')

'CHICAGO PEACE'

ORIGIN **Johnston, US, 1962**
FLOWER SIZE **5.1in (13cm)**
FLOWERING **Recurrent**
HEIGHT/SPREAD **3.9ft (1.2m)/3.3ft (1m)**
HARDINESS **Zone 5**
AWARDS **Portland GM 1962**

'CLIMBING PEACE'

Climbing Hybrid Tea
ORIGIN **Kordes, Germany, 1951**
FLOWER SIZE **6.3in (16cm)**
FLOWERING **Repeats intermittently**
HEIGHT/SPREAD **16.4ft (5m)/8.2ft (2.5m)**

'KRONENBOURG'

syn. 'FLAMING PEACE'
ORIGIN **McGredy, Northern Ireland, 1966**
FLOWER SIZE **5.1in (13cm)**
FLOWERING **Recurrent**
HEIGHT/SPREAD **4.1ft (1.25m)/3.3ft (1m)**
HARDINESS **Zone 5**

'CHICAGO PEACE'

'CLIMBING PEACE'

'KRONENBOURG'

'MLLE. FRANZISKA KRÜGER'

Tea Rose

ORIGIN **Nabonnand, France, 1880**
PARENTAGE **'Catherine Mermet' × 'Général Schablikine'**
FLOWER SIZE **3.5in (9cm)**
SCENT **Fairly strong and tealike**
FLOWERING **Repeats constantly**
HEIGHT/SPREAD **4.9ft (1.5m)/4.1ft (1.25m)**
HARDINESS **Zone 6**

'Mlle. Franziska Krüger' is a very beautiful Tea rose, with all the strengths and weaknesses of its race. Its elegant buds open out flat into lightly cupped flowers, with a quartered shape and swirls of quilled petals. The color is variable, but usually very pale, silky pink with a hint of salmon and buff toward the center. The petal backs are darker, which means that a multitude of subtle tints, hues, and shades are reflected between the petals. The flowers are borne singly or in small clusters on slender stems that hang, making them better as garden plants than for cutting. The plant has dark leaves, rather narrow leaflets and flowers incessantly – for 12 months of the year in hot climates – but it is susceptible to mildew and occasionally to blackspot, and its flower buds ball in humid weather.

'MLLE. FRANZISKA KRÜGER'

'Mme. Abel Chatenay'

'Mme. Abel Chatenay'

Hybrid Tea

ORIGIN **Pernet-Ducher, France, 1895**
PARENTAGE **'Victor Verdier' x 'Dr. Grill'**
FLOWER SIZE **4.3in (11cm)**
SCENT **Strong and tealike**
FLOWERING **Repeats constantly**
HEIGHT/SPREAD **3.3ft (1m)/2.7ft (80cm)**
HARDINESS **Zone 7**

Few Hybrid Teas can claim to be over 100 years old and still as widely grown as 'Mme. Abel Chatenay'. It has been consistently popular over the years for its vigor and floriferousness – as well as the sheer loveliness of its flowers. These are a beautiful silky pink, with much deeper petal backs (dark carmine) and a darker shadow toward the center. They roll back their petals in such a way that the buds are especially elegant and the open flowers seem all the more substantial. They are borne singly and in clusters of up to five, almost without interruption, until the first frosts of winter; in hot areas 'Mme. Abel Chatenay' flowers year-round. The plant has small leaves, crimson when young, and is fairly healthy, especially in dry climates. Its scent is delicious. Mme. Abel Chatenay (1857–1928) was the wife of a distinguished French nurseryman and horticulturist who was secretary-general and vice-president of the National Horticultural Society of France.

'Mme. Alfred Carrière'

Noisette

ORIGIN **Schwartz, France, 1879**
FLOWER SIZE **3.9in (10cm)**
SCENT **Strong and sweet**
FLOWERING **Early, and almost continuous**
HEIGHT/SPREAD **16.4ft (5m)/6.6ft (2m)**
HARDINESS **Zone 7**

This famous Noisette rose is popular around the world, and will flower for 12 months of the year in mild climates. Elsewhere, it is one of the earliest of all roses to flower. Its long, elegant buds are delicate pink as they unscroll. The flowers of 'Mme. Alfred Carrière' are palest pink at first, especially in cool weather, though normally they pass quickly to brilliant white and remain on the plant for a long time. They are lightly cupped, with ruffled petals when fully opened out. They come on long, straight stems in loose clusters of 3–9 flowers, and are excellent as cut flowers. The plant has large, droopy, pale green leaves. It is vigorous, with a lot of slender, upright stems, and few thorns. It tolerates a certain degree of shade: in cool countries it is sometimes grown on a dark wall, and in hot ones it lights up a cool, shady place. It is healthy, except for a little mildew. It was named after an amateur rosarian in the Dauphiné.

'Mme. Alice Garnier'

'Mme. Alice Garnier'

Wichurana Rambler

ORIGIN **Fauque, France, 1906**
PARENTAGE ***Rosa wichurana* x 'Mme. Charles'**
FLOWER SIZE **1.8in (4.5cm)**
SCENT **Strong and fruity**
FLOWERING **Almost constant**
HEIGHT/SPREAD **9.8ft (3m)/6.6ft (2m)**
HARDINESS **Zone 6**

Such a pretty rose as 'Mme. Alice Garnier' should be in every garden. It is small and neat in all its characteristics, and lacks the intense vigor of most Wichurana ramblers. It is perfect for small gardens and flowers continuously. In fact, it was the first continually flowering Wichurana rambler to be introduced. Its flowers are fully double with neat, quilled petals that reflex as they expand. Their overall color is apricot, with deep terracotta at the center, and paler, pinker edges. The petal backs are darker, so the flowers appear to fade to a much softer shade of pink as they open out. They have a delicious scent of ripe peaches and come in clusters of 3–15. The plant has dark pink stems and small, neat, glossy, medium-dark green leaves. Its long, slender, often prostrate stems will eventually reach 9.8ft (3m). And it flowers right through to late autumn.

'Mme. Alfred Carrière'

'Mme. Caroline Testout'

Hybrid Tea

ORIGIN **Pernet-Ducher, France, 1890**
PARENTAGE **'Mme. de Tartras' x 'Lady Mary Fitzwilliam'**
FLOWER SIZE **4.7in (12cm)**
SCENT **Medium and sweet**
FLOWERING **Repeats well**
HEIGHT/SPREAD **3.3ft (1m)/2.7ft (80cm)**
HARDINESS **Zone 6**

This must once have been the most popular rose in the world. 'Mme. Caroline Testout' was planted in such quantities along the sidewalks of Portland, Oregon, that it became known as "America's Rose City." It is still one of the greatest garden roses, especially in its climbing form. The flowers are large and globular, with a mass of short, broad petals that roll back at their edges and endow the flower with an air of blowsy opulence. The flowers are bright silvery pink, slightly darker on the reverses, and stand up well to rain despite their size. They last a long time, are always well formed, and shatter neatly when they die. They come singly or in clusters of 3–5, and sometimes nod their heads a little. The plant has many large prickles and mid-green leaves with large, round leaflets. It is remarkably healthy, though the flower buds may ball in damp weather. It is a thrifty grower and very long-lived: some of Portland's bushes are now 100 years old.

Even more extensively grown is the climbing form, **'Climbing Mme. Caroline Testout'**, whose flowers are yet larger and very profusely carried in the first, main flowering, and then intermittently until autumn. The plant is rather lanky and prickly, but vigorous, and will quickly climb 16.4ft (5m) up a house, though it is then slow to make new basal growths. It is said that the original Mme. Caroline Testout was a milliner, who bought the name of the rose to promote her business.

'Mme. Caroline Testout'

'Climbing Mme. Caroline Testout'

Sport of 'Mme. Caroline Testout'

'Climbing Mme. Caroline Testout'

Climbing Hybrid Tea
ORIGIN **Chauvry, France, 1901**
FLOWER SIZE **5.5in (14cm)**
HEIGHT/SPREAD **16.4ft (5m)/8.2ft (2.5m)**

'Mme. Bérard'

Tea Rose

ORIGIN **Levet, France, 1870**
PARENTAGE **'Mme. Falcot' x 'Gloire de Dijon'**
FLOWER SIZE **4.3in (11cm)**
SCENT **Strong, sweet, and tealike**
FLOWERING **Repeats constantly**
HEIGHT/SPREAD **9.8ft (3m)/6.6ft (2m)**
HARDINESS **Zone 7**

'Mme. Bérard' was introduced as an improved 'Gloire de Dijon', which is still a fair judgement, though it is not as widely grown as its more famous parent. The buds are more pointed and the colors are richer, though, as with 'Gloire de Dijon', they are variable. The buds are rich pink, almost pale crimson, and this color, though fading with age, stays on the petal backs to create pretty contrasts with the deep, buff yellow of the open flowers. The flowers come singly and in twos and threes, on long, slender stems; sometimes they nod their heads, but it makes a good cutting rose, not least for its strong scent. When they

'Mme. Bérard'

M

open out, the flowers are full of quilled petals in a quartered form. The plant, though hardy for a Tea rose, does best in mild or warm climates. Its stems and young foliage are reddish or bronzy, with a few large prickles and large, glossy leaves.

'Mme. Butterfly'

see 'Ophelia'

'Mme. de la Roche-Lambert'

Moss Rose

ORIGIN **Robert, France, 1851**
FLOWER SIZE **2.8in (7cm)**
SCENT **Moderate and sweet**
FLOWERING **Remontant**
HEIGHT/SPREAD **4.1ft (1.25m)/3.3ft (1m)**
HARDINESS **Zone 5**

'Mme. de la Roche-Lambert' is the best of the crimson Damask Perpetual Moss roses. The flowers open out from small buds and quickly develop into a muddled mass of small petals in a lightly cupped arrangement. Later they reflex into a pompon rosette. They are rich cherry crimson with paler reverses. The buds and sepals are fringed with lots of very pretty light green, feathery moss on them. The flowers come on short stems in tight clusters of 3–5, with a leafy ruff of petals below the flower in the Portland manner. The plant has light green new leaves and round leaflets, together with heavily mossed stems, which later harden into a mass of prickles. The leaves, too, darken with age, until the bush as a whole seems rather recessive in color: it looks best with pale companion plantings. Although it tends to flop over under the weight of its flowers, the plant is not especially floriferous: the flowers come in a series of flushes rather than in one mighty display. Sometimes it suffers from mildew, especially on the mossy pedicels.

'Mme. Driout'

'Mme. Driout'

Climbing Tea Rose

ORIGIN **Thirat, France, 1902**
PARENTAGE **Sport of 'Reine Marie Henriette'**
FLOWER SIZE **4.3in (11cm)**
SCENT **Light and sweet**
FLOWERING **Early, and repeats well**
HEIGHT/SPREAD **9.8ft (3m)/6.6ft (2m)**
HARDINESS **Zone 6**

'Mme. Driout' is a striped sport of a crimson climbing Tea rose called 'Reine Marie Henriette', which was known as the red 'Gloire de Dijon' – very popular, early flowering, and floriferous. 'Mme. Driout' is predominantly pink, slightly darker on the petal backs, with irregular splashes and stripes of pale crimson or cerise. The flowers are large, shapely, and long-petaled, and hang down under their own weight. They come in clusters of 3–7 and reflex prettily as they open. The plant is somewhat thorny and has large, handsome leaves, but it is very susceptible to blackspot, mildew, and rust. It is surprisingly hardy, but only really suited to hot, dry climates, where its enormous buds can unfold without balling – the petals are thin. There is less variegation in autumn. Given much pampering, or good luck with the weather, it is a rose of supreme beauty and something of a rarity – a striped Tea rose. It also roots easily from cuttings.

'Mme. de la Roche-Lambert'

'Mme. Gabriel Luizet'

Hybrid Perpetual

ORIGIN **Liabaud, France, 1877**
PARENTAGE **'Jules Margottin' seedling**
FLOWER SIZE **4.3in (11cm)**
SCENT **Strong and sweet**
FLOWERING **Repeats**
HEIGHT/SPREAD **5.7ft (1.75m)/3.3ft (1m)**
HARDINESS **Zone 5**

This is a rose that turns up time and again in old abandoned settlements in hot climates: one of the great qualities of 'Mme. Gabriel Luizet' is its tolerance of heat and drought. The flowers are silvery pink, with rose pink on the backs of the petals, and a rounded shape, almost globular. Beautiful pink shadows form between the many petals. It is one of the earlier Hybrid Perpetuals to flower, and one of the most prolific, though it is a shy repeat flowerer. The flowers are borne singly or in rather tight clusters of up to five flowers. The plant has mid-green leaves and a sturdy, upright habit. Mildew can be a problem.

'Magna Charta', a sport of 'Mme. Gabriel Luizet', is a sumptuous, dark Hybrid Perpetual, which was a popular exhibition rose in its day. The full, plump buds open out to large, pale, cherry pink flowers with silvery pink backs to the petals. The flowers are borne singly, on short, stiff stems. The plant has long, pale green leaves, quite a lot of prickles, and a vigorous, upright habit of growth: in hot climates it will grow to 9.8ft (3m).

'Mme. Gabriel Luizet'

'Magna Charta'

It flowers very freely in midseason, but not reliably later in the year. It may suffer a little from mildew, and, in damp weather, the flowers may not open properly. Its name commemorates a document of King John of England (1215), of importance to English constitutional history.

Sport of 'Mme. Gabriel Luizet'

'Magna Charta'

ORIGIN **W. Paul, Britain, 1876**
SCENT **Light and sweet**
FLOWERING **Once abundantly, occasionally in autumn**
HEIGHT/SPREAD **4.9ft (1.5m)/3.3ft (1m)**

'Mme. Ernst Calvat'

see 'Mme. Isaac Pereire'

'Mme. Ferdinand Jamin'

see 'American Beauty'

'Mme. Georges Bruant'

Rugosa Hybrid

ORIGIN **Bruant, France, 1887**
PARENTAGE ***Rosa rugosa* × 'Sombreuil'**
FLOWER SIZE **3.1in (8cm)**
SCENT **Strong and sweet**
FLOWERING **Repeats well**
HEIGHT/SPREAD **6.6ft (2m)/4.9ft (1.5m)**
HARDINESS **Zone 5**

For many years, 'Mme. Georges Bruant' was the best of the white flowered Rugosas. It was also one of the first to be bred. Its flowers are pure white, and, though not much more than semi-double, are full of delicate, papery petals. These are fairly loosely held, so that the flower may appear somewhat formless, especially after rain, but there is always a ring of pale yellow stamens to give a focal point at the centre. The flowers come singly and, more often, in clusters of up to about seven, and look very attractive against the background of the bright green leaves. Sometimes the flowers are followed by hips. 'Mme. Georges Bruant' makes a tall bush, fairly healthy, but extremely prickly. It is a reliable repeat flowerer, producing its flowers well into autumn. Georges Bruant was a nurseryman from Poitiers and named this rose after his wife.

'Mme. Georges Bruant'

'MME. GRÉGOIRE STAECHELIN'

'MME. GRÉGOIRE STAECHELIN'

Modern Climber

ORIGIN **Dot, Spain, 1927**
PARENTAGE **'Frau Karl Druschki' x 'Château de Clos Vougeot'**
FLOWER SIZE **5.1in (13cm)**
SCENT **Strong and sweet**
FLOWERING **Once only, fairly early in season**
HEIGHT/SPREAD **13.1ft (4m)/8.2ft (2.5m)**
HARDINESS **Zone 6**

'Mme. Grégoire Staechelin' is very popular – and rightly so – all over the world. It is one of the most spectacular early-flowering climbers in cool climates and one of the most reliable everywhere. The flowers open from pendulous crimson buds, long and elegant like a Hybrid Tea's. As the flowers expand, they develop a distinct ruffle to their petals that shows off their unique combination of pink shades – flesh pink, with paler edges and darker petal backs. They come singly or in small clusters (rarely of more than four), which hang down in such a way that you can look straight into the heart of the flower and wonder at its long, wavy petals and myriad shades of pink. They are most profusely carried and noticeably early in the season, except in subtropical areas. Later come large, orange pink, pear-shaped hips. The leaves are large, glossy, and healthy. 'Mme. Grégoire Staechelin' is a blowsy beauty, but a very vigorous and reliable performer.

'MME. HARDY'

Damask Rose

ORIGIN **Hardy, France, 1832**
FLOWER SIZE **2.8in (7cm)**
SCENT **Moderate and sweet**
FLOWERING **Once only**
HEIGHT/SPREAD **6.6ft (2m)/4.9ft (1.5m)**
HARDINESS **Zone 5**

An iconic rose, 'Mme. Hardy' sums up all that is most beautiful and desirable in old roses. The form of the flowers is exquisite, and their scent (though light) is delicious. Although the purest of all white roses when fully open, there is a hint of pink in the bud. The outermost petals reflex slightly to surround an almost perfect circle of short, ruffled petals, quartered around a characteristic green eye. The flowers come in clusters of 3–5, occasionally singly, and may be damaged by rain. The leafy sepals are very distinctive. 'Mme. Hardy' is fairly vigorous and bushy, with lots of fresh green leaves, generally healthy except for an occasional brush with blackspot. The stems are moderately prickly. The rose was named after Félicité, wife of the introducer, Alexandre Hardy, director of the Jardin du Luxembourg in Paris.

'MME. HARDY'

'MME. JOSEPH SCHWARTZ'

see 'DUCHESSE DE BRABANT'

'MME. ISAAC PEREIRE'

Bourbon Rose

ORIGIN **Garçon, France, 1881**
FLOWER SIZE **3.5in (9cm)**
SCENT **Very strong and sweet**
FLOWERING **Repeats in flushes**
HEIGHT/SPREAD **8.2ft (2.5m)/6.6ft (2m)**
HARDINESS **Zone 6**

'Mme. Isaac Pereire' represents all the strengths and the weaknesses of the late 19th-century shrub roses. It is capable of producing some of the most opulent flowers, enriched by one of the most sumptuous scents of all roses. It is also a scraggy, thorny plant, a martyr to blackspot, and most inconsistent in the quality of its flowers. Even the color of 'Mme. Isaac Pereire' is controversial. At best, the flowers are rich, pale crimson, fading to lilac pink or silver at the edges: at worst, they are what the English breeder Jack Harkness described as a "strident pink [which] fights a losing battle against the inroads of magenta." "Raspberry," "cerise rose," "bright fuchsia," and "purplish rose madder" are other descriptions. The flowers are substantial and weighty. The first bloom is often disappointing. Sometimes the entire crop of flowers is deformed by a form of proliferation in which the stamens metamorphose into green carpels. More often, the flowers are short on petals and leave a hole at the center as they slowly reflex into giant pompon whorls. In autumn, the center is full of uniformly dark pink petals, beautifully arranged so as to create a quartered flower, and neatly rolled back at the tips. The flowers emerge from small, stubby buds and are borne singly or in clusters of up to five. The leaves are small, and few in number: the vigor of the plant seems quite unaffected by these shortcomings or by defoliation by blackspot. The bush throws out long, gawky stems, which flower at the tips but are then best tied down so that they break into flower all along their length next year. They also blend very well in a mixed border with white, blue, purple, and silvery colors.

'Mme. Ernst Calvat' is a sport of 'Mme. Isaac Pereire', and is similar in everything except its color. The flowers are soft pink, with darker petal backs, which give some pretty pink shadings at the center. The outer petals are nearly white.

Sport of 'Mme. Isaac Pereire'

'MME. ERNST CALVAT'

ORIGIN **Schwartz, France, 1888**

'MME. ISAAC PEREIRE'

'MME. ERNST CALVAT'

'MME. JULES BOUCHÉ'

'MME. JULES BOUCHÉ'

Hybrid Tea

ORIGIN **Croibier, France, 1911**
PARENTAGE **'Pharisäer' x seedling**
FLOWER SIZE **4.7in (12cm)**
SCENT **Medium and tealike**
FLOWERING **Repeats**
HEIGHT/SPREAD **4.9ft (1.5m)/3.3ft (1m)**
HARDINESS **Zone 6**

Few Hybrid Tea roses have remained popular for so long as 'Mme. Jules Bouché': its pale beauty is as captivating now as when it was first introduced nearly 100 years ago. The flowers open from high-pointed buds and are white with a hint of buff or yellow at the center. They have a lot of long petals, which reflex elegantly at the edges, and long, purple stems – good for cutting. The plant is somewhat prone to mildew, but grows vigorously. A climbing form, 'Climbing Mme. Jules Bouché', has even larger flowers, but does not bloom as repeatedly as the bush form.

'MME. JULES GRAVEREAUX'

Climbing Tea Rose

ORIGIN **Soupert & Notting, Luxembourg, 1901**
PARENTAGE **'Rêve d'Or' x 'Viscountess Folkestone'**
FLOWER SIZE **3.9in (10cm)**
SCENT **Strong and tealike**
FLOWERING **Repeats well**
HEIGHT/SPREAD **9.8ft (3m)/6.6ft (2m)**
HARDINESS **Zone 7**

It is hardier than most Tea climbers, so 'Mme. Jules Gravereaux' offers a chance to grow Tea roses where they might

'MME. JULES GRAVEREAUX'

otherwise not survive. The flowers are large and very full, with petals that are buff or pale apricot, but noticeably darker toward the center and paler at the edges. The petal backs are pinker, and darker. The combination of colors and shades is typical of the best Tea roses. The flowers develop from long, elegant buds and come both singly and in clusters (of up to seven). 'Mme. Jules Gravereaux' makes a vigorous, lanky plant with large prickles and medium-sized leaves. It grows vigorously and repeats constantly, especially in hot climates where it will flower year-round. Elsewhere, it can also be pruned back to about 3.3ft (1m) and grown as a vigorous bush rose. Mme Jules Gravereaux was the wife of the Parisian businessman who commissioned the famous rose garden at L'Haÿ-les-Roses.

'Mme. Knorr'

Portland

ORIGIN **Verdier, France, 1855**
FLOWER SIZE **3.9in (10cm)**
SCENT **Strong and sweet**
FLOWERING **Repeats**
HEIGHT/SPREAD **4.1ft (1.25m)/3.3ft (1m)**
HARDINESS **Zone 5**

The Portland roses are valued because they have all the characteristics of the old-fashioned, early 19th-century roses, but flower more than once. 'Mme. Knorr' has large, strongly scented flowers, full of petals in a somewhat muddled rosette shape. The petals are a good, rich pink, with silvery pink backs; when the flowers open out flat there is a pretty contrast where some of the petals are curled or twisted over. The flowers come singly and in fairly tight clusters of up to three or four. 'Mme. Knorr' makes a sturdy, upright plant, with a lot of prickles on its thick stems, but a slender overall habit of growth. Its leaves are mid-green, large, and lush. It is a reliable repeat flowerer, sending out a new flush of flowers every six weeks or so. Its great hardiness makes it especially useful in areas where the winters are too cold for modern roses like the English Roses.

'Mme. L. Dieudonné'

'Mme. L. Dieudonné'

Hybrid Tea

ORIGIN **Meilland, France, 1949**
PARENTAGE **('Mme. Joseph Perraud' × 'Brasier') × ('Charles P. Kilham' × 'Capucine Chambard')**
FLOWER SIZE **4.7in (12cm)**
SCENT **Medium and fruity**
FLOWERING **Repeats well**
HEIGHT/SPREAD **4.1ft (1.25m)/3.3ft (1m)**
HARDINESS **Zone 5**

'Mme. L. Dieudonné' is a good example of a Pernetiana rose – one of the race of red and yellow roses that resulted from early 20th-century efforts to bring the bright yellow colors of *Rosa foetida* into our garden roses. In fact, many people would say that 'Mme. L. Dieudonné' is the best of them all. It is a very handsome bicolor, with bright red on the upper sides of the petals, bright yellow on the undersides, and orange tinges where the colors seem to run into each other. As the flowers age, the yellow fades, and the red becomes more crimson, but it remains a striking shade. The flowers come singly and in clusters of up to three, and are well set off by handsome, dark leaves and bronzy new growths. Mildew may be a problem in damp climates, but 'Mme. L. Dieudonné' flourishes in hot, dry parts of the world.

'Mme. Laurette Messimy'

'Mme. Laurette Messimy'

China Rose

ORIGIN **Guillot fils, France, 1887**
PARENTAGE **('Rival de Paestum' × 'Mme. Falcot') × 'Mme. Falcot'**
FLOWER SIZE **2.8in (7cm)**
SCENT **Medium and tealike**
FLOWERING **Repeats constantly**
HEIGHT/SPREAD **4.1ft (1.25m)/3.3ft (1m)**
HARDINESS **Zone 7**

Most Tea and China roses darken as they age, but 'Mme. Laurette Messimy' fades from salmon pink to rose pink. The flowers are a complex mixture of colors at first – pale coral, pink, apricot, yellow, and cream, giving rise to beautiful shades and shadows across the whole flower. They open from long, elegant buds, and have attractively reflexed petals. By the time they have opened completely, they are semidouble, lightly cupped, and pink with a white patch at the center. They come singly or in small clusters (rarely of more than four flowers) and flower repeatedly, so that in hot climates there is scarcely a week when the bush does not have at least one flower on it. 'Mme. Laurette Messimy' has dark leaves, slender stems, a few large prickles, and a bushy habit of growth. It is fairly healthy, especially in hot, dry climates, where it is a most dependable performer.

'Mme. Lauriol de Barny'

Bourbon Rose

ORIGIN **Trouillard, France, 1868**
FLOWER SIZE **4.3in (11cm)**
SCENT **Strong and sweet**
FLOWERING **Once only**
HEIGHT/SPREAD **6.6ft (2m)/6.6ft (2m)**
HARDINESS **Zone 5**

No one knows the parents of 'Mme. Lauriol de Barny', but it is probably a hybrid between a Bourbon rose and a once-flowering Damask rose. It is a vigorous, lanky grower, whose long, slender, supple stems are best pegged down or tied into a trellis, whereupon they will break abundantly into flower at every node. If trained as a climber, it will reach 9.8ft (3m). The flowers are large, rich pink, and full of neatly folded petals arranged in a quartered shape. The petals are broad but short, which means that the flowers are unusually flat when they open out. They come in clusters of 3–7, giving a succession of flowers and creating an effect of abundance that lasts for weeks on end. Few roses can match its loveliness. Alas, 'Mme. Lauriol de Barny' flowers only once a year.

'Mme. Legras de St Germain'

Alba Rose

ORIGIN **France, c.1846**
FLOWER SIZE **3.5in (9cm)**
SCENT **Strong and sweet**
FLOWERING **Once only**
HEIGHT/SPREAD **8.2ft (2.5m)/4.9ft (1.5m)**
HARDINESS **Zone 5**

Ancient, thornless, and mysterious, 'Mme. Legras de St. Germain' fits easily into no category. It is best thought of as an Alba hybrid. The pale, gray green leaves, the white flowers, and the sweet scent are Alba attributes. The flower opens from a slender bud (note the long, leafy sepals) to reveal a mass of creamy-white petals spiraling around a button eye. Later it reflexes into a pompon, leaving a hole at the center. The flowers come in loose clusters of 3–9 and look nice against the neat, soft leaves. The plant is tall, hardy, healthy, and vigorous, and will grow to 16.4ft (5m) if trained as a climber. Its supple stems and lack of thorns make it easy to train.

'Mme. Knorr'

'Mme. Lauriol de Barny'

'Mme. Legras de St Germain'

'Mme. Lombard'

'Mme. Louis Laperrière'

'Mme. Plantier'

'Mme. Lombard'

Tea Rose

ORIGIN **Lacharme, France, 1878**
PARENTAGE **'Mme. de Tartas' seedling**
FLOWER SIZE **3.9in (10cm)**
SCENT **Medium and tealike**
FLOWERING **Continuous**
HEIGHT/SPREAD **4.1ft (1.25m)/3.3ft (1m)**
HARDINESS **Zone 7**

Few roses bloom so continuously as 'Mme. Lombard'. In warm climates it will flower for 12 months of the year. Its long, pointed crimson buds spiral open into elegant flowers, whose complex mixture of pink, apricot, orange, and yellow is enhanced by a silky sheen. The yellow shades fade and the pink hues intensify as the flowers open out completely, until the outer petals are pale magenta while the inner ones are still peach colored or salmon. The colors are darker and redder in autumn. The flowers come singly or in small clusters (of up to four) on slender, nodding stems, and last well if cut. 'Mme. Lombard' has large, dark green, healthy leaves and a lot of large prickles. It is naturally vigorous, but its eventual size depends upon growing conditions. In hot climates it will eventually reach 6.6ft (2m) if fed and watered, but it is often seen in cool climates as a thin bush no more than 2.5ft (75cm) high. 'Mme. Lombard' will also survive for many years on poor soil, with no watering, and complete neglect. It requires little pruning and roots easily from cuttings.

M

'Mme. Louis Laperrière'

Hybrid Tea

ORIGIN **Laperrière, France, 1951**
PARENTAGE **'Crimson Glory' seedling**
FLOWER SIZE **3.9in (10cm)**
SCENT **Very strong and sweet**
FLOWERING **Repeats**
HEIGHT/SPREAD **2.7ft (80cm)/2.7ft (80cm)**
HARDINESS **Zone 6**

In the years after World War II, there was a race among rose breeders to create the Hybrid Tea that would take over from the 1930s 'Crimson Glory' as everyone's favorite fragrant crimson rose. The main competitor to the English-raised 'Ena Harkness' and 'Josephine Bruce' came from France, where both 'Charles Mallerin' and 'Mme. Louis Laperrière' were introduced in 1951. 'Mme. Louis Laperrière' is a wonderful rose by any standards. The flowers are not large, but they are full of dark crimson petals, which keep their color very well and are very freely produced. The plant does not appear to be a strong grower, but the speed with which it reflowers is evidence of its true vigor. It flowers early in the season and makes an excellent bedding rose. The bush has small, mid-green leaves, which are healthy in dry climates but may suffer from blackspot in wet weather.

'Mme. Louis Lévêque'

Moss Rose

ORIGIN **Lévêque, France, 1898**
FLOWER SIZE **3.9in (10cm)**
SCENT **Strong and sweet**
FLOWERING **Remontant**
HEIGHT/SPREAD **4.9ft (1.5m)/3.3ft (1m)**
HARDINESS **Zone 5**

Many would say that 'Mme. Louis Lévêque' is the best of all the repeat flowering Moss roses. The flowers are certainly the largest, and it is a reliable repeat flowerer, as well as having a delicious, strong scent. The flowers are rose pink, with slightly paler undersides to the petals, which are often visible because the globular flowers are full of ruffled little petals, roughly arranged in a quartered shape. They keep their color well and come both singly and in clusters of up to four. They are not the mossiest of roses, but lightly covered with green moss, especially on the buds and sepals. The plant is vigorous, upright, fairly healthy, and covered in long, lush, mid-green leaves. The flowers may spoil in rain, so 'Mme. Louis Lévêque' does best in dry weather and, being very hardy, is useful in hot summers and cold winters.

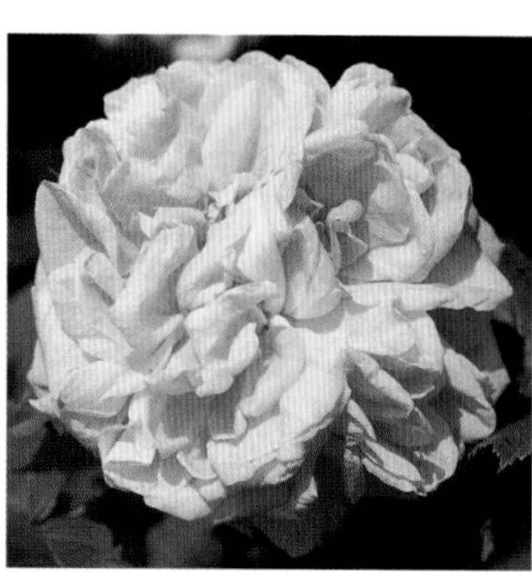

'Mme. Louis Lévêque'

'Mme. Marie Curie'

see 'Québec'

'Mme. Pierre Oger'

see 'Reine Victoria'

'Mme. Plantier'

Alba-Noisette Hybrid

ORIGIN **Plantier, France, 1835**
FLOWER SIZE **2.8in (7cm)**
SCENT **Light, musky, and green**
FLOWERING **Once only**
HEIGHT/SPREAD **13.1ft (4m)/8.2ft (2.5m)**
HARDINESS **Zone 4**

'Mme. Plantier' combines the grace and profusion of the Noisette roses with the hardiness and beauty of the Albas. It is a vigorous plant, sometimes grown as a loose, freestanding shrub, but more suitable for training around a pole or tripod as a pillar rose. It is most remarkable for its hardiness and its

'Mme. Pierre S. du Pont'

syn. 'Mrs. Pierre S. du Pont'

Hybrid Tea

ORIGIN **Mallerin, France, 1929**
PARENTAGE **('Ophelia' × 'Rayon d'Or') × ('Ophelia' × ['Constance' × 'Souvenir de Claudius Pernet'])**
FLOWER SIZE **3.9in (10cm)**
SCENT **Strong and fruity**
FLOWERING **Repeats well**
HEIGHT/SPREAD **3.3ft (1m)/3.3ft (1m)**
HARDINESS **Zone 6**

The flowers of 'Mme. Pierre S. du Pont' open from red or orange buds, but are pure bright yellow at first, fading only slightly to mid-yellow. The petal backs are always a richer, darker yellow. The flowers are elegant in bud and as they open out, but pleasantly disorganized when fully expanded, because they are only lightly double and the petals are loosely held. The flowers are usually borne singly but occasionally in clusters of up to about five on fairly strong stems. They are well set off by dark, glossy leaves.

The sport, **'Climbing Mme. Pierre S. du Pont'**, is an even better plant, flowering very early and abundantly, and repeating all through the summer and into autumn. It is one of the most floriferous of all Climbing Hybrid Teas and has kept its popularity against competition for many years. It is sensational in the gardens of Bagatelle in Paris. Pierre S. du Pont (1870–1954) was an American chemicals millionaire: he and his wife created the gardens at Longwood in Pennsylvania.

'Mme. Pierre S. du Pont'

'Climbing Mme. Pierre S. du Pont'

Sport of 'Mme. Pierre S. du Pont'

'Climbing Mme. Pierre S. du Pont'

Climbing Hybrid Tea
ORIGIN **Buisman, Netherlands, 1937**
FLOWER SIZE **4.3in (11cm)**
HEIGHT/SPREAD **16.4ft (5m)/9.8ft (3m)**

adaptability to different climates – hardy in St. Petersburg, but used as a rootstock in 19th-century Florida. The flowers are very beautiful, pale pink at first (but quickly turning pure white), and fully double, sometimes with a button eye. They are borne in clusters of 5–20 flowers on a vigorous, bushy, thornless shrub with small, pale green leaves. If 'Mme. Plantier' flowered more than once, it would be the world's favorite rose.

'Mme. Sancy de Parabère'

Boursault

ORIGIN **Bonnet, France, 1874**
FLOWER SIZE **4.3in (11cm)**
SCENT **Light and clovelike**
FLOWERING **Once, early in season**
HEIGHT/SPREAD **13.1ft (4m)/9.8ft (3m)**
HARDINESS **Zone 4**

The Boursault roses are all thornless, very hardy, and very early flowering. 'Mme. Sancy de Parabère' is the best pink Boursault rose and widely offered by nurseries throughout the world, though it is not as popular as it should be. Its flowers have a distinctive shape, like some peonies and camellias, with a circle of flat guard petals splayed out around the outside and a rounded ruffle of smaller petals at the center. They are a bright rose pink and generously borne in small clusters (of 3–5 flowers). Their petals are thin and soft, which makes them susceptible to wind and rain damage. That said, a perfectly shaped flower is extremely beautiful and a plant in full bloom is very effective from a distance. The leaves are small and the smooth stems are crimson on the sunny side. 'Mme. Sancy de Parabère' grows to about 13.1ft (4m).

'Mme. Zöetmans'

'Mme. Zöetmans'

Damask Rose

ORIGIN **Marest, France, 1830**
FLOWER SIZE **3.1in (8cm)**
SCENT **Strong and sweet**
FLOWERING **Once only**
HEIGHT/SPREAD **4.1ft (1.25m)/4.9ft (1.5m)**
HARDINESS **Zone 5**

The beauty of the Damask roses is perfectly revealed in 'Mme. Zöetmans'. It is a rose without flaw. The flowers are palest pink at first – especially in cool climates – but fade quickly to white, and full of quilled petals laid in a swirling rosette around a distinct button eye. They are among the first of the old roses to flower, and come both singly and in clusters of up to five – usually three. The flowers tend to hang down a little, which is an attractive habit, against a background of pale green leaves. 'Mme. Zöetmans' is a lax grower, with slender, bristly stems and masses of fresh and healthy leaves. It is fairly vigorous but tends to spread sideways rather than upward.

'Mme. Sancy de Parabère'

'Mojave'

Modern Art

see Prince de Monaco

'Mojave'

Hybrid Tea

ORIGIN **Swim, US, 1954**
PARENTAGE **'Charlotte Armstrong' × 'Signora Piero Puricelli'**
FLOWER SIZE **5.5in (14cm)**
SCENT **Medium and fruity**
FLOWERING **Repeats**
HEIGHT/SPREAD **4.9ft (1.5m)/3.3ft (1m)**
HARDINESS **Zone 6**
AWARDS **Bagatelle GM 1953; Geneva GM 1953; AARS GM 1954**

Its color gave 'Mojave' its name – orange, with tinges of pink and crimson, like the rocks of the Mojave Desert. In hot weather it eventually fades to pale buff pink, but not before the flower has opened completely and revealed its large crimson filaments. When well grown, the flowers can be as much as 5.9in (15cm) across, which made it a popular rose for cutting and exhibition in the 1950s and 1960s. The flowers are usually borne singly, but occasionally in twos and threes. Its main fault as a garden rose is its weakness for mildew and blackspot, but these are not a problem in those hot, dry climates where 'Mojave' is still a popular, rewarding rose to grow.

'Moje Hammarberg'

Rugosa Hybrid

ORIGIN **Hammarberg, Sweden, 1931**
FLOWER SIZE **3.1in (8cm)**
SCENT **Strong and sweet**
FLOWERING **Repeats well**
HEIGHT/SPREAD **3.3ft (1m)/4.1ft (1.25m)**
HARDINESS **Zone 4**

There are many Rugosa hybrids with handsome magenta flowers. The features that distinguish 'Moje Hammarberg' are its early flowering (one of the earliest of all shrub roses) and lax habit of growth. It usually extends in width more than height, and has even been recommended as a groundcover rose, though landscape planting would be more appropriate. The flowers are loosely double, with pale yellow stamens and a delicious, sweet scent. They come in clusters of 3–5 and are succeeded by large, vermilion, tomato-shaped hips. The plant has very

'Moje Hammarberg'

prickly stems and bright green, healthy, pleated, wrinkled leaves. It is extremely hardy and repeats constantly, so that the later flowers associate with the first hips.

Molineux

syn. 'AUSmol'

Shrub Rose

ORIGIN **Austin, Britain, 1994**
PARENTAGE **'Golden Showers' seedling × seedling**
FLOWER SIZE **3.1in (8cm)**
SCENT **Strong and fruity**
FLOWERING **Repeats well**
HEIGHT/SPREAD **2.5ft (75cm)/2.5ft (75cm)**
HARDINESS **Zone 6**
AWARDS **Edland FA 1996; RNRS PIT 1996; Glasgow GM 1999**

Although it may grow as much as 6.6ft (2m) high in a hot climate, Molineux is entirely much more compact – and freer flowering – than David Austin's earlier yellow roses like Graham Thomas. The flowers are golden yellow with rich apricot markings, an occasional dark pink patch at the center, and a lot of petals. They open into lightly cupped rosettes and fade to lemon yellow, with creamy edges: the color is always quite variable. They come in clusters of 3–9. The plant is fairly healthy: it has middling to dark green leaves and a few prickles. It does very well in both cool climates and hot, and will produce flowers right through the hottest summer months.

Molineux

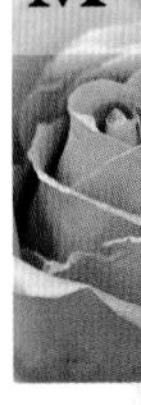

MON CHÉRI

MONIKA

'MONSIEUR TILLIER'

MON CHÉRI

syn. 'AROCHER'
Hybrid Tea

ORIGIN **Christensen, US, 1981**
PARENTAGE **('White Satin' x 'Bewitched') x Double Delight**
FLOWER SIZE **4.7in (12cm)**
SCENT **Light and fruity**
FLOWERING **Repeats well**
HEIGHT/SPREAD **3.9ft (1.2m)/3.3ft (1m)**
HARDINESS **Zone 6**
AWARDS **AARS 1982**

Mon Chéri is most remarkable for its coloring. The outer petals are a good bright crimson, but the inner ones open pale buff yellow. As the flower matures, the inner petals fade to cream for a while, but the crimson area expands toward the center, so that the inner petals then turn to deep pink and crimson. It is a most unusual sequence among roses, and not to everyone's taste. The flowers are broad, flat, and opulent: they come, usually singly, on long stems. The plant has a lot of prickles and fairly ordinary (but healthy) leaves. It is rather a gawky grower but does especially well in hot climates.

MON JARDIN ET MA MAISON

syn. 'MEICHAVRIN'
Modern Climber

ORIGIN **Meilland, France, 1998**
PARENTAGE **(Margaret Merril x Bonica 82) x 'Pascali'**
FLOWER SIZE **3.9in (10cm)**
SCENT **Light and sweet**
FLOWERING **Repeats**
HEIGHT/SPREAD **6.6ft (2m)/3.3ft (1m)**
HARDINESS **Zone 6**

Mon Jardin et Ma Maison – named after a French lifestyle magazine – is a splendid shrub rose or short climber. Its fat, round buds elongate as they open and reveal a large, many-petaled, cream colored flower, with a cupped and quartered shape. The petals are white at the edges of the flower but produce a rich buff suffusion at the center, reminiscent of old Tea roses. The color fades to palest lemon pink, but is never lost completely and gives a depth to the flower as a whole at every stage of its development. The flowers come singly or in clusters of up to about six, and are well set off by strong, healthy, dark green leaves.

MONIKA

syn. 'TANAKNOM', Monica
Hybrid Tea

ORIGIN **Tantau, Germany, 1985**
FLOWER SIZE **4.3in (11cm)**
SCENT **Light**
FLOWERING **Repeats well**
HEIGHT/SPREAD **5.7ft (1.75m)/3.3ft (1m)**
HARDINESS **Zone 6**

Monika is a very striking red and yellow Hybrid Tea. The flowers are at their most stunning when they are in the process of unfurling from their long, slim buds. Then there is a remarkable contrast between the orange vermilion color of the petals and the yellow petal backs. The flower is duller when it opens out flat and the yellow contrast is lost from sight. They are borne, usually singly, on very long, upright stems, making Monika a good rose for cutting. The plant has good, healthy, dark, glossy leaves and makes a tall, vigorous, upright bush – as much as 6.6ft (2m) high in a hot climate, but is usually pruned to less than 3.3ft (1m) in its native Germany.

'MONSIEUR TILLIER'

Tea Rose

ORIGIN **Bernaix, France, 1891**
FLOWER SIZE **2.8in (7cm)**
SCENT **Strong and tealike**
FLOWERING **Repeats constantly**
HEIGHT/SPREAD **6.6ft (2m)/3.3ft (1m)**
HARDINESS **Zone 7**

Several different roses are sold and grown as 'Monsieur Tillier', including the Tea roses properly known as 'Archiduc Joseph' and 'Duchesse de Brabant'. Some authorities claim that the confusion exists principally in England, but the truth is that all three roses are almost unknown there, because the English climate is too cool. In the US and Australia, however, it pays to see what you are getting before you buy 'Monsieur Tillier'. The flowers are dark coral pink at first, but darken and lose their yellow tints as they age, so that the outer petals end up almost crimson while the inner ones still have a suggestion of orange. They are full of quill-shaped petals at first but hold their petals more loosely as they open out and reflex. Their scent of tea is delicious. The plant is tall and vigorous, with slender, prickly, crimson stems and small, green brown leaves. It grows vigorously to at least 6.6ft (2m), but is usually cut back to about half that height. In hot climates it flowers year-round.

'MONTANA'

syn. 'ROYAL OCCASION'
Floribunda

ORIGIN **Tantau, Germany, 1974**
PARENTAGE **'Walzertraum' x 'Europeana'**
FLOWER SIZE **2.8in (7cm)**
SCENT **Light and sweet**
FLOWERING **Repeats well**
HEIGHT/SPREAD **4.1ft (1.25m)/2.5ft (75cm)**
HARDINESS **Zone 5**
AWARDS **ADR 1974**

This rose has nothing to do with the American state, but is named after the German fashion designer Claude Montana. It is a very fine, vigorous, healthy scarlet Floribunda. The flowers open out nicely almost flat, and informally shaped. They are a very cheerful bright, unfading color and borne in large, eye-catching clusters (somewhat crowded) of 5–25. It is not a rose of any great subtlety, but is good in public parks where color is required, and it remains deservedly popular in Germany. The plant has large, thick, medium-dark leaves and bronzy new growths. It stands up well to rain, and will grow well in poor soils. It is both floriferous and a good repeater.

MON JARDIN ET MA MAISON

'MONTANA'

'MONTEZUMA'

MOONBEAM

'MOONLIGHT'

'MONTEZUMA'

Grandiflora

ORIGIN **Swim, US, 1955**
PARENTAGE **'Fandango' x 'Floradora'**
FLOWER SIZE **4.3in (11cm)**
SCENT **Light and fruity**
FLOWERING **Repeats**
HEIGHT/SPREAD **4.1ft (1.25m)/3.3ft (1m)**
HARDINESS **Zone 6**
AWARDS **Geneva GM 1955; NRS GM 1956; Portland GM 1957**

The picture above shows 'Montezuma' at its best – a startling contrast between coral pink and orange yellow. However, the yellow tints fade quickly from the opening bud, so that by the time the flower is fully open, the color has changed to a uniform salmon pink. The flowers are elegantly shaped, long-stemmed, well held, and usually borne singly, making them popular for cutting and exhibition. Some flowers are borne in clusters of up to six – it is classified not as a Hybrid Tea but as a Grandiflora. The plant is vigorous, prickly, and bushy. It is a good repeater and a quick grower, best in hot, dry climates where mildew is not a problem.

MOON SHADOW

syn. 'JACLAF'

Hybrid Tea

ORIGIN **Warriner, US, 1996**
PARENTAGE **Blue Ribbon seedling**
FLOWER SIZE **4.7in (12cm)**
SCENT **Strong and sweet**
FLOWERING **Repeats**
HEIGHT/SPREAD **4.9ft (1.5m)/3.3ft (1m)**
HARDINESS **Zone 6**

California rose breeders have introduced dozens of mauve Hybrid Teas in recent years: Moon Shadow is a good example, with an intense, piercingly sweet scent. The flowers are large, with thick petals which are gray mauve, with some somewhat more lilac pink patches toward the center. They are pretty both as buds and as fully open flowers. They usually come in clusters of 3–5, but sometimes also singly, on long, stout stems that are good for cutting. Moon Shadow has glossy, dark green leaves and a scattering of prickles. It makes a vigorous plant that performs well in hot climates: mildew may be a problem elsewhere.

MOONBEAM

syn. 'AUSBEAM'

Shrub Rose

ORIGIN **Austin, Britain, 1983**
FLOWER SIZE **3.1in (8cm)**
SCENT **Strong**
FLOWERING **Repeats well**
HEIGHT/SPREAD **3.9ft (1.2m)/4.9ft (1.5m)**
HARDINESS **Zone 6**

The delicacy of David Austin's lightly-petaled roses makes a rare contrast to the more commonly introduced full-flowered ones. Moonbeam has large semisingle, mother-of-pearl flowers – pale apricot in bud – that fade to a ghostly white after the golden stamens turn brown. They come in long-stemmed clusters of 5–7 and are very freely produced. The plant also repeats well, so that it is rarely without flowers, especially in warm climates where it is most appreciated. Moonbeam is upright, but bushy and robust, with pale green, disease-resistant foliage and some prickles. Its pale coloring is very effective in shaded corners of the garden.

'MOONLIGHT'

Hybrid Musk

ORIGIN **Pemberton, Britain, 1913**
PARENTAGE **'Trier' x 'Sulphurea'**
FLOWER SIZE **2in (5cm)**
SCENT **Medium, musky, and sweet**
FLOWERING **Repeats well**
HEIGHT/SPREAD **5.7ft (1.75m)/6.6ft (2m)**
HARDINESS **Zone 7**

'Moonlight' is a handsome, vigorous shrub or pillar rose, which is often confused with 'Trier'. Its buds are cream colored and open to translucent, creamy white flowers that have more petals than 'Trier' and are larger, too. The flowers are cupped, with a small brush of light gold stamens at the center. They come in spacious clusters of 5–25, but in autumn the clusters are much larger (up to 60 flowers), and the flowers are sometimes followed by round hips. The plant makes an open, healthy bush, with glossy, dark green leaves which are red or maroon when young – as are the stems and flower stalks. It has quite a lot of large prickles and flowers in a series of flushes, with occasional blooms in between. It is a great favorite among gardeners as a specimen shrub or in mixed plantings.

'MOONSPRITE'

Floribunda

ORIGIN **Swim, US, 1956**
PARENTAGE **'Sutter's Gold' x 'Ondine'**
FLOWER SIZE **2.8in (7cm)**
SCENT **Strong, sweet, and fruity**
FLOWERING **Repeats**
HEIGHT/SPREAD **3.3ft (1m)/2.7ft (80cm)**
HARDINESS **Zone 6**
AWARDS **Baden-Baden GM 1955; Rome GM 1956**

The flowers of 'Moonsprite' are perfect rosettes, full of petals in the old-fashioned style made popular by David Austin in the 1980s. The many-petaled form was not at all fashionable when 'Moonsprite' came out in 1956, but it achieved a degree of popularity almost immediately and has remained fairly widely available in cultivation ever since. The flowers open bright yellow, but fade quickly to lemon, cream, and white: the typical 'Moonsprite' flower has a brilliant yellow center and a white edge, all in a pompon shape. They fade quickest in hot weather. The flowers usually come in loose clusters of 3–7. 'Moonsprite' has small, dark, healthy leaves and is fairly vigorous, but it is not a tall grower, so is useful where space or height is limited. It flowers in a series of flushes every six weeks or so. It is, however, a rose that performs much better in hot, dry climates and seems to lack vigor in cool, damp conditions.

MOON SHADOW

'MOONSPRITE'

MOONSTONE

syn. 'WEKCRYLAND', Cadillac de Ville
Hybrid Tea

ORIGIN **Carruth, US, 1998**
PARENTAGE Crystalline x Lynn Anderson
FLOWER SIZE **5.5in (14cm)**
SCENT **Medium, sweet, and fruity**
FLOWERING **Repeats**
HEIGHT/SPREAD **4.9ft (1.5m)/3.3ft (1m)**
HARDINESS **Zone 6**

The color of Moonstone is variable. The American Rose Society describes it as white, but pink and white would be more accurate – the petals are white on the reverse and pink inside, and usually have dark pink edges too. The flowers change to pearly pink as they age, but only in very hot weather do they fade completely to white. They open from fat buds and have a lot of long petals. Moonstone is a prize winning exhibition rose and is excellent as a cut-flower rose: the flowers come usually singly, sometimes in small clusters, on long stout stems. They are most abundantly borne in a series of flushes. Moonstone has large, healthy, matte leaves and an upright habit of growth. Although unusually hardy, it does best in dry weather: its long petals and full flowers suffer in rain.

MOONSTONE

'MORDEN AMORETTE'

Shrub Rose

ORIGIN **Marshall, Canada, 1977**
PARENTAGE **('Sondermeldung' x ['Donald Prior' x *Rosa arkansana*]) x ('Fire King' x ['J.W. Fargo' x 'Assiniboine'])**
FLOWER SIZE **2.8in (7cm)**
SCENT **Little or none**
FLOWERING **Repeats**
HEIGHT/SPREAD **3.3ft (1m)/3.3ft (1m)**
HARDINESS **Zone 4**

The Parkland series of roses, bred to withstand the Canadian winters, are excellent plants in all climates. They also vary in their performance: 'Morden Amorette', for example, grows no more than 1.6ft (50cm) in Manitoba, but reaches 9.8ft (3m) in southern California. The flowers are the same everywhere – bright pink, with a hint of purple, and a white patch at the center. The petals have white undersides and tend to fade to cream at the edges

RALPH MOORE

THE KING OF MINIATURE ROSES, MOORE HAS BRED A DIVERSE RANGE INCLUDING MINIATURE HYBRID TEAS, MOSSES, AND CLIMBERS

RALPH MOORE has been the leading raiser and popularizer of miniature roses for over 50 years. His rose-breeding goes back still further. Born in 1907, Moore raised his first rose ('Lois Crouse') in 1927, started his own rose nursery in 1937, and, now in his 90s, is still issuing new miniature roses today.

RALPH MOORE

Most of the Ralph Moore roses listed in this encyclopedia are miniatures, but they are immensely diverse and variable. By crossing his original hybrids with Hybrid Teas, he introduced tiny, elegant, perfect miniature Hybrid Teas. Likewise, his crosses with Floribundas produced miniatures with large clusters of flowers in the Floribunda style, but all scaled down to miniature stature. The influential 'Little Buckaroo' (1956) and the attractive 'Rose Hills Red' (1978) both have 'Floradora' (Tantau, 1944) in their immediate ancestry.

Climbing miniatures began with 'Candy Cane' (1958). Blue roses were represented by 'Mr. Bluebird' (1960) and yellows by 'Yellow Doll' (1962), followed by the incomparable 'Rise 'n' Shine' (1977). Striped roses reached their finest development in 'Stars 'n' Stripes' (1975), the result of working with the old striped Hybrid Perpetual rose 'Ferdinand Pichard' (Tanne, 1921). By crosses with 19th-century Moss roses, Moore raised miniature Moss roses, both the simple Moss 'Fairy Moss' (1969) and crested hybrids that came from 'Cristata' and produced 'Crested Jewel' (1971), quickly followed by the first yellow-flowered miniature Moss, 'Goldmoss' (1972).

Meanwhile, Ralph Moore and his Sequoia Nursery in California continue to bring out miniatures of supreme quality, such as 'Orange Parfait' (1998). But it is worth remembering that not all Moore's roses are miniatures – witness his stunning vermilion Floribunda 'Playtime' (1989), the Rugosa Hybrid 'Linda Campbell' (1990), and the patio rose 'Golden Gardens' (1988).

'GOLDEN GARDENS' AT BARROSA, SOUTH AUSTRALIA

M

'MORDEN AMORETTE'

– an attractive combination of colors. They are borne singly and in clusters of up to seven. 'Morden Amorette' has small leaves which are healthy in dry climates but sometimes suffer from mildew and blackspot in Canada. It is a reliable reflowerer, if the first crop of flowers is deadheaded. In Canada the plant is neat and compact in its habit of growth, but in hot climates it makes a loose, open shrub.

'MORDEN BLUSH'

Shrub Rose

ORIGIN **Collicutt & Marshall, Canada, 1988**
PARENTAGE **('Prairie Princess' × 'Morden Amorette') × ([(*Rosa arkansana* × 'Assiniboine') × 'White Bouquet'] × 'Prairie Princess')**
FLOWER SIZE **2.4in (6cm)**
SCENT **Light and sweet**
FLOWERING **Repeats well**
HEIGHT/SPREAD **3.3ft (1m)/3.3ft (1m)**
HARDINESS **Zone 4**

The flowers of 'Morden Blush' are a beautiful pale pink, with hints of dark pearl pink at the center and creamy white outer petals – pinker in cool weather. It has a delicacy and charm which belie its origin: all the Morden series of Parkland roses were bred to withstand the bitter winters of central Canada. 'Morden Blush' is the most floriferous of them all, and the most popular. The flowers are fully double, with rows and rows of neat, frilly petals opening from buds that resemble small Hybrid Teas. They keep their shape for a long time, as much as two weeks, and the pale open flowers contrast attractively with the deep pink buds: the flowers are borne both singly and in clusters of up to about six. 'Morden Blush' has dark, glossy leaves that are healthy in dry weather, but susceptible to blackspot in damp conditions. It also tolerates great heat, growing to 6.6ft (2m) in the southern States, but remaining short, compact, and no more than 2.5ft (75cm) in Canada. It flowers continuously and profusely through to the first frost of winter.

'MORDEN CENTENNIAL'

Shrub Rose

ORIGIN **Marshall, Canada, 1980**
PARENTAGE **'Prairie Princess' × ('White Bouquet' × ['J.W. Fargo' × 'Assiniboine'])**
FLOWER SIZE **3.1in (8cm)**
SCENT **Light and sweet**
FLOWERING **Repeats**
HEIGHT/SPREAD **5.7ft (1.75m)/4.1ft (1.25m)**
HARDINESS **Zone 4**

The Morden roses come from Agriculture Canada's breeding station at Morden, Manitoba. All are excellent, and 'Morden Centennial' is one of the best. Its flowers are pale crimson at first, but fade to bright mid-pink as they open out attractively double. They come singly or in clusters of up to 15 (typically 3–7), and are followed by long-lasting red hips. The first flowering is very abundant, but the plant always has a few flowers until its second big flush arrives in autumn. Deadheading improves the quantity of its second coming. The plant has dark, shiny leaves that are healthy (except for a little blackspot), and a vigorous habit of growth. Pruning makes 'Morden Centennial' bushier and may increase flower production. The town of Morden was founded in 1880.

'MORDEN FIREGLOW'

Shrub Rose

ORIGIN **Collicutt & Marshall, Canada, 1989**
PARENTAGE **seedling × 'Morden Cardinette'**
FLOWER SIZE **2.4in (6cm)**
SCENT **Light and sweet**
FLOWERING **Once profusely, then intermittently**
HEIGHT/SPREAD **3.3ft (1m)/2.7ft (80cm)**
HARDINESS **Zone 4**

'MORDEN FIREGLOW'

This Canadian rose is popular for its great hardiness and its unusual color. No other Explorer or Parkland rose has the same glowing red flowers as 'Morden Fireglow'. Close examination reveals that the petals are bright orange red, with scarlet reverses. The flowers are loosely double and cupped. They come singly or in clusters of up to five and are followed by large, round hips. The bush has medium-dark leaves, which may attract a little mildew and blackspot in damp climates, but is otherwise healthy. Its first flowering is very profuse, but its flower production thereafter is only intermittent. The flowers ball in wet weather. In the coldest of climates, however, 'Morden Fireglow' is useful because it is a good substitute for Floribundas that will not survive a harsh winter.

'MORDEN RUBY'

Shrub Rose

ORIGIN **Marshall, Canada, 1977**
PARENTAGE **'Fire King' × (*Rosa arkansana* × 'J.W. Fargo' × 'Assiniboine')**
FLOWER SIZE **2.8in (7cm)**
SCENT **Light and musky**
FLOWERING **Repeats**
HEIGHT/SPREAD **4.1ft (1.25m)/4.1ft (1.25m)**
HARDINESS **Zone 4**

'Morden Ruby' is a sister seedling to 'Adelaide Hoodless', and equally popular. Its flowers are dark pink or pale crimson and fully double. However, it is actually a sport from a single-flowered seedling that was never introduced, and may sometimes revert back to this single form. Careful scrutiny reveals that the petals have lots of crimson dots against a deep pink background. The flowers come in clusters of 5–10 on long, slender

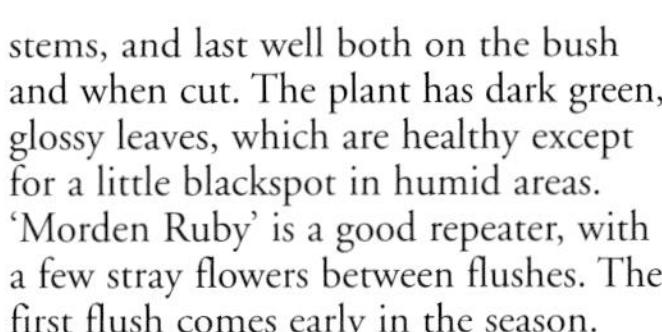

stems, and last well both on the bush and when cut. The plant has dark green, glossy leaves, which are healthy except for a little blackspot in humid areas. 'Morden Ruby' is a good repeater, with a few stray flowers between flushes. The first flush comes early in the season.

'MORLETII'

see 'INERMIS MORLETII'

'MORNING JEWEL'

Modern Climber

ORIGIN **Cocker, Britain, 1968**
PARENTAGE **'New Dawn' × 'Red Dandy'**
FLOWER SIZE **3.1in (8cm)**
SCENT **Medium and sweet**
FLOWERING **Repeats well**
HEIGHT/SPREAD **13.1ft (4m)/8.2ft (2.5m)**
HARDINESS **Zone 5**
AWARDS **ADR 1975**

This Scottish rose has always been popular in Germany, where it won a coveted ADR award. The flowers are semidouble, with large, strong, weatherproof petals that are often somewhat lopsided – which gives them a special charm. They open out to a lightly cupped shape. The flowers are a beautiful rich, dark, luminous pink, paler on their undersides and white toward the center. They come on long stems either singly or in clusters of up to seven, and are useful for cutting. 'Morning Jewel' is rarely without flowers after its first fine blooming, and the leaves are dark, glossy, and healthy.

'MORSDAG'

see 'DICK KOSTER'

'MORNING JEWEL'

'MORDEN BLUSH'

'MORDEN RUBY'

ROSA MOSCHATA

Rosa moschata

Wild Rose

FLOWER SIZE **1.6in (4cm)**
SCENT **Strong and musky**
FLOWERING **Once only, late in season**
HEIGHT/SPREAD **11.5ft (3.5m)/8.2ft (2.5m)**
HARDINESS **Zone 7**

Rosa moschata is similar to the wild Musk rose *Rosa brunonii*. It is fairly variable in its characteristics, and probably has a dash of the China rose in its makeup. All forms have pure white flowers, which are borne in loose corymbs and do not start into flower until very late in the season. They have handsome, wavy, pale yellow stamens and a conspicuously long style at the center. *Rosa moschata* flowers so late, and for such a long period, that it is sometimes thought – mistakenly – to be repeat flowering. Occasionally the flowers are semi-double. Their scent is delicious, especially in the evening. *Rosa moschata* is vigorous but fairly short: it can be grown as a 6.6ft (2m) shrub rather than a climber. The plant has few thorns. The leaves are long, gray green, and very healthy.

'Moth'

syn. 'The Moth'

Shrub Rose

ORIGIN **Austin, Britain, 1983**
FLOWER SIZE **4.7in (12cm)**
SCENT **Light and fresh**
FLOWERING **Remontant**
HEIGHT/SPREAD **3.9ft (1.2m)/3.3ft (1m)**
HARDINESS **Zone 6**

'Moth'

The qualities of this very floriferous David Austin rose have never been fully appreciated in its native England. In hot, dry climates it is one of the most beautiful of roses, and immensely floriferous in its first flowering. The buds are long, elegant, and buff or apricot colored. They open out quickly into huge, lightly cupped, loosely semidouble flowers, which are an intriguing color – pale velvety pink with a hint of gray or suede, fading quickly to ashy white. The delicate petals are set off by yellow stamens and red stigmas. The flowers come in small clusters, typically of about five. The plant is prickly, stout-stemmed, and a little ungainly, but vigorous. It is a little slow to repeat, but flowers much more frequently in hot climates.

'Mother's Day'

see 'Dick Koster'

Mottisfont Abbey

The best collection of old roses in the United Kingdom is at this National Trust garden in Hampshire, England

Mottisfont Abbey's rose garden may not be a match for the big collections on the European mainland, but it is charmingly laid out, well-labeled, and maintained to a very high standard by its owner, the National Trust. Mottisfont Abbey itself is a large, brick-built country house in majestic parkland: a tributary of the River Test surges out of the ground nearby. The rose garden was begun in 1972 to display the collection brought together over many years by the English rose expert Graham Stuart Thomas. It is best seen in June, when nearly 1,000 different cultivars are in flower in the two, adjacent, walled gardens.

Almost all the roses at Mottisfont were bred before 1900, and there is an emphasis upon Gallicas, Damasks, Moss roses, and Bourbons. On the walls are climbers and ramblers of every kind – Noisettes, Wichuranas, Teas, and Multifloras. The design of the garden is formal, with straight paths, box-edged beds, and geometric lawns. At the center of the larger walled garden is a low fountain in a pool whose sides are draped with 'Raubritter'. Over one of the principal paths is an arch of 'Adélaïde d'Orléans', while another focuses on a Lutyens-style seat behind which 'Constance Spry' has been trained against an old brick wall. Within the smaller garden is a circular arcade planted with 'Debutante' and 'Bleu Magenta'.

'Raubritter'

Roses of the same class are often planted together. There is, for example, an area devoted to China roses, another to early Rugosa hybrids, and a third to Tea roses. This helps visitors to study, compare, and learn.

Mixed borders at Mottisfont

What makes the garden so exciting, however, are the English-style companion plantings, with herbaceous plants weaving around the rose bushes. Chosen for their harmony under the soft English light, the combinations are a model of their kind: yellow *Digitalis grandiflora* around the purple shrub rose 'Zigeunerknabe' for example, and drifts of pink or purple *Linaria grandiflora* almost naturalized among the Gallicas.

MOUNT HOOD

MOUNTAIN SNOW

MOUNT HOOD

syn. 'MACMOUHOO', Foster's Wellington Cup

Grandiflora

ORIGIN McGredy, US, 1988
PARENTAGE Sexy Rexy x Pot o' Gold
FLOWER SIZE 3.9in (10cm)
SCENT Light and sweet
FLOWERING Repeats
HEIGHT/SPREAD 4.9ft (1.5m)/3.3ft (1m)
HARDINESS Zone 6
AWARDS NZ GM 1992; AARS 1996

This seedling of Sexy Rexy is similar to its parents: certainly, it has the same small, dark, wavy leaves that Sexy Rexy has and they are a very good foil for the flowers. Mount Hood has large white flowers in clusters of 3–8. They are pure white except for a hint of pink (in cool weather) or yellow (in hot) at the center. The petals have a distinct and attractive wave to their outline as the flowers open out, but they are beautiful in both shape and color at every stage of their growth. The plant is healthy, tall, and vigorous, sending up a constant stream of flowers. In New Zealand the plant is known as Foster's Wellington Cup, but it is now much more widely grown in the warmer parts of the US.

'MOUNT SHASTA'

Grandiflora

ORIGIN Swim & Weeks, US, 1963
PARENTAGE 'Queen Elizabeth' x 'Blanche Mallerin'
FLOWER SIZE 5.1in (13cm)
SCENT Medium and sweet
FLOWERING Repeats
HEIGHT/SPREAD 6.6ft (2m)/3.3ft (1m)
HARDINESS Zone 6

'Mount Shasta' is a very vigorous Grandiflora rose with all the characteristics of an unusually strong and tall Hybrid Tea. Its buds are very long and elegant, and the flowers retain that elegance as they open out, cupped at first and then reflexed to show their crimson stamens. The flowers have just a hint of pink as they open, but soon turn to pure, brilliant white. They are almost always borne singly, on very long, upright stems, making them very popular for cutting. The plant has large, dark leaves and a very upright habit.

MOUNTAIN SNOW

syn. 'AUSSNOW'

Wichurana Hybrid

ORIGIN Austin, Britain, 1985
FLOWER SIZE 2in (5cm)
SCENT Medium and sweet
FLOWERING Once only
HEIGHT/SPREAD 13.1ft (4m)/8.2ft (2.5m)
HARDINESS Zone 6

David Austin is best known for his roses in the old-fashioned style, which he calls English Roses. However, from time to time he releases a rose that is quite different from his main line of rose breeding, but which he considers an unusual and worthy addition to our gardens. Mountain Snow is an example. Little is known of its origins, but this is a rambler of Wichurana descent. Its flowers are semidouble and bright white, with a good circle of dark yellow stamens at the center. They come in clusters of 10–30 and are well set off by the dark, glossy leaves. Mountain Snow is particularly good in dry climates. Elsewhere it holds its petals, dies badly, and blotches to crimson in rain.

MOUNTBATTEN

syn. 'HARMANTELLE'

Floribunda

ORIGIN Harkness, Britain, 1982
PARENTAGE 'Peer Gynt' x (['Anne Cocker' x 'Arthur Bell'] x 'Southampton')
FLOWER SIZE 3.1in (8cm)
SCENT Strong, sweet, and fruity
FLOWERING Repeats
HEIGHT/SPREAD 4.9ft (1.5m)/3.3ft (1m)
HARDINESS Zone 6
AWARDS Belfast GM 1982; Orléans GM 1982; ROTY 1982; Courtrai GM 1986; Golden Rose of the Hague 1986

Mountbatten leaped to fame in Britain when it formed part of Princess Diana's wedding bouquet in 1981. It was named after Louis, Earl Mountbatten, a great-uncle of Prince Charles, who had been murdered in 1979. Its flowers are a rich, glowing yellow, with a pink tinge to the petal tips at first, later fading to lemon yellow. The flowers are cup-shaped, with outer petals that reflex, though all the petals have a ruffled movement to them, coming from a nick at their tips. They are borne in long clusters of 5–11. The plant is vigorous and upright, with fairly healthy, tough leaves. It is tall and needs pruning back to encourage more flowers.

'MOUNT SHASTA'

'MOUSSELINE'

see 'ALFRED DE DALMAS'

'MOUSSEUX DU JAPON'

syn. 'MUSCOSA JAPONICA'

Moss Rose

FLOWER SIZE 2in (5cm)
SCENT Light
FLOWERING Once only
HEIGHT/SPREAD 4.9ft (1.5m)/4.9ft (1.5m)
HARDINESS Zone 5

'Mousseux du Japon' is a curiosity, of little intrinsic beauty but universally acknowledged as the mossiest of all Moss roses. Its origins are unknown, except that it has no connection with Japan, but dates more probably from mid-19th-century France. The moss is bright, reptilian green, and does not cover just the sepals and receptacle, but also extends right down the stems and up into some of the leaf stalks. In fact, the moss is intrusive and detracts from the flowers, which are small and somewhat constricted by the sepals. They have difficulty opening out, and, when they do so, are fairly shapeless. Their color is variable, but usually deep pink, fading to pale pink, with much paler petal backs: the petals are small and thin. The plant has small, dark, crinkled leaves and is no stranger to mildew.

MOUNTBATTEN

'MOUSSEUX DU JAPON'

ROSA MOYESII

ROSA MOYESII

Wild Rose

FLOWER SIZE **2in (5cm)**
SCENT **Light and sweet**
FLOWERING **Once only**
HEIGHT/SPREAD **13.1ft (4m)/13.1ft (4m)**
HARDINESS **Zone 5**

Rosa moyesii became very popular in Western gardens immediately after it was introduced from China in the early 20th century: it is still one of the most widely grown shrubby species. Its flowers are any shade between rose pink, blood red, and dark crimson, but all have deep yellow anthers, loaded with pale pollen around a disk at the center. *Rosa moyesii* is however grown mainly for its hips, which are large (2–2.4in/5–6cm long), bright orange vermilion, and flagon-shaped. They festoon the branches from late summer onward. The plant makes a large shrub, and its branches arch out and over to cover a large area – very impressive in a large-scale woodland garden but not suitable for small-scale gardens. It has long leaves with a lot of little leaflets, and large, ferocious prickles. It is a variable species, and some of the named forms are worth seeking out, including 'Geranium' and 'Highdownensis'.

'MOZART'

Hybrid Musk

ORIGIN **Lambert, Germany, 1937**
PARENTAGE **'Robin Hood' × 'Rote Pharisäer'**
FLOWER SIZE **1.2in (3cm)**
SCENT **Strong, sweet, and musky**
FLOWERING **Almost continuous**
HEIGHT/SPREAD **3.9ft (1.2m)/6.6ft (2m)**
HARDINESS **Zone 5**

'MR. BLUEBIRD'

This was the last of Peter Lambert's Hybrid Musks to be released: it is one of the simplest and one of the best, though its published parentage is questionable. The flowers are pink and white. They have a large white center, surrounded at first by a thick cherry crimson edge that fades quickly to pink and then continues to dissolve away more slowly until the flower is almost completely white. They come in large and highly decorative clusters of 20–50 flowers and make a splendid massed effect when well cultivated. The overall effect is somewhere between 'Ballerina' and 'Marjorie Fair', but 'Mozart' is quite distinct and better in several ways: the large green leaves of 'Mozart' are far finer and it is not susceptible to blackspot. In hot climates it can be grown as a 9.8ft (3m) climber.

'MR. BLUEBIRD'

Miniature Rose

ORIGIN **Moore, US, 1960**
PARENTAGE **'Oakington Ruby' × 'Old Blush'**
FLOWER SIZE **1.4in (3.5cm)**
SCENT **Light and sweet**
FLOWERING **Repeats well**
HEIGHT/SPREAD **2ft (60cm)/1.3ft (40cm)**
HARDINESS **Zone 6**

Variously described as a Polyantha and a miniature rose, 'Mr. Bluebird' is a neat, pretty rose that fits well in containers and is useful at the front of a mixed border. Its flowers are magenta with a hint of purple and white centers. As it ages, it takes on the softer tones of lilac and mauve. They are lightly cupped and semidouble, and have that excellent quality in any rose of shedding its petals cleanly when it has finished flowering. The flowers come in small clusters (typically of 5–10) on a compact, bushy plant with dark leaves that are somewhat large for a miniature. 'Mr. Bluebird' is a very good repeat flowerer and grows readily from cuttings, so it is easy to build up a large stock to use as edging.

'MRS. ANTHONY WATERER'

'MRS. ANTHONY WATERER'

Rugosa Hybrid

ORIGIN **Waterer, Britain, 1898**
PARENTAGE ***Rosa rugosa* × 'Général Jacqueminot'**
FLOWER SIZE **2.8in (7cm)**
SCENT **Strong and sweet**
FLOWERING **Early, and then intermittently**
HEIGHT/SPREAD **4.9ft (1.5m)/4.9ft (1.5m)**
HARDINESS **Zone 5**

'Mrs. Anthony Waterer' was one of the earliest Rugosas bred in England. Its bright, mid-crimson flowers glow with color when they first emerge from the bud, but then acquire a duller sheen. The petals are somewhat loosely arranged, but the bright yellow stamens shine at the center. The flowers are produced, early in the season, singly or in clusters of 3–5 flowers. The wrinkly leaves ("rugose" is the botanical word for their corrugated surface) are fairly susceptible to blackspot and rust. The bush has very prickly stems and tends to send out long, arching stems that flower only at their ends. Young plants in a vigorous state of growth perform better and bear more flowers in autumn.

'MRS. B. R. CANT'

Tea Rose

ORIGIN **Cant, Britain, 1901**
FLOWER SIZE **3.1in (8cm)**
SCENT **Medium and tealike**
FLOWERING **Almost continuous**
HEIGHT/SPREAD **8.2ft (2.5m)/8.2ft (2.5m)**
HARDINESS **Zone 6**

Although bred in England, and named for the raiser's wife, 'Mrs. B. R. Cant' is a hot climate rose, and much more widely grown these days in the US and Australia. The flowers are silvery pink with darker petal backs, cupped, and full of petals, occasionally with a quartered center. They come singly or in small clusters on long stems, making it a useful cut flower. The plant has a lot of medium-sized, dark, healthy leaves and a vigorous, bushy habit of growth – often as wide as it is high. It tolerates poor soils, but responds to feeding and watering. It flowers until the first frost – nonstop in frost-free areas – and often produces its finest flowers in autumn. Cuttings root quickly and easily.

'MRS. B. R. CANT'

MRS. DOREEN PIKE

syn. 'AUSDOR'

Rugosa Hybrid

ORIGIN **Austin, Britain, 1994**
PARENTAGE **'Martin Frobisher' × 'Roseraie de l'Haÿ'**
FLOWER SIZE **2.4in (6cm)**
SCENT **Moderate and sweet**
FLOWERING **Repeats well**
HEIGHT/SPREAD **3.3ft (1m)/4.1ft (1.25m)**
HARDINESS **Zone 4**

David Austin is an adventurous breeder, who does not confine himself to raising ever more perfect English Roses. His work with 'Martin Frobisher' has produced a number of Hybrid Rugosas with all the charm associated with his roses, but also with a hardiness that makes them invaluable in such climates as Scandinavia and Canada. The flowers of Mrs. Doreen Pike are very dark pink or pale crimson rosettes, fading to pale mauve pink at the edges, and with much paler backs to the petals. They come in small clusters (of 3–7 flowers) and are very full of petals, sometimes arranged in a button eye, and set off by small, rough leaves that may (like many Rugosas) suffer from chlorosis. The plant is compact, bushy, prickly, and wider than tall. It is an excellent border plant in any climate, and useful too for landscaping and groundcover plans.

MRS. DOREEN PIKE

'MOZART'

'Mrs. Dudley Cross'

Tea Rose

ORIGIN **W. Paul, Britain, 1907**
FLOWER SIZE **3.9in (10cm)**
SCENT **Strong and tealike**
FLOWERING **Repeats continuously**
HEIGHT/SPREAD **2.7ft (80cm)/3.3ft (1m)**
HARDINESS **Zone 7**

'Mrs. Dudley Cross' is still popular and widely grown in the southern states of the US. It is an excellent rose that represents the culmination of years of Tea-rose breeding. Its color is infinitely variable, but always a combination of buff yellow, pink, and cream – classic Tea rose colors. It is usually pinker in cool weather, and when cut for the house, and more yellow or cream in hot weather. The flowers are full of petals, usually rosette-shaped, and occasionally quartered, with a fragrance that travels on the air. They are borne singly or in clusters of 3–5. The plant has pretty new stems, almost thornless, and healthy, handsome foliage, which is red when young. It is a good survivor, tolerating poor soil, drought, and years of neglect. With good cultivation it will reach 6.6ft (2m), but is usually pruned to about half that height.

'Mrs. Dudley Cross'

'Mrs. Fred Danks'

Hybrid Tea or Pillar Rose

ORIGIN **Clark, Australia, 1951**
FLOWER SIZE **3.5in (9cm)**
SCENT **Strong and tealike**
FLOWERING **Fully recurrent**
HEIGHT/SPREAD **6.6ft (2m)/4.9ft (1.5m)**
HARDINESS **Zone 8**

'Mrs. Fred Danks' – introduced posthumously and named after a friend of Alister Clark – is a vigorous, repeat flowering bush or pillar rose of *Rosa gigantea* origins. Such is the vigor of its long, slender branches that it is often pegged down so that flowering spurs break out along its whole length and not just at the top. The tall, elegant buds are pale crimson, but the flowers open lilac pink with paler pink petal backs, and a creamy white center. They fade to pale pink and sometimes bleach somewhat unattractively in hot sun. The flowers usually come in small clusters (up to five flowers) and flower almost ceaselessly in warm climates. The leaves are reddish at first and occasionally go down with mildew, but they are fairly resistant to blackspot.

'Mrs. Fred Danks'

'Mrs. F. W. Flight'

Multiflora Rambler

ORIGIN **Cutbush, US, 1905**
PARENTAGE **'Turner's Crimson Rambler' × 'The Garland'**
FLOWER SIZE **1.8in (4.5cm)**
SCENT **Musky**
FLOWERING **Once, fairly early in season**
HEIGHT/SPREAD **13.1ft (4m)/9.8ft (3m)**
HARDINESS **Zone 5**

A plant of 'Mrs. F. W. Flight' in peak condition is a sight of stunning beauty: there is a famous avenue of this immensely vigorous rambler wound around 16.4ft (5m) cones at L'Haÿ-les-Roses, alternating with 'Paul's Scarlet Climber' treated in the same way. The individual flowers open dark pink but soon fade to pale pink and have a small white patch at the center, but the overall effect is of pure, radiant, soft pink. The flowers are borne in large clusters of 30–50, and in such quantities as to cover the entire surface of the plant in full bloom. It is one of the most floriferous of all roses. The plant has lush, pale green, Multiflora foliage and thick, vigorous stems, but it flowers only once. It roots easily and quickly from cuttings.

A sport known as **'White Flight'** is just as arresting in full flower as its pink-flowered parent. The whole plant seems to be covered in large clusters of small, semidouble, wavy flowers. It is identical to its parent in all respects apart from its color. The buds have a hint of creamy pink on their backs, but the flowers are pure white. As they age, they acquire a somewhat ghostly green tinge, and they hang on to the bush until they are quite brown – but that does not detract from the sight of a well-trained plant at the peak of its flowering. It occasionally reverts to 'Mrs. F. W. Flight', and the plant looks even better for the touch of pink.

'Mrs. F. W. Flight'

'White Flight'

Sport of 'Mrs. F. W. Flight'

'White Flight'

syn. 'White Mrs. Flight', 'Astra Desmond'
ORIGIN **Rockford, Britain, 1916**

'Mrs. Herbert Stevens'

Hybrid Tea

ORIGIN **McGredy, Northern Ireland, 1910**
PARENTAGE **'Frau Karl Druschki' × 'Niphetos'**
FLOWER SIZE **4.7in (12cm)**
SCENT **Strong and tealike**
FLOWERING **Repeats well**
HEIGHT/SPREAD **4.1ft (1.25m)/3.3ft (1m)**
HARDINESS **Zone 7**

Sometimes a bush rose is overshadowed by its climbing sport. 'Mrs. Herbert Stevens' is a good example, because it is now rarely seen (though still sold), whereas its sport, **'Climbing Mrs. Herbert Stevens'**, is widely grown all over the world, and especially in hot, dry climates where its delicate petals can open out to perfection. 'Mrs. Herbert Stevens' is sometimes described as a Tea rose, but it is best thought of as a somewhat tender Hybrid Tea with some of the best characteristics of the Teas. Its flowers are pure white, except for a yellow shadow at the center of the bud and a hint of green on the outer petals. The petals are noticeably long, though also soft and thin, which means that they spoil quickly in rain and brown off in damp weather. The flowers of 'Mrs. Herbert Stevens' are fully double, and hang down on weak pedicels, which is a fault in the bush form but an asset in the climber. The petals reflex very attractively in the opening bud, while the fully open flower has a mass of loose petals. The plant has large leaves and a tendency to mildew – not a problem in dry, warm areas. It repeats extremely well. The same is true of 'Climbing Mrs. Herbert Stevens', though it is not such a constant repeater as the original bush form. It is, however, much more vigorous, and will grow in hot climates to a great height – as much as 26.2ft (8m). Its flowers are larger than the bush form's, but otherwise identical in all details. Both have a delicious tea scent and thrive even in poor soils.

'Mrs. Herbert Stevens'

'Climbing 'Mrs. Herbert Stevens'

Sport of 'Mrs. Herbert Stevens'

'Climbing Mrs. Herbert Stevens'

Climbing Hybrid Tea
ORIGIN **Pernet-Ducher, France, 1922**
FLOWER SIZE **5.5in (14cm)**
FLOWERING **Repeats well for a climbing sport**
HEIGHT/SPREAD **16.4ft (5m)/9.8ft (3m)**

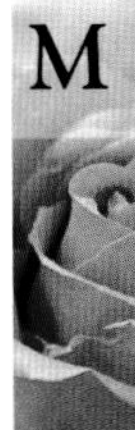

'MRS. JOHN LAING'

'MRS. OAKLEY FISHER'

'MRS. PAUL'

'MULLARD JUBILEE'

'MRS. JOHN LAING'

Hybrid Perpetual

ORIGIN **Bennett, Britain, 1887**
PARENTAGE **'François Michelon' x unknown**
FLOWER SIZE **4.3in (11cm)**
SCENT **Strong and sweet**
FLOWERING **Repeats well**
HEIGHT/SPREAD **4.9ft (1.5m)/4.9ft (1.5m)**
HARDINESS **Zone 5**

The fat, wide flowers of 'Mrs. John Laing' are very beautiful. The buds are cabbagelike, but they open into large, loose flowers, almost blowsy when fully open. They are mid-pink at first, fading to pale lilac pink, with silver reverses to the petals, and they stand out well against the mid-green, matte leaves. They are borne singly or in clusters of 3–5 on stout stalks that hold the flowers well above the leaves. The plant has an upright habit, but its long stems (nearly thornless) bow over under the weight of their flowers and then break into flower all along their length. 'Mrs. John Laing' is one of the most floriferous of all Hybrid Perpetuals and flowers especially well in autumn. It tolerates poor soils, but also responds well to feeding, and it is almost invariably healthy and vigorous.

'MRS. OAKLEY FISHER'

Hybrid Tea

ORIGIN **Cant, Britain, 1921**
FLOWER SIZE **3.1in (8cm)**
SCENT **Medium and sweet**
FLOWERING **Repeats constantly**
HEIGHT/SPREAD **4.9ft (1.5m)/4.1ft (1.25m)**
HARDINESS **Zone 6**

Single-flowered Hybrid Teas enjoyed a short-lived vogue in the 1920s. 'Mrs. Oakley Fisher' is the best of them, and has remained popular ever since. The flowers have an extraordinary loveliness of color and grace of carriage. They are a mixture of copper, orange, and apricot – paler and more yellow toward the center, but pinker and darker toward the edges. Their finest feature is the large circle of crimson stamens, all of different lengths, at their center. It gives the flowers their defining beauty. The flowers open lightly cupped and close up again at night. When the sun shines through their petals, the surface of the bush seems to dance with color. The plant is vigorous and healthy, especially in warm climates, with large prickles, dark green leaves, and crimson new growth. It is excellent for borders because it mixes well with most colors.

'MRS. PAUL'

Bourbon Rose

ORIGIN **W. Paul, Britain, 1891**
PARENTAGE **'Mme. Isaac Pereire' seedling**
FLOWER SIZE **3.9in (10cm)**
SCENT **Strong and sweet**
FLOWERING **Repeats**
HEIGHT/SPREAD **4.9ft (1.5m)/4.1ft (1.25m)**
HARDINESS **Zone 6**

This unusual rose was bred to translate the good qualities of 'Mme. Isaac Pereire' (tough petals, size, and scent) into other colors and forms. The color is bright pink at first, but eventually a soft pink, with shining mother-of-pearl edges. There are some patches of dark pink within the flower – a few petals here and there – and the petal backs are paler. Its imbricated shape resembles a camellia at first, before it reflexes to a pompon, with layer upon layer of frilly guard petals and a mass of small quilled ones at the center. The flowers come singly, or in clusters of up to five, on a fairly vigorous bush with large, dark leaves and big prickles.

MRS. PIERRE S. DU PONT

see 'MME. PIERRE S. DU PONT'

'MULLARD JUBILEE'

syn. 'ELECTRON'

Hybrid Tea

ORIGIN **McGredy, Northern Ireland, 1970**
PARENTAGE **'Paddy McGredy' x 'Prima Ballerina'**
FLOWER SIZE **5.1in (13cm)**
SCENT **Very strong and sweet**
FLOWERING **Repeats well**
HEIGHT/SPREAD **3.3ft (1m)/2.5ft (75cm)**
HARDINESS **Zone 6**
AWARDS **RNRS GM 1969; The Hague GM 1970; Belfast GM 1972; AARS 1973; Portland GM 1973**

'Mullard Jubilee' was bred in Northern Ireland but has proved a satisfactory rose in a wide variety of climates and conditions. It has been especially popular in the US, where it is known as 'Electron'. It is a tough, large Hybrid Tea, with a proper sweet Damask scent. The flower is a rich glowing pink, prettiest when the bud is just past the half open stage. It is a popular rose for cut flowers and for exhibition, where its thick, solid petals and habit of opening slowly are advantages. The flowers also hold their color well, fading only slightly at the edges. Eventually they open out into a big cup shape, with the petals reflexed. The flowers are almost always borne singly, occasionally in twos or threes, on strong stalks. The plant is vigorous but compact, with very prickly stems and dark green, glossy leaves. It is very healthy in cold climates, but occasionally susceptible to fungal diseases in warmer areas.

ROSA MULLIGANII

syn. *ROSA LONGICUSPIS*

Wild Rose

FLOWER SIZE **1.6in (4cm)**
SCENT **Strong, fruity, and musky**
FLOWERING **Once only**
HEIGHT/SPREAD **16.4ft (5m)/9.8ft (3m)**
HARDINESS **Zone 6**

The Synstylae roses from China and the Himalayas – the wild ones with huge clusters of small white flowers – are very variable and difficult to separate out. *Rosa mulliganii* is a case in point. It occurs all over southeast Asia, but merges imperceptibly with other species

'MRS. SAM MCGREDY'

Hybrid Tea

ORIGIN **McGredy, Northern Ireland, 1929**
PARENTAGE **('Donald MacDonald' x 'Golden Emblem') x (seedling x 'The Queen Alexandra Rose')**
FLOWER SIZE **3.9in (10cm)**
SCENT **Strong, rich, and fruity**
FLOWERING **Repeats well**
HEIGHT/SPREAD **3.3ft (1m)/2.7ft (80cm)**
HARDINESS **Zone 5**

The bush form of 'Mrs. Sam McGredy' is now rarely seen, though it is still available in England. It was named after the wife of Sam McGredy III and enjoyed an especially long fashion as a garden rose. It remained in the British list of the Top Ten roses for almost 30 years. The British *Rose Annual* reported in 1929 that its color was "somewhat difficult to describe – orange red, shaded apricot, reverse of petals red." Later it turns to salmon or pink, while keeping its orange red backs.

Much more widely known and grown is the climbing sport, **'Climbing Mrs. Sam McGredy'**. The flowers are large, little more than semidouble, and open out to reveal very handsome, large, crimson filaments. The plant has crimson new growth and big prickles. It is one of the first to bloom in spring. The individual flowers are not long-lived, but their beauty and vivid color are a great joy. 'Climbing Mrs. Sam McGredy' forms a very prickly, lanky plant, not excessively vigorous, but very free flowering. It has two weaknesses: first, it may pick up a little blackspot in areas where this is a problem (though the disease seems to do no damage to the plant); second, it is surprisingly difficult for nurserymen to propagate. This may limit its availability. However, both forms – 'Mrs. Sam McGredy' and 'Climbing Mrs. Sam McGredy' – are first-rate, free flowering roses.

'MRS. SAM MCGREDY'

Sport of 'Mrs. Sam McGredy'

'CLIMBING MRS. SAM MCGREDY'

Climbing Hybrid Tea
ORIGIN **1937**
FLOWER SIZE **4.7in (12cm)**
FLOWERING **Repeats well (for a climbing sport)**
HEIGHT/SPREAD **9.8ft (3m)/5.7ft (1.75m)**

ROSA MULLIGANII

at the edges of its natural distribution and is sometimes split up by botanists into a confusion of subspecies, varieties, and forms. So it is a good idea to see it in bloom before acquiring it. That said, almost all the forms of *Rosa mulliganii* on the market are excellent garden plants. The flowers are pure white and borne on long pedicels in loose, open clusters of 5–20 in great profusion. The most distinctive features of the plant are its dark mahogany red stems and its numerous, stout prickles. The leaves are large and dark green and the red hips, at 0.8in (2cm), are among the largest for this sort of rose.

ROSA MULTIBRACTEATA

Wild Rose

FLOWER SIZE **1.4in (3.5cm)**
SCENT **Little or none**
FLOWERING **Once only**
HEIGHT/SPREAD **9.8ft (3m)/9.8ft (3m)**
HARDINESS **Zone 6**

This handsome species was used by Tantau to breed the popular shrub rose 'Cerise Bouquet', but *Rosa multibracteata* is a thoroughly garden worthy plant in its own right. Its flowers are small, but abundantly carried all along the long arching branches, and usually in clusters of up to seven. They are bright pink and backed by attractive leafy bracts which set them off well. They are followed in due course by small (0.6in/1.5cm), egg-shaped fruits, which turn to orange only rather late in the season. The plant is late to flower, too. Its leaves are small, rarely more than 2.4in (6cm) long, with leaflets that are green on top and gray underneath.

ROSA MULTIBRACTEATA

Rosa multibracteata comes from western China and is very variable in the wild, as it is in cultivation.

ROSA MULTIFLORA

Wild Rose

FLOWER SIZE **0.4in (1cm)**
SCENT **Strong and musky**
FLOWERING **Once only, early to midseason**
HEIGHT/SPREAD **9.8ft (3m)/9.8ft (3m)**
HARDINESS **Zone 5**

Rosa multiflora is one of the most important wild rose species, partly because it is widely used as a rootstock on which to graft other roses – it roots very easily from cuttings – but more because it is an ancestor of the Multiflora ramblers, the Polyantha roses, the Floribundas, and the Grandifloras. The flowers of *Rosa multiflora* are small and white but carried in erect panicles containing as many as 500 flowers – the epithet *multiflora* refers to the sheer number of flowers that it produces. Each has a puff of dark yellow stamens and an exserted style. They are followed by small (0.3in/0.7cm), round hips. The plant is vigorous and strong-growing, with thick stems that arch over and root where they touch the ground, but will also climb up a small tree to 16.4ft (5m) or more. It has few prickles, though they are large. The leaves are very attractive – large, pale green, and lush, with ciliate stipules, a dominant characteristic seen in many of its descendants. *Rosa multiflora* has hybridized extensively in the wild. In its purest form it is native to northern Japan and parts of Korea. Forms with larger flowers or pink flowers are of hybrid origin. *Rosa multiflora* is a useful garden plant because it is happy in extreme heat and cold, and will grow in both dry and wet conditions.

ROSA MULTIFLORA

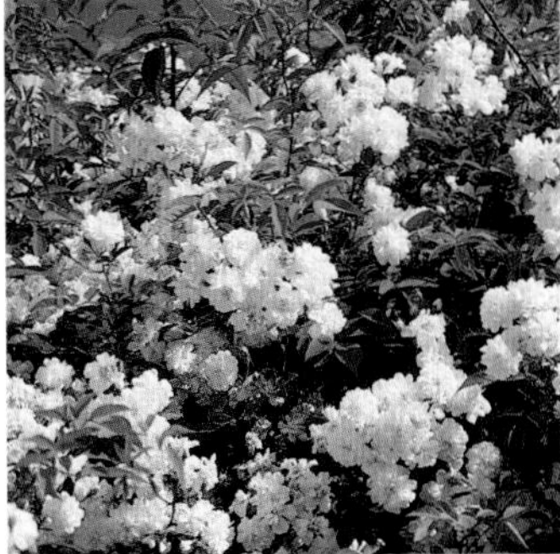

ROSA MULTIFLORA 'CARNEA'

ROSA MULTIFLORA 'CARNEA'

Multiflora Rambler

ORIGIN **1804**
FLOWER SIZE **1.6in (4cm)**
SCENT **Strong and musky**
FLOWERING **Once only, midseason**
HEIGHT/SPREAD **13.1ft (4m)/8.2ft (2.5m)**
HARDINESS **Zone 5**

'Carnea' was the first cultivar of *Rosa multiflora* to be introduced to Europe and North America from China. It was brought to England by Thomas Evans in 1804 and was later painted by Redouté. It is a hybrid, with *Rosa chinensis* in its ancestry. The flowers are very pretty and abundant, fully double, pearly pink fading to white: the central petals are always slightly darker than the outer ones. There seem to be a number of clones in cultivation under this name. When 'Carnea' was first offered for sale in Philadelphia, $20 was frequently paid for a single plant.

ROSA MULTIFLORA VAR. PLATYPHYLLA

see 'GREVILLEI'

'ROSA MUNDI'

see 'OFFICINALIS'

'MUTABILIS'

China Rose

ORIGIN **Italy, c.1900**
FLOWER SIZE **2.4in (6cm)**
SCENT **Light**
FLOWERING **Continuous**
HEIGHT/SPREAD **6.6ft (2m)/8.2ft (2.5m)**
HARDINESS **Zone 7**

The origins of 'Mutabilis' are obscure. It was introduced commercially in 1933 from a plant given to the Swiss nurseryman Henri Corrévon by the Borromeos, who own Isola Bella on Lake Maggiore and who called it 'Tipo Ideale'. It is now a widely grown and popular rose in warm regions – never without flowers. The flowers open orange or buff yellow, before turning to pink and ending up a dull, pale crimson: in hot weather they pass quickly to crimson and the color is darker. The graceful

'MUTABILIS'

petals rarely overlap but reflex in innumerable different, elegant ways. The flowers are carried in small clusters on long, slender, crimson stems. The young leaves too are crimson (later bronzy and dark green), as are the large prickles. 'Mutabilis' may be trained as a climber, but looks best as a shrub. It roots quickly from cuttings and needs very little pruning: a thinning every three or four years is enough. Surprisingly, it does not transmit its changing colors to its seedlings.

'MY CHOICE'

Hybrid Tea

ORIGIN **Le Grice, Britain, 1958**
PARENTAGE **'Wellworth' × 'Ena Harkness'**
FLOWER SIZE **5.1in (13cm)**
SCENT **Very strong and sweet**
FLOWERING **Repeats**
HEIGHT/SPREAD **3.3ft (1m)/2.7ft (80cm)**
HARDINESS **Zone 6**
AWARDS **RNRS GM 1958; Portland GM 1962**

This Hybrid Tea was bred in England, but does best in warm, dry climates where 'My Choice' can open out its flowers undamaged by rain, and its large leathery leaves are not susceptible to mildew or blackspot. The flowers are large, full of petals, and very beautiful when they open out – pink, with pale yellow petal backs, which make a striking contrast, especially in cool weather when the colors are freshest. Their beauty is heightened by the way the petals curl back their edges and enhanced by the penetrating Damask scent. The plant is strong, vigorous, and healthy in warm climates, where it will quickly reach 4.9ft (1.5m) and produce a succession of exhibition-standard flowers on long stems.

'MY CHOICE'

'Nancy Hayward'

Hybrid Gigantea

ORIGIN **Clark, Australia, 1937**
PARENTAGE **'Jessie Clark' × unknown**
FLOWER SIZE **4.3in (11cm)**
SCENT **Light**
FLOWERING **Continuous**
HEIGHT/SPREAD **19.7ft (6m)/13.1ft (4m)**
HARDINESS **Zone 9**

'Nancy Hayward' has been widely grown in its native Australia ever since its introduction. It is probably the most popular climber in every part of the country. The reason is simple: as well as flowering spectacularly in spring, an established plant is never without a flower, even in winter. The flowers are a particularly vivid, glowing shade of deep pink on both sides of the petals. It also makes an excellent cut flower: the color looks good under artificial light and the flowers last for much longer than many full-petaled roses. One of Alister Clark's aims in breeding with *Rosa gigantea* was to produce repeat-flowering roses that flourished in the hot, dry Australian climate. It was in these second generation hybrids that he achieved his greatest successes. It is said, however, that Nancy Hayward, the friend of Clark after whom the rose was named, disliked her namesake intensely.

'Narrow Water'

Noisette

ORIGIN **Daisy Hill, Northern Ireland, 1883**
FLOWER SIZE **1.2in (3cm)**
SCENT **Strong and musky**
FLOWERING **Repeats continually**
HEIGHT/SPREAD **13.1ft (4m)/8.2ft (2.5m)**
HARDINESS **Zone 6**

'Narrow Water' was introduced as a foundling, and is probably a much earlier rose whose real name has long since been forgotten. It was found at Narrow Water Castle, an 1830s country house at Warrenpoint in County Down, Northern Ireland. It is one of the most reliable, beautiful, and hardy of all the small-flowered Noisettes. Its pink buds open out flat to reveal the handsome stamens. The flowers are small, semidouble, pale mauve pink (fading to cream and white), and nicely held on sturdy, upright stalks in large, airy clusters of up to 40 flowers. The plant has dark leaves and a few large thorns. It makes a freestanding bush about 6.6ft (2m) high, or a leggy climber reaching 16.4ft (5m) up a tree. It puts out flush after flush of flowers all through the year in hot climates.

'Nancy Hayward'

'Nastarana'

Noisette

ORIGIN **W. Paul, Britain, 1879**
FLOWER SIZE **2in (5cm)**
SCENT **Strong and musky**
FLOWERING **Repeats well**
HEIGHT/SPREAD **6.6ft (2m)/6.6ft (2m)**
HARDINESS **Zone 7**

Nastarana has medium-sized clusters of medium-small, pale pink flowers, which fade quickly to white. They are fully double, but almost all the stamens make little petaloids, which give the flowers a form that is unique among roses. The flowers drop their petals cleanly: long, slender hips follow. The leaves are attractively glaucous. 'Nastarana' is probably a hybrid between *Rosa moschata* and a China rose, which would explain why it is a reliable repeat flowerer, starting late into bloom, but then continuing until almost all other roses have ceased to flower. More than one cultivar is sold under this name.

Natchez

see Little Bo-Peep

'Nathalie Nypels'

see 'Mevrouw Nathalie Nypels'

'Nastarana'

'National Trust'

syn. 'Bad Nauheim'

Hybrid Tea

ORIGIN **McGredy, Northern Ireland, 1970**
PARENTAGE **'Evelyn Fison' × 'King of Hearts'**
FLOWER SIZE **4.3in (11cm)**
SCENT **Light and sweet**
FLOWERING **Repeats well**
HEIGHT/SPREAD **2.7ft (80cm)/2ft (60cm)**
HARDINESS **Zone 6**

This short-growing, bright red Hybrid Tea enjoyed a degree of popularity in the 1970s, but was always overshadowed by better contemporaries like Alec's Red. The flowers of 'National Trust' are pretty as they open: the outer petals fold back to a point, giving a spiky effect to contrast with the unraveling whorls of the inner petals. Sometimes they produce a split center – this is essentially a garden rose, not suitable for exhibition. The color is variable too, being only a dark pink in some soils. The flowers are borne on strong, upright stems, usually singly, sometimes in clusters of 3–5. The thick petals stand up well to rain. The plant is healthy and bushy, with lots of dull green leaves, and flowers well into autumn, when some of its best blooms appear. The National Trust is a conservation foundation in England and Wales: it owns such gardens as Sissinghurst Castle and Hidcote Manor.

'National Trust'

NDR 1 Radio Niedersachsen

syn. 'KORELEDAS', Centenary, Heartache

Floribunda

ORIGIN **Kordes, Germany, 1996**
FLOWER SIZE **2.4in (6cm)**
SCENT **Light and musky**
FLOWERING **Repeats constantly**
HEIGHT/SPREAD **4.9ft (1.5m)/3.3ft (1m)**
HARDINESS **Zone 6**

Vigor is the quality that NDR 1 Radio Niedersachsen has in abundance. It grows quickly and lustily, never too high or too wide but, perhaps more than any other rose, it exudes energy. The flowers are beautiful: semidouble and wide open, with rippling petals and a pretty contrast between the mid-pink upper sides and the dark pink backs. They are borne in amazing profusion in clusters of 7–15 all over the surface of the plant, and repeat so quickly that it seems always in flower. The plant has large, glossy, healthy leaves, and a good bushy habit. It is perfect for landscaping, mixed plantings, or hedging. NDR Radio 1 Niedersachsen is a leading radio station in Germany; the rose is known as Centenary or Heartache elsewhere.

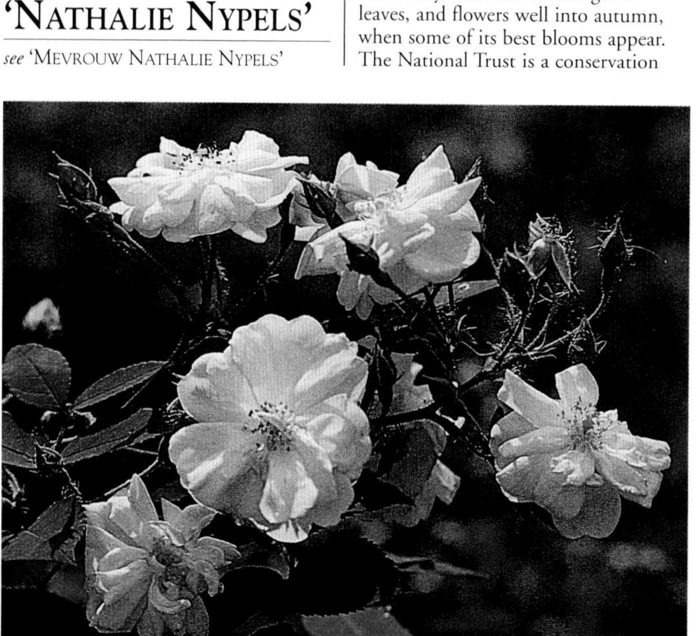

'Narrow Water'

NDR 1 Radio Niedersachsen

'NEARLY WILD'

'NEARLY WILD'

Shrub Rose

ORIGIN **Brownell, US, 1941**
PARENTAGE **'Dr. W. Van Fleet' × 'Leuchstern'**
FLOWER SIZE **2.4in (6cm)**
SCENT **Light and sweet**
FLOWERING **Almost continuous**
HEIGHT/SPREAD **2ft (60cm)/2.7ft (80cm)**
HARDINESS **Zone 5**

The Brownells were always willing to make unconventional crosses in their search for new roses that would survive a New England winter. The ancestry of 'Nearly Wild' makes it a Wichurana shrub rose. It has pretty, single, pink flowers that increase considerably in size as they open, from 2in (5cm) to 3.1in (8cm). They are a clear, dark rose pink at first, with a slightly paler center. As the flower matures, this pale center fades to white and then grows in size, so that eventually there is more white on the flower than pink. The petals have a nick in their outer edge, which gives them a little ripple, and the stamens are a very pretty golden yellow when they open, though they shrivel and shrink to brown somewhat quickly. The flowers come in clusters of 3–9 and do indeed resemble a wild rose. The plant is low-growing, flowers nearly perpetually, has dark Wichurana leaves, and seems immune to all diseases.

'NEIGE D'AVRIL'

Multiflora Rambler

ORIGIN **Robichon, France, 1908**
FLOWER SIZE **1.8in (4.5cm)**
SCENT **Strong and musky**
FLOWERING **Once only, early in season**
HEIGHT/SPREAD **13.1ft (4m)/9.8ft (3m)**
HARDINESS **Zone 5**

No one knows the origin of this charming Multiflora rambler: it was a by-product of the Robichons' efforts to breed dwarf Polyantha roses. It has two outstanding characteristics: its thornlessness and its early flowering, about a month before most other ramblers. It also lasts a long time in bloom. The flowers are pure white, with crinkly petals, and open out to reveal dark yellow stamens. They come in clusters of 5–30, which are well set off by the large, fresh, pale leaves. The plant is vigorous, healthy, and easy to grow. It is also fairly hardy, surviving the winter in New Hampshire without protection. The Robichon family were nurserymen at Pithiviers, southwest of Paris: they also bred apples.

'NEIGE D'AVRIL'

'NESTOR'

Gallica

ORIGIN **Vibert, France, 1834**
FLOWER SIZE **3.9in (10cm)**
SCENT **Strong and sweet**
FLOWERING **Once only**
HEIGHT/SPREAD **4.1ft (1.25m)/3.3ft (1m)**
HARDINESS **Zone 5**

In ancient Greek legend, King Nestor was the son of Chloris, the husband of Eurydice, and the father of Perseus. His rose is a handsome, rich, dark pink Gallica. It opens out (from crimson buds) to form a roughly quartered shape and a swirling mass of petals – the smallest are quilled and lie over the larger petals to give the rose its shape and character. The flowers are borne singly or in clusters of up to four, and fade at the edges as they age. The plant has bright green leaves – generally healthy – and little prickles. It grows fairly vigorously but sometimes bends over under the weight of its flowers – 'Nestor' is one of those Gallicas that are improved by staking. It is, however, a good and unfussy grower and thrives on poor soils.

'NESTOR'

'NEVADA'

Shrub Rose

ORIGIN **Dot, Spain, 1927**
PARENTAGE **'La Giralda' × 'Altaica'**
FLOWER SIZE **3.9in (10cm)**
SCENT **Light and sweet**
FLOWERING **Early, then intermittently**
HEIGHT/SPREAD **9.8ft (3m)/13.1ft (4m)**
HARDINESS **Zone 4**

In cool climates, this beautiful shrub rose flowers very early in the season: 'Nevada' and the Frühlings series are the first to bloom in late spring. The flowers are large, almost single, with loose and lovely petals of pale cream, passing quickly to pure white. The yellow stamens complete a vision of beauty. The plant has long, arching stems, curving out most gracefully as they grow, and its large saucers of glowing white are thickly poised along their entire length. The plant takes a few years to build up to achieve a critical mass, but it will reach 16.4ft (5m) in a hot climate, while its hardiness recommends itself to rose lovers in cold climates like Scandinavia. Its leaves are small and may suffer from blackspot. The rose has nothing to do with the American state, except that both owe their name to their Spanish ancestry ("*nevada*" means "snowy"). The parentage of this most lovely of roses has long been disputed. Pedro Dot distributed it as a hybrid of *Rosa moyesii*, but its round black hips prove it a seedling of *Rosa spinosissima*. In hot weather, the flowers sometimes turn pink as they age.

'NEVADA'

'MARGUERITE HILLING'

In 1959, T. Hilling & Co. of Chobham in England (for whom Graham Thomas worked) introduced a pure pink sport called **'Marguerite Hilling'**, which is now as widely grown and popular as 'Nevada' itself. The roses are identical in everything except color.

Sport of 'Nevada'

'MARGUERITE HILLING'

Shrub Rose
ORIGIN **Hilling, Britain, 1959**

'NEW DAWN'

see 'DR. W. VAN FLEET'

NEW DAY

see MABELLA

NEW FACE

syn. 'INTERCLEM'

Shrub Rose

ORIGIN **Interplant, Netherlands, 1978**
FLOWER SIZE **2in (5cm)**
SCENT **Light, musky, and sweet**
FLOWERING **Repeats constantly**
HEIGHT/SPREAD **6.6ft (2m)/4.9ft (1.5m)**
HARDINESS **Zone 6**
AWARDS **Bagatelle GM 1981**

New Face is a tall, slender, upright shrub, which is absolutely covered in flowers almost continuously through until late autumn. The flowers are fairly unusual – the narrow petals are white with bright pink edges but rarely wide enough to overlap each other. They are cream colored for a day or so when they first open, before fading to white. But the flowers come in very large and spacious clusters (typically of 10–50, sometimes more). The plant has many long, upright, and noticeably slender stems, each terminating in a cluster of flowers. It also has quite a number of large prickles on those long main growths, while the flowering stems are absolutely covered in much smaller prickles. Nevertheless, the clusters are excellent for cutting. The plant has healthy, medium-dark green leaves.

NEW FACE

NEW YEAR

NEW YEAR

syn. 'MACNEWYE', Arcadian

Grandiflora

ORIGIN **McGredy, New Zealand, 1983**
PARENTAGE **'Mary Sumner' seedling**
FLOWER SIZE **4.3in (11cm)**
SCENT **Medium and fruity**
FLOWERING **Repeats well**
HEIGHT/SPREAD **4.9ft (1.5m)/3.3ft (1m)**
HARDINESS **Zone 6**
AWARDS **AARS 1987**

The flowers of New Year have three distinct colors beautifully blended within them – crimson, vermilion, and orange. When they open out – they are unusual among Grandifloras for looking their best when fully expanded – the inner petals are pale orange with darker undersides, while the outer ones have crimson edges. They have an attractive roll to their outline, which adds enormously to their character and charm. They are usually borne singly early in the season and in clusters of up to five later. The plant has mid-green, healthy, glossy leaves and a dense, compact shape. New Year repeats well, and quickly.

'NEWS'

Floribunda

ORIGIN **Le Grice, Britain, 1968**
PARENTAGE **'Lilac Charm' x 'Tuscany'**
FLOWER SIZE **3.5in (9cm)**
SCENT **Light and sweet**
FLOWERING **Repeats**
HEIGHT/SPREAD **2.7ft (80cm)/2ft (60cm)**
HARDINESS **Zone 5**
AWARDS **RNRS GM 1970**

'News' created a sensation when it first appeared: here, for the first time, was a purple Floribunda, bred by back-crossing to an old Gallica rose. The English breeder Edward le Grice specialized in breeding roses with unusual colors, especially mauves, lilacs, purple, browns, and tans. 'News' was his masterpiece. Its buds have a hint of crimson, but open quickly to bright purple flowers that

'NEWS'

keep their color well, losing only some of the brightness of the young flower as they age and fade to lilac. They are large for a Floribunda, and semidouble, with slightly ruffled petals, and open out flat around a big patch of golden stamens. The stamens and the wavy petals add enormously to the beauty of the flower. The flowers come in clusters of 5–9 and are held well above the leaves on strong, upright stems. The leaves are dark and the plant fairly vigorous – it is a good, reliable repeater – apart from an occasional brush with rust.

NIAGARA

see AVON

NICCOLO PAGANINI

syn. 'MEICAIRMA', Courage, Paganini

Floribunda

ORIGIN **Meilland, France, 1991**
FLOWER SIZE **2.8in (7cm)**
SCENT **Medium and sweet**
FLOWERING **Repeats well**
HEIGHT/SPREAD **4.1ft (1.25m)/3.3ft (1m)**
HARDINESS **Zone 6**
AWARDS **Geneva 1989; La Plus Belle Rose de France 1990; Lyon Rose of the Century 1990**

This handsome, velvety, red Floribunda has sold especially well wherever Meilland has a strong market presence. However, Niccolo Paganini deserves to be yet more widely grown, especially in warm climates, because its flowers tolerate heat better than many red roses and it is extraordinarily floriferous. The

NICCOLO PAGANINI

flowers have short petals, but a lot of them, and they open out fairly quickly, keeping their shape and color for an unusually long time. The flowers come in clusters of 5–12, occasionally more, on a compact, healthy plant with large, dark leaves. Niccolo Paganini is an excellent bedding rose where a sustained show of red is required. It was named after the virtuoso violinist and composer (1782–1840).

NICE DAY

syn. 'CHEWSEA', Patio Queen

Miniature Climber

ORIGIN **Warner, Britain, 1992**
PARENTAGE **Seaspray x Warm Welcome**
FLOWER SIZE **1.6in (4cm)**
SCENT **Light and sweet**
FLOWERING **Repeats constantly**
HEIGHT/SPREAD **8.2ft (2.5m)/4.9ft (1.5m)**
HARDINESS **Zone 6**

The flowers of Nice Day are unusual and attractive. They open out in such a way that their petals are arranged in neatly imbricated circles. Their charm comes from the way in which each petal reflexes along its sides to form a pointed tip. The flowers are salmon pink, fading gently to a paler shade of pink from the outside of the flower, so that the inner petals are always darker and create a contrast. At the center is a cushion of pale stamens. The petal backs are darker at first, and more orange, but the flowers lose their brightness fairly quickly. They come in small, spacious clusters (typically 3–8) on long stems, and are borne in a series of flushes until well into autumn. Nice Day has neat, small, dark leaves (bronzy at first), a lot of long stems, a dense, bushy habit, and few prickles.

NICE DAY

NEW ZEALAND

syn. 'MACGENEV', Aotearoa

Grandiflora

ORIGIN **McGredy, New Zealand, 1989**
PARENTAGE **Harmonie x Auckland Metro**
FLOWER SIZE **4.7in (12cm)**
SCENT **Very strong and sweet**
FLOWERING **Repeats well**
HEIGHT/SPREAD **3.9ft (1.2m)/2.7ft (80cm)**
HARDINESS **Zone 5**
AWARDS **Portland GM & FA 1995**

Sam McGredy gave this rose a double name – Aotearoa New Zealand – to celebrate both the Maori and the European cultures in his adopted homeland on the occasion of its sesquicentenary, or 150th anniversary. It is one of the most beautiful and easiest of all roses to grow. The flowers open from high-pointed, deep pink buds. They are large, strongly scented, and pale pink in color. Close examination shows that the petals are actually blush pink on their upper sides, and slightly darker, a true peach pink, on the reverse. Sometimes the coloring is a little blotchy, but this adds to the charm of the rose: the combination of shape and color is very pretty indeed. The flowers are large and come singly or in clusters of 3–7 on long, strong stems, which makes them useful for cutting and exhibition. The plant has dark, glossy,

NEW ZEALAND

healthy leaves and flowers almost continuously. It is one of the most beautiful of all modern roses.

McGredy also introduced a pure white sport of New Zealand called Land of the Long White Cloud in 1998. It is exactly the same, except for its color, which sometimes has just a hint of yellow at the center. It is proving popular in its own country and in the US, where it is known as Full Sail.

Sport of New Zealand

LAND OF THE LONG WHITE CLOUD

syn. 'MACLANOFLON', FULL SAIL
Hybrid Tea
ORIGIN **McGredy, New Zealand, 1998**
HEIGHT/SPREAD **4.1ft (1.25m)/2.7ft (80cm)**

NICOLE

syn. 'KORICOLE', Tabris, 'KORTABRIS'

Floribunda

ORIGIN **Kordes, Germany, 1985**
PARENTAGE **seedling × 'Bordure Rose'**
FLOWER SIZE **3.5in (9cm)**
SCENT **Light and greeny**
FLOWERING **Repeats very well**
HEIGHT/SPREAD **6.6ft (2m)/5.7ft (1.75m)**
HARDINESS **Zone 6**

In the 1980s, the great German rose breeders W. Kordes & Sohne introduced three spectacular bicolored Floribundas – Hannah Gordon (1983), Nicole (1985), and Tabris (1986). They were very similar to each other – so similar in cultivation, in fact, that they began to be mistaken for each other. Hannah Gordon is distinct enough to be treated as a cultivar, but Nicole and Tabris are so alike that it is best to treat them as synonyms for one another. Nicole takes precedence as a name, since it was issued earlier. It is a stupendous shrubby Floribunda, with large, milk white flowers liberally dipped in a bright, lurid pink. The short, wavy petals have paler backs, but keep their color well, and the flowers are borne in clusters of 3–10. Nicole makes a vigorous, spreading bush, with very healthy leaves (except for an occasional dab of blackspot in cool climates) and thorny stems. A winner, whatever its name.

NIGHT LIGHT

syn. 'POULLIGHT'

Pillar or Shrub Rose

ORIGIN **Poulsen, Denmark, 1982**
PARENTAGE **'Westerland' × 'Pastorale'**
FLOWER SIZE **3.5in (9cm)**
SCENT **Moderate and fruity**
FLOWERING **Repeats well**
HEIGHT/SPREAD **8.2ft (2.5m)/8.2ft (2.5m)**
HARDINESS **Zone 6**

Night Light is a fine example of the 'Masquerade' type of rose, whose color changes from yellow to red as it matures, though Night Light is a very vigorous shrub or short climber. Its flowers open butter yellow, with pink tinges on the petal edges. Those edges then deepen to raspberry crimson and grow thicker. The color changes more quickly in hot weather, when the yellow changes more to vermilion than crimson. Much of the distinctive charm of this variety – despite its fairly shocking color scheme – comes from its ruffled petals: they have a wave to their outline that looks almost artificial and gives much character to the bloom. The flowers come in long-stemmed clusters of 5–15 and stand up well to rain. The plant is a stiff, gawky shrub as much as 6.6ft (2m) tall (more as a climber), with large, dark, glossy leaves and horrendously prickly stems.

NIGHT LIGHT

NICOLE

'NIL BLEU'

syn. 'BLUE NILE'

Hybrid Tea

ORIGIN **Delbard, France, 1976**
PARENTAGE **(['Holstein' × 'Bayadère'] × 'Prélude') × 'St. Exupéry'**
FLOWER SIZE **4.7in (12cm)**
SCENT **Strong and sweet**
FLOWERING **Repeats**
HEIGHT/SPREAD **4.9ft (1.5m)/3.3ft (1m)**
HARDINESS **Zone 6**

The large, many-petaled flowers of 'Nil Bleu' have a stupendous scent and keep their lilac mauve color right through their flowering. They are elegantly shaped as they open and borne both singly and in twos and threes. They come on long stems, which makes them useful for cutting and for exhibition, especially in warm climates where they grow most vigorously. 'Nil Bleu' has a stout, upright habit of growth, a lot of prickles and noticeably large, dark leaves. In cool climates it is usually pruned back to about 2.5ft (75cm) but, in warm areas, it flowers best at twice that height. It is a good rose everywhere.

'NIL BLEU'

'NINA WEIBULL'

'NINA WEIBULL'

Floribunda

ORIGIN **Poulsen, Denmark, 1962**
PARENTAGE **'Fanal' × 'Masquerade'**
FLOWER SIZE **2.4in (6cm)**
SCENT **Light and sweet**
FLOWERING **Repeats well**
HEIGHT/SPREAD **2.5ft (75cm)/1.6ft (50cm)**
HARDINESS **Zone 4**

More than 40 years after it was first introduced, 'Nina Weibull' is still by far the most popular red Floribunda in Scandinavia. It is widely grown from Finland to Iceland and universally praised for its health and hardiness. Yet it is almost unknown in North America – even in the coldest areas. The flowers are bright, dark red, and keep their color well. They usually come in clusters of 3–10, but occasionally in vast bouquets of up to 30. They stand up well to rain and flower almost continuously until the first frost. 'Nina Weibull' has dark, glossy leaves, a fair ration of large prickles, and a vigorous, bushy habit. It never grows very tall, which makes it useful for mass bedding: all the plants flower at the same height. And it is a splendid, cheerful garden plant.

'NIPHETOS'

Tea Rose

ORIGIN **Bougère, France, 1843**
FLOWER SIZE **3.5in (9cm)**
SCENT **Strong tea scent**
FLOWERING **Repeats constantly**
HEIGHT/SPREAD **2.7ft (80cm)/2ft (60cm)**
HARDINESS **Zone 7**

This famous old rose has a curiously modern look, with long, pointed flower buds which curl back at the edges, a trait that comes directly down the generations to the roses of today. The flowers of 'Niphetos' are pure white, except for a hint of lemon at the base to start with and a pink tinge just before they drop their petals. They come on long purple stems, usually singly, but sometimes in clusters of up to five, and were a popular greenhouse and commercial cut-flower rose in the 19th century. They have a habit, common to many Tea roses, of nodding their flowers as they open out. They are prettiest at the half open stage: they lose control when fully open, and the petals seem less neat. The plant is compact, with pale green leaves and a few large prickles. 'Climbing Niphetos' occurred as a spontaneous sport in Salisbury, England, in 1889. It is identical to the bush form except for having slightly larger flowers and repeat flowering less. Both grow best in hot, dry climates.

'NIPHETOS'

ROSA NITIDA

ROSA NITIDA

Wild Rose

FLOWER SIZE **2in (5cm)**
SCENT **Light and sweet**
FLOWERING **Once only, fairly late in season**
HEIGHT/SPREAD **2.7ft (80cm)/2ft (60cm)**
HARDINESS **Zone 4**

"Nitidus" is the Latin word for "shining," and *Rosa nitida* gets its name from its glossy leaves. It is by far the best short-growing wild rose for small gardens. It comes from New England and eastern Canada, so it is exceptionally hardy. The flowers are a very bright pink, sometimes with a white eye but always with a thick cluster of pale yellow stamens. They usually come singly, but occasionally in twos and threes, and are followed by round, bristly, vermilion hips (0.4in/1cm in diameter). The leaves are healthy and very attractive, with narrow leaflets that turn brilliant red and yellow in autumn. The plant is a thicketing mass of very prickly, russet brown stems, beautiful even in winter. It is very tolerant of heat and cold, dry soil, and poor drainage. It has even been planted to consolidate embankments.

NOBLE ANTONY

syn. 'AUSWAY'

Shrub Rose

ORIGIN **Austin, Britain, 1995**
PARENTAGE **('Lilian Austin' x 'The Squire') x ('Duftwolke' x 'Glastonbury')**
FLOWER SIZE **3.9in (10cm)**
SCENT **Strong and sweet**
FLOWERING **Repeats**
HEIGHT/SPREAD **3.3ft (1m)/3.3ft (1m)**
HARDINESS **Zone 5**

Noble Antony – the name is a quotation from Shakespeare's *Julius Caesar* – has deep pink flowers with a hint of magenta. It is sometimes a somewhat blotchy color, made up of dark veins on a paler ground. The petal backs are paler and the flowers have a lot of petals, which reflex and build up like a large pompon. They are borne singly or in small clusters on a slightly sparse looking, prickly bush with dark, glossy leaves. Blackspot can be a problem. Although not perhaps among the best of David Austin's English Roses, it is useful for its compact habit, which recommends it for forward positions in mixed borders.

WERNER NOACK

A FREQUENT AWARD WINNER, GERMANY'S NOACK HAS ALSO HAD MAJOR SUCCESS WITH HIS FLOWER CARPET SERIES

WHAT SETS Werner Noack (b.1927) apart is his original approach to both breeding and promoting roses. Right from the start, he set out to breed healthy roses. This requirement was preeminent: roses must be free from rust and stand up well to mildew. They should also be hardy, colorful, and free flowering, with handsome foliage.

REINHARD AND WERNER NOACK

Noack's best are groundcover, Floribunda, and shrub roses. He has raised a few short-growing climbers – of which **Momo** (1994) is outstanding – and a handful of Hybrid Teas, which are not well known, though **Samara** (1989) and **Focus** (1997) are good. Noack's first rose to win the top prize at the German ADR rose trials was **Ravensberg** in 1986. Between then and 2002, he and his son Reinhard won more ADR awards than any other breeder – more even than Kordes, including no fewer than five in 1995, and again in 1999. Some of these winners are widely grown all over the world, but others are little known. The spectacular **Apfelblüte** (1992) and **Wildfang** (1989), for example, each won an ADR award in 1991, but have never been widely promoted or grown.

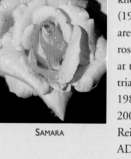

SAMARA

Noack's Flower Carpet series was given very different treatment. The plants were marketed as being of exceptional value and were sold in attention grabbing pink pots. This exercise in branding, advertising, and public relations began with **Heidetraum**, launched as **Pink Flower Carpet**. In its first year in the US, Noack sold 15 times more plants than for a normal introduction. This success was followed by **Schneeflocke (White Flower Carpet)** and **Celina (Yellow Flower Carpet)**. Others in the series include **Alcantara (Red Flower Carpet)**, **Alfabia (Coral Flower Carpet)**, and **Sommermelodie (Appleblossom Flower Carpet)**.

WILDFANG

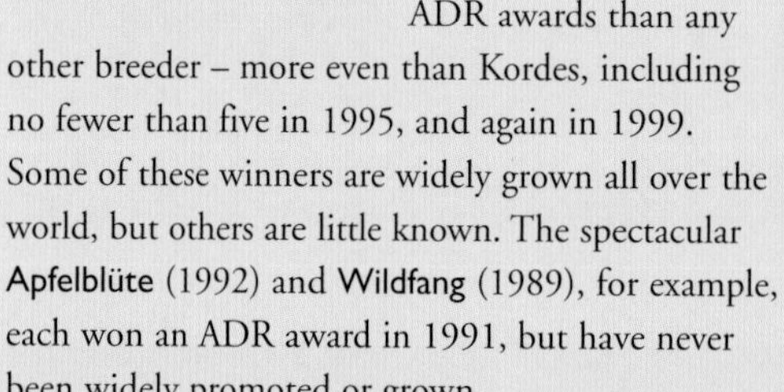

NOBLE ANTONY

'NOËLLA NABONNAND'

Tea Rose

ORIGIN **Nabonnand, France, 1901**
PARENTAGE **'Reine Marie Henriette' x 'Bardou Job'**
FLOWER SIZE **5.1in (13cm)**
SCENT **Strong and sweet**
FLOWERING **Almost continuous**
HEIGHT/SPREAD **9.8ft (3m)/5.7ft (1.75m)**
HARDINESS **Zone 7**

It was introduced in 1901, but the flowers of 'Noëlla Nabonnand' are large even by today's standards. They are also richly scented and produced in great

'NOËLLA NABONNAND'

quantity. Although only lightly double, the flowers hold their petals somewhat loosely (and shed them cleanly), which creates the effect that they are full of petals. They are deep, bright crimson, losing their brightness but keeping their color as they age, with nearly white backs to the petals – a striking contrast. The petals are unusually long, and the buds therefore very elegant. 'Noëlla Nabonnand' makes a vigorous, leafy bush with thick stems, stout prickles, and fairly healthy leaves. It has been a firm favorite in hot climates ever since it was first introduced.

'NOISETTE CARNÉE'

syn. 'BLUSH NOISETTE'

Noisette

ORIGIN **Noisette, US, 1817**
PARENTAGE **'Champney's Pink Cluster' self-pollinated seedling**
FLOWER SIZE **1.6in (4cm)**
SCENT **Strong and distinctive**
FLOWERING **Repeats constantly**
HEIGHT/SPREAD **8.2ft (2.5m)/4.9ft (1.5m)**
HARDINESS **Zone 5**

America's first repeat flowering rose was the founder of an entirely new race of roses – the Noisettes. The lilac pink flowers of 'Noisette Carnée' are well held on long stems in large clusters of 20–50. They open from crimson buds and fade almost to white at the edges. The long, slender calyces are very distinctive. The leaves are dark, with crimson midribs, and the reddish stems are nearly thornless. The plant is not especially vigorous, and takes some years to build up to its eventual height, while most of its energy goes into the continuous production of new flowering stems. It will flower year-round in warm climates, though it is also remarkably hardy. It is very healthy. Although thousands of modern roses claim it as a distant ancestor, 'Noisette Carnée' (or 'Blush Noisette' in America) is still a first-rate rose in its own right, whether it is grown as a freestanding bush or a short climber.

'NOISETTE CARNÉE'

'NORWICH CASTLE'

Shrub Rose

ORIGIN **Beales, Britain, 1976**
PARENTAGE **'Whisky' × 'Arthur Bell'**
FLOWER SIZE **5.1in (13cm)**
SCENT **Medium and musky**
FLOWERING **Repeats**
HEIGHT/SPREAD **5.7ft (1.75m)/3.3ft (1m)**
HARDINESS **Zone 6**

It was introduced as a Floribunda, but 'Norwich Castle' is closer to a Grandiflora because it has large flowers in clusters on a vigorous, tall plant. The flowers are apricot colored, with darker petal backs – a coppery orange color that fades only slightly with age. The orange shadows that form in the opening bud as the long, elegant petals unfurl are especially beautiful. The flowers come singly or in strong, sturdy clusters of up to five, which make excellent cut flowers. The plant has large, stout stems and large, healthy, dark green leaves. In hot climates it will reach as much as 6.6ft (2m), but little more than 4.1ft (1.25m) in its native eastern England. Norwich Castle has one of the finest Norman keeps in Europe.

'NORWICH CASTLE'

NOSTALGIE

syn. 'TANEIGLAT'

Hybrid Tea

ORIGIN **Tantau, Germany, 1996**
FLOWER SIZE **4.3in (11cm)**
SCENT **Strong and sweet**
FLOWERING **Repeats**
HEIGHT/SPREAD **3.3ft (1m)/2.7ft (80cm)**
HARDINESS **Zone 6**

The striking colors of Nostalgie catch the eye from far away. The nose is then beguiled by its strong, sweet scent. It is an excellent Hybrid Tea, especially popular in its native Germany. The flowers are large and somewhat cupped, with a swirl of creamy white petals at the center and bright cherry crimson at the edges. The flowers open only slowly, which means that they last a long time if cut for the house and keep their color well. Eventually the petals take on a wavy outline, so that the flower is attractive at every stage of its development. Nostalgie is a neat, compact plant, not too tall, with strong, dark, shiny, healthy leaves. It repeats well, and makes a good display as a bedding rose.

NOSTALGIE

'NOVA ZEMBLA'

see 'CONRAD FERDINAND MEYER'

NOVAÏA

syn. 'ORAGOFÉ'

Floribunda

ORIGIN **Orard, France, 1997**
FLOWER SIZE **2.4in (6cm)**
SCENT **Light, sweet, and musky**
FLOWERING **Repeats constantly**
HEIGHT/SPREAD **3.3ft (1m)/2.7ft (80cm)**
HARDINESS **Zone 6**
AWARDS **Courtrai GM 1997; Geneva GM 1997; Paris GM 1997; Plus Belle Rose de France 1997**

The bicolored flowers of Novaïa are red and white, but the distribution of the colors is quite unusual because the petal backs (which are what you see as the bud starts to open) have only a tinge of crimson along their edges and the rest is white. However, the upsides of the petals are mostly crimson, with only a small patch of white at the center. So the rose gives the impression of darkening as it matures. The petals also take on an attractive waviness, which adds to their character. The flowers are very prolifically borne – Novaïa is an excellent bedding rose – in large, loose clusters, typically of 8–15. The plant is a vigorous grower, with stout stems and medium-sized leaves, mid-green and unexciting, but healthy.

NOVAÏA

'NOZOMI'

'NOZOMI'

syn. 'HEIDERÖSLEIN NOZOMI'

Ground Cover

ORIGIN **Onodera, Japan, 1968**
PARENTAGE **'Fairy Princess' x 'Sweet Fairy'**
FLOWER SIZE **0.8in (2cm)**
SCENT **Light and musky**
FLOWERING **Once only**
HEIGHT/SPREAD **1.6ft (50cm)/4.9ft (1.5m)**
HARDINESS **Zone 6**

There is no denying the popularity of 'Nozomi', though there are many better roses. Its main attraction is the simplicity of its flowers and its compact habit. It is sometimes said to be the smallest of groundcover roses, which makes it suitable for containers. Its prostrate habit and strangely zigzag stems also recommend it for rock gardens and Japanese gardens. 'Nozomi' is itself of Japanese raising. Its flowers have narrow, pearly pink petals (darker pink on the backs), which are not wide enough to overlap, and a cluster of golden stamens at the center. These emerge from every node, but there is only one flowering. Sometimes it also produces tiny, red hips. The plant has very small, dark, shiny leaves and is fairly healthy.

'NUITS DE YOUNG'

Moss Rose

ORIGIN **Laffay, France, 1845**
FLOWER SIZE **1.6in (4cm)**
SCENT **Strong and sweet**
FLOWERING **Once only, midseason**
HEIGHT/SPREAD **4.9ft (1.5m)/3.3ft (1m)**
HARDINESS **Zone 4**

There is nothing in the world of roses to match 'Nuits de Young'. It is the darkest and the smallest of all the old Moss roses. The flowers are darkest purple, with a hint of dark crimson toward the center at first, but always with dark, nearly black shadows between the petals. The stamens are rich golden yellow and set the whole flower in relief. The flowers are heavily covered in very dark moss – the buds, sepals, receptacles, and flower stems. The flowers come on long stems, in clusters of 3–9, and are useful for cutting. The plant has very thin, wiry stems and a naturally upright and slender habit of growth – a useful rose for narrow spaces. The leaves too are small, and dark green with crimson

'NUITS DE YOUNG'

edges. The plant tolerates poor soil and, if grown on its own roots, will naturally form a useful thicket. 'Nuits de Young' owes its unusual name to the English poet Edward Young (1683–1765), whose *Night Thoughts* were once popular in French translation.

'NUR MAHAL'

Hybrid Musk

ORIGIN **Pemberton, Britain, 1923**
PARENTAGE **'Château de Clos Vougeot' x seedling**
FLOWER SIZE **2.8in (7cm)**
SCENT **Light and musky**
FLOWERING **Repeats well**
HEIGHT/SPREAD **9.8ft (3m)/6.6ft (2m)**
HARDINESS **Zone 6**

This is one of the least known of the Pemberton Musks but one of the brightest and easiest to grow. All it lacks is strong scent. The flowers are semi-double, with an attractive roll to the petals, and a bright purplish crimson color. The color is set off by golden stamens, a white center, and white streaks in the petals. The flowers come in large, open clusters, typically of 10–25 during the first flowering, and at least twice as many in autumn. The bush has a naturally lax habit, with arching stems and dark, glossy leaves. It is fairly healthy. Like all the other Pemberton Musks, 'Nur Mahal' can be trained as a short climber in hot climates, where its nearly continuous flowering is a great asset.

'NUR MAHAL'

'NYMPHENBURG'

Shrub Rose

ORIGIN **Kordes, Germany, 1954**
PARENTAGE **'Sangerhausen' x 'Sunmist'**
FLOWER SIZE **3.1in (8cm)**
SCENT **Strong and fruity**
FLOWERING **Repeats well**
HEIGHT/SPREAD **5.7ft (1.75m)/4.1ft (1.25m)**
HARDINESS **Zone 5**

Although sometimes classified among the Hybrid Musks, it is best to think of 'Nymphenburg' as a vigorous shrub in the Floribunda style. Three of its four grandparents were Floribundas. Its flowers are fairly large and double, salmon pink at first, fading to rose pink, but always pinker at the edges of the petals and paler toward the center, which is pale yellow, fading to cream. They hold their petals somewhat loosely, but the flowers are always attractively shaped and borne in clusters of 3–10.

'NYMPHENBURG'

'Nymphenburg' has a lot of large, dark, healthy leaves and a few large prickles. It grows strongly and upright, and will make a short, leggy climber 8.2ft (2.5m) high in hot climates. The whole plant exudes toughness and vigor. And the scent of the flowers is delicious.

'NYVELDT'S WHITE'

Rugosa Hybrid

ORIGIN **Nyveldt, Netherlands, 1955**
PARENTAGE **(*Rosa rugosa* 'Rubra' x *Rosa cinnamomea*) x *Rosa nitida***
FLOWER SIZE **3.1in (8cm)**
SCENT **Medium and sweet**
FLOWERING **Continuous**
HEIGHT/SPREAD **6.6ft (2m)/4.1ft (1.25m)**
HARDINESS **Zone 4**

Although it boasts three rose species in its putative ancestry, 'Nyveldt's White' most resembles a Rugosa hybrid. It is popular with landscapers who want a hardy, rugged hedge that looks slightly more refined than the undiluted forms of *Rosa rugosa*. Its flowers are white, single, and fairly large, with a ring of deep yellow stamens at the center and sometimes an attractive twist to the petals. They are borne singly or in small clusters continuously through until late autumn. They are followed by fine orange hips (0.6in/1.5cm in diameter) with long, persistent sepals. The leaves are light green, wrinkly, attractive, slightly grayer underneath, with foliolate stipules, savage little barbs, and long, elegant leaflets. The plant is upright, very prickly, and much more leggy than most Rugosa roses. Rust is a problem unless preventative action is taken early in the season.

'NYVELDT'S WHITE'

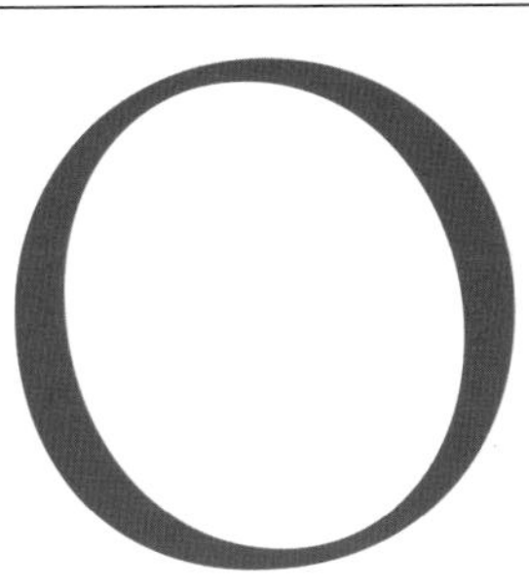

'OCEANA'

see 'OSIANA'

OCTAVIA HILL

syn. 'HARZEAL'
Floribunda

ORIGIN **Harkness, Britain, 1993**
PARENTAGE **Armada x 'Compassion'**
FLOWER SIZE **3.1in (8cm)**
SCENT **Medium, sweet, and Damask**
FLOWERING **Repeats well**
HEIGHT/SPREAD **4.9ft (1.5m)/3.3ft (1m)**
HARDINESS **Zone 6**

OCTAVIA HILL

The flowers of Octavia Hill are very full of petals, sometimes arranged in a roughly quartered shape. They are pale creamy pink, with a darker pink patch at the base of the petal backs, which gives a pink flush to the whole flower. The flowers come in small clusters, typically of 3–5, on long stems. Octavia Hill – the rose was named after an English social reformer (1838–1912) – has dark, healthy, semiglossy leaves and a bushy habit of growth. It is a very free-flowering plant, seemingly never out of flower until late autumn, provided it is deadheaded.

'OFFICINALIS'

Gallica

ORIGIN **c.1400**
FLOWER SIZE **3.9in (10cm)**
SCENT **Very strong and sweet**
FLOWERING **Once only**
HEIGHT/SPREAD **4.1ft (1.25m)/3.3ft (1m)**
HARDINESS **Zone 5**

The red rose of Lancaster is an early cultivated variety of *Rosa gallica*. It probably arose in France in about 1400: earlier Gallicas were simpler and closer to the wild species. It was widely grown right from the start for medicine, perfume, and preserves, as well as for its supreme intrinsic beauty. The flowers are large even by modern standards and, on well-grown plants, can reach 4.7–5.1in (12–13cm). They are semidouble and bright magenta pink, fading a little as they age. The petals open out fairly flat around a large mass of bright yellow stamens. The flowers come in clusters of up to five and are followed by dull red hips. The plant has large, mid-green leaves, somewhat rough to the touch, and a vigorous, bushy, branching habit. It has quite a lot of small bristles but only a few real prickles. The plant roots easily from hardwood cuttings and, if grown on its own roots (always to be recommended), suckers readily and builds up into a fine thicket. It sometimes gets a little mildew on the pedicels and receptacles, but never enough to do harm. Perhaps the most remarkable quality of 'Officinalis' is that such an ancient rose should still be of high ornamental value today, quite apart from being fairly healthy and vigorous. Many rose growers still rate it among their top ten garden roses. In the mid-16th century, probably in Norwich, England, a sport of 'Officinalis' occurred, which has white stripes irregularly splashed across the petals. This is known as **'Versicolor'** or 'Rosa Mundi' and is in every other way identical to 'Officinalis'. 'Versicolor' is as popular and widely grown as its parent, to which a few flowers or a branch will occasionally revert.

'OFFICINALIS'

'VERSICOLOR'

Sport of 'Officinalis'

'VERSICOLOR'

syn. 'ROSA MUNDI'
ORIGIN **Britain, c.1560**

'OKLAHOMA'

OCTOBERFEST

see LANTERN

'OKLAHOMA'

Hybrid Tea

ORIGIN **Swim & Weeks, US, 1964**
PARENTAGE **'Chrysler Imperial' x 'Charles Mallerin'**
FLOWER SIZE **5.1in (13cm)**
SCENT **Very strong and sweet**
FLOWERING **Repeats well**
HEIGHT/SPREAD **6.6ft (2m)/4.1ft (1.25m)**
HARDINESS **Zone 6**
AWARDS **Japan GM 1963**

'Oklahoma' is a large, vigorous, deep crimson Hybrid Tea. It shares the same parents as 'Mister Lincoln' and 'Papa Meilland', and is the darkest of the three. The flowers open from large buds and expand their petals slowly. They are globular at first, but later cupped – attractive at all stages. The petals have velvety, nearly black markings on their upper sides. The flowers are usually borne singly on long, strong stems that are excellent for cutting. 'Oklahoma' does best in dry climates: the flowers ball in damp conditions but thrive in heat. The plant is fairly healthy, with large, fairly ordinary leaves and large prickles. In hot climates it can reach 8.2ft (2.5m).

'OLD BLUSH'

see page 290

'OLD CRIMSON CHINA'

see 'SLATER'S CRIMSON'

'OLD MASTER'

Floribunda

ORIGIN **McGredy, New Zealand, 1974**
PARENTAGE **('Maxi' x 'Evelyn Fison') x ('Orange Sweetheart' x 'Frühlingsmorgen')**
FLOWER SIZE **4.3in (11cm)**
SCENT **Strong**
FLOWERING **Repeats well**
HEIGHT/SPREAD **2.7ft (80cm)/2ft (60cm)**
HARDINESS **Zone 5**

'Old Master' is one of Sam McGredy's earliest "hand-painted" roses, and still one of the best. The flowers are dark, glowing, and crimson red, but even more eye-catching are the pure white centers, the narrow white piping along the edge of the petals, and the pure white petal backs. Although the exact pattern of red and white differs from flower to flower, it is always very striking. White streaks break out of the center and run into the red parts of the petals; usually one very long streak stretches to the edge of the petal. The flowers have fine golden stamens and come in clusters of 3–11. The plant has dense foliage, very glossy leaves, and horrendous prickles. It is fairly healthy and notably hardy.

'OLD MASTER'

OLD PORT

syn. 'MACKATI'
Floribunda

ORIGIN **McGredy, New Zealand, 1990**
PARENTAGE **(['Anytime' x 'Eyepaint'] x 'Purple Splendour') x Stephens' Big Purple**
FLOWER SIZE **3.9in (10cm)**
SCENT **Strong and sweet**
FLOWERING **Repeats well**
HEIGHT/SPREAD **3.3ft (1m)/2.7ft (80cm)**
HARDINESS **Zone 6**

In cool climates, Old Port is the best of the purple Floribundas. It is particularly popular in Germany. It is a sumptuous dark purple (though the petal backs are paler), and its rich color is attractive from quite a distance. Despite their dark coloring, the flowers seem to glow. In hot conditions, they turn quickly to lilac, like some of the Gallica roses in their ancestry. Old Port also has an old-fashioned shape, which has become popular in recent years – the flowers are seen at their best not in bud (as Hybrid Teas are) but when they open out. The plant has medium-dark, glossy leaves and a short, compact habit of growth.

OLD PORT

OLYMPIAD

syn. 'MACAUCK'

Hybrid Tea

ORIGIN **McGredy, New Zealand, 1982**
PARENTAGE **'Red Planet' x 'Pharaon'**
FLOWER SIZE **5.5in (14cm)**
SCENT **Light and sweet**
FLOWERING **Repeats**
HEIGHT/SPREAD **4.9ft (1.5m)/3.3ft (1m)**
HARDINESS **Zone 6**
AWARDS **AARS 1984; Portland GM 1995**

The name of Olympiad was chosen to honor the Los Angeles Olympic Games in 1984. It is a fine, dark red Hybrid Tea with huge flowers on long, strong stems, which have won many prizes at shows and exhibitions. The flowers are full of thick petals, and last well as cut flowers. They also stand up well to heat, unlike many dark red roses that burn in the sun. They are usually borne singly, but occasionally come in clusters of up to four flowers. The plant is somewhat rigid and upright in growth, with mid-green leaves that stand up well to mildew but are susceptible to blackspot, especially in damp climates. The natural vigor of Olympiad makes it a good bedding rose.

OLYMPIAD

OLYMPIC GOLD

see GOLDENER OLYMP

'OMAR KHAYYÁM'

Damask Rose

ORIGIN **Britain, 1893**
FLOWER SIZE **2.4in (6cm)**
SCENT **Strong and sweet**
FLOWERING **Once only, in midsummer**
HEIGHT/SPREAD **6.6ft (2m)/6.6ft (2m)**
HARDINESS **Zone 5**

There is an interesting story behind this old Damask rose. The Persian poet Omar Khayyám was famous in Victorian England because of Edward Fitzgerald's translation of the *Rubáiyát*. In 1884, an English artist called William Simpson visited the poet's grave in Nashipur, and brought back hips of a rose growing over it. The seeds were sown and, in due course, a cutting of the best seedling was planted on Fitzgerald's grave at Boulge in Suffolk. That rose is now known as 'Omar Khayyám'. It is a fairly primitive Damask, closely related to 'Quatre Saisons' but once flowering. Its small flowers have a ragged shape, quilled petals, and a button eye. The petals show quite a variation in color, some being mid-pink and others pale. The flowers have the characteristic long sepals of the Damasks. The large, scrawny bush has a lot of prickles and beautiful light green leaves. More of a curiosity than a rose of intrinsic merit, 'Omar Khayyám' also suffers from blackspot.

'OMAR KHAYYÁM'

OPEN ARMS

syn. 'CHEWPIXCEL'

Rambler

ORIGIN **Warner, Britain, 1995**
PARENTAGE Mary Sumner x Laura Ashley
FLOWER SIZE **1.6in (4cm)**
SCENT **Light and musky**
FLOWERING **Repeats constantly**
HEIGHT/SPREAD **8.2ft (2.5m)/6.6ft (2m)**
HARDINESS **Zone 6**

This pretty patio rambler is an excellent plant for small gardens. Open Arms produces its flowers almost continuously on a compact, attractive, easy to grow plant. The flowers are pale salmon pink when they first open, fading quickly to pure rose-pink, and with a patch of

OPEN ARMS

'OLD BLUSH'

syn. 'PARSON'S PINK'

China Rose

ORIGIN **Britain, c.1750**
FLOWER SIZE **2.8in (7cm)**
SCENT **Medium and tealike**
FLOWERING **Continuous**
HEIGHT/SPREAD **3.3ft (1m)/3.3ft (1m)**
HARDINESS **Zone 6**

No rose has been so important in the development of our modern roses as 'Old Blush'. It is an old China rose, which has been grown in China, and possibly Japan, for at least 1,000 years. It was valued because it flowered continuously, unlike the wild roses from which it was descended. The same quality of perpetual flowering distinguished it when 'Old Blush' was brought to the West, probably in about 1750. It was crossed with the roses grown in Europe, especially Damasks and Gallicas, to produce the Bourbon roses and Hybrid Perpetuals. Its genes are present in all modern roses. It is still an excellent garden rose in its own right, with medium-sized, loosely double flowers, which open pale pink (from red buds) and darken to deep pink as they age. Sometimes they are followed by small red hips. The plant has slender green stems, a sprinkling of prickles, mid-green leaves, and crimson new growth. It flowers perpetually in warm climates. In cold climates, where it is forced into winter dormancy, it is one of the first to flower again in spring and one of the last to give up in late autumn.

No one knows when or where the climbing form, **'Climbing Old Blush'** was first recorded, but it is one of the best of all climbers. The flowers are noticeably larger than in the bush form, and they nod down on their slender stalks, which is an attractive habit. Their color is a wonderful combination of silvery pink and mauve, all the more beautiful for the extra size. They come singly or (more usually) in clusters of up to about five, and start to flower very early in the season. They are then never without at least a few flowers until winter sets in, and will continue through to spring in warm climates.

Another sport is **'Viridiflora'** – a real green rose in which all the parts of the flowers have been transformed into photosynthesizing structures. The petals, anthers, and styles are all leafy derivatives. Its mutation from 'Old Blush' is so slight that geneticists have not yet identified the gene responsible for the change. The flowers are green at first, but fade to a very pleasant coppery shade as they age, and then remain upon the bush for many weeks instead of dropping their "petals." In every other respect, 'Viridiflora' is still 'Old Blush' – same leaves, same prickles, same hardiness, same vigorous branching habit. It is not easy to spot the flowers from a distance, but they look very good surrounded by gray leaved plants like artemisias, and make quite a conversation piece if cut for the house.

'OLD BLUSH'

'CLIMBING OLD BLUSH'

'VIRIDIFLORA'

Sports of 'Old Blush'

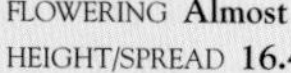

'CLIMBING OLD BLUSH'

Climbing China Rose

ORIGIN **c.1750**
FLOWER SIZE **3.1in (8cm)**
SCENT **Light and tealike**
FLOWERING **Almost continuous**
HEIGHT/SPREAD **16.4ft (5m)/8.2ft (2.5m)**

'VIRIDIFLORA'

syn. 'GREEN ROSE'

ORIGIN **Bambridge & Harrison, Britain, c.1845**
FLOWER SIZE **2.4in (6cm)**
SCENT **None**
HEIGHT/SPREAD **3.3ft (1m)/2.7ft (80cm)**
HARDINESS **Zone 5**

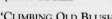

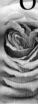

white toward the center. They are semi-double, with handsome yellow stamens at the center. They come in clusters of 5–20 at the ends of the branches. This means that the flowers multiply year by year as each stem throws out more side stems bearing their clusters of flowers at the end. Open Arms grows into a bushy climber, nearly thornless and a pillar of color from top to bottom. The leaves are small, neat, dark, shiny, and healthy, except for a little blackspot later in the season.

Opening Night

syn. 'JACOLBER'

Hybrid Tea

ORIGIN **Zary, US, 1998**
PARENTAGE Olympiad x Ingrid Bergman
FLOWER SIZE **5.1in (13cm)**
SCENT **Light but sweet**
FLOWERING **Repeats well**
HEIGHT/SPREAD **4.9ft (1.5m)/3.3ft (1m)**
HARDINESS **Zone 5**
AWARDS **AARS 1998**

Keith Zary bred Opening Night to combine the long stems, bright red flowers, and elegant shape of Olympiad with the handsome leaves and health of Ingrid Bergman. Its flowers open from nearly black buds and are bright crimson red, with a velvety sheen at first. Later the whorled petals open out and fade to dark cherry crimson. They are borne singly on long stems (up to 1.6ft/50cm) and are full of large, thick petals, which makes it an excellent, long-lasting cutting rose. Its floriferousness also makes it an excellent garden plant, probably the best red Hybrid Tea of recent years. The leaves are crimson when young but then turn dark, glossy green. The plant is healthy, strong-growing and upright, but broad too, which gives it the structure to produce a large quantity of flowers.

Oregold

see Anneliese Rothenberger

Oxford

see L'Aimant

Opening Night

'Ophelia'

'Ophelia'

Hybrid Tea

ORIGIN **W. Paul, Britain, 1912**
FLOWER SIZE **3.9in (10cm)**
SCENT **Strong and sweet**
FLOWERING **Repeats very well**
HEIGHT/SPREAD **3.3ft (1m)/2.7ft (80cm)**
HARDINESS **Zone 6**

No one knows where 'Ophelia' came from. One theory is that it was a seedling that turned up in a batch of 'Antoine Rivoire' that William Paul & Son bought in from Pernet-Ducher in Lyon. The Pauls realized that it was something different, and somewhat promising, so they propagated it and named it 'Ophelia'. Its long, slender buds became the industry standard for Hybrid Teas: it was the perfect form to which all should aspire. The flowers are not too full, but have large outer petals and smaller inner ones. The bud forms a perfect conical shape and the petals reflex elegantly as they unfurl. The flowers of 'Ophelia' are pale salmon flesh, shaded with rose, and with an apricot heart. They are abundantly produced on long, straight stems, usually singly, but sometimes in clusters of up to five, and on rare occasions in huge clusters, which may contain as many as 20 flowers. The plant has an air of delicacy and refinement at all times. The flowers are borne on a vigorous, erect plant, which may sometimes be susceptible to blackspot. Thrips, too, can spoil the flowers.

In due course, 'Ophelia' became a prolific parent and an ancestor of 'Mme. A. Meilland' ('Peace'). It was also widely grown as a cut flower under glass, in conditions where color sports and mutations were noticed, propagated, and introduced as new roses. 'Ophelia' proved to be unusually sportive, and is credited with about 30 sports (or sports of sports), which were commercially introduced.

One of the best known sports is **'Mme. Butterfly'** (a paler pink with a hint of yellow at the center). Also still quite widely available are **'Lady Sylvia'** (a deeper pink) and 'Golden Ophelia' (pale yellow), though all the sports are somewhat mixed up in many nurseries now. All four also produced climbing sports, of which **'Climbing Ophelia'**, **'Climbing Mme. Butterfly'**, and **'Climbing Lady Sylvia'** are all quite widely available.

'Climbing Ophelia'

'Mme. Butterfly'

'Climbing Mme. Butterfly'

'Lady Sylvia'

'Climbing Lady Sylvia'

Sports of 'Ophelia'

'Climbing Ophelia'

Climbing Hybrid Tea
ORIGIN **Dickson, Northern Ireland, 1920**
FLOWER SIZE **4.7in (12cm)**
HEIGHT/SPREAD **13.1ft (4m)/6.6ft (2m)**

'Mme. Butterfly'

ORIGIN **Hill, US, 1918**

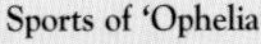

Sports of 'Mme. Butterfly'

'Climbing Mme. Butterfly'

Climbing Hybrid Tea
ORIGIN **Smith, 1926**
FLOWER SIZE **4.7in (12cm)**
HEIGHT/SPREAD **13.1ft (4m)/6.6ft (2m)**

'Lady Sylvia'

ORIGIN **Stevens, Britain, 1926**

Sport of 'Lady Sylvia'

'Climbing Lady Sylvia'

Climbing Hybrid Tea
ORIGIN **Stevens, Britain, 1933**
FLOWER SIZE **4.7in (12cm)**
HEIGHT/SPREAD **13.1ft (4m)/6.6ft (2m)**

'ORANGE HONEY'

'ORANGE HONEY'

Miniature Rose

ORIGIN **Moore, US, 1979**
PARENTAGE **'Rumba' x 'Over the Rainbow'**
FLOWER SIZE **1.6in (4cm)**
SCENT **Light and fruity**
FLOWERING **Repeats well**
HEIGHT/SPREAD **2ft (60cm)/1.3ft (40cm)**
HARDINESS **Zone 6**

'Orange Honey' is classed as a miniature rose, but it can get up to 2.7ft (80cm) and is therefore best thought of as a small shrub for the front of a bright border. The flowers open quickly from high-centered buds to cup-shaped flowers in clusters of 3–11. They are pale orange, with yellow backs and a yellow center, but lose their yellow coloring, so that the rose becomes crimson and white before the red too fades, and the flowers end up pink and white. But the overall impression given by 'Orange Honey' is of vibrant, cheerful orange. The bush has neat, dark, glossy, Wichurana foliage and a dense, upright habit of growth.

ORANGE MEILLANDINA

SYN. 'MEIJIKATAR', Orange Sunblaze

Miniature Rose

ORIGIN **Meilland, France, 1979**
PARENTAGE **Parador x (Baby Bettina x 'Mevrouw van Straaten van Nes')**
FLOWER SIZE **1.6in (4cm)**
SCENT **Light and sweet**
FLOWERING **Repeats constantly**
HEIGHT/SPREAD **1.6ft (50cm)/10in (25cm)**
HARDINESS **Zone 6**

ORANGE MEILLANDINA

The first thing to note about Orange Meillandina is that it is not orange, but red. The flowers are a bright, eye-catching vermilion right from the start, and turn duller and redder as they age. They are small, double, shapely, and borne either singly or in small clusters of up to five. Orange Meillandina has small, neat, medium-dark leaves, and flowers so well as to be almost continuously in bloom. It makes a good container plant, as well as providing color at the front of a border. Meilland introduced a climbing form in 1985 as Grimpant Orange Meillandina. It is the same as the dwarf form, but grows to 8.2ft (2.5m) and flowers somewhat more intermittently after the first extravagant display.

'ORANGE MORSDAG'

see 'DICK KOSTER'

'ORANGE SENSATION'

Floribunda

ORIGIN **de Ruiter, Belgium, 1961**
PARENTAGE **'Amor' x 'Fashion'**
FLOWER SIZE **3.1in (8cm)**
SCENT **Medium and fruity**
FLOWERING **Repeats well**
HEIGHT/SPREAD **3.3ft (1m)/2.7ft (80cm)**
HARDINESS **Zone 6**
AWARDS **NRA GM 1961; Golden Rose of the Hague 1968**

This deep orange Floribunda has been deservedly popular ever since it was introduced more than 40 years ago.

'ORANGE SENSATION'

'Orange Sensation' has a hint of yellow at the center, and fades eventually to pale crimson, but the overall impression is of brilliant, dark orange. The flowers are no more than semidouble, which means that they stand up well to rain. However, the petals reflex along their sides in such a way that the flowers appear more substantial than they really are. They have a small tuft of dark stamens at the center and, usually, a few white streaks. The flowers come in large, spacious clusters, typically of 7–15, on strong stems. The plant has healthy, mid-green leaves and repeats quickly, so that the bush is rarely without flowers.

ORANGE SUNBLAZE

see ORANGE MEILLANDINA

'ORANGE TRIUMPH'

Polyantha

ORIGIN **Kordes, Germany, 1937**
PARENTAGE **'Eva' x 'Solarium'**
FLOWER SIZE **1.6in (4cm)**
SCENT **Little or none**
FLOWERING **Repeats well**
HEIGHT/SPREAD **4.9ft (1.5m)/3.9ft (1.2m)**
HARDINESS **Zone 5**
AWARDS **NRS GM 1937**

It should be explained from the outset that 'Orange Triumph' is *not* orange, but deep coral and dull pink. Orange was a very rare and desirable color among roses in the 1930s, and a number were introduced that seem red or pink to later generations. The flowers of 'Orange Triumph' are cupped, with a somewhat tight and shapeless arrangement of petals, but they come in large, showy, open clusters of 10–40 flowers and repeat well all through the summer and autumn. The flowers are also very rain resistant. The plant has a vigorous, upright habit and lots of glossy, healthy, dark leaves. It roots easily from cuttings. It is easy to grow and survives neglect and competition well, so that it is often found in neglected gardens more than half a century old.

'ORANGEADE'

Floribunda

ORIGIN **McGredy, Northern Ireland, 1959**
PARENTAGE **'Orange Sweetheart' x 'Kordes' Sondermeldung'**
FLOWER SIZE **3.1in (8cm)**
SCENT **Light and fruity**
FLOWERING **Repeats well**
HEIGHT/SPREAD **4.9ft (1.5m)/3.3ft (1m)**
HARDINESS **Zone 6**
AWARDS **NRS GM 1959**

This dazzling orange Floribunda is still one of the best. The brilliant nasturtium orange flowers have no trace of any other color, apart from a small circle of short yellow stamens. They are semisingle and cupped in shape, occasionally borne singly, but more usually in long-stemmed clusters of 3–11. The plant is vigorous – it will grow to 6.6ft (2m) in a hot climate, though usually less than half that height – and repeats very well. It also stands up well to rain in cool climates. The large dark leaves are bronzy when young

'ORANGE TRIUMPH'

'ORANGEADE'

– a good contrast to the flowers – with broad leaflets. They may attract blackspot in susceptible areas.

ORANGES 'N' LEMONS

syn. 'MACORANLEM', Papagena
Floribunda

ORIGIN **McGredy, New Zealand, 1992**
PARENTAGE **New Year x Freude seedling**
FLOWER SIZE **3.1in (8cm)**
SCENT **Light and fruity**
FLOWERING **Repeats well**
HEIGHT/SPREAD **4.9ft (1.5m)/3.3ft (1m)**
HARDINESS **Zone 6**

ORANGES 'N' LEMONS

Oranges 'n' Lemons is a very handsome modern rose with stripes of brilliant vermilion orange and bright lemon yellow. The stripes are very irregular, but there is about twice as much lemon in the flower as orange. The colors are very striking and remain on the bush for many days, still looking good when at last they fade to salmon and cream. The opening buds are neat and shapely, but the flowers open almost flat to reveal a muddle of variegated petals. The flowers come in clusters of 3–7 and stand up very well to rain. They are set off by magnificent mahogany red new foliage, which eventually turns dark green, though the stems and (rather few) thorns are also red at first. The bush is healthy, strong, and vigorous, with long, arching branches, that will reach 6.6ft (2m) or more in a hot climate. The best colors and most blooms come in cool weather.

'ORLÉANS ROSE'

Polyantha

ORIGIN **Levavasseur, France, 1909**
PARENTAGE **'Mme. Norbert Levavasseur' x unknown**
FLOWER SIZE **1.4in (3.5cm)**
SCENT **Light**
FLOWERING **Repeats continuously**
HEIGHT/SPREAD **2.3ft (70cm)/1.6ft (50cm)**
HARDINESS **Zone 5**

'Orléans Rose' is a classic Polyantha, with large clusters of 10–30 neat flowers. The flowers open cherry crimson with a white center, but fade to carmine and lilac pink. The flower stalks are covered with brown, glandular bristles, which emit a resinous aroma when touched. The plant has bright green leaves with crimson stalks and midribs. 'Orléans Rose' is an important rose – it appears in the ancestry of almost every subsequent Polyantha and Floribunda – but it is still a good rose in its own right. It is vigorous and healthy, except for an occasional brush with mildew, and it roots very easily from cuttings. There is a second rose grown as 'Orléans Rose' in some parts of the world, which has nearly single, pink and white flowers.

'Orléans Rose' proved an extremely sportive rose: over 20 distinct sports of it were named and introduced in the 50 years following its introduction.

In 1917, de Ruiter introduced a sport with slightly darker flowers, and named it **'Miss Edith Cavell'**. This was a brave action in the middle of World War I, because Cavell was an English nurse who had been shot by the Germans for spying, and the Netherlands were technically neutral.

'ORLÉANS ROSE'

'MISS EDITH CAVELL'

Sport of 'Orléans Rose'

'MISS EDITH CAVELL'

syn. 'EDITH CAVELL'
ORIGIN **de Ruiter, Netherlands, 1917**

OREGOLD

see ANNELIESE ROTHENBERGER

'ORPHELINE DE JUILLET'

Gallica

ORIGIN **France, c.1837**
FLOWER SIZE **2.8in (7cm)**
SCENT **Medium and sweet**
FLOWERING **Once only**
HEIGHT/SPREAD **4.9ft (1.5m)/5.7ft (1.75m)**
HARDINESS **Zone 5**

The flowers of 'Orpheline de Juillet' are deep purple, with nearly white backs, and a hint of bright crimson at the base of the petals, turning to gray as they age. The inner petals also have a few white streaks radiating out from the center. They are fully double, and sometimes display a quartered center and/or button eye. They usually come in clusters of about three, sometimes more. 'Orpheline de Juillet' is fairly lax and sprawling in habit, with prickly, slender stems. The leaves which are small and mid-green are somewhat susceptible to mildew.

'ORPHELINE DE JUILLET'

'OSIANA'

'OSIANA'

syn. 'OCEANA'
Hybrid Tea

ORIGIN **Tantau, Germany, 1988**
FLOWER SIZE **4.3in (11cm)**
SCENT **Medium and fruity**
FLOWERING **Repeats**
HEIGHT/SPREAD **5.7ft (1.75m)/4.1ft (1.25m)**
HARDINESS **Zone 6**

Ivory, pale apricot, salmon pink, and peachy champagne – these are some of the colors used to describe the pastel shades of **'Osiana'**. Most of the flowers' color lies toward the center, and they fade as they age, especially at the edges, until the fully open flower is little more than mother-of-pearl. **'Osiana'** is essentially a rose for cutting – not for the florist industry but for home use. The flowers are shapely and full of petals. They are borne singly on long, strong stems and last many days in water. **'Osiana'** has large, healthy, mid-green leaves and handsome crimson new growth. It is a rose that responds well to good cultivation. If fed and nurtured, it will grow to a great height and reward you with large flowers of exhibition quality.

Othello

Othello

syn. 'AUSlo'

Shrub Rose

ORIGIN **Austin, Britain, 1986**
PARENTAGE **'Lilian Austin' × 'The Squire'**
FLOWER SIZE **3.9in (10cm)**
SCENT **Strong, sweet, and fruity**
FLOWERING **Repeats**
HEIGHT/SPREAD **4.1ft (1.25m)/3.3ft (1m)**
HARDINESS **Zone 6**

Othello is a big, bold rose, as dark and deep as its name suggests. The flowers are crimson, with dark pink petal backs and hints of cherry, purple, and red according to the season and the weather. The darkest colors come in cool weather and the edges of the flowers are always paler. The flowers are cabbagelike at first, but eventually open out to a lightly cupped shape enclosing a large quantity of short petals. The flowers are borne singly or in small clusters and are held erect on stout stems, which make them good for cutting. The plant has many large prickles and tough, dark green foliage, sometimes susceptible to mildew. It repeats fairly well, except in hot weather. It will grow to 6.6ft (2m) in hot climates, where flowering can be encouraged by pegging down long stems.

Our Lady of Guadalupe

syn. 'JACveryp', Shining Hope

Floribunda

ORIGIN **Zary, US, 2000**
FLOWER SIZE **2.8in (7cm)**
SCENT **Light and sweet**
FLOWERING **Repeats well**
HEIGHT/SPREAD **3.3ft (1m)/2.7ft (80cm)**
HARDINESS **Zone 6**

Jackson & Perkins introduced this rose as Shining Hope but changed it to Our Lady of Guadalupe and allocated some of the proceeds of sale to support the Hispanic College Fund. It is a charming pink Floribunda, with long petals and a distinctive elegance. The flowers open from crimson buds, and the petal backs remain darker than the upsides, so there is always a hint of dark pink in the shadows at the center of the flower, even when the pink has started to fade. They come in open clusters of 3–10 and make a fine display as a bedding rose – not too tall, even in California, but vigorous. The plant has dark, healthy, shiny leaves and a neat, bushy habit of growth.

Our Molly

'Our Rosamond'

Our Molly

syn. 'DICreason'

Shrub Rose

ORIGIN **Dickson, Northern Ireland, 1994**
FLOWER SIZE **2in (5cm)**
SCENT **Little or none**
FLOWERING **Repeats constantly**
HEIGHT/SPREAD **4.1ft (1.25m)/4.1ft (1.25m)**
HARDINESS **Zone 6**
AWARDS **Glasgow GM 1996**

Few roses are as floriferous as Our Molly. It is an extremely useful rose where brilliant color is needed. The flowers are single, and not large, but carried in extraordinary profusion all over the surface of the bush. They are red and white – deep, blood red, with white centers, dark yellow stamens, and occasional streaks of white running out into the red parts of the petals. They come in clusters of 5–20 and are followed by small red hips. Our Molly makes a lax, spreading bush, somewhat like a Hybrid Musk, with reddish stems, a lot of prickles, and ordinary, mid-green leaves. Deadheading helps to increase the number of flowers produced in the later flushes. The rose commemorates Molly Frizzell, sometime president of the Rose Society of Northern Ireland.

'Our Rosamond'

Hybrid Tea

ORIGIN **Bell, Australia, 1983**
PARENTAGE **'Daily Sketch' seedling × 'Red Planet'**
FLOWER SIZE **4.7in (12cm)**
SCENT **Light, but sweet**
FLOWERING **Fully remontant**
HEIGHT/SPREAD **3.9ft (1.2m)/3.3ft (1m)**
HARDINESS **Zone 6**

'Our Rosamond' was raised by a distinguished Australian amateur, Ron Bell, from Berwick, Victoria. It is essentially an exhibition rose for warm, dry climates. The long-stemmed flowers are large and very full of long, wide petals, which start to reflex as soon as they have space to do so. This gives the flowers a distinctive elegance right from the start. Their color is pale, silky pink, but variable: sometimes the petals have a touch of deeper pink along their edges. They are also slightly darker on their backs, which gives the flowers a great depth of pink shading between the petals. The plant is a good grower, upright in habit, fairly healthy, and blessed with only a few prickles. It is just one of many Australian roses that should be more widely grown abroad.

Our Lady of Guadalupe

Outta the Blue

syn. 'WEKstephitsu'

Shrub Rose

ORIGIN **Carruth, US, 2001**
PARENTAGE **Stephen's Big Purple × (International Herald Tribune × *Rosa soulieana* seedling)**
FLOWER SIZE **3.9in (10cm)**
SCENT **Strong, sweet, and spicy**
FLOWERING **Repeats well**
HEIGHT/SPREAD **4.9ft (1.5m)/4.1ft (1.25m)**
HARDINESS **Zone 6**

The sumptuous color of its flowers guaranteed popularity to Outta the Blue as soon as it was introduced. They are rich purple, with darker velvet patches. When they open out, there is also a hint of yellow at the center, but the deep plum purple color of the petals predominates all the time. In hot weather, as the flowers age, they fade to lavender and cream. They are large and rounded, with short petals (but lots of them), and they come in clusters of 5–15. Outta the Blue makes an upright, bushy plant, with healthy, dark green leaves. It is a quick repeat flowerer, so that it seems to be in flower almost continuously. The scent is distinctly delicious.

Oxfordshire

see Sommermorgen

Outta the Blue

P

PALMENGARTEN FRANKFURT

PANTHÈRE ROSE

'PADERBORN'

see 'BISCHOFSSTADT PADERBORN'

'PAESTANA'

see 'PORTLAND ROSE'

PALMENGARTEN FRANKFURT

syn. 'KORSILAN', Beauce, Country Dream, Our Rosy Carpet

Ground Cover

ORIGIN **Kordes, Germany, 1988**
PARENTAGE **('The Fairy' × 'Temple Bells') × ('Bubble Bath' × 'Lilli Marleen')**
FLOWER SIZE **2.4in (6cm)**
SCENT **Little or none**
FLOWERING **Continuous**
HEIGHT/SPREAD **2.7ft (80cm)/4.1ft (1.25m)**
HARDINESS **Zone 5**
AWARDS **ADR 1992**

Palmengarten Frankfurt is a very good Ground cover rose. Its value lies not so much in the beauty of the individual blooms but in the massed effect of the bush as a whole. It is usually planted in large quantities as a landscaping or groundcover rose. The flowers, which are pink with a hint of mauve, cupped, and loosely and lightly double, are reminiscent of the early Polyantha roses. They come in large, open clusters of 10–30 and are borne very profusely. The plant has neat, healthy, dark, small, Wichurana type leaves and is both hardy and tolerant of poor cultivation. Palmengarten Frankfurt tends to grow sideways as much as upward, and makes a fine informal hedge or edging in the garden. Palmengarten is the name of a great botanical and horticultural display garden in Frankfurt, Germany.

PANACHE

see TOP HIT

PANTHÈRE ROSE

syn. 'MEICAPINAL', Pink Panther, Aachener Dom

Hybrid Tea

ORIGIN **Meilland, France, 1982**
PARENTAGE **Coppélia 76 × Romantica 76**
FLOWER SIZE **4.3in (11cm)**
SCENT **Strong and sweet**
FLOWERING **Repeats well**
HEIGHT/SPREAD **4.1ft (1.25m)/3.3ft (1m)**
HARDINESS **Zone 6**
AWARDS **The Hague GM 1981**

This handsome Hybrid Tea would be called a Grandiflora in North America, because its flowers, although large, usually come in clusters. The flowers of Panthère Rose are a beautiful salmon pink, slightly more orange at first and pinker later, but always an attractive shade. They stand up very well to both sun and rain. The plant is hardy and strong-growing, with beautiful crimson new growth, slightly glaucous leaves, and broad leaflets. It is one of a line bred by Meilland for its resistance to blackspot in the mild, wet conditions of northern Europe. Panthère Rose is especially popular in Germany, where it is known as Aachener Dom. It has the unusual quality of growing to much greater heights in tropical climates, quickly reaching 13.1ft (4m), while usually pruned back to 2.7ft (80cm) in northern Europe.

'PAPA HÉMERAY'

China Rose

ORIGIN **Hémeray-Aubert, France, 1912**
PARENTAGE **'Hiawatha' × 'Old Blush'**
FLOWER SIZE **1.6in (4cm)**
SCENT **Light and musky**
FLOWERING **Repeats**
HEIGHT/SPREAD **4.1ft (1.25m)/3.3ft (1m)**
HARDINESS **Zone 6**

Although usually classified as a China rose, it is best to think of 'Papa Hémeray' as a Polyantha. The simple crimson and white flowers are very like those of its parent 'Hiawatha' and, although slightly larger, they are borne in large clusters, typically of 5–20 flowers. On the other hand, it has the typically angular growth of China roses and flowers liberally in flush after flush until the first frost – or year-round in hot climates. The crimson coloring fades to dark pink as the flowers age, and the stamens brown quickly. 'Papa Hémeray' makes a dense, vigorous bush, with dark, glossy leaves and few prickles. It needs only the lightest of pruning – and the offcuts can easily be rooted as cuttings.

'PAPA HÉMERAY'

'PAPA MEILLAND'

Hybrid Tea

ORIGIN **Meilland, France, 1963**
PARENTAGE **'Chrysler Imperial' × 'Charles Mallerin'**
FLOWER SIZE **5.1in (13cm)**
SCENT **Strong and sweet**
FLOWERING **Repeats well**
HEIGHT/SPREAD **4.1ft (1.25m)/3.3ft (1m)**
HARDINESS **Zone 6**
AWARDS **Baden-Baden GM 1962; Gamble FA 1974; World's Favourite Rose 1988**

'PAPA MEILLAND'

Many would say that 'Papa Meilland' is the best crimson Hybrid Tea in the world. It is certainly one of the most fragrant, with a rich, penetrating, sweet scent, which has won it international prizes. The buds are elegant and pointed before opening to reveal dark velvety crimson blooms with slightly more scarlet centers and an exquisite shape as they open out. They are borne singly on long stems and last well, which makes them good for cutting and exhibition, and, unlike so many crimson Hybrid Teas, they are held well erect, instead of drooping. They also drop their petals cleanly. The upright, prickly plant does best in warm climates, where it grows fairly vigorously. The leaves are nondescript and susceptible to mildew in some places. 'Papa Meilland' is not the most prolific bearer of blooms, but their quality is unsurpassed.

The climbing form, called **'Climbing Papa Meilland'**, is identical to 'Papa Meilland', except for its height and its pattern of intermittent flowering after the first fine showing.

Sport of 'Papa Meilland'

'CLIMBING PAPA MEILLAND'

Climbing Hybrid Tea

ORIGIN **Stratford, Britain, 1970**
FLOWER SIZE **5.9in (15cm)**
FLOWERING **Spectacular first flowering, then intermittently**
HEIGHT/SPREAD **13.1ft (4m)/6.6ft (2m)**

'PAPILLON'

'PARADE'

PARADISE

'PAPILLON'

Tea Rose

ORIGIN **Nabonnand, France, 1881**
FLOWER SIZE **3.1in (8cm)**
SCENT **Light and tealike**
FLOWERING **Repeats constantly**
HEIGHT/SPREAD **4.9ft (1.5m)/3.3ft (1m)**
HARDINESS **Zone 7**

The flowers of 'Papillon' are a rich mixture of coppery pink shades, with a hint of white at the base of the petals and deep orange pink shadows. Somewhat cupped at first, the flowers later open out and display their ragged petals in such a way that they resemble the wings of butterflies – hence the name. They are generously borne both singly and in clusters, and well set off by rich coppery new leaves and growth. The plant grows slowly but will eventually reach 9.8ft (3m) in hot climates and can be treated as a climber or pillar rose. Normally, however, it is seen as a bush about 3.3ft (1m) high. 'Papillon' is a reliable repeater.

'PARA TI'

syn. 'POUR TOI'

Miniature Rose

ORIGIN **Dot, Spain, 1946**
PARENTAGE **'Eduardo Toda' x 'Pompon de Paris'**
FLOWER SIZE **1in (2.5cm)**
SCENT **Light and sweet**
FLOWERING **Repeats constantly**
HEIGHT/SPREAD **11.8in (30cm)/0.7ft (20cm)**
HARDINESS **Zone 6**

Every flower of 'Para Ti' is a miniature Hybrid Tea, though the lightly double buds expand quickly and the fully open flowers are much more conspicuous than the slender, unopened buds. They are pure white, except for a hint of green at the base of the buds and the yellow stamens at the center. They are held erect, straining cheerfully toward the sun, and usually carried in sufficient quantities to make quite an impact, even though the flowers are so small. They are well complemented by the small, dark, shiny leaves. 'Para Ti' makes a small, bushy, upright plant and is still one of the best miniature roses. It is especially useful for mixing with other colors and for providing brightness in semishady sites.

'PARADE'

Modern Climber

ORIGIN **Boerner, US, 1953**
PARENTAGE **'New Dawn' seedling x 'Minna Kordes'**
FLOWER SIZE **3.9in (10cm)**
SCENT **Strong and sweet**
FLOWERING **Repeats well**
HEIGHT/SPREAD **9.8ft (3m)/6.6ft (2m)**
HARDINESS **Zone 6**

'Parade' is one of the best of all climbing roses for small gardens. It has huge flowers, never stops flowering, and does not grow too tall. The flowers are bright deep pink or cherry carmine, paler toward the edge of the flower and sometimes with a hint of purple toward the center. The petal backs are slightly paler and more silvery. The flowers are cupped, and so heavy with petals that they often nod over. This is a good thing because it means that rain does not spoil them but you can look up into them. They come singly or in clusters of up to five. The plant has lots of large, dark green leaves: the influence of 'New Dawn' is visible here and in its resistance to disease. It grows vigorously and is very floriferous, both in its first flowering and thereafter until late autumn.

'PARA TI'

PARADISE

syn. 'WEZEIP', Burning Sky

Hybrid Tea

ORIGIN **Weeks, US, 1978**
PARENTAGE **'Swarthmore' x 'Angel Face' seedling**
FLOWER SIZE **4.7in (12cm)**
SCENT **Very strong and sweet**
FLOWERING **Repeats**
HEIGHT/SPREAD **4.1ft (1.25m)/3.3ft (1m)**
HARDINESS **Zone 5**
AWARDS **AARS 1979; Portland GM 1979**

The color of this beautiful Hybrid Tea was considered a breakthrough when it was first introduced: lilac mauve with crimson edges. Paradise also has a very strong scent, large flowers, and a lot of them. The color is variable, and depends upon temperature – the crimson edging is strongest in hot weather but the lavender also fades slightly in the sun. The flowers are beautifully shaped, with petals that curl back at the edges, and come singly or in clusters of up to three. It is useful for cutting and exhibition. The plant has a lot of prickles, a sturdy, upright habit of growth, and healthy, dark green leaves. It is also one of the hardiest Hybrid Teas.

PARIS D'YVES SAINT LAURENT

syn. 'MEIVAMO'

Hybrid Tea

ORIGIN **Meilland, France, 1994**
PARENTAGE **'Silva' sport x Rouge Meilland 84**
FLOWER SIZE **5.1in (13cm)**
SCENT **Light and sweet**
FLOWERING **Repeats**
HEIGHT/SPREAD **4.1ft (1.25m)/3.3ft (1m)**
HARDINESS **Zone 6**

Although widely promoted and grown for the cut-flower trade, Paris d'Yves Saint Laurent is also an excellent garden rose. It does especially well in dry weather, when its large, many-petaled flowers can open out undamaged. They are rose pink, with bright pink petal backs and a distinctive roll to the long petals, which gives the whole flower its characteristic charm. The flowers are usually borne singly on long stems, fairly regularly until the first frosts. Paris d'Yves Saint Laurent has large, dark, healthy leaves and a moderately vigorous habit. Since it is named after the French fashion house, one might have expected the flowers to be more strongly scented.

PARIS D'YVES SAINT LAURENT

'PARKDIREKTOR RIGGERS'

'PARKDIREKTOR RIGGERS'

Kordesii Hybrid

ORIGIN **Kordes, Germany, 1957**
PARENTAGE **'Kordesii' x 'Crimson Glow'**
FLOWER SIZE **2in (5cm)**
SCENT **Little or none**
FLOWERING **Repeats well**
HEIGHT/SPREAD **13.1ft (4m)/6.6ft (2m)**
HARDINESS **Zone 4**
AWARDS **ADR 1960**

The hard red flowers of 'Parkdirektor Riggers' need bright light to show them to advantage. They lack luminescence, so that in dull weather their color is strangely recessive. When illuminated by brilliant sunshine, however, they can be the brightest flowers in the whole garden, especially when an entire cluster of up to 30 is in full flower. The individual flowers are a deep, unfading red, uniform across every part of the petals, apart from occasional white flecks at the base. There is a small ring of greeny yellow stamens at the center. The plant has dark, glossy, healthy leaves and a good, well-branched habit of growth. It is very free-flowering, and just as happy in tropical gardens as in the subzero temperatures for which the Kordesii climbers were bred.

'PARKZAUBER'

Shrub Rose

ORIGIN **Kordes, Germany, 1956**
PARENTAGE **'Kordes' Sondermeldung' x 'Nuits de Young'**
FLOWER SIZE **3.9in (10cm)**
SCENT **Strong and sweet**
FLOWERING **Once only**
HEIGHT/SPREAD **6.6ft (2m)/4.9ft (1.5m)**
HARDINESS **Zone 5**

Wilhelm Kordes experimented with many old roses in the course of his long and distinguished career as a hybridizer. 'Parkzauber' was a cross between a fashionable orange Floribunda and a small purple Moss rose – two roses as different from each other as it is possible to imagine. The flowers are dark pink or cherry colored, with a muddle of quilled petals settling nicely around the center as they open out. They are usually borne in clusters of 3–7, but always very profusely. 'Parkzauber' is a vigorous shrub, upright at first but more arching in habit later, with coarse, dark leaves (sometimes with only three leaflets) and quite a covering of moss on the receptacles and flower stems. Kordes released it five years before David Austin introduced 'Constance Spry'; it is interesting to consider how different would have been the story of roses late in the 20th century if Kordes had continued to develop his old/new hybrids.

'PARKZIERDE'

Bourbon Hybrid

ORIGIN **Geschwind, Hungary, 1909**
FLOWER SIZE **3.1in (8cm)**
SCENT **Strong and sweet**
FLOWERING **Once only**
HEIGHT/SPREAD **5.7ft (1.75m)/4.9ft (1.5m)**
HARDINESS **Zone 5**

Although it was raised by Rudolph Geschwind, 'Parkzierde' was actually introduced by Peter Lambert in Germany, who passed it off as one of his own roses. Only recently has it been possible to restore the credit for this and other roses to the great Hungarian breeder. 'Parkzierde' is a once-flowering Bourbon hybrid, a by-product of Geschwind's work to make garden roses more hardy. The flowers are cupped, well scented, and full of petals, pale crimson in color, but fading as they age, with hints of purple and violet in the outer petals. They usually come in long-stemmed clusters of 3–5. The plant is vigorous, with healthy, soft green leaves and an arching habit of growth.

'PARKZAUBER'

'PARKZIERDE'

'PARSON'S PINK'

see 'OLD BLUSH'

'PARTRIDGE'

see 'WEISSE IMMENSEE'

'PASCALI'

Hybrid Tea

ORIGIN **Lens, Belgium, 1963**
PARENTAGE **'Queen Elizabeth' x 'White Butterfly'**
FLOWER SIZE **4.7in (12cm)**
SCENT **Light and sweet**
FLOWERING **Repeats very well**
HEIGHT/SPREAD **5.7ft (1.75m)/2.7ft (80cm)**
HARDINESS **Zone 6**
AWARDS **The Hague GM 1963; Portland GM 1967; AARS 1969; World's Favourite Rose 1991**

Louis Lens bred many magnificent Hybrid Teas before he devoted himself to the development of Musk roses. 'Pascali' is one of his best. It is a shapely, strong-growing white rose, with tough petals, an upright habit of growth, and a fair amount of good health. The flowers are pure white, with ivory white backs, which gives rise to cream colored reflections in the shadows between the petals. The flowers are slow to open and are borne singly on long stems, which makes them popular for exhibition and cutting. The easy to grow plant is tall and narrow, with large dark leaves. It produces its flowers in great abundance.

'PASCALI'

PAT AUSTIN

syn. 'AUSMUM'

Shrub Rose

ORIGIN **Austin, Britain, 1995**
PARENTAGE **Graham Thomas x Abraham Darby**
FLOWER SIZE **4.7in (12cm)**
SCENT **Strong and fruity**
FLOWERING **Repeats**
HEIGHT/SPREAD **4.1ft (1.25m)/4.1ft (1.25m)**
HARDINESS **Zone 6**

Pat Austin was a shock when it first came out: here was a David Austin rose in copper, coral, and amber, quite different from the muted pastel shades of typical English Roses. It is actually a very good rose, with large, cupped flowers and wonderful contrasts between the coral petals and their pale yellow backs. It opens out into a loose flower, with rich red stamens at the center and always a few little petals waywardly curling in to give contrast and character. Eventually the orange fades to pink and the yellow to cream. The flowers are loosely held in clusters of 3–7, starting early in the season, and contrast well with the dark, handsome leaves. Pat Austin is David Austin's wife; their garden at Albrighton is designed around her sculptures.

PATIO QUEEN

see NICE DAY

PAT AUSTIN

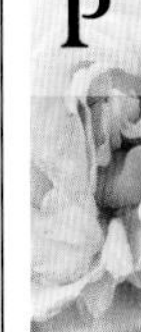
P

'PAUL CRAMPEL'

'PAUL CRAMPEL'

Polyantha

ORIGIN **Kersbergen, 1930**
PARENTAGE **sport of 'Superb'**
FLOWER SIZE **1.2in (3cm)**
SCENT **Light and musky**
FLOWERING **Repeats well**
HEIGHT/SPREAD **2ft (60cm)/2ft (60cm)**
HARDINESS **Zone 6**

'Paul Crampel' is an important rose in the history of gardening. It was the first to contain the pelargonidin molecules that give modern orange roses their extraordinary brilliance. Pelargonidin is not naturally found in roses, but it is common in red geraniums and is what gives them their peculiar brightness of color. 'Paul Crampel' the rose is named after a pelargonium of the same name, introduced by Lemoine in 1889 to commemorate the French explorer Paul Crampel (1864–91). The rose was a sport of a crimson Polyantha called 'Superb', to which it sometimes reverts, but the presence of pelargonidin in 'Paul Crampel' was used to breed bigger and better roses with the same brilliant orange sheen, which is now so common in modern roses that we take it for granted. 'Paul Crampel' has semidouble, cupped flowers, with a small white patch at the center, in large clusters of 10–30. It is a typical Polyantha, hardy and healthy, and produces its flowers in flush after flush through until the first frost – or constantly in hot climates.

'PAUL NEYRON'

Hybrid Perpetual

ORIGIN **Levet, France, 1869**
PARENTAGE **'Victor Verdier' x 'Anna de Diesbach'**
FLOWER SIZE **5.5in (14cm)**
SCENT **Light**
FLOWERING **Remontant**
HEIGHT/SPREAD **4.9ft (1.5m)/3.3ft (1m)**
HARDINESS **Zone 5**

One hundred years ago, 'Paul Neyron' was universally accepted as by far the largest rose ever known, its flowers reaching as much as 6.3–6.7in (16–17cm) in favorable conditions. Such was its fame that it gave its name, "Neyron-pink," to a particularly glowing shade of pale carmine. The flowers are deep rose pink, with a suggestion of lilac, and pale silver backs. Its globular buds open out to huge cupped flowers,

'PAUL NEYRON'

very full of petals, with a ruffled formation like a peony. The flowers are held well up on strong stems, and come usually singly, but occasionally in twos and threes. It has large, matte green leaves, occasionally liable to blackspot, but 'Paul Neyron' is one of those roses that respond well to good cultivation. Given food and water in a hot, dry climate, it will produce a prodigious crop of flowers every six weeks or so. Paul Neyron, who died young, was a friend of Levet's family.

'PAUL NOËL'

Wichurana Rambler

ORIGIN **Tanne, France, 1913**
PARENTAGE ***Rosa wichurana* x 'Monsieur Tillier'**
FLOWER SIZE **2.4in (6cm)**
SCENT **Medium and tealike**
FLOWERING **Once, early in season, with a few later flowers**
HEIGHT/SPREAD **9.8ft (3m)/6.6ft (2m)**
HARDINESS **Zone 7**

'Paul Noël' is a widely grown first-generation Wichurana rambler, with the long, slender branches that are so well adapted to training, or to weeping standards. The flowers are a striking coral pink, with a hint of yellow around the central button eye, and slightly paler pink on their undersides. They open quickly into a starburst of sharply quilled petals, rolled back along their sides like a cactus dahlia. They come in small clusters, of rarely more than five at a time, and produce a few flowers later in the year after the first burst of color. The leaves are small, tough, and quite dark in the Wichurana way, but susceptible to mildew. Paul Noël was a friend of Rémy Tanne and director of the Jardin des Plantes in Rouen, Tanne's home town.

PAUL RICARD

syn. 'MEINIVOZ', Summer's Kiss, Spirit of Peace

Hybrid Tea

ORIGIN **Meilland, France, 1991**
PARENTAGE **(Michel Hidalgo x 'Mischief') x Ambassador**
FLOWER SIZE **3.9in (10cm)**
SCENT **Strong, sweet, and spicy**
FLOWERING **Repeats**
HEIGHT/SPREAD **3.3ft (1m)/2.7ft (80cm)**
HARDINESS **Zone 6**
AWARDS **Rome GM 1991**

Of the many superb roses bred and introduced by Meilland in the last 20 years, Paul Ricard is among the best. Its flowers are handsome, full of large petals, and a beautiful shade of buff or pale apricot, with darker backs to the petals – the color of copper or caramel. They are

PAUL RICARD

usually borne singly, though sometimes in small clusters, on long, strong stems, that make them perfect for cutting. Their scent is a great bonus: Paul Ricard has won prizes for its fragrance, as well as for all-around garden performance. The plant is vigorous and repeats quickly, without ever growing too tall. The fine green leaves withstand blackspot and stand up fairly well to mildew. It is a rose that responds well to good cultivation – feed it, and it will reward you.

'PAUL RICAULT'

Hybrid China

ORIGIN **Portemer, France, 1845**
FLOWER SIZE **4.3in (11cm)**
SCENT **Strong and sweet**
FLOWERING **Once only**
HEIGHT/SPREAD **5.7ft (1.75m)/4.9ft (1.5m)**
HARDINESS **Zone 5**

Rose experts argue about the origins of 'Paul Ricault' – is it a Centifolia or a Hybrid China? – but all are agreed that it is a beautiful and rewarding garden rose. The flowers open from crimson buds. They are large, cupped, and full of dark pink or pale crimson petals, which are slightly rolled back at their tips, while at the same time arranged in an attractive quartered shape within the outer guard petals. The color fades from the outside as the flower opens and matures, so that it ends up dark pink with a tinge of mauve, while keeping its color well toward the center of the flower. The flowers come in clusters of 3–7 and cut well: their scent is delicious. The bush is vigorous, with smooth China leaves and large prickles. It is inclined to become a little lanky and bare at the bottom. The long, vigorous growth arches over attractively under the weight of the flowers. If pegged down in winter, they will flower all along their length.

'PAUL NOËL' *(as a weeping standard)*

'PAUL RICAULT'

William Paul and Family

TWO GENERATIONS OF THE PAUL FAMILY PRODUCED FOUR EMINENT AND VERSATILE ROSE BREEDERS, WHO ALSO WROTE BOOKS ABOUT THEIR SKILLS AND KNOWLEDGE

William Paul (1823–1905) was the founder of the British rose industry. His influential book, *The Rose Garden*, was first published in 1848 when he was barely 25, and was revised and reprinted 11 times until 1910.

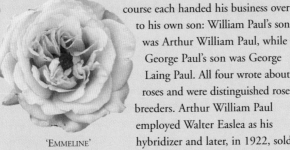

'Emmeline'

William Paul was a nurseryman's son from Cheshunt in Hertfordshire. He ran the business with his brother George after their father's death in 1847. Later they started separate nurseries and in due course each handed his business over to his own son: William Paul's son was Arthur William Paul, while George Paul's son was George Laing Paul. All four wrote about roses and were distinguished rose breeders. Arthur William Paul employed Walter Easlea as his hybridizer and later, in 1922, sold the business to Chaplin Brothers.

'Lady Godiva'

The Pauls bred roses of every kind: Bourbons like 'Vivid' (1853); Hybrid Perpetuals like 'Black Prince' (1866); Hybrid Teas like 'Dawn' (1898) and 'Emmeline' (1921); Multiflora Ramblers like 'Lilliput' (1897) and 'Lady Godiva' (1908), a pale pink sport of 'Dorothy Perkins'. They also experimented with unusual species: 'Una' (1898) is a hybrid of the dog rose, *Rosa canina*, and 'Mermaid' (1918) of *Rosa bracteata*.

Both branches of the family used "Paul" as a prefix to rose names – for example, 'Paul's Lemon Pillar' (G.L. Paul, 1915) and 'Paul's Scarlet Climber' (A.W. Paul, 1916). This was an early exercise in branding, and each benefited from the other's publicity, but it also confused their separate identities, so that few people realize just how many gifted nurserymen traded under the name of "Paul."

'Lilliput'

Paul Shirville

syn. 'HARqueterwife', Heart Throb

Hybrid Tea

ORIGIN **Harkness, Britain, 1981**
PARENTAGE **'Compassion' x 'Mischief'**
FLOWER SIZE **3.1in (8cm)**
SCENT **Very strong and sweet**
FLOWERING **Repeats well**
HEIGHT/SPREAD **3.3ft (1m)/2.5ft (75cm)**
HARDINESS **Zone 5**
AWARDS **Edland FA 1982; Golden Rose of Courtrai 1989; The Hague FA 1990; Auckland FA 1991**

Paul Shirville is a splendid all-purpose modern rose, equally useful for bedding and picking. It combines the shape of the Hybrid Teas with the profuse flowering of the Floribundas. The flowers are pink, with a yellow flush at the back of the petals, which creates a salmon pink glow at first. The color varies in depth, but there is always a warmth to the pinkness of Paul Shirville. Its scent has won it several international prizes. The flowers are carried singly or in clusters of up to five, and produced with great freedom. They are excellent for cutting as well as garden display. Their only weakness is a tendency to ball in wet weather. The plant has a lot of prickles, together with glossy, dark green leaves (bronze red when new) and a slight susceptibility to blackspot where this is prevalent.

Paul Shirville

'Paul Transon'

Wichurana Rambler

ORIGIN **Barbier, France, 1900**
PARENTAGE ***Rosa wichurana* x 'L'Idéal'**
FLOWER SIZE **2.4in (6cm)**
SCENT **Strong and tealike**
FLOWERING **Once, midseason, then intermittently**
HEIGHT/SPREAD **13.1ft (4m)/8.2ft (2.5m)**
HARDINESS **Zone 6**

There is considerable confusion between 'Paul Transon' and 'Paul Noël'. Most of the plants grown, sold, and admired in Europe as 'Paul Transon' are, in fact, 'Paul Noël'. 'Paul Transon' has cupped flowers and incurved petals, whereas 'Paul Noël' has a starburst of quilled petals radiating out from the centre. 'Paul Transon' has dark pink buds, which open to pale salmon pink flowers with a much deeper center, almost coppery or terracotta pink. Later they fade to flesh pink. They are borne singly and in clusters of up to five. Although never a profuse flowerer, 'Paul Transon' does produce a few flowers almost continuously into autumn. The plant is vigorous, with dark green, glossy foliage and purplish red young stems. It may get a little mildew late in the year, but never enough to affect its health.

'Paul Transon'

'PAUL'S HIMALAYAN MUSK RAMBLER'

'PAUL'S HIMALAYAN MUSK RAMBLER'

Hybrid Musk

ORIGIN **W. Paul, Britain, 1916**
FLOWER SIZE **1.2in (3cm)**
SCENT **Strong and musky**
FLOWERING **Once, quite late in season**
HEIGHT/SPREAD **16.4ft (5m)/9.8ft (3m)**
HARDINESS **Zone 6**

The rose now widely grown as 'Paul's Himalayan Musk' is one of the most vigorous of all ramblers. Its flowers are small and their petals are very prettily arranged in a loose rosette. They open soft lilac pink, but fade over the next couple of days to white. They are strongly scented of musk, offset by lush, pale green leaves, and borne in large, spacious clusters of 30–50. The popularity of this rose since its re-introduction in the 1970s rests as much on its vigor and zest for life as it does on its flowers. Planted in the most unpromising of situations at the foot of a fairly tall tree, it will make its way up in a few years and cascade out of the branches in eye-catching profusion.

'PAUL'S LEMON PILLAR'

Tea-Noisette

ORIGIN **G. Paul, Britain, 1915**
PARENTAGE **'Frau Karl Druschki' x 'Maréchal Niel'**
FLOWER SIZE **4.7in (12cm)**
SCENT **Strong and sweet**
FLOWERING **Once only, fairly early in season**
HEIGHT/SPREAD **11.5ft (3.5m)/6.6ft (2m)**
HARDINESS **Zone 7**
AWARDS **NRS GM 1915**

'Paul's Lemon Pillar' is neither lemon colored, nor a pillar rose, but it is still one of the most beautiful white climbers of the 20th century. There is a hint of lemon at the center of the pendulous flowers as they open from long, elegant white buds, but it soon fades to cream and white. And it will quickly grow to 13.1ft (4m) – and much more up a wall or tree. The flowers hang down under their own weight, though the stems that support them are long and strong: the whole growth of the plant is strong, stiff, and upright in its carriage. The thick, lanky stems are prickly, but the plant covers itself with sweet-smelling flowers, which last a long time if cut and taken indoors. The petals, though large and exquisitely rolled back at the edges, are sensitive to rain damage, so this is a rose that does best in hot, dry climates. Large red hips follow in autumn.

'PAUL'S SCARLET CLIMBER'

'PAUL'S SCARLET CLIMBER'

Modern Climber

ORIGIN **W. Paul, Britain, 1916**
FLOWER SIZE **2.8in (7cm)**
SCENT **Light**
FLOWERING **Once spectacularly, then occasionally**
HEIGHT/SPREAD **8.2ft (2.5m)/4.9ft (1.5m)**
AWARDS **NRS GM 1915; Bagatelle GM 1918**
HARDINESS **Zone 5**

'Paul's Scarlet Climber' has been popular across the world, in hot climates and in cold, ever since its introduction. It took over from 'Excelsa' as everyone's favorite red climber, and in due course passed the baton on to 'Danse du Feu' and 'Dublin Bay'. Its flowers are vivid crimson, with a scarlet sheen at first, but they later pick up a slightly purple cast and fade to cherry red. They are borne in clusters of 3–15 in great profusion, and are carried on long stems, which are good for cutting and immune to sunshine or rain. The plant is very hardy, healthy, thick stemmed, fairly prickly, and moderately vigorous. 'Paul's Scarlet Climber' thrives in poor soil and is a long-lived, enduring plant everywhere, cheerfully covering itself in flowers year after year.

'PAULII'

Rugosa Hybrid

ORIGIN **G. Paul, Britain, 1903**
PARENTAGE ***Rosa rugosa* x *Rosa arvensis***
FLOWER SIZE **2.8in (7cm)**
SCENT **Light and sweet**
FLOWERING **Continuous**
HEIGHT/SPREAD **3.3ft (1m)/13.1ft (4m)**
HARDINESS **Zone 5**

There is some slight uncertainty about the origins of 'Paulii', but it is a hybrid of *Rosa rugosa*, with either *Rosa arvensis* or *Rosa multiflora* as the other parent. It is a modest trailing rose, with small clusters of single, white, crinkly flowers, which appear in small clusters intermittently throughout the summer and autumn. The narrow petals have an elegant and distinctive outline, but the plant is extremely prickly. It forms a low thicket and has bright green, crinkly leaves. It is too wild for all but the largest gardens, but is widely planted in western Europe as a hardy ground-covering landscape rose.

'Paulii Rosea' is a pink sport, and sometimes reverts to the original white form. Both are more widely grown than their value merits.

'PAULII'

'PAULII ROSEA'

Sport of 'Paulii'

'PAULII ROSEA'

ORIGIN **G. Paul, Britain, 1910**

'PAX'

Hybrid Musk

ORIGIN **Pemberton, Britain, 1918**
PARENTAGE **'Trier' x 'Sunburst'**
FLOWER SIZE **3.9in (10cm)**
SCENT **Strong, sweet, and musky**
FLOWERING **Repeats well**
HEIGHT/SPREAD **6.6ft (2m)/4.9ft (1.5m)**
HARDINESS **Zone 6**
AWARDS **NRS GM 1918**

Of all the Pemberton Hybrid Musk roses, none has such elegant buds as 'Pax'. They are long and slender, and nod attractively on their short stalks. They are cream colored or ivory at this early stage, but turn pure white when they open out to reveal a semi-double flower with a good cluster of golden stamens at the center. The petals are thicker and more substantial than most Musk roses. The flowers come in long clusters of 5–7 early in the year, but up to 30 later, when the plant produces long new shoots from near the ground. The leaves are a beautiful foil to the flowers, being dark and glossy, with crimson edges at first. The new growths are also crimson. 'Pax' has an open, arching habit of growth, and will reach 13.1ft (4m) if grown as a climber against a wall.

'PEACE'

see 'MME. A. MEILLAND'

'PAX'

'PAUL'S LEMON PILLAR' ▶

PEACEKEEPER

PEACEKEEPER

syn. 'HARBELLA'
Floribunda

ORIGIN Harkness, Britain, 1994
PARENTAGE 'Dame of Sark' x Bright Smile
FLOWER SIZE 3.5in (9cm)
SCENT Strong and sweet
FLOWERING Repeats well
HEIGHT/SPREAD 2.7ft (80cm)/2ft (60cm)
HARDINESS Zone 6
AWARDS Geneva 1995

This scented Floribunda goes on flowering and flowering. Indeed, Peacekeeper seems never to be out of flower. The flowers are unusually beautiful too – fairly large and lightly double, with elegantly pointed petals and a handsome ring of stamens at the center. They are apricot colored, with a large patch of rich yellow toward the base of the petals. The flowers are handsome at every stage of their development, and the buds are attractive even before they open. They are borne in clusters of 3–8, but very profusely, by the well-branched plant. Peacekeeper has medium-sized, medium-dark leaves, which stand up well to disease, and an upright, bushy habit of growth. Although bred in England, it performs well in hot climates and is popular in Australia and parts of the US.

PEACH BLOSSOM

syn. 'AUSBLOSSOM'
Shrub Rose

ORIGIN Austin, Britain, 1990
PARENTAGE 'The Prioress' x Mary Rose
FLOWER SIZE 2.4in (6cm)
SCENT Light and fruity
FLOWERING Repeats
HEIGHT/SPREAD 4.9ft (1.5m)/4.9ft (1.5m)
HARDINESS Zone 6

This rose takes its name from a character in Shakespeare's *A Midsummer Night's Dream.* The flowers of Peach Blossom are semidouble, cupped, and borne in clusters. They are palest pink, with a creamy yellow base, darker petal backs, and an attractive mass of stamens at the center of every flower. They are very generously produced in tight clusters of 3–10 and followed by red hips. Regular deadheading helps to promote further flowering, which will continue well into autumn. The plant has healthy, mid-green, glossy leaves and a fair share of prickles.

'PEARL DRIFT'

PEACH SUNBLAZE

see PÊCHE MEILLANDINA

'PEARL DRIFT'

Hybrid Tea

ORIGIN Le Grice, Britain, 1981
PARENTAGE 'Mermaid' x 'New Dawn'
FLOWER SIZE 3.5in (9cm)
SCENT Light and musky
FLOWERING Continuous
HEIGHT/SPREAD 3.3ft (1m)/6.6ft (2m)
HARDINESS Zone 6

It was truly an inspired act of experimentation that induced Edward Le Grice to bring together two of the most vigorous and famous of modern climbers – one hardy, one tender – to see what might emerge from the cross. Little did he anticipate that the result would be a low-growing shrub, wider than it is high: a prototype groundcover rose. Moreover, 'Pearl Drift' has exceptionally fine, dark, glossy leaves, which are the darkest of all roses. The flowers are semidouble, lightly cupped, and a beautiful mother-of-pearl color, suffused with pink. They have a small, almost constricted, central boss of pale stamens, which is quite distinctive. The plant has thick, short-jointed, pale green stems, which branch frequently, so that it quickly builds up a dense structure. It is hardy and fairly healthy, and may grow to a height of as much as 13.1ft (4m) in hot climates. It is early into bloom and flowers very freely over a long period.

PEARL MEIDILAND

see PERLE MEILLANDÉCOR

PEACH BLOSSOM

PEARLY GATES

see AMERICA

PEAUDOUCE

see ELINA

PÊCHE MEILLANDINA

syn. 'MEIXERUL', Peach Meillandina, Peach Sunblaze
Patio Rose

ORIGIN Meilland, France, 1991
FLOWER SIZE 2in (5cm)
SCENT Light, sweet, and fruity
FLOWERING Repeats very well
HEIGHT/SPREAD 1.3ft (40cm)/1.3ft (40cm)
HARDINESS Zone 6

One of the prettiest of the Meillandina series, Pêche Meillandina is also one of the shortest – a Floribunda so short and compact as to qualify as a patio rose. The flowers are a very beautiful, pale, peach pink, uniformly colored on both sides, with a little more yellow toward the center of the flower at first. They are very prettily shaped like rosettes, and open from equally charming buds. They come singly or in clusters, typically of 3–5 flowers but sometimes more. The plant is vigorous, neat, and healthy, with small, dark leaves and a fair measure of prickles. It is a very useful plant for containers or the front of a border.

PEEK-A-BOO

syn. 'DICGROW', Brass Ring
Patio Rose

ORIGIN Dickson, Northern Ireland, 1981
PARENTAGE Memento x 'Nozomi'
FLOWER SIZE 1.8in (4.5cm)
SCENT Light and sweet
FLOWERING Repeats well
HEIGHT/SPREAD 1.6ft (50cm)/1.6ft (50cm)
HARDINESS Zone 6

PÊCHE MEILLANDINA

This cheerful little patio rose seems constantly in flower. The flowers of Peek-a-Boo are quite small, but they are carried in large clusters, typically of 10–20, all over the surface of the plant. They are a wonderful cinnamon color as the buds expand, then pale orange with a good yellow patch toward the center when they first open out to reveal their golden stamens. Later the flowers lose their yellow tints and change to pink and white, but the colors all combine harmoniously in their clusters and make a fine impact. Peek-a-Boo has small, mid-green leaves and a bushy, arching habit. It can be planted in quantity as a groundcover rose but looks very good at the front of a border and in containers.

'PEER GYNT'

Hybrid Tea

ORIGIN Kordes, Germany, 1968
PARENTAGE 'Königin der Rosen' x 'Goldrausch'
FLOWER SIZE 3.5in (9cm)
SCENT Light and fruity
FLOWERING Repeats
HEIGHT/SPREAD 4.1ft (1.25m)/3.3ft (1m)
HARDINESS Zone 6
AWARDS Belfast GM 1970

Although classified among the Hybrid Teas, 'Peer Gynt' is actually intermediate between them and the

PEEK-A-BOO

'PEER GYNT'

Floribundas. Its flowers, for example, open out flat or slightly cupped like a Floribunda's, and come in clusters of up to ten – only a few flowers are singly borne. They open out pure lemon yellow, with golden stamens. The petals are short and broad, with a slight wave to their outline. Occasionally, when they come to the end of their flowering, they also acquire a pink tinge to their tips. The flowers last well if cut for the house. 'Peer Gynt' is one of the few Hybrid Teas to have a compact, upright, but bushy habit, with thick, strong stems. It is also fairly prickly. The leaves are large, glossy, and fairly dark green. It is one of the hardiest yellow Hybrid Teas and keeps its leaves well into winter – at least in its native Denmark, where it flowers right through until the first frost.

PEGASUS

syn. 'AUSMOON'

Shrub Rose

ORIGIN **Austin, Britain, 1995**
PARENTAGE **Graham Thomas x 'Pascali'**
FLOWER SIZE **3.9in (10cm)**
SCENT **Medium and fruity**
FLOWERING **Repeats**
HEIGHT/SPREAD **4.1ft (1.25m)/3.3ft (1m)**
HARDINESS **Zone 6**

The flowers of Pegasus are very beautiful – large, full of petals, and a charming soft apricot color. The petals pale at the edges to ivory or cream, and reflex their edges so that the fully open flower is a mass of small, quilled, inner petals against the larger outer ones. They are borne singly and in small clusters, first at the end of the new stems and then where they break into leaf all along their length. Pegasus has a leafy, arching habit of growth, which shows off the flowers well, but does not require staking. The leaves are large, dark, and fairly glossy – a very good foil for the flowers – and stand up well to disease. The plant has few prickles and makes a thick shrub. The individual flowers also last well if cut for the house.

PEGASUS

JOSEPH PEMBERTON

AN AMATEUR ROSARIAN, PEMBERTON, OF ESSEX, ENGLAND, WAS RESPONSIBLE FOR POPULARIZING HYBRID MUSKS

JOSEPH PEMBERTON (1852–1926) was an Anglican clergyman and a keen amateur rosarian. He was a successful exhibitor, the author of a best-selling book on roses and eventually president of the National Rose Society of Great Britain. When he retired from his religious ministry, he started to breed his own roses, searching for the old-fashioned qualities of the "Grandmother's Roses" that had seemed so full of scent and beauty to him as a boy.

JOSEPH PEMBERTON

The pillars of his hybridizing were the Lambertiana rose 'Trier' (Lambert, 1904) and the Polyantha 'Marie-Jeanne' (Turbat, 1913). Pemberton crossed them with the leading Hybrid Teas of the day, and selected the best seedlings for their vigor, floriferousness, and scent. At first he called them Hybrid Teas, but was later persuaded to call them 'Hybrid Musks' instead. The best are 'Penelope' (1924), 'Cornelia' (1925), and 'Felicia' (1928). In England they grow as lax shrubs 4.9–6.6ft (1.5–2m) tall, but in hot climates they are true climbers reaching as much as 16.4ft (5m). Not all are widely grown: the purple 'Sammy' (1921) and white 'Maid Marion' (1930) for example, are rarely seen in gardens today.

Pemberton also bred a number of straightforward Hybrid Teas, some of which are preserved at the Europas Rosarium in Sangerhausen, Germany. One of the best is 'I Zingari' (1925), a striking Pernetiana rose with crimson petals and yellow backs. Sangerhausen also features a good collection of Pemberton's climbers and ramblers, a by-product of his breeding of Hybrid Musks. 'Pemberton's White Rambler' (1914) and 'Sea Spray' (1923) are both excellent Multiflora ramblers: the pink-flowered 'Queen Alexandra' (1915) performs well in dry climates.

'MAID MARION'

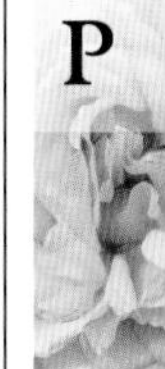
P

'PÉLISSON'

Moss Rose

ORIGIN **Vibert, France, 1848**
FLOWER SIZE **3.1in (8cm)**
SCENT **Strong and sweet**
FLOWERING **Once only**
HEIGHT/SPREAD **4.1ft (1.25m)/3.3ft (1m)**
HARDINESS **Zone 5**

It is not the mossiest of Moss roses, but 'Pélisson' is an excellent once flowering rose. Its flowers are a medium-dark pink, and they hold that color well, except for a little fading at the edges as they age. They open out lightly cupped, with a swirling arrangement of quilled petals and sometimes a rough button eye. The sepals, receptacles, and flower stems have a sprinkling of dark khaki moss, which is sticky and fragrant to the touch. The plant is sturdy and upright, with small, dark leaves and a light covering of tiny bristles where the moss runs out and the prickles begin. 'Pélisson' is only moderately vigorous, but responds well to good cultivation by producing large flowers, and more of them.

'PÉLISSON'

ROSA PENDULINA

ROSA PENDULINA

Wild Rose

FLOWER SIZE **2in (5cm)**
SCENT **Little or none**
FLOWERING **Once, early in season**
HEIGHT/SPREAD **5.7ft (1.75m)/4.9ft (1.5m)**
HARDINESS **Zone 3**

The alpine rose is extremely hardy and thornless. Its flowers are among the first to appear, and its fruit among the most handsome. And yet it is far too rarely grown in gardens. The flowers are a good deep pink, with crimson sepals and nearly white anthers providing a striking contrast. The leaves are small, neat, and glabrous, and the smooth stems are a rich crimson brown. The hips are orange, long, and flagon-shaped. It is a variable species. Only the more vigorous forms reach any great height, while the subspecies sometimes known as *Rosa pyrenaica* is rarely more than 1.6ft (50cm) tall. All have a gently suckering habit without ever being invasive.

P

'PENELOPE'

Hybrid Musk

ORIGIN **Pemberton, Britain, 1924**
PARENTAGE **'Trier' x 'Ophelia'**
FLOWER SIZE **2.8in (7cm)**
SCENT **Strong: a mixture of musk and sweetness**
FLOWERING **Repeats well**
HEIGHT/SPREAD **6.6ft (2m)/6.6ft (2m)**
HARDINESS **Zone 7**
AWARDS **NRS GM 1925**

'Penelope' is one of the best known and most popular of the Hybrid Musks. Its charm lies in the massed effect of its prolific flowering rather than the beauty of its individual blooms. Its flowers are shell pink, with golden centers at first, fading quickly to white; the buds and petal backs are a somewhat darker peach pink. The petals are slightly ruffled and the flowers have prominent lemon yellow stamens. They look good if large clusters are picked for the house. They have short stems, and occur in dense, loose, pendulous clusters of 5–10 flowers, or more in autumn, when the clusters appear at the end of long, new growths and may contain as many as 60 flowers. 'Penelope' is a shy autumn-flowerer, unless deadheaded earlier. If left, the flowers are followed by large, coral pink hips – a very unusual color. In hot climates, the bush will produce two crops of flowers before the hips; in cool countries, only one. The foliage is plum red at first, and later dark, shiny, and somber. The plant makes good mounded, rounded, spreading growth, and resents pruning. In hot climates it becomes a climber 13.1– 16.4ft (4–5m) high. It is generally healthy, tolerant of shade and poor soils, and easily propagated by cuttings.

'PENELOPE'

PENNY LANE

syn. 'HARDWELL'

Modern Climber

ORIGIN **Harkness, Britain, 1998**
PARENTAGE **'New Dawn' seedling**
FLOWER SIZE **4.3in (11cm)**
SCENT **Medium and sweet**
FLOWERING **Repeats**
HEIGHT/SPREAD **13.1ft (4m)/8.2ft (2.5m)**
HARDINESS **Zone 5**
AWARDS **ROTY 1998**

Climbers and ramblers are popular again, and Penny Lane was the first of a new generation of Harkness climbers with smaller flowers and an old-fashioned shape. As with many of the best modern repeat-flowering ramblers, it is a hybrid between 'New Dawn' and a modern bush rose. Its flowers are large, loosely double, and very beautiful, with lots of petals. They are apricot buff in color at the center, paling to ivory at the edges. They come in small clusters (typically of 3–5 flowers) and repeat well, but Penny Lane is not the most free-flowering of ramblers. The plant has dark, shiny, healthy, Wichurana leaves and slender stems, which make it easy to train.

PENNY LANE

PENTHOUSE

syn. 'MACNGAURU', West Coast

Hybrid Tea

ORIGIN **McGredy, New Zealand, 1987**
PARENTAGE **(['Yellow Pages' x 'Kabuki'] x 'Golden Gate') x (seedling x 'Picasso')**
FLOWER SIZE **5.1in (13cm)**
SCENT **Medium and sweet**
FLOWERING **Repeats well**
HEIGHT/SPREAD **4.1ft (1.25m)/3.3ft (1m)**
HARDINESS **Zone 6**

Sam McGredy regards this blowsy pink beauty as the healthiest rose he has ever raised. It is a large-flowered Hybrid Tea, which seems never to be out of flower. The flowers are pale pink, with deep pink backs, but the deep pink is hidden underneath as the flowers open and expand. The petals sometimes acquire a scalloped edge and a wave to their bearing. The flowers are almost invariably borne singly, on long, strong stems, which makes this an excellent rose for cutting. The plant is vigorous and productive, with large, dark, healthy leaves. When you compare the qualities of this rose with the Hybrid Teas that were produced 50 years ago, you realize just how enormous have been the improvements in modern roses since then. A winner.

PENTHOUSE

PERCEPTION

PERCEPTION

syn. 'HARZIPPEE', LeAnn Rimes

Hybrid Tea

ORIGIN **Harkness, Britain, 1997**
PARENTAGE **Dr. Darley x Sweetheart**
FLOWER SIZE **4.7in (12cm)**
SCENT **Strong Damask sweetness**
FLOWERING **Repeats well**
HEIGHT/SPREAD **3.3ft (1m)/2.7ft (80cm)**
HARDINESS **Zone 6**

Perception is a large and richly scented Hybrid Tea, beautiful at all stages of its development. The bud is long and elegant: the petals are large and there are a lot of them. It unfurls slowly into a creamy white flower with a deep pink edging. There is a hint of butter yellow at the center, but the colors run into each other, so that the edges seem to have been stained with raspberry juice. The flowers are borne, mostly singly, on long stems: they are good for cutting and exhibition. The plant has large, dark green, glossy leaves and a tall, upright habit of growth. In hot climates it will reach as much as 5.7ft (1.75m) and may even become somewhat leggy, in which case it is best planted at the back of a border where it is surrounded by other plants.

PERDITA

syn. 'AUSPERD'

Shrub Rose

ORIGIN **Austin, Britain, 1983**
PARENTAGE **'The Friar' x (seedling x 'Schneewittchen')**
FLOWER SIZE **3.1in (8cm)**
SCENT **Strong and spicy**
FLOWERING **Repeats well**
HEIGHT/SPREAD **3.3ft (1m)/2.5ft (75cm)**
HARDINESS **Zone 6**
AWARDS **Edland FA 1984**

When in bud, Perdita looks like an ordinary Hybrid Tea. It is only when the flower is fully opened out that its true character is revealed – a beautiful quartered arrangement of richly colored little petals surrounded by large, flat,

PERDITA

milk white guard petals. The center is a glowing pink, with a hint of apricot in warm weather. This effect comes from the petal backs, which are pale salmon, in contrast to ivory white on the upper sides. The delicate combination of colors is very useful in flower arrangements. The flowers come in small clusters of 3–7 on a prickly plant with large, dark green leaves, which are susceptible to fungal diseases in the autumn. The bush needs light pruning for several years while it builds up its structure. An established plant in a warm climate, where rust and blackspot are less of a problem, may be as much as 6.6ft (2m) tall. Perdita was the shepherd princess in Shakespeare's *A Winter's Tale.*

PERESTROIKA

see SONNENKIND

PERFECT MOMENT

syn. 'KORWILMA'

Hybrid Tea

ORIGIN **Kordes, Germany, 1989**
PARENTAGE **(Mabella x Mercedes) x seedling**
FLOWER SIZE **4.3in (11cm)**
SCENT **Slight**
FLOWERING **Repeats well**
HEIGHT/SPREAD **4.1ft (1.25m)/2.5ft (75cm)**
HARDINESS **Zone 5**
AWARDS **AARS 1991**

Perfect Moment is a magnificent bicolor rose in rich velvety crimson and bright egg yolk yellow. In hot weather, the petal tips have markings that are almost black. The color contrasts are particularly striking when the swirling buds are only half unfolded. Later, the colors fade, so that although they retain a dark spot at the tip, the petals are pale crimson with a creamy yellow base. The flowers open

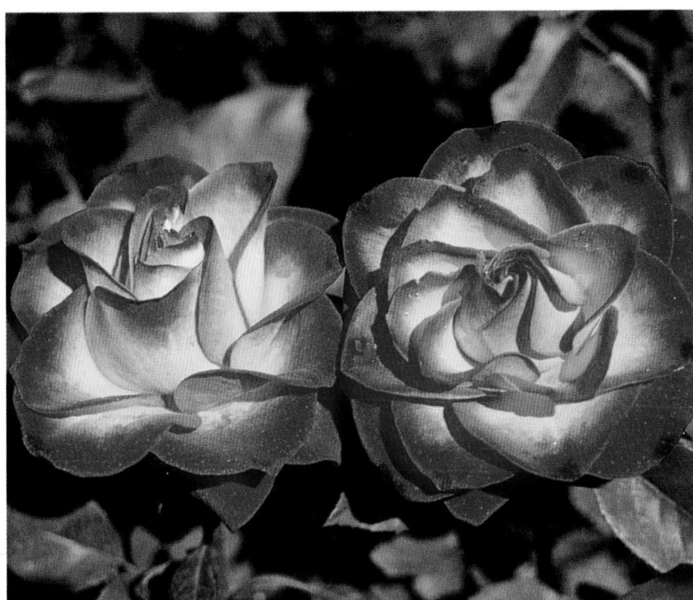

PERFECT MOMENT

'PERFUME DELIGHT'

out into classic Hybrid Teas, good for exhibition and borne singly on long, straight stems, occasionally in clusters. The leaves are dark, semiglossy, mid-green, and healthy. The plant is extremely thorny. It has an uneven habit of growth, but is upright and bushy. It flowers throughout the year in hot climates.

'PERFUME DELIGHT'

Hybrid Tea

ORIGIN **Swim & Weeks, US, 1973**
PARENTAGE **'Mme. A. Meilland' x (['Rouge Meilland' x 'Chrysler Imperial'] x 'El Capitan')**
FLOWER SIZE **4.7in (12cm)**
SCENT **Strong and sweet**
FLOWERING **Repeats**
HEIGHT/SPREAD **4.9ft (1.5m)/3.3ft (1m)**
HARDINESS **Zone 6**
AWARDS **AARS 1974**

This American Hybrid Tea is popular in the US and Australia, but almost unknown in Europe. 'Perfume Delight' has large, shapely flowers, which open dark pink and fade to pale pink. The petals have paler backs and a hint of mauve toward the edges. They are also long, strong, and rain resistant. The flowers come singly (occasionally in small clusters) on long stems, making them useful for cutting. The rich Damask scent is powerfully exhaled indoors. The plant is vigorous, upright, strong-growing, free-flowering, and moderately healthy. Its leaves are large and dark. 'Perfume Delight' repeats regularly until late autumn, though it is not the most abundant of roses. Quantity is the price you pay for quality.

'PERGOLÈSE'

Portland

ORIGIN **Robert & Moreau, France, 1860**
FLOWER SIZE **2.8in (7cm)**
SCENT **Strong and sweet**
FLOWERING **Remontant**
HEIGHT/SPREAD **4.1ft (1.25m)/2.7ft (80cm)**
HARDINESS **Zone 5**

The Portland roses often make up in floriferousness what they lack in vigor. 'Pergolèse' is not a strong grower, but it is a reliable repeat flowerer and responds very positively to good cultivation – especially deadheading. The flowers are a rich purple crimson, fading to dark cherry red as they open out almost flat to reveal a mass of neat petals arranged in a quartered shape. Later they fade

'PERGOLÈSE'

further, to dark pink, starting from the edges. Sometimes a green carpel peeps through at the center. The flowers come singly and in twos and threes and show up well against the neat, matte, mid-green leaves. The plant has an upright, branching habit of growth, and mixes especially well with herbaceous plants.

'PERLA DE ALCAÑADA'

Miniature Rose

ORIGIN **Dot, Spain, 1944**
PARENTAGE **'Perle des Rouges' x 'Pompon de Paris'**
FLOWER SIZE **1in (2.5cm)**
SCENT **Light and sweet**
FLOWERING **Repeats well**
HEIGHT/SPREAD **11.8in (30cm)/10in (25cm)**
HARDINESS **Zone 6**

The year 1944 was not a good time to introduce a new rose – all the Western world was at war – but 'Perla de Alcañada' was a success right from the start and is still widely grown. It also appears in the ancestry of many of the best modern miniature roses. The flowers are small, but elegantly shaped like tiny Hybrid Teas, and profusely carried all over the surface of the dense, neat bush. They are a bright, slightly purplish crimson and sometimes have tiny flecks of white running through the petals. 'Perla de Alcañada' is compact and twiggy, with lots of small, dark leaves and more than a scattering of prickles. The foliage and the bushiness of the plant make a good foil for the flowers. The leaves are fairly susceptible to blackspot, but this does not appear to affect the capacity of the plant to grow larger every year. 'Perla de Alcañada' also roots quickly from cuttings, so it is easy to propagate enough to make a tiny hedge or edging.

'PERLA DE ALCAÑADA'

'PERLE D'OR'

'PERLE D'OR'

Polyantha

ORIGIN **Rambaux, France, 1883**
PARENTAGE **unnamed Polyantha x 'Mme. Falcot'**
FLOWER SIZE **1.6in (4cm)**
SCENT **Sweet and fruity**
FLOWERING **Repeats very well**
HEIGHT/SPREAD **3.3ft (1m)/3.3ft (1m)**
HARDINESS **Zone 6**

When the first Polyanthas were crossed with Tea roses, their offspring combined the delicate size of the former with the subtle colors of the latter. 'Perle d'Or' is an excellent example and a rose of outstanding beauty and charm. Its flowers open from small, elegant, vermilion buds and are deep apricot pink at first, paling to mother-of-pearl from the outside. The petal backs are always darker, and create rich shadowy tones within the half-open flower. In hot weather the flowers open out loosely and reflex into a mass of small, straplike petals. If the plant is poorly grown, the flowers have fewer petals and a brush of stamens at the center. They come in large, long-stemmed, spacious clusters, typically of 5–25 flowers. The plant has red new growth, a few large prickles, and small, dark, healthy leaves. In hot climates it is almost always in flower. It needs little or no pruning.

P

'PERLE DES PANACHÉES'

Gallica

ORIGIN **Vibert, France, 1845**
FLOWER SIZE **2.8in (7cm)**
SCENT **Medium and sweet**
FLOWERING **Once, midseason**
HEIGHT/SPREAD **4.9ft (1.5m)/5.7ft (1.75m)**
HARDINESS **Zone 5**

'PERLE DES PANACHÉES'

This pretty and distinctive striped Gallica has pale pink flowers with pale crimson stripes, flakes, and slashes – all very irregularly sized and shaped, though there is about twice as much pale coloring on every flower as there is dark. The flowers of 'Perle des Panachées' hold their petals loosely but open out nearly flat, then fade to white and dark pink. They display themselves well in slightly pendulous clusters of 3–5 on an attractive and somewhat spreading bush with slender stems. The leaves are a refreshing bright pale green (bronzy when young) with long, pointed leaflets, but often only three of them.

PERLE MEILLANDÉCOR

syn. 'MEIPLATIN', Pearl Meidiland
Ground Cover

ORIGIN **Meilland, France, 1989**
FLOWER SIZE **2in (5cm)**
SCENT **Little or none**
FLOWERING **Repeats**
HEIGHT/SPREAD **2.5ft (75cm)/3.3ft (1m)**
HARDINESS **Zone 6**

It may have no fragrance, but Perle Meillandécor is one of the best of the modern groundcover roses. Its dense, lax growth really does smother weeds, and there is no match for the sheer volume of its flowers during its first flowering. The flowers are pale, translucent pink – pearly perhaps, or silky – with a hint of pale salmon pink toward the center at first, and fading to white at the edges. They are fully double, and carried in clusters of 5–25 in such quantities that the bush catches the eye from a great distance. They are also very beautiful close-up. The leaves are dark, glossy, and tough, with *Rosa wichurana* in the background. Perle Meillandécor is also very disease resistant, hardy, and tolerant of heat. It has a mounding habit of growth, spreading sideways rather than upward. It is not a continuous flowerer, but produces a series of lesser flushes after the spectacular first blooming.

PERLE MEILLANDÉCOR

'PERLE DES JARDINS'

Tea Rose

ORIGIN **Levet, France, 1874**
FLOWER SIZE **3.1in (8cm)**
SCENT **Strong and tealike**
FLOWERING **Almost continuous**
HEIGHT/SPREAD **4.1ft (1.25m)/3.3ft (1m)**
HARDINESS **Zone 7**

Many of the 19th-century Tea roses that were bred in the south of France are now more common in hot, dry areas of Australia and the US. 'Perle des Jardins' is a good example. In damp conditions, the buds ball, the flowers crumple, and the leaves attract mildew, but see it in Perth or Las Vegas and there is no finer rose. The globular buds are buff yellow, with hints of apricot and pink toward the center. They open out roughly quartered and absolutely packed with tissue paper petals, canary yellow toward the center, and cream or white at the edges. The colors are darker in cool weather, and fade more quickly in hot, but are always delicate and attractive. The flowers come singly or in clusters of up to four on strong stems – unlike most Tea roses. 'Perle des Jardins' is vigorous, upright, and bushy, with slender branches, purple crimson when young. The leaves are dark, glossy, and slightly wavy.

'PERLE DES JARDINS'

The New York florist Peter Henderson introduced **'Climbing Perle des Jardins'** in 1889. It is identical to the bush form except that its flowers are slightly larger, the plant grows to 9.8ft (3m) (or more), and it flowers only spasmodically after the spectacular first flowering in spring.

Sport of 'Perle des Jardins'

'CLIMBING PERLE DES JARDINS'

Climbing Tea
ORIGIN **Henderson, US, 1890**
FLOWER SIZE **3.5in (9cm)**
FLOWERING **Once abundantly, then intermittently**
HEIGHT/SPREAD **13.1ft (4m)/6.6ft (2m)**

'PERLE VON WEISSENSTEIN'

Gallica

ORIGIN **Schwartzkopf, Germany, 1773**
FLOWER SIZE **2.8in (7cm)**
SCENT **Very strong and sweet**
FLOWERING **Once only**
HEIGHT/SPREAD **8.2ft (2.5m)/4.9ft (1.5m)**
HARDINESS **Zone 5**

The importance of 'Perle von Weissenstein' is historical: it was the first Gallica rose to be raised and named in Germany. Schwartzkopf was head gardener to Landgrave Friedrich II of Hesse at Kassel, and Weissenstein was then the name for the palace of Wilhelmshöhe. 'Perle von Weissenstein' is probably a hybrid between a Gallica and a Centifolia – the leaves, prickles, and flower shape would all come from its Centifolia parent. The flowers are medium-sized, deep pink with a lilac tinge, cupped and tightly packed with little petals. They tend to ball in damp weather, and even in its native Kassel 'Perle von Weissenstein' rarely opens up and flowers satisfactorily. Year after year, the entire crop is lost to rot. It is, however, a most lusty grower, sending out long, scrawny shoots whose large leaves are separated by armies of prickles. When it does flower successfully, and opens out fully, it is a plant of rare beauty.

'PERLE VON WEISSENSTEIN'

JOSEPH PERNET-DUCHER

THE LEGENDARY FRENCH ROSE BREEDER PERNET-DUCHER WAS RESPONSIBLE FOR TRANSFORMING THE YELLOW ROSES OF THE WORLD

OF ALL THE DISTINGUISHED nurserymen and breeders who gave the city of Lyon its dominant position within the rose industry in the second half of the 19th century, Joseph Pernet-Ducher (1859–1928) was undoubtedly the most able and achieved most for the advance of roses.

Roses were in his blood. His father, Jean Pernet (1832–1896), was a Lyon nurseryman who bred the Hybrid Perpetual 'Baronne Adolphe de Rothschild' (1868) and the perpetually flowering Moss rose 'Louis Gimard' (1877). His father-in-law Claude Ducher (1820–1874) raised the fine purple Hybrid Perpetual 'Gloire de Ducher' and two very important Tea roses, 'Marie van Houtte' (1871) and 'Anna Olivier' (1872).

Joseph Pernet-Ducher was one of the first breeders to commit his energies to developing the new class of Hybrid Teas. He used controlled pollination to raise them – not by any means a universal practice at that time. When still a young man, Pernet-Ducher introduced two of the most famous and beautiful of all the old Hybrid Teas: 'Mme. Caroline Testout' (1890) and 'Mme. Abel Châtenay' (1895).

Pernet-Ducher was not a great experimenter with unusual species, but he did decide early on that he wanted to transfer the bright unfading yellow of *Rosa foetida* into hardy garden roses. The only yellow shades to date had been the pale buff yellows of Tea roses and Noisettes. Pernet-Ducher used the pollen of

'JULIEN POTIN'

JOSEPH PERNET-DUCHER

'Persiana' on the red Hybrid Perpetual 'Antoine Ducher' and raised just one seedling from the cross, which he planted out in his garden. Two years later, another seedling appeared alongside it. Its flowers were large, full of petals and a remarkable combination of yellow, apricot, peach, and pink. He named this second seedling 'Soleil d'Or' and released it on November 1, 1900: all our modern yellow roses descend from it.

'Soleil d'Or' was in need of further development. Pernet-Ducher crossed it with selected Hybrid Teas to improve its floriferousness and separate out its yellow coloring. 'Lyon Rose' (1907) and 'Rayon d'Or' (1910) were steps along the way. But many of Pernet-Ducher's seedlings were orange, like 'Angèle Pernet' (1924) while others faded to pink – 'Souvenir de Georges Pernet' is an example. The descendants of 'Soleil d'Or' became known as the Pernetiana roses and were generally treated as a distinct class until the introduction of 'Julien Potin' in 1927, by which time they were fully integrated into the mainstream of Hybrid Teas. 'Mme. A. Meilland' and all the yellow and orange roses of the 20th century would not have been possible without 'Soleil d'Or'. Nor would the fruity scent of so many modern roses: this too can be traced back to *Rosa foetida*, and is the result of mixing the fetid smell of the Persian rose with the Damask scents of old European roses.

'Soleil d'Or' was not the only outcome of Pernet-Ducher's experiments with *Rosa foetida*. Also in 1900, he introduced another seedling of the Persian rose called 'Rhodophile Gravereaux' and, many years later, in 1923, he released two handsome climbing yellow roses, 'Le Rêve' and 'Lawrence Johnston' which initially he had not thought good enough for introduction. Nor was he the only rosarian to succeed at breeding hardy yellow roses from *Rosa foetida*: the Bavarian Hermann Müller had raised several seedlings in the 1880s, and in 1894 introduced a repeat flowering bush rose with a complicated parentage called 'Gottfried Keller'. But 'Soleil d'Or' is a better rose.

Joseph Pernet-Ducher was a simple man of little education. His knowledge of roses was legendary but based only on observation and memory. He wrote no books and sought no fame, yet in the years following 1900 he soon became the most revered rose breeder of his time. He was the man whose yellow roses had transformed the gardens of the whole world: Joseph Pernet-Ducher was the "Wizard of Lyon."

'SOUVENIR DE GEORGES PERNET'

'Pernille Poulsen'

'Pernille Poulsen'

Floribunda

ORIGIN **Poulsen, Denmark, 1965**
PARENTAGE **'Ma Perkins' x 'Columbine'**
FLOWER SIZE **3.1in (8cm)**
SCENT **Medium and refreshing**
FLOWERING **Repeats almost continuously**
HEIGHT/SPREAD **2.7ft (80cm)/2ft (60cm)**
HARDINESS **Zone 5**

'Pernille Poulsen' is a low-growing Floribunda, attractive in small gardens as well as useful in landscaping plans. Its lightly double flowers are salmon pink, with white at the center, and have yellow stamens. The color fades slightly as the flowers age, and becomes more pink, less salmon. The flowers come in clusters of 3–7, flowering very heavily fairly early in the season and then keeping up a good succession of flowers right through until late autumn. The bush is twiggy (hence its abundant flowering) and fairly healthy. Pernille Poulsen is the daughter of the breeder, and, together with her husband Mogens Olesen, has kept up the family tradition and is now directly involved in rose breeding herself.

P

'Persetosa'

Wild Rose

ORIGIN **1914**
FLOWER SIZE **0.6in (1.5cm)**
SCENT **Little**
FLOWERING **Once, early in season**
HEIGHT/SPREAD **6.6ft (2m)/11.5ft (3.5m)**
HARDINESS **Zone 6**

Although sometimes known as *Rosa farreri* 'Persetosa', this plant is in fact a cultivar of the rarely seen *Rosa elegantula*. It was collected by the English botanist Reginald Farrer in western China in 1915, and selected from a batch of seedlings by the English plantsman E. A. Bowles. It does not come true from seed. 'Persetosa' is very beautiful early in the year, when the long, prickly shoots are studded with tiny, dark pink flowers (with white stamens) all along their length. The flowers are followed by bright red, glistening, top-shaped hips, and fat new growth completely covered in crimson bristles. The leaves are long and narrow (the leaflets are very small) and turn crimson in autumn. It is a charming and unusual shrub.

'Peter Benjamin'

'Peter Benjamin'

Hybrid Tea

ORIGIN **Allender, Australia, 1978**
PARENTAGE **'Peter Frankenfeld' x 'Benjamin Franklin'**
FLOWER SIZE **4.7in (12cm)**
SCENT **Strong and sweet**
FLOWERING **Fully recurrent**
HEIGHT/SPREAD **4.1ft (1.25m)/3.3ft (1m)**
HARDINESS **Zone 6**

'Peter Benjamin' gets its name from its parents. The petals are slightly on the short side, but there are plenty of them and the big buds eventually open out into broad, cabbage-shaped flowers. Their color is rose pink, with slightly more coral pink on the backs, which give the center of the flower a pretty salmon pink suffusion. The petals are, however, sensitive to rain – they become spotted where the rain has fallen – so 'Peter Benjamin' does best in hot, dry climates like that of its native Australia.

'Peter Frankenfeld'

Hybrid Tea

ORIGIN **Kordes, Germany, 1966**
FLOWER SIZE **5.5in (14cm)**
SCENT **Good and sweet**
FLOWERING **Repeats**
HEIGHT/SPREAD **4.9ft (1.5m)/4.1ft (1.25m)**
HARDINESS **Zone 6**

'Persetosa'

'Peter Frankenfeld'

In 'Peter Frankenfeld' we have one of the great exhibition Hybrid Teas – its flowers are enormous and borne singly on long stems, which also make it good for flower arrangements. The flowers are bright, deep pink – a somewhat loud color – with long, reflexed petals and high centers. The bush is vigorous, and blessed with large, dark, healthy leaves. It does particularly well in hot, dry climates: it is widely sold in California and much of Australia. In the US it grows best in cool, wet areas. Peter Frankenfeld (1913– 79) was a German comic actor.

'Petite de Hollande'

Centifolia

ORIGIN **c.1800**
FLOWER SIZE **2in (5cm)**
SCENT **Strong and sweet**
FLOWERING **Once, midseason**
HEIGHT/SPREAD **3.9ft (1.2m)/3.3ft (1m)**
HARDINESS **Zone 5**

'Petite de Hollande'

The origins of 'Petite de Hollande' are obscure: it is probably a hybrid of 'Centifolia', and best thought of as a scaled-down relative of it, but it is certainly not a sport of another Centifolia. Its buds are small and round, with long, leafy sepals. The flowers are small, delicately pretty, neat, and round. They usually open flat, with a swirl of petals around a button eye. They are borne singly or, more commonly, in clusters of up to six, and are deep rose pink at the center, paler at the edges. The plant has a lot of prickles and light green foliage, which is large in proportion to the flowers. It makes a more dense bush than most Centifolias and is more resistant to disease. Although it flowers only once, the season of bloom lasts over several weeks. It is fairly easy to root from cuttings and forms a neatly suckering shrub, which suggests an affinity to the Gallica roses.

'Petite Lisette'

Damask Rose

ORIGIN **Vibert, France, 1817**
FLOWER SIZE **2.4in (6cm)**
SCENT **Medium and sweet**
FLOWERING **Once only**
HEIGHT/SPREAD **4.1ft (1.25m)/4.9ft (1.5m)**
HARDINESS **Zone 5**

Ever since 'Petite Lisette' was introduced, people have argued about how to categorize it. Some consider it a dwarf Centifolia rose, but the safer course of action is to treat it as a Damask of sorts. Its flowers are small but complete replicas of full-size Damask flowers, with a rosette of little petals contained within larger guard petals. Sometimes it tends toward a quartered shape and a rough button eye. The flowers are rich pink at the center and paler at the edges. They have conspicuously leafy sepals and are usually borne in clusters of 3–10.

'Petite Lisette'

'Petite Lisette' has small, bristly prickles, a loose, arching habit of growth, and healthy gray green leaves. If grown on its own roots, it suckers around and forms thickets.

'Petite Orléanaise'

Gallica

FLOWER SIZE **2.4in (6cm)**
SCENT **Strong and sweet**
FLOWERING **Once only**
HEIGHT/SPREAD **4.9ft (1.5m)/3.3ft (1m)**
HARDINESS **Zone 5**

Its origins are obscure – it is variously placed with the Gallicas and the Centifolias – but 'Petite Orléanaise' is an attractive old rose with a lot of fairly small flowers. They are deep pink, with silver pink undersides and a pronounced button eye when they open out. The flowers often have long, leafy sepals, like some of the Damask roses, and are richly scented. They come in large clusters, typically of 5–10, which is much more usual among the old roses. The plant has surprisingly large leaves, which serve to emphasize the daintiness of the flowers. Blackspot and mildew may be a problem in damp climates, but not in dry ones nor, apparently, in very cold areas: in Montreal, for example, 'Petite Orléanaise' is regarded as one of the healthiest of all roses.

'Petite Orléanaise'

Pheasant

see Heidekönigin

Philippe Noiret

syn. 'MEIzoele', Glowing Peace

Hybrid Tea

ORIGIN **Meilland, France, 1999**
PARENTAGE **'Sun King 74' x Roxane**
FLOWER SIZE **5.9in (15cm)**
SCENT **Light and sweet**
FLOWERING **Repeats**
HEIGHT/SPREAD **4.1ft (1.25m)/3.3ft (1m)**
HARDINESS **Zone 6**
AWARDS **AARS 2001**

In North America this vigorous Hybrid Tea is known as Glowing Peace, and one can see the resemblance to the original 'Peace' ('Mme. A. Meilland'). However, Philippe Noiret has a more intense color and keeps its deep pink edges as its petals fade. It also has shorter petals and more of them. The flowers open from classically elegant (but slightly plump) buds, which are crimson and yellow on the outside. When they open out you can see the dark yellow stamens at the center. They are borne singly and in clusters of up to five on long, strong stems that are good for cutting. Philippe Noiret has large dark leaves (which are not completely disease-free) and a dense, bushy shape. It makes a very vigorous plant, and sends up new flowering stems with speed and enthusiasm, so that it appears to be continuously in flower. It won the top prize at the All-America Rose Selections in 2001, and has sold especially well in America. And yet, many would say that the original 'Mme. A. Meilland', introduced as long ago as 1945, is still a better rose.

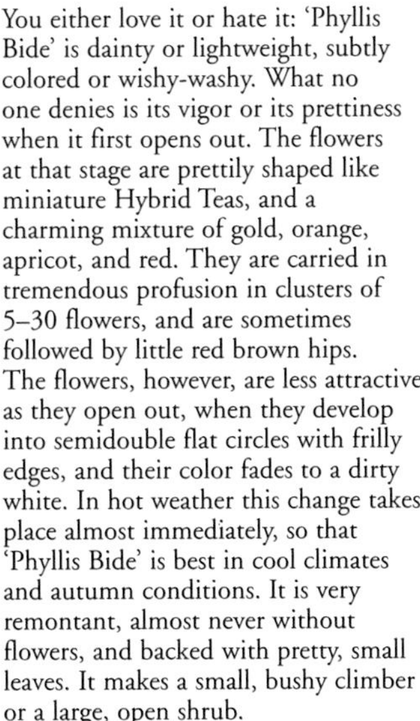

Philippe Noiret

'Phyllis Bide'

'Phyllis Bide'

Polyantha-type Climber

ORIGIN **Bide, Britain, 1923**
PARENTAGE **'Perle d'Or' x 'Gloire de Dijon'**
FLOWER SIZE **1.6in (4cm)**
SCENT **Light and sweet**
FLOWERING **Repeats**
HEIGHT/SPREAD **9.8ft (3m)/6.6ft (2m)**
HARDINESS **Zone 6**
AWARDS **NRS GM 1924**

You either love it or hate it: 'Phyllis Bide' is dainty or lightweight, subtly colored or wishy-washy. What no one denies is its vigor or its prettiness when it first opens out. The flowers at that stage are prettily shaped like miniature Hybrid Teas, and a charming mixture of gold, orange, apricot, and red. They are carried in tremendous profusion in clusters of 5–30 flowers, and are sometimes followed by little red brown hips. The flowers, however, are less attractive as they open out, when they develop into semidouble flat circles with frilly edges, and their color fades to a dirty white. In hot weather this change takes place almost immediately, so that 'Phyllis Bide' is best in cool climates and autumn conditions. It is very remontant, almost never without flowers, and backed with pretty, small leaves. It makes a small, bushy climber or a large, open shrub.

'Picasso'

syn. MACpic

Floribunda

ORIGIN **McGredy, Northern Ireland, 1971**
PARENTAGE **'Marlena' x ('Evelyn Fison' x ['Frühlingsmorgen' x 'Orange Sweetheart'])**
FLOWER SIZE **3.1in (8cm)**
SCENT **Light**
FLOWERING **Repeats well**
HEIGHT/SPREAD **3.3ft (1m)/3.3ft (1m)**
HARDINESS **Zone 6**
AWARDS **Belfast GM 1973; NZ GM 1973**

'Picasso' was the first of Sam McGredy's "hand-painted" roses to be released, and its genes turn up in many later roses. It is not, however, the best of plants to grow in Northern Ireland, where it was bred, since it suffers from blackspot in damp climates. On the other hand, the distinctive markings – and especially the irregular white edges to the petals – are not quite so developed in hot, dry climates. The flowers are full of petals but open out flat to reveal dark red petals with silvery white backs. White streaks run out from the small white circle that surrounds the yellow stamens at the center. The stamens themselves quickly turn brown. In some conditions, the petals also have a regular white margin. The plant has small dark leaves and makes short bushy growth – it is best when only lightly pruned.

'Picasso'

'PICCADILLY'

Hybrid Tea

ORIGIN **McGredy, Northern Ireland, 1960**
PARENTAGE **'McGredy's Yellow' x 'Karl Herbst'**
FLOWER SIZE **3.9in (10cm)**
SCENT **Light and sweet**
FLOWERING **Repeats well**
HEIGHT/SPREAD **4.1ft (1.25m)/2.7ft (80cm)**
HARDINESS **Zone 5**
AWARDS **Madrid GM 1960; Rome GM 1960**

This is one of the great classic Hybrid Teas, still widely grown and sold many years after it was introduced. 'Piccadilly' has large red and yellow flowers, brighter and scarlet at first, then crimson and cream colored as it ages. The flowers are always shapely and stand up well to rain. They are often borne in clusters as well as singly; disbudding produces flowers large enough to win prizes at shows. 'Piccadilly' is vigorous and a good repeat flowerer. Its leaves are dark green and glossy, but reddish when young. Blackspot may be a problem in damp weather, but the plant may grow as high as 6.6ft (2m) in hot climates.

'Piccadilly' produced a sport known as **'Harry Wheatcroft'** in which the orange parts are shot through with streaks of the yellow. The color contrast is intensified by the thick boss of stamens with red filaments and golden anthers. Its name commemorates a flamboyant English nurseryman.

'PICCADILLY'

'HARRY WHEATCROFT'

Sport of 'Piccadilly'

'HARRY WHEATCROFT'

syn. 'CARIBIA'
Hybrid Tea
ORIGIN **Wheatcroft, Britain, 1972**
HEIGHT/SPREAD **3.3ft (1m)/2.7ft (80cm)**

'PICTURE'

Hybrid Tea

ORIGIN **McGredy, Northern Ireland, 1932**
FLOWER SIZE **3.9in (10cm)**
SCENT **Medium and sweet**
FLOWERING **Repeats**
HEIGHT/SPREAD **3.3ft (1m)/2.7ft (80cm)**
HARDINESS **Zone 6**

Old rose enthusiasts have begun to discover the early Hybrid Teas: 'Picture' is one that is increasingly widely grown once again. It was popular in the 1930s and 1940s, especially in cool climates, where its lightly double flowers opened out slowly and stood up well to rain. The flowers are deep pink, with pale outer petals and creamy reverses. They start as elegant, conical buds, whose petals curl back at their edges in the characteristic style of Hybrid Teas. Later, they open out and display a better form than many. They come on long stems (good for cutting) on a fairly compact bush whose dark leaves are healthy for an old rose. It is no match for modern Hybrid Teas, but 'Picture' has a period charm that makes it well worth growing.

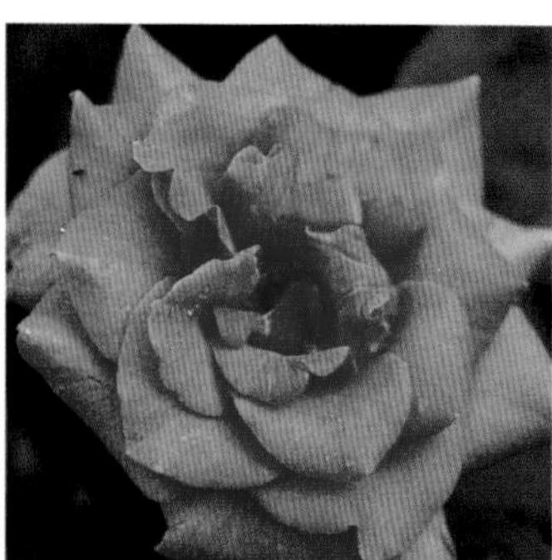

'PICTURE'

PIERETTE

syn. 'UHLWE'
Rugosa Hybrid

ORIGIN **Uhl, Germany, 1987**
FLOWER SIZE **3.9in (10cm)**
SCENT **Strong and sweet**
FLOWERING **Repeats**
HEIGHT/SPREAD **3.3ft (1m)/3.3ft (1m)**
HARDINESS **Zone 4**

Rosa rugosa has been widely used in recent years to breed roses that will stand up to extreme cold. Pierette is a fine example: bred in Germany to challenge the freezing winters in northern Europe, it has also proved popular in the colder parts of North America. The flowers are dark magenta pink and full of petals, but they open out enough to reveal their dark yellow stamens. Sometimes they have a button eye. They are borne singly and in clusters of up to five, and are followed by vermilion hips. Pierette is a good repeater, so the first hips are always accompanied by later flowers, even in very cold areas with a short flowering season. The plant is prickly, with healthy, wrinkled, mid-green leaves and a spreading, procumbent habit, which makes it useful as a landscaping or groundcover plant.

PIERETTE

PIERRE DE RONSARD

syn. 'MEIVIOLIN', Eden Rose 88
Shrub Rose

ORIGIN **Meilland, France, 1987**
PARENTAGE **('Danse des Sylphes' x 'Handel') x 'Kalinka'**
FLOWER SIZE **3.9in (10cm)**
SCENT **Light and sweet**
FLOWERING **Repeats**
HEIGHT/SPREAD **9.8ft (3m)/6.6ft (2m)**
HARDINESS **Zone 6**

There is an old-fashioned charm to the flowers of Pierre de Ronsard, even though it was bred exclusively from modern antecedents. The flowers are large, cupped, and full of large, long petals, which take many days to unfurl. Indeed, in cool, wet climates they rarely open out at all, but Pierre de Ronsard is essentially a rose for Mediterranean climates, and warmer. The flowers are cream colored or ivory, with deep pink edges to the petals, but the exact coloring is very variable, and sometimes the pink is more obvious toward the center of the flowers and the white at the outside edges. There is often a hint of green on the outer petals, too. The flowers are heavy, and tend to nod under their own weight – an attractive feature. Pierre de Ronsard is a compact grower, not very vigorous, which builds up only slowly. Its leaves are healthy, dark, tough, and shiny; the stems have only a very few prickles. Its first flowering is remarkably abundant and covers the plant from top to bottom; thereafter the flowers come in much smaller numbers, but continuously.

PIGALLE 84

syn. 'MEICLOUX', Chacok, Jubilee 150
Floribunda

ORIGIN **Meilland, France, 1984**
PARENTAGE **'Prince Igor' x (['Zambra' x 'Suspense'] x 'King's Ransom')**
FLOWER SIZE **3.9in (10cm)**
SCENT **Light and sweet**
FLOWERING **Repeats well**
HEIGHT/SPREAD **4.1ft (1.25m)/2.5ft (75cm)**
HARDINESS **Zone 6**

Pigalle 84 is a bold combination of vermilion, orange, and yellow. The exact mixture differs, and there is more orange and vermilion in hot weather. The contrast comes from having yellow petals at the center and bright vermilion at the outside, but sometimes the inner petals also take on an apricot or orange glow, while the petal backs remain yellow. It is quite a full flower for a

PIERRE DE RONSARD *(at Meilland's nursery in Provence)*

P

PIGALLE 84

Floribunda, but the clusters are not large – usually 5–9 flowers. They last a long time and keep their color surprisingly well, both in the garden and as a cut flower. The plant has mid-green, matte leaves and is fairly unmemorable except for its brilliant flowers. The name commemorates the French sculptor Jean-Baptiste Pigalle (1714–85), after whom the Place Pigalle in Paris was named.

PILLOW FIGHT

syn. 'WEKPIPOGOP'

Shrub Rose

ORIGIN **Carruth, US, 1999**
PARENTAGE Pink Polyanna x Gourmet Popcorn
FLOWER SIZE **2.4in (6cm)**
SCENT **Fairly strong: a mixture of musk and sweetness**
FLOWERING **Repeats constantly**
HEIGHT/SPREAD **3.3ft (1m)/3.3ft (1m)**
HARDINESS **Zone 6**

The name Pillow Fight refers to a sackful of feathers, a resemblance that is immediately seen in the dense clusters of small, white, ruffled flowers that this rose produces in great abundance. When they first open, the flowers are cupped, with a hint of amber at the center, which comes in part from the golden stamens. They soon open out flat and turn to a ghostly white that shines in even the dullest weather. The flowers are borne in compact clusters of 20–40 and are set off by neat, dark green, glossy leaves. The flowers have rather soft petals, so this rose does best in hot, dry climates.

ROSA PIMPINELLIFOLIA

see ROSA SPINOSISSIMA

PILLOW FIGHT

PINK BELLS

PINK BELLS

syn. 'POULBELLS'

Ground Cover

ORIGIN **Poulsen, Denmark, 1983**
FLOWER SIZE **1.2in (3cm)**
SCENT **Light and musky**
FLOWERING **Once strongly, then intermittently**
HEIGHT/SPREAD **3.3ft (1m)/5.7ft (1.75m)**
HARDINESS **Zone 5**

Pink Bells is a very floriferous groundcover rose. The flowers are small but carried in amazing profusion, and each one is crammed with little petals. They are bright pink at first, and in cool or overcast weather, but fade to pale pink after they open out, while retaining a darker shade on the petal backs. They come in large clusters, stand up well to rain, and are supported by small, dark, shiny, healthy leaves. The plant grows densely and can reach 5.7ft (1.75m) high and twice as wide in hot climates.

'PINK CHEROKEE'

see 'ANEMONENROSE'

'PINK CLOUD'

Modern Climber

ORIGIN **Boerner, US, 1952**
PARENTAGE **'New Dawn' seedling**
FLOWER SIZE **3.1in (8cm)**
SCENT **Medium and tealike**
FLOWERING **Repeats**
HEIGHT/SPREAD **9.8ft (3m)/6.6ft (2m)**
HARDINESS **Zone 5**

Eugene Boerner used 'New Dawn' to breed many of the best modern climbers – perpetual-flowering, prolific, and hardy. 'Pink Cloud' is an outstanding example. Its flowers are dark pink, full of petals, deliciously scented, and borne in large clusters of 5–15 – so large, in fact, that they tend to hang down attractively under their own weight. The plant flowers very profusely during its first flowering, and then on a lesser scale until well into autumn. 'Pink Cloud' is a vigorous, speedy, upright grower, with dark, glossy, healthy, Wichurana foliage. It is still widely grown and sold all over the world, and rightly so.

'PINK FAVORITE'

Hybrid Tea

ORIGIN **Von Abrams, US, 1956**
PARENTAGE **'Juno' x ('Georg Arends' x 'New Dawn')**
FLOWER SIZE **4.3in (11cm)**
SCENT **Medium, spicy, and sweet**
FLOWERING **Repeats**
HEIGHT/SPREAD **4.1ft (1.25m)/3.3ft (1m)**
HARDINESS **Zone 6**
AWARDS **Portland GM 1957**

The unusual ancestry of this fine, pink Hybrid Tea produced a few surprises. The flowers are pleasant enough – creamy pink with darker backs, and borne in clusters of three or more – and it has fine, dark, glossy leaves. But, after it had been grown for a few years, people began to realize that 'Pink Favorite' was by far the most resistant of all Hybrid Teas to both mildew and blackspot. Breeders tried crossing it to raise a new race of healthy roses, but 'Pink Favorite' never seemed to pass on its good qualities. Its best offspring was a color sport introduced as 'Honey Favorite' (Abrams, 1962), which is a rich butterscotch color, fading to fawn. Both fare best in cool climates, where their flowers last a long time and seem impervious to rain. And they are still remarkably healthy.

'PINK GROOTENDORST'

see 'F. J. GROOTENDORST'

'PINK CLOUD'

'PINK FAVORITE'

PINK LA SÉVILLANA

see LA SÉVILLANA

PINK MEIDILAND

syn. 'MEIPOQUE', Schloss Heidegg

Shrub Rose

ORIGIN **Meilland, France, 1984**
PARENTAGE Anne de Bretagne x Nirvana
FLOWER SIZE **2.4in (6cm)**
SCENT **Light and musky**
FLOWERING **Almost continuous**
HEIGHT/SPREAD **4.9ft (1.5m)/5.7ft (1.75m)**
HARDINESS **Zone 6**
AWARDS **ADR 1987**

This was the first of the Meidiland Shrub roses to be introduced. Although promoted for landscaping, Pink Meidiland makes an excellent shrub for gardens, and flowers continuously until late autumn. The flowers are very pretty, single, and deep pink with a white center and white petal backs. The petals have an attractive ripple to their shape, and the long stamens at the center have red filaments. The flowers come in clusters of 3–15 and are followed by vermilion hips. Deadheading helps to promote quick reflowering, but the plant is never without flowers. Pink Meidiland is bushy, prickly, compact, and extremely healthy, with handsome, clean, mid-green leaves and bronzy new growth. The flowers attract bees and stand up well to rain.

PINK PANTHER

see PANTHÈRE ROSE

PINK MEIDILAND

'PINK PARFAIT'

'PINK PARFAIT'

Grandiflora

ORIGIN **Swim, US, 1960**
PARENTAGE **'First Love' x 'Pinocchio'**
FLOWER SIZE **4.7in (12cm)**
SCENT **Light and sweet**
FLOWERING **Repeats well and quickly**
HEIGHT/SPREAD **4.1ft (1.25m)/3.3ft (1m)**
HARDINESS **Zone 5**
AWARDS **Baden-Baden GM 1959; Portland GM 1959; AARS 1961; NRS GM 1992**

Although registered as an American Grandiflora rose, 'Pink Parfait' is closer to a Floribunda in height and character – and an excellent garden plant. It has large flowers, which are lightly double and open out fully. They start a rich pink and pale to flesh pink as they age. They are deeper pink at the edges and ivory white at the center, but the color varies according to the climate and weather from season to season. The flowers are particularly elegant when half open, though that stage does not last long because they expand somewhat quickly: in fact, the flower is attractive at every stage of development. The flowers come in large, open clusters of anything from 3–20. The plant has large, healthy, medium-dark leaves and exudes vigor.

'PINK PERPÊTUE'

Modern Climber

ORIGIN **Gregory, Britain, 1965**
PARENTAGE **'Danse du Feu' x 'New Dawn'**
FLOWER SIZE **2.8in (7cm)**
SCENT **Light to medium**
FLOWERING **Repeats well**
HEIGHT/SPREAD **9.8ft (3m)/6.6ft (2m)**
HARDINESS **Zone 5**

'Pink Perpêtue' is a short climber or pillar rose for cool climates: it flowers especially well and shows its richest colors in a temperate autumn. The flowers have short petals, clear pink on their upper sides and carmine on the backs, but sometimes the colors blotch in rain and bleach in sun. At their peak in summer, the flowers seem to glow with color and stand out from a distance. They come in strong, upright clusters (typically of 5–7 flowers). The plant is a little stiff for easy training, and thorny, but it flowers well in autumn, especially if deadheaded after its first flowering. The leaves are dark with somewhat rounded leaflets and an occasional touch of blackspot.

'PINK PERPÊTUE'

'PINK PROSPERITY'

Hybrid Musk

ORIGIN **Bentall, Britain, 1931**
PARENTAGE **'Prosperity' x unknown**
FLOWER SIZE **2in (5cm)**
SCENT **Strong and delicious: a mixture of musk and sweetness**
FLOWERING **Repeats well**
HEIGHT/SPREAD **5.7ft (1.75m)/4.9ft (1.5m)**
HARDINESS **Zone 6**

Many of the plants labeled in gardens as 'Pink Prosperity' are, in fact, plain 'Prosperity', which has a pink tinge when it first opens. They are somewhat mixed up commercially, but 'Pink Prosperity' has smaller flowers, with more petals and a neater shape. They open from crimson buds and are a deep rose pink at first, even though they turn to white as they expand and open out. They have neat imbricated petals around the yellow stamens, and the flowers come in long clusters, which open over a long period. Indeed, some of the later-flowering buds are barely formed when the first flowers in a cluster start to open. This makes for sustained color and continuity. There are usually 10–25 flowers in a cluster. The leaves are mid-green, and may need some protection against blackspot. They have the characteristically fringed stipules and zigzag stems of the Multiflora Hybrids. The plant has large thorns and an attractive, open, arching habit. It repeats very well and is free with its scent even on cool or windy days.

PINK ROBUSTA

PINK ROBUSTA

syn. 'KORPINROB', The Seckford Rose

Shrub Rose

ORIGIN **Kordes, Germany, 1986**
PARENTAGE **('Zitronenfalter' x 'Cläre Grammerstorf') x Robusta**
FLOWER SIZE **3.9in (10cm)**
SCENT **Light and sweet**
FLOWERING **Repeats well**
HEIGHT/SPREAD **4.9ft (1.5m)/4.1ft (1.25m)**
HARDINESS **Zone 4**

This is not a pink sport of the popular red Rugosa hybrid Robusta, but a seedling of it. The flowers of Pink Robusta are rose pink and semidouble, with a patch of white toward the center, and pale stamens. The petals are large, and have a charming ruffle, which gives the flowers much of their character. They are carried very profusely in clusters of 3–7 (sometimes more, or less) almost without interruption until the first frost. Pink Robusta has a lot of large, dark, healthy, glossy leaves and fewer prickles than its parent. Its hardiness makes it popular in Canada, Scandinavia, and central Europe. It is a large shrub, and excellent for plantings in public parks and landscaping. When a bush is in full flower, it draws you over from quite a distance to admire it close-up.

'PINK PEACE'

Hybrid Tea

ORIGIN **Meilland, France, 1959**
PARENTAGE **('Mme. A. Meilland' x 'Monique') x ('Mme. A. Meilland' x 'Mrs. John Laing')**
FLOWER SIZE **5.1in (13cm)**
SCENT **Strong and sweet**
FLOWERING **Repeats well**
HEIGHT/SPREAD **4.9ft (1.5m)/4.1ft (1.25m)**
HARDINESS **Zone 6**
AWARDS **Geneva GM 1959; Rome GM 1959**

It is pink and closely related to 'Mme. A. Meilland', but 'Pink Peace' is a descendant of 'Peace', not a sport. Its flowers are large, with a lot of long petals curling back attractively at their edges. Their color is a distinctive dark pink or pale crimson, a somewhat uncompromising shade. The flowers are borne singly and in clusters of up to five on long, strong stems, which make them good for cutting. Their size has also made 'Pink Peace' popular with exhibitors. The flowers last well in water. 'Pink Peace' is, however, essentially a rose for the garden, where it grows vigorously and tolerates poor soils. Its leaves are a somewhat ordinary green, and susceptible to rust. Its thick, stiff stems will reach at least 6.6ft (2m) if grown in a hot climate and left unpruned.

'Candy Stripe' is a sport of 'Pink Peace' and is exactly the same as its parent in all respects except for the color of its flowers, which are splashed and spattered with palest pink.

'PINK PEACE'

'CANDY STRIPE'

Sport of 'Pink Peace'

'CANDY STRIPE'

ORIGIN **McCummings, US, 1963**

'PINK PROSPERITY'

'PINKIE'

Polyantha

ORIGIN **Swim, US, 1947**
PARENTAGE **'China Doll' seedling**
FLOWER SIZE **2in (5cm)**
SCENT **Fairly strong and sweet**
FLOWERING **Repeats constantly**
HEIGHT/SPREAD **3.3ft (1m)/2.7ft (80cm)**
HARDINESS **Zone 6**
AWARDS **AARS 1948**

This wonderful rose is still grown in America and popular in Australia, but 'Pinkie' is almost unknown elsewhere. Its flowers are loose, semidouble, reflexed, and dainty, opening from elegantly scrolled buds. They are a good, mid-pink color, fading slightly in hot sunshine. Small (0.4in/1cm), round, vermilion hips follow in due course. The flowers are borne in clusters of 5–25 in amazing profusion, hiding the leaves from sight. In hot climates, it flowers continuously. 'Pinkie' makes a short and slender plant, with a lot of small twiggy stems and a lax habit of growth. Its leaves are bright green, thin, and glossy. It is easily propagated from cuttings.

It is sometimes said that 'Pinkie' was named after a 1940s movie in which the actress Jeanne Crain starred. That cannot be correct, however: the film was called *Pinky*, not *Pinkie*, and it was made in 1949, two years after 'Pinkie' was introduced.

The climbing sport **'Climbing Pinkie'** is an immensely floriferous rose, flowering from late spring right through to early winter in warm climates. The plant is completely thornless, with flexible stems – ideal for training over arches and pergolas. It is very popular in Australia, where it may flower all year round.

Sport of 'Pinkie'

'CLIMBING PINKIE'

Climber
ORIGIN **Dering, US, 1952**
FLOWER SIZE **2.4in (6cm)**
FLOWERING **Repeat-flowering**
HEIGHT/SPREAD **9.8ft (3m)/6.6ft (2m)**

'PINKIE' (*in hot weather*)

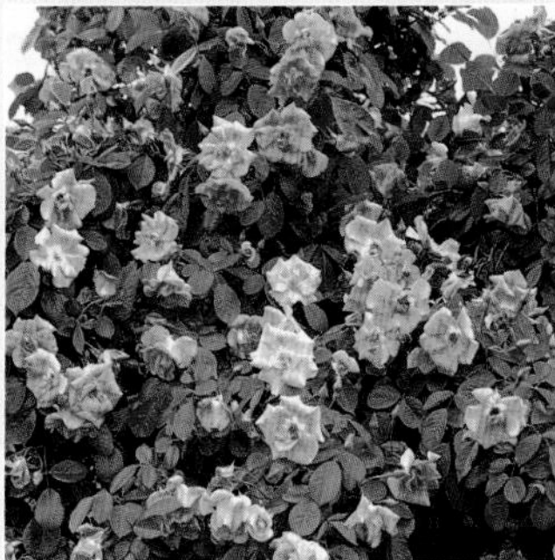
'CLIMBING PINKIE' (*in cool weather*)

PINK SPRAY

PINK SPRAY

syn. 'LENSPRA'
Ground Cover

ORIGIN **Lens, Belgium, 1980**
PARENTAGE ***Rosa wichurana* form x *Rosa multiflora* var. *adenochaeta***
FLOWER SIZE **0.6in (1.5cm)**
SCENT **Light and musky**
FLOWERING **Once only**
HEIGHT/SPREAD **1.6ft (50cm)/4.9ft (1.5m)**
HARDINESS **Zone 6**

Louis Lens was a most adventurous breeder who raised many unusual Musk roses from *Rosa multiflora* var. *adenochaeta*. But they are mostly 6.6ft (2m) shrubs, whereas Pink Spray is a dwarf procumbent creeper. No other rose resembles it, except its sister seedling White Spray. The flowers of Pink Spray are tiny, dark pink at first, fading to pale pink, with a bright white center and a tuft of yellow stamens at the middle. The petals have a distinct roll, which adds to the character of the flowers, but the most remarkable characteristic of Pink Spray is its sheer floriferousness. At the height of its flowering, it is completely covered in small clusters of flowers, hiding the small, dark leaves and the dense, twiggy structure of the bush. The flowers are followed by tiny vermilion hips. It is an excellent rose for rock gardens and for trailing down low walls.

PINK SYMPHONIE

syn. 'MEITONJE', Pretty Polly, Sweet Sunblaze
Patio Rose

ORIGIN **Meilland, France, 1987**
PARENTAGE **'Darling Flame' x Air France**
FLOWER SIZE **2in (5cm)**
SCENT **Light and musky**
FLOWERING **Almost continuous**
HEIGHT/SPREAD **1.6ft (50cm)/1.6ft (50cm)**
HARDINESS **Zone 6**
AWARDS **RNRS PIT 1989; Glasgow GM 1992**

A patio rose, a miniature, a shrub rose: Pink Symphonie has been called all of these, but it is a unique little rose, which

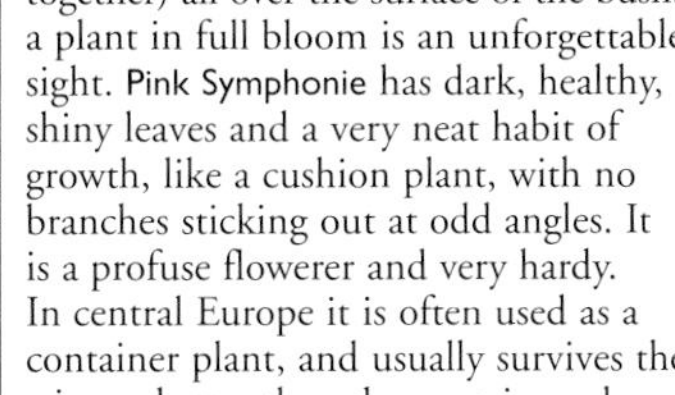

once won the top prize at the British rose trials. The flowers are soft pink with darker pink petal backs, lightly double, and very pretty. They come in small clusters (rarely of more than three flowers together) all over the surface of the bush: a plant in full bloom is an unforgettable sight. Pink Symphonie has dark, healthy, shiny leaves and a very neat habit of growth, like a cushion plant, with no branches sticking out at odd angles. It is a profuse flowerer and very hardy. In central Europe it is often used as a container plant, and usually survives the winters better than the containers do.

'PINK WONDER'

see 'KALINKA'

PLAY ROSE

see DÉBORAH

PINK SYMPHONIE

'PLAYBOY'

Floribunda

ORIGIN **Cocker, Britain, 1976**
PARENTAGE **'City of Leeds' x ('Chanelle' x 'Piccadilly')**
FLOWER SIZE **2.8in (7cm)**
SCENT **Light**
FLOWERING **Repeats well**
HEIGHT/SPREAD **3.3ft (1m)/2.7ft (80cm)**
HARDINESS **Zone 6**
AWARDS **Portland GM 1989**

'Playboy' is a flashy red and yellow Floribunda, guaranteed to brighten up a garden. The flowers are bright golden yellow with a thick, dark orange edging: the exact color varies a little from flower to flower and becomes redder as they age, especially in hot weather. The flowers have yellow petal backs and handsome golden stamens. They are lightly double, with wavy edges to the petals, which emphasize the striking color contrasts. The flowers come in spacious clusters of 3–7 and last a long time both on the bush and as cut flowers: 'Playboy' is also popular as an exhibition Floribunda. The plant has dark, healthy, glossy leaves and is one of the easiest to grow and most rewarding of all roses.

'PLAYBOY'

PLAYGIRL

PLAYGIRL

syn. 'MORPLAG'

Floribunda

ORIGIN **Moore, US, 1986**
PARENTAGE **'Angel Face' × 'Playboy'**
FLOWER SIZE **2.8in (7cm)**
SCENT **Light, sweet, and fruity**
FLOWERING **Repeats well**
HEIGHT/SPREAD **2.7ft (80cm)/2ft (60cm)**
HARDINESS **Zone 5**

Playgirl is a very beautiful Ralph Moore rose that has a unique quality. Its flowers are light purple crimson at first, with very ruffled petals around a strikingly large boss of yellow stamens. These are characteristics inherited from 'Angel Face', but in the case of Playgirl they are also very reminiscent of a single-flowered camellia. The coloring runs all through the flower, with little variation; later it fades to bright pink and lilac mauve. The flowers come on long stems, occasionally singly but usually in clusters of up to seven. The plant has very glossy, dark green leaves and is very healthy – an excellent choice for the front of a border.

PLEINE DE GRÂCE

syn. 'LENGRA'

Shrub Rose

ORIGIN **Lens, Belgium, 1983**
PARENTAGE **'Ballerina' × *Rosa filipes***
FLOWER SIZE **1.6in (4cm)**
SCENT **Strong and musky**
FLOWERING **Once only**
HEIGHT/SPREAD **9.8ft (3m)/13.1ft (4m)**
HARDINESS **Zone 6**

Pleine de Grâce – the name is taken from the Ave Maria – is an immensely floriferous and outsize shrub. It seldom grows much higher than 13.1ft (4m), but then it begins to grow sideways and covers its frame from top to bottom with thousands of flowers. These open from creamy white buds and are reminiscent of *Rosa filipes* in their shape: the petals do not quite overlap, so you can see through the tiny gaps they leave between each other. They have long stamens, which turn brown very quickly. The flowers come in huge clusters (typically of 50–100) and are followed by large quantities of tiny orange hips, which stay on the bush until after the leaves have dropped. Every year the plant, which is very prickly and has dark red stems, sends up new growths, perhaps 6.6ft (2m) long, on which the next year's bounty of flowers will be borne. The leaves are healthy and bright green, and have very long, narrow leaflets.

PLEINE DE GRÂCE

POETRY IN MOTION

POETRY IN MOTION

syn. 'HARÉLAN', Gift of Life

Hybrid Tea

ORIGIN **Harkness, Britain, 1997**
PARENTAGE **Dr. Darley x Elina**
FLOWER SIZE **3.9in (10cm)**
SCENT **Medium, sweet, and fruity**
FLOWERING **Repeats well**
HEIGHT/SPREAD **4.1ft (1.25m)/2.7ft (80cm)**
HARDINESS **Zone 6**
AWARDS **Belfast GM 1999**

The flowers of Poetry in Motion are lemon yellow, with a hint of peach on the backs of the petals. They are also slightly darker toward their centers, where the golden stamens send out darker, richer shadows between the petals. The flowers are not especially large, as Hybrid Teas go, but they are elegantly shaped and are borne singly at the ends of long stems, which makes them useful as cut-flower roses. They also stand up well to rain. Poetry in Motion has large, healthy, medium-dark leaves and large prickles. The plant is upright in growth and perhaps a little stiff in habit, but it is a sturdy grower and a good repeater.

POKER

POKER

syn. 'MEIPAZDIA'

Hybrid Tea

ORIGIN **Meilland, France, 1998**
FLOWER SIZE **4.3in (11cm)**
SCENT **Strong and sweet**
FLOWERING **Repeats**
HEIGHT/SPREAD **4.1ft (1.25m)/2.7ft (80cm)**
HARDINESS **Zone 6**

Meilland no longer stock this white Hybrid Tea, even though they introduced it as recently as 1998. However, Poker is still widely available from other nurseries, especially in France. The flowers are classic, elegant, and strongly scented. There is a hint of pink at the center of the opening bud, but the flowers turn quickly to pure white. They are borne singly on long, straight stems and are excellent for cutting. Poker has medium-sized, dark green leaves and a sturdy, upright habit of growth. It deserves a longer stay in our gardens than it has enjoyed in Meilland's catalogue.

POLAR STAR

see POLARSTERN

'POLAREIS'

Rugosa Hybrid

ORIGIN **Germany, 1991**
FLOWER SIZE **2in (5cm)**
SCENT **Light and musky**
FLOWERING **Continuous**
HEIGHT/SPREAD **5.7ft (1.75m)/6.6ft (2m)**
HARDINESS **Zone 4**

No one can remember the origins of 'Polareis'. It was imported into western Europe from the Leningrad (St. Petersburg) Botanic Garden in the 1960s. Its original name had already been lost, so 'Polareis' is a provisional name, which it received when Strobel and Meilland reintroduced it simultaneously in 1991. It is an extremely hardy Hybrid Rugosa, with many-petaled, pale pink flowers that fade to white at the edges. The flowers have soft petals and are profusely borne in dense clusters of 7–15. The plant is very prickly, with healthy, green Rugosa leaves. It may get a touch of mildew from time to time, but usually grows out of it. It is an eye-catching addition to the Rugosas and the first to have two colors within the flower.

POLARSTERN

syn. 'TANLARPOST', Polar Star

Hybrid Tea

ORIGIN **Tantau, Germany, 1982**
FLOWER SIZE **5.5in (14cm)**
SCENT **Light and pleasantly sweet**
FLOWERING **Continuous**
HEIGHT/SPREAD **3.3ft (1m)/2.5ft (75cm)**
HARDINESS **Zone 5**
AWARDS **ROTY 1985**

'POLAREIS'

POLARSTERN

Polarstern is a handsome, creamy white Hybrid Tea. It is a big, solid, dependable rose, somewhat short on charm. The bud is cream or ivory colored. At the half open stage there is often a hint of lemon at the center, but the fully open flower is a luminous creamy white. The flower has a lot of petals, which reflex prettily. They are very thick and strong, so the flower stands up well to rain, but it also means that the bud is globular and opens slowly. In hot weather, the rose actually opens out completely and shows its golden stamens. All the stages of its development are attractive. The flowers are borne, almost always singly but occasionally in quite large clusters, on long, strong, stiff stems: as well as being a first-rate garden rose, it is a consistent prizewinner at shows. The bush has large dark leaves and is healthy apart from an occasional brush with mildew. Polarstern produces its flowers in great quantities, so that although, like all Hybrid Teas, they come in flushes, it is never without a flower in between those flushes until late into autumn.

POLKA 91

syn. 'MEITOSIER', Lord Byron, Twilight Glow

Modern Climber

ORIGIN **Meilland, France, 1992**
PARENTAGE **'Golden Showers' x 'Lichtkönigin Lucia'**
FLOWER SIZE **4.7in (12cm)**
SCENT **Light**
FLOWERING **Repeats well**
HEIGHT/SPREAD **9.8ft (3m)/6.6ft (2m)**
HARDINESS **Zone 5**

Polka 91 is a most unusual and beautiful rose, which can be grown either as a short climber or as a large, arching shrub. The flowers are exquisite: deep apricot, fading to palest buff at the edges, with darker petal backs, which add more hues and shades to the flower as a whole. The petals have frilly edges, which are deeply lobed and indented, as well as a distinct ruffle in the way they display themselves like layers of crêpe paper. The flowers come singly or in small clusters – of seldom more than three at a time – and are very pretty when picked for indoor arrangements. They are not borne constantly but in a succession of flowering flushes (two in a cool climate, three in warmer areas), with occasional flowers interspersed between. The leaves are large, dark, glossy, and fairly healthy.

POLKA 91

POLLUCE

POLLUCE

syn. 'BARPOLL'

Shrub Rose

ORIGIN **Barni, Italy, 1987**
FLOWER SIZE **1.8in (4.5cm)**
SCENT **Musky**
FLOWERING **Almost continuous**
HEIGHT/SPREAD **2.7ft (80cm)/4.1ft (1.25m)**
HARDINESS **Zone 5**

Barni introduced Polluce at the same time as its heavenly twin Castore. Both are absolutely first-rate shrub roses, which should properly be classified among the Hybrid Musks. Many would say that, of the two, Polluce has the edge over its brother – the flowers are slightly larger and it seems to flower even more continuously, if such were possible. Polluce has bright crimson, semidouble flowers with a patch of white toward the center. They come in large clusters (typically 20–60 flowers) and repeat quickly, with always a few flowers between the main flushes. Small orange hips follow in autumn. Polluce has small, glossy, Wichurana leaves and an open, arching habit, so that its flowering sprays appear right down to ground level. In hot climates it can be trained as a 6.6ft (2m) pillar rose, but it is a valuable plant in cool and continental climates, too. It is vigorous and generally healthy – a winner.

'POLSTJÄRNAN'

Rambler

ORIGIN **Wasast-Järna, Finland, 1937**
PARENTAGE ***Rosa beggeriana* hybrid**
FLOWER SIZE **1in (2.5cm)**
SCENT **Light, sweet, and pleasant**
FLOWERING **Once only, early in season**
HEIGHT/SPREAD **16.4ft (5m)/9.8ft (3m)**
HARDINESS **Zone 3**

'POLYANTHA GRANDIFLORA'

'POLSTJÄRNAN'

In places as cold as Alaska and northern Russia, there is only one climbing rose worth growing – 'Polstjärnan'. Its name means "polar star" and it survives the bitterest of winters. The flowers are small, white, and only semidouble, but attractively shaped and carried in large, open clusters, typically of 20–60 flowers. Each flower is set off by a cluster of golden stamens. A plant in full flower is a stunning sight: it is a rose that is widely grown in much milder climates because it matches the best ramblers for sheer flower power. It sends up long, slender branches, lightly covered with small, dark leaves. It can also be grown as a billowing bush, 9.8ft (3m) high and wide.

'POLYANTHA GRANDIFLORA'

syn. Rosa x *gentiliana*

Hybrid Multiflora

ORIGIN **Bernaix, France, 1886**
FLOWER SIZE **1.8in (4.5cm)**
SCENT **Strong and musky**
FLOWERING **Once, midseason**
HEIGHT/SPREAD **13.1ft (4m)/9.8ft (3m)**
HARDINESS **Zone 6**

'Polyantha Grandiflora' is a rose of great beauty, and most profuse in its single flowering. The individual flowers are larger than most wild looking ramblers, pure white, and with a handsome brush of orange stamens, which lights up the whole of the newly opened flower. The stamens are of uneven length, which gives them their distinctive character. The flowers are carried in large clusters (20–60 flowers) and beautifully set off by red brown stalks and bristly stems. The leaves, too, are handsome – bright green, large, and glossy, with crimson midribs when they are young. The flowers are followed by masses of plump little hips. Because it sets so many seeds, 'Polyantha Grandiflora' has been recommended as a source of seedling rootstocks, which may explain why more than one cultivar is grown under this name.

ROSA POMIFERA

see ROSA VILLOSA

'Pompon Blanc Parfait'

'Pompon Blanc Parfait'

Alba/Noisette cross

ORIGIN **Verdier, France, 1876**
FLOWER SIZE **2in (5cm)**
SCENT **Strong and musky**
FLOWERING **Occasionally remontant**
HEIGHT/SPREAD **6.6ft (2m)/3.3ft (1m)**
HARDINESS **Zone 5**

Although often described as an Alba rose, the hybrid origin of 'Pompon Blanc Parfait' can be deduced from its small flowers, its narrow, upright habit, and its tendency to produce a few flowers in autumn. They are palest pink at first, but fade to white as they open out to neat and perfect rosettes, sometimes with a button eye at the center. They come singly or, more usually, in overcrowded clusters of up to about ten flowers. The scent is quite delicious. 'Pompon Blanc Parfait' is tall and very slender – almost fastigiate – with short, leafy side growth and handsome gray green leaves. The stems of the plant are smooth when young, but develop prickles during their second year.

'Pompon de Bourgogne'

syn. 'Burgundy', 'Parvifolia'

Centifolia

ORIGIN **France, 1684**
FLOWER SIZE **0.8in (2cm)**
SCENT **Light**
FLOWERING **Once, midseason**
HEIGHT/SPREAD **2.5ft (75cm)/2ft (60cm)**
HARDINESS **Zone 5**

Nothing is known of the origins of this miniature old rose, though 'Pompon de Bourgogne' may be as much as 400 years old. Its history is complicated by the fact that several different forms of it are in cultivation. Usually, it makes a small, compact plant, which is a perfect miniature in everything – especially its flowers and leaves. The flowers are deep crimson with pink backs, fading to mauve purple. They have a button eye, where the pale petal backs are curled back toward the center, and a lot of tiny, shell-shaped petals so neatly arranged as a rosette that the appearance is stylized – almost heraldic. The flowers come singly or in clusters of 3–5 at the tips of the stems. 'Pompon de Bourgogne' is strong-growing and makes a mass of slender, erect branchlets with only a few prickles. It is best pruned back immediately after flowering to prevent it from getting too leggy. Left unpruned, the plant will eventually attain quite a height – even as much as 4.9ft (1.5m).

'Pompon Panachée'

Gallica

ORIGIN **Moreau & Robert, France**
FLOWER SIZE **2.4in (6cm)**
SCENT **Medium and sweet**
FLOWERING **Once only**
HEIGHT/SPREAD **4.9ft (1.5m)/3.3ft (1m)**
HARDINESS **Zone 5**

'Pompon Panachée'

Little is known about the history of 'Pompon Panachée'. It is not the oldest of striped roses, nor the largest, nor the most fragrant, nor in any way exceptional, though it is an agreeable plant and has its place in any collection of old roses. The flowers are white or pale pink, irregularly splashed with dark pink or crimson. They are cupped at first but later reflex like little pompons, while retaining a loose button eye. Sometimes they also have a green pointel at the center. They come singly or in twos and threes on a plant that has pale green leaves and can grow almost to 6.6ft (2m).

'Pompon de Bourgogne'

'Pompon de Paris'

syn. Rouletii

China Rose

FLOWER SIZE **1.2in (3cm)**
SCENT **Light and tealike**
FLOWERING **Repeats constantly**
HEIGHT/SPREAD **1.6ft (50cm)/1.3ft (40cm)**
HARDINESS **Zone 6**

The origins of 'Pompon de Paris' and its sport, 'Climbing Pompon de Paris', are unknown. The bush form is said to have been popular as a pot plant in Paris in the 19th century. It may be an older rose renamed, perhaps one introduced from China, or it may be one of the many China rose seedlings raised in Italy in the 1820s and 1830s. It was probably the first ever miniature to be bred. The flowers of 'Pompon de Paris' are small, double, and bright pink. They start to flower early in the season and continue until late. The leaves are neat, small, mid-green, shiny, and borne at short intervals on somewhat zigzag stems. The plant is vigorous and fairly healthy, and roots very easily from cuttings. It has a scattering of stout prickles.

'Climbing Pompon de Paris' flowers with great profusion very early in the season, but produces only a few flowers later on. In all other details it is exactly the same as the dwarf form. It will reach well over 16.4ft (5m) if grown against a wall or up a tree. Its long wands are slender and flexible, so they tend to arch over when covered with flowers – an unforgettable sight.

'Pompon de Paris'

'Climbing Pompon de Paris'

Sport of 'Pompon de Paris'

'Climbing Pompon de Paris'

Climbing China

ORIGIN **c.1839**
FLOWERING **Once spectacularly, then only intermittently**
HEIGHT/SPREAD **13.1ft (4m)/6.6ft (2m)**

'POPCORN'

Miniature Rose

ORIGIN **Morey, US, 1973**
PARENTAGE **'Katharina Zeimet' x 'Diamond Jewel'**
FLOWER SIZE **0.8in (2cm)**
SCENT **Slight and musky**
FLOWERING **Almost continuous**
HEIGHT/SPREAD **11.8in (30cm)/2ft (60cm)**
HARDINESS **Zone 6**

The old Polyanthas continue to produce wonderful seedlings for modern gardens. 'Popcorn' was bred from 'Katharina Zeimet', which was introduced as long ago as 1901. Its buds are cream colored, but they change quickly to pure white as they open up. They are semidouble, with an attractive wave to the petals, and a tiny boss of yellow stamens at the center. They come in large clusters – typically of 10–30 flowers – which make a magnificent display at first though, unfortunately, they hold onto their dead petals later and do not shed them cleanly. The plant has large, mid-green leaves which stand up well to disease. It roots easily from cuttings, so you can quickly build up enough plants for a complete edging.

Gourmet Popcorn is a sport of 'Popcorn' with slightly larger flowers. It is an excellent garden rose, which seems never to be out of flower. The individual flowers are not especially exciting, though they open from attractive creamy buds. The newly opened flowers are cupped and have golden stamens, which infuse the flowers with a creamy glow, but the stamens soon turn brown and the flowers open out pure white. Gourmet Popcorn looks well at the front of a border and as a landscaping rose.

Sport of 'Popcorn'

GOURMET POPCORN

syn. 'WEOPOP', Summer Snow
ORIGIN **Desamero, US, 1986**
FLOWER SIZE **1in (2.5cm)**

'POPCORN'

GOURMET POPCORN

'PORTRAIT'

It is a tall, vigorous plant, with a lot of flowers – good as a bedding rose and superb for cutting. The flowers are rose pink with darker, mid-pink backs to the petals, which give rise to attractive dark shadows within the expanding flower. Later the petals open out and lie flat in an attractive shape. The flowers sometimes come singly but, more usually, in clusters of 3–7 on long, strong stems. 'Portrait' is a vigorous grower, pushing up new stems with more flowers very quickly, so that it seems to be always in flower. It has large, glossy, dark, leaves (but watch out for blackspot), and grows as well in cold climates as hot ones.

'POPPY FLASH'

see 'RUSTICANA'

'PORTLAND ROSE'

syn. 'DUCHESS OF PORTLAND', 'PAESTANA'

Portland

ORIGIN **Portland, Britain, c.1750**
FLOWER SIZE **2.8in (7cm)**
SCENT **Medium and sweet**
FLOWERING **Remontant**
HEIGHT/SPREAD **2.7ft (80cm)/2ft (60cm)**
HARDINESS **Zone 5**

The origins of the 'Portland Rose' have intrigued people for over 200 years. Its importance lies in its ability to reflower time and again throughout the growing season. It became the founder of a race of remontant roses known as the Portland roses. Recent DNA work has established that it is a cross between a Gallica rose and a Damask. It is called "Portland" because it was once attributed to an English Duchess of Portland. Its flowers are semidouble, dark pink or pale crimson, with a small white patch toward the center, and a large ring of stamens, heavy with golden pollen. The petals are often ragged and irregular in shape, with occasional white streaks running out from the middle. The leaves are green, like a Gallica's, and susceptible to blackspot. The hips are long like a Damask's. The plant is not vigorous, but forms a low thicket of slender stems.

'PORTLAND ROSE'

PORTMEIRION

syn. 'AUSGUARD'

Shrub Rose

ORIGIN **Austin, Britain, 1999**
FLOWER SIZE **3.9in (10cm)**
SCENT **Strong and myrrhlike**
FLOWERING **Repeats**
HEIGHT/SPREAD **4.9ft (1.5m)/3.3ft (1m)**
HARDINESS **Zone 6**

The flowers of Portmeirion are lightly cupped and very attractive, each a well-formed rosette. They open deep pink (though the petals have slightly paler backs) and fade to mid-pink. Usually, they also have a white patch at the center and a scattering of rich yellow stamens, visible when they open out. They are carried singly or in clusters of up to seven on long, willowy, prickly stems. Sometimes the individual flowers nod over on their thin stalks. Portmeirion has an upright, slender habit of growth. Its leaves are mid-green, large, and fairly sparse; they may attract a little mildew late in the season. Portmeirion is said to be a short-growing rose, seldom more than 3.3ft (1m) high, but in David Austin's own garden it reaches 5.7ft (1.75m), and in hot climates can be even taller.

'PORTRAIT'

syn. 'STÉPHANIE DE MONACO'

Hybrid Tea

ORIGIN **Meyer, US, 1971**
PARENTAGE **'Pink Parfait' x 'Pink Peace'**
FLOWER SIZE **4.7in (12cm)**
SCENT **Strong and sweet**
FLOWERING **Repeats**
HEIGHT/SPREAD **4.9ft (1.5m)/3.3ft (1m)**
HARDINESS **Zone 6**
AWARDS **AARS 1972**

This charming Hybrid Tea – 'Portrait' in the US but 'Stéphanie de Monaco' in much of Europe – was the first amateur-raised rose to win the top All-America Rose Selection award.

PORTMEIRION

POT O' GOLD

syn. 'DICDIVINE'

Hybrid Tea

ORIGIN **Dickson, Northern Ireland, 1980**
PARENTAGE **'Eurorose' x 'Whisky'**
FLOWER SIZE **3.9in (10cm)**
SCENT **Medium, sweet, and fruity**
FLOWERING **Repeats well**
HEIGHT/SPREAD **3.3ft (1m)/2.7ft (80cm)**
HARDINESS **Zone 6**

The flowers explain the name of Pot o' Gold: they are bright yellow, with a hint of apricot or gold at the center. Later they fade to lemon, though the color is always darker in the middle. The flowers open from pointed buds and have a lot of petals, so that they remain very pretty when they open out. They are borne sometimes singly and sometimes in clusters of up to seven – Pot o' Gold has the Floribunda 'Eurorose' as one of its parents. The plant is very vigorous, with mid-green leaves (they have crimson edges at first) and a bushy habit of growth. Blackspot can be a problem in autumn, but Pot o' Gold is a fine, not too short bedding rose.

POT O' GOLD

'Pour Toi'

see 'Para Ti'

'Prairie Dawn'

Setigera Hybrid

ORIGIN **Morden, US, 1959**
PARENTAGE **'Prairie Youth' x ('Ross Rambler' x ['Dr. W. Van Fleet' x 'Altaica'])**
FLOWER SIZE **3.1in (8cm)**
SCENT **Medium and sweet**
FLOWERING **Repeats**
HEIGHT/SPREAD **4.9ft (1.5m)/4.1ft (1.25m)**
HARDINESS **Zone 4**

This was an important rose when first introduced: 'Prairie Dawn' was hardy in some of the coldest parts of the world, yet its flowers were of good size and produced almost continuously. In due course, it was much used for further breeding, so that it turns up in the ancestry of many subzero hybrids. The flowers are lightly double and come in clusters of 3–6 at the ends of the branches. They are a wonderful rich, warm, glowing pink at first, fading slightly as they age, especially in hot sunshine. 'Prairie Dawn' has small, dark green, glossy leaves and a graceful, airy, upright habit of growth. It is susceptible to blackspot, but this does not affect the plant's vigor, and it can be considered a low-care rose. In warmer climates it is a climber or pillar rose 9.8ft (3m) tall.

'Prairie Dawn'

'Prairie Harvest'

Shrub Rose

ORIGIN **Buck, US, 1985**
PARENTAGE **'Carefree Beauty' x Friesia**
FLOWER SIZE **3.9in (10cm)**
SCENT **Good: musky with a hint of sweetness**
FLOWERING **Repeats constantly**
HEIGHT/SPREAD **4.9ft (1.5m)/4.1ft (1.25m)**
HARDINESS **Zone 5**

The 'Prairie' roses were bred to resist the bitter Iowa winters: 'Prairie Harvest' is one the best – hardy, healthy, vigorous, and constantly in bloom until the first frost. The flowers open from small, neat, conical buds. They are lemon yellow at first, fading to cream and white as they expand into a loosely double shape. They are carried on long stems, singly or in clusters of up to seven. The plant is very vigorous, reaching 9.8ft (3m) in southern

'Prairie Harvest'

California. If left unpruned, the stems may bow under the weight of the flowers. The plant has large, dark, healthy leaves, but the lower parts are bare of foliage. It has an erect habit, unlike 'Prairie Princess', which is more spreading.

'Prairie Joy'

Shrub Rose

ORIGIN **Collicut, Canada, 1985**
PARENTAGE **'Prairie Princess' x 'Morden Cardinette'**
FLOWER SIZE **2.8in (7cm)**
SCENT **Light and sweet**
FLOWERING **Once spectacularly, then intermittently**
HEIGHT/SPREAD **4.9ft (1.5m)/4.1ft (1.25m)**
HARDINESS **Zone 3**

P

The Poulsen Family

POULSEN, SCANDINAVIA'S LARGEST ROSE NURSERY, PRODUCED ITS FIRST CLASSICS ALMOST A CENTURY AGO – AND IS STILL BREEDING PRIZE-WINNERS TODAY

The Poulsen nursery was founded in 1878 by Dorus Theus Poulsen (1850–1925). His three sons worked with him, and it was the eldest, Dines (1879–1940), who bred the first Poulsen roses – 'Ellen Poulsen' in 1911 and 'Rödhätte' in 1912. 'Rödhätte' was a cross between a Polyantha and a Hybrid Tea, and a taste of the Poulsen roses that were to make the family name famous.

Dines's younger brother, Svend (1884–1974), then took over the rose breeding. His aim was to breed roses that would be hardy in the cold Danish climate and flower continuously throughout the short Scandinavian summer. His first achievement was to introduce 'Else Poulsen' and 'Kirsten Poulsen' in 1924 – bred, like 'Rödhätte', by crossing Polyantha roses with Hybrid Teas. Svend's later achievements included the first yellow Floribunda, 'Poulsen's Yellow' (1938), and the excellent 'Poulsen's Crimson' (1950). Further success came with the exquisite white 'Irene av Denmark' and the cheerful multicolored 'Rumba' (1958).

Kalmar

Svend Poulsen was succeeded by his son Niels (b.1919), whose first roses included three beauties: 'Hakuun' (1962), 'Nina Weibull' (1962), and 'Chinatown' (1963). His cut-flower rose 'Nordia' (1967) proved a popular moneymaker.

Svend Poulsen (left) and son Niels

Today the company is run by Niels Poulsen's daughter, Pernille, and her husband Mogens N. Olesen. Their bestsellers include Ingrid Bergman (1984) and three of the best groundcover roses, White Bells (1980), Pink Bells (1983), and Kent (1988). Poulsen is still breeding modern roses of exquisite beauty, like Kalmar (1996), and winning major prizes at international trials for new roses: Amber Cover won the top award at Bagatelle in 2001. Poulsen also produces two-thirds of all the roses sold as house plants around the world: that rose on your windowsill probably started life in Denmark.

'PRAIRIE JOY'

'PRÉSIDENT DE SÈZE'

PRÉSIDENT LEOPOLD SENGHOR

Introduced as a hedging rose, 'Prairie Joy' is an excellent garden rose, too. Its flowers are a good size, and full of petals in a old-fashioned, button-eyed shape, opening mid-pink from darker buds and fading to pale pink. The flowers come singly and in clusters of up to six, and are followed by small orange hips. 'Prairie Joy' has a vigorous, branching habit and a lot of healthy foliage. It grows quickly, pushing up strong new shoots, which then arch over when they flower. It is very easy to grow – plant it and forget about it. 'Prairie Joy' was bred from a Griffith Buck rose and a Morden rose, so its hardiness is exceptional.

'PRAIRIE PRINCESS'

Shrub Rose

ORIGIN **Buck, US, 1972**
PARENTAGE **'Carrousel' x ('Morning Stars' x 'Suzanne')**
FLOWER SIZE **3.9in (10cm)**
SCENT **Good and sweet**
FLOWERING **Repeats well**
HEIGHT/SPREAD **6.6ft (2m)/6.6ft (2m)**
HARDINESS **Zone 4**

'Prairie Princess' was one of the first roses bred by Dr. Griffith Buck of Iowa State University to withstand the freezing temperatures of a Midwest winter. It has also been widely used to breed further superhardy roses. The flowers of 'Prairie Princess' open mid-pink from darker buds and are lightly double and cupped, with yellow stamens, which keep their color for a long time. The flowers come in clusters of 3–7. The bush is disease resistant and vigorous, growing tall enough to be treated as a short climber in warm climates. But in areas with subzero winters, 'Prairie Princess' is just a very good shrub rose – simple, floriferous, pretty, and sturdy.

'PRECIOUS PLATINUM'

syn. 'RED STAR'
Hybrid Tea

ORIGIN **Dickson, Northern Ireland, 1974**
PARENTAGE **'Red Planet' x 'Franklin Engelmann'**
FLOWER SIZE **4.7in (12cm)**
SCENT **Light and fruity**
FLOWERING **Repeats**
HEIGHT/SPREAD **3.9ft (1.2m)/3.3ft (1m)**
HARDINESS **Zone 6**

'Precious Platinum' is a fairly ordinary red Hybrid Tea that has never reached the highest ranks of popularity. It is pretty as a half-open bud, and makes a good lasting rose for cutting or exhibition. The flowers are borne, almost always singly, on long, strong stems. They are bright crimson, very full of petals, but only slightly scented and quick to spoil in rain. 'Precious Platinum' fares better in hot climates, where the flowers open right out and keep their color well, and the plant reaches 4.9ft (1.5m) or more. It is late to start into flower, and there are pauses between flushes. Nevertheless, 'Precious Platinum' makes a useful bedding plant, generally healthy, though sometimes susceptible to mildew.

'PRÉSIDENT DE SÈZE'

Gallica

ORIGIN **Hébert, France, 1836**
FLOWER SIZE **3.1in (8cm)**
SCENT **Strong and sweet**
FLOWERING **Once only**
HEIGHT/SPREAD **4.1ft (1.25m)/3.3ft (1m)**
HARDINESS **Zone 5**

The color changes of 'Président de Sèze' as the flowers open and develop have fascinated rose growers for many years. The fat buds open cherry crimson with pink petal backs, but the flowers then fade to magenta, mauve, lilac, gray and parchment white. The process starts with the outer petals, so that a fully expanded flower runs from bright crimson at the center to ash white at the edge. The flowers open out flat, with a neat mass of quilled petals and a quartered shape around a green eye. They come in twos and threes on short stems, surrounded by pale green leaves. The bush is healthier and more prickly than most Gallicas. Romain de Sèze (1748–1828) was one of three advocates who represented Louis XVI at his trial.

PRÉSIDENT LEOPOLD SENGHOR

syn. 'MEILUMINAC'
Hybrid Tea

ORIGIN **Meilland, France, 1979**
PARENTAGE **('Samouraï' x 'Imperator') x 'Pharaon'**
FLOWER SIZE **4.7in (12cm)**
SCENT **Little**
FLOWERING **Repeats**
HEIGHT/SPREAD **4.1ft (1.25m)/2.7ft (80cm)**
HARDINESS **Zone 6**
AWARDS **La Plus Belle Rose de France 1977**

There are many classic Hybrid Teas with dark red flowers. Président Leopold Senghor has been popular in France ever since it was introduced, but it has never been widely grown elsewhere. The buds are crimson, and open eventually to dark red – dark scarlet toward the center of the flower and more crimson toward the edges. The petals have beautiful velvety black markings on them. The flowers are borne singly, occasionally in twos and threes, but sometimes somewhat sparingly. The plant is vigorous and healthy, with pale green leaves, bronzy when young, and a fair amount of prickles. Léopold Senghor was the first President of Senegal.

'PRAIRIE PRINCESS'

'PRECIOUS PLATINUM'

Prestige de Lyon

Pretty Jessica

'Prima Ballerina'

Prestige de Lyon

syn. MEInimo, Regatta

Hybrid Tea

ORIGIN **Meilland, France, 1992**
PARENTAGE **Coppélia 76 x (seedling x Laura 81)**
FLOWER SIZE **3.9in (10cm)**
SCENT **Strong and fruity**
FLOWERING **Repeats**
HEIGHT/SPREAD **4.1ft (1.25m)/3.3ft (1m)**
HARDINESS **Zone 6**
AWARDS **Geneva FA 1992**

Few roses are perfect: Prestige de Lyon is not as floriferous as some Hybrid Teas and it makes a somewhat scraggy plant, but it also has great qualities. The flowers are extremely beautiful at all stages, from the classically elegant buds to the fully open flowers. They are salmon pink at the first flowering and deep rose pink in the autumn, but always fading gradually from the edges to a pale rose pink, and with paler, creamy pink petals and a hint of orange at the center. The open flower is often imbricated in shape, like a magnolia, with a lot of petals lying down neatly over each other. The plant has few prickles and large, healthy, dark green leaves, crimson when young. It is useful in mixed plantings or in massed displays.

Pretty Jessica

syn. 'AUSjess'

Shrub Rose

ORIGIN **Austin, Britain, 1983**
PARENTAGE **'Wife of Bath' x seedling**
FLOWER SIZE **2.8in (7cm)**
SCENT **Strong and sweet**
FLOWERING **Repeats well**
HEIGHT/SPREAD **2.5ft (75cm)/2ft (60cm)**
HARDINESS **Zone 6**

Pretty Jessica is a very useful short-growing rose and popular for small gardens. Its flowers are not especially distinctive, but they do embody completely the charm of David Austin's English Roses. The buds are crimson, but the petals roll back their tips as they open to pale pink flowers, with darker backs. The flowers are very full – globular at first – before they flatten out to reveal a mass of little petals in the old-fashioned style, all retained by large, pale guard petals around the outside. The inside petals curl over and wave and twist in no discernible pattern. The plant is nearly thornless. Unlike many David Austin roses, it remains neat and compact even in hot, dry climates, where its weakness for fungal diseases (rust, mildew, and blackspot) is less of a problem. "Pretty Jessica" – so-called by her suitor Lorenzo – was Shylock's daughter in *The Merchant of Venice.*

Pretty Lady

syn. 'SCRivo'

Floribunda

ORIGIN **Scrivens, Britain, 1996**
PARENTAGE **(seedling x [*Rosa davidii* var. *elongata* x seedling]) x (['Troika' x 'Alpine Sunset'] x Freedom)**
FLOWER SIZE **3.9in (10cm)**
SCENT **Medium and sweet**
FLOWERING **Repeats well**
HEIGHT/SPREAD **4.1ft (1.25m)/3.3ft (1m)**
HARDINESS **Zone 6**

The English amateur breeder Len Scrivens used a little-known species *Rosa davidii* var. *elongata* to develop this disease-free Floribunda: the mid-green leaves of Pretty Lady are resistant to blackspot even in the damp English climate. The flowers are a very beautiful pale apricot color – creamy white on the upper sides of the petals and apricot on the backs, with hints of peach and pink in the shadows between the petals. Pretty Lady is intermediate between the Floribundas and Hybrid Teas, bearing medium–large flowers both singly and in clusters of up to about six. The plant is somewhat prickly – but healthy, vigorous, and easy to grow.

Pretty Lady

Pretty Polly

see Pink Symphonie

'Prima Ballerina'

Hybrid Tea

ORIGIN **Tantau, Germany, 1957**
PARENTAGE **seedling x 'Mme. A. Meilland'**
FLOWER SIZE **4.3in (11cm)**
SCENT **Strong and sweet**
FLOWERING **Repeats well**
HEIGHT/SPREAD **3.3ft (1m)/2.5ft (75cm)**
HARDINESS **Zone 6**

'Prima Ballerina' is one of the best of the many seedlings of 'Mme. A. Meilland'. Its large-petaled flowers are held at an attractive angle and are pretty at all stages of their development. The buds are dark pink, long, and elegant. The flowers are large, lightly double, and bright pink overall: shades of mid-pink and dark pink merge imperceptibly within each flower. The petals are thick and have a reflective sheen all over their surfaces. The flowers come singly or in clusters of 3–5. The plant is a sturdy, vigorous grower, with glossy, bronzy leaves, which are large and healthy, except for an occasional touch of mildew. It is an excellent garden plant as well as being good for picking. It flowers heavily in a series of flushes, with a few blooms in between.

'Primevère'

Wichurana Rambler

ORIGIN **Barbier, France, 1927**
PARENTAGE ***Rosa wichurana* x 'Constance'**
FLOWER SIZE **2.8in (7cm)**
SCENT **Moderate**
FLOWERING **Once, midseason, then sporadically until winter**
HEIGHT/SPREAD **13.1ft (4m)/8.2ft (2.5m)**
HARDINESS **Zone 5**

The flat flowers of 'Primevère' are so full of petals that they seem much larger than they really are. It is the best large-flowered yellow Wichurana rambler. The flowers have quilled and muddled centers, but are blessed with a deep, lasting yellow color, which fades only slowly from bright yellow to lemon yellow. The individual roses last for several days and are good for cutting: they come singly or in long-stemmed clusters of up to five flowers. The leaves are dark and glossy in the Wichurana manner, and the plant produces long, vigorous growth with a lot of prickles, which helps it to climb.

'Primevère'

ROSA PRIMULA

ROSA PRIMULA

Wild Rose

FLOWER SIZE 1.4in (3.5cm)
SCENT Light and sweet
FLOWERING Once only, early in season
HEIGHT/SPREAD 8.2ft (2.5m)/8.2ft (2.5m)
HARDINESS Zone 5

The best thing about *Rosa primula* is the scent of its leaves – a strong smell of incense, freely dispersed on the air in humid weather and when you crush a leaflet. It is also useful for its early flowering, health, and hardiness. The flowers are pale yellow and carried on side shoots all along the main stems, right at the start of the rose season. They are followed in due course by round, red hips. The dainty, fernlike leaves are long, with as many as 15 little leaflets. The plant has slender, russet brown stems and a lot of prickles. It is somewhat too large for most gardens, but looks good in a woodland setting.

'PRINCE CAMILLE DE ROHAN'

Hybrid Perpetual

ORIGIN Verdier, France, 1861
PARENTAGE 'Général Jacqueminot' × unknown
FLOWER SIZE 3.1in (8cm)
SCENT Medium and sweet
FLOWERING Some repeating in autumn
HEIGHT/SPREAD 4.1ft (1.25m)/3.3ft (1m)
HARDINESS Zone 6

'PRINCE CAMILLE DE ROHAN'

'ROGER LAMBELIN'

The color of 'Prince Camille de Rohan' is superb – a rich, dark crimson with velvety black markings and hints of maroon and dark red. The flowers are large, too, and full of petals. In hot weather they have difficulty reflecting the sun's rays, and can scorch at the edges. They come either singly or in small, tight clusters, and are sometimes held somewhat feebly, so that the flowers seem to nod on their short stems. The plant has small, pale, convex leaves (strongly susceptible to blackspot) and a gently arching habit of growth. It is a rose that responds well to feeding, watering, and disease prevention.

'Prince Camille de Rohan' has given rise to an interesting sport called **'Roger Lambelin'**, whose petals are heavily streaked with white flashes. They run from the center of the flower to the petal edges and have the effect of shortening the petals and giving them a picotee edge. It is a type of variegation that is not found in any other rose and, though the effect is striking, it is not exactly beautiful. In all other respects 'Roger Lambelin' is identical to 'Prince Camille de Rohan' and shares its weakness for blackspot.

Sport of 'Prince Camille de Rohan'

'ROGER LAMBELIN'

ORIGIN Schwartz, 1890, probably in France
FLOWER SIZE 2.8in (7cm)

'PRINCE CHARLES'

'PRINCE CHARLES'

Bourbon Rose

ORIGIN Hardy, France, 1842
FLOWER SIZE 2.8in (7cm)
SCENT Medium and sweet
FLOWERING Once only
HEIGHT/SPREAD 4.9ft (1.5m)/4.1ft (1.25m)
HARDINESS Zone 5

Experts say that 'Prince Charles' cannot be a Bourbon rose, because it flowers only once. However, no one can think of a better classification for this beautiful old rose. Its flowers are medium-sized, but carried in great abundance. Their color is very variable – at its best, deepest purple, but often pale crimson or lilac colored. The variation is not related to temperature or sunshine, but depends upon how well it is growing: deep colors mean that you are feeding it well and it is growing happily, while pale colors indicate a plant under stress. In any event, the petals often have darker stripes in them. The flowers are double, but cup-shaped, so that the stamens at the center are usually visible. 'Prince Charles' has large dark leaves (watch out for blackspot) and sturdy, upright stems with very few prickles. If grown on its own roots, the plant suckers around agreeably and eventually builds up into a spectacular thicket of color.

PRINCE DE MONACO

syn. 'POULART', Modern Art

Hybrid Tea

ORIGIN Olesen, Denmark, 1983
FLOWER SIZE 2.8in (7cm)
SCENT Light
FLOWERING Repeats
HEIGHT/SPREAD 3.3ft (1m)/2.7ft (80cm)
HARDINESS Zone 6
AWARDS Rome GM 1984

Prince de Monaco is not an obvious member of the "hand-painted" group of roses, despite its other name of Modern Art. It opens from an unexciting bud into a fairly conventional flower, bright orange vermilion or smoky red, with a white center and paler petal backs. Then, as it matures, it acquires a pretty ruffling to its petals (like a geranium red gardenia), and finally develops "hand-painted" mottlings in a shade of maroon or oxblood just before the petals fade and drop. The plant is unexceptional, with fairly dark leaves, an upright habit, and prickles.

'PRINCEPS'

'PRINCEPS'

Modern Climber or Pillar Rose

ORIGIN Clark, Australia, 1942
FLOWER SIZE 4.7in (12cm)
SCENT Strong and sweet
FLOWERING Sometimes recurrent
HEIGHT/SPREAD 11.5ft (3.5m)/8.2ft (2.5m)
HARDINESS Zone 7

'Princeps' is a classic crimson Hybrid Tea type pillar rose, and very sweetly scented. It was unusual when it first appeared for having really strong, upright stems, so that the flowers did not hang their heads as almost every other red rose did at that time. The flowers come singly or in small clusters of up to about five. They have a fine, large mass of golden stamens at the center, and fade slightly to cherry red. The petal backs are always slightly paler, too. 'Princeps' is one of the first roses to flower in spring and grows vigorously, with smooth, mid-green foliage and many prickles. More than one rose can be seen under this name in Australian gardens.

PRINCESS ALEXANDRA

see ALEXANDRA RENAISSANCE

PRINCE DE MONACO

Mottisfont Abbey, Hampshire, England ▶

PRINCESS ALICE

PRINCESS ALICE

syn. 'HARTANNA', Zonta Rose, Brite Lites

Floribunda

ORIGIN **Harkness, Britain, 1985**
PARENTAGE **Judy Garland x Anne Harkness**
FLOWER SIZE **2.4in (6cm)**
SCENT **Light and fruity**
FLOWERING **Repeats well**
HEIGHT/SPREAD **4.9ft (1.5m)/2.7ft (80cm)**
HARDINESS **Zone 6**
AWARDS **Dublin GM 1984**

Princess Alice is a vigorous and prolific yellow rose, somewhat short on charm. Its ruffled flowers are fairly small, but carried in large clusters (typically of 7–20) at the end of an ungainly, lanky, awkward, upright, prickly, stiff, and slender shrub. The flowers are golden yellow at first and hold their color well, turning to lemon yellow only very slowly, even in hot climates. It repeats well, so that it is often in flower when there is little else to admire in the rose garden. The flowers also last a long time when cut for the house. The bush is healthy and vigorous, with bright green leaves and prickly stems. And it is rarely out of flower. It was named after Princess Alice, Duchess of Gloucester, an aunt of Queen Elizabeth II.

PRINCESS OF WALES

syn. 'HARDINKUM'

Floribunda

ORIGIN **Harkness, Britain, 1997**
FLOWER SIZE **2.8in (7cm)**
SCENT **Medium and sweet**
FLOWERING **Repeats well**
HEIGHT/SPREAD **2.7ft (80cm)/2ft (60cm)**
HARDINESS **Zone 6**

This beautiful white Floribunda was chosen by the late Diana, Princess of Wales, to bear her name. The deal was that some of the proceeds of sale would go to a charity that she patronized – which they did. The trouble is that the princess was no judge of excellence in roses, and Princess of Wales is not a very good one. It does better in dry climates, where it is less liable to succumb to disease and its thin petals can open out successfully, but in its native England it is a martyr to blackspot and its flowers crumple in the rain. Its buds are creamy white, but the flowers open pure white and are generously borne all over the surface of the bush, usually in clusters of 3–8. Princess of Wales is a short, compact, not very vigorous bush that repeats well and fairly quickly.

PRINCESSE DE MONACO

syn. 'MEIMAGARMIC'

Hybrid Tea

ORIGIN **Meilland, France, 1982**
PARENTAGE **Ambassador x 'Mme. A. Meilland'**
FLOWER SIZE **5.1in (13cm)**
SCENT **Light and fruity**
FLOWERING **Repeats well**
HEIGHT/SPREAD **3.3ft (1m)/2.7ft (80cm)**
HARDINESS **Zone 5**

This beautiful Hybrid Tea won several prizes when it was first introduced. It is still widely grown all over the world. The flowers are creamy white, with a pink edge to their petals. The fat opening buds look as if they have been dipped in pink, but the color darkens to crimson and spreads as the flowers expand. They usually come singly on fairly long stems, and last well as cut flowers. In fact, they never seem to open out completely. Although said to be good for exhibition, the flowers often have split centers. Princesse de Monaco is very hardy and healthy, and exceptionally resistant to disease in most climates and situations. It is sturdy, healthy, and upright in habit, with dark, glossy leaves. It is one of the shorter Hybrid Teas, and particularly useful for small gardens.

PRINCESSE DE MONACO

'PRINCESSE DE NASSAU'

Noisette

ORIGIN **Laffay, France, 1835**
FLOWER SIZE **2.4in (6cm)**
SCENT **Strong and musky**
FLOWERING **Repeats**
HEIGHT/SPREAD **9.8ft (3m)/6.6ft (2m)**
HARDINESS **Zone 7**

The rose now in cultivation as 'Princesse de Nassau' was reintroduced by the Englishman Graham Thomas in the 1970s. It has pink buds, but the flowers are cream at first and fade to white. They are fully double but open out flat, with a beautiful contrast between the creamy white petals and the deep golden stamens. The strong musk scent is delicious. The flowers come in somewhat long clusters of 5–30. The pale green leaves are a good foil for them. 'Princesse de Nassau' has even paler green new growth, somewhat zigzag stems, a scattering of prickles, and a bushy habit.

'PRINCESSE DE NASSAU'

'PRINCESSE LOUISE'

Sempervirens Hybrid

ORIGIN **Jacques, France, 1829**
PARENTAGE ***Rosa sempervirens* x 'Old Blush'**
FLOWER SIZE **2.4in (6cm)**
SCENT **Strong, sweet, and musky**
FLOWERING **Once only**
HEIGHT/SPREAD **16.4ft (5m)/9.8ft (3m)**
HARDINESS **Zone 6**

It is clear that, within a very few years of its introduction, no less than three different roses were circulating as 'Princesse Louise'. This remains the situation today – one is white (still found in Italy), one is pink (grown and sold in much of France), and the third is white with pink petal backs (most commonly seen elsewhere). It is the latter that is illustrated here, but only because it is the most widely grown. Either of the others may be the "true" 'Princesse Louise': more historic research is needed before a definitive naming can be made. The rose pictured below has crimson buds, which open to neat, pale pink, ruffled flowers that turn quickly to white, while crimson remains on the tips of the outer petals. The flowers come in clusters of 5–20 and are set off well by the neat, dark leaves. The name commemorates Princesse Louise d'Orléans (1812–50), eldest daughter of King Louis-Philippe, who married King Léopold I of the Belgians in 1832.

PRINCESS OF WALES

'PRINCESSE LOUISE'

P

'PRINCESSE MARGARET D'ANGLETERRE'

Hybrid Tea

ORIGIN **Meilland, France, 1968**
PARENTAGE **'Queen Elizabeth' x ('Mme. A. Meilland' x 'Michèle Meilland')**
FLOWER SIZE **4.7in (12cm)**
SCENT **Light and sweet**
FLOWERING **Repeats well**
HEIGHT/SPREAD **3.3ft (1m)/2.7ft (80cm)**
HARDINESS **Zone 6**
AWARDS **Portland GM 1977**

This vigorous Hybrid Tea has been consistently popular ever since it was introduced. The flowers of 'Princesse Margaret d'Angleterre' are a rich, bright pink, with strong petals and a shape that is attractive at all stages of its development. They keep their color well, and are usually borne singly on long, strong stems. It is an excellent cutting rose and lasts well both in a vase and in the garden. 'Princesse Margaret d'Angleterre' is a vigorous, upright grower with large, dark leaves and a lot of prickles. It is not tall, but a good repeater: an established bush is rarely out of flower. It was named after Princess Margaret of England (1930–2002).

'PRINCESSE MARGARET D'ANGLETERRE'

'PRINCESSE MARIE'

Hybrid Sempervirens

ORIGIN **Jacques, France, 1829**
PARENTAGE ***Rosa sempervirens* x 'Old Blush'**
FLOWER SIZE **2.4in (6cm)**
SCENT **Strong and musky**
FLOWERING **Once only, fairly late in season**
HEIGHT/SPREAD **16.4ft (5m)/9.8ft (3m)**
HARDINESS **Zone 6**

Several different roses go under the name of 'Princesse Marie', and all of them claim to be the original one. It has been confused with 'Ethel', 'Reine des Belges', and a mysterious seedling from Ireland called 'Belvedere'. The true 'Princesse Marie' is a palest pink hybrid of *Rosa sempervirens*, fairly similar in general appearance to its sister seedlings 'Adélaïde d'Orléans', 'Félicité et Perpétue', and 'Princesse Louise'. Its flowers are very double, quartered, and cupped at first, but opening out flat later. They come in large, open clusters that fade quickly to pearl and white. The plant has large dark leaves and impressive prickles. There is no problem identifying the lady after whom it was named: Princesse Marie, second daughter of King Louis-Philippe, was born in 1813, married Duke Alexander of Württemberg in 1837, and died of consumption two years later.

'PRINCESSE MARIE'

PRISCILLA BURTON

syn. 'MACRAT'

Floribunda

ORIGIN **McGredy, New Zealand, 1978**
PARENTAGE **Old Master x seedling**
FLOWER SIZE **2.4in (6cm)**
SCENT **Light and pleasant**
FLOWERING **Repeats well**
HEIGHT/SPREAD **3.3ft (1m)/2.5ft (75cm)**
HARDINESS **Zone 6**
AWARDS **RNRS PIT 1976**

Like most of the early "hand-painted" roses, Priscilla Burton is bright crimson with a silvery white center, but the color is extremely variable. Usually, the white area runs up into the crimson and creates a feathery pattern where they meet. As the flowers age, the white turns to pink and the crimson recedes even further. But there are other variations and patterns, according to the climate, weather, and time of year. Priscilla Burton is semisingle, with red filaments and pale anthers. The flowers come in strong, upright clusters of 3–11. The plant has handsome dark foliage and bright crimson new growths. It is sometimes subject to a little mildew.

PRISCILLA BURTON

PRISTINE

syn. 'JAXCPICO'

Hybrid Tea

ORIGIN **Warriner, US, 1978**
PARENTAGE **'White Masterpiece' x 'First Prize'**
FLOWER SIZE **6.3in (16cm)**
SCENT **Strong, sweet, and musky**
FLOWERING **Repeats**
HEIGHT/SPREAD **4.9ft (1.5m)/3.3ft (1m)**
HARDINESS **Zone 6**
AWARDS **Edland FA 1979; Portland GM 1979**

This is an outsize rose in all its features – flowers, leaves, even its prickles are large. It is also blessed with exceptional elegance and a strong scent, which won it the top prize for fragrance in the English rose trials. Pristine is, above all, a rose for cutting or exhibition, because its stems are very long and its flowers are always borne singly. The flowers are mother-of-pearl with a white center. The color comes from a pale pink blush on the edges of the petal backs. When the flowers open out, they take on a neatly imbricated shape like a magnolia. The plant has crimson new growths and prickles, and healthy, dark green leaves. It is remarkably vigorous and a good repeater – and deservedly popular, especially in hot climates.

PRISTINE

'PROBUZENÍ'

see 'DR. W. VAN FLEET'

PROMINENT

Grandiflora

ORIGIN **Kordes, Germany, 1971**
PARENTAGE **'Königin der Rosen' x 'Zorina'**
FLOWER SIZE **3.5in (9cm)**
SCENT **Light**
FLOWERING **Repeats constantly**
HEIGHT/SPREAD **6.6ft (2m)/4.1ft (1.25m)**
HARDINESS **Zone 5**
AWARDS **ADR 1971; Portland GM 1975; AARS 1977**

Prominent is vigorous, easy to grow, and a very arresting color. Its flowers open slowly from perfect buds – long and elegant – and its outer petals reflex almost to a point, as if to emphasize the beauty of its shape. The flowers are fluorescent vermilion orange, with a hint of yellow at the center when eventually they open out. Its strong stems, ability to last a long time in water, and profuse blooming make it a popular cut-flower rose. Despite its propensity for sending up "split" blooms, it has been grown commercially. Its bright color and tolerance of poor soils also make it popular in the garden. Prominent is vigorous, with dull leaves, a few prickles, upright growth, and an occasional brush with mildew.

PROMINENT

'PROSPERITY'

PROUD TITANIA

'PROSPERITY'

Hybrid Musk

ORIGIN **Pemberton, Britain, 1917**
PARENTAGE **'Marie Jeanne' x 'Perle des Jardins'**
FLOWER SIZE **2.4in (6cm)**
SCENT **Medium, musky, and sweet**
FLOWERING **Repeats well**
HEIGHT/SPREAD **4.9ft (1.5m)/4.1ft (1.25m)**
HARDINESS **Zone 6**

Many consider 'Prosperity' the best of the white Hybrid Musks. Its flowers are among the largest, and they are very abundantly borne. Individually, they are charming enough, with creamy white petals and golden stamens, but the massed effect of their large, open clusters is mighty impressive. During the first flowering the clusters are medium-sized but cover the whole bush; later flushes tend to have larger, arching clusters but fewer of them. 'Prosperity' has healthy, handsome, dark, glossy leaves and reddish new growth. It has an upright habit and can be trained up to 8.2ft (2.5m) as a pillar rose. Its flowers come in flush after flush throughout the growing season. It is easily propagated from cuttings.

PROSPERO

syn. 'AUSPERO'
Shrub Rose

ORIGIN **Austin, Britain, 1983**
PARENTAGE **'The Knight' x 'Château de Clos Vougeot'**
FLOWER SIZE **3.5in (9cm)**
SCENT **Strong and sweet**
FLOWERING **Repeats**
HEIGHT/SPREAD **3.3ft (1m)/3.3ft (1m)**
HARDINESS **Zone 6**

Prickly, disease-prone, and none-too-vigorous, Prospero is nevertheless an excellent rose for small gardens. It does especially well in hot, dry climates, where disease is not a problem. The flowers are worth all the effort you can put into making the plant happy: large, deep crimson, beautifully shaped, and intensely fragrant. They have a mass of small, ruffled petals at the center, and reflex from bright crimson rosettes to sober purple pompons as they age. They come on short stems, usually in clusters of 3–4, reminiscent of an old Portland rose. The plant is compact and leafy, with small, deep green leaves. Being short, it adapts well to containers. It responds well to feeding and watering.

PROUD TITANIA

syn. 'AUSTANIA'
Shrub Rose

ORIGIN **Austin, Britain, 1983**
FLOWER SIZE **3.9in (10cm)**
SCENT **Medium and sweet**
FLOWERING **Repeats**
HEIGHT/SPREAD **4.1ft (1.25m)/4.1ft (1.25m)**
HARDINESS **Zone 5**

Proud Titania has been widely criticized in England – and rightly – for its tendency to ball and its susceptibility to mildew and rust. However, it remains popular in hot, dry climates, where these shortcomings are not a problem. Its flowers are large and borne in great profusion, covering the bush with nodding blooms at its first, main flowering. They are creamy white at first, with palest pink on the petal backs, but fade to white with just a hint of pink or buff at the center. They open out fairly flat, with a mass of small quilled petals at the center and many layers of broader petals around the outside. The flowers come either singly or in small clusters on an arching bush with small, glossy leaves. Proud Titania takes its name from William Shakespeare's comedy *A Midsummer Night's Dream*, in which the fairy King Oberon greets his wife "Ill met by moonlight, proud Titania."

PROSPERO

PUR CAPRICE

PUR CAPRICE

syn. 'DELJAVERT'
Shrub Rose

ORIGIN **Delbard, France, 1997**
FLOWER SIZE **2.8in (7cm)**
SCENT **Light and sweet**
FLOWERING **Repeats very well**
HEIGHT/SPREAD **2.7ft (80cm)/2ft (60cm)**
HARDINESS **Zone 6**
AWARDS **Baden-Baden GM 1996; Bagatelle GM 1996; Rome GM 1996**

The flowers of Pur Caprice are unusual in shape and color. When they first open, they are rich golden yellow. Then they pick up a broad red edging and start to lose their yellowness. By the time the flowers have turned to parchment white, the red edges have changed – to green. The shape of the petals makes this change of color all the more dramatic: they are extremely crinkled and held at an angle that is very un-roselike. The plant is quite short and bushy, but tough and healthy enough. It flowers almost continuously and holds on to its petals for weeks after they have turned green.

'PURPLE PAVEMENT'

see 'ROTES MEER'

PURPLE TIGER

syn. 'JACPURR', Impressionist
Floribunda

ORIGIN **Christensen, US, 1991**
PARENTAGE **Intrigue x Pinstripe**
FLOWER SIZE **3.5in (9cm)**
SCENT **Light and sweet**
FLOWERING **Repeats**
HEIGHT/SPREAD **3.3ft (1m)/2.3ft (70cm)**
HARDINESS **Zone 6**

Striped roses were one of the great discoveries in the 1980s and 1990s. Everyone seemed to produce them, so they had to be good to do well. Purple Tiger is unique in its coloring – an extraordinary whirl of purple and white, flecked and splashed, very inconstant and irregular, and often mixed with pink and lilac too. But purple is the dominant color, and it is a gift to flower arrangers. The flowers usually come in clusters of 3–5 and the plant repeats quickly, so that it is in flower almost without interruption throughout the season. Purple Tiger has

PURPLE TIGER

mid-green leaves (blackspot can be a problem) and a noticeably upright habit of growth, while remaining bushy and compact. A final bonus – it has almost no prickles.

'PUSSTA'

syn. 'NEW DAILY MAIL'

Floribunda

ORIGIN **Tantau, Germany, 1972**
PARENTAGE **'John Dijkstra' × 'Walzertraum'**
FLOWER SIZE **3.1in (8cm)**
SCENT **Light and sweet**
FLOWERING **Repeats well**
HEIGHT/SPREAD **1.3ft (40cm)/1.6ft (50cm)**
HARDINESS **Zone 6**
AWARDS **ADR 1973**

'Pussta' is a very short Floribunda, with scarlet flowers in small clusters of 2–5, somewhat loosely and feebly held. The flowers are rain resistant and shed their petals cleanly when they are spent. The leaves are handsome, mid-green in color, and healthy. It is popular in northern and western Europe for its its floriferousness. There is nothing to match it as a short bedding rose in red, but it can also be used as an accent plant in mixed borders. The Pussta is the name of the flat, steppelike plain of Hungary.

'PUSSTA'

'QUÉBEC'

syn. 'MME. MARIE CURIE'

Hybrid Tea

ORIGIN **Gaujard, France, 1943**
FLOWER SIZE **3.9in (10cm)**
SCENT **Light and fruity**
FLOWERING **Repeats well**
HEIGHT/SPREAD **3.3ft (1m)/2.7ft (80cm)**
HARDINESS **Zone 6**
AWARDS **AARS 1944**

The year 1943 was not a good time in France to bring out a new rose, but 'Québec' traveled to the US and won the top prize in the international trials known as the All-America Rose Selections. It changed its name to 'Mme. Marie Curie' and sold well all over North America. 'Québec' is a good, rich yellow rose that keeps its color and has the classic shape of the best Hybrid Teas – a long, elegant, conical bud, slowly unfurling its shapely petals. It is still pretty when it opens out to reveal dark pollen and stamens. The plant is vigorous, and reflowers fairly quickly, with large, dark leaves and no disease problems in the areas where it fares best – the Mediterranean parts of France and the hotter, drier parts of the US.

'QUÉBEC'

QUEEN MARGRETHE

see DRONNING MARGRETHE

QUEEN MOTHER

syn. 'KORQUEMU'

Miniature Rose

ORIGIN **Kordes, Germany, 1991**
FLOWER SIZE **2in (5cm)**
SCENT **Light**
FLOWERING **Continuous**
HEIGHT/SPREAD **2ft (60cm)/2.7ft (80cm)**
HARDINESS **Zone 5**
AWARDS **ADR 1996**

For several years Queen Mother has been the most widely sold rose in England. It was named to commemorate the 90th birthday of Queen Elizabeth, widow of George VI of England and mother of Queen Elizabeth II. The flowers are pale soft pink, with deeper pink toward the center and richer colors in cool weather. They open out to a neat, circular shape surrounding a pretty boss of stamens of different lengths. The flowers have a slightly wild look to them, but are borne in clusters with unbelievable profusion all over the bush and right through until late autumn. Queen Mother is an extremely healthy plant and full of vitality, with dark green Wichurana leaves and a lax habit of growth. It is excellent both as a landscaping rose and in mixed plantings in small gardens, where it is a very reliable performer, well deserving of its popularity.

QUEEN MOTHER

'QUATRE SAISONS'

syn. Rosa damascena 'BIFERA', Autumn Damask

Damask Rose

ORIGIN **c.1660**
FLOWER SIZE **2.8in (7cm)**
SCENT **Strong, sweet, and delicious**
FLOWERING **In flushes, continuously**
HEIGHT/SPREAD **6.6ft (2m)/4.9ft (1.5m)**
HARDINESS **Zone 5**

The autumn-flowering Damask is one of the most important historic roses. It is the oldest European rose that flowers more than once, in a series of flushes at roughly six-week intervals right through until late autumn. In Italy it was known in the 17th century as *la rosa d'ogni mese* ("the monthly rose"). It is genetically indistinguishable from the ordinary once-flowering Damask rose, from which it is presumably a seedling or mutation. The flowers are loosely double and deep pink, fading to rose pink, and blessed with the sweetest scent imaginable. They have long, slender receptacles, shaped like narrow funnels, and long, slender sepals. They are borne in tight, erect clusters of 3–10. The leaves are soft green, matte-surfaced, and conspicuously serrated. The stems are covered in long, downward-facing prickles of every size. The bush is naturally fairly open, even lanky, but can easily be pruned back to a more compact shape in winter. 'Quatre Saisons' also responds well to deadheading, to encourage the next flush of flowers.

'Quatre Saisons Blanc Mousseux' is a white, mossy sport of 'Quatre Saisons', which Laffay is credited with introducing. It must have raised many questions at the time: how could a rose change from pink to white, and simultaneously acquire a covering of bronzy green moss all over its sepals, receptacles, and flower stems? We know now that it is so similar to 'Quatre Saisons' that genetic analysis cannot separate them. We also know that parts of a plant frequently revert from being white and mossy to pink and plain. However 'Quatre Saisons Blanc Mousseux' is as good a garden plant as its parent, with the same constant flowering and intense, sweet scent. If you have to choose between them, opt for 'Quatre Saisons Blanc Mousseux', because sooner or later a twig or two will revert to 'Quatre Saisons' and you will have two roses for the price of one.

'QUATRE SAISONS'

'QUATRE SAISONS BLANC MOUSSEUX'

Sport of 'Quatre Saisons'

'QUATRE SAISONS BLANC MOUSSEUX'

Damask Moss Rose

ORIGIN **Laffay, France, c.1837**

'Queen Elizabeth'

syn. 'The Queen Elizabeth Rose'
Grandiflora

ORIGIN **Lammerts, US, 1954**
PARENTAGE **'Charlotte Armstrong' × 'Floradora'**
FLOWER SIZE **3.9in (10cm)**
SCENT **Medium and sweet**
FLOWERING **Repeats very well**
HEIGHT/SPREAD **8.2ft (2.5m)/3.3ft (1m)**
HARDINESS **Zone 6**
AWARDS **Portland GM 1954; AARS 1955; NRS PIT 1955; ARS GM 1957; Golden Rose of the Hague 1968; World's Favourite Rose 1979**

This popular rose was named in honor of Queen Elizabeth II, who ascended the British throne in 1952. It was raised in the US but is widely grown throughout the world. It thrives in England, where its tough petals are unaffected by rain. The flowers are a warm, pale pink, with not too many petals, and darker pink petal backs. In hot climates they fade to pale pink, but keep their color well elsewhere. The flowers are of Hybrid Tea shape – slender and elegant – but usually borne in large, spacious clusters of 3–15, which led to 'Queen Elizabeth' being called the first of a new class – the Grandiflora roses. Although this class is not recognized outside the US, 'Queen Elizabeth' is still its finest representative. In fact, the flowers are sometimes borne singly, as also happens with Floribundas. Its long, strong, upright stems make it ideal for cutting. As the outer petals reflex, they acquire a slight ruffle and reveal a layer of smaller inner petals, but these too open out eventually, until the flower is quite flat. The plant has large, strong, dark leaves with rounded leaflets. Although rust may be a problem in some areas, 'Queen Elizabeth' is fairly disease-resistant. Its narrow, upright habit makes it useful where space is limited. It is vigorous, with thick stems and large prickles, but will grow well in poor soil.

Several color sports have been introduced over the years, of which 'Yellow Queen Elizabeth' (Vlaeminck, 1964) and **'White Queen Elizabeth'** are the most widely available. They are the same as the original in every detail except their color. Other sports still occasionally seen include 'Shell Queen' (Allen, 1961), 'Pearly Queen' (North Hill, 1963), 'Royal Queen' (Verschuren, 1965), 'Ivory Queen' (Delforge, 1965), 'Flamingo Queen' (Chan, 1972), and 'Blushing Queen' (Baker, 1976).

Much more popular is the climbing sport, **'Climbing Queen Elizabeth'**, which is possessed of such vigor that its flowers are borne too high to be appreciated. It has the stiff, upright growth of the bush form, which makes it very difficult to train sideways like other climbing sports. But it is widely grown all over the world.

'Queen Elizabeth'

Sports of 'Queen Elizabeth'

'Climbing Queen Elizabeth'

Climbing Grandiflora
ORIGIN **Wisler, US, 1957**
FLOWERING **Once heavily, then intermittently**
HEIGHT/SPREAD **19.7ft (6m)/4.9ft (1.5m)**

'Climbing Queen Elizabeth'

'White Queen Elizabeth'

syn. 'Blanc Queen Elizabeth'
ORIGIN **Banner, Britain, 1965**

'White Queen Elizabeth'

Queen Nefertiti

syn. 'AUSap'
Shrub Rose

ORIGIN **Austin, Britain, 1988**
PARENTAGE Lilian Austin × Tamora
FLOWER SIZE **3.5in (9cm)**
SCENT **Fairly strong mix of sweetness and tea**
FLOWERING **Repeats very well**
HEIGHT/SPREAD **3.3ft (1m)/2.7ft (80cm)**
HARDINESS **Zone 6**

It is not one of David Austin's best roses but Queen Nefertiti remains popular. The flowers tend to have a somewhat irregular rosette shape, and, although they open a pretty, glowing, peachy yellow, they pale with age and acquire unattractive hints of pink. That said, they mix well with a wide variety of other roses, shrubs, and herbaceous plants. Queen Nefertiti has its strong points: it is a quick and prolific reflowerer and is easy to grow. Its name commemorates the Egyptian queen.

Queen Nefertiti

'Queen of Denmark'

see 'Königin von Dänemark'

Queen of Hearts

Modern Climber

ORIGIN **Clark, Australia, 1920**
PARENTAGE **'Gustav Grünerwald' × 'Rosy Morn'**
FLOWER SIZE **4.3in (11cm)**
SCENT **Strong**
FLOWERING **Occasionally recurrent**
HEIGHT/SPREAD **13.1ft (4m)/9.8ft (3m)**
HARDINESS **Zone 6**

The sight of Queen of Hearts covered in flowers is a spectacle never forgotten, but such profusion is rarely followed by more flowers later in the year. The flowers are a fine pink with deeper pink petal backs and a variable shape, but they usually open to reveal their stamens and a muddle of petals around them. The outer petals fade a little, so there is a contrast between the bright pink centers and the paler pink outsides. The flowers are carried singly, very occasionally in clusters of 2–3. The plant makes sturdy, upright, vigorous, leafy, growth, with smooth, mid-green foliage and a lot of large prickles. It is fairly free from fungal diseases. It is one of the best of the large-flowered, once-flowering climbers so popular in the mid-20th century.

Queen of Hearts

'Queen of Hearts'

see 'Dame de Coeur'

'Queen of the Musks'

Hybrid Musk

ORIGIN **G. Paul, Britain, 1913**
FLOWER SIZE **2in (5cm)**
SCENT **Strong and musky**
FLOWERING **Repeats constantly**
HEIGHT/SPREAD **6.6ft (2m)/4.9ft (1.5m)**
HARDINESS **Zone 6**

Although it is almost forgotten in England, where it was bred, 'Queen of the Musks' is a splendid Musk rose, widely grown all over the world and especially popular in France. The flowers have red buds and pale pink and white flowers, with deep pink petal backs. The flowers open completely flat and display striking orange stamens. They are borne in open clusters of 10–30. The plant has shiny, mid- to dark green leaves with elongated leaflets, and a tendency to produce a lot of small bristly prickles on some of the flowering stems – especially the thicker ones. 'Queen of the Musks' is usually pruned quite hard, and grown as a bush about 3.3ft (1m) tall, but it is best when allowed to build up a permanent structure of branches and reach 6.6ft (2m) – or 13.1ft (4m) up a wall. It is vigorous, floriferous, and remontant.

'Queen of the Musks'

'RADIANCE'

Hybrid Tea

ORIGIN **Cook, US, 1908**
PARENTAGE **'Enchanter' × 'Cardinal'**
FLOWER SIZE **4.7in (12cm)**
SCENT **Strong and sweet**
FLOWERING **Repeats well**
HEIGHT/SPREAD **4.9ft (1.5m)/4.1ft (1.25m)**
HARDINESS **Zone 6**

'Radiance' was one of the roses that made the Hybrid Teas so popular in the early years of the 20th century. It has large flowers and a good scent, and it repeats reliably. It is also extremely adaptable and easy to grow in widely different conditions. The flowers are a very attractive soft pink, with slightly darker backs to the petals. They have a slightly rounded or globular shape – the conical shape was not confirmed as the ideal of beauty among Hybrid Teas until the 1920s – but the flowers are well held on long, strong, slender stems and their petals reflex attractively. 'Radiance' was at first widely grown under glass as a cut flower in New England, partly because it is a quick and reliable repeat flowerer. The plant has large leaves, moderate vigor, and a gawky habit of growth.

RADIO TIMES

syn. 'AUSSAL'

Shrub Rose

ORIGIN **Austin, Britain, 1994**
FLOWER SIZE **3.1in (8cm)**
SCENT **Strong and sweet**
FLOWERING **Repeats well**
HEIGHT/SPREAD **2.7ft (80cm)/2.7ft (80cm)**
HARDINESS **Zone 5**

Radio Times is a short and pretty English Rose from David Austin, very useful for the front of a border. The flowers are pale rose pink, paler at the edges and

RADIO TIMES

'RADIANCE'

pinker at the center – a shade that manages to be both rich and fresh. The flowers are round, flat, rosette-shaped, and full of quilled petals with a pleat down the middle. Sometimes they have a button eye. They are usually borne in small clusters – typically of 3–5 flowers. The plant has prickly stems, mid-green leaves, a bushy habit, and attractive, arching growth, but all within scale.

RADOX BOUQUET

syn. 'HARMUSKY'

Floribunda

ORIGIN **Harkness, Britain, 1980**
PARENTAGE **('Alec's Red' × 'Piccadilly') × ('Southampton' × ['Cläre Grammerstorf' × 'Frühlingsmorgen'])**
FLOWER SIZE **3.1in (8cm)**
SCENT **Strong and sweet**
FLOWERING **Repeats very well**
HEIGHT/SPREAD **4.9ft (1.5m)/3.3ft (1m)**
HARDINESS **Zone 6**
AWARDS **Geneva FA 1980; Belfast FA 1983**

This vigorous, stylish, pink Floribunda has proved very popular. Radox Bouquet has large, double flowers of mid-pink, with a hint of salmon toward the center at first, and paler pink petal backs. They open out lightly cupped, sometimes with an old-fashioned arrangement of petals at the center. They come singly or in dense clusters of 3–5 early in the season, but have up to 12 in the cluster later. They also shatter and drop their petals cleanly when they are spent, which means that the clusters always look neat. The flower stems are strong, thick, upright, and good for cutting. Radox Bouquet has a lot of large, healthy, glossy, mid-green leaves and a vigorous habit of growth. It is easy to grow and repeats very well. It has also won prizes for its scent.

RAINBOW'S END

RAINBOW'S END

syn. 'SAVALIFE'

Miniature Rose

ORIGIN **Saville, US, 1984**
PARENTAGE **'Rise 'n' Shine' × 'Watercolor'**
FLOWER SIZE **1.6in (4cm)**
SCENT **Light and fruity**
FLOWERING **Repeats**
HEIGHT/SPREAD **1.3ft (40cm)/1.3ft (40cm)**
HARDINESS **Zone 6**
AWARDS **AoE 1986**

Bright colors and beautiful form have ensured that Rainbow's End is one of the most popular miniature roses in North America, although it is little known elsewhere. The flowers are each like perfect Hybrid Teas, with high centers and elegantly reflexing petals, but tiny, and usually carried in small clusters. They are rich yellow at first, but gradually take on a red tinge that works its way inward from the petal tips until the fading flower is almost completely red. The flowers last for up to a week if picked for the house. Rainbow's End has crimson stems and a lot of dark but slightly glaucous leaves. It is bushy and compact, but a little susceptible to blackspot. A climbing form, which has recently been introduced as Climbing Rainbow's End, will grow to 13.1ft (4m).

'RAMBLING RECTOR'

Multiflora Rambler

ORIGIN **Daisy Hill, Northern Ireland, c.1900**
FLOWER SIZE **1.6in (4cm)**
SCENT **Strong, musky, and delicious**
FLOWERING **Once only, midseason**
HEIGHT/SPREAD **11.5ft (3.5m)/6.6ft (2m)**
HARDINESS **Zone 6**

No one knows the origins of this popular climbing rose, which will reach up to 19.7ft (6m) up a tree. The Daisy Hill nurseries at Newry in Northern Ireland never bred roses, but they did introduce occasional foundlings, of which this is one. Presumably it was found in an Irish rectory garden and is an older rose renamed. 'Rambling Rector' produces large, airy clusters of 10–50 little semidouble roses. They open creamy white, with bright yellow stamens at the center, but fade to pure white, just as the stamens quickly turn brown. The flowers are followed by masses of small orange hips. The pale green leaves are very beautiful. The plant is vigorous and healthy, and roots very easily from cuttings. It can also be cut back and grown as a vigorous 6.6ft (2m) shrub.

RADOX BOUQUET

'RAMBLING RECTOR'

RAMIRA

RAMIRA

syn. 'KORMEITA', Agatha Christie

Modern Climber

ORIGIN **Kordes, Germany, 1988**
FLOWER SIZE **4.3in (11cm)**
SCENT **Light and sweet**
FLOWERING **Repeats well**
HEIGHT/SPREAD **9.8ft (3m)/6.6ft (2m)**
HARDINESS **Zone 6**

Its parentage is unknown, but Ramira is a vigorous bicolor climber of the 'Handel' type. Its coloring is, however, deeper and richer, and its flowers are slightly larger. It is pretty at all stages of its development, both in bud, when it resembles a Hybrid Tea, and after it has opened out and its petals flutter like a Floribunda's. The flowers come singly and in clusters of 3–4, occasionally more, and stand up well to sun and rain. Ramira has handsome, healthy, dark, shiny leaves and a vigorous, upright habit of growth. It performs well in almost any climate, and is especially satisfactory in cool, wet areas.

'RAMONA'

see 'ANEMONENROSE'

'RAUBRITTER'

Shrub Rose

ORIGIN **Kordes, Germany, 1936**
PARENTAGE **'Daisy Hill' x 'Solarium'**
FLOWER SIZE **2.4in (6cm)**
SCENT **Light and musky**
FLOWERING **Once, midseason**
HEIGHT/SPREAD **8.2ft (2.5m)/8.2ft (2.5m)**
HARDINESS **Zone 5**

'RAUBRITTER'

An interesting and distinct rose, 'Raubritter' is the product of Wilhelm Kordes's experimental breeding with the dog rose *Rosa canina.* When the flowers open from their small, pointed buds, they are completely globular, with a small gap at the top. The petals are rich pink, but this color is hidden inside the flower: the visible parts are the petal backs, which are pale silvery pink. The flowers are held in large, loose clusters (10–40 flowers) and carried in great profusion, but their petals are thin and soft, so they do best in dry weather. The plant has small thin leaves (fairly susceptible to mildew and blackspot), slender, prickly stems, and a lax habit of growth. 'Raubritter' may be grown as a tall climber, a medium-sized mounded shrub, or a low landscaping ground-cover rose. A scrambling specimen above a small pool is the focal point of the rose garden at Mottisfont Abbey in England.

'RAYMOND CHENAULT'

Kordesii Hybrid

ORIGIN **Kordes, Germany, 1960**
PARENTAGE **'Kordesii' x 'Montezuma'**
FLOWER SIZE **3.9in (10cm)**
SCENT **Light or slight**
FLOWERING **Repeats well**
HEIGHT/SPREAD **11.5ft (3.5m)/6.6ft (2m)**
HARDINESS **Zone 5**

'Raymond Chenault' is a first-rate Kordesii climber, which can also be grown as a vigorous shrub. Its flowers are semisingle, with wavy petals and a circle of rich yellow stamens at the center. The color of the flowers is very variable however – anything from rich, velvety crimson to cherry or bright scarlet – and it seems to vary according to the season as well as from year to year, with no ready explanation. The flowers come in long, spacious clusters of 3–7, which are good for cutting and last well. The leaves are handsome, healthy, dark green, and glossy. Raymond Chenault was a distinguished French plant breeder and a friend of Wilhelm Kordes for more than 50 years.

'RAYMOND CHENAULT'

RECONCILIATION

RECONCILIATION

syn. 'HARTILLERY'

Hybrid Tea

ORIGIN **Harkness, Britain, 1995**
FLOWER SIZE **5.5in (14cm)**
SCENT **Strong and sweet**
FLOWERING **Repeats**
HEIGHT/SPREAD **4.1ft (1.25m)/3.3ft (1m)**
HARDINESS **Zone 6**

Modern Hybrid Teas do not come better than Reconciliation: its flowers are enormous and its scent is delicious. The buds are most elegantly shaped as the flowers start to unfurl and beautiful still when fully open. Their color is amber or buff at first, but fading to peach and pink as the flowers open and age. The change begins with the outer petals, so that there is a gentle grading of shades from the center outward. They are borne, usually singly but sometimes in twos and threes, on long, strong stems that are good for cutting. Reconciliation also makes a good bedding rose, with a vigorous, upright habit of growth and healthy, dark leaves.

RED BALLERINA

see MARJORIE FAIR

RED BELLS

syn. 'POULRED'

Ground Cover

ORIGIN **Poulsen, Denmark, 1980**
PARENTAGE **'Mini-Poul' x 'Temple Bells'**
FLOWER SIZE **1.6in (4cm)**
SCENT **Light and sweet**
FLOWERING **Once heavily, and then intermittently**
HEIGHT/SPREAD **2.7ft (80cm)/3.3ft (1m)**
HARDINESS **Zone 6**

The Danish rose-breeding family of Poulsen was one of the first to breed good ground-cover roses. These were developed from Poulsen's miniature roses and have the scaled-down neatness of true miniatures, but with larger flowers and a denser habit of growth. Red Bells is a good example – a thoroughly useful rose, both in small gardens, where a single specimen provides spectacular color, and in large landscaping designs, where it can be planted in hundreds. The flowers are lightly double, cupped (almost bell-shaped), with golden stamens and crimson red coloring. Red Bells covers itself with flowers during its main flowering, but produces only a few flowers thereafter. The plant has a compact, slightly spreading habit and handsome, healthy, dark, glossy leaves.

RED BELLS

RED BLANKET

RED BLANKET

syn. 'INTERCEL'

Ground Cover

ORIGIN **Ilsink, Netherlands, 1979**
PARENTAGE **'Yesterday' seedling**
FLOWER SIZE **1.6in (4cm)**
SCENT **Light, musky, and sweet**
FLOWERING **Repeats**
HEIGHT/SPREAD **3.3ft (1m)/3.3ft (1m)**
HARDINESS **Zone 6**

This is one of those lax, low shrub roses that are generally described as groundcover roses. However, Red Blanket is also an excellent plant for containers, where its lax habit is shown to advantage, and useful in mixed borders, too. The flowers are pale crimson red and semidouble, with a white patch toward the center, bright yellow stamens, and an occasional white streak worked into the red part of the petals. They come in open clusters of 5–20 on a floriferous small shrub that has a lot of prickles and handsome, dark, Wichurana leaves. Red Blanket is vigorous and a reliable repeater, suitable for almost any position and tolerant of poor soils.

'RED CASCADE'

syn. 'MOORCAP'

Miniature Climber

ORIGIN **Moore, US, 1976**
PARENTAGE **(*Rosa wichurana* × 'Floradora') × 'Magic Dragon'**
FLOWER SIZE **1.2in (3cm)**
SCENT **Light and musky**
FLOWERING **Almost continuous**
HEIGHT/SPREAD **6.6ft (2m)/3.3ft (1m)**
HARDINESS **Zone 6**

A groundcover plant or a climber? 'Red Cascade' can be grown as either. If grown in the open, it mounds up into a loose, low shrub. Sometimes it is recommended for hanging baskets: it hangs down prettily, but quickly grows too large. Its size depends upon climate: heat makes for larger plants. Despite these contradictions, 'Red Cascade' is a beautiful, popular, and useful rose. Its tiny, dark red flowers, cupped and packed with petals, are produced in thousands and continue in flower until the first frost. The flowers last well if cut for the house. They come in large clusters of 5–25. 'Red Cascade' has a lot of tiny, dark, glossy, healthy, Wichurana leaves, and is thickly clothed with ferocious prickles. If grown as a groundcover, it roots as it creeps along. It also comes very easily from cuttings.

'RED DEVIL'

syn. 'COEUR D'AMOUR'

Hybrid Tea

ORIGIN **Dickson, Northern Ireland, 1967**
PARENTAGE **'Silver Lining' × 'Prima Ballerina'**
FLOWER SIZE **5.5in (14cm)**
SCENT **Strong and sweet**
FLOWERING **Repeats**
HEIGHT/SPREAD **5.7ft (1.75m)/3.3ft (1m)**
HARDINESS **Zone 5**
AWARDS **Japan 1967; Belfast GM 1969; Portland GM 1970**

This large red Hybrid Tea is still the most popular exhibition rose in Britain, and widely grown all over the world. The flowers of 'Red Devil' open from large, fat buds. They are no more than light crimson at first, because the undersides of the petals are paler than the upper sides. A slightly darker shade of crimson appears when the petals start to unroll and reflex their edges. The flowers are borne singly on long stems but they spoil easily in rain, so this is a rose that does better in dry weather. That said, 'Red Devil' is a very good and vigorous, easy to grow garden rose. The plant has healthy, medium-dark green leaves and will reach 8.2ft (2.5m) if grown in a hot climate and left unpruned.

'RED DEVIL'

'RED FOUNTAIN'

RED FLOWER CARPET

see ALCANTARA

'RED FOUNTAIN'

Modern Climber

ORIGIN **Williams, US, 1975**
PARENTAGE **'Don Juan' × 'Blaze'**
FLOWER SIZE **2in (5cm)**
SCENT **Medium and sweet**
FLOWERING **Repeats**
HEIGHT/SPREAD **13.1ft (4m)/6.6ft (2m)**
HARDINESS **Zone 6**

The flowers of 'Red Fountain' are dark red, almost crimson at first, and hold their color well. They come in clusters, typically of 5–7 flowers, and they also have the short-petaled, open, cupped shape of a Floribunda. They are borne on long stems and last well as cut flowers – and on the bush, too, eventually dropping their petals cleanly. 'Red Fountain' makes a good climber, with an arching habit of growth, but it can also be pruned back and grown as a shrub no more than 6.6ft (2m) tall. It has large, dark, healthy leaves and repeats well. When well grown, it is rarely out of flower. It was bred in Maryland by J. Benjamin Williams, so its hardiness is another asset.

RED MAX GRAF

see ROTE MAX GRAF

RED MEIDILAND

see ROUGE MEILLANDÉCOR

'RED NEW DAWN'

see 'ETENDARD'

RED RASCAL

syn. 'JACBED'

Patio Rose

ORIGIN **Warriner, US, 1986**
FLOWER SIZE **2in (5cm)**
SCENT **Little or none**
FLOWERING **Repeats well**
HEIGHT/SPREAD **2.7ft (80cm)/3.3ft (1m)**
HARDINESS **Zone 6**

It is classified as a patio rose, and is very useful where a small, compact red rose is needed, but Red Rascal is also useful as a landscaping rose. It is spectacular planted in masses. Red Rascal has small, double, shapely, bright red flowers, beautifully set off by small, medium-dark, shiny leaves. The flowers are abundantly borne both singly and in small clusters (of up to about five flowers), and the plant sheds them cleanly when they have finished flowering. Red Rascal is a good repeater.

RED RASCAL

'Redcoat'

syn. 'AUScoat'
Shrub Rose

ORIGIN **Austin, Britain, 1973**
PARENTAGE **'Parade' x seedling**
FLOWER SIZE **3.9in (10cm)**
SCENT **Light, but sweet**
FLOWERING **Repeats well**
HEIGHT/SPREAD **6.6ft (2m)/4.9ft (1.5m)**
HARDINESS **Zone 6**

'Redcoat'

'Redcoat' was one of David Austin's early introductions, and very different from his later series of old-fashioned-style roses known as English Roses. The flowers are single, occasionally with a few extra petals, and loosely held. They open bright scarlet, with good yellow stamens at first that shine out against a small white patch at the center of the flower. Later the flowers change to dull crimson. They come in clusters of 3–9, held well above the leaves. The bush is very floriferous, especially in hot climates, and is a magnificent sight when the whole bush is in full flower. 'Redcoat' is vigorous, robust, and healthy. It becomes very bushy at the top, and makes a good hedge or pillar rose.

David Austin introduced a pink-flowered sport of 'Redcoat' in 1983 called Dapple Dawn, which is exactly the same as its parent in everything except its color. It opens dark pink and fades to rose pink, but is always pale pink, almost white, at the center. Both have proved popular and successful roses all around the world.

Dapple Dawn

Sport of 'Redcoat'

Dapple Dawn

syn. 'AUSapple'
ORIGIN **Austin, Britain, 1983**

'Redgold'

'Redgold'

syn. 'Rouge et Or'
Floribunda

ORIGIN **Dickson, Northern Ireland, 1971**
PARENTAGE **(['Karl Herbst' x 'Masquerade'] x 'Faust') x 'Piccadilly'**
FLOWER SIZE **3.1in (8cm)**
SCENT **Light and fruity**
FLOWERING **Repeats**
HEIGHT/SPREAD **4.1ft (1.25m)/3.3ft (1m)**
HARDINESS **Zone 6**
AWARDS **Portland GM 1969; AARS 1971**

This brilliantly colored Floribunda remains popular all over the world more than 30 years after it was introduced. 'Redgold' describes its color well: the flowers are dark yellow at first, with red edges to the petals and a suggestion of gold where the colors overlap. As the flowers open and develop, the red deepens and runs down toward the center, so that eventually the yellow is swamped by red. It is a striking and attractive change, provided you like hot colors. The flowers come singly and in clusters, typically of 3–5, and last very well both when cut and in the garden. 'Redgold' has large leaves and a vigorous, upright habit of growth. It is very floriferous and repeats quickly.

Redouté

see Mary Rose

R

Pierre Joseph Redouté

HIGHLY SKILLED IN THE TECHNIQUE OF COLOR STIPPLING, REDOUTÉ CAPTURED THE QUALITIES OF OLD ROSES PERFECTLY IN HIS DRAWINGS

Pierre Joseph Redouté (1759–1840) was born in the Austrian Netherlands (now Belgium), but worked in Paris for most of his life. In his 20s he trained as a botanical illustrator, working for the distinguished amateur botanist L'Héritier and later with professionals like Augustin de Candolle. In 1798, the future Empress Josephine employed him to record her plant collection at Malmaison, near Paris. This led to Redouté's *Description des Plantes rares cultivées à Malmaison et à Navarre* – his earliest success. But it is for his depictions of roses that he is best remembered, especially his three volumes of *Les Roses,* published between 1817 and 1824.

Pierre Joseph Redouté

Redouté used color stippling – etched dots that define the shape, substance, and texture of a subject. He so perfected this technique that he was able to capture not only the form and colors of each rose but also its intrinsic qualities. As his fame and his enterprizes multiplied, Redouté did less drawing and became more involved in directing the teams of painters and engravers working for him. His studio's work contributed much to the growing popularity of roses in the first half of the 19th century. It has also proved a valuable record of contemporary rose collections – especially the Empress's – for modern historians concerned with the identification and naming of old roses.

Rosa damascena

REGENSBERG

syn. 'MACYOUMIS'

Patio Rose

ORIGIN **McGredy, New Zealand, 1979**
PARENTAGE **Geoff Boycott x Old Master**
FLOWER SIZE **3.9in (10cm)**
SCENT **Light, but sweet**
FLOWERING **Repeats well**
HEIGHT/SPREAD **2.5ft (75cm)/3.3ft (1m)**
HARDINESS **Zone 6**
AWARDS **Baden-Baden 1980**

Regensberg is one of the best of the "hand-painted" roses, of an unusually low-growing and compact habit. Its flowers open quickly to bright cerise or hot-pink – a slightly bluish crimson – with a very abrupt contrast provided by a brilliant white center and white streaks that stretch up into the petals. The backs of the petals are also white, though the red coloring on the other side can be seen through them. Although they have a good number of petals, the flowers open out so flat that they appear only semidouble, with pale yellow stamens. They come in crowded, short-stemmed clusters of 3–7. The plant has healthy, glossy leaves, small and very dark, with dark bronze new growth. It grows to little more than 11.8in (30cm) in a cool climate, where the flowers are also larger, and makes an ideal front of the border or patio rose, almost never without flowers. Regensberg (the historical Ratisbon) is a famous university city in Germany.

'REINE DE L'ILE DE BOURBON'

syn. 'BOURBON QUEEN'

Bourbon Rose

ORIGIN **Mauget, France, 1834**
FLOWER SIZE **3.1in (8cm)**
SCENT **Strong and sweet**
FLOWERING **Repeats very occasionally**
HEIGHT/SPREAD **5.7ft (1.75m)/4.9ft (1.5m)**
HARDINESS **Zone 5**

This early-flowering favorite is often found in old gardens. Its flowers are a slightly purple pink, with a white patch toward the center and much paler petal backs. It has white streaks on the inner petals, and paler petal edges, too. The petals are wide but short and, although there are many of them, they curl around the yellow stamens and make the flowers appear no more than semidouble. They are generously borne in small clusters all along the long, prickly stems: 'Reine de l'Ile de Bourbon' is one of the most floriferous of the old roses. The flowers are followed by large orange hips. The plant is hardy, vigorous, and tolerant of poor soils and neglect. The leaves are large and dark, with rounded leaflets. They may attract a little blackspot, but are usually healthy. It is effectively only once-flowering, but every so often (not every year) it produces one or two flowers in autumn. In hot climates it can be trained up to 13.1ft (4m).

'REINE DE L'ILE DE BOURBON'

REGENSBERG

'REINE DES CENTFEUILLES'

Centifolia

ORIGIN **France, 1824**
FLOWER SIZE **2.8in (7cm)**
SCENT **Medium and sweet**
FLOWERING **Once only**
HEIGHT/SPREAD **5.7ft (1.75m)/4.9ft (1.5m)**
HARDINESS **Zone 5**

This Queen of the Centifolias is of unknown hybrid origin, lumped with the Centifolia roses because of its name. It is, however, a rose of great beauty, whose single flowering lasts for a long time. The flowers are rich mid-pink with darker backs to the petals. They are cup-shaped, and exceptionally full of petals, folded and pleated into a loose rosette, sometimes with a button eye. They usually come in clusters (typically of 3–7) on slightly weak stems, so that they hang sideways a little and sway in the wind. The plant has small, dark, smooth leaves and a lot of prickles.

'REINE DES CENTFEUILLES'

'REINE DES VIOLETTES'

Hybrid Perpetual

ORIGIN **Millet-Malet, France, 1860**
PARENTAGE **'Pié IX' x unknown**
FLOWER SIZE **3.9in (10cm)**
SCENT **Strong and sweet**
FLOWERING **Repeats well**
HEIGHT/SPREAD **6.6ft (2m)/4.9ft (1.5m)**
HARDINESS **Zone 5**

The popularity of 'Reine des Violettes' almost amounts to a cult. Its great quality is the color of its flowers, but this varies enormously according to the year, place, soil, and climate. It is usually rich purple at first, before fading to lilac mauve. The undersides of the petals, however, are pale silvery pink, and set up very beautiful contrasts within the quartered flower. This is especially notable on the button eye that forms around the center. The buds are nondescript: it is the fully open flower that calls for praise, though it does shatter and die very promptly – almost too soon. The flowers come in tight clusters, with short stems and a ruff of leaves similar to that of a Portland rose. 'Reine des Violettes' has matte, dull, unexciting leaves and smooth stems – no prickles. The plant responds especially well to good cultivation (feeding and the prevention of fungal infections) and performs best in hot, dry weather.

'REINE DES VIOLETTES'

Relax Meillandécor

syn. 'MEIdarwet'

Shrub Rose

ORIGIN **Meilland, France, 1993**
FLOWER SIZE **2.4in (6cm)**
SCENT **Light and musky**
FLOWERING **Constantly in flower**
HEIGHT/SPREAD **2.7ft (80cm)/4.1ft (1.25m)**
HARDINESS **Zone 6**

This handsome, healthy groundcover rose should be grown more widely, though it is popular in northwestern Europe. Relax Meillandécor has red buds and salmon pink semidouble flowers, which fade quickly to pure pink but keep darker pink patches toward the center. They come in clusters, typically of 4–10 flowers, and are followed by small red hips. Nevertheless, it is a good repeat-flowerer, even if it is not deadheaded. Relax Meillandécor grows vigorously and has a broad, spreading habit of growth, which makes it excellent for use in containers as well as in mixed borders and also as a landscaping rose. It has small, medium-dark, shiny, healthy leaves, which last well into winter and suggest some Wichurana ancestry.

Relax Meillandécor

Remember Me

syn. 'COCdestin'

Hybrid Tea

ORIGIN **Cocker, Britain, 1984**
PARENTAGE **'Ann Letts' x ('Dainty Maid' x 'Pink Favorite')**
FLOWER SIZE **4.3in (11cm)**
SCENT **Rich and fruity**
FLOWERING **Repeats well**
HEIGHT/SPREAD **4.1ft (1.25m)/3.3ft (1m)**
HARDINESS **Zone 6**
AWARDS **Belfast GM 1986; James Mason GM 1995**

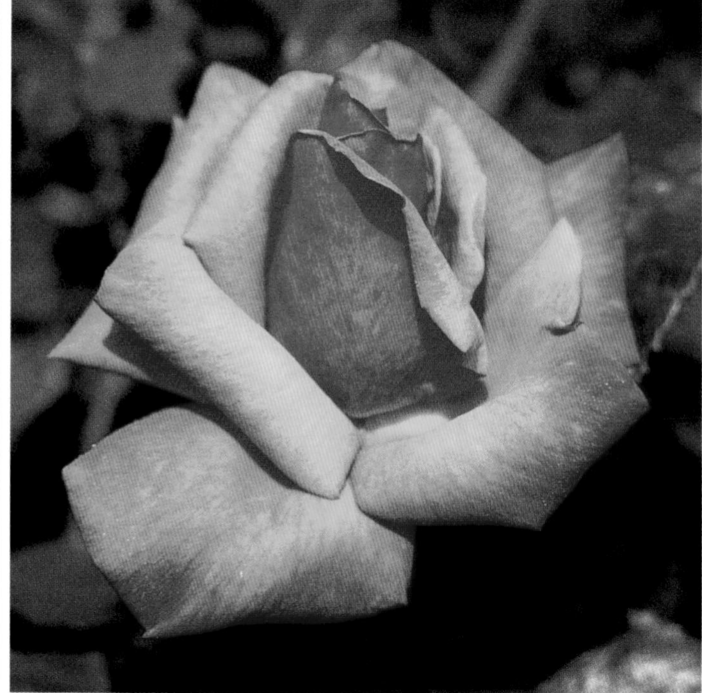

Remember Me

'Reine Victoria'

syn. 'La Reine Victoria'

Bourbon Rose

ORIGIN **Schwartz, France, 1872**
FLOWER SIZE **2.8in (7cm)**
SCENT **Medium and sweet**
FLOWERING **Repeats**
HEIGHT/SPREAD **6.6ft (2m)/2.5ft (75cm)**
HARDINESS **Zone 6**

Although placed among the Bourbon roses, 'Reine Victoria' is quite distinctive. Many consider its delicate charm the epitome of Victorian beauty. Its flowers are so cupped in shape as to appear almost spherical when they first open. They are made up of many short, strongly incurved petals colored deep lilac pink, with paler silvery reverses. The petals are thin, almost translucent, and sensitive to rain. The flowers come in clusters of 3–9 both early and late in the season, repeating at regular intervals until late autumn, with a few odd blooms in between. The bush is very slim and erect, growing vigorously, with pretty, pale green leaves. It is, however, very susceptible to both blackspot and mildew, and therefore fares better in hot, dry climates.

A sport is rarely more highly esteemed than the original from which it sported, but **'Mme. Pierre Oger'** is an exception. The two roses are exactly the same in all respects except color. 'Mme. Pierre Oger' has flesh pink petals, tipped with crimson, and, since they are paler than the petals of 'Reine Victoria', they appear even more delicate and translucent. It has the same slender, erect habit as its parent and, unfortunately, the same propensity to mildew and blackspot, which is so serious that in damp climates it is almost impossible to grow this rose without taking measures to prevent the spread of fungal infection.

'Reine Victoria'

'Mme. Pierre Oger'

Sport of 'Reine Victoria'

'Mme. Pierre Oger'

ORIGIN **Oger, France, 1878**

The buds of Remember Me are dark orange-brown, and open to peach colored flowers that fade eventually to pink. But there are many other shades and tints within the petals – admirers mention orange, yellow, fawn, cream, salmon, amber, beige, brown, copper, cinnamon, tan, and rust. The flowers are large, beautifully formed, and usually borne singly, only occasionally in clusters of 3–4. The plant is bushy, prickly, dense, and compact, with small, strong, dark, glossy, healthy leaves. It is vigorous and free-flowering, too. It grows everywhere, but Remember Me produces its largest flowers and richest colors in cool weather and in climates like that of its native Scotland.

Remembrance

syn. 'HARxampton'

Floribunda

ORIGIN **Harkness, Britain, 1992**
PARENTAGE **'Trumpeter' x 'Southampton'**
FLOWER SIZE **3.1in (8cm)**
SCENT **Light and sweet**
FLOWERING **Repeats**
HEIGHT/SPREAD **2.7ft (80cm)/2ft (60cm)**
HARDINESS **Zone 6**
AWARDS **Glasgow GM 1995**

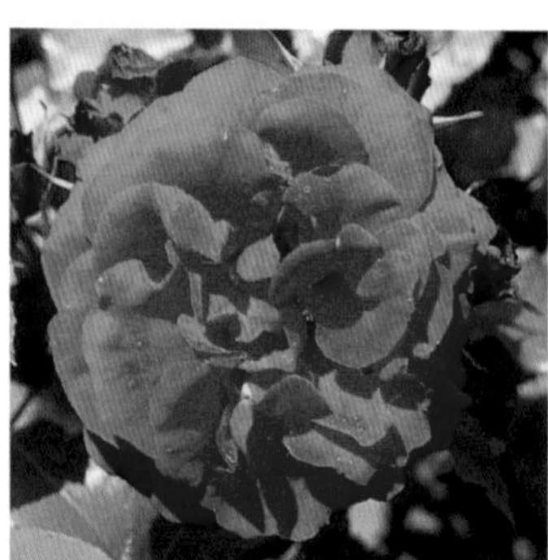

Remembrance

It is difficult to better Remembrance as a short-growing Floribunda. Its flowers are a bright red or scarlet, a very vivid shade, and quite large. They come in clusters – typically of 3–5 flowers but occasionally more – and sometimes singly too. The plant is dense and compact, which means that the whole surface seems to be covered in color when it is in midbloom. Remembrance has dark, glossy, healthy leaves and a neat, bushy habit of growth. Its size makes it useful in small gardens and containers. It is also a good repeater.

'Renae'

Climbing Floribunda-type

ORIGIN **Moore, US, 1954**
PARENTAGE **'Etoile Luisante' x unknown**
FLOWER SIZE **2.4in (6cm)**
SCENT **Strong, sweet, and spicy**
FLOWERING **Constantly in flower**
HEIGHT/SPREAD **9.8ft (3m)/6.6ft (2m)**
HARDINESS **Zone 6**

'Renae'

'Renae' has loads of character: it flowers continuously and its stems are thornless. The flowers open from pointed buds and are clear rose pink at first, before fading to white. They have a clean, circular outline and are cupped in shape, usually with yellow stamens when they open out but sometimes with a button eye. The flowers come in compact clusters of 3–15 and drop their petals cleanly as soon as they have finished flowering. They are good for cutting. The plant has shiny, healthy, evergreen, mid-green leaves with slender, drooping leaflets. 'Renae' makes a tall, loose shrub, a fine pillar rose, and a good weeping standard. It is a particularly popular rose in the US and Australia, but should be much more widely grown elsewhere.

RENAISSANCE

syn. 'HARZART'

Floribunda

ORIGIN **Harkness, Britain, 1994**
PARENTAGE **Amber Queen x Margaret Merril**
FLOWER SIZE **2.8in (7cm)**
SCENT **Strong and sweet**
FLOWERING **Repeats very well**
HEIGHT/SPREAD **3.3ft (1m)/2ft (60cm)**
HARDINESS **Zone 6**
AWARDS **Belfast FA 1995; Glasgow FA 1996**

With two of Harkness's own best roses for parents, Renaissance is also a supremely beautiful creation. Its flowers are elegant both in bud and when they open out. Renaissance has long, broad outer petals and shorter inner ones: all have a charming wave to their carriage, which adds grace and character to the flower as a whole. They are palest creamy pink, with slightly darker backs – rose pink at most – and the yellow stamens at the center are enough to create a pale salmon glow at the heart of the half-open flower. The flowers come singly or in clusters of up to seven on long stems that are held well above the large, dark, glossy leaves. The plant is very healthy, vigorous, and floriferous, producing its flowers almost continuously until at least late autumn. It is a good cut flower but even better as a garden plant, when the flowers seem to hover over the bushy plant. A modern classic.

RENDEZ-VOUS

RENDEZ-VOUS

syn. 'MEIPOBIL'

Hybrid Tea

ORIGIN **Meilland, France, 1987**
FLOWER SIZE **5.1in (13cm)**
SCENT **Strong, sweet, and fruity**
FLOWERING **Repeats**
HEIGHT/SPREAD **4.1ft (1.25m)/2.7ft (80cm)**
HARDINESS **Zone 6**
AWARDS **Belfast FA 1990**

The great French house of Meilland continues to produce stupendous traditional Hybrid Teas. Rendez-vous is a fine example – not too tall, but elegant, prolific, and vigorous. The flowers are somewhere between dark pink and pale crimson in color, with a hint of rich magenta, and they have noticeably long petals that curl back along their edges. They are borne usually singly, but occasionally in clusters of 3–4, and their scent is delicious. Rendez-vous has mid-green leaves, quite a number of prickles, and a neat habit of growth. It is a good repeater, too, pushing up new flowers until the first frost.

'RENÉ ANDRÉ'

Wichurana Rambler

ORIGIN **Barbier, France, 1901**
PARENTAGE ***Rosa wichurana* x 'L'Idéal'**
FLOWER SIZE **2.4in (6cm)**
SCENT **Light and tealike**
FLOWERING **Once early in season, then intermittently**
HEIGHT/SPREAD **13.1ft (4m)/6.6ft (2m)**
HARDINESS **Zone 6**

'René André' was one of the first three Wichurana ramblers issued by Barbier of Orléans, and at the time considered better even than 'Albéric Barbier'. Its loosely semidouble flowers have a wonderful mixture of colors when they first open – pink, saffron, carmine, and bronze – before the yellow tones fade away through cream to white, leaving the flowers pale pink, with traces of crimson. They come in clusters of 3–11 and keep their color well if cut and taken indoors. The plant has prickly stems and dark, glossy, bronzy-green leaves. It is sometimes liable to attract mildew. René André was the son of Edouard André, the French garden designer and editor of the prestigious *Revue Horticole*.

'RENÉ D'ANJOU'

'RENÉ D'ANJOU'

Moss Rose

ORIGIN **Robert, France, 1853**
FLOWER SIZE **2.8in (7cm)**
SCENT **Strong and sweet**
FLOWERING **Once only**
HEIGHT/SPREAD **5.7ft (1.75m)/4.1ft (1.25m)**
HARDINESS **Zone 5**

"Good" King René d'Anjou (1409–80) was a soldier, poet, patron, and romantic. His rose is a deep pink Moss, bred at the height of the 19th century. The flowers are full of petals, arranged in a muddled, swirling shape around the center, and showing tints of pale pink and purple as well as the deep rich pink overall. In hot weather they fade to pink and lilac. The flowers come singly and, more often, in clusters of 3–7, and are well covered with dark, brown green, sticky moss. 'René d'Anjou' has bright green leaves (bronzy when young), bristly stems, and an open, bushy habit of growth. It is vigorous, without growing too tall, and a reliable, unfussy garden plant. If only it repeated its flowering, it would be the perfect old rose.

RENAISSANCE

'RENÉ ANDRÉ'

'RÊVE D'OR'

'RÉVEIL DIJONNAIS'

'RICHARDII'

'RÊVE D'OR'

Noisette

ORIGIN **Ducher, France, 1869**
PARENTAGE **'Mme. Schultz' x unknown**
FLOWER SIZE **2.4in (6cm)**
SCENT **Strong and tealike**
FLOWERING **Repeats constantly**
HEIGHT/SPREAD **13.1ft (4m)/6.6ft (2m)**
HARDINESS **Zone 7**

'Rêve d'Or' is a vigorous, fast-growing Noisette, one of the best climbing roses for warm climates. Its buds are the only shortcoming – somewhat stumpy, with red tips, which remain on the outer petals. The flowers are golden yellow, with pale yellow edges and apricot petal backs: the overall impression is of buff gold. Although the exact shade differs from season to season, it keeps its color better than many roses of this color. The flowers come singly or in clusters of up to 15. The plant has a lot of large, deep green, glossy, nearly evergreen leaves, which are red at first and clothe the plant down to ground level. It is immensely floriferous in its first flowering, but repeats intermittently thereafter until early winter.

'RÉVEIL DIJONNAIS'

Climbing Hybrid Tea

ORIGIN **Buatois, France, 1931**
PARENTAGE **'Eugen Fürst' x 'Constance'**
FLOWER SIZE **3.9in (10cm)**
SCENT **Medium and fruity**
FLOWERING **Some repeat flowering**
HEIGHT/SPREAD **9.8ft (3m)/6.6ft (2m)**
HARDINESS **Zone 5**
AWARDS **Portland GM 1929**

Some roses fare better in hot, dry climates. 'Réveil Dijonnais' is one of them, for it is neither vigorous nor healthy in cool, wet conditions. At its best, however, it is a most striking and exciting short climber. The flowers are single, with a few extra petals, and open out to a lightly cupped shape like wild roses do. It is their coloration that is so unusual – bright crimson overlaid with bright yellow to produce bright orange around a golden yellow center. Then the yellow tints fade from the whole flower, leaving the orange parts more red and the yellow center cream colored. The petal backs and edges are also yellow. The flowers are borne singly or in short-stemmed clusters of up to five. The leaves are thick, glossy, and bronzy green. The plant flowers early and fairly profusely, then more occasionally. It makes thick brown stems and bears short prickles.

'RHONDA'

Modern Climber

ORIGIN **Lissemore, US, 1968**
PARENTAGE **'New Dawn' x 'Spartan'**
FLOWER SIZE **3.9in (10cm)**
SCENT **Light and sweet**
FLOWERING **Repeats well**
HEIGHT/SPREAD **9.8ft (3m)/6.6ft (2m)**
HARDINESS **Zone 5**

This excellent climbing rose is popular in the US, and should be better known elsewhere. 'Rhonda' has large flowers that are full of petals and shapely, both in the bud and when fully opened out. They are a good deep rich pink and keep their color well. They are profusely borne, both singly and in well-spaced clusters, which can hold as many as 15 flowers, though 3–7 is more normal. When they age, they drop their petals cleanly. 'Rhonda' was raised by an amateur, and one of its parents is 'New Dawn', from which it inherits its glossy, dark green, Wichurana leaves. The plant is moderately vigorous, with a lot of flowers, good continuity, and heavy repeat flowering. It is generally healthy, though it may get a little mildew late in the season in damp climates. It is also somewhat prickly.

'RHONDA'

'RICHARDII'

syn. ROSA SANCTA

Hybrid Canina

ORIGIN **c.1890**
FLOWER SIZE **2.4in (6cm)**
SCENT **Light and musky**
FLOWERING **Once only**
HEIGHT/SPREAD **2.7ft (80cm)/6.6ft (2m)**
HARDINESS **Zone 6**

'Richardii' is reputed to be so old that it can be identified from Egyptian tombs as far back as 200AD. Unfortunately, it is not recorded any earlier than about 1890. It is a pleasant scrambling rose, probably a hybrid between *Rosa gallica* and *Rosa arvensis*. The elegant, pale pink, single flowers each have a large ring of golden stamens around a long style. Their petals have a silky sheen and a slightly crumpled texture, suggestive of fragility and transience, which add enormously to their attraction. They are generously borne in large, loose clusters (typically of 5–10 flowers) over a period of several

RIMOSA 79

syn. 'MEIGRONURI', Gold Bunny

Floribunda

ORIGIN **Meilland, France, 1978**
PARENTAGE **'Rusticana' x ('Charleston' x 'Allgold')**
FLOWER SIZE **3.1in (8cm)**
SCENT **Light and fruity**
FLOWERING **Repeats well**
HEIGHT/SPREAD **3.3ft (1m)/2.7ft (80cm)**
HARDINESS **Zone 6**

RIMOSA 79

This French-raised Floribunda, which is known as Rimosa 79 in France, Gold Badge in the US, and Gold Bunny almost everywhere else in the world, is especially popular in Australia. It produces shapely flowers that open bright yellow and hold their color well in cool climates, fading only slowly (to lemon yellow) in hot ones. The flowers open out attractively to show their golden stamens and are borne both singly and in clusters of up to seven. The double flowers have fairly long stems (for a short bush) and are useful for picking. They are most freely produced on the bush, almost without interruption, until early winter: Rimosa 79 is one of the most floriferous of all Floribundas. The plant is neat and compact, with light green leaves. Blackspot may be a problem in damp weather. It fares especially well in warm climates.

Meilland introduced a climbing form of Rimosa 79 in 1986 called Grimpant Rimosa (elsewhere known as Climbing Rimosa, Climbing Gold Badge, and Climbing Gold Bunny), which has all the qualities of the bush form and is unusually floriferous for a climbing sport. It flowers very profusely at the start of the season, but also repeats well thereafter.

GRIMPANT RIMOSA

Sport of Rimosa 79

GRIMPANT RIMOSA

syn. 'MEIGRO-NURISAR', Climbing Rimosa, Climbing Gold Bunny

Climbing Floribunda

ORIGIN **Meilland, France, 1991**
HEIGHT/SPREAD **13.1ft (4m)/6.6ft (2m)**
AWARDS **Baden-Baden GM 1991; Saverne GM 1991**

RING OF FIRE

weeks. The plant has a lax habit with slender stems and Gallica type leaves. Powdery mildew can be a problem later in the year.

RINA HUGO

syn. 'DORVISO'

Hybrid Tea

ORIGIN: **Dorieux, France, 1993**
FLOWER SIZE **5.9in (15cm)**
SCENT **Light and sweet**
FLOWERING **Repeats well**
HEIGHT/SPREAD **5.7ft (1.75m)/4.1ft (1.25m)**
HARDINESS **Zone 6**

This French-bred Hybrid Tea, which is named for a South African singer, has become extremely popular as an exhibition rose in the US. Its flowers are large, shapely, full of petals, and slow to open – which means that they keep their shape well – and are usually borne singly on long, strong stems. They are a glorious, glowing deep pink, with a hint of magenta that is very attractive. Rina Hugo makes a vigorous, strong-growing bush, with large, dark, healthy leaves. It grows especially well in hot, dry climates and responds to good cultivation by throwing up flush after flush of sumptuous flowers.

RING OF FIRE

syn. 'MORFIRE'

Miniature Rose

ORIGIN **Moore, US, 1986**
PARENTAGE **'Pink Petticoat' x Rimosa 79**
FLOWER SIZE **1.6in (4cm)**
SCENT **Light, musky, and fruity**
FLOWERING **Repeats well**
HEIGHT/SPREAD **2ft (60cm)/1.3ft (40cm)**
HARDINESS **Zone 6**
AWARDS **AoE 1987**

When the flowers of Ring of Fire open, they are bright yellow with a vermilion edge to the petals. The overall effect is of quite a hard orange. As the flowers age, the yellow fades to cream and white, and the vermilion takes on a red or crimson hue. The petals also develop an attractive frill as the whole flower acquires the pompon shape of a dahlia or African marigold. Ring of Fire is no more than a miniature rose, with a somewhat open habit – not as bushy as many of Ralph Moore's other introductions. However, it is a good repeater, and the flowers stand up well to both sun and rain. The small, neat leaves are healthy, too.

'RINGLET'

Modern Climber or Pillar Rose

ORIGIN **Clark, Australia, 1922**
PARENTAGE **'Ernest Morel' x 'Betty Berkeley'**
FLOWER SIZE **2.2in (5.5cm)**
SCENT **Light**
FLOWERING **Fully remontant**
HEIGHT/SPREAD **9.8ft (3m)/8.2ft (2.5m)**
HARDINESS **Zone 6**

'Ringlet' is a pretty and unusual rose, somewhat different than Alister Clark's other hybrids. Its flowers open out from dark pink buds and are white with a broad band of dark pink around the edge. This band is often flecked with crimson, and those crimson patches persist even when the pink edges fade away. The newly opened flower is enlivened by bright yellow stamens, but the petals stay on the flowers (and look good) long after the stamens turn brown. The flowers come in clusters of 3–15 and are set off by light or mid-green leaves. The plant is best treated as a pillar rose, or a lax, sprawling shrub, somewhat like the Pemberton Musks. It has only a few thorns and is much hardier than most Clark roses: it has survived for many years at Europa-Rosarium, Sangerhausen.

RIO SAMBA

'RINGLET'

RIO SAMBA

syn. 'JACRITE'

Floribunda

ORIGIN **Warriner, US, 1991**
PARENTAGE **seedling x Sunbright**
FLOWER SIZE **3.9in (10cm)**
SCENT **Light**
FLOWERING **Repeats regularly**
HEIGHT/SPREAD **4.1ft (1.25m)/2.5ft (75cm)**
HARDINESS **Zone 6**
AWARDS **AARS 1993**

Rio Samba is a very bright red and yellow bicolor. The buds are red on the outside but pure yellow inside, with a red edging. The colors fade and change, but not unattractively, so that the red parts get larger and paler as the flower matures. The fully open bloom has a reddish pink color wash with a pale yellow center and base to the petals. The flowers are borne singly or in small clusters on strong, upright stems. The bush is upright, tall, and fairly prickly, with small dark leaves. An excellent bedding rose.

'RISE 'N' SHINE'

syn. 'GOLDEN SUNBLAZE'

Miniature Rose

ORIGIN **Moore, US, 1977**
PARENTAGE **'Little Darling' x 'Yellow Magic'**
FLOWER SIZE **1.6in (4cm)**
SCENT **Strong and musky**
FLOWERING **Repeats well**
HEIGHT/SPREAD **2ft (60cm)/1.3ft (40cm)**
HARDINESS **Zone 6**
AWARDS **AoE 1978**

Popular all over the world, 'Rise 'n' Shine' is still the most widely grown yellow miniature rose and sets the standard against which all others are judged. The whorled buds are yolk yellow, with slightly paler petal backs, but open to a pure bright yellow color before fading to lemon and cream. Their beauty is greatly enhanced when newly open by the deep yellow stamens at the center. The flowers come singly and in nicely spaced clusters of up to seven. 'Rise 'n' Shine' makes a dense, bushy plant with small, dark, healthy leaves and narrow leaflets. It is vigorous and repeats so quickly as to seem perpetually flowering.

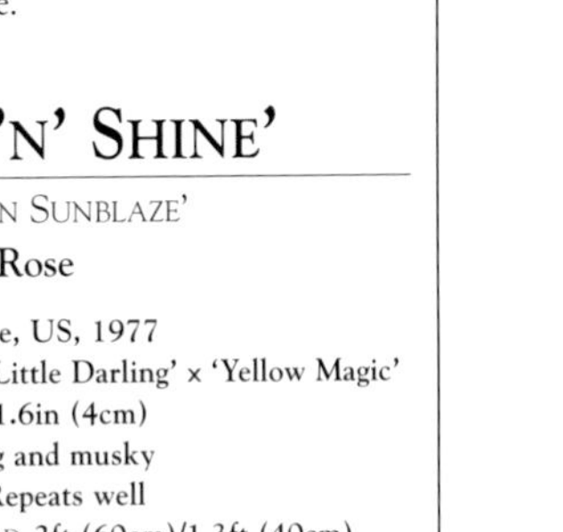

'RISE 'N' SHINE'

'RITTER VON BARMSTEDE'

'RITTER VON BARMSTEDE'

Kordesii Hybrid

ORIGIN **Kordes, Germany, 1959**
PARENTAGE **'Kordesii' x unknown**
FLOWER SIZE **2.8in (7cm)**
SCENT **Light and sweet**
FLOWERING **Repeats well**
HEIGHT/SPREAD **13.1ft (4m)/6.6ft (2m)**
HARDINESS **Zone 5**

Wilhelm Kordes crossed 'Kordesii' with an unnamed Polyantha to obtain this vigorous, strongly remontant climber. 'Ritter von Barmstede' has lightly double flowers, which are carmine pink with a small white circle at the center. The petal backs are slightly paler. The flowers have a distinctive wave to their petals, which is much stronger than is usually found in flowers whose petals are normally stacked flat. It holds on to its petals for a long time, so that the clusters (typically of 5–15 flowers) may become somewhat crowded. The plant is vigorous, with healthy, mid-green, glossy leaves. The Knights of Barmstede were powerful local landowners in Holstein in the 12th–14th centuries.

R

'RIVAL DE PAESTUM'

Tea Rose

ORIGIN **Béluze, France, 1841**
FLOWER SIZE **2.4in (6cm)**
SCENT **Light and tealike**
FLOWERING **Constantly in flower**
HEIGHT/SPREAD **3.3ft (1m)/3.3ft (1m)**
HARDINESS **Zone 7**

Virgil's *Georgics* refers to the twice-flowering roses of Paestum, an image that haunts horticulturists. When repeat flowering roses first occurred in western Europe in the 18th century, they were often compared to their classical forebears. 'Portland Rose' was sometimes known as 'Paestana', and clearly Jean Béluze considered his perpetually flowering China-Tea rose a fair match for it. In fact, 'Rival de Paestum' is a modest rose, with small, loose, ivory white flowers that droop down on weak pedicels. They have the elegant buds of the Teas and Chinas and soft petals that spoil in rain. Sometimes the flowers have a hint of pink at the center. 'Rival de Paestum' makes a neat, dense bush, thickly covered in small dark leaves – watch out for mildew. It is only moderately vigorous, but it flowers and flowers year-round.

'RIVAL DE PAESTUM'

'ROB ROY'

'ROB ROY'

Floribunda

ORIGIN **Cocker, Britain, 1970**
PARENTAGE **'Evelyn Fison' x 'Wendy Cussons'**
FLOWER SIZE **3.5in (9cm)**
SCENT **Light**
FLOWERING **Repeats well**
HEIGHT/SPREAD **4.1ft (1.25m)/3.3ft (1m)**
HARDINESS **Zone 6**

'Rob Roy' is a good example of a Floribunda whose flowers are individually shaped like a Hybrid Tea's. They are fairly large and well petaled, but open out quickly from scrolled buds. Their color is a brilliant rich red, which they hold until shortly before they drop their petals. They are borne singly and in well-spaced clusters (typically of 3–5 flowers) on a vigorous, upright plant that seems to flower almost continuously, and certainly late into the autumn, even in cool climates. The leaves are glossy and dark, but bronzy red when young. They may need a little protection from blackspot in some years.

'ROBERT LE DIABLE'

Gallica Hybrid

ORIGIN **France, c.1831**
FLOWER SIZE **2.8in (7cm)**
SCENT **Moderate and sweet**
FLOWERING **Once only, fairly late in season**
HEIGHT/SPREAD **4.1ft (1.25m)/2.7ft (80cm)**
HARDINESS **Zone 5**

'ROBERT LE DIABLE'

Although not the most spectacular of old roses, 'Robert le Diable' has a distinct charm of its own. It is also useful as a late flowerer to extend the season for once-flowering roses. The flowers open from attractive, pointed buds – unusual for a Gallica and suggestive of China rose ancestry. They reflex their petals as they expand, ending up almost pompon-shaped. They are a fine purple crimson color at first, and keep that dark shade in cool weather. However, 'Robert le Diable' really comes into its own in hot weather, when its flowers change from purple to cerise, magenta, lilac, and gray, while always retaining darker shadings and highlights. The plant forms a thicket of dark, slender, wiry stems that flop over under the weight of their flowers. Its long leaves are resistant to disease in areas with cold winters or dry summers, but susceptible to blackspot in mild, damp parts of the world. No one knows its parents, breeder, or date, but Meyerbeer's influential opera *Robert le Diable* was first performed in 1831.

'ROBERT LÉOPOLD'

Moss Rose

ORIGIN **Buatois, France, 1941**
FLOWER SIZE **3.5in (9cm)**
SCENT **Very sweet**
FLOWERING **Some repeat flowering**
HEIGHT/SPREAD **9.8ft (3m)/13.1ft (4m)**
HARDINESS **Zone 5**

Emmanuel Buatois was a very inventive breeder, and this salmon pink Moss rose created quite a sensation when it was first introduced. Traditional Moss roses were white, pink, or crimson: 'Robert Léopold' was the first to have so much yellow in its makeup. The flowers are semidouble and lightly cupped, with pretty stamens at the center. After a couple of days, they fade to rose pink. They come singly or (more usually) in clusters of up to five on strong, erect stems. Their sepals are extremely mossy, and the moss runs down the stems until gradually it is represented instead by a mass of small prickles. The whole plant is extremely prickly: the prickles are soft and crimson

'ROBERT LÉOPOLD'

when new, but hard and gray as they age. The plant is very vigorous, and quickly makes long, gawky stems, which are best pegged down so that they break into flower all along their arching lengths. It is extremely beautiful in full flower, and the moss itself is strongly scented.

'Robin Hood'

Hybrid Musk

ORIGIN **Pemberton, Britain, 1927**
PARENTAGE **seedling x 'Miss Edith Cavell'**
FLOWER SIZE **0.8in (2cm)**
SCENT **Light or slight**
FLOWERING **Repeats well**
HEIGHT/SPREAD **4.9ft (1.5m)/3.9ft (1.2m)**
HARDINESS **Zone 6**

Unlike most of his Musks, Pemberton bred 'Robin Hood' from a Polyantha. Although the flowers are very small, they compensate by coming in large clusters and flowering repeatedly all through the growing season. The individual flowers are very variable, even within the same cluster: some are single, others are semi-double. All are crimson or cherry red with a white center and a lot of white streaks breaking into the red parts of the flowers. At the center are handsome golden stamens, but they do not last long before turning brown. The flowers have brown pedicels and come in dense clusters, often forming themselves into tight balls of crimson. The leaves are dark green with slender leaflets. The plant is fairly prickly, healthy, and vigorous: it often bows over under the weight of its large flower trusses. Wilhelm Kordes used 'Robin Hood' as the basis for breeding his own race of Musk roses and Floribundas, hardy in the climate of continental Europe.

Robin Redbreast

syn. 'INTERROB'

Ground Cover

ORIGIN **Interplant, Netherlands, 1983**
PARENTAGE **seedling x 'Eyepaint'**
FLOWER SIZE **1.6in (4cm)**
SCENT **Little or none**
FLOWERING **Repeats**
HEIGHT/SPREAD **2.5ft (75cm)/4.1ft (1.25m)**
HARDINESS **Zone 6**

The flowers of Robin Redbreast are so spectacular that they have been used as a substitute for bright summer bedding. They are carried in immense profusion in clusters of 10–20 all over the surface of the plant. The contrast between the dark red petals, the pure white center, and the silvery petal backs makes a particularly brilliant impression. This is even greater when the newly opened flowers have golden stamens at the center. Robin Redbreast has a lax habit of growth, a lot of medium prickles, and small, mid-green, glossy leaves. It is especially useful in containers, in bright-colored plantings, and as a landscape rose on a large scale.

Robin Redbreast

'Robin Hood'

Robusta

syn. 'KORGOSA'

Rugosa Hybrid

ORIGIN **Kordes, Germany, 1979**
PARENTAGE ***Rosa rugosa* var. *regeliana* seedling**
FLOWER SIZE **2.8in (7cm)**
SCENT **Light**
FLOWERING **Continuous**
HEIGHT/SPREAD **6.6ft (2m)/4.9ft (1.5m)**
HARDINESS **Zone 4**
AWARDS **ADR 1980**

Few Rugosa roses have such a bright coloring as Robusta: its dark scarlet flowers glow with brightness. It is also unusually tall and vigorous, being grown as a short climber at Bagatelle in Paris. The flowers are single and uniformly colored, and sometimes have a small tuft of stamens at the center, though occasionally this is so rudimentary as to be insignificant; many Rugosa roses are completely sterile. The flowers open from long buds and come in short-stemmed clusters of 5–10. The plant is extremely prickly – so covered in long prickles that it is impossible to handle without thick gloves – but the large, bright green, wrinkly foliage is a splendid foil for the brilliant red flowers. It grows well in poor soils and is very hardy. Although Robusta is liable to blackspot in some areas, this should not deter anyone from growing it.

Robusta

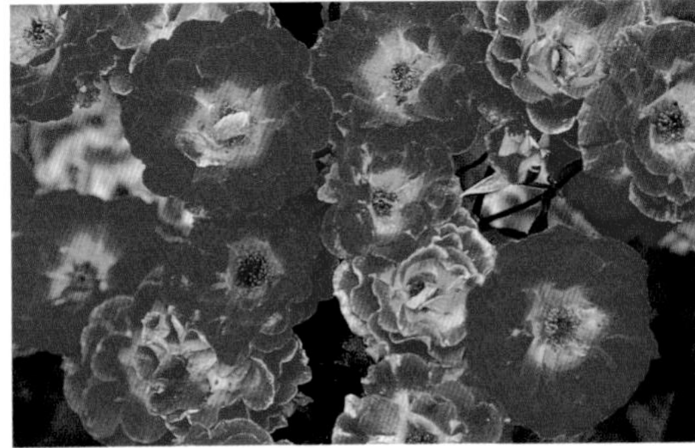
Rock 'n' Roll

Rock 'n' Roll

syn. 'MACFIRWAL', Stretch Johnson, Tango

Shrub Rose

ORIGIN **McGredy, New Zealand, 1988**
PARENTAGE **Sexy Rexy x Maestro**
FLOWER SIZE **2.8in (7cm)**
SCENT **Light and sweet**
FLOWERING **Repeats**
HEIGHT/SPREAD **4.9ft (1.5m)/3.3ft (1m)**
HARDINESS **Zone 6**
AWARDS **RNRS GM 1988; Golden Rose of the Hague 1993**

Rock 'n' Roll is one of those vigorous, bushy Floribundas that gets classified as a shrub rose. The flowers open out quickly to reveal their bright vermilion petals, with a patch of yellow at the center and orange yellow backs to the petals. The yellow pigment fades quickly, leaving the flowers red and white but no less striking – the color hits you in the eye at all stages of its development. Occasionally the flowers also have a few white stripes – Rock 'n' Roll is a descendant of McGredy's "hand-painted" series. The flowers have wavy edges and come in clusters of 5–20. The leaves are dark, shiny, and fairly healthy. The plant is vigorous and bushy, though it may be trained as a short climber in hot climates.

Rody

syn. 'TANYDOR'

Ground Cover

ORIGIN **Tantau, Germany, 1994**
FLOWER SIZE **2in (5cm)**
SCENT **Little or none**
FLOWERING **Repeats continuously**
HEIGHT/SPREAD **2ft (60cm)/4.1ft (1.25m)**
HARDINESS **Zone 6**

Tantau Rosen, who bred this splendid ground-cover rose, described the color of Rody as "raspberry red." It is an accurate observation, though alas the flowers do not have a scent to match their fruity color. They are more than semidouble, but not overly full of petals, though the flowers arrange themselves in a pattern that makes them look very double, and they come in clusters of 3–12 flowers. When in full flower, they hide almost completely the small, dark, glossy, Wichurana leaves. Rody is hardy, vigorous, and healthy, with short, arching branches that then flop down under the weight of their flowers, so that the plant grows sideways faster than it climbs heavenward. It is sometimes promoted as a landscaping rose, but it is also very useful in containers and as a specimen plant in mixed borders.

'Roger Lambelin'

see 'Prince Camille de Rohan'

Rody

ROKOKO

ROKOKO

syn. 'TANOKOR'

Shrub Rose

ORIGIN **Tantau, Germany, 1987**
FLOWER SIZE **3.1in (8cm)**
SCENT **Light and musky**
FLOWERING **Repeats well**
HEIGHT/SPREAD **4.9ft (1.5m)/3.3ft (1m)**
HARDINESS **Zone 5**

There are two roses in Germany called Rokoko. One is a short, workmanlike, pink Rugosa introduced by Baum in 1990; the other is a beautiful, aristocratic, pale apricot pink shrub rose in the Floribunda style, introduced by Tantau in 1987. The two cultivars are fairly confused in the trade, even in Germany, so it is important to know which one you are getting. Tantau's Rokoko is the better of the two and the most widely available – a tall, vigorous plant, with clusters of large, exquisitely ruffled flowers. They are fully double, but stand up well to rain, and open out to show their orange stamens at the center. Their color is apricot in the bud and fades gently through a spectrum of pastel shades to a pearly cream color as they open and age. Rokoko has a lot of dark green leaves, reddish new growth, and makes a good, bushy plant.

R

ROMANTIC DAYS

see HONORÉ DE BALZAC

ROMANZE

syn. 'TANEZAMOR'

Shrub Rose

ORIGIN **Tantau, Germany, 1985**
FLOWER SIZE **2.4in (6cm)**
SCENT **Light and sweet**
FLOWERING **Repeats well**
HEIGHT/SPREAD **4.9ft (1.5m)/4.1ft (1.25m)**
HARDINESS **Zone 6**
AWARDS **Baden-Baden GM 1985; ADR 1986**

Part Floribunda, part shrub, part landscape rose – Romanze is wholly German. It is the epitome of the modern German Park roses, which are hardy, healthy, weather resistant, easy to grow, and brilliantly floriferous. Its flowers are mid-pink, with deepest pink petal backs, and are lightly scented. The flower is double and blessed with tough, strong petals that give a spectacular display of color. They are sometimes borne singly but more often in clusters of 5–15 and show up well against the large dark leaves. The new growth is rich crimson and an even better foil for the flowers. Romanze is an excellent garden plant, but better still when densely planted in big masses. Then it becomes the one rose that everyone is drawn to and wants to know its name.

ROMANZE

'ROSA MUNDI'

see ROSA OFFICINALIS

'ROSA ZWERG'

syn. 'DWARF PAVEMENT'

Rugosa Hybrid

ORIGIN **Baum, Germany, 1984**
FLOWER SIZE **2.8in (7cm)**
SCENT **Strong and sweet**
FLOWERING **Repeats well**
HEIGHT/SPREAD **2.7ft (80cm)/2.7ft (80cm)**
HARDINESS **Zone 4**

In cold climates, 'Rosa Zwerg' is one of the best roses for landscaping and ground cover. Its tight, low-growing habit makes it useful, too, in private gardens. It is not among the most ornamental of roses, but it is healthy, thrifty, and highly scented. 'Rosa Zwerg' has semidouble, pale pink flowers with a hint of mauve in them and a ring of yellow stamens. In North America, it is sold as 'Dwarf Pavement' and promoted (together with other Baum roses) as the Pavement series of hardy Rugosas, with bigger flowers than usual. However, the flowers of 'Rosa Zwerg' are no larger than average among Rugosas. They are followed by quantities of large red hips, and, since it reflowers well, the bush is still blooming when the first hips are ripe. Like most Rugosas, 'Rosa Zwerg' will grow equally well in hot, dry climates and stands up well to wind and salt.

ROSABELL

ROSABELL

syn. 'COCCELESTE'

Patio Rose

ORIGIN **Cocker, Britain, 1986**
PARENTAGE **('National Trust' x 'Wee Man') x 'Darling Flame'**
FLOWER SIZE **2in (5cm)**
SCENT **Light and sweet**
FLOWERING **Repeats**
HEIGHT/SPREAD **1.6ft (50cm)/11.8in (30cm)**
HARDINESS **Zone 6**

The charm of Rosabell lies in the way the breeders have been able to put old-fashioned flowers on the neat, dwarf habit of a Patio rose. The flowers open from plump buds and are bright rose pink, with slightly darker petal backs. The petals are numerous, and the inner ones are quilled, giving the rose its 19th-century look. The flowers come in clusters of 3–15 and are very freely produced. Rosabell has shiny, healthy, mid-green leaves and repeats well. It is a very useful free flowering rose for containers and small borders.

ROSALIE CORAL

syn. 'CHEWALLOP'

Patio Climber

ORIGIN **Warner, Britain, 1991**
PARENTAGE **('Elizabeth of Glamis' x ['Galway Bay' x 'Sutter's Gold']) x Anna Ford**
FLOWER SIZE **1.6in (4cm)**
SCENT **Light and fruity**
FLOWERING **Repeats well**
HEIGHT/SPREAD **6.6ft (2m)/3.3ft (1m)**
HARDINESS **Zone 6**

ROSALIE CORAL

A plant of Rosalie Coral in full flower is a breathtaking sight. It is covered from top to bottom in brilliant orange flowers. The flowers have a yellow eye and bright yellow petal backs, which make the orange seem even brighter. They are carried in clusters of 3–8 flowers, sometimes singly, and the first, spectacular flowering lasts for several weeks. Thereafter, the plant is never without a few flowers until the next full flush arrives. Rosalie Coral has neat little leaves – dark, shiny, and copious – which are a good foil for the radiant flowers. It makes a vigorous, twiggy, prickly plant that is generally healthy, though blackspot may be a problem in autumn.

Rosarium Uetersen

syn. 'KORtersen'

Modern Climber

ORIGIN **Kordes, Germany, 1977**
PARENTAGE **'Karlsruhe' seedling**
FLOWER SIZE **3.5in (9cm)**
SCENT **Medium and sweet**
FLOWERING **Repeats well**
HEIGHT/SPREAD **11.5ft (3.5m)/8.2ft (2.5m)**
HARDINESS **Zone 5**

The popularity of this shrubby climber has grown consistently since it was introduced in 1977. The flowers of Rosarium Uetersen were considered too old-fashioned at the time, but now that its qualities are recognized, it is widely grown all over the world. The flowers are large, loosely quartered, and very full of petals. The clusters are large, too: a plant in full fling, rustling its dark pink, ruffled petals, is a vision of supreme loveliness. The undersides of the petals are a more silvery pink, and the flowers fade slightly as they age, which intensifies the beauty of the new flowers and the clusters as a whole. The flowers are produced profusely at first, then somewhat more intermittently. They stand up surprisingly well to wind and rain. The leaves are many, large, glossy, healthy, and mid-green. The plant can be trained either as a climber or as a shrub. Its name honors the great rose garden at Uetersen near the Kordes' nursery in Holstein.

Rosarium Uetersen

'Rose à Parfum de l'Haÿ'

Rugosa Hybrid

ORIGIN **Gravereaux, France, 1901**
PARENTAGE **('Kazanlik' × 'Général Jacqueminot') × *Rosa rugosa***
FLOWER SIZE **3.1in (8cm)**
SCENT **Very strong and sweet**
FLOWERING **Repeats**
HEIGHT/SPREAD **5.7ft (1.75m)/4.9ft (1.5m)**
HARDINESS **Zone 5**

Pretty purple flowers and a sumptuous scent are the main strengths of 'Rose à Parfum de l'Haÿ'; mildew, prickliness, and no hips are its weaknesses. The cupped flowers are purple pink or magenta, turning bluer as they age, loosely double, and sometimes revealing yellow stamens at the center. They come singly or in short-stalked clusters of up to four, but the flowers are sterile, so the plant never bears hips. The leaves are not rugose but smooth, pale, and glossy. Mildew can be a problem. The plant has an upright habit of growth and thick stems, and is very vigorous – good on poor soils and very hardy. But 'Roseraie de l'Haÿ' is a better plant.

'Rose d'Amour'

see Rosa virginiana 'Plena'

'Rose de Meaux'

Centifolia

ORIGIN **France, 1789**
FLOWER SIZE **1.2in (3cm)**
SCENT **Light and sweet**
FLOWERING **Once only, fairly early in season**
HEIGHT/SPREAD **3.3ft (1m)/2.7ft (80cm)**
HARDINESS **Zone 5**

Too different to be a sport of it, this scaled-down smaller rose is probably related to 'Centifolia'. The flowers of 'Rose de Meaux' are small, and carried either singly or in clusters of up to five. Cupped at first, they later open out almost flat, with large, paler petals around the outside and a mass of tiny, darker petals within. The petals have a soft, silky look, and are very thin, which makes them susceptible to rain damage. In humid weather, the buds ball. It makes a pretty plant, and responds well to feeding and watering, but it is out of scale in a mixed rose garden.

'Rose de Meaux'

'Rose de Rescht'

'Rose de Rescht'

Portland

ORIGIN **France, c.1840**
FLOWER SIZE **2.4in (6cm)**
SCENT **Strong and sweet**
FLOWERING **Remontant**
HEIGHT/SPREAD **3.3ft (1m)/2.5ft (75cm)**
HARDINESS **Zone 5**

The true name of this popular Portland rose is lost, but it has been grown as 'Rose de Rescht' since an English nurserywoman named Nancy Lindsay reintroduced it. Lindsay claimed to have found it near Rescht in Persia, but she was notoriously untruthful, and this claim can be discounted. It is certainly not a Persian rose – more probably of French origin. Its flowers open from completely spherical buds. They are pale crimson, but slightly more purple in cool weather, with a lot of neatly arranged little petals. Sometimes they have a button eye. They come in tight clusters of 3–7 on short stems and are surrounded by a ruff of leaves: 'Rose de Rescht' has the Portland habit of producing ever shorter internodes on its flowering stems, so that the whole bush appears very thick and leafy. Those leaves are pale green, with a slightly rugose surface. The plant repeats regularly, at approximately six-week intervals, provided it is deadheaded after each flush or rejuvenated by a hard annual pruning. 'Rose de Rescht' makes a neat, small, compact bush. It may suffer from a little blackspot late in the season.

'Rose des Maures'

syn. 'Sissinghurst Castle'

Gallica

ORIGIN **France, c.1850**
FLOWER SIZE **2.8in (7cm)**
SCENT **Light and sweet**
FLOWERING **Once only**
HEIGHT/SPREAD **4.9ft (1.5m)/3.3ft (1m)**
HARDINESS **Zone 5**

No one knows the origins of this rose, which was found by the English writer Vita Sackville-West in her garden at Sissinghurst Castle and somehow identified as 'Rose des Maures'. It has small purple flowers with somewhat rounded petals arranged around a few golden stamens. Sometimes a few white flecks spread out from the center into the purple petals. The flowers may come singly or in clusters of up to eight, but typically in threes. 'Rose des Maures' is an upright grower, with long, thin, unbranched stems, few prickles, and mid-green leaves. The plant flourishes in poor soil, survives neglect, and, if grown on its own roots, makes a good thicket.

'Rose des Maures'

'Rose du Roi'

'Rose du Roi'

Portland

ORIGIN **Lélieur, France, 1815**
FLOWER SIZE **3.5in (9cm)**
SCENT **Strong, rich, and sweet**
FLOWERING **Remontant**
HEIGHT/SPREAD **4.9ft (1.5m)/4.9ft (1.5m)**
HARDINESS **Zone 6**

It is one of the earliest Portland roses or Damask Perpetuals, but 'Rose du Roi' is also one of the best. It repeats its flowering reliably every six weeks or so until the first frost. The flowers are very beautiful – deep magenta and fully petaled. Some show their stamens, but others have a button eye instead. The flowers usually come singly, but occasionally in clusters of up to three. The receptacles and capsules are long and slender like a Damask's. The leaves are mid-green, with a slightly rough surface, and fairly healthy, except for a little mildew and blackspot in cool, damp conditions. The stems are covered in bristles, but the plant has no real prickles. 'Rose du Roi' is somewhat mixed up commercially with 'Rose du Roi à Fleurs Pourpres', but both are first-rate old garden roses.

'Rose du Roi à Fleurs Pourpres'

Portland

ORIGIN **France, 1819**
FLOWER SIZE **3.1in (8cm)**
SCENT **Strong and sweet**
FLOWERING **Repeats**
HEIGHT/SPREAD **4.9ft (1.5m)/3.3ft (1m)**
HARDINESS **Zone 5**

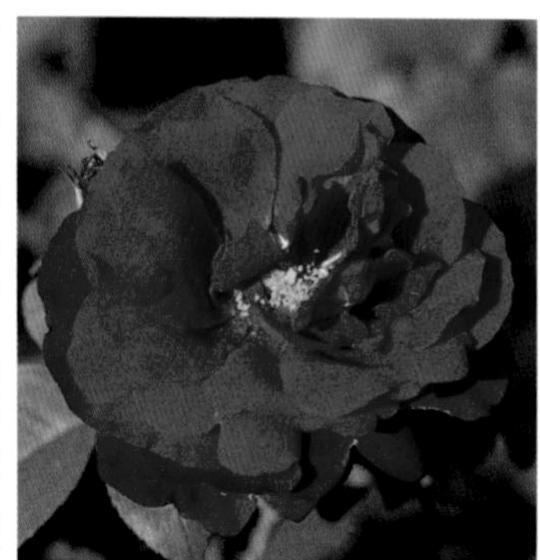
'Rose du Roi à Fleurs Pourpres'

This is one of those rich purple Portland roses like 'Pergolèse' and 'Arthur de Sansal'. It is not a sport of 'Rose du Roi', but may be a seedling of it: we do not know. 'Rose du Roi à Fleurs Pourpres' has rich purple flowers, with a tinge of bright crimson at first, but turning duller, bluer, and grayer as they age. The flowers open out flat and full of petals, often with a button eye. They come singly or in twos and threes. The flowers are surrounded by leaves because the internodes get progressively shorter as the stems grow up. The plant has dark, matt leaves and a lot of small bristles, but few of them are large enough to amount to real prickles. The plant is fairly vigorous and healthy, by the standards of old roses, but grows best in hot climates. In cool conditions it may struggle to reach more than 2.7ft (80cm).

'Rose Gaujard'

Hybrid Tea

ORIGIN **Gaujard, France, 1957**
PARENTAGE **'Mme. A. Meilland' x 'Opéra' seedling**
FLOWER SIZE **3.5in (9cm)**
SCENT **Light and sweet**
FLOWERING **Repeats**
HEIGHT/SPREAD **4.1ft (1.25m)/3.3ft (1m)**
HARDINESS **Zone 6**
AWARDS **NRS GM 1958**

Jean Gaujard took over the famous nursery of Joseph Pernet-Ducher in Lyon, and 'Rose Gaujard' is his best-known hybrid, still widely available all around the world nearly 50 years after it was first introduced. It is a vigorous, upright Hybrid Tea, with large flowers of exhibition quality borne singly on long, strong stems. The flowers are a remarkable color: bright carmine or cherry pink, with nearly white backs to the petals. The contrast is dramatic and exciting. The buds have the classic long, conical shape of the Hybrid Tea, and are very beautiful as they start to unfold. The open flower, too, has a good shape. The foliage is large, dark green, and healthy. It is a most reliable repeat flowerer: sometimes the largest and most sumptuous flowers are borne in autumn.

'Rose Gaujard'

'Rosemarie Viaud'

'Rosemarie Viaud'

Multiflora Rambler

ORIGIN **Igoult, France, 1924**
PARENTAGE **'Veilchenblau' x unknown**
FLOWER SIZE **1.4in (3.5cm)**
SCENT **Little or none**
FLOWERING **Once, midseason**
HEIGHT/SPREAD **13.1ft (4m)/9.8ft (3m)**
HARDINESS **Zone 5**

'Rosemarie Viaud' is probably an open-pollinated seedling of 'Veilchenblau', one of about a dozen that were introduced in the 1910s and 1920s, often by nurserymen in search of the perfect rootstock for budding other roses. 'Rosemarie Viaud' is suitable because it is very vigorous, it roots quickly from cuttings, and it is completely thornless. As a climbing rose, it is distinct and valuable for its large clusters of pretty flowers – crimson purple at first, but quickly losing their redness and fading to a beautiful dusky Parma violet, enlivened at all times by stripes and flecks of white running out into the petals. 'Rosemarie Viaud' is best grown in an open position, where it is less likely to attract mildew until after it has flowered. However, the disease, which is common to many Multiflora ramblers, never seems to dampen its vigor. It has tiny bristly glands on the pedicels, which, when rubbed, give off a pleasant resinous scent.

Rosemary Harkness

syn. 'HARrowbond'
Floribunda

ORIGIN **Harkness, Britain, 1985**
PARENTAGE **'Compassion' x 'Basildon Bond' x 'Grandpa Dickson'**
FLOWER SIZE **3.1in (8cm)**
SCENT **Strong and sweet**
FLOWERING **Repeats**
HEIGHT/SPREAD **3.3ft (1m)/2.7ft (80cm)**
HARDINESS **Zone 5**
AWARDS **Belfast GM & FA 1987; Glasgow FA 1991**

There is a feeling among British rose growers that Rosemary Harkness has not had the success it deserves. It has a beautiful array of colors, a strong scent, and a good compact habit. It is grown all over the world, but in no country is it on every good rose nursery's list. Yet the color alone is enough to recommend it – salmon, orange, peach, pink, and yellow all prettily blended together, then taking on softer, muted tones as the flower ages and fades, until the petals are almost translucent. Although classified among the Floribundas, each flower has the shape of a Hybrid Tea at first, but acquires a ruffled form to its petals as it opens out. The scent is stupendous, and it is equally good as a bedding rose and a cut rose. It flowers early, but may be a little slow to repeat. The bush is dense and compact, with dark, shiny leaves. Rosemary is Peter Harkness's daughter.

Rosemary Harkness

'Rosemary Rose'

Floribunda

ORIGIN **de Ruiter, Netherlands, 1954**
PARENTAGE **'Gruss an Teplitz' seedling**
FLOWER SIZE **2.8in (7cm)**
SCENT **Strong and sweet**
FLOWERING **Repeats constantly**
HEIGHT/SPREAD **2.7ft (80cm)/2ft (60cm)**
HARDINESS **Zone 6**
AWARDS **NRS GM 1954; Rome GM 1954**

From time to time during the mid-20th century, when gardens were dominated by Hybrid Teas and Floribundas, a rose was introduced that had an interesting, old-fashioned shape. 'Rosemary Rose' is a good example, but it never elicited the enthusiasm that David Austin's English Roses sparked in the 1980s. The flowers of 'Rosemary Rose' are dark pink or pale crimson and full of petals laid out in a rosette shape. They come in clusters of 3–7 and are well set off by the crimson new leaves and stems of the plant itself. 'Rosemary Rose' is a good repeater, but it is not as tall as its parent 'Gruss an Teplitz', from which most of its good character descends.

'ROSEMARY ROSE' *(at Hever Castle, Kent)*

'Roseraie de l'Haÿ'

Rugosa Hybrid

ORIGIN **Gravereaux, France, 1901**
FLOWER SIZE **3.5in (9cm)**
SCENT **Strong, sweet, and fruity**
FLOWERING **Almost continuous**
HEIGHT/SPREAD **5.7ft (1.75m)/6.6ft (2m)**
HARDINESS **Zone 4**

Many Hybrid Rugosas were bred in the years around 1900, and 'Roseraie de l'Haÿ' is one of the best. The rich French amateur Jules Gravereaux was the breeder, and he named it after his soon to be famous garden. It has long, scrolled buds that open bright purple, fading eventually to a paler shade that combines well with soft colors. It is very shapely: its ruffled petals are a statement of conspicuous opulence. It has pale stamens and an extravagant scent. It repeats so constantly that it is rarely out of flower until late autumn. It does produce hips, but they are small and few. The plant has bright green, healthy, Rugosa leaves (pleated, rough, and veined) and good autumn color. Its stems are very prickly.

'ROSERAIE DE L'HAŸ'

Rosenstädte and Rosendörfer

"ROSE TOWNS" AND "ROSE VILLAGES" IN GERMANY MAKE A FEATURE OF ROSES WITH ABUNDANT PLANTINGS IN GARDENS, ON VERGES, AND IN PUBLIC SPACES

Roses are extremely popular in Germany: the rose is its national flower. One unique aspect of the German rose scene is the system of "rose towns" and "rose villages" run by the Verein Deutscher Rosenfreunde, the German Rose Society. Towns and villages that wish to take part decide to make roses a feature of their amenity and private plantings. They plant their roadside verges, front gardens, and public places with thousands of roses to improve the appearance of the local area and attract the attention of tourists and visitors. This allows such places to be recognized as a "Rosenstadt" or "Rosendorf" ("Rose town" or "Rose village") and to prefix their names with this title. There are some 15 such rose-bedecked locations throughout Germany, from little villages such as Rosendorf Seppenrade in the Münsterland to large industrial towns such as Rosenstadt Zweibrücken in the Pfalz and Rosenstadt Dortmund in Westphalia. Almost all have a substantial public rose garden at their center, usually with recreational and wedding facilities. One of the most charming is the rosarium at Uetersen, which was founded in the 1930s as a display garden by the three great Holstein rose nurseries of the day – Kordes, Tantau, and Krause.

THE HISTORIC ROSARIUM IN ROSENSTADT UETERSEN

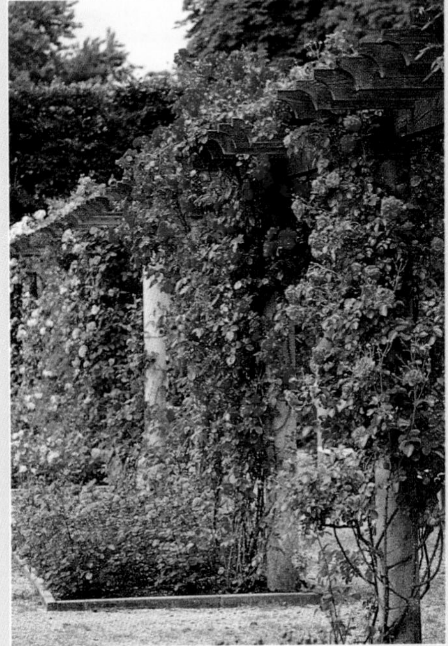

PILLAR ROSES IN ROSENSTADT BADEN-BADEN

R

Roseromantic

syn. 'KORsommer'

Shrub Rose

ORIGIN **Kordes, Germany, 1984**
PARENTAGE **seedling x 'Tornado'**
FLOWER SIZE **2.8in (7cm)**
SCENT **Light and sweet**
FLOWERING **Repeats well**
HEIGHT/SPREAD **4.9ft (1.5m)/6.6ft (2m)**
HARDINESS **Zone 6**
AWARDS **Baden-Baden GM 1982**

Its flowers are single, pink and white, and only lightly scented: at first acquaintance you might be tempted to think that Roseromantic is not much of a rose. In fact, its flowers are extremely beautiful, partly because they have long, wispy stamens with a crimson base, and partly because they are carried very profusely in large clusters on long stems. The flowers are followed by large, round, vermilion hips, though deadheading does help to promote reflowering. Roseromantic has small, dark, glossy leaves and a bushy, spreading habit of growth. In Germany, it is normally seen as a groundcover plant 2–2.7ft (60–80cm) high, but in hot climates it will reach nearly 6.6ft (2m) and make an arching shrub nearly 9.8ft (3m) wide.

'Rosette Delizy'

Tea Rose

ORIGIN **Nabonnand, France, 1922**
PARENTAGE **'Général Galliéni' x 'Comtesse Bardi'**
FLOWER SIZE **3.5in (9cm)**
SCENT **Strong and tealike**
FLOWERING **Continuous**
HEIGHT/SPREAD **6.6ft (2m)/8.2ft (2.5m)**
HARDINESS **Zone 7**

'Rosette Delizy' is pretty at all stages of its growth and development – a "must-have" rose for all who garden in warm climates. The long-pointed bud is bright yellow (this is the darkest yellow of all Tea roses) with crimson edges, but the buds soon open out almost flat. Then the outer petals are grayed pink and the inner ones lemon yellow, with still quite a lot of rich rich yellow at the center. The colors are darker and yellower in cool weather, and paler and pinker in hot. The flower has a muddled center, though some petals are quill-shaped. The plant has mid-green, glossy leaves on a vigorous bush capable of reaching 9.8ft (3m), but usually attaining only about half that height. The scent is delicious.

Roseromantic

Rosie O'Donnell

syn. 'WEKwinwin', New Era

Hybrid Tea

ORIGIN **Winchel, US, 1998**
FLOWER SIZE **4.7in (12cm)**
SCENT **Light and sweet**
FLOWERING **Repeats**
HEIGHT/SPREAD **4.9ft (1.5m)/3.3ft (1m)**
HARDINESS **Zone 6**

When the flowers of Rosie O'Donnell are expanding, they exhibit a striking contrast between the bright red petals and their pale yellow undersides. This lessens as the flowers open out and the yellow fades first to cream and then to white. The red parts also lose their brightness, and turn to pale crimson. However, the flowers are large and shapely, and usually borne singly on long stems, excellent for cutting, especially as they last well in water. Rosie O'Donnell has dark, bronzy green leaves (quite an unusual color), and may be susceptible to blackspot in some places. It grows vigorously, and blooms in a series of flushes until the weather turns too cold. The flowers are largest in cool weather, and tend to fade quickly in heat. Rosie O'Donnell (b.1962) is a comedienne and talk show host.

Rosy Carpet

Rosy Carpet

syn. 'INTercarp'

Ground Cover

ORIGIN **Interplant, Netherlands, 1983**
PARENTAGE **'Yesterday' seedling**
FLOWER SIZE **2in (5cm)**
SCENT **Light, sweet, and musky**
FLOWERING **Repeats**
HEIGHT/SPREAD **2.7ft (80cm)/4.9ft (1.5m)**
HARDINESS **Zone 5**

This seedling of 'Yesterday' has proved popular as a garden plant, as well as being a fine groundcover rose for large landscaping plans. The flowers of Rosy Carpet are pale crimson, fading slightly to dark pink, with a patch of white at the center and bright yellow stamens. They come in long-stemmed clusters of 5–15, and are very liberally borne. Rosy Carpet makes a lax, arching plant, with small, dark, healthy, glossy leaves and a profusion of prickles. It is a good repeat flowerer and useful in containers, where its loose habit is shown to advantage.

'Rosy Cushion'

syn. 'INTerall'

Ground Cover

ORIGIN **Interplant, Netherlands, 1979**
PARENTAGE **'Yesterday' seedling**
FLOWER SIZE **2in (5cm)**
SCENT **Light and musky**
FLOWERING **Repeats constantly**
HEIGHT/SPREAD **3.3ft (1m)/4.9ft (1.5m)**
HARDINESS **Zone 6**

'Rosy Cushion' was one of the first modern groundcover roses. It is still among the best and most popular. Its flowers are very simple – pink, with a white center and a good circle of golden stamens. They are pale pink inside, and darker pink on the petal backs, with just a few more petals than a single flower would normally have. The flowers come in clusters of 5–25 and are very freely borne all over the surface of the plant. 'Rosy Cushion' has handsome dark leaves (very healthy) and a lot of little prickles. It makes a dense plant, wider than tall, and is very useful in mixed borders, where it can be used to underplant and fill spaces between other plants. It is almost constantly in flower through until late autumn.

'Rosette Delizy'

'Rosy Cushion'

Rosy Future

Rosy Future

syn. 'HARwaderox'

Patio Rose

ORIGIN **Harkness, Britain, 1991**
PARENTAGE **Radox Bouquet x Anna Ford**
FLOWER SIZE **2.4in (6cm)**
SCENT **Strong and sweet**
FLOWERING **Repeats well**
HEIGHT/SPREAD **2.7ft (80cm)/2ft (60cm)**
HARDINESS **Zone 6**

There are several contradictions about Rosy Future. Its flowers are much bigger than the leaves, which would be more in scale on a miniature rose. And it was issued as a patio rose, or dwarf Floribunda, yet in hot climates it will grow quickly to 8.2ft (2.5m). Nevertheless, it is a good rose in any conditions. The loose, semidouble flowers are pale crimson or dark pink, with a white patch at the center and white streaks making their way up into the petals. The center is crowned with a ring of golden stamens. The flowers come in clusters of up to ten. Rosy Future has neat, glossy, little leaves, few prickles, and a compact, upright habit of growth. In hot climates it remains compact, but the stems arch over somewhat more. The first flowering is immensely profuse, but Rosy Future is a good repeater and there are always a few flowers on the bush between flushes.

'Rosy Mantle'

Modern Climber

ORIGIN **Cocker, Britain, 1968**
PARENTAGE **'New Dawn' x 'Prima Ballerina'**
FLOWER SIZE **5.1in (13cm)**
SCENT **Fairly strong and sweet**
FLOWERING **Repeats very well**
HEIGHT/SPREAD **9.8ft (3m)/6.6ft (2m)**
HARDINESS **Zone 5**

Bred to withstand the cold, wet weather of Scotland, 'Rosy Mantle' combines the toughness of 'New Dawn' with the elegance of 'Prima Ballerina'. The petals are large and reflex prettily, but the flowers are only lightly double, so they open quickly and do not spoil. Coral-pink at first, they lose their yellow tints and turn a good deep pink. They keep their color best in cool climates. The long flower stems are good for cutting, and the flowers are usually borne in small clusters – typically of 3–5 at a time. 'Rosy Mantle' is a reliable repeat flowerer and has large, dark, glossy leaves – in short, the perfect modern pillar rose and far superior to the better-known Compassion.

'Rote Apart'

'Rote Apart'

syn. 'Scarlet Pavement'

Shrub Rose

ORIGIN **Uhl, Germany, 1991**
FLOWER SIZE **2.4in (6cm)**
SCENT **Strong and sweet**
FLOWERING **Repeats**
HEIGHT/SPREAD **4.1ft (1.25m)/3.3ft (1m)**
HARDINESS **Zone 4**

This Rugosa rose is promoted as a groundcover rose, but in warm climates it quickly reaches 4.9ft (1.5m) and makes a fine freestanding shrub. The flowers of 'Rote Apart' are semi-double, dark crimson purple, with incurved petals and pale golden stamens at the center. They come in clusters of up to about eight, and are followed by handsome, bright red hips. However, the plant continues to push out its flowers until the first frost, so that the hips are accompanied by yet more flowers. 'Rote Apart' has bright, mid-green leaves with the typical pleated leaflets of Rugosa roses, and good autumn color. The flowers are thin-petaled and suffer in rain, but it is an excellent garden rose for really cold climates.

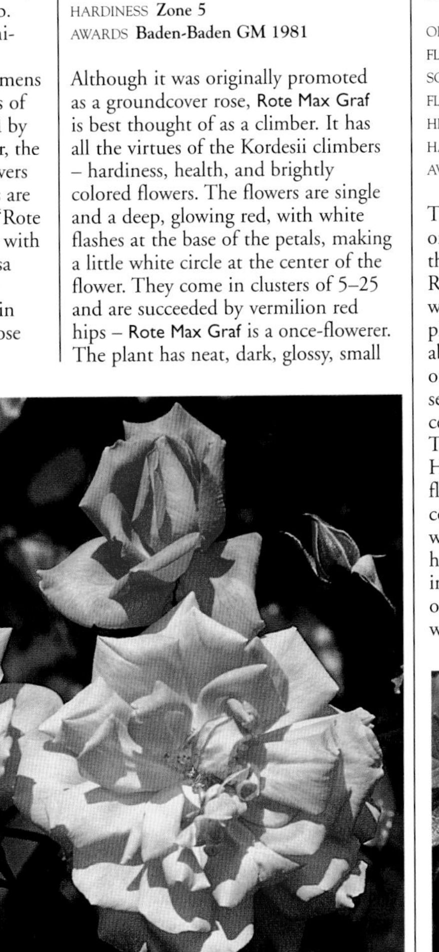

'Rosy Mantle'

Rote Max Graf

Rote Max Graf

syn. 'KORmax', Red Max Graf

Ground Cover

ORIGIN **Kordes, Germany, 1980**
PARENTAGE **'Kordesii' seedling**
FLOWER SIZE **2.8in (7cm)**
SCENT **Light and musky**
FLOWERING **Once only**
HEIGHT/SPREAD **13.1ft (4m)/8.2ft (2.5m)**
HARDINESS **Zone 5**
AWARDS **Baden-Baden GM 1981**

Although it was originally promoted as a groundcover rose, Rote Max Graf is best thought of as a climber. It has all the virtues of the Kordesii climbers – hardiness, health, and brightly colored flowers. The flowers are single and a deep, glowing red, with white flashes at the base of the petals, making a little white circle at the center of the flower. They come in clusters of 5–25 and are succeeded by vermilion red hips – Rote Max Graf is a once-flowerer. The plant has neat, dark, glossy, small leaves, a lot of prickles, slender stems and a lax habit. It will root where it touches the ground if grown as a scrambling shrub, and so is best tied in like a rambler.

'Rotes Meer'

syn. 'Purple Pavement'

Rugosa Hybrid

ORIGIN **Baum, Germany, 1984**
FLOWER SIZE **2.4in (6cm)**
SCENT **Very strong, sweet, and rich**
FLOWERING **Repeats constantly**
HEIGHT/SPREAD **4.1ft (1.25m)/3.3ft (1m)**
HARDINESS **Zone 4**
AWARDS **ADR 1994**

This modern Rugosa rose is outstanding on two counts: first, 'Rotes Meer' has the darkest crimson purple flowers of all Rugosas; second, it has a compact habit, which is unusual and makes it a suitable plant for groundcover. It also has in abundance the delicious, heady scent of the best Rugosas. The flowers are semidouble, with golden stamens at the center, and come in clusters of 3–9. They are followed by bright red hips. However, 'Rotes Meer' is a good repeat flowerer and produces its flowers continuously until the first frost of winter. The plant has bright green, healthy, crinkled leaves (bright yellow in autumn) and a low, rounded habit of growth. It is an excellent hedger as well as a garden plant.

'Rotes Meer'

ROUGE MEILLAND 84

syn. 'MEIMALYNA'

Hybrid Tea

ORIGIN **Meilland, France, 1984**
PARENTAGE **(['Queen Elizabeth' x 'Karl Herbst'] x 'Pharaon') x Antonia Ridge**
FLOWER SIZE **4.7in (12cm)**
SCENT **Medium and sweet**
FLOWERING **Repeats**
HEIGHT/SPREAD **4.1ft (1.25m)/3.3ft (1m)**
HARDINESS **Zone 6**

The original 'Rouge Meilland' was an important rose in Europe: it was the first to be patented in France, on September 19, 1951. François Meilland had fought long and hard to protect the rights of breeders. His masterpiece, 'Mme. A. Meilland', produced substantial royalties for him in the US, where plant patents had been in existence since 1930, but nothing at all in Europe. Rouge Meilland 84 reuses the name, but is quite a different plant. Its flowers are bright red (like redcurrants, according to Meilland) and classically elegant in the bud. They are usually borne singly on long stems, which make them good for cutting, and they repeat flower regularly through until autumn. The plant has healthy, mid-green leaves and a strong, vigorous, upright habit of growth. It is a fine and popular rose, if a little short on personality.

ROUGE MEILLAND 84

'ROUNDELAY'

ROSA ROXBURGHII

Species Hybrid

FLOWER SIZE **3.1in (8cm)**
SCENT **Light**
FLOWERING **Almost continuous**
HEIGHT/SPREAD **9.8ft (3m)/9.8ft (3m)**
HARDINESS **Zone 7**

This is the "double form" of *Rosa roxburghii*, which, by a quirk of botanical nomenclature, is treated as the "type" for the species, while the wild single-flowered form is known as *Rosa roxburghii normalis*. The double form is probably a hybrid with *Rosa chinensis*. It opens out almost flat, with a muddled collection of petals at the center – dark pink with lilac tints at the center of the petals, and paler both at the edges and on the backs of the petals. The plant has long, straight leaves with as many leaflets as the wild form, large prickles, and gray brown flaking bark. The flowers are carried on the old wood in great profusion right through until early winter. It is less hardy than the wild form, but a plant of great loveliness. There are several hybrids of *Rosa roxburghii* in cultivation, all of them beautiful garden plants.

Rosa roxburghii normalis is one of the most beautiful and distinctive of all wild roses. Its pale green leaves, for example, are long and slender, with 10–18 pairs of leaflets, instead of the two or three seen on most cultivated roses, and they seem almost to surround the short-stemmed flowers. The fruits, too, are unique, being covered in long green spines, and turning just slightly yellow when ripe, never becoming red. They fall off when they are ripe, instead of remaining on the bush as other rose-hips do. The flowers are variable in color, but usually dark pink with a central white patch, and have loosely held petals and a circle of pale, short stamens. The plant has very flaky, peeling, gray bark, which gives it interest even in winter, and a few hefty prickles, usually borne in pairs. It will grow to 9.8ft (3m) high and 16.4ft (5m) wide, though usually less in cultivation.

ROSA ROXBURGHII

ROSA ROXBURGHII NORMALIS

Hybrid of *Rosa roxburghii*

ROSA ROXBURGHII NORMALIS

Wild Rose

FLOWER SIZE **2.8in (7cm)**
SCENT **Light and sweet**
FLOWERING **Once only**
HEIGHT/SPREAD **6.6ft (2m)/6.6ft (2m)**
HARDINESS **Zone 6**

ROUGE MEILLANDÉCOR

syn. 'MEINEBLE', Red Meidiland

Shrub Rose

ORIGIN **Meilland, France, 1989**
PARENTAGE **'Sea Foam' x ('Picasso' x 'Eyepaint')**
FLOWER SIZE **2.8in (7cm)**
SCENT **Light and musky**
FLOWERING **Repeats well**
HEIGHT/SPREAD **3.3ft (1m)/6.6ft (2m)**
HARDINESS **Zone 5**

This is the finest shrub rose of modern times. Rouge Meillandécor has single, cupped, large, bright, velvety red flowers, with a white eye and yellow stamens. They are borne with extraordinary profusion all over the surface of the plant in loose clusters of 5–15. They are followed by small, round, vermilion hips, but the plant is a quick and generous repeater, so the floral display also continues until late autumn. Rouge Meillandécor makes a dense, rounded plant, wider than tall, and capable of growing to 4.9ft (1.5m), but often seen pruned back to 1.4ft (40cm). It has dark, glossy leaves, is apparently immune to disease, and is also unusually hardy for such a beautiful rose. It is useful for all purposes from groundcover to filling containers, but it is above all a wonderful garden plant, full of flower and color for much of the gardening year.

ROULETTI

see 'POMPON DE PARIS'

'ROUNDELAY'

Grandiflora

ORIGIN **Swim, US, 1954**
PARENTAGE **'Charlotte Armstrong' x 'Floradora'**
FLOWER SIZE **3.5in (9cm)**
SCENT **Medium and fruity**
FLOWERING **Repeats**
HEIGHT/SPREAD **4.9ft (1.5m)/3.3ft (1m)**
HARDINESS **Zone 6**
AWARDS **Geneva GM 1954**

The flowers of 'Roundelay' are an unusually dark brilliant red – cardinal red, blood red, and strawberry red are some of the terms used to describe them. They are fine, classic Hybrid Teas, with long petals and an elegant reflexing shape as they expand. Later the flowers open out flat and take on a distinctive ripple to their petals. They are borne singly and in clusters of up to five on a vigorous plant that will grow to 4.9ft (1.5m) in hot climates, but is usually pruned back to half that height in cooler parts of the world. 'Roundelay' has large, dark, tough, healthy leaves, stout stems, and an upright habit of growth.

ROXANE

syn. 'LAPDAL'

Hybrid Tea

ORIGIN **Laperrière, France, 1990**
FLOWER SIZE **4.7in (12cm)**
SCENT **Light and sweet**
FLOWERING **Repeats**
HEIGHT/SPREAD **4.1ft (1.25m)/3.3ft (1m)**
HARDINESS **Zone 6**

It is little known outside France, but Roxane is deservedly popular in its native land. The flowers are large and elegant in the classic Hybrid Tea fashion, with long buds whose petals unfurl slowly. They are pale yellow, fading to cream, with a bright crimson edge that passes to pink as the flowers age. The flowers are borne both singly, and in clusters of up to four, on long stems that last well if cut for the house. The plant is bushy and upright, with healthy, mid-green leaves. A climbing form, Climbing Roxane, was introduced in 2000 and is also proving very popular in France.

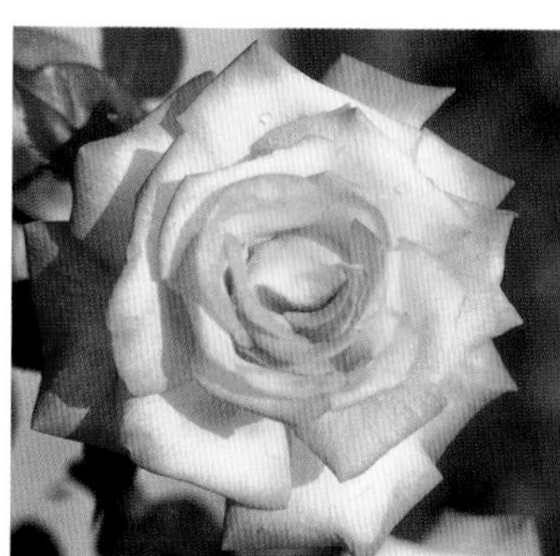

ROXANE

ROUGE MEILLANDÉCOR ▶

ROYAL BASSINO

'ROYAL GOLD'

'ROYAL HIGHNESS'

ROYAL BASSINO

syn. 'KORFUNGO', Country Prince

Ground Cover

ORIGIN **Kordes, Germany, 1990**
FLOWER SIZE **2in (5cm)**
SCENT **Light or slight**
FLOWERING **Repeats well**
HEIGHT/SPREAD **1.6ft (50cm)/3.3ft (1m)**
HARDINESS **Zone 6**

Royal Bassino is an excellent groundcover or landscaping rose, which, being wider than it is high, is also extremely useful in small gardens. It bears masses of semisingle bright red flowers with shining yellow stamens and little or no white at the center – a uniform and highly satisfactory red, even though some flowers eventually fade to crimson. They come in clusters of 10–25 and never cease to flower until late autumn. The plant has dark, shiny, Wichurana leaves and is remarkably vigorous and healthy.

ROYAL BONICA

see BONICA 82

'ROYAL DANE'

see 'TROIKA'

'ROYAL EDWARD'

Miniature Rose

ORIGIN **Ogilvie, Canada, 1994**
PARENTAGE **'Kordesii' x ('Kordesii' x [('Red Dawn' x 'Suzanne') x 'Zeus'])**
FLOWER SIZE **2in (5cm)**
SCENT **Light and musky**
FLOWERING **Repeats**
HEIGHT/SPREAD **1.6ft (50cm)/2ft (60cm)**
HARDINESS **Zone 4**

The Explorer roses were bred to supply Canadians with perpetually flowering roses that could withstand the worst of their winters. All are vigorous, large-flowered, and a snub to the Arctic winds. All, that is, except 'Royal Edward', which is small and modest – the only miniature rose that will grow in the Yukon. The simple, semisingle flowers are pink, fading to pale pink, with creamy yellow stamens. They come singly or in clusters of up to seven flowers. The leaves are dark, glossy, and healthy in the colder parts of Canada, but they are susceptible to blackspot in mild areas like Vancouver. The plant repeats on and off until the first frosts. The name "Royal Edward" refers to Queen Victoria's father, the Duke of Kent, who was Commander-in-Chief of the British forces in North America in the 1790s.

'ROYAL GOLD'

Modern Climber

ORIGIN **Morey, US, 1957**
PARENTAGE **'Climbing Goldilocks' x 'Lydia'**
FLOWER SIZE **3.9in (10cm)**
SCENT **Medium and fruity**
FLOWERING **Repeats**
HEIGHT/SPREAD **9.8ft (3m)/6.6ft (2m)**
HARDINESS **Zone 6**

This yellow-flowered modern climber has been popular since its introduction in the 1950s. William Kordes called 'Royal Gold' "the most perfect yellow rose flower you can think of." Its flowers are fully double, deep golden yellow, and very shapely, like Hybrid Teas, though they open out eventually to display conspicuous yellow stamens. They are borne singly or in small clusters on long stems that last well when cut. The plant has glossy green leaves and grows moderately vigorously. It does repeat its first, fine flowering, but on a lesser scale and only after a long interval. 'Royal Gold' is most vigorous and healthy in a warm climate.

'ROYAL HIGHNESS'

Hybrid Tea

ORIGIN **Swim & Weeks, US, 1962**
PARENTAGE **'Virgo' x 'Mme A. Meilland'**
FLOWER SIZE **4.7in (12cm)**
SCENT **Strong and sweet**
FLOWERING **Repeats well**
HEIGHT/SPREAD **5.7ft (1.75m)/4.1ft (1.25m)**
HARDINESS **Zone 6**
AWARDS **Portland GM 1961; Madrid GM 1962; AARS 1963**

The popularity of 'Royal Highness' is easy to explain: no other Hybrid Tea has such large and elegant, sweet-scented, pale pink flowers. They are invariably carried singly on long stems, which makes them very useful as cut flowers and also popular for exhibition. The petals are creamy white with pink undersides, and the exquisite shade of palest pink comes from the shadows that form between the opening petals. The flowers spoil quickly in rain, so this is a rose that performs best in hot climates. The plant is a strong grower and a good repeater. The strong, sweet scent is a bonus.

'ROYAL OCCASION'

see 'MONTANA'

ROYAL PAGEANT

see DELLA BALFOUR

'ROYAL SUNSET'

Modern Climber

ORIGIN **Morey, US, 1960**
PARENTAGE **'Sungold' x 'Sutter's Gold'**
FLOWER SIZE **5.5in (14cm)**
SCENT **Strong, sweet, and fruity**
FLOWERING **Repeats**
HEIGHT/SPREAD **16.4ft (5m)/9.8ft (3m)**
HARDINESS **Zone 7**
AWARDS **Portland GM 1960**

'Royal Sunset' is popular in the US, especially in California, but unknown in other parts of the world. It is a very vigorous climbing rose, with massive stems and outsize flowers. They are long and elegant in the Hybrid Tea style, but not too full of petals, so that they also open out nicely to a beautifully cupped shape. The color is a glowing pale orange, with hints of gold and yellow at the base of the petals – darker outside and paler inside. They are borne singly and in small clusters (typically of three flowers) on long, strong stems that last well if cut and are useful for lavish

'ROYAL EDWARD'

'ROYAL SUNSET'

'RUBENS'

arrangements. 'Royal Sunset' has large, healthy, deep green leaves and big prickles, and will grow to 32.8ft (10m) in a hot climate.

ROYAL WILLIAM

see DUFTZAUBER 84

'RUBENS'

Tea Rose

ORIGIN **Moreau-Robert, France, 1859**
FLOWER SIZE **3.1in (8cm)**
SCENT **Strong and tealike**
FLOWERING **Continuous**
HEIGHT/SPREAD **3.3ft (1m)/4.1ft (1.25m)**
HARDINESS **Zone 7**

The flowers of 'Rubens' are creamy white, with just a hint of pink reflected from the petal backs. It is an exquisite combination of shades, especially when the stamens suggest a touch of yellow at the center. As the flowers open and age, the pink tints fade to white. The flowers are long, slender, and delicately scrolled, and they hang down on their stalks in the fashion of Tea roses. They are usually borne singly but occasionally in twos and threes. 'Rubens' has fine, dark, healthy leaves, reddish prickles, and a lax, spreading habit of growth: the bush is normally wider than it is high. Its petals are damaged by heavy rain, but it can hardly be beat as a rose for hot climates.

ROSA *RUBIGINOSA*

syn. ROSA *EGLANTERIA*

Wild Rose

FLOWER SIZE **1.2in (3cm)**
SCENT **Light**
FLOWERING **Once only**
HEIGHT/SPREAD **8.2ft (2.5m)/6.6ft (2m)**
HARDINESS **Zone 5**

The sweet briar is a relation of the dog rose, *Rosa canina*, and occurs naturally all through Europe on calcareous (alkaline) soils. It was once much esteemed for the scent of its leaves, which emit a light, sweet, fruity fragrance when crushed between the fingers. Not everyone can detect it, but the scent is freely carried on the air after rain and in humid weather. Some people say it reminds them of apples. The flowers of *Rosa rubiginosa* are smaller than the dog rose's, and darker. They come in clusters of 3–7 flowers and are succeeded by handsome, scarlet, oval hips. The leaves are lightly toothed, slender, and bright mid-green. The plant has a lot of ferocious prickles, hooked back like a scimitar. It is at home in a wild garden or hedgerow.

ROSA *RUBRIFOLIA*

see ROSA *GLAUCA*

'RUBROTINCTA'

syn. 'HEBE'S LIP'

Damask Rose

ORIGIN **Lee, Britain, 1846**
FLOWER SIZE **2.8in (7cm)**
SCENT **Strong and myrrhlike**
FLOWERING **Once only**
HEIGHT/SPREAD **6.6ft (2m)/3.3ft (1m)**
HARDINESS **Zone 5**

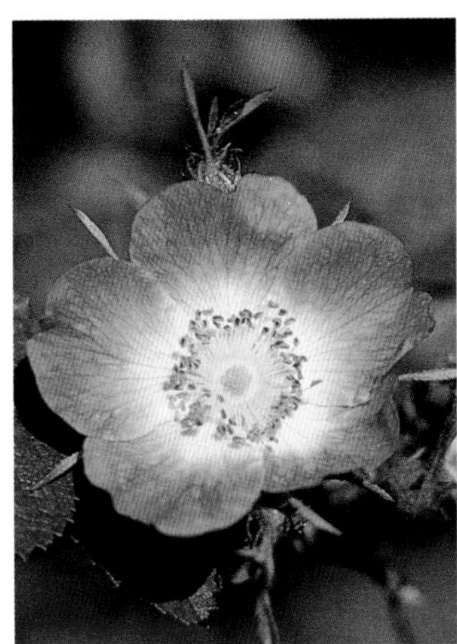
ROSA *RUBIGINOSA*

'RUBROTINCTA'

'Rubrotincta' is an unusual rose. It is probably a hybrid between *Rosa arvensis* and a Damask rose. It has the musk-myrrh scent, long stigma, and scandent habit of *Rosa arvensis*, with the pale leaves and many hooked prickles of the Damasks. The buds are bright pale crimson. The flowers, when they open, are semidouble and creamy white (fading to pure white), with a smudge of red on the tips of the outer petals, left over from the buds. Inside the beautifully cupped flower is a large, airy ring of golden stamens. The flowers come in clusters of 3–10, though their season of flowering is short. Sometimes the flowers are followed by orange hips. Despite the fragile beauty of its flowers, 'Rubrotincta' is a tough and hardy bush. It thrives in poor soil, jostles happily with other shrubs, and will climb up a small tree to 13.1ft (4m).

RUBY ANNIVERSARY

syn. 'HARBONNY'

Floribunda

ORIGIN **Harkness, Britain, 1993**
FLOWER SIZE **2.4in (6cm)**
SCENT **Light and sweet**
FLOWERING **Repeats well**
HEIGHT/SPREAD **2.7ft (80cm)/2ft (60cm)**
HARDINESS **Zone 6**
AWARDS **Belfast GM 1995**

The popularity of Ruby Anniversary is confined mainly to Britain, where its name celebrates a 40th wedding anniversary. The flowers are small and not exactly ruby colored but more turkey red, with slightly paler backs to the petals. The flowers have little scent but come in fairly large clusters (of 5–12 flowers) and make a fine display both as a bedding rose and when cut. Ruby Anniversary has small, dark, healthy, glossy leaves and makes a short, compact plant. It repeats its flowering quickly and looks good in containers as well as at the front of a mixed planting.

RUBY ANNIVERSARY

'RUBY WEDDING'

Hybrid Tea

ORIGIN **Gregory, Britain, 1979**
FLOWER SIZE **3.9in (10cm)**
SCENT **Light and sweet**
FLOWERING **Repeats**
HEIGHT/SPREAD **4.1ft (1.25m)/2.7ft (80cm)**
HARDINESS **Zone 6**

Almost every rose nursery in Britain stocks 'Ruby Wedding': it is often given as a present to celebrate 40 years of marriage. The rose – like the expression "ruby wedding" itself – is unknown elsewhere. 'Ruby Wedding' has bright dark pink or pale crimson flowers with a lot of short petals, which open out loosely and keep their color well. They come singly and in clusters of up to five, and the plant repeats quickly. 'Ruby Wedding' has handsome, glossy, dark green foliage and crimson new growth. It is a vigorous grower with a dense, branching structure. Blackspot may be a problem in autumn.

'RUBY WEDDING'

RUGELDA

syn. 'KORRUGE'

Rugosa Hybrid

ORIGIN **Kordes, Germany, 1989**
PARENTAGE **seedling x Robusta**
FLOWER SIZE **3.1in (8cm)**
SCENT **Light, but sweet**
FLOWERING **Repeats well**
HEIGHT/SPREAD **4.9ft (1.5m)/4.1ft (1.25m)**
HARDINESS **Zone 5**
AWARDS **ADR 1992**

Rugelda is the best yellow Rugosa rose, blessed with great vigor and spectacular when in full flower. The flowers open from scarlet buds and are lemon yellow, with a reddish edge, fading to cream and pink, though their exact color does vary a bit according to the weather.

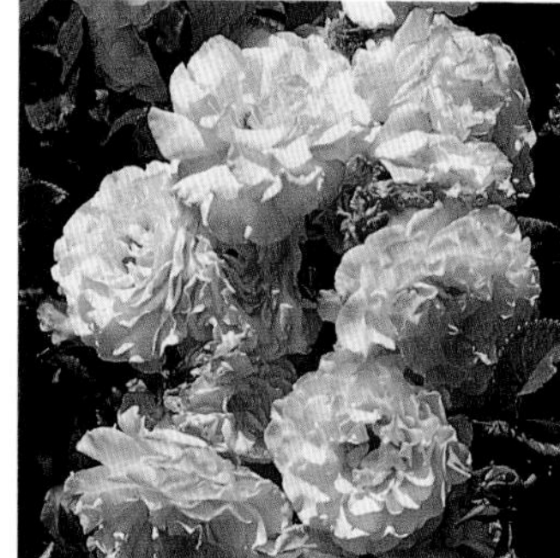

RUGELDA

They have ruffled petals and eventually open out like pompons. They come in large clusters, typically of 5–20 flowers, usually at the tips of the stems. Those

'RUMBA'

stems are ferociously prickly, but vigorous, thick, and a beautiful purple color when young. The leaves are large, slightly wrinkled, and very glossy, with long terminal leaflets. The bush is fairly healthy and will grow to more than 6.6ft (2m) in a hot climate, but benefits from being cut back to 4.9ft (1.5m) in spring to encourage new flowering stems.

ROSA RUGOSA

Wild Rose

FLOWER SIZE **3.1in (8cm)**
SCENT **Strong and very sweet**
FLOWERING **Intermittent until late autumn**
HEIGHT/SPREAD **4.1ft (1.25m)/4.9ft (1.5m)**
HARDINESS **Zone 3**

Rosa rugosa has some of the largest flowers of all wild roses. It is native to China and Japan, where cultivated forms have also been grown for hundreds of years. It is among the hardiest of all roses, and actually grows taller in cold areas than warm ones. It is also unusual among wild roses for continuing to flower right through until autumn, when the first flush of hips are already ripe. Those flowers open from long buds into sumptuous, magenta pink, crinkly petaled beauties, with a large circle of bright yellow stamens at the center. They are borne singly or in small clusters (of 2–5 flowers) at the ends of short side-branches. The hips, which follow quickly, are large, fat, bright red, and shaped like tomatoes. The leaves are bright green, with a lot of pleats and wrinkles on the leaflets – "rugose" is the botanical name for it. They turn a beautiful deep golden yellow in autumn. Sometimes they are also somewhat yellow in cultivation: this is usually due to a manganese deficiency. The plant has pale green stems that are absolutely covered in long prickles, making this a difficult rose to handle. It is extremely drought-tolerant, wind-resistant, and healthy, though its hybrids are often susceptible to rust. It spreads by suckering and has even been used to stabilize coastal sand dunes.

***Rosa rugosa* 'Alba'** is a white-flowered form that comes true from seed, while **'Rubra'** is darker. Both are otherwise identical to the species.

ROSA RUGOSA

Hybrids of *Rosa rugosa*

ROSA RUGOSA 'ALBA'

ORIGIN **c.1800**

ROSA RUGOSA 'RUBRA'

ROSA RUGOSA 'ALBA'

ROSA RUGOSA 'RUBRA'

'RUMBA'

Floribunda

ORIGIN **Poulsen, Germany, 1958**
PARENTAGE **'Masquerade' x ('Poulsen's Bedder' x 'Floradora')**
FLOWER SIZE **2.4in (6cm)**
SCENT **Light and fruity**
FLOWERING **Repeats well**
HEIGHT/SPREAD **1.6ft (50cm)/1.6ft (50cm)**
HARDINESS **Zone 6**

'Rumba' was one of the first roses to bring the brilliant but changeable colors of 'Masquerade' to a short-growing Floribunda. Its flowers open yellow but acquire bright vermilion edges to their petals, which later turn to dull crimson as the yellow tinges fade. They also have yellow petal backs and retain a yellow center throughout. They are rosette shaped and stand up well to wet weather, but do not drop their petals cleanly, which detracts from their usefulness as a bedding rose. They come in clusters of 3–15 on a sturdy, compact bush with glossy, mid-green leaves, and repeat well. Although superseded many times since it was first introduced, 'Rumba' remains popular and widely grown, especially in northwestern Europe.

RUSH

syn. 'LENMOBRI'

Shrub Rose

ORIGIN **Lens, Belgium, 1983**
PARENTAGE **'Ballerina' x 'Britannia'**
FLOWER SIZE **2in (5cm)**
SCENT **Moderate and musky**
FLOWERING **Repeats**
HEIGHT/SPREAD **2.5ft (75cm)/2.5ft (75cm)**
HARDINESS **Zone 6**
AWARDS **Lyon Rose of the Century 1983; Düsseldorf GM 1997**

Rush is a very striking modern shrub rose, with masses of pink and white flowers and a lot of Hybrid Musk character. The flowers are single (five petals) and white, with a broad pink

RUSH

edging – deep pink, fading to pale pink and receding as it does so, so that the edging gets narrower with age. The filaments around the stigma form a rich crimson circle at the center that draws the eye and provides a focus for the radiating white petals. The flowers come in large, billowing clusters (typically of 10–25 flowers). The leaves are long, dark green, and healthy. Rush will grow to as much as 6.6ft (2m) in hot climates, and is a very good garden plant, mixing well with other plants and flowering profusely through to late autumn.

'RUSSELLIANA'

Multiflora Rambler

ORIGIN **Cormack & Sinclair, Britain, c.1826**
FLOWER SIZE **2.2in (5.5cm)**
SCENT **Light**
FLOWERING **Once, early in season**
HEIGHT/SPREAD **13.1ft (4m)/6.6ft (2m)**
HARDINESS **Zone 5**

'Russelliana' is a curious rose – and not entirely attractive. It has buds like miniature kohlrabies. The flowers open dark crimson and fade to mauve pink, but are shot through by white stripes, which also have the effect of twisting and deforming the petals. These are paler at the edges, and notched at the tips. Few of the flowers have any individual beauty, but the overall effect of a plant in full bloom is impressive. The flowers come in large, open clusters and are full of their small, untidy petals. The bush has large, sparse, coarse, dark leaves and a great number of prickles. It grows well in poor soil and comes quickly from cuttings. It is thought to be a hybrid between a form of *Rosa multiflora* and a Gallica rose. Mildew and blackspot are its constant companions.

'RUSSELLIANA'

'RUSTICANA'

syn. 'POPPY FLASH'

Floribunda

ORIGIN **Meilland, France, 1971**
PARENTAGE **'Dany Robin' × 'Fire King'**
FLOWER SIZE **4.7in (12cm)**
SCENT **Medium and fruity**
FLOWERING **Repeats well**
HEIGHT/SPREAD **4.1ft (1.25m)/3.3ft (1m)**
HARDINESS **Zone 6**
AWARDS **Geneva GM 1970; Rome GM 1972**

The flowers of 'Rusticana' are a brilliant smoky orange. It is an eye-catching shade, and well shown when the flowers open to reveal a bright yellow patch at the center and golden stamens. The flowers are only lightly double, so they open out well. The undersides of the petals are a slightly pinker orange – dark salmon or vermilion lake – and the flowers tend to lose their yellow tones as they age, until they appear more red than orange overall. By that time the stamens have turned to brown and the petals have acquired a slight wave to their outline.

'RUSTICANA'

'GRIMPANT RUSTICANA'

The flowers sometimes come singly but usually in fairly tight clusters of 3–7 on long stems, and repeat well throughout the growing season. The leaves are large, handsome, healthy, medium-dark, and semiglossy – and there are a lot of them. The bush carries its flowers in great quantities: flowering stems appear all over its surface, more like a shrub than a Floribunda.

Meilland introduced a climbing form as **'Grimpant Rusticana'** in 1975. It is exactly the same as the bush form, but grows to about 13.1ft (4m). It does not flower as repeatedly as the bush form, but the flowers are finely shaped and very attractive when they hang down slightly from an arch or wall.

Sport of 'Rusticana'

'GRIMPANT RUSTICANA'

syn. MEILÉNASAR, 'CLIMBING POPPY FLASH', 'CLIMBING RUSTICANA'

Climbing Floribunda

ORIGIN **Meilland, France, 1975**
FLOWER SIZE **5.1in (13cm)**
FLOWERING **Repeats a little**
HEIGHT/SPREAD **13.1ft (4m)/8.2ft (2.5m)**

DAVID RUSTON

IN HIS GARDEN IN SOUTHERN AUSTRALIA, ROSARIAN DAVID RUSTION GROWS SOME 35,000 ROSES – THE LARGEST COLLECTION IN THE SOUTHERN HEMISPHERE

DAVID RUSTON is Australia's most distinguished rosarian – his garden in the South Australian Riverland has the largest collection of roses in the southern hemisphere. There are roses of every kind, and many that are rarely seen elsewhere. Some of the cultivars are unknown to visitors from cold climates because of their reputation for tenderness, which is not a problem in Australia. Others are sports that Ruston has found, propagated, and preserved: he has introduced some 30 climbing sports alone, including 'Climbing Lady X' and 'Climbing Dearest', both of which originated in his garden.

In his 27-acre (11-hectare) garden at Renmark, Ruston grows some 35,000 roses. The natural rainfall is less than 11.8in (30cm) a year, but the garden is irrigated from the mighty Murray River and thus receives some 98.4in (250cm) of water a year. This is essential in a climate where the temperature reaches a daily average of 104°F (40°C) and stays at this extreme for some three months. But the climate is also very dry, so that fungal diseases are not a problem: "There is very little blackspot, next to no rust, and mildew occurs mainly in early autumn," says Ruston. As a result, he can demonstrate that there are many first-rate roses wrongly written off by European and American writers and nurserymen as too disease-ridden to persist with.

DAVID RUSTON

ROSE FIELDS AT RENMARK

The entire length of the 3,280ft (1km) road frontage at Renmark is lined by different climbing roses. In the more ornamental parts of the garden are features like the arch of 'Bloomfield Courage' (Thomas, 1925), which has become a fashion icon for Australian gardeners, as well as old roses like the stunning 'Mme. Henri Guillot' (Meilland, 1942) that are no longer sold commercially, but offer a quality unsurpassed by that of modern roses.

However, Ruston is a keen collector of roses both new and old. It is important for him to evaluate the merit of individual cultivars as garden plants and as cut flowers – he is both the largest supplier of budwood in the southern hemisphere, as well as a major supplier of roses for commercial floristry. Ignoring fashion, he tries to find out which plants will really flourish in the hot, dry conditions of South Australia. Ruston uses row upon row of cultivars in his business. David Austin's English Roses, for example, are splendid for floral arrangements and remain in flower for 12 months of the year: Ruston has planted a full 5 acres (2 hectares) of them.

'MME. HENRI GUILLOT'

'Sadlers Wells'

Shrub Rose

ORIGIN **Beales, Britain, 1983**
PARENTAGE **'Penelope' x 'Rose Gaujard'**
FLOWER SIZE **3.1in (8cm)**
SCENT **Light and musky**
FLOWERING **Repeats**
HEIGHT/SPREAD **4.1ft (1.25m)/3.3ft (1m)**
HARDINESS **Zone 6**

'Sadlers Wells'

Peter Beales, the breeder of 'Sadler's Wells', classifies it as a Hybrid Musk, along with its parent 'Penelope', but it is best considered a shrub rose: it has a stiffer, more upright habit of growth than the true Musks, and lacks their great grace. The flowers are lightly semidouble and white, with crimson edges and a nice ruffle to the petals. They come in clusters of 5–10 and have attractive golden stamens at the center. The plant has handsome dark leaves like those of 'Penelope'. It is a fine sight when covered in flowers, especially if several are planted together, but the individual flowers are somewhat ordinary. In hot climates the first display is the best; in England, where it was bred, the autumn blooming produces larger clusters and richer colors.

Sahara

syn. 'TANARASAH'

Shrub Rose

ORIGIN **Tantau, Germany, 1996**
FLOWER SIZE **2.8in (7cm)**
SCENT **Light and fruity**
FLOWERING **Repeats constantly**
HEIGHT/SPREAD **5.7ft (1.75m)/4.9ft (1.5m)**
HARDINESS **Zone 6**

Sahara

Too vigorous to be a Floribunda, Sahara makes a spectacular show where sheer bulk and brilliant color are required. It arches over under the weight of its flower trusses and repeats quickly, so that there is a good display until the end of the season. The flowers are rich yellow, with pale orange shades towards the center – a wonderful color – then fade to lemon yellow or buff, while a pale crimson marking develops on the edge of the petals. They come in large clusters for such a large-flowered rose, sometimes as many as 15 flowers together, but typically 5–10. Sahara has healthy, mid-green, shiny leaves and a strong, bushy habit of growth. It is popular in western Europe but rarely seen elsewhere. It should not be confused with Sahara de Meilland, which is a cream colored Hybrid Tea grown for the cut-flower trade, much less dramatic than Tantau's Sahara.

'Salet'

Moss Rose

ORIGIN **Lacharme, France, 1854**
FLOWER SIZE **3.1in (8cm)**
SCENT **Strong and sweet**
FLOWERING **Repeats very well**
HEIGHT/SPREAD **4.9ft (1.5m)/4.1ft (1.25m)**
HARDINESS **Zone 5**

'Salet' is one of the most free flowering Moss roses and consequently one of the most popular. It repeats its flowering liberally and regularly until late autumn. The flowers are a pretty rose pink – darker at the center and paler at the edges, and darker, too, in cool weather. The large guard petals enclose a mass of small pleated petals in a somewhat disorganized shape that resembles a loose rosette. Sometimes they have a rough button eye at the center. The flowers open from globular buds, lightly covered in pale green moss, and are attractive at all stages of their development. They come singly and in clusters of up to five. 'Salet' has pale, soft leaves, a lot of bristles on the stems, and a neat, upright, leafy habit of growth. It is an excellent choice for gardens big or small.

Salita

Salita

syn. 'KORMORLET'

Modern Climber

ORIGIN **Kordes, Germany, 1987**
FLOWER SIZE **3.9in (10cm)**
SCENT **Light and sweet**
FLOWERING **Repeats constantly**
HEIGHT/SPREAD **13.1ft (4m)/6.6ft (2m)**
HARDINESS **Zone 5**

The Kordes family has a long tradition of breeding repeat flowering climbing roses. Salita is a good example, for it also has the bright colors that are popular in Germany. The flowers are vermilion with a hint of coral – an unusual blend of red and orange before fading to dark pink. They shine with brilliance when the sun lights them up. Each is shaped like a Hybrid Tea and produced singly and in well-spaced clusters of up to five on long, strong stems. Salita has large, healthy, glossy leaves and crimson new growth. It climbs only slowly in Germany and is sometimes grown as a shrub, but in hot climates it is a vigorous grower. It is especially good as a pillar rose, because it produces its flowers at different levels, and not just up at the top.

'Salet'

'Safrano'

Tea Rose

ORIGIN **Beauregard, France, 1839**
FLOWER SIZE **3.1in (8cm)**
SCENT **Good: a mixture of tea and cloves**
FLOWERING **Constantly in flower**
HEIGHT/SPREAD **4.9ft (1.5m)/3.3ft (1m)**
HARDINESS **Zone 8**

Although its parents are not recorded, 'Safrano' is generally regarded as a seedling of an old Chinese garden rose – 'Parks' Yellow' Tea rose – which was introduced to Europe in the 1820s. 'Safrano' is therefore one of the earliest European-bred Tea roses. Its flowers are rarely more than semi-double, but its petals reflex prettily and the central ones are sometimes arranged in an attractive but informal rosette. They come singly or in small clusters (of rarely more than three flowers) and have the Tea habit of hanging down, which is variously explained by the slenderness of its flower stalks or the weight of its flowers. The saffron color of its name is seldom seen: 'Safrano' is usually buff or fawn colored, fading quickly to cream. The plant has thin, dark leaves, maroon stems, a few prickles, and no great resistance to cold or to fungal infections.

'Safrano'

'Isabella Sprunt' is a color sport of 'Safrano'. Its flowers are somewhat more yellow than fawn, but fade quickly to cream. Some people maintain that it has fuller flowers than 'Safrano', but this is not always obvious. This aside, it is otherwise identical in every way to its parent.

Sport of 'Safrano'

'Isabella Sprunt'

ORIGIN **Sprunt, US, 1855**
SCENT **Good and spicy**

'SALLY HOLMES'

'SALLY HOLMES'

Shrub Rose

ORIGIN **Holmes, Britain, 1976**
PARENTAGE **'Ivory Fashion' × 'Ballerina'**
FLOWER SIZE **3.1in (8cm)**
SCENT **Light and musky**
FLOWERING **Repeats well**
HEIGHT/SPREAD **4.9ft (1.5m)/6.6ft (2m)**
HARDINESS **Zone 5**
AWARDS **Baden-Baden GM 1980; Portland GM 1993**

'Sally Holmes', named after the breeder's wife, is the sort of inspired hybrid that amateur breeders sometimes produce from parents that professionals would never dream of crossing. Its flowers come in enormous clusters, like its Musk parent 'Ballerina', but have the size and diameter of its Floribunda parent 'Ivory Fashion'. Although bred in England, 'Sally Holmes' fares best in hot climates, where it will reach 13.1ft (4m) as a climber and 6.6ft (2m) as a dense, billowing shrub. The flowers are cream at first, with a hint of pink from the unopened buds, and have long golden stamens. The stamens soon die and the petals turn a ghostly white, picking up pink blotches in rainy weather, but the flowers last a long time in both rain and heat. They come in long-stemmed clusters of 10–40. The plant needs staking in windy positions, otherwise the new growth snaps off at ground level. The leaves are fairly ordinary – mid-green and semi-glossy – and the plant repeat flowers quickly and reliably and is fairly disease resistant, except for an occasional brush with blackspot.

'SAMANTHA'

Hybrid Tea

ORIGIN **Warriner, US, 1974**
PARENTAGE **'Bridal Pink' seedling**
FLOWER SIZE **3.9in (10cm)**
SCENT **Light and sweet**
FLOWERING **Repeats well**
HEIGHT/SPREAD **4.9ft (1.5m)/3.3ft (1m)**
HARDINESS **Zone 6**

This shapely Hybrid Tea has only a light scent, but the cut flowers last a long time in water: 'Samantha' is an excellent florist's rose. Its flowers are bright red at first, fading to crimson but keeping their form for many days – ideal for cutting. They are usually borne singly, but occasionally come in twos and threes, on long, strong stems. The plant has large, medium-dark leaves: blackspot may be a problem in autumn. It repeats well and makes a reliable bedding rose, vigorous and eye-catching.

SAMARITAN

syn. 'HARVERAG', King Arthur

Hybrid Tea

ORIGIN **Harkness, Britain, 1988**
PARENTAGE **'Silver Jubilee' × 'Dr. A. J. Verhage'**
FLOWER SIZE **3.9in (10cm)**
SCENT **Medium and fruity**
FLOWERING **Repeats well**
HEIGHT/SPREAD **4.1ft (1.25m)/2.7ft (80cm)**
HARDINESS **Zone 6**
AWARDS **Orléans Rose d'Or 1990**

The English rose-breeding dynasty of Harkness has been introducing a series of old/new roses under the "English Legend" banner. Samaritan is a good example: it combines the shape and scent of the old roses with the colors and abundance of the new. The flowers are arranged as roughly quartered rosettes,

'SAMANTHA'

SAMARITAN

and filled with many small quilled petals. They are a beautiful soft apricot color, fading slightly to buff pink at the edges as they mature. They are usually borne singly but sometimes in small, long-stemmed clusters. Samaritan makes a vigorous, upright plant with mid- to dark green, glossy leaves. It repeats quickly and copiously: in hot climates it will flower almost throughout the year.

'SAMOURAÏ'

syn. 'SCARLET KNIGHT'

Grandiflora

ORIGIN **Meilland, France, 1966**
PARENTAGE **('Rouge Meilland' × 'Kordes' Sondermeldung') × 'Sutter's Gold'**
FLOWER SIZE **3.9in (10cm)**
SCENT **Light and sweet**
FLOWERING **Repeats**
HEIGHT/SPREAD **4.9ft (1.5m)/3.3ft (1m)**
HARDINESS **Zone 6**
AWARDS **Madrid GM 1966; AARS 1968**

The buds of 'Samouraï' are so dark as to be almost black: even when fully open, the flowers are an extremely dark shade of red. It is a handsome Hybrid Tea, with thick, strong petals that stand up to sun and rain. The flowers usually come singly but sometimes in small clusters (of up to four flowers together), on firm, stout stems. 'Samouraï' is an excellent bedding rose, with dark, shiny leaves, large prickles, and great vigor. It sends up new flowers all through the growing season. If it only had a stronger scent it would be the perfect red rose.

'SAMOURAÏ'

'SAMUEL HOLLAND'

see 'CAPTAIN SAMUEL HOLLAND'

ROSA SANCTA

see 'RICHARDII'

'SANDER'S WHITE RAMBLER'

Wichurana Rambler

ORIGIN **Sander, Britain, 1912**
FLOWER SIZE **1.2in (3cm)**
SCENT **Strong and sweet**
FLOWERING **Once, quite late in season**
HEIGHT/SPREAD **13.1ft (4m)/9.8ft (3m)**
HARDINESS **Zone 5**

'Sander's White Rambler' is a very beautiful Wichurana rambler of the 'Dorothy Perkins' type – long, slender, well-spaced clusters that arch outward over dark, lustrous leaves. The individual flowers open flat and are packed with little petals that form a perfect rosette. It is unusual for its good rain resistance and very strong scent. There are about 10–20 flowers in a cluster. The plant is very vigorous and easy to grow (and roots quickly from cuttings), sending up every year a forest of vigorous new long stems from near the base of the plant. Untrained, it soon forms a sprawling mass on a rough piece of ground or bank. Grafted high, it makes an elegant weeping standard.

'SANDER'S WHITE RAMBLER'

Sangerhausen

A FASCINATING TREASURE TROVE OF EARLY 20TH-CENTURY ROSES NESTLES AMID THE INDUSTRIAL SLAG HEAPS OF EASTERN GERMANY'S COMMUNIST PAST

THE EUROPEAN ROSE GARDEN at Sangerhausen in Germany features the largest collection of different rose cultivars in the world. It boasts more than 7,000 species and cultivars and 60,000 rose bushes. The rosarium, which was originally intended as a repository for every new rose introduced into commerce, was founded by the German Rose Society in 1898. Peter Lambert was a promoter and the amateur Albert Hoffmann donated his extensive collection of *Rosa* species before the garden opened to the public five years later. The collection thrived in the difficult era of National Socialism and survived the invasion of 1945. It was also well maintained (and expanded) during the Communist years, when the town of Sangerhausen was systematically spoiled and proletarianized by the digging of unprofitable coal mines: peaked slag heaps are now the focal point of the garden's views across the Saxon countryside.

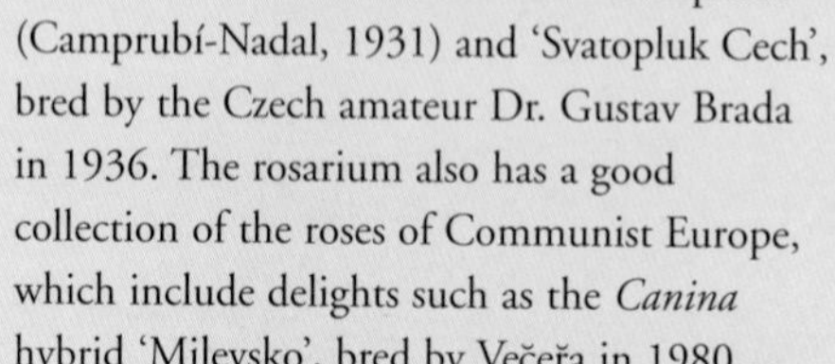
PLAQUE PAYING TRIBUTE TO ALBERT HOFFMANN

Although the rosarium did not fulfil its purpose as a repository, and acquired few new varieties from 1950–90, it is nevertheless an unrivaled reference collection of all the roses of the first half of the 20th century – a living encyclopedia of our horticultural heritage.

Certain classes of roses are particularly well represented, notably Polyanthas, Hybrid Perpetuals, Noisette hybrids, and ramblers of every kind. Here you can see such rarities as the white sport of 'Turner's Crimson Rambler' known as 'Fernande Krier' (Walter, 1925) and the Noisette sport 'Gruss an Friedberg' (Rogmanns, 1902). The oldest Hybrid Teas like 'Dr. A. Hermans' (Verschuren, 1907) appear, along with roses from countries with small rose industries like the Spanish 'Recuerdo de Felio Camprubí' (Camprubí-Nadal, 1931) and 'Svatopluk Cech', bred by the Czech amateur Dr. Gustav Brada in 1936. The rosarium also has a good collection of the roses of Communist Europe, which include delights such as the *Canina* hybrid 'Milevsko', bred by Večeřa in 1980.

The fluid design takes visitors around the pool and formal display gardens near the entrance, where the "black" rose 'Nigrette' and the "green" rose *Rosa chinensis* 'Viridiflora' are displayed as curiosities, then up past ranks of ramblers and climbers, through the collections of Damasks, Bourbons, and Rugosa hybrids, to the many rows of early Polyantha roses at the very top of the garden, beyond which another extension has recently been added.

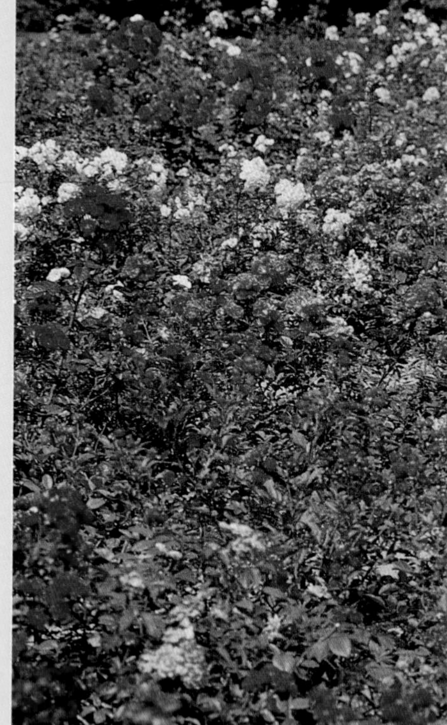
POLYANTHA BEDS

The garden lies in a cold region of central Europe, where winter temperatures have been known to drop to -13°F (-25°C). It is some 660ft (200m) above sea level and receives little more than 1.6ft (50cm) rain a year. The soil is thin, cold, light, sandy, and neutral. Although the rosarium covers some 37 acres (15 hectares), it feels smaller and more intimate. Space is at a premium, so bush roses are pruned to keep them small and climbers are tied in every year to a single post. The administrators are extremely generous in sharing budwood with other leading rose collections all over the world; nonetheless, some 2,000 cultivars remain unique to Sangerhausen.

THE ROSE COLLECTION FLOURISHES AMID A BLEAK POST-INDUSTRIAL LANDSCAPE

'SANGUINEA'

'SANGUINEA'

China Rose

ORIGIN **c.1824**
FLOWER SIZE **2.4in (6cm)**
SCENT **Medium and tealike**
FLOWERING **Continuous**
HEIGHT/SPREAD **4.1ft (1.25m)/4.1ft (1.25m)**
HARDINESS **Zone 7**

Several different roses go under the name of 'Sanguinea': all are single-flowered China roses. It is best considered as a group of closely related roses that come fairly true from seed. They all have striking, blood red flowers that fade to a more crimson shade as they age. Their most distinctive characteristic is the way the petals are irregularly reflexed, so that the flowers seem to be held at unusual angles all over the surface of the plant. Sometimes they have a tiny patch of white at the center, behind the wispy stamens. The plant is a bushy grower that will make a twiggy structure in hot climates and build up to as much as 6.6ft (2m) in all directions, but it is more usually seen pruned much lower. It rarely exceeds 2.3ft (70cm) in cool climates. The leaves are dark and small, and the flowers are followed by small orange hips. 'Sanguinea' flowers continuously, through every month of the year.

'SANTA CATALINA'

Modern Climber

ORIGIN **McGredy, Northern Ireland, 1970**
PARENTAGE **'Paddy McGredy' × 'Gruss an Heidelberg'**
FLOWER SIZE **3.9in (10cm)**
SCENT **Light and sweet**
FLOWERING **Repeats**
HEIGHT/SPREAD **13.1ft (4m)/6.6ft (2m)**
HARDINESS **Zone 6**

This beautiful rose is popular in France, but rarely seen elsewhere, which is a shame, because 'Santa Catalina' is one of the best early flowering climbers. The flowers are semidouble and a very attractive shade of milky pink, with pale salmon colored petal backs. At the center is a circle of long stamens, with a hint of crimson at their base, which sets off the entire flower perfectly. The petals take on a charming and distinctive roll as they age. The flowers come in mighty clusters of 3–10 and are very profusely borne in the first flowering and on a lesser scale thereafter, but enough to make a good display through until

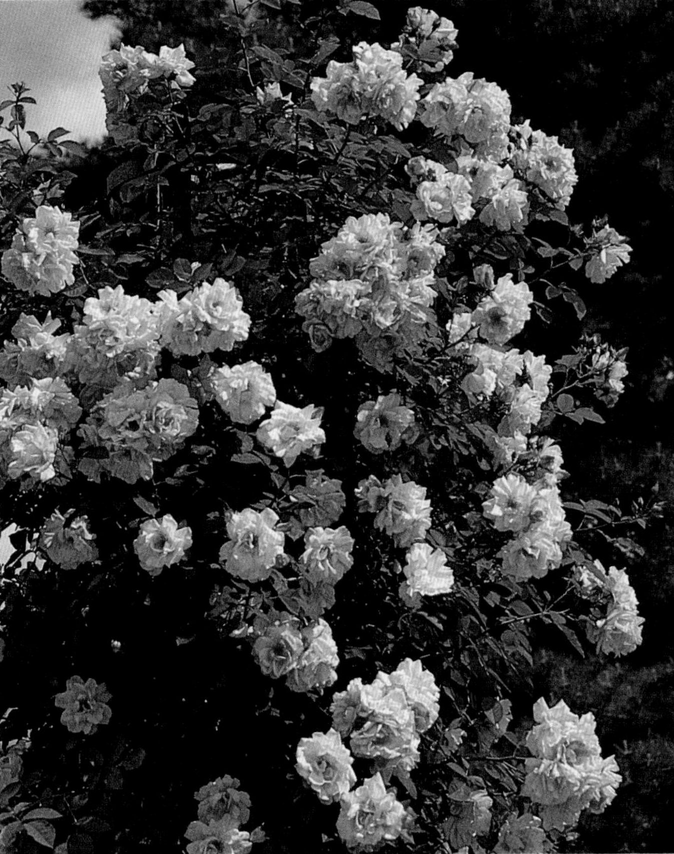
'SANTA CATALINA'

autumn. The plant is vigorous, upright, and fairly healthy, with mid-green leaves and a lot of new growth coming up from near the base to ensure that it never becomes leggy. An excellent rose.

SANTANA

syn. 'TANKLSEANT'

Modern Climber

ORIGIN **Tantau, Germany, 1985**
FLOWER SIZE **3.9in (10cm)**
SCENT **Little or none**
FLOWERING **Repeats well**
HEIGHT/SPREAD **9.8ft (3m)/6.6ft (2m)**
HARDINESS **Zone 5**

Its glossy leaves and hardiness proclaim Santana a Kordesii climber – as does its lack of scent. It is, however, an excellent

SANTANA

and prolific rose. The flowers are lightly double and attractive at all stages of their development. They are a rich, glowing, blood red color, weatherproof, and long lasting. They come in small clusters (typically of 3–7 flowers) not just at the top but all over the plant. Santana has very healthy, tough, mid-green leaves and an upright habit of growth. It is a good repeater and produces a steady supply of flowers in its native Germany until the first frost of winter. It can be grown as a freestanding bush, but also looks good when treated as a pillar rose.

'SARABANDE'

Floribunda

ORIGIN **Meilland, France, 1957**
PARENTAGE **'Cocorico' × 'Moulin Rouge'**
FLOWER SIZE **2.8in (7cm)**
SCENT **Light and fruity**
FLOWERING **Repeats well**
HEIGHT/SPREAD **2.7ft (80cm)/2ft (60cm)**
HARDINESS **Zone 6**
AWARDS **Bagatelle GM 1957; Geneva GM 1957; Rome GM 1957; Portland GM 1958; AARS 1960**

This short Floribunda remains a popular bedding rose long after it was first introduced. 'Sarabande' has semi-single, lightly cupped flowers of the most brilliant orange vermilion imaginable. They often have a slightly irregular outline, which gives a particular charm to the flowers – as do the paler patch toward the center and the ring of golden stamens. The flowers come in clusters of 5–12 and make a rewarding

'SARABANDE'

display. 'Sarabande' has medium-dark leaves, large prickles, and a low, open habit of growth. The plant is very hardy, and widely grown in central Europe still, but also performs surprisingly well in hot climates, where it is rarely out of bloom.

SARAH

see JARDINS DE BAGATELLE

'SARAH VAN FLEET'

Rugosa Hybrid

ORIGIN **Van Fleet, US, 1926**
PARENTAGE ***Rosa rugosa* × 'My Maryland'**
FLOWER SIZE **3.5in (9cm)**
SCENT **Strong and sweet**
FLOWERING **Once generously, then intermittently**
HEIGHT/SPREAD **6.6ft (2m)/4.9ft (1.5m)**
HARDINESS **Zone 4**

The flowers of 'Sarah Van Fleet' are very inviting as they open out to reveal a mass of pale yellow stamens surrounded by crinkly, mauve pink petals. They come in small clusters somewhat early in the season, and repeat thereafter through until late autumn. Unusually for a Rugosa rose, the flowers are not followed by hips. 'Sarah Van Fleet' is a lanky grower that tends to become bare at the base of its thick (and very prickly) stems. Its leaves are pale green and wrinkled, and they emerge early in the season, but are prone to mildew and rust later. It grows vigorously and makes a fierce hedge. Although it is very hardy, it also performs well in hot climates like Texas, where it continues to flower, even in the heat of midsummer. A white sport of 'Sarah Van Fleet' called 'Mary Manners' is sometimes seen; it is exactly the same as its parent in everything except color.

'SARAH VAN FLEET'

'Satchmo'

'Satchmo'

Floribunda

ORIGIN **McGredy, Northern Ireland, 1970**
PARENTAGE **'Evelyn Fison' x 'Diamant'**
FLOWER SIZE **3.1in (8cm)**
SCENT **Little or none**
FLOWERING **Repeats well**
HEIGHT/SPREAD **2.5ft (75cm)/2.5ft (75cm)**
HARDINESS **Zone 6**
AWARDS **The Hague GM 1970**

'Satchmo' is a brilliant red, short-growing Floribunda with a lot of character. Its flowers are bright vermilion or orange-scarlet and are particularly useful for big bedding displays. They are borne singly or in small clusters (typically of 3–9 flowers) on upright stems. Although bred to be rainproof, the flowers also perform well in hot, dry climates. The leaves are mid-green and occasionally subject to mildew, but 'Satchmo' is an easy to grow rose that produces its flowers with excellent continuity right through until late autumn.

Savoy Hotel

syn. 'HARvintage'
Hybrid Tea

ORIGIN **Harkness, Britain, 1987**
PARENTAGE **'Silver Jubilee' x Amber Queen**
FLOWER SIZE **5.1in (13cm)**
SCENT **Medium and sweet**
FLOWERING **Repeats well**
HEIGHT/SPREAD **3.3ft (1m)/2.5ft (75cm)**
HARDINESS **Zone 6**
AWARDS **Dublin GM 1988**

Large-flowered, thick-petaled, healthy, and vigorous: Savoy Hotel is one of the best modern Hybrid Teas. Its silvery pink petals have pale raspberry pink backs, and much of the beauty of the opening flower comes from the shades reflected in the shadows between the many petals, as well as its elegant, swirling shape. The flowers come on long stems, usually singly, which makes them good for both exhibition and flower arrangements. The bush is somewhat unremarkable, though it is vigorous, prolific, and healthy. It was named to commemorate the centenary of a famous London hotel.

Savoy Hotel

'Scabrosa'

'Scabrosa'

Rugosa Hybrid

ORIGIN **Harkness, Britain, 1950**
FLOWER SIZE **4.7in (12cm)**
SCENT **Strong, sweet, and spicy**
FLOWERING **Repeats well**
HEIGHT/SPREAD **4.9ft (1.5m)/4.9ft (1.5m)**
HARDINESS **Zone 4**

The Harknesses, who introduced 'Scabrosa', are the first to admit that they have no idea where this rose came from. They were not involved in rose-breeding at the time, so they think it was a foundling, but they cannot say who found it, when, or where. 'Scabrosa' is a very fine form or hybrid of *Rosa rugosa*. The flowers are large, single, and bright magenta, with large, wavy petals and pale, creamy stamens. They come in clusters of up to about ten and are followed by large, tomato-shaped hips, though the plant continues to flower well into autumn, so flowers and hips sit alongside each other for several months. The plant has rough, crinkly leaves, lots of prickles, and good autumn colour. It is very healthy and vigorous, but difficult to associate well with other plants in the garden, making it best on its own or in wilder areas.

'Scarlet Fire'

see 'Scharlachglut'

'Scarlet Gem'

syn. 'Scarlet Pimpernell'
Miniature Rose

ORIGIN **Meilland, France, 1961**
PARENTAGE **('Moulin Rouge' x 'Fashion') x ('Perla de Montserrat' x 'Perla de Alcañada')**
FLOWER SIZE **1.6in (4cm)**
SCENT **Light and musky**
FLOWERING **Repeats well**
HEIGHT/SPREAD **1.3ft (40cm)/11.8in (30cm)**
HARDINESS **Zone 6**

The flowers of 'Scarlet Gem' are lightly cupped at first, then open out almost flat to show that they are very full of petals. At this stage they have a very neat, rounded outline, unusual among miniature roses. They are vermilion initially, but fade to salmon and pink as they age, especially in sunny weather. They come in open clusters of 5–15 flowers on a sturdy, bushy, upright plant with medium-dark, glossy leaves.

'Scarlet Gem'

'Scarlet Knight'

see 'Samouraï'

Scarlet Meillandécor

syn. 'MEIkrotal', Scarlet Meidiland
Ground Cover

ORIGIN **Meilland, France, 1987**
PARENTAGE **seedling x 'Clair Matin'**
FLOWER SIZE **1.6in (4cm)**
SCENT **Light and musky**
FLOWERING **Constantly in flower**
HEIGHT/SPREAD **4.1ft (1.25m)/6.6ft (2m)**
HARDINESS **Zone 6**
AWARDS **Frankfurt GM 1989**

Health, vigor, adaptability, and toughness are essential to the Meilland family of ground-cover roses, and Scarlet Meillandécor has them all. Its flowers are small and bright red, with ruffled petals. The plant produces arching new growth that are often weighed down with flowers but also build up into a mounding shrub. The flowers do not drop their petals cleanly, but "hold their dead." It is a rose that needs no pruning, though tidy gardeners may wish to deadhead it and cut out the dead wood underneath. The plant has dark, glossy, healthy, Wichurana leaves, and continues to flower right through the summer and autumn.

Scarlet Meillandécor

'Scarlet Pavement'

see 'Rote Apart'

'Scarlet Pimpernel'

see 'Scarlet Gem'

'Scarlet Queen Elizabeth'

Floribunda

ORIGIN **Dickson, Northern Ireland, 1963**
PARENTAGE **'Korona' seedling × 'Queen Elizabeth'**
FLOWER SIZE **3.1in (8cm)**
SCENT **Very light and fruity**
FLOWERING **Repeats well**
HEIGHT/SPREAD **6.6ft (2m)/4.1ft (1.25m)**
HARDINESS **Zone 6**
AWARDS **Golden Rose of the Hague 1973**

The brilliant coloring of 'Scarlet Queen Elizabeth' comes from the stunning (but scentless) 1950s Floribunda 'Korona', now rarely seen. 'Scarlet Queen Elizabeth' is a stout, vigorous grower, and must be pruned hard to keep it to an acceptable height in the garden, because its flowers come at the end of very long stems. The flowers are a bright, pale vermilion and freely borne in clusters of up to 12, but they have short, incurved petals that curve so far over the center that they seem never to open properly. They also react to rain by erupting into red spots. The plant is an upright grower with dark, healthy foliage.

Scentimental

syn. 'WEKplapep'

Floribunda

ORIGIN **Carruth, US, 1996**
PARENTAGE **'Playboy' × Peppermint Twist**
FLOWER SIZE **4.7in (12cm)**
SCENT **Strong and sweet**
FLOWERING **Repeats well**
HEIGHT/SPREAD **4.1ft (1.25m)/3.3ft (1m)**
HARDINESS **Zone 6**
AWARDS **AARS 1997**

Scentimental is one of the best modern striped roses. Although classified as a Floribunda, its flowers come only in

'Scarlet Queen Elizabeth'

small clusters and are as large as the flowers of any Hybrid Tea. Their most noticeable characteristic, except for their wonderful scent, is the variation in the stripes on their handsome, thick petals. Some petals are cherry crimson with a few white stripes, while other petals show a few flecks of dark pink on an otherwise completely white flower. Most fall somewhere in between, since every petal is different. The flowers, which hold their color well, are fairly double and open out large and flat, with a few petaloids in the center that sometimes hide the central stamens. The plant is shapely, healthy, and fairly vigorous, with slightly ridged foliage. Scentimental repeats well, but produces its largest flowers and richest colors in cool conditions.

Scentsation

syn. 'FRYromeo'

Hybrid Tea

ORIGIN **Fryer, Britain, 1998**
FLOWER SIZE **4.3in (11cm)**
SCENT **Very strong and sweet**
FLOWERING **Repeats well**
HEIGHT/SPREAD **4.9ft (1.5m)/3.3ft (1m)**
HARDINESS **Zone 6**

If scent were the only quality sought in a good rose, Scentsation would be in every garden. Its scent is rich, strong, and pervasive – a sheer delight. But Scentsation is not so blessed with the other qualities that go to make a top rose. Its color is pale apricot, a pretty shade until it fades and loses its yellow hues and ends up a wishy-washy pink. The flowers tend to come in clusters of 5–9, but occasionally singly, and have long stems for cutting. The plant

Scepter'd Isle

is stiff, gawky, and upright in habit, with pale green foliage that is no stranger to blackspot. On the plus side, Scentsation has vigor and floriferousness, but the flowers can be disappointing, except for their wonderful scent.

Scepter'd Isle

syn. 'AUSland'

Shrub Rose

ORIGIN **Austin, Britain, 1996**
FLOWER SIZE **4.3in (11cm)**
SCENT **Strong, sweet, and myrrhlike**
FLOWERING **Repeats well**
HEIGHT/SPREAD **3.3ft (1m)/2.5ft (75cm)**
HARDINESS **Zone 6**

Scepter'd Isle – Shakespeare's description of England in *Henry V* – is a neat, short-growing rose in its native country, but will grow to nearly 6.6ft (2m) in a hot climate. The flowers are very cupped, so that they never open out fully but enclose their stamens within rose pink petals. They are paler pink on the petal backs and creamy toward the center. The flowers come in long-stemmed clusters of 3–11, held well above the leaves, and are borne almost continuously. Their myrrh scent is both powerful and delicious. The plant makes fairly upright growth, with dark green leaves and some prickles.

'Scharlachglut'

syn. 'Scarlet Fire'

Shrub Rose

ORIGIN **Kordes, Germany, 1952**
PARENTAGE **'Poinsettia' × 'Alika'**
FLOWER SIZE **4.7in (12cm)**
SCENT **Light and sweet**
FLOWERING **Once only**
HEIGHT/SPREAD **9.8ft (3m)/6.6ft (2m)**
HARDINESS **Zone 4**

Twice a year this is one of the most beautiful roses in the garden – first, in midseason, when 'Scharlachglut' covers itself in large scarlet flowers, and second, later in the year, when it is decked with very large, orange, pear-shaped fruits. In between these two high points it has little to offer. 'Scharlachglut' is a cross between a Russian form of *Rosa gallica* called 'Alika' and a red Hybrid Tea. Its flowers are single, with perhaps an extra petal or two, and sometimes with a white streak working out from the center. The large stamens are very attractive. The flowers come singly or in small clusters and are freely borne. 'Scharlachglut' makes an arching shrub 8.2ft (2.5m) high or 13.1ft (4m) trained as a climber up a wall. It is hardy and healthy, with medium-dark leaves and a scattering of large prickles. It blooms only once, but that flowering lasts a long time.

Scentimental

Scentsation

'Scharlachglut'

SCHNEEFLOCKE

SCHNEEFLOCKE

syn. 'NOASCHNEE', White Flower Carpet

Ground Cover

ORIGIN **Noack, Germany, 1991**
PARENTAGE Heidetraum x Margaret Merril
FLOWER SIZE **3.9in (10cm)**
SCENT **Strong and sweet**
FLOWERING **Repeats constantly**
HEIGHT/SPREAD **2.7ft (80cm)/4.1ft (1.25m)**
HARDINESS **Zone 5**
AWARDS **ADR 1991; RNRS GM 1991; Golden Rose of the Hague 1995**

The German house of Noack has promoted some of its groundcover roses outside Germany as the Flower Carpet series. Schneeflocke is widely known as White Flower Carpet, and many would say that it is the best of the series. Its semidouble flowers are large and pure, brilliant white, with a circle of yellow stamens and a light ruffle to the outer petals when they open out. They come in clusters of 3–15, make an enormous impact when a plant is in full flower, and last a long time. They are followed by small, orange yellow hips. Schneeflocke makes a broad, compact, bushy plant, with shiny, medium-dark leaves that are very resistant to blackspot and rust. It is a very versatile rose that can be used for groundcover, mixed beds, landscaping, and containers. In Germany it blooms continuously throughout the season, with surges of flowers appearing right through until late autumn.

S

SCHNEEKÖNIGIN

syn. 'TANIGINO', Magic Blanket, Neige d'Eté

Shrub Rose

ORIGIN **Tantau, Germany, 1992**
FLOWER SIZE **2in (5cm)**
SCENT **Light and musky**
FLOWERING **Continuous**
HEIGHT/SPREAD **2.7ft (80cm)/4.9ft (1.5m)**
HARDINESS **Zone 6**
AWARDS **ADR 1995**

Many evergreen groundcover roses were bred from *Rosa wichurana* in the 1990s; Schneekönigin is one of the best and won the prestigious German ADR award. Its flowers open from pale buff buds and are creamy white at first, before fading to pure white. They are semidouble, with a handsome boss of pale yellow stamens at the center. They come in long clusters that open their flowers over a lengthy period, so that the surface of the shrub seems always to be in bloom. The plant has a lax habit of growth and small, dark, healthy leaves. Like all groundcover roses, Schneekönigin is excellent, too, for landscape planting and as a shrub for mixed borders in private gardens. It flowers right through until late autumn.

SCHNEEKÖNIGIN

'SCHNEEKOPPE'

syn. 'SNOW PAVEMENT'

Rugosa Hybrid

ORIGIN **Baum, Germany, 1984**
FLOWER SIZE **2.8in (7cm)**
SCENT **Strong and sweet**
FLOWERING **Repeats well**
HEIGHT/SPREAD **3.3ft (1m)/3.3ft (1m)**
HARDINESS **Zone 4**

This outstanding Rugosa hybrid is a useful and popular rose. The flowers of 'Schneekoppe' are lightly double, with long, papery petals and pretty yellow stamens. They are white with a hint of pink or lilac within, and are followed by fine, vermilion, tomato-shaped hips. Actually, the plant goes on producing flowers right through until the first frost, so that the later flowers appear alongside the first hips. The flowers (and hips) come in small clusters and are well set off by the wrinkled, pale green leaves. 'Schneekoppe' grows laxly and is usually wider than it is tall. Both its hardiness and tolerance of poor soils make 'Schneekoppe' especially suitable for landscaping, hedging, and groundcover, but the beauty of its flowers entitles it to a place in the garden.

'SCHNEEKOPPE'

SCHNEESTURM

SCHNEESTURM

syn. 'TANMURSE', Blenheim

Ground Cover

ORIGIN **Tantau, Germany, 1990**
FLOWER SIZE **1.6in (4cm)**
SCENT **Medium and sweet**
FLOWERING **Almost continuous**
HEIGHT/SPREAD **3.3ft (1m)/4.1ft (1.25m)**
HARDINESS **Zone 5**
AWARDS **RNRS PIT 1992; ADR 1993**

This handsome groundcover rose won top prizes in Germany as Schneesturm and in Britain as Blenheim. The flowers are double and creamy white – white at the edges and cream toward the center, where the yellow stamens glow. They come in large clusters, typically of 10–20 flowers but sometimes more. Schneesturm has small, tough, dark, glossy leaves, indicating *Rosa wichurana* somewhere in its ancestry, and quite a lot of prickles. The plant has a loose habit of growth, with lax stems that tend to become more procumbent as they develop and fill out. It is hardy, healthy, and very adaptable – useful for lighting up a shady corner but good for everything from container planting to landscaping.

SCHNEEWALZER 87

syn. 'TANREZLAW', Snow Waltz

Modern Climber

ORIGIN **Tantau, Germany, 1987**
FLOWER SIZE **5.5in (14cm)**
SCENT **Medium and sweet**
FLOWERING **Repeats**
HEIGHT/SPREAD **13.1ft (4m)/6.6ft (2m)**
HARDINESS **Zone 6**

This fine modern climbing rose is popular in both western Europe and Scandinavia. Schneewalzer 87 has large flowers of Hybrid Tea shape. They are palest lemon, with a mother-of-pearl center at first, before fading to pure white. They are usually borne singly on long stems, but sometimes come in twos or threes. They are not carried too stiffly, but instead bend slightly sideways, which means that their flowers may be seen even though the plant climbs to 13.1ft (4m) or more. The plant has dark, healthy leaves and a vigorous, branching habit of growth. Its many-petaled flowers are borne almost continuously. They spoil in rain, so Schneewalzer 87 should to be grown more widely in warm, dry climates, where it will thrive.

SCHNEEWALZER 87

'SCHNEEWITTCHEN'

'SCHNEEWITTCHEN'

Polyantha

ORIGIN **Lambert, Germany, 1901**
PARENTAGE **'Aglaia' × ('Pâquerette' × 'Souvenir de Mme. Levet')**
FLOWER SIZE **2.8in (7cm)**
SCENT **Medium and musky**
FLOWERING **Continuous**
HEIGHT/SPREAD **4.9ft (1.5m)/2.7ft (80cm)**
HARDINESS **Zone 5**

This 'Schneewittchen' is the "original" one, a Polyantha introduced by Peter Lambert in 1901. Once almost extinct, it is now fairly widely available again. The flowers open cream colored at first, with a hint of pink, but quickly fade to pure white. They have bright yellow stamens, but, by the time the flowers have opened out enough to show them, the stamens have turned to brown. The double flowers come in clusters of 5–25 on a very free flowering, compact, small bush. The leaves are dark green and the stems have few prickles, sometimes none. 'Schneewittchen' is an excellent subject for the front of a border, where it combines with everything and flowers ceaselessly through until late autumn.

'SCHNEEZWERG'

Rugosa Hybrid

ORIGIN **Lambert, Germany, 1912**
PARENTAGE ***Rosa rugosa* seedling**
FLOWER SIZE **2.8in (7cm)**
SCENT **Strong, sweet, and spicy**
FLOWERING **Repeats well**
HEIGHT/SPREAD **5.7ft (1.75m)/4.1ft (1.25m)**
HARDINESS **Zone 4**

It would be impossible to improve upon 'Schneezwerg' as an all-round garden shrub: it flowers continuously; it is very hardy and healthy; it has vermilion hips that appear quite early on and remain on the plant until winter; it offers splendid pale yellow leaf color in autumn; and it is easy to grow. The flowers are semidouble and luminous white (especially in the evening), with a neatly cupped arrangement of petals around a circle of deep yellow stamens. They come in small clusters (typically of 3–4 flowers) and stand up well to rain. The leaves are pleated in the Rugosa manner, pale green, and glossy on their upper sides. 'Schneezwerg' has a neater, denser habit of growth than most Rugosa roses, and its stems have a thick covering of prickles.

'SCHNEEZWERG'

'SCHOENER'S NUTKANA'

Shrub Rose

ORIGIN **Schoener, US, 1930**
PARENTAGE ***Rosa nutkana* × 'Paul Neyron'**
FLOWER SIZE **3.1in (8cm)**
SCENT **Light**
FLOWERING **Once only, midseason**
HEIGHT/SPREAD **4.9ft (1.5m)/4.9ft (1.5m)**
HARDINESS **Zone 5**

'SCHOENER'S NUTKANA'

This rose commemorates Father Georg Schoener, a German Catholic priest who emigrated to the US and immersed himself in experimental rose breeding. The flowers of 'Schoener's Nutkana' are single, with five petals (plus an occasional extra one or two), and have a large circle of pale stamens at the center. The petals turn back along their sides, which gives them a somewhat square appearance and a distinctive shape to the flowers, which are deep cyclamen pink. 'Schoener's Nutkana' makes a sprawling shrub with nearly thornless stems and a dense covering of small, pale green leaves. Schoener's intention was to use native American species to breed a race of roses suited to American growing conditions.

'SCHNEEWITTCHEN'

syn. 'FÉE DES NEIGES', 'ICEBERG'

Floribunda

ORIGIN **Kordes, Germany, 1958**
PARENTAGE **'Robin Hood' × 'Virgo'**
FLOWER SIZE **2.8in (7cm)**
SCENT **Light, sweet, and attractive**
FLOWERING **Continuous**
HEIGHT/SPREAD **4.9ft (1.5m)/3.3ft (1m)**
HARDINESS **Zone 5**
AWARDS **Baden-Baden GM 1958; NRS GM 1958; World's Favourite Rose 1983**

'Schneewittchen' is the world's most popular and widely grown rose – and one of the most beautiful. In Britain, Australia, and the US it is known as 'Iceberg', which is a better name, because Peter Lambert's Polyantha 'Schneewittchen' is still grown. Kordes's 'Schneewittchen' is classified as a Floribunda, but is actually the result of crossing a Hybrid Musk with a Hybrid Tea. It is exceptionally hardy and floriferous, flowering for 12 months of the year in hot climates. The buds are long, sometimes greenish or pink, and open into lightly double, pure white flowers, with just a hint of pink at first in cool weather. The flowers are very long lasting, both in the garden and when cut, with stamens that keep their yellow color for many days. They are very prolifically borne in open clusters of 3–15, and drop their petals cleanly when spent. The plant is bushy and vigorous, with distinctive pale green stems, a scattering of prickles and pale, shiny, thin leaves. It will grow to 6.6ft (2m) in a hot climate but is usually pruned to half that height. Blackspot is a problem in wet weather, but 'Schneewittchen' is regarded as one of the healthiest of all roses in dry climates like that of Australia. It is widely used as hedging, in massed bedding, and in specimen plantings.

Sports of 'Schneewittchen'

BRILLIANT PINK ICEBERG

syn. 'PROBRIL'
ORIGIN **Weatherley, Australia, 1999**

'CLIMBING ICEBERG'

Climbing Floribunda
ORIGIN **Cants, Britain, 1968**
FLOWER SIZE **3.1in (8cm)**
HEIGHT/SPREAD **13.1ft (4m)/6.6ft (2m)**

'SCHNEEWITTCHEN'

BRILLIANT PINK ICEBERG

'CLIMBING ICEBERG'

S

'SCHOOLGIRL'

'SCHOOLGIRL'

Modern Climber

ORIGIN **McGredy, Northern Ireland, 1964**
PARENTAGE **'Coral Dawn' x 'Belle Blonde'**
FLOWER SIZE **4.7in (12cm)**
SCENT **Strong and sweet**
FLOWERING **Repeats**
HEIGHT/SPREAD **11.5ft (3.5m)/6.6ft (2m)**
HARDINESS **Zone 6**

The color of 'Schoolgirl' is unusual among large-flowered climbers, and very attractive. The outer petals are pink, with peachy petal backs, while the inner petals are pale coral, with dark apricot reverses. The long Hybrid Tea-style buds open out as full and shapely flowers with a crown of red filaments at the center. At all stages, even when they fade to salmon pink, the flowers are attractively shaped and charmingly colored. They are large, lightly double, richly scented, and usually carried singly like Hybrid Teas. The plant itself is less attractive, however: the prickles are large and plentiful; the dark green, glossy foliage is prone to blackspot; the stems are apt to become bare and leggy at the base; and, although it is strongly recurrent, 'Schoolgirl' is not the most productive of modern climbers.

S

SCHWARZE MADONNA

syn. 'KORSCHWAMA', Barry Fearn
Hybrid Tea

ORIGIN **Kordes, Germany, 1992**
FLOWER SIZE **4.3in (11cm)**
SCENT **Light and sweet**
FLOWERING **Repeats**
HEIGHT/SPREAD **4.9ft (1.5m)/4.1ft (1.25m)**
HARDINESS **Zone 6**

This vigorous Hybrid Tea is probably the darkest crimson rose to be introduced in modern times. Unfortunately, Schwarze Madonna does not have a scent to match. In all other respects, however, it is an excellent rose. The flowers are large, many-petaled, and very dark crimson, with black velvety patches, especially on the outer petals. They keep their color well – indeed, the flowers last a long time both on the bush and when cut for the house. They come on long stems and are usually borne singly. Schwarze Madonna is a vigorous, tall bush with dark, healthy, shiny leaves that are a good foil for the flowers. It has a good branching habit,

SCHWARZE MADONNA

which means that it becomes quite a broad mass of long stems, each of them bearing a sumptuous flower.

'SCORCHER'

Modern Climber

ORIGIN **Clark, Australia, 1922**
PARENTAGE **'Mme. Abel Chatenay' x unknown**
FLOWER SIZE **3.5in (9cm)**
SCENT **Light**
FLOWERING **Occasionally remontant**
HEIGHT/SPREAD **11.5ft (3.5m)/8.2ft (2.5m)**
HARDINESS **Zone 6**

'Scorcher' is a brilliant deep scarlet climber: its vibrant color was quite unlike any other rose when it was first introduced. The flowers are barely semidouble, and are borne usually singly but sometimes in small clusters – and always most profusely – somewhat early in the season. The petals are large, loose, and wavy, with white bases and occasional white streaks. The small, glossy leaves indicate *Rosa wichurana* in its ancestry. New growth is orange red at first. The long, prickly stems are rather bare and respond well to being tied down, so that they flower all along their length.

'SCORCHER'

'SEA FOAM'

'SEA FOAM'

Shrub Rose

ORIGIN **Schwartz, US, 1964**
PARENTAGE **('White Dawn' x 'Pinocchio') self-pollinated seedling**
FLOWER SIZE **2in (5cm)**
SCENT **Light and musky**
FLOWERING **Repeats constantly**
HEIGHT/SPREAD **3.3ft (1m)/6.6ft (2m)**
HARDINESS **Zone 5**
AWARDS **Rome GM 1963**

There has always been some controversy about how to categorize 'Sea Foam'. It is probably best thought of as a shrub that can be trained as a groundcover or a short climber. The flowers are white, with a pink and pearly tinge at the center that fades quickly. They have an old-fashioned shape and are very full of soft petals. The flowers therefore fare best in dry weather, though they are larger in cool, wet climates. The plant is late to start into bloom but then continues through until late autumn. 'Sea Foam' has long, lax stems that will trail for about 3.3ft (1m) in cool areas but climb to 9.8ft (3m) in a hot climate. It makes a good weeping standard. The plant has a lot of prickles and small, dark green, healthy leaves. It comes easily and quickly from cuttings. An excellent rose, deservedly popular.

'SEA PEARL'

Floribunda

ORIGIN **Dickson, Northern Ireland, 1964**
PARENTAGE **'Kordes' Perfecta' x 'Montezuma'**
FLOWER SIZE **3.5in (9cm)**
SCENT **Light and fetid**
FLOWERING **Repeats well**
HEIGHT/SPREAD **4.9ft (1.5m)/3.3ft (1m)**
HARDINESS **Zone 6**

The pink buds of 'Sea Pearl' open pale salmon, with a pale yellow flush at the base of the petals and pale yellow petal backs. They have long petals and a long pointed shape, like a Hybrid Tea. The flowers open out semidouble, though in dull weather they tend to keep a more closed, cupped shape. They also darken very considerably, so that they end up deep pink, almost crimson. The flowers

'SEA PEARL'

come in slender, elegant, open clusters of 3–15 on strong, upright stems. 'Sea Pearl' has an upright habit of growth: it is not very bushy, but its slender stems are very prickly. The leaves are medium-dark (crimson when young), leathery, and not especially glossy. They may get a touch of blackspot late in the year.

'SEAGULL'

Wichurana Rambler

ORIGIN **Pritchard, Britain, 1907**
FLOWER SIZE **1.2in (3cm)**
SCENT **Strong and musky**
FLOWERING **Once, early in season**
HEIGHT/SPREAD **13.1ft (4m)/9.8ft (3m)**
HARDINESS **Zone 5**

One of the most floriferous of all climbers, a plant of 'Seagull' in the middle of its display is a billowing mass of white, scented, lightly semidouble flowers. Its origins are unknown, but it is very much a Multiflora rambler and close to 'Rambling Rector'. Indeed, the two are sometimes mixed up by nurseries. The flowers of 'Seagull' come in large, upright panicles, typically of 30–50 flowers, and have bright golden stamens at the center, though they do turn to brown fairly early on. They are followed by small red hips. 'Seagull' has large pale leaves, big thorns, and vigorous, thick stems. It is a particularly good rambler for tumbling out of a small tree, like an apple or an olive. There are records of it growing as much as 26.2ft (8m) high.

'SEAGULL'

'SEASHELL'

'SEASHELL'

Hybrid Tea

ORIGIN **Kordes, Germany, 1976**
PARENTAGE **seedling x 'Königin der Rosen'**
FLOWER SIZE **4.3in (11cm)**
SCENT **Light and fruity**
FLOWERING **Repeats**
HEIGHT/SPREAD **4.1ft (1.25m)/3.3ft (1m)**
HARDINESS **Zone 6**
AWARDS **AARS 1976**

The flowers of 'Seashell' are full of petals, and they open out almost flat: sometimes you can see the carpels at the center. The flowers are orange when they first open, then take on a pink tinge, passing through bright salmon to pale apricot pink – but attractive at all stages. They are usually borne singly and last a long time, both in the garden and when cut for the house. 'Seashell' has large, healthy, medium-dark leaves and an upright habit of growth. It is fairly vigorous, but you may have to wait a while for the next flush of flowers. The plant responds well to good cultivation.

SEBASTIAN KNEIPP

syn. 'KORPASTATO', Fragrant Memories
Shrub Rose

ORIGIN **Kordes, Germany, 1995**
FLOWER SIZE **3.9in (10cm)**
SCENT **Medium and sweet**
FLOWERING **Repeats well**
HEIGHT/SPREAD **4.9ft (1.5m)/4.1ft (1.25m)**
HARDINESS **Zone 6**

SEBASTIAN KNEIPP

SECRET

Sebastian Kneipp has lightly cupped flowers, with a mass of small petals in a muddled but pretty arrangement. The flowers are mother-of-pearl at first, but turn to white, while usually keeping a hint of pearl at the center. They come singly or, more usually, in clusters of up to seven, well set off by dark green leaves. The bush is vigorous, healthy, floriferous, and fairly prickly. It grows to 6.6ft (2m) in hot climates.

SECRET

syn. 'HILAROMA'
Hybrid Tea

ORIGIN **Tracy, US, 1992**
PARENTAGE **Pristine x Friendship**
FLOWER SIZE **4.3in (11cm)**
SCENT **Strong and fruity**
FLOWERING **Repeats well**
HEIGHT/SPREAD **4.1ft (1.25m)/3.3ft (1m)**
HARDINESS **Zone 6**
AWARDS **AARS 1994; Portland GM 1998**

This beautiful pink and white Hybrid Tea has white petals with pink-dipped tips. Secret is prettiest when the bud starts to open and the petals swirl out from the center. The flowers are still pretty when they reflex further, but have a rather muddled arrangement of petals when fully open. They are borne usually singly on long, strong stems. The leaves are large, healthy, dark, and fairly glossy, and carried on a prickly, gawky bush.

SELFRIDGES

see BEROLINA

SENATOR BURDA

see VICTOR HUGO

SENTEUR ROYALE

see DUFTRAUSCH

ROSA SERICEA 'PTERACANTHA'

Wild Rose

FLOWER SIZE **2in (5cm)**
SCENT **Little or none**
FLOWERING **Once, early in season**
HEIGHT/SPREAD **9.8ft (3m)/8.2ft (2.5m)**
HARDINESS **Zone 6**

Rosa sericea 'Pteracantha' is the only rose that is grown principally for the beauty of its prickles. These are large, flat, broad at the base, and brilliant blood red in color when young. The plant is best placed so that the sun shines through the prickles and illuminates them, preferably during the early morning or late afternoon. They can be as much as 1.6in (4cm) long at the base. The flowers are four-petaled, cream colored or white, and carried singly or in small clusters. In cool climates it is often the first of all roses to flower. 'Pteracantha' has small, healthy, ferny, gray -green leaves. It tolerates poor soils but gives of its best when pruned in winter, then fed and watered to encourage lush growth. The prickles turn to gray as the stems harden toward the end of the season.

ROSA SERRATIPETALA

see 'CRAMOISI SUPÉRIEUR'

ROSA SETIGERA

Wild Rose

FLOWER SIZE **6cm (2.4in)**
SCENT **Medium and musky**
FLOWERING **Once only, fairly late in season**
HEIGHT/SPREAD **16.4ft (5m)/9.8ft (3m)**
HARDINESS **Zone 4**

The great value of *Rosa setigera* is its hardiness and adaptability. It is native to most of North America – from freezing Ontario to steamy Florida – and is by far the hardiest of all the wild climbing roses. Few Americans esteem it as a garden plant: for most, it is a curiosity, not a rose for beautiful gardens. In fact, the flowers are a handsome bright pink, a very striking color, fading to pale pink or nearly white. They come in loose clusters of 5–15 and are followed by round, bristly, vermilion hips (0.4in/1cm across). *Rosa setigera* has large, rough, bramblelike leaves, usually with only three leaflets. Its autumn leaf color is among the best of all roses. The plant makes a loose, spreading shrub, with slender, flexible stems that extend rapidly, building a freestanding shrub (6.6ft/2m high and 16.4ft/5m across), or climbing higher up into trees. It flowers very late and for a long period, filling the space between the first and second bloomings of most remontant roses. It was widely used in the 19th century to breed hardy rambling roses.

ROSA SERICEA 'PTERACANTHA'

ROSA SETIGERA

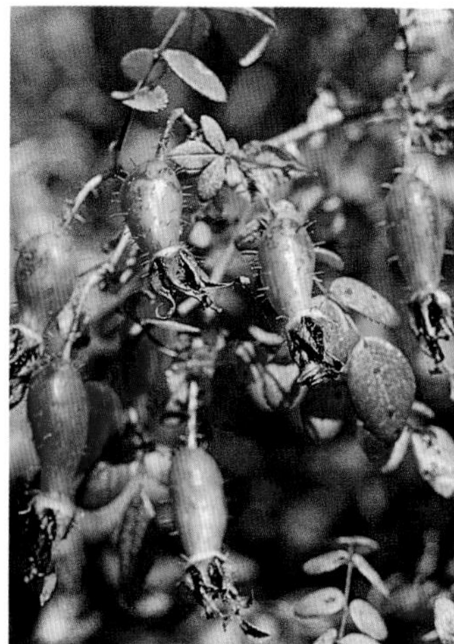
ROSA SETIPODA

SEXY REXY

ROSA SETIPODA

Wild Rose

FLOWER SIZE **1.6in (4cm)**
SCENT **Light and fruity**
FLOWERING **Once only**
HEIGHT/SPREAD **9.8ft (3m)/6.6ft (2m)**
HARDINESS **Zone 5**

The main reason for growing *Rosa setipoda* is its large, red, flagon-shaped hips. They are extremely handsome and last long enough to be a striking feature in the garden. They weigh the branches down and shine in the late summer sun. Sometimes they are as long as 2.4in (6cm). The flowers are attractive, if short-lived: they are dark purple pink, grading to pure white at the center, with pale yellow stamens and large bracts below the sepals. They come in clusters of about 20 flowers. The plant is a gawky grower, with a lot of thorns and long, healthy leaves. It makes a good specimen plant in any garden and is very impressive planted in masses in a large woodland setting. It comes from China and was first introduced to the West in 1901.

S

'SEVEN SISTERS'

see 'GREVILLEI'

SEXY REXY

syn. 'MACREXY', Heckenzauber

Floribunda

ORIGIN **McGredy, New Zealand, 1984**
PARENTAGE **Seaspray x Träumerei**
FLOWER SIZE **2.8in (7cm)**
SCENT **Light**
FLOWERING **Late in season, but repeats**
HEIGHT/SPREAD **2.5ft (75cm)/2ft (60cm)**
HARDINESS **Zone 6**
AWARDS **NZ GM 1984; Orléans GM 1988; Glasgow GM 1989; Auckland GM 1990; Portland GM 1990; James Mason GM 1996**

No one knows whether its name has been an advantage or a handicap to this beautiful Floribunda. The flowers of Sexy Rexy open nearly flat (except for a light ruffling), and lay themselves out formally like camellias. They are rose pink, with darker petal backs and paler edges to the flowers – a very pretty grading of colors and petal sizes. The flowers come in large clusters of 5–15 on strong, straight stems: Sexy Rexy is a good exhibition rose and a long-lasting cut flower. The plant has a dense, low habit and dark, healthy leaves. Its first flowering, fairly late in the season, is long and heavy but it may be slow to repeat. Deadheading helps it to rebloom more quickly and heavily. It is a good bedding rose and unusually successful in a mixed border.

'SHADOW'

Hybrid Tea

ORIGIN **Dawson, Australia, 1966**
FLOWER SIZE **3.9in (10cm)**
SCENT **Moderate**
FLOWERING **Repeats well**
HEIGHT/SPREAD **4.9ft (1.5m)/4.1ft (1.25m)**
HARDINESS **Zone 6**

This dark, velvety crimson Hybrid Tea was George Dawson's first hybrid, introduced commercially in the year he retired as a market gardener. The buds are almost black and the flowers are borne on stiff, strong stems, usually singly but occasionally in clusters of up to three. The new leaves are purple crimson, before turning to dark green. The plant is vigorous and healthy. 'Shadow' is a good exhibition rose and lasts well as a cut flower. However, it has less scent than many Hybrid Teas and is sometimes somewhat slow to repeat.

'SHADOW'

'SHAILER'S WHITE MOSS'

see 'CENTIFOLIA'

'SHALOM'

Shrub Rose

ORIGIN **Poulsen, Denmark, 1973**
PARENTAGE **'Korona' seedling**
FLOWER SIZE **3.1in (8cm)**
SCENT **Light and sweet**
FLOWERING **Repeats**
HEIGHT/SPREAD **6.6ft (2m)/4.9ft (1.5m)**
HARDINESS **Zone 6**

The flowers of 'Shalom' are vermilion colored and full of petals. The color is an unusually bright shade, which means that the plant stands out from quite a distance. They come in somewhat dense clusters of 3–10 (sometimes singly, too) and hold their color well. 'Shalom' starts into flower later than most roses but continues until the first frosts – or well into winter in hot climates. The bush is upright and vigorous, with mid-green leaves and reddish new growth. It is one of those shrub roses that most closely resembles an unusually vigorous Floribunda.

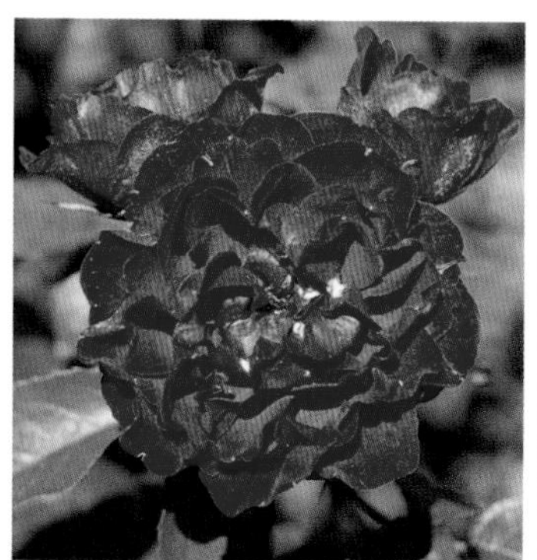
'SHALOM'

SHARIFA ASMA

syn. 'AUSREEF'

Shrub Rose

ORIGIN **Austin, Britain, 1989**
PARENTAGE **Mary Rose x Admired Miranda**
FLOWER SIZE **3.5in (9cm)**
SCENT **Strong, sweet, and musky**
FLOWERING **Repeats**
HEIGHT/SPREAD **4.1ft (1.25m)/3.3ft (1m)**
HARDINESS **Zone 6**

The popularity of Sharifa Asma rests partly on the beauty of its pale pink flowers and partly on its compact shape and manageable size. It is one of the best of David Austin's English Roses for small gardens. The flowers fade to white from their edges, turning first to blush pink and mother-of-pearl, while keeping a hint of palest yellow at the center. They are very full of petals, and somewhat cupped at first, before reflexing to form an informal rosette. They come in small, dense clusters, typically of 3–4 flowers. The scent is complex, with a hint of myrrh and damask as well as musk and sweetness. Sharifa Asma has large, healthy, mid-green, semiglossy leaves and a lot of prickles. It makes a short, sturdy, upright bush, with none of the long sprawling stems of some English Roses. The flowers come in a series of flushes, even in the hottest weather, until late autumn. Thrips may be a problem.

SHARIFA ASMA

SHEER BLISS

SHEER BLISS

syn. 'JACTRO'

Hybrid Tea

ORIGIN **Warriner, US, 1985**
PARENTAGE **'White Masterpiece' x 'Grand Masterpiece'**
FLOWER SIZE **5.5in (14cm)**
SCENT **Strong and sweet**
FLOWERING **Repeats**
HEIGHT/SPREAD **5.7ft (1.75m)/3.3ft (1m)**
HARDINESS **Zone 6**
AWARDS **Japan GM 1984; AARS 1987**

Large, pink, and sweetly scented: Sheer Bliss is a classic Hybrid Tea. Its buds are large and elegant, with long petals that slowly unfurl and reflex their edges. The flowers are full of petals and fade to white as they age, while always retaining a slight pink edge to the petals. They are usually borne singly (sometimes in small clusters) on long stems, which make them good for cutting. The size of the flowers is popular with exhibitors. Sheer Bliss makes an upright, strong-growing bush, especially in the hot climates it prefers, with mid-green, healthy leaves and large prickles. It is popular in the US, Australia, and New Zealand, but almost unknown in Europe, where it would grow well in Mediterranean countries.

SHEILA'S PERFUME

syn. 'HARSHERRY'

Floribunda

ORIGIN **Sheridan, Britain, 1982**
PARENTAGE **'Peer Gynt' x ('Daily Sketch' x ['Paddy McGredy' x 'Prima Ballerina'])**
FLOWER SIZE **3.1in (8cm)**
SCENT **Strong and sweet**
FLOWERING **Repeats**
HEIGHT/SPREAD **4.9ft (1.5m)/3.3ft (1m)**
HARDINESS **Zone 6**
AWARDS **Edland FA 1981; Glasgow FA 1989**

This rose was bred by an English amateur and named Sheila's Perfume after his wife. It is attractively colored, shapely, and strongly scented, though there is some doubt as to whether to call it a Floribunda or a Hybrid Tea. The flowers are large, long-petaled, and elegant, basically buff yellow with a heavy edging of bright cherry crimson. Both colors take on a more muted shade as they age, ending up white and pink. This happens most quickly in hot weather: Sheila's Perfume is one of those roses that produce their largest flowers and richest colors in cool climates. The flowers come singly and in clusters of up to five. The bush is upright, fairly dense, and a quick repeater. The leaves are dark and handsome, but crimson at first, and susceptible to blackspot.

SHINE ON

SHINE ON

syn. 'DICTALENT'

Patio Rose

ORIGIN **Dickson, Northern Ireland, 1994**
PARENTAGE **Sweet Magic seedling**
FLOWER SIZE **2.8in (7cm)**
SCENT **Light**
FLOWERING **Repeats well**
HEIGHT/SPREAD **2.3ft (70cm)/1.6ft (50cm)**
HARDINESS **Zone 6**

Shine On is a cheerful, compact patio rose. The flowers are bright vermilion at first, with somewhat more yellow on the petal backs. However, the yellow tints fade away as the flowers age, and they end up pink all over. They are full of short, neat, reflexed petals and come in clusters of 5–15 flowers. The plant is very floriferous and repeats quickly. It has small, dark, glossy leaves, a scattering of prickles, and a compact habit of growth. It is an excellent rose for containers, rarely out of flower.

SHINING HOPE

see OUR LADY OF GUADALUPE

SHINING HOUR

syn. 'JACYEF'

Grandiflora

ORIGIN **Warriner, US, 1989**
PARENTAGE **Sunbright x Sun Flare**
FLOWER SIZE **4.3in (11cm)**
SCENT **Medium, sweet, and fruity**
FLOWERING **Repeats**
HEIGHT/SPREAD **4.1ft (1.25m)/3.3ft (1m)**
HARDINESS **Zone 6**
AWARDS **AARS 1991**

SHEILA'S PERFUME

SHINING HOUR

In Shining Hour we have a deep lemon yellow Grandiflora (of the Hybrid Tea type) that holds its color well, fading only when the flowers are fully open. The buds are small, but the flowers swell and grow as they open, and have large petals that are tiered up like the layers of a ruff when fully expanded. They come both singly and in small clusters (typically of 4–5 flowers) on an upright bush with long stems and prickles. The plant has healthy, glossy, dusky green leaves and purple new growth.

SHOCKING BLUE

syn. 'KORBLUE'

Floribunda

ORIGIN **Kordes, Germany, 1974**
PARENTAGE **seedling x 'Silver Star'**
FLOWER SIZE **3.9in (10cm)**
SCENT **Strong and sweet, with a hint of lemon**
FLOWERING **Repeats well**
HEIGHT/SPREAD **3.3ft (1m)/2.5ft (75cm)**
HARDINESS **Zone 6**

This is a very good rose with an unusual color, but Shocking Blue does not really live up to its name. The flowers are fuchsia pink with magenta petal backs: the shades reflected in the shadows between the ruffled petals are dark lilac and purple. The flowers are large and shaped like those of a Hybrid Tea, but borne in clusters of 3–9. Its long stems make it excellent for cutting and flower arranging: it is also grown commercially as a cut flower. Its narrow habit of growth also commends it to florists. Shocking Blue is intensely fragrant. Its leaves are dark, glossy, tough, and healthy. The bush grows quickly and responds well to pruning by producing new flowers all the more quickly. The best flowers, for size and color, come in cool conditions.

SHOCKING BLUE

'Shot Silk'

Hybrid Tea

ORIGIN **Dickson, Northern Ireland, 1924**
PARENTAGE **'Hugh Dickson' seedling x 'Sunstar'**
FLOWER SIZE **4.3in (11cm)**
SCENT **Strong and sweet**
FLOWERING **Repeats**
HEIGHT/SPREAD **4.1ft (1.25m)/3.3ft (1m)**
HARDINESS **Zone 6**
AWARDS **NRS GM 1923**

When it was first issued, 'Shot Silk' was popular because it was one of the first "Pernetiana" Hybrid Teas (i.e. those with yellow or orange in their coloring) that was also strongly scented. The flowers are true Hybrid Teas, with long, elegant buds borne singly or in small clusters (of up to four flowers) on strong, upright stems. However, the inner petals are few and short, so that the open flower is decidedly inelegant, and the individual flowers do not last long. The color of 'Shot Silk' is very variable – basically bright cherry red, flushed with salmon and orange, but sometimes more orange or yellow than red, and always more pink as the flowers fade. The best colors come in dull weather and cool climates (the flowers stand up very well to rain) and fade quickly in sunny weather and hot climates. The plant has good, medium-dark leaves but very few prickles. 'Shot Silk' is fairly healthy, and its natural vigor throws off fungal disease, though it grows measurably better if well fed and watered. The plant repeats constantly until late autumn.

The beautiful climbing sport, **'Climbing Shot Silk'**, is more popular now than the bush form. It flowers very prolifically early in the season and then intermittently. An established plant is rarely without flowers until late autumn.

Sport of 'Shot Silk'

'Climbing Shot Silk'

Climbing Hybrid Tea
ORIGIN **Knight, Britain, 1931**
FLOWERING **Repeats a little after the first spectacular flowering**
HEIGHT/SPREAD **13.1ft (4m)/8.2ft (2.5m)**

'SHOT SILK' *(in cool weather)*

'CLIMBING SHOT SILK' *(in hot weather)*

SIESTA

Showbiz

see INGRID WEIBULL

Shreveport

syn. 'KORpesh'
Grandiflora

ORIGIN **Kordes, Germany, 1981**
PARENTAGE **'Zorina' x 'Uwe Seeler'**
FLOWER SIZE **4.7in (12cm)**
SCENT **Medium and fruity**
FLOWERING **Repeats well**
HEIGHT/SPREAD **4.9ft (1.5m)/4.1ft (1.25m)**
HARDINESS **Zone 6**
AWARDS **AARS 1982**

Shreveport is the city in Louisiana where the American Rose Society has its headquarters. However, the Shreveport rose is German, the brainchild of the house of Kordes. It is a tall, vigorous Grandiflora of the Hybrid Tea type, with large, shapely flowers borne singly or in clusters of up to four. They are a cheerful mixture of orange and coral pink, slightly paler on the petal backs, and hold their color well. The flowers, on long stems, are good enough for exhibition. The plant is very upright in habit, vigorous, and well branched, with small prickles and large, healthy leaves.

'Shropshire Lass'

Shrub Rose

ORIGIN **Austin, Britain, 1968**
PARENTAGE **'Mme. Butterfly' x 'Mme. Legras de St Germain'**
FLOWER SIZE **3.9in (10cm)**
SCENT **Medium and sweet**
FLOWERING **Once only**
HEIGHT/SPREAD **6.6ft (2m)/5.7ft (1.75m)**
HARDINESS **Zone 5**

This was one of David Austin's earliest shrub roses, and, although it would probably not be introduced if it were bred today, 'Shropshire Lass' is still very popular. It flowers only once, but most abundantly, and there is a wonderful grace to a mature bush covered by the luminous pearl pink flowers. Each flower has a large boss of golden stamens at the center and fades eventually to white. As it is once-flowering, there is no need to deadhead the flowers: besides, handsome large orange hips follow in autumn. The plant has thin, wild looking leaves and quite a lot of small prickles on its slender stems. It is a thrifty grower, reaching 13.1ft (4m) in hot climates, and very hardy.

Siesta

syn. 'MEIcascal'
Shrub Rose

ORIGIN **Meilland, France, 2001**
FLOWER SIZE **1.6in (4cm)**
SCENT **Light and musky**
FLOWERING **Continuous**
HEIGHT/SPREAD **2.5ft (75cm)/2.5ft (75cm)**
HARDINESS **Zone 6**

Siesta is one of a new style of shrubby landscaping roses that also look good in a garden. Meilland calls them "*farniente*" roses, which indicates that they need no maintenance. The flowers of Siesta are single (five petals), pale crimson or dark pink, with a cheerful white eye. They come in big, spacious clusters of 15–40. The glossy, mid-green leaves are very healthy – health and hardiness being two of the most important criteria when breeding a "no trouble" rose like this. Siesta has proved very popular in the short time since its introduction.

Signature

syn. 'JACnor'
Hybrid Tea

ORIGIN **Warriner, US, 1996**
PARENTAGE **Honor x 'First Federal's Renaissance'**
FLOWER SIZE **4.7in (12cm)**
SCENT **Medium and sweet**
FLOWERING **Repeats well**
HEIGHT/SPREAD **4.9ft (1.5m)/3.3ft (1m)**
HARDINESS **Zone 6**

Signature is a very elegant, deep pink Hybrid Tea; a good exhibition rose with a luminous quality that makes it stand out in the garden, too. The flowers are deep pink, with cream toward the base of the petals. The buds unfurl slowly in a perfect cone of thick, strong petals, just slightly rolled back at their edges; in cool weather the creamy undersides provide an especially handsome contrast. The flowers are borne singly on long, sturdy stems and repeat quickly. The plant has many prickles and large, dark green, glossy leaves that may need to be treated to prevent blackspot and mildew. Signature grows quickly and vigorously: left unpruned it will reach 6.6ft (2m).

SHREVEPORT

'SHROPSHIRE LASS'

SIGNATURE

'Signora Piero Puricelli'

syn. 'Signora'

Hybrid Tea

ORIGIN **Aicardi, Italy, 1936**
PARENTAGE **'Julien Potin' x 'Sensation'**
FLOWER SIZE **4.7in (12cm)**
SCENT **Strong and fruity**
FLOWERING **Repeats well**
HEIGHT/SPREAD **4.9ft (1.5m)/4.1ft (1.25m)**
HARDINESS **Zone 6**
AWARDS **Portland GM 1937**

The name of 'Signora Piero Puricelli' was shortened to 'Signora' outside Italy, and ensured that this stupendous rose remained a favorite both for cutting and for bedding for over 20 years. The flowers are a wonderful combination of orange, yellow, and pink – basically orange, with yellow petal backs and dark pink tips to the outer petals. But the colors run into each other to produce an immensely variable mix of apricot, peach, coral, gold, and salmon pink. The strongly scented flowers come abundantly, but usually singly, on stout, straight stems. They are unusually good in hot weather, while also standing up well to rain. The plant has large, glossy leaves that may be susceptible to blackspot in cool conditions. Domenico Aicardi, the breeder, lived at Poggio di Sanremo on the Italian Riviera and in the 1930s bred roses for the Mediterranean climate.

'Signora Piero Puricelli'

'Ambossfunken'

'Ambossfunken' is a popular sport with irregular yellow stripes radiating from the center of the petals.

Sport of 'Signora Piero Puricelli'

'Ambossfunken'

syn. 'Anvil Sparks'

Hybrid Tea

ORIGIN **Meyer, South Africa, 1961**

Silver Anniversary

see Karen Blixen

'Silver Jubilee'

Hybrid Tea

ORIGIN **Cocker, Britain, 1978**
PARENTAGE **(['Highlight' x 'Königin der Rosen'] x ['Parkdirektor Riggers' x 'Piccadilly']) x 'Mischief'**
FLOWER SIZE **4.7in (12cm)**
SCENT **Light, but sweet**
FLOWERING **Repeats well**
HEIGHT/SPREAD **4.1ft (1.25m)/3.3ft (1m)**
HARDINESS **Zone 6**
AWARDS **RNRS PIT 1977; Belfast GM 1980; Portland GM 1981; James Mason GM 1985**

Although 'Silver Jubilee' was for many years the most popular Hybrid Tea in Britain – its flowers are very rain resistant – it has made comparatively little impression on rose gardeners in other countries. The flowers are a beautiful confection of apricot and pink. The outer petals are pale pink, the inner ones dark pink, and the ones in between tend to be apricot. The petal backs are darker, which creates beautiful shadows between the petals. The flowers are also perfectly shaped, opening out only slowly from broad, peaked buds. They come singly or in clusters of up to five, and are excellent cut roses. The plant is compact and prickly, with fine, dense, dark bronzy green leaves that are disease-free except for a little blackspot. The name of the rose commemorates the Silver Jubilee (25th anniversary) of the accession to the throne by Queen Elizabeth II of England.

'Silver Jubilee'

'Silver Moon'

Wichurana Rambler

ORIGIN **Van Fleet, US, 1910**
PARENTAGE **(*Rosa wichurana* x 'Devoniensis') x unknown**
FLOWER SIZE **3.9in (10cm)**
SCENT **Strong and musky**
FLOWERING **Once, midseason or slightly later**
HEIGHT/SPREAD **16.4ft (5m)/9.8ft (3m)**
HARDINESS **Zone 7**

'Silver Moon'

It was long believed that Walter Van Fleet used *Rosa laevigata*, the Cherokee rose of Georgia, as one of the parents of 'Silver Moon', but modern DNA analysis has shown that it played no part in the breeding of this rose. Nevertheless, 'Silver Moon' quickly became the most popular climbing rose in warm regions of the US, more popular even than 'American Pillar'. Its unopened buds are creamy yellow, but the flowers are silvery white, very large, almost single (just a few extra petals), and lightly cupped, with large, golden yellow stamens at the center. They come in clusters of 3–10. The leaves are bronzy green at first, then a good, dark, glossy green, and are almost evergreen. The plant is very healthy and resistant to disease, and it grows with exceptional vigor. It is not a rose for small gardens, unless it scrambles up a tall, slender evergreen, such as a cypress. Although hardy in mild climates, it needs a hot summer to flower well.

Simba

see Helmut Schmidt

'Simon Fraser'

Shrub Rose

ORIGIN **Ogilvie, Canada, 1992**
PARENTAGE **(Bonanza x ['Arthur Bell' x ('Red Dawn' x 'Suzanne')]) x (seedling x [('Red Dawn' x 'Suzanne') x 'Champlain'])**
FLOWER SIZE **2in (5cm)**
SCENT **Light and musky**
FLOWERING **Repeats**
HEIGHT/SPREAD **2.5ft (75cm)/3.3ft (1m)**
HARDINESS **Zone 4**

Hardiness and charm it may have in abundance, but 'Simon Fraser' can also bring mildew and blackspot. This weakness is very unusual among the Explorer roses, but take precautions against disease and you will be richly rewarded. The flowers are bright pink, with a fine white patch at the center, and a small patch of stamens. They are usually semidouble, but not always: sometimes they will also be fully double, and sometimes nearly single. The petals have a distinctive roll to their carriage, which gives a lot of character to the flower. The flowers come in clusters of 3–7 all over the surface of the low, spreading bush. 'Simon Fraser' has dark, glossy leaves and a fair covering of prickles. It is a reliable repeater that flowers more or less continuously from summer to autumn in Canada, but both earlier and later in kinder climates. Simon Fraser explored modern day British Columbia in 1805–7 and journeyed down the river that bears his name to reach the Pacific.

'Simon Fraser'

Simplicity

syn. 'JACink', Pink Simplicity

Shrub Rose

ORIGIN **Warriner, US, 1978**
PARENTAGE **'Schneewittchen' seedling**
FLOWER SIZE **2.8in (7cm)**
SCENT **Light and sweet**
FLOWERING **Almost constant**
HEIGHT/SPREAD **4.9ft (1.5m)/3.3ft (1m)**
HARDINESS **Zone 6**
AWARDS **NZ GM 1976**

This seedling of 'Schneewittchen' has been introduced all over the world (except Europe) as a healthy, fast-growing, easy to grow landscaping rose. Like its parent, Simplicity may suffer a little from blackspot, but it is extremely free flowering. In hot climates it flowers year-round. The flowers are semidouble, lightly cupped, and pink, with a tendency for the pink coloring to vary from petal to petal within each flower – an attractive feature. The flowers come in clusters of 5–15 and are very freely borne. Simplicity is vigorous and somewhat upright in its habit of growth. It is sometimes recommended as a hedging plant, but is not so suitable a choice as some of the modern landscaping roses from France and Germany, such as Pink Meidiland and Mainaufeuer.

Singin' in the Rain

see Spek's Centennial

Simplicity

'Sir Cedric Morris'

'Sir Cedric Morris'

Species Hybrid

ORIGIN **Morris, Britain, 1979**
FLOWER SIZE **1.6in (4cm)**
SCENT **Strong and musky**
FLOWERING **Once, somewhat late in season**
HEIGHT/SPREAD **26.2ft (8m)/13.1ft (4m)**
HARDINESS **Zone 6**

It is said that this enormous climbing rose was discovered by the English painter Sir Cedric Morris (1889–1982) in a batch of *Rosa glauca* seedlings. However, there is no trace of the blue-leaved shrub in this tearaway rambler, and it is much more likely to be a hybrid between *Rosa soulieana* and another Synstylae species like *Rosa mulliganii*. The creamy white single flowers come in large clusters of 20–30, which are very profusely borne. They are followed by small, round hips that last well into late autumn. 'Sir Cedric Morris' has large gray leaves with long, slender leaflets and a lot of large thorns. It is especially useful for being late flowering.

Sir Clough

syn. 'AUSclough'
Shrub Rose

ORIGIN **Austin, Britain, 1983**
PARENTAGE **'Chaucer' x 'Conrad Ferdinand Meyer'**
FLOWER SIZE **4.7in (12cm)**
SCENT **Strong, sweet, and delicious**
FLOWERING **Repeats**
HEIGHT/SPREAD **4.9ft (1.5m)/4.1ft (1.25m)**
HARDINESS **Zone 5**

This is a simple, vigorous English Rose from David Austin. The flowers of Sir Clough are only lightly double, and a very bright pink, with a white patch and beautiful golden stamens at the center. The buds are coral colored. The flowers come singly and (more frequently) in clusters of 3–7 and are followed by orange hips. Sir Clough is a lanky grower that will quickly reach 8.2ft (2.5m) in a hot climate and is everywhere a tall, arching shrub. It is best layered to maximize the number of flowers, though its ferocious prickles discourage close contact. Its mid-green leaves (bronzy when young) may pick up a little blackspot later in the year. It was named after the Welsh architect Sir Clough Williams-Ellis (1883–1978).

Sir Clough

Sir Edward Elgar

syn. 'AUSprima'
Shrub Rose

ORIGIN **Austin, Britain, 1992**
PARENTAGE **Mary Rose x 'The Squire'**
FLOWER SIZE **2.8in (7cm)**
SCENT **Light and sweet**
FLOWERING **Repeats**
HEIGHT/SPREAD **3.3ft (1m)/2ft (60cm)**
HARDINESS **Zone 6**

The beautiful, richly colored flowers of Sir Edward Elgar combine well with other plants in mixed plantings. The flowers are bright cherry pink at first, fading to dull lilac pink, with pale pink at the very edges of the petals. They are lightly cupped, with a lot of petals in a loose, muddled center. Later they reflex into a pompon. They are borne singly, or occasionally in twos and threes, and repeat well. The plant has a lot of small prickles, a good upright habit of growth, and mid-green leaves with slightly puckered leaflets. In hot countries Sir Edward Elgar will grow to 4.9ft (1.5m) high and wide. It was named after the English composer (1857–1934).

Sir Edward Elgar

'Sir Thomas Lipton'

Rugosa Hybrid

ORIGIN **Van Fleet, US, 1900**
PARENTAGE ***Rosa rugosa* 'Alba' x 'Clothilde Soupert'**
FLOWER SIZE **2.8in (7cm)**
SCENT **Strong and very sweet**
FLOWERING **Repeats**
HEIGHT/SPREAD **6.6ft (2m)/6.6ft (2m)**
HARDINESS **Zone 5**

Many consider this to be the best of the early Rugosa hybrids. The flowers of 'Sir Thomas Lipton' are pure white, semidouble to double, with a somewhat disorganized mass of thin petals and a cluster of golden stamens at the center. The flowers come in clusters of 3–7 and are carried continuously after the first prolific bloom. The plant has a lot of long prickles, bright, mid-green, wrinkly leaves, and an arching habit of growth. It is generally healthy, but may suffer from blackspot and rust in areas where these are prevalent. It is very tolerant of heat, cold, dryness, and damp. Sir Thomas Lipton (1850–1931) was a rich British grocer whose yacht, *Shamrock I*, challenged for the America's Cup in 1899.

'Sir Thomas Lipton'

Sir Walter Raleigh

syn. 'AUSpry'
Shrub Rose

ORIGIN **Austin, Britain, 1985**
PARENTAGE **'Lilian Austin' x 'Chaucer'**
FLOWER SIZE **3.9in (10cm)**
SCENT **Strong and sweet**
FLOWERING **Remontant**
HEIGHT/SPREAD **4.1ft (1.25m)/3.3ft (1m)**
HARDINESS **Zone 6**

Sir Walter Raleigh is not the best of David Austin's pink English Roses, but it is still widely grown. Its flowers are among the largest and come in small clusters of 3–5. They open bright gentle pink, with paler petal backs, and are lightly cupped, with a great number of loosely held incurved petals and a bunch of golden stamens at the center, reminiscent of a tree peony. The plant is prickly, with fairly ordinary leaves and a stoloniferous habit of growth. It is not a reliable repeater and is sometimes susceptible to mildew and rust. Sir Walter Raleigh (1554–1618) was an English explorer and politician.

'Sissinghurst Castle'

see 'Rose des Maures'

Sir Walter Raleigh

'SLATER'S CRIMSON'

SMARTY

SNOW GOOSE

'SKYROCKET'

see 'WILHELM'

'SLATER'S CRIMSON'

syn. 'OLD CRIMSON CHINA', 'SEMPERFLORENS'

China Rose

ORIGIN **China**
FLOWER SIZE **2.4in (6cm)**
SCENT **Strong and tealike**
FLOWERING **Continuous**
HEIGHT/SPREAD **4.1ft (1.25m)/3.3ft (1m)**
HARDINESS **Zone 6**

'Slater's Crimson' is the oldest documented garden rose in this book – and probably the oldest in cultivation. DNA analysis shows it to be one of the parents of 'Old Blush', which can be identified in Chinese paintings from the 9th century. So 'Slater's Crimson' must be even older than that. Certainly, no European rose cultivar can safely be traced back to before *c.*1400. 'Slater's Crimson' was introduced to Britain from China in the late 18th century. It is a bright dark red, with the distinctive white streaks running through the inner petals that still feature in many of its descendants, our modern roses. It opens pink, even pale pink, but darkens with age, as many Tea roses do. The flowers come singly or in small clusters (typically of three) on a dense, twiggy bush that is slow-growing at first and takes time to build up to its full size. It is susceptible to mildew, and fairly tender, but a common rose in hot climates, flowering all year-round. More than one rose is grown and sold under this name. Many are open-pollinated seedlings of the original.

SMARTY

syn. 'INTERSMART'

Ground Cover

ORIGIN **Ilsink, Netherlands, 1979**
PARENTAGE **'Yesterday' × seedling**
FLOWER SIZE **2in (5cm)**
SCENT **Light, sweet, and musky**
FLOWERING **Continuous**
HEIGHT/SPREAD **4.9ft (1.5m)/6.6ft (2m)**
HARDINESS **Zone 5**

Smarty is an excellent shrub, always in bloom until late autumn. In hot climates it will flower year-round. The flowers are palest rose pink, fading to mother-of-pearl and white. They have handsome yellow stamens and are very attractive to bees. They come in large clusters, typically of 5–25 flowers. The plant has a lot of small prickles, bright green leaves, and a good branching habit of growth. It spreads attractively, quickly becoming wider than tall. Smarty is the perfect groundcover.

SNOW CARPET

syn. 'MACCARPE'

Miniature Rose

ORIGIN **McGredy, New Zealand, 1980**
PARENTAGE **'New Penny' × 'Temple Bells'**
FLOWER SIZE **0.8in (2cm)**
SCENT **Light and musky**
FLOWERING **Repeats**
HEIGHT/SPREAD **1.3ft (40cm)/4.1ft (1.25m)**
HARDINESS **Zone 5**
AWARDS **Baden-Baden GM 1982**

Few of the so-called groundcover roses really suppress the weeds. Snow Carpet is one of the best: its dense, matted habit of growth overcomes almost all competition. The plant has a thick mass of thin, wiry stems that trail along the ground and spread naturally. Its flowers are cream colored at first, fading quickly to white, with a hint of yellow at the center where the stamens are hidden by the inner petals. In their first flowering, the flowers seem to cover the surface of the plant. The leaves are healthy, minute, dark, glossy, and neat. The ultimate size of Snow Carpet depends on the climate. It is taller in hot climates and ventures further along the ground. It also makes a good weeping standard.

SNOW GOOSE

syn. 'AUSPOM'

Shrub Rose

ORIGIN **Austin, Britain, 1996**
FLOWER SIZE **1.6in (4cm)**
SCENT **Light and musky**
FLOWERING **Repeats well**
HEIGHT/SPREAD **8.2ft (2.5m)/4.9ft (1.5m)**
HARDINESS **Zone 6**

The origins of this pretty climber are not yet known, but it bears a close resemblance to Francine Austin, which is a hybrid of the old Noisette rose 'Alister Stella Gray'. Snow Goose has ivory white flowers that fade quickly to pure white and have a lot of narrow, straplike petals toward the center, in the same way as some Noisettes. They come in clusters of 5–20 and are freely borne – almost continuously in hot climates. Snow Goose has small, dark, shiny, healthy leaves, only a few prickles, and a bushy habit of growth. It is best grown as a pillar rose, where it will flower almost down to ground level. It can grow to 16.4ft (5m) in hot countries.

SNOW PAVEMENT

see SCHNEEKOPPE

'SNOWDON'

Rugosa Hybrid

ORIGIN **Austin, Britain, 1989**
FLOWER SIZE **2.4in (6cm)**
SCENT **Strong and sweet**
FLOWERING **Repeats constantly**
HEIGHT/SPREAD **8.2ft (2.5m)/6.6ft (2m)**
HARDINESS **Zone 5**

This tall, white-flowered Rugosa rose has proved popular as a more floriferous alternative to 'Sir Thomas Lipton'. The flowers of 'Snowdon' are no more than medium-sized, but full of delicate white petals that glow when the sun shines through them. In rainy weather they tend to ball. They come singly and in large clusters, sometimes of up to 15 flowers, and are produced constantly until the end of the growing season. Deadheading helps to ensure that the reflowering is strong and continuous. 'Snowdon' has attractive, pale green leaves and thick, prickly stems. It grows to at least 8.2ft (2.5m), and needs a lot of space, so it is best in large gardens.

SNOW CARPET

'SNOWDON'

'SNOWFIRE'

'SNOWFIRE'

Hybrid Tea

ORIGIN **Kordes, Germany, 1970**
PARENTAGE **'Kordes' Brillant' x 'Freiheitsglocke'**
FLOWER SIZE **5.1in (13cm)**
SCENT **Light and fruity**
FLOWERING **Repeats**
HEIGHT/SPREAD **3.3ft (1m)/2.7ft (80cm)**
HARDINESS **Zone 6**

There is an unusually striking contrast between the two sides of the petals of 'Snowfire'. The upper sides are deep, rich red, and the undersides are pure white. There is no mixing or merging of the colors: the two sides are as different and distinct as possible. The contrast is most visible when the bud starts to expand: by the time it is fully open, the white parts of the flower are hidden. The flowers are usually borne singly, but occasionally in clusters. The plant has large, dark, healthy leaves and a lot of prickles. It is an upright grower, and fairly vigorous, especially in hot climates.

'SNOWLINE'

see 'EDELWEISS'

S

'SOFTEE'

Miniature Rose

ORIGIN **Moore, US, 1983**
FLOWER SIZE **1.2in (3cm)**
SCENT **Moderate and musky**
FLOWERING **Repeats continuously**
HEIGHT/SPREAD **2.7ft (80cm)/4.9ft (1.5m)**
HARDINESS **Zone 6**

'SOFTEE'

The flowers of 'Softee' have a hint of apricot when the bud starts to expand, but they open out very quickly and turn to pure white. Although fully double, the petals arrange themselves neatly around the yellow stamens (which quickly turn to brown). The flowers are carried in clusters of 10–30 with quite extraordinary abundance, and remain in good condition for many days. 'Softee' is not the most miniature of roses – these days we might call it a groundcover rose – but it is fairly compact, with small, dark leaves and very few prickles. It is vigorous, healthy, and a good repeater, wonderful when planted as a low hedge.

SOIRÉE DE BONHEUR

syn. 'CROEST'

Modern Climber

ORIGIN **Croix, France, 1993**
FLOWER SIZE **3.1in (8cm)**
SCENT **Light and sweet**
FLOWERING **Repeats**
HEIGHT/SPREAD **8.2ft (2.5m)/4.9ft (1.5m)**
HARDINESS **Zone 6**
AWARDS **Baden-Baden GM 1996; Geneva GM 1996; Saverne GM 1996**

SOIRÉE DE BONHEUR

This pretty climbing rose is popular in France but little known elsewhere. It is sometimes difficult for a small-scale rose breeder like Croix to compete against the mega-nurseries, no matter how good his roses may be. Soirée de Bonheur has flowers in the Floribunda style. They are short-petaled but fully double, with a cupped shape and a boss of dark yellow stamens at the center. Salmon pink when they first open, they fade to an attractive rose pink over the next few days. They come in loose clusters of 3–8 and are freely borne in a succession of flushes until late autumn. The plant has large, matte, mid-green leaves, a scattering of prickles, and a fairly vigorous habit.

'SOLEIL D'OR'

Fetida Hybrid

ORIGIN **Pernet-Ducher, France, 1900**
PARENTAGE **('Antoine Ducher' x 'Persiana') self-pollinated seedling**
FLOWER SIZE **2.4in (6cm)**
SCENT **Strong and fruity**
FLOWERING **Remontant**
HEIGHT/SPREAD **4.9ft (1.5m)/3.3ft (1m)**
HARDINESS **Zone 5**

This was an epoch-making rose – the first hardy, repeat-flowering orange yellow rose. Every modern yellow rose owes its coloring to Pernet-Ducher's cross. It was the result of 15 years' work with the brilliant yellow, once-flowering 'Persiana', whose pollen was barely viable. 'Soleil d'Or' has an extraordinary combination of colors. The outer petals are apricot yellow, and the inner ones are rich, sun ripened, apricot pink. The petals incurve slightly, and their paler yellower reverses contrast well with the pinker inner colors. They are neatly cup-shaped, and very pretty as they open, though less attractive when fully expanded, and untidy when they fade. The plant has a prickly, gawky, upright habit, with strong stems covered in large, stout thorns. The flowers are borne on short stems off these long branches. The plant has a reputation for weak growth, and fares best in hot climates. It is susceptible to blackspot, but this is not a problem in dry areas. 'Soleil d'Or' was quickly crossed with the Hybrid Teas to breed a race that became known as "Pernetiana" roses in honour of Pernet-Ducher. They were the first hardy yellow or orange garden roses, and by the 1920s they were completely absorbed into the Hybrid Teas. 'Soleil d'Or' remains popular with rose lovers all over the world, partly for its remarkable colouring and partly because of its importance in the history of roses.

'SOLEIL D'OR'

SOLITAIRE

syn. 'MACYEFRE', Chartreuse

Hybrid Tea

ORIGIN **McGredy, New Zealand, 1978**
PARENTAGE **Freude x Benson & Hedges Gold**
FLOWER SIZE **13cm (5.1in)**
SCENT **Light and fruity**
FLOWERING **Repeats**
HEIGHT/SPREAD **4.9ft (1.5m)/3.3ft (1m)**
HARDINESS **Zone 6**
AWARDS **RNRS PIT 1985**

Solitaire is not unlike a richer version of 'Mme. A. Meilland'. The ground color is lemon yellow, with an amber flush toward the center of the flower and cherry red edgings that fade to dark pink as they age. The flowers are large and beautifully formed, with thick, strong petals that stand up well to wind and rain. The red edging emphasizes their shapeliness at every stage of their development, from classic Hybrid Tea bud to wide open flower. Solitaire has large dark leaves, bronzy when young, and healthy. It is a vigorous, upright grower that repeats quickly. In hot climates it will reach at least 6.6ft (2m).

SOLITAIRE

'SOMBREUIL'

'SOMBREUIL'

Tea Rose

ORIGIN **Robert, France, 1850**
FLOWER SIZE **3.5in (9cm)**
SCENT **Strong, sweet, and tealike**
FLOWERING **Repeats constantly**
HEIGHT/SPREAD **13.1ft (4m)/6.6ft (2m)**
HARDINESS **Zone 6**

'Sombreuil' is a very popular and hardy Tea-Noisette whose elegant buds open out to beautiful flat flowers with a quartered mass of quilled petals and, sometimes, a green eye. The flowers are creamy white, with a hint of pale pink at the center, and are held fairly upright in small clusters (usually of three flowers) or sometimes singly. It flowers profusely, almost continuously, and sheds its faded petals naturally. The petals are somewhat soft, which means that it performs better in dry, warm weather. The flowers last well when cut. The plant has attractive dark leaves and the leaflets have pointed tips. It will grow to as much as 32.8ft (10m). Some authorities call it 'Mlle. de Sombreuil' and believe that it was named after the daughter of the Comte de Sombreuil, who was governor of Les Invalides at the time of the French Revolution. His daughter saved him from prison, and almost certain death.

SOMMERDUFT

syn. 'TANFUDERMOS', Summer Fragrance

Hybrid Tea

ORIGIN **Tantau, Germany, 1985**
FLOWER SIZE **4.7in (12cm)**
SCENT **Medium and sweet**
FLOWERING **Repeats well**
HEIGHT/SPREAD **4.1ft (1.25m)/3.3ft (1m)**
HARDINESS **Zone 6**

SOMMERDUFT

This is a splendid dark red Hybrid Tea with a good, rich scent. Sommerduft has nearly black buds and sumptuous, deep red flowers that keep their bold coloring until just before they drop their petals. They have the classic elegance of the traditional Hybrid Tea as they open out, and are borne singly on long, strong stems, which makes them good for cutting. The flowers are not too full of petals, so this is a rose that stands up well to wet climates. Sommerduft is a sturdy, bushy, upright plant with large, dark, healthy leaves. It grows vigorously and repeats well, which makes it a good bedding rose as well as a pleasure to pick.

SOMMERMÄRCHEN

syn. 'KORPINKA', Berkshire, Country Touch, Summer Fairytale, Xenia

Ground Cover

ORIGIN **Kordes, Germany, 1992**
PARENTAGE Weisse Immensee x Heidekönigin
FLOWER SIZE **2in (5cm)**
SCENT **Light and fruity**
FLOWERING **Almost continuous**
HEIGHT/SPREAD **2.7ft (80cm)/4.9ft (1.5m)**
HARDINESS **Zone 5**
AWARDS **Baden-Baden GM 1992; Geneva GM 1992; Glasgow GM 1996**

This is one of the most eye-catching of all the many ground-cover roses introduced in recent years. It is grown under many different names all over the world: Sommermärchen is its original German name. The contrast between its sumptuous, magenta pink flowers and its golden stamens is what first draws your attention. Then you notice the scalloped edge to the petals and the sheer abundance of its flowers, which are held in clusters of 5–15 and appear continuously until late in the season. Sommermärchen also has fine, dark, glossy leaves, which are a good foil for the flowers. It makes a compact but spreading bush, valuable for everything from landscaping to container planting. It is best of all as a garden plant.

SOMMERMÄRCHEN

SOMMERMORGEN

SOMMERMORGEN

syn. 'KORFULLWIND', Oxfordshire, Baby Blanket

Shrub Rose

ORIGIN **Kordes, Germany, 1991**
PARENTAGE Weisse Immensee x Goldmarie 82
FLOWER SIZE **2.4in (6cm)**
SCENT **Light and musky**
FLOWERING **Repeats constantly**
HEIGHT/SPREAD **2.5ft (75cm)/4.9ft (1.5m)**
HARDINESS **Zone 6**
AWARDS **Golden Rose of Courtrai 1993; RNRS GM 1993; Monza GM 1995**

The development of groundcover roses has been one of the most promising horticultural developments of recent years. Sommermorgen is a first-rate example of a plant that is useful for groundcover or landscaping, but is an excellent rose for the garden, too. Wider than high, it is perfect at the front of a mixed border, and flowers nonstop until late autumn. The flowers are pale pink, with dark pink petal backs and often with frilly edges, too. They open out to show a cluster of dark, rich yellow stamens against a small white patch at the center. They are borne in clusters of up to 15 (usually 4–7), held well above the dark, glossy, healthy foliage. The bush has small leaves, few prickles, and a compact habit.

SOMMERWIND

SOMMERWIND

syn. 'KORLANUM', Surrey, Vent d'Été

Shrub Rose

ORIGIN **Kordes, Germany, 1985**
PARENTAGE **'The Fairy' seedling**
FLOWER SIZE **2in (5cm)**
SCENT **Light and musky**
FLOWERING **Almost continuous**
HEIGHT/SPREAD **2.7ft (80cm)/4.1ft (1.25m)**
HARDINESS **Zone 6**
AWARDS **ADR 1987; Baden-Baden GM 1987; RNRS GM 1987; Genoa GM 1989**

This seedling of 'The Fairy' has become one of the most popular of the modern groundcover roses. The flowers of Sommerwind open dark pink and fade to pale pink as their stamens darken and their petals take on an attractive ruffle. They are profusely carried in clusters of 5–25 all over the surface of the plant. Although the flowers are individually attractive close-up, it is the sheer profusion of their first flowering that is outstanding, and the fact that the plant continues in flower thereafter for the rest of the season. Sommerwind has small, medium-dark, semiglossy leaves and a lax, bushy habit of growth. It is immensely vigorous and healthy. Its uses are many: excellent for landscaping, good in containers, useful as an edging, stupendous in combination with other shrubs, and a good filler anywhere.

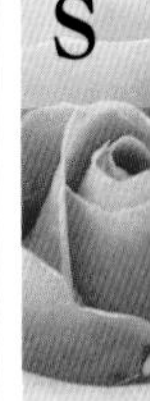

SONIA MEILLAND

SONNENKIND

'SOPHIE'S PERPETUAL'

SONIA MEILLAND

syn. 'MEIHELVET', Sweet Promise, Sonia

Grandiflora

ORIGIN **Meilland, France, 1974**
PARENTAGE **'Zambra' x ('Baccará' x 'White Knight')**
FLOWER SIZE **4.3in (11cm)**
SCENT **Strong, rich, and sweet**
FLOWERING **Repeats well**
HEIGHT/SPREAD **3.3ft (1m)/2.7ft (80cm)**
HARDINESS **Zone 6**

Named after Alain Meilland's daughter, Sonia Meilland has been a leading cut-flower rose in Europe ever since its introduction. The flowers have long, slender, pretty buds that are warm coral pink. They last a long time as buds, but eventually open out to pale salmon or flesh pink flowers with a muddled, old-fashioned shape that is quite unexpected but equally attractive. The flowers have lots of petals and long stems for cutting: they are good at all stages of their development. They are most freely produced and set off by dark, glossy leaves. Their color tends to fade in hot weather, and the flowers dislike rain, but Sonia Meilland has proved to be one of the most successful of all greenhouse roses.

S

SONIA RYKIEL

syn. 'MASDOGUI'

Shrub Rose

ORIGIN **Guillot-Massad, France, 1995**
FLOWER SIZE **3.1in (8cm)**
SCENT **Strong, sweet, and fruity**
FLOWERING **Repeats**
HEIGHT/SPREAD **4.9ft (1.5m)/6.6ft (2m)**
HARDINESS **Zone 6**

Jean-Pierre Guillot has developed his race of Generosa roses as a specifically French reinterpretation of the old rose virtues – scent, shapeliness, and continuous flowering. Sonia Rykiel is probably the best known, and its name pays tribute to a leading French fashion house. Its flowers are pink at the edges and coral or amber toward the center – a very beautiful combination of shades – and the pointed petals are exquisitely arranged as a dense, quartered rosette. They are borne usually singly but sometimes in twos and threes, and are well set off by the neat, dark leaves. Their scent is delicious and has won an important prize in France. However, Sonia Rykiel is not a rose without faults. The flowers tend to bend over on their stems and hang their heads. The plant has a wayward habit of growth, which means that it occasionally sends out long stems (up to 8.2ft/2.5m) that are out of proportion to the rest.

SONNENKIND

syn. 'KORHITOM', Perestroika

Patio Rose

ORIGIN **Kordes, Germany, 1986**
PARENTAGE **seedling x Goldmarie 82**
FLOWER SIZE **2.4in (6cm)**
SCENT **Light and sweet**
FLOWERING **Repeats well**
HEIGHT/SPREAD **2.3ft (70cm)/1.6ft (50cm)**
HARDINESS **Zone 6**

Sonnenkind resembles a scaled-down Hybrid Tea. Some experts actually call it a short Hybrid Tea and others a large miniature, but the consensus seems to be that it fits best into the inbetween category of patio rose. The flowers are elegantly shaped and often borne singly. They are pure, rich yellow in color, and show up beautifully against the dark, glossy leaves. They also drop cleanly when they have finished flowering. The plant is healthy, bushy, and very floriferous, flowering all over its surface and rarely out of flower. Its neat stature makes it ideal for containers.

SONNENSCHIRM

syn. 'TANMIRSCH', Broadlands, Canicule, Golden Touch

Shrub Rose

ORIGIN **Tantau, Germany, 1993**
FLOWER SIZE **2.8in (7cm)**
SCENT **Light**
FLOWERING **Continuous through until late autumn**
HEIGHT/SPREAD **2.5ft (75cm)/4.1ft (1.25m)**
HARDINESS **Zone 5**
AWARDS **RNRS PIT 1995**

This excellent small shrub rose has proved popular and successful in many different growing conditions all around the world, from Manitoba to Melbourne. Sonnenschirm is covered in pale yellow, double, rounded flowers for months on end. Its lax habit and mounded shape, broader than it is high, make it useful for groundcover and landscaping, but it is also a good specimen rose or standard rose in the garden. The flowers, which are slightly cupped, have long, pointed sepals and golden stamens. They come singly or in clusters of up to five flowers. The plant has dense, healthy, glossy foliage with a hint of Rugosa in its ancestry. Sonnenschirm grows particularly well on poor soil and, although vigorous enough, makes none of those long growths that have to be pruned into shape.

'SOPHIE'S PERPETUAL'

Hybrid China

ORIGIN **France, c.1860**
FLOWER SIZE **2.8in (7cm)**
SCENT **Musky and tealike**
FLOWERING **Repeats constantly**
HEIGHT/SPREAD **4.9ft (1.5m)/4.1ft (1.25m)**
HARDINESS **Zone 7**

One of the differences between China roses and old garden roses of the Western world is the way that European roses fade as they age but oriental ones darken. 'Sophie's Perpetual' is a good example of this darkening process, and does it with style. The flowers are pale China pink at first – a slightly blue pink that is palest toward the center – but they turn to crimson as they age. This can happen very abruptly in hot weather, so that there is a striking contrast between the pale pink inner petals

SONIA RYKIEL

SONNENSCHIRM

and the dark crimson outer ones. The flowers come in clusters of 3–7 on short but sturdy stems. The plant has dark China-rose leaves and a few stout prickles and is very healthy. It is best pruned lightly, so that it builds up a permanent structure of branches. 'Sophie's Perpetual' is a temporary name given by the rosarian Humphrey Brooke, who reintroduced it, pending the correct identification.

Sophy's Rose

syn. 'AUSlot'

Shrub Rose

ORIGIN **Austin, Britain, 1997**
FLOWER SIZE **3.1in (8cm)**
SCENT **Light and musky**
FLOWERING **Repeats**
HEIGHT/SPREAD **4.1ft (1.25m)/3.3ft (1m)**
HARDINESS **Zone 6**

One of the outstanding qualities of Sophy's Rose is that it remains short and compact even in hot climates. It also has flowers of quite extraordinary beauty. They are pale crimson purple, with paler undersides to the petals – especially noticeable at the center of the flower, where the petals fold over to form a neat button eye. Each flower has a great number of petals, and they are reflexed along their edges so that they form a point at their tips, not unlike a dahlia. The flowers come in small clusters, typically of 3–5, and are well set off by the healthy, medium-dark leaves. Sophy's Rose has a dense, twiggy, neat structure and few prickles. It is a reliable repeat flowerer.

Rosa soulieana

Wild Rose

FLOWER SIZE **1.6in (4cm)**
SCENT **Light and fruity**
FLOWERING **Once only, fairly late in season**
HEIGHT/SPREAD **13.1ft (4m)/8.2ft (2.5m)**
HARDINESS **Zone 6**

This is one of the best species roses – beautiful in flower, leaf, and fruit. The flowers are pale yellow in bud, opening cream, and produced rather late in the season in large clusters (typically of 15–30 flowers). They have golden stamens and a prominent stigma that sticks out in the center. The hips that follow are small (0.4in/1cm), round, vermilion red, and long-lasting. Not all plants produce hips: there is a tendency for some plants of *Rosa soulieana* to be all male. Anyway, the leaves are almost the best part of *Rosa soulieana* – healthy, large, glaucous, gray green, and well complemented by white stems with large, pale, hooked prickles. The plant is vigorous, and quickly forms a thuggish thicket if grown as a shrub, but its long, arching stems make it ideal for training as a climber. It has seldom been used in hybridizing, and the best of its offspring is a similarly vigorous climber called 'Wickwar' (Steadman, *c.*1960), a probable hybrid with *Rosa brunonii*. It has slightly larger flowers (2in/5cm) and the same glorious gray glaucous foliage.

Rosa soulieana

Sophy's Rose

'Soupert et Notting'

Moss Rose

ORIGIN **Pernet père, France, 1874**
FLOWER SIZE **3.5in (9cm)**
SCENT **Medium and sweet**
FLOWERING **Repeats a little in autumn**
HEIGHT/SPREAD **3.9ft (1.2m)/3.3ft (1m)**
HARDINESS **Zone 5**

'Soupert et Notting' was named by Claude Pernet in honor of an important Luxembourg firm of rose growers and breeders. It is an old-fashioned Damask Moss rose that repeats its flowering, provided it is deadheaded and well fed immediately after its first flush of flowers has faded. The flowers are mid-pink, fading to pale pink, with slightly paler backs to the petals. They are somewhat globular at first, then no more than slightly cupped, sometimes quartered, and occasionally showing a button eye. The mid-green moss is lightly applied but found especially on the receptacles and pedicels. The flowers come in somewhat short-stemmed, dense clusters of up to five. The plant has the ever-shortening internodes on the flowering stems that characterize the Damask Mosses and Portland roses. The leaves of 'Soupert et Notting' are slightly gray green in color and healthy.

'Soupert et Notting'

'Sourire d'Orchidée'

Shrub Rose

ORIGIN **Croix, France, 1985**
FLOWER SIZE **2.4in (6cm)**
SCENT **Strong, sweet, and musky**
FLOWERING **Repeats continuously**
HEIGHT/SPREAD **8.2ft (2.5m)/6.6ft (2m)**
HARDINESS **Zone 5**
AWARDS **Geneva GM 1985**

This shrubby climber is very popular in France, and appreciated wherever it is grown elsewhere in Europe. 'Sourire d'Orchidée' has semidouble flowers of great grace and beauty: they open pale pink and fade to white, though the overall effect is of mother-of-pearl. The petals are slightly darker underneath and the unopened buds are pink. The flowers have handsome stamens of uneven length and a delicious scent. They come in very large and spacious clusters of up to 30 flowers – typically 6–12 – and are borne with great freedom until the first frost of winter. In hot climates 'Sourire d'Orchidée' would probably flower all the year round. The plant is bushy, vigorous, and fairly healthy, with large pale leaves: it can be trained as a shrub, a short climber (9.8–13.1ft/3–4m), or a loose hedging rose.

'Sourire d'Orchidée'

'Southampton'

Floribunda

ORIGIN **Harkness, Britain, 1971**
PARENTAGE **('Ann Elizabeth' x 'Allgold') x 'Yellow Cushion'**
FLOWER SIZE **2.8in (7cm)**
SCENT **Medium and sweet**
FLOWERING **Repeats well**
HEIGHT/SPREAD **4.9ft (1.5m)/3.3ft (1m)**
HARDINESS **Zone 6**
AWARDS **Belfast GM 1974**

The Mayor and Corporation of Southampton did well to acquire this stunning Floribunda from Harkness's nursery: for some years afterward it was considered the best of all Floribundas in England. The flowers are apricot, orange, or salmon, paling slightly and becoming pinker as they age, but a handsome shade at all times. The petals have flushes of scarlet on their backs, which are always slightly darker, too. The flowers are lightly double and stand up well to wind and rain – often a problem in England. Although not especially distinguished in their shape, the flowers are most abundantly produced, usually in flat-topped clusters of 3–11 but sometimes singly. They are large enough to resemble a Hybrid Tea when they first open. They come on long stems, which makes them good for cutting. The plant is very vigorous and tall, with small dark leaves. It is still a good rose and one of the best in its color range.

'Southampton'

'SOUVENIR D'ADOLPHE TURC'

'Souvenir d'Adolphe Turc'

Polyantha

ORIGIN **Turc, France, 1924**
FLOWER SIZE **1.2in (3cm)**
SCENT **Light and musky**
FLOWERING **Repeats constantly**
HEIGHT/SPREAD **2ft (60cm)/2.7ft (80cm)**
HARDINESS **Zone 6**

A few of the Polyanthas bred at the start of the 20th century have never faded from popularity: 'Souvenir d'Adolphe Turc' is one. Its flowers are an unusual strong, pale coral color, before passing to fresh pink and fading to a lighter shade. They are loosely semidouble and borne in large, open clusters of 5–30 flowers – very beautiful as they arch out over the neat little plant. 'Souvenir d'Adolphe Turc' has light green foliage, somewhat bristly stems, and a few prickles. It is useful in containers and in the garden and does best in cool climates, where its colors are most intense.

'SOUVENIR D'ELISE VARDON'

'Souvenir de la Malmaison'

Bourbon Rose

ORIGIN **Béluze, France, 1843**
PARENTAGE **Probably 'Mme. Desprez' x 'Devoniensis'**
FLOWER SIZE **4.7in (12cm)**
SCENT **Strong, sweet, and fruity**
FLOWERING **Almost continuous**
HEIGHT/SPREAD **3.3ft (1m)/3.3ft (1m)**
HARDINESS **Zone 6**

Famous in its own right for its beauty and its very name, 'Souvenir de la Malmaison' has also spawned four distinct and desirable sports: a climbing form, a dark pink one, a pure white, and a semisingle one. The flowers of 'Souvenir de la Malmaison' (named after the Empress Josephine's country house) are soft flesh pink, paling to cream at the edges, cupped when opening, and full of beautifully arranged little petals – "quilled and quartered" is the traditional description. They closely resemble many of the modern English Roses bred by David Austin in the way the outer guard petals enclose the mass of neat little petals within. Through its most famous offspring, 'Gloire de Dijon', it is indeed an ancestor of many of these modern beauties. 'Souvenir de la Malmaison' has thin, soft petals, so they spoil quickly in wet weather and the unopened buds ball. All the 'Souvenir de la Malmaison' tribe fare better in hot, dry climates, where they also grow much taller – as much as 6.6ft (2m) for the bush forms (twice as high as in cool climates). 'Souvenir de la Malmaison' is not notably vigorous, needing some years to build up to a good size, and requiring only minimal pruning. The leaves, which are large and glossy, and sometimes attract mildew and blackspot in cool, damp climates, are perhaps a little stiff and prickly.

The sports are identical in every way except for color: **'Leweson Gower'** is mid-pink, and **'Kronprinzessin Viktoria'** (named after Queen Victoria's eldest daughter [1840–1901], who married Emperor Frederick III of Germany) is white with pale yellow reflections from its stamens. **'Souvenir de St Anne's'** is a semisingle sport, whose petals glow with translucent loveliness: it was found in St Anne's Park, Dublin. The climbing sport, **'Climbing Souvenir de la Malmaison'**, has slightly larger flowers than the bush form and grows to 13.1ft (4m), but it flowers less abundantly – there are periods between flushes when it carries no flowers, and the later flushes are always less spectacular than the first of the year. But all the 'Malmaison' roses are worth growing for their exquisite beauty.

'SOUVENIR DE LA MALMAISON'

Sports of 'Souvenir de la Malmaison'

'Leweson Gower'

syn. 'SOUVENIR DE LA MALMAISON ROUGE'
ORIGIN **Béluze, France, 1845**

'Kronprinzessin Viktoria'

ORIGIN **Volvert, Germany, 1887**

'Souvenir de St. Anne's'

ORIGIN **Hilling, Britain, 1950**

'Climbing Souvenir de la Malmaison'

Climbing Bourbon
ORIGIN **Bennett, Britain, 1893**
FLOWER SIZE **5.1in (13cm)**
FLOWERING **Once, followed by lesser flushes**
HEIGHT/SPREAD **13.1ft (4m)/3.3ft (1m)**

'KRONPRINZESSIN VIKTORIA'

'SOUVENIR DE ST ANNE'S'

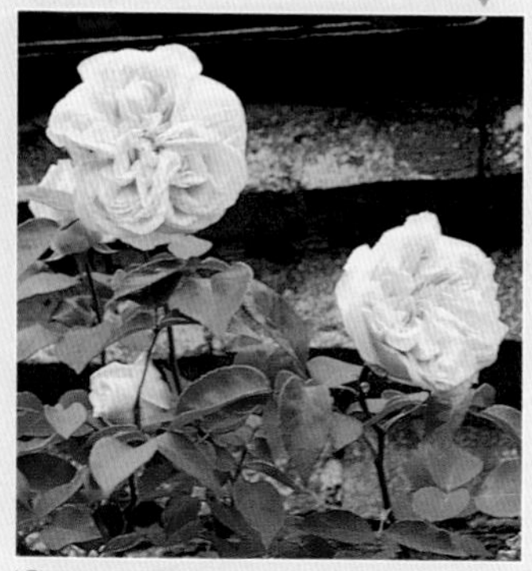

'CLIMBING SOUVENIR DE LA MALMAISON'

'Souvenir d'Elise Vardon'

Tea Rose

ORIGIN **Marest, France, 1855**
FLOWER SIZE **3.5in (9cm)**
SCENT **Strong, tealike, and fruity**
FLOWERING **Continuous**
HEIGHT/SPREAD **3.3ft (1m)/2.7ft (80cm)**
HARDINESS **Zone 7**

'Souvenir d'Elise Vardon' has all the virtues of the old Tea roses: exquisite shape, enchanting colors, and perpetual flowering. The flowers are large, elegant in the bud, globular as they expand, and attractive when fully opened out. They are a wonderful mixture of pink, cream, apricot, lemon, and buff, though the yellow tints fade as they age, and the flowers tend to end up pale pink and cream with only a hint of buff still at the center. They are produced singly and in small clusters all over the surface of the plant: no Hybrid Tea can match this rose for sheer floriferousness. The plant is small, compact, and fairly prickly, with dark leaves. In hot climates, it will flower year-round.

'Souvenir de la Malmaison Rouge'

see 'LEWESON GOWER'

'Souvenir de Claudius Denoyel'

Climbing Hybrid Tea

ORIGIN **Chambard, France, 1920**
PARENTAGE **'Château de Clos Vougeot' x 'Commandeur Jules Gravereaux'**
FLOWER SIZE **4.3in (11cm)**
SCENT **Medium and sweet**
FLOWERING **Repeats**
HEIGHT/SPREAD **9.8ft (3m)/6.6ft (2m)**
HARDINESS **Zone 6**

'Souvenir de Claudius Denoyel' is a short-growing climber or pillar rose that has remained popular despite being superseded by better roses. Its flowers

'Souvenir de Claudius Denoyel'

are usually bright crimson, but the color is variable and sometimes they are little more than carmine colored. They are lightly double, with strong, thick petals surrounding a large boss of bright yellow stamens. The flowers come singly or in pendulous clusters of up to five, and sometimes repeat later in the season. The plant is a slow grower, and responds to good cultivation, especially feeding and watering. It is sometimes liable to attract blackspot. Chambard of Lyon-Vénissieux specialized in new roses, but bred few of his own. Claudius Denoyel was his niece's husband, who died young.

'Souvenir de Mme. Auguste Charles'

Bourbon Rose

ORIGIN **Moreau-Robert, France, 1866**
FLOWER SIZE **4.7in (12cm)**
SCENT **Light**
FLOWERING **Remontant**
HEIGHT/SPREAD **6.6ft (2m)/4.9ft (1.5m)**
HARDINESS **Zone 5**

This opulent old Bourbon rose has large flowers that open out flat and later reflex into a pompon: 'Souvenir de Mme. Auguste Charles' needs hot, dry weather at flowering time to give of its best. The petals are quilled, pleated, and pointed but, contrary to some authorities, never fimbriated. Their color is quite uneven: most of the petals are very pale at their edges, but many conceal traces of a rich deep pink within the folds of their pleats. The flowers are borne singly or in clusters of up to four on a lanky plant that will make 6.6ft (2m) in a hot climate, but is best pegged down so that it flowers all along its thick, strong stems.

'Souvenir de Mme. Léonie Viennot'

Climbing Tea-type

ORIGIN **Bernaix, France, 1898**
FLOWER SIZE **3.9in (10cm)**
SCENT **Strong and tealike**
FLOWERING **Almost continuous**
HEIGHT/SPREAD **9.8ft (3m)/8.2ft (2.5m)**
HARDINESS **Zone 7**

'Souvenir de Mme. Léonie Viennot' is widely grown in warm areas, where it will flower for 12 months of the year. Its flowers open flat and very full, with recurved petals like a peony. Their coloring is unusual: they are deep peach pink at first, especially on the tips of their petals, but the flowers turn pinker and paler as they age. The outer petals fade to pale pink and the petal backs change from creamy yellow to silver pink. A fully open flower is a muddle of pink, crimson, cream, and buff. The flowers are borne singly or in strong, upright clusters of up to five. They are well set off by the crimson new growth of the plant. The dark green, drooping leaves have long leaflets and red midribs. They are susceptible to mildew, but this does not affect the plant's capacity to flower incessantly. The scent of the flowers is very strong and floats freely on the air. 'Souvenir de Mme. Léonie Viennot' comes easily from cuttings and the plant has little or no need of pruning.

'Souvenir de Philèmon Cochet'

see 'Blanc Double de Coubert'

'Souvenir de Thérèse Levet'

'Souvenir de St. Anne's'

see 'Souvenir de la Malmaison'

'Souvenir de Thérèse Levet'

Tea Rose

ORIGIN **Levet, France, 1886**
PARENTAGE **'Adam' seedling**
FLOWER SIZE **2.4in (6cm)**
SCENT **Light and tealike**
FLOWERING **Constantly in flower**
HEIGHT/SPREAD **5.7ft (1.75m)/4.9ft (1.5m)**
HARDINESS **Zone 7**

There are few really red Tea roses: 'Souvenir de Thérèse Levet' has somewhat more China genes in its makeup than most. Its leaves, in particular, are small and dark like a China rose. Its flowers are a somewhat ordinary, bright cherry crimson, with a few white streaks at the center. They are only lightly double, and you may search a long time before finding a perfectly shaped flower, but they open neatly and have a handsome cluster of dark yellow stamens at the center. They also last well when cut for the house. The flowers normally come singly – occasionally in twos and threes – and repeat well. The plant has large prickles and dense, twiggy growth. Mildew can be a problem.

'Souvenir du Docteur Jamain'

Hybrid Perpetual

ORIGIN **Lacharme, France, 1865**
PARENTAGE **'Général Jacqueminot' × 'Charles Lefèbvre'**
FLOWER SIZE **3.1in (8cm)**
SCENT **Strong and sweet**
FLOWERING **Remontant**
HEIGHT/SPREAD **9.8ft (3m)/8.2ft (2.5m)**
HARDINESS **Zone 6**

Deep, rich crimson, with a "true" rose scent to match – it is no wonder that 'Souvenir du Docteur Jamain' remains consistently popular so many years after it was first introduced. The flowers are darkest red, with black velvety markings on the upper sides of the petals, which give them their crimson overlay. Sometimes the inner petals have a streak of white in them, which serves to emphasize the dark richness of the rest of the flower, as do the bright yellow stamens at the center. 'Souvenir du Docteur Jamain' is a lanky grower, almost thornless, whose flexible stems make it easy to train as a short climber or to peg down to break into flower all along its length. The leaves are bronzy at first, later mid-green, and susceptible to mildew and blackspot. It does best in hot, dry climates, but responds well to good cultivation anywhere. It was a favorite of Vita Sackville-West at Sissinghurst.

'Souvenir de Mme. Auguste Charles'

'Souvenir de Mme. Léonie Viennot'

'Souvenir du Docteur Jamain'

'Sparkling Scarlet'

see 'Iskra'

Sparkling Yellow

see Yellow Cover

'Spartan'

Floribunda

ORIGIN **Boerner, US, 1955**
PARENTAGE **'Geranium Red' x 'Fashion'**
FLOWER SIZE **3.1in (8cm)**
SCENT **Strong, sweet, and fruity**
FLOWERING **Repeats well**
HEIGHT/SPREAD **3.3ft (1m)/2.7ft (80cm)**
HARDINESS **Zone 6**
AWARDS **NRS PIT 1954; Portland GM 1955**

This was an important rose: a Floribunda with large flowers and a lot of petals. 'Spartan' also flowered from top to bottom, and not just at the tips of the stems. This was an innovation when it was introduced in 1955. The flowers are a striking color, a deep, radiant coral pink, though the exact tone differs from season to season: it is usually more orange in warm climates and pinker in cool. The flowers come singly and in clusters of up to seven, and are regularly produced right through until the end of the season. They often have an old-fashioned, muddled arrangement of petals when they open out fully.

'Spartan'

'Spartan' makes a vigorous, rounded, bushy plant with a lot of glossy green leaves and thick growth. Blackspot may affect it in autumn.

Special Occasion

syn. 'FRYyoung'
Hybrid Tea

ORIGIN **Fryer, Britain, 1995**
FLOWER SIZE **4.7in (12cm)**
SCENT **Medium, sweet, and fruity**
FLOWERING **Repeats**
HEIGHT/SPREAD **4.1ft (1.25m)/2.7ft (80cm)**
HARDINESS **Zone 6**
AWARDS **Genoa GM 1995**

The exquisite color and form of Special Occasion are typical of the best modern Hybrid Teas, of which the breeder Gareth Fryer is the leading English exponent. The flowers are large, full of petals, but elegantly shaped as an

Special Occasion

unfurling bud and beautiful at every stage until it is fully open. They are a ravishing shade of apricot, paler at the edges and darker toward the center of the flower as well as on the petal backs. Coppery pink shadows appear between the petals. The flowers usually come singly on stout stems but occasionally in clusters, too. Special Occasion is usually among the first Hybrid Teas to flower, and it repeats regularly (and quickly) until the end of the growing season. It makes a neat, bushy plant with dark, healthy, glossy leaves.

'Spectabilis'

Sempervirens Hybrid

ORIGIN **c.1833**
FLOWER SIZE **2.4in (6cm)**
SCENT **Strong, musky, and myrrhlike**
FLOWERING **Once only, fairly late in season**
HEIGHT/SPREAD **8.2ft (2.5m)/6.6ft (2m)**
HARDINESS **Zone 6**

The flowers of 'Spectabilis' open from fat little crimson buds, and it is immediately obvious that every flower is delicately formed into a perfect formal rosette, with a button eye and a hint of the green carpel at the center. The color contrast is equally exquisite: shell pink with a white center, not just where the white petal backs have curled over to make the eye, but also in the surrounding petals. Later they reflex

Spek's Centennial

right back into a pompon. The flowers have quite an unusual, but delicious, scent. They come in large clusters, typically of 10–30, and have a few late flowers after the first, profuse flowering. The plant has neat, small, dark, evergreen leaves and long, slender stems with some prickles.

'Spectacular'

see 'Danse du Feu'

Spek's Centennial

syn. 'MACivy', Singin' in the Rain
Floribunda

ORIGIN **McGredy, New Zealand, 1991**
PARENTAGE **Sexy Rexy x Pot o' Gold**
FLOWER SIZE **2.8in (7cm)**
SCENT **Strong, sweet, and fruity**
FLOWERING **Repeats freely**
HEIGHT/SPREAD **4.1ft (1.25m)/3.3ft (1m)**
HARDINESS **Zone 6**
AWARDS **RNRS GM 1991; AARS 1995**

The flowers of Spek's Centennial are very shapely and a very unusual color. Although classified as a Floribunda, the flowers come both singly and in clusters of up to five, and the individual flowers have all the elegance and petalage of a Hybrid Tea. They are variable in color, but usually smoky pink (sometimes more apricot) with copper brown petal backs. They also have deeper pink petal

'Sparrieshoop'

Shrub Rose

ORIGIN **Kordes, Germany, 1953**
PARENTAGE **('Baby Château' x 'Else Poulsen') x 'Magnifica'**
FLOWER SIZE **3.5in (9cm)**
SCENT **Medium**
FLOWERING **Repeats well**
HEIGHT/SPREAD **4.9ft (1.5m)/4.9ft (1.5m)**
HARDINESS **Zone 5**
AWARDS **Portland GM 1971**

'Sparrieshoop' is one of the Kordes hybrids descended from the sweetbriar *Rosa rubiginosa*, and is named after a small town near the breeders' nursery. It is a rose of simple loveliness, opening from long, slender buds to large, well-scented, clear pink flowers with a white center and golden stamens. They are single, with a few extra petals, lightly cupped, and most abundantly borne in upright, well-held clusters of 3–11. After the first, spectacular flowering, the plant carries a few flowers right through until autumn. It makes a mounded shrub or – in hot climates – a 9.8ft (3m) climber. It is sometimes a little susceptible to mildew in autumn.

Kordes introduced a white sport in 1962 as **'Weisse aus Sparrieshoop'**; it is exactly the same as 'Sparrieshoop' in all respects except for its color.

'Sparrieshoop'

'Weisse aus Sparrieshoop'

Sport of 'Sparrieshoop'

'Weisse aus Sparrieshoop'

syn. 'White Sparrieshoop'
ORIGIN **Kordes, Germany, 1962**
HEIGHT/SPREAD **4.9ft (1.5m)/3.3ft (1m)**

'Spectabilis'

S

'SQUATTER'S DREAM'

tips and paler centers, almost cream colored. Spek's Centennial has dark, healthy leaves and a thick, upright habit of growth. It is a fairly good repeat flowerer and grows vigorously. In hot climates the plant may reach 6.6ft (2m).

SPELLBOUND

see FLORA DANICA

'SPENCER'

see 'BARONNE ADOLPHE DE ROTHSCHILD'

ROSA SPINOSISSIMA 'ALTAICA'

see 'ALTAICA'

ROSA SPINOSISSIMA 'DUNWICHENSIS'

see 'DUNWICH'

'SPLENDENS'

see 'AYRSHIRE SPLENDENS'

'SPONG'

see 'CENTIFOLIA'

'SPRAY CÉCILE BRUNNER'

see 'CÉCILE BRUNNER'

'SQUATTER'S DREAM'

Shrub Rose

ORIGIN **Clark, Australia, 1923**
PARENTAGE ***Rosa gigantea* hybrid x unknown**
FLOWER SIZE **3.5in (9cm)**
SCENT **Medium and sweet**
FLOWERING **Fully recurrent**
HEIGHT/SPREAD **4.9ft (1.5m)/4.9ft (1.5m)**
HARDINESS **Zone 8**

'Squatter's Dream' is a second-generation Gigantea Hybrid – exactly the kind of Australian rose that Alister Clark sought to create – a bushy, perpetually flowering shrub that would cope with the hot, dry climate of inland Victoria. Tough though it is, 'Squatter's Dream' resembles a more delicate, paler version of 'Mrs. Oakley Fisher'. The long, slender, orange buds open out to saffron yellow flowers with apricot backs to the petals. The color is creamier at the edges and more yellow at the center. The flowers are almost single, with beautiful red gold stamens. They are carried singly or in clusters of up to five. The plant is vigorous and rounded in habit, with few prickles. Its leaves are dark and bronzy at first, later turning richly green with purple stalks and stems.

'SPEK'S YELLOW'

syn. 'GOLDEN SCEPTER'

Hybrid Tea

ORIGIN **Verschuren-Pechtold, Netherlands, 1950**
PARENTAGE **'Geheimrat Duisberg' seedling**
FLOWER SIZE **3.9in (10cm)**
SCENT **Strong and fruity**
FLOWERING **Repeats well**
HEIGHT/SPREAD **4.9ft (1.5m)/4.1ft (1.25m)**
HARDINESS **Zone 5**

'SPEK'S YELLOW'

The flowers of 'Spek's Yellow' are pretty. The buds are long, slender, and rich, deep yellow. They open into loosely double flowers and hold their color well. In hot weather they reflex their petals and resemble spiky yellow starbursts. The flowers are sometimes borne individually but more often in spacious clusters, which may be large (as many as 15 flowers), on long, strong stems. They make excellent cut flowers and are freely produced. 'Spek's Yellow' is a good garden plant that grows vigorously (somewhat lankily) and reflowers well. It also survives heat, cold, and neglect. Its leaves are dark, medium-sized, and few, and its stems very prickly – not a pretty plant, but redeemed by the quantity and quality of its flowers.

A climbing form, **'Climbing Spek's Yellow'**, was introduced in 1956 and is popular in Britain. (The bush form is now most usually seen in the US, where it is known as 'Golden Scepter'.) It grows vigorously to at least 13.1ft (4m), but is an ungainly grower with big prickles, few leaves, and rigid, upright growths. It needs to be covered with complementary plants such as clematis to hide its stems and prolong the season: 'Climbing Spek's Yellow' has only a few flowers after the first flowering.

Sport of 'Spek's Yellow'

'CLIMBING SPEK'S YELLOW'

syn. 'CLIMBING GOLDEN SCEPTER'
Climbing Hybrid Tea
ORIGIN **Walters, 1956**
FLOWER SIZE **4.3in (11cm)**
FLOWERING **Once well, early in season, then only occasionally**
HEIGHT/SPREAD **16.4ft (5m)/8.2ft (2.5m)**

ROSA SPINOSISSIMA

syn. *ROSA PIMPINELLIFOLIA*

Wild Rose

FLOWER SIZE **1.6in (4cm)**
SCENT **Light and fetid**
FLOWERING **Once only, usually early in season**
HEIGHT/SPREAD **3.3ft (1m)/3.3ft (1m)**
HARDINESS **Zone 3**

There is no mistaking *Rosa spinosissima*. It has black hips, masses of prickles, and dainty little leaves. It is native to a large part of Europe from Ireland to the Caucasus, occurring naturally from seaside sand dunes to Alpine mountains. The flowers are creamy white and lightly cupped, with a fine crown of yellow stamens at the center. They are borne singly in the axils all over the bush, and make a fine display early on in the season in the wild, but late when it is grown in hot climates. The hips are maroon black, shiny, and round. The leaves are small, at most 2.4in (6cm) long, with 5–9 small, thin, rounded leaflets. *Rosa spinosissima* has slender brown stems covered in long, slender prickles. It is naturally stoloniferous and suckers around when grown on its own roots. This is very welcome if you intend it to make an impenetrable hedge, but *Rosa spinosissima* is better grafted on a nonsuckering rootstock if it is required to keep to its allotted space in the garden. It is very hardy and tolerant of poor soil. Many distinct forms are available, including 'Altaica' and 'Dunwich', and many hybrids too.

***Rosa spinosissima* 'Double White'** may be a hybrid of the species, not just a form. Its flowers are pure white and globular, enclosing deep yellow stamens within a strongly cupped form, and are especially beautiful when the sun shines through them. It is taller than most forms of the species, and sets only a few hips. Otherwise it resembles its parent in all respects except one – it has a sweet scent of lily-of-the-valley, a delicious fragrance shared by no other rose.

Hybrid of *Rosa spinosissima*

ROSA SPINOSISSIMA 'DOUBLE WHITE'

ORIGIN **c.1800**
FLOWER SIZE **1.4in (3.5cm)**
SCENT **Strong, sweet, and floral**
FLOWERING **Once only**
HEIGHT/SPREAD **5.7ft (1.75m)/4.1ft (1.25m)**
HARDINESS **Zone 5**

ROSA SPINOSISSIMA

ROSA SPINOSISSIMA 'DOUBLE WHITE'

S

St. Cecilia

St. Cecilia

syn. 'AUSmit'

Shrub Rose

ORIGIN **Austin, Britain, 1987**
PARENTAGE **'Wife of Bath' x seedling**
FLOWER SIZE **3.9in (10cm)**
SCENT **Medium, sweet, and myrrhlike**
FLOWERING **Late in season, repeats**
HEIGHT/SPREAD **3.3ft (1m)/2.5ft (75cm)**
HARDINESS **Zone 6**

St. Cecilia is a beautiful English Rose, never more than 3.3ft (1m) tall in England, but twice as high in hot climates. Its flowers are pale pearl pink or cream, with a hint of buff at the center, but the color can vary from pale apricot to pure white, according to the season and the stage of their development. They are cupped, with a muddled mass of incurved petals at the center that contrast with the flat, outer, guard petals. They are borne usually singly, sometimes in twos and threes, on weak pedicels, so that the flowers nod over gracefully. Nevertheless, their long stems make them useful for cutting. The plant has many small brown prickles, dark green leaves (not too many), and a bushy habit of growth. It sometimes needs protection from rust and mildew.

'St. Nicholas'

Damask Rose

ORIGIN **Hilling, Britain, 1950**
FLOWER SIZE **3.1in (8cm)**
SCENT **Strong and sweet**
FLOWERING **Once, midseason**
HEIGHT/SPREAD **4.9ft (1.5m)/4.1ft (1.25m)**
HARDINESS **Zone 5**

This charming and distinctive rose occurred as a seedling in a garden called St. Nicholas in Yorkshire, England, which belonged to the Hon. Robert James, after whom the climbing rose 'Bobbie James' was named. It is different from other Damask roses, and fits neatly into no obvious category. The loosely semidouble flowers, which quickly open out flat, are rose pink with a white center and have sumptuous stamens that light it up. The flowers come in larger clusters than other Damasks (up to 15) and flower over a long period. In autumn 'St. Nicholas' carries long-lasting, round, red hips that are closer to those of *Rosa gallica* than to the Damasks. The plant has fine, light green leaves (with a slight gloss to their surface), densely covering the bush like a Gallica rose.

St. Patrick

St. Patrick

syn. 'WEKamanda', Limelight

Hybrid Tea

ORIGIN **Strickland, US, 1995**
PARENTAGE **Brandy x Gold Medal**
FLOWER SIZE **5.1in (13cm)**
SCENT **Light**
FLOWERING **Repeats well**
HEIGHT/SPREAD **4.1ft (1.25m)/3.3ft (1m)**
HARDINESS **Zone 6**

St. Patrick was bred by a Californian amateur and opens so slowly that it is suited only to hot, dry climates, where long-lasting yellow roses are few. Actually, its buds are green – hence the name – and the flowers keep a green shading at the edges that is accentuated in hot weather. They have unusually long petals, which are golden yellow at the base and keep their color very well, as well as the greenish tinge. Indeed, they last for a long time both as cut flowers and in the garden: sometimes the petals remain erect and the flowers never open out fully. They are abundantly carried on long, stout stems. St. Patrick makes a vigorous and healthy plant, and repeats well, even in the hottest conditions.

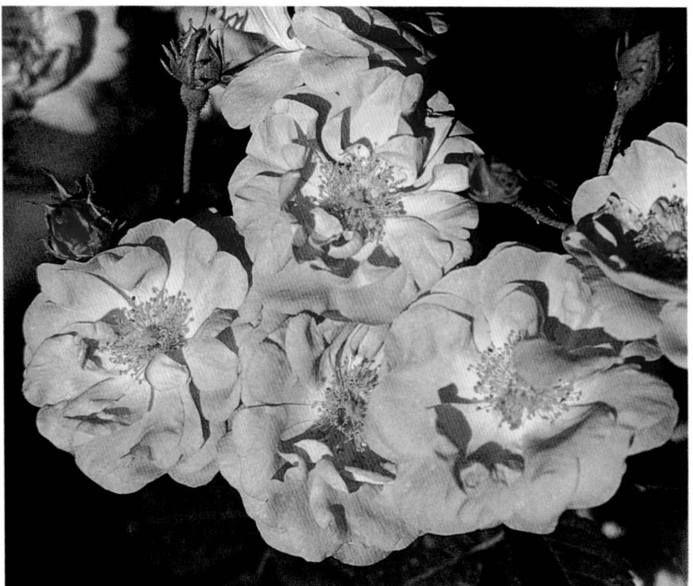
'St. Nicholas'

St. Swithun

syn. 'AUSwith'

Shrub Rose

ORIGIN **Austin, Britain, 1994**
PARENTAGE **Mary Rose x ('Chaucer' x 'Conrad Ferdinand Meyer')**
FLOWER SIZE **3.5in (9cm)**
SCENT **Strong, myrrhlike, and delicious**
FLOWERING **Repeats**
HEIGHT/SPREAD **4.9ft (1.5m)/3.3ft (1m)**
HARDINESS **Zone 5**

Some English Roses grow much taller in unEnglish climates. St. Swithun makes just about 4.9ft (1.5m) high in northern Europe, but reaches twice that height in California or Australia, where it is grown as a climber. The flowers are large and milky pink, with darker petal backs and paler edges, fading to white at the edges. Sometimes there is a hint of pale yellow at the center, though this may be obscured by a loose button eye. The flowers are lightly cupped and very full of petals: when well grown, the flowers can be as much as 5.5in (14cm) across. They are borne singly or in small clusters (of up to five flowers) on a prickly plant that reflowers quickly. The leaves are large, mid-green (bronzy at first), semiglossy, and fairly healthy. St. Swithun is vigorous, with an open habit that sends up long, arching growth. Pruning will keep it more compact in cool climates.

St. Swithun

Stadt Würzburg

syn. 'KORgust', Sunsation, Veldfire

Hybrid Tea

ORIGIN **Kordes, Germany, 1987**
FLOWER SIZE **4.7in (12cm)**
SCENT **Light and fruity**
FLOWERING **Repeats**
HEIGHT/SPREAD **4.9ft (1.5m)/4.1ft (1.25m)**
HARDINESS **Zone 6**

This is a big, shrubby Hybrid Tea that exudes vigor and good health. Stadt Würzburg has large flowers borne singly on long, straight stems. They are excellent for cutting, and make a fine display as a bedding rose. They are also popular with exhibitors. Their color is deep orange at first, with yellow patches on the petal backs. As they age, the flowers tend to lose their yellow tints and become more red, with creamy backs, but the color contrasts are always striking. Stadt Würzburg is a broad, bushy plant with healthy, medium-dark, glossy leaves. It is a prolific flowerer and performs as well in hot climates as it does in its native Germany.

Stadt Würzburg

STAINLESS STEEL

STAINLESS STEEL

syn. 'WEKBLUSI'

Hybrid Tea

ORIGIN **Carruth, US, 1991**
PARENTAGE **'Blue Nile' x Silverado**
FLOWER SIZE **4.3in (11cm)**
SCENT **Strong and sweet**
FLOWERING **Repeats well**
HEIGHT/SPREAD **6.6ft (2m)/4.1ft (1.25m)**
HARDINESS **Zone 6**

Rose breeders have for many years sought the "perfect" mauve or lilac Hybrid Tea, and many consider that Stainless Steel is a useful step on the way. It has a blue white tint reminiscent of steel and an excellent strong, sweet scent. The flowers open from green white buds with a pink edge, and begin to be pretty when they unfold and reveal silvery gray petals with lavender on the petal backs and mauve reflections in the center. The colors are never very deep, but the petals have a brilliance that is almost luminescent. The flowers are borne on long stems, either singly or in spacious clusters of up to five, and make a good display in the garden as well as being a first-rate cut-flower and exhibition rose. The flowers last a long time, but their color and size are best in cool weather. The plant is vigorous, upright, and somewhat scraggy, with only a few stout stems and large, deep green foliage.

'STANWELL PERPETUAL'

Spinosissima Hybrid

ORIGIN **Lee, Britain, 1838**
FLOWER SIZE **3.1in (8cm)**
SCENT **Strong and sweet**
FLOWERING **Early in season, then almost continuous**
HEIGHT/SPREAD **6.6ft (2m)/4.9ft (1.5m)**
HARDINESS **Zone 4**

'Stanwell Perpetual' was found in a cottage garden as a spontaneous seedling. No one has identified its parents, but they are thought to be a form of *Rosa spinosissima* and a Perpetual Damask. It certainly has the foliage of the former – small and gray with many leaflets – and a thick covering of prickles (reddish at first, later gray) that envelops its stems. It flowers early and then continuously until early winter. Its flowers are shell pink, with paler reverses, fading to white, and opening out flat and quartered with a pretty arrangement of quilled petals. They are carried singly on short stems, but do not last as cut flowers. The plant is slow to establish but thrives in poor soil and needs minimum pruning as it builds up its size. When established, it throws out huge, arching wands as high as 6.6ft (2m) or more. Then all it needs is for the old, dead, or dying wood to be cut out. The bush has an airy look, which comes from the neat little leaves; these may get blackspot, but never seriously. Occasionally it produces a maroon red hip or two, but these are invariably empty of seeds.

'STANWELL PERPETUAL'

'STARINA'

Miniature Rose

ORIGIN **Meilland, France, 1965**
PARENTAGE **('Dany Robin' x 'Fire King') x 'Perla de Montserrat'**
FLOWER SIZE **1.2in (3cm)**
SCENT **Medium and sweet**
FLOWERING **Repeats well**
HEIGHT/SPREAD **1.3ft (40cm)/11.8in (30cm)**
HARDINESS **Zone 6**
AWARDS **Japan GM 1968; ADR 1971**

This was the rose that put the miniatures into every rose garden: 'Starina' is still one of the most widely grown of all roses. The opening buds are like tiny Hybrid Teas, with all their elegance scaled down. The flowers are bright vermilion, grading through orange to yellow at the base of the petals. The petal backs are yellow, too. Its shape and color make 'Starina' a favorite exhibition variety, useful as a cut flower and perfect for growing in containers. It has neat, small, dark leaves and repeats well. A very satisfactory and showy small rose.

STARRY NIGHT

see ANITA PEREIRE

'STARS 'N' STRIPES'

Miniature Rose

ORIGIN **Moore, US, 1975**
PARENTAGE **'Little Chief' x ('Little Darling' x 'Ferdinand Pichard')**
FLOWER SIZE **0.8in (2cm)**
SCENT **Light and musky**
FLOWERING **Repeats well, almost continuous**
HEIGHT/SPREAD **1.6ft (50cm)/11.8in (30cm)**
HARDINESS **Zone 6**

This perky miniature was the first of the modern striped roses. Ralph Moore used the old striped Hybrid Perpetual 'Ferdinand Pichard' to introduce stripes into his miniature roses, and in due course other breeders used 'Stars 'n' Stripes' as the basis of the hundreds of striped roses that have been launched since the 1980s. The flowers of 'Stars 'n' Stripes' are mostly white with crimson splashes. They come on long, slender spikes composed of clusters of 3–5 flowers all down the stems. The plant has neat, dark leaves and few prickles (often none). Its slender, erect habit of growth is very distinctive, and there are records of 'Stars 'n' Stripes' growing to 4.9ft (1.5m) in hot climates. Its main weakness is that the flowers hold on to their petals for too long after they have turned brown and withered.

'STARS 'N' STRIPES'

'STARINA'

ROSA STELLATA

Wild Rose

FLOWER SIZE **5cm (2in)**
SCENT **Little or none**
FLOWERING **Once only**
HEIGHT/SPREAD **3.3ft (1m)/3.3ft (1m)**
HARDINESS **Zone 7**

Rosa stellata is an unusual wild rose, so much on the botanical fringes of the genus *Rosa* that some people think it should be put in its own closely related genus. It is a very pretty, prickly shrub, building up into a wiry mass, and suckering pleasantly if grown on its own roots. It has tiny, crinkly leaves like a gooseberry's, and comparatively large flowers, borne singly all over the surface of the plant. They are bright magenta at first, but fade to pale pink at the edges. The ring of creamy white stamens lightens up the center and adds greatly to its distinctive character. The plant is native to the southwestern US, where it grows in very dry positions. *Rosa stellata* will survive temperatures of -4°F (-20°C) in winter if kept dry at the roots, but needs a hot position if it is to flower well.

ROSA STELLATA

Stephens' Big Purple

syn. 'STEbigpu', Big Purple, Nuit d'Orient

Hybrid Tea

ORIGIN **Stephens, New Zealand, 1985**
PARENTAGE **seedling x 'Purple Splendour'**
FLOWER SIZE **4.7in (12cm)**
SCENT **Very strong and sweet**
FLOWERING **Repeats well**
HEIGHT/SPREAD **5.7ft (1.75m)/3.3ft (1m)**
HARDINESS **Zone 6**

This sumptuous purple Hybrid Tea was raised by an amateur: Pat Stephens was secretary of the New Zealand Rose Society. The flowers of Stephens' Big Purple are not only large and beautifully shaped but also very sweetly scented. The buds unfurl their many petals slowly. As the flowers are usually borne singly on very long stems, they are excellent for flower arrangements: their remarkable dark color is much admired. However, the color does differ according to the season, and may on occasions be more crimson than purple. The flowers are rain sensitive, too, so this is a rose that does best in dry climates. Stephens' Big Purple has dark, healthy leaves and a vigorous, upright habit of growth.

Stephens' Big Purple

'Sterling Silver'

Hybrid Tea

ORIGIN **Fisher, Britain, 1957**
PARENTAGE **seedling x 'Mme. A. Meilland'**
FLOWER SIZE **3.5in (9cm)**
SCENT **Strong, rich, and sweet**
FLOWERING **Repeats**
HEIGHT/SPREAD **4.1ft (1.25m)/2.7ft (80cm)**
HARDINESS **Zone 6**

This was the first lavender mauve Hybrid Tea to become widely popular, especially in the US, although not everyone approved of its color. The very sweetly scented flowers are usually borne singly on long stems and, when perfectly formed, are among the most beautiful of all roses. 'Sterling Silver' is, however, not an easy rose to grow well – it is a miserly bloomer, not very vigorous, and susceptible to mildew and blackspot. It needs a warm climate in which to build up a bushy structure, after which it will flower much more profusely, especially if it is fertilized and an effort is made to prevent fungal infections.

'Strawberry Ice'

see 'Bordure Rose'

Stretch Johnson

see Rock 'n' Roll

Success Story

see Weight Watchers Success

Suffolk

see Bassino

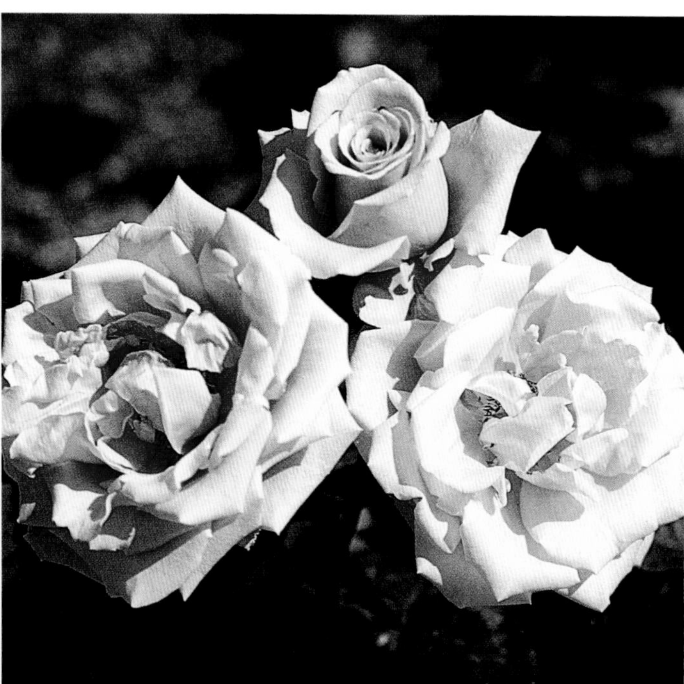
'Sterling Silver'

'Suitor'

Polyantha

ORIGIN **Clark, Australia, 1942**
FLOWER SIZE **1.6in (4cm)**
SCENT **Medium and musky**
FLOWERING **Repeats well**
HEIGHT/SPREAD **2ft (60cm)/3.3ft (1m)**
HARDINESS **Zone 7**

'Suitor' is a bushy Polyantha of *Rosa wichurana* descent. Its pretty, round buds open out to masses of small, neat, round flowers that are deep pink at first, but soon fade to mid-pink and then (more slowly) almost to white: it seems that every imaginable shade of pink is present on the bush at any one time. The petals have paler backs, with white flecks and a white base. The flowers are borne in large clusters, typically of 10–40. The plant has mid-green leaves, small leaflets, few prickles, and a spreading habit that makes it very suitable for the front of a border or for landscaping. It is fully recurrent, especially if deadheaded. As with most of Alister Clark's excellent hybrids, 'Suitor' is virtually unknown outside its native Australia.

'Suma'

Ground Cover

ORIGIN **Onodera, Japan, 1989**
PARENTAGE **'Nozomi' seedling**
FLOWER SIZE **1.4in (3.5cm)**
SCENT **Medium and sweet**
FLOWERING **Repeats**
HEIGHT/SPREAD **2.7ft (80cm)/3.3ft (1m)**
HARDINESS **Zone 6**

If you like small, scrambling, ground-cover roses, then 'Suma' is well worth growing. Its flowers are small, double, scented, and cherry red, fading to dark pink, with a white patch at the center and somewhat wavy petals. The flowers come in clusters of 5–20 all over the lax plant. 'Suma' has small, healthy, neat, dark leaves. If you train it up, it can be treated as a miniature climber and may reach 4.9ft (1.5m), but it is best grown as a lax groundcover plant or in a container. It repeats fairly well.

'Suma'

Summer Fragrance

see Sommerduft

Summer Gold

see Marselisborg

Summer Lady

syn. 'TANydal'

Hybrid Tea

ORIGIN **Tantau, Germany, 1991**
FLOWER SIZE **4.7in (12cm)**
SCENT **Medium and sweet**
FLOWERING **Repeats**
HEIGHT/SPREAD **4.1ft (1.25m)/2.7ft (80cm)**
HARDINESS **Zone 6**

Summer Lady is a popular modern exhibition rose whose elegant, slender buds are borne on long stems, which make them perfect for large floral arrangements. The flowers themselves are also large and carried both singly and in clusters of up to four. They are pale pink, with a slightly deeper shade of salmon pink on the backs of the petals, which gives a warm glow to the whole flower. Summer Lady makes a sturdy, vigorous, upright plant with large, healthy, leathery leaves. Its slender shape makes it a good choice for small gardens.

Summer Lady

'SUMMER SNOW'

'SUMMER SNOW'

Floribunda

ORIGIN **Couteau, France, 1936**
PARENTAGE **'Tausendschön' x unknown**
FLOWER SIZE **2in (5cm)**
SCENT **Medium and musky**
FLOWERING **Once, quite early in season**
HEIGHT/SPREAD **9.8ft (3m)/6.6ft (2m)**
HARDINESS **Zone 5**

'Summer Snow' is probably an open-pollinated seedling of 'Tausendschön', which it resembles in its lush, bright green leaves and its thornlessness. The flowers are paper white, and open very cupped to a mass of crinkly petals around a boss of stamens that very quickly turn brown. They come in somewhat congested clusters of 10–40. 'Summer Snow' is one of those roses that look better from a distance than close-up. The petals are thin and easily rain-damaged, so the plant is at its best in dry weather. It flowers very profusely over a long period repeating later. The climber, however, does not.

SUMMER SNOW

see 'POPCORN'

'SUMMER SUNSHINE'

Hybrid Tea

ORIGIN **Swim, US, 1962**
PARENTAGE **'Buccaneer' x 'Lemon Chiffon'**
FLOWER SIZE **4.7in (12cm)**
SCENT **Medium and fruity**
FLOWERING **Repeats well**
HEIGHT/SPREAD **4.9ft (1.5m)/4.1ft (1.25m)**
HARDINESS **Zone 6**

'SUMMER SUNSHINE'

Although 'Summer Sunshine' is more than 40 years old now, its popularity remains undiminished. It has the reputation of being the earliest and latest Hybrid Tea to flower, and is among the best of all yellow roses for keeping its color. The flowers are mid-yellow, opening from long, elegant buds. They are lightly double and open out to expose golden stamens and crimson filaments. As they are usually borne singly on long stems, the flowers are especially popular as cutting roses. The plant has large, matte, mid-green leaves, crimson new foliage, and large crimson prickles. It is vigorous and upright, and flowers not continuously but in a series of flushes.

'SUMMER WIND'

Shrub Rose

ORIGIN **Buck, US, 1975**
PARENTAGE **('Fandango' x 'Florence Mary Morse') x 'Applejack'**
FLOWER SIZE **3.9in (10cm)**
SCENT **Light and fruity**
FLOWERING **Repeats**
HEIGHT/SPREAD **4.9ft (1.5m)/4.1ft (1.25m)**
HARDINESS **Zone 5**

This is one of Griffith Buck's earliest hardy hybrids and not so widely grown these days as his later, fuller roses. The flowers of 'Summer Wind' are no more than semidouble, but they are large and richly colored – pale crimson, with an orange wash toward the center that fades as the flowers age. They often have a small misshapen petal near the center, which actually gives extra character to the bloom as a whole. The flowers are borne singly and in clusters of up to about eight. 'Summer Wind' has a lot of healthy, dark green leaves and large thorns. It is a sturdy grower and quite upright, but also bushy. It repeats until the first frost of winter in its native Iowa.

'SUMMER WIND'

SUMMER WINE

SUMMER WINE

syn. 'KORIZONT'
Modern Climber

ORIGIN **Kordes, Germany, 1985**
FLOWER SIZE **3.1in (8cm)**
SCENT **Medium and sweet**
FLOWERING **Repeats well**
HEIGHT/SPREAD **13.1ft (4m)/6.6ft (2m)**
HARDINESS **Zone 6**

The flowers of Summer Wine are no more than semidouble at best, yet this climber has become one of the most popular in western Europe. Once seen, everyone is captivated. The flowers open from long, slender buds whose bright coral color sets off the gentle salmon pink of the open flowers. These have yellow centers and fade to pink and white, but the eye is seized by the long crimson filaments and yellow anthers of the stamens in the middle. They are simply unique in their beauty. The flowers are lightly cupped and come in small clusters (typically of 3–5), repeating well until late autumn. The plant has stout, prickly stems and large, fairly ordinary leaves. It will reach 2m (6.6ft) as a freestanding bush, or twice that height as a climber.

SUMMER'S KISS

see PAUL RICARD

SUN FLARE

syn. 'JACJEM'
Floribunda

ORIGIN **Warriner, US, 1981**
PARENTAGE **Friesia x seedling**
FLOWER SIZE **3.5in (9cm)**
SCENT **Light and fruity**
FLOWERING **Repeats well**
HEIGHT/SPREAD **2.5ft (75cm)/2.5ft (75cm)**
HARDINESS **Zone 6**
AWARDS **Japan GM 1981; AARS 1983; Portland GM 1985**

Sun Flare is a good, short, yellow Floribunda that can also be used in landscaping. The flowers are lightly double, open out nicely, and hold their petals loosely. They are a very bright yellow at first and keep their color well: they fade to a good pale yellow but never to white. The stamens also hold their color quite well and intensify the yellowness of the flowers, which are abundantly carried in clusters of 3–10. The bush has reddish prickles, a compact habit, and small, glossy, healthy leaves. Sometimes it also produces clusters of red hips.

SUN FLARE

SUN HIT

SUN HIT

syn. 'POULHIT'

Patio Rose

ORIGIN **Poulsen, Denmark, 1994**
FLOWER SIZE **2in (5cm)**
SCENT **Light and fruity**
FLOWERING **Repeats very well**
HEIGHT/SPREAD **2ft (60cm)/1.6ft (50cm)**
HARDINESS **Zone 6**

When allowed to grow to its full size, Sun Hit is naturally a patio rose. However, it was originally developed for the potted rose market, where Poulsen is a major player, and so it is usually seen as several rooted cuttings growing in a small pot and flowering spectacularly. It is just as good as a garden plant. The shapely flowers are fully double and a good lemon yellow, with hints of amber and peach toward the center. They come singly and in small clusters, rarely with more than five flowers, but generously carried all over the surface of the plant. Sun Hit has small, healthy, dark green leaves, a few small prickles, and a vigorous habit of growth. It is a quick and reliable repeat flowerer.

SUN SPRINKLES

syn. 'JACHAL'

Miniature Rose

ORIGIN **Walden, US, 1999**
PARENTAGE **Yellow Jacket seedling**
FLOWER SIZE **1.8in (4.5cm)**
SCENT **Light and fruity**
FLOWERING **Repeats well**
HEIGHT/SPREAD **2.7ft (80cm)/2ft (60cm)**
HARDINESS **Zone 6**
AWARDS **AARS 2001**

It is classified as a miniature rose, but Sun Sprinkles will grow to 2.7ft (80cm) in hot climates. Its flowers are a good, rich, golden yellow, fading to pale yellow, but lasting a long time on the plant and when cut for the house. They are lightly double and borne both singly and in small clusters. The flowers look especially intensely colored against the small, dark, glossy foliage. Sun Sprinkles usually makes a compact, vigorous little bush, though sometimes the new growths shoot up through the flowers and spoil the effect. It is useful wherever its bright color is welcome, from large landscaping designs to single plants in containers.

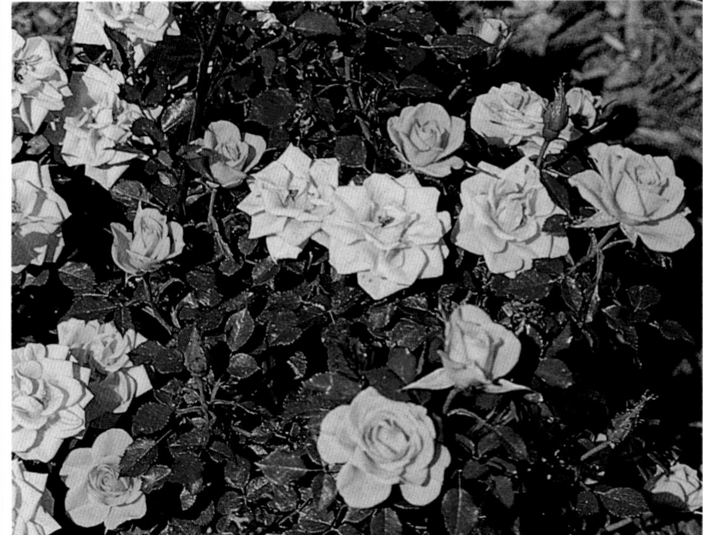
SUN SPRINKLES

'SUNBLEST'

see 'LANDORA'

'SUNLIT'

Hybrid Tea

ORIGIN **Clark, Australia, 1937**
FLOWER SIZE **2.8in (7cm)**
SCENT **Medium**
FLOWERING **Fully recurrent**
HEIGHT/SPREAD **3.3ft (1m)/3.3ft (1m)**
HARDINESS **Zone 8**

Its ancestry is unknown, but 'Sunlit' is exactly the sort of Hybrid Tea rose descended from *Rosa gigantea* that Alister Clark sought to develop for the Australian climate. It is a very handsome color: rich apricot, aging to pink and mother-of-pearl, with striking purple red stamens. The petal backs are much darker than the upper sides – dark pinky apricot – which means that they contrast with the much paler upper sides and create beautiful dark shades at the center of the flower. The plant has broad leaflets, smooth leaves, few prickles, and a very compact habit of growth. It is very floriferous, flowering all year in hot climates.

SUN SPRITE

see FRIESIA

'SUNNY JUNE'

Shrub Rose

ORIGIN **Lammerts, US, 1952**
PARENTAGE **'Crimson Glory' x 'Captain Thomas'**
FLOWER SIZE **2.8in (7cm)**
SCENT **Light and fruity**
FLOWERING **Repeats well**
HEIGHT/SPREAD **6.6ft (2m)/4.9ft (1.5m)**
HARDINESS **Zone 5**

'Sunny June' can be summed up as a yellow version of 'Mrs. Oakley Fisher' or a hardy 'Captain Thomas'. Its flowers are single, with an occasional extra petal or two. The petals are quite narrow, so they rarely overlap and the background is visible between them. They open from long, pointed buds and are pure dark yellow all through, except for a large copper red circle of stamens. The dark, glossy, healthy leaves are an excellent foil for the small clusters of flowers on long stems that are produced incessantly until late autumn. 'Sunny June' is an upright shrub or pillar rose, but will make 13.1ft (4m) up a wall in hot areas.

'SUNNY JUNE'

'SUNLIT'

'SUNNY SOUTH'

Hybrid Tea

ORIGIN **Clark, Australia, 1918**
PARENTAGE **'Gustav Grünerwald' x 'Betty Berkeley'**
FLOWER SIZE **3.1in (8cm)**
SCENT **Medium and sweet**
FLOWERING **Fully recurrent**
HEIGHT/SPREAD **6.6ft (2m)/6.6ft (2m)**
HARDINESS **Zone 8**

'Sunny South' is a popular rose in Australia, where it was once widely used for ornamental hedges. It is a vigorous, upright bush or pillar rose that pushes up a mass of long, slender flowering stems like a modern Grandiflora rose. The slim, elegant buds open out very prettily to well-spaced flowers that are rich pink (fading to pale pink), flushed with carmine, and peach pink or yellow at the base of the petals. They are lightly double, with prominent stamens and a good scent. The flowers are borne singly or, more usually, in clusters of up to six. 'Sunny South' produces very handsome, purple new growth and has a long flowering period.

SUNSATION

see STADT WÜRZBURG

SUNSEEKER

see DUCHESS OF YORK

'SUNNY SOUTH'

SUNSET BOULEVARD

SUNSET BOULEVARD

syn. 'HARBABBLE'
Floribunda

ORIGIN **Harkness, Britain, 1997**
PARENTAGE **Harold Macmillan x Fellowship**
FLOWER SIZE **4.3in (11cm)**
SCENT **Light**
FLOWERING **Repeats well**
HEIGHT/SPREAD **3.3ft (1m)/2.7ft (80cm)**
HARDINESS **Zone 6**
AWARDS **ROTY 1997; Glasgow GM 1998**

The qualities of Sunset Boulevard have yet to be widely appreciated in the US. It is a vibrant and very floriferous orange yellow Floribunda. It opens from shapely Hybrid Tea buds, though their strawberry red color is unusual. The loosely double flowers are apricot orange with hints of coral, fading eventually to pinker tones. They are borne on strong stems singly or in clusters of up to nine. The plant has handsome, glossy, healthy leaves. It is a glorious sight when planted in large numbers as a bedding rose – but not for lovers of muted tones.

SUPER DOROTHY

SUNSET CELEBRATION

see WARM WISHES

SUNSHINE

see CELINA

SUPER DOROTHY

syn. 'HELDORO'
Wichurana Rambler

ORIGIN **Hetzel, Germany, 1986**
PARENTAGE **'Dorothy Perkins' seedling**
FLOWER SIZE **1.8in (4.5cm)**
SCENT **Little or none**
FLOWERING **Repeats well**
HEIGHT/SPREAD **9.8ft (3m)/6.6ft (2m)**
HARDINESS **Zone 5**

Karl Hetzel bred Super Dorothy as an improved 'Dorothy Perkins' – repeat-flowering and free from mildew. Its flowers are slightly darker than those of 'Dorothy Perkins', but a good deep pink with paler petal backs and a white patch at the center. Super Dorothy's flowers fade as they age, and particularly where the petals are directly exposed to sunlight. They come in large, loose panicles, typically of 20–40 flowers. The leaves are small, mid-green, glossy, and healthy, except for an occasional brush with blackspot. Super Dorothy has pale green stems, a smattering of prickles, and a loose habit. It is not as vigorous as 'Dorothy Perkins', but its lax habit makes it suitable for training as a good weeping standard. Super Dorothy starts into flower fairly late, but is then a good and quick repeater, rarely out of flower for long until the first frost.

SUPER EXCELSA

syn. 'HELEXA'
Wichurana Shrub

ORIGIN **Hetzel, Germany, 1986**
PARENTAGE **'Excelsa' x unknown**
FLOWER SIZE **1.4in (3.5cm)**
SCENT **Light**
FLOWERING **Repeats well**
HEIGHT/SPREAD **6.6ft (2m)/6.6ft (2m)**
HARDINESS **Zone 5**
AWARDS **ADR 1992**

SUPER EXCELSA

Karl Hetzel bred Super Excelsa as an improved version of the popular, hardy old rambler 'Excelsa'. It was the first of his hybrids to win the prestigious ADR award – healthier than 'Excelsa', and repeat flowering. It produces large clusters of fully double, carmine crimson flowers, with a white center and occasional white streaks through the petals. They fade to a more purple color as they age, and have paler, more silvery, backs to the petals. The plant is not as vigorous as 'Excelsa', and can barely be called a climber, but it produces its flowers repeatedly after the first heavy flowering in midseason. It has dark, Wichurana leaves and a lax habit. It makes a good pillar or groundcover rose, and a magnificent tall weeping standard. It is very hardy, but good in hot climates, too, though it may get mildew.

SUPER FAIRY

syn. 'HELSUFAIR'
Multiflora Rambler

ORIGIN **Hetzel, Germany, 1992**
FLOWER SIZE **1.4in (3.5cm)**
SCENT **Light and musky**
FLOWERING **Repeats**
HEIGHT/SPREAD **13.1ft (4m)/8.2ft (2.5m)**
HARDINESS **Zone 5**

This is the tallest of the Hetzel climbers, which aim to combine the abundance of the old ramblers with the ability to flower again and again. Super Fairy has rich pink flowers that fade to light pink and have a brush of golden stamens at the center. They are borne in large clusters, typically of 10–20 flowers, right through until late autumn, though the first flowering is still the most spectacular. The clusters also last surprisingly well as cut flowers. Super Fairy is a vigorous plant, with long, slender, flexible stems and small, bright, healthy leaves. Its lax habit of growth and ability to reflower make it a useful weeping standard.

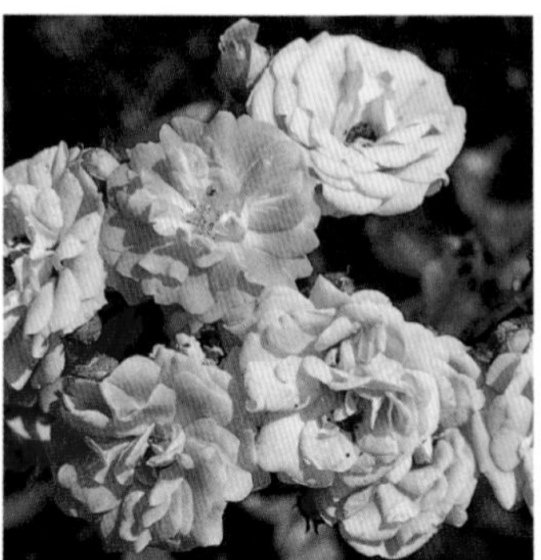
SUPER FAIRY

'SUPER STAR'

syn. 'TROPICANA'
Hybrid Tea

ORIGIN **Tantau, Germany, 1960**
PARENTAGE **'Mme. A. Meilland' seedling x 'Alpenglühen' seedling**
FLOWER SIZE **5.1in (13cm)**
SCENT **Strong, sweet, and fruity**
FLOWERING **Repeats very well**
HEIGHT/SPREAD **4.9ft (1.5m)/3.3ft (1m)**
HARDINESS **Zone 6**
AWARDS **NRS PIT 1960; Portland GM 1961; AARS 1963; ARS GM 1967**

'SUPER STAR'

'CLIMBING SUPER STAR'

'Super Star' was a sensation when it was first introduced, especially in North America, where it was renamed 'Tropicana'. It carried the bright geranium red pigment known as pelargonidin, which is not natural to roses, but which gives modern cultivars their extraordinary brilliance. Its flowers are large and perfectly shaped, very strongly scented, vigorous, and healthy. They are very freely borne on long stems, singly and in clusters of up to five. In fact, 'Super Star' was a popular, long lasting rose for cutting and exhibition, as well as being a first-rate garden performer. The flowers are shades of orange, vermilion, and coral, with slightly more salmon pink petal backs, but all imbued with the vivid intensity of geraniums. The plant has large leaves and more than a scattering of large prickles. It is almost constantly in flower. Some years after it was first introduced, however, the super-healthy 'Super Star' began to be badly affected by mildew. This was not the fault of the rose, but may be the result of a mutation of the mildew fungus. The popularity of 'Super Star' took a knock, and so did the popularity of all roses as easy to grow, no-work garden plants. Ever since that date (*c.*1970), breeders have concentrated above all upon the production of disease free roses, and with great success. That said, 'Super Star' is still healthy in dry climates. The climbing sport, known as **'Climbing Super Star'** is similar in most respects apart from its vigorous climbing habit. Like many climbing sports, its flowers are slightly larger than the bush form and very freely borne in their first flush.

Sport of 'Super Star'

'CLIMBING SUPER STAR'

syn. 'CLIMBING TROPICANA'
Climbing Hybrid Tea
ORIGIN **Boerner, US, 1971**
FLOWER SIZE **5.5in (14cm)**
FLOWERING **Copious first flowering, then intermittently**
HEIGHT/SPREAD **13.1ft (4m)/8.2ft (2.5m)**

S

'SURPASSE TOUT'

Gallica

ORIGIN **Hardy, France, c.1823**
FLOWER SIZE **2.8in (7cm)**
SCENT **Very strong and sweet**
FLOWERING **Once only**
HEIGHT/SPREAD **4.1ft (1.25m)/3.3ft (1m)**
HARDINESS **Zone 5**

Although 'Surpasse Tout' does not really live up to its name, nevertheless it is a very beautiful Gallica rose. The flowers are a bright dark pink or cherry color, with slightly paler backs to the petals and a wonderful scent. The flowers have a lot of petals, a flat or lightly cupped shape, and, usually, a large button eye. They come in clusters of 3–7, with quite long stems and stalks. The plant is vigorous, with a lot of bushy branches and only a few prickles. Its leaves are large, mid-green, and typical of the Gallica roses, with slender leaflets and a ridged surface.

'SURPASSE TOUT'

SURREY

see SOMMERWIND

'SUSAN HAMPSHIRE'

Hybrid Tea

ORIGIN **Paolino, France, 1972**
PARENTAGE **('Monique' × 'Symphonie') × 'Maria Callas'**
FLOWER SIZE **5.1in (13cm)**
SCENT **Strong and sweet**
FLOWERING **Repeats**
HEIGHT/SPREAD **4.1ft (1.25m)/3.3ft (1m)**
HARDINESS **Zone 6**

The flowers of 'Susan Hampshire' are large, and so full of petals that they take a long time to open out. They are deep magenta pink, fading only slightly as they age, and shapely both as opening buds and when fully expanded. They are usually borne singly on long stems, and are very sweetly scented. 'Susan Hampshire' makes a vigorous and free flowering plant, with lots of large, dull, mid-green leaves. It does best in dry, warm climates and responds well to feeding. At their best, the flowers are nothing short of sumptuous. Susan Hampshire is an English actress, popular for her part in a television adaption of *The Forsyte Saga*.

'SUSAN HAMPSHIRE'

'SUSAN LOUISE'

Hybrid Gigantea

ORIGIN **Adams, US, 1929**
FLOWER SIZE **4.3in (11cm)**
SCENT **Light and tealike**
FLOWERING **Continuous**
HEIGHT/SPREAD **4.9ft (1.5m)/4.9ft (1.5m)**
HARDINESS **Zone 9**

There is some debate about the origins of 'Susan Louise'. Everyone agrees that it is related to the magnificent 'Belle Portugaise' – one of the most popular climbers in California, where 'Susan Louise' comes from – but no one knows whether it is a sport or a seedling of it. In any event, it helps to think of 'Susan Louise' as a short, bushy, repeat flowering version of 'Belle Portugaise'. Its buds are long, slender, elegant, and dark pink. They open out paler, a soft, creamy pink with a hint of apricot at the center. Like 'Belle Portugaise', the flowers often have a few small petals folded over the center and hiding the pale stamens. 'Susan Louise' has long leaves with slender leaflets that droop in the elegant manner of *Rosa gigantea*. In hot climates it flowers all the year through, and, if fed and left unpruned, will eventually make an enormous shrub at least 9.8ft (3m) high and wide.

'SUSAN LOUISE'

SUSSEX

syn. 'POULAVE'

Ground Cover

ORIGIN **Poulsen, Denmark, 1991**
FLOWER SIZE **2in (5cm)**
SCENT **Light and sweet**
FLOWERING **Almost continuous**
HEIGHT/SPREAD **2ft (60cm)/4.1ft (1.25m)**
HARDINESS **Zone 6**

SUSSEX

This has proved one of the most popular of modern groundcover roses. At their best, the flowers of Sussex are exquisite in both shape and color: fully double, imbricated, and rich apricot, fading to buff at the edges, with a golden flush on the innermost petals. Such perfection lasts for no more than a day: thereafter the flowers fade to pink and dirty white, the stamens turn brown, and the petals reflex to a commonplace shape. However, the flowers are borne in long lasting clusters of 3–10, and there are always fresh flowers to take the place of the spent ones. Sussex has dark green leaves, bronzy new growth, and an open, spreading habit of growth. It is a very good repeat flowerer, which gives of its best in cool climates like that of England or its native Denmark.

'SUTTER'S GOLD'

Hybrid Tea

ORIGIN **Swim, US, 1950**
PARENTAGE **'Charlotte Armstrong' × 'Signora Piero Puricelli'**
FLOWER SIZE **5.5in (14cm)**
SCENT **Strong, sweet, and fruity**
FLOWERING **Repeats well**
HEIGHT/SPREAD **4.9ft (1.5m)/4.1ft (1.25m)**
HARDINESS **Zone 6**
AWARDS **Portland GM 1946; Bagatelle GM 1948; Geneva GM 1949; AARS 1950**

'SUTTER'S GOLD'

The middle years of the 20th century were the high point for Hybrid Teas. 'Sutter's Gold' is one of many stunning roses from that period that have remained intensely popular to this day. The long-petaled flowers are deep golden yellow at first, fading to lemon yellow. They open from red buds, and keep the red splashes on the backs of their outer petals, though they usually fade to pink. Sometimes, especially in hot weather, the red intensifies, but, however the coloring is distributed, it is always vivid and attractive. The flowers have long, elegant buds but open out lightly double and, in dry weather, may eventually reflex their petals into spiky tips. The flowers are almost always borne singly on a vigorous, quick growing, and quick repeating plant. They come very early in the season and are often the first of all the Hybrid Teas to open. 'Sutter's Gold' has dark green leaves (fairly healthy) and a lot of prickles. It is a first-rate garden plant in almost any climate. When especially well grown, the flowers can reach as much as 6.3in (16cm). When not so happy, they have fewer petals, but the plant never stops producing them.

Weeks produced a climbing form in 1954, which is a vigorous, prickly grower and can reach 13.1ft (4m). **'Climbing Sutter's Gold'** flowers very early in the season, and profusely, but only intermittently thereafter.

Sport of 'Sutter's Gold'

'CLIMBING SUTTER'S GOLD'

Climbing Hybrid Tea
ORIGIN **Weeks, US, 1950?**
HEIGHT/SPREAD **13.1ft (4m)/8.2ft (2.5m)**

Swan

'Swan Lake'

Swan

syn. 'AUSwhite'

Shrub Rose

ORIGIN **Austin, Britain, 1987**
PARENTAGE **'Charles Austin' x (seedling x 'Schneewittchen')**
FLOWER SIZE **3.5in (9cm)**
SCENT **Light**
FLOWERING **Repeats well**
HEIGHT/SPREAD **4.9ft (1.5m)/4.9ft (1.5m)**
HARDINESS **Zone 5**

Swan is one of those David Austin roses that does best in hot, dry climates: in its native England, it balls and spots in the rain, as well as attracting mildew and rust. The buds are long and elegant like a Hybrid Tea's, but the open flower is a complete contrast – full of quilled petals, rosette-shaped, sometimes quartered, and always exquisitely beautiful. The flowers are lemon yellow at first, with hints of buff at the center, but soon fade to cream and white. They come singly or in clusters of 3–5, excellent for cutting, with very long stems. The flowers open slowly and last well in water. The plant has ordinary Hybrid Tea-like leaves and a vigorous, upright habit of growth. With good cultivation, it repeats very quickly.

'Swan Lake'

Modern Climber

ORIGIN **McGredy, Northern Ireland, 1968**
PARENTAGE **'Memoriam' x 'Gruss an Heidelberg'**
FLOWER SIZE **3.1in (8cm)**
SCENT **Light and sweet**
FLOWERING **Repeats**
HEIGHT/SPREAD **9.8ft (3m)/6.6ft (2m)**
HARDINESS **Zone 6**

The flowers of 'Swan Lake' are elegantly shaped and very full of petals, but their greatest quality is that they stand up well to rain, which makes this short-growing climber a good choice for damp climates. The flowers are white, with a beautiful flush of pink at the center, and usually come in small clusters (of 3–7 flowers), but are occasionally borne singly. The stems are long, which makes them good for picking: the individual flowers are quite small, but a cluster looks good in a specimen vase and lasts well. The plant is fairly vigorous, but not a tall grower, so 'Swan Lake' can also be grown as a bush rose. It has a lot of healthy, dark green leaves and repeats very well.

Swany

syn. 'MEIburenac'

Ground Cover

ORIGIN **Meilland, France, 1978**
PARENTAGE ***Rosa sempervirens* hybrid x 'Mlle. Marthe Carron'**
FLOWER SIZE **2.4in (6cm)**
SCENT **Light and musky**
FLOWERING **Repeats**
HEIGHT/SPREAD **2ft (60cm)/4.9ft (1.5m)**
HARDINESS **Zone 6**

This was an important rose – Meilland's first entry into the new market for groundcover roses, and still one of the best. Swany combines the genes of two evergreen roses, *Rosa sempervirens* and (through 'Mlle. Marthe Carron') *Rosa wichurana*, but, instead of being a vigorous climber, it remains a lax, repeat flowering shrub. The flowers are pure white, with just a shadow of palest pink as they open, and full of petals neatly arranged as a rosette. They come in clusters of 5–20 on fairly long stems. The leaves are very handsome – dark, small, glossy, and evergreen. Swany has a loose, open habit and is extremely useful scrambling down a bank or over an old tree stump. It can also be trained as a short pillar rose.

Swany *(grown as a standard at Bagetelle, Paris)*

Sweet Chariot

syn. 'MORchari'

Polyantha

ORIGIN **Moore, US, 1984**
PARENTAGE **'Little Chief' x 'Violette'**
FLOWER SIZE **1.2in (3cm)**
SCENT **Strong and sweet**
FLOWERING **Repeats well**
HEIGHT/SPREAD **2ft (60cm)/2ft (60cm)**
HARDINESS **Zone 6**

One of the parents of Sweet Chariot is 'Violette', the most purple of all the old ramblers. The flowers of Sweet Chariot share this rich, dark color when they open, then fade to lilac: the contrast between the two shades is very beautiful. The flowers form very double, neat rosettes, and the strong Damask scent is most unusual among short roses. The flowers come in large clusters, usually of 5–15, and are borne in great quantity all over the surface of the bush. Sweet Chariot is also a quick and bountiful repeat flowerer. It has a lax habit, which means that it is good in containers, but it is probably seen at its best as a garden plant when surrounded by complementary color plantings. The small, neat, mid-green leaves are a good complement, but they sometimes suffer from blackspot. This is not a problem in dry climates.

Sweet Chariot

Sweet Dream

syn. 'FRYminicot'

Patio Rose

ORIGIN **Fryer, Britain, 1988**
PARENTAGE **seedling x (['Anytime' x 'Liverpool Echo']) x (['New Penny' x seedling])**
FLOWER SIZE **2.4in (6cm)**
SCENT **Good, sweet, and fruity**
FLOWERING **Repeats well**
HEIGHT/SPREAD **2.7ft (80cm)/1.6ft (50cm)**
HARDINESS **Zone 6**
AWARDS **ROTY 1988; James Mason GM 1998**

This short Floribunda has been a bestseller in England ever since its introduction. The flowers are a beautiful apricot, fading to buff, and it combines very well in the garden with other colors and plantings. They are very cupped, with a lot of petals and a delicious scent. They are borne in slightly congested clusters (typically of 5–15 flowers). The plant is fairly bushy, with a narrow, erect habit of growth and dark, healthy, glossy leaves. It is small enough to be grown in containers, but is more widely used as a permanent planting at the front of a border. It is extremely profuse and flowers continuously until late autumn.

Sweet Dream

SWEET INSPIRATION

SWEET JULIET

SWEET INSPIRATION

syn. 'JACSIM'

Floribunda

ORIGIN **Warriner, US, 1991**
PARENTAGE Sun Flare x Simplicity
FLOWER SIZE **3.1in (8cm)**
SCENT **Light**
FLOWERING **Repeats well**
HEIGHT/SPREAD **2.7ft (80cm)/2ft (60cm)**
HARDINESS **Zone 6**
AWARDS **AARS 1993**

Sweet Inspiration is a beautiful, low-growing Floribunda. The flowers are soft sugar pink, with cream and white at the base of the petals and toward the center of the flower. They look best as they open out, when they have an attractive Hybrid Tea shape, and somewhat more ordinary when their petals open out fully. They come in small clusters – typically of 3–7 flowers, but sometimes singly – and in great profusion, so that the bushes seems to be covered in flowers during their first, main flowering. Re-bloom is good. The bush has fairly ordinary but healthy, mid-green leaves, few prickles, and a compact habit of growth. It is easy to grow and looks good both in massed plantings and as a single plant in a mixed border.

SWEET JULIET

syn. 'AUSLEAP'

Shrub Rose

ORIGIN **Austin, Britain, 1989**
PARENTAGE Graham Thomas x Admired Miranda
FLOWER SIZE **2.4in (6cm)**
SCENT **Strong and fruity**
FLOWERING **Repeats well, with brief gaps between flowerings**
HEIGHT/SPREAD **3.9ft (1.2m)/3ft (90cm)**
HARDINESS **Zone 6**
AWARDS **Belfast FA 1992**

The small buds of Sweet Juliet open out to flat, pretty rosettes and an irregular mass of short petals at the center of the flowers. Sometimes they have a button eye. Their color is a combination of apricot, buff, peach, and pink – an unusually complex mixture – but the petal backs are always darker and the pinks lose their yellow tinges with age. The guard petals are always much paler. The flowers come singly or in clusters of up to seven. The plant makes a leafy bush (mildew may be a problem in damp climates) with large leaves and pointed leaflets. In fact, it has a tendency to produce leaves at the expense of flowers. It performs best, and repeats quickly, in hot climates when it is well fed and watered. Then it will make a good pillar rose up to 8.2ft (2.5m) tall. "Sweet Juliet," implored Romeo, "make me immortal with a kiss."

SWEET MAGIC

syn. 'DICMAGIC'

Miniature Rose

ORIGIN **Dickson, Northern Ireland, 1986**
PARENTAGE Peek-a-Boo x Bright Smile
FLOWER SIZE **1.6in (4cm)**
SCENT **Moderate and sweet**
FLOWERING **Repeats well**
HEIGHT/SPREAD **2ft (60cm)/2ft (60cm)**
HARDINESS **Zone 6**
AWARDS **ROTY 1987**

Sweet Magic is a short, cheerful, orange miniature, still popular in Britain. Its flowers have a much more regular shape than most small roses: it has what rose breeders call "good form." The flowers are bright orange at first, with a yellow center and a light gold wash on the petal backs. Later on, the orange fades to pink, but the flower retains its good shape and remains eye-catching. The plant is fairly compact, with small, dark, neat, glossy leaves that are in proportion to the flowers and set them off well. It is generally healthy, though blackspot may be a problem.

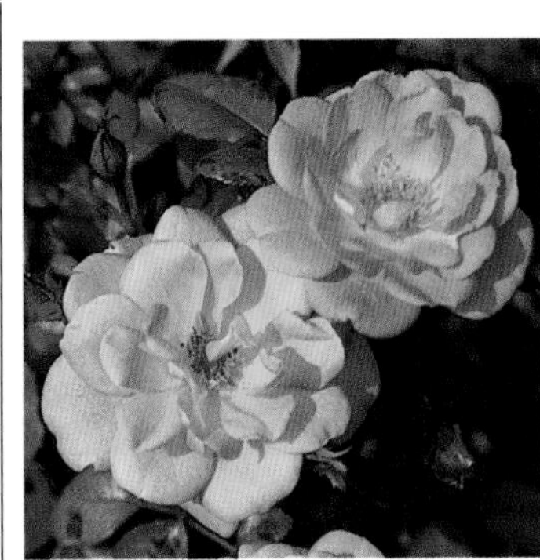
SWEET MAGIC

SWEET SUNBLAZE

see PINK SYMPHONIE

'SWEET SURRENDER'

Hybrid Tea

ORIGIN **Weeks, US, 1983**
PARENTAGE **seedling x 'Tiffany'**
FLOWER SIZE **4.7in (12cm)**
SCENT **Strong, sweet, and Damasky**
FLOWERING **Repeats**
HEIGHT/SPREAD **4.1ft (1.25m)/3.3ft (1m)**
HARDINESS **Zone 6**
AWARDS **AARS 1983**

Large pink Hybrid Teas are always popular, but 'Sweet Surrender' also has a slightly old-fashioned look reminiscent of the great Hybrid Perpetuals of the 19th century. The flowers open from surprisingly small (but elegant) buds, and go on growing as they expand their many petals. Sometimes the flowers become so large and heavy with petals that they nod over. They are a clear mid-pink in color, fading to pale creamy pink, with slightly darker petal backs. The colors are strongest in warm weather, but the flowers are at least always pink at the center. They are borne usually singly, on long stems, but occasionally in clusters of up to four. The plant has mid-green, healthy leaves and repeats well.

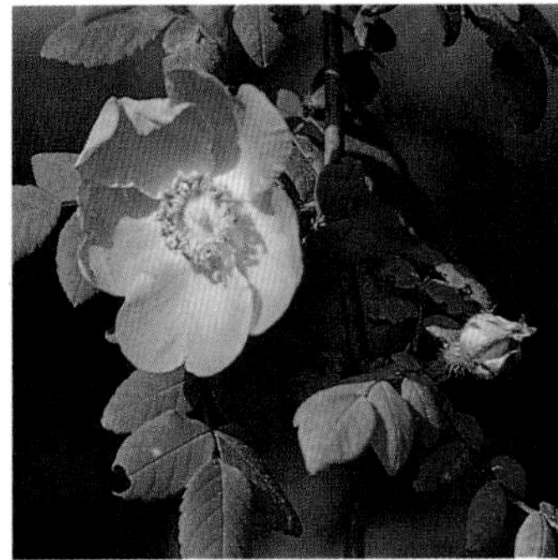
ROSA SWEGINZOWII

ROSA SWEGINZOWII

Wild Rose

FLOWER SIZE **1.6in (4cm)**
SCENT **Light and sweet**
FLOWERING **Once only**
HEIGHT/SPREAD **9.8ft (3m)/6.6ft (2m)**
HARDINESS **Zone 5**

Rosa sweginzowii is grown for its handsome prickles and long hips. Its flowers are pretty, but fleeting – pale pink with pale stamens, and borne either singly or in twos and threes. The sepals and calyx have tiny aromatic hairs, which emit the same pinewood scent as Moss roses exude when rubbed. The hips are vermilion, long, and waisted, with the sepals persisting at the base. The prickles are large, triangular, and glowing crimson when young, later gray. *Rosa sweginzowii* also has long, attractive leaves with as many as 13 leaflets. It is native to quite a large area of northwestern China, and shows much variability in the wild. It also merges with *Rosa moyesii*. A form called *Rosa sweginzowii* 'Macrocarpa' (which is probably of hybrid origin), with larger hips, is particularly popular in Germany.

'SWEET SURRENDER'

'SYDONIE'

'SYDONIE'

Portland

ORIGIN **Dorisy, France, 1846**
FLOWER SIZE **3.1in (8cm)**
SCENT **Strong and sweet**
FLOWERING **Remontant**
HEIGHT/SPREAD **4.9ft (1.5m)/3.3ft (1m)**
HARDINESS **Zone 5**

At first sight, 'Sydonie' is almost indistinguishable from 'Jacques Cartier', another Portland rose of the mid-19th century. Its flowers are full and flat, rose pink at the center and pale pink at the edges. The many petals are larger around the edge of the flower and smaller, nibbed, and pleated toward the center. They form a rough button eye around the stigma, and come in short-stalked clusters of 3–5 flowers. Like all Portlands, 'Sydonie' has thick, sturdy stems and very short internodes that shorten toward the tips, so that the flowers seem to be surrounded by a ruff of leaves. The leaves are larger than those of 'Jacques Cartier' and the leaflets rounder. The stems, too, are more prickly. But the two roses never flower at quite the same time, so you can extend the season usefully by growing both.

SYLVIA

syn. 'KORLIFT', Congratulations
Floribunda

ORIGIN **Kordes, Germany, 1979**
PARENTAGE **'Carina' seedling**
FLOWER SIZE **4.7in (12cm)**
SCENT **Medium and sweet**
FLOWERING **Repeats**
HEIGHT/SPREAD **6.6ft (2m)/4.1ft (1.25m)**
HARDINESS **Zone 6**
AWARDS **ADR 1977**

The English name of Sylvia is Congratulations, which guarantees its popularity in Britain. It is very widely grown in Europe and Australia, but has never been introduced into the US. Sylvia has large, elegant, silvery pink flowers that open slowly from classic, mid-pink, Hybrid Tea buds. When eventually the flowers open out completely, the petals are fully (and neatly) reflexed, and a creamy yellow flush is sometimes discernible at the center. The flowers are usually borne singly (occasionally in twos and threes) on long stems, which make them useful for cutting. They last a long time both on the bush and as cut flowers. Sylvia is vigorous, upright, and fairly healthy (watch out for mildew), with large, mid-green, semiglossy leaves. It repeats regularly through until autumn.

SYLVIA

'SYLVIE VARTAN'

Polyantha

ORIGIN **Eve, France, 1969**
FLOWER SIZE **2.4in (6cm)**
SCENT **Light and sweet**
FLOWERING **Repeats well**
HEIGHT/SPREAD **2.7ft (80cm)/2.7ft (80cm)**
HARDINESS **Zone 6**

This was the first rose to be bred and introduced by André Eve, the French nurseryman who was largely responsible for starting the Old Rose movement in France. 'Sylvie Vartan' has remained one of Eve's most popular roses. It is a bright pink Polyantha of the Floribunda type. Its flowers are full of petals, charming in shape, and borne in clusters of 5–10. They show up well against the handsome, healthy, dark green leaves. 'Sylvie Vartan' is low-growing and compact, but vigorous, and throws out a constant succession of beautiful flowers until late in the year. Its name honors one of the great French chanteuses of the 20th century.

'SYLVIE VARTAN'

'SYMPATHIE'

Kordesii Hybrid

ORIGIN **Kordes, Germany, 1964**
PARENTAGE **'Wilhelm Hansmann' x 'Don Juan'**
FLOWER SIZE **3.9in (10cm)**
SCENT **Light and sweet**
FLOWERING **Repeats well**
HEIGHT/SPREAD **11.5ft (3.5m)/6.6ft (2m)**
HARDINESS **Zone 5**

'SYMPATHIE'

This is a second-generation Kordesii Hybrid. 'Sympathie' combines the hardiness of the Kordesii race with the elegant shape of the Hybrid Teas. The flowers are double and high-centered, with elegantly reflexing petals. They are a sumptuous rich red, with a dark crimson overlay in places, which gives a velvety sheen. Some of the petals have an occasional white fleck at their bases. The flowers are freely borne in clusters of 3–10: the lavish main flowering is followed by a series of smaller ones, so that the plant is rarely without flowers until late autumn. The flowers seem to stand up well to wind and rain. 'Sympathie' makes a bushy, vigorous plant with healthy, glossy, rich green leaves and a lot of new stems coming up from the bottom.

SYMPHONY

syn. 'AUSLETT'
Shrub Rose

ORIGIN **Austin, Britain, 1986**
PARENTAGE **'The Friar' x 'Yellow Cushion'**
FLOWER SIZE **3.1in (8cm)**
SCENT **Medium and sweet**
FLOWERING **Repeats**
HEIGHT/SPREAD **3.3ft (1m)/3.3ft (1m)**
HARDINESS **Zone 5**

This is a good yellow English Rose from David Austin, though much more popular in hotter climates than in England itself. Symphony has fairly large flowers in tight clusters of up to seven. They have a beautiful old-fashioned shape, usually quartered and lightly cupped, with a mass of small petals held within broad guard petals. The flowers are yellow at first, fading to cream and white from the outside inward. The outer petals later take on a pink tinge as they age. The plant has large, medium-dark, glossy leaves and an upright habit of growth. Symphony is a good flowerer, starting early and continuing almost without interruption until late autumn. Its flowers spoil in damp climates like England's, but are superb in much of California and most of Australia.

SYMPHONY

TABOO

see BARKAROLE

TABRIS

see NICOLE

'TALISMAN'

Hybrid Tea

ORIGIN **Montgomery, US, 1929**
PARENTAGE **'Ophelia' x 'Souvenir de Claudius Pernet'**
FLOWER SIZE **3.5in (9cm)**
SCENT **Medium and sweet**
FLOWERING **Repeats**
HEIGHT/SPREAD **4.1ft (1.25m)/3.3ft (1m)**
HARDINESS **Zone 6**
AWARDS **ARS GM 1929**

In the 1930s, 'Talisman' was one of the world's most popular roses. The flowers are not large, but an unusual and attractive combination of colors: red, yellow, pink, and white at various stages of their development, always very variable but mainly reddish with yellow on the petal backs. They start from pointed buds and eventually open out almost completely flat. The flowers are borne singly on long, slender stems. The plant has mid-green leaves and lots of thin, upright stems. It flowers early and repeats well.

TALL STORY

syn. 'DICKOOKY'

Shrub Rose

ORIGIN **Dickson, Northern Ireland, 1984**
PARENTAGE **Friesia x 'Yesterday'**
FLOWER SIZE **2in (5cm)**
SCENT **Strong and fruity**
FLOWERING **Repeats well**
HEIGHT/SPREAD **5.7ft (1.75m)/4.1ft (1.25m)**
HARDINESS **Zone 6**

'TALISMAN'

Tall Story is the result of an unusual cross that gives it considerable originality and hybrid vigor. Its flowers are produced in great quantities in upright clusters of 5–15. They open lemon yellow and fade to white and are carried on graceful, arching stems. Their fragrance carries on the air and is particularly strong at night. The flowers are well shown off by the pale but bright green leaves, which also have good disease resistance. It makes a lax shrub that, left to its own devices, tends to grow wider than high, so that it can be used as groundcover. It is best if loosely tied to a stake or other support, when its remarkable ability to flower right down to ground level can be appreciated. It will then reach about 6.6ft (2m) and flower continuously until late autumn.

TAMORA

syn. 'AUSTAMORA'

Shrub Rose

ORIGIN **Austin, Britain, 1983**
PARENTAGE **'Chaucer' x 'Conrad Ferdinand Meyer'**
FLOWER SIZE **3.5in (9cm)**
SCENT **Strong and myrrhlike**
FLOWERING **Repeats**
HEIGHT/SPREAD **3.3ft (1m)/2.5ft (75cm)**
HARDINESS **Zone 6**

Tamora is one of those David Austin roses that thrive better in warm climates than in England itself. The flowers are pale apricot, fading to buff and mother-of-pearl, with darker backs to the petals. They come singly or in clusters of 3–7. Slightly cupped at first, they open out later as informal rosettes with a lot of short, broad petals in an old rose confusion of color and form. The plant has fairly prickly, slender stems and small, dark green leaves like a Floribunda. It seldom exceeds 3.3ft (1m), usually keeping closer to 2.5ft (75cm).

TALL STORY

TAMORA

It is good at the front of a mixed border and, because of its floriferousness and repeat flowering, in massed plantings, too. It is healthy in hot, dry climates, but also in Montreal, where tests at the Botanical Garden showed Tamora to have a high degree of resistance to blackspot, powdery mildew, and rust. It is very free with its fragrance.

'TAPIS VOLANT'

Ground Cover

ORIGIN **Lens, Belgium, 1982**
PARENTAGE ***Rosa luciae* var. *onoei* x (*Rosa multiflora* var. *adenochaeta* x 'Ballerina')**
FLOWER SIZE **1.6in (4cm)**
SCENT **Light, musky, and fruity**
FLOWERING **Repeats**
HEIGHT/SPREAD **2.7ft (80cm)/4.1ft (1.25m)**
HARDINESS **Zone 6**
AWARDS **Courtrai GM 1987**

This lax, perpetually flowering shrub has a complex ancestry that includes rare forms of oriental species. 'Tapis Volant' is typical of the breeder Louis Lens's originality. The flowers are pink and white, small, single, and deliciously scented. They come in very large clusters – typically of 30–50 flowers – that explode along the ground like pink clouds. The flowers are very attractive to bees, so they are duly followed by small vermilion hips, though the flowers (and the bees) continue to appear until autumn draws in. 'Tapis Volant' has healthy, bright green leaves and a habit of spreading sideways rather than upward. It is extremely easy to grow.

'TAPIS VOLANT'

'TATJANA'

Hybrid Tea

ORIGIN **Kordes, Germany, 1970**
PARENTAGE **'Liebeszauber' x 'Präsident Dr. H. C. Schröder'**
FLOWER SIZE **4.3in (11cm)**
SCENT **Strong and sweet**
FLOWERING **Repeats**
HEIGHT/SPREAD **2.7ft (80cm)/2ft (60cm)**
HARDINESS **Zone 6**

'Tatjana' is a handsome dark red Hybrid Tea – the sort of rose that is popular in Germany, where many of the best examples have for long originated. Both its parents, as well as 'Tatjana' itself, were raised by Kordes in Holstein, north of Hamburg. The flowers are a bright dark red, with nearly black velvety markings on some of the petals and an occasional white streak. They open from elegant buds into shapely flowers, well held on strong stems. 'Tatjana' has large dark leaves, big prickles, and a branching, upright habit of growth. It is short, compact, and very hardy in its native Germany, but will grow to at least 3.3ft (1m) in hot climates like that of Australia, where it is also popular.

'TATJANA'

MATTHIAS TANTAU AND SON

THE TANTAUS FOUNDED THEIR NURSERY IN UETERSEN, GERMANY, IN 1906, AND FROM THE 1930S ONWWARD ESTABLISHED A REPUTATION FOR INNOVATION

THE TANTAUS founded their nursery in 1906 and have been eminent rose breeders since the 1930s – second only to their neighbors, the Kordes family.

Matthias Tantau Senior was an innovative breeder with a particular interest in breeding Floribundas. Two of them, 'Tantau's Triumph' (1945) and 'Fanal' (1946), helped the nursery to recover from World War II, as did the brilliant white climber 'Direktor Benschop' (1945).

MATTHIAS TANTAU JUNIOR

Tantau's son, Matthias Tantau Junior, continued to breed a few climbers, like the rich yellow, large-flowered 'Dukat' (1955) and a series of bright Floribundas, which were immensely popular in Germany: examples are 'Lichterloh' (1955), 'Lagerfeuer' (1958), 'Rosali' (1972), and 'Mio Mac' (1973). However, Tantau Junior was also interested in Hybrid Teas, and from the mid-1950s onward bred some of the most famous roses of the day: 'Prima Ballerina' (1957), 'Super Star' (1960), 'Caramba' (1967), 'Duftwolke' (1967), 'Whisky' (1967), 'Anneliese Rothenberger' (1970), 'Mildred Scheel' (1977), Pfälzer Gold (1982), and Polarstern (1982). Almost all were very strongly scented, shapely, healthy, and brilliantly colorful. The Tantaus rarely revealed the parentage of their roses – and kept their commercial advantage. They were active, too, in other markets: their 'Garnette' (1947) rose was one of the most popular cut-flower roses of the 1950s and 1960s.

'LAGERFEUER'

Tantau Junior retired in 1985, and sold the business to a long-time colleague, Hans Jürgen Evers. The company has flourished, and Evers has proved a successful and innovative breeder. His introductions include miniatures like Orange Baby (1994), groundcover roses like Red Haze (1998), and modern large-flowered shrub roses like Ashram (1998) and Augusta Luise (1999).

'TAUSENDSCHÖN'

Multiflora Rambler

ORIGIN **Kiese, Germany, 1906**
PARENTAGE **'Daniel Lacombe' x 'Weisser Herumstreicher'**
FLOWER SIZE **2.4in (6cm)**
SCENT **Light and musky**
FLOWERING **Once only**
HEIGHT/SPREAD **16.4ft (5m)/9.8ft (3m)**
HARDINESS **Zone 5**

It is not hard to see why 'Tausendschön' was an immediate success: it was very hardy, thornless, and healthy, and laden with many-colored flowers. The "thousand beauties" referred to in its name are tints of white, pale pink, rose pink, and cream. The flowers are deep rose pink when they open, and fade to paler pink, though the petals toward the center of the flowers usually open creamy and remain pale throughout the long flowering period. The flowers are double, with distinctively ruffled petals, and come in large, strong-stemmed clusters (of 20–40 flowers). The leaves, which are an attractive, soft green, are a good foil to the cascade of gentle hues and tints of the flowers, while the smooth stems are much more pliable than many Multifloras and make 'Tausendschön' a good subject for training.

'TAUSENDSCHÖN'

TCHAIKOVSKI

syn. 'MEICHIBON'

Shrub Rose

ORIGIN **Meilland, France, 2000**
FLOWER SIZE **3.5in (9cm)**
SCENT **Light and sweet**
FLOWERING **Repeats well**
HEIGHT/SPREAD **2.7ft (80cm)/2ft (60cm)**
HARDINESS **Zone 6**

In recent years, the great French house of Meilland has branded some of its new introductions as "farniente" roses. The name identifies them as easy-care roses – very hardy, very healthy, and best left unpruned. Tchaikovski is a good example of the type. It has elegant buds like a Hybrid Tea and the flowers open to an old-fashioned shape, but the plant needs no spraying, deadheading, or pruning. The flowers are a beautiful creamy color with pale buff petal backs, which gives rise to hints of apricot and pale yellow at the center. They are very full of petals, and are well set off by the dark leaves and the dense structure of the plant. If it is left to grow naturally, Tchaikovski will eventually reach as much as 4.9ft (1.5m) in a hot climate.

TCHAIKOVSKI

'TEA RAMBLER'

Multiflora Rambler

ORIGIN **G. Paul, Britain, 1904**
PARENTAGE **'Turner's Crimson Rambler' x unknown Tea rose**
FLOWER SIZE **2in (5cm)**
SCENT **Strong and sweet**
FLOWERING **Once only**
HEIGHT/SPREAD **16.4ft (5m)/9.8ft (3m)**
HARDINESS **Zone 6**

The opening flowers of 'Tea Rambler' are neatly scrolled like tiny Tea roses. When they open out, they have a more muddled shape, but the loose way in

'TEA RAMBLER'

Tchin-Tchin

syn. 'MEIchanso', Parador

Floribunda

ORIGIN **Paolino, France, 1978**
PARENTAGE **('Sarabande' seedling × ['Alain' × 'Orange Triumph']) × 'Diablotin'**
FLOWER SIZE **3.1in (8cm)**
SCENT **Light and musky**
FLOWERING **Repeats well**
HEIGHT/SPREAD **3.3ft (1m)/2.7ft (80cm)**
HARDINESS **Zone 6**
AWARDS **Geneva GM 1978; Tokyo GM 1978**

Tchin-Tchin

Its complicated parentage tells us that Tchin-Tchin was the end product of a lengthy program to produce the perfect orange Floribunda. The market agreed, and Tchin-Tchin has remained popular ever since its introduction, especially in its native France. The flowers are large for a Floribunda and fully double, with pure vermilion orange petals. Eventually they open to reveal their stamens and an occasional white stripe at the base of the petals. The flowers come in clusters of 3–10 and fade to red as they age. The plant has dark leaves and a sprinkling of prickles. It is a good repeater, rarely out of flower until late autumn.

Meilland introduced a climbing form as Grimpant Tchin-Tchin in 1996, and it, too, has enjoyed success. It is exactly the same as the bush form, except for its climbing habit. The brilliance of the flowers attracts your attention from quite a distance.

Sport of Tchin-Tchin

Grimpant Tchin-Tchin

syn. 'MEIchanso-Sar'

Climbing Floribunda

ORIGIN **Meilland, France, 1995**
FLOWER SIZE **3.5in (9cm)**
FLOWERING **Once superbly, then intermittently**
HEIGHT/SPREAD **9.8ft (3m)/6.6ft (2m)**

which they hold their petals is both distinctive and attractive. The flowers are pale salmon pink, fading to pure silver pink, but the petal backs are always darker, almost coppery pink at first. They come in loose clusters of 5–15 and give an impression of profusion. 'Tea Rambler' is a very vigorous grower. Its stems are supple but fat, with lush new growth, soft young leaves, and glossy, bright green, older leaves. The plant grows vigorously to as much as 16.4ft (5m) in height.

Tear Drop

syn. 'DICOMO'

Patio Rose

ORIGIN **Dickson, Northern Ireland, 1988**
PARENTAGE **Pink Spray × Bright Smile**
FLOWER SIZE **2in (5cm)**
SCENT **Light and musky**
FLOWERING **Repeats well**
HEIGHT/SPREAD **1.6ft (50cm)/1.3ft (40cm)**
HARDINESS **Zone 6**

This was the first white groundcover rose bred in the British Isles. Tear Drop performs wonderfully in cool, wet climates: its flowers open quickly, and are unaffected by rain. They are pure white and semidouble, with an unusually handsome splash of rich yellow stamens at the center. The petals are brilliant white, and glow brightly when the sun shines through them. They come in clusters of 3–10 and are followed by small red hips. Tear Drop has small, dark, healthy leaves and a low, compact habit of growth. The plant is very vigorous and repeats so quickly and fully as to seem a continuous flowerer.

Teasing Georgia

syn. 'AUSbaker'

Shrub Rose

ORIGIN **Austin, Britain, 1998**
PARENTAGE **'Charles Austin' seedling**
FLOWER SIZE **3.5in (9cm)**
SCENT **Very strong, sweet, and fruity**
FLOWERING **Repeats**
HEIGHT/SPREAD **4.9ft (1.5m)/3.3ft (1m)**
HARDINESS **Zone 6**

The soft colors of this exquisite English Rose are very beautiful. The flowers of Teasing Georgia are creamy white at the edges and golden yellow at the center, with shades of honey, buff, and lemon in between. They are extremely full of petals, cupped but quartered, and sometimes hang down slightly under their own weight. They are usually borne singly but occasionally in small clusters, and always exude an air of elegance. Teasing Georgia makes a lax shrub that needs good pruning to keep it compact; in hot climates it will make a fine and vigorous pillar rose 6.6ft (2m) high. It has mid-green, semi-glossy, healthy leaves and few prickles. The scent is delicious.

Tear Drop

Teasing Georgia

Téquila

syn. 'MEIgavesol'

Floribunda

ORIGIN **Meilland, France, 1978**
PARENTAGE **'Rusticana' × 'Rumba' seedling**
FLOWER SIZE **2.8in (7cm)**
SCENT **Light and fruity**
FLOWERING **Repeats**
HEIGHT/SPREAD **5.7ft (1.75m)/3.3ft (1m)**
HARDINESS **Zone 6**

There are two roses from Meilland called Téquila. One is an unusual orange and brown florists' rose, introduced in 1998 with the registered name of 'MEIstefy'. The other is an excellent garden rose that came out in 1978 under the name of 'MEIgavesol' and is grown all over the world, but not in the US or Canada. It is a brilliant orange Floribunda with cupped, semidouble flowers, red edges to the outer petals, and a large circle of dark stamens. The flowers come in long-stemmed clusters of 3–8 and last well if cut for the house. Téquila has dark, glossy leaves, bronzy new growth, and a vigorous habit of growth. It is a good repeater and, in hot climates, will flower until early winter.

Téquila

Tequila Sunrise

syn. 'DICobey'

Hybrid Tea

ORIGIN **Dickson, Northern Ireland, 1988**
PARENTAGE **'Bonfire Night' × Freedom**
FLOWER SIZE **4.3in (11cm)**
SCENT **Light and fruity**
FLOWERING **Repeats well**
HEIGHT/SPREAD **4.9ft (1.5m)/4.1ft (1.25m)**
HARDINESS **Zone 6**
AWARDS **RNRS GM 1988; Belfast GM 1989**

Its showy colors, good shape, and vigor have rightly made Tequila Sunrise popular. The flowers open deep yellow, but pick up a coral red edging as they develop and expand, so that a bush in full flower is a dazzling mixture of red and yellow. The flowers are full of short petals, arranged so that they seem to be swirling out from the center. They also have crinkled edges. The overall effect is distinctive and attractive. The flowers are normally borne singly on stout, upright stems. It makes a dense, broad, but vigorous bush, with dark leaves and red new growth. It is usually very healthy.

Tequila Sunrise

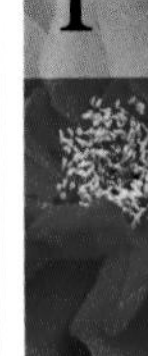

Tess of the d'Urbervilles

syn. 'AUSmove'

Shrub Rose

ORIGIN **Austin, Britain, 1998**
PARENTAGE **'The Squire' seedling**
FLOWER SIZE **4.7in (12cm)**
SCENT **Light and sweet**
FLOWERING **Repeats well**
HEIGHT/SPREAD **5.7ft (1.75m)/4.1ft (1.25m)**
HARDINESS **Zone 6**

The buds of Tess of the d'Urbervilles are almost black, and the flowers are glowing, dark crimson when they start to open. At this stage there is no more beautiful rose in the garden. Then the flowers start to lose their charm: they fade to crimson and cerise; they open out and turn back their petals like a pompon; and they hang their heads so that all you see is the back of the flower as it flops down on to the leaves below. In hot climates, however, Tess of the d'Urbervilles makes an attractive pillar rose and will reach 8.2ft (2.5m). Then the lax habit becomes an asset, and the flowers flop down at eye level. The flowers grow considerably in size as they mature – no more than 3.5in (9cm) large to start with, they expand until eventually they reach 4.7in (12cm). They are usually borne singly but sometimes in clusters of up to four. Tess of the d'Urbervilles has large dark leaves and somewhat broad leaflets. Its stems are very prickly.

Tess of the d'Urbervilles

Texas

syn. 'POULtex'

Patio Rose

ORIGIN **Poulsen, Denmark, 1984**
FLOWER SIZE **1.6in (4cm)**
SCENT **Light and fruity**
FLOWERING **Repeats**
HEIGHT/SPREAD **2ft (60cm)/1.6ft (50cm)**
HARDINESS **Zone 6**

There are two roses called Texas. One is a greenhouse rose, bred by Kordes in Germany and grown for the cut-flower market, with yellow flowers and pink edges. The other, shown here, is a handsome miniature introduced as a garden rose by Poulsen in Denmark, with cupped, semidouble yellow flowers that run from rich yellow at the center to pale lemon yellow at the edges of the petals. Texas has a fine brush of stamens at the center of the flower when the petals first open out, though they look less attractive when the stamens turn brown. The flowers come in clusters of 3–10 on a compact bush with small, dark, healthy leaves. The plant is a quick repeater.

Texas

'Thalia'

Multiflora Rambler

ORIGIN **Schmitt, Germany, 1895**
PARENTAGE **'Ma Pâquerette' x unknown**
FLOWER SIZE **1.2in (3cm)**
SCENT **Strong and musky**
FLOWERING **Once only**
HEIGHT/SPREAD **13.1ft (4m)/8.2ft (2.5m)**
HARDINESS **Zone 5**

Parc de la Tête d'Or

One of the largest and finest public parks in Europe, Lyon's Parc de la Tête d'Or has two rose collections of great beauty

The Parc de la Tête d'Or was laid out in the English landscape style in the 1850s and is immensely popular with the people of Lyon. Within its 290 acres (117 hectares) are two rose collections of great beauty. One is the extensive "new" rose garden, created in 1964, which has 60,000 bushes representing 320 cultivars. The roses come from all over the world, but the modern French roses are especially interesting. Examples include the handsome Floribunda Vanille-Groseille (Delbard, 2000) and the rarely-seen Hybrid Tea 'Nona' (Clause, 1995).

'Nona'

The other collection is at Lyon's Botanic Garden, situated within the grounds of the Parc de la Tête d'Or. The Botanic Garden has a historic collection of 570 rose cultivars, many of them chosen to represent the work of Lyon's rose breeders in the 19th century. It also boasts a well-displayed collection of some 100 rose species.

Trials take place in yet another part of the Parc de la Tête d'Or set out in display beds around a beautiful colonnade hung with climbing roses. The winner each year is awarded the prize of "La Plus Belle Rose de France".

Vanille-Groseille

Climbing roses on colonnade

T

'THALIA'

A small-time nurseryman in Alsace bred 'Thalia', but it was bought and distributed by Peter Lambert, then at the start of his career as a rose breeder. It has small, white, semidouble flowers in large clusters (typically of 20–50), and is not dissimilar to many of the simpler Multiflora ramblers. The plant grows vigorously, sending up juicy young stems from the base with bright green leaves and few prickles. It roots very easily from cuttings and is easy to cultivate. It is a particular feature of the famous rose garden at L'Haÿ-les-Roses.

THAT'S JAZZ

see JAZZ

THE ALEXANDRA ROSE

syn. 'AUSDAY', Alexandra Rose

Shrub Rose

ORIGIN **Austin, Britain, 1994**
PARENTAGE **'Shropshire Lass' x Heritage**
FLOWER SIZE **2in (5cm)**
SCENT **Slight**
FLOWERING **Repeats**
HEIGHT/SPREAD **4.9ft (1.5m)/4.1ft (1.25m)**
HARDINESS **Zone 5**

The Alexandra Rose – named after Queen Alexandra (1844–1925), wife of King Edward VII of England – is not a typical David Austin rose. It is single-flowered, like an improved "wild" rose. The flowers open a pretty, fresh salmon pink (from coppery buds), with a cream center at first, but these colors later turn to pale pink and white. The pale stamens are also pretty. The flowers come in airy clusters of 3–20 and associate well with other plantings. The plant has few prickles, a lax habit of growth, and fairly ordinary, mid-green, glossy leaves. It is healthy and repeats well, so that it seems never to be without flowers until late autumn.

'THE BISHOP'

see 'LE ROSIER ÉVÊQUE'

THE CHILDREN'S ROSE

see GINA LOLLOBRIGIDA

THE COUNTRYMAN

syn. 'AUSMAN', Countryman

Shrub Rose

ORIGIN **Austin, Britain, 1987**
PARENTAGE **'Lilian Austin' x 'Comte de Chambord'**
FLOWER SIZE **3.1in (8cm)**
SCENT **Strong and sweet**
FLOWERING **Remontant**
HEIGHT/SPREAD **4.1ft (1.25m)/3.3ft (1m)**
HARDINESS **Zone 5**

The Countryman closely resembles the Portland roses to which its parent 'Comte de Chambord' belongs: it is a genuinely new "old" rose. Its flowers are flat and full of pretty, narrow, ruffled pink petals, deep glowing pink at first, fading to rose pink. The petals have paler backs and edges and a hint of cream at the base. The flowers come in short-stalked clusters of 3–7 and are held upright on short, leafy stems. Round hips follow in autumn if the plant is not deadheaded; otherwise it will bloom until the first frost. The leaves are healthy and dark, with narrow leaflets and pale undersides. The plant makes a leafy bush, with the stout growth, prickly stems, and short nodes of the Portlands. Although naturally erect, the stems sometimes flop over, especially in hot climates, where The Countryman grows taller (6.6ft/2m) and is a good candidate for pegging down.

THE COUNTRYMAN

THE DARK LADY

syn. 'AUSBLOOM', Dark Lady

Shrub Rose

ORIGIN **Austin, Britain, 1991**
PARENTAGE **Mary Rose x Prospero**
FLOWER SIZE **3.1in (8cm)**
SCENT **Strong and sweet**
FLOWERING **Repeats**
HEIGHT/SPREAD **2.7ft (80cm)/3.3ft (1m)**
HARDINESS **Zone 6**

Despite its name, The Dark Lady is not conspicuously dark – at best bright crimson, slightly paler on the petal backs, and no more than dark pink in hot climates. But the large, loose flowers are very beautiful and very sweetly scented. They open out flat, full, and loosely rosette-shaped, usually with a rough button eye. The outer petals curve down very early on and create a billowing effect: later the whole flower reflexes into a pompon. The flowers are borne singly or in small clusters, typically of 2–3 flowers. The plant has mid-green leaves, thin leaflets (watch out for mildew), and quite a lot of prickles. It is only moderately vigorous, and has a somewhat spreading habit, but responds well to good cultivation and flowers again more quickly if deadheaded. In hot climates the plant will reach 4.9ft (1.5m). The "Dark Lady" was the inspiration for some of Shakespeare's sonnets.

THE DARK LADY

THE ALEXANDRA ROSE

'THE DOCTOR'

Hybrid Tea

ORIGIN **Howard, 1936**
PARENTAGE **'Mrs. J.D. Eisele' x 'Los Angeles'**
FLOWER SIZE **6.3in (16cm)**
SCENT **Strong and sweet**
FLOWERING **Repeats**
HEIGHT/SPREAD **3.3ft (1m)/2.7ft (80cm)**
HARDINESS **Zone 6**
AWARDS **NRS GM 1938**

Who was "The Doctor"? He was Jean Henri Nicolas (1875–1937), a Frenchman living in the US, who was a much loved rosarian and friend of the breeder Fred Howard. His rose was highly prized in England, where it was by far the most popular Hybrid Tea for many years, partly because it stands up well to rain. The flowers are among the largest ever raised – huge, sumptuous, seductive roses of rich deep pink, elegant in the bud and opening their vast petals in an unconventional shape that serves to emphasize their sheer size. Later, a climbing form with even larger flowers appeared. 'The Doctor' is a sturdy, upright plant, with a fair number of prickles and pale leaves: blackspot can be a problem.

THE DOVE

see LA PALOMA 85

'THE DOCTOR'

T

'The Fairy'

syn. 'Féerie'

Polyantha

ORIGIN **Bentall, Britain, 1932**
PARENTAGE **'Paul Crampel' x 'Lady Gay'**
FLOWER SIZE **1.6in (4cm)**
SCENT **Little or none**
FLOWERING **Late in season, then intermittently**
HEIGHT/SPREAD **2.5ft (75cm)/4.1ft (1.25m)**
HARDINESS **Zone 6**

'The Fairy' is the world's most popular and widely grown Polyantha rose, and one of the easiest to grow. Its flowers are a cheerful mid-pink, fading to pale pink and eventually almost to white (the color holds best in cool weather). They have a frilly, ruffled demeanor and come in long, airy clusters of 10–40 flowers, starting rather late in the season but continuing thereafter until late autumn. Sometimes they are followed by small, round, orange hips. The plant has pale, glossy leaves and a naturally loose habit, which means that it spreads sideways as it grows. In damp weather it is susceptible to mildew and blackspot, but these never seem to affect its vigor and can safely be ignored. It roots quickly and well from cuttings, and people sometimes use it as a low edging by lining out cuttings where it is intended to grow. It is an excellent groundcover and landscaping plant, but even better as a patio rose or a small plant in mixed borders.

In 1990, Vurens-Spek in the Netherlands introduced a darker sport of 'The Fairy' as Lovely Fairy. The flowers are a rich, pale crimson, with paler hints toward the center, but otherwise identical. It is arguably a better color than 'The Fairy' itself, and has quickly become widely sold all over the world.

'The Fairy'

Lovely Fairy

Sport of 'The Fairy'

Lovely Fairy

syn. 'SPEvu'
ORIGIN **Vurens-Spek, Netherlands, 1990**

'The Garland'

'The Friar'

Shrub Rose

ORIGIN **Austin, Britain, 1969**
PARENTAGE **'Ivory Fashion' seedling**
FLOWER SIZE **3.5in (9cm)**
SCENT **Strong and fruity**
FLOWERING **Repeats**
HEIGHT/SPREAD **3.3ft (1m)/2.7ft (80cm)**
HARDINESS **Zone 6**

'The Friar' fares much better in hot climates than cool, and it needs a régime of feeding, watering, and disease prevention to be at its best. The flowers are pale blush pink with a hint of buff yellow toward the center and white edges to the petals. They have an attractive quartered shape and are borne both singly and in small clusters. The plant has the habit of a Hybrid Tea, with upright growth, quite a lot of prickles, dark leaves, and bronzy new growth. Mildew and blackspot may visit it from time to time. It is a good repeater, providing it is grown well.

'The Friar'

'The Garland'

Multiflora Rambler

ORIGIN **Wells, Britain, 1835**
PARENTAGE ***Rosa moschata* x *Rosa multiflora***
FLOWER SIZE **1.6in (4cm)**
SCENT **Strong and musky**
FLOWERING **Once, midseason**
HEIGHT/SPREAD **13.1ft (4m)/9.8ft (3m)**
HARDINESS **Zone 6**

Gertrude Jekyll had no doubts about the merits of this beautiful and vigorous rambler: "It is well worth getting up at 4am on a mid-June morning to see the tender loveliness of the newly opening buds; for, beautiful though they are at noon, they are better still when just awakening after the refreshing influence of the short summer night." One reason is that the opening flowers are pale peach pink, but the color passes and fades to white as they open out fully. The slender buds turn into small, elegant, upward-facing, semidouble flowers on long stems and are usually carried in very large, conical clusters of up to 40, sometimes more. Two characteristics distinguish 'The Garland' from every other climbing rose: the petals are distinctively reflexed along their sides, and the stamens at the center form a crown around the stigma. The plant is exceptionally vigorous, fairly late to flower, and very free flowering. The stems are very prickly and the prickles are large.

The Herbalist

syn. 'AUSsemi'

Shrub Rose

ORIGIN **Austin, Britain, 1991**
PARENTAGE **seedling x 'Louise Odier'**
FLOWER SIZE **2.8in (7cm)**
SCENT **Light and sweet**
FLOWERING **Repeats almost continuously**
HEIGHT/SPREAD **4.1ft (1.25m)/3.3ft (1m)**
HARDINESS **Zone 6**

David Austin named this rose The Herbalist because it reminded him of 'Officinalis', the old apothecaries' rose. The color is certainly a good match, being very dark pink or pale cherry crimson, with rose pink undersides, before fading to mid-pink. The flowers are semidouble, with loosely incurved and wavy petals partly hiding a large brush of golden stamens. They come in small clusters (typically of 5–7 flowers) and are succeeded by scarlet hips, though deadheading improves the reflowering. The plant has healthy, dark leaves, quite a lot of prickles, and a dense, twiggy habit of growth. It is one of the few David Austin roses that remain small and neat when grown in a hot climate.

The Herbalist

'The Hunter'

see 'Hunter'

The Jacobite Rose

see 'Alba Maxima'

The Lady

syn. 'FRYjingo'

Hybrid Tea

ORIGIN **Fryer, Britain, 1985**
PARENTAGE **'Pink Parfait' x 'Redgold'**
FLOWER SIZE **3.9in (10cm)**
SCENT **Light and fruity**
FLOWERING **Repeats**
HEIGHT/SPREAD **4.9ft (1.5m)/3.3ft (1m)**
HARDINESS **Zone 6**
AWARDS **Baden-Baden GM 1987**

The elegant shape and soft colors of The Lady are very attractive. The flowers are pale peach at first, with primrose yellow petal backs and a pink tinge to the edges. Later they open out and fade to cream and white, but retain a yellow flush at the center, which sets off the crimson stamens. The flowers usually come singly, on long stems, and are good for cutting. They also stand up well to rain. The plant carries healthy but fairly ordinary green leaves and bronzy new growth. It has a vigorous, bushy, and upright habit of growth and a scattering of large prickles. It is easy to grow and a good repeater.

The Lady

T

THE MCCARTNEY ROSE

THE MCCARTNEY ROSE

syn. 'MEIZELI'

Hybrid Tea

ORIGIN **Meilland, France, 1991**
PARENTAGE **(Nirvana x 'Papa Meilland') x First Prize**
FLOWER SIZE **4.7in (12cm)**
SCENT **Very strong and sweet**
FLOWERING **Repeats well**
HEIGHT/SPREAD **4.9ft (1.5m)/2.5ft (75cm)**
HARDINESS **Zone 6**
AWARDS **Bagatelle FA 1988; Geneva GM 1988; Le Rœulx GM & FA 1988; Madrid FA 1988; Monza GM & FA 1988; Paris GM 1988; Belfast FA 1993; Durbanville FA 1993; Paris FA 1993**

Few roses have a stronger scent than The McCartney Rose. When it won the Nantes award for fragrance, its scent was described as "fruity, lemony, limey, spicy … and remarkably fresh." The flowers are massive, though they open from long, narrow-waisted buds and their size is not really apparent until they open out as cup-shaped flowers. The petals are very broad, too. The flowers are deep shocking pink at first, fading gently to mid-pink. They come usually singly, but sometimes in clusters of up to five. Rather surprisingly, they do not last well as cut flowers. The plant has large, mid-green, shiny leaves that do occasionally get blackspot. If unpruned it will easily reach 6.6ft (2m) in a hot climate, but is usually seen as a bush pruned to no more than 3.3ft (1m). It flowers almost continuously until early winter.

'THE MILLER'

Shrub Rose

ORIGIN **Austin, Britain, 1970**
PARENTAGE **'Baronne Adolphe de Rothschild' x 'Chaucer'**
FLOWER SIZE **3.5in (9cm)**
SCENT **Light and sweet**
FLOWERING **Repeats**
HEIGHT/SPREAD **5.7ft (1.75m)/4.1ft (1.25m)**
HARDINESS **Zone 5**

This tall and vigorous English Rose is not as good as later examples from David Austin, but is still widely grown. The flowers of 'The Miller' are a fine mid-pink, fading slightly toward the edges, and full of petals. They come both singly and in clusters of up to about four and repeat well. The plant is tough and hardy, reaching as much as 8.2ft (2.5m) in a hot climate, but generally pruned back to half that height elsewhere. It has a lot of prickles and pale green leaves, fairly closely spaced on the stems, which gives a leafy look to the plant as a whole.

THE MOTH

see MOTH

'THE NEW DAWN'

see 'DR. W. VAN FLEET'

THE NUN

syn. 'AUSNUN'

Shrub Rose

ORIGIN **Austin, Britain, 1987**
PARENTAGE **'The Prioress' seedling**
FLOWER SIZE **2.4in (6cm)**
SCENT **Moderate, sweet, and myrrhlike**
FLOWERING **Repeats**
HEIGHT/SPREAD **4.9ft (1.5m)/3.3ft (1m)**
HARDINESS **Zone 6**

This rose has its champions, but The Nun is unusual in several ways and not everyone's taste. Its flowers are so cupped that they never open out, which means that you have to peer into them to see the golden stamens – "like a tulip," its supporters say. The petals are pale buff fading to dirty white, at which stage its admirers compare its color to eggshells. The flowers are held in uneven clusters of 3–7 on a gawky, prickly plant with a sparse covering of leaves that are subject to mildew and sometimes rust. In hot climates The Nun will grow to 6.6ft (2m); in its native England it is usually pruned back to 3.3ft (1m).

'THE MILLER'

THE NUN

THE PILGRIM

syn. 'AUSWALKER', Gartenarchitekt Günther Schulze

Shrub Rose

ORIGIN **Austin, Britain, 1991**
PARENTAGE **Graham Thomas x 'Yellow Button'**
FLOWER SIZE **3.5in (9cm)**
SCENT **Strong: a mixture of musk and fruit**
FLOWERING **Repeats well**
HEIGHT/SPREAD **4.9ft (1.5m)/4.1ft (1.25m)**
HARDINESS **Zone 6**

You can recognize a bed of The Pilgrim in full flower from a long distance: no other rose produces such a dense mass of yellow color. It is exceptionally floriferous – the result of combining large clusters (typically of 15 flowers) with large, flat-topped, individual flowers. The color varies according to the climate: it fades quickly in hot sun, but in cooler conditions the whole flower is a good ripe yellow at first. It fades from the edges inward, passing to lemon and cream, but always with beautiful contrasts between the pale outer petals and the bright inner ones. The flowers are each a mass of little petals – quilled, tightly packed, neat, and small – very occasionally with a button eye. They are good in arrangements and combine well with other plants in the garden. The plant is strong and robust, growing vigorously, with a few large thorns, bright green leaves, and strong, upright stems. In hot climates it will quickly reach 8ft (2.5m) and is grown as a short climber. Deadheading helps it to rebloom continuously through to autumn.

THE PRINCE

THE PRINCE

syn. 'AUSVELVET'

Shrub Rose

ORIGIN **Austin, Britain, 1991**
PARENTAGE **'Lilian Austin' x 'The Squire'**
FLOWER SIZE **3.1in (8cm)**
SCENT **Strong and sweet**
FLOWERING **Remontant**
HEIGHT/SPREAD **2.5ft (75cm)/3.3ft (1m)**
HARDINESS **Zone 6**

The Prince is an English Rose of royal distinction. Indeed, it closely resembles a short-growing, 19th-century Hybrid Perpetual. The flowers open from globular buds, almost black in color. They are rich, dark crimson at first – later more purple – rosette-shaped, quartered, and full of small petals. Eventually they reflex into pompons. The plant is prickly, low, and spreading, with dark Hybrid Tea-type leaves (bronzy at first). It bears its flowers singly on stems that are long but weak, so that the flowers nod their heads. The plant is by no means a weakling, however, though it responds to good cultivation: repeat flowering is improved by deadheading. Mildew can be a problem in damp conditions.

THE PILGRIM

'THE PRIORESS'

'THE PRIORESS'

Shrub Rose

ORIGIN **Austin, Britain, 1969**
PARENTAGE **'Ma Perkins' × 'Mme. Pierre Oger'**
FLOWER SIZE **2.8in (7cm)**
SCENT **Moderate and fruity**
FLOWERING **Repeats**
HEIGHT/SPREAD **4.9ft (1.5m)/4.9ft (1.5m)**
HARDINESS **Zone 6**

Although now overtaken by better examples, this early English Rose still has its followers. The flowers of 'The Prioress' are blush pink or mother-of-pearl and globular in shape, with just enough of an opening at the top to espy the golden stamens within. They rarely, if ever, open out fully but are borne in tight clusters of up to about ten, where they are perhaps too squashed against each other to show to advantage. The plant is a stiff, prickly, gawky grower, but vigorous and fairly healthy, except for a weakness for mildew. It will grow to 6.6ft (2m) in hot climates, where it is more widely appreciated than in Britain.

'THE REEVE'

syn. AUSREEVE

Shrub Rose

ORIGIN **Austin, Britain, 1979**
PARENTAGE **'Lilian Austin' × 'Chaucer'**
FLOWER SIZE **3.1in (8cm)**
SCENT **Strong mixture of sweetness and musk**
FLOWERING **Repeats**
HEIGHT/SPREAD **4.1ft (1.25m)/4.1ft (1.25m)**
HARDINESS **Zone 5**

'The Reeve', named after a character in Chaucer's *The Canterbury Tales*, has pale crimson buds that open to mid-pink flowers and fade to pale pink. The influence of one of Chaucer's parents, 'Constance Spry', is apparent from the very globular shape of the flowers, with just a glimpse of golden stamens at the center. Later they are more shallowly cupped, with a lot of incurved petals, reminiscent of the old Centifolia roses, and a source of "old Dutch" style flowers for year-round arrangements. The flowers come in tight, nodding clusters of 3–7. The bush has dark green leaves (bronzy at first), a fairly spreading habit (almost messy), long, slender stems, a tendency to mildew, and a lot of small red prickles.

'THE SQUIRE'

THE SECKFORD ROSE

see PINK ROBUSTA

'THE SQUIRE'

Shrub Rose

ORIGIN **Austin, Britain, 1976**
PARENTAGE **'The Knight' × 'Château de Clos Vougeot'**
FLOWER SIZE **4.3in (11cm)**
SCENT **Strong and sweet**
FLOWERING **Repeats**
HEIGHT/SPREAD **3.3ft (1m)/2.5ft (75cm)**
HARDINESS **Zone 6**

When it was first introduced, 'The Squire' was widely hailed as the perfect new "old" crimson rose, but David Austin believes it has now been superseded by better English Roses. The squat buds open into lightly cupped, rosette-shaped flowers with many quilled petals. They are bright dark crimson, with occasional patches of darker coloring, almost black. However, the color does fade, especially in hot sun, and may end up no more than dark pink. The flowers come singly or in small clusters (of up to five flowers). They are good to pick, and last well, both in water and on the bush. The plant is fairly upright and not very vigorous. It has a lot of fierce prickles and dull, dark green leaves. It is susceptible to mildew but reflowers better than many of David Austin's earlier roses.

'THE REEVE'

THE TEMPTATIONS

THE TEMPTATIONS

syn. 'WEKAQ'

Hybrid Tea

ORIGIN **Winchel, US, 1990**
PARENTAGE **Paradise × 'Admiral Rodney'**
FLOWER SIZE **3.9in (10cm)**
SCENT **Medium and sweet**
FLOWERING **Repeats well**
HEIGHT/SPREAD **4.1ft (1.25m)/3.3ft (1m)**
HARDINESS **Zone 6**
AWARDS **ARS GM 1989**

The color of The Temptations is somewhat variable. Sometimes the flowers are pale pink, with a darker edge to the petals. Often, however, they are creamy white, with pale pink edges to some of the outer petals and a hint of buff toward the center. This inconsistency sometimes surprises their owners, but the colors are usually deepest in autumn and cool weather. The petals reflex sharply, so the opening bud is especially handsome. The flowers are borne singly on long stems, and, though not the largest of specimens, they are good for exhibition as well as flower arrangements. The plant is fairly tall, and upright in habit, with dark green leaves and red new growth. The Temptations is the name of an American singing group.

THE TIMES ROSE

see MARIANDEL

'THE WIFE OF BATH'

see 'WIFE OF BATH'

THE WORLD

see DIE WELT

'THE YEOMAN'

Shrub Rose

ORIGIN **Austin, Britain, 1969**
PARENTAGE **'Ivory Fashion' × ('Constance Spry' × 'Monique')**
FLOWER SIZE **3.1in (8cm)**
SCENT **Strong and fruity**
FLOWERING **Repeats**
HEIGHT/SPREAD **2.5ft (75cm)/2ft (60cm)**
HARDINESS **Zone 6**

'The Yeoman' was a great success when it was first introduced: here was a short-growing plant with large, richly scented, salmon apricot flowers in the old-fashioned style. Alas, it turned out to be a poor grower, lacking in vigor and subject to mildew, blackspot, and rust. Nevertheless, it has its adherents still and it responds well to good cultivation. The flowers open peach pink, with pinker petal tips and yellow backs and bases. Then the yellow tints fade, leaving an altogether pinker flower. Nurseries often advise people to plant several plants of a particular rose together to maximize its effect. Although this advice is not correct for all roses, it is right for 'The Yeoman': three or five plants at the front of a border are needed to make an impact. And it looks well with companion plantings of almost any color.

'THE YEOMAN'

'THÉRÈSE BUGNET'

Rugosa Hybrid

ORIGIN **Bugnet, Canada, 1950**
PARENTAGE **([*Rosa acicularis* x *Rosa rugosa kamtchatica*] x [*Rosa amblyotis* x *Rosa rugosa* 'Plena']) x 'Betty Bland'**
FLOWER SIZE **2.8in (7cm)**
SCENT **Strong, sweet, and rich**
FLOWERING **Continuously**
HEIGHT/SPREAD **6.6ft (2m)/3.3ft (1m)**
HARDINESS **Zone 4**

The novelist Georges Bugnet (1879–1981) spent 25 years breeding roses to survive the cold winters of Alberta: 'Thérèse Bugnet' is his non-literary masterpiece. Its flowers are bright pink, fading to pale pink, and arrange their petals in such a way as to give them a beautiful, muddled, old-fashioned look. They are generously borne, singly and in clusters of up to five, on a very handsome bush that – unusually for a Rugosa hybrid – is almost completely thornless. It flowers until the first frost, especially if the plant is deadheaded. 'Thérèse Bugnet' has handsome leaves (bronzy when young; dark yellow in autumn), and red stems, which are especially attractive when the winter sun shines upon them. It is healthy, easy to grow, and exceptionally hardy, but, like so many subzero roses, will also grow happily in warm climates, like that of southern California.

'THÉRÈSE BUGNET'

GRAHAM THOMAS

THE WRITINGS OF HORTICULTURIST GRAHAM THOMAS BROUGHT OLD ROSES BACK INTO FASHION

GRAHAM STUART THOMAS (1909–2003) was the catalyst for the growing interest in the conservation of old roses. He was also a powerful individual in British horticulture through the latter half of the 20th century, due to his position as gardens adviser to the National Trust in England and Wales, and to his influential writings. He became interested in old roses in the 1930s, when he began to assemble a collection of Gallicas, Damasks, and Centifolias whose existence was threatened by the success of Hybrid Tea roses. He extolled the merits of these 19th-century roses in three books: *The Old Shrub Roses* (1955), *Shrub Roses of Today* (1962), and *Climbing Roses Old and New* (1965). These books, and the aesthetic they articulated, brought about a change of public perception. Old roses became fashionable again, in England and then throughout the world.

'SOUVENIR DE ST. ANNE'S'

Thomas's eye for a good rose was not confined to old roses. During his years working for two leading nurseries in Surrey, Thomas introduced several popular new shrub roses and climbers, including 'Abbotswood', 'Bobbie James', 'St. Nicholas', and 'Souvenir de St. Anne's'. He is commemorated by the spectacular yellow English Rose, Graham Thomas, bred by David Austin and introduced in 1983.

GRAHAM THOMAS, AND THE ROSE NAMED AFTER HIM, AT MOTTISFONT ABBEY

'THISBE'

Shrub Rose

ORIGIN **Pemberton, Britain, 1918**
PARENTAGE **'Marie-Jeanne' x 'Perle des Jardins'**
FLOWER SIZE **2.4in (6cm)**
SCENT **Medium, sweet, and musky**
FLOWERING **Repeats well**
HEIGHT/SPREAD **4.9ft (1.5m)/4.1ft (1.25m)**
HARDINESS **Zone 6**

Although often described as a Hybrid Musk, 'Thisbe' was actually bred by crossing a Polyantha with a Noisette. The flowers open primrose yellow from golden yellow buds, and fade to cream and white. They are loosely semidouble and have a circle of rich orange stamens around the prominent pistil. They come in dense clusters of 5–15, but more in autumn, at the ends of the new growth. The plant has dark, glossy leaves like a Noisette, and small, narrow leaflets. It is bushy and, unlike the Hybrid Musks, does not grow as a climber in hot climates. It is, however, very healthy, needs little or no pruning, and flowers almost continuously until late autumn.

THOMAS BARTON

see CHARLOTTE RAMPLING

'THISBE'

'TIFFANY'

Hybrid Tea

ORIGIN **Lindquist, US, 1954**
PARENTAGE **'Charlotte Armstrong' x 'Girona'**
FLOWER SIZE **4.3in (11cm)**
SCENT **Strong, sweet, and fruity**
FLOWERING **Repeats well**
HEIGHT/SPREAD **4.9ft (1.5m)/3.3ft (1m)**
HARDINESS **Zone 6**
AWARDS **Portland GM 1954; AARS 1955; Gamble FA 1962**

'TIFFANY'

Any rose that is widely grown 50 years after its first introduction has got to be special: 'Tiffany' has a wonderful scent, great elegance of form, and a lazy beauty that is seen to perfection in hot climates. The flowers open from long, slender buds. They are pink with a suggestion of salmon at first, and paler backs to the petals. When they open out, they have a pale yellow flush toward the center that greatly enhances the beauty of the whole flower. The flowers are not overly full of petals, but they take their time to open out and are beautiful at all stages of their development. The flowers come singly or in small clusters (usually of 3–4 flowers) on fairly long, strong stems. The plant has dark green leaves and a vigorous, strong habit of growth, unless it is badly grown, in which case the stems are sometimes too thin to support the flowers. It repeats well, in a series of flushes through until late autumn. Its long petals may suffer in rain, but it is supremely lovely in warm, dry weather.

Lindquist also introduced a climbing form in 1957. It has never been as universally popular as the bush form, but **'Climbing Tiffany'** is still fairly widely sold and grown. It has only a few flowers after its first, big flowering each year. It is almost identical to the bush form except for growing to about 13.1ft (4m) high.

Sport of 'Tiffany'

'CLIMBING TIFFANY'

Climbing Hybrid Tea
ORIGIN **Lindquist, US, 1958**
FLOWER SIZE **5.1in (13cm)**
FLOWERING **Once well, thereafter only a little**
HEIGHT/SPREAD **13.1ft (4m)/8.2ft (2.5m)**

TIMELESS

'TIKI'

Floribunda

ORIGIN **McGredy, Northern Ireland, 1964**
PARENTAGE **'Mme. Léon Cuny' x 'Spartan'**
FLOWER SIZE **3.1in (8cm)**
SCENT **Strong and sweet**
FLOWERING **Repeats well**
HEIGHT/SPREAD **4.1ft (1.25m)/3.3ft (1m)**
HARDINESS **Zone 6**

This beautiful rose was an early example of the sort of rose that is halfway between a Floribunda and a Hybrid Tea. 'Tiki' has fair-sized flowers borne sometimes singly and sometimes in clusters of up to about eight. They are individually shaped like a Hybrid Tea, with elegant, conical buds opening to flowers that are also attractive when they expand into perfectly circular semidouble blooms. Their color is also very beautiful – apricot pink at first, fading to rose pink and mother-of-pearl, before picking up a tinge of deeper pink as they age. The plant is tall, shrubby, and fairly healthy.

'TIKI'

TIMELESS

syn. 'JACECOND'
Hybrid Tea

ORIGIN **Zary, US, 1998**
PARENTAGE **Spirit of Glasnost x Kardinal 85**
FLOWER SIZE **4.3in (11cm)**
SCENT **Light and sweet**
FLOWERING **Repeats**
HEIGHT/SPREAD **4.1ft (1.25m)/3.3ft (1m)**
HARDINESS **Zone 6**
AWARDS **AARS 1997**

Although it is classified as a Hybrid Tea, Timeless has the vigor and clustered inflorescence seen in the American Grandifloras. The flowers are a clear crimson red, opening from classically perfect buds. They are carried both singly and in clusters, on long, straight, strong stems, which make them good for cutting. They also last a long time in water – as much as ten days. Timeless has mid- to dark green, shiny leaves, a lot of prickles, and an upright, bushy habit of growth, though its height depends upon growing conditions. It is vigorous, and repeats well.

'TINEKE'

Hybrid Tea

ORIGIN **Select, 1989**
FLOWER SIZE **4.7in (12cm)**
SCENT **Little or none**
FLOWERING **Repeats very quickly**
HEIGHT/SPREAD **4.9ft (1.5m)/3.3ft (1m)**
HARDINESS **Zone 6**

Although essentially a rose for the cut-flower trade, 'Tineke' also does well as a garden rose in hot, dry climates and in periods of dry weather elsewhere. The flowers are large and very full of petals, neatly arranged in fat buds that take several days to unfold. They are creamy white in color, with pure white outer petals and a hint of lemon at the center. The flowers come singly on very long stems (2–2.7ft/60–80cm) and last over a week in water. They spoil in rain, but in ideal growing conditions they grow quickly and produce flush after flush of exhibition-quality blooms. The foliage is large, dark, and healthy, and the plant has a vigorous, upright habit.

'TINEKE'

TINO ROSSI

syn. 'MEICELNA', Your Garden
Hybrid Tea

ORIGIN **Meilland, France, 1980**
FLOWER SIZE **3.9in (10cm)**
SCENT **Strong, sweet, and lemony**
FLOWERING **Repeats**
HEIGHT/SPREAD **3.3ft (1m)/2.7ft (80cm)**
HARDINESS **Zone 7**
AWARDS **Bagatelle GM 1989**

This rose was chosen by his friends to honor the French singer and crooner Tino Rossi (1907–83). It was a color he

TINO ROSSI

particularly liked – deep, rich pink. The flowers are shapely, with large petals and pale crimson undersides. Their scent won them a prize at Bagatelle. They usually come singly and are very abundantly borne throughout the growing season. Tino Rossi is as good as a cut flower as it is in the garden. It has large, dark, shiny, healthy leaves and a vigorous habit of growth. It is extremely popular in Europe and Australia, but little known in North America.

TINTINARA

syn. 'DICUPTIGHT'

Hybrid Tea

ORIGIN **Dickson, Northern Ireland, 1996**
PARENTAGE **Melody Maker seedling**
FLOWER SIZE **4.7in (12cm)**
SCENT **Moderate and sweet**
FLOWERING **Repeats**
HEIGHT/SPREAD **3.3ft (1m)/2.7ft (80cm)**
HARDINESS **Zone 6**
AWARDS **The Hague GM 1994**

The flowers of Tintinara are a brilliant scarlet when they first open, and they seem all the hotter for the yellow tints at the base of the petals. Later on, they lose their yellow tints and the flowers end up a geranium lake color or salmon pink. But it is a striking sight to see a bush of large, glowing flowers in its full glory. Tintinara is a short-growing Hybrid Tea that makes a good bedding plant as well as producing flowers that are good for cutting and of elegant shape at every stage of their development. They are not too full of petals, which means that the flowers of Tintinara fare well in wet climates. The bush is vigorous, strong-growing, upright, compact, and healthy.

'TITIAN'

'TITIAN'

Floribunda

ORIGIN **Riethmüller, Australia, 1950**
FLOWER SIZE **3.9in (10cm)**
SCENT **Medium and sweet**
FLOWERING **Repeats well**
HEIGHT/SPREAD **4.1ft (1.25m)/4.9ft (1.5m)**
HARDINESS **Zone 6**

This is one of the few Australian-bred roses to have been made widely available in Europe. Frank Riethmüller (1885–1966) was a German immigrant who lived at Turramurra in Queensland. 'Titian' was his first hybrid, bred in 1934, and distributed in Europe by Kordes in 1950. Kordes also introduced a climbing sport in 1964. The flowers are semi-double and open out flat to a muddled center and a somewhat old-fashioned shape, like a Bourbon rose. The outer petals are pale crimson, and contrast nicely with the bright cerise pink colors toward the center of the flower. The flowers are borne singly and in clusters of up to five. The plant has a spreading habit of growth, bright green leaves, and broad leaflets. It makes an excellent ever-blooming pillar rose in warm climates like Australia's, and a sturdy, tall bush in cool climates like northern Europe's.

TINTINARA

TIVOLI 150

syn. 'POULDUCE', Tivoli Gardens, Château Pavié

Hybrid Tea

ORIGIN **Poulsen, Denmark, 1994**
FLOWER SIZE **4.7in (12cm)**
SCENT **Light and sweet**
FLOWERING **Repeats well**
HEIGHT/SPREAD **2.7ft (80cm)/2ft (60cm)**
HARDINESS **Zone 5**

Tivoli 150 is a good, modern, yellow Hybrid Tea, best known in Scandinavia and western Europe. The flowers are large, full of petals, and pretty at all stages of their development. The long, elegant bud opens out somewhat slowly. The flower is lemon yellow, with slightly deeper yellow on the petal backs, which gives it a golden center. Eventually it opens out into an old-fashioned, muddled rosette of many petals, and starts to fade at the edges. The flowers come usually singly, occasionally in twos and threes, and repeat well. The leaves are generally unexceptional, but the plant is hardy and healthy. It flowers well until late autumn. The name of the rose honors the 150th anniversary of the Tivoli Gardens in Copenhagen.

TIVOLI 150

'TOBY TRISTRAM'

Hybrid Filipes

ORIGIN **Targett, Britain, c.1970**
FLOWER SIZE **1.2in (3cm)**
SCENT **Moderate and musky**
FLOWERING **Once, midseason**
HEIGHT/SPREAD **16.4ft (5m)/9.8ft (3m)**
HARDINESS **Zone 6**

The origins of 'Toby Tristram' are obscure: it is thought to be a cross between 'Kiftsgate' and a Multiflora hybrid that turned up in an English garden during the 1970s. It is now very popular in western Europe. The flowers open pale creamy pink from pink buds, but fade quickly to white. They are carried in enormous profusion in large, spacious clusters of 50 or more, and are followed in autumn by equally prolific quantities of small, pendulous, red hips. The plant has large, mid-green leaves, with bronzy tips at first. It is very vigorous and grows to a considerable height, pushing out new growth 19.7ft (6m) long every year, and quickly climbing to 32.8ft (10m) up a house or tree. There is a particularly fine archway of 'Toby Tristram' at L'Haÿ-les-Roses in Paris.

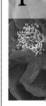

'TOBY TRISTRAM'

'TOM TOM'

'TOM TOM'

Floribunda

ORIGIN Lindquist, US, 1957
PARENTAGE 'Improved Lafayette' x 'Floradora'
FLOWER SIZE 3.1in (8cm)
SCENT Light and fruity
FLOWERING Repeats
HEIGHT/SPREAD 2.7ft (80cm)/2ft (60cm)
HARDINESS Zone 6

'Tom Tom' is a semidouble pink Floribunda, with a patch of white at the center and dark yellow stamens. It is still popular so many years after it was bred because it is an easy to grow plant and a tireless performer. The buds and flowers are larger than most Floribunda's and borne in unusually large clusters, typically of 8–20, which are very impressive when in full bloom. The autumn flowering is very heavy, and the pink of the flowers is darker in cool weather, taking on a saturated tone. 'Tom Tom' is a sturdy, upright grower, not too tall, but healthy and hardy. The leaves are dark and shiny.

TOMMELISE

syn. KORTENAY, Hertfordshire, Sandefjord

Ground Cover

ORIGIN Kordes, Germany, 1989
FLOWER SIZE 1.2in (3cm)
SCENT Little or none
FLOWERING Repeats well
HEIGHT/SPREAD 1.6ft (50cm)/3.3ft (1m)
HARDINESS Zone 5

It may not be the best modern groundcover rose, but Tommelise is popular in Scandinavia (where it is very hardy) and in England (where it is known as Hertfordshire). The flowers are deep pink (darker in autumn) and single, with a white patch at the center and a circle of bright yellow stamens that fade to brown soon after the flowers open out. The flowers come in large clusters, typically of 20–30, and stand up well to rain. Tommelise is a sprawling plant with neat little dark leaves and a fair scattering of prickles. It is a good repeater and healthy, and makes a cheerful rose for growing either in containers or at the front of a border.

TOMMELISE

'TONNER'S FANCY'

Modern Climber

ORIGIN Clark, Australia, 1928
PARENTAGE *Rosa gigantea* seedling x unknown
FLOWER SIZE 3.9in (10cm)
SCENT Moderate, but sweet and pleasant
FLOWERING Once only, early in season
HEIGHT/SPREAD 16.4ft (5m)/9.8ft (3m)
HARDINESS Zone 8

'Tonner's Fancy' is a very pretty Hybrid Gigantea, somewhat transitory in flower. The flowers are a pale apricot or blush color, fading to cream, with darker petal backs and deep pink tones at the center. They are only lightly double and especially pretty when they are opening out. The petals reflex nicely and the stamens at the center have handsome red filaments. The plant has the beautiful drooping leaves of *Rosa gigantea*, which are bronzy red when young. It grows vigorously and is healthy, but suitable only for warm climates. 'Tonner's Fancy' takes its name from one of Alister Clark's racehorses.

'TONNER'S FANCY' *(the original plant at Alister Clark's estate near Melbourne)*

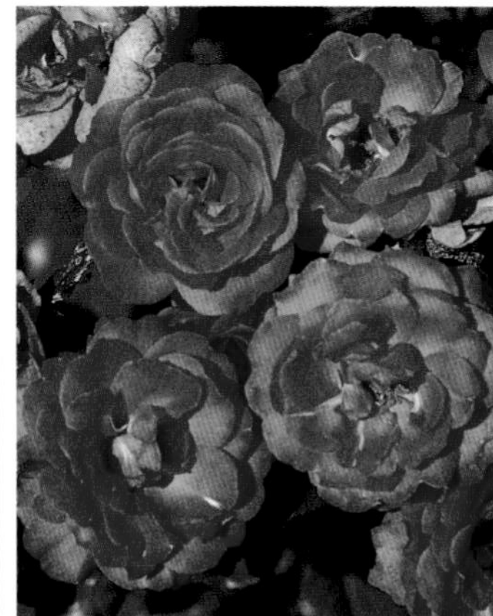
TOP HIT

TOP HIT

syn. 'POULTOP', Brilliant Hit, Carrot Top, Panache

Miniature Rose

ORIGIN Poulsen, Denmark, 1991
FLOWER SIZE 2in (5cm)
SCENT Light and musky
FLOWERING Repeats well
HEIGHT/SPREAD 2ft (60cm)/1.6ft (50cm)
HARDINESS Zone 6

Top Hit has several synonyms, all of which hint at the brilliance of its bright orange flowers. They have a fluorescence and vibrancy that have never been bettered by any other rose. Furthermore, Top Hit keeps its color right through until it drops its petals. The flowers are shapely, double, and abundantly borne in clusters of 5–10 flowers throughout the season. Top Hit makes a short, compact plant with healthy, dark leaves and reddish new growth. It is an excellent plant for containers but is at its best when closely spaced in mass plantings.

TOP MARKS

TOP MARKS

syn. 'FRYMINISTAR'

Patio Rose

ORIGIN Fryer, Britain, 1992
FLOWER SIZE 1.4in (3.5cm)
SCENT Light and musky
FLOWERING Repeats well
HEIGHT/SPREAD 2.3ft (70cm)/1.6ft (50cm)
HARDINESS Zone 6
AWARDS RNRS GM 1990; ROTY 1992

Top Marks is a very useful, bright vermilion patio rose that keeps its color well. The flowers are fully double, open out well, and last a long time on the bush. They come in clusters of 3–15 and repeat quickly, so that the plant appears always to be in flower. Top Marks makes a dense, compact bush with prickly stems and small, medium-dark, healthy leaves. It is very useful in containers and small-scale gardens where a reliable patch of brilliant color is required.

TOPAZ JEWEL

syn. 'MORYELRUG', Gelbe Dagmar Hastrup, Yellow Dagmar Hastrup, Rustica 91

Rugosa Hybrid

ORIGIN Moore, US, 1987
PARENTAGE 'Golden Angel' x 'Belle Poitevine'
FLOWER SIZE 3.1in (8cm)
SCENT Moderate, sweet, and spicy
FLOWERING Repeats well
HEIGHT/SPREAD 4.1ft (1.25m)/4.9ft (1.5m)
HARDINESS Zone 5

Topaz Jewel was introduced as a yellow Rugosa hybrid, of which there are few. Its flowers are yolk yellow at first, fading quickly to lemon, cream, and white, though there is always some color left at the center of the flower, sometimes even a hint of buff. In hot weather the flowers take on a greenish tinge. They are lightly double, with loose petals and pretty stamens, and come in tight clusters of 5–9 flowers, sometimes slightly smothered by leaves. The bush is very hardy, very prickly, and useful both for groundcover (or landscaping) and as a garden plant. The leaves are dark, veined, rugose, and fairly healthy, though traces of blackspot and mildew may sometimes be found. Unlike most Rugosas, it does not set hips.

TOPAZ JEWEL

TOPKAPI PALACE

syn. 'POULTHE'

Miniature Rose

ORIGIN **Poulsen, Denmark, 1996**
FLOWER SIZE **2in (5cm)**
SCENT **Medium and sweet**
FLOWERING **Repeats well**
HEIGHT/SPREAD **1.6ft (50cm)/1.6ft (50cm)**
HARDINESS **Zone 5**

Topkapi Palace is a very attractive large miniature or patio rose. The flowers have a charming arrangement of petals as they unfold, which gives them a distinctly old-fashioned shape. They are bright, deep pink at first (with slightly darker petal backs), and are at their loveliest as they start to bloom. Later they fade to pale pink, which gives rise to striking contrasts of color within an individual cluster. In hot weather they may bleach unattractively almost to white, making this a rose for cooler climates. The flowers come in clusters of 5–20, opening over a long period and repeating quickly, so that the bush seems never to be out of flower. The plant has small, glossy, Wichurana leaves and appears very healthy. Topkapi is the Ottoman Imperial Palace in Istanbul.

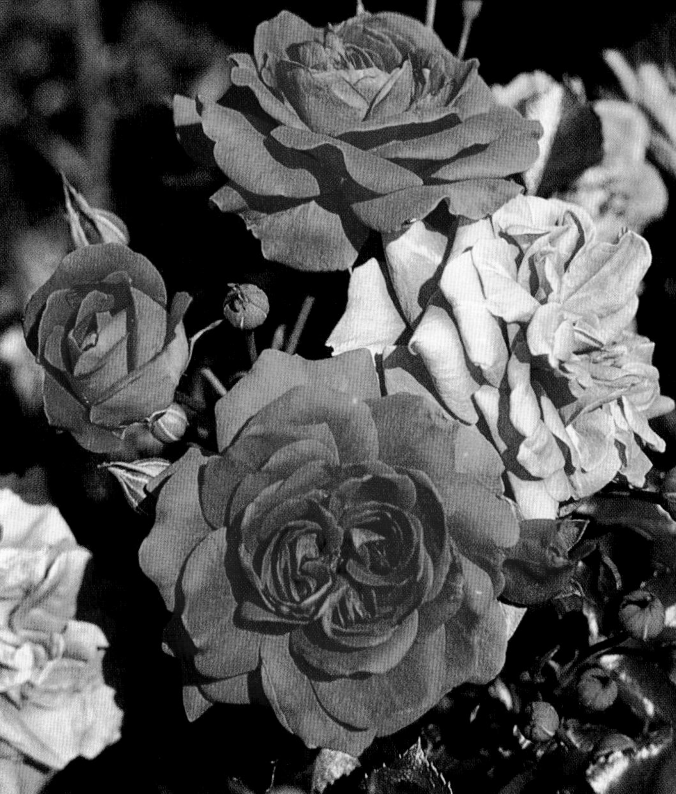
TOPKAPI PALACE

'TORO'

see 'UNCLE JOE'

TOUCH OF CLASS

see MARÉCHAL LECLERC

TOULOUSE-LAUTREC

syn. 'MEIREVOLT'

Shrub Rose

ORIGIN **Meilland, France, 1993**
PARENTAGE **Ambassador x ('King's Ransom' x 'Landora')**
FLOWER SIZE **3.9in (10cm)**
SCENT **Strong and sweet**
FLOWERING **Repeats**
HEIGHT/SPREAD **4.9ft (1.5m)/4.1ft (1.25m)**
HARDINESS **Zone 6**
AWARDS **Monza FA 1993**

It is classified as a shrub, but Toulouse-Lautrec looks like a large Hybrid Tea with old-fashioned flowers. They are rich yellow, fading at the edges, and full of petals, somewhat like a Gallic version of Graham Thomas. In hot climates like that of Los Angeles it quickly reaches 6.6ft (2m). The flowers are cupped and roughly quartered, with a mass of small, quilled petals at the center. They are borne singly, but fairly generously, and their stems are long enough to make a useful cut flower. Toulouse-Lautrec has medium-dark, glossy leaves – a good foil for the bright flowers – but watch out for blackspot.

'TOUR DE MALAKOFF'

Hybrid China

ORIGIN **Soupert & Notting, Luxembourg, 1856**
FLOWER SIZE **3.9in (10cm)**
SCENT **Strong and sweet**
FLOWERING **Once only**
HEIGHT/SPREAD **8.2ft (2.5m)/4.9ft (1.5m)**
HARDINESS **Zone 5**

Like 'Fantin Latour'and 'Paul Ricault', 'Tour de Malakoff' is one of those hybrids between an old European rose and a China rose. They fit into no category, but have an abundance of hybrid vigor that renders them exceptional garden roses. The globular buds and mauve petals that show as they unfold give no hint of the glories to follow, because it is only when the flowers are fully expanded that 'Tour de Malakoff' shows its true colors – darkest plum purple at the center, fading to pale lilac gray at the edges, and with every imaginable shade of lavender, crimson, and blackcurrant in between. The petals are thin, loose, and wayward: the overall effect is rich and voluptuous. The flowers come singly, or in clusters of up to five, all along the long, lanky stems. It makes a lax, sprawling shrub with large prickles and small, smooth leaves that may need protection from mildew and blackspot. Alexandre Chauvelot built the Tour de Malakoff on the edge of Paris in 1855 as a Crimean War Memorial. It was demolished in 1870 but its memory lives on in the name of a suburb.

TOURNAMENT OF ROSES

TOURNAMENT OF ROSES

syn. 'JACIENT', Poésie, Berkeley

Grandiflora

ORIGIN **Warriner, US, 1988**
PARENTAGE **Impatient x seedling**
FLOWER SIZE **3.5in (9cm)**
SCENT **Little or none**
FLOWERING **Repeats almost constantly**
HEIGHT/SPREAD **4.1ft (1.25m)/3.3ft (1m)**
HARDINESS **Zone 6**
AWARDS **AARS 1989**

Tournament of Roses is a big Floribunda-type rose with fat, swirling, individual flowers shaped like Hybrid Teas, reminiscent of 'Queen Elizabeth'. The flowers have several shades of pink within them – deep pink at the center, pale pink (almost white) at the edges, and darker petal backs (the buds are red). They come in long-stemmed clusters of 5–7 and are excellent for exhibiting and cutting. The bush has dark green, glossy leaves, large prickles, and a fairly upright habit of growth, though it is not among the most vigorous of roses. It produces flowers well into winter in hot climates, and very freely in both its first flowering and thereafter. Of all roses, it is said to be one of the most resistant to blackspot, mildew, and rust. The Tournament of Roses is a festival of flowers (plus music and football) held annually on New Year's Day in Pasadena, California.

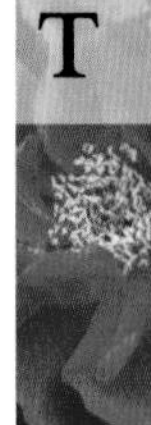

TOULOUSE-LAUTREC

'TOUR DE MALAKOFF'

TRADESCANT

TOYNBEE HALL

see BELLA ROSA

TRADESCANT

syn. 'AUSDIR'

Shrub Rose

ORIGIN **Austin, Britain, 1994**
PARENTAGE **Prospero x seedling**
FLOWER SIZE **2.4in (6cm)**
SCENT **Medium and sweet**
FLOWERING **Repeats**
HEIGHT/SPREAD **3.3ft (1m)/2.7ft (80cm)**
HARDINESS **Zone 6**

Inbreeding diminishes vigor, which may explain why Tradescant is a weak grower. The flowers are by far the darkest of David Austin's English Roses – a shade that seems to recede into the shadows – and the rose needs careful planting to ensure that it is seen to advantage. Nevertheless, the petals are redder at the edges and turn purple with age. The flowers open out lightly cupped, quilled, and sometimes quartered; later they flatten out and their outer petals acquire an attractive wave. They come in clusters, typically of 5–10 flowers, on a slender bush whose stems arch over. The leaves are medium-sized, dark green, and sometimes susceptible to blackspot, though Tradescant is healthier when well fed. The amazing dark crimson flowers justify every labor spent upon this rose's cultivation.

TRADITION 95

syn. 'KORKELTIN'

Modern Climber

ORIGIN **Kordes, Germany, 1995**
FLOWER SIZE **3.1in (8cm)**
SCENT **Light and sweet**
FLOWERING **Continuous**
HEIGHT/SPREAD **8.2ft (2.5m)/6.6ft (2m)**
HARDINESS **Zone 5**

Tradition 95 is very hardy, flowers continuously, and keeps its color well. It is an excellent short climber. The flowers are slightly more than semi-double and a glowing crimson red with bright golden stamens. They come in large clusters of 5–20 flowers like a vigorous Floribunda, and stand up well to rain. Tradition 95 is bushy, too, which means that it can be grown not only as a freestanding shrub or a pillar rose, but also as a well-furnished climber. The leaves are dark, healthy, and very glossy – the parentage of Tradition 95 has not yet been published, but it clearly has 'Kordesii' in its ancestry. It is a vigorous grower that pushes out a large number of new (and very prickly) stems every year on which to carry its profuse flushes of flowers.

TRADITION 95

'TRÄUMEREI'

syn. 'RÊVERIE'

Floribunda

ORIGIN **Kordes, Germany, 1974**
PARENTAGE **'Königin der Rosen' seedling**
FLOWER SIZE **3.5in (9cm)**
SCENT **Strong and sweet**
FLOWERING **Repeats**
HEIGHT/SPREAD **3.3ft (1m)/2.7ft (80cm)**
HARDINESS **Zone 6**

It was bred as long ago as 1974, but 'Träumerei' has remained consistently popular, especially in its native Germany. It is a fine, dark, glowing salmon pink Floribunda with a delicious scent. The flowers are large and fairly full of petals for a Floribunda. They are produced most generously in clusters of 3–8 flowers that are good for cutting, even though 'Träumerei' is essentially a garden rose. The flowers stand up well to rain, but also perform successfully in hot climates. 'Träumerei' makes a broad, well-branched, upright plant, with strong, dark leaves that are generally very healthy. It is vigorous and quick to repeat.

'TRÄUMEREI'

TRAVIATA

syn. 'MEILAVIO'

Hybrid Tea

ORIGIN **Meilland, France, 1998**
PARENTAGE **(Porta Nigra x Paola) x William Shakespeare**
FLOWER SIZE **4.7in (12cm)**
SCENT **Light and fruity**
FLOWERING **Repeats**
HEIGHT/SPREAD **4.9ft (1.5m)/3.3ft (1m)**
HARDINESS **Zone 6**

Meilland used the David Austin rose William Shakespeare to bring some old-fashioned charm to this Hybrid Tea in the Romantica series. The result is a fat, Turkey red flower with a lot of small petals, sometimes arranged in a quartered shape. At their best they are exquisite, though the flowers may ball in damp weather, spoil in rain, and burn in hot sun. When they open out, the flowers have a few white flecks toward the center. They lose their brightness and fade to crimson with age. They are borne, usually singly, on long stems that are good for cutting and last well in water. Traviata is vigorous, with thick, sturdy stems, large, dark, glossy leaves, and rounded leaflets. The plant produces its flowers prolifically in a series of flushes that last right through until late autumn.

TRAVIATA

'TREASURE TROVE'

Filipes Rambler

ORIGIN **Treasure, Britain, 1977**
PARENTAGE ***Rosa filipes* x unknown**
FLOWER SIZE **2.4in (6cm)**
SCENT **Moderate and sweet**
FLOWERING **Once, somewhat late in season**
HEIGHT/SPREAD **16.4ft (5m)/9.8ft (3m)**
HARDINESS **Zone 6**

John Treasure, who found this chance seedling in 1961, was a gentleman nurseryman with a clematis nursery and a beautiful garden at Tenbury Wells in England. Although 'Treasure Trove' is said to be a cross between 'Kiftsgate' and 'Apricot Silk', there is no firm evidence for either parent. It is an extremely vigorous and healthy climbing rose, capable of reaching 26.2ft (8m) or more. The flowers have the beautiful coloring of a Noisette – copper and pink at first, but fading to buff, cream, mother-of-pearl, and white. They open out loosely double and come in large, airy clusters of 10–25 flowers. The foliage is large, and the new growth and limp young leaves are a beautiful rich crimson. 'Treasure Trove' is one of the most beautiful of all once-flowering climbing roses.

'TREASURE TROVE'

T

TREVOR GRIFFITHS

TREVOR GRIFFITHS

syn. 'AUSOLD'

Shrub Rose

ORIGIN **Austin, Britain, 1994**
PARENTAGE **'Wife of Bath' x Hero**
FLOWER SIZE **3.1in (8cm)**
SCENT **Strong and sweet**
FLOWERING **Repeats**
HEIGHT/SPREAD **4.9ft (1.5m)/4.1ft (1.25m)**
HARDINESS **Zone 5**

Trevor Griffiths is one of the prettiest of David Austin's pink English Roses, and very strongly scented, too. The flowers open fairly flat to an irregular mass of petals reminiscent of old Damask roses. Warm pink at the center, and paler at the edges and on the petal backs, they come in short-stemmed clusters of 3–7. The plant is covered in masses of small red prickles. The dark green leaves have a rough old-rose texture and may be susceptible to blackspot. The bush looks excellent in mixed plantings of roses and herbaceous plants. Trevor Griffiths was a New Zealand nurseryman whose books did much to popularize old roses.

'TRICOLORE DE FLANDRE'

Gallica

ORIGIN **Van Houtte, Belgium, 1846**
FLOWER SIZE **2.4in (6cm)**
SCENT **Moderate and sweet**
FLOWERING **Once only**
HEIGHT/SPREAD **3.3ft (1m)/2.7ft (80cm)**
HARDINESS **Zone 5**

Any Gallica introduced as late as 1846 had to be a good one in order to compete with the repeat flowering Bourbons and Hybrid Perpetuals that were beginning to dominate the market for new roses. 'Tricolore de Flandre' is an excellent striped rose that has the advantage these days of being one of the smallest and most compact of old roses. The flowers are neat, but very full of petals, and have a green button eye that sticks up in the middle. Their coloring and striping vary greatly according to the weather, but are usually dark crimson on a pink ground, fading to purple and even Parma violet on white as the flowers age. When grown on its own roots (which is always best with Gallicas), 'Tricolore de Flandre' spreads into a mighty mass of dark green leaves, studded with beautiful flowers. It has only a few thorns and takes to pot culture better than most Gallicas.

'TRICOLORE DE FLANDRE'

'TRIER'

Multiflora Rambler

ORIGIN **Lambert, Germany, 1904**
PARENTAGE **'Aglaia' x unknown**
FLOWER SIZE **1.4in (3.5cm)**
SCENT **Strong, musky, and sweet**
FLOWERING **Repeats continuously**
HEIGHT/SPREAD **6.6ft (2m)/8.2ft (2.5m)**
HARDINESS **Zone 6**

Peter Lambert knew that 'Trier' was a good rose, which is why he named it after his home town in Germany, but he would be surprised to learn that his shrub is treated as a 16.4ft (5m) climber in hot climates, and that it became the foundation of a whole new race of roses called the Hybrid Musks. There is only a trace of *Rosa moschata* in 'Trier' – it is best thought of as a repeat flowering Multiflora hybrid, not a dwarf Polyantha or a lank rambler, but intermediate in size. The flowers open from pink buds. They are white, with a large brush of rich golden stamens. They are very freely borne in large, loose clusters of 5–50 flowers at first, but up to 100 in late summer and autumn. Small red hips follow. The flowers are set off by dark, glossy, green leaves. There are a few down-curved, red prickles. The plant is healthy, vigorous, and surprisingly hardy.

'TRIER'

TRIER 2000

TRIER 2000

syn. 'KORMETTER', Anna Livia, Sandton Smile

Floribunda

ORIGIN **Kordes, Germany, 1985**
PARENTAGE **(seedling x 'Tornado') x seedling**
FLOWER SIZE **3.1in (8cm)**
SCENT **Light and fruity**
FLOWERING **Repeats well**
HEIGHT/SPREAD **5.7ft (1.75m)/4.1ft (1.25m)**
HARDINESS **Zone 6**
AWARDS **Orléans GM 1987; Golden Rose of the Hague 1989; Glasgow GM 1991**

Trier 2000 is a 1980s Floribunda whose popularity enjoyed a surge at the millennium. It was originally named to commemorate the start of Roman rule in the city of Trier 2,000 years ago. The shapely flowers are salmon pink, but paler and whiter toward the center, opening semidouble, with pretty stamens. One curious attribute they share with many roses is a tendency for the flowers to assume red blotches after rain, as if injured by the raindrops. They come in clusters of 5–15, with very long stems that make them good for cutting. The plant has long prickles, medium-dark leaves (not immune to blackspot), and a bushy habit of growth. The new leaves and growth are bronzy red when young. Trier 2000 is very floriferous and looks good in a mixed border.

'TRIGINTIPETALA'

see 'KAZANLIK'

'TRIOMPHE DU LUXEMBOURG'

Tea Rose

ORIGIN **Hardy, France, 1840**
FLOWER SIZE **4.7in (12cm)**
SCENT **Medium and sweet**
FLOWERING **Remontant**
HEIGHT/SPREAD **4.1ft (1.25m)/4.9ft (1.5m)**
HARDINESS **Zone 7**

This vigorous Tea rose has certain characteristics of the Bourbon roses – including a globular shape as it opens, and a sweet scent that lacks the tarry aroma of tea. The fat, cabbagelike, mid-pink buds of 'Triomphe du Luxembourg' are bursting with petals that start to reflex quite early, showing that the petals are creamy flesh pink but the backs are clear rose pink. Then the flowers open out wide, and lightly cupped, to reveal a lot of little petals with pretty, deep shadows between them. The flowers usually come singly, occasionally in twos and threes. The plant has purplish stems, quite a lot of thorns, and small, rounded leaflets. It was named after the Luxembourg gardens in Paris where Hardy worked.

'TRIOMPHE DU LUXEMBOURG'

'TROIKA'

TROPICAL SUNSET

'TRUE LOVE'

'TROIKA'

syn. 'ROYAL DANE'

Hybrid Tea

ORIGIN **Poulsen, Denmark, 1971**
PARENTAGE **('Super Star' x ['Baccará' x 'Prinsesse Astrid af Norge']) x 'Hanne'**
FLOWER SIZE **4.7in (12cm)**
SCENT **Medium and sweet**
FLOWERING **Repeats**
HEIGHT/SPREAD **4.1ft (1.25m)/2.5ft (75cm)**
HARDINESS **Zone 6**
AWARDS **James Mason GM 1992**

'Troika' has been a much loved rose for many years. This is due in part to its beautiful coloring: the flowers are pure salmon pink, with darker shades on the petal backs, a yellow flush at the base, and splashes of rose red on the edges of the outer petals. It is a warm and attractive combination of colors. The flowers have the classic shape of the large-flowered Hybrid Teas. They come singly on long, elegant stems and are very pretty at all stages of growth. The plant has large dark leaves and is both vigorous and healthy. It repeats well and is useful in large bedding plans. In hot climates it will grow to 6.6ft (2m).

TROILUS

syn. 'AUSOIL'

Shrub Rose

ORIGIN **Austin, Britain, 1983**
PARENTAGE **('Duchesse de Montebello' x 'Chaucer') x 'Charles Austin'**
FLOWER SIZE **3.1in (8cm)**
SCENT **Strong and sweet**
FLOWERING **Repeats**
HEIGHT/SPREAD **4.1ft (1.25m)/3.3ft (1m)**
HARDINESS **Zone 6**

This is a David Austin rose for warm climates. In its native England, the flowers of Troilus are tightly cupped and spoil in rain, but in hot conditions its flowers are larger, more open, and more intensely colored. At their best, the flowers are buff colored, with hints of apricot, pink, and cream, and richer, darker shadows toward the center. They come in large, heavy clusters, often somewhat tight and overly full of flowers. However, they are good for picking in hot climates and give useful bulk to big arrangements. Troilus is vigorous, narrow, and upright, with large, dark green, fairly glossy leaves and quite a few prickles. It is a slow repeater in cool climates but repeats well elsewhere, especially if deadheaded, fed, and watered.

TROPICAL SUNSET

syn. 'MACTAURANG', Marvelle

Hybrid Tea

ORIGIN **McGredy, New Zealand, 1998**
PARENTAGE **Louise Gardner x (Auckland Metro x 'Stars 'n' Stripes' seedling)**
FLOWER SIZE **4.7in (12cm)**
SCENT **Medium and fruity**
FLOWERING **Repeats well**
HEIGHT/SPREAD **5.7ft (1.75m)/4.1ft (1.25m)**
HARDINESS **Zone 6**

Sam McGredy has issued a number of striped roses: Tropical Sunset is perhaps the best, and is particularly popular in the milder parts of the US. The flowers come singly, on long stems, and are bright yellow, splashed with orange. The stripes appear more clearly on the upper sides of the petals – the reverses remain yellow. Later, the yellow fades to cream and the orange turns crimson, but the overall effect remains charming. The flowers come on a vigorous, upright plant with large prickles and healthy, medium-dark leaves.

'TROPICANA'

see 'SUPER STAR'

'TRUE LOVE'

syn. 'YORKSHIRE BANK'

Hybrid Tea

ORIGIN **de Ruiter, 1979**
PARENTAGE **'Pascali' x 'Peer Gynt'**
FLOWER SIZE **4.7in (12cm)**
SCENT **Medium and sweet**
FLOWERING **Repeats**
HEIGHT/SPREAD **4.1ft (1.25m)/2.7ft (80cm)**
HARDINESS **Zone 6**
AWARDS **Geneva GM 1979; NZ GM 1979**

The large, elegant flowers of 'True Love' are very beautiful. They are creamy white, with hints and flushes of buff, pink, and palest yellow at the center. The combination of many-petaled shapeliness and subtle coloring is exquisite, and has ensured the continuing popularity of 'True Love' for many years, especially in Europe. The flowers come sometimes singly and sometimes in clusters of up to five, on long stems that are perfect for cutting and indeed for exhibition. The plant has a vigorous, open habit of growth and dark, healthy leaves. It is usually pruned hard to maximize the size of the flowers, but 'True Love' can also be allowed to build up into a bushy shrub and will cover itself all over with its superbly beautiful blooms.

'TRUMPETER'

syn. MACTRUM

Floribunda

ORIGIN **McGredy, New Zealand, 1977**
PARENTAGE **'Satchmo' seedling**
FLOWER SIZE **2.8in (7cm)**
SCENT **Light**
FLOWERING **Almost constant**
HEIGHT/SPREAD **2ft (60cm)/1.6ft (50cm)**
HARDINESS **Zone 6**
AWARDS **NZ GM 1977; James Mason GM 1991**

The popularity of this neat, compact, vermilion Floribunda is well deserved: 'Trumpeter' goes on flowering abundantly and ceaselessly right

TROILUS

'TRUMPETER'

TURBO

through until late autumn. The flowers are a very brilliant color, sometimes described as dark orange or scarlet, and fully double. They open out lightly cupped and come in clusters of 3–15. Since the plants are so short, they seem to be covered in their spectacular, fluorescent flowers all the time. 'Trumpeter' is an excellent choice for a short bedding rose or for planting in containers. The plant has dark, healthy, glossy foliage, with a purplish tinge at first and a slightly lax habit of growth.

TURBO

syn. 'MEIROZRUG', Turbo Meidiland

Rugosa Hybrid

ORIGIN **Meilland, France, 1993**
PARENTAGE **('Fru Dagmar Hastrup' x Manou Meilland) x 'Pink Grootendorst'**
FLOWER SIZE **2.4in (6cm)**
SCENT **Light or slight**
FLOWERING **Repeats well**
HEIGHT/SPREAD **3.3ft (1m)/3.3ft (1m)**
HARDINESS **Zone 5**

This floriferous modern Rugosa hybrid is useful for landscaping as well as for garden plantings. The flowers of Turbo open rich cherry pink and fade to pale rose pink, passing through every possible shade and tone between them. The petal backs are always slightly paler, and there is also a hint of white at the center. The flowers are only lightly double, and the petals lie flat to reveal a small patch of pale stamens. The flowers come in large, tight, terminal clusters at the end of the new wood (usually 10–20 flowers in a cluster) on short, weak stems, which means that they hang down like cherries. The plant is healthy, tough, compact, and very prickly. The leaves are pale, smooth, and glossy (which is unexpected for a Rugosa hybrid), and tinged with red when young. It repeats well.

'TURNER'S CRIMSON RAMBLER'

syn. 'CRIMSON RAMBLER'

Multiflora Rambler

ORIGIN **Turner, Britain, 1893**
FLOWER SIZE **1.6in (4cm)**
SCENT **Little or none**
FLOWERING **Once only**
HEIGHT/SPREAD **13.1ft (4m)/9.8ft (3m)**
HARDINESS **Zone 5**

'Turner's Crimson Rambler' changed the whole history of our garden roses. It is an old Chinese garden rose that was introduced to Europe in 1878 and was popularized by an English nurseryman called Turner. Its origins are unknown, but it has *Rosa multiflora*, *Rosa wichurana*, and *Rosa chinensis* in its ancestry. The flowers are small, double, and bright, unfading crimson. They are borne in vast quantities in large, loose, pendulous clusters, typically of 20–30 flowers, somewhat late in the season. It is hard to overestimate its outstanding floriferousness. Small, round, orange hips follow in due course. The plant is very vigorous, with pale green wood and glossy evergreen leaves, which are these days somewhat susceptible to mildew. It grows to about 16.4ft (5m). A vast number of open-pollinated seedlings were introduced in the 1900s and 1910s, including such famous ramblers as 'Dorothy Perkins' and 'Excelsa'. 'Turner's Crimson Rambler' also contributed substantially to the development of Polyantha roses: almost every Polyantha claims it as an ancestor.

'TUSCANY'

Gallica

ORIGIN **c.1600**
FLOWER SIZE **2.4in (6cm)**
SCENT **Strong and sweet**
FLOWERING **Once only**
HEIGHT/SPREAD **4.1ft (1.25m)/2.5ft (75cm)**
HARDINESS **Zone 5**

'TURNER'S CRIMSON RAMBLER'

'TUSCANY'

No one knows the origin of this beautiful dark Gallica rose. Some believe it to be the same as the "Old Velvet" rose described by the English plantsman John Gerard in 1596. All are agreed that 'Tuscany' is a rose of rare but simple beauty. Its flowers are rich, dark crimson, with occasional white flecks. They are lightly double, with a glowing ring of golden stamens that emphasizes the opulence of the rose and its color. They come in clusters of 3–7. The plant is very upright in habit, almost without prickles, with slender stems, small dark leaves, and somewhat rounded leaflets.

'TUSCANY SUPERB'

Gallica

ORIGIN **Rivers, Britain, 1837**
PARENTAGE **'Tuscany' x unknown**
FLOWER SIZE **2.8in (7cm)**
SCENT **Light and sweet**
FLOWERING **Once only**
HEIGHT/SPREAD **4.9ft (1.5m)/4.1ft (1.25m)**
HARDINESS **Zone 5**

'TUSCANY SUPERB'

The main interest surrounding 'Tuscany Superb' is that it was one of the few Gallicas bred in England. The raiser, Thomas Rivers (1798–1877), was a distinguished breeder of fruit trees. Although branded "superb," it has one serious weakness, which is that the petals tend to fold over toward the center (the photograph above is an exception), instead of lying back and forming a pretty rosette like most old roses do. It is also only lightly scented. On the other hand, the flowers are larger and fuller than 'Tuscany', and they are a stupendously rich color – deeper purple than 'Tuscany' and intensified by yellow stamens and a few white streaks on some of the inner petals. The leaves, too, are larger and more luxuriant. The flowers come singly or in twos and threes on a vigorous bush that has a few prickles.

'TUTU MAUVE'

Floribunda

ORIGIN **Delbard-Chabert, France, 1963**
FLOWER SIZE **3.9in (10cm)**
SCENT **Light and sweet**
FLOWERING **Repeats well**
HEIGHT/SPREAD **3.3ft (1m)/2.7ft (80cm)**
HARDINESS **Zone 6**
AWARDS **Madrid 1962**

This vigorous Floribunda has been popular ever since it was introduced. 'Tutu Mauve' has lilac mauve flowers, with a deeper shade of the same color on the petal backs. They fade slightly as they age, and sometimes take on a pink tinge, but the mauve usually lasts well. The flowers are full of short petals and come in clusters of up to about seven. The plant is healthy, compact, and easy to grow. It combines well in mixed borders. The flowers crumple in the rain, so this is a rose for dry climates. It is especially popular in Australia.

'TUTU MAUVE'

'Ulrich Brunner Fils'

Hybrid Perpetual

ORIGIN **Levet, France, 1881**
PARENTAGE **'Paul Neyron' x unknown**
FLOWER SIZE **4.7in (12cm)**
SCENT **Strong and sweet**
FLOWERING **Remontant**
HEIGHT/SPREAD **5.7ft (1.75m)/4.1ft (1.25m)**
HARDINESS **Zone 5**

'Ulrich Brunner Fils' was one of few Hybrid Perpetuals bred by Antoine Levet of Lyon, a man who never introduced a disappointing rose. It has bright cherry pink flowers – very large and very full of petals. The petal backs are pale pink, and the color as a whole fades as it ages. The flowers are fairly globular – incurved toward the center and more reflexed toward the outside – and borne singly or in twos and threes, held well above the leaves on upright stems. They are good for picking and have a rich scent, but they do suffer in rain. The leaves are large, mid-green, and shiny. The plant has a strong, slender, upright habit and few thorns. It is one of the easiest of old roses to grow. If its long shoots are pegged down, they will break into flower all along their length.

Ultimate Pink

syn. 'JACVAL'

Hybrid Tea

ORIGIN **Zary, US, 1998**
PARENTAGE **seedling x 'Jadis'**
FLOWER SIZE **4.7in (12cm)**
SCENT **Little or none**
FLOWERING **Repeats well**
HEIGHT/SPREAD **4.9ft (1.5m)/3.3ft (1m)**
HARDINESS **Zone 6**

'Ulrich Brunner Fils'

Ultimate Pink

It has a beautiful color and an exquisite shape, but can any rose claim to be the ultimate rose without a scent to match? Ultimate Pink has little or no scent at all. However, its buds are very elegant, long, and tapered, and they spiral out into flawless, long-petaled flowers. The color is clear, pure pink, almost translucent, and fades only very slightly as it ages. The flowers are borne usually singly but occasionally in clusters – always well held on strong, upright stems. The plant is vigorous and healthy, with only a few prickles and large, mid-green leaves.

'Uncle Joe'

syn. 'TORO', 'EL TORO'

Hybrid Tea

ORIGIN **Kern, US, 1972**
PARENTAGE **('Mirandy' x 'Charles Mallerin') x seedling**
FLOWER SIZE **5.1in (13cm)**
SCENT **Light and sweet**
FLOWERING **Repeats**
HEIGHT/SPREAD **6.6ft (2m)/4.1ft (1.25m)**
HARDINESS **Zone 6**

It has many synonyms, but there is no mistaking 'Uncle Joe': its flowers last longer than those of any other red Hybrid Tea. They are large and very full of petals, but take an unconscionable time to open. In damp spells the flowers ball, and in wet weather they spoil, but in warm, dry weather 'Uncle Joe' will go on opening its large, pointed buds for days on end. It is the exhibitor's dream rose. Eventually the flowers open out cherry crimson, with quite a number of white stripes at the center, but still they do not drop their petals, preferring instead to wither on the bush. They are borne singly on stout, long stems, which makes them popular for cutting; indeed, 'Uncle Joe' is also grown commercially as a cut flower. It has dark, medium-sized leaves and a tall, upright habit. Later on, this laid-back beauty gets around to blooming again.

'Uncle Joe'

'Uncle Walter'

Hybrid Tea

ORIGIN **McGredy, Northern Ireland, 1963**
PARENTAGE **'Schlosser's Brilliant' x 'Gruss an Heidelberg'**
FLOWER SIZE **4.3in (11cm)**
SCENT **Little or none**
FLOWERING **Repeats**
HEIGHT/SPREAD **6.6ft (2m)/3.3ft (1m)**
HARDINESS **Zone 6**

It is difficult to categorize 'Uncle Walter': it could be considered an outsize Hybrid Tea, a bushy climber, or a shrub rose of sorts. The flowers are large and shapely Hybrid Teas of a pure, unfading blood red, except for an occasional white streak and a glimpse of the yellow stamens when they open out. They come singly and, more often, in long-stemmed clusters of up to nine flowers, and are carried all over the surface of the plant. The leaves of 'Uncle Walter' are medium-dark and undistinguished, and it has a scattering of large prickles. It makes a lax plant that needs support: one way to achieve this is to grow it as a hedge; another is to tie it into a fence about 3.3ft (1m) high. When well grown, 'Uncle Walter' is a stupendous sight. It was named after Sam McGredy IV's uncle, Walter Johnston, who ran the family nursery in Northern Ireland during the 19 years of Sam's minority.

'Unique'

see 'CENTIFOLIA'

'Unique Panachée'

see 'CENTIFOLIA'

'Uncle Walter'

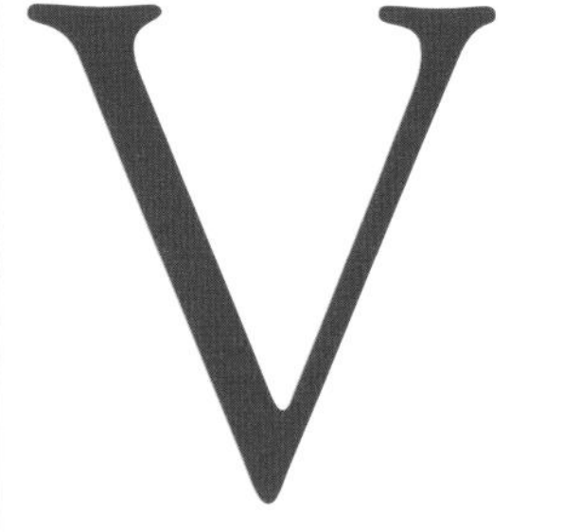

Valencia '89

syn. 'KOREKLIA'

Hybrid Tea

ORIGIN **Kordes, Germany, 1989**
FLOWER SIZE **5.1in (13cm)**
SCENT **Very strong and sweet**
FLOWERING **Repeats well**
HEIGHT/SPREAD **4.1ft (1.25m)/3.3ft (1m)**
HARDINESS **Zone 6**
AWARDS **Durbanville GM 1988; Edland FA 1989**

Valencia '89 is the best apricot colored Hybrid Tea, and is also blessed with a wonderful fragrance. The flowers are large, and open from long buds. They are old-gold in color, with bronzy apricot backs and thick velvety petals. The flowers pale as they open out, especially at the edges, so that eventually the outer petals are pale pink, while the inner ones remain a deep apricot colour. They are borne, usually singly, on long, strong stems – good for exhibition and long lasting when cut for the house. The plant is both vigorous and healthy, with large dark leaves, and a lot of them. All in all, Valencia '89 can be recommended as an excellent performer and a good repeater.

Valentine Heart

syn. 'DICOGLE'

Floribunda

ORIGIN **Dickson, Northern Ireland, 1989**
PARENTAGE **'Shona' x Pot o' Gold**
FLOWER SIZE **2.8in (7cm)**
SCENT **Strong and sweet**
FLOWERING **Almost continuous**
HEIGHT/SPREAD **4.1ft (1.25m)/2.5ft (75cm)**
HARDINESS **Zone 6**

Valencia '89

VALENTINE HEART

The flowers of Valentine Heart have a hint of red at their center – hence its name. The flowers are actually a two-tone pink: rich dark pink on the petal backs and pale rose pink within. The buds are dark, too – pale red before they open out. The flowers are lightly double, in the best Dickson tradition of breeding roses that tolerate the rain of Ireland – "weather resistant" is the usual euphemism – but pretty, too. They come in spacious clusters of 5–15 flowers, well held on long stems. Their sweet scent is a great bonus. The plant has dense, mid-green leaves (purple when young) and a bushy habit of growth. It flowers almost continuously. In every respect, Valentine Heart is a very attractive garden plant with the added advantage that it doubles up as a good cutting rose.

'VANGUARD'

Rugosa Hybrid

ORIGIN **Stevens, US, 1932**
PARENTAGE **(*Rosa rugosa* 'Alba' × *Rosa wichurana*) × 'El Dorado'**
FLOWER SIZE **5.1in (13cm)**
SCENT **Strong, sweet, and fruity**
FLOWERING **Repeats**
HEIGHT/SPREAD **8.2ft (2.5m)/6.6ft (2m)**
HARDINESS **Zone 5**

The breeder of this remarkable rose was a gifted young amateur who died shortly after it was introduced. He sought to combine the hardiness and scent of *Rosa rugosa* with the vigor of *Rosa wichurana* and the colors and size of a Hybrid Tea. He was completely successful, and yet nothing resembling 'Vanguard' followed for another 20 years. The flowers of 'Vanguard' open from long scarlet or coral buds. They are large, very full of petals, and apricot, peach, or salmon colored at first, with hints of scarlet, too. Over the next few days, and especially in hot weather, they fade to beautiful shades of pale pink, pearl, and cream. The petals arrange themselves beautifully at all stages of this development. The flowers come singly, or occasionally in twos and threes, and tend to nod their heads, which is just as well since the plant can grow very tall – as much as 13.1ft (4m) in hot climates, though 6.6ft (2m) is normal elsewhere. 'Vanguard' has very glossy rugose foliage (rust can be a problem) and bronzy new growth. It makes a huge, lanky bush.

'VANGUARD'

WALTER VAN FLEET

AFTER PRACTICING AS A DOCTOR, VAN FLEET TURNED HIS HAND TO BREEDING ROSES, PRODUCING SOME OF AMERICA'S BEST-LOVED HYBRIDS

WALTER VAN FLEET (1857–1922) studied medicine and practiced as a doctor. Later, he worked as a plant breeder for the US Department of Agriculture. Van Fleet was the first American to hybridize *Rosa wichurana* and *Rosa rugosa* – and very successfully. 'New Century' (1900) and 'Sarah Van Fleet' are fine examples of his Rugosa roses; 'May Queen' and 'Mary Lovett' (1915) of his excellent Wichuranas. Van Fleet also used 'Turner's Crimson Rambler' to breed 'Philadelphia Rambler' (1904), a great improvement on its parent. By the 1920s the three most popular climbing roses in the US were all raised by Van Fleet: 'Dr. W. Van Fleet', 'Silver Moon', and 'American Pillar'.

WALTER VAN FLEET

After he died, the American Rose Society turned Van Fleet into a popular hero – the champion of every garden owner, America's greatest rose hybridist, perhaps the greatest plant breeder America had ever known. Van Fleet had been the dreamer who wanted to put roses in every American yard, however modest it might be. Many of his hybrids, still under trial, would be of inestimable benefit to American gardeners. The society would negotiate with the Department of Agriculture to release the best of Van Fleet's orphaned seedlings. The editor of the *American Rose Annual* summed up the society's marketing strategy in words that were calculated to thrill every American: Dr. Van Fleet "had never cared to undertake the breeding of the ordinary Hybrid Tea roses, the petted darlings of the French and English favored climates. Dr. Van Fleet wanted roses that could stand with the lilacs and the spireas and the mock oranges, and with all the other hardy shrubs of American home-grounds." As a result, the ARS distributed in 1924 the first of Van Fleet's "dooryard" roses, the splendid pink climber 'Mary Wallace' and followed it up with such important roses as 'Breeze Hill' and 'Glenn Dale' (1927).

'NEW CENTURY'

'PHILADELPHIA RAMBLER'

'VANITY'

'VARIEGATA DI BOLOGNA'

VELVET FRAGRANCE

'VANITY'

Hybrid Musk

ORIGIN **Pemberton, Britain, 1920**
PARENTAGE **'Château de Clos Vougeot' seedling**
FLOWER SIZE **2.8in (7cm)**
SCENT **Medium and musky**
FLOWERING **Repeats well**
HEIGHT/SPREAD **6.6ft (2m)/4.9ft (1.5m)**
HARDINESS **Zone 6**

Although widely sold and grown, 'Vanity' is sometimes overlooked in favor of more glamorous Hybrid Musks. This is a mistake, for it has a usefulness and a beauty of its own. The flowers are all but single, with a charming wave to their petals. Their color is bright cherry pink or magenta at first, but fades to lilac pink as they age. They have a very small white patch at the base of the petals and a crown of dark yellow stamens. They are somewhat loosely borne in large, open clusters, and make quite an impact on the garden, though 'Vanity' can be a difficult color to mix well. Round orange hips follow in due course. The plant has an open habit of growth and can be trained as a 13.1ft (4m) climber in hot climates. Its leaves are large and somewhat sparse, but healthy enough.

'VARIEGATA DI BOLOGNA'

Bourbon Rose

ORIGIN **Bonfiglioli, Italy, 1909**
PARENTAGE **sport of 'Victor Emmanuel'**
FLOWER SIZE **3.1in (8cm)**
SCENT **Strong and sweet**
FLOWERING **Once, midseason, then sporadically**
HEIGHT/SPREAD **9.8ft (3m)/6.6ft (2m)**
HARDINESS **Zone 5**

'Variegata di Bologna' has always been popular, partly perhaps due to its exotic name. It is a pale rose pink with a few crimson purple flecks and stripes. In hot weather the stripes are paler, but so, too, is the pink background. It is thought to be a sport from 'Victor Emmanuel', which is a purple rose, so the stripes are a reminder of its parent. The flowers are fat, cupped, full, and occasionally quartered. They come in tight clusters (the flowers have short pedicels) of 3–5, but ball in damp weather. The plant has large, thin, lush, mid-green leaves, which sometimes show a little blackspot. However, the plant is also very vigorous, sending up long stems that have to be tied in to keep it neat. The flowers make good potpourri because the striping is preserved on the dried petals. Sometimes part of the plant reverts to 'Victor Emmanuel'.

'VATERTAG'

see 'DICK KOSTER'

'VEILCHENBLAU'

Multiflora Rambler

ORIGIN **Kiese, Germany, 1909**
PARENTAGE **'Turner's Crimson Rambler' × 'Erinnerung an Brod'**
FLOWER SIZE **1.4in (3.5cm)**
SCENT **Sweet and fruity**
FLOWERING **Once only, early in season**
HEIGHT/SPREAD **9.8ft (3m)/6.6ft (2m)**
HARDINESS **Zone 5**

'Veilchenblau' is the best known and most widely grown of the purple flowered ramblers. Its flowers are reddish purple at first, then lose their red tints and turn a dark blue violet, before fading to lilac gray, especially in hot weather. The flowers tend to stay on the plant for a long time, so all these different hues are usually present together. Most of the flowers also have broad white streaks in them, running right from the white center to the tips of the petals. They are carried in open clusters of 10–30 flowers and followed by small orange hips in autumn. The stems are thick and thornless, with long internodes between the large, lush, pale green leaves. The plant grows vigorously and roots quickly from cuttings (it has been used as a rootstock). It grows well in extremes of both cold and heat, and tolerates shade. 'Veilchenblau' was the mother of a small brood of purple ramblers that appeared in the 1910s and 1920s. Some, like 'Rosemarie Viaud' and Violette', are still widely grown, while other, perhaps better, examples are seen only in old rose collections, including 'Donau' (Praskac, 1913), 'Schloss Friedenstein' (Schmidt, 1915), and 'Mosel' (Lambert, 1920).

VELDFIRE

see STADT WÜRZBURG

VELVET FRAGRANCE

syn. 'FRYPERDEE', Velours Parfumé

Hybrid Tea

ORIGIN **Fryer, Britain, 1988**
PARENTAGE **'Mildred Scheel' × 'Duftwolke'**
FLOWER SIZE **5.5in (14cm)**
SCENT **Very strong and sweet**
FLOWERING **Repeats well**
HEIGHT/SPREAD **5.7ft (1.75m)/4.1ft (1.25m)**
HARDINESS **Zone 6**
AWARDS **Edland FA 1987; Baden-Baden FA 1990**

Velvet Fragrance is one of the most popular crimson Hybrid Teas of today, and its scent is as strong and delicious as any. The flowers are very large, full of petals, and elegantly formed, and at their best in hot, dry weather. They are a silky, dark crimson, with nearly black markings and a velvety sheen on the tips of the petals. The flowers are borne singly on long, strong stems that are excellent for cutting, and the plant continues to produce new flowers right through until late autumn. Sometimes these come on exceptionally vigorous new growth, along which many long-stemmed flowers are borne individually at the ends of lateral growth. Velvet Fragrance has large, dark green, semiglossy leaves, healthy except for a weakness for blackspot in areas where this is a problem. The plant is vigorous and upright, and its new growth is crimson.

'VENUSTA PENDULA'

Ayrshire

ORIGIN **Britain**
FLOWER SIZE **2.8in (7cm)**
SCENT **Strong, musky, with myrrh**
FLOWERING **Once only**
HEIGHT/SPREAD **13.1ft (4m)/9.8ft (3m)**
HARDINESS **Zone 5**

This is an old rose, discovered and renamed when it was reintroduced by Kordes in 1928. It is probably an

'VEILCHENBLAU'

'VENUSTA PENDULA'

Ayrshire Rambler of British origin. The flowers are fairly full, white with pink markings, and open out to show their yellow stamens. They are carried in small clusters all along the long, slender growth, and are followed by red hips. Their scent is very strong and pervasive, freely released on the air. The plant has small, dark green leaves and crimson new stems. It is prickly and fairly healthy, although it does suffer from a weakness for mildew in cool climates. 'Venusta Pendula' is extremely hardy in central Europe, where it is very popular. It deserves to be more widely grown in cold parts of other continents.

'VERSICOLOR'

see 'OFFICINALIS'

'VESPER'

'VESPER'

Floribunda

ORIGIN **Le Grice, Britain, 1966**
FLOWER SIZE **2.8in (7cm)**
SCENT **Light**
FLOWERING **Repeats well**
HEIGHT/SPREAD **2.7ft (80cm)/2.3ft (70cm)**
HARDINESS **Zone 6**

'Vesper' is an orange Floribunda, which, in some conditions, is tinged and washed by tints of brown. This usually occurs in cool weather, and mainly on the petal backs. If it is well grown, and the flowers have a lot of petals, there are beautiful hints of butterscotch and mahogany in the shadows between them – otherwise it appears wishy-washy. The flowers are borne singly or in small, loose clusters in the first flowering, and subsequently in larger clusters (of 5–10 flowers). The leaves are undistinguished, except for a bronzy tint when young, and are prone to blackspot. The plant is fairly vigorous, and takes several years to build up to a good size. It is best only lightly pruned.

JEAN-PIERRE VIBERT

MANY OF THE ROSES BRED BY THE FRENCH NURSERYMAN VIBERT IN THE 19TH CENTURY ARE STILL AVAILABLE TODAY

JEAN-PIERRE VIBERT (1777–1866) was the first French nurseryman to specialize exclusively in roses. He took over the business of Descemet, the raiser of 'Chloris' and 'Impératrice Joséphine', in 1815, just as the rose was beginning to acquire popularity as a garden flower. Vibert prospered. During the 1830s his annual catalogue offered over 1,000 different roses for sale.

PORTRAIT OF JEAN-PIERRE VIBERT BY HIS GRANDSON, JEHAN GEORGES VIBERT

Vibert was a prolific breeder of roses, and an opinionated writer who tended to make enemies. His introductions came to some 600 new cultivars, of which about 60 are still in cultivation. Gallicas were his great speciality; Vibert bred some of the most exquisite and sophisticated of the old roses: 'Duchesse d'Angoulême', 'Duchesse de Buccleuch', 'Nestor', 'Perle des Panachées', and 'Ypsilanti' are among his many creations. Other good Gallicas include 'Duc d'Orléans' (1830) and the striped 'Mécène' (1845) – Vibert liked striped roses. He also bred Albas, Damasks (including the incomparable 'Ville de Bruxelles'), and Mosses. Toward the end of his career, he began to understand the value of repeat flowering roses, and bred a few Portland roses (including 'Yolande d'Aragon'), Hybrid Chinas like 'Belmont' (1846), and such Hybrid Perpetuals as 'Dembrowski' (1849). In 1851, at the age of 74, Vibert retired. He sold his business to his nursery foreman, Robert, who continued to trade until the 1890s, breeding some of the most beautiful Moss roses and Portlands.

'DUC D'ORLÉANS'

VETERAN'S HONOR

syn. 'JACOPPER', Lady in Red, City of Newcastle Bicentenary

Hybrid Tea

ORIGIN **Zary, US, 1995**
PARENTAGE **Showstopper x (seedling x 'Royalty')**
FLOWER SIZE **5.1in (13cm)**
SCENT **Medium and sweet**
FLOWERING **Repeats**
HEIGHT/SPREAD **4.9ft (1.5m)/3.3ft (1m)**
HARDINESS **Zone 6**

Like most new roses bred in the US, Veteran's Honor comes from southern California. It performs best in hot, dry climates, where its layer upon layer of long petals can open out slowly. Rain spoils it. The buds are tall, conical, and elegant. The large flowers are a beautiful scarlet crimson at first and, though they lose their brilliance with age, they remain a good, dark cherry crimson. They are borne singly on long, straight stems – perfect for large flower arrangements. The plant has medium-dark leaves, crimson new growth, a scattering of prickles, and a vigorous, upright habit of growth.

'VICK'S CAPRICE'

see 'ARCHIDUCHESSE ELISABETH D'AUTRICHE'

VETERAN'S HONOR

'Vîcomtesse Pierre du Fou'

'Vîcomtesse Pierre du Fou'

Modern Climber

ORIGIN **Sauvageot, France, 1923**
PARENTAGE **'L'Idéal' x 'Joseph Hill'**
FLOWER SIZE **4.3in (11cm)**
SCENT **Medium, sweet, and tealike**
FLOWERING **Repeats freely**
HEIGHT/SPREAD **9.8ft (3m)/9.8ft (3m)**
HARDINESS **Zone 7**

There are few large-flowered repeat-flowering climbers from the 1920s, but 'Vîcomtesse Pierre du Fou' is a good rose by any standard. It is a cross between a Climbing Tea and a bushy Hybrid Tea, and combines the best of both. Its flowers are pink with a hint of copper at first. The petal backs are paler and there is a suggestion of cream toward the center. The flowers have a quartered shape as they start to open but continue to reflex their petals along their sides, so that eventually the flowers look rather spiky. They hang their heads on weak pedicels and come in clusters of up to seven. The plant has large, medium-dark leaves, with red new growth. It is rather a lanky grower, but vigorous and very free flowering.

Victor Borge

syn. 'POULvue', Michael Crawford, Medima

Hybrid Tea

ORIGIN **Poulsen, Denmark, 1991**
FLOWER SIZE **3.9in (10cm)**
SCENT **Light and fruity**
FLOWERING **Repeats**
HEIGHT/SPREAD **4.1ft (1.25m)/3.3ft (1m)**
HARDINESS **Zone 6**

Orange, apricot, peach, salmon, pink, and yellow are all present in the flowers of Victor Borge. The dominant color is apricot pink, but the petals have yellow backs. The flowers lose some of their yellow tones as they age, becoming progressively more pink, until eventually they open out to reveal large yellow centers. Victor Borge is a Hybrid Tea and has the conical buds of the type, but the flowers are often carried in clusters, sometimes containing as many as ten flowers. It is a vigorous plant that flowers more or less continuously, though it has an ungainly habit when young until it has established its naturally broad structure. It has large, healthy, glossy, medium-dark leaves and crimson new growth. The rose was named after Victor Borge, a Danish entertainer.

Victor Borge

Victor Hugo

syn. MEIvestal, Senator Burda

Hybrid Tea

ORIGIN **Meilland, France, 1988**
PARENTAGE **('Karl Herbst' x ['Royal Velvet' x 'Suspense']) x 'Erotika'**
FLOWER SIZE **5.5in (14cm)**
SCENT **Medium and sweet**
FLOWERING **Repeats**
HEIGHT/SPREAD **5.7ft (1.75m)/4.1ft (1.25m)**
HARDINESS **Zone 6**

This traditional Hybrid Tea won a prize for its scent at the international trials at The Hague in 1985. Its flowers are not exceptional as they start to unfurl, but they expand in size and are very fine by the time they open out fully. They are bright dark red at first, changing to crimson as they age, and borne on long stems, usually singly but occasionally in clusters of up to five. The plant is very vigorous, with large leaves and large prickles. It is healthy and repeats its flowering quickly.

Victorian Spice

see L'Aimant

'Victoriana'

Floribunda

ORIGIN **Le Grice, Britain, 1977**
FLOWER SIZE **4.3in (11cm)**
SCENT **Light and sweet**
FLOWERING **Repeats well**
HEIGHT/SPREAD **3.3ft (1m)/2.7ft (80cm)**
HARDINESS **Zone 6**

Victor Hugo

'Victoriana'

Edward Le Grice was an English rose breeder who specialized in unusual colors: 'Victoriana' was one of his last raisings, introduced in the year of his death. Its flowers are a remarkable rich, rusty orange color overall, but close examination shows it to be made up of brown or maroon patches on a salmon pink ground. The petal backs are white, with pink edges, and this confusion of shades is accentuated by the waviness of the petals' shape. The flowers come singly, or in clusters of up to five, on a vigorous, shapely, healthy plant. The color is always variable, but the dark overtones last longer in cool climates.

'Village Maid'

see 'Centifolia'

'Ville de Bruxelles'

syn. 'La Ville de Bruxelles'

Damask Rose

ORIGIN **Vibert, France, 1836**
FLOWER SIZE **4.3in (11cm)**
SCENT **Strong and sweet**
FLOWERING **Once only**
HEIGHT/SPREAD **5.7ft (1.75m)/4.9ft (1.5m)**
HARDINESS **Zone 5**

Even within such a beautiful race as the Damasks, 'Ville de Bruxelles' stands out as an exceptional rose. The flowers are a uniformly deep rose pink color, fading only a little at the edges, and roughly quartered around a button eye. They are lightly cupped at first, but open flat and later reflex their outer petals, while still retaining the mass of little quilled, folded, pleated petals that fill the center of the flower. The flowers are large, too, and seem to grow in size as they mature They are wonderfully supported by large, lush, soft, pale green leaves that droop delicately as they open and expand. The plant is vigorous and beautifully clothed by its healthy leaves, while the stems are smooth, except for masses of tiny bristles. 'Ville de Bruxelles' grows expansively and gives pleasure even when not in flower.

'Ville de Bruxelles'

Rosa villosa

syn. *Rosa pomifera*

Wild Rose

FLOWER SIZE **1.6in (4cm)**
SCENT **Light and sweet**
FLOWERING **Once only**
HEIGHT/SPREAD **6.6ft (2m)/6.6ft (2m)**
HARDINESS **Zone 5**

Rosa villosa is a very pretty but variable species. It is grown mainly for the beauty of its glaucous leaves, but also for its large hips. It is sometimes known as *Rosa pomifera*, meaning "apple-bearing" – a reference to the size (1.2–1.6in/3–4cm) and edibility of the hips, which are dark red and usually bristly. *Rosa villosa* does, however, merge into another species called *Rosa mollis*, whose hips are smooth. Both plants are native to a large part of central and southern Europe. The single flowers are small and pale pink, sometimes with a white center and pale yellow stamens. They are borne singly or in clusters of up to three, rarely more, and show up well against the gray green leaves.

'Violacea'

see 'La Belle Sultane'

Rosa villosa

'VIOLET CARSON'

'VIOLET CARSON'

Floribunda

ORIGIN **McGredy, Northern Ireland, 1964**
PARENTAGE **'Mme. Léon Cuny' x 'Spartan'**
FLOWER SIZE **3.1in (8cm)**
SCENT **Medium, sweet, and musky**
FLOWERING **Repeats well**
HEIGHT/SPREAD **4.1ft (1.25m)/3.3ft (1m)**
HARDINESS **Zone 6**

'Violet Carson' has elegant flowers in large, open clusters of 3–15. They are shrimp pink at first, with creamy centers and paler petal backs, before fading to pink and white. They have a lot of petals, and each flower reflexes attractively as it develops. The plant has dark, slightly glaucous leaves and crimson new growths. It has only a few prickles, sometimes none. Violet Carson (1898–1983) was a popular British character actress.

VIOLETTA

see INTERNATIONAL HERALD TRIBUNE

'VIOLETTE'

Multiflora Rambler

ORIGIN **Turbat, France, 1921**
FLOWER SIZE **1.2in (3cm)**
SCENT **Light and musky**
FLOWERING **Once, midseason**
HEIGHT/SPREAD **9.8ft (3m)/6.6ft (2m)**
HARDINESS **Zone 6**

'VIOLETTE'

'Violette' is one of the darkest of the "blue" ramblers bred in France and Germany in the 1910s and 1920s. The flowers are a rich purple, with pale lilac backs to the petals, occasional white streaks, and bright golden stamens. The color is best appreciated when 'Violette' is grown next to its putative parent 'Veilchenblau', which appears pinky mauve by comparison. The densely double flowers are small and borne in clusters of 10–30. The plant has bright, pale green leaves, slender growths (for a Multiflora), and few thorns. It is less vigorous than 'Veilchenblau', but shares its slight susceptibility to mildew in autumn.

VIOLETTE PARFUMÉE

syn. 'DORIENT', Mélodie Parfumée
Grandiflora

ORIGIN **Dorieux, France, 1995**
FLOWER SIZE **4.7in (12cm)**
SCENT **Strong, rich, and fruity**
FLOWERING **Repeats**
HEIGHT/SPREAD **5.7ft (1.75m)/3.3ft (1m)**
HARDINESS **Zone 6**
AWARDS **Baden-Baden GM & FA 1995; Bagatelle GM & FA 1995**

This beautiful purple Hybrid Tea has won many prizes in Europe for its scent. Violette Parfumée is said to be reminiscent of cloves, lemons, Damask roses, and spices. The flowers are large, with long petals. They open bright crimson, but fade to violet and lilac and mauve pink as they age. The petal backs are always paler, too. When the flowers open out fully, you can see a white patch at the center and a thick circle of golden stamens. The flowers are heavily streaked with white – not enough for them to be considered striped, but much more than is usual among red and purple roses. Violette Parfumée is a vigorous grower, with large, dull green leaves and a strong, upright habit of growth.

VIOLETTE PARFUMÉE

VIOLON D'INGRES

syn. 'MEIBOSNIO'
Hybrid Tea

ORIGIN **Meilland, France, 2001**
PARENTAGE **Pigalle 84 x (Paloma Blanca x 'Carefree Beauty')**
FLOWER SIZE **4.3in (11cm)**
SCENT **Little or none**
FLOWERING **Repeats**
HEIGHT/SPREAD **3.3ft (1m)/2.7ft (80cm)**
HARDINESS **Zone 5**

This important new rose indicates a change in direction for European rose breeding: Violon d'Ingres is bred largely from the super hardy American roses of Griffith Buck, but it has an old-fashioned form like David Austin's English Roses. Its cupped flowers are large and deep yellow, with an amber heart and pink edges to the petals. They have a mass of quilled petals arranged in a quartered form and are very beautiful when they open out. They are usually borne singly on long stems, and are good for cutting – they are already grown commercially for the cut-flower market, though Violon d'Ingres is chiefly a garden rose. It is vigorous, healthy, and a good repeater, with an upright habit of growth. The name refers to the painter Ingres's passion for music, and has come to mean any hobby or interest that absorbs a person's leisure time.

VIOLON D'INGRES

ROSA VIRGINIANA

Wild Rose

FLOWER SIZE **2in (5cm)**
SCENT **Light and sweet**
FLOWERING **One long, late flowering**
HEIGHT/SPREAD **4.9ft (1.5m)/4.9ft (1.5m)**
HARDINESS **Zone 4**

Rosa virginiana is the best all-around among the wild roses. Its flowers are handsome and deep, bright pink – they radiate color when newly opened, before losing their glow after a day or so. They come singly or in small clusters (of up to four flowers) and have a fine ring of yellow stamens at the center. They are followed by conspicuous, round red hips, which will last, in some areas, right through until late winter. In autumn comes the best leaf color of all roses, when the whole plant turns yellow, orange, scarlet, crimson, and brown for weeks on end. And in winter the plant is revealed to be covered in bright red brown prickles that light up the landscape. The plant forms a thicketing mass of glittering dark green leaves and seems immune to all diseases. It is extremely hardy and tolerant of poor soils.

There are a number of forms in cultivation, including *Rosa virginiana* 'Alba', an exceptionally handsome variety with pure white flowers. ***Rosa virginiana* 'Plena'** is probably a hybrid of the species, though it is very ancient, being recorded from the mid-18th century. It has slightly duller leaves, less autumn color, and fewer prickles than pure *Rosa virginiana*, but the buds are most elegantly scrolled and they open into exquisite rosettes. The flowers were once much valued as buttonholes.

ROSA VIRGINIANA

ROSA VIRGINIANA 'PLENA'

Hybrid of *Rosa virginiana*

ROSA VIRGINIANA 'PLENA'

syn. 'ROSE D'AMOUR'
Species Hybrid
FLOWER SIZE **2.4in (6cm)**
SCENT **Slight**
FLOWERING **Once only**
HEIGHT/SPREAD **9.8ft (3m)/6.6ft (2m)**
HARDINESS **Zone 5**

'VIRGO'

'VIRGO'

Hybrid Tea

ORIGIN **Mallerin, France, 1947**
PARENTAGE **'Blanche Mallerin' x 'Neige Parfum'**
FLOWER SIZE **4.3in (11cm)**
SCENT **Light and sweet**
FLOWERING **Repeats**
HEIGHT/SPREAD **2.7ft (80cm)/2ft (60cm)**
HARDINESS **Zone 6**
AWARDS **NRS GM 1949**

It has become fashionable to decry 'Virgo' as too mildew prone for today's gardens, but the truth is that it grows extremely well everywhere except in very damp climates, where its petals crumple in rain. In dry areas it is still one of the best of all Hybrid Teas. Its continued popularity means that it is sold and grown all around the world. The flowers are long, slender, elegant, and white. In cool climates they sometimes have a hint of pink in the buds, and in hot ones a suggestion of yellow at the center, but they open out pure white. The flowers come singly or in clusters of up to four, on stems that are fairly long, considering that the plant is tall-growing only in hot climates (where it may reach 4.9ft/1.5m). The plant has dark leaves, a few large prickles, and an open habit of growth.

'VIRIDIFLORA'

see 'OLD BLUSH'

V

'VIVID'

Bourbon Rose

ORIGIN **A. Paul, Britain, 1853**
FLOWER SIZE **3.1in (8cm)**
SCENT **Moderate and sweet**
FLOWERING **Occasionally remontant**
HEIGHT/SPREAD **5.7ft (1.75m)/3.3ft (1m)**
HARDINESS **Zone 5**

This is one of the few English-raised Bourbon roses, but it is not one of the best. The flowers are handsome enough: 'Vivid' lives up to its name by producing bright crimson red flowers, which are cupped and full of petals arranged in an attractively quartered form. It is a somewhat brilliant a hue among the old roses, but fades to dark magenta as it ages. The flowers come singly and in tight clusters of up to five. 'Vivid' makes a vigorous, lanky, prickly shrub, with pale green leaves that are susceptible to blackspot. It is an erratic repeat flowerer. In fact, it is best to think of it as a once-flowerer, and then you will be pleased every few years when it produces a few autumn flowers.

'VIVID'

VOGELPARK WALSRODE

syn. 'KORLOMET', Kookaburra

Shrub Rose

ORIGIN **Kordes, Germany, 1988**
PARENTAGE **(['Lampion' x Träumerei] x 'Shrubby Pink') x 'New Dawn'**
FLOWER SIZE **3.1in (8cm)**
SCENT **Light and sweet**
FLOWERING **Repeats well**
HEIGHT/SPREAD **4.9ft (1.5m)/6.6ft (2m)**
HARDINESS **Zone 5**
AWARDS **ADR 1989**

Vogelpark Walsrode, named after the largest bird sanctuary in the world, is a very fine shrub rose. The flowers are palest pink, fading to white, lightly and loosely double, with handsome golden stamens. The petals are somewhat irregular in shape and outline, so the plant is best seen at a distance. The flowers come on long stems in loose, Floribunda-style clusters of 3–9, sometimes more. The dark, shiny foliage is healthy except for occasional blackspot, but it is otherwise a very hardy, thrifty, easy to grow, and beautiful plant.

VOGELPARK WALSRODE

'VOL DE NUIT'

'VOL DE NUIT'

Hybrid Tea

ORIGIN **Delbard, France, 1970**
PARENTAGE **('Holstein' x ['Bayadère' x 'Prélude']) x 'Saint-Exupéry'**
FLOWER SIZE **3.9in (10cm)**
SCENT **Strong and sweet**
FLOWERING **Repeats well**
HEIGHT/SPREAD **4.9ft (1.5m)/3.3ft (1m)**
HARDINESS **Zone 6**
AWARDS **Rome GM 1970**

'Vol de Nuit' is one of the most vigorous and satisfactory of the mauve Hybrid Teas. The flowers are pale lilac pink, with plum crimson reverses, and purple shadows between the petals. The flowers are especially pretty when the outer petals reflex elegantly but the inner ones are still whorled into a dark bud. The petals are broad and thick, and the flowers are possessed of a wonderful strong scent. They come usually singly, but sometimes in twos and threes, and always on long stems, excellent for cutting and exhibition. The plant is vigorous and fairly bushy, with dark, healthy leaves.

VOODOO

syn. 'AROMICLEA'

Hybrid Tea

ORIGIN **Christensen, US, 1984**
PARENTAGE **(['Camelot' x 'First Prize'] x 'Typhoo Tea') x 'Lolita'**
FLOWER SIZE **5.5in (14cm)**
SCENT **Moderate and sweet**
FLOWERING **Repeats**
HEIGHT/SPREAD **4.9ft (1.5m)/3.3ft (1m)**
HARDINESS **Zone 6**
AWARDS **AARS 1986**

Voodoo is a very healthy, handsome, deep salmon pink Hybrid Tea. The flowers are large and full of different shades of salmon, yellow, orange, crimson, and pink. They are not especially shapely in the bud, but pleasant and full of large petals as they open out, and they have a fine scent. They are borne singly on long, strong stems, which are ideal for cutting, but they also make a good display in the garden. Voodoo is an upright grower, with dark, glossy leaves that are exceptionally healthy: their health is almost the first thing you notice about them. The plant is a vigorous grower and a quick repeater, especially in hot climates.

VOODOO

Wandering Minstrel

syn. 'HARQUINCE', Daniel Gélin

Floribunda

ORIGIN **Harkness, Britain, 1986**
PARENTAGE **'Dame of Sark' x 'Silver Jubilee'**
FLOWER SIZE **3.9in (10cm)**
SCENT **Light and fruity**
FLOWERING **Repeats well**
HEIGHT/SPREAD **3.3ft (1m)/2.3ft (70cm)**
HARDINESS **Zone 6**

This highly colorful, short Floribunda is most popular in France, where its name Daniel Gélin commemorates the actor (1921–2002). The flowers of Wandering Minstrel are a bright shade of orange, with yellow petal backs and hints of peach pink as the petals age and lose some of their yellowness. They are attractively semidouble and shapely, with a distinct roll to their edges and a pale yellow ring of stamens at the center. They come in clusters of 5–10. Their brilliant, glowing orange color stands out from quite a distance. Wandering Minstrel is a vigorous, healthy, bushy plant with handsome dark leaves. It will grow to about 3.3ft (1m), but is usually seen pruned back to half that height.

'Waitziana'

see 'MACRANTHA'

Wapiti

syn. 'MEINAGRE', Dazzla, Laurence Olivier

Floribunda

ORIGIN **Meilland, France, 1988**
FLOWER SIZE **2.8in (7cm)**
SCENT **Light and sweet**
FLOWERING **Repeats well**
HEIGHT/SPREAD **3.3ft (1m)/2ft (60cm)**
HARDINESS **Zone 6**
AWARDS **Geneva GM 1987; Monza GM 1987; Rome GM 1987**

Wapiti

Wandering Minstrel

Wapiti is a lightly double, scarlet Floribunda. The flowers open out quickly to reveal their bright, velvety petals, struck through with an occasional white stripe, and handsome yellow stamens at the center. The flowers are not especially large (2.8–3.1in/7–8cm), but they have ruffled petals and come in clusters of 4–10, so they make a considerable impact. Wapiti has large, dark, glossy leaves – blackspot can be a problem – and a bushy habit of growth. It will eventually grow to 3.3ft (1m), but is generally seen pruned to half that height. It is a good repeater.

Warm Welcome

syn. 'CHEWIZZ'

Climbing Miniature-type Rose

ORIGIN **Warner, Britain, 1991**
PARENTAGE **('Elizabeth of Glamis' x ['Galway Bay' x 'Sutter's Gold']) x Anna Ford**
FLOWER SIZE **1.6in (4cm)**
SCENT **Light**
FLOWERING **Continuous**
HEIGHT/SPREAD **8.2ft (2.5m)/4.9ft (1.5m)**
HARDINESS **Zone 6**
AWARDS **NZ GM 1987; RNRS PIT 1988**

Warm Welcome was the first of the patio climbers bred by Chris Warner: all have a neat, narrow habit of growth, healthy leaves, bright colors, and good repeat flowering. The popularity of Warm Welcome when introduced was instant and sensational. Its flowers are nearly single and brilliant, glowing orange vermilion, with a yellow center and petal bases. They come on long pedicels in long, open clusters of 5–30 flowers, and repeat so quickly that the plant seems always to be in full flower. The flower clusters cover the plant from head to foot – a very unusual and desirable habit among roses. The beautiful leaves are dark green (crimson at first), small, and neat. Warm Welcome is vigorous and healthy, perfect for small gardens – if only the flowers were more strongly scented.

Warm Welcome

Warm Wishes

Warm Wishes

syn. 'FRYXOTIC', Sunset Celebration

Hybrid Tea

ORIGIN **Fryer, Britain, 1994**
PARENTAGE **'Pot o' Gold' seedling x Cheshire Life**
FLOWER SIZE **4.7in (12cm)**
SCENT **Medium and fruity**
FLOWERING **Repeats well**
HEIGHT/SPREAD **3.3ft (1m)/2.5ft (75cm)**
HARDINESS **Zone 6**
AWARDS **Belfast GM 1996; Golden Rose of the Hague 1997; AARS 1998**

Warm Wishes has won prizes in test gardens in very different growing conditions all over the world. It is a traditional Hybrid Tea of great elegance and vigor. Its charm lies in its color and shape. Its color is a mixture of apricot and pink, though the exact shade differs according to the weather and climate – always darker toward the center of the flower and on the petal backs, but darker, too, in cool weather. In hot weather it fades quickly to pink and cream. The flowers open from large, pointed buds and keep this shape for a long time as the petals open out and curve back. They come, usually singly, on long stems that last a long time when cut. Warm Wishes has healthy, dark green foliage, and repeat flowers very quickly.

'Warrawee'

Hybrid Tea

ORIGIN **Fitzhardinge, Australia, 1935**
PARENTAGE **'Padre' x 'Rev. F. Page-Roberts'**
FLOWER SIZE **4.3in (11cm)**
SCENT **Strong and sweet**
FLOWERING **Fully remontant**
HEIGHT/SPREAD **4.1ft (1.25m)/4.1ft (1.25m)**
HARDINESS **Zone 6**

'Warrawee' was the first hybrid bred by the Australian Olive Rose Fitzhardinge (1881–1956). The flowers are soft pink or mother-of-pearl in color, with mid-pink petal backs. It is very pretty in bud, and as a half-open flower, when the dark petal backs reflect deep colors into the center of the bloom. Once they open out, the flowers are inclined to become more ragged. They come singly or in clusters of up to five on a stout, vigorous plant. The leaves have broad leaflets and a liability to blackspot and mildew. 'Warrawee' is named after the town in New South Wales where Mrs. Fitzhardinge lived.

'Warrawee'

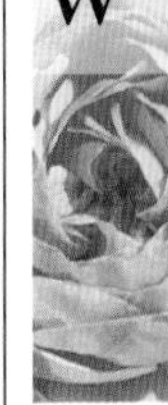

'WARRIOR'

WARWICK CASTLE

'WARRIOR'

Floribunda

ORIGIN **Le Grice, Britain, 1977**
PARENTAGE **'City of Belfast' x 'Ronde Endiablée'**
FLOWER SIZE **2.8in (7cm)**
SCENT **Little or none**
FLOWERING **Repeats well**
HEIGHT/SPREAD **3.3ft (1m)/1.6ft (50cm)**
HARDINESS **Zone 6**

This is a useful, short Floribunda with bright vermilion flowers – blood red, the breeder thought, which suggested the name 'Warrior'. They are fully double, with a mass of ruffled petals, but neat and round in outline. Sometimes you can catch a glimpse of the yellow stamens at the center. The flowers come usually in small clusters, typically of 3–5, but occasionally more, and sometimes singly. Their stems are not long, but they last well if cut. 'Warrior' is best of all as a bedding rose. It packs a lot of color into its small stature and compact shape, and repeats its flowering both liberally and quickly. It has small, medium-dark leaves and is very healthy, except for a touch of blackspot in damp climates late in the year.

WARWICK CASTLE

syn. 'AUSLIAN'
Shrub Rose

ORIGIN **Austin, Britain, 1986**
PARENTAGE **'The Reeve' x 'Lilian Austin'**
FLOWER SIZE **3.1in (8cm)**
SCENT **Medium and sweet**
FLOWERING **Repeats**
HEIGHT/SPREAD **3.3ft (1m)/4.1ft (1.25m)**
HARDINESS **Zone 6**

At its best, Warwick Castle is a rose of exceptional beauty. The flowers are bright carmine pink, with a great number of petals forming a loose rosette. They are profusely carried in clusters of 3–7. The bush has a lax habit of growth, so that one way of growing it is as a groundcover or open shrub, from which new growth arches up and over. The leaves are mid-green (bronzy red when young), but susceptible to mildew and rust. In damp weather the flowers tend to ball. Warwick Castle is one of David Austin's English Roses that do better in a warmer, drier climate than that of England.

ROSA WEBBIANA

Wild Rose

FLOWER SIZE **1.6in (4cm)**
SCENT **Light and sweet**
FLOWERING **Once only, fairly early in season**
HEIGHT/SPREAD **6.6ft (2m)/4.9ft (1.5m)**
HARDINESS **Zone 5**

Rosa webbiana is one of the daintiest of wild roses, with pretty flowers, neat leaves, and handsome hips. Like so many species roses, it is fairly variable in nature and there are several different forms of it in cultivation. The flowers are pink, usually with a white center and a ring of pale stamens. They are borne singly in the leaf axils all along the branches and are perfectly complemented by the leaves, which have small, widely spaced leaflets. The hips are long, flagon-shaped, and bright orange or vermilion. The plant has slender, arching branches and long,

WEEKS ROSES

THIS CALIFORNIA-BASED COMPANY BRED SOME OF THE BEST ROSES OF THE '60S AND '70S AND, WITH TOM CARRUTH, IS STILL PRODUCING WINNERS TODAY

WEEKS ROSES was founded as a wholesale producer by Ollie and Verona Weeks in Ontario, California, in 1938. The company flourished, especially after it began to breed its own roses. Today, Weeks claims to offer the widest selection of popular and unusual varieties in the industry – some 250 cultivars – and has a well-founded reputation for excellence. Research and rose breeding are carried out at Upland; the growing grounds (about 650 acres/263 hectares) are at Wasco, in the San Joaquin Valley.

Ollie Weeks collaborated with Herb Swim of Armstrong Nurseries (see p.40) to produce some of the best roses of the 1960s and 1970s, including classic Hybrid Teas like 'Royal Highness' (1962) and 'Paloma' (1968). There were a few unconventional beauties along the way: muddled centers were not fashionable when 'Angel Face' came out in 1968, and 'Old Smoothie' in 1970.

'PALOMA'

Working on his own, Weeks introduced more exquisite Hybrid Teas like 'Alabama' (1976), Paradise (1979), and Silver Spoon (1985), and two very fine crimson roses – The Senator (1980) and nearly black Night Time (1983).

Tom Carruth joined Weeks Roses in 1988 and is widely considered the most inventive breeder in the US today. Columbus (1990) was one of his early successes, followed by Stainless Steel (1991) and a series of All-America Rose Selection winners including Scentimental (1996), Betty Boop (1999), and Fourth of July (1999).

HERB SWIM (LEFT) AND OLLIE WEEKS

Carruth combines an insistence on healthiness (Barbra Streisand is the only exception) with an enterprising and creative approach to rose breeding. He has issued – and is still producing – some of the best new roses in the world. Three or four are introduced every year, out of a total of about 200,000 seedlings actually raised. The only American-born rose to receive an award from the All-America Rose Selections trials in 2003 was Carruth's new Floribunda Hot Cocoa, an ever-changing, smoky blend of tan, chocolate, orange, apricot, and russet.

THE SENATOR

ROSA WEBBIANA

straight prickles. It flowers early, and its graceful beauty heralds the start of the rose season.

'WEDDING DAY'

Wild Rose

ORIGIN **Stern, Britain, 1950**
PARENTAGE ***Rosa mulliganii* var. *sinowilsonii* seedling**
FLOWER SIZE **1.2in (3cm)**
SCENT **Strong and fruity**
FLOWERING **Once only**
HEIGHT/SPREAD **26.2ft (8m)/16.4ft (5m)**
HARDINESS **Zone 6**

This rampant once-flowering climber occurred as a chance seedling in the garden of a wealthy British banker named Sir Frederic Stern. He named the rose 'Wedding Day' because it first flowered on June 26, his own wedding anniversary. It is said to be a hybrid between *Rosa mulliganii* var. *sinowilsonii* and *Rosa moyesii*, but it is difficult to detect the influence of the latter species. The flowers of 'Wedding Day' open from pale apricot buds and are creamy yellow before fading to pure white; they are carried with enormous profusion in clusters of 20–40. The flowers pick up crimson markings as they fade, and are succeeded by little scarlet hips. The plant is prickly, with medium-dark leaves and long new growth. In some parts of the world, the rose grown as 'Wedding Day' is, in fact, 'Polyantha Grandiflora'.

WEIGHT WATCHERS SUCCESS

syn. 'JACBITOU', Success Story
Hybrid Tea

ORIGIN **Zary, US, 1999**
PARENTAGE **Henry Fonda x French Perfume**
FLOWER SIZE **5.9in (15cm)**
SCENT **Strong and sweet**
FLOWERING **Repeats well**
HEIGHT/SPREAD **4.9ft (1.5m)/3.3ft (1m)**
HARDINESS **Zone 6**

WEIGHT WATCHERS SUCCESS

This enormous rose was promoted by Sarah, Duchess of York, as an elegant symbol for the attainment of weight-loss goals through the well-known diet organization's program. The flowers are beautiful, large and fat, cream with pink edges and a lemon flush at the center. They hold their colors well, even in hot sun, and are usually borne singly, occasionally in twos and threes. They come on long stems, which makes them excellent for exhibition or cutting: the scent is rich and pervasive. Weight Watchers Success has a vigorous, upright habit of growth, few prickles, and dark leaves. It tends to fare best in warm climates where the sumptuous flowers will not be injured by rain or wind.

'WEISSE AUS SPARRIESHOOP'

see 'SPARRIESHOOP'

WEISSE IMMENSEE

syn. 'KORWEIRIM', Partridge
Ground Cover

ORIGIN **Kordes, Germany, 1982**
PARENTAGE ***Rosa wichurana* x 'The Fairy'**
FLOWER SIZE **1.6in (4cm)**
SCENT **Medium and musky**
FLOWERING **Once only**
HEIGHT/SPREAD **1.6ft (50cm)/16.4ft (5m)**
HARDINESS **Zone 6**

WEISSE IMMENSEE

The dimensions given above for Weisse Immensee assume that it is grown as a groundcover rose. It was introduced as a trailing rose, but, as many have discovered, it is, in fact, a Wichurana rambler. Compared to all the other Wichurana ramblers that will trail along as groundcover plants, Weisse Immensee is fairly unexciting – once-flowering, with small single flowers. They open white from pale pink buds and have a loose brush of golden stamens at the center. They come in clusters of 5–10 and are followed by little red hips. The leaves are small, dark, glossy, and healthy, and the plant is prickly. Weisse Immensee roots as it spreads if planted to grow along the ground, but its long, slender stems will climb 16.4ft (5m) up a small tree.

'WEISSE NEW DAWN'

see 'DR. W. VAN FLEET'

'WEDDING DAY'

WEISSE WOLKE

WELWYN GARDEN GLORY

WEISSE WOLKE

syn. 'KORSTACHA', Nuage Blanc, White Cloud

Shrub Rose

ORIGIN **Kordes, Germany, 1993**
FLOWER SIZE **3.1in (8cm)**
SCENT **Moderate and sweet**
FLOWERING **Repeats well**
HEIGHT/SPREAD **9.8ft (3m)/6.6ft (2m)**
HARDINESS **Zone 6**

This splendid modern climber can be grown as a short climber and as a vigorous shrub. Weisse Wolke has handsome, pure white, lightly double flowers that open out almost flat to reveal a brush of golden stamens. They come in clusters of 3–10. They emerge not only at the tips of the stems but also on short laterals all along the old wood, which means that the display is extremely profuse. Weisse Wolke has long, thick, arching canes and a lot of healthy, large, dark, glossy leaves. It repeats quickly, and seems to be almost continuously in flower. Its height depends on how it is grown and trained: 6.6ft (2m) as a shrub in Germany, but up to 16.4ft (5m) as a climber in Australia. In English-speaking countries it is known as White Cloud. Unfortunately, so too is another Kordes rose, a Rugosa called Gletscherfee, and the two are confused.

WELWYN GARDEN GLORY

syn. 'HARZUMBER', Garden Glory

Floribunda

ORIGIN **Harkness, Britain, 1996**
FLOWER SIZE **4.3in (11cm)**
SCENT **Light and sweet**
FLOWERING **Repeats well**
HEIGHT/SPREAD **4.1ft (1.25m)/2.7ft (80cm)**
HARDINESS **Zone 6**

Modern Harkness roses are very distinctive, especially the Hybrid Teas and Floribundas. Many have a special wave or roll to their petals when the flower opens out, and this gives immense character and charm to them all. Welwyn Garden Glory has large apricot colored flowers, with slightly darker petal backs to create beautiful deep shadows between the petals. They fade slowly through buff to pale parchment pink, but always retain a dark color toward the center of the flower. The flowers are produced usually singly, but occasionally in twos and threes, and are excellent as cut roses. The plant is sturdy, vigorous, narrow, and upright, with medium-dark, healthy leaves.

'WENDY CUSSONS'

'WESTERLAND'

Shrub Rose

ORIGIN **Kordes, Germany, 1969**
PARENTAGE **'Friedrich Wörlein' × 'Circus'**
FLOWER SIZE **4.3in (11cm)**
SCENT **Strong and fruity**
FLOWERING **Repeats constantly**
HEIGHT/SPREAD **6.6ft (2m)/4.9ft (1.5m)**
HARDINESS **Zone 5**
AWARDS **ADR 1974**

'WESTERLAND'

The renown of 'Westerland' continues to spread. At first it was grown only as a shrub rose in Germany. It did not receive its ADR award until five years after it was introduced. Now its unique qualities are appreciated by gardeners all over the world, and it is widely planted as a short climber, in hot areas. Its only problem (if problem it be) is its color – a glowing mixture of vermilion, crimson, orange, pink, yellow, and amber – which is difficult to handle in a small garden. The flowers are large and semidouble, with wavy petals, and are borne in large, loose clusters of 5–10. It starts into flower early and repeats well until late autumn. Its flushes last a long time, so that it is rarely without flowers. 'Westerland' has long, healthy leaves, with large leaflets and a dark surface that is a good complement to the brightly colored flowers. The plant is vigorous, upright, well branched, and fairly thorny.

'Autumn Sunset' is a paler sport of 'Westerland', with fewer petals. The flowers are soft yellow with a salmon flush and dark apricot or orange petal backs. The colors are richer in cool weather, but fade in any event to buff. It is rarely seen outside the US, where it originated.

Sport of 'Westerland'

'AUTUMN SUNSET'

ORIGIN **Lowe, US, 1986**

'WENDY CUSSONS'

Hybrid Tea

ORIGIN **Gregory, Britain, 1963**
PARENTAGE **'Kordes' Sondermeldung' × 'Eden Rose'**
FLOWER SIZE **5.1in (13cm)**
SCENT **Strong and sweet**
FLOWERING **Repeats**
HEIGHT/SPREAD **4.1ft (1.25m)/3.3ft (1m)**
HARDINESS **Zone 6**
AWARDS **NRS PIT 1959; Golden Rose of the Hague 1964; Portland GM 1964**

The flowers of 'Wendy Cussons' are pretty at all stages, from the unfurling bud to the fully opened bloom. They also grow in size, starting with small buds and enlarging as the flowers expand. They are cherry pink at first, with slightly paler petal backs, and fade to pink as they age. It is an unusual color that was previously rare among Hybrid Teas because nurseries considered it unlikely to prove popular. The commercial success of 'Wendy Cussons' made them change their minds. The petals are tough and stand up well to rain. They reflex attractively, which contributes much to the charm of the rose. The plant is vigorous and healthy, except for an occasional touch of blackspot late in the year, with a good, branching habit and fairly prickly stems. It is an excellent rose to pick for the house.

WENLOCK

syn. 'AUSWEN'

Shrub Rose

ORIGIN **Austin, Britain, 1984**
PARENTAGE **'The Knight' × 'Glastonbury'**
FLOWER SIZE **3.1in (8cm)**
SCENT **Strong and sweet**
FLOWERING **Repeats well**
HEIGHT/SPREAD **4.9ft (1.5m)/4.9ft (1.5m)**
HARDINESS **Zone 5**

Wenlock is one of those English Roses that are a neat shrub in the cool growing conditions of England, but vigorous enough to be called a climber in hot climates like the southern States. The flowers are full of crimson petals, sometimes with a white streak or two toward the center. They come singly and in small clusters (typically of 3–5

WENLOCK

W

WESTFALENPARK

FOUNDED IN THE COLD WAR, THIS EXTENSIVE MODERN GARDEN CONTAINS MORE THAN 3,000 DIFFERENT ROSES AND SOME 38 THEMED ROSE GARDENS

WESTFALENPARK IN DORTMUND is a huge, modern public amenity garden, with no less than 173 acres (70 hectares) of horticultural display. It was developed in 1969 as the West German National Rosarium when the rose collection at Sangerhausen was lost to East Germany. It contains over 3,000 different roses, used in such diverse ways that the number of rose bushes in Westfalenpark is closer to 50,000. All are accommodated within a fluid contemporary design that is a pleasure to walk through. There is a good display of cultivars from German breeders and abroad. The collections are kept up to date: recent additions include the cultivars 'Shogun' (Tantau, 2000) and 'Fair Lady' (Rosenunion, 2000). Westfalenpark incorporates a sequence of some 38 themed rose gardens, starting with a Romantic Garden, a Jugendstil Garden, and a Medieval Garden, and ending with the huge Rosengarten in Kaiserhain at the northeastern end, which is one of the most beautiful modern rose gardens in the world. It relies for its effect partly upon the spacious design, which has generated a very charming sequence of angles and levels, but even more upon the skillful grading of colors and shades, and the way in which roses are combined with shrubs and herbaceous plants. There is much to learn from and admire throughout Westfalenpark.

MIXED PLANTINGS IN THE KAISERHAIN AT WESTFALENPARK

'SHOGUN'

flowers) on short stems and are followed by large red hips. Deadheading removes the hips but also helps to ensure good reflowering – in favorable conditions Wenlock can be a constant bloomer. The flowers fade to cherry pink as they age. They also have weak necks and spoil in the rain, but they are very beautiful. Wenlock has large dark leaves, somewhat susceptible to blackspot. Its stems are very prickly and grow to 9.8ft (3m) in a hot climate. Elsewhere it is more bushy, but upright, and always vigorous.

WESTFALENPARK

syn. 'KORPLAVI', Chevreuse

Shrub Rose

ORIGIN **Kordes, Germany, 1986**
PARENTAGE **seedling x Las Vegas**
FLOWER SIZE **3.1in (8cm)**
SCENT **Light**
FLOWERING **Repeats well**
HEIGHT/SPREAD **6.6ft (2m)/6.6ft (2m)**
HARDINESS **Zone 6**

Westfalenpark is a vigorous shrub rose or a bushy climber with flowers of Hybrid Tea quality. They come singly or in handsome, open clusters of 3–7 flowers. They are a fine shade of amber, with slightly darker, more coppery backs to the petals, and darker shadows toward the center of the flower. The edges of the flowers take on a pinker tinge as they fade – all in all a most unusual and attractive color combination. The plant is healthy, with a lax habit of growth and a fair amount of large thorns. The leaves are large, glossy, and dark green, bronzy at first. Westfalenpark is a huge public park in Germany featuring themed rose gardens (see above).

'WHISKY'

syn. 'WHISKY MAC'

Hybrid Tea

ORIGIN **Tantau, Germany, 1967**
PARENTAGE **seedling × 'Dr. A. J. Verhage'**
FLOWER SIZE **4.3in (11cm)**
SCENT **Very strong, sweet, and fruity**
FLOWERING **Repeats quickly**
HEIGHT/SPREAD **2.7ft (80cm)/2.7ft (80cm)**
HARDINESS **Zone 6**

This is a rose that the rose trade loves to hate. Critics point out that it has never won any international awards, it suffers from mildew, and it dies when hard pruned. The answer is that 'Whisky' has very beautiful flowers and a delicious scent, and not every garden suffers from mildew; and anyway, traditional pruning is no longer recommended for garden roses. The flowers are apricot pink, with yellow petal backs and bases, and hints of crimson and orange at first. In hot climates the colors are much paler, typically buff yellow – 'Whisky' is a rose that is at its best in cool conditions. The flowers have long petals and open from elegant buds to stylishly cupped flowers with wavy petals. They stand up to rain and last well as cut flowers. The plant has dark green leaves (bright bronze crimson when young), a fair number of prickles, and a low, spreading habit of growth. In England the rose is called 'Whisky Mac'.

'WHITE BATH'

see 'CENTIFOLIA'

WESTFALENPARK

'WHISKY'

White Bells

syn. 'POULwhite'

Ground Cover

ORIGIN **Poulsen, Denmark, 1980**
PARENTAGE **'Mini-Poul' x 'Temple Bells'**
FLOWER SIZE **1.6in (4cm)**
SCENT **Light and sweet**
FLOWERING **Once heavily, then intermittently**
HEIGHT/SPREAD **2.7ft (80cm)/3.3ft (1m)**
HARDINESS **Zone 6**

White Bells is a good groundcover rose. It does not grow very high, but it has a mounded, trailing habit that makes it extremely useful on awkward areas like steep banks. It is also good in containers. The flowers open quite a bright yellow but fade very quickly to pure white. The process starts at the edges, so that the freshly opened flowers have yellow centers and white outer petals. The flowers are double, rosette-shaped, round, and full of petals. They are produced in small, tight clusters all over the surface of the bush at the first flowering and intermittently thereafter. White Bells has small, dark, neat, glossy leaves of the Wichurana type, and is very healthy. It looks especially handsome when grown as a weeping standard, unforgettable in full flower.

'White Cécile Brunner'

see 'Cécile Brunner'

White Cloud

see Weisse Wolke

'White Cockade'

Modern Climber

ORIGIN **Cocker, Britain, 1969**
PARENTAGE **'New Dawn' x 'Circus'**
FLOWER SIZE **3.1in (8cm)**
SCENT **Medium and sweet**
FLOWERING **Repeats well**
HEIGHT/SPREAD **9.8ft (3m)/6.6ft (2m)**
HARDINESS **Zone 5**

'White Cockade'

White Bells

This was one of the first roses bred by Alec Cocker in the 1960s: he foresaw a need for compact, repeat flowering climbers for small, modern gardens. 'White Cockade' is still one of the best, and remains very popular in the UK. The flowers are creamy white at first, quickly turning to pure white, with tough, short petals that resist the Scottish rain very well. They come on short stems in clusters of 3–15 and are well set off by dark, glossy, Wichurana leaves. The plant is thick-stemmed and somewhat inflexible, which means that it makes a good self-supporting shrub. It has a quite a lot of large prickles and is susceptible to blackspot, but usually not until late in the season. A white cockade was the symbol of the Jacobites: "Follow my white cockade" was Bonnie Prince Charlie's rallying cry.

White Diamond

'White Dawn'

'White Dawn'

syn. 'White New Dawn'

Modern Climber

ORIGIN **Longley, US, 1949**
PARENTAGE **'New Dawn' x 'Lily Pons'**
FLOWER SIZE **2.8in (7cm)**
SCENT **Moderate and sweet**
FLOWERING **Repeats well**
HEIGHT/SPREAD **13.1ft (4m)/8.2ft (2.5m)**
HARDINESS **Zone 6**

'White Dawn' is an American seedling of 'New Dawn', and is not to be confused with 'Weisse New Dawn' – a true sport of 'New Dawn' and popular in Europe. The flowers of 'White Dawn' are fully double, with imbricated petals like a gardenia or camellia. The color is pure white, with none of the pale pink tints of 'Weisse New Dawn', and the flowers are fuller, too. They come singly or in clusters of up to seven and show up well against the dark, glossy foliage. The plant is very thorny and vigorous, but susceptible to mildew in autumn.

White Diamond

syn. 'INTeramon'

Floribunda

ORIGIN **Interplant, Netherlands, 1994**
FLOWER SIZE **2in (5cm)**
SCENT **Light and sweet**
FLOWERING **Repeats quickly**
HEIGHT/SPREAD **2.7ft (80cm)/2ft (60cm)**
HARDINESS **Zone 6**

This is a small, shrubby Floribunda with brilliant white flowers. White Diamond covers itself in flowers and repeats so quickly that it is never out of flower until late in the year. The flowers are double, but open out so that the petals are arranged around the outside with a small center of golden stamens. These turn brown, but the petals remain pure white. The flowers of White Diamond are very generously borne in clusters of 3–10 all over the plant, and are set off by dark, glossy, healthy leaves. The plant is vigorous, compact, and bushy.

'White Dorothy'

see 'Dorothy Perkins'

'White Duchesse de Brabant

see 'Duchesse de Brabant'

White Flower Carpet

see Schneeflocke

'White Grootendorst'

see 'F. J.Grootendorst'

W

WHITE LIGHTNIN'

WHITE LIGHTNIN'

syn. 'AROWHIF'
Grandiflora

ORIGIN **Swim & Christensen, US, 1980**
PARENTAGE **'Angel Face' x 'Misty'**
FLOWER SIZE **4.3in (11cm)**
SCENT **Strong, sweet, and fruity**
FLOWERING **Repeats**
HEIGHT/SPREAD **4.1ft (1.25m)/3.3ft (1m)**
HARDINESS **Zone 6**
AWARDS **AARS 1981**

Although classified in the US as a Grandiflora rose, White Lightnin' is no taller than most Floribundas. Its flowers are pure white, except for a hint of yellow at the center at first. They have ruffled petals and, in good weather, may open out cup-shaped to show their pale yellow stamens. Sometimes the outer petals acquire a tinge of pink just before dropping. The flowers come singly or, more often, in clusters of up to seven, and have a delicious scent. White Lightnin' has lush, shiny, healthy, mid-green leaves and a broad but upright habit of growth. Its flowers come in a series of flushes right through until late autumn.

'WHITE MAMAN COCHET'

see 'MAMAN COCHET'

'WHITE MASTERPIECE'

Hybrid Tea

ORIGIN **Boerner, US, 1969**
FLOWER SIZE **5.1in (13cm)**
SCENT **Light and sweet**
FLOWERING **Repeats**
HEIGHT/SPREAD **4.1ft (1.25m)/3.3ft (1m)**
HARDINESS **Zone 6**

This is very much a rose for hot, dry climates. The long petals of 'White Masterpiece' bruise in rain and wind, but the flowers are a favorite for exhibition in areas where it can be grown well. It certainly responds to good cultivation – feeding and spraying – though mildew is a problem in damp areas. The flowers are large and fully petaled, with just a hint of yellow at the center when the long, large buds start to unfurl. When they open out, the flowers are white with only a hint of cream at the centre, and carried singly on long, straight stems – perfect for cutting. 'White Masterpiece' has large, mid-green leaves and a fair sprinkling of prickles. It is neither quick to reflower nor a generous bearer of blooms, but the autumn flowers can be of amazing size and beauty.

'WHITE MASTERPIECE'

WHITE MEIDILAND

see ALBA MEIDILAND

'WHITE MRS FLIGHT'

see 'MRS F. W. FLIGHT'

'WHITE NEW DAWN'

see 'WHITE DAWN'

'WHITE PET'

see 'FÉLICITÉ ET PERPÉTUE'

'WHITE QUEEN ELIZABETH'

see 'QUEEN ELIZABETH'

WHITE SIMPLICITY

syn. 'JACSNOW'
Floribunda

ORIGIN **Jackson & Perkins, US, 1991**
FLOWER SIZE **3.5in (9cm)**
SCENT **Light and sweet**
FLOWERING **Repeats constantly**
HEIGHT/SPREAD **4.9ft (1.5m)/4.1ft (1.25m)**
HARDINESS **Zone 6**

Although it was introduced as a hedging rose, White Simplicity is a good choice for mixed plantings. Its brilliant white flowers and glossy leaves combine with everything, and the flowers are produced very generously right through until late autumn. They open out to show a mass of loosely held petals around a tuft of deep yellow stamens. The plant is healthy, vigorous, and compact, and has the happy habit of shedding its flowers as soon as they have finished flowering. It is a lovely rose to have in the garden.

WHITE SIMPLICITY

WHITE SPRAY

WHITE SPRAY

syn. 'LENPLI'
Ground Cover

ORIGIN **Lens, Belgium, 1980**
PARENTAGE ***Rosa wichurana* form x *Rosa multiflora* var. *adenochaeta***
FLOWER SIZE **0.8in (2cm)**
SCENT **Light and musky**
FLOWERING **Repeats well**
HEIGHT/SPREAD **11.8in (30cm)/3.3ft (1m)**
HARDINESS **Zone 5**

This small, white, groundcover plant is the twin of 'Pink Spray'. It shares all the virtues of its pink sibling except one: White Spray suffers from rainfall – the tiny petals assume ugly crimson blotches and the flowers disintegrate. But in fine weather it forms a creeping cascade of foaming white flowers like an alpine plant. Its habit of growth is small, compact, prostrate, or weeping. The small, neat, dark green, Wichurana leaves are the perfect foil to the pure white, five-petaled flowers. The flowers get their distinctive charm from the narrowness of their petals – not quite wide enough to meet and overlap each other: the result is that each tiny petal is outlined against a dark background. The flowers come in small clusters and are followed by very small vermilion hips.

'White Wings'

Rosa wichurana

'Wife of Bath'

'WHITE WINGS'

Hybrid Tea

ORIGIN **Krebs, US, 1947**
PARENTAGE **'Dainty Bess' seedling**
FLOWER SIZE **3.1in (8cm)**
SCENT **Medium and sweet**
FLOWERING **Almost continuous**
HEIGHT/SPREAD **4.9ft (1.5m)/4.1ft (1.25m)**
HARDINESS **Zone 6**

The beauty of 'White Wings' rests entirely on the contrast between the white single flowers and the long crimson or maroon anthers. Imagine it with pale yellow stamens at the center, and its character would change completely. The anthers are the making of 'White Wings' and the best gene it has inherited from its famous parent 'Dainty Bess'. The flowers of 'White Wings' open from pale coral pink buds. They come in clusters, typically of 3–7, and are borne with great freedom, so that the supply of flowers is almost continuous. It copes well with rain and thrives in hot, dry climates, where it will eventually reach 6.6ft (2m). It is best pruned as little as possible, and should be allowed to build up a permanent structure of branches in order to maximize the production of flowers. It is an excellent rose for mixed borders, combining well with all pale and pastel shades.

W

ROSA WICHURANA

Wild Rose

FLOWER SIZE **1.6in (4cm)**
SCENT **Strong, sweet, and musky**
FLOWERING **Once only, fairly late in season**
HEIGHT/SPREAD **16.4ft (5m)/9.8ft (3m)**
HARDINESS **Zone 6**

Rosa wichurana changed the history of rose breeding. It was the progenitor of all the Wichurana ramblers that poured out of the nurseries of the world in the early part of the 20th century. Its genes have now found their way into many of our modern bush roses. It is a cheerful, scrambling, evergreen species from parts of China, Taiwan, Korea, and Japan. Its flowers are small, single, white, and carried in panicles of 5–10. The leaves usually have nine small leaflets that are distinctly dark and glossy – this is the famous Wichurana foliage seen in many of the best modern roses. The plant sends out long, procumbent shoots, which root as they progress, but will clamber up trees and bushes to quite a height. Every leaf-node has two fierce, curved prickles on it. *Rosa wichurana* has considerable merit as an ornamental: it flowers late and profusely; it is a fine groundcover plant; it is insensible to disease; and its glittering evergreen leaves are a delight.

'WIENER CHARME'

syn. 'VIENNA CHARM'

Hybrid Tea

ORIGIN: **Kordes, Germany, 1963**
PARENTAGE **'Chantré' x 'Goldene Sonne'**
FLOWER SIZE **5.9in (15cm)**
SCENT **Medium and fruity**
FLOWERING **Repeats well**
HEIGHT/SPREAD **4.9ft (1.5m)/3.3ft (1m)**
HARDINESS **Zone 6**

The size of its flowers and their beautiful coppery gold color made 'Wiener Charme' a popular rose in Europe right from the start. The flowers are not too full of petals but borne singly or in small clusters throughout the growing season. The petals are more yellow on their upper sides and redder underneath. 'Wiener Charme' has handsome deep green leaves, which are dark coppery red at first. The plant is vigorous and healthy in hot, dry climates and remains a great favorite in Australia and parts of the US, but is now susceptible to blackspot in the damp, cool parts of Europe.

'Wiener Charme'

'WIFE OF BATH'

syn. 'GLÜCKSBURG', 'THE WIFE OF BATH'

Shrub Rose

ORIGIN **Austin, Britain, 1969**
PARENTAGE **'Mme. Caroline Testout' x ('Ma Perkins' x 'Constance Spry')**
FLOWER SIZE **2.8in (7cm)**
SCENT **Strong, sweet, and myrrhlike**
FLOWERING **Repeats well**
HEIGHT/SPREAD **3.3ft (1m)/2.5ft (75cm)**
HARDINESS **Zone 6**

'Wife of Bath' – named after a character in Chaucer's *The Canterbury Tales* – was one of David Austin's first repeat flowering English Roses and is still one of the most popular. Its full, cupped flowers open from red buds and are deep pink at the center and palest pink at the outermost petals, though the petal backs are always paler. This creates a very pretty contrast, since the outer petals are flat guard petals and the inner ones are small, muddled, and many. The flowers come in clusters of 3–9 and repeat well until late autumn. 'Wife of Bath' has small, mid-green leaves and a neat habit of growth. It is a tough, reliable rose for the front of a border.

'WILHELM'

syn. 'SKYROCKET'

Hybrid Musk

ORIGIN **Kordes, Germany, 1934**
PARENTAGE **'Robin Hood' x 'J.C. Thornton'**
FLOWER SIZE **2.8in (7cm)**
SCENT **Medium and musky**
FLOWERING **Repeats well**
HEIGHT/SPREAD **13.1ft (4m)/6.6ft (2m)**
HARDINESS **Zone 6**

Wilhelm Kordes used the Pemberton Musks to build a race of hardy shrub roses that would survive the winter anywhere in Germany and flower continuously in summer. 'Wilhelm' was his masterpiece: a vigorous shrub whose bright crimson flowers appear continuously until late autumn. They are semidouble, with a few white streaks toward the center and a good tuft of golden stamens. The flowers come in loose and spacious clusters of 5–25 on a vigorous bush that is no more than a shrub in Germany but widely used as a 13.1ft (4m) climber in hot climates. The plant has large, mid-green leaves, pale green stems, an open, branching habit, and a few prickles. It is both vigorous and healthy.

When Graham Thomas was working for the English nurserymen T. Hilling & Co., he introduced a lighter red sport of 'Wilhelm', which he called 'Will Scarlet'. It has never been as popular as the original, and tends to fade to lilac-pink in hot weather. In all other respects, however, it is identical to 'Wilhelm' and especially valuable for its floriferousness and good health.

'Wilhelm'

Sport of 'Wilhelm'

'WILL SCARLET'

ORIGIN **Hilling, Britain, 1948**

PARK WILHELMSHÖHE: ROSENINSEL

WITHIN THE GARDENS OF GERMANY'S SCHLOSS WILHELMSHÖHE IS A ROSE GARDEN FEATURING SOME 1,500 ROSES FROM THE 18TH AND 19TH CENTURIES

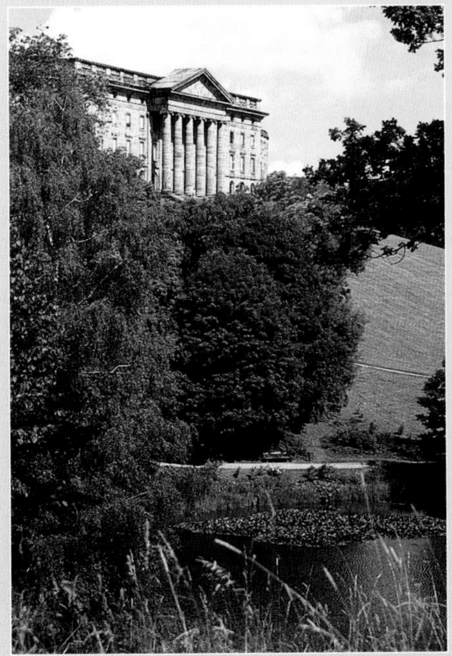
VIEW OF THE SCHLOSS FROM THE ROSE GARDEN

WILHELMSHÖHE WAS THE PALACE and park of the Landgraves and Electors of Hessen. It occupies an entire mountainside above the city of Kassel and extends to nearly 2,470 acres (1000 hectares). Within it are magnificent gardens from every period: the newest is the Roseninsel Park, founded in 1977. It was the brainchild of Hedi and Wernt Grimm, who were leading lights of the Heritage Rose movement in Germany and lived nearby. The Grimms' aim was to fill the landscape around one of the lakes at Wilhelmshöhe with roses from the 18th and 19th centuries – and they succeeded triumphantly.

The collection at Wilhelmshöhe now has some 1,500 different old rose cultivars, including 'Perle von Weissenstein', the first rose to be bred in Germany. The shrub roses are especially impressive: the garden has a nearly complete collection of roses by Rudolph Geschwind, including the rare purple pink Hybrid Perpetual 'Anna Scharsach' (1890). Almost all the Hybrid Musks are grown, including some unnamed hybrids bred by Louis Lens by crossing 'Trier' with 'Mutabilis'. Modern German breeders are well represented: the Kordes shrub roses include the rarely seen 'Burg Baden' (1955) and the rose of the garden itself, **Park Wilhelmshöhe** (1987). It is a place of rare enchantment on a warm June afternoon.

PARK WILHELMSHÖHE

'WILL ALDERMAN'

Rugosa Hybrid

ORIGIN **Skinner, US, 1954**
PARENTAGE **(*Rosa rugosa* x *Rosa acicularis*) x seedling**
FLOWER SIZE **2.8in (7cm)**
SCENT **Strong and sweet**
FLOWERING **Repeats**
HEIGHT/SPREAD **4.1ft (1.25m)/4.1ft (1.25m)**
HARDINESS **Zone 4**

This superhardy Rugosa rose was bred by the Canadian plant breeder Dr. Frank Skinner to withstand the Manitoba winters and to give flowers that were significantly superior to *Rosa rugosa* itself. 'Will Alderman' has semi-double flowers that open out to a neat, round outline. They are magenta pink, with a small white patch at the center, and dark yellow stamens. They come singly and in clusters of up to five flowers. Their scent is delicious. 'Will Alderman' makes a compact and manageable shrub, with a lot of healthy, pale green, corrugated foliage, a dense habit of growth, and considerable vigor. It is a good repeat flowerer, bearing its flowers until the first frost, when the leaves turn bright yellow and the plant is shown to have handsome russet stems in winter. Like so many roses bred for subArctic conditions, 'Will Alderman' also flourishes in hot climates like that of southern California.

'WILL ALDERMAN'

'WILL SCARLET'

see 'WILHELM'

'WILLIAM ALLEN RICHARDSON'

Noisette

ORIGIN **Ducher, France, 1878**
PARENTAGE **'Rêve d'Or' x unknown**
FLOWER SIZE **2.8in (7cm)**
SCENT **Moderate and tealike**
FLOWERING **Almost continuous**
HEIGHT/SPREAD **13.1ft (4m)/6.6ft (2m)**
HARDINESS **Zone 7**

Few roses change color so quickly as 'William Allen Richardson'. The buds are the richest orange apricot color imaginable, but by the time they have fully opened out into flat and somewhat irregular flowers they are at best creamy white. A popular buttonhole rose for many years, it is perhaps prettiest when half-open. Then the center of the flower is still deeply colored and contrasts with the buff yellow around it and the white of the outer petals. It keeps its color better in cool, overcast weather, and has the great quality of shedding its petals as soon as they have faded. The flowers come in clusters of 5–20 and are repeated right through until early winter. The plant is very vigorous, with dark green, glossy leaves and occasionally a little blackspot. William Allen Richardson was a wealthy Kentucky amateur rosarian who traveled to Lyon to choose his rose.

'WILLIAM ALLEN RICHARDSON'

'WILLIAM BAFFIN'

WILLIAM BOOTH

'WILLIAM BAFFIN'

Kordesii Hybrid

ORIGIN **Svejda, Canada, 1983**
PARENTAGE **'Kordesii' × ('Red Dawn' × 'Suzanne')**
FLOWER SIZE **2.8in (7cm)**
SCENT **Little or none**
FLOWERING **Fairly continuous**
HEIGHT/SPREAD **6.6ft (2m)/6.6ft (2m)**
HARDINESS **Zone 3**

'William Baffin' is probably the most vigorous, dependable, and hardy of the Explorer roses raised at Ottawa to withstand Canadian winters. It is named after the English Arctic explorer (*c.*1584–1622) who discovered Baffin Bay. The loose, semidouble flowers are deep pink, with golden stamens, white flashes at the base of the petals, and paler reverses (often visible when the petals curve over). They come in clusters of 10–30 and appear more or less continuously throughout the growing season. The overall effect of a plant in full flower is reminiscent of a superior wild rose. The foliage is dark, thick, glossy, and resistant to blackspot, mildew, and rust in Ottawa and Montreal but not always in milder climates. It responds well to feeding and comes easily from softwood cuttings.

WILLIAM BOOTH

Kordesii Hybrid

ORIGIN **L'Assomption, Canada, 1999**
PARENTAGE **('Kordesii' × 'Max Graf') × ('Arthur Bell' × 'Applejack')**
FLOWER SIZE **2in (5cm)**
SCENT **Light and musky**
FLOWERING **Almost continuous**
HEIGHT/SPREAD **4.9ft (1.5m)/6.6ft (2m)**
HARDINESS **Zone 4**

This is one of the latest Explorer roses, and named not after a Canadian pioneer but to commemorate the founder of the Salvation Army. William Booth has small, single flowers that open deep crimson but fade to cerise and have paler petal backs as well as a small white patch at the center and a handsome circle of yellow stamens. They come in clusters of 5–10 and appear almost continuously until the first frost. William Booth makes a lax, arching, mounding shrub that can either be allowed to flop around as a landscaping shrub or be tied up as a pillar rose. In hot climates it is a tall climber. In its native Québec, William Booth is a vigorous grower, with a scattering of prickles and healthy, dark, glossy leaves. It roots easily from cuttings and needs no pruning.

'WILLIAM III'

Spinosissima Hybrid

ORIGIN **Britain, c.1910**
FLOWER SIZE **1.2in (3cm)**
SCENT **Light and fruity**
FLOWERING **Once only, somewhat early in season in most places**
HEIGHT/SPREAD **2.7ft (80cm)/2ft (60cm)**
HARDINESS **Zone 5**

There are many forms and hybrids of the Scotch *Rosa spinosissima*, and they all inherit the dense, prickly, thicketing habit of the species. 'William III' is no exception, but its color is unmatched by any of the others and is assumed to have come from a cross or back-cross to one of the deep purple Gallica roses. The flowers are single, with a few extra petals, and very bright crimson at first, with purple undertones and a white patch at the center around the bright yellow stamens. Contrast comes from the white streaks that run out into the petals from the center and from the nearly white petal backs. It flowers profusely and vividly early in the season (except in hot climates, where it is a midseason flowerer), and is succeeded by small black hips like blackcurrants. The plant has small, neat foliage and a slender, twiggy habit of growth. It will make a very useful small, impenetrable hedge if grown on its own roots and allowed to sucker.

'WILLIAM III'

'WILLIAM LOBB'

Moss Rose

ORIGIN **Laffay, France, 1855**
FLOWER SIZE **2.8in (7cm)**
SCENT **Strong and sweet**
FLOWERING **Once only**
HEIGHT/SPREAD **8.2ft (2.5m)/4.9ft (1.5m)**
HARDINESS **Zone 5**

This great purple Moss rose is surpassed in height (but not in color) only by 'Comtesse de Murinais'. It has great vigor and sends up long, lanky, bristly stems that terminate in large, heavily mossed clusters of crimson flowers. As they age, the flowers turn to purple, magenta, lilac, lavender, mauve, and gray, all contained within heavily mossed, bright green sepals. Some of the petals fold over to reveal paler backs of reflective pink. The thick green moss runs down the stems until it turns into soft crimson prickles. The leaves are large and fairly healthy, though occasionally susceptible to blackspot, just as the sepals are liable to attract mildew. Since they are so tall, the stems need support, though they break into flower very nicely all along their length if pegged down or allowed to flop over. William Lobb (1809–63) was a Cornish plant collector.

WILLIAM MORRIS

syn. AUSWILL

Shrub Rose

ORIGIN **Austin, Britain, 1998**
PARENTAGE **Abraham Darby seedling**
FLOWER SIZE **3.1in (8cm)**
SCENT **Medium and fruity**
FLOWERING **Repeats**
HEIGHT/SPREAD **5.7ft (1.75m)/4.1ft (1.25m)**
HARDINESS **Zone 6**

The apricot flowers of William Morris are extremely beautiful. They have a mass of small petals, neatly arranged in a formal rosette and carried in clusters of 3–7. The petal backs are pale pink and the apricot tones also fade to pink as the flowers mature, so there is always a gentle contrast of colors within the clusters. The plant has dark, glossy leaves, a few large prickles, and a lax habit of growth. In hot countries like Australia William Morris makes a tall, arching shrub and can be trained as a short climber. It repeats well everywhere. The English artist and designer William Morris (1834–96) was a central figure of the Pre-Raphaelite movement.

WILLIAM MORRIS

'WILLIAM LOBB' ►

WILLIAM SHAKESPEARE

ROSA WILLMOTTIAE

WILTSHIRE

WILLIAM SHAKESPEARE

syn. 'AUSROYAL'

Shrub Rose

ORIGIN **Austin, Britain, 1987**
PARENTAGE **'The Squire' x Mary Rose**
FLOWER SIZE **3.5in (9cm)**
SCENT **Strong and sweet**
FLOWERING **Repeats well**
HEIGHT/SPREAD **4.9ft (1.5m)/4.1ft (1.25m)**
HARDINESS **Zone 6**

A few years after this sumptuous crimson rose was introduced, William Shakespeare started to show a susceptibility to rust and blackspot in its native England. Austin's response was to withdraw it and substitute another one, called William Shakespeare 2000. However, the original William Shakespeare continues to be an excellent, healthy garden rose in much of the world – and much more widely sold than its putative successor. Its flowers open dark red with purple undertones and a massive rosette of little petals, quilled and quartered around a button eye. The color is slightly brighter and more scarlet toward the center, but the overall impression is of deepest richest crimson. The flowers come singly or in clusters of up to four and have long stems, good for cutting. The plant has quite a few prickles, dark leaves, and a rounded, bushy habit. William Shakespeare is very free flowering, though it takes a few years to settle in and show its potential. The flowers come biggest and best in cool autumn weather.

'WILLIAMS' DOUBLE YELLOW'

Spinosissima Hybrid

ORIGIN **Williams, Britain, 1828**
PARENTAGE ***Rosa spinosissima* x *Rosa foetida***
FLOWER SIZE **2.4in (6cm)**
SCENT **Medium and fruity**
FLOWERING **Once only, early in season**
HEIGHT/SPREAD **4.1ft (1.25m)/4.1ft (1.25m)**
HARDINESS **Zone 4**

There are two yellow hybrids of the ancient Scots rose *Rosa spinosissima* – the well-known, popular 'Harison's Yellow' and the little-known 'Williams' Double Yellow'. They are remarkably similar: rose experts point to only one certain distinguishing feature – the presence of green carpels at the center of the flowers of 'Williams' Double Yellow'. It is a hybrid with a form of *Rosa foetida*, though it is not possible to say which cultivars were involved in the cross. Its flowers are fairly double, and bright, clear yellow, paling just a little at the edges. The plant has small leaves like the Scots rose and a suckering habit. It flourishes on poor soils and is extremely adaptable as to climate: it performs well in hot regions but was also carried across much of Canada by early settlers.

ROSA WILLMOTTIAE

Wild Rose

FLOWER SIZE **1.6in (4cm)**
SCENT **Little or none**
FLOWERING **Once, fairly early in season**
HEIGHT/SPREAD **6.6ft (2m)/6.6ft (2m)**
HARDINESS **Zone 5**

There are few more attractive sights early in the season than a young bush of *Rosa willmottiae* in full flower. It is the embodiment of beauty when the arching branches are covered in rich pink flowers with a hint of lilac in their petals. It is one of the few wild roses that merits a place in a mixed border or even as a specimen shrub, rather than being banished to a less prominent part of the garden. Its flowers are not especially large, but they come on short laterals all over the surface of the plant, set off by pale stamens and dainty, fernlike foliage. Later the leaves grow longer (though rarely more than 2.4in/6cm) and the flowers are followed by round red hips.

'WILLIAMS' DOUBLE YELLOW'

WILTSHIRE

syn. 'KORMUSE'

Ground Cover

ORIGIN **Kordes, Germany, 1993**
PARENTAGE **Heidekönigin x seedling**
FLOWER SIZE **2.8in (7cm)**
SCENT **Light and fruity**
FLOWERING **Continuous**
HEIGHT/SPREAD **3.3ft (1m)/2.5ft (75cm)**
HARDINESS **Zone 6**

In the 1980s, the English nursery of Mattocks had the idea of introducing good small shrubs and groundcover roses from mainland European breeders like Kordes, Tantau, and Poulsen, and naming them after British counties. Some had already been introduced under other names, but not Wiltshire, which is one of the best and is now widely grown around the world. Its flowers are deep pink, with a hint of coral that fades away as they age. They come in loose clusters of 5–30 and are very profusely borne from midseason through until late autumn. The leaves are dark, glossy, and large (for a short plant), and the stems have a few prickles. The plant has a lax habit of growth, which means that it grows up at first and then bends over as the flowers develop. Wiltshire is an excellent shrub for groundcover, in pots, at the front of a border, or in large landscaping plans.

WINCHESTER CATHEDRAL

see MARY ROSE

WINDRUSH

syn. 'AUSRUSH'

Shrub Rose

ORIGIN **Austin, Britain, 1984**
PARENTAGE **seedling x ('Canterbury' x 'Golden Wings')**
FLOWER SIZE **3.9in (10cm)**
SCENT **Strong**
FLOWERING **Repeats**
HEIGHT/SPREAD **4.9ft (1.5m)/4.9ft (1.5m)**
HARDINESS **Zone 5**

David Austin introduced Windrush as an improved version of 'Golden Wings', which is a fair description, though Windrush lacks the glorious red stamens of its grandparent. Its pale lemon yellow flowers float over the surface of the lax plant, and quickly turn to cream and white, starting at the edges and moving toward the center, where there is a large boss of yellow stamens. The flowers come in upright clusters of 3–11 and are followed by large, round hips: deadheading is essential to ensure that it continues to flower. The prickly plant has medium-sized, mid-green leaves and is healthy, except for an occasional touch of mildew. It is very floriferous and one of the first of all roses to bloom in cool climates – a characteristic inherited from its ancestor 'Altaica'.

WINDRUSH

'WINNIPEG PARKS'

Shrub Rose

ORIGIN **Collicutt, Canada, 1990**
PARENTAGE **('Prairie Princess' x 'Cuthbert Grant') x (seedling x 'Morden Cardinette')**
FLOWER SIZE **3.1in (8cm)**
SCENT **Light and musky**
FLOWERING **Repeats almost continuously**
HEIGHT/SPREAD **2.7ft (80cm)/2.7ft (80cm)**
HARDINESS **Zone 4**

One of the prettiest and one of the hardiest of the Canadian roses – that is the general opinion of 'Winnipeg Parks'. Its flowers are a luminous cherry red – sometimes more red and sometimes more pink, but always somewhere between the two colors. The individual flowers do not last long, but are very freely borne all season long. They are semidouble and cupped, with yellow stamens, and come singly or in small clusters of up to five. The overall effect is like a Floribunda. 'Winnipeg Parks' has a lot of dark, healthy, semi-glossy leaves (reddish when young) and makes a dense bush. It is an excellent bedding rose for the coldest of climates.

WISE PORTIA

syn. 'AUSPORT'

Shrub Rose

ORIGIN **Austin, Britain, 1982**
PARENTAGE **'The Knight' x 'Glastonbury'**
FLOWER SIZE **3.1in (8cm)**
SCENT **Strong and sweet**
FLOWERING **Repeats**
HEIGHT/SPREAD **3.3ft (1m)/2.7ft (80cm)**
HARDINESS **Zone 6**

Although it is never the most vigorous of David Austin's English Roses, Wise Portia is one that does better in hotter, drier climates than in England. Then it is a healthy grower, untroubled by blackspot and mildew. The flowers are deep magenta or pale crimson, fading with age to deep pink mauve or lilac, especially in hot weather. They open as loose rosettes and last well as cut flowers. Their large size and unusual color make them useful in arrangements, too, though the flowers are sometimes too heavy for their stems. Wise Portia is neat and compact, with somewhat thin, spindly growth and not enough foliage, though the leaves are a good dark green – bronzy red when young. It responds to good cultivation and is a quick repeater.

WISE PORTIA

'WINNIPEG PARKS'

'WOBURN ABBEY'

WISHING

syn. 'DICKERFUFFLE', Georgie Girl

Floribunda

ORIGIN **Dickson, Northern Ireland, 1985**
PARENTAGE **'Silver Jubilee' x Bright Smile**
FLOWER SIZE **2.8in (7cm)**
SCENT **Light and fruity**
FLOWERING **Repeats well**
HEIGHT/SPREAD **2.7ft (80cm)/2ft (60cm)**
HARDINESS **Zone 6**

This is a very useful, short-growing Floribunda. The flowers of Wishing are handsome, full of petals, and shaped like little Hybrid Teas. They are also an unusual orange peach color, with yellow toward the center, though they lose their yellow flush as they age and turn pink from the edges inward. Eventually the flowers are more pink than apricot. Wishing makes a compact plant, with quite a covering of prickles, bronzy new growth, and mid-green, semiglossy leaves. It is a good repeater and acceptably healthy. Above all, it is very good value where a small rose with a lot of elegant, colorful flowers is required.

WISHING

'WOBURN ABBEY'

Floribunda

ORIGIN **Sidey & Cobley, Britain, 1962**
PARENTAGE **'Masquerade' x 'Fashion'**
FLOWER SIZE **2.4in (6cm)**
SCENT **Medium and fruity**
FLOWERING **Repeats well**
HEIGHT/SPREAD **3.3ft (1m)/2.7ft (80cm)**
HARDINESS **Zone 6**

Some roses become much more popular abroad than in their country of origin. 'Woburn Abbey' is a good example. It was bred in England, and grown there for a few years without ever becoming very popular, and then it faded to near obscurity, perhaps because of its weakness for mildew and blackspot. Meanwhile, it acquired a strong following in Australia, where such diseases are not a big problem and where 'Woburn Abbey' is still widely known and grown today. Its flowers are a fine tangerine orange color, merging toward bright yellow at the center and with tints of amber and occasional red flushes – a stunning combination, especially since the flowers come in clusters of 3–10. 'Woburn Abbey' makes a vigorous, bushy plant with handsome, dark leaves and bronzy new growth. It flowers almost continuously.

WOODS OF WINDSOR

see BELAMI

ROSA WOODSII

Wild Rose

FLOWER SIZE **1.6in (4cm)**
SCENT **Light and sweet**
FLOWERING **Once only**
HEIGHT/SPREAD **4.9ft (1.5m)/4.1ft (1.25m)**
HARDINESS **Zone 4**

Rosa woodsii is native to a very large area of North America, from Alaska to northern Mexico: the epicenter of its natural distribution is in Alberta and Montana, where it often occurs on wetland sites. Its flowers are simple but beautiful: dark rose pink, with a neat circle of yellow stamens at the center. They come in clusters of 3–6 and are followed by small (0.4in/1cm) round hips. The leaves are also small, with seven leaflets close together. The stems are slender and lightly covered in prickles. *Rosa woodsii* is a naturally suckering plant and spreads vigorously, unless grafted on a more stationary rootstock. However, the unwanted suckers can easily be pulled out if the plant should prove invasive.

ROSA WOODSII

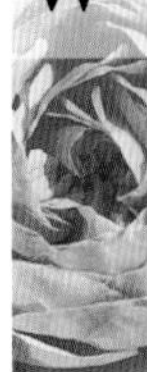

Rosa xanthina 'Canary Bird'

see 'Canary Bird'

Yakimour

syn. 'MEIpsilon'

Hybrid Tea

ORIGIN **Meilland, France, 1985**
FLOWER SIZE **4.3in (11cm)**
SCENT **Little or none**
FLOWERING **Repeats**
HEIGHT/SPREAD **4.1ft (1.25m)/2.7ft (80cm)**
HARDINESS **Zone 6**
AWARDS **Baden-Baden 1985**

Yakimour is a striking bicolor Hybrid Tea. The flowers are bright scarlet, with yellow backs to the petals. The contrast between the two colors is most obvious and enjoyable when the bud is unfurling. Then the yellow fades to creamy white and the scarlet darkens to crimson. By the time the flower has opened out fully, the undersides are hidden from view. The flowers come usually singly, but sometimes in small clusters. They are complemented by dark, glossy leaves that are unfortunately somewhat susceptible to blackspot and mildew. Nevertheless, Yakimour is still quite widely available in France, but is not so readily found elsewhere.

Yakimour

'Yellow Button'

Yellow Cover

'Yellow Button'

Shrub Rose

ORIGIN **Austin, Britain, 1975**
PARENTAGE **'Wife of Bath' x 'Chinatown'**
FLOWER SIZE **2.4in (6cm)**
SCENT **Light, fruity, and musky**
FLOWERING **Repeats**
HEIGHT/SPREAD **2.7ft (80cm)/3.3ft (1m)**
HARDINESS **Zone 5**

'Yellow Button' was the first of David Austin's English Roses in yellow. The flowers are rich yolk yellow when they first open, but soon fade quickly to white, starting at the edges. This sets up a wonderful contrast between the bright yellow center and the white outer petals. The flowers are rosette-shaped, with masses of pretty petals – some quill-like, some folded – and often a button eye. Eventually the whole flower fades to white and then reflexes into a pompon. The flowers come in clusters of 3–9. The plant has fairly ordinary dark leaves and few thorns, and is healthy, except for occasional blackspot. Its lax habit makes it useful at the front of a bed. It performs best in cool climates, fading too quickly in hot sun.

Yellow Charles Austin

see 'Charles Austin'

Yellow Cover

syn. 'POULgode', Golden Cover, Lexington, Sparkling Yellow

Ground Cover

ORIGIN **Poulsen, Denmark, 1993**
FLOWER SIZE **1.6in (4cm)**
SCENT **Light and sweet**
FLOWERING **Repeats constantly**
HEIGHT/SPREAD **2ft (60cm)/2.7ft (80cm)**
HARDINESS **Zone 5**

This groundcover rose has its admirers. Yellow Cover has pale yellow flowers that fade to cream. They are no more than semidouble, but they have a fine crown of golden stamens at the center. They come in clusters of 3–15, and are followed by little red hips. It flowers well, and repeats so quickly that it seems to be continuously flowering. It is not a tight, weed suppressing groundcover rose, but more of an open, Polyantha style shrub. Its leaves are small, medium-dark, and glossy in the Wichurana style, but unfortunately prone to blackspot.

Yellow Dagmar Hastrup

see Topaz Jewel

'Yellow Doll'

Miniature Rose

ORIGIN **Moore, US, 1962**
PARENTAGE **'Golden Glow' x 'Zee'**
FLOWER SIZE **1.6in (4cm)**
SCENT **Light and fruity**
FLOWERING **Repeats**
HEIGHT/SPREAD **1.3ft (40cm)/11.8in (30cm)**
HARDINESS **Zone 5**

Everyone agrees that 'Yellow Doll' is still one of the best of the yellow miniatures. Ralph Moore, the king of miniature roses, used the superhardy "subzero" rambler 'Golden Glow' as one of its parents, and the result is a little shrub of great hardiness with dark, Wichurana type leaves. The flowers of 'Yellow Doll' open from pointed buds and are full of narrow petals, though they open out flat to reveal a large boss of deep golden stamens at the center. The flowers are primrose yellow, fading to cream at the edges, but they come in clusters of 3–10 and are borne very freely. 'Yellow Doll' is a neat, short plant with tiny, healthy leaves and a vigorous habit of growth.

Yellow Fairy

syn. 'POULfair'

Ground Cover

ORIGIN **Olesen, Denmark, 1988**
PARENTAGE **Texas x 'The Fairy'**
FLOWER SIZE **1.6in (4cm)**
SCENT **Light and musky**
FLOWERING **Repeats well**
HEIGHT/SPREAD **2.7ft (80cm)/2ft (60cm)**
HARDINESS **Zone 6**
AWARDS **Madrid GM 1988**

This is a good modern Polyantha, though Yellow Fairy is promoted as a groundcover rose. Its flowers are fully double and borne in clusters of 3–8 all over the surface of the plant. They are a good bright yellow when they first open, with hints of gold and amber

'Yellow Doll'

X

Yellow Fairy

toward the center, but fade over the next few days to lemon and cream. **Yellow Fairy** does not shed its spent flowers cleanly, but this is not a huge defect because there are always other roses to take their place. It is an open shrub of attractive shape, with handsome, healthy, small, dark leaves in the Wichurana style.

Yellow Romantica

see Colette

'Yellowhammer'

Floribunda

ORIGIN **McGredy, Northern Ireland, 1956**
PARENTAGE **'Poulsen's Yellow' seedling**
FLOWER SIZE **2.4in (6cm)**
SCENT **Strong and fruity**
FLOWERING **Repeats**
HEIGHT/SPREAD **2.7ft (80cm)/2ft (60cm)**
HARDINESS **Zone 6**
AWARDS **NRS GM 1954**

'Yellowhammer' had a long run as a short, yellow Floribunda and is still fairly widely grown. Its flowers are full of petals (too many 1950s Floribundas were no more than single or semisingle). They open a deep golden yellow and, though they eventually fade slightly at the edges of the petals, they always keep a rich dark yellow toward the center. The flowers come in clusters of 3–5 and the plant repeats well. 'Yellowhammer' has dark green leaves and a bushy habit of growth. There is a climbing form that is occasionally seen in Europe, especially in France: it was introduced by Dorieux in 1976.

'Yellowhammer'

'Yesterday'

Yellowstone

see Marselisborg

'Yesterday'

syn. 'Tapis d'Orient'

Polyantha

ORIGIN **Harkness, Britain, 1974**
PARENTAGE **('Phyllis Bide' × 'Shepherd's Delight') × 'Ballerina'**
FLOWER SIZE **1.8in (4.5cm)**
SCENT **Light and musky**
FLOWERING **Repeats very well**
HEIGHT/SPREAD **3.3ft (1m)/3.3ft (1m)**
HARDINESS **Zone 5**
AWARDS **Monza GM 1974; Baden-Baden GM 1975; ADR 1978**

Jack Harkness called this rose 'Yesterday' because all its ancestors had been bred and introduced many years previously. In the event, it sparked a renewed interest in the historic Polyanthas that were bred in the first half of the 20th century. 'Yesterday' has pale purple crimson flowers with a white center and a neat tuft of golden stamens that keep their color well. The flowers fade to pink but are borne in clusters of 5–25 over a long period, so the effect is always colorful. The plant also repeats quickly, so that it is almost continuously in flower until late autumn. It has small, healthy, glossy leaves and a neat habit of growth, which makes it a good combiner with herbaceous plants in a mixed border. This is an excellent all-around rose.

'Yolande d'Aragon'

'Yolande d'Aragon'

Portland

ORIGIN **Vibert, France, 1843**
FLOWER SIZE **3.9in (10cm)**
SCENT **Strong and sweet**
FLOWERING **Remontant**
HEIGHT/SPREAD **4.1ft (1.25m)/3.3ft (1m)**
HARDINESS **Zone 5**

'Yolande d'Aragon' is a magnificent, large, intensely scented, repeat-flowering rose that conquers the heart of all rose growers. Its flowers are lightly cupped, with a neat, circular outline composed of pale, silky guard petals enclosing a mass of smaller, darker petals, many of them quilled. It is deep pink, with slightly paler edges and a hint of magenta at the center. The plant has small, smooth, pale green leaves that show its China rose ancestry. It has a sturdy, upright habit of growth and repeats regularly throughout the summer and autumn, provided it is deadheaded. It also responds to feeding and watering. Yolande d'Aragon (1379– 1442) was the queen of four kingdoms (Sicily, Naples, Jerusalem, and Aragon), Duchess of Anjou, and Countess of Provence, "the wisest and most beautiful princess in Christendom."

'York and Lancaster'

syn. Rosa damascena 'Versicolor'

Damask Rose

ORIGIN **Britain, c.1550**
FLOWER SIZE **2.8in (7cm)**
SCENT **Strong and sweet**
FLOWERING **Once only**
HEIGHT/SPREAD **8.2ft (2.5m)/8.2ft (2.5m)**
HARDINESS **Zone 4**

Many old striped roses bear the name 'York and Lancaster', but this is the correct one – a Damask that can be traced back at least as far as 1551. Legend maintains that it appeared as a symbol of peace at the end of the 15th-century Wars of the Roses in England, but this story can be neither proved nor disproved. 'York and Lancaster' is not much of a plant by modern standards – its best characteristic is its soft, lush, blue green leaves – but the somewhat undersized flowers also have a certain intrinsic charm. They are either pure rose pink, or pure white, or blessed with petals of both colors. Sometimes a few petals are variously striped and mottled in pink and white. Neither color predominates, and their distribution appears to be quite random. All three types frequently appear in the same cluster, typically of 3–5 flowers. This is well illustrated by the photograph shown below. Their scent is invariably delicious.

Yorkshire Bank

see True Love

'York and Lancaster'

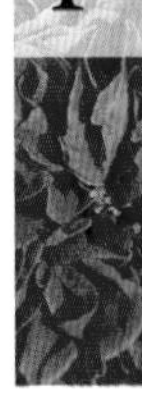

'Ypsilanti'

Yves Piaget

'Ypsilanti'

syn. 'Ipsilanté'

Gallica

ORIGIN **Vibert, France, 1821**
FLOWER SIZE **4.5in (11cm)**
SCENT **Strong and sweet**
FLOWERING **Once only, fairly late in season**
HEIGHT/SPREAD **4.9ft (1.5m)/3.3ft (1m)**
HARDINESS **Zone 5**

The unusual name of this handsome Gallica rose commemorates Alexander Ypsilanti, a hero of the Greek War of Independence. Its flowers open out flat and double, a swirl of roughly quartered petals around a small green eye. They open from red buds but are dark purple pink at first, fading to paler pinkand eventually to lavender gray at the edges. The contrast of colors in'Ypsilanti' is not the most abrupt among Gallicas, but distinct and distinctive nevertheless. The flowers are borne sometimes singly, but usually in twos or threes, and last well, both on the branches and as cut flowers. The plant makes a lax, leafy, floppy bush, with pale green leaves and few prickles. It is healthy except for an occasional touch of mildew later. It is also a thrifty and vigorous grower, one of many Gallicas that will give an excellent performance even on poor soils.

Yves Piaget

syn. 'MEIvildo', Queen Adelaide, Royal Brompton Rose

Hybrid Tea

ORIGIN **Meilland, France, 1985**
PARENTAGE **(['Pharaon' x 'Mme. A. Meilland'] x ['Chrysler Imperial' x 'Charles Mallerin']) x 'Tamango'**
FLOWER SIZE **4.7in (12cm)**
SCENT **Strong: a mixture of sweetness and fruit**
FLOWERING **Repeats well**
HEIGHT/SPREAD **2.5ft (75cm)/1.6ft (50cm)**
HARDINESS **Zone 6**
AWARDS **Geneva GM & FA 1982; Le Roeulx GM & FA 1982; Bagatelle FA 1992**

Yves Piaget was the rose that set the House of Meilland on to breeding its race of Romantica roses. Actually, it was issued as a Hybrid Tea, but its peony-shaped flowers, with their frilly, waved petals, were clearly the beginning of something new. The flowers of Yves Piaget are fat and round. They are pale rose pink at the edges and rich mid-pink toward the center, with irregular, indented petal ends as well as the characteristic ruffling. They come singly or in twos and threes on long, strong stems, good for cutting, and have an amazing scent. Although short, the plant has an upright and bushy habit, with only a few thorns. It responds well to warmth, feeding, and watering. Its handsome, mid-green leaves have good disease resistance in warm, dry climates, but may be susceptible to fungal diseases in cool, wet ones. It is a most abundant and continuous bloomer. Yves Piaget is a Swiss horologist.

'Yvonne Rabier'

Polyantha

ORIGIN **Turbat, France, 1910**
FLOWER SIZE **1.2in (3cm)**
SCENT **Light, sweet, and musky**
FLOWERING **Continuous**
HEIGHT/SPREAD **2ft (60cm)/2ft (60cm)**
HARDINESS **Zone 5**

'Yvonne Rabier'

In hot climates, this famous old Polyantha is always in flower. The flowers of 'Yvonne Rabier' are white, with just a hint of palest yellow at the center at first. They are very double and full of petals, though they do open out eventually. They come in large, open clusters, typically of 10–30 flowers, which make a great show in the garden. However, the petals are soft and easily injured by rain, so this rose is at its best only in dry weather. 'Yvonne Rabier' has dark, rough, glossy leaves: its parents are not known, but these leaves show that it certainly has both Multifloras and Wichuranas among its ancestors. It is extremely easy to grow: it comes quickly from cuttings; it tolerates poor soil; and it is very hardy and healthy. It is an excellent groundcover rose that can also be used in containers. If left unpruned, it will eventually reach 4.9–6.6ft (1.5–2m) in hot climates.

Zambra 93

syn. 'MEIcurbos', Magic Fire

Floribunda

ORIGIN **Meilland, France, 1992**
FLOWER SIZE **3.5in (9cm)**
SCENT **Light and fruity**
FLOWERING **Repeats well**
HEIGHT/SPREAD **2.7ft (80cm)/2ft (60cm)**
HARDINESS **Zone 7**
AWARDS **Bagatelle GM 1992; Baden-Baden GM 1993**

There are two roses called "Zambra." The first was a famous old orange Floribunda introduced by Meilland in 1961; it was popular for many years all over the world and much used as a parent to breed new roses. The second is called Zambra 93 to distinguish it from the older cultivar. It, too, is an orange Floribunda, and has become popular and widely available – but only in France. Its flowers are bright orange when they first open, with a patch of yellow at the center. As the flowers age, the yellow starts to fade, which means that they become redder, starting at the edges of the petals, which also start to reflex. The flowers come in tight clusters of 3–10 and make a very fine display as a bedding rose. Zambra 93 has a compact habit, medium-dark leaves, and a lot of prickles. It is very vigorous and a quick repeat flowerer.

Zambra 93

'Zara Hore-Ruthven'

Hybrid Tea

ORIGIN **Clark, Australia, 1932**
PARENTAGE **'Mme. Abel Chatenay' × 'Scorcher'**
FLOWER SIZE **3.9in (10cm)**
SCENT **Light**
FLOWERING **Fully recurrent**
HEIGHT/SPREAD **4.1ft (1.25m)/3.3ft (1m)**
HARDINESS **Zone 6**

This lightly petaled Hybrid Tea is very pretty in bud, but less attractive when it opens out. The flowers are rich pink, with a few white flecks, and the petals seem to grow at irregular angles: it has a slightly ungroomed look to it, quite unlike a classic Hybrid Tea. The flowers are carried singly or in clusters of up to three. The plant is fairly healthy

'Zara Hore-Ruthven'

and vigorous, with gray green leaves and very thorny stems. Lady (Zara Eileen) Hore-Ruthven was the wife of the Governor of South Australia (1928– 34), later Governor-General of Australia and 1st Earl of Gowrie.

'Zigeunerknabe'

syn. 'Gipsy Boy'

Shrub Rose

ORIGIN **Geschwind, Hungary, 1909**
FLOWER SIZE **2.4in (6cm)**
SCENT **Light and sweet**
FLOWERING **Once only**
HEIGHT/ SPREAD **4.9ft (1.5m)/6.6ft (2m)**
HARDINESS **Zone 4**

For many years this rose was known as 'Gipsy Boy' and attributed to the German breeder Peter Lambert: now we know that its original name was 'Zigeunerknabe' and that it was bred by the Hungarian Rudolph Geschwind as a by-product of his experiments in breeding hardy climbers. It probably has *Rosa setigera* and various Gallica roses in its background. The flowers open from round buds. They have a lot of small

'Zigeunerknabe'

petals laid out in neat circles around a glimpse of golden stamens at the center. They are dark crimson at first, losing their brightness and turning purple as they age. They also have white flecks in the petals and a small white eye behind the stamens. The plant has small, dark, wrinkly leaves with rounded leaflets, somewhat susceptible to blackspot. 'Zigeunerknabe' has a habit of sending out new branches somewhat more sideways than upward. They are thick, sturdy, and covered in prickles. Despite its faults 'Zigeunerknabe' remains a popular rose.

'Zéphirine Drouhin'

Bourbon Rose

ORIGIN **Bizot, France, 1868**
FLOWER SIZE **3.5in (9cm)**
SCENT **Very strong and sweet**
FLOWERING **Continuous**
HEIGHT/SPREAD **9.8ft (3m)/6.6ft (2m)**
HARDINESS **Zone 5**

This is often believed to be the only "thornless" rose, and, although there are many others without prickles, 'Zéphirine Drouhin' is by far the best known and most widely grown. It is probably a cross between a Boursault and a Hybrid Perpetual. The flowers of 'Zéphirine Drouhin' are bright cherry pink, not especially shapely, but loosely double, with white streaks running into the colored parts from the white center around the stamens. They come singly or in small clusters (typically of 3–5 flowers) and are extremely freely borne – 'Zéphirine Drouhin' is one of the first and last roses to bloom, and it does so continuously. The scent is delicious. The plant is fairly vigorous, with smooth crimson stems, red new growth, and dull green leaves. Blackspot, mildew, and rust can all be a problem. It may be grown as a bush, a pillar rose, or a climber against a wall. Zéphirine Drouhin was the wife of a French amateur rose lover from Sémur-en-Auxois on the Côte d'Or.

Two pink sports are known. **'Kathleen Harrop'** has fewer petals and is slightly less vigorous, but can nevertheless be grown as a climber. Its petals are rose pink with dark backs, as are those of the other sport, **'Marthe'**, but 'Marthe' has fuller flowers, so the petal backs reflect deeper tones into the heart of the flower.

Sports of 'Zéphirine Drouhin'

'Kathleen Harrop'

ORIGIN **Dickson, Northern Ireland, 1919**
HEIGHT/SPREAD **8.2ft (2.5m)/6.6ft (2m)**

'Marthe'

ORIGIN **Zeiner, 1911**

'Zéphirine Drouhin'

'Kathleen Harrop'

'Marthe'

'Zitronenfalter'

Shrub Rose

ORIGIN **Tantau, Germany, 1956**
PARENTAGE **'Märchenland' × 'Mme. A. Meilland'**
FLOWER SIZE **2.8in (7cm)**
SCENT **Light and fruity**
FLOWERING **Repeats well**
HEIGHT/SPREAD **6.6ft (2m)/4.1ft (1.25m)**
HARDINESS **Zone 6**

This handsome shrub rose takes its name from a species of butterfly, the Brimstone Yellow, that is native to Germany. Its wings are an exact match for the color of 'Zitronenfalter'. The flowers are a soft primrose yellow, lightly double and cupped, but set off by beautiful stamens, which have golden anthers and pretty red filaments of differing lengths. The flowers come in clusters of 3–9 and are followed by round orange hips. 'Zitronenfalter' makes a vigorous, upright bush, with dark, glossy, green leaves and a scattering of prickles.

'Zitronenfalter'

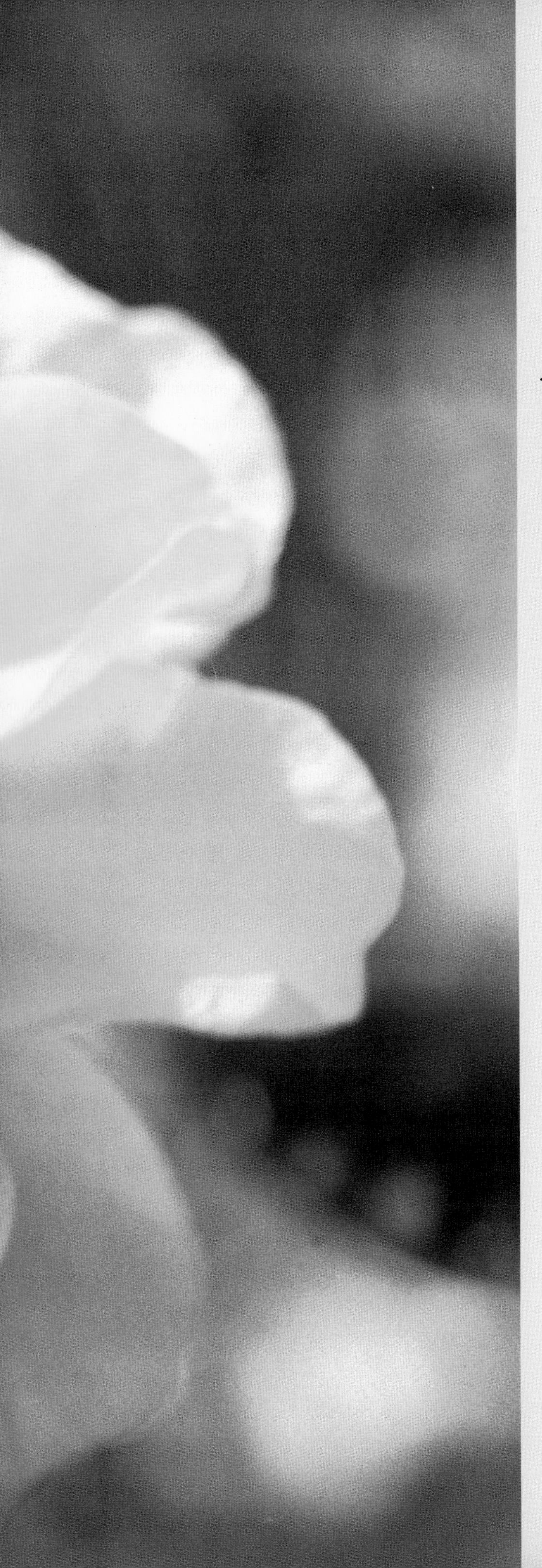

CULTIVATING ROSES

Despite being an enormously diverse group of plants, all roses are easy to grow and care for. This section, with practical advice and illustrated step-by-step sequences, provides all the help you need in order to grow healthy, floriferous plants.

USING ROSES IN YOUR GARDEN

ROSES ARE GARDEN SHRUBS and as such they are easy to grow and rewarding. Most roses produce large flowers in a wide color range for many months of the year. Their length of flowering time is the principal difference between roses and other shrubs.

There are many ways of growing roses in the garden – in beds and borders, against walls, over pergolas and arches, through trees, as groundcover, as hedges, and in containers. In large gardens they have traditionally been planted in masses – large quantities of just one variety in a bed of its own. Used in mixed borders, companion planting helps to prolong the season of interest.

This encyclopedia will help you to choose the best roses for your garden conditions, or you can approach one of the leading specialized societies. Almost all national rose societies publish a list of rose varieties that fare well in their country and its climate.

How to Buy Roses

The rose trade is unique in the way it sells, in that a large proportion of its sales are ordered from a catalogue or website, or by mail. These roses are delivered by mail or carrier as bare-root plants in the dormant season. Bare-root plants are inexpensive and they usually represent good value. Nurseries send these plants out at the right time for planting in their particular locality.

Mail order, however, gives you no control over the quality of the roses you buy. The alternative is to select your roses in pots from a garden center. This enables you to choose well-grown, healthy specimens and, if they are in flower at the time of your visit, to see exactly what you are getting. The roses sold in garden centers may be of variable quality, so it is important to choose carefully – look for a network of healthy roots that almost fill the pot. Otherwise you may find yourself with one of the "seconds" or "leftovers" which remain unsold at the end of the bare-root mailing season and are then sold on to garden centers to be potted up for sale.

Today's trend is toward growing roses on their own roots, rather than on a budded stock. Most roses used for landscaping are pot-grown and sold on their own roots, and they make much better plants than budded ones. Budded roses growing in containers are best bought fairly early in the season when you have a better selection and when you can see that they are growing well.

BUYING HEALTHY PLANTS

Always buy your roses from a reputable grower. Look for a sturdy, fibrous root system and thick, vigorous stems. Good nurseries keep their bare-root plants in cold storage for weeks or months, releasing them to customers only when the weather is suitable for planting.

Look for health, freshness, and vigor in container-grown roses too. They should have plenty of new growth from the stems or branches.

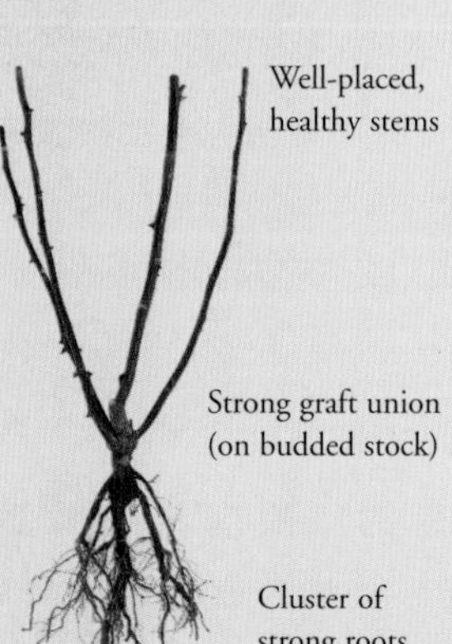

BARE-ROOT ROSE

CONTAINER-GROWN ROSE

Dedicated Rose Gardens

Dedicated rose gardens date back at least to the 18th century but became popular during the 20th century once the new Wichurana climbers and Hybrid Teas started to be produced in great numbers. When Floribundas arrived in the 1950s, offering color for months on end, it was usual to plant vast numbers of a single cultivar each in a special bed. The formula works less well with old garden roses, many of which flower

only once. But rose gardens remain popular in warm climates where the season for Floribundas and Hybrid Teas starts early and lasts until autumn.

Many of the world's most beautiful rose gardens have been laid out as hundreds of beds, each planted with a different rose. The famous gardens at l'Haÿ-les-Roses and Bagatelle are classic examples of this formal style. But new roses also suit a more fluid modernist layout: examples include Descanso Gardens at La Cañada, Flintridge, in California and the great Roseraie at Parc de la Tête d'Or, Lyon, in France.

A FORMAL ROSE GARDEN
In this rose garden the beds are edged by low box hedges and given further structure by pergolas clothed in climbing roses.

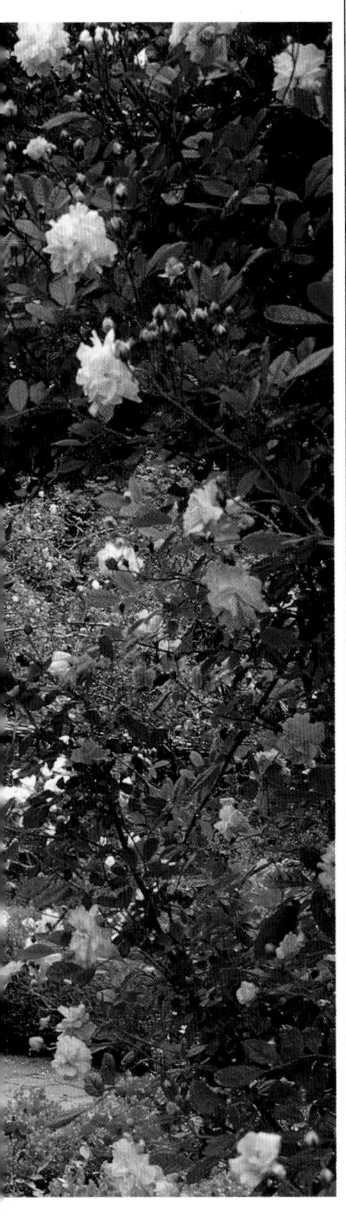

Mixed Plantings

The modern trend is to treat roses as garden shrubs and interplant them with other shrubs and herbaceous plants. This helps to prolong the roses' season of interest – important for once-flowering roses – and creates pleasing plant combinations. The foliage of some roses provides beautiful colors throughout the growing season: the blue leaves of *Rosa glauca* and the gray of *Rosa fedtschenkoana* are wonderful foils for mixed plantings.

It used to be thought that other plants compete with the roses by taking too much goodness from the soil. We now know that all roses are happy to combine with other plants and that a dense cover of mixed plantings helps to conserve moisture in the soil. It also presents endless opportunities to create beautiful effects through contrasts and harmonies of color and shape.

In cool climates, herbaceous plants are often chosen as companions so that their flowering coincides with the first blooming of the roses. The pastel shades of foxgloves, alchemilla, campanulas, and geraniums look most effective with the pinks and purples of old-fashioned roses. Pinks, diascias, cistus, and lavender achieve the same effects in warmer climates. Some of the best mixed borders are made in hot climates by interplanting bright red or yellow roses with hibiscus, lantanas, aloes, and pelargoniums.

Another purpose of mixed planting is to ensure color in the garden at all times of year. Winter- and autumn-flowering bulbs such as snowdrops, bluebells, and colchicums make excellent plantings in cool climates, as do watsonias, freesias, and clivias in hot. Some herbaceous plants also add autumn interest, notably Michaelmas daisies and Japanese anemones in cool climates. Subshrubby salvias are spectacular in warmer areas.

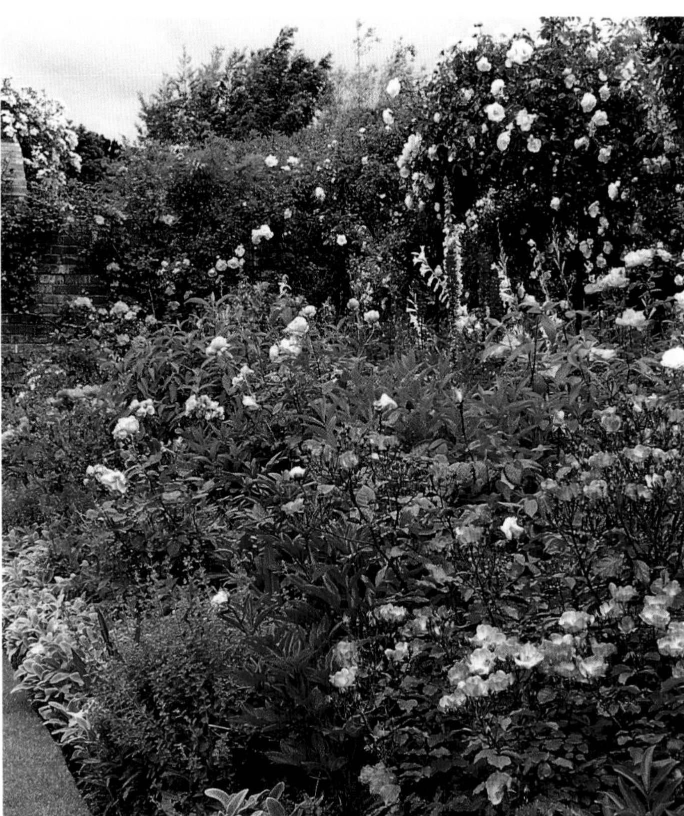

ROSES IN A MIXED PLANTING
In a wide border, shrub roses are a key element of the mixed planting, giving shape and form as well as colorful flowers.

Roses as Hedging

A rose hedge in full flower is a spectacular garden feature. Choose the right cultivar, and the hedge can be a formal edging 7.8in (20cm) high or a dense screen over 6.6ft (2m) tall. It is best to use one cultivar only: mixed hedges lack the impact of repetition.

Consider the purpose of the hedge. Most serve to divide up a garden into smaller spaces and enclose them. But roses do not respond well to close clipping, like yew or box. They have a looser, more natural habit of growth. Some of the best hedges are made from lax growers, like the Hybrid Musks, tied into a framework of wires or wood. This gives the structure and formality needed to act as a boundary. Few rose hedges are impenetrable, though the Sweetbriar hybrids can present a formidable obstacle. Some of the best hedges consist of vigorous Floribundas like 'Schneewittchen', which flower almost constantly and can be pruned frequently.

USING ROSES FOR A HEDGE
The Hybrid Musk 'Felicia' has been used to make a productive and attractive hedge that responds well to frequent pruning.

Planting and Growing Roses

The requirements of roses are exactly the same as those of other garden shrubs. All prefer a deep, rich, fertile soil, but roses will grow well enough and give satisfaction in a wide variety of soils and situations. Roses prefer a sunny position but tolerate some shade, especially if they can climb up toward the light. They prefer a soil that is neither too acid nor too alkaline, but most roses will thrive even in these conditions. Roses will not flourish in drafty situations or in standing water, however. If you have a high water table, plant roses on top of a small mound or in raised beds.

Always prepare the soil with compost or other organic matter although, recent tests by the Royal National Rose Society in England suggest that after three years it is impossible to tell how thoroughly the soil was prepared before planting.

Planting Bare-root Roses

After preparing soil by adding compost, organic matter, sand, or other amendments, rose bushes are ready to plant.

When growing roses in groups, you need to decide how close to plant them. This encyclopedia gives the height and spread of individual roses, and the distance you choose will depend on whether you want to interplant your roses with shrubs and herbaceous plants. The trend in recent years has been to plant roses more densely, even in dedicated rose beds. Some gardeners no longer wish to see each plant separated from another by a large area of bare earth.

Before planting, cut off any spindly or broken branches and prune back the rest to approximately half their length, so that the plant does not have too much top growth for the roots to support. Dig a hole large enough to accommodate the roots of the plant comfortably and incorporate some manure, leaf mold, or fertilizer in the bottom. If the roots all point in one direction, dig a hole to fit their shape, rather than spreading them out by force. Push the soil back over the roots once the rose is planted. In the northern US, always plant budded bare-root roses so that the bud or graft union, the visible "union" where the branches meet the roots, is 2–4in (5–10cm) below ground level. In the southern US, however, and in many of the coastal areas, the bud union is planted at ground level or above ground level. Water the rose well after you have planted it and keep an eye on its water requirements during the first few months, while it is establishing itself.

If the weather or soil is unsuitable for planting when your bare-root roses arrive, it is best to "heel them in." This involves digging a shallow trench, laying out the roses, covering their roots with soil, and watering them from time to time until you are ready to transplant them into their permanent positions. Bare-root plants will always benefit from having their roots immersed in water – typically overnight – just before planting.

1 Cut back the top growth, first by removing spindly, dead, or damaged branches. Prune back all remaining branches to about half their length.

2 Dig a hole that will accommodate the rose with its roots spread out. Make it deep enough for the bud union to be 2–4in (5–10cm) below the surface.

3 Mix super phosphate or bone meal into the bottom of the hole and place the rose. Using a stick laid across the top, check the level of bud union.

4 Refill the hole with soil, making sure there are no big air pockets. Gently firm soil to leave a slight depression in the center. Water well.

Planting Container-grown Roses

Pot-grown and own-root roses should also be planted with the bud union between the stems and the roots just below surface level. Dig a hole to accommodate the pot, take out the rose and its pot-shaped root ball and place it at the bottom of the hole. Tease some of the compost off the sides of the root ball and mix in the soil you have taken from the hole, as you fill up the sides and press the rose firmly in the ground. Pot-grown roses can be planted at any time; if they are in growth, remove any open flowers.

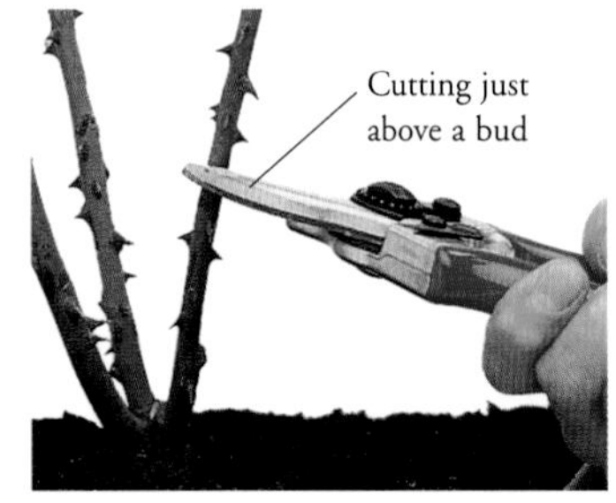

Pruning a dormant rose
Prune back a newly planted container-grown rose to within 3–6in (8–15cm) above ground level to promote a strong root system and vigorous growth in spring.

Growing in Containers

Most roses can be grown in pots like any other plant, and this is a very satisfactory way of growing patio and groundcover roses. Pot-grown roses need constant care to ensure that they receive the right amount of water and regular feeding. They also appreciate rich, free-draining compost. The best roses for containers are those that don't get too tall since strong winds can knock over badly balanced containers.

Planting and Staking Standard Roses

Plant standard roses in exactly the same way as other roses, but without burying the bud union at the base of the main stem below the ground. Check that the final soil level corresponds with the old soil mark. Firm staking is essential. The stake is normally put in place before the roots are covered with soil, at the same time as the rose is placed in its hole. Drive a strong stake into the base of the hole for about 20in (50cm), until it feels firm. It should then reach to the top of the stem, just below the top graft union. Complete the planting and tie the stem firmly to the top and middle part of the stake with rubber tree ties.

1 Drive in the wooden stake, next to the root ball, and check that it comes up to the level of the graft union at the top of the stem.

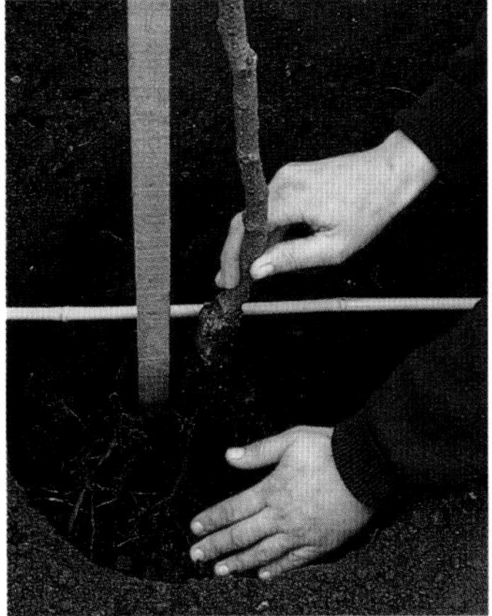

2 Plant the rose so that the earth reaches the old soil mark, and with the stake on the windward side so the rose does not lean into it in strong gusts.

3 Attach the stem firmly to the top of the stake with a rubber tree tie, just below the graft union. Secure with a second tie halfway up the stake.

Feeding and Routine Care

In open ground, roses are excellent garden shrubs and they will continue to flower even when neglected in badly maintained gardens or a wilderness. But to be at their best, roses generally respond well to feeding, pruning, training, and spraying. From time to time many roses suffer from fungal diseases, but this is more likely to happen if the plant is weakened by bad cultivation; if its needs are met, there is no reason for the disease to recur the following year.

Feeding helps roses to grow more quickly as well as making them better able to resist disease. Nutrients, whether in the form of organic manure or inorganic fertilizer, should ideally be applied just before and during the main growing season. The best way to feed roses is to scatter a rose fertilizer, available from garden centers or in larger quantities from agricultural suppliers, on the ground around the roots in spring and early summer. Mulches are very useful too, both for helping a new rose to get started and for the continued health of established roses. They help to conserve water below the ground, and to deter weeds which compete with roses for the nutrients in the soil. Organic manures, like well-rotted compost, make a good mulch, but so does woven plastic sheeting, available from garden centers

Roses do not need protection from sun and heat, but they respond well to watering by putting on new growth. Watering is therefore advisable in hot, dry climates: it prevents summer dormancy, and ensures that the plants continue to flower. Watering is also crucial for newly planted roses while they are becoming established. Soak each plant thoroughly, all around the root area, preferably in the evenings when evaporation from the soil surface is reduced.

The new growth on climbers and rambers should be tied in regularly during the summer months to prevent these roses from becoming straggly and outgrowing their space.

In cold climates, roses may need protection in winter. There are two principal ways of minimizing the risk of death or damage from winter conditions and both are laborious. One method is to wrap the plants with protective cladding: straw, leaves, and evergreen conifer branches are traditional materials, but horticultural fleece is now widely used. The other method involves earthing over the roses completely until spring.

It is always wise, and certainly less arduous, to choose roses that are suited to your climatic conditions. This encyclopedia makes it clear that there is a great choice of roses for subzero climates (for example, the Explorer roses bred in Ottawa) as well as for hot, dry conditions (such as the Gigantea hybrids bred by Alister Clark in Australia).

DETACHING SUCKERS

Budded roses sometimes throw up undesirable suckers from the rootstock below ground. Suckers are clearly distinguishable from the "true" rose stems, because the leaves and stem are different in color, size, and shape. Detach them as low down below the soil surface as possible.

Tracing the sucker
Scrape away the soil to reveal the top of the rootstock. Check that the suspect shoot arises from below the bud union.

Removing the sucker
Pull the sucker sharply away from the rootstock to deter regrowth, then refill the hole and firm the soil.

Winter protection
In very cold climates, it is usual to insulate roses against the worst of the winter weather. Straw and conifer branches are the traditional materials, but horticultural fleece is more commonly used today. In extreme conditions, roses may have to be earthed over.

Pruning Roses

THERE ARE TWO reasons for pruning rose bushes: the first is to encourage them to flower better and the second is to keep them to the size and shape that you want in your garden. You cannot underprune a rose, but you can most certainly overprune one, and more roses are killed by overly enthusiastic pruning than by anything else. Hard pruning was popular when Hybrid Teas and Hybrid Perpetuals were grown principally for exhibition. It is not suitable for garden roses. Pruners will cut through newish wood but you may need to use loppers for older, harder wood.

The natural instinct of a rose bush is to produce seed and, unless the plant is once-flowering, it will produce a new crop of flowers more quickly if it is deadheaded after the first flowering. This involves snapping or cutting off the flowers when they have died. Remove as little of the plant as possible – just the flowers, their receptacles, and their stems. Try not to cut out any leaves, since they all help to strengthen the plant for a quick reblooming. For some of the older roses, like the Portlands and the Bourbons, deadheading leads to a much improved second flowering.

Pruning Bush and Shrub Roses

Roses can be pruned and shaped at any time, though cutting them back when they are in full growth is not a good idea since it will delay flowering. It is easiest to neaten roses in winter when the plants are leafless and you can see their structures clearly. First, cut out any branches that seem to be dying back – stems that are beginning to look woody and threadbare. Then prune the rest of the bush, depending on the type of rose (see below).

The Royal National Rose Society in England has conducted extensive trials on pruning and deadheading, which disprove much traditional advice on pruning. For example, it is shown to be unnecessary to cut the stems immediately above a bud. Nor should we cut out any "blind" non-flowering shoots: they help the plant to build up its strength and produce more flowers on other stems. Indeed, the trials showed that a rough trim with hedge trimmers gave better results than "traditional" pruning.

Most shrub roses, old garden roses, and rose species need little or no pruning, and they should not be touched until they have built up their strength and structure for at least four years. Pruning should then be limited to cutting out the oldest wood, right down to ground level, to encourage newer, free flowering growth. Try not to remove more than one-third of a bush in the course of a year unless it is getting too tall for its position.

When Floribundas and Hybrid Teas are grown principally for garden display, they can be pruned in the same manner by cutting out old, dying wood and trimming back the rest of the bush by about one-third. This is enough to ensure that the bush throws up strong new wood which will bear flowers. The same applies to patio roses and miniatures.

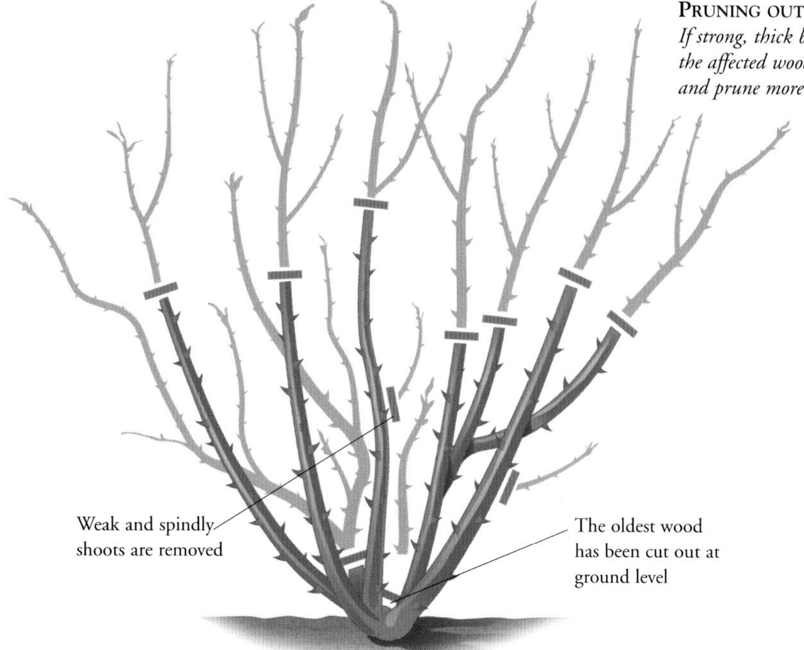
Weak and spindly shoots are removed
The oldest wood has been cut out at ground level

Pruning a shrub rose
One or two of the oldest branches should be cut out completely and the rest of the shrub pruned by about one-third overall.

Pruning out dead wood
If strong, thick branches die back, cut out the affected wood, feed the plants well, and prune more lightly in future.

Deadheading

Deadheading means picking off the faded flowers. This is useful in repeat flowering roses, to speed up the arrival of the next flowers and prevent the plant from producing hips. It is especially effective with Hybrid Teas. Floribundas (above) may be deadheaded if the leading flower, as it fades, appears unsightly and spoils the look of the cluster.

Using Hedgetrimmers to Prune Roses
The fastest effective way of pruning roses is to use electric hedgetrimmers, though some people consider the result unsightly. Hybrid Teas and Floribundas are cut straight to the desired height; older roses are best cut to a more rounded form.

Pruning and Training Climbers and Ramblers

The same pruning principles apply to ramblers and climbers as to all other roses. The traditional advice was to cut the long branches of old ramblers down to the ground after they had borne the current year's flowers. This is an unnecessary chore, since these long wands will, in any case, flower again next year, though less freely than the newer growth. The best advice is to wait until winter, then cut out any wood that is seen to be dying back or growing where it is not welcome. If the ramblers are trained to a support, this is also a good time to tie them in.

Climbers take longer to develop a permanent framework than ramblers. Pruning should involve no more than the periodical removal of any stems that are dying back or exceeding the climber's bounds. The received wisdom is that one should encourage new growth to sprout low down on the plant, but there is no sure way of doing this without pruning the whole plant very severely, which is just as likely to kill it off. Many climbers in fact flower very well for years on end with no pruning at all. When you resume pruning, you may want to cut them back slightly harder, in order to encourage them to regenerate.

Most climbing roses need some type of support and this can take the form of poles, pyramids, obelisks, and trees, as well as fan training against walls and fences. Flat, vertical surfaces such as walls will need to be provided with wires spaced about 18in (45cm) apart and secured to the wall with vine eyes. Using soft garden twine, tie in the flexible new shoots as close to horizontal as possible in order to encourage flowering on the new side shoots. With upright structures such as poles and obelisks, tie in the shoots at intervals. Check all supports from time to time and replace any ties that have broken or frayed. Where ramblers have been encouraged to grow into trees, they will do this freely, without being tied in.

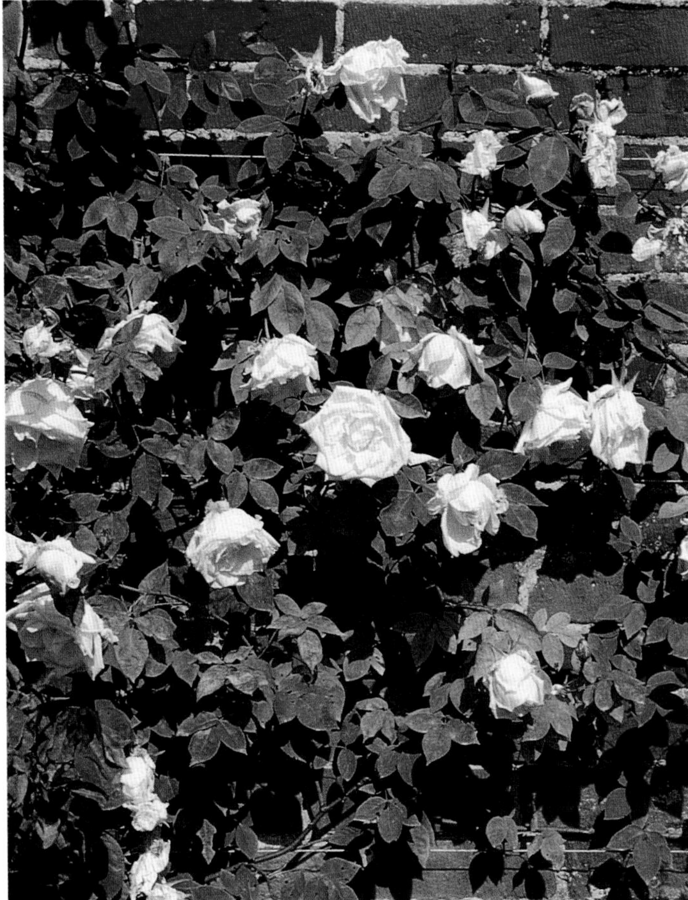

Covering a Wall
Ramblers and climbing roses should be tied in to a framework of horizontal wires attached to walls and fences. This will encourage them to grow sideways to cover the entire area. After that, simply tip back the main shoots when they extend too far.

Training Climbing Roses
Space out the main stems, train them sideways, and then prune roses grown against a wall or fence in order to maximize the display of flowers.

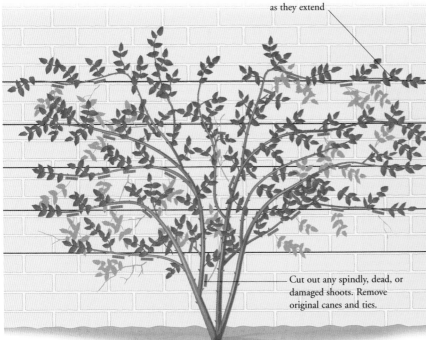

Tie in new growth to build a framework, training shoots so they will grow sideways; tie them to wires as they extend

Cut out any spindly, dead, or damaged shoots. Remove original canes and ties.

Cutting Out Diseased Growth
The periodical removal of dead, diseased, and twiggy growth will encourage climbers and ramblers to send up strong, healthy stems from below ground level.

Tying In
On walls and fences, when the new growth is green and can be easily bent, tie in the main shoots as close to horizontal as possible to metal wires.

PROPAGATING ROSES

ALL PLANT PROPAGATION is a race between decomposition and the healthy establishment of a new young plant, so hygiene is all-important. The easist way for amateurs to propagate roses is by cuttings. Almost every variety will root easily and quickly. If you trim rose prunings in autumn and stick them in the ground, some offcuts will even form roots and develop into new plants. The success rate with Multiflora ramblers is almost 100 percent.

There are two main types of cutting: hardwood and semiripe, or softwood. Shrub, Floribunda, rambler, and climbing roses can be propagated from hardwood cuttings. Semiripe cuttings are successful with Hybrid Perpetuals, Hybrid Teas, Bourbons, and China roses, although there is a risk that these may fail to make enough woody growth in their first few months to carry them safely through the first winter. The solution is to keep them somewhat dry in winter and delay potting until spring.

It is easy to raise roses from seed, but only the wild rose species will come true. Hybrids will never turn identical to their parents and therefore must be propagated by other means.

Taking Hardwood Cuttings

Many types of rose can be grown from hardwood cuttings. These usually root easily and the resulting plants grow on their own roots, so there will be no problem with suckers. Take the cuttings outside in late autumn and early winter. The ideal conditions are a light, warm soil and a sheltered site. Choose ripe wood, preferably from a strong sideshoot with a woody base, that will not rot. The best cuttings have several dormant buds near the base, which are rich in auxins, the hormones that promote rooting. Rooting hormone powder, available from garden centers, is an optional extra, which may help difficult varieties to root faster.

Trim the cuttings with pruners, discarding the soft growth at the tip. Their length will depend on the variety: 3in (7cm) is long enough for a miniature but the cuttings may be as long as 14in (35cm) for a lanky grower like 'William Lobb'. If they have leaves, retain them.

Cuttings need air and water in order to root well. Insert them into the soil to roughly half their length. This is just enough to ensure that they are firmly anchored and do not rock in the wind, so that the new roots are not broken off. Placing them at a slight angle helps to make the cuttings more secure. Replace the soil and tread it firmly round the cuttings, then water thoroughly. In dry climates, continue to keep the cuttings well watered.

You can usually tell by the spring whether a cutting has taken, if it looks green and is starting to grow leaves. By summer, there should be signs of strong new growth breaking from one or more of the axillary buds hidden below ground level. If they look strong and healthy, the cuttings should be ready to transplant by the autumn, so dig them up carefully and move them to their permanent positions. Some may need another year in which to establish themselves.

1 Take your cuttings in autumn when the soil is warm but moist and the weather is not too dry. Choose wood that has been produced during the course of the year and is well-ripened.

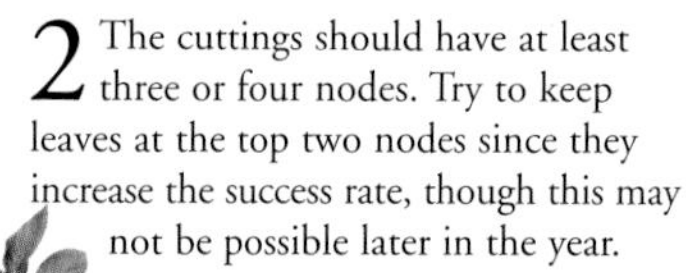

2 The cuttings should have at least three or four nodes. Try to keep leaves at the top two nodes since they increase the success rate, though this may not be possible later in the year.

3 Insert the cuttings vertically into the soil so that they are held firmly and will not be blown out by the wind. Long cuttings can be inserted at an angle of up to 45 degrees. Water well.

4 Most cuttings, especially those of vigorous roses like ramblers, can be dug up and transplanted into their new positions 12 months later. Some may need up to another year, however.

Dividing Roses

Some roses produce useful suckers – and not just from their understocks. When you pull them up, you will find that they are attached by long stoloniferous roots that run just below the soil surface. If you chop off one of the suckers with a piece of root attached and replant it elsewhere, it will grow into a new plant.

Sometimes the whole bush forms a close thicket of stems. Gallicas roses and Scotch roses are good examples of thicket-forming shrubs. These can be divided in winter in the same way as herbaceous plants. Simply dig up the whole plant and cut off about two-thirds of the top growth to ensure that the roots of the new plants are not put under strain by too much leaf and flower in the first year. Use a pair of pruners to separate out the tangle of roots and branches. Each small part can then be replanted.

This technique can only be used on roses which are grown on their own roots and is of no use to grafted plants. It is a good way of building up a large stock to create a hedge.

DIVIDING A ROSE
A thicket of own-root roses can be pulled apart, divided into smaller pieces, and replanted. Each division will form an entirely new plant.

Taking Softwood Cuttings

Softwood cuttings can be taken at any time of year from early spring onward. A good time is shortly after the plants have had their first flowering. Choose material with a number of closely spaced axillary buds near the base. These will break to form new growth from beneath the soil surface and help the cutting to develop into a sturdy, well-shaped bush. Always include at least one leaf; you may need to trim off some of the leaflets if the leaf is so big that it makes the cutting unstable when inserted into the compost.

Place cuttings in a propagating frame – a mist unit or closed frame with a soil-warming cable – or cover each pot with a plastic bag, snipping a corner to let in more air once rooted.

1 Choose young wood, but not too sappy or it will rot off easily. Trim just below a leaf joint, where the harder wood is rich in root-promoting auxins.

2 Using a sharp knife, cut off the softest growth at the top so that the finished cutting has a firm base and a pair of leaves at the top.

3 Dip the base in a rooting hormone powder containing fungicide to stop the stem from rotting. Place in well-drained sterile compost and water.

4 Cover the pot with a plastic bag and place in a warm, semishaded position, like a windowsill, which receives little or no direct sunlight.

Raising Roses from Seed

Seed is by far the best way to raise large quantities of species roses for hedging or as rootstocks. All need a period of chilling before they will germinate, but some alpine species like *Rosa glauca* need at least two years outside, exposed to all the elements, before they will germinate.

It is best to take the seeds out of their fleshy hips before sowing them, and to cover pots or trays with wire mesh to deter rodents. Leave the pots outside throughout the winter for the rain and cold to break down the natural dormancy of the seeds, then bring them into a cool greenhouse or unheated indoor room when you see the first seedlings germinate.

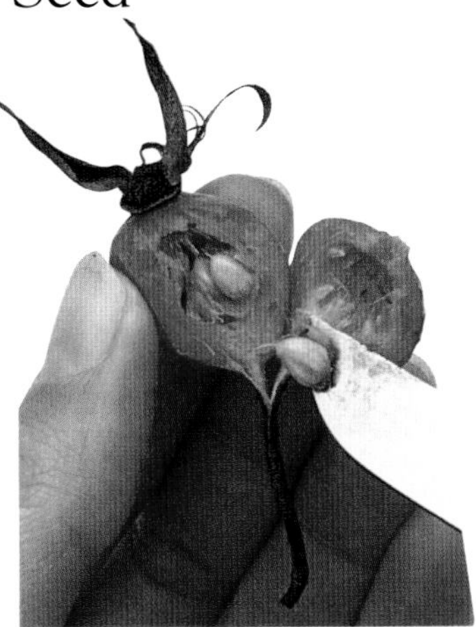

1 The seeds of most roses are hard white pits inside the fleshy hips. Extract them in autumn, in readiness for sowing, and discard the hips.

2 Sow seeds in a sterile, free-draining compost, and cover lightly with gravel or an inert preparation to prevent them from being washed out by rain.

3 Pot up seedlings individually when the first leaves appear in spring. Those sown in individual cells can be grown until taller to transplant better.

Other Methods of Propagation

Some other forms of propagating, like budding and micropropagation, are principally for commercial producers. Budding remains the nurseryman's preferred means of propagating roses, because only one eye is needed for a new plant. Other uses include new hybrids that can be bulked up quickly for trial and rampant suckering roses like the Scotch roses can be prevented from spreading.

This delicate operation joins a bud from a chosen variety onto the root system (rootstock) of a wild rose, which ensures vigorous growth. The technique requires a lot of skill, however, and the best way to learn about budding is to watch a professional budder at work.

Micropropagation, by contrast, requires a considerable understanding of biochemistry and is not a practical proposition for amateurs.

Alternative amateur methods of propagating roses include root cuttings, which are most practicable for old roses like Gallicas which spread around on their own roots. Layering branches is another option for climbers, ramblers, and shrub roses in cool climates, while air layering is a possibility in humid tropical countries.

Any rose with flexible enough stems can be layered in autumn. Choose a strong branch that can be bent easily to meet the ground, and make a horizontal cut in its underside to produce a 4in (10cm) "tongue" of stem. Wedge this cut open with a sturdy twig and place the cut section into forked-over soil a little way from the parent rose. Hold it down with bent wire or a stone, then cover with a mound of soil. Tie the tip of the stem to an upright cane and water the whole area, then leave in place for about 12 months.

The following autumn, check that the layer has rooted, then sever it carefully from the parent plant and transplant it into its new home.

Keeping Roses Healthy

All plants are susceptible to pests and diseases, and roses are no exception. Good cultivation is the best way to prevent or deal with them. Insects which prey on roses differ from country to country but include aphids, thrips, saw-flies, and rose-beetle.

The three principal diseases to affect roses are blackspot, rust, and mildew. These fungal infections are unsightly, but they never kill a well-established plant. Their virulence differs from place to place, season to season, and year to year. Blackspot, for example, is rare in hot, dry climates. A plant may be covered in mildew one year because it is weakened by bad cultivation, but it will not suffer the following year if its needs are properly met.

If disease is a problem in your area, choose roses that are not notably susceptible. This encyclopedia draws attention to especially healthy roses. Modern breeders recognize the importance of disease-resistance and rose specialists, nurserymen, and knowledgeable gardeners can tell you what does well for them. Rose societies, organic institutes, and horticultural organizations often conduct trials and research, and publish their findings.

Taking Preventative Measures

Insects and fungal diseases can be discouraged by preventative sprays. There is a wide choice of natural, chemical, and nonresidual remedies. The trend toward minimum use of chemicals is well established, though you can rest assured that any substance approved by a national government for retail use will have undergone rigid safety tests before being authorized.

If you wish to use approved chemicals, there are two golden rules. First, choose a systemic chemical one that will prevent infection; second, apply it as early in the season as you can. Prevention is always better than cure. Recent trials by the Royal National Rose Society in England have shown that a preventative spray applied in late winter, when the dormant leaf buds are just starting to expand, followed by another spray one month later, will increase chances of protection from fungal infection. If you need to spray during the flowering season, do it in the evening when the bees will have returned to their hives.

In general, you should not spray if the weather is sunny or windy, and the leaves must be dry. Use a trigger sprayer for a minor problem, or a compression sprayer for a larger area, and spray the top and underside of the foliage thoroughly until the liquid runs off the leaves.

Roses rarely suffer long-term damage, and natural controls (such as birds and other insects) tend to keep infestations under control. Predators are now available commercially to control particular pests like spider mite. To reduce the incidence of disease, always keep your garden free of debris and remove dead leaves that may harbor disease.

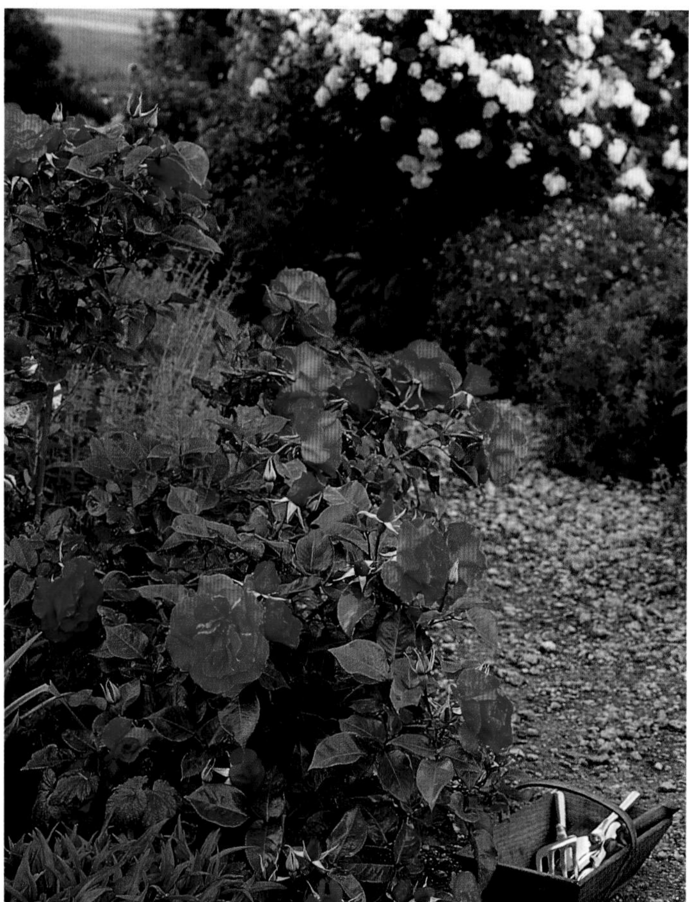

Thriving in the garden
A well-grown rose plant – one that is adequately fed, well-watered, and lightly pruned – will be more resistant to diseases and pests than one which is under stress.

Roses and Disease Resistance

No garden plant is entirely free from the danger of infection by such organisms as fungi and bacteria. Roses are no exception, but some roses are more susceptible than others to the classic ills of blackspot, mildew, and rust. It is impossible to draw up a list of "disease-resistant roses" because the nature and severity of disease varies enormously according to the climate. Many superhealthy roses bred for hardiness in Canada succumb to mildew and blackspot in warmer, humid climates, while blackspot is virtually unknown in dry climates.

The encyclopedia's A–Z section indicates which individual roses have a reputation for good health in a variety of conditions. The best way to choose healthy roses for your area is to seek and follow local advice. Modern roses are generally healthier than old ones, though diseases may be less disfiguring on older cultivars.

Schneeflocke
Also known as White Flower Carpet, *this is one of the most disease-resistant of the modern ground-cover roses.*

'American Beauty'
This crimson Hybrid Perpetual rose is notoriously susceptible to blackspot, mildew, and rust.

Dealing with Pests and Diseases

Rose growers need to know how to recognize the main pests and diseases, how to minimize damage, and where to get advice. Prevention is always better than cure, and there is a range of traditional organic and chemical options available to gardeners. Good cultivation, including feeding and manuring, helps to build up healthy disease-resistance.

Aphids

Aphids – often known as greenfly – are small insects that suck the sap of tender plant growth. They are often seen clustering on young, unopened rosebuds, but even more commonly on the undersides of young leaves. Their activity never kills established rose bushes but often distorts the buds and leaves they feed upon. Aphids also excrete honeydew, which attracts an unsightly black fungus called sooty mold. If undetected, they quickly form large colonies and may cause damage to young plants. Small infestations can be removed manually. There are many antiaphid preparations available to gardeners, usually in the form of sprays. These include contact insecticides and modern systemic aphicides.

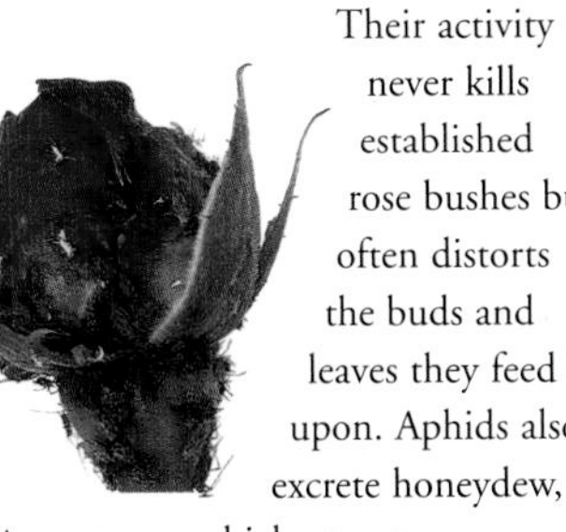

APHIDS

Blackspot

Blackspot (*Diplocarpon rosae*) is a well-known fungal disease of roses. It is not a serious problem in dry climates, but almost ubiquitous in warm, damp conditions. It shows up literally as black spots in the rose leaves, which then turn yellow before the leaves drop off. Severe infections may defoliate the plant completely. Blackspot also infests other parts of the plant and overwinters on the stems, which makes it difficult to prevent new infections next year. The spores are carried in the wind and germinate in wet weather. Blackspot weakens an established rose plant, and it has been known to kill a young one outright. Some roses are more susceptible than others – ask your local supplier for advice before you buy – but healthy plants in an active state of growth are always less vulnerable. Prevention is infinitely better than cure: most commercial growers use systemic sprays as soon as the first leaves appear.

BLACKSPOT

Mildew

The word "mildew" covers two distinct diseases. "Downy" mildew (*Peronospora sparsa*) is characterized by brown-gray pustules on the undersides of the rose leaves. It can be a serious pest of cut-flower roses grown under glass, but occurs less in gardens. "Powdery" mildew (*Sphaerotheca pannosa* var. *rosa*) is a more common disorder, easily identified by the way it covers young growth with its white mycelium. Older leaves are generally resistant to mildew, but young growth, including the buds and pedicels, may become distorted and stunted. The disease is spread by spores in the wind. Its development is encouraged by dryness at the plant's roots, poor air circulation, and cool, wet weather. Climbing roses growing against walls are particularly susceptible to mildew. The disease spreads fast and is unattractive, but fortunately, it is rarely fatal. Fungicidal spays are the usual remedy, but prevention is better still.

Rose Balling

Balling is an old and perplexing problem for rose lovers. It is not as common as mildew or blackspot, but it affects the flowers directly. It is caused by a form of *Botrytis cinerea*, which is not usually a serious pest of roses but does develop in cool, damp conditions. Most gardeners are unaware of its presence until the damage is done. Balling affects the flowers as they prepare to open, and shows as an invisible covering of mycelium that sticks the surface of the petals together. The bud appears ready to open, but fails to expand and eventually rots off and drops. Sometimes it is possible to break open the bud by gentle massaging – usually only the outer petals are infected – otherwise the only hope is better weather. Balling affects roses with many, thin petals, especially some of the older roses ('Impératrice Joséphine' and 'Perle von Weissenstein' are notorious examples) and hybrids of *Rosa spinosissima* and *R. rugosa*. Most modern roses have thick, sturdy petals and are less troubled by balling.

ROSE BALLING

Rust

Rust is another serious fungal infection of roses, and the only one where there is a serious danger that the plant may die. Bright orange pustules erupt on both sides of the leaves, and spread to other parts of a bush. It travels most virulently in cool, damp climates. The disease is caused by species of *Phragmidium*, most notably *P. tuberculatum*, one of thousands of rusts which affect the entire plant world. Rose rust is hard to eradicate because it overwinters as spores on fallen leaves, in soil, and on other plants. Fresh infection will be introduced by spores carried in the wind. Chemical control offers the only effective prevention and most large-scale rose nurseries spray with a systemic fungicide early in the season.

However, some cultivars are much more susceptible to rust than others; most vulnerable are some of the older Rugosa hybrids like 'Conrad Ferdinand Meyer'.

Thrips

A multitude of tiny insects go by the name of "thrips." Several species feed on rose flowers, both as winged adults and as larvae, but roses are only one of their hosts. The adult thrips are carried on the wind and seem especially attracted to pale roses – white, yellow, and pink. The larvae dig deep into the bud and eat the tissues of the petals. As the flowers expand, they are seen to be damaged and deformed, with brown edges to the petals. Control is a problem and natural predators are rarely enough to control thrips. Insecticides may help, and many thrips are killed in the process of treating roses for other insects, like aphids. Thrips have a short life cycle, which is shortest in hot weather. They are a particular nuisance for rose lovers in North America and Australia.

MILDEW

RUST

THRIPS

GLOSSARY

Italicized words have their own entry.

Agatha rose A group of roses bred 1760–1830 which are sometimes included among the Gallica roses.

Aggregate species A group of closely related species that are so similar in their botanical characteristics that they may all be grouped together as one species.

Anther The pollen-bearing tip of the stamen.

Attar of roses A scent distilled from rose petals.

Axil The angle between a leaf and a stem where an axillary bud develops.

Ayrshire roses Hybrids of *Rosa arvensis* that generally make useful groundcover plants and are also good for growing up into the branches of trees.

Balled Of a flower that does not open properly and rots when still in bud (*see* p.443).

Bare-root Of plants sold with their roots bare of soil.

Bedding rose A rose whose principal use is as a colorful garden plant, often planted in large numbers for effect.

Bicolored Of a flower that has two different shades of color, often sharply contrasting.

Blackspot Disease affecting leaves and stems of roses (*see* p.443).

Boss The cluster of stamens at the flower center.

Boursault rose A small race of early-flowering, hardy, thornless roses, mostly climbers, first bred by a Frenchman named Boursault in about 1820.

Bract A leaf that looks like a green petal and serves to protect the opening bud – not to be confused with a *sepal.*

Buds of classical shape There are several classical shapes among roses; perhaps the best-known is the elegant conical shape of an opening Hybrid Tea.

Button eye/center Some roses, especially the older cultivars, have a circle of petals at the center, turned over and raised up like an old button.

Carpel A *pistil*, the female part of a flower.

Compacta rose A small group of Polyantha roses bred by de Ruiter in the 1950s.

Corymb The arrangement of flowers in a loose cluster of flowers typical of roses.

Cultivar A "cultivated variety" of a plant arising or maintained in cultivation. Many popular roses are cultivars, for example *Rosa* 'New Dawn', and their name is shown thus in single quotes.

Deadheading The process of removing spent flowers.

Diploid Diploid plants have two sets of chromosomes.

Disbudding Removing unopened flower buds; a technique employed to ensure that the remaining buds open up into larger than normal flowers.

Double Of a flower that has many rows of petals. Double rose flowers are divided into three categories: semidouble (10–20 petals), double (20–40 petals), and very double (over 40 petals).

Dooryard roses A term used by American rosarians in the early 20th century to describe their ideal of hardy, healthy, free-flowering roses for American gardens.

English Rose The name used to describe those roses bred by David Austin that combine the best qualities of old roses and modern ones, i.e., scent, floral beauty, vigor, and repeat-flowering.

Explorer rose A series of superhardy roses, bred by the Canadian Department of Agriculture to survive the worst Canadian winters.

Exserted stigma When the *stigma* of a rose sticks out and projects from the center of the flower, it is said to be exserted.

Filament The lower part, or stalk, of a stamen, which joins it to and supports the anther.

Foliolate Resembling a leaf.

Frühlings rose A series of shrub roses bred by Wilhelm Kordes in the 1930s and 1940s by crossing *Rosa* 'Altaica' with various Hybrid Teas.

Fully double Very full of petals.

Glaucous Blue green, blue gray, or white with a bluish, grayish, or whitish bloom.

Groundcover Usually low-growing plants that quickly cover the soil surface and suppress weeds.

Guard petals Outer petals.

Habit The characteristic growth or general appearance of a plant.

Hardwood cutting A method of propagation in which a cutting is taken from ripe wood that feels firm to the touch (*see* p.440).

Heritage roses Older roses – those bred before about 1914 – are sometimes referred to as Heritage (or Historic) Roses

High-centered buds Long, conical-shaped buds, typically associated with Hybrid Teas.

Hip The fruit of the rose, which is large and decorative in some varieties.

Imbricated Of petals that are neatly overlapping.

Incurved Applied to petals and florets that curve inward to form a compact, rounded shape.

Internode The section of stem between two *nodes*.

Leaflet What many people think of as a rose leaf is actually a leaflet, or a subdivision of the compound leaf. Rose leaves are pinnate, with pairs of leaflets along a central leaf-blade and a single leaflet at the end.

Node The point at which a leaf or sideshoot joins a stem

Pedicel A flower stalk.

Petalage The number or arrangement of petals in a flower.

Petaloid Resembling a petal.

Pistil The female part of the flower consisting of *stigma*, *style*, and ovary.

Powdery mildew A disease affecting roses (*see* p.443).

Quartered Of flowers, especially those of old rose cultivars, that are roughly divided into quarters when they open out.

Rambler A vigorous climbing rose with a loose, lax arrangement of stems.

Receptacle The part of a rose between its *sepals* and its *pedicel*. Later it turns into a *hip*.

Recurrent Repeat flowering.

Reflexed Of petals whose edges are turned back away from the center of the flower.

Remontant Flowering more than once in successive bursts.

Reverse The side of the petal that faces away from the center.

Revert To return to normal, such as when a sport starts to produce the same growth as its parent.

Romantica rose A series of roses bred and introduced since the mid-1980s by Meilland in France, and combining (like *English Roses*) the best qualities of old roses and modern ones.

Rosette A flower shape characterized by radiating circles of petals.

Seedling A plant grown from seed; the offspring of a named variety.

Sepal The five, green, petallike parts of a rose that enclose a bud.

Single A rose flower with no more than five petals.

Sport A mutation, caused by an induced or spontaneous genetic change, which may produce shoots with different characteristics, or flowers of a different color from the parent plant.

Stamen The male part of a flower, consisting of a stalk (*filament*) and the pollen-bearing part (*anther*).

Standard A standard rose is formed by grafting a desirable cultivar, which forms the head, on a tall stem. A rambler forms the head of a weeping standard.

Stigma The tip of a *pistil*, which receives the pollen when a flower is fertilized.

Style The central part of a *pistil*, between the *stigma* and the ovary.

Sucker A shoot arising from the roots of a rose.

Tetraploid Tetraploid plants have four sets of chromosomes.

Triploid Triploid plants have three sets of chromosomes. Triploid roses tend not to produce seed.

Truss A compact cluster of fruits or flowers, often large and showy.

Weeping Of roses whose branches or branchlets assume a pendulous habit of growth, such as ramblers with a loose, lax habit that are grafted high on a standard stem.

Wichurana-type Of leaves or foliage that are distinctively hard, dark, healthy, glossy, as are those of *Rosa wichurana* and its descendants.

Index to Species

The names of rose species have undergone a number of changes over the years and this index is included to facilitate use of the encyclopedia. See also the notes on nomenclature on p.4.

Rose Societies Around the World

Australia
The National Rose Society of Australia
29 Columbia Crescent
Modbury North, SA 5092
Tel: (61) 8 8264 0084

Austria
Österreichische Rosenfreunde in der
Österreichischen Gartenbau-Gesellschaft
Parkring 12, A-1010 Vienna
Tel: (43) 1 512 84 16
Fax: (43) 1 512 84 16/17

Belgium
Société Royale Nationale "Les Amis de la Rose"/
Koninklijke Nationale Maat Schappij
"De Vrienden van de Roos"
Korte Aststraat 12, B-9750 Huise Zingem
Fax: (32) (0)9 384 83 39

Canada
The Canadian Rose Society
3272 Valmarie Drive, Mississauga,
Ontario L5C 2A8
Tel: (1) 905 275 7089
Email: crs@mirror.org
www.mirror.org/groups/crs/

Czech Republic
Czech Rosa Club
Ceskomalínská 17
160 00 Praha 6
Tel: (420) 221 624 508
Email: josef.thomas@sujb.cz
www.zahradkari.cz/czs/szo/rosaklub

Denmark
Det Danske Rosenselskab (DDRS)
Kirkedalsvej 63, Raarup,
DK-7130 Juelsminde
Tel: (45) 7568 5232
Fax: (45) 7569 5746
Email: post@rosenselskabet.dk
www.rosenselskabet.dk

Finland
Suomen Ruususeura r.y. -
Finska Rosensällskapet r.f.
Mynttiläntie 18,
02780 Espoo
Tel: (358) 9 811053 or (358) 40 5336339
Email: tuuli.lahdentausta@lyocentre-nordic.fi
www.puutarha.net/ruususeura

France
Société Française des Roses "Les Amis des Roses"
Roseraie du Parc de la Tête d'Or
F-69459 Lyon Cédex 06
Tel: (33) (0) 474 94 04 36
Fax: (33) (0) 474 95 54 16

Germany
Verein Deutscher Rosenfreunde
Waldseestrasse 14
D-76530 Baden-Baden
Tel: (49) 7221/31302
Fax: (49) 7221/38337
Email: info@rosenfreunde.de
www.rosenfreunde.de

Greece
The Hellenic Rose Society
Akti Miaouli 93
Piraeus 185-38
Tel: (30) 210-4290620-5
Fax: (30) 210-4290375
Email: damianou@otenet.gr

Italy
Associazione Italiana della Rosa (AIR)
Roseto "Niso Fumagalli"
Villa Reale, 20052 Monza (MI)
Tel: (39) 039-320-994
Fax: (39) 039-2086-237
Email: info@airosa.it
www.airosa.it

Netherlands
De Nederlandse Rozenvereniging
Hofstad 2, 5298 AP, Liempde
Tel: (31) 0345-558465
Email: info@rozenvereniging.nl
www.rozenvereniging.nl

Norway
The Norwegian Rose Society (NRS)
Storgata 12
N-3484 Holmsbu
Tel: (47) 32 79 88 50
Email: leonardl@online.no

New Zealand
The National Rose Society
of New Zealand Inc.
P. O. Box 66,
Bunnythorpe
Tel/fax: (64) 63 292 700
www.nzroses.org.nz

Northern Ireland
The Rose Society of Northern Ireland
15 Carnduff Road, Larne,
Co. Antrim BT40 3NJ
Tel: (44) 028 2827 2658
Email: info@rosemerald.co.uk
www.rosemerald.co.uk

South Africa
The Federation of Rose Societies
of South Africa (ROSA)
P. O. Box 28188, 0132 Sunnyside,
Pretoria
Tel: (27) 12 544 0144
Fax: (27) 12 544 0813
Email: ROSA@ludwigsroses.co.za
www.ludwigsroses.co.za

Roses on the Worldwide Web

www.ars.org
The site of the American Rose Society, which is dedicated to the enjoyment, enhancement, and promotion of the rose. The site, and those of its affiliate local societies, provide a wealth of technical literature and inspirational photography of roses and gardens.

www.rose.org
The All-America Rose Selections web site. The AARS is a nonprofit association, founded in 1938, of rose growers and introducers dedicated to the introduction and promotion of exceptional roses. The AARS awards recognize outstanding new rose varieties that have withstood the test of time.

www.rhs.org.uk
The site of the UK's Royal Horticultural Society offers advice and inspiration on all aspects of gardening and horticulture as well as access to a large database of plant and gardening information.

www.helpmefind.com/rose
A web site devoted to roses and all that is rose related, including selecting, buying, caring for, and exhibiting roses. The site features lists of roses, show results, suppliers, gardens, organizations, books, events, and a comprehensive glossary.

www.worldrose.org
The web site of the World Federation of Rose Societies, an association of the national rose societies of 36 countries around the world, representing more than 100,000 rose lovers. The federation's goal is to expand contact among their member societies and increase the flow of knowledge about the rose.

www.rosarian.com
A site for gardeners who grow roses, offering a compendium of the various resources at GardenWeb related to roses, such as forums, frequently asked questions about roses, and articles on roses in literature and art.

Spain
Asociación Española de la Rosa
Oficina Técnica del Plan Verde
Av. Primado Reig, 70, 46010 Valencia
Tel: (34) 96 362 92 66
Fax: (34) 96 362 20 51

Sweden
Svenska Rosensällskapet
Bomullsgången 15
S 611 37 Nyköping
Fax: (46) 155 21 64 29
Email: srs@svenskarosensallskapet.org
www.svenskarosensallskapet.org

Switzerland
Gesellschaft Schweizerischer
Rosenfreunde (GSRF)
Bahnhofstr. 11
CH-8640 Rapperswil
Tel: (41) 055/210 24 09
www.rosenfreunde.ch

United Kingdom
The Royal National Rose Society
The Gardens of the Rose
Chiswell Green, St. Albans,
Hertfordshire AL2 3NR
Tel: (44) 1727 850461
Fax: (44) 1727 850360
Email: helpline@rosesociety.org.uk
www.rosesociety.org.uk

United States of America
The American Rose Society
P. O. Box 30,000, Shreveport,
Louisiana 71130-0030
Tel: (1) (318) 938-5402
Fax: (1) (318) 938-5405
Email: ars@ars-hq.org
www.ars.org

General Index

Acknowledgments

The authors would like to thank the following friends and acquaintances for the help they have given us in the course of writing this book:

David Austin Jr., Beatrice Barni, Christopher Blair, Helle Brumme, Tom Carruth, Derek Coombes, Paul David, Coen Decoster, Guy Delbard, Brent Elliott, André Eve, Barry Futter, Bill Grant, Lee Griffiths, Peter Harkness, Lita Johansen, Ian Kennedy of BARB, Anna Kruger, David Lamb, Mandy Lebentz, Barbara Levy, Tony Lord, Clair Martin, Michael Marriott, Jacques Mouchotte, Trevor Nottle, Elena Pizzi, Chris Reid, Madeline Quest-Ritson, Martyn Rix, Peter Schneider, David Stone, Barbara Tchertoff, Erich Unmuth, Ghislain d'Ursel, Rudy Velle, William Waterfield, James Young, Maryly Young, and Keith Zary.

We would particularly like to thank the following garden owners, many of them also friends of ours, in whose gardens some of the photographs in this book were taken: Marylyn Abbott, David Austin, Peter Beales, Walter Branchi, Maria Chaworth-Musters, Walter Duncan, André Eve, Gianfranco Fineschi, Maurice & Rosemary Foster, François Joyaux, Raymond & Thérèse Loubert, Gregg Lowery, Keith & Margaret Marshall, Clair Martin, Georges & Odile Masquelier, Jon Nieuwesteeg, Martin & Victoria Nye, Roger & Nicky Phillips, Martyn & Alison Rix, Henry & Susie Robinson, Ruth Rundle and Barbara & Philip Stockitt. We owe a special debt to The National Trust, The National Trust for Scotland, The Royal Horticultural Society, and The Royal National Rose Society for their fine gardens and their skilful cultivation of roses.

In addition we would like to thank the owners of the following nurseries and gardens, in which many more of our photographs were taken. Argentina: El Rosedal, Buenos Aires. Australia: Adelaide Botanic Garden; Brundrett's Nursery; Carrick Hill; Château Barrosa; Mount Lofty Botanic Garden; Ross Roses; Ruston's Nursery; Urrbrae; Werribee Park. Austria: Park Weikersdorf, Baden bei Wien. Belgium: Park Coloma, Sint-Pieters-Leeuw. Germany: Gönneranlage, Baden-Baden; Insel Mainau; W. Kordes & Söhne, Sparrieshoop; Europa-Rosarium, Sangerhausen; Rosarium Uetersen; Westfalenpark, Dortmund; Europas Rosengarten, Zweibrücken. Denmark: Rosenpark Gerlev. France: Jardins de Bagatelle, Paris; Jardin des Roses, Doué; Les Chemins de la Rose, Doué; Roseraie Départmentale du Val-de-Marne, L'Haÿ-les-Roses; Jardin Verger Delbard, Malicorne; Meilland Richardier, Le Luc; Parc Floral, Olivet; Parc de la Tête d'Or, Lyon; Roseraie de Saverne; United Kingdom: Queen Mary's Rose Garden, Regent's Park. Italy: La Landriana, Torsanlorenzo; Villa Hanbury, La Mortola; I Giardini di Ninfa; Rose Barni, Pistoia; Roseto di Firenze. United States: Balboa Park, San Diego; Berkeley Rose Garden; Descanso Gardens, La Cañada; Flower Fields, Carlsbad; Huntington Botanical Gardens, San Marino; Quarry Hill Botanical Garden, Sonoma; Rose Hills Memorial Park, Whittier; San José Heritage Rose Garden; Mission Gardens, Santa Barbara.

General index Hilary Bird
Illustrations (pp.436–7) John Woodcock
Proofreading Patsy North, Helen Ridge
Additional photography (pp.434–441) Peter Anderson
Picture research Celia Dearing, Franzisca Marking
Picture librarian Lucy Claxton

Picture Credits

All photographs have been supplied by the author unless otherwise stated. The publisher would like to thank the following for their kind permission to reproduce their photographs:
(Abbreviations key: t=top, b=bottom, r=right, l=left, c=centre)

1: Steve Wooster; **2**: Flowerphotos/Carol Sharp; **3**: Steve Wooster; **6–7**: Flowerphotos/Dave Tully; **8**: Lindley Library; **9**: Bridgeman Art Library, London/New York/Noortman (London) Ltd (br); **10**: Bridgeman Art Library, London /New York/Chateau de Malmaison, Paris; **11**: Bridgeman Art Library, London /New York/Agnew & Sons, UK Ltd; **13**: John Glover (b); **16–17**: Flowerphotos/Carol Sharp; **20**: Garden World Images (tr); **20**: Photos Horticultural (br); **20**: RoseExpert (bc); **24**: RoseExpert (tcl); **25**: RoseExpert (tl); **26**: Garden Picture Library/ Christi Carter (bc); **29**: Holt Studios International/ M.Szadzuik/R.Zinck (tr); **29**: Weeks Roses (trb); **32**: RoseExpert (tr); **36**: Roger's Plants Ltd/Bill Grant (br); **40**: Armstrong Garden Centers (br); **45**: Andrew Lawson (tl); **47**: Garden World Images (tl, tr); **51**: Photos Horticultural (crb); **59**: Photos Horticultural (tc); **61**: Jerry Pavia Photography Inc.(tl); **61**:Treloar Roses/Tracey Treloar (bc); **62–63**: Steve Wooster; **64**: Andrew Lawson (tc); **64**: RoseExpert (br); **67**: RoseExpert (tc); **74**: Courtesy Mary Eileen Buck (br); **75**: Garden Picture Library/David Cavagnaro (bc); 77: RoseExpert (br); **87**: Garden World Images (br); **88**: A–Z Botanical Collection (tr); **94**: Photos Horticultural (tr); **105**: Garden World Images (br); **106**: Garden World Images (tl); **108–109**: Steve Wooster; **112**: Garden World Images (br); **115**: Garden Picture Library/Howard Rice (br); **116**: Studio Valois, Paris (bl); **118**: Garden Picture Library/David Cavagnaro (tr); **120**: Steven's Studios, Newtownards (cr); **121**: Jerry Pavia Photography Inc. (tc); **122**: Photographer unknown (bl); **138**: Photos Horticultural (bl); **143**: Garden Picture Library/Christi Carter (tc); **144**: Agriculture & Agrifood Canada, Morden Research Station (cr, bl); **147**: DK Picture Library (bl) **147**: Garden Picture Library/Steven Wooster (tr); **151**: Photos Horticultural (tl); **152–153**: Jerry Harpur/Marcus Harpur; **156**: Garden Picture Library/Densey Clyne (tr); **161**: Garden World Images (tr); **166**: Andrew Lawson (tr); **169**: Meilland International (tl); **179**: Photos Horticultural (tr); **180**: Andrew Lawson (tc); **182**: RoseExpert (br); **185**: Courtesy Peter Harkness (c); **186**: Jerry Pavia Photography Inc. (tr); **189**: John Glover/Mannington Garden, Norfolk (tc); **189**: Andrew Lawson (br); **189**: Garden World Images (tl); **191**: Holt Studios International/Alan & Linda Detrick (bl); **195**: Garden Picture Library/Jerry Pavia (bl); **198** RoseExpert: (bl); **202**: Roger's Plants Ltd (bl); **203**: Courtesy Jackson & Perkins Company, Newark, NY/R.E.Briggs (tl); **206**: Tiny Petals Nursery (bc); **208–209**: Garden Picture Library/JS Sira; **218**: Photos Horticultural (br); **218**: Garden World Images (bc); **221**: Photographer unknown (bl); **223**: Jerry Pavia Photography Inc. (tl); **226**: James Young (br); **227**: Royal National Rose Society (cl); **231**: Photos Horticultural (tr); **232**: Photographer unknown (c); **242**: Garden World Images (cb); **255**: Leslie Stuart (c); **256**: Garden World Images (tl); **257**: Photographer unknown (t); **266–267**: Steve Wooster; **274**: Bob Bauer (cl); **275**: RoseExpert (tr, bl, bc); **278**: Jerry Pavia Photography Inc. (tr); **278**: Garden World Images (tcl); **286**: Noack Rosen (tr); **286**: Garden World Images (tl); **293**: Garden Picture Library /Brian Carter (br); **300**: A–Z Botanical Collection (br); **303**: Royal National Rose Society (tr); **305**: Jerry Pavia Photography Inc. (tc); **307**: Lindley Library (t); **312**: Roger's Plants Ltd (tr); **318**: Photographer unknown (br); **321**: James Young (ca); **322–323** Clive Nichols; **328**: Garden World Images (t); **330**: RoseExpert (tl); **331**: Photos Horticultural (br); **332**: Bridgeman Art Library, London /New York/Musee de Meudon, France (bl), Royal Botanical Gardens, Kew (br); **364–365**: Jerry Harpur; **367**: Garden and Wildlife Matters (br); **367**: James Young (c); **369**: Photos Horticultural (bl); **379**: Garden World Images (tr); **384** Garden World Images: (cr); **390**: Photographer unknown (tl); **391**: Photos Horticultural (bl); **395**: Photos Horticultural (tc); **397**: Andrew Lawson (bl); **397**: Garden World Images (c, br); **402–403**: Steve Wooster; **409**: Lindley Library (c); **411**: Brent C. Dickerson (c); **412**: Garden World Images (tcr); **416**: Gordon Ayers Photography (c); **417**: RoseExpert (tr); **422**: Photos Horticultural (tl); **422**: Garden World Images (bl); **427**: Garden World Images (tc); **432–433**: Flowerphotos/ Ashton; **434**: DK Picture Library (bl); **434–435**: Steve Wooster; **435**: John Glover (br); **435**: Steve Wooster/Ethridge Gardens, Timaru, NZ. Design: Nan Raymond (tr); **436**: DK Picture Library; **437**: DK Picture Library (t); **437**: RoseExpert (br); **438**: DK Picture Library (cl); **438**: Hamilton Photography/Stephen Hamilton (tr); **438**: Royal National Rose Society (br); **439**: DK Picture Library (cr, br); **440**: DK Picture Library; **441**: DK Picture Library; **442**: Garden Picture Library/ Mayer/Le Scanff (bl); **443**: DK Picture Library (cl, cr); **443**: Garden Picture Library/ Lamontagne (bc)/ Neil Holmes (t); **443**: Holt Studios/Nigel Cattlin (br); **443**: Oxford Scientific Films/Geoff Kid (bl).

Every effort has been made to trace the copyright holders and we apologize in advance for any unintentional omissions.